HEATH
ALGEBRA 1
AN INTEGRATED APPROACH

LARSON, KANOLD, STIFF

COMPLETE SOLUTIONS
MANUAL

McDougal Littell
Evanston, Illinois • Boston • Dallas

International Standard Book Number: 0-669-43425-6

3 4 5 6 7 8 9 10 HWI 01 00 99 98

Chapter 1

Connections to Algebra

1.1 Numbers and Number Operations

Communicating about Algebra

A. Round numbers to make calculations easier. (Answers vary.)

$$\begin{aligned}[413.2 \div (12.5 - 6.1)] - 2.6 &\approx [420 \div (12 - 6)] - 3 \\ &= [420 \div 6] - 3 \\ &= 70 - 3 \\ &= 67\end{aligned}$$

B. Round numbers to make calculations easier. (Answers vary.)

$$\begin{aligned}0.45 \cdot (1.92 - 0.84) \cdot 17.6 &\approx \tfrac{1}{2} \cdot (2 - 1) \cdot 18 \\ &= \tfrac{1}{2} \cdot 1 \cdot 18 \\ &= 9\end{aligned}$$

EXERCISES

1. California

2. California has a larger population.

3. 59,000

4. **c.** 7000

5. Add the total number of teams from each state. Subtract the total number of teams in Florida from the total number of teams in New York.

6. 7300

7. $4 + 9 = 13$

8. $12 + 6 = 18$

9. $8 - 7 = 1$

10. $9 - 2 = 7$

11. $4 \cdot 6 = 24$

12. $7 \cdot 3 = 21$

13. $16 \div 4 = 4$

14. $5 \div 1 = 5$

15. $$\begin{aligned}[8 - 3(2)] \cdot 6 &= [8 - 6] \cdot 6 \\ &= 2 \cdot 6 \\ &= 12\end{aligned}$$

16. $$\begin{aligned}12 - [(4)(2) + 2] &= 12 - [8 + 2] \\ &= 12 - 10 \\ &= 2\end{aligned}$$

17. $[3(6) + 2] + 4 = [18 + 2] + 4$
$= 20 + 4$
$= 24$

18. $4 - [(2 \cdot 9) - 17] = 4 - [18 - 17]$
$= 4 - 1$
$= 3$

19. $24 \div [10 - (4 \div 2)] = 24 \div [10 - 2]$
$= 24 \div 8$
$= 3$

20. $12 + [16 \div (3 + 1)] = 12 + [16 \div 4]$
$= 12 + 4$
$= 16$

21. $10 + [9 \div (1 + 2)] = 10 + [9 \div 3]$
$= 10 + 3$
$= 13$

22. $[12 \div (1 + 5)] - 2 = [12 \div 6] - 2$
$= 2 - 2$
$= 0$

23. $18 \div [(8)(2) - 7] = 18 \div [16 - 7]$
$= 18 \div 9$
$= 2$

24. $[(10 \cdot 3) - 10] \div 4 = [30 - 10] \div 4$
$= 20 \div 4$
$= 5$

25. $[12 \div (3 \cdot 2)] + 4 = [12 \div 6] + 4$
$= 2 + 4$
$= 6$

26. $16 - [54 \div (3)(3)] = 16 - [54 \div 9]$
$= 16 - 6$
$= 10$

27. $\dfrac{10}{(4 - 3) \cdot 2} = \dfrac{10}{1 \cdot 2}$
$= \dfrac{10}{2}$
$= 5$

28. $\dfrac{28}{(4)(2) - 4} = \dfrac{28}{8 - 4}$
$= \dfrac{28}{4}$
$= 7$

29. $[52.4 - (16.1 \div 3.6)] - 30.2 \approx 17.73$

30. $13.9 \div [(7.4 - 6.2) + 4.9] \approx 2.28$

31. $42.1 \div [(3.2 \cdot 6.1) - 1.3] \approx 2.31$

32. $[(16.0)(7.2 \div 3.9) + 6.2] - 29.8 \approx 5.94$

33. $[439.9 + (12.9 \div 4.1)] - (42.2)(6.1) \approx 185.63$

34. $(9.4 \div 2.7) + [(4.3)(16.1) - 17.7] \approx 55.01$

35. Area = (Length)(Width)
= (4)(4)
= 16 square feet

36. Area = (Length)(Width)
= (5)(3)
= 15 square meters

37. Area = $\frac{1}{2}$ (Base)(Height)
= $\frac{1}{2}(8)(5)$
= (4)(5)
= 20 square inches

38. Cost = (Length of fence)(Cost per meter)
Cost per meter = $13
Length of fence = $2(2 + 6 + 2) + 2(2 + 5 + 2)$
$= 2(10) + 2(9)$
$= 20 + 18$
= 38 meters
Cost = (38)(13) = $494

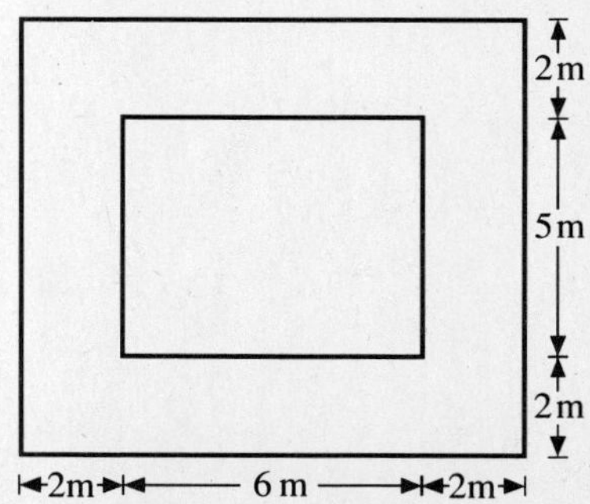

39. $\text{Area} = (\text{Length})(\text{Width})$
$= (15)(2.5)$
$= 37.5$ square yards

40. $C = (\pi)(d)$
$\approx (3.14)(200)$
$= 628$ feet

41. $\text{Total value} = (\text{Value per card})(\text{Number of cards})$
$= (110{,}000)(50)$
$= \$5{,}500{,}000$

42. $\text{Total value} = (2)(17{,}000) + (3)(14{,}000)$
$= 34{,}000 + 42{,}000$
$= \$76{,}000$

43. $\frac{6}{5} = 1.2$

44. $50\% = \frac{50}{100} = \frac{1}{2}$

45. $\frac{3}{4} = 0.75 = 75\%$

46. $60\% = 0.60$

47. $0.32 = \frac{8}{25}$

48. $0.07 = 7\%$

49. $\frac{4}{9} \approx 0.44$

50. $\frac{7}{6} \approx 1.17$

51. $100 - (19 + 15 + 10 + 2 + 29) = 100 - 75$
$= 25\%$

52. $100 - (34 + 12 + 10 + 21) = 100 - 77$
$= 23\%$

53. $\text{Area} = (9)(3) + (3)(3)$
$= 27 + 9$
$= 36$

54. $\text{Area} = (12)(8) + (8)(4)$
$= 96 + 32$
$= 128$

55. $50.00 + 50.00 = \$100.00$

56. $100.00 + 0.37 = \$100.37$

57. $100.37 - 30.00 = \$70.37$

58. $70.37 + 0.58 = \$70.95$

1.2 Variables in Algebra

Communicating about Algebra

A. $2a = b$

$2 \cdot 1 \stackrel{?}{=} 2$

$2 = 2$

Statement is true.

B. $5a = b + 3$

$5 \cdot 1 \stackrel{?}{=} 2 + 3$

$5 = 5$

Statement is true.

C. $5c - x = 4b$

$5 \cdot 3 - 8 \stackrel{?}{=} 4 \cdot 2$

$15 - 8 \stackrel{?}{=} 8$

$7 \neq 8$

Statement is false.

Statement is true if $x = 7$. (Answers vary.)

D. $7b - x = 2c$

$7 \cdot 2 - 8 \stackrel{?}{=} 2 \cdot 3$

$14 - 8 \stackrel{?}{=} 6$

$6 = 6$

Statement is true.

E. $7 + b = x + a$

$7 + 2 \stackrel{?}{=} 8 + 1$

$9 = 9$

Statement is true.

F. $8 + b = 7 + x$

$8 + 2 \stackrel{?}{=} 7 + 8$

$10 \neq 15$

Statement is false.

Statement is true if $b = 7$. (Answers vary.)

EXERCISES

1. r divided by the product of 3 and s

2. $6x + y$

3. $8x = 8(3)$
$= 24$

4. $9a - 2 = 9(1) - 2$
$= 9 - 2$
$= 7$

5. $a - b = 10 - 3$
$= 7$

6. $2x + 4y = 2(2) + 4(3)$
$= 4 + 12$
$= 16$

Other values of x and y:
$x = 0,\ y = 4$
$x = 4,\ y = 2$
$x = 6,\ y = 1$
$x = 8,\ y = 0$

7. $2x + 1 = 2(4) + 1$
$= 8 + 1$
$= 9$

8. $x - 9 = 21 - 9$
$= 12$

9. $2r - s + 4 = 2(4) - 5 + 4$
$= 8 - 5 + 4$
$= 3 + 4$
$= 7$

10. $3a + b = 3(2) + 1$
$= 6 + 1$
$= 7$

11. $(a - 2) + 4a = (4 - 2) + 4(4)$
$= 2 + 16$
$= 18$

12. $6a - (1 + a) = 6(3) - (1 + 3)$
$= 18 - 4$
$= 14$

13. $3x(4 + x) = 3(2)(4 + 2)$
$= 3(2)(6)$
$= 6(6)$
$= 36$

14. $5y + 4(y - 3) = 5(4) + 4(4 - 3)$
$= 5(4) + 4(1)$
$= 20 + 4$
$= 24$

15. $x \div (3y - 4) = 6 \div [3(2) - 4]$
$= 6 \div (6 - 4)$
$= 6 \div 2$
$= 3$

16. $[9 - (x \div 4)] + y = 9 - (8 \div 4) + 7$
$= 9 - 2 + 7$
$= 7 + 7$
$= 14$

17. $24 \div (x + 2) = 24 \div (2 + 2)$
$= 24 \div 4$
$= 6$

18. $24 \div (x+2) = 24 \div (0+2)$
$= 24 \div 2$
$= 12$

19. $24 \div (x+2) = 24 \div (4+2)$
$= 24 \div 6$
$= 4$

20. $24 \div (x+2) = 24 \div (10+2)$
$= 24 \div 12$
$= 2$

21. $4.97a + 9.21 = 4.97(6.21) + 9.21$
≈ 40.07

22. $3.2(2.1a - 4.3) = 3.2(2.1 \cdot 4.8 - 4.3)$
≈ 18.50

23. $6.9(x - 3.2y) - 56.2 = 6.9(19.1 - 3.2 \cdot 1.1) - 56.2$
≈ 51.30

24. $15.9 \div (x+y) = 15.9 \div (3.2 + 3.4)$
≈ 2.41

25. $L = 110$ meters, $W = 49$ meters
$A = L \cdot W$
$= 110 \cdot 49$
$= 5390$ square meters

26. $P = \$80$, $r = 6\% = 0.06$, $t = \frac{9}{12} = 0.75$ (in years)
$I = Prt$
$= 80(0.06)(0.75)$
$= 4.8(0.75)$
$= \$3.60$

27. $r = 72$ km/hr, $t = 2$ hr
$d = rt$
$= 72(2)$
$= 144$ kilometers

28. $r = 300$ ft/min, $t = 1$ hr $= 60$ min
$d = rt$
$= 300(60)$
$= 18{,}000$ feet

29. $6 + 11 = 17$

30. $14 - 9 = 5$

31. $6 \cdot 8 = 48$

32. $27 \div 3 = 9$

33. $42.6 + 9.3 = 51.9$

34. $21.3 - 16.8 = 4.5$

35. $9.39 \div 6.12 \approx 1.53$

36. $3.9 \cdot 6.4 = 24.96$

37. $10 - [8 \div (4-2)] = 10 - [8 \div 2]$
$= 10 - 4$
$= 6$

38. $6 \cdot (12 \div 4) + 9 = 6 \cdot 3 + 9$
$= 18 + 9$
$= 27$

39. $[(9-5) \cdot 4] \div 4 = [4 \cdot 4] \div 4$
$= 16 \div 4$
$= 4$

40. $(16+4) \div (2 \cdot 5) = 20 \div 10$
$= 2$

41. $30 - [(36 \div 3) + 6] = 30 - [12 + 6]$
$= 30 - 18$
$= 12$

42. $(12 \cdot 2) + (12 - 10) = 24 + 2$
$= 26$

43. $P = a + b + c$

a. $P = a + b + c = 2 + 3 + 4$
$= 5 + 4$
$= 9$

b. $P = a + b + c = 3 + 4 + 5$
$= 7 + 5$
$= 12$

c. $P = a + b + c = 4 + 5 + 6$
$= 9 + 6$
$= 15$

44. $C = 2\pi r$

a. $C = 2\pi r \approx 2(3.14)(2)$
$= (6.28)(2)$
$= 12.56$

b. $C = 2\pi r \approx 2(3.14)(3)$
$= (6.28)(3)$
$= 18.84$

c. $C = 2\pi r \approx 2(3.14)(4)$
$= (6.28)(4)$
$= 25.12$

45. The perimeter increases by 3 units.

46. The circumference increases by a factor of 2π or approximately 6.28.

47. 1983 $D = 270(3) - 200$
$= 810 - 200$
$= 610$

1984 $D = 270(4) - 200$
$= 1080 - 200$
$= 880$

1985 $D = 270(5) - 200$
$= 1350 - 200$
$= 1150$

1986 $D = 270(6) - 200$
$= 1620 - 200$
$= 1420$

1987 $D = 270(7) - 200$
$= 1890 - 200$
$= 1690$

1988 $D = 270(8) - 200$
$= 2160 - 200$
$= 1960$

1989 $D = 270(9) - 200$
$= 2430 - 200$
$= 2230$

1990 $D = 270(10) - 200$
$= 2700 - 200$
$= 2500$

Year	1983	1984	1985	1986	1987	1988	1989	1990
t	3	4	5	6	7	8	9	10
D	610	880	1150	1420	1690	1960	2230	2500

48.

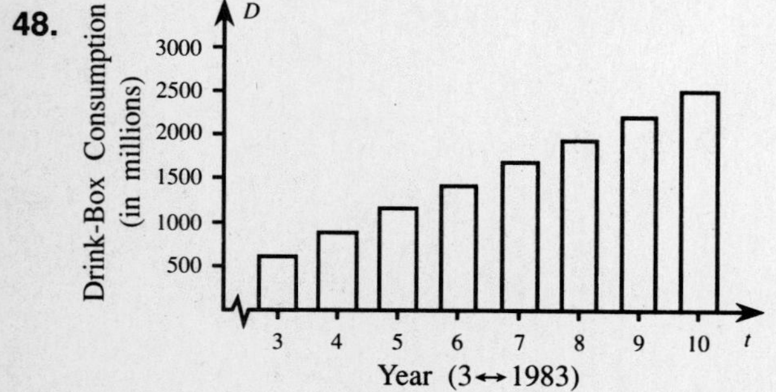

Each year the consumption increases by the same amount.

49. Consumption per person $= \frac{2500}{250} \approx 10$ drink-boxes per person.

50. In 1983 the population was about 234 million. The per person consumption of drink-boxes that year was $\frac{610}{234} \approx 2.6$. Thus, the per person consumption did increase.

Mixed REVIEW

1. $17 - 9 + 28 = 8 + 28$
$= 36$

2. $\frac{2}{3} + 3 = \frac{2}{3} + \frac{9}{3}$
$= \frac{11}{3}$

3. $(0.10)(245) = \$24.50$

4. 0.75 is greater than $\frac{1}{2}$, or 0.5.

5. $(9)(4) = 36$

6. $13 - 5 = 8$

7. $9 \div [3 + (11 - 5)] = 9 \div [3 + 6]$
$= 9 \div 9$
$= 1$

8. $[(7 \cdot 3) - 2] + (8 \div 4) = [21 - 2] + 2$
$= 19 + 2$
$= 21$

9. $21 \div 7 = 3$

10. $x - 2y = 14 - 2(3)$
$= 14 - 6$
$= 8$

11. $3x + 1 = 3(2) + 1$
$= 6 + 1$
$= 7$

12. $3x + 2 = 3(2) + 2$
$= 6 + 2$
$= 8$

13. $\frac{1}{2}(x - 7) = \frac{1}{2}(11 - 7)$
$= \frac{1}{2}(4)$
$= 2$

14. $\frac{x}{2} + \frac{x}{4} = \frac{1}{2} + \frac{1}{4}$
$= \frac{3}{4}$

15. $P = 4x$

16. $P = 2(103) + 2(210)$
$= 206 + 420$
$= 626$ feet

17. $1.4x + 7.4 = 1.4(3.2) + 7.4$
$= 11.88$

18. $\frac{72 + 68 + 60 + 76 + 64}{5} = \frac{340}{5}$
$= 68$ inches

19. $\frac{1}{2}(2a - 3b) = \frac{1}{2}(2 \cdot 9 - 3 \cdot 4)$
$= \frac{1}{2}(18 - 12)$
$= \frac{1}{2}(6)$
$= \frac{6}{2}$
$= 3$

1.3 Exponents and Powers

Communicating about Algebra

A. $r = \frac{1}{2}d = \frac{1}{2}(165) = 82.5$

$S = 4\pi r^2 \approx 4 \cdot 3.14 \cdot (82.5)^2 = 85{,}486.5$ square feet

B. $S = 4\pi r^2 \approx 4 \cdot 3.14 \cdot (6370)^2 = 509{,}645{,}864$ square kilometers

C. $(509{,}645{,}864)(0.292) \approx 148{,}816{,}592$ square kilometers

D. $509{,}645{,}864 - 148{,}816{,}592 = 360{,}829{,}272$ square kilometers

EXERCISES

1. Eighteen to the third power
Eighteen cubed

2. 18 is called the base.

3. 3 is called the exponent.

4. $18^3 = 5832$

5. x^2 is the area of a square with side x.

6. y^3 is the volume of a cube with edge y.

7. 2^3

8. x^2

9. 9^y

10. y^9

11. 3^4

12. y^2

13. a^6

14. 4^3

15. $(2x)^3$

16. $y^2 = 9^2$
$= 81$

17. $a^4 = 3^4$
$= 81$

18. $a^2 - 3 = 3^2 - 3$
$= 9 - 3$
$= 6$

19. $16 + x^3 = 16 + 2^3$
$= 16 + 8$
$= 24$

20. $(x + y)^2 = (3 + 4)^2$
$= 7^2$
$= 49$

21. $x^2 + y^2 = 2^2 + 6^2$
$= 4 + 36$
$= 40$

22. $(2a)^2 - b = (2 \cdot 4)^2 - 10$
$= 8^2 - 10$
$= 64 - 10$
$= 54$

23. $(6x + y)^2 = (6 \cdot 1 + 4)^2$
$= (6 + 4)^2$
$= 10^2$
$= 100$

24. $3r^2 + 6s = 3 \cdot 2^2 + 6 \cdot 3$
$= 3 \cdot 4 + 6 \cdot 3$
$= 12 + 18$
$= 30$

25. $4x - 3y^3 = 4 \cdot 7 - 3 \cdot 2^3$
$= 4 \cdot 7 - 3 \cdot 8$
$= 28 - 24$
$= 4$

26. $9^5 = 59{,}049$

27. $13^4 = 28{,}561$

28. $5^9 = 1{,}953{,}125$

29. $3^{11} = 177{,}147$

30. $A = s^2$
$= 8^2$
$= 64$ square inches

31. $V = s^3$
$= 11^3$
$= 1331$ cubic inches

32. $A = \pi r^2$
$\approx (3.14)(60)^2$
$= 11{,}304$ square feet

33. $r = \frac{1}{2}d = \frac{1}{2}(6.67) = 3.335$
$S = 4\pi r^2$
$\approx 4(3.14)(3.335)^2$
$= 139.7$ square centimeters

34. After 1 year: $A = 1000(1 + 0.06)^1$
$= 1000(1.06)$
$= \$1060.00$

After 10 years: $A = 1000(1 + 0.06)^{10}$
$= 1000(1.06)^{10}$
$= \$1790.85$

After 20 years: $A = 1000(1 + 0.06)^{20}$
$= 1000(1.06)^{20}$
$= \$3207.14$

35. $V = \frac{1}{3}hb^2$
$= \frac{1}{3}(20.6)(35)^2$
≈ 8411.67 cubic meters

36. $V = s^3$
$= 12^3$
$= 1728$ cubic inches

37. $1.6^5 \approx 10.49$

38. $3.9^3 \approx 59.32$

39. $6.9^2 = 47.61$

40. $4.3^4 \approx 341.88$

41. $x^2 + 1 = 10$
$x^2 = 9$
$x = 3$

42. $x^3 - 3 = 5$
$x^3 = 8$
$x = 2$

43. 1st paper takes $1\frac{1}{2}$ hours.
2nd paper takes $3 \cdot 1\frac{1}{2}$ hours.
3rd paper takes $3 \cdot 3 \cdot 1\frac{1}{2}$ hours.
$T = 3^2 \cdot \frac{3}{2} = 9 \cdot \frac{3}{2} = \frac{27}{2} = 13\frac{1}{2}$ hours

44. 1st day $= 1¢$
2nd day $= 2 \cdot 1¢ = 2^1 \cdot 1$
3rd day $= 2 \cdot 2 \cdot 1¢ = 2^2 \cdot 1$
$\vdots$
30th day $= 2^{29} \cdot 1¢ \approx \$5{,}368{,}709.12$

45.

9^1	9^2	9^3	9^4	9^5	9^6	9^7	9^8
9	81	729	6561	59,049	531,441	4,782,969	43,046,721

The pattern for the last digit is "9, 1, 9, 1, ..."

46.

8^1	8^2	8^3	8^4	8^5	8^6	8^7	8^8
8	64	512	4096	32,768	262,144	2,097,152	16,777,216

The pattern for the last digit is "8, 4, 2, 6, 8, 4, 2, 6, ..."

7^1	7^2	7^3	7^4	7^5	7^6	7^7	7^8
7	49	343	2401	16,807	117,649	823,543	5,764,801

The pattern for the last digit is "7, 9, 3, 1, 7, 9, 3, 1, ..."

Programming a Calculator

	x = 0	x = 1	x = 2	x = 5.36
1. $x^2 + 2x$	0	3	8	39.45
3. $0.5x + 10$	10	10.5	11	12.68
5. x^2	0	1	4	28.73
7. $3x^2 + 8x$	0	11	28	129.07

	x = 0	x = 1	x = 2	x = 5.36
2. $60 - 9x$	60	51	42	11.76
4. $\frac{1}{3}x$	0	0.33	0.67	1.79
6. $x^2 + 1$	1	2	5	29.73
8. $5x^2$	0	5	20	143.65

1.4 Order of Operations

Communicating about Algebra

A. $100 - 50 - 10 = 100 - 40 = 60$ *Incorrect*
$100 - 50 - 10 = 50 - 10 = 40$ *Correct*

B. $4 + 3 \cdot 5 - 2 = 7 \cdot 5 - 2 = 35 - 2 = 33$ *Incorrect*
$4 + 3 \cdot 5 - 2 = 7 \cdot 5 - 2 = 7 \cdot 3 = 21$ *Incorrect*
$4 + 3 \cdot 5 - 2 = 4 + 15 - 2 = 19 - 2 = 17$ *Correct*
$4 + 3 \cdot 5 - 2 = 4 + 15 - 2 = 4 + 13 = 17$ *Incorrect*
$4 + 3 \cdot 5 - 2 = 4 + 3 \cdot 3 = 7 \cdot 3 = 21$ *Incorrect*
$4 + 3 \cdot 5 - 2 = 4 + 3 \cdot 3 = 4 + 9 = 13$ *Incorrect*

C. $18 - 6 + 5 - 4 = 12 + 5 - 4 = 17 - 4 = 13$ *Correct*
$18 - 6 + 5 - 4 = 12 + 5 - 4 = 12 + 1 = 13$ *Incorrect*
$18 - 6 + 5 - 4 = 18 - 11 - 4 = 7 - 4 = 3$ *Incorrect*
$18 - 6 + 5 - 4 = 18 - 11 - 4 = 18 - 7 = 11$ *Incorrect*
$18 - 6 + 5 - 4 = 18 - 6 + 1 = 12 + 1 = 13$ *Incorrect*
$18 - 6 + 5 - 4 = 18 - 6 + 1 = 18 - 7 = 11$ *Incorrect*

D. $24 \div 4 \div 2 = 6 \div 2 = 3$ *Correct*
$24 \div 4 \div 2 = 24 \div 2 = 12$ *Incorrect*

EXERCISES

1. The exponent operation is performed first.

2. The leftmost operation is performed first.

3. $4 + (16 \div 8) - 2$

4. $3 + (4 \cdot 9) = 3 + 36$ $\quad (3 + 4) \cdot 9 = 7 \cdot 9$
$= 39 \quad = 63$

$3 + 4 \cdot 9 = 3 + (4 \cdot 9)$

5. $4 + 2 - 1 = (4 + 2) - 1$
$= 6 - 1$
$= 5$

6. $3 \cdot 1 + 4 = (3 \cdot 1) + 4$
$= 3 + 4$
$= 7$

7. $8 \div 4 + 4 \cdot 2 = (8 \div 4) + (4 \cdot 2)$
$= 2 + 8$
$= 10$

8. $5 + 8 \cdot 3 + 2 = 5 + (8 \cdot 3) + 2$
$= 5 + 24 + 2$
$= (5 + 24) + 2$
$= 29 + 2$
$= 31$

9. $14 \div 7 + 3^2 = 14 \div 7 + 9$
$= (14 \div 7) + 9$
$= 2 + 9$
$= 11$

10. $2 \cdot 3^2 - 9 = 2 \cdot 9 - 9$
$= (2 \cdot 9) - 9$
$= 18 - 9$
$= 9$

11. $10 \cdot (3 + 1) - 16 = 10 \cdot 4 - 16$
$= (10 \cdot 4) - 16$
$= 40 - 16$
$= 24$

12. $13 + (3 \cdot 2)^2 - 8 = 13 + 6^2 - 8$
$= 13 + 36 - 8$
$= (13 + 36) - 8$
$= 49 - 8$
$= 41$

13. $10 - 3 \cdot 2 = 10 - 6 = 4$

14. $15 - 2 \cdot 2 = 15 - 4 = 11$

15. **b.** $\dfrac{8 \cdot 3}{4 + 3^2 - 1} = 8 \cdot 3 \div (4 + 3^2 - 1)$

16. **b.** $\dfrac{(4 - 2)^2 + 5}{3} = [(4 - 2)^2 + 5] \div 3$

17. $2 + 2x^3 = 2 + 2(2)^3$
$= 2 + 2 \cdot 8$
$= 2 + 16$
$= 18$

18. $16 - x^2 \div 12 = 16 - 6^2 \div 12$
$= 16 - 36 \div 12$
$= 16 - 3$
$= 13$

19. $x^2 + 2x + 1 = 5^2 + 2 \cdot 5 + 1$
$= 25 + 2 \cdot 5 + 1$
$= 25 + 10 + 1$
$= 35 + 1$
$= 36$

20. $x^3 - 4x + 9 = 4^3 - 4 \cdot 4 + 9$
$= 64 - 4 \cdot 4 + 9$
$= 64 - 16 + 9$
$= 48 + 9$
$= 57$

21. $2l + 2w = 2 \cdot 3 + 2 \cdot 19$

$= 6 + 38$

$= 44$

22. $4r^2 - s = 4 \cdot 4^2 - 14$

$= 4 \cdot 16 - 14$

$= 64 - 14$

$= 50$

23. $\frac{2x + y}{7} = \frac{2 \cdot 12 + 11}{7}$

$= \frac{24 + 11}{7}$

$= \frac{35}{7}$

$= 5$

24. $6 + \frac{x}{y} \cdot 4 = 6 + \frac{8}{4} \cdot 4$

$= 6 + 2 \cdot 4$

$= 6 + 8$

$= 14$

25. Calculator 1

16 [−] [(] [(] 4 [÷] 2 [)] [×] 5 [)] [=]

26. Calculator 2

15 [−] [(] 6 [÷] 3 [)] [−] 2 [=]

27. Calculator 2

10 [+] [(] 15 [÷] 5 [)] [+] 16 [=]

28. Calculator 1

[(] 4 [×] 3 [)] [+] [(] 6 [÷] 2 [)] [=]

29. Calculator 1

[(] 12 [÷] 3 [)] [+] [(] 16 [÷] 4 [)] [=]

30. Calculator 2

8 [+] 22 [−] [(] 15 [÷] 5 [)] [=]

31. 159,327.5 feet is not the correct perimeter. The department did not follow the correct order of operations.

32. $(35.99 + 42.99)(0.07) = (78.98)(0.07)$

$= \$5.53$

Cashier did not follow the correct order of operations.

33. $\frac{1248 + 741 + 402}{3} = \frac{1989 + 402}{3}$

$= \frac{2391}{3}$

$= 797$

34. $\frac{87 + 92 + 81}{3} = \frac{179 + 81}{3}$

$= \frac{260}{3}$

$= 86\frac{2}{3}$

35. $2x + 3x + 4x = (2)(12.9) + (3)(12.9) + (4)(12.9)$

$= 25.8 + 38.7 + 51.6$

$= 116.1$ centimeters

36. $x + 1.5x + 2x + 3x = 4.2 + (1.5)(4.2) + (2)(4.2) + (3)(4.2)$

$= 4.2 + 6.3 + 8.4 + 12.6$

$= 10.5 + 8.4 + 12.6$

$= 18.9 + 12.6$

$= 31.5$ feet

37. $2 \cdot (2.9)^2 = 2(8.41)$

$= 16.82$ square units

38. $2 \cdot (2.9)^3 = 2(24.389)$

$= 48.778$ cubic units

39. $2\pi r^2$

40. $(360 + 20 + 20) \cdot (160 + 64 + 64) = (400) \cdot (288)$
$= 115,200$ square feet

41. $4.3 + (6.9 \div 2.3)$

42. $9.6 \cdot 1.3 - (3.6 \div 2.4)$

43. $6.2 \div 3.1 + (4.7 \cdot 5.3)$

44. $9.3 + (5.4 \cdot 1.1)$

45. $A = \frac{1}{2}h(b_1 + b_2)$
$= \frac{1}{2} \cdot 2 \cdot (6 + 10)$
$= \frac{1}{2} \cdot 2 \cdot 16$
$= 1 \cdot 16$
$= 16$ square meters

Mid-Chapter SELF-TEST

1. 0.625

2. 20%

3. $\frac{1}{2} + \frac{1}{4} = \frac{2}{4} + \frac{1}{4} = \frac{3}{4}$

4. $6 - 2 = 4$

5. $1 \cdot 8 = 8$

6. $7 \div 21 = \frac{7}{21} = \frac{1}{3}$

7. $2[3(4 \div 2) + 6] - 5 = 2[3(2) + 6] - 5$
$= 2[6 + 6] - 5$
$= 2 \cdot 12 - 5$
$= 24 - 5$
$= 19$

8. $3 + [(4 - 1) \cdot 5] = 3 + [3 \cdot 5]$
$= 3 + 15$
$= 18$

9. $3 \cdot 8 \div 2 - 9 \div 3 = 24 \div 2 - 9 \div 3$
$= 12 - 9 \div 3$
$= 12 - 3$
$= 9$

10. $9 - 3 \cdot 2 + 1 \div 2 = 9 - 6 + 1 \div 2$
$= 9 - 6 + \frac{1}{2}$
$= 3 + \frac{1}{2}$
$= 3\frac{1}{2}$

11. $12 \div (5x - y) = 12 \div (5 \cdot 2 - 1)$
$= 12 \div (10 - 1)$
$= 12 \div 9$
$= \frac{12}{9}$
$= 1\frac{3}{9}$
$= 1\frac{1}{3}$

12. $(3x + 2) \cdot y = (3 \cdot 1 + 2) \cdot 4$
$= (3 + 2) \cdot 4$
$= 5 \cdot 4$
$= 20$

13. $13 - 2x^2 \div 8 = 13 - 2 \cdot 6^2 \div 8$
$= 13 - 2 \cdot 36 \div 8$
$= 13 - 72 \div 8$
$= 13 - 9$
$= 4$

14. $9x^2 - x \div 2 = 9 \cdot 6^2 - 6 \div 2$
$= 9 \cdot 36 - 6 \div 2$
$= 324 - 3$
$= 321$

15. $1.3x + 0.75 = 1.3 \cdot 2.7 + 0.75$
$= 4.26$

16. $3.47 - 2.3y = 3.47 - 2.3 \cdot 1.25$
$= 0.595$

17. Area = (Length)(Width)
Length = $2 \cdot$ Width
Width = 4
Length = $2 \cdot 4 = 8$
Area = $8 \cdot 4 = 32$ square meters

18. x^3

19. Amount of fencing $= 2 \cdot x + 250 + (250 - 150)$
$= 2x + 250 + 100$
$= 2x + 350$
When $x = 75$ feet:
$2x + 350 = 2 \cdot 75 + 350$
$= 150 + 350$
$= 500$ feet

20. $A = \frac{1}{2}bh$
$= \frac{1}{2}(40.5)(35)$
$= (20.25)(35)$
$= 708.75$ square inches

21. $s = \frac{1}{2}(4\pi r^2) \approx 0.5(4 \cdot 3.14 \cdot 3^2)$
$= 0.5(4 \cdot 3.14 \cdot 9)$
$= 0.5(12.56 \cdot 9)$
$= 0.5(113.04)$
$= 56.52$ square meters

1.5 Equations and Inequalities

Communicating about Algebra

A.

$(1)^2 + 8 - 5(1) \stackrel{?}{=} 2$	$(2)^2 + 8 - 5(2) \stackrel{?}{=} 2$	$(3)^2 + 8 - 5(3) \stackrel{?}{=} 2$	$(4)^2 + 8 - 5(4) \stackrel{?}{=} 2$
$1 + 8 - 5 \stackrel{?}{=} 2$	$4 + 8 - 10 \stackrel{?}{=} 2$	$9 + 8 - 15 \stackrel{?}{=} 2$	$16 + 8 - 20 \stackrel{?}{=} 2$
$9 - 5 \stackrel{?}{=} 2$	$12 - 10 \stackrel{?}{=} 2$	$17 - 15 \stackrel{?}{=} 2$	$24 - 20 \stackrel{?}{=} 2$
$4 \neq 2$	$2 = 2$	$2 = 2$	$4 \neq 2$

2 and 3 are solutions.

B. 1. **b.** $x = 4$ is the only solution.
2. **c.** x may have any value and the equation is true.
3. **a.** No number will satisfy this equation.

EXERCISES

1. This is an equation because there is an equal sign placed between the two expressions.

2. This is an expression because there is no equal sign or inequality symbol placed between two expressions.

3. This is an expression because there is no equal sign or inequality symbol placed between two expressions.

4. This is an equation because there is an equal sign placed between the two expressions.

5. This is an inequality because there is an inequality symbol placed between the two expressions.

6. This is an inequality because there is an inequality symbol placed between the two expressions.

7. Left: $13 + 4x$
Right: $2x + 1$

8. **b.**

9.
$$3x + 1 = 13$$
$$3 \cdot 4 + 1 \stackrel{?}{=} 13$$
$$12 + 1 \stackrel{?}{=} 13$$
$$13 = 13$$
4 is a solution.

10.
$$3 + 2x = 9$$
$$3 + 2 \cdot 2 \stackrel{?}{=} 9$$
$$3 + 4 \stackrel{?}{=} 9$$
$$7 \neq 9$$
2 is not a solution.

11.
$$4y + 2 = 2y + 8$$
$$4 \cdot 3 + 2 \stackrel{?}{=} 2 \cdot 3 + 8$$
$$12 + 2 \stackrel{?}{=} 6 + 8$$
$$14 = 14$$
3 is a solution.

12.
$$2y + y = 2y + 5$$
$$2 \cdot 5 + 5 \stackrel{?}{=} 2 \cdot 5 + 5$$
$$10 + 5 \stackrel{?}{=} 10 + 5$$
$$15 = 15$$
5 is a solution.

13.
$$5x - 2 = 11$$
$$5 \cdot 2 - 2 \stackrel{?}{=} 11$$
$$10 - 2 \stackrel{?}{=} 11$$
$$8 \neq 11$$
2 is not a solution.

14.
$$6x - 4 = 3$$
$$6 \cdot 1 - 4 \stackrel{?}{=} 3$$
$$6 - 4 \stackrel{?}{=} 3$$
$$2 \neq 3$$
1 is not a solution.

15. What number can be added to 4 to obtain 7?
Answer: 3

16. What number can be added to 6 to obtain 11?
Answer: 5

17. What number can 2 be subtracted from to obtain 5?
Answer: 7

18. What number can 5 be subtracted from to obtain 1?
Answer: 6

19. What number can be multiplied by 3 to obtain 12?
Answer: 4

20. What number can be multiplied by 2 to obtain 6?
Answer: 3

21. What number can be divided by 5 to obtain 4?
Answer: 20

22. What number can be divided by 4 to obtain 5?
Answer: 20

23. What number can be multiplied by 2 and the result added to 1 to obtain 7?
Answer: 3

24. What number can be multiplied by 2 and have 1 subtracted from the result to obtain 9?
Answer: 5

25. What number can be cubed to obtain 27?
Answer: 3

26. What number can be cubed to obtain 1?
Answer: 1

27. $x - 2 < 6$

$7 - 2 \stackrel{?}{<} 6$

$5 < 6$

7 is a solution.

28. $5 + x > 8$

$5 + 4 \stackrel{?}{>} 8$

$9 > 8$

4 is a solution.

29. $6 + 2x \geq 10$

$6 + 2 \cdot 2 \stackrel{?}{\geq} 10$

$6 + 4 \stackrel{?}{\geq} 10$

$10 \geq 10$

2 is a solution.

30. $3x - 1 \geq 7$

$3 \cdot 3 - 1 \stackrel{?}{\geq} 7$

$9 - 1 \stackrel{?}{\geq} 7$

$8 \geq 7$

3 is a solution.

31. $4x - 3 < 0$

$4 \cdot 1 - 3 \stackrel{?}{<} 0$

$4 - 3 \stackrel{?}{<} 0$

$1 \not< 0$

1 is not a solution.

32. $x - 7 \geq 11 - x$

$9 - 7 \stackrel{?}{\geq} 11 - 9$

$2 \geq 2$

9 is a solution.

33. 20 represents the number of square feet needed for each station.

x represents the number of computer stations.

400 represents the area available for computer stations.

34. 8 represents the number of complete screens needed to receive an energy bar.

x represents the number of extra energy bars.

96 represents the number of screens completed.

35. 18 represents the cost of filling the tank one time.

x represents the number of times you can completely fill the tank.

y represents the amount of money you have leftover.

65 represents the total amount of money you have available for gas.

36. 5 represents the amount you save each week.

n represents the number of weeks.

m represents the amount of money left.

18.75 represents the cost of the T-shirts.

37. $6 + 5 = 11$

38. $15 - 9 = 6$

39. $4 \cdot 8 = 32$

40. $12 \div 3 = 4$

41. $6 - [(3 \cdot 8) - 21] = 6 - [24 - 21]$

$= 6 - 3$

$= 3$

42. $[18 \div (3 + 3)] + 5 = [18 \div 6] + 5$

$= 3 + 5$

$= 8$

43. $7 + [12 - (3)(4)] = 7 + [12 - 12]$

$= 7 + 0$

$= 7$

44. $16 - (12 \div 2) = 16 - 6$

$= 10$

45. $x + 11 = 14 + 11$

$= 25$

46. $2n - 3 = 2 \cdot 9 - 3$

$= 18 - 3$

$= 15$

47. $3y + 2x = 3 \cdot 7 + 2 \cdot 2$
$= 21 + 4$
$= 25$

48. $7a - 4b = 7 \cdot 2 - 4 \cdot 1$
$= 14 - 4$
$= 10$

49. $(x + y)^2 = (8 + 4)^2$
$= 12^2$
$= 144$

50. $3s^2 + 6r^3 = 3 \cdot 5^2 + 6 \cdot 1^3$
$= 3 \cdot 25 + 6 \cdot 1$
$= 75 + 6$
$= 81$

51. $x + 15 < 29$

52. $9y = 72$

53. $x - 4 = 18$

54. $n \div 3 \geq 4$

55. $3x + 12 = 32$

56. $x = 20 + y$

57. $V = 380 + 100$

58. The Boeing 747 wing span is 1.2 times the length. A Boeing 747 is wider than it is long.

59. $61 + 57 + x = 180$
$x = 62$

d. 62°

60. $x = 6$ and $x = 6$
Both equations have 6 as a solution.

61. $y = 18$ and $y = 18$
Both equations have 18 as a solution.

62. $x = 2$ and $x = 2$
Both equations have 2 as a solution.

63. $a = 2$ and $a = 2$
Both equations have 2 as a solution.

64. The tail is 1.8 times the length of the body.

65. $y = 1.8x$
$= 1.8 \cdot 30$
$= 54$

Length of tail is 54 centimeters.

66. $y = 1.8x$
$18 = 1.8x$
$x = 10$

Length of body is 10 inches.

1.6 Verbal Models and Algebraic Models

Communicating about Algebra

A. $30x$, $\dfrac{\text{milligrams}}{\text{ounce}} \times \text{ounce} = \text{milligrams}$

B. $30 \cdot 1 = 30$ milligrams

EXERCISES

1. Subtraction

2. $8 - x$

3. Yes

4. 1. Write a verbal model.
2. Assign labels.
3. Write an algebraic model.

5. $x + 5 = 12$

6. $4n < 36$

7. $m - 5 < 20$

8. $10 \div y = 5$

9. $x + 12$

10. $2y + 5$

11. $\frac{1}{2}m$

12. $4n - 3$

13. $11 + r \div 7$

14. $x \div 6$

15. **d.**

16. **a.**

17. **e.**

18. **f.**

19. **b.**

20. **c.**

21. $s + 16 = 36$

22. $10 < 3b$

23. $25 - y = 10.5$

24. $17n = 1$

25. $8 + 12 + (x + 4) + 8 + 6 + 2x$

26. (Area large circle) − (Area small circle)
$\pi \cdot 12^2 - \pi \cdot 4^2$

27. Correct

28. Incorrect, $3x - 7 = 8$

29. Incorrect, $3(2 - y) = 4$

30. Correct

31. **b.** $\frac{1}{4}p = 2.30$

32. **a.** $\frac{1}{10}L = 45$

33. $(w - 4)$ is the number of red cars.
a. $w + (w - 4) = 24$

34. **b.** $c + 6 = 50$

35. x^7

36. 8^3

37. y^6

38. 12^4

39.
$$\frac{4x + 2y}{5} = \frac{4 \cdot 1 + 2 \cdot 8}{5} = \frac{4 + 16}{5} = \frac{20}{5} = 4$$

40.
$$6 + \frac{x + 2}{y} = 6 + \frac{7 + 2}{3} = 6 + \frac{9}{3} = 6 + 3 = 9$$

41.
$$3y^2 - w = 3 \cdot 8^2 - 27 = 3 \cdot 64 - 27 = 192 - 27 = 165$$

42.
$$2x^3 - 3y = 2 \cdot 4^3 - 3 \cdot 6 = 2 \cdot 64 - 3 \cdot 6 = 128 - 18 = 110$$

43. $7y + 2 = 4y + 8$

$7(2) + 2 \stackrel{?}{=} 4(2) + 8$

$14 + 2 \stackrel{?}{=} 8 + 8$

$16 = 16$

2 is a solution.

44. $5x - 1 = 3x + 2$

$5(4) - 1 \stackrel{?}{=} 3(4) + 2$

$20 - 1 \stackrel{?}{=} 12 + 2$

$19 \neq 14$

4 is not a solution.

45. $32 - 5y > 11$

$32 - 5(3) \stackrel{?}{>} 11$

$32 - 15 \stackrel{?}{>} 11$

$17 > 11$

3 is a solution.

46. $7m + 2 < 12$

$7(1) + 2 \stackrel{?}{<} 12$

$7 + 2 \stackrel{?}{<} 12$

$9 < 12$

1 is a solution.

47. $s - 7 \geq 12 - s$

$9 - 7 \stackrel{?}{\geq} 12 - 9$

$2 \ngeq 3$

9 is not a solution.

48. $n + 2 \leq 2n - 2$

$4 + 2 \stackrel{?}{\leq} 2(4) - 2$

$6 \stackrel{?}{\leq} 8 - 2$

$6 \leq 6$

4 is a solution.

49. 5 decreased by 2 times a number

50. 3 times a number, less 4

51. 6 times the sum of 3 and a number

52. A number times the sum of another number and 6

53. 2 less than the product of 5 and a number equals 14.

54. The difference between 15 and the product of 2 and a number equals 7.

55. Let y represent the attendance at Super Bowl XXIII.
$y = x - 6141$

56. $y = 81{,}270 - 6141$
$y = 75{,}129$

Mixed REVIEW

1. $17 - 5 + 3 = 12 + 3$
$= 15$

2. $x^2 - 2 = 7^2 - 2$
$= 49 - 2$
$= 47$

3. $4 + 8 \cdot 4 - 1 = 4 + 32 - 1$
$= 36 - 1$
$= 35$

4. $22 - 4^2 \div 2 = 22 - 16 \div 2$
$= 22 - 8$
$= 14$

5. $2x^3 + x = 2 \cdot 3^3 + 3$
$= 2 \cdot (27) + 3$
$= 54 + 3$
$= 57$

6. $16 + x^2 \div 4 = 17$
$16 + 2^2 \div 4 \stackrel{?}{=} 17$
$16 + 4 \div 4 \stackrel{?}{=} 17$
$16 + 1 \stackrel{?}{=} 17$
$17 = 17$

2 is a solution.

7. $x^2 - 4 = 5$
$3^2 - 4 \stackrel{?}{=} 5$
$9 - 4 \stackrel{?}{=} 5$
$5 = 5$

3 is a solution.

8. $2x - 9 = 13$
$2(11) - 9 \stackrel{?}{=} 13$
$22 - 9 \stackrel{?}{=} 13$
$13 = 13$

11 is a solution.

9. $x = 6$

10. $x = 1$

11. $2x - 3 < 15$
$2(9) - 3 \stackrel{?}{<} 15$
$18 - 3 \stackrel{?}{<} 15$
$15 \not< 15$

9 is not a solution.

12. $3 + 7x \geq 13$
$3 + 7(2) \stackrel{?}{\geq} 13$
$3 + 14 \stackrel{?}{\geq} 13$
$17 \geq 13$

2 is a solution.

13. $3x + 4 \leq 16$
$3(2) + 4 \stackrel{?}{\leq} 16$
$6 + 4 \stackrel{?}{\leq} 16$
$10 \leq 16$

2 is a solution.

$3x + 4 \leq 16$
$3(4) + 4 \stackrel{?}{\leq} 16$
$12 + 4 \stackrel{?}{\leq} 16$
$16 \leq 16$

4 is a solution.

$3x + 4 \leq 16$
$3(6) + 4 \stackrel{?}{\leq} 16$
$18 + 4 \stackrel{?}{\leq} 16$
$22 \not\leq 16$

6 is not a solution.

14. $3.8 + 18.2 \div 7 - 1.6 = 4.8$

15. $149.95(0.07) = \$10.50$ sales tax
$149.95 + 10.50 = \$160.45$ keyboard & sales tax

16. x = number of drink-boxes
y = number of submarine sandwiches
$0.25x + 0.40y$

1.7 A Problem-Solving Plan

Communicating about Algebra

A. Sales tax is too high. If the sales tax is 7%, the cologne would cost about $565.

B. Area is too big. This kitchen would be 27 feet by 27 feet.

C. Interest is too much. Interest would be less than 1% ($20) for a one month time period.

D. Time is too little. At a distance of about 3000 miles the plane would have to travel at 2000 miles per hour.

EXERCISES

1. [Profit per box] • [Boxes of greeting cards sold] = [Amount of money raised]

2. Profit per box = 1.50 (dollars per box)
Boxes of greeting cards sold = x (boxes)
Amount of money raised = 1800 (dollars)

3. $1.50x = 1800$

4. $x = 1200$

5. The club needs to sell 1200 greeting cards.

6. Multiply $1.50 by 1200.

7. $(15 - 3) + 8 = 12 + 8$
$= 20$ minutes

8. [Time to walk home] • [Your walking speed] = [Distance from home]

9. Time to walk home = t (hours)
Your walking speed = 4 (miles per hour)
Distance from home = 1 (miles)

10. $t \cdot 4 = 1$ or
$t \cdot \frac{1}{15} = 1$

11. $t = \frac{1}{4}$ hour or
$t = 15$ minutes

12. Walk, it takes less time.

13. $150

14. [Extra money needed] = [Number of contributors] • [Suggested contribution amount]

15. Extra money needed = 150 (dollars)
Number of contributors = y (people)
Suggested contribution amount = 0.75 (dollars per person)

16. $150 = y \cdot 0.75$

17. $y = 200$ people

18. 200 people must contribute $0.75.

19. 6 hours round trip

20. [Available driving hours] • [Speed of uncle's car] = [Distance to and from grandmother's house]

21. Available driving hours = 6 (hours)
Speed of uncle's car = 50 (miles per hour)
Round trip to grandmother's = x (miles)

22. $6 \cdot 50 = x$

23. $x = 300$ miles round trip

24. Yes. Round trip to your grandmother's house is 200 miles which is less than 300 miles.

25. [Number of weeks worked] $\cdot$ [Amount you save each week] = [Price of stereo with compact disk player]

26. Number of weeks worked = 12 (weeks)
Amount you save each week = m (dollars per week)
Price of stereo with compact disk player = 432 (dollars)

27. $12m = 432$

28. You would have to save $36 each week to be able to buy the stereo with the compact disk player.

29. The suspect would have 18 minutes to go from the robbery site to the gas station.

30. [Travel time] $\cdot$ [Rate of travel] = [Distance of robbery site to gas station]

31. Time to travel $= \frac{18}{60} = \frac{3}{10}$ (hours)
Rate of travel = x (miles per hour)
Distance of robbery site to gas station = 12 (miles)

32. $\frac{3}{10}x = 12$

33. $x = 40$ miles per hour

34. No, the suspect could have traveled by car at $\frac{2}{3}$ mile per minute or 40 miles per hour.

35. $412 + 613 + 510 + 620 + x \geq 2500$

$2155 + x \geq 2500$

Smallest value of $x = 345$.

36. $95 + x > \frac{1}{2}(95 + 120 + 45)$

$95 + x > \frac{1}{2}(260)$

$95 + x > 130$

Smallest value of x is 36.

37. You need 4 hours to reach your goal.

38. [Time to travel] $\cdot$ [Rate of travel] = [Distance]

39. Time to travel = 4 (hours)
Rate of travel = x (miles per hour)
Distance = 640 (miles)

40. $4x = 640$

41. $x = 160$ miles per hour

42. No, the chances of your maintaining an average of 160 mph for 4 hours are very slight.

The Problem-Solving Process: Developing Strategies

1. Make a table.

$(2l + 2w = 24)$

Width	Length	Area
0	12	0
1	11	11
2	10	20
3	9	27
4	8	32
5	7	35
6	6	36

The greatest area occurs when the rectangle is 6 cm by 6 cm.

2. Guess, check, and revise.

$3 + (3 \div 3) \cdot (3 + 3) \cdot 3 - 3 = 18$

3. Make a table.

Teams	128	64	32	16	8	4	2
Number of games	64	32	16	8	4	2	1

$64 + 32 + 16 + 8 + 4 + 2 + 1 = 127$ games

4. Draw a diagram.

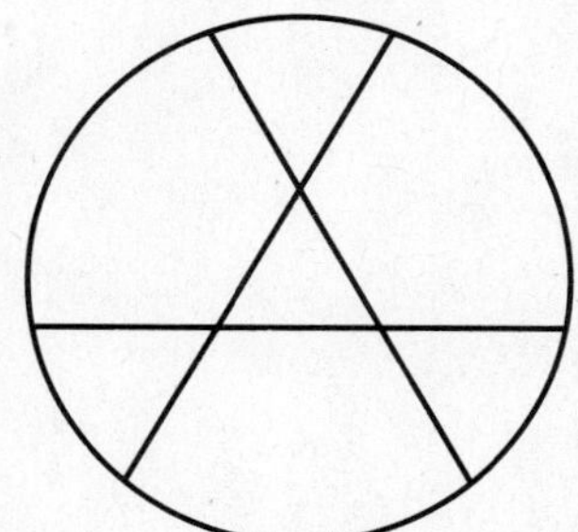

1.8 Exploring Data: Tables and Graphs

Communicating about Algebra

A. Resting: $\frac{350}{1.1} \approx 318$ minutes

Walking: $\frac{350}{5.5} \approx 64$ minutes

Swimming: $\frac{350}{10.9} \approx 32$ minutes

Running: $\frac{350}{14.7} \approx 24$ minutes

B. 1970: 23 million

1980: 32 million

1990: 42 million

C. Add the numbers. Divide the sum by 30.

Average: $\frac{110}{30} = \frac{11}{3} = 3\frac{2}{3}$

EXERCISES

1. Data means information, facts, or numbers that describe something.

2. Yes, by placing the numbers in a table, patterns or trends are more apparent.

3. A frequency distribution is a collection of possible numbers written in order, with tally marks used to count how many times each number occurs in the collection.

4. Yes, the frequency distribution tally mark count is equivalent to the height of the corresponding bar of the bar graph.

5. First way—list the place of the record down the left-hand column and list the events across the top.

Second way—list the events down the left-hand column and list the place of the record across the top.

6. No, they are equal in readability.

7. Compact disc sales surpassed cassette sales in 1992. The first bar graph is easier to use.

8. Compact disc sales increased. No. The first bar graph is easier to use.

9. The lower stacked bar graph shows the total sales for all three types of recordings.

10. Total sales were approximately the same in 1990 (740 million) and 1992 (746 million). The second bar graph is easier to use.

11. b. \$0.30,
since $1.89 \div 6 = 0.315$.

12. b. \$6.68,
since $3.59 + 1.89 + 3(0.40) = \$6.68$.

13.

Number	Tally	Frequency
0	|	1
1	|	1
2	||	2
3	||	2
4	||	2
5	||	2
6	|||	3
7	|||||	5
8	||	2
9	|	1
10	||	2
11	|	1
12	||	2
13	|	1
14		0
15	|	1
16		0
17	|	1
18	|	1

14.
$$\begin{aligned}\tfrac{1}{30}(0 \cdot 1 + 1 \cdot 1 + \cdots + 18 \cdot 1) &= \tfrac{1}{30}(0 + 1 + \cdots + 18)\\ &= \tfrac{1}{30}(225)\\ &= 7.5 \text{ hours}\end{aligned}$$

15. 12 hours should have two ×'s.
13 hours should have one ×.

16.

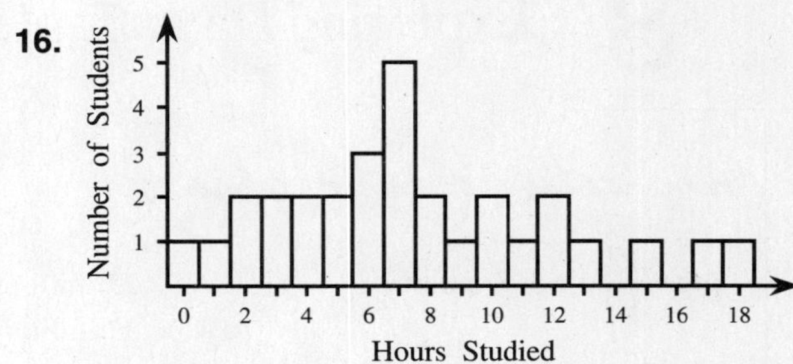

17. −23° C to −18° C

18. −18° C to −12° C

19. $2W + 2L = 120$

20.

Width (feet)	10	15	20	25	30	35	40	45	50
Length (feet)	50	45	40	35	30	25	20	15	10
Area (sq ft)	500	675	800	875	900	875	800	675	500

21. b. A rectangle whose width is equal to its length, (a square).
With a fixed length perimeter, the largest area results from a 30 feet by 30 feet square.

22.

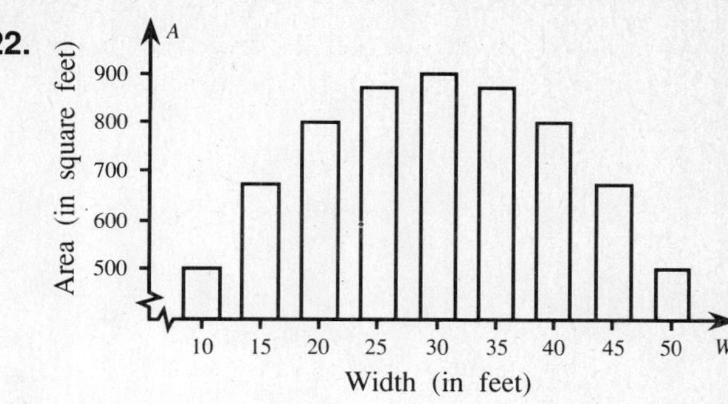

23. Bike riding and swimming

24. Approximately 45

Chapter REVIEW

1. $\frac{1}{8} = 0.125$

2. $\frac{2}{5} = 0.4 = 40\%$

3. $0.75 = \frac{75}{100} = \frac{3}{4}$

4. $0.33 = 33\%$

5. $10\% = 0.10$

6. $25\% = 0.25 = \frac{25}{100} = \frac{1}{4}$

7. $5 + \frac{3}{2} = \frac{10}{2} + \frac{3}{2} = \frac{13}{2}$

8. $9 \cdot 9 = 81$

9. $23 - 7 = 16$

10. $14 \div 4 = \frac{14}{4} = \frac{7}{2}$

11. $$\begin{aligned} 3 - [(4 \div 2) + 1] &= 3 - [2 + 1] \\ &= 3 - 3 \\ &= 0 \end{aligned}$$

12. $$\begin{aligned} 3(7) + [9 - (18 \div 6)] &= 21 + [9 - 3] \\ &= 21 + 6 \\ &= 27 \end{aligned}$$

13. $$\begin{aligned} [(4 + 16) \div 5] - 2 &= [20 \div 5] - 2 \\ &= 4 - 2 \\ &= 2 \end{aligned}$$

14. $$\begin{aligned} \frac{(3)(5)}{(8-7) \cdot 3} &= \frac{(3)(5)}{1 \cdot 3} \\ &= \frac{15}{3} \\ &= 5 \end{aligned}$$

15. 1.5125

16. 41.19

17. $$\begin{aligned} 2s - 3 &= 2 \cdot 14 - 3 \\ &= 28 - 3 \\ &= 25 \end{aligned}$$

18. $$\begin{aligned} (x + 4) \div 9 &= (23 + 4) \div 9 \\ &= 27 \div 9 \\ &= 3 \end{aligned}$$

19. $$\begin{aligned} 2x - 3y + 2 &= 2 \cdot 4 - 3 \cdot 1 + 2 \\ &= 8 - 3 + 2 \\ &= 5 + 2 \\ &= 7 \end{aligned}$$

20. $$\begin{aligned} (3x - 5)(y + 2) &= (3 \cdot 3 - 5)(2 + 2) \\ &= (9 - 5)(4) \\ &= (4)(4) \\ &= 16 \end{aligned}$$

21. $2.6 + (3.9 \div 1.5) = 5.2$

22. $3.7 \cdot 5.5 - 6.2 \cdot 1.9 = 8.57$

23. x^5

24. 9^7

25. $4 + 21 \div 3 - 3^2 = 4 + 21 \div 3 - 9$
$= 4 + 7 - 9$
$= 11 - 9$
$= 2$

26. $(12 - 7)^2 + 5 = 5^2 + 5$
$= 25 + 5$
$= 30$

27. $\frac{6 + 2^2}{17 - 6 \cdot 2} = \frac{6 + 4}{17 - 12}$
$= \frac{10}{5}$
$= 2$

28. $\frac{9 - 1 \cdot 7}{42} = \frac{9 - 7}{42}$
$= \frac{2}{42}$
$= \frac{1}{21}$

29. $12 - 2x^2 = 12 - 2 \cdot 2^2$
$= 12 - 2 \cdot 4$
$= 12 - 8$
$= 4$

30. $x^3 + x - 7 = 3^3 + 3 - 7$
$= 27 + 3 - 7$
$= 30 - 7$
$= 23$

31. $\frac{x - 3y}{6} = \frac{15 - 3 \cdot 2}{6}$
$= \frac{15 - 6}{6}$
$= \frac{9}{6}$
$= \frac{3}{2}$

32. $\frac{x^2}{y^2} + 4 = \frac{4^2}{2^2} + 4$
$= \frac{16}{4} + 4$
$= 4 + 4$
$= 8$

33. $x = 4$

34. $x = 8$

35. $x = 4$

36. $x = 0$

37. $x^2 - x + 2 = 44$
$7^2 - 7 + 2 \stackrel{?}{=} 44$
$49 - 7 + 2 \stackrel{?}{=} 44$
$42 + 2 \stackrel{?}{=} 44$
$44 = 44$
7 is a solution.

38. $2x - 3 = 2$
$2 \cdot 4 - 3 \stackrel{?}{=} 2$
$8 - 3 \stackrel{?}{=} 2$
$5 \neq 2$
4 is not a solution.

39. $9x - 3 > 24$
$9 \cdot 3 - 3 \stackrel{?}{>} 24$
$27 - 3 \stackrel{?}{>} 24$
$24 \not> 24$
3 is not a solution.

40. $13 + 2x \leq 25$
$13 + 2 \cdot 6 \stackrel{?}{\leq} 25$
$13 + 12 \stackrel{?}{\leq} 25$
$25 \leq 25$
6 is a solution.

41. 4 represents the amount of money saved each week.
x represents the number of weeks.
y represents the amount of extra money.
15.90 represents the cost of the compact disc.

42. 0.35 represents the cost of each bottle of juice.
a represents the number of bottles of juice.
b represents the amount of extra money.
65 represents the amount of money available to buy juice.

43. $x^2 + 6$

44. $\frac{1}{2}y - 9$

45. $x \div 2 > 7$

46. $9 + 6y \leq 20$

47. $x^3 - y = 60$

48. $m - 2n = 10$

49. $180x + 200y$

50. $0.02x + 3.50y$

51. One person was going to St. Ives.

52. $\frac{3}{180} = \frac{1}{60}$ hour or 1 minute

53. s^2
$s^2 = 9^2$
$= 81$ square inches

54. $2 \cdot (2w) + 2 \cdot (3w) = 4w + 6w = 10w$
$10w = 10 \cdot 4 = 40$ inches

55. $[(20)(25) - (19.5)(24)] + 1 = [500 - 468] + 1$
$= 32 + 1$
$= 33$

56. Approximately 11.5% were unemployed in 1986.

57. The unemployment rate was decreasing from 1986 to 1989.

58. $100(7\%) = 100(.07) = 7$ people

Chapter TEST

1. $2(x - 3) + x^2 \div 4 = 2(6 - 3) + 6^2 \div 4$
$= 2(3) + 36 \div 4$
$= 6 + 9$
$= 15$

2. $9(x - y^2) = 9(6 - 2^2)$
$= 9(6 - 4)$
$= 9(2)$
$= 18$

3. False
$(3 \cdot 4)^2 \stackrel{?}{=} 3 \cdot 4^2$
$12^2 \stackrel{?}{=} 3 \cdot 16$
$144 \neq 48$

4. False
$\frac{2}{6} \stackrel{?}{=} 3$
$\frac{1}{3} \neq 3$

5. False
$4 - 3 \stackrel{?}{=} 3 - 4$
$1 \neq -1$

6. True
$5 \div (3 - 1) + 1 \stackrel{?}{>} 5 - 3 \cdot 4 \div 6$
$5 \div 2 + 1 \stackrel{?}{>} 5 - 12 \div 6$
$\frac{5}{2} + 1 \stackrel{?}{>} 5 - 2$
$\frac{7}{2} > 3$

7. False
$0.10(27) \stackrel{?}{=} 0.27$
$2.70 \neq 0.27$

8. True
$14 - x^2 \leq 7$
$14 - 3^2 \stackrel{?}{\leq} 7$
$14 - 9 \stackrel{?}{\leq} 7$
$5 \leq 7$

9. $x = 3$

10. $x = 3$

11. $(13 + 7) \cdot 4 \div 2 = 40$
$20 \cdot 4 \div 2 = 40$
$80 \div 2 = 40$
$40 = 40$

12. $(2x + 2) \cdot (4 - 3) = 12$
$(2 \cdot 5 + 2) \cdot (4 - 3) = 12$
$(10 + 2) \cdot (4 - 3) = 12$
$12 \cdot 1 = 12$
$12 = 12$

13. $d = r \cdot t$
$= 35 \cdot 2\frac{1}{2}$
$= 35 \cdot \frac{5}{2}$
$= \frac{175}{2}$
$= 87.5$ miles
Yes, it is enough time.

14. $2x - (y^2 + 2)$

15. $V = \pi r^2 h$

$= \pi(\frac{16}{2})^2(10)$

$\approx 3.14(8)^2(10)$

$= 3.14(64)(10)$

$= 200.96(10)$

$= 2009.6$ cubic feet

16. $(1.2)(0.5)(20) = (0.6)(20)$

$= 12$ square yards

17. $90 + 90 + 90 + 90 = 180 + 90 + 90$

$= 270 + 90$

$= 360$ feet

18. $\frac{3920}{35} = 112$ students

19. **a.** Approximately 25 million

b. Cats and birds

Chapter 2

Rules of Algebra

2.1 The Real Number Line

Communicating about Algebra

A. False. Zero is an integer and is neither positive nor negative.

B. True. The absolute value is the distance between the origin and the point representing the real number. Distance is positive.

C. False. If a is negative, the expression $-a$ is positive.

D. True. Any negative number is less than a positive number.

E. True. If two numbers are not equal to each other, then one number must be larger than the other number.

EXERCISES

1. Five is less than six.
Five is to the left of six on the real number line.

2. $2 > -3$

3. False, true, true, true

4. -10

5. 6

6. -2

7. 4 is greater.

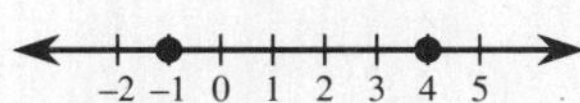

8. 3 is greater.

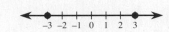

9. 2 is greater.

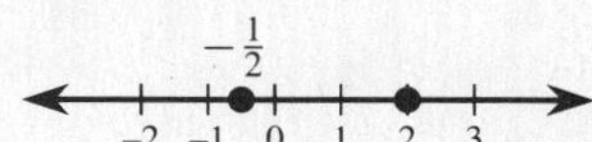

10. 2.5 is greater.

11. 4.5 is greater.

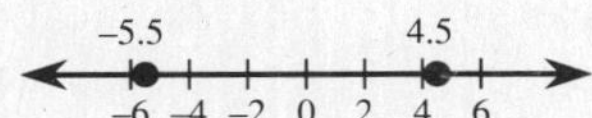

12. 2.1 is greater.

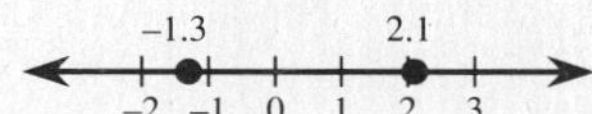

13. $\frac{3}{4}$ is greater.

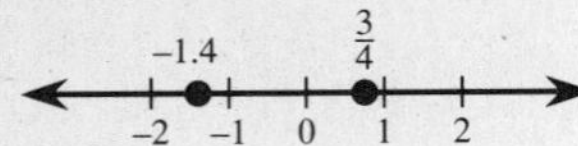

14. $-\frac{2}{3}$ is greater.

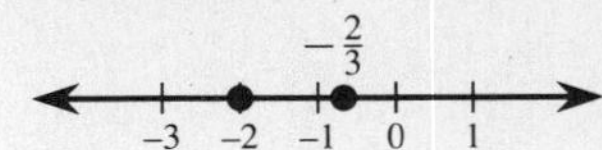

15. $-1.9,\ -\frac{1}{2},\ 0,\ \frac{1}{2},\ 3.1,\ 4$

16. $-4.6,\ -\frac{3}{4},\ -\frac{1}{2},\ \frac{1}{3},\ 1.5,\ 6$

17. -6

18. 10

19. 2.4

20. -1.9

21. 9

22. -3.6

23. 0

24. 1

25. 5

26. 3

27. $\frac{4}{5}$

28. $\frac{1}{2}$

29. 3.2

30. 4.1

31. 0

32. 16.3

33. Sun

34. Deneb and Beta Crucis

35. Libya and Ireland

36. Japan

37. Chile, Ireland, and Mexico

38. Libya, Israel, Kenya, Japan, Pakistan

39. $v = \dfrac{-240 \text{ feet}}{20 \text{ seconds}} = -12$ feet per second

$s = |v| = |-12| = 12$ feet per second

40. $s = \dfrac{4600 \text{ feet}}{8 \text{ minutes}} = 575$ feet per minute

41.
$$\begin{aligned} 4x + 3y &= 4(2) + 3(1) \\ &= 8 + 3 \\ &= 11 \end{aligned}$$

42.
$$\begin{aligned} 2a - b &= 2(6) - 3 \\ &= 12 - 3 \\ &= 9 \end{aligned}$$

43.
$$\begin{aligned} \tfrac{1}{4}x - y &= \tfrac{1}{4}(9) - 5 \\ &= \tfrac{9}{4} - \tfrac{20}{4} \\ &= -\tfrac{11}{4} \end{aligned}$$

44.
$$\begin{aligned} \tfrac{1}{2}a + 4b &= \left(\tfrac{1}{2}\right)(10) + (4)(3) \\ &= 5 + 12 \\ &= 17 \end{aligned}$$

45.
$$\begin{aligned} |-4| + |3| &= 4 + 3 \\ &= 7 \end{aligned}$$

46.
$$\begin{aligned} |6| - |-1| &= 6 - 1 \\ &= 5 \end{aligned}$$

47.
$$\begin{aligned} |x| + |y| &= |-3| + |-1| \\ &= 3 + 1 \\ &= 4 \end{aligned}$$

48.
$$\begin{aligned} |y| - |x| &= |-7| - |3| \\ &= 7 - 3 \\ &= 4 \end{aligned}$$

49. $a = 4$

50. $a = 9$

51. $x = 8$

52. $y = 8$

53. $x = 2$ or $x = -2$; Both values are two units from the origin.

54. $x = 0$; There is only one solution since the opposite of 0 is 0.

55. No solution; The absolute value of a number is always nonnegative.

56. Any real number; A number and its opposite are the same distance from the origin.

2.2 Addition of Real Numbers

Communicating about Algebra

A. $-4+3=-1$

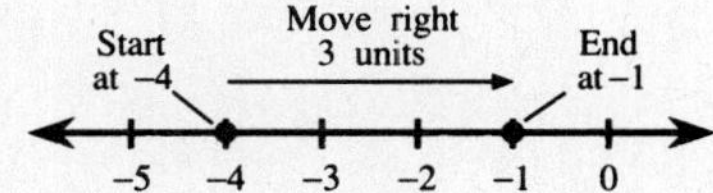

$3+(-4)=-1$

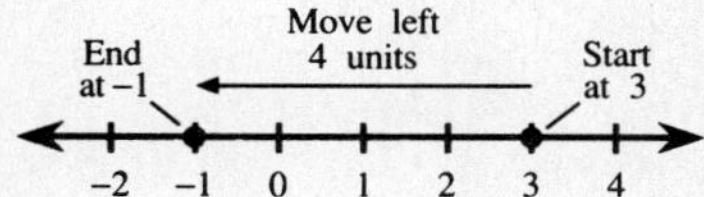

B. $-3+2+(-1)=-2$

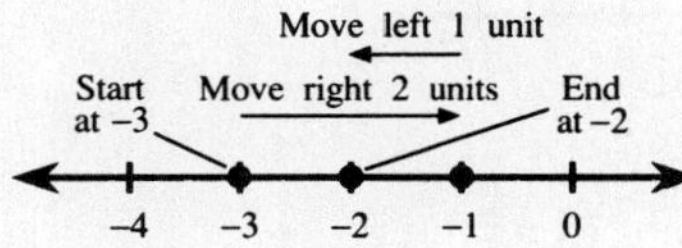

$-3+(-1)+2=-2$

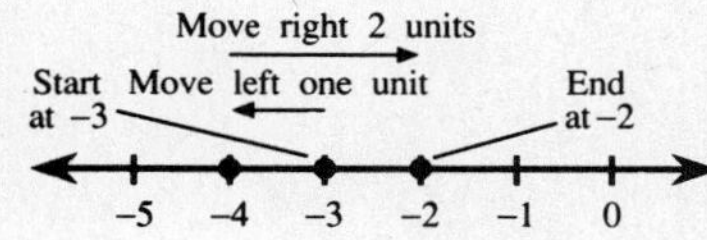

$-1+(-3)+2=-2$

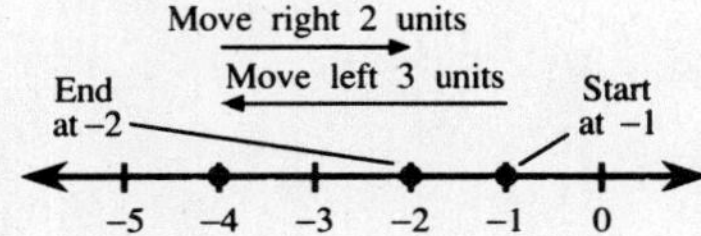

$-1+2+(-3)=-2$

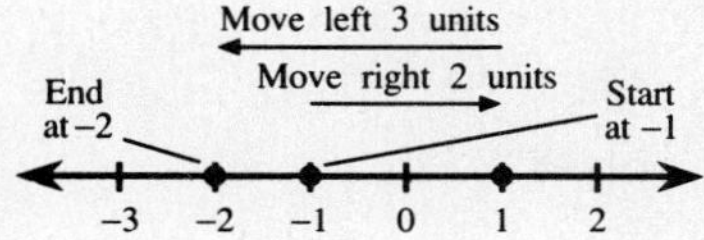

$2+(-3)+(-1)=-2$

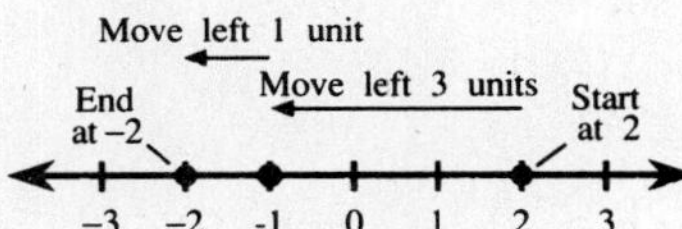

$2+(-1)+(-3)=-2$

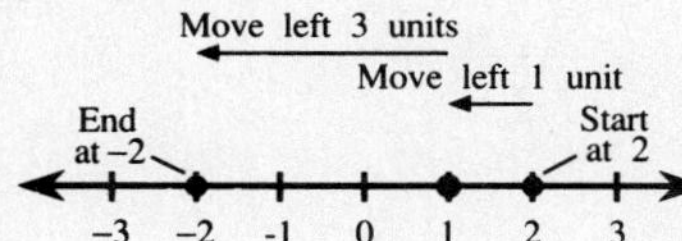

EXERCISES

1. False

2. True

3. No

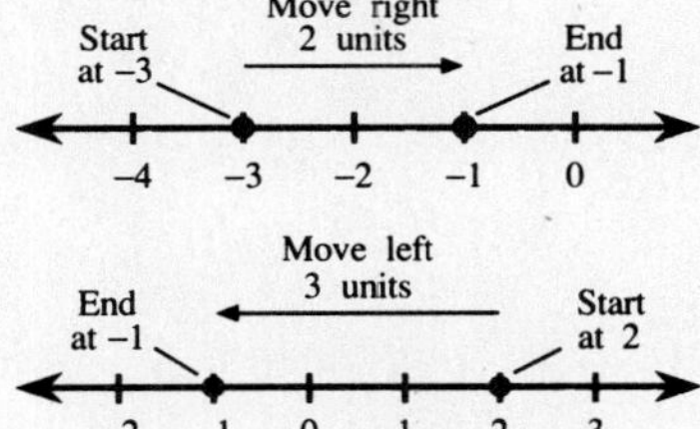

4. Any number added to zero is that same number.

5. 4

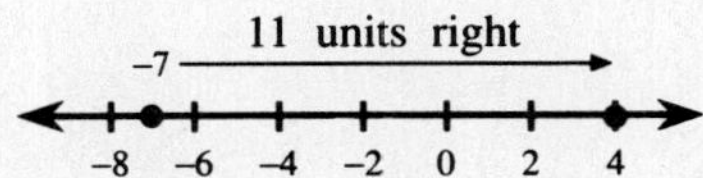

6. -1

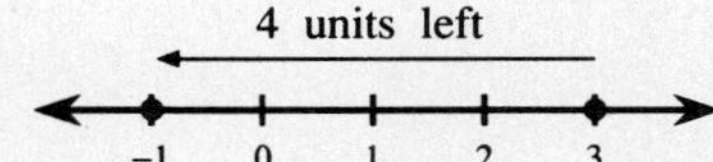

7. $\frac{1}{2}$

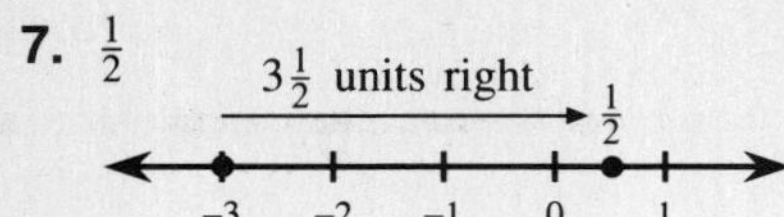

8. -10

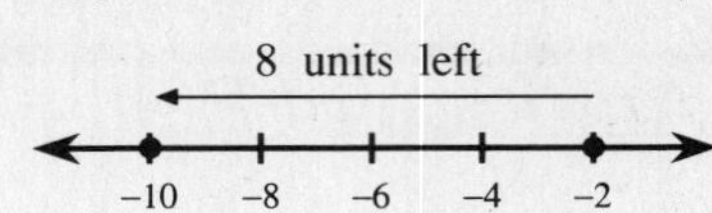

9. 1

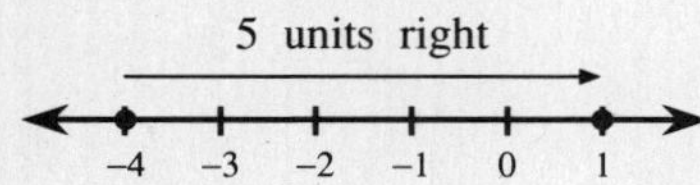

10. -1

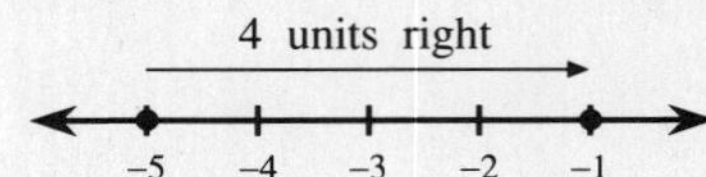

11. 1

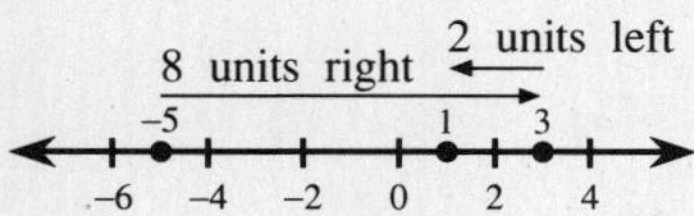

12. -6

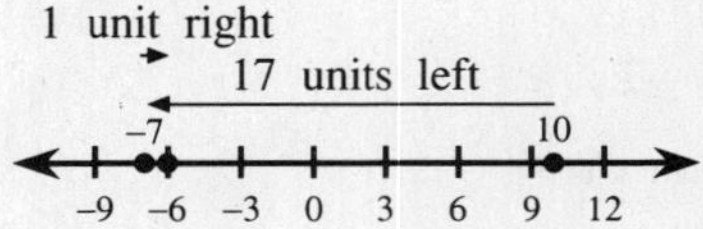

13. $-4 + 2 = -2$

14. $6 + 3 = 9$

15. $7 + 0 = 7$

16. $0 + (-6) = -6$

17. $-11 + (-4) = -15$

18. $12 + (-9) = 3$

19. $5 + (-10) + (-3) = (-5) + (-3)$
$= -8$

20. $-2 + 11 + (-7) = 9 + (-7)$
$= 2$

21. $-(8 + 5) = -(13)$
$= -13$
$-(8 + 5) = (-8) + (-5)$
$= -13$

22. $-[-(4 + 3)] = +(4 + 3)$
$= 7$
$-[-(4 + 3)] = -[-7]$
$= 7$

23. $-[12 + (-6)] = -[6]$
$= -6$
$-[12 + (-6)] = -12 + 6$
$= -6$

24. $-[1 - (-3)] = -1 + (-3)$
$= -4$
$-[1 - (-3)] = -[1 + 3]$
$= -4$

25. -7.2

26. 1.7

27. 3.1

28. -5.8

29. $3 + x + (-8) = x + 3 + (-8)$
$= x - 5$

30. $2x + 8 + (-8) = 2x$

31. $-6 + x + 2 = x + (-6) + 2$
$= x - 4$

32. $3 + (-2) + p + 19 = 3 + (-2) + 19 + p$
$= 1 + 19 + p$
$= 20 + p$

33. $37 + (-15) = 22$ yards

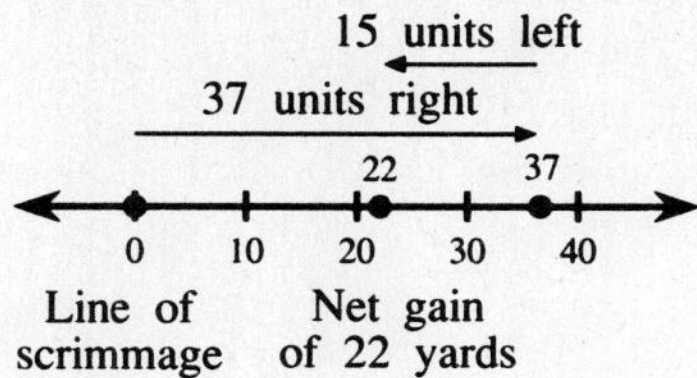

34. Your team won because it gained enough yardage to make it to the goal line and score a touchdown.

6 units right
2 units right
4 units left
8 units right
0 2 4 6 8 10 12
Line of scrimmage
Net gain of 12 yards

35.
$-10 + 11 = +1$ Ion
$-11 + 11 = 0$ Atom
$-9 + 9 = 0$ Atom
$-10 + 9 = -1$ Ion

36.
Na: 2nd
Na^{+1}: 1st
F^{-1}: 4th

37. $3412.53 + 5784.25 + (-9013.86) = 182.92$

The result is positive so the company made a profit.

38. $-5519.80 + 2337.06 + 3615.11 = 432.37$

The result is positive so the company made a profit.

39. $2{:}00 + 3$ hours $= 5{:}00$ P.M.

40. $(7 + 3) + 6\frac{3}{4} + 2(1\frac{1}{2}) - 12 = 7{:}45$ P.M.

41. 16

42. 0

43. 7

44. 11

45.
$$\begin{aligned} a^2 - 5 &= 3^2 - 5 \\ &= 9 - 5 \\ &= 4 \end{aligned}$$

46.
$$\begin{aligned} 3x^3 - 9 &= 3(2)^3 - 9 \\ &= 3(8) - 9 \\ &= 24 - 9 \\ &= 15 \end{aligned}$$

47.
$$\begin{aligned} (6s - t)^2 &= (6 \cdot 3 - 9)^2 \\ &= (18 - 9)^2 \\ &= 9^2 \\ &= 81 \end{aligned}$$

48.
$$\begin{aligned} 17 - (3m + 1)^2 &= 17 - (3 \cdot 1 + 1)^2 \\ &= 17 - (3 + 1)^2 \\ &= 17 - 4^2 \\ &= 17 - 16 \\ &= 1 \end{aligned}$$

49. $x = 3$

50. $x = 3$

51. **a.** $x + 3.8 = 5$, **c.** $5 - 3.8 = x$, and **d.** $5 - x = 3.8$

You need 1.2 kilograms.

52. Both equations correctly describe the relationship.

a. The sum of the 5 smaller areas equals the total area.

b. The total area minus the sum of the known smaller areas equal the unknown smaller area.

$$\begin{aligned} (26)(30) - (192 + 140 + 100 + 12) &= x \\ 780 - 552 &= x \\ x &= 228 \text{ square feet} \end{aligned}$$

53.

Round	You	Sister
1st	+8	+6
2nd	+3	+4
3rd	?	+3
Total	11+?	13

No. A hole in one (par 2 for the round) will give you the win for the 3rd round and a tie overall. A score of 2 (par 3 for the round) will tie you for the round while your sister wins overall. Otherwise, your sister wins the round and overall.

54. $x = -9$

55. $x = 45$

56. $x = -41$

57. a. $[16(0.30) - 2]x + [60(0.15) - 5]x \geq 29.95$

$$2.8x + 4x \geq 29.95$$
$$6.8x \geq 29.95$$
$$x \geq 4.4$$

Since $x \geq 4.4$, the smallest integer value is 5.

Mixed REVIEW

1. $2y + 14 = 2 \cdot 5 + 14$
$= 10 + 14$
$= 24$

2. $(4 \div 2) + 3(8 - 7) = 2 + (3)(1)$
$= 2 + 3$
$= 5$

3. $\frac{3}{8} = 0.375$
$= 37.5\%$

4. $-\frac{1}{2}$

5. s^5

6. $2r^2 + 5y^3 = 2 \cdot (4)^2 + 5 \cdot (2)^3$
$= 2 \cdot 16 + 5 \cdot 8$
$= 32 + 40$
$= 72$

7. $t = 3$, using guess and check.

$3^3 - 4 = 27 - 4$
$= 23$

8. $|-4.3| = 4.3$

9. $x \div 4 + 3 \geq 5$
$8 \div 4 + 3 \overset{?}{\geq} 5$
$2 + 3 \overset{?}{\geq} 5$
$5 \geq 5$

8 is a solution.

10. $6y = 20 + 2y$
$6 \cdot 5 \overset{?}{=} 20 + 2 \cdot 5$
$30 \overset{?}{=} 20 + 10$
$30 = 30$

5 is a solution.

11. $8 \cdot 3 = 24$

12. $3 \div 4 = \frac{3}{4}$

13. 43.56

14. 8

15. −8, −5, −2, 0, 1, 3, 4

16. $\pi r^2 = \pi(6)^2$
$\approx 3.14 \cdot 36$
$= 113.04$ square centimeters

17. $x^3 = 5^3$
$= 125$ cubic inches

18. $3n - 8 < 20$

2.3 Subtraction of Real Numbers

Communicating about Algebra

A. Equivalent

B. Not equivalent for any number but 0.

C. Not equivalent for any number.

EXERCISES

1. True

2. True

3. First term: $-x$
Second term: -3

4. Yes; $4 - 3 = 1$,
$3 - 4 = -1$

5. $-3 - (-2) - (-1) = -3 + 2 + 1$
$= 0$

6. Yes; $-(6 - 3) = -(3) = -3$,
$-6 + 3 = -3$

7. $3 - 8 = -5$

8. $12 - 8 = 4$

9. $7 - 4 = 3$

10. $4 - 7 = -3$

11. $\frac{6}{2} - \frac{3}{2} = \frac{3}{2}$

12. $\frac{2}{3} - \frac{12}{3} = -\frac{10}{3}$

13. $-1 - 5 = -6$

14. $-9 - 6 = -15$

15. $8 - |-6| = 8 - 6$
$= 2$

16. $12 - |-7| = 12 - 7$
$= 5$

17. $-6 - |4| = -6 - 4$
$= -10$

18. $-3 - |5| = -3 - 5$
$= -8$

19. $|10| - 6.5 = 10 - 6.5$
$= 3.5$

20. $|15| - 2.4 = 15 - 2.4$
$= 12.6$

21. $\left|-\frac{3}{4}\right| - \frac{7}{4} = \frac{3}{4} - \frac{7}{4}$
$= -\frac{4}{4} = -1$

22. $\left|-\frac{7}{4}\right| - \frac{3}{4} = \frac{7}{4} - \frac{3}{4}$
$= \frac{4}{4}$
$= 1$

23. $2 - (-6) - 7 = 2 + 6 - 7$
$= 8 - 7$
$= 1$

24. $3 + (-4) - 2 = -1 - 2$
$= -3$

25. $-6 + 5 - 4 = -1 - 4$
$= -5$

26. $-11 - (-12) + 1 = -11 + 12 + 1$
$= 1 + 1$
$= 2$

27. $5 - 3 + 12 - 9 = 2 + 12 - 9$
$= 14 - 9$
$= 5$

28. $10 - 4 - 9 + 2 = 6 - 9 + 2$
$= -3 + 2$
$= -1$

29. 5.7

30. 1.8

31. 1.04

32. 2.27

33. 6.8

34. -13.1

35. $4 - (1 + x) = 4 - (1 + 2)$
$= 4 - 3$
$= 1$

$4 - (1 + x) = 4 - 1 - x$
$= 3 - x$
$= 3 - 2$
$= 1$

36. $2 - (4 - t) = 2 - (4 - 1)$
$= 2 - 3$
$= -1$

$2 - (4 - t) = 2 - 4 + t$
$= -2 + t$
$= -2 + 1 = -1$

37. $15 - (-x) + 7 = 15 - [-(-6)] + 7$
$= 15 - 6 + 7$
$= 9 + 7$
$= 16$

$15 - (-x) + 7 = 15 + x + 7$
$= x + 22$
$= -6 + 22$
$= 16$

38. $12 - (-x) - 5 = 12 - [-(-2)] - 5$
$= 12 - 2 - 5$
$= 10 - 5$
$= 5$

$12 - (-x) - 5 = 12 + x - 5$
$= 7 + x$
$= 7 + (-2)$
$= 5$

39. $-9 - (-13) - p = -9 - (-13) - (-7)$
$= -9 + 13 + 7$
$= 4 + 7$
$= 11$

$-9 - (-13) - p = -9 + 13 - p$
$= 4 - p$
$= 4 - (-7)$
$= 11$

40. $-8 - (-5) - r = -8 - (-5) - (-3)$
$= -8 + 5 + 3$
$= -3 + 3$
$= 0$

$-8 - (-5) - r = -8 + 5 - r$
$= -3 - r$
$= -3 - (-3)$
$= -3 + 3$
$= 0$

41. $-x - (3 - 8) + 4 = -10 - (3 - 8) + 4$
$= -10 - (-5) + 4$
$= -10 + 5 + 4$
$= -5 + 4$
$= -1$

$-x - (3 - 8) + 4 = -x - (-5) + 4$
$= -x + 5 + 4$
$= -x + 9$
$= -10 + 9$
$= -1$

42. $-x-(7+6)+2 = -9-(7+6)+2$
$= -9-13+2$
$= -22+2$
$= -20$

$-x-(7+6)+2 = -x-13+2$
$= -x-11$
$= -9-11$
$= -20$

43. Money received: $200+300 = \$500$
Money spent: $4(115)+8(40) = 460+320 = \$780$
Net: $500-780 = -\$280$

You lost money on this trip around the board since you spent more money than you received.

44. (Peak of hill) − (Foot of hill) = $515-325 = 190$ feet
The hill is 190 feet high.
From A to B: $275-300 = -25$ feet
From B to C: $325-275 = 50$ feet
From C to D: $515-325 = 190$ feet
From D to E: $440-515 = -75$ feet
From E to F: $210-440 = -230$ feet
$-25+50+190+(-75)+(-230) = -90$ feet net change

45.

Month	J	F	M	A	M	J	J	A	S	O	N	D
Change in percentage	−2%	−1%	3%	−2%	7%	1%	0%	−3%	1%	5%	−7%	−2%

46. $-2-1+3-2+7+1 = 6\%$
$0-3+1+5-7-2 = -6\%$
$6-6 = 0\%$

47. $-5,\ -3,\ -2\frac{1}{2},\ -1.25,\ 1,\ 2\frac{1}{2},\ 4.3$

48. $-2\frac{1}{2}$ -1.25 $2\frac{1}{2}$ 4.3
−5 −4 −3 −2 −1 0 1 2 3 4 5

49. $-2\frac{1}{2},\ -1.25,\ 1,\ 2\frac{1}{2}$

50. $-5,\ 4.3$

51. $6+(1-3) = 6+(-2)$
$= 4$

52. $-5+11 = 6$

53. $-12+4 = -8$

54. $8+(-2) = 6$

55. $x = 18$

56. $x = -15$

57. $x = 24$

58. $x = -3$

59. $-x+(-x) = -2x$
$-x+(-x)+(-x) = -3x$

60. $-x+(-2x) = -3x$
$-2x+(-3x)+(-4x) = -9x$

61. $4+(-x)+(-2x) = 4+(-3x)$
$= 4-3x$

62. $3-[-x+(-x)] = 3-(-2x)$
$= 3+2x$

63. Each quarter rest gets 1 beat.
The half note gets 2 beats.
$1 + 2 + 1 = 4$ beats

64. Each eighth rest gets $\frac{1}{2}$ beat.
Each eighth note gets $\frac{1}{2}$ beat.
$\frac{1}{2} + \frac{1}{2} + \frac{1}{2} + \frac{1}{2} + \frac{1}{2} + \frac{1}{2} + \frac{1}{2} + \frac{1}{2} = \frac{8}{2} = 4$ beats

65. 1st measure: The half note gets 2 beats.
The quarter note gets one beat.
$2 + 1 = 3$ beats
2nd measure: Each quarter note gets 1 beat.
The dotted eighth note gets $\frac{3}{4}$ beat.
The sixteenth note gets $\frac{1}{4}$ beat.
$1 + 1 + \frac{3}{4} + \frac{1}{4} = 3$ beats

66. The dotted eighth note gets $\frac{3}{4}$ beat.
The sixteenth note gets $\frac{1}{4}$ beat.
Each quarter note gets 1 beat.
$\frac{3}{4} + \frac{1}{4} + 1 + 1 = 3$ beats

2.4 Exploring Data: Matrices

Communicating about Algebra

$$\begin{bmatrix} 16 & 3 & 2 & 13 \\ 5 & 10 & 11 & 8 \\ 9 & 6 & 7 & 12 \\ 4 & 15 & 14 & 1 \end{bmatrix}$$

Each number from 1 to 16 is used once. Each row, column, and diagonal add up to 34.

EXERCISES

1. 3 rows
2 columns

2. -3

3. $a = 1$ $\quad b = 3$
$c = -1$ $\quad d = 0$

4. $$\begin{bmatrix} -1 & 0 & -4 \\ 2 & -3 & 0 \end{bmatrix} + \begin{bmatrix} 3 & -2 & 0 \\ -2 & 1 & -4 \end{bmatrix} = \begin{bmatrix} 2 & -2 & -4 \\ 0 & -2 & -4 \end{bmatrix}$$
$$\begin{bmatrix} -1 & 0 & -4 \\ 2 & -3 & 0 \end{bmatrix} - \begin{bmatrix} 3 & -2 & 0 \\ -2 & 1 & -4 \end{bmatrix} = \begin{bmatrix} -4 & 2 & -4 \\ 4 & -4 & 4 \end{bmatrix}$$

5. Can be added

6. Cannot be added

7. Cannot be added

8. Can be added

9. $$\begin{bmatrix} 4 & -1 \\ 6 & 0 \end{bmatrix} + \begin{bmatrix} 4 & -3 \\ -7 & 2 \end{bmatrix} = \begin{bmatrix} 4+4 & -1+(-3) \\ 6+(-7) & 0+2 \end{bmatrix} = \begin{bmatrix} 8 & -4 \\ -1 & 2 \end{bmatrix}$$

10. $$\begin{bmatrix} 6 & -3 \\ -4 & -2 \end{bmatrix} + \begin{bmatrix} -5 & 3 \\ 4 & 3 \end{bmatrix} = \begin{bmatrix} 6+(-5) & -3+3 \\ -4+4 & -2+3 \end{bmatrix} = \begin{bmatrix} 1 & 0 \\ 0 & 1 \end{bmatrix}$$

11. $$\begin{bmatrix} 2 & 1 & -2 \\ 3 & 0 & 3 \end{bmatrix} + \begin{bmatrix} 1 & -3 & 4 \\ 2 & 5 & -5 \end{bmatrix} = \begin{bmatrix} 2+1 & 1+(-3) & -2+4 \\ 3+2 & 0+5 & 3+(-5) \end{bmatrix} = \begin{bmatrix} 3 & -2 & 2 \\ 5 & 5 & -2 \end{bmatrix}$$

12. $$\begin{bmatrix} 2 & 9 & -3 \\ 1 & 8 & -2 \\ -4 & 1 & 0 \end{bmatrix} + \begin{bmatrix} -1 & -6 & 4 \\ -1 & 2 & 6 \\ 2 & -4 & 2 \end{bmatrix} = \begin{bmatrix} 2+(-1) & 9+(-6) & -3+4 \\ 1+(-1) & 8+2 & -2+6 \\ -4+2 & 1+(-4) & 0+2 \end{bmatrix} = \begin{bmatrix} 1 & 3 & 1 \\ 0 & 10 & 4 \\ -2 & -3 & 2 \end{bmatrix}$$

13. $\begin{bmatrix} -1.3 & 2.4 & -6.9 \\ 15.8 & 0 & -3.4 \end{bmatrix} + \begin{bmatrix} 2.6 & 2.3 & -6.9 \\ 1.7 & 3.2 & -5.8 \end{bmatrix} = \begin{bmatrix} -1.3+2.6 & 2.4+2.3 & -6.9+(-6.9) \\ 15.8+1.7 & 0+3.2 & -3.4+(-5.8) \end{bmatrix}$

$= \begin{bmatrix} 1.3 & 4.7 & -13.8 \\ 17.5 & 3.2 & -9.2 \end{bmatrix}$

14. $\begin{bmatrix} 6.1 & -1.7 \\ -1.3 & 4.4 \\ 3.2 & -5.9 \end{bmatrix} + \begin{bmatrix} 1.5 & 9.1 \\ -6.4 & 4.9 \\ 5.4 & -3.3 \end{bmatrix} = \begin{bmatrix} 6.1+1.5 & -1.7+9.1 \\ -1.3+(-6.4) & 4.4+4.9 \\ 3.2+5.4 & -5.9+(-3.3) \end{bmatrix} = \begin{bmatrix} 7.6 & 7.4 \\ -7.7 & 9.3 \\ 8.6 & -9.2 \end{bmatrix}$

15. $\begin{bmatrix} 9 & -4 \\ 2 & -4 \end{bmatrix} - \begin{bmatrix} 6 & 6 \\ -2 & -4 \end{bmatrix} = \begin{bmatrix} 9-6 & -4-6 \\ 2-(-2) & -4-(-4) \end{bmatrix} = \begin{bmatrix} 3 & -10 \\ 4 & 0 \end{bmatrix}$

16. $\begin{bmatrix} 6 & 4 \\ 10 & -5 \end{bmatrix} - \begin{bmatrix} 7 & 1 \\ -1 & -6 \end{bmatrix} = \begin{bmatrix} 6-7 & 4-1 \\ 10-(-1) & -5-(-6) \end{bmatrix} = \begin{bmatrix} -1 & 3 \\ 11 & 1 \end{bmatrix}$

17. $\begin{bmatrix} -3 & 1 \\ 0 & -9 \\ 1 & 7 \end{bmatrix} - \begin{bmatrix} 6 & 4 \\ -5 & 8 \\ -1 & 4 \end{bmatrix} = \begin{bmatrix} -3-6 & 1-4 \\ 0-(-5) & -9-8 \\ 1-(-1) & 7-4 \end{bmatrix} = \begin{bmatrix} -9 & -3 \\ 5 & -17 \\ 2 & 3 \end{bmatrix}$

18. $\begin{bmatrix} -5 & 12 & -1 \\ -10 & 4 & 0 \end{bmatrix} - \begin{bmatrix} -3 & 0 & 1 \\ 9 & 2 & -2 \end{bmatrix} = \begin{bmatrix} -5-(-3) & 12-0 & -1-1 \\ -10-9 & 4-2 & 0-(-2) \end{bmatrix} = \begin{bmatrix} -2 & 12 & -2 \\ -19 & 2 & 2 \end{bmatrix}$

19. $2a = 10$ $\quad 3b = 9$ $\quad c - 4 = 16$

$a = 5$ $\quad b = 3$ $\quad c = 20$ $\quad d = -4$

20. $b + 1 = 9$ $\quad 4c = 12$ $\quad d - 1 = 16$

$a = 4$ $\quad b = 8$ $\quad c = 3$ $\quad d = 17$

21.

	New releases	Regular selections
Comedy	25	215
Drama	30	350
Horror	25	180

25 newly released comedy videos

22.

	Sale price titles	Regular price titles
Tapes	45	3000
Compact disks	20	2500

20 compact disk titles on sale

23. Yes. The sum of the wins and losses/ties is 16 for each team each year.

$$\begin{bmatrix} 10 & 14 & 10 & 13 \\ 3 & 6 & 5 & 4 \\ 10 & 6 & 6 & 7 \\ 11 & 12 & 8 & 7 \end{bmatrix} + \begin{bmatrix} 6 & 2 & 6 & 3 \\ 13 & 10 & 11 & 12 \\ 6 & 10 & 10 & 9 \\ 5 & 4 & 8 & 9 \end{bmatrix} = \begin{bmatrix} 10+6 & 14+2 & 10+6 & 13+3 \\ 3+13 & 6+10 & 5+11 & 4+12 \\ 10+6 & 6+10 & 6+10 & 7+9 \\ 11+5 & 12+4 & 8+8 & 7+9 \end{bmatrix}$$

$$= \begin{bmatrix} 16 & 16 & 16 & 16 \\ 16 & 16 & 16 & 16 \\ 16 & 16 & 16 & 16 \\ 16 & 16 & 16 & 16 \end{bmatrix}$$

24.

RAISES	0-1 yr	2-3 yr	4 + yr
Grade Level 4	0.50	0.50	0.50
Grade Level 5	0.75	0.75	0.75
Grade Level 6	1.00	1.00	1.00

$$\begin{bmatrix} 8.00 & 9.00 & 9.50 \\ 10.00 & 10.50 & 11.00 \\ 11.50 & 12.00 & 12.50 \end{bmatrix} + \begin{bmatrix} 0.50 & 0.50 & 0.50 \\ 0.75 & 0.75 & 0.75 \\ 1.00 & 1.00 & 1.00 \end{bmatrix} = \begin{bmatrix} 8.00+0.50 & 9.00+0.50 & 9.50+0.50 \\ 10.00+0.75 & 10.50+0.75 & 11.00+0.75 \\ 11.50+1.00 & 12.00+1.00 & 12.50+1.00 \end{bmatrix}$$

$$= \begin{bmatrix} 8.50 & 9.50 & 10.00 \\ 10.75 & 11.25 & 11.75 \\ 12.50 & 13.00 & 13.50 \end{bmatrix}$$

25. $\begin{bmatrix} 33 & 15 \\ 38 & 30 \\ 65 & 18 \end{bmatrix} + \begin{bmatrix} 39 & 18 \\ 29 & 23 \\ 78 & 21 \end{bmatrix} = \begin{bmatrix} 33+39 & 15+18 \\ 38+29 & 30+23 \\ 65+78 & 18+21 \end{bmatrix} = \begin{bmatrix} 72 & 33 \\ 67 & 53 \\ 143 & 39 \end{bmatrix}$

Burrito profit: $72 - 33 = \$39$

Taco profit: $67 - 53 = \$14$

Cheeseburger profit: $143 - 39 = \$104$

Total profit: $39 + 14 + 104 = \$157$

26. No, you did not raise enough money.

27. $\begin{bmatrix} 2 & -1 \\ 3 & 6 \end{bmatrix} + \begin{bmatrix} 6 & 10 \\ -1 & -6 \end{bmatrix} = \begin{bmatrix} 2+6 & -1+10 \\ 3+(-1) & 6+(-6) \end{bmatrix} = \begin{bmatrix} 8 & 9 \\ 2 & 0 \end{bmatrix}$

28. $\begin{bmatrix} -4 & 5 \\ 6 & 2 \end{bmatrix} - \begin{bmatrix} 3 & -1 \\ -5 & 6 \end{bmatrix} = \begin{bmatrix} -4-3 & 5-(-1) \\ 6-(-5) & 2-6 \end{bmatrix} = \begin{bmatrix} -7 & 6 \\ 11 & -4 \end{bmatrix}$

29. $\frac{1}{2}x + 1 = \frac{1}{2} \cdot \frac{1}{2} + 1$
$= \frac{1}{4} + 1$
$= 1\frac{1}{4}$

30. $6x - 1 = 6 \cdot \frac{1}{3} - 1$
$= \frac{6}{3} - 1$
$= 2 - 1$
$= 1$

31. $x = 27$

32. $x = 9$

33.

INCOMES ($)	May	June
Store 1	98,000	81,500
Store 2	61,800	72,900

34.

PROFITS ($)	May	June
Store 1	16,500	10,500
Store 2	9,600	10,600

35. $\begin{bmatrix} 98{,}000 & 81{,}500 \\ 61{,}800 & 72{,}900 \end{bmatrix} - \begin{bmatrix} 16{,}500 & 10{,}500 \\ 9{,}600 & 10{,}600 \end{bmatrix} = \begin{bmatrix} 98{,}000 - 16{,}500 & 81{,}500 - 10{,}500 \\ 61{,}800 - 9{,}600 & 72{,}900 - 10{,}600 \end{bmatrix} = \begin{bmatrix} 81{,}500 & 71{,}000 \\ 52{,}200 & 62{,}300 \end{bmatrix}$

EXPENSES ($)	May	June
Store 1	81,500	71,000
Store 2	52,200	62,300

36. $52,200 in May
$62,300 in June
$52{,}200 + 62{,}300 = \$114{,}500$ in May and June

Programming a Calculator

1. $\begin{bmatrix} 1 & 2 & 5 \\ -2 & 0 & -3 \end{bmatrix} + \begin{bmatrix} 0 & -4 & -2 \\ 2 & 0 & 3 \end{bmatrix} = \begin{bmatrix} 1+0 & 2+(-4) & 5+(-2) \\ -2+2 & 0+0 & -3+3 \end{bmatrix} = \begin{bmatrix} 1 & -2 & 3 \\ 0 & 0 & 0 \end{bmatrix}$

$\begin{bmatrix} 1 & 2 & 5 \\ -2 & 0 & -3 \end{bmatrix} - \begin{bmatrix} 0 & -4 & -2 \\ 2 & 0 & 3 \end{bmatrix} = \begin{bmatrix} 1-0 & 2-(-4) & 5-(-2) \\ -2-2 & 0-0 & -3-3 \end{bmatrix} = \begin{bmatrix} 1 & 6 & 7 \\ -4 & 0 & -6 \end{bmatrix}$

2. $\begin{bmatrix} -3 & 4 & 2 \\ 6 & 1 & -4 \\ 0 & -2 & -5 \end{bmatrix} + \begin{bmatrix} 2 & 0 & -1 \\ -4 & 5 & 0 \\ 0 & -3 & 9 \end{bmatrix} = \begin{bmatrix} -3+2 & 4+0 & 2+(-1) \\ 6+(-4) & 1+5 & -4+0 \\ 0+0 & -2+(-3) & -5+9 \end{bmatrix} = \begin{bmatrix} -1 & 4 & 1 \\ 2 & 6 & -4 \\ 0 & -5 & 4 \end{bmatrix}$

$\begin{bmatrix} -3 & 4 & 2 \\ 6 & 1 & -4 \\ 0 & -2 & -5 \end{bmatrix} - \begin{bmatrix} 2 & 0 & -1 \\ -4 & 5 & 0 \\ 0 & -3 & 9 \end{bmatrix} = \begin{bmatrix} -3-2 & 4-0 & 2-(-1) \\ 6-(-4) & 1-5 & -4-0 \\ 0-0 & -2-(-3) & -5-9 \end{bmatrix} = \begin{bmatrix} -5 & 4 & 3 \\ 10 & -4 & -4 \\ 0 & 1 & -14 \end{bmatrix}$

Mid-Chapter SELF-TEST

1. -4

2. $-\frac{1}{2}$

3. 6

4. $-\frac{3}{2}$

5. 4

6. $-3\frac{1}{3}$

7. $7 + (-5) = 2$

8. $-6 + 2 = -4$

9. $-\frac{1}{2} + \frac{3}{2} + \left(-\frac{3}{4}\right) = 1 + \left(-\frac{3}{4}\right)$
$= \frac{1}{4}$

10. $9 + 7 + (-6.5) + 1.1 = 16 + (-6.5) + 1.1$
$= 9.5 + 1.1$
$= 10.6$

11. 3.4

12. -7.7

13. 5.4

14. 0

15. $2 - (x - 3) = 2 - x + 3$
$= 5 - x$
$= 5 - 4$
$= 1$

16. $3 - (-x) - \left(-\frac{1}{2}\right) = 3 + x + \frac{1}{2}$
$= 3\frac{1}{2} + x$
$= 3\frac{1}{2} + 1$
$= 4\frac{1}{2}$

17. $-[y + (-6)] - (y + 4) = -y + 6 - y - 4$
$= -2y + 2$
$= -2(-1) + 2$
$= 2 + 2$
$= 4$

18. $|r| - (r + 3) = |r| - r - 3$
$= |-5| - (-5) - 3$
$= 5 + 5 - 3$
$= 10 - 3$
$= 7$

19. $s + (7 - s) - 4 = s + 7 - s - 4$
$= 3$

20. $s + \left|-\frac{3}{2}\right| - (8 - s) = s + \frac{3}{2} - 8 + s$
$= 2s + \frac{3}{2} - \frac{16}{2}$
$= 2s - \frac{13}{2}$
$= 2(-2) - \frac{13}{2}$
$= -4 - \frac{13}{2}$
$= -\frac{8}{2} - \frac{13}{2}$
$= -\frac{21}{2}$

21. $$\begin{bmatrix} 3 & 6 & 7 \\ 4 & 0 & 8 \\ -1 & 2 & -4 \end{bmatrix} + \begin{bmatrix} -3 & 6 & 0 \\ 1 & 8 & 4 \\ 1 & 6 & 5 \end{bmatrix} = \begin{bmatrix} 3+(-3) & 6+6 & 7+0 \\ 4+1 & 0+8 & 8+4 \\ -1+1 & 2+6 & -4+5 \end{bmatrix} = \begin{bmatrix} 0 & 12 & 7 \\ 5 & 8 & 12 \\ 0 & 8 & 1 \end{bmatrix}$$

22. $$\begin{bmatrix} -\frac{1}{2} & 3 & \frac{3}{4} \\ 10 & -7 & 4 \\ 6 & 9 & 0 \end{bmatrix} - \begin{bmatrix} \frac{1}{2} & 8 & \frac{3}{4} \\ 2 & 1 & 5 \\ 0 & -1 & -3 \end{bmatrix} = \begin{bmatrix} -\frac{1}{2} - \frac{1}{2} & 3-8 & \frac{3}{4} - \frac{3}{4} \\ 10-2 & -7-1 & 4-5 \\ 6-0 & 9-(-1) & 0-(-3) \end{bmatrix} = \begin{bmatrix} -1 & -5 & 0 \\ 8 & -8 & -1 \\ 6 & 10 & 3 \end{bmatrix}$$

23. -15 feet per second
15 feet per second

24. $60 + 2 + 2 + 2 + 2 + (-5) = 63°\text{F}$

25.

	Income	**Expense**
Bowlathon	384	192
Car wash	150	10
Sub sale	400	200

Total Income: $384 + 150 + 400 = 934$
Total Expense: $192 + 10 + 200 = 402$
$934 - 402 = \$532$ raised, \$32 over.
Yes, there was enough money.

26.

	Feet	**Meters**
Sears Tower	1454	443
World Trade Center	1350	411
Empire State Building	1250	381
Amoco Building	1136	346
John Hancock Center	1127	344

2.5 Multiplication of Real Numbers

Communicating about Algebra

A. (4 downs) $\left(-3 \dfrac{\text{yards}}{\text{down}}\right) = -12$ yards

B. (3000 baskets) $\left(-0.15 \dfrac{\text{dollars}}{\text{basket}}\right) = -450$ dollars

EXERCISES

1. False. The product of $-a$ and b is the opposite of ab.

2. False. The product of 0 and any number is 0.

3. True. This is the Commutative Property of multiplication. The order of multiplication does not change their product.

4. True. This is a rule for simplifying products with 3 or more factors.

5. No. This is the Commutative Property of multiplication.

6. $\left(\frac{\text{feet}}{\text{second}}\right) \cdot (\text{second}) = \text{feet}$

7. -48

8. -9

9. -28

10. -18

11. $-x$

12. $-60p$

13. $-48a$

14. $-10c$

15. $|(-5)|(6) = (5)(6)$
$= 30$

16. $(6)|(-5)| = (6)(5)$
$= 30$

17. $|(-2)(21)| = |-42|$
$= 42$

18. $|(8)(-9)| = |-72|$
$= 72$

19. 9

20. -16

21. $-8x^3$

22. $-3x^2$

23. -30

24. -80

25. $-48x$

26. $20x$

27. $168x^2$

28. $330y$

29. $\left(\frac{1}{3}a\right)\left(-\frac{2}{5}a\right)\left(\frac{3}{4}a\right) = -\frac{6}{60}a^3 = -\frac{1}{10}a^3$

30. $\left(-\frac{1}{4}b\right)\left(-\frac{1}{5}b\right)\left(\frac{1}{2}b\right) = \frac{1}{40}b^3$

31. 70.62

32. -45.96

33. 353.01

34. 1417.93

35. $2x^2 - 4x = 2(-3)^2 - 4(-3)$
$= 18 - (-12)$
$= 30$

36. $3x + x^2 = 3(-7) + (-7)^2$
$= -21 + 49$
$= 28$

37. $-2x - 5x = -2(4) - 5(4)$
$= -8 - 20$
$= -28$

38. $-6x + x = -6(9) + 9$
$= -54 + 9$
$= -45$

39. $-2(|x - 7|) = -2(|-3 - 7|)$
$= -2(|-10|)$
$= -2(10)$
$= -20$

40. $-5(|a - 4|) = -5(|-4 - 4|)$
$= -5(|-8|)$
$= -5(8)$
$= -40$

41. $(|9 - y|)(-1) = (|9 - (-5)|)(-1)$
$= (|14|)(-1)$
$= (14)(-1)$
$= -14$

42. $(|12 - m|)(-3) = (|12 - 6|)(-3)$
$= (|6|)(-3)$
$= (6)(-3)$
$= -18$

43. $-2x^2 + 3x + 1 = -2(5)^2 + 3(5) + 1$
$= -50 + 15 + 1$
$= -34$

44. $-7x - (-4x^3) = -7(4) - (-4(4)^3)$
$= -28 - (-256)$
$= 228$

45. $T + 5(-2) = T - 10$

$T - 10 = 82 - 10 = 72°$

Day	0	1	2	3	4	5
Temp	82°	80°	78°	76°	74°	72°

46. $x + (-1.8)(1992 - 1988) = x - 7.2$

$x - 7.2 = 76 - 7.2$

$= 68.8$ centimeters

Year	1988	1989	1990	1991	1992
Length	76 cm	74.2 cm	72.4 cm	70.6 cm	68.8 cm

47. c.

$6 + (6 - \frac{1}{2}) + [6 - 2(\frac{1}{2})] = 6 + 6\frac{1}{2} + 5$

$= 16\frac{1}{2}$ feet

No, this did not beat the record.

48. The expression represents the amount of money in dollars that the store lost due to the price reduction on health bars.

49. a. $80(0.6) = 48$ kilometers

50. $\left(20\ \frac{\text{miles}}{\text{hour}}\right)(1.5 \text{ hours}) = 30 \text{ miles}$

$\left(17\ \frac{\text{miles}}{\text{hour}}\right)(1.5 \text{ hours}) = 25.5 \text{ miles}$

$30 - 25.5 = 4.5$ miles behind

51. 2.5

52. -11

53. $-3^2 + 4 = -9 + 4$

$= -5$

54. $-5 + (-2)^3 = -5 + (-8)$

$= -13$

55. 3

56. -3

57. $|-3| - 7 = 3 - 7$

$= -4$

58. $4 - |-8| = 4 - 8$

$= -4$

59. $a + 3 = 10$ $\quad -4 + b = 6$ $\quad 0 + c = 8$ $\quad 1 + 4 = d$

$a = 7$ $\quad b = 10$ $\quad c = 8$ $\quad 5 = d$

60. $\begin{bmatrix} -6 & 2 & |4| \\ 0 & -9 & 18 \end{bmatrix} - \begin{bmatrix} -6 & (-1)^5 & 0 \\ 3 & 14 & |-5| \end{bmatrix} = \begin{bmatrix} -6-(-6) & 2-(-1) & 4-0 \\ 0-3 & -9-14 & 18-5 \end{bmatrix} = \begin{bmatrix} 0 & 3 & 4 \\ -3 & -23 & 13 \end{bmatrix}$

61. $-3\begin{bmatrix} 2 & 6 \\ -1 & -8 \end{bmatrix} = \begin{bmatrix} (-3)2 & (-3)(6) \\ (-3)(-1) & (-3)(-8) \end{bmatrix} = \begin{bmatrix} -6 & -18 \\ 3 & 24 \end{bmatrix}$

62. $-7\begin{bmatrix} -2 & 0 & 3 \\ 2^2 & -11 & -8 \end{bmatrix} = \begin{bmatrix} (-7)(-2) & (-7)(0) & (-7)(3) \\ (-7)(4) & (-7)(-11) & (-7)(-8) \end{bmatrix} = \begin{bmatrix} 14 & 0 & -21 \\ -28 & 77 & 56 \end{bmatrix}$

63. $-1\begin{bmatrix} 2x & -5y \\ -10m & 13n \end{bmatrix} = \begin{bmatrix} (-1)(2x) & (-1)(-5y) \\ (-1)(-10m) & (-1)(13n) \end{bmatrix} = \begin{bmatrix} -2x & 5y \\ 10m & -13n \end{bmatrix}$

64. $2\begin{bmatrix} x & 2y \\ -3m & 12n \end{bmatrix} = \begin{bmatrix} (2)(x) & (2)(2y) \\ (2)(-3m) & (2)(12n) \end{bmatrix} = \begin{bmatrix} 2x & 4y \\ -6m & 24n \end{bmatrix}$

65. The product represents the amount of sales tax for each item at each store.

66. $(0.05)(32.95) = \$1.65$

67. The product represents the total wholesale cost of all the T-shirts at the stores.

68. $(10.50)(10) = \$105.00$

2.6 The Distributive Property

Communicating about Algebra

Use the Distributive Property.

$$y = 2x - 3$$
$$-2y = -2(2x - 3)$$
$$-2y = -4x + 6$$

EXERCISES

1. Not true; $2(4 + 6) = 2(4) + 2(6)$

2. True; application of Distributive Property

3. True; application of Distributive Property

4. Not true; $(3 - 2)16 = 3(16) - 2(16)$

5. Distributive Property

6. $3x - 5 - 2x = x - 5$

7. $2(x - 3) + x = 2x - 6 + x$
$= 3x - 6$

8. $-(x - 1) + 2x = -x + 1 + 2x$
$= x + 1$

9. $3(y + 6) = 3y + 3(6)$
$= 3y + 18$

10. $(x + 1)11 = x(11) + 1(11)$
$= 11x + 11$

11. $(4 - x)7 = 4(7) - x(7)$
$= 28 - 7x$

12. $-4(y - 2) = -4(y) - (-4)(2)$
$= -4y + 8$

13. $(x + 5)(-2) = x(-2) + 5(-2)$
$= -2x - 10$

14. $10(y - 6) = 10(y) - 10(6)$
$= 10y - 60$

15. $x(8 + x) = x(8) + x(x)$
$= 8x + x^2$

16. $(x - 14)x = x(x) - 14(x)$
$= x^2 - 14x$

17. $-y(y - 9) = -y(y) - 9(-y)$
$= -y^2 + 9y$

18. $-x(8 + x) = -x(8) + (-x)(x)$
$= -8x - x^2$

19. $a(a - 2) = a(a) - a(2)$
$= a^2 - 2a$

20. $(3 + y)y = 3(y) + y(y)$
$= 3y + y^2$

21. $4(10 - 3x) = 4(10) - (4)(3x)$
$= 40 - 12x$

22. $(16 + 3t)t = 16(t) + 3t(t)$
$= 16t + 3t^2$

23. $(4s + 3)(-5) = 4s(-5) + 3(-5)$
$= -20s - 15$

24. $-13(1 - x) = -13(1) - (-13)(x)$
$= -13 + 13x$

25. $(6x+9)x = 6x(x) + 9(x)$
$= 6x^2 + 9x$

26. $4x(x-20) = 4x(x) - 4x(20)$
$= 4x^2 - 80x$

27. $(4-3x)(-6x) = 4(-6x) - 3x(-6x)$
$= -24x + 18x^2$

28. $-5s(s+2) = -5s(s) + (-5s)2$
$= -5s^2 - 10s$

29. $2x(9+x) = 2x(9) + 2x(x)$
$= 18x + 2x^2$

30. $(12+9y)6 = 12(6) + 9y(6)$
$= 72 + 54y$

31. $(12-5y)y = 12(y) - 5y(y)$
$= 12y - 5y^2$

32. $(5-2x)(-10x) = 5(-10x) - 2x(-10x)$
$= -50x + 20x^2$

33. $-8y(2y+7) = (-8y)(2y) + (-8y)(7)$
$= -16y^2 - 56y$

34. $x(18+2x) = x(18) + x(2x)$
$= 18x + 2x^2$

35. $-4a(3a-4) = -4a(3a) - (-4a)(4)$
$= -12a^2 + 16a$

36. $-a(5-2a) = -a(5) - (-a)(2a)$
$= -5a + 2a^2$

37. $4 + x - 1 = 3 + x$

38. $x + 5 + x = 2x + 5$

39. $2x^2 + 9x^2 + 4 = 11x^2 + 4$

40. $10x - 4 - 5x = 5x - 4$

41. $-3(x+1) - 2 = -3x - 3 - 2$
$= -3x - 5$

42. $(2x-1)(2) + x = 4x - 2 + x$
$= 5x - 2$

43. $11x + (8-x)3 = 11x + 24 - 3x$
$= 8x + 24$

44. $7x(2-x) - 4x = 14x - 7x^2 - 4x$
$= 10x - 7x^2$

45. $-6x(x-1) + x^2 = -6x^2 + 6x + x^2$
$= -5x^2 + 6x$

46. $x^2 - (4 + x^2) = x^2 - 4 - x^2$
$= -4$

47. $15 + x + 0.06(15 + x) \le 42$
$15 + x + 0.90 + 0.06x \le 42$
$1.06x + 15.90 \le 42$

48. $1.06(25) + 15.9 = 26.5 + 15.9$
$= 42.40$

No, you do not have enough money. The most the jeans could cost would be \$24.62.

49. **a.** and **b.**

50.

Average (*A*)	120	130	140	150	160	170	180	190	200
***H* = 0.8 (200 – *A*)**	64	56	48	40	32	24	16	8	0
***H* = 0.9 (180 – *A*)**	54	45	36	27	18	9	0	0	0

Advantage of 90% handicap: Better for leagues with greater range of averages.

Disadvantages of 90% handicap: A low-average bowler has a greater likelihood for exceeding a low average by a large amount than a good bowler has for exceeding a high average by a large amount, thereby giving the low-average bowler an unfair advantage on occasion.

Advantage of 80% handicap: Better for leagues with a smaller range of averages and with the averages tending towards those of an average bowler (120–180).

Disadvantage of 80% handicap: Does not serve to "equalize" better bowlers with averages in the 180–200 range.

51. $2[x + (x - 7)] = 2[2x - 7] = 4x - 14$

52. $(x - 2) + (x + 11) + (2x + 3) = 4x + 12$

53. $a(b + c) = ab + ac$

54. The area of the blue rectangle is $a(b - c)$, or the area of the whole rectangle minus the white rectangle is $ab - ac$.

$a(b - c) = ab - ac$

55. $$\begin{aligned} 3.6(x - 1.2) &= 3.6(x) - 3.6(1.2) \\ &= 3.6x - 4.32 \end{aligned}$$

56. $$\begin{aligned} 9.1(4.3 + 1.1x) &= 9.1(4.3) + 9.1(1.1x) \\ &= 39.13 + 10.01x \end{aligned}$$

57. $$\begin{aligned} (6.1 - 32.3x)(-2) &= 6.1(-2) - 32.3x(-2) \\ &= -12.2 + 64.6x \end{aligned}$$

58. $$\begin{aligned} -6.6(10.9 - 3.5x) &= -6.6(10.9) - (-6.6)(3.5x) \\ &= -71.94 + 23.1x \end{aligned}$$

59. $$\begin{aligned} &-4.1x(2.1x - 40.9) \\ &= -4.1x(2.1x) - (-4.1x)(40.9) \\ &= -8.61x^2 + 167.69x \end{aligned}$$

60. $$\begin{aligned} (3.3 - 0.9x)(-2x) &= 3.3(-2x) - (0.9x)(-2x) \\ &= -6.6x + 1.8x^2 \end{aligned}$$

61. $$\begin{aligned} 6x - 3x &= 12 \\ 3x &= 12 \\ x &= 4 \end{aligned}$$

62. $$\begin{aligned} 8y - 4y &= 48 \\ 4y &= 48 \\ y &= 12 \end{aligned}$$

63. $$\begin{aligned} 6y + 3 - y &= 8 \\ 5y + 3 &= 8 \\ y &= 1 \end{aligned}$$

64. $$\begin{aligned} 4 + 2y - 4 &= 16 \\ 2y &= 16 \\ y &= 8 \end{aligned}$$

65. $$\begin{aligned} -z + 4z &= 27 \\ 3z &= 27 \\ z &= 9 \end{aligned}$$

66. $$\begin{aligned} 4x - 8 - x &= 1 \\ 3x - 8 &= 1 \\ x &= 3 \end{aligned}$$

67. $$4\left(\begin{bmatrix} 2 & -1 \\ 4 & -6 \end{bmatrix} + \begin{bmatrix} -4 & 6 \\ 2 & 9 \end{bmatrix}\right) = 4\begin{bmatrix} -2 & 5 \\ 6 & 3 \end{bmatrix} = \begin{bmatrix} -8 & 20 \\ 24 & 12 \end{bmatrix}$$

$$4\begin{bmatrix} 2 & -1 \\ 4 & -6 \end{bmatrix} + 4\begin{bmatrix} -4 & 6 \\ 2 & 9 \end{bmatrix} = \begin{bmatrix} 8 & -4 \\ 16 & -24 \end{bmatrix} + \begin{bmatrix} -16 & 24 \\ 8 & 36 \end{bmatrix} = \begin{bmatrix} -8 & 20 \\ 24 & 12 \end{bmatrix}$$

Multiplication of a matrix by a real number is distributive over a matrix addition.

68. $$2\left(\begin{bmatrix} -1 & 0 \\ 6 & 4 \end{bmatrix} - \begin{bmatrix} 3 & 6 \\ -7 & 1 \end{bmatrix}\right) = 2\begin{bmatrix} -4 & -6 \\ 13 & 3 \end{bmatrix} = \begin{bmatrix} -8 & -12 \\ 26 & 6 \end{bmatrix}$$

$$2\begin{bmatrix} -1 & 0 \\ 6 & 4 \end{bmatrix} - 2\begin{bmatrix} 3 & 6 \\ -7 & 1 \end{bmatrix} = \begin{bmatrix} -2 & 0 \\ 12 & 8 \end{bmatrix} - \begin{bmatrix} 6 & 12 \\ -14 & 2 \end{bmatrix} = \begin{bmatrix} -8 & -12 \\ 26 & 6 \end{bmatrix}$$

Multiplication of a matrix by a real number is distributive over a matrix subtraction.

69. Substituting any two numbers except 0 for x and y will show that the equality is not true.

Mixed REVIEW

1. $3 \div (4-1) = 3 \div 3$
$= 1$

2. $[10-(4 \cdot 2)] \cdot 7 = [10-8] \cdot 7$
$= 2 \cdot 7$
$= 14$

3. 19

4. $\frac{2}{5} = 0.4 = 40\%$

5. $\frac{1}{4}\left(-\frac{1}{2}\right) + 2 = -\frac{1}{8} + \frac{16}{8}$
$= 1\frac{7}{8}$

6. $11 - [54 \div (2)(9)] = 11 - (54 \div 18)$
$= 11 - 3$
$= 8$

7. $2x^3 = 2(5)^3$
$= 2(125)$
$= 250$

8. $8x - 3y = 8(-1) - 3(3)$
$= -8 - 9$
$= -17$

9. $\dfrac{x+4}{5} = \dfrac{-3+4}{5} = \dfrac{1}{5}$

10. $|x| - 1 + (-x) = |-3| - 1 + (-(-3))$
$= 3 - 1 + 3 = 5$

11. $3 \cdot (6-2) + 17 = 3 \cdot 4 + 17$
$= 12 + 17$
$= 29$

$3 \cdot 6 - 2 + 17 = 18 - 2 + 17$
$= 16 + 17$
$= 33$

No, they are not equal.

12. $4x + x^2 > 6x$
$4(-2) + (-2)^2 \stackrel{?}{>} 6(-2)$
$-8 + 4 \stackrel{?}{>} -12$
$-4 > -12$

-2 is a solution.

13. $3x - (-8) \le -9$
$3(-1) + 8 \stackrel{?}{\le} -9$
$-3 + 8 \stackrel{?}{\le} -9$
$5 \not\le -9$

-1 is not a solution.

14. $-4x + 3 - 2(1-x) = -4x + 3 - 2 + 2x$
$= -2x + 1$

15. $(-11)(-3) + 12(-2) = 33 - 24$
$= 9$

16. -0.912

17. $-2\frac{1}{2}, -\frac{4}{3}, \frac{1}{3}, \frac{5}{8}, 2$

$-2\frac{1}{2}$ $-\frac{4}{3}$ $\frac{1}{3}$ $\frac{5}{8}$

−3 −2 −1 0 1 2 3

18. $3 \cdot 3 \cdot 3 = 3^3$

2.7 Division of Real Numbers

Communicating about Algebra

A. -0.125 is the reciprocal of -8. The product of a number and its reciprocal is 1.

B. There are fewer keys to press when using the division key.

EXERCISES

1. False; dividing by a number is the same as multiplying by the reciprocal of the number, not its opposite.

2. True, by definition of reciprocal.

3. $\frac{1}{22}$

4. $-\frac{1}{17}$

5. $\frac{5}{4}$

6. $-\frac{2}{7}$

7. 0

8. Yes; zero

9. $16 \cdot \frac{1}{4}$

10. $24 \cdot \frac{1}{8}$

11. $2x \cdot 9$

12. $\frac{1}{2}x \cdot \frac{1}{3}$

13. $\frac{4}{9} \cdot \frac{1}{6}$

14. $12x \cdot \frac{3}{2}$

15. $48 \cdot 2$

16. $4 \cdot \frac{4}{3}$

17. $6 \div 3 = 6 \cdot \frac{1}{3}$
$= 2$

18. $27 \div 9 = 27 \cdot \frac{1}{9}$
$= 3$

19. $9 \div \frac{1}{2} = 9 \cdot 2$
$= 18$

20. $8 \div \frac{1}{5} = 8 \cdot 5$
$= 40$

21. $\dfrac{92}{\frac{1}{2}} = 92 \cdot 2$
$= 184$

22. $\dfrac{16}{\frac{4}{9}} = 16 \cdot \dfrac{9}{4}$
$= 36$

23. $-8 \div 4 = -8 \cdot \frac{1}{4}$
$= -2$

24. $36 \div -6 = (36)\left(-\frac{1}{6}\right)$
$= -6$

25. $8 \div -9 = (18)\left(-\frac{1}{9}\right)$
$= -2$

26. $-64 \div 16 = -64 \cdot \frac{1}{16}$
$= -4$

27. $-10 \div \frac{1}{9} = -10 \cdot 9$
$= -90$

28. $-33 \div -\frac{1}{2} = (-33)(-2)$
$= 66$

29. $-\frac{1}{7} \div -3 = \left(-\frac{1}{7}\right)\left(-\frac{1}{3}\right)$
$= \frac{1}{21}$

30. $-\frac{3}{4} \div 4 = -\frac{3}{4} \cdot \frac{1}{4}$
$= -\frac{3}{16}$

31. $\dfrac{x}{4} \div 3 = \dfrac{x}{4} \cdot \dfrac{1}{3}$
$= \dfrac{x}{12}$

32. $\dfrac{2x}{3} \div \dfrac{1}{2} = \dfrac{2x}{3} \cdot 2$
$= \dfrac{4x}{3}$

33. $35x \div \frac{1}{7} = 35x \cdot 7$
$= 245x$

34. $4x \div -\frac{1}{2} = (4x)(-2)$
$= -8x$

35. $84x \div -\frac{4}{5} = (84x)\left(-\frac{5}{4}\right)$
$= -105x$

36. $-\frac{x}{4} \div 3 = -\frac{x}{4} \cdot \frac{1}{3}$
$= -\frac{x}{12}$

37. $\frac{9x - 27}{3} = (9x - 27)\frac{1}{3}$
$= 9x\left(\frac{1}{3}\right) - 27\left(\frac{1}{3}\right)$
$= 3x - 9$

38. $\frac{24x + 18}{-2} = (24x + 18)\left(-\frac{1}{2}\right)$
$= 24x\left(-\frac{1}{2}\right) + 18\left(-\frac{1}{2}\right)$
$= -12x - 9$

39. $\frac{-32 + x}{-8} = (-32 + x)\left(-\frac{1}{8}\right)$
$= (-32)\left(-\frac{1}{8}\right) + x\left(-\frac{1}{8}\right)$
$= 4 - \frac{1}{8}x$

40. $\frac{45 - 9x}{9} = (45 - 9x)\left(\frac{1}{9}\right)$
$= 45\left(\frac{1}{9}\right) - 9x\left(\frac{1}{9}\right)$
$= 5 - x$

41. $\frac{x - y}{6} = \frac{12 - 0}{6}$
$= 12 \cdot \frac{1}{6}$
$= 2$

42. $\frac{r - 4}{s} = \frac{24 - 4}{\frac{1}{2}}$
$= 20 \cdot 2$
$= 40$

43. $\frac{3a - b}{a} = \frac{3\left(\frac{1}{3}\right) - (-2)}{\frac{1}{3}}$
$= (1 + 2) \cdot 3$
$= 3 \cdot 3$
$= 9$

44. $\frac{16 - 4x}{y} = \frac{16 - 4(2)}{\frac{1}{2}}$
$= (16 - 8) \cdot 2$
$= 8 \cdot 2$
$= 16$

45. $\frac{15x - 10}{y} = \frac{15(3) - 10}{\frac{2}{3}}$
$= (45 - 10) \cdot \frac{3}{2}$
$= 35 \cdot \frac{3}{2}$
$= \frac{105}{2}$

46. $\frac{3a - 4b}{ab} = \frac{3\left(-\frac{1}{3}\right) - 4\left(\frac{1}{4}\right)}{\left(-\frac{1}{3}\right)\left(\frac{1}{4}\right)}$
$= \frac{-1 - 1}{-\frac{1}{12}}$
$= -2 \cdot (-12)$
$= 24$

47. $\frac{ab}{2a - 8} = \frac{8 \cdot 10}{2 \cdot 8 - 8} = \frac{80}{16 - 8}$
$= \frac{80}{8} = 80 \cdot \frac{1}{8}$
$= 10$

48. $\frac{x}{4y + 6} = \frac{\frac{3}{5}}{4\left(\frac{1}{2}\right) + 6}$
$= \frac{\frac{3}{5}}{2 + 6}$
$= \frac{\frac{3}{5}}{8}$
$= \frac{3}{5} \cdot \frac{1}{8}$
$= \frac{3}{40}$

49. $\frac{60}{\frac{5}{4}} = 60 \cdot \frac{4}{5}$
$= \frac{240}{5}$
$= 48$ breadsticks

50. $\frac{126}{4\frac{1}{2}} = \frac{126}{\frac{9}{2}}$
$= 126 \cdot \frac{2}{9}$
$= \frac{252}{9}$
$= 28$ birdhouses

51. $15 - \frac{32}{28} = 15 - 1.14$

$= \$13.86$ per birdhouse

52. $\frac{13.86}{2} = (13.86)\left(\frac{1}{2}\right)$

$= \$6.93$ per hour

53. $\frac{1}{1400 \cdot 1000} = \frac{1}{1{,}400{,}000}$ second

54. $\frac{1}{92.3 \cdot 1{,}000{,}000} = \frac{1}{92{,}300{,}000}$ second

55. $\frac{1}{\frac{1}{90{,}000{,}000}} = 90{,}000{,}000$ per second

Since the frequency is between 88,000,000 and 108,000,000 vibrations per second, this is an FM station with a radio station setting at 90.0 FM.

56. $\frac{1}{\frac{1}{905{,}000}} = 905{,}000$ per second

Since the frequency is between 535,000 and 1,705,000 vibrations per second, this is an AM station with a radio station setting of 905 AM.

57. -6

58. 2

59. 12

60. 16

61. $4 \div \frac{1}{2} + 9 - 12 = 4 \cdot 2 + 9 - 12$

$= 8 + 9 - 12$

$= 5$

62. $6 + 9 \div \frac{1}{4} - 14 = 6 + 9 \cdot 4 - 14$

$= 6 + 36 - 14$

$= 28$

63. $8 - 14 \div 2 \cdot 4 = 8 - 7 \cdot 4$

$= 8 - 28$

$= -20$

64. $3 - 6^2 \div 2 = 3 - 36 \div 2$

$= 3 - 18$

$= -15$

65. $\left(-4 \div \frac{1}{3}\right)^2 - 9 = (-4 \cdot 3)^2 - 9$

$= (-12)^2 - 9$

$= 144 - 9$

$= 135$

66. $14 - \left(2 \div -\frac{1}{4}\right)^2 = 14 - (2 \cdot -4)^2$

$= 14 - (-8)^2$

$= 14 - 64$

$= -50$

67. $|-2| - |-4| = 2 - 4$

$= -2$

68. $2|-1| - |-3| = 2(1) - 3$

$= 2 - 3$

$= -1$

69. $-x \div \frac{1}{2} = -6 \div \frac{1}{2}$

$= -6 \cdot 2$

$= -12$

70. $14 \div y + 2 = 14 \div \frac{2}{3} + 2$

$= 14 \cdot \frac{3}{2} + 2$

$= 21 + 2$

$= 23$

71. $\frac{x}{2} \div 8 = \frac{4}{2} \div 8$

$= \frac{4}{2} \cdot \frac{1}{8}$

$= \frac{4}{16}$

$= \frac{1}{4}$

72. $2 \div \frac{x}{9} = 2 \div \frac{3}{9}$
$= 2 \div \frac{1}{3}$
$= 2 \cdot \frac{3}{1}$
$= 6$

73. $x \div 2 = \frac{1}{4} \div 2$
$= \frac{1}{4} \cdot \frac{1}{2}$
$= \frac{1}{8}$

74. $8 \cdot x = 8 \cdot \frac{1}{8} = 1$

75.

$\frac{x}{1}$	$\frac{x}{0.1}$	$\frac{x}{0.01}$	$\frac{x}{0.001}$	$\frac{x}{0.0001}$	$\frac{x}{0.00001}$
x	$10x$	$100x$	$1000x$	$10000x$	$100{,}000x$

There is one zero in the answer for every decimal place in the original expression. $1{,}000{,}000x$

76.

$\frac{(-1)^1}{(-1)^1}$	$\frac{(-1)^1}{(-1)^2}$	$\frac{(-1)^2}{(-1)^1}$	$\frac{(-1)^2}{(-1)^2}$	$\frac{(-1)^3}{(-1)^1}$	$\frac{(-1)^3}{(-1)^2}$	$\frac{(-1)^3}{(-1)^3}$
1	-1	-1	1	1	-1	1

When the sum of the exponents is odd, the answer is negative. When the sum is even, the answer is positive.

77. -1

78. 1

79. -1

80. 1

81. $\frac{110{,}757 \text{ dollars}}{7872 \text{ pounds}} = 14.07$ dollars per pound

$14.07 \cdot (1 - 0.8) = 14.07 \cdot 0.2$
$= 2.81$ dollars per pound

2.8 Exploring Data: Rates and Ratios

Communicating about Algebra

A. $\pi \approx 3.141592654$

3.1416

$\frac{22}{7} \approx 3.142857143$

$\frac{355}{113} \approx 3.14159292$

In increasing order: π, $\frac{355}{113}$, 3.1416, $\frac{22}{7}$

B. $\frac{355}{113}$

EXERCISES

1. Rate compares two quantities measured in different units.

Ratio compares two quantities measured in the same unit.

2. Rate

3. Ratio; π

4. Rate; ratio

5. $\dfrac{440 \text{ miles}}{3 \text{ gallons}} \approx 146.7$ miles per gallon

6. $\dfrac{460 \text{ miles}}{12 \text{ gallons}} \approx 38.3$ miles per gallon

7. $\dfrac{85 \text{ dollars}}{20 \text{ hours}} = \$4.25$ per hour

8. $\dfrac{127.50 \text{ dollars}}{30 \text{ hours}} = \$4.25$ per hour

9. $\dfrac{80 \text{ kilometers}}{\frac{3}{4} \text{ hours}} = 80 \cdot \dfrac{4}{3}$

≈ 106.7 kilometers per hour

10. $\dfrac{m \text{ miles}}{\frac{3}{4} \text{ hours}} = m \cdot \dfrac{4}{3}$

$= \dfrac{4}{3}m$ miles per hour

11. $\dfrac{4.99 \text{ dollars}}{3 \text{ videos}} = \$1.66$ per video

$1.79 - 1.66 = \$0.13$ per video

12. $\dfrac{\$1.20}{5} = \$0.24$ per bar

$\dfrac{\$1.59}{7} = \$0.227$ per bar

Box of 7 for $1.59 is a better buy.

13. $\dfrac{83 \text{ strokes}}{18 \text{ holes}} \approx 4.6$ strokes per hole

$\dfrac{44 \text{ strokes}}{9 \text{ holes}} \approx 4.9$ strokes per hole

The average of 4.6 strokes per hole is better.

14. $\dfrac{10{,}513 \text{ books}}{255 \text{ shelves}} \approx 41.2$ books per shelf

$\dfrac{659 \text{ books}}{41.2 \text{ books per shelf}} \approx 16$ shelves

Use 16 shelves.

15. $\dfrac{127 \text{ CD's}}{35 \text{ CD's per case}} \approx 3.6$ cases or 4 cases

$35 \cdot 4 - 127 = 140 - 127 = 13$ compact disks

16. $\dfrac{888{,}045}{365} = 2433$ automobiles stolen per day

17. $\dfrac{352{,}225{,}000}{365} = 965{,}000$ colas drunk for breakfast per day

18. $\dfrac{1{,}572{,}481{,}430}{365} = 4{,}308{,}168$ credit card purchases per day

19. $\dfrac{12{,}045}{365} = 33$ new consumer products introduced per day

20. $\dfrac{350{,}000{,}000{,}000}{365} = 958{,}904{,}110$ photocopies made per day

21. $\dfrac{450{,}000{,}000}{365} \approx \$1{,}232{,}877$ spent on sun-care products per day

22. $\dfrac{88{,}695}{365} = 243$ patents issued per day

23. $\dfrac{20{,}440}{365} = 56$ fires started by arson per day

24. $\dfrac{13{,}140{,}000{,}000}{365} = 36{,}000{,}000$ postage stamps printed per day

25. $\dfrac{24{,}820}{365} = 68$ animals treated with acupuncture per day

26. $\dfrac{2.50}{50} = \dfrac{1}{20}$

27. $\frac{72}{70} = \frac{36}{35}$

28. $\dfrac{3\frac{1}{2}}{3} = \dfrac{\frac{7}{2}}{3} = \dfrac{7}{2} \cdot \dfrac{1}{3} = \dfrac{7}{6}$

$\dfrac{3}{3\frac{1}{2}} = \dfrac{3}{\frac{7}{2}} = 3 \cdot \dfrac{2}{7} = \dfrac{6}{7}$

They are reciprocals.

29. Ratio: $\dfrac{15}{225} = \dfrac{1}{15}$

$\dfrac{225 \text{ dogs}}{12 \text{ weeks}} = 18.75$ dogs per week

No, the shelter is slower than normal.

30. $\frac{8}{32} = 25\%$

31. $\dfrac{90 \cdot 90}{270 \cdot 270} = \dfrac{8100}{72{,}900} = \dfrac{1}{9}$

32. Wins to total games ratio: $\frac{80}{120} = \frac{2}{3}$

Losses to total games ratio: $\frac{40}{120} = \frac{1}{3}$

33. High School: $\frac{8}{12} = \frac{2}{3}$

Associate: $\frac{8}{14} = \frac{4}{7}$

Bachelor's: $\frac{8}{16} = \frac{1}{2}$

Master's: $\frac{8}{18} = \frac{4}{9}$

Doctor's: $\frac{8}{20} = \frac{2}{5}$

34. In 1980: $\dfrac{227{,}757{,}000}{4{,}477{,}000{,}000} \approx 0.051$

In 1989: $\dfrac{248{,}231{,}000}{5{,}239{,}000{,}000} \approx 0.047$

U.S. population is decreasing compared to the world population.

35. The engine gear has 6 teeth.

The axle gear has 24 teeth.

Gear ratio: $\frac{6}{24} = \frac{1}{4}$

36. 1st Gear: $\frac{52}{28} = \frac{13}{7}$

2nd Gear: $\frac{52}{24} = \frac{13}{6}$

3rd Gear: $\frac{52}{20} = \frac{13}{5}$

4th Gear: $\frac{52}{17}$

5th Gear: $\frac{52}{14} = \frac{26}{7}$

The first gear, because the lower the gear ratio, the easier it is to turn the axle.

37. e.

38. h.

39. a.

40. f.

41. g.

42. d.

43. b.

44. c.

45. $-3 - (-2) = -3 + 2$
$= -1$

46. $5 - (3 + 7) = 5 - 10$
$= -5$

47. $2 + |-3| - 12 = 2 + 3 - 12$
$= -7$

48. $11 - 4 + |-8| = 11 - 4 + 8$
$= 15$

49. $6x - 4x = 2x$

50. $-5y + 2y = -3y$

51. $4^3 - 8x = 64 - 8 \cdot 7$
$= 64 - 56$
$= 8$

52. $\frac{1}{12}(-11 - t^2) = \frac{1}{12}[-11 - (2)^2]$
$= \frac{1}{12}[-11 - 4]$
$= \frac{1}{12}(-15)$
$= -\frac{15}{12}$
$= -\frac{5}{4}$

53. $\frac{1}{8}[m + (-5)] = \frac{1}{8}[21 + (-5)]$
$= \frac{1}{8}[16]$
$= 2$

54. $63x \div -3 = 63 \cdot 7 \div -3$
$= 441 \div -3$
$= -147$

55. $49y \div \frac{7}{3} = 49(-1) \div \frac{7}{3}$
$= -49 \cdot \frac{3}{7}$
$= -21$

56. $-3x - (-6)^2 = -3(-9) - 36$
$= 27 - 36$
$= -9$

57. $\frac{3.9 \text{ cm}}{2.9 \text{ cm}} = 1.34$ for width
$\frac{5.1 \text{ cm}}{3.8 \text{ cm}} = 1.34$ for length
Approximately $\frac{4}{3}$

58. $\left(\frac{1}{2} \text{ inch}\right)\left(200 \ \frac{\text{miles}}{\text{inch}}\right) \approx 100$ miles

59. $\frac{y}{x} = \frac{2}{5}$
$\frac{12}{x} = \frac{2}{5}$
$\frac{12}{x}(5) = 2$
$\frac{60}{x} = 2$
$60 = 2x$
$x = 30$ cousins

Chapter REVIEW

1. 1

2. $-2, -\frac{2}{3}, 0, \frac{1}{2}, \frac{5}{3}$

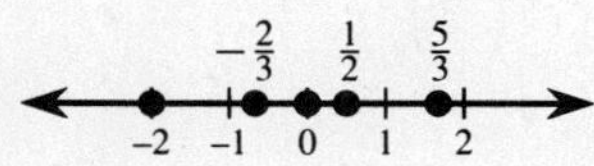

3.

4.

5. $|-1.1| = 1.1$

6. $|4.5| = 4.5$

7. $8 + (-4) = 4$

8. $-5 + (-3) + 4 = -8 + 4$
$= -4$

9. $|-5| - 4 = 5 - 4$
$= 1$

10. $10 - (-2) - |5| = 10 + 2 - 5$
$= 12 - 5$
$= 7$

11. $-[(-7)+8] = -[1]$
$= -1$

12. $-[3+(-4)] = -[-1]$
$= 1$

13. -13.6

14. 16.8

15. $(-14)(-2) = 28$

16. $(-9)(-2)\left(-\frac{1}{3}\right) = (18)\left(-\frac{1}{3}\right)$
$= -6$

17. $\frac{3}{8} \div \frac{1}{2} = \frac{3}{8} \cdot 2$
$= \frac{6}{8}$
$= \frac{3}{4}$

18. $-16 \div -4 = -16 \cdot -\frac{1}{4}$
$= 4$

19. $\frac{1}{3}m - m^2 = \frac{1}{3}\left(\frac{1}{2}\right) - \left(\frac{1}{2}\right)^2$
$= \frac{1}{6} - \frac{1}{4}$
$= \frac{4}{24} - \frac{6}{24}$
$= -\frac{2}{24}$
$= -\frac{1}{12}$

20. $-6x + 2|x-3| = -6(-3) + 2|-3-3|$
$= 18 + 2|-6|$
$= 18 + 2 \cdot 6$
$= 18 + 12$
$= 30$

21. $\dfrac{3r-6s}{3} = \dfrac{3(1)-6(2)}{3}$
$= \dfrac{3-12}{3}$
$= \dfrac{-9}{3} = -3$

22. $\dfrac{xy}{3x+4y} = \dfrac{4\left(\frac{1}{2}\right)}{3(4)+4\left(\frac{1}{2}\right)}$
$= \dfrac{2}{12+2}$
$= \dfrac{2}{14} = \dfrac{1}{7}$

23. $4 + (-x) + 10 = 14 - x$
$= 14 - 5$
$= 9$

24. $|m| - m + 3 = \left|\frac{1}{2}\right| - \frac{1}{2} + 3$
$= \frac{1}{2} - \frac{1}{2} + 3$
$= 3$

25. $7(y-1) + 10 = 7y - 7 + 10$
$= 7y + 3$

26. $3m^2 - (1 + 2m^2) = 3m^2 - 1 - 2m^2$
$= m^2 - 1$

27. $\dfrac{4x-16}{2} = (4x-16) \cdot \dfrac{1}{2}$
$= 4x\left(\dfrac{1}{2}\right) - 16\left(\dfrac{1}{2}\right)$
$= 2x - 8$

28. $\dfrac{-45+15y}{-5} = (-45+15y)\left(-\dfrac{1}{5}\right)$
$= -45\left(-\dfrac{1}{5}\right) + 15y\left(-\dfrac{1}{5}\right)$
$= 9 - 3y$

29. $$\begin{bmatrix} 3 & -\frac{1}{2} \\ 4 & 0 \\ 1 & -5 \end{bmatrix} + \begin{bmatrix} -4 & \frac{5}{2} \\ 6 & -3 \\ 7 & 2 \end{bmatrix} = \begin{bmatrix} 3+(-4) & -\frac{1}{2}+\frac{5}{2} \\ 4+6 & 0+(-3) \\ 1+7 & -5+2 \end{bmatrix} = \begin{bmatrix} -1 & 2 \\ 10 & -3 \\ 8 & -3 \end{bmatrix}$$

30. $$\begin{bmatrix} -\frac{3}{4} & \frac{1}{2} & \frac{3}{2} \\ \frac{5}{4} & \frac{1}{8} & \frac{3}{4} \end{bmatrix} - \begin{bmatrix} \frac{1}{4} & -\frac{3}{2} & 0 \\ -\frac{1}{4} & \frac{3}{8} & 1 \end{bmatrix} = \begin{bmatrix} -\frac{3}{4}-\frac{1}{4} & \frac{1}{2}-\left(-\frac{3}{2}\right) & \frac{3}{2}-0 \\ \frac{5}{4}-\left(-\frac{1}{4}\right) & \frac{1}{8}-\frac{3}{8} & \frac{3}{4}-1 \end{bmatrix} = \begin{bmatrix} -1 & 2 & \frac{3}{2} \\ \frac{3}{2} & -\frac{1}{4} & -\frac{1}{4} \end{bmatrix}$$

31.

	Nov	Dec	Jan	Feb	Mar	Apr
High	64	57	56	59	61	63
Low	45	45	40	43	44	45

32. November through April

33. January through September

34. September and October: difference of 20°
December: difference of 12°

35. Speed = 20 feet per second.
c. $h = 20 \cdot 60$

36. $60(3) = 180$ miles
c. $4r = 180$

37. $7 + 6 + (-3) = 10$ A.M.

38. $-1002.91 + (-565.77) + 14{,}232.01 + 3{,}027.88 = \$15{,}691.21$

39. $-12 + 0 + 12 = 0$; Atom

40. $-10 + 0 + 12 = 2$; Ion

41. $-10 + 0 + 11 = 1$; Ion

42. Exercise 40

43. Elk Island: $\dfrac{48{,}000}{750} = 64$ acres per buffalo

Wood Buffalo: $\dfrac{11{,}072{,}000}{3375} \approx 3,280.6$ acres per buffalo

Wind Cave: $\dfrac{28{,}300}{325} \approx 87.1$ acres per buffalo

Yellowstone: $\dfrac{2{,}219{,}800}{2850} \approx 778.9$ acres per buffalo

44. Wood Buffalo National Park

45. Elk Island National Park

46. $(2000)(0.147) = 294$

47. $(3500)(0.085) = 298$

48. $(1500)(0.196) - (1500)(0.054) = 294 - 81$
$= 213$

49. **a.** and **b.** In **a.**, the number who have not worked for pay is subtracted from 1500. In **b.**, the fraction who have worked for pay is multiplied by 1500.

50. Chamber 1: 1
Chamber 2: $(1)(1.063)$
Chamber 3: $(1)(1.063)(1.063) = (1.063)^2$
$= 1.129969$
≈ 1.13

So Chamber 3 ≈ 13.0% larger than Chamber 1.

51. $\dfrac{1}{1.063} \approx 0.941$ or 94.1%
Chamber 1 is approximately 94.1% of Chamber 2 or 1 − 94.1% = 5.9% smaller.

52. $3 \cdot (1.063)^3 \approx 3.6$ cubic centimeters

53. **a.** $(1.06)^{18} \approx 2.85$
Chamber 0 = 1
Chamber 1 = $(1.06)^1$
Chamber 2 = $(1.06)^2$
⋮
Chamber 18 = $(1.06)^{18}$

54. UNH: $\frac{37}{184}$, UCSB: $\frac{2}{17}$, MIT: $\frac{24}{126} = \frac{4}{21}$, WVU: $\frac{36}{144} = \frac{1}{4}$, TA&M: $\frac{48}{134} = \frac{24}{67}$

West Virginia University's $\frac{1}{4}$ ratio is closest.

55. $$(3 \text{ knots})\left(\frac{1\frac{\text{n. mi}}{\text{hr}}}{1 \text{ knot}}\right)\left(\frac{6080 \text{ ft}}{1 \text{ n.mi}}\right)\left(\frac{1 \text{ mi}}{5280 \text{ ft}}\right) = (3)\left(1\frac{\text{n. mi}}{\text{hr}}\right)\left(\frac{6080}{1 \text{ n. mi}}\right)\left(\frac{1 \text{ mi}}{5280}\right) \approx 3.45 \text{ miles per hour}$$

56. $(2)(0.3) = 0.6$ horsepower

57. $\left(\frac{2 \text{ foot pedal}}{1 \text{ paddle axle}}\right)$(70 paddle axle revolutions per minute) = 140 foot pedal revolutions per minute

Chapter TEST

1. $-\frac{5}{2}, -\frac{5}{4}, \frac{3}{4}$

2. b.

3. $9 + (-10) + 2 = -1 + 2$
$= 1$

4. $-2.97 - 3.20 - (-0.02) = -6.15$

5. $(-6)(4)(-1) = (-24)(-1) = 24$

6. $72 \div (-12) = -6$

7. $$\frac{4-x}{-3} = \frac{4-(-1)}{-3} = \frac{4+1}{-3} = -\frac{5}{3}$$

8. $$1 - 2x^2 = 1 - 2(-2)^2 = 1 - 2(4) = 1 - 8 = -7$$

9. $-2x + 3 + 3x - 9 = x - 6$

10. $3 - 4(x-2) = 3 - 4x + 8$
$= 11 - 4x$

11. $$\begin{bmatrix} 3 & -7 \\ \frac{1}{2} & 6 \\ 0 & 2 \end{bmatrix} + \begin{bmatrix} -4 & 2 \\ -\frac{1}{2} & 4 \\ 5 & \frac{1}{4} \end{bmatrix} = \begin{bmatrix} 3+(-4) & -7+2 \\ \frac{1}{2}+\left(-\frac{1}{2}\right) & 6+4 \\ 0+5 & 2+\frac{1}{4} \end{bmatrix} = \begin{bmatrix} -1 & -5 \\ 0 & 10 \\ 5 & 2\frac{1}{4} \end{bmatrix}$$

12. $$\begin{bmatrix} 2 & -\frac{2}{3} & 4 \\ 5 & 16 & -7 \end{bmatrix} - \begin{bmatrix} 5 & \frac{1}{3} & -1 \\ -2 & 8 & 4 \end{bmatrix} = \begin{bmatrix} 2-5 & -\frac{2}{3}-\frac{1}{3} & 4-(-1) \\ 5-(-2) & 16-8 & -7-4 \end{bmatrix} = \begin{bmatrix} -3 & -1 & 5 \\ 7 & 8 & -11 \end{bmatrix}$$

13. True

14. False

15. True

16. False

17. False

18. True

19. $100\left(3\frac{1}{2}\right) = 100\left(\frac{7}{2}\right) = 350$ kilometers

20. $2189.70 + 1527.11 - 502.18 - 266.54 = \$2948.09$

21. $300 \cdot \frac{27}{1} = \$8100$ (Taiwanese)

22. $\frac{3+2}{36} = \frac{5}{36} = \frac{1}{7.2}$; Yes

23. $\frac{0.99}{1}$

$\frac{1.79}{1.75} = \frac{1.02}{1}$

The one liter bottle is the better buy.

24.

	9th	10th	11th	12th
Males	307	323	290	289
Females	331	300	270	312

There are 323 male students in the 10th grade.

25. Velocity = -15 feet per second

Speed = 15 feet per second

$\frac{1800}{15} = 120$ seconds or 2 minutes

Chapter 3

Solving Linear Equations

3.1 Solving Equations Using One Transformation

Communicating about Algebra

A. Multiply both sides by $\frac{3}{2}$.

B. Yes; 5 is a solution because it checks.

$\frac{1}{7}(5) \stackrel{?}{=} \frac{5}{7}$

$\frac{5}{7} = \frac{5}{7}$

No; there are no other solutions. To confirm this, solve the equation.

$7 \cdot \frac{1}{7}x = 7 \cdot \frac{5}{7}$

$x = 5$

C. Add 5 to both sides of the equation to isolate the variable.

D. Multiplying both sides of the equation by $-\frac{5}{3}$ gives the solution because it isolates the variable on the left side of the equation.

$\left(-\frac{5}{3}\right)\left(-\frac{3}{5}\right)x = \left(-\frac{5}{3}\right)81$

$x = -135$

EXERCISES

1. True

2. True

3. False, the number must be nonzero.

4. Addition and subtraction are inverses.
Multiplication and division are inverses.

5. $2x = 6$ *Divide both side by 2.*
$x - 5 = 11$ *Add 5 to both sides.*
$2 + n = 5$ *Subtract 2 from both sides.*
$\frac{1}{4}s = 3$ *Multiply both sides by 4.*

6. 1. If $a = b$, then $a + c = b + c$. *Addition Property*
2. If $a = b$, then $a - c = b - c$. *Subtraction Property*
3. If $a = b$, then $ca = cb$. *Multiplication Property*
4. If $a = b$, and $c \neq 0$, then $\frac{a}{c} = \frac{b}{c}$. *Division Property*

7. Equations are equivalent.

8. Equations are not equivalent.

9. Subtract 31

10. Add 27

11. Divide by -2

12. Multiply by 5

13.
$$4 + t = 13$$
$$4 + t - 4 = 13 - 4$$
$$t = 9$$

14.
$$m + 15 = -3$$
$$m + 15 - 15 = -3 - 15$$
$$m = -18$$

15.
$$w - 5 = 11$$
$$w - 5 + 5 = 11 + 5$$
$$w = 16$$

16.
$$x - (-3) = 4$$
$$x + 3 = 4$$
$$x + 3 - 3 = 4 - 3$$
$$x = 1$$

17.
$$y + 7 = -5$$
$$y + 7 - 7 = -5 - 7$$
$$y = -12$$

18.
$$6 + n = 0$$
$$6 + n - 6 = 0 - 6$$
$$n = -6$$

19.
$$14 = b + 4$$
$$14 - 4 = b + 4 - 4$$
$$10 = b$$

20.
$$-3 = 7 + a$$
$$-3 - 7 = 7 + a - 7$$
$$-10 = a$$

21.
$$|-3| + n = 0$$
$$3 + n = 0$$
$$3 + n - 3 = 0 - 3$$
$$n = -3$$

22.
$$|-9| + z = -5$$
$$9 + z = -5$$
$$z = -5 - 9$$
$$z = -14$$

23.
$$22 = s + 7$$
$$22 - 7 = s + 7 - 7$$
$$15 = s$$

24.
$$37 = r - (-8)$$
$$37 = r + 8$$
$$37 - 8 = r + 8 - 8$$
$$29 = r$$

25.
$$10x = 100$$
$$\frac{10x}{10} = \frac{100}{10}$$
$$x = 10$$

26.
$$-21m = 42$$
$$\frac{-21m}{-21} = \frac{42}{-21}$$
$$m = -2$$

27.
$$16 = -2a$$
$$\frac{16}{-2} = \frac{-2a}{-2}$$
$$-8 = a$$

28.
$$15b = 5$$
$$\frac{15b}{15} = \frac{5}{15}$$
$$b = \frac{1}{3}$$

29.
$$256 = 16c$$
$$\frac{256}{16} = \frac{16c}{16}$$
$$16 = c$$

30.
$$-4m = -16$$
$$\frac{-4m}{-4} = \frac{-16}{-4}$$
$$m = 4$$

31.
$$400 = 25n$$
$$\frac{400}{25} = \frac{25n}{25}$$
$$16 = n$$

32.
$$330 = -15p$$
$$\frac{330}{-15} = \frac{-15p}{-15}$$
$$-22 = p$$

33.
$$\tfrac{1}{2}x = -40$$
$$\left(\tfrac{2}{1}\right)\left(\tfrac{1}{2}\right)x = \left(\tfrac{2}{1}\right)(-40)$$
$$x = -80$$

34.
$$\tfrac{1}{3}z = 78$$
$$\left(\tfrac{3}{1}\right)\left(\tfrac{1}{3}\right)z = \left(\tfrac{3}{1}\right)78$$
$$z = 234$$

35.
$$0 = \tfrac{3}{5}t$$
$$\left(\tfrac{5}{3}\right)(0) = \left(\tfrac{5}{3}\right)\left(\tfrac{3}{5}\right)t$$
$$0 = t$$

36.
$$-x = 4$$
$$(-1)(-x) = (-1)(4)$$
$$x = -4$$

37. $-\frac{3}{4}L = 75$

$\left(-\frac{4}{3}\right)\left(-\frac{3}{4}\right)L = \left(-\frac{4}{3}\right)(75)$

$L = -100$

38. $-\frac{4}{5}c = 20$

$\left(-\frac{5}{4}\right)\left(-\frac{4}{5}\right)c = \left(-\frac{5}{4}\right)(20)$

$c = -25$

39. $\frac{1}{3}y = 3\frac{2}{3}$

$\frac{1}{3}y = \frac{11}{3}$

$\left(\frac{3}{1}\right)\left(\frac{1}{3}\right)y = \left(\frac{3}{1}\right)\left(\frac{11}{3}\right)$

$y = 11$

40. $\frac{3}{4}z = -5\frac{1}{2}$

$\frac{3}{4}z = -\frac{11}{2}$

$\left(\frac{4}{3}\right)\left(\frac{3}{4}\right)z = \left(\frac{4}{3}\right)\left(-\frac{11}{2}\right)$

$z = -\frac{22}{3}$

41. $-\frac{2}{5}x = -4$

$\left(-\frac{5}{2}\right)\left(-\frac{2}{5}\right)x = \left(-\frac{5}{2}\right)(-4)$

$x = 10$

42. $-\frac{2}{3}y = -4$

$\left(-\frac{3}{2}\right)\left(-\frac{2}{3}\right)y = \left(-\frac{3}{2}\right)(-4)$

$y = 6$

43. $\frac{x}{4} = 2$

$\left(\frac{4}{1}\right)\left(\frac{x}{4}\right) = \left(\frac{4}{1}\right)(2)$

$x = 8$

44. $\frac{c}{7} = 15$

$\left(\frac{7}{1}\right)\left(\frac{c}{7}\right) = \left(\frac{7}{1}\right)(15)$

$c = 105$

45. $\frac{x}{2} = -3$

$\left(\frac{2}{1}\right)\left(\frac{x}{2}\right) = \left(\frac{2}{1}\right)(-3)$

$x = -6$

46. $\frac{n}{-1} = -2$

$-n = -2$

$(-1)(-n) = (-1)(-2)$

$n = 2$

47. $\frac{t}{-2} = \frac{1}{2}$

$\left(-\frac{2}{1}\right)\left(-\frac{t}{2}\right) = \left(-\frac{2}{1}\right)\left(\frac{1}{2}\right)$

$t = -1$

48. $\frac{m}{-4} = -\frac{3}{4}$

$\left(-\frac{4}{1}\right)\left(-\frac{m}{4}\right) = \left(-\frac{4}{1}\right)\left(-\frac{3}{4}\right)$

$m = 3$

49. a. $x + 47 = 53$

$x + 47 - 47 = 53 - 47$

$x = 6$

50. b. $x + 7 = 83$

$x + 7 - 7 = 83 - 7$

$x = 76$

51. $\frac{x}{5} = \frac{3}{7}$

$5 \cdot \frac{x}{5} = 5 \cdot \frac{3}{7}$

$x = \frac{15}{7}$ feet

52. $\frac{x}{5} = \frac{12}{8}$

$5 \cdot \frac{x}{5} = 5 \cdot \frac{12}{8}$

$x = \frac{60}{8}$

$= \frac{15}{2}$ centimeters

53. $\frac{50}{70} = \frac{x}{6}$

$50 \cdot 6 = 70 \cdot x$

$\frac{1}{70} \cdot 300 = x$

$x = \frac{30}{7}$

$= 4\frac{2}{7}$ feet

54. $\frac{x}{2} = \frac{300}{100}$

$100 \cdot x = 300 \cdot 2$

$100x = 600$

$x = 600 \cdot \frac{1}{100}$

$x = 6$ feet

55. a. $\frac{x}{2} = \frac{4(1/2)}{6}$

$6 \cdot \frac{x}{2} = \frac{4(1/2)}{6} \cdot 6$

$3x = \frac{9}{2}$

$x = \frac{3}{2}$

56. b. $\frac{x}{3} = 41$

$\left(\frac{3}{1}\right)\left(\frac{x}{3}\right) = \left(\frac{3}{1}\right)(41)$

$x = 123$

57. $1.9x = 95$ or $\frac{x}{95} = \frac{100}{190}$

$\frac{1.9x}{1.9} = \frac{95}{1.9}$ $\quad x = \left(\frac{10}{19}\right)95$

$x = 50$ $\quad x = 50$

58. $\frac{14}{29} \cdot 87 = x$

$\frac{1218}{29} = x$

$42 = x$

59. $-8 - 4 = -12$

60. $-3 + 7 = 4$

61. $-9 + 5 = -4$

62. $-5 + 9 = 4$

63. $3(6 - 2) = 3(4)$
$= 12$

64. $(-4 + 1)(-2) = (-3)(-2)$
$= 6$

65. $(7 - 11)4 = (-4)(4)$
$= -16$

66. $-5(8 + 2) = (-5)(10)$
$= -50$

67. $(-12)\left(\frac{3}{2}\right) = -18$

68. $(8)\left(-\frac{1}{2}\right) = -4$

69. $(-5)(-11) = 55$

70. $(6)(-13) = -78$

71. $\left(-\frac{3}{2}\right)\left(-\frac{2}{3}\right) = 1$

72. $\left(\frac{4}{3}\right)\left(-\frac{3}{4}\right) = -1$

73. $\left(\frac{1}{2}\right)\left(\frac{6}{4}\right) = \frac{3}{4}$

74. $\left(\frac{2}{7}\right)\left(\frac{7}{4}\right) = \frac{1}{2}$

75. $-8 \div 2 = -4$

76. $18 \div 6 = 3$

77. $3.75 \div 0.25 = 15$

78. $10.6 \div 0.4 = 26.5$

79. $2x + 2(3x) = 168$

$2x + 6x = 168$

$8x = 168$

$x = 21$

Length $= 3(21)$

$= 63$

Width $= 21$

80. Area $= (10 - x)(2x - 3)$

When $x = 3$, $A = (10 - 3)[2(3) - 3] = 21$

When $x = 5$, $A = (10 - 5)[2(5) - 3] = 35$

When $x = 7$, $A = (10 - 7)[2(7) - 3] = 33$

The greatest area occurs when $x = 5$.

81. $-(-x) = 15$

$x = 15$

82. $-(-3x) = -21$

$3x = -21$

$\frac{3x}{3} = -\frac{21}{3}$

$x = -7$

83. $-3 = x - (-7)$

$-3 = x + 7$

$-3 - 7 = x + 7 - 7$

$-10 = x$

84. $-|-8| = 15 - x$

$-8 = 15 - x$

$-8 - 15 = 15 - x - 15$

$-23 = -x$

$(-1)(-23) = (-1)(-x)$

$23 = x$

3.2 Solving Equations Using Two or More Transformations

Communicating about Algebra

A. $2(x - 3) = 5$

$2x - 6 = 5$

$2x = 11$

$x = \frac{11}{2}$

In expanding $2(x - 3)$, your friend should have multiplied 2 times x and 2 times -3.

B. $5 - 3x = 10$

$-3x = 5$

$x = -\frac{5}{3}$

Your friend should have subtracted 3 from 5 because 5 is not a coefficient of x.

C. $\frac{1}{4}x - 2 = 7$

$x - 8 = 28$

$x = 36$

Your friend should have multiplied 4 times -2.

EXERCISES

1. Subtract 1 from both sides.

2. $2x + 4 = -2$

$2(-3) + 4 \stackrel{?}{=} -2$

$-6 + 4 \stackrel{?}{=} -2$

$-2 = -2$

Yes, -3 is a solution.

3. $10x + 8 = -2$

$10x = -10$

$x = -1$

Error: 8 added to right side instead of subtracted

4. Either step could be done first, but by multiplying by the reciprocal of $\frac{4}{3}$ (step b) you would remove the fraction from the problem.

5. $x - 10 = 16$

$6 - 10 \stackrel{?}{=} 16$

$-4 \neq 16$

6 is not a solution.

6. $\frac{1}{2}x - 9 = -2$

$\frac{1}{2}(14) - 9 \stackrel{?}{=} -2$

$7 - 9 \stackrel{?}{=} -2$

$-2 = -2$

14 is a solution.

7. $\frac{2}{3}x + 1 = -5$

$\frac{2}{3}(-9) + 1 \stackrel{?}{=} -5$

$-6 + 1 \stackrel{?}{=} -5$

$-5 = -5$

-9 is a solution.

8. $4x - \frac{1}{2} = -\frac{3}{2}$

$4\left(-\frac{1}{2}\right) - \frac{1}{2} \stackrel{?}{=} -\frac{3}{2}$

$-\frac{4}{2} - \frac{1}{2} \stackrel{?}{=} -\frac{3}{2}$

$-\frac{5}{2} \neq -\frac{3}{2}$

$-\frac{1}{2}$ is not a solution.

9. $\frac{3x}{5} + 1 = 7$

$\frac{3(-10)}{5} + 1 \stackrel{?}{=} 7$

$-6 + 1 \stackrel{?}{=} 7$

$-5 \neq 7$

-10 is not a solution.

10. $-4 - \frac{x}{9} = -8$

$-4 - \frac{36}{9} \stackrel{?}{=} -8$

$-4 - 4 \stackrel{?}{=} -8$

$-8 = -8$

36 is a solution.

11. $3x - 7 = 23$

$3x = 30$

$x = 10$

12. $2x + 5 = 9$

$2x = 4$

$x = 2$

13. $\frac{1}{4}x + 2 = 3$

$\frac{1}{4}x = 1$

$x = 4$

14. $\frac{1}{2}x - 1 = -1$

$\frac{1}{2}x = 0$

$x = 0$

15. $6 = 14 - 2x$

$-8 = -2x$

$4 = x$

16. $9 - \frac{2}{3}x = -1$

$-\frac{2}{3}x = -10$

$x = 15$

17. $-4 + \frac{4}{5}x = -6$

$\frac{4}{5}x = -2$

$x = -\frac{5}{2}$

18. $3x + \frac{1}{2} = -1$

$3x = -\frac{3}{2}$

$x = -\frac{1}{2}$

19. $\frac{4x}{3} + 5 = -3$

$\frac{4x}{3} = -8$

$x = -6$

20. $16 = 2 - \frac{2x}{5}$

$14 = -\frac{2x}{5}$

$-35 = x$

21. $4x - 3x = 9$

$x = 9$

22. $-6x + 4x = 2$

$-2x = 2$

$x = -1$

23. $x + 5x - 5 = 1$

$6x = 6$

$x = 1$

24. $3x - 7 + x = 5$

$4x = 12$

$x = 3$

25. $-2 = \frac{2x}{3} - x$

$-2 = -\frac{1}{3}x$

$6 = x$

26. $-10 = \frac{1}{2}x + x$

$-10 = \frac{3}{2}x$

$-\frac{20}{3} = x$

27. $3(x - 2) = 18$

$x - 2 = 6$

$x = 8$

28. $12(2 - x) = 6$

$2 - x = \frac{1}{2}$

$-x = -\frac{3}{2}$

$x = \frac{3}{2}$

29. $19 = 2(x + 1) - x$

$19 = 2x + 2 - x$

$19 = x + 2$

$17 = x$

30. $6 = \frac{3}{2}x + \frac{1}{2}(x - 4)$

$6 = \frac{3}{2}x + \frac{1}{2}x - 2$

$6 = 2x - 2$

$8 = 2x$

$4 = x$

31. $3x + \frac{3}{2}(2x - 1) = 2$

$3x + 3x - \frac{3}{2} = 2$

$6x - \frac{3}{2} = 2$

$6x = \frac{7}{2}$

$x = \frac{7}{12}$

32. $55x - 3(9x + 12) = -64$

$55x - 27x - 36 = -64$

$28x - 36 = -64$

$28x = -28$

$x = -1$

33. $\frac{9}{2}(x + 3) = 27$

$x + 3 = 6$

$x = 3$

34. $\frac{4}{9}(2x - 4) = 48$

$2x - 4 = 108$

$2x = 112$

$x = 56$

35. $32x + 285 = 357$

$32x = 72$

$x = 2\frac{1}{4}$ hours

36. $2600 = 12x - 3640$

$6240 = 12x$

$x = 520$ boxes

37. $0 = -32t + 28$

$-28 = -32t$

$t = \frac{7}{8}$ second

38. Rate for 1st machine $= 300$ (pages per hour)
Rate for 2nd machine $= 500$ (pages per hour)
Time to complete $= t$ (hours)
Total pages $= 6 \cdot 500$ (pages)

$300t + 500t = 6 \cdot 500$

$800t = 3000$

$t = 3\frac{3}{4}$ hours

39. It would take the first person 6 hours to complete the project, and it would take the second person 8 hours.

$\frac{1}{8}t + \frac{1}{6}t = 1$

$\frac{3}{24}t + \frac{4}{24}t = 1$

$\frac{7}{24}t = 1$

$t = \frac{24}{7}$ or $3\frac{3}{7}$ hours

40. $F = \frac{9}{5}C + 32$

$57 = \frac{9}{5}C + 32$

$25 = \frac{9}{5}C$

$C \approx 13.9^\circ$

41. $P = 2w + 2(3w)$

$16 = 2w + 6w$

$16 = 8w$

$w = 2$ meters

42. $7 + 6x = 19$

$6x = 12$

$x = 2$

43. $2x + 4x = 6x$

$= 6(4)$

$= 24$

44. $91y - 4 - 62y = 29y - 4$

$= 29(2) - 4$

$= 58 - 4$

$= 54$

45. $s^2 - 2s + 1 = 3^2 - 2(3) + 1$

$= 9 - 6 + 1$

$= 3 + 1$

$= 4$

46. $42 - t^2 = 42 - 8^2$

$= 42 - 64$

$= -22$

47. $16 + 9x - 12y - x = 16 + 8x - 12y$

$= 16 + 8(1) - 12(2)$

$= 16 + 8 - 24$

$= 24 - 24$

$= 0$

48. $3x - 4y + 9 = 3(4) - 4(4) + 9$

$= 12 - 16 + 9$

$= -4 + 9$

$= 5$

49. $4.9s - 12.1 + 9.7t = 4.9(3.2) - 12.1 + 9.7(1.7)$

$= 20.07$

50. $61.5 - 48.1x + 48.1y = 61.5 - 48.1(2.2) + 48.1(0.3)$

$= -29.9$

51. e. $\frac{m}{x} - 1$

Since $x(p+1) = m$

$p + 1 = \frac{m}{x}$

$p = \frac{m}{x} - 1$

52. No; 12 was not subtracted from both sides.

$6x + 12 = 18$

$6x = 6$

$x = 1$

53. $\frac{2}{3}x + 1 = \frac{1}{3}$ $\qquad$ $\frac{2}{3}x + 1 = \frac{1}{3}$

$2x + 3 = 1$ $\qquad$ $\frac{2}{3}x = -\frac{2}{3}$

$2x = -2$ $\qquad$ $x = -1$

$x = -1$

Multiplying by 3 gets rid of the fraction.

54. $\frac{1}{2}x - \frac{1}{4} = \frac{3}{4}$ $\qquad$ $\frac{1}{2}x - \frac{1}{4} = \frac{3}{4}$

$2x - 1 = 3$ $\qquad$ $\frac{1}{2}x = 1$

$2x = 4$ $\qquad$ $x = 2$

$x = 2$

Multiplying by 4 gets rid of the fraction.

55. $\frac{1}{2}(3x - 7) = 4$ $\qquad$ $\frac{1}{2}(3x - 7) = 4$

$3x - 7 = 8$ $\qquad$ $\frac{3}{2}x - \frac{7}{2} = 4$

$3x = 15$ $\qquad$ $\frac{3}{2}x = \frac{15}{2}$

$x = 5$ $\qquad$ $x = \frac{15}{2}\left(\frac{2}{3}\right)$

$= 5$

Multiply by the reciprocal to get rid of the fraction.

56. $\frac{6}{11}(x - 4) = -36$ $\qquad$ $\frac{6}{11}(x - 4) = -36$

$x - 4 = -66$ $\qquad$ $\frac{6}{11}x - \frac{24}{11} = -36$

$x = -62$ $\qquad$ $\frac{6}{11}x = -\frac{372}{11}$

$x = -62$

Multiply by the reciprocal to get rid of the fraction.

57. $-56 = \frac{8}{9}(4 - x)$ $\qquad$ $-56 = \frac{8}{9}(4 - x)$

$-63 = 4 - x$ $\qquad$ $-56 = \frac{32}{9} - \frac{8}{9}x$

$-67 = -x$ $\qquad$ $-\frac{536}{9} = -\frac{8}{9}x$

$67 = x$ $\qquad$ $67 = x$

Multiply by the reciprocal to get rid of the fraction.

58. $-9 = \frac{3}{7}(-2x + 5)$ $\qquad$ $-9 = \frac{3}{7}(-2x - 5)$

$-21 = -2x + 5$ $\qquad$ $-9 = -\frac{6}{7}x + \frac{15}{7}$

$-26 = -2x$ $\qquad$ $-\frac{78}{7} = -\frac{6}{7}x$

$13 = x$ $\qquad$ $13 = x$

Multiply by the reciprocal to get rid of the fraction.

3.3 Solving Equations with Variables on Both Sides

Communicating about Algebra

A.

$$\begin{aligned} -3x + 5 &= 9x - 19 & \\ -3x + 5 + 3x &= 9x - 19 + 3x & \textit{Add 3x to both sides} \\ 5 &= 12x - 19 & \textit{Simplify} \\ 5 + 19 &= 12x - 19 + 19 & \textit{Add 19 to both sides} \\ 24 &= 12x & \textit{Simplify} \\ \frac{24}{12} &= \frac{12x}{12} & \textit{Divide both sides by 12} \\ x &= 2 & \textit{Simplify} \end{aligned}$$

Check: $-3(2) + 5 \stackrel{?}{=} 9(2) - 19$

$-6 + 5 \stackrel{?}{=} 18 - 19$

$-1 = -1$

B. Write $-(3y - 6)$ as $-3y + 6$ to combine like terms.

EXERCISES

1. False. Collect the variables on the side with the larger to have a positive variable coefficient.

2. True

$x = 2x$

$x - x = 2x - x$

$0 = x$

3. Use the Distributive Property.

$81 - 9x = 4x - 10$

4. Add $9x$ to both sides to have a positive coefficient.

$81 = 13x - 10$

5. Add 10 to both sides.

$91 = 13x$

6. $x = 7$

Check:

$(9 - 7)9 \stackrel{?}{=} 4(7) - 10$

$(2)9 \stackrel{?}{=} 28 - 10$

$18 = 18$

7. Subtract x from both sides.

8. Add $4x$ to both sides.

9. Add 18 to both sides.

10. Add 16 to both sides.

11. Use the Distributive Property.

12. Use the Distributive Property.

13. $4x + 27 = 3x$

$x + 27 = 0$

$x = -27$

14. $8y + 14 = 6y$

$2y + 14 = 0$

$2y = -14$

$y = -7$

15. $-2m = 16m - 9$

$0 = 18m - 9$

$9 = 18m$

$\frac{1}{2} = m$

16. $7n = -35n - 6$

$42n = -6$

$n = -\frac{6}{42}$

$n = -\frac{1}{7}$

17. $12c - 4 = 4c$

$8c - 4 = 0$

$8c = 4$

$c = \frac{1}{2}$

18. $-25d + 10 = 15d$

$10 = 40d$

$\frac{10}{40} = d$

$\frac{1}{4} = d$

19. $5r + 6 = -14r - 13$

$19r + 6 = -13$

$19r = -19$

$r = -1$

20. $7s - 8 = 10s + 1$

$-8 = 3s + 1$

$-9 = 3s$

$-3 = s$

21. $12p - 7 = -3p + 8$

$15p - 7 = 8$

$15p = 15$

$p = 1$

22. $-6q + 8 = 4q - 12$

$8 = 10q - 12$

$20 = 10q$

$2 = q$

23. $-7 + 4m = 6m - 5$

$-7 = 2m - 5$

$-2 = 2m$

$-1 = m$

24. $-9 + 13g = 11 - g$

$-9 + 14g = 11$

$14g = 20$

$g = \frac{20}{14}$

$g = \frac{10}{7}$

25. $8 - 9t = 21t - 17$

$8 = 30t - 17$

$25 = 30t$

$\frac{25}{30} = t$

$\frac{5}{6} = t$

26. $20 + 8r = -4 + 5r$

$20 + 3r = -4$

$3r = -24$

$r = -8$

27. $6(3 - x) = 3x$

$18 - 6x = 3x$

$18 = 9x$

$2 = x$

28. $-2(x - 5) = -x$

$-2x + 10 = -x$

$10 = x$

29. $(-4 + y)10 = 2y$

$-40 + 10y = 2y$

$-40 + 8y = 0$

$8y = 40$

$y = 5$

30. $(-6a - 2)4 = 16a$

$-24a - 8 = 16a$

$-8 = 40a$

$-\frac{8}{40} = a$

$-\frac{1}{5} = a$

31. $9(b - 4) = 5(3b - 2)$

$9b - 36 = 15b - 10$

$-36 = 6b - 10$

$-26 = 6b$

$-\frac{26}{6} = b$

$-\frac{13}{3} = b$

32. $-4(3 - n) = 11(4n - 3)$

$-12 + 4n = 44n - 33$

$-12 = 40n - 33$

$21 = 40n$

$\frac{21}{40} = n$

33. $\frac{1}{2}(8n - 2) = 16 - 30n$

$4n - 1 = 16 - 30n$

$34n - 1 = 16$

$34n = 17$

$n = \frac{1}{2}$

34. $\frac{1}{3}(42 - 18z) = 2(8 - 4z)$

$14 - 6z = 16 - 8z$

$14 + 2z = 16$

$2z = 2$

$z = 1$

35. $\frac{1}{4}(100 + 36s) = 15 - 4s$

$25 + 9s = 15 - 4s$

$25 + 13s = 15$

$13s = -10$

$s = -\frac{10}{13}$

36. $\frac{2}{3}(24t - 9) = 8t + 23$

$16t - 6 = 8t + 23$

$8t - 6 = 23$

$8t = 29$

$t = \frac{29}{8}$

37. $5 \cdot t = 3 \cdot t + 28$

$2t = 28$

$t = 14$ times

You would need to use the trail 15 or more times to justify buying your own equipment.

38. Tony's height now = 60 (inches)
Tony's rate of growth = $2\frac{1}{3}$ (inches per year)
Number of years = y (years)
Kate's height now = 63 (inches)
Kate's rate of growth = $\frac{1}{3}$ (inch per year)

$60 + \frac{7}{3} \cdot y = 63 + \frac{1}{3}y$

$60 + 2y = 63$

$2y = 3$

$y = \frac{3}{2}$

$y = 1\frac{1}{2}$ years

39. a. $s + 80 = 3s$

40. $s + 80 = 3s$

$80 = 2s$

$40 = s$

If you go swimming more than 40 times, you will benefit by buying a membership.

41. c. $18n = 13n + 2000$

42. $18n = 13n + 2000$

$5n = 2000$

$n = 400$

The Fast Track Company must sell 400 cars a day to break even.

43. $x - 2(x - 1) = x - 2x + 2$

$= -x + 2$

44. $4 - 3(2x - 2) = 4 - 6x + 6$

$= -6x + 10$

45. $2(6 + 3x) - 8 = 12 + 6x - 8$

$= 6x + 4$

46. $-4(2 + 5y) + 10 = -8 - 20y + 10$

$= -20y + 2$

47. $7x[2 - (-5)] - 3x = 7x[7] - 3x$

$= 49x - 3x$

$= 46x$

48. $-4m[-2 - (-6)] - 11(m + 1) = -4m[4] - 11(m + 1)$

$= -16m - 11m - 11$

$= -27m - 11$

49. $8(2 - x) = -4x$

$8(2 - 4) \stackrel{?}{=} -4(4)$

$8(-2) \stackrel{?}{=} -16$

$-16 = -16$

4 is a solution.

50. $-6(7 - a) = 4a$

$-6(7 - 5) \stackrel{?}{=} 4(5)$

$-6(2) \stackrel{?}{=} 20$

$-12 \neq 20$

5 is not a solution.

51. $\frac{1}{3}x + 10 = -12$

$\frac{1}{3}(7) + 10 \stackrel{?}{=} -12$

$\frac{7}{3} + \frac{30}{3} \stackrel{?}{=} -12$

$\frac{37}{3} \neq -12$

7 is not a solution.

52. $12 - \frac{1}{4}x = 32$

$12 - \frac{1}{4}(-80) \stackrel{?}{=} 32$

$12 + 20 \stackrel{?}{=} 32$

$32 = 32$

-80 is a solution.

53. $\frac{1}{2}x - 8 = \frac{1}{2}(x - 8)$

$\frac{1}{2}(18) - 8 \stackrel{?}{=} \frac{1}{2}(18 - 8)$

$9 - 8 \stackrel{?}{=} \frac{1}{2}(10)$

$1 \neq 5$

18 is not a solution.

54. $27 + 6x = 3x - 9$

$27 + 6(-6) \stackrel{?}{=} 3(-6) - 9$

$27 - 36 \stackrel{?}{=} -18 - 9$

$-9 \neq -27$

-6 is not a solution.

55. $20x - 4 = 6$

$20x = 10$

$x = \frac{1}{2}$

56. Correct

57. $-3(y + 12) = 51$

$-3y - 36 = 51$

$-3y = 87$

$y = -29$

58. $(b - 4)8 = -12$

$8b - 32 = -12$

$8b = 20$

$b = \frac{20}{8}$

$b = \frac{5}{2}$

59. $8y(4 - 1) = 2y - 6$

$24y = 2y - 6$

$22y = -6$

$y = -\frac{6}{22}$

$y = -\frac{3}{11}$

60. $(c + 6)7 = (4 - c)3$

$7c + 42 = 12 - 3c$

$10c + 42 = 12$

$10c = -30$

$c = -3$

61. $3(4 - x) = -2x + 12 - x$

$12 - 3x = -3x + 12$

$0 = 0$

The equation has many solutions.

62. $8x - [4 - (-2)] = 8x$

$8x - [6] = 8x$

$-6 = 0$

The equation has no solution.

63. $2a - 3 = -4a + 7$

$6a - 3 = 7$

$6a = 10$

$a = \frac{10}{6}$

$a = \frac{5}{3}$

$-4b + 2 = 6b - 23$

$2 = 10b - 23$

$25 = 10b$

$\frac{25}{10} = b$

$b = \frac{5}{2}$

$-17c + 7 = 93c - 153$

$7 = 110c - 153$

$160 = 110c$

$\frac{160}{110} = c$

$c = \frac{16}{11}$

$3d - 19 = 14 - 3(d - 1)$

$3d - 19 = 14 - 3d + 3$

$3d - 19 = 17 - 3d$

$6d - 19 = 17$

$6d = 36$

$d = 6$

Mixed **REVIEW**

1. $5\% = \frac{5}{100} = \frac{1}{20}$

2. $67\% = 0.67$

3. $27 \div 3 = 9$

4. $\frac{4}{3}(9) = \frac{36}{3} = 12$

5. $\frac{1}{3}(6 - 2x) - 4\left(1 + \frac{1}{3}x\right) = 2 - \frac{2}{3}x - 4 - \frac{4}{3}x$

$= -2 - \frac{6}{3}x$

$= -2 - 2x$

6. $\left(3x \div \frac{1}{2}\right) \div 6 = (3x \cdot 2) \div 6$

$= 6x \div 6$

$= x$

7. $(3)^2 \cdot x^3$

8. $|-32| = 32$

9. $-\frac{7}{2}$

10. -15.3

11. $3x - 4 \le 6$

$3(3) - 4 \overset{?}{\le} 6$

$9 - 4 \overset{?}{\le} 6$

$5 \le 6$

3 is a solution.

$3x - 4 \le 6$

$3(4) - 4 \overset{?}{\le} 6$

$12 - 4 \overset{?}{\le} 6$

$8 \not\le 6$

4 is not a solution.

12. $\frac{1}{2}(y+6) \cdot 4y = \frac{1}{2}(1+6) \cdot 4(1)$

$= \frac{1}{2}(7)(4)$

$= \frac{7}{2}(4)$

$= \frac{28}{2}$

$= 14$

13. $2 \cdot \frac{7}{2}w + 2 \cdot w = 9w$

14. $(-9+4) \cdot (x-6) = (-9+4) \cdot (11-6)$

$= (-5)(5)$

$= -25$

15. $3x - 2 < 12$

16. $x + 5y$

3.4 Linear Equations and Problem Solving

Communicating about Algebra

A. Verbal Model:

[Top margin] + [Bottom margin] + 4 · [Picture space] + 5 · [Picture length] = [Total length]

Labels:

Top margin $= \frac{7}{8}$	(inches)
Bottom margin $= \frac{7}{8}$	(inches)
Picture-space length $= \frac{3}{16}$	(inches)
Picture length $= x$	(inches)
Total length $= 11$	(inches)

Equation:

$\frac{7}{8} + \frac{7}{8} + 4\left(\frac{3}{16}\right) + 5x = 11$

$\frac{10}{4} + 5x = 11$

$5x = 11 - \frac{5}{2}$

$5x = \frac{17}{2}$

$x = \frac{17}{10}$ or $1\frac{7}{10}$ inches

B. $\dfrac{\text{width}}{\text{height}} = \dfrac{3/2}{17/10}\left(\dfrac{10}{10}\right) = \dfrac{15}{17}$

C. No. $\dfrac{\text{width}}{\text{height}} = \dfrac{8}{10} = \dfrac{4}{5} \ne \dfrac{15}{17}$

Yes, you will have to crop photos.

EXERCISES

1. Rate of 1st runner $= 10$ (kilometers per hour)
Time after 2nd runner starts $= t$ (hours)
Distance advantage of 1st runner $= 7$ (kilometers)
Rate of 2nd runner $= 15$ (kilometers per hour)

2. $10t + 7 = 15t$

3. $10t + 7 = 15t$

$7 = 5t$

$\frac{7}{5} = t$

$t = \frac{7}{5}$ hours

From the instant the second runner started running, each runner ran for $\frac{7}{5}$ hours.

4. Distance $=$ (rate of 2nd runner) • (time after 2nd runner starts)

$= 15 \cdot \frac{7}{5}$

Distance $= 21$ kilometers

5. | Rate of stray elephant | • | Time to catch up | = | Rate of herd of elephants | • | Time to catch up | + | Distance from elephant to herd |

6. Rate of stray elephant $= 25$ (miles per hour)
Time to catch up $= \frac{1}{12}$ (hour)
Rate of herd of elephants $= 10$ (miles per hour)
Distance from elephant to herd $= d$ (miles)

7. $25\left(\frac{1}{12}\right) = 10\left(\frac{1}{12}\right) + d$

8. $25\left(\frac{1}{12}\right) = 10\left(\frac{1}{12}\right) + d$

$\frac{25}{12} = \frac{10}{12} + d$

$\frac{15}{12} = d$

$d = 1\frac{1}{4}$ miles

The herd had traveled $1\frac{1}{4}$ miles when the stray elephant became frightened.

9. | Population of western region | + | Rate of western increase | • | Number of years | = | Population of midwest region | + | Rate of midwest increase | • | Number of years |

10. Population of western region $= 50,679,000$ (people)
Rate of western increase $= 982,000$ (people per year)
Population of midwest region $= 58,878,000$ (people)
Rate of midwest increase $= 222,000$ (people per year)
Number of years $= y$ (years)

11. $50,679,000 + 982,000y = 58,878,000 + 222,000y$

12. $50,679,000 + 982,000y = 58,878,000 + 222,000y$

$760,000y = 8,199,000$

$y \approx 10.8$ years

$1988 + 11 = 1999$

13.

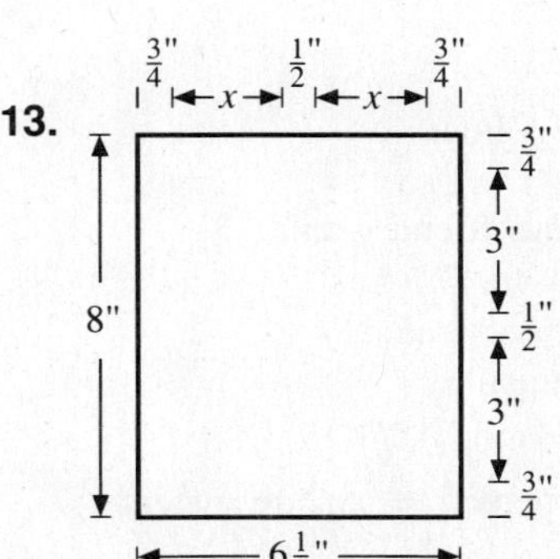

14. $2 \cdot$ [Picture width] $+$ [Gutter width] $+ 2 \cdot$ [Margin width] $=$ [Cover width]

15. Picture width $= x$ (inches)
Gutter width $= \frac{1}{2}$ (inch)
Margin width $= \frac{3}{4}$ (inch)
Cover width $= 6\frac{1}{2}$ (inches)

16. $2x + \frac{1}{2} + 2 \cdot \frac{3}{4} = 6\frac{1}{2}$

17.
$$2x + \frac{1}{2} + 2 \cdot \frac{3}{4} = 6\frac{1}{2}$$
$$2x + 2 = \frac{13}{2}$$
$$2x = \frac{9}{2}$$
$$x = \frac{9}{4}$$
$$x = 2\frac{1}{4} \text{ inches}$$

You should make the pictures $2\frac{1}{4}$ inches wide.

18. [Your current amount of money] $+$ [Money you save each week] $\cdot$ [Number of weeks] $=$ [Sister's current amount of money] $-$ [Additional money spent] $\cdot$ [Number of weeks]

19.

Your current amount of money = 60	(dollars)
Money you save each week = 5	(dollars per week)
Number of weeks = w	(weeks)
Sister's current amount of money = 135	(dollars)
Additional money spent = 10	(dollars per week)

20. $60 + 5w = 135 - 10w$

21.
$$60 + 5w = 135 - 10w$$
$$60 + 15w = 135$$
$$15w = 75$$
$$w = 5 \text{ weeks}$$

You will have as much money as your sister in 5 weeks.

22. [Greenville temperature] $+$ [Rate of temperature increase] $\cdot$ [Number of hours] $=$ [Waterloo temperature] $-$ [Rate of temperature decrease] $\cdot$ [Number of hours]

23.

Greenville temperature = 69	(°F)
Rate of temperature increase = 2	(°F per hour)
Number of hours = h	(hours)
Waterloo temperature = 84	(°F)
Rate of temperature decrease = 3	(°F per hour)

24. $69 + 2h = 84 - 3h$

25.
$$69 + 2h = 84 - 3h$$
$$69 + 5h = 84$$
$$5h = 15$$
$$h = 3 \text{ hours}$$

You and your friend would have to talk for 3 hours before the temperature would be equal.

26. $\frac{\text{miles}}{\text{hour}} \cdot \text{hours} = \text{miles}$

27. $\frac{\text{feet}}{\text{minute}} \cdot \text{minutes} = \text{feet}$

28. meters $\cdot$ meters $=$ square meters

29. liters $-$ liters $=$ liters

30. $\frac{\text{hours}}{\text{day}} \cdot \text{days} = \text{hours}$

31. $\frac{\text{inches}}{\text{foot}} \cdot \text{feet} = \text{inches}$

32. centimeters + centimeters = centimeters

33. hours ÷ day = hours per day

34. $t = \frac{d}{r}$

$= \frac{30 \text{ feet}}{25 \text{ feet/second}}$

$= \frac{6}{5} \text{ seconds}$

35. $\frac{(30 + x) \text{ feet}}{50 \text{ feet/second}}$

36. $\frac{30 + x}{50} = \frac{6}{5}$

$30 + x = 60$

$x = 30$

37. The coyote must be less than 30 feet from the rabbit to catch him before he reaches his burrow.

Mid-Chapter SELF-TEST

1. $3m = 18$

$m = 6$

2. $\frac{1}{4}p = 7$

$p = 28$

3. $y - 6 = 7$

$y = 13$

4. $x + \frac{1}{2} = 3$

$x = \frac{5}{2}$

5. $3s + 2 = 17$

$3s = 15$

$s = 5$

6. $\frac{x}{4} + 10 = \frac{3}{4}$

$x + 40 = 3$

$x = -37$

7. $16(x - 2) - (x - 3) = 29$

$16x - 32 - x + 3 = 29$

$15x - 29 = 29$

$15x = 58$

$x = \frac{58}{15}$

8. $\frac{1}{4}(y + 8) + 6 = 10$

$\frac{1}{4}y + 2 + 6 = 10$

$\frac{1}{4}y + 8 = 10$

$\frac{1}{4}y = 2$

$y = 8$

9. $12n + 2 - 3n = 5 - (n - 2)$

$9n + 2 = 5 - n + 2$

$10n + 2 = 7$

$10n = 5$

$n = \frac{1}{2}$

10. $y + 2 = 2y - 4$

$2 = y - 4$

$6 = y$

11. $\frac{1}{2}(x - 2) = 3 - x$

$x - 2 = 6 - 2x$

$3x - 2 = 6$

$3x = 8$

$x = \frac{8}{3}$

12. $3p - 2 = \frac{1}{3}(6p + 5)$

$3p - 2 = 2p + \frac{5}{3}$

$p - 2 = \frac{5}{3}$

$p = \frac{11}{3}$

13. $-2(x + 3) = 3x + 1$

$-2x - 6 = 3x + 1$

$-6 = 5x + 1$

$-7 = 5x$

$-\frac{7}{5} = x$

14. Correct

15. Correct

16. **c.** $4x = 12$

17. **a.** $5x = 35$

c. $x = \frac{1}{5}(35)$

18. $\frac{6}{4} = \frac{3}{2}$ ratio, **b.** $\frac{H}{20} = \frac{6}{4}$

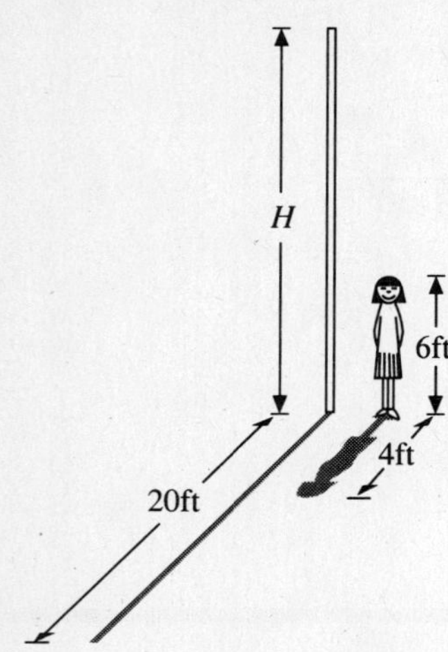

19. $\frac{H}{20} = \frac{6}{4}$

$H = \frac{6}{4} \cdot 20$

$H = 30$ feet

20. c. $n + 2 + 5 = 2n + 2$

3.5 Solving Equations That Involve Decimals

Communicating about Algebra

A. Charge for 1st minute $= 0.44$ (dollars)
Rate for additional minutes $= 0.28$ (dollars per minute)
Total cost $= 5.26$ (dollars)

B. $0.44 + 0.28x = 5.26$

$0.28x = 4.82$

$x \approx 17.21$

After the first minute, you can talk for an additional 17 minutes. Thus, you can talk for 18 minutes.

EXERCISES

1. $\frac{20.00}{3} = 6.666\ldots \approx 6.67$

$(6.67)(3) = 20.01$

2. b. 80.5
Uses the same amount of decimal places.

3. Multiply both sides of the equation by ten.

4. b. The solution is $x \approx 0.43$.

5. -367.8

6. 83.7

7. 63.6

8. 2.2

9. 14.6

10. 1.4

11. 5.36

12. -2.50

13. $-41.287 - 3.382 = -44.669$

≈ -44.67

14. $11.051(3.467) \approx 38.31$

15. $-23.981(-4.598) \approx 110.26$

16. $15.953 \div 3.476 \approx 4.59$

17. $17x - 33 = 114$
$17x = 147$
$x \approx 8.65$

18. $-3x + 51 = 104$
$-3x = 53$
$x \approx -17.67$

19. $-18 + 41a = 57$
$41a = 75$
$a \approx 1.83$

20. $31 = 44 - 12m$
$-13 = -12m$
$1.08 \approx m$

21. $25 = 14 - 10d$
$11 = -10d$
$-1.1 = d$

22. $99 = 100t + 56$
$43 = 100t$
$0.43 = t$

23. $238 = 79z - 43$
$281 = 79z$
$3.56 \approx z$

24. $28 - 68c = 241$
$-68c = 213$
$c \approx -3.13$

25. $3(31 - 12x) = 82$
$93 - 36x = 82$
$-36x = -11$
$x \approx 0.31$

26. $5(-8x + 15) = 49$
$-40x + 75 = 49$
$-40x = -26$
$x = 0.65$

27. $2(-5x + 4) = -x$
$-10x + 8 = -x$
$8 = 9x$
$0.89 \approx x$

28. $-(x - 3) = 2(3x + 1)$
$-x + 3 = 6x + 2$
$1 = 7x$
$0.14 \approx x$

29. $15.74 - 2.36x = 18.66x - 12.23$
$15.74 = 21.02x - 12.23$
$27.97 = 21.02x$
$1.33 \approx x$

30. $5.423 - 6.411x = 8.213x + 3.081$
$5.423 = 14.624x + 3.081$
$2.342 = 14.624x$
$0.16 \approx x$

31. $2.7 - 3.6x = 8.4 + 23.7x$
$2.7 = 8.4 + 27.3x$
$-5.7 = 27.3x$
$-0.21 \approx x$

32. $5.3 + 9.2x = 7.4x - 8.8$
$5.3 + 1.8x = -8.8$
$1.8x = -14.1$
$x \approx -7.83$

33. $6(3.14 + 1.59x) = 12.29x - 4.37$
$18.84 + 9.54x = 12.29x - 4.37$
$18.84 = 2.75x - 4.37$
$23.21 = 2.75x$
$8.44 = x$

34. $18(1.01 - 2.30x) = 4.93x + 6.22$
$18.18 - 41.40x = 4.93x + 6.22$
$-46.33x = -11.96$
$x \approx 0.26$

35. $18.41x - 12.75 = (4.32 - 6.81)3$
$18.41x - 12.75 = 12.96x - 20.43$
$5.45x - 12.75 = -20.43$
$5.45x = -7.68$
$x \approx -1.41$

36. $25.79x - 18.24 = (7.77 - 13.91x)(-6)$
$25.79x - 18.24 = -46.62 + 83.46x$
$-18.24 = -46.62 + 57.67x$
$28.38 = 57.67x$
$0.49 \approx x$

37. $38.5x + 2.4 = -31.7 + 41.8x$

$2.4 = -31.7 + 3.3x$

$34.1 = 3.3x$

$10.33 \approx x$

38. $26.4x - 3.2 = 5.9x - 32.1$

$20.5x - 3.2 = -32.1$

$20.5x = -28.9$

$x \approx -1.41$

39. $x + 0.05x = 32.14$

$1.05x = 32.14$

$x = \$30.61$

40. $x + 0.15x = 6.46$

$1.15x = 6.46$

$x = \$5.62$

41. a. $42.5r = 10.3$

42. $42.5r = 10.3$

$r \approx 0.2$ kilometers per minute

43. $0.26l = w$

$0.26l = 23.5$

$l \approx 90.4$ inches

44. $0.25l = w$

$0.25l = 31.5$

$l = 126.0$ inches

45. [Rate of cold water] • [Amount of time for cold water] = [Rate of hot water] • [Amount of time for hot water]

46. Rate of hot water = 7.8 (liters per minute)
Rate of cold water = 12.3 (liters per minute)
Amount of time for cold water = t (minutes)
Amount of time for hot water = $t + 2$ (minutes)

47. $12.3t = 7.8(t + 2)$

48. $12.3t = 7.8t + 15.6$

$4.5t = 15.6$

$t \approx 3.5$ minutes

49. $150 + 0.38x = 300$

$0.38x = 150$

$x = \$394.74$

50. $150 + 0.38x = 500$

$0.38x = 350$

$x = \$921.05$

51. $|-3| + n = 15$

$3 + n = 15$

$n = 12$

52. $2n + |-8| = 22$

$2n + 8 = 22$

$2n = 14$

$n = 7$

53. $5x + (-4)^2 = 21$

$5x + 16 = 21$

$5x = 5$

$x = 1$

54. $-(6)^2 + 19x = 15$

$-36 + 19x = 15$

$19x = 51$

$x = \frac{51}{19}$

55. $3t - (-2t) + 14 = 6$

$3t + 2t + 14 = 6$

$5t + 14 = 6$

$5t = -8$

$t = -\frac{8}{5}$

56. $7t + (-3t) - 8 = 16$

$4t - 8 = 16$

$4t = 24$

$t = 6$

57. $3(10y - 12) + 15y = 54$

$30y - 36 + 15y = 54$

$45y - 36 = 54$

$45y = 90$

$y = 2$

58. $x - 8 = 2 + 4x$

$-8 = 2 + 3x$

$-10 = 3x$

$x = -\frac{10}{3}$

59. $12 + 2x = 8 - 5x$

$12 + 7x = 8$

$7x = -4$

$x = -\frac{4}{7}$

60. $-2a = 3.9$

$a = -1.95$

$3.1b = -2.6b + 5$

$5.7b = 5$

$b \approx 0.88$

$0.57c = -8.6$

$c \approx -15.09$

$3.2(d + 48) = -d + 1.7$

$3.2d + 153.6 = -d + 1.7$

$4.2d + 153.6 = 1.7$

$4.2d = -151.9$

$d \approx -36.17$

61. $\frac{15(0.20)}{15+5} = \frac{3}{20}$

$= 0.15$

$= 15\%$

c. 15.0

62. Let x represent the least number of households with dogs. Of the 56,000 households, 30% have dogs. In a red county the number is 20% or higher.

$x = [(56{,}000)(0.30)](1.20)$

$x = 20{,}160$ households

63. Let y represent the greatest number of households with cats. Of the 112,000 households, 22% have cats. A blue county is below average so the greatest number of households with cats will be one less than the average.

$y = (112{,}000)(0.22) - 1$

$y = 24{,}639$ households

64. Let z represent the least number of households in a county. Since a yellow county may have up to 20% more pets, the least number of households will be one less than would occur at 20% above average.

$[(z - 1)(0.22)](1.2) = 74{,}000$

$0.264(z - 1) = 74{,}000$

$z - 1 \approx 280{,}303$

$z \approx 280{,}304$ households

65. Let x represent the least number of households in a county. Since a red county may have 20% to 100% more pets, the least number of households will occur when there are 100% more pets.

$[x(0.3)](1 + 1.00) = 23{,}000$

$0.6x = 23{,}000$

$x \approx 38{,}333$ households

3.6 Literal Equations and Formulas

Communicating about Algebra

A. $V = \frac{1}{3}hs^2$

$\frac{3V}{s^2} = h$

B. $h = \frac{3 \cdot 90{,}000{,}000}{750^2}$

$= 480$ feet

EXERCISES

1. False

2. **b.** $a - 6 = 3b + 9$

c. $4s + 9t = 16$

These are literal equations because each uses more than one letter as a variable.

3. $3n + 4m = 9$

$4m = 9 - 3n$

$m = \frac{9 - 3n}{4}$

4. $I = Prt$

$\frac{I}{Pt} = r$

$r = \frac{I}{Pt}$

5. $A = \frac{1}{2}bh$

$2A = bh$

$\frac{2A}{b} = h$

6. $P = 2L + 2W$

$P - 2W = 2L$

$\frac{P - 2W}{2} = L$

7. $V = LWH$

$\frac{V}{WH} = L$

8. $V = \pi r^2 h$

$\frac{V}{\pi r^2} = h$

9. $S = C + rC$

$S = C(1 + r)$

$\frac{S}{(1 + r)} = C$

10. $S = L - rL$

$S = L(1 - r)$

$\frac{S}{(1 - r)} = L$

11. $A = P + Prt$

$A - P = Prt$

$\frac{A - P}{Pt} = r$

12. $A = P(1 + r)^t$

$\frac{A}{(1 + r)^t} = P$

13. $A = \frac{1}{2}h(b_1 + b_2)$

$\frac{2A}{h} = b_1 + b_2$

$\frac{2A}{h} - b_2 = b_1$

14. $S = \frac{rL - a}{r - 1}$

$S(r - 1) = rL - a$

$Sr - S = rL - a$

$Sr - rL = S - a$

$r(S - L) = S - a$

$r = \frac{S - a}{S - L}$

15. $L = a + (n - 1)d$

$L - a = (n - 1)d$

$\frac{L - a}{d} = n - 1$

$\frac{L - a}{d} + 1 = n$

16. $S = \frac{n}{2}[2a + (n - 1)d]$

$\frac{2}{n}S = 2a + (n - 1)d$

$\frac{2}{n}S - (n - 1)d = 2a$

$\frac{1}{2}\left[\frac{2}{n}S - (n - 1)d\right] = a$

$\frac{S}{n} - (n - 1)\frac{d}{2} = a$

17. $lwh = V$

$h = \frac{V}{lw}$

$h = \frac{9.4}{(12)(3)}$

$h \approx 0.26$ feet

18. $V = \pi r^2 h$

$\frac{V}{\pi r^2} = h$

$\frac{48\pi}{\pi(2)^2} = h$

$\frac{48}{4} = h$

$h = 12$ centimeters

19. $L = 1.5W$

$P = 2L + 2W$

$P = 2(1.5)W + 2W$

$P = 5W$

$W = \frac{P}{5}$

$W = \frac{75}{5}$

$W = 15$ inches

20. $W = 0.62L$

$P = 2W + 2L$

$P = 2(0.62L) + 2L$

$P = 3.24L$

$L = \frac{P}{3.24}$

$L = \frac{3}{3.24}$

$L \approx 0.93$ feet

21.
$$P \approx \frac{1.2w}{H^2}$$
$$PH^2 \approx 1.2w$$
$$\frac{PH^2}{1.2} \approx w$$
$$\frac{45 \cdot 2^2}{1.2} \approx w$$
$$w \approx 150 \text{ pounds}$$

22.
$$F = MA$$
$$A = \frac{F}{M}$$
$$A = \frac{20}{10}$$
$A = 2$ meters per second per second

23.
$$A = P(1+r)^t$$
$$P = \frac{A}{(1+r)^t}$$
$$P = \frac{324.75}{(1+0.072)^2}$$
$$P = \$282.59$$
$$P = \frac{324.75}{(1+0.053)^2}$$
$$P = \$292.88$$
$$324.75 - 282.59 = \$42.16$$
$$324.75 - 292.88 = \$31.87$$
$$42.16 + 31.87 = \$74.03$$

24.
$$A = P + Prt$$
$$\frac{A-P}{Pt} = r$$
$$r = \frac{428 - 400}{400 \cdot 1}$$
$$r = \frac{28}{400}$$
$$r = 0.07$$
$$r = 7\%$$

25.
$$A = P(1+r)^t$$
$$P = \frac{A}{(1+r)^t}$$
$$P = \frac{179.20}{(1+.06)^2}$$
$$P = \frac{179.20}{1.1236}$$
$$P = \$159.49$$

26.
$$A = P + Prt$$
$$A - P = Prt$$
$$t = \frac{A-P}{Pr}$$
$$t = \frac{396.80 - 320}{320(0.12)}$$
$$t = \frac{76.80}{38.4}$$
$$t = 2 \text{ years}$$

27.
$$4t - 1 = 7$$
$$4t = 8$$
$$t = 2$$

28.
$$s - 35 + 9 = 10 - s$$
$$s - 26 = 10 - s$$
$$2s - 26 = 10$$
$$2s = 36$$
$$s = 18$$

29.
$$3(x-1) = x + 9$$
$$3x - 3 = x + 9$$
$$2x - 3 = 9$$
$$2x = 12$$
$$x = 6$$

30.
$$\tfrac{1}{2}\left(\tfrac{1}{2}a + 4\right) = 8 - \tfrac{3}{4}a$$
$$\tfrac{1}{2}a + 4 = 16 - \tfrac{3}{2}a$$
$$2a + 4 = 16$$
$$2a = 12$$
$$a = 6$$

31.
$$4V - 3H + 9 = 4\left(\tfrac{1}{2}\right) - 3(4) + 9$$
$$= 2 - 12 + 9$$
$$= -10 + 9$$
$$= -1$$

32.
$$9x + 36 - 4y = 9(2) + 36 - 4(14)$$
$$= 18 + 36 - 56$$
$$= 54 - 56$$
$$= -2$$

33.
$$(1.2x - 1)^4 - 0.1 = (1.2 \cdot 1.1 - 1)^4 - 0.1$$
$$= (0.32)^4 - 0.1$$
$$\approx 0.01 - 0.1$$
$$= -0.09$$

34.
$$\tfrac{1}{2}(x-y)^2 = \tfrac{1}{2}(2-4)^2$$
$$= \tfrac{1}{2}(-2)^2$$
$$= \tfrac{1}{2}(4)$$
$$= 2$$

35.
$$A = P(1.08)^t$$
$$\frac{A}{(1.08)^t} = P$$

36.
$$P = \frac{10{,}000}{(1.08)^1}$$
$$= \$9259.26$$

37.
$$P = \frac{10{,}000}{(1.08)^5}$$
$$= \$6805.83$$

38.

10 years	\$4,631.94
15 years	\$3,152.42
20 years	\$2,145.49
30 years	\$ 993.78
50 years	\$ 213.22
100 years	\$ 4.55
180 years	\$ 0.01

39. $A = 5000(1.05)^{100} = \$657,506.29$ in 1890

Assume \$257,506.29 was used at this time.

$A = 400,000(1.05)^{100} = \$52,600,503.14$ could be available in 1990.

Boston used part of this money to establish the Franklin Technical Institute, a trade school in Boston.

Philadelphia used the money to establish the Franklin Institute, founded in 1824, as a nonprofit scientific and educational institution.

Mixed REVIEW

1. $(-37.2)(0.23) - 18.2 \div 4.9 \approx -12.3$

2. $\frac{3x}{4y} - \frac{1}{2}x = \frac{3\left(\frac{1}{3}\right)}{4(2)} - \frac{1}{2}\left(\frac{1}{3}\right)$

$= \frac{1}{8} - \frac{1}{6}$

$= \frac{3}{24} - \frac{4}{24}$

$= -\frac{1}{24}$

3. $\frac{1}{8} + \frac{3}{4} = \frac{1}{8} + \frac{6}{8}$

$= \frac{7}{8}$

4. $3 - (-7) = 3 + 7$

$= 10$

5. $3x(x-4) + 2(1-x) = 3x^2 - 12x + 2 - 2x$

$= 3x^2 - 14x + 2$

6. $x^4 = 3^4$

$= 81$

7. $-4 + 2x + (-12) = 2x - 16$

8. $3 \div \left(\frac{4}{3} \cdot \frac{3}{8}\right) - 7 = 3 \div \left(\frac{1}{2}\right) - 7$

$= 3 \cdot 2 - 7$

$= 6 - 7$

$= -1$

9. $7x - 2x + 3 = 8$

$5x + 3 = 8$

$5x = 5$

$x = 1$

10. $3x - 4 = 4$

$3x = 8$

$x = \frac{8}{3}$

11. $\frac{4x}{3} - 5 = 7$

$\frac{4}{3}x = 12$

$x = 9$

12. $6x + 29 = -4x - 1$

$10x + 29 = -1$

$10x = -30$

$x = -3$

13. $24 = 7n + 3$

14. $2x + 2 \cdot 3y < 20$

15. $(x+6)\left(\frac{1}{4}\right)$

16. $4 - x = x$

3.7 Exploring Data: Scatter Plots

Communicating about Algebra

A. (29.8, 80.6) (33.2, 82.0) (35.5, 77.0) (37.7, 73.6) (39.1, 76.1) (41.2, 73.0) (43.5, 68.4) (46.8, 64.3)

T
84 80 76 72 68 64
Temperature (°F)
28 32 36 40 44 48 L
Latitude (°N)

B. As the latitude increases, the temperature decreases.

C. The latitude of St. Louis is approximately 39°.

EXERCISES

1. **b.** an ordered pair of real numbers

2. 3 is the horizontal coordinate.
7 is the vertical coordinate.

3. A(2, 3) B(−1, 4) C(0, 0)
D(3, 0) E(−2, −2) F(2, −3)

4. The point lies below the horizontal axis and right of the vertical axis.

5.

(−3, 4) (0, 3) (2, 2) (4, 0) (−3, −1) (2, −1)

6. A (−3, 2)
B (1, −2)
C (2, 0)
D (2, 3)
E (−2, −1)
F (0, −3)

7. A (2, 4)
B (1, 2)
C (−2, 3)
D (−1, 0)
E (0, −1)
F (4, −2)

8. A (−3, 0)
B (−4, −4)
C (−2, −3)
D (2, −2)
E (1, 1)
F (0, 2)

9.

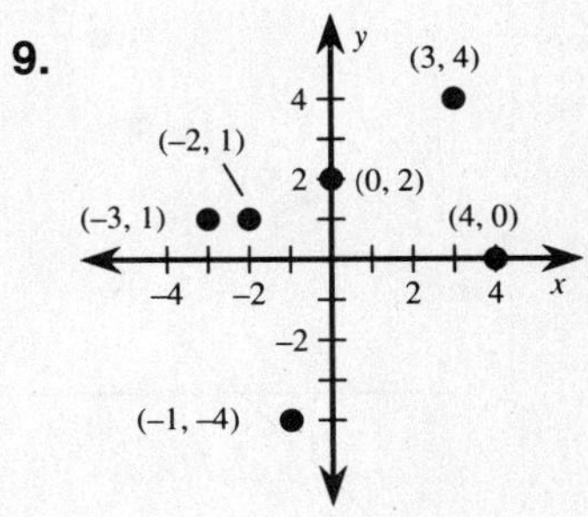

10.

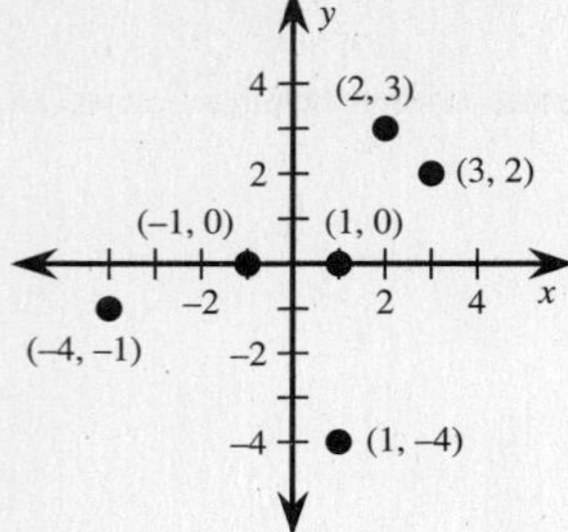

11.

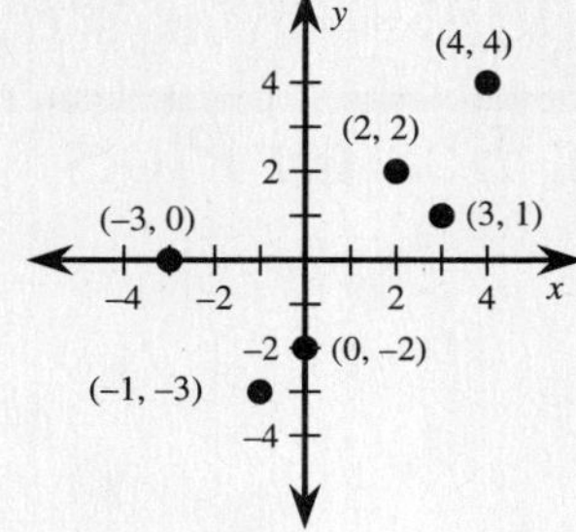

12.

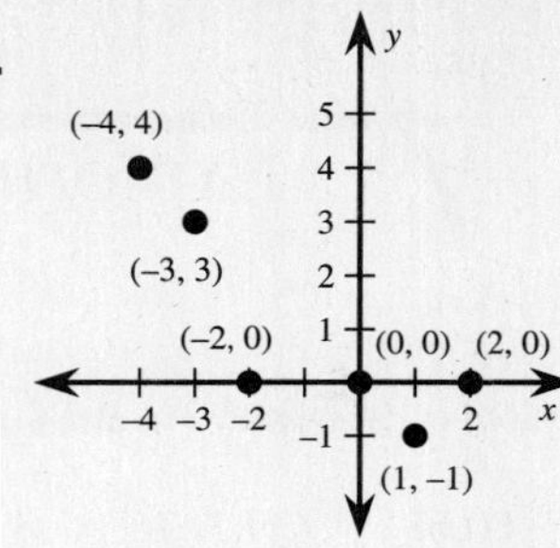

13. The value of t is 1990.

The value of C is 5.

14. The horizontal axis is in years.

The vertical axis is in dollars.

15. **c.** C increases as t increases

16. x is 3.

y is 6.

17. The horizontal axis is in inches.

The vertical axis is in inches.

18. **a.** y decreases as x increases

19.

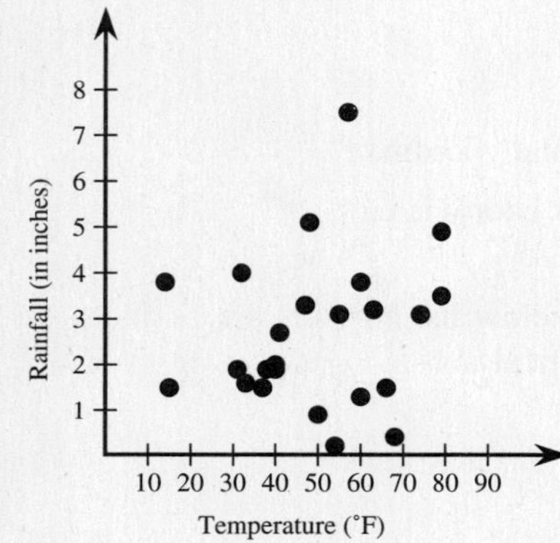

20. There is no relationship between temperature and rainfall.

21. Cluster around (38, 1.9) represents the cities with similar January climates.

22. The lowest temperature is 14° F.

The highest temperature is 79° F.

23.

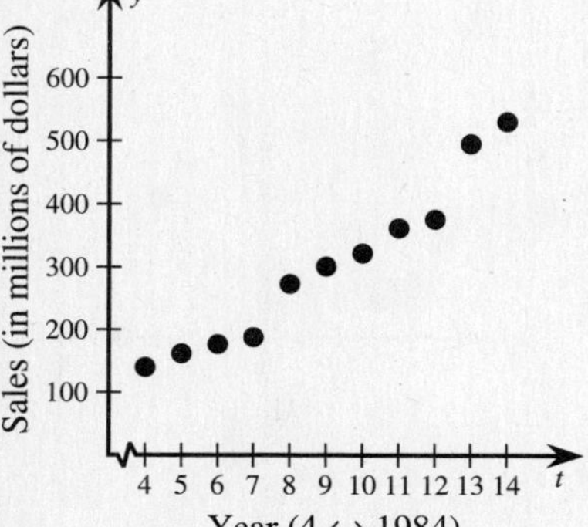

24. Sales generally increased from 1984 to 1994.

25.

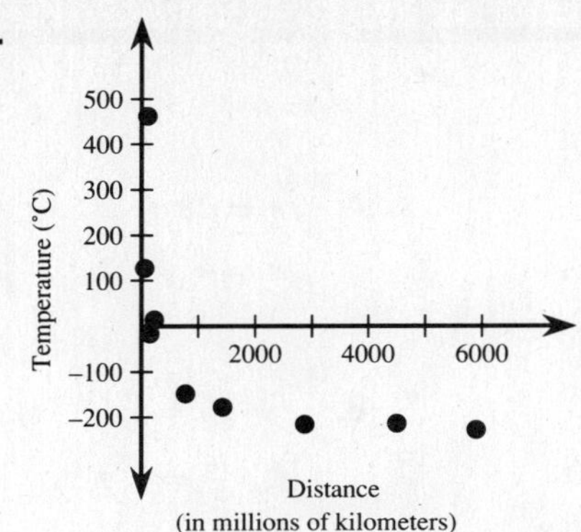

26. As the distance from the sun increases, the tendency is for the temperature to decrease. Planets further away receive less energy from the sun to heat its surface. Note: Mercury 127° and Venus 462° show an exemption.

27. $2y + x = 4$

$x = 4 - 2y$

28. $2y + x = 4$

$2y = 4 - x$

$y = \frac{1}{2}(4 - x)$

29. $3b - (-2a) + 9 = -7$

$3b + 2a = -16$

$2a = -16 - 3b$

$a = \frac{1}{2}(-16 - 3b)$

30. $3b - (-2a) + 9 = -7$

$3b + 2a = -16$

$3b = -16 - 2a$

$b = \frac{1}{3}(-16 - 2a)$

31. $5m + 3n + 4 = -2n$

$5m + 5n + 4 = 0$

$5n = -5m - 4$

$n = -m - \frac{4}{5}$

32. $12t - 2(3s) = 5t$

$12t - 5t = 6s$

$7t = 6s$

$\frac{7}{6}t = s$

33. $3a - (-21) = 7a - 7$

$3a + 21 = 7a - 7$

$28 = 4a$

$7 = a$

34. $-18 - 4c = 5 + 9c$

$-23 = 13c$

$-\frac{23}{13} = c$

35. $5m - 3^2 = -4m - 18$

$9m - 9 = -18$

$9m = -9$

$m = -1$

36. Answer depends on student's choices.

37. Answer depends on student's choices.

Using a Graphing Calculator

1.

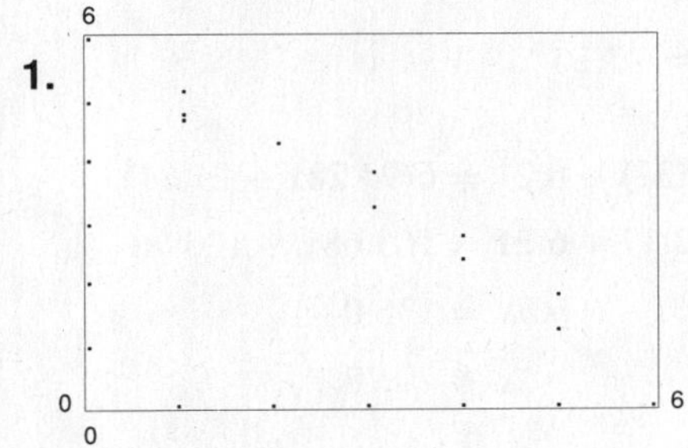

2.

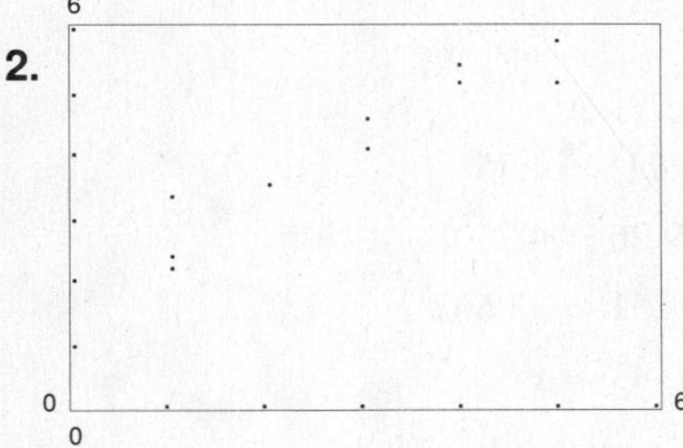

Chapter REVIEW

1. $12 = x - 2$

$14 = x$

2. $y + 4 = -6$

$y = -10$

3. $\frac{m}{8} = \frac{1}{4}$

$m = 2$

4. $7n = 28$

$n = 4$

5. $3p - (-4) = 13$

$3p + 4 = 13$

$3p = 9$

$p = 3$

6. $\frac{x}{6} + \frac{1}{3} = \frac{1}{2}$

$\frac{x}{6} = \frac{1}{2} - \frac{1}{3}$

$\frac{x}{6} = \frac{1}{6}$

$x = 1$

7. $\frac{1}{4}(y + 8) = 0$

$y + 8 = 0$

$y = -8$

8. $16 = 5(1 - x)$

$\frac{16}{5} = 1 - x$

$\frac{16}{5} + x = 1$

$x = 1 - \frac{16}{5}$

$x = -\frac{11}{5}$

9. $9p + 7(p + 1) = 17 - 4p$

$9p + 7p + 7 = 17 - 4p$

$9p + 7p + 4p = 17 - 7$

$20p = 10$

$p = \frac{1}{2}$

10. $\frac{1}{5}x - 3x + 2 = \frac{2}{5}x + 18$

$x - 15x + 10 = 2x + 90$

$-14x + 10 = 2x + 90$

$-80 = 16x$

$-\frac{80}{16} = x$

$-5 = x$

11. $\frac{2}{3}(x - 4) = 3(x + 6)$

$2(x - 4) = 9(x + 6)$

$2x - 8 = 9x + 54$

$-62 = 7x$

$-\frac{62}{7} = x$

12. $\frac{1}{4}x + 16 = 3\left(\frac{1}{4}x + \frac{4}{3}\right)$

$\frac{1}{4}x + 16 = \frac{3}{4}x + 4$

$x + 64 = 3x + 16$

$48 = 2x$

$24 = x$

13. $5(x - 2) = -3(7 - 4x)$

$5x - 10 = -21 + 12x$

$11 = 7x$

$1.57 \approx x$

14. $\frac{4}{9}y = 6(y + 6)$

$4y = 54(y + 6)$

$4y = 54y + 324$

$-324 = 50y$

$-6.48 = y$

15. $13.7t - 4.7 = 9.9 + 8.1t$

$137t - 47 = 99 + 81t$

$56t = 146$

$t \approx 2.61$

16. $4.6(2a + 3) = 3.7a - 4$

$46(2a + 3) = 37a - 40$

$92a + 138 = 37a - 40$

$55a = -178$

$a \approx -3.24$

17. $-6(5.61x - 3.21) = 4.75$

$-33.66x + 19.26 = 4.75$

$14.51 = 33.66x$

$0.43 \approx x$

18. $7(81.74x - 0.31) - 6.21 = 6(94.28x + 21.11)$

$572.18x - 2.17 - 6.21 = 565.68x + 126.66$

$6.5x = 135.04$

$x \approx 20.78$

19. $4x - 3y = 2$

$4x - 2 = 3y$

$\frac{1}{3}(4x - 2) = y$

20. $4x - 3y = 2$

$4x = 2 + 3y$

$x = \frac{1}{4}(2 + 3y)$

21. $A = \frac{1}{2}bh$

$A = \frac{h}{2}b$

$\frac{2}{h}A = b$

22.
$$A = \frac{1}{2}h(b_1 + b_2)$$
$$\frac{2}{h}A = b_1 + b_2$$
$$\frac{2}{h}A - b_1 = b_2$$

23. $12 + \frac{3}{2}t = 6 + 2t$
$$24 + 3t = 12 + 4t$$
$$t = 12 \text{ weeks}$$

24. $66{,}035.8 - 65{,}660.1 = r(8)$
$$375.7 = 8r$$
$$r \approx 47.0 \text{ mph}$$
$$\text{average speed } \approx 47.0 \text{ mph}$$

$$66{,}035.8 - 65{,}660.1 = r(8 - 1)$$
$$375.7 = 7r$$
$$r \approx 53.7 \text{ mph}$$
$$\text{average driving speed } \approx 53.7 \text{ mph}$$

25.
$$\frac{2\frac{1}{2}}{2} = \frac{x}{5}$$
$$\frac{\frac{5}{2}}{2} \cdot 5 = \frac{x}{5} \cdot 5$$
$$\frac{5}{2} \cdot \frac{1}{2} \cdot 5 = x$$
$$x = \frac{25}{4} \text{ or } 6\tfrac{1}{4} \text{ cups flour}$$

$$\frac{\frac{1}{3}}{2} = \frac{x}{5}$$
$$\frac{1}{3} \cdot \frac{1}{2} = \frac{x}{5}$$
$$\frac{1}{6} \cdot 5 = \frac{x}{5} \cdot 5$$
$$\frac{5}{6} = x$$
$$x = \frac{5}{6} \text{ cup raisins}$$

26. $12 \cdot 30 = r \cdot (30 + 5)$
$$360 = 35r$$
$$r \approx 10.3 \text{ kilometers per hour}$$

27. $2[35{,}000{,}000 - 78{,}000t] = 39{,}400{,}000 + 50{,}000t$
$$70{,}000{,}000 - 156{,}000t = 39{,}400{,}000 + 50{,}000t$$
$$30{,}600{,}000 = 206{,}000t$$
$$t \approx 148.5 \text{ years}$$

28. $20(.20) + 10(.30) = 4 + 3$
$$= 7 \text{ milliliters of acid}$$

$$\frac{7}{20 + 10} = \frac{7}{30}$$
$$\approx .233$$
$$= 23.3\%$$

29. Total amount of 22% mixture = $x + 20$ milliliters
$$(0.2)(20) + (0.3)(x) = (0.22)(x + 20)$$
$$4 + 0.3x = 0.22x + 4.4$$
$$0.08x = 0.4$$
$$x = 5 \text{ milliliters}$$

30. $25 - [0.65p + (0.07)(0.65p)] = 3.13$
$$25 - [0.65p + 0.0455p] = 3.13$$
$$25 - 0.6955p = 3.13$$
$$25 - 3.13 = 0.6955p$$
$$21.87 = 0.6955p$$
$$31.45 = p$$

31. There was a trade surplus in 1975.
There was a trade deficit from 1976–1988.

32. The greatest trade deficit was during 1986 and 1987.

33. Imports 1987 = \$405 billion.
Exports 1987 = \$255 billion.
Total traded = \$660 billion.

The estimate agrees with the bar chart.

34. $350 - 129 = 221$ billion exported
Japan had a trade surplus.

35.
$x =$ imported
$x + 60 =$ exported

$$470 = (x + 60) + x$$
$$470 = 2x + 60$$
$$410 = 2x$$
$$205 = x$$

Imported \$205 billion
Exported \$265 billion

36.
$x =$ imported
$x - 4.5 =$ exported

$$280 = x + (x - 4.5)$$
$$280 = 2x - 4.5$$
$$284.5 = 2x$$
$$142.25 = x$$

Imported \$142.25 billion
Exported \$137.75 billion

Chapter TEST

1. $3c = 36$
$c = 12$

2. $\frac{x}{4} = 20$
$x = 80$

3. $4y - 3(y + 8) = 12$
$4y - 3y - 24 = 12$
$y - 24 = 12$
$y = 36$

4. $\frac{1}{4}m + 3 = 2$
$\frac{1}{4}m = -1$
$m = -4$

5. $6 + 9x - 2 = 7x + (-2x) + 8$
$9x + 4 = 5x + 8$
$4x = 4$
$x = 1$

6. $\frac{3}{4}x - 6 = x - 8$
$2 = \frac{1}{4}x$
$8 = x$

7. $\frac{3}{8}(p - 8) + \frac{1}{8}p = -\frac{1}{2}(p - 7)$
$\frac{3}{8}p - 3 + \frac{1}{8}p = -\frac{1}{2}p + \frac{7}{2}$
$\frac{1}{2}p - 3 = -\frac{1}{2}p + \frac{7}{2}$
$p = \frac{7}{2} + 3$
$p = \frac{13}{2}$

8. $(3 \div 4) - r\left(r - \frac{1}{2}\right) = r(3 - r)$
$\frac{3}{4} - r^2 + \frac{1}{2}r = 3r - r^2$
$\frac{3}{4} + \frac{1}{2}r = 3r$
$3 + 2r = 12r$
$3 = 10r$
$r = \frac{3}{10}$

9. $19x - 12 = 4(6 - 4x)$
$19x - 12 = 24 - 16x$
$35x = 36$
$x \approx 1.03$

10. $\frac{18y}{3} - 7 = 7y$
$18y - 21 = 21y$
$-21 = 3y$
$y = -7$

11. $27.3m - 45.1 = -13.2 + 6.8m$
$20.5m = 31.9$
$m \approx 1.56$

12. $7(8.65x - 37.61) = (28.45 + 3.75x)(-4)$
$60.55x - 263.27 = -113.8 - 15x$
$75.55x = 149.47$
$x \approx 1.98$

13. $C = 2\pi r$

$\dfrac{C}{2\pi} = r$

14. $S = 2\pi r^2 + 2\pi rh$

$S - 2\pi r^2 = 2\pi rh$

$\dfrac{S - 2\pi r^2}{2\pi r} = h$

15. $44.2 = 2(0.7)L + 2L$

$44.2 = 1.4L + 2L$

$44.2 = 3.4L$

$L = 13$ centimeters

$W = 0.7L$

$W = 0.7(13)$

$W = 9.1$ centimeters

9.1 centimeters × 13 centimeters

16. [Money earned babysitting per week] • [Number of weeks] + [Bonus] + 7 = [[Money earned mowing lawns per week] + [Money earned running errands per week]] • [Number of weeks]

Money earned babysitting = 15	(dollars per week)
Money earned mowing lawns = 10	(dollars per week)
Money earned running errands = 8	(dollars per week)
Bonus = 5	(dollars)
Number of weeks = w	(weeks)

$15w + 5 + 7 = (10 + 8)w$

$15w + 12 = 18w$

$12 = 3w$

$w = 4$ weeks

17. $A = P + Prt$

$314.70 = 300 + 300r(1)$

$14.70 = 300r$

$r = 0.049$

$= 4.9\%$

18.

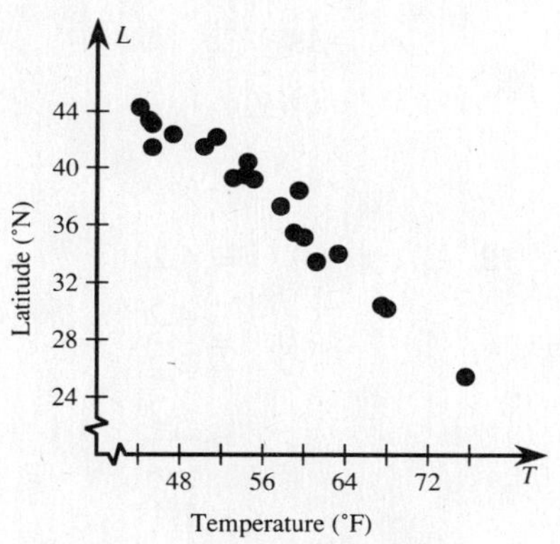

Higher temperatures correspond to a lower latitude.

Cummulative REVIEW

1. $3 + 2(24 \div 6) = 3 + 2(4)$

$= 3 + 8$

$= 11$

2. $4.9 \div (4 + 3) + 0.6 = 4.9 \div 7 + 0.6$

$= 0.7 + 0.6$

$= 1.3$

3. $[(13 - 8)^2 + 2] \div 3 = [5^2 + 2] \div 3$

$= [25 + 2] \div 3$

$= 27 \div 3$

$= 9$

4. $32 \div (-4) - (2 - 8) = 32 \div (-4) - (-6)$

$= -8 + 6$

$= -2$

5. $|3 - 10| - 3.7(4) = |-7| - 14.8$

$= 7 - 14.8$

$= -7.8$

6. $(6.8)^2 - |11.1 - 2.2| = 46.24 - |8.9|$

$= 46.24 - 8.9$

$= 37.34$

7. $(47 - 36.5)9 + 6.1 = (10.5)9 + 6.1$
$= 94.5 + 6.1$
$= 100.6$

8. $(29 + 1) \div (-5) = 30 \div (-5)$
$= -6$

9. $\dfrac{4(3-2)}{(6)(3)} = \dfrac{4(1)}{18}$
$= \dfrac{2}{9}$

10. $\dfrac{3^2 \cdot 4}{(42 - 21)} = \dfrac{9 \cdot 4}{21}$
$= \dfrac{36}{21}$
$= \dfrac{12}{7}$

11. $\dfrac{3^2 - 8(6)}{7} = \dfrac{9 - 48}{7}$
$= \dfrac{-39}{7}$

12. $\dfrac{8 + 2(-4)}{6(-6)} = \dfrac{8 + (-8)}{-36}$
$= \dfrac{0}{-36}$
$= 0$

13. $4(x - 2) = 3^2 - x$
$4x - 8 = 9 - x$
$5x = 17$
$x = \frac{17}{5}$

14. $\frac{1}{3}n + 3 = n - 2$
$n + 9 = 3n - 6$
$15 = 2n$
$\frac{15}{2} = n$

15. $9(2p + 1) - 3p > 4p - 6$
$18p + 9 - 3p > 4p - 6$
$11p > -15$
$p > -\frac{15}{11}$

16. $(q - 12)3 \leq 5q + 2$
$3q - 36 \leq 5q + 2$
$-38 \leq 2q$
$-19 \leq q$

17. $\dfrac{2y}{3} = \dfrac{8}{27}$
$y = \dfrac{8}{27}\left(\dfrac{3}{2}\right)$
$y = \dfrac{4}{9}$

18. $\dfrac{m}{12} + \dfrac{5}{6} = \dfrac{5}{24}$
$2m + 20 = 5$
$2m = -15$
$m = -\dfrac{15}{2}$

19. $3.2(x - 0.1) = 4.2$
$x - 0.1 = \dfrac{4.2}{3.2}$
$x = \dfrac{4.2}{3.2} + 0.1$
$x \approx 1.41$

20. $(19.8 - r)6.2 = 37.7r - 49.2$
$122.76 - 6.2r = 37.7r - 49.2$
$171.96 = 43.9r$
$r \approx 3.92$

21. $18t(4.2 - 36.1) < -86.13$
$18t(-31.9) < -86.13$
$t > \dfrac{-86.13}{18(-31.9)}$
$t > 0.15$

22. $41.2(2a - 0.6) > (0.25a + 3)99.9$
$82.4a - 24.72 > 24.975a + 299.7$
$57.425a > 324.42$
$a > 5.65$

23. $$\begin{bmatrix} 47 & -3 & 22 \\ 6 & -17 & 9 \end{bmatrix} + \begin{bmatrix} -33 & 18 & 10 \\ 44 & -24 & -44 \end{bmatrix} = \begin{bmatrix} 47 + (-33) & -3 + 18 & 22 + 10 \\ 6 + 44 & -17 + (-24) & 9 + (-44) \end{bmatrix} = \begin{bmatrix} 14 & 15 & 32 \\ 50 & -41 & -35 \end{bmatrix}$$

24. $$\begin{bmatrix} 4 & 10 \\ -6 & 18 \\ 29 & -14 \end{bmatrix} - \begin{bmatrix} 56 & 2 \\ 4 & -11 \\ 29 & 7 \end{bmatrix} = \begin{bmatrix} 4 - 56 & 10 - 2 \\ -6 - 4 & 18 - (-11) \\ 29 - 29 & -14 - 7 \end{bmatrix} = \begin{bmatrix} -52 & 8 \\ -10 & 29 \\ 0 & -21 \end{bmatrix}$$

25. $3n - 27$

26. $\dfrac{65}{n} < 14$

27. $(n + 27)\frac{1}{2} = 37$

28. $n^2 + 18 \geq 87$

29. $|n| < \frac{36}{5}$

30. $(2n - 40)^2$

31. Let x represent the number of orders of wrapping paper.

$$1(x) + 50(3) = 550$$
$$x + 150 = 550$$
$$x = 400 \text{ orders of wrapping paper}$$

32.

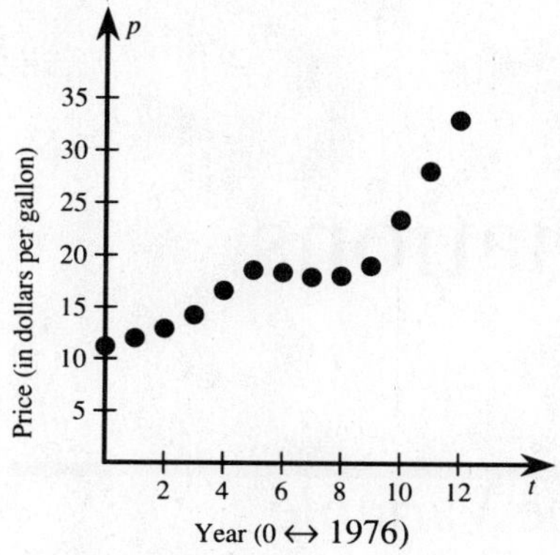

(0, 11.20) (1, 12.00) (2, 12.93) (3, 14.26) (4, 16.64) (5, 18.60) (6, 18.39) (7, 17.95) (8, 18.08) (9, 19.05) (10, 23.45) (11, 28.10) (12, 33.00)

33. $\dfrac{\text{Area of new table}}{\text{Area of old table}} = \dfrac{(2)(8)}{(2)(6)} = \dfrac{4}{3}$

34. Let x represent the number of old tables.

$$(2)(6)x = (2)(8)(24)$$
$$12x = 384$$
$$x = 32 \text{ tables}$$

35. $\dfrac{\text{Number of words found}}{\text{Time to find words}} = \dfrac{30}{15} = 2$ words per minute

36. $\dfrac{\text{Number of words found}}{\text{Time to find words}} = \dfrac{18}{8} = 2\frac{1}{4}$ words per minute

She found the words faster in the newspaper.

37. Let p represent the percent discount.

$$21.95(1 - p) = 17.56$$
$$1 - p = \frac{17.56}{21.95}$$
$$p = 1 - \frac{17.56}{21.95}$$
$$p = 0.2 \text{ or } 20\%$$

38.

$$V = \pi r^2 h$$
$$42.4 = 3.14(1.5)^2 h$$
$$h = \frac{42.4}{3.14(1.5)^2}$$
$$h \approx 6 \text{ inches}$$

Chapter 4

Graphing Linear Equations

4.1 Graphing Linear Equations in One Variable

Communicating about Algebra

A.

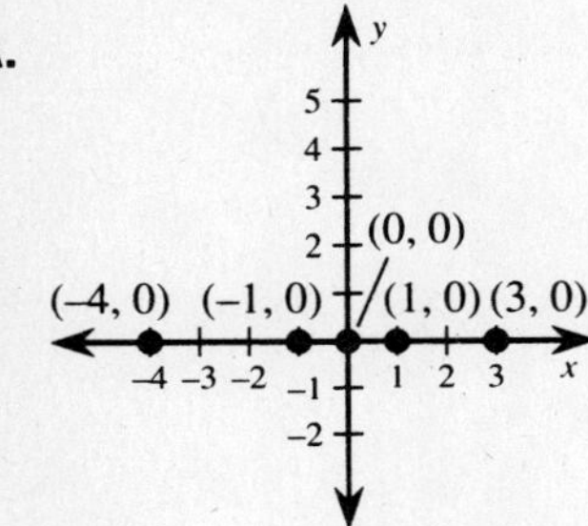

B. The second coordinate is zero.
The equation for the x-axis is $y = 0$.

C.

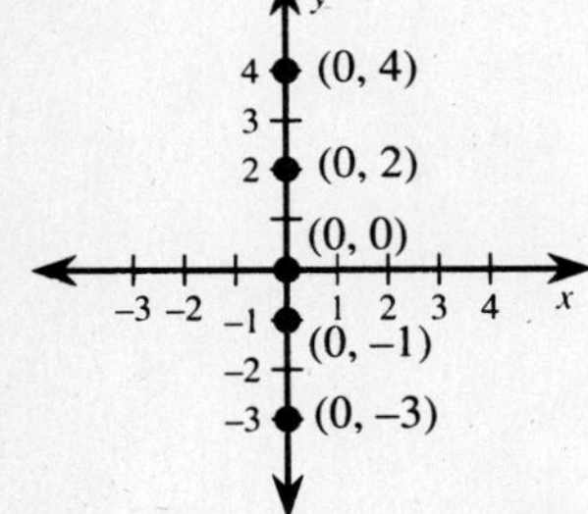

The first coordinate is zero.
The equation for the y-axis is $x = 0$.

D. (0, 0)

E. $x = -4$

F. The x-coordinate is 1 for all points on the line $x = 1$.

EXERCISES

1. 2

2. −3

3. False; the graph of $x = 4$ consists of all points with x-coordinate 4. This is a vertical line.

4. True

5. 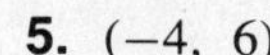 $(-4, 6)$

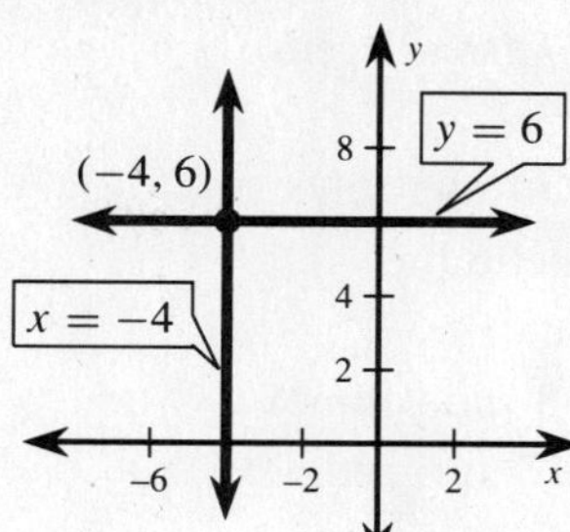

6. $y = -2$
$x = 3$

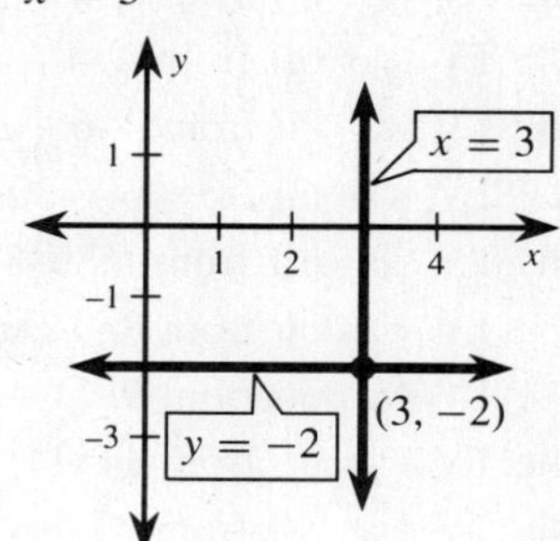

7. **c.**

8. **a.**

9. **d.**

10. **b.**

11. $(6, -1)$

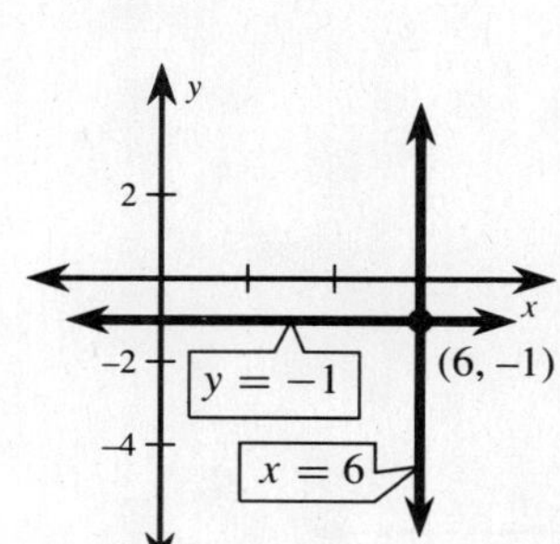

12. $(7, 3)$

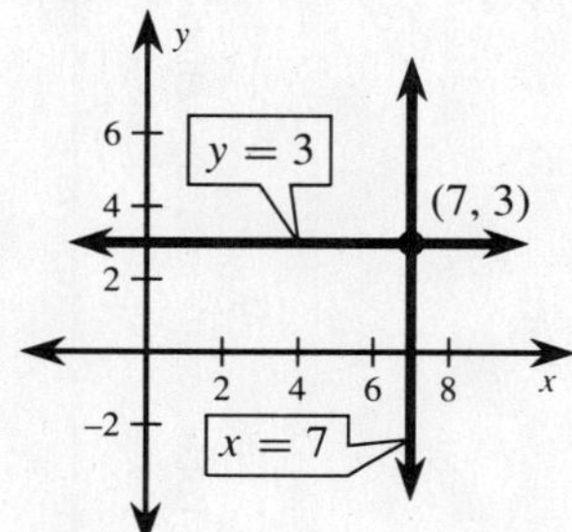

13. $(-4, -5)$

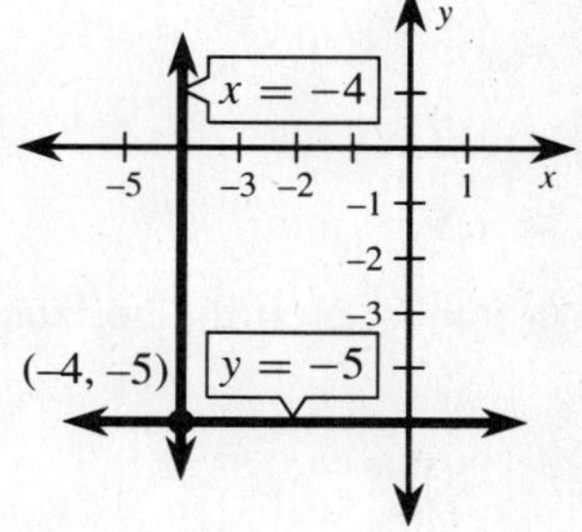

14. $(-8, 2)$

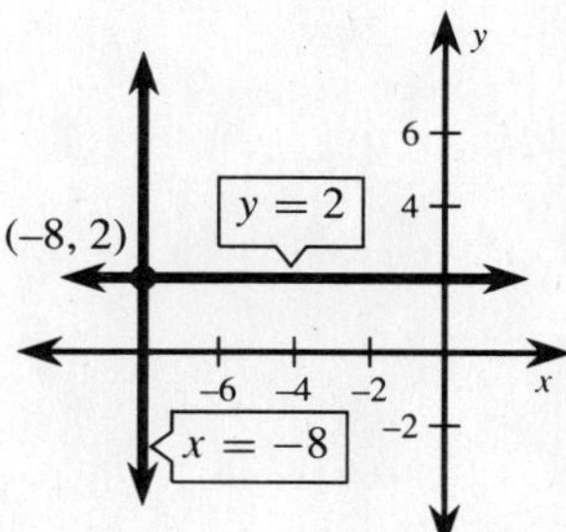

15. Yes

16. No

17. No

18. Yes

19. $x = 2$

20. $y = 4$

21. $y = -72$

22. $x = -1$

23. $x = 10$
$y = -6$

24. $x = 8$
$y = -3$

25. $x = -21$
$y = -15$

26. $x = -4$
$y = -17$

27. $x = -5$
$y = 12$

28. $x = -9$
$y = 11$

29. $x = 3$
$y = 0$

30. $x = 0$
$y = -1$

31. The TV was off from noon until 1 P.M..
The TV was on from 1–2 P.M. on Channel 4 (soap opera).
The TV was off from 2–4 P.M..
The TV was on from 4–6 P.M. on Channel 7 (after school).
The TV was on from 6–6:30 P.M. on Channel 6 (news).
The TV was off from 6:30–8 P.M. (dinnertime).
The TV was on from 8–9 P.M. on Channel 8 (primetime).
The TV was on from 9–11 P.M. on Channel 7 (primetime).
The TV was on from 11–11:30 P.M. on Channel 6 (news).
The TV was off from 11:30–midnight (bedtime).

32. The TV was on 7 hours.

33. Channel 7 was on the most. Each of its segments is longer than any other segment.

34. $\frac{72}{48} = 1.5$ Bass
$\frac{48}{32} = 1.5$ Cello
$\frac{36}{24} = 1.5$ Viola
$\frac{26}{17} \approx 1.5$ Violin
The points lie on the horizontal line $y = 1.5$.

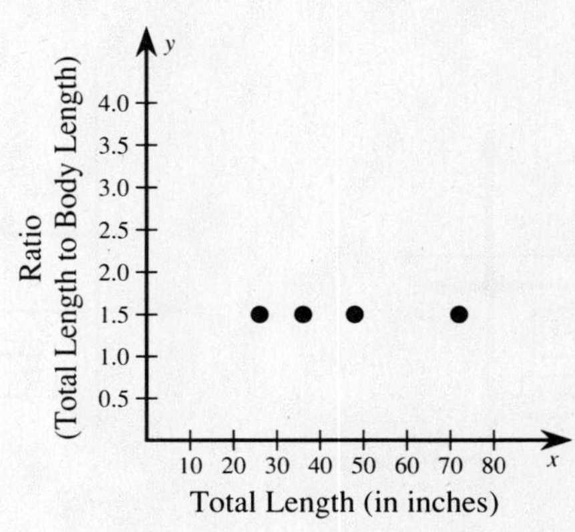

35. $\frac{28}{44} \approx 0.6$ Bass
$\frac{17}{29} \approx 0.6$ Cello
$\frac{13}{21} \approx 0.6$ Viola
$\frac{10}{17} \approx 0.6$ Violin
The points lie on the horizontal line $y = 0.6$.

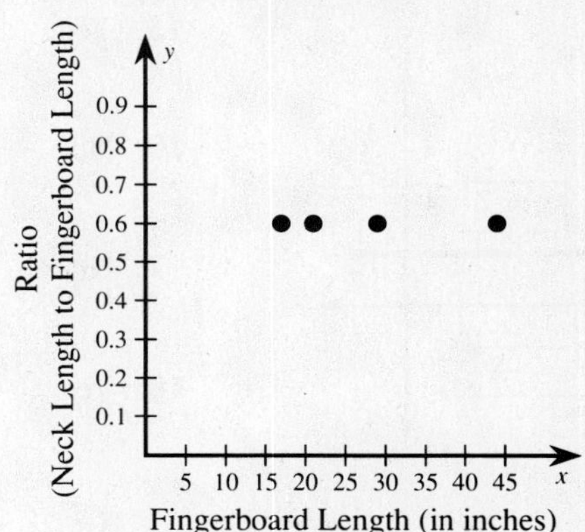

36. Total length to fingerboard ≈ 1.6
Body to fingerboard ≈ 1.1

37.

Year	1980	1981	1982	1983	1984	1985	1986	1987	1988
Total in U.S.	1572	1572	1572	1572	1572	1572	1572	1572	1572

38.

Number of Symphony Orchestras

1600
1400
1200
1000
800
600
400
200

1 2 3 4 5 6 7 8 t

Year (0 ↔ 1980)

★ College/Community
● Urban/Major
■ Total

39. The total number of orchestras lie on the line $y = 1572$. When the number of college orchestras increased, the number of urban orchestras decreased. When the number of college orchestras decreased, the number of urban orchestras increased.

40. Air

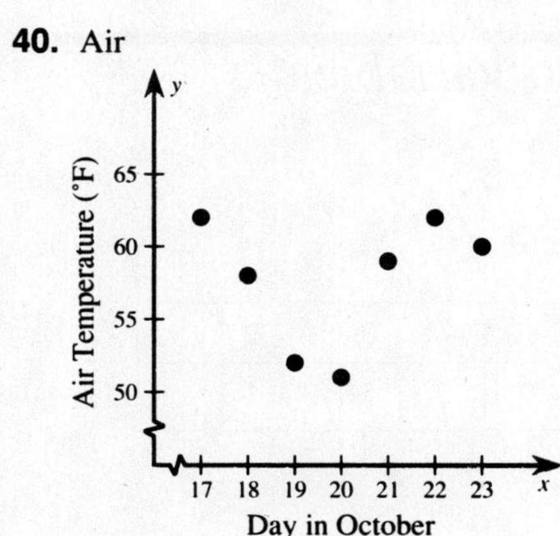

Water

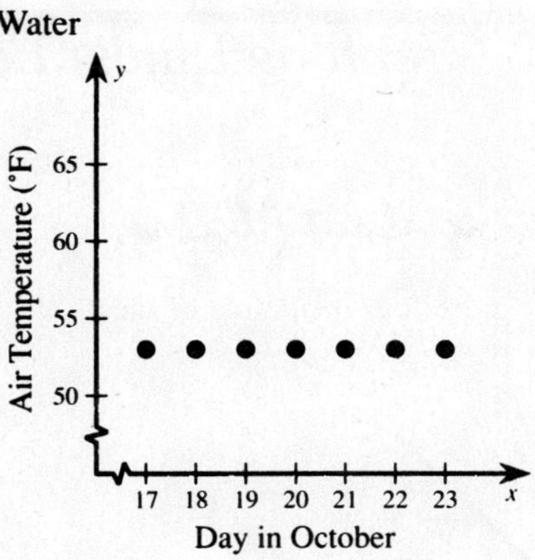

41. The points on the water temperature graph have the same second coordinate.

42. Air temperatures vary more than water temperatures.

43.
$$2x + 5y = 10$$
$$5y = 10 - 2x$$
$$y = \tfrac{1}{5}(10 - 2x)$$

44.
$$4y - 6x = 3$$
$$4y = 3 + 6x$$
$$y = \tfrac{1}{4}(3 + 6x)$$

45.
$$2y - 5x = 14$$
$$2y = 14 + 5x$$
$$y = \tfrac{1}{2}(14 + 5x)$$

46.
$$-6y - 8x = 22$$
$$-6y = 22 + 8x$$
$$y = -\tfrac{1}{6}(22 + 8x)$$
$$y = -\tfrac{1}{3}(11 + 4x)$$

47.
$$3x - 7y = -2x + 19$$
$$-7y = -5x + 19$$
$$y = \tfrac{1}{7}(5x - 19)$$

48.
$$9y + 10x = 21 + 18x$$
$$9y = 21 + 8x$$
$$y = \tfrac{1}{9}(21 + 8x)$$

49. No, they are not solutions.
$$3x - y = 17$$
$$3(0) - 8 \stackrel{?}{=} 17$$
$$-8 \neq 17$$

50. Yes, they are solutions.
$$2y - x = 21$$
$$2(13) - 5 \stackrel{?}{=} 21$$
$$26 - 5 \stackrel{?}{=} 21$$
$$21 = 21$$

51. Yes, they are solutions.

$$4y - 7x = -20$$
$$4(9) - 7(8) = 36 - 56$$
$$= -20$$

52. No, they are not solutions.

$$5x - 2y = 30$$
$$5(4) + 2(0) = 20 + 0$$
$$= 20$$

53. $(-3+2,\ -4+5) = (-1,\ 1)$
$(-2+2,\ -1+5) = (0,\ 4)$
$(1+2,\ -3+5) = (3,\ 2)$

54. $(-5+6,\ 2-3) = (1,\ -1)$
$(-3+6,\ 5-3) = (3,\ 2)$
$(-1+6,\ 2-3) = (5,\ -1)$
$(-3+6,\ -1-3) = (3,\ -4)$

4.2 Graphing Linear Equations in Two Variables

Communicating about Algebra

A. The graphs bisect the four quadrants of the plane.

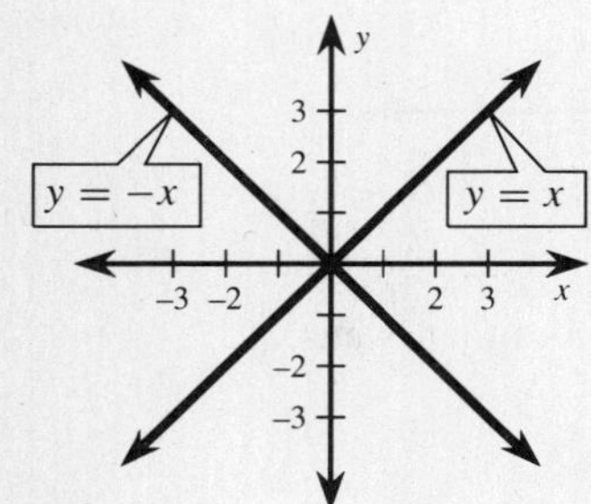

B.

x	−3	−2	−1	0	1	2	3
y	11	9	7	5	3	1	−1

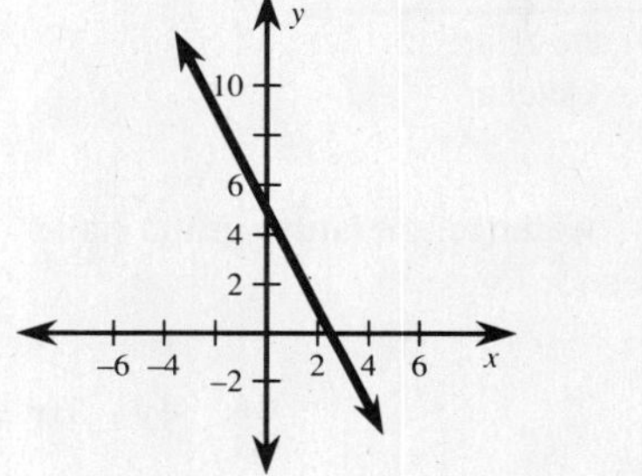

C. Two points are needed to determine a line. If two points are plotted and a line drawn, the remaining points will fall on the line.

D. x would be multiples of 4 so that y would be an integer value.

EXERCISES

1. A number pair that makes the equation true.

2. The graph of an equation is the collection of all points $(x,\ y)$ that are solution points of the equation.

3. **c.** and **d.**

4. $4y - 6x = 10$

$4y = 6x + 10$ — *Add 6x to both sides to isolate the y-term.*

$y = \frac{1}{4}(6x + 10)$ — *Multiply both sides by $\frac{1}{4}$ to get a y-coefficient of 1.*

$y = \frac{3}{2}x + \frac{5}{2}$ — *Simplify*

5. a. $(2, 2)$

$$\begin{aligned} 2x + 3y &= 10 \\ 2(2) + 3(2) &\stackrel{?}{=} 10 \\ 4 + 6 &\stackrel{?}{=} 10 \\ 10 &= 10 \end{aligned}$$

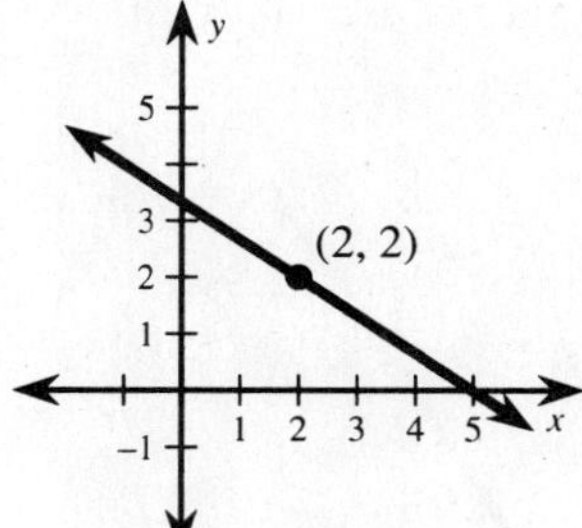

6. b. $(-1, 1)$

$$\begin{aligned} 2y - 4x &= 6 \\ 2(1) - 4(-1) &\stackrel{?}{=} 6 \\ 2 + 4 &\stackrel{?}{=} 6 \\ 6 &= 6 \end{aligned}$$

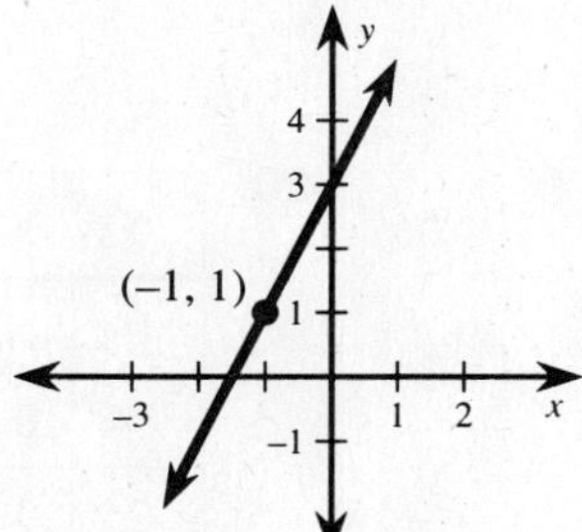

7. a. $(3, 0)$

$$\begin{aligned} 6y - 3x &= -9 \\ 6(0) - 3(3) &\stackrel{?}{=} -9 \\ 0 - 9 &\stackrel{?}{=} -9 \\ -9 &= -9 \end{aligned}$$

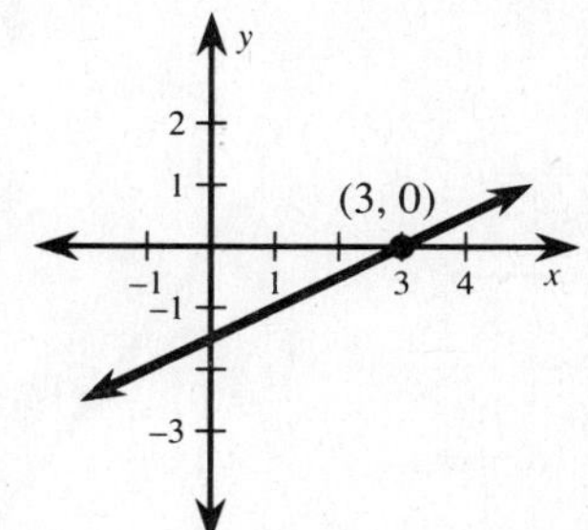

8. a. $(-3, 0)$

$$\begin{aligned} -5x - 8y &= 15 \\ -5(-3) - 8(0) &\stackrel{?}{=} 15 \\ 15 - 0 &\stackrel{?}{=} 15 \\ 15 &= 15 \end{aligned}$$

9.

x	*y*
−1	−6
0	−4
2	0

$(-1, -6)$
$(0, -4)$
$(2, 0)$

10.

x	*y*
−1	−8
0	5
2	−1

$(-1, 8)$
$(0, 5)$
$(2, -1)$

11.

x	*y*
−1	−9
0	−3
1	3

$(-1, -9)$
$(0, -3)$
$(1, 3)$

12.

x	*y*
−1	5
0	3
1	1

$(-1, 5)$
$(0, 3)$
$(1, 1)$

13.

x	*y*
−1	3
0	2
1	1

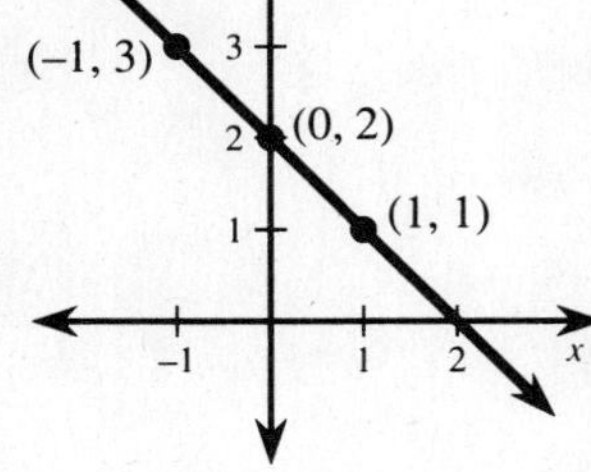

14.

x	*y*
−1	9
0	5
1	1

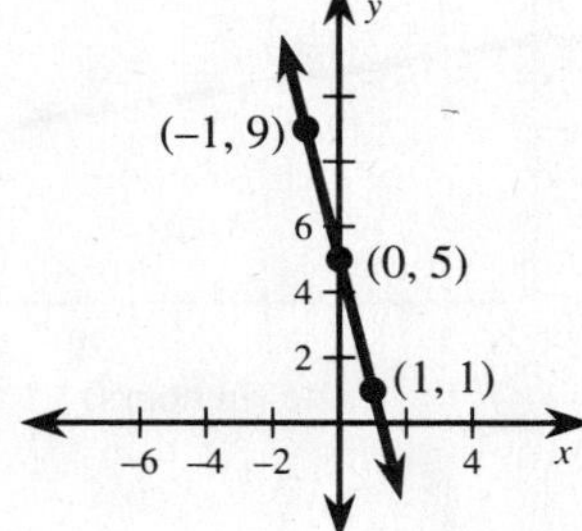

15.

x	*y*
−1	−3
0	−2
1	−1

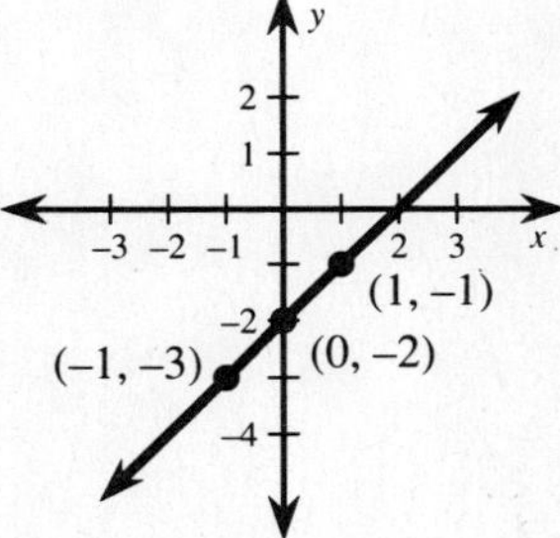

16.

x	*y*
−1	−4
0	−6
1	−8

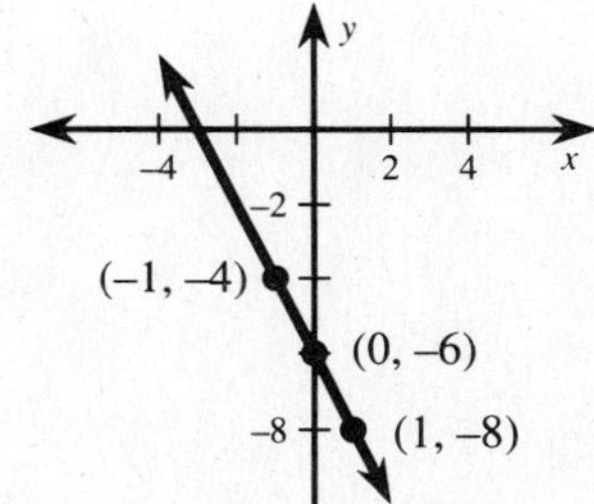

17.

x	y
−2	3
0	4
2	5

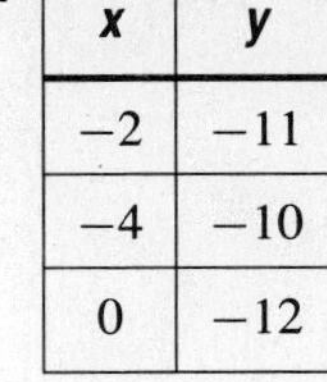

18.

x	y
−2	−11
−4	−10
0	−12

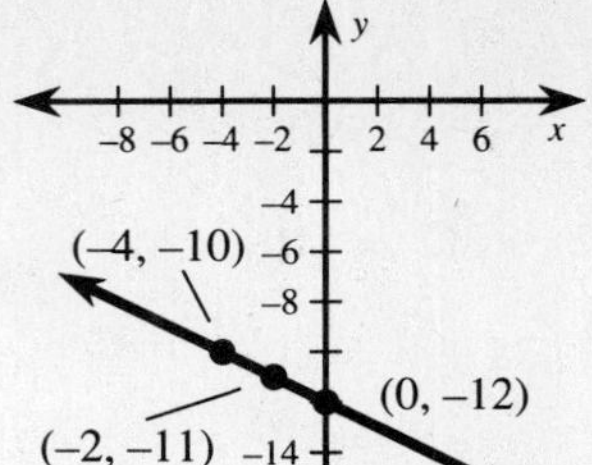

19.

x	y
0	8
6	0
3	4

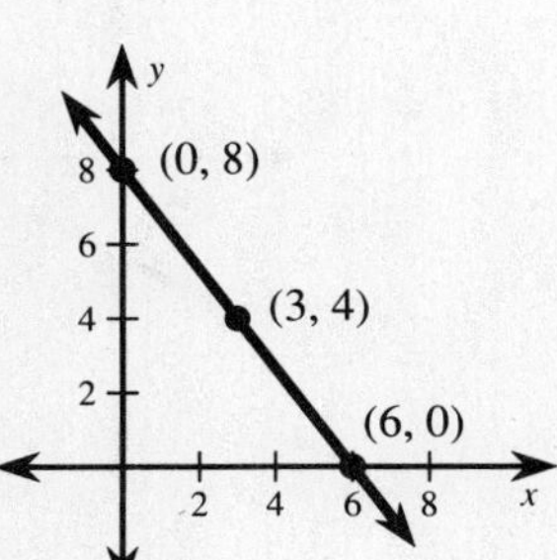

20.

x	y
0	6
−4	0
2	9

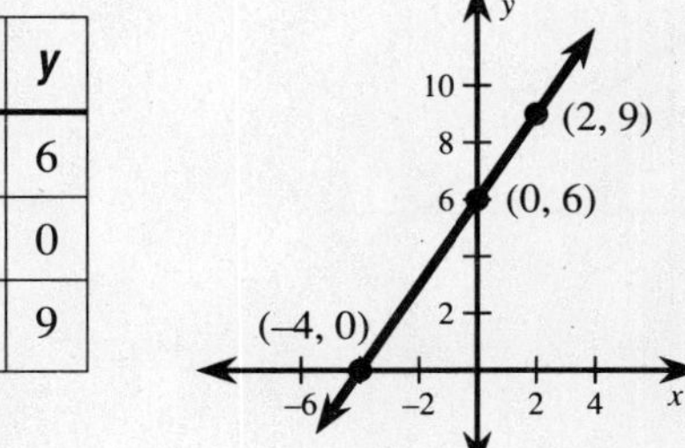

21. b.

22. d.

23. a.

24. c.

25.
$$F^\circ = \tfrac{9}{5}(C^\circ) + 32$$
$$F^\circ = \tfrac{9}{5}(-40) + 32$$
$$F^\circ = -72 + 32$$
$$F^\circ = -40^\circ$$
$$-40^\circ F = -40^\circ C$$

26. The graph on the right is misleading. A decrease of \$1000 per \$3 million or more is not dramatic.

27.

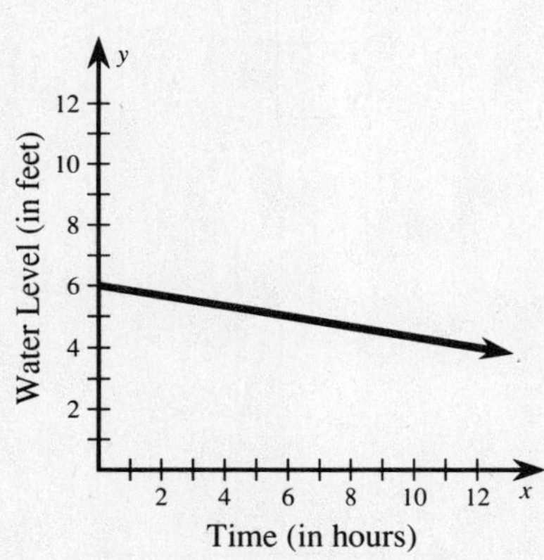

28.
$$y = 6 - \tfrac{1}{6}t$$
$$0 = 6 - \tfrac{1}{6}t$$
$$\tfrac{1}{6}t = 6$$
$$t = 36 \text{ hours}$$

29. a.

30. b.

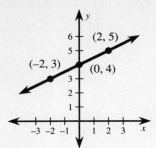

31. 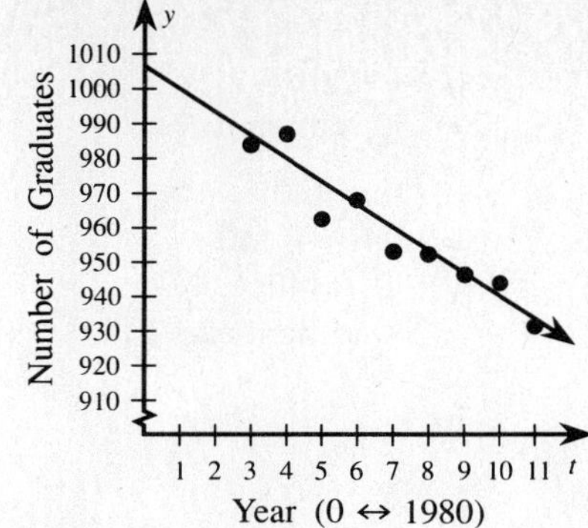

$y = -6.5t + 1006$

$y = -6.5(12) + 1006$

$y = -78 + 1006$

$y = 928$ graduates

32. 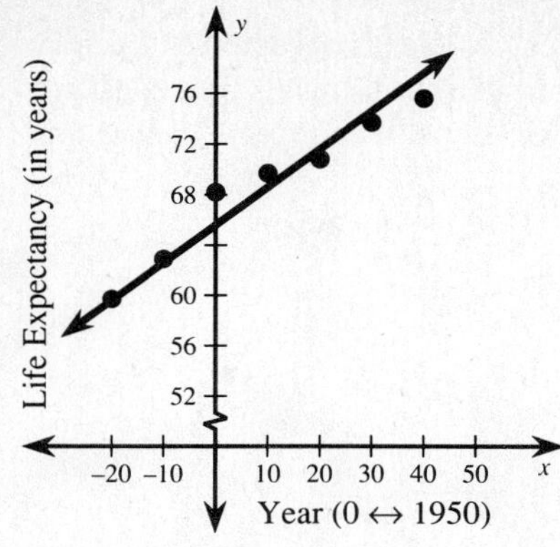

$y = 0.3t + 65.6$

$y = 0.3(50) + 65.6$

$y = 15 + 65.6$

$y = 80.6$

33. 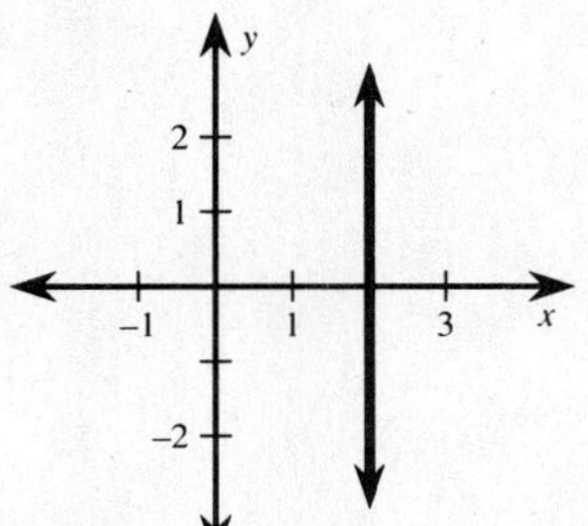

34. 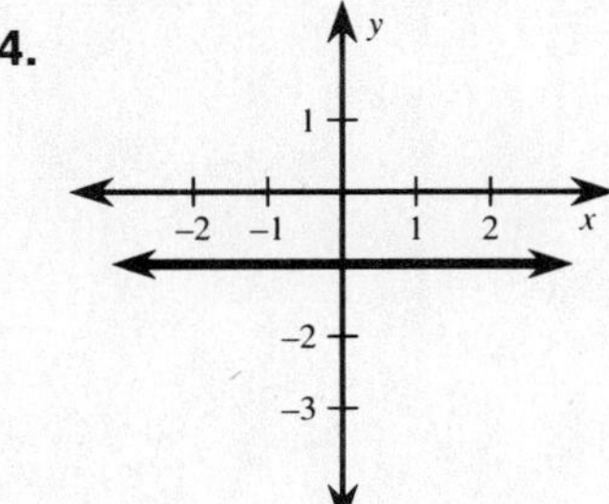

35. 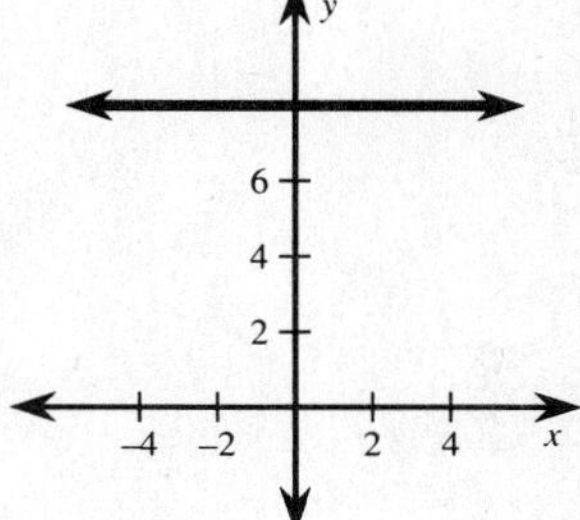

36. 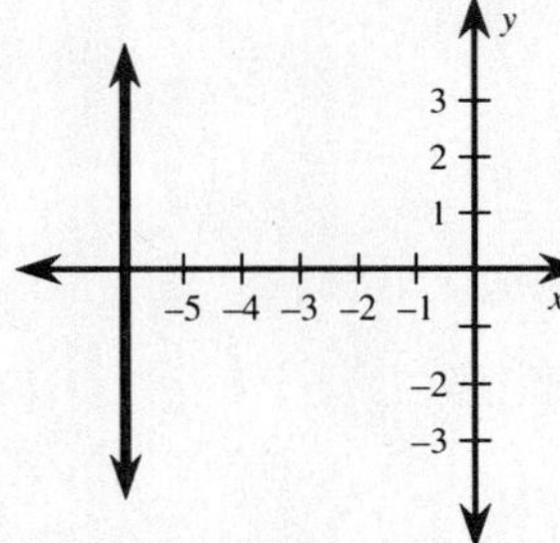

37. $(-4,\ 7)$

38. $(11, 5)$

39. $(-10,\ -12)$

40. $(6,\ -18)$

41. $x = 6$
$y = -3$

42. $x = -12$
$y = -15$

43. $x = 8$
$y = 21$

44. $x = -7$
$y = 9$

45. 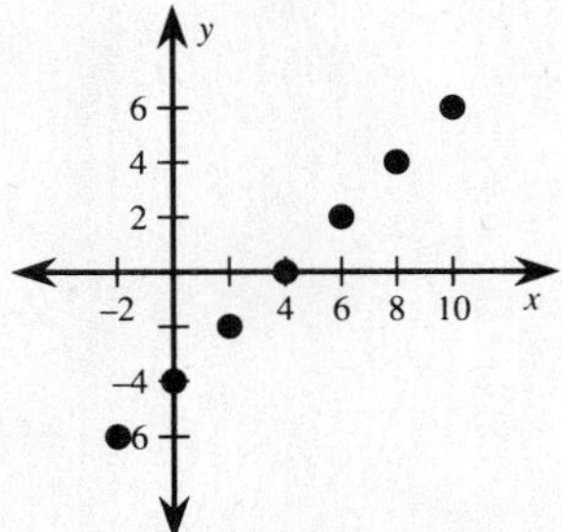

As x increases, y increases.

$y = x - 4$

46. 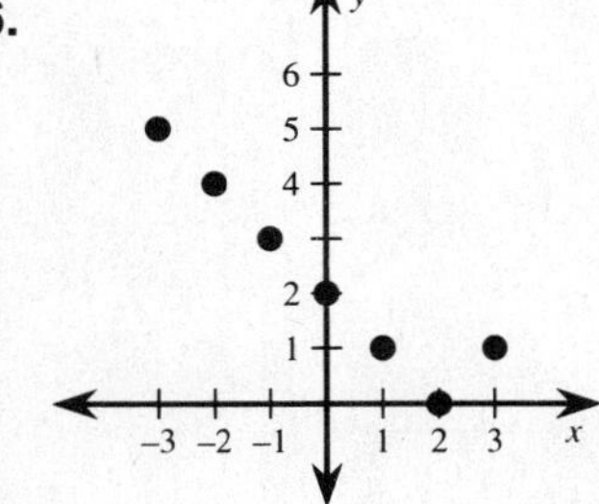

From -3 to 2, x increases as y decreases. From 2 to 3, x increases as y increases.

$y = |x - 2|$ or $y = |2 - x|$

47. Any of the three vehicles is acceptable. Each vehicle increases its speed, travels at a constant rate, slows down, stops, then repeats the pattern.

48. U.S. in 1980

$$y = 4(10) + 110$$
$$y = 40 + 110$$
$$y = 150 \text{ million cars}$$

World in 1980 (excluding U.S.)

$$y = 12t + 140$$
$$y = 12(10) + 140$$
$$y = 120 + 140$$
$$y = 260 \text{ million cars}$$

$$\frac{150}{260 + 150} = \frac{150}{410} \approx 36.6\%$$

Using a Graphing Calculator

1.

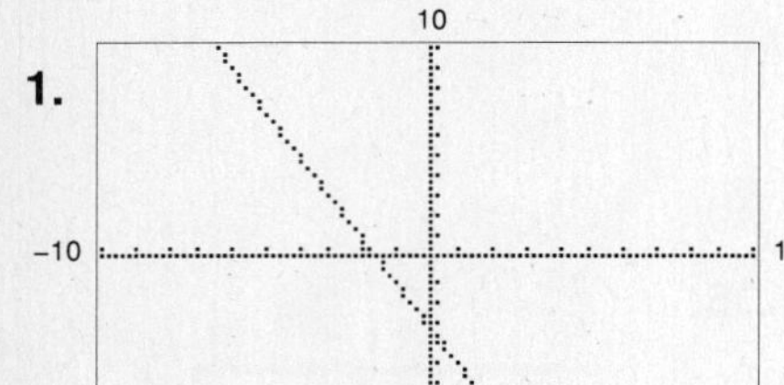

2.

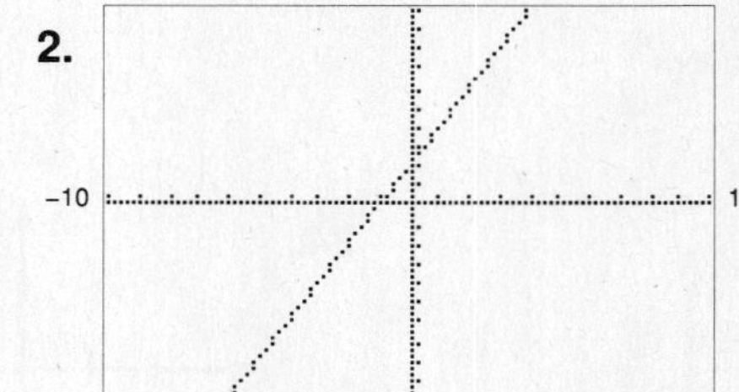

3.

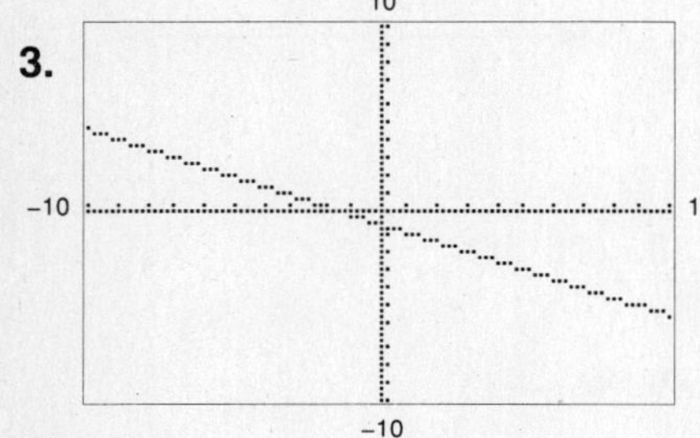

4.

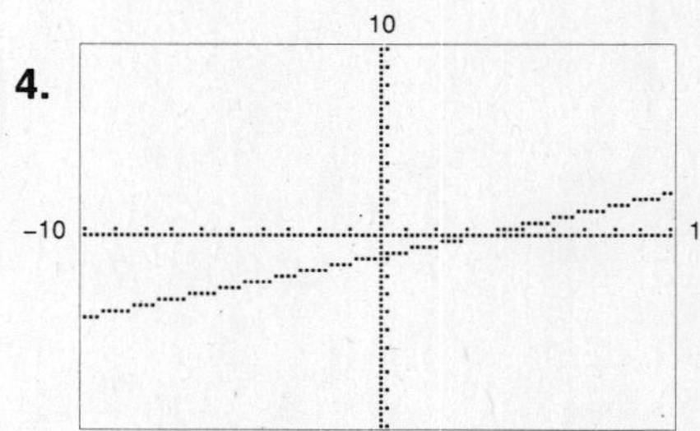

5.

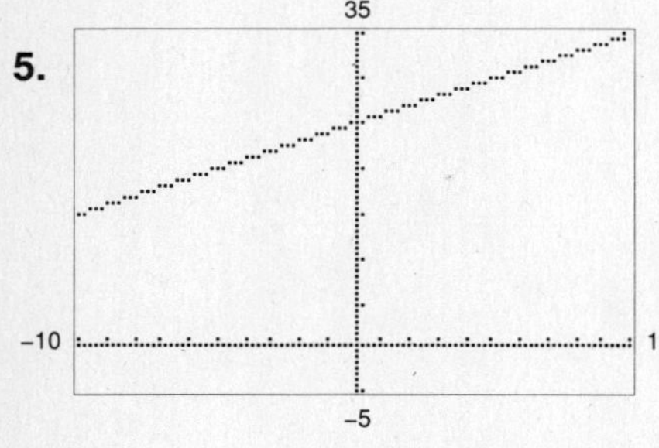

6.

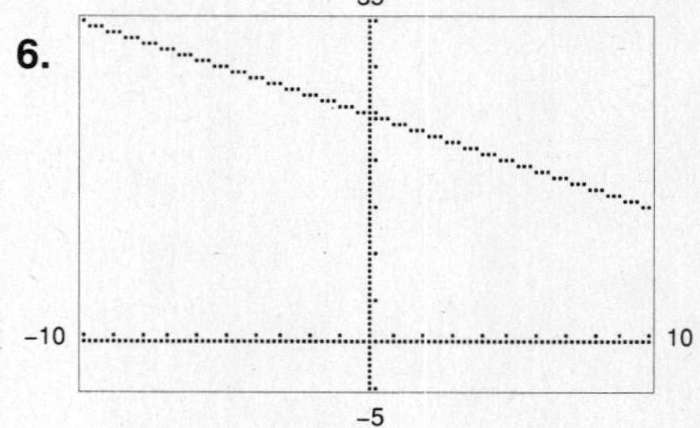

7.

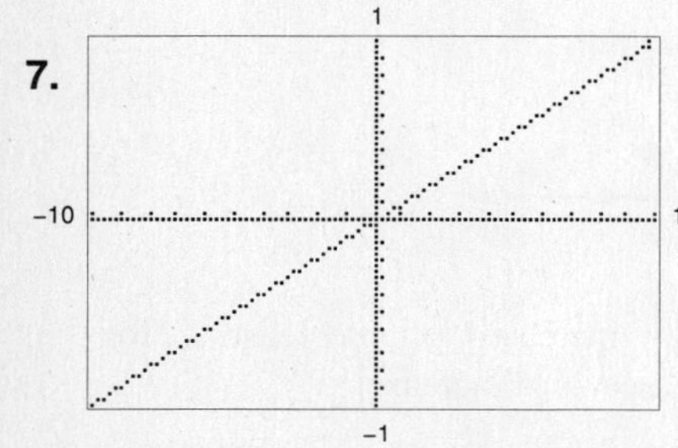

8.

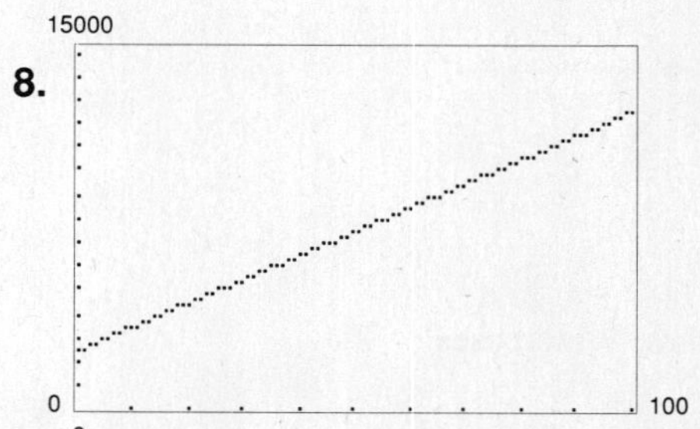

4.3 Quick Graphs Using Intercepts

Communicating about Algebra

A. x-intercept: $(-19,\ 0)$
y-intercept: none

B. x-intercept: none
y-intercept: $(0,\ 615)$

C. x-intercept: $(0,\ 0)$
y-intercept: $(0,\ 0)$
Find the point where they each occur: $(0,\ 0)$

D. Horizontal lines, vertical lines, and lines that pass through the origin have only one point as an intercept instead of the two needed to do a quick graph.

EXERCISES

1. True

2. Two, because only 1 line can be drawn between 2 points.

3. Set $y = 0$ and solve for x.

4. Set $x = 0$ and solve for y.

5. -8 is the x-intercept of the line.

$$0 = \tfrac{1}{2}x + 4$$
$$-4 = \tfrac{1}{2}x$$
$$-8 = x$$

6. -4 is the y intercept of the line.

$$y = 6x - 4$$
$$y = 6 \cdot 0 - 4$$
$$y = -4$$

7. **c.**

8. **a.**

9. **d.**

10. **b.**

11. x-intercept: 2
y-intercept: 3

12. x-intercept: -2
y-intercept: 4

13. x-intercept: -4
y-intercept: -1

14. x-intercept: -5
y-intercept: 2

15.

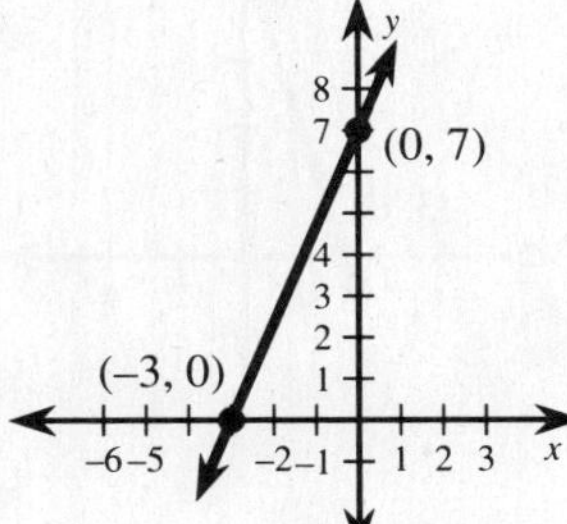

16.

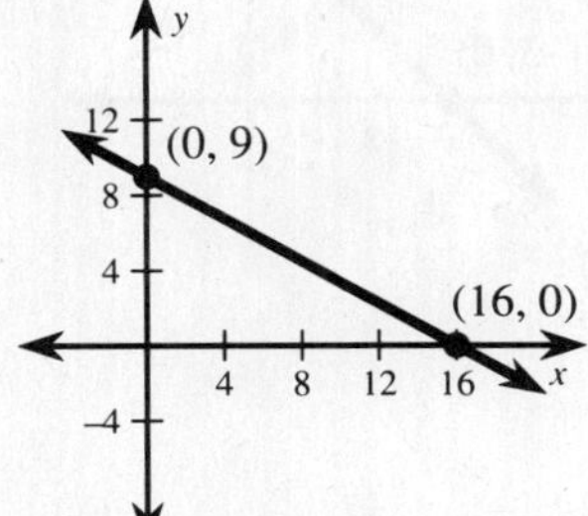

17.

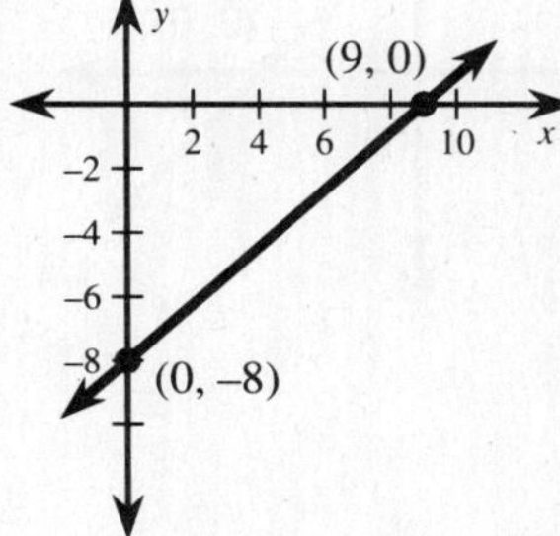

18.

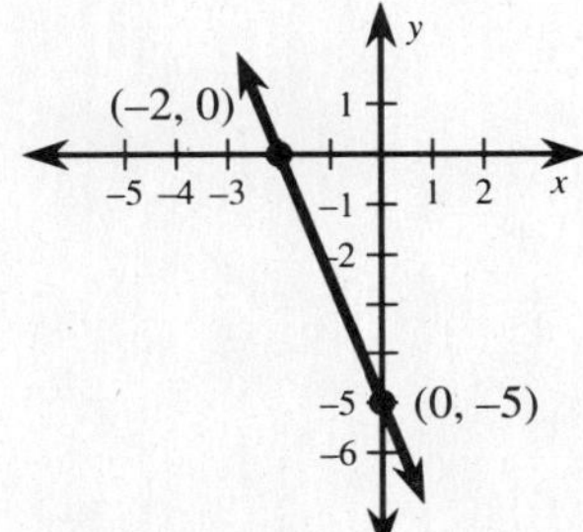

19.

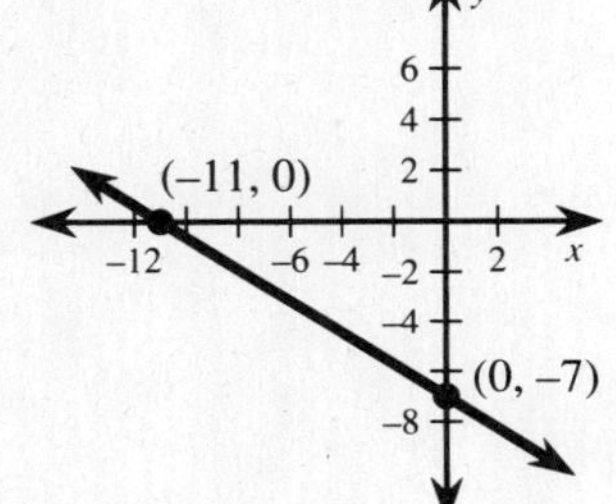

20.

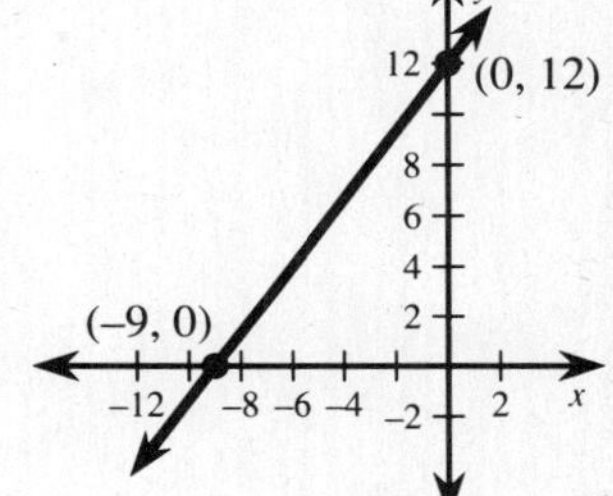

21. $x - 2y = 4$
$x - 2(0) = 4$
$x = 4$

22. $x + 4y = -2$
$x + 4(0) = -2$
$x = -2$

23. $2x - 3y = 6$
$2x - 3(0) = 6$
$2x = 6$
$x = 3$

24. $5x + 6y = 95$
$5x + (6)(0) = 95$
$5x = 95$
$x = 19$

25. $-6x - 4y = 42$
$-6x - 4(0) = 42$
$-6x = 42$
$x = -7$

26. $9x - 4y = 54$
$9x - 4(0) = 54$
$9x = 54$
$x = 6$

27. $-x - 5y = 12$
$-x - 5(0) = 12$
$-x = 12$
$x = -12$

28. $-13x - y = 39$
$-13x - 0 = 39$
$-13x = 39$
$x = -3$

29. $y = 4x - 2$
$y = 4(0) - 2$
$y = -2$

30. $y = -3x + 7$
$y = -3(0) + 7$
$y = 7$

31. $y = 13x + 26$
$y = 13(0) + 26$
$y = 26$

32. $y = 6x - 24$
$y = 6(0) - 24$
$y = -24$

33. $3x - 4y = 16$
$3(0) - 4y = 16$
$-4y = 16$
$y = -4$

34. $2x - 17y = -51$
$2(0) - 17y = -51$
$-17y = -51$
$y = 3$

35. $-x + 8y = 40$
$-0 + 8y = 40$
$8y = 40$
$y = 5$

36. $6x + 9y = -81$
$6(0) + 9y = -81$
$9y = -81$
$y = -9$

37. x-intercept: $0 = 2 - x$
$x = 2$

y-intercept: $y = 2 - 0$
$y = 2$

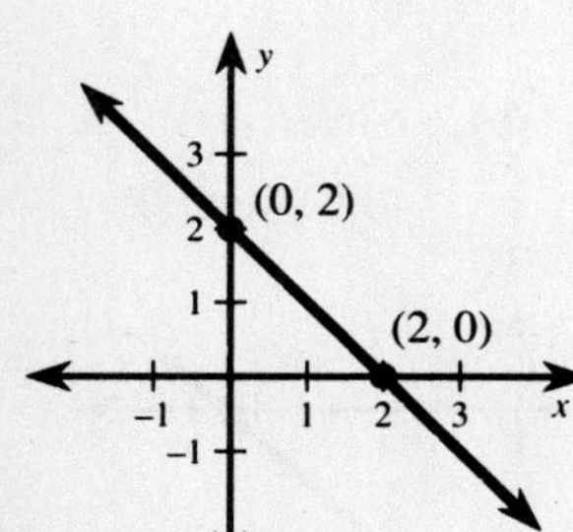

38. x-intercept: $0 = x + 3$
$x = -3$

y-intercept: $y = 0 + 3$
$y = 3$

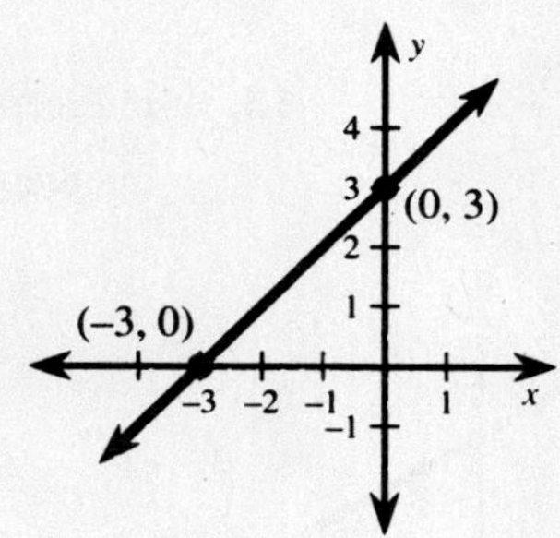

39. x-intercept: $0 = 3x + 9$

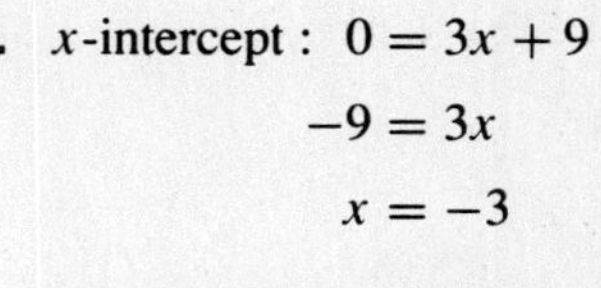

$-9 = 3x$
$x = -3$

y-intercept: $y = 3(0) + 9$
$y = 9$

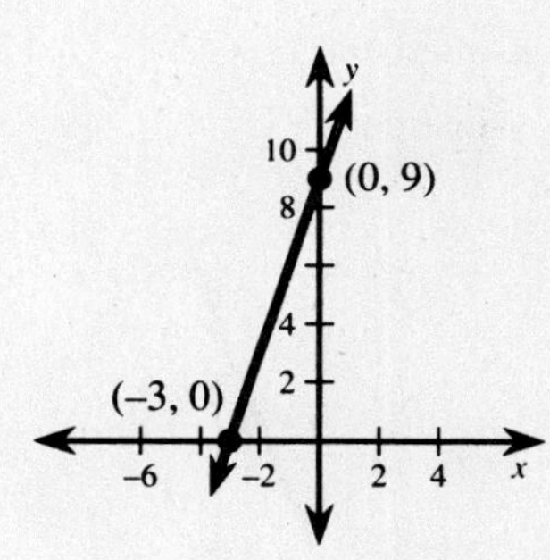

40. x-intercept : $0 = -4 + 2x$

$4 = 2x$

$x = 2$

y-intercept : $y = -4 + 2(0)$

$y = -4$

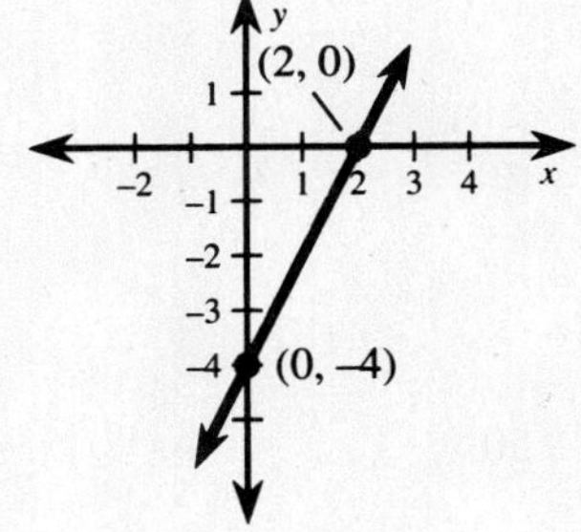

41. x-intercept : $3x + 5(0) = 15$

$3x = 15$

$x = 5$

y-intercept : $3(0) + 5y = 15$

$5y = 15$

$y = 3$

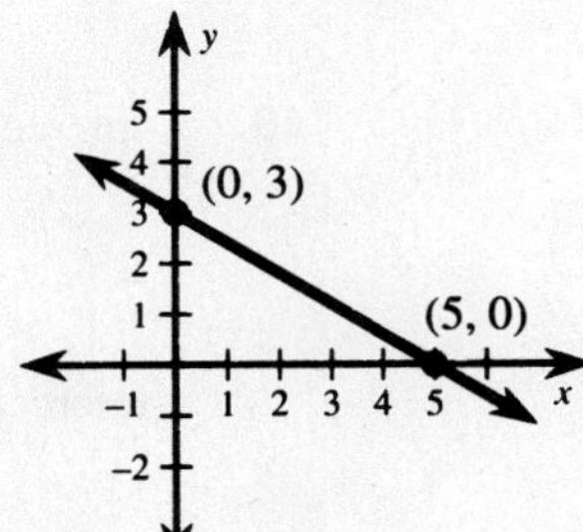

42. x-intercept : $4x + 3(0) = 24$

$4x = 24$

$x = 6$

y-intercept : $4(0) + 3y = 24$

$3y = 24$

$y = 8$

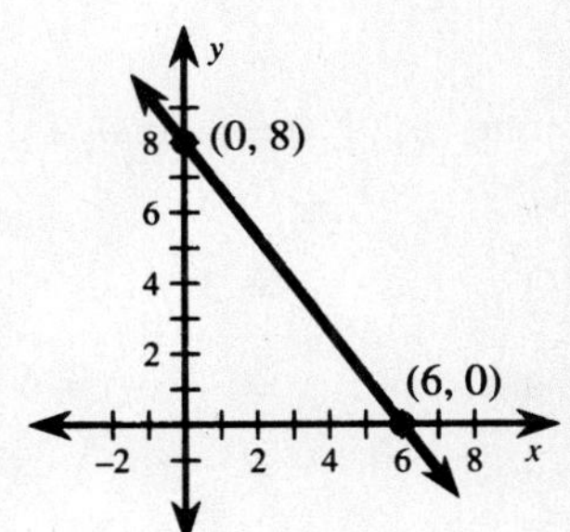

43. x-intercept : $-9x + 2(0) = 36$

$-9x = 36$

$x = -4$

y-intercept : $-9(0) + 2(y) = 36$

$2y = 36$

$y = 18$

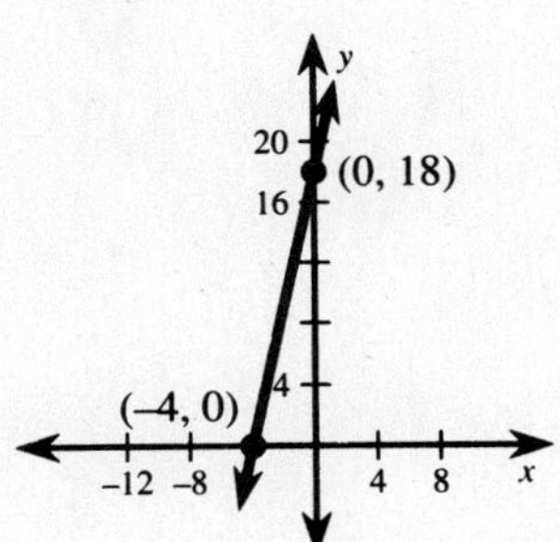

44. x-intercept : $x - 6(0) = 36$

$x = 36$

y-intercept : $0 - 6y = 36$

$-6y = 36$

$y = -6$

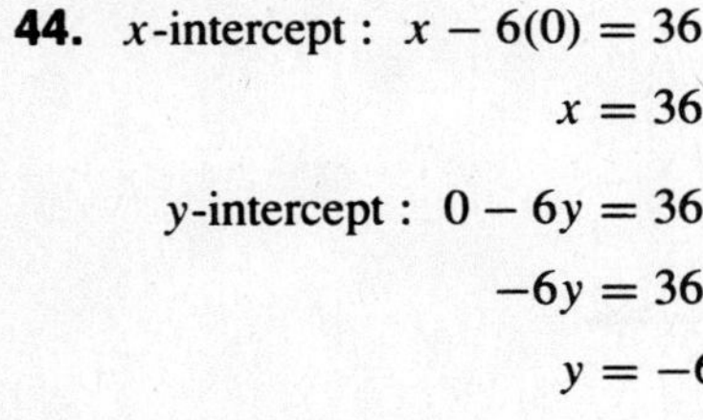

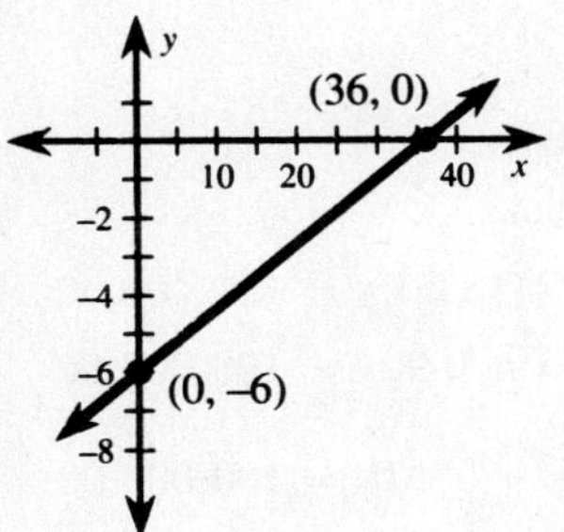

45. x-intercept : $5x - 0 = 35$

$5x = 35$

$x = 7$

y-intercept : $5(0) - y = 35$

$-y = 35$

$y = -35$

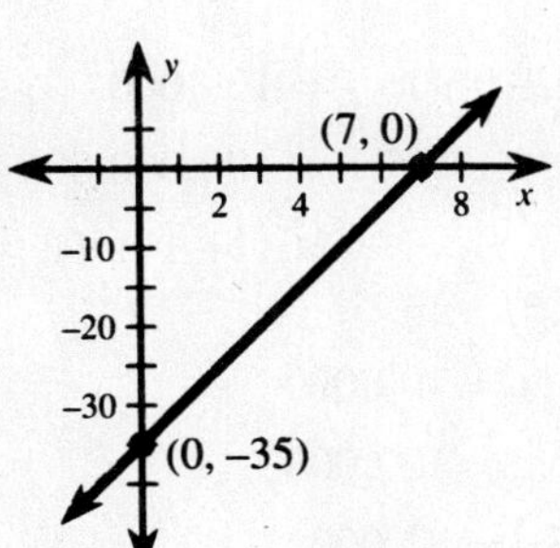

46. x-intercept: $10x + (7)(0) = -140$

$$10x = -140$$

$$x = -14$$

y-intercept: $10(0) + 7y = -140$

$$7y = -140$$

$$y = -20$$

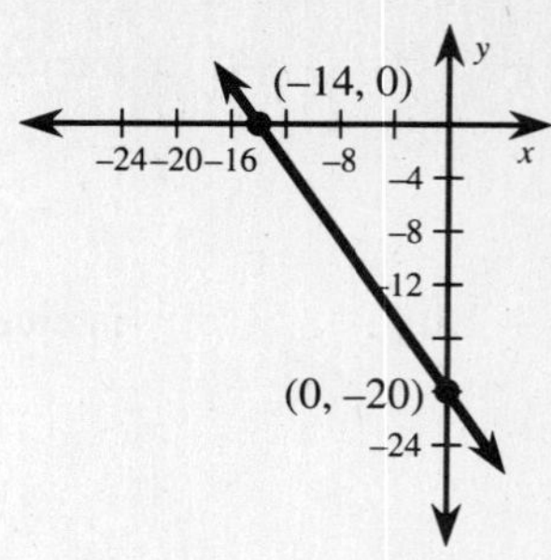

47. x-intercept: $0 = -3x + 9$

$$3x = 9$$

$$x = 3$$

y-intercept: $y = -3(0) + 9$

$$y = 9$$

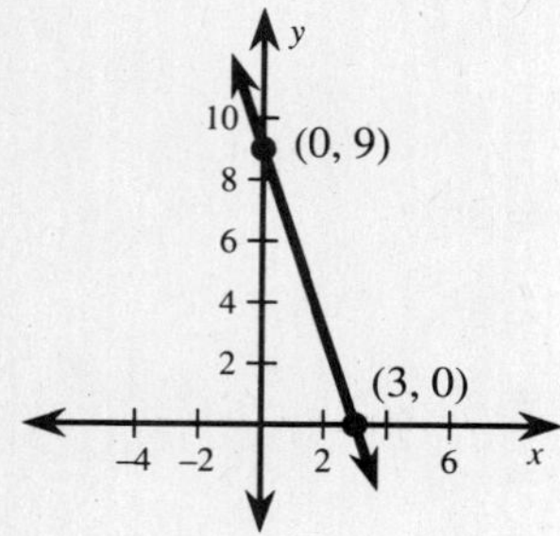

48. x-intercept: $0 = 10(x) + 50$

$$-50 = 10x$$

$$x = -5$$

y-intercept: $y = 10(0) + 50$

$$y = 50$$

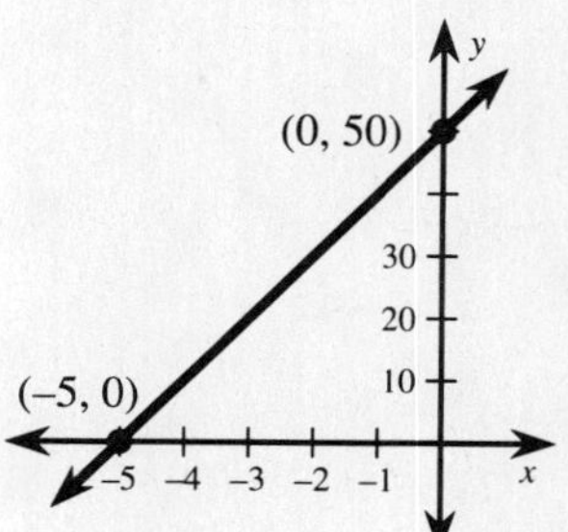

49. x = number of paperbacks.
y = number of hardbacks.

$$(0.05)(5.00)x + (0.05)(18.00)y = 100{,}000.00$$

$$0.25x + 0.90y = 100{,}000.00$$

$$0.25x + 0.9(0) = 100{,}000.00$$

$$0.25x = 100{,}000.00$$

$$x = 400{,}000$$

$$0.25(0) + 0.90(y) = 100{,}000.00$$

$$0.90y = 100{,}000.00$$

$$y = 111{,}111.11$$

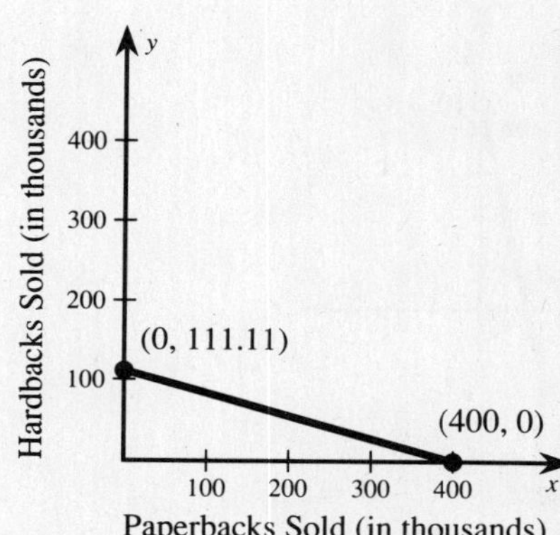

50. $0.05(18 \cdot 20{,}000 + 5x) = 100{,}000$

$$18{,}000 + 0.25x = 100{,}000$$

$$0.25x = 82{,}000$$

$$x = 328{,}000 \text{ paperbacks}$$

Alicia will receive 5% of the total book sales. The total book sales will be \$18 times the number of hardcover books sold plus \$5 times the number of paperbacks sold.

51. $x =$ number of people before 6 P.M.

$y =$ number of people after 6 P.M.

$4x + 7y = 11{,}228$

x-intercept: $4x + 7(0) = 11{,}228$

$4x = 11{,}228$

$x = 2807$

y-intercept: $4(0) + 7y = 11{,}228$

$7y = 11{,}228$

$y = 1604$

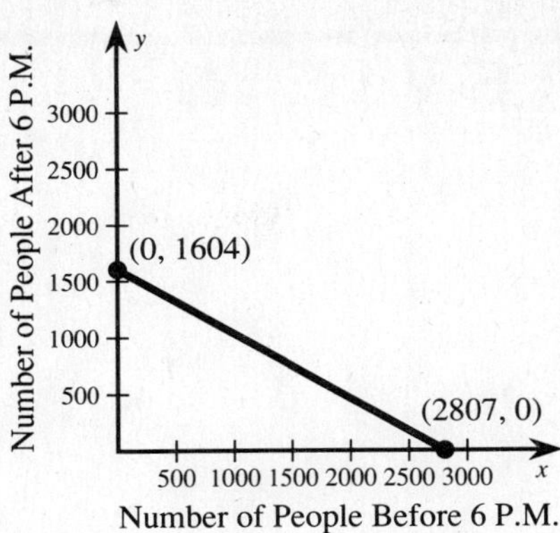

52. $4x + 7y = 11{,}228$

$4(0) + 7y = 11{,}228$

$7y = 11{,}228$

$y = 1604$ people

53. $4x - 3y = -5$

$4(1) - 3(-3) \stackrel{?}{=} -5$

$4 + 9 \stackrel{?}{=} -5$

$13 \neq -5$

$(1, -3)$ is not a solution.

54. $-5x - 4y = 9$

$-5(-5) - 4(4) \stackrel{?}{=} 9$

$25 - 16 \stackrel{?}{=} 9$

$9 = 9$

$(-5, 4)$ is a solution.

55. $6x + 2y = 18$

$2y = 18 - 6x$

$y = \frac{1}{2}(18 - 6x)$

$y = 9 - 3x$

56. $4x - y = 7$

$4x = 7 + y$

$4x - 7 = y$

$y = 4x - 7$

57. $-9x - 3y = 2$

$-9x = 2 + 3y$

$-9x - 2 = 3y$

$\frac{1}{3}(-9x - 2) = y$

$y = -3x - \frac{2}{3}$

58. $5x + 20y = 10$

$x + 4y = 2$

$4y = 2 - x$

$y = \frac{1}{4}(2 - x)$

59. $30x + 60y = 1800$

$x + 2y = 60$

$x + 2(0) = 60$ $\quad$ $0 + 2y = 60$

$x = 60$ $\quad$ $y = 30$

$(60, 0), (0, 30)$

60. The distance between the adjacent tick marks on both the x and y axis is 10 units.

61. $64x - 16y = 256$

$4x - y = 16$

$4x - 0 = 16$ $\quad$ $4(0) - y = 16$

$x = 4$ $\quad$ $y = -16$

$(4, 0), (0, -16)$

62. The distance between the adjacent tick marks on both the x and y axis is 2 units.

63. $(28, 21.34)$

64. No, there is some unknown limit between 21.34 and 0 that will take longer and longer to reach.

Mixed REVIEW

1. $3x + 7 = 3(0) + 7$
$= 7$

2. $\frac{1}{3} \cdot 6a(4 - b) = \frac{1}{3} \cdot 6 \cdot 1(4 - 3)$
$= 2 \cdot 1 \cdot 1$
$= 2$

3. $4(x - 1) = 2y$
$2(x - 1) = y$

4. $\frac{10}{9}x = 3x + y$
$10x = 27x + 9y$
$0 = 17x + 9y$
$-9y = 17x$
$x = -\frac{9}{17}y$

5. 3.2

6. $|-3(-10)| = |30|$
$= 30$

7. $(3^2 - 1) \div 2^3 = (9 - 1) \div 8$
$= 8 \div 8$
$= 1$

8. $4[(-5)^2 + (-10) - 7] = 4(25 - 10 - 7)$
$= 4(8)$
$= 32$

9. $3(x^2 - 1) - 4(x - x^2) = 3x^2 - 3 - 4x + 4x^2$
$= 7x^2 - 4x - 3$

10. $x(x - 1) - (2 + x^2) = x^2 - x - 2 - x^2$
$= -x - 2$

11. $4 \cdot x + 3 \div 2 = 4x + \frac{3}{2}$
$4 \cdot (x + 3) \div 2 = (4x + 12) \div 2$
$= 2x + 6$

No, they are not equal.

12. $\frac{1}{5}(16x + 2) = \frac{16}{5}x + \frac{2}{5}$
$(16x + 2) \div 5 = \frac{16x + 2}{5}$
$= \frac{16}{5}x + \frac{2}{5}$

Yes, they are equal.

13. $$\begin{bmatrix} 0.4 & 9.2 \\ 6.3 & 7.8 \end{bmatrix} + \begin{bmatrix} -4.3 & 1.8 \\ -2.2 & 2.2 \end{bmatrix} = \begin{bmatrix} 0.4 - 4.3 & 9.2 + 1.8 \\ 6.3 - 2.2 & 7.8 + 2.2 \end{bmatrix} = \begin{bmatrix} -3.9 & 11.0 \\ 4.1 & 10.0 \end{bmatrix}$$

14. $$\begin{bmatrix} \frac{1}{4} & -\frac{3}{2} \\ \frac{3}{8} & \frac{7}{8} \end{bmatrix} - \begin{bmatrix} \frac{1}{8} & -\frac{3}{2} \\ -\frac{1}{8} & \frac{3}{4} \end{bmatrix} = \begin{bmatrix} \frac{1}{4} - \frac{1}{8} & -\frac{3}{2} + \frac{3}{2} \\ \frac{3}{8} + \frac{1}{8} & \frac{7}{8} - \frac{3}{4} \end{bmatrix} = \begin{bmatrix} \frac{1}{8} & 0 \\ \frac{1}{2} & \frac{1}{8} \end{bmatrix}$$

15. $14x - 10 \geq 3x + 2$

$14(0) - 10 \overset{?}{\geq} 3(0) + 2$

$-10 \not\geq 2$

0 is not a solution.

16. $\frac{1}{2}(1 - x) < -2$

$\frac{1}{2}(1 - 3) \overset{?}{<} -2$

$\frac{1}{2}(-2) \overset{?}{<} -2$

$-1 \not< -2$

3 is not a solution.

17. $4y^2 - 3 = 1$

$4(-1)^2 - 3 \overset{?}{=} 1$

$4(1) - 3 \overset{?}{=} 1$

$4 - 3 \overset{?}{=} 1$

$1 = 1$

-1 is a solution.

18. $-3(a - 9.5) = -12$

$-3(5.5 - 9.5) \overset{?}{=} -12$

$-3(-4) \overset{?}{=} -12$

$12 \neq -12$

5.5 is not a solution.

19. $2x - y = 5$

$2(2) - (-1) \overset{?}{=} 5$

$4 + 1 \overset{?}{=} 5$

$5 = 5$

$(2, -1)$ is a solution.

20. $y = 4$

$4 = 4$

$(0, 4)$ is a solution.

4.4 The Slope of a Line

Communicating about Algebra

A. $m = \frac{90 - 0}{5 - 3}$

$= \frac{90}{2}$

$= 45$ miles per hour

B. $m = \frac{63 - 45}{7 - 10}$

$= \frac{18}{-3}$

$= -6$°F per hour

EXERCISES

1. The student did not use the same order of subtraction for both the numerator and denominator.

2. The numerator is called the rise.

3. The denominator is called the run.

4. Since the x-coordinates have the same value, the denominator for the slope formula is zero.

5. The slope of a horizontal line is zero.

6. **b.**, If the slope is interpreted as steepness;
c., if the slope is interpreted as a number.

7. True

8. Miles per hour, dollars per pound

9. a: -1
b: 1

10. a: $-\frac{1}{3}$
b: -3

11. a: -2
b: undefined

12. a: 0
b: 2

13.

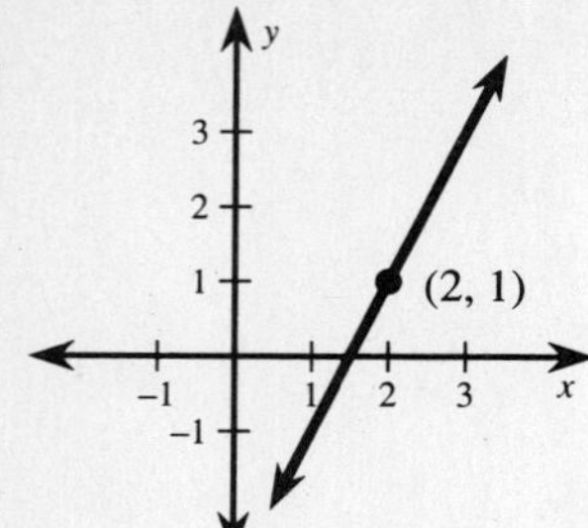

14.

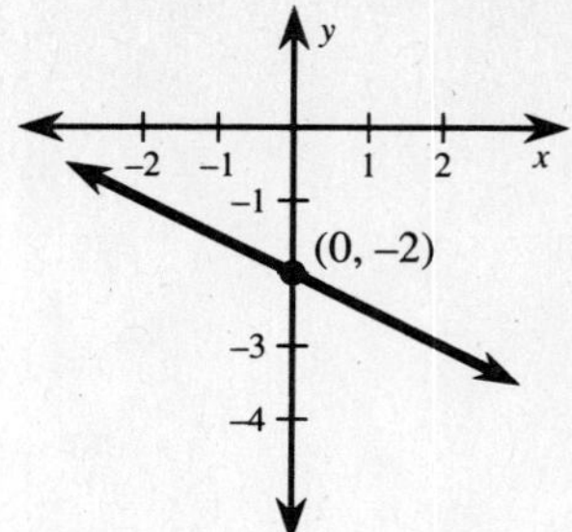

15.

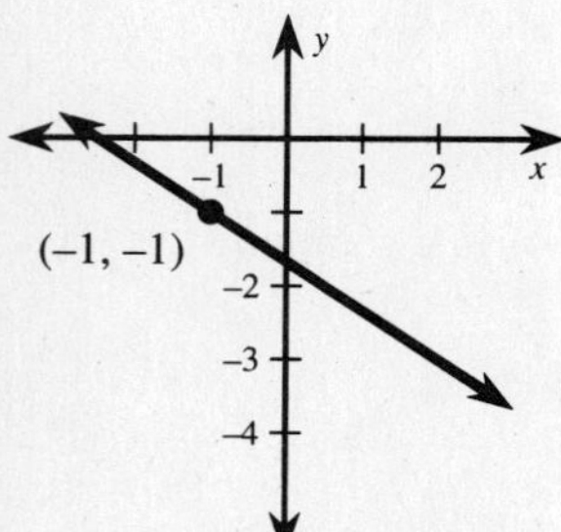

16.

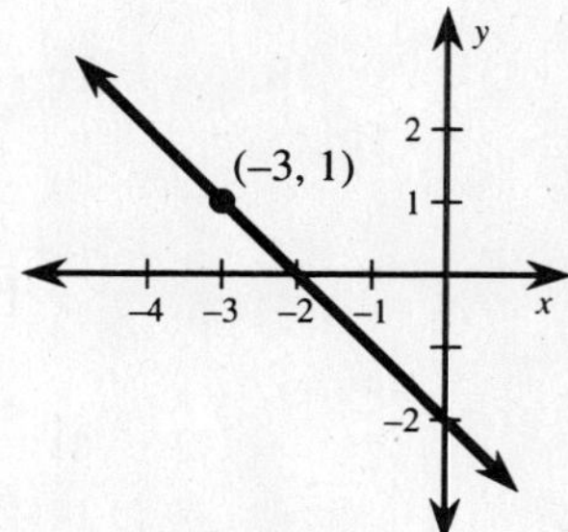

17. $m = \dfrac{5-0}{4-0}$

$= \dfrac{5}{4}$

18. $m = \dfrac{0-(-3)}{0-(-1)}$

$= \dfrac{3}{1}$

$= 3$

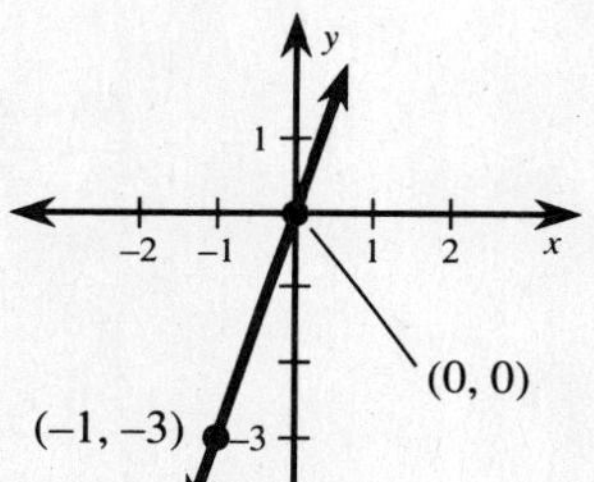

19. $m = \dfrac{6-(-2)}{1-(-3)}$

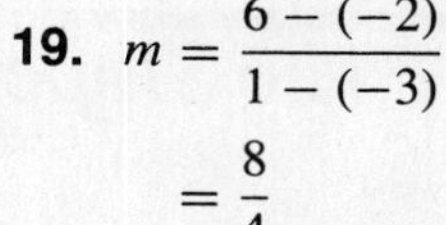

$= \dfrac{8}{4}$

$= 2$

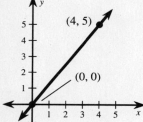

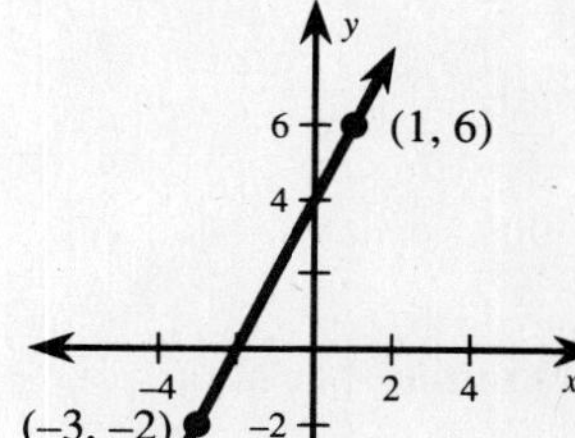

20. $m = \dfrac{0-(-6)}{8-0}$

$= \dfrac{6}{8}$

$= \dfrac{3}{4}$

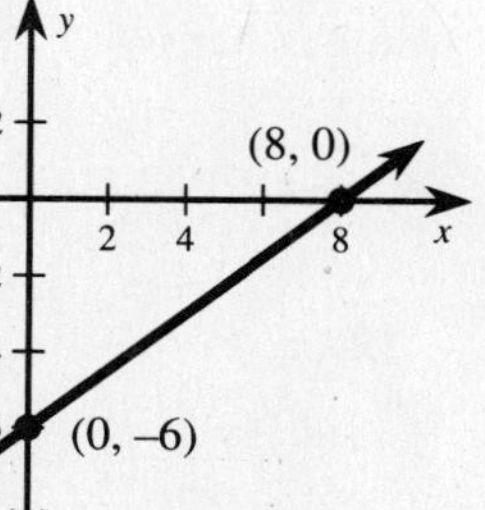

21. $m = \dfrac{0-6}{8-0}$

$= \dfrac{-6}{8}$

$= -\dfrac{3}{4}$

22. $m = \dfrac{-4-4}{4-2}$

$= \dfrac{-8}{2}$

$= -4$

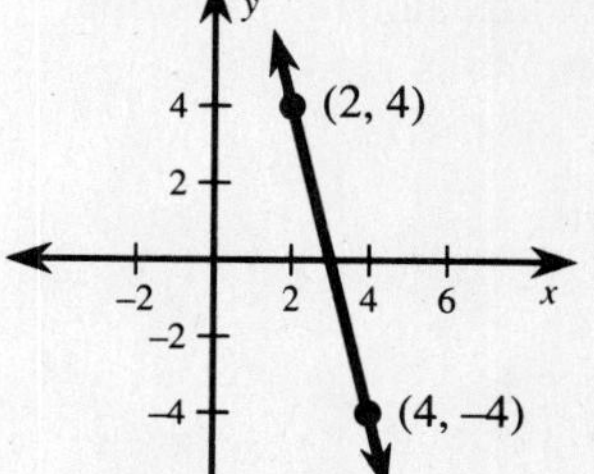

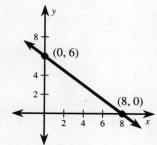

23. $m = \frac{4-(-1)}{-6-(-6)}$

$= \frac{5}{0}$ (undefined)

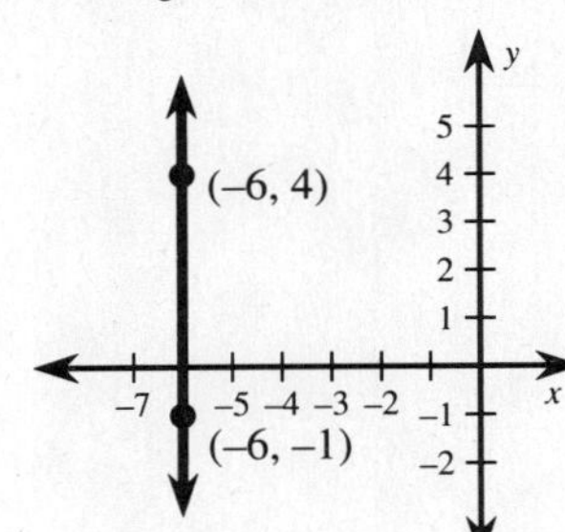

24. $m = \frac{0-(-10)}{-4-0}$

$= \frac{10}{-4}$

$= -\frac{5}{2}$

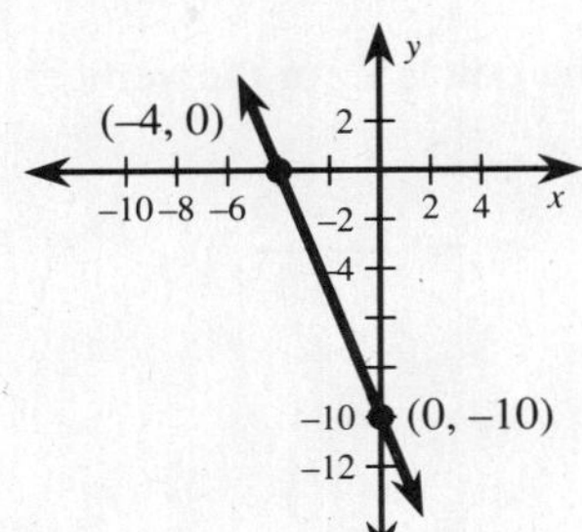

25. $m = \frac{-2-(-2)}{-2-1}$

$= \frac{0}{-3}$

$= 0$

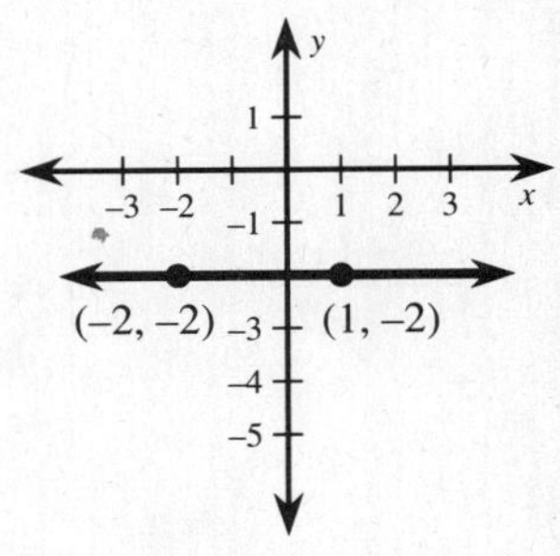

26. $m = \frac{0-6}{3-3}$

$= \frac{-6}{0}$ (undefined)

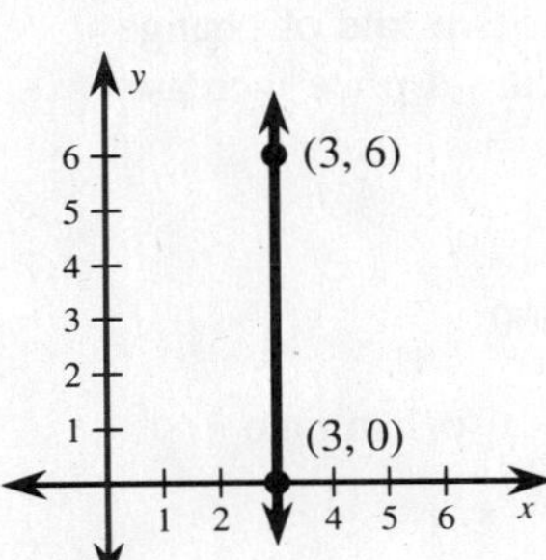

27. $m = \frac{5-2}{-3-2}$

$= \frac{3}{-5}$

$= -\frac{3}{5}$

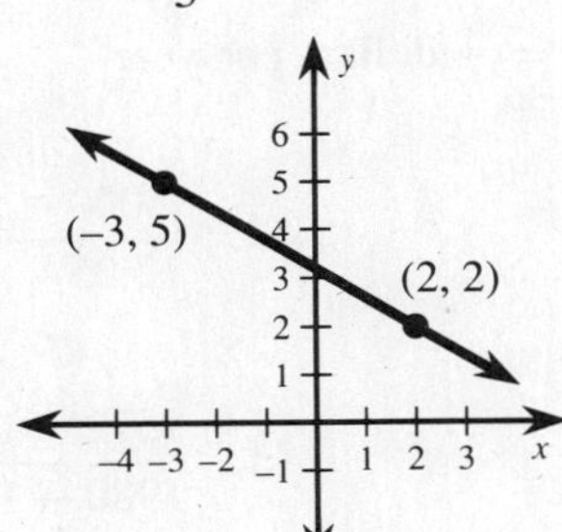

28. $m = \frac{1-1}{6-4}$

$= \frac{0}{2}$

$= 0$

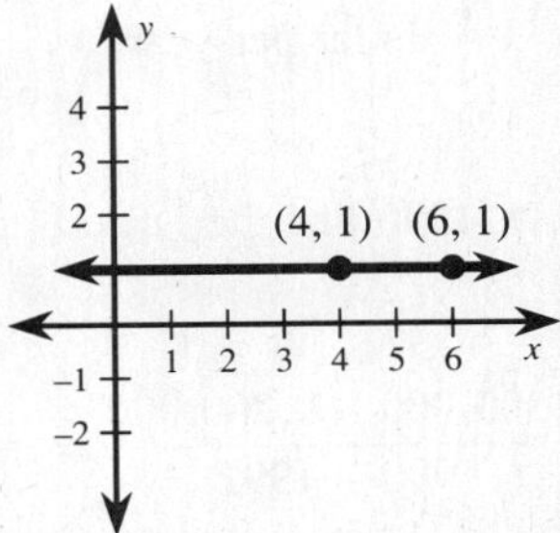

29. $m = \frac{9-3}{6-4}$

$= \frac{6}{2}$

$= 3$

Line rises to the right.

30. $m = \frac{4-8}{7-(-1)}$

$= \frac{-4}{8}$

$= -\frac{1}{2}$

Line falls to the right.

31. $m = \frac{10-(-4)}{5-5}$

$= \frac{14}{0}$ (undefined)

Line is vertical.

32. $m = \frac{1-8}{-3-9}$

$= \frac{-7}{-12}$

$= \frac{7}{12}$

Line rises to the right.

33. $m = \frac{1-(-3)}{1-4}$

$= \frac{4}{-3}$

$= -\frac{4}{3}$

Line falls to the right.

34. $m = \frac{7-7}{-6-1}$

$= \frac{0}{-7}$

$= 0$

Line is horizontal.

35. $m = \frac{2-23}{2-9}$

$= \frac{-21}{-7}$

$= 3$ inches per minute

36. $m = \dfrac{5 - 69}{3 - 11}$

$= \dfrac{-64}{-8}$

$= 8$ dollars per year

37. $m = \dfrac{1 - 2}{-2 - 1} = \dfrac{-1}{-3} = \dfrac{1}{3}$ $\quad m = \dfrac{1 - 3}{-2 - 3} = \dfrac{-2}{-5} = \dfrac{2}{5}$ $\quad m = \dfrac{2 - 3}{1 - 3} = \dfrac{-1}{-2} = \dfrac{1}{2}$

The points form the vertices of a triangle.

38. $m = \dfrac{-4 - (-2)}{-2 - 2} = \dfrac{-2}{-4} = \dfrac{1}{2}$ $\quad m = \dfrac{-4 - 0}{-2 - 6} = \dfrac{-4}{-8} = \dfrac{1}{2}$ $\quad m = \dfrac{-2 - 0}{2 - 6} = \dfrac{-2}{-4} = \dfrac{1}{2}$

The points lie on the same line.

39. $m = \dfrac{8 - 18}{1950 - 1980}$

$= \dfrac{-10}{-30}$

$= \dfrac{1}{3}$ dollar per year

40. $m = \dfrac{18 - 30}{1980 - 1990}$

$= \dfrac{-12}{-10}$

$= \dfrac{6}{5}$ dollars per year

41. All 5 year periods have a positive rate of change. Positive rate of change means a price increase.

42. 1985–1990 had the largest price increase.

43. $\dfrac{8000 - 5400}{12{:}05 - 12{:}08} = \dfrac{-2600}{3}$ feet per minute

44. $\dfrac{1{,}300{,}000 - 1{,}200{,}000}{1990 - 1992} = \dfrac{100{,}000}{-2}$

$= -50{,}000$ dollars per year

45. $\dfrac{1572 - 1572}{1980 - 1987} = \dfrac{0}{-7}$

$= 0$ symphony orchestras per year

46. $\dfrac{67 - 31}{1980 - 1987} = \dfrac{-36}{7}$ new productions per year

(Note: 5.14 fewer productions per year)

47. $\dfrac{591{,}000 - 727{,}700}{1980 - 1990} = \dfrac{-136{,}700}{-10}$

$= 13{,}670$ people per year

48. $\dfrac{100{,}300 - 132{,}200}{1980 - 1990} = \dfrac{-31{,}900}{-10}$

$= 3190$ people per year

49. San Diego: $\dfrac{1{,}876{,}900 - 2{,}461{,}100}{1980 - 1990} = \dfrac{-584{,}200}{-10}$

$= 58{,}420$ people per year

Tijuana: $\dfrac{480{,}000 - 742{,}600}{1980 - 1990} = \dfrac{-262{,}600}{-10}$

$= 26{,}260$ people per year

San Diego had the greater rate of change.

50. Tucson: $\dfrac{534{,}500 - 655{,}000}{1980 - 1990} = \dfrac{-120{,}500}{-10}$

$= 12{,}050$ people per year

Nogales: $\dfrac{71{,}000 - 107{,}100}{1980 - 1990} = \dfrac{-36{,}100}{-10}$

$= 3610$ people per year

Tucson had the greater rate of change.

51. $9x - 2y = 14$

$-2y = 14 - 9x$

$y = -\frac{1}{2}(14 - 9x)$

52. $5x + 9y = 18$

$9y = 18 - 5x$

$y = \frac{1}{9}(18 - 5x)$

53. $-6x + 3y = 18$

$-2x + y = 6$

$y = 6 + 2x$

54. $-2x - 2y = 7$

$-2x - 7 = 2y$

$y = -\frac{1}{2}(2x + 7)$

55. $3x - 12(0) = 16$

$x = \frac{16}{3}$

$3(0) - 12y = 16$

$y = -\frac{16}{12}$

$= -\frac{4}{3}$

$\left(\frac{16}{3}, 0\right), \left(0, -\frac{4}{3}\right)$

56. $-2x + 4(0) = 16$

$x = -8$

$-2(0) + 4y = 16$

$y = 4$

$(-8, 0), (0, 4)$

57. $-14x + 3(0) = -42$

$x = 3$

$-14(0) + 3y = -42$

$y = -14$

$(3, 0), (0, -14)$

58. $x - 21(0) = 7$

$x = 7$

$0 - 21y = 7$

$y = \frac{7}{-21}$

$= -\frac{1}{3}$

$(7, 0), \left(0, -\frac{1}{3}\right)$

59. $\dfrac{4 - 6}{3 - x} = -\dfrac{2}{5}$

$5(4 - 6) = -2(3 - x)$

$-10 = -6 + 2x$

$-4 = 2x$

$x = -2$

60. $m = \dfrac{0 - (-17)}{0 - 5}$

$m = -\dfrac{17}{15}$

61. $4x + 5y = 50$

$5y = 50 - 4x$

$y = 10 - \frac{4}{5}x$

$y = 10 - \dfrac{4}{5}(5)$

$= 10 - 4$

$= 6$

$(5, 6)$

$y = 10 - \dfrac{4}{5}(10)$

$= 10 - 8$

$= 2$

$(10, 2)$

$m = \dfrac{6 - 2}{5 - 10}$

$= -\dfrac{4}{5}$

Solve the equation for y. For each point, pick a value for the x-coordinate and evaluate the equation to determine its y-coordinate. Use the slope formula to determine the slope of the line.

62. $y = -\frac{1}{2}(2) + 3$

$= -1 + 3$

$= 2$

$(2, 2)$

$y = -\frac{1}{2}(4) + 3$

$= -2 + 3$

$= 1$

$(4, 1)$

$m = \dfrac{1-2}{4-2}$

$= -\dfrac{1}{2}$

63. $y = 2x + 2 : 2$

$y = x + 1 : 1$

$y = \frac{1}{2}x - 1 : -1$

$y = \frac{3}{5}x - 3 : -3$

The y-intercept is the constant term in the equation.

Mid-Chapter SELF-TEST

1.

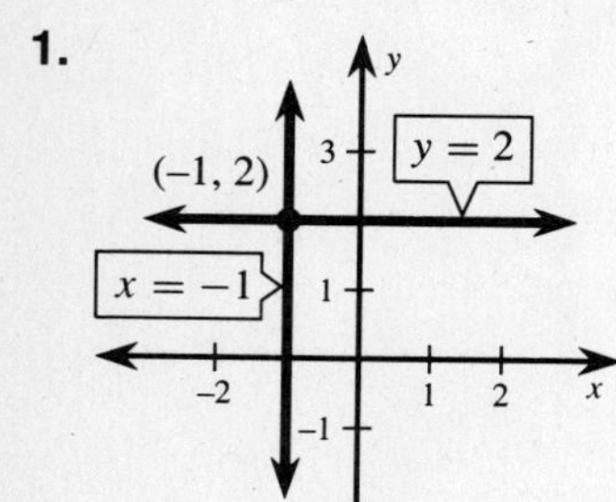

2. $x = 4, y = -6$

3. $6x + \frac{1}{3}y = 9$

$\frac{1}{3}y = 9 - 6x$

$y = 27 - 18x$

4. $x + \frac{3}{4}y = 4$

$\frac{3}{4}y = 4 - x$

$y = \frac{4}{3}(4 - x)$

5. $\frac{12}{5}x - y = 4$

$\frac{12}{5}x - 4 = y$

x	y
0	−4
$\frac{5}{3}$	0
5	8

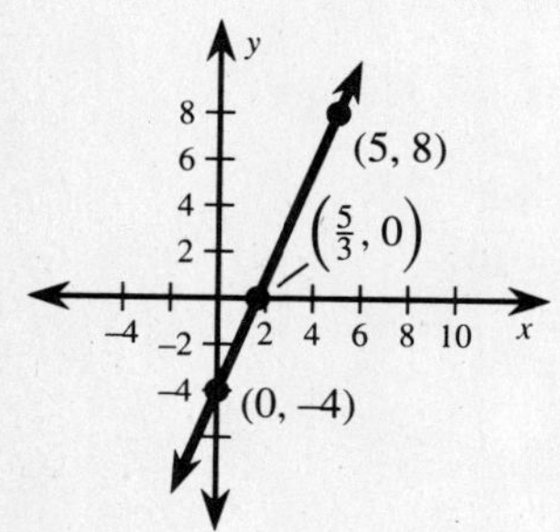

6. $3x + 4y = 3$

$4y = 3 - 3x$

$y = \frac{1}{4}(3 - 3x)$

x	y
1	0
0	$\frac{3}{4}$
−1	$\frac{3}{2}$

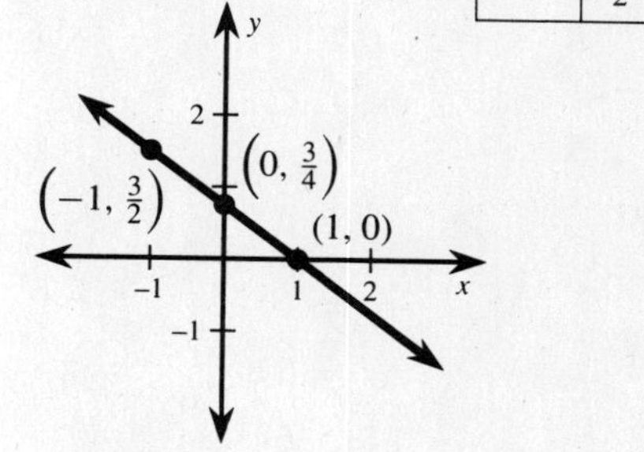

7. $5x + 3y = 11$

$5(3) + 3\left(-\frac{4}{3}\right) \stackrel{?}{=} 11$

$15 - 4 \stackrel{?}{=} 11$

$11 = 11$

$\left(3, -\frac{4}{3}\right)$ is a solution.

8. $\frac{9}{2}x - y = 20$

$\frac{9}{2}(3) - 5 \stackrel{?}{=} 20$

$\frac{27}{2} - \frac{10}{2} \stackrel{?}{=} 20$

$\frac{17}{2} \neq 20$

(3, 5) is not a solution.

9. $5x - 3(0) = 15$ $\quad$ $5(0) - 3y = 15$

$x = 3$ $\quad$ $y = -5$

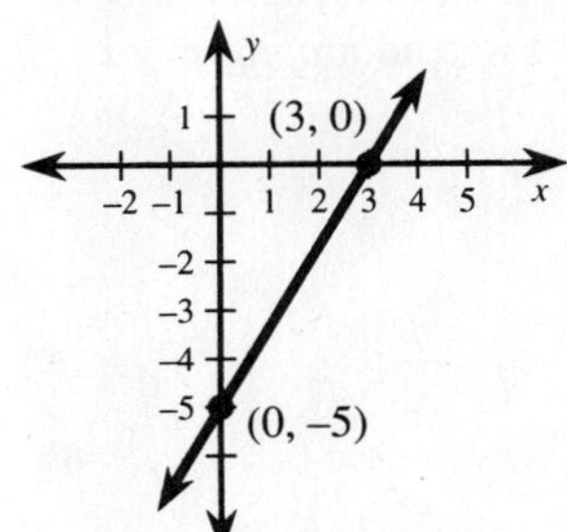

10. $-7x + 4(0) = 28$ $\quad$ $-7(0) + 4y = 28$

$x = -4$ $\quad$ $y = 7$

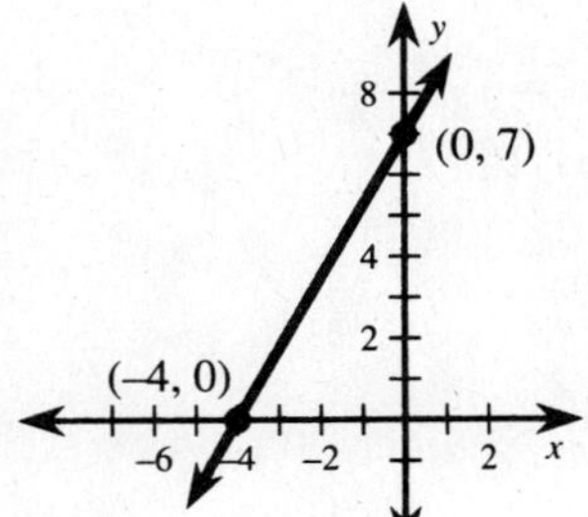

11. c.

12. b.

13. -3

14. 3

15. $m = \dfrac{1 - 15}{-1 - 20}$

$= \dfrac{-14}{-21}$

$= \dfrac{2}{3}$

16. $m = \dfrac{2 - 6}{\frac{4}{3} - \frac{2}{3}}$

$= \dfrac{-4}{\frac{2}{3}}$

$= \dfrac{-12}{2}$

$= -6$

17. $\dfrac{3.75 - 5.95}{2.5 - 4.0} = \dfrac{-2.20}{-1.5}$

$= \dfrac{22}{15}$ dollars per pound

18. $\dfrac{200 - 1000}{\frac{1}{2} - 2} = \dfrac{-800}{-\frac{3}{2}}$

$= \dfrac{1600}{3}$ people per square mile

19. $x =$ number of baskets of apples

$y =$ number of baskets of strawberries

$4x + 6y = 336$

$4x + 6(0) = 336$

$x = 84$

$4.0 + 6y = 336$

$y = 56$

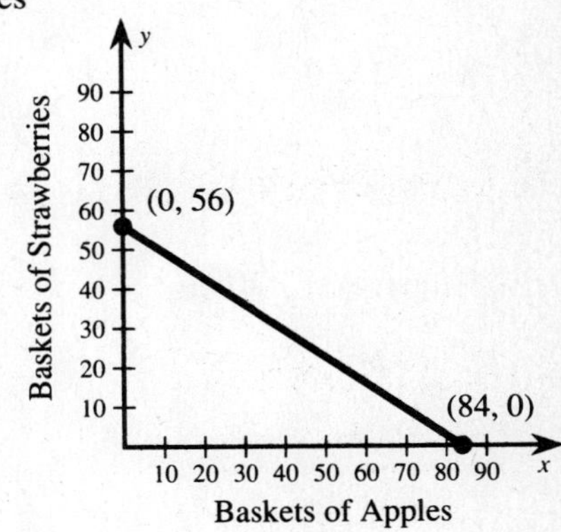

20. $\dfrac{1450 - 1140}{4 - 1} = \dfrac{310}{3}$

$= \$103.33$ dollars per month

4.5 Quick Graphs Using Slope-Intercept Form

Communicating about Algebra

A. The C-intercepts represent the base cost of the printing. The slopes represent the cost per book.

B. $C = 750 + 2(500) = 1750$

Full-color cost per book $= \frac{1750}{500} = \$3.50$

$C = 250 + 1.75(500) = 1125$

Single-color cost per book $= \frac{1125}{500} = \$2.25$

C. Full-color cost per book $= \frac{2250}{750} = \$3.00$

Single-color cost per book $= \frac{1562.5}{750} \approx \$2.09$

You could charge less per book. The base cost of the printing would be spread among more copies.

EXERCISES

1. Yes; the slope of the line does not change.

2. m is the slope. b is the y-intercept.

3. Two different lines that have the same slope are parallel.

4. $3x + 2y = 1$

$2y = -3 + 1$

$y = -\frac{3}{2}x + \frac{1}{2}$

The slope is $-\frac{3}{2}$.
The y-intercept is $\frac{1}{2}$.

5. $5x + 7y = 0$

$7y = -5x$

$y = -\frac{5}{7}x$

6. $2x - 4y = 0$

$2x = 4y$

$y = \frac{1}{2}x$

7. $3x + 4y = 12$

$4y = -3x + 12$

$y = -\frac{3}{4}x + 3$

8. $-4x + 5y = 8$

$5y = 4x + 8$

$y = \frac{4}{5}x + \frac{8}{5}$

9. $y + 10 = 0$

$y = -10$

10. $y - 12 = 0$

$y = 12$

11. Slope: -2
y-intercept: 1

12. Slope: 3
y-intercept: -6

13. Slope: -8
y-intercept: -4

14. Slope: 4
y-intercept: -20

15. $x - y = 3x + 4$

$-y = 2x + 4$

$y = -2x - 4$

Slope: -2
y-intercept: -4

16. $2y - x = 7x - 9$

$2y = 8x - 9$

$y = 4x - \frac{9}{2}$

Slope: 4
y-intercept: $-\frac{9}{2}$

17. $2x - y - 3 = 0$

$2x - 3 = y$

$y = 2x - 3$

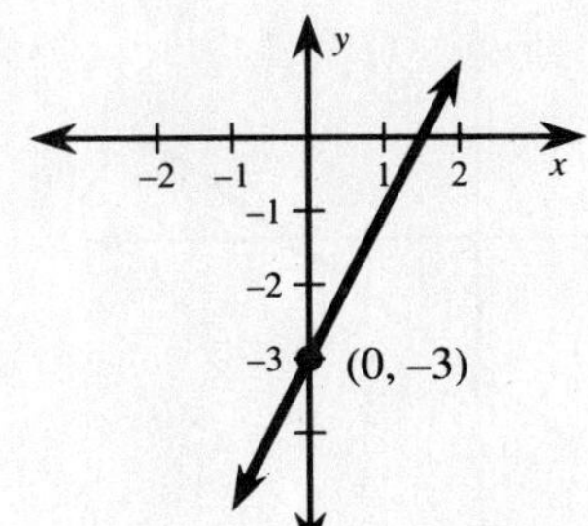

18. $x - y + 2 = 0$

$x + 2 = y$

$y = x + 2$

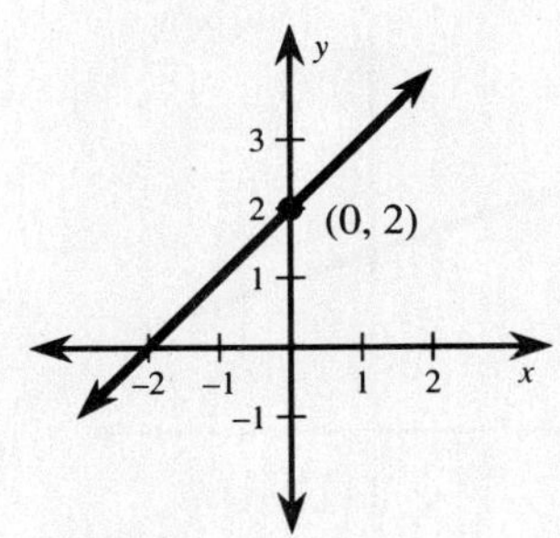

19. $x + y = 0$

$y = -x$

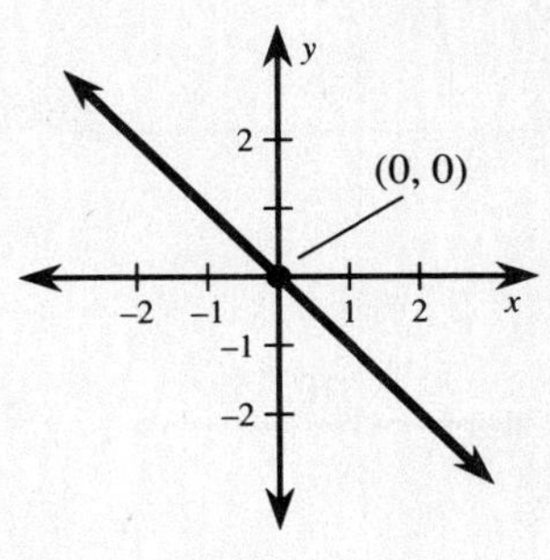

20. $x - y = 0$

$y = x$

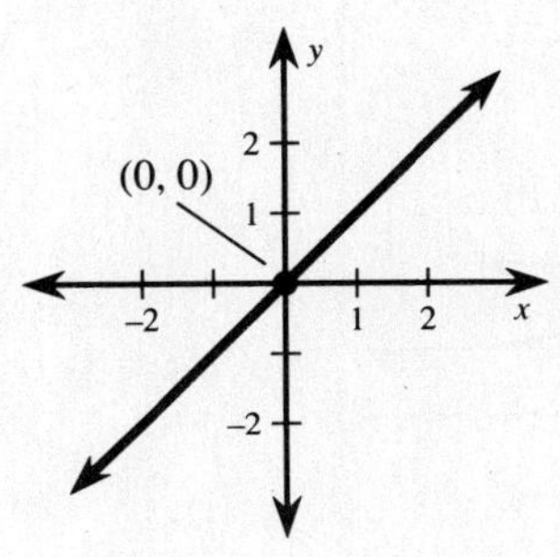

21. $x + 2y - 2 = 0$

$2y = -x + 2$

$y = -\frac{1}{2}x + 1$

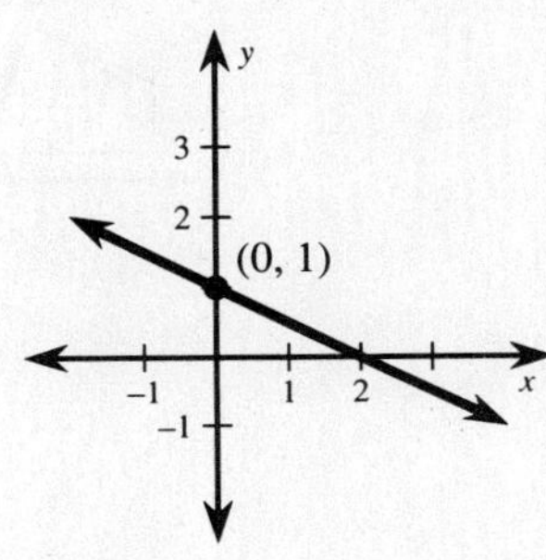

22. $3x - 2y - 2 = 0$

$3x - 2 = 2y$

$\frac{3}{2}x - 1 = y$

$y = \frac{3}{2}x - 1$

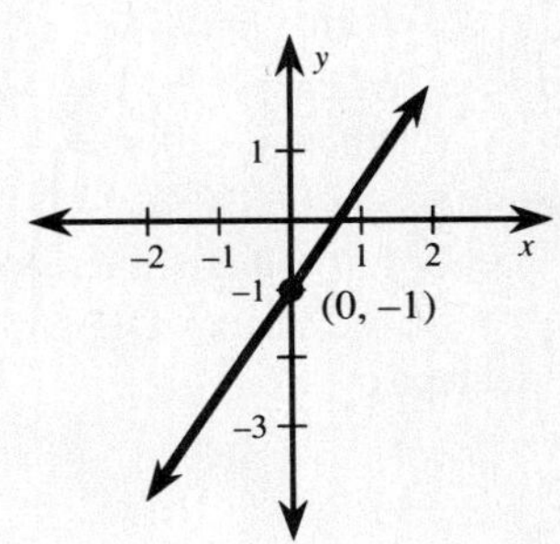

23. $3x - 4y + 2 = 0$

$3x + 2 = 4y$

$\frac{3}{4}x + \frac{1}{2} = y$

$y = \frac{3}{4}x + \frac{1}{2}$

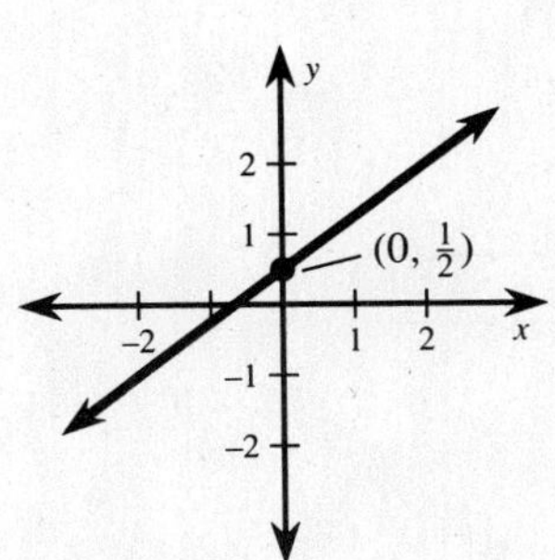

24. $10x + 6y - 3 = 0$

$6y = -10x + 3$

$y = -\frac{5}{3}x + \frac{1}{2}$

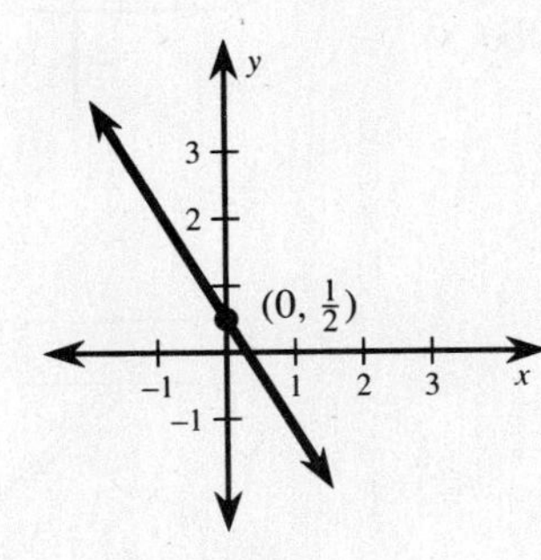

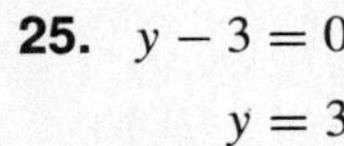

25. $y - 3 = 0$

$y = 3$

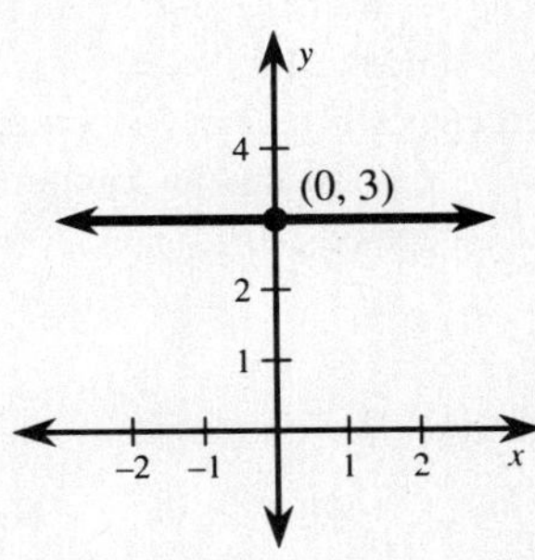

26. $y + 5 = 0$

$y = -5$

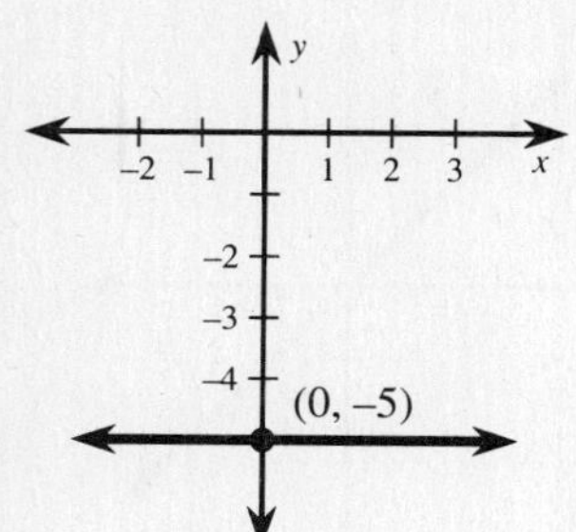

27. $2x + 3y - 4 = x + 5$

$3y = -x + 9$

$y = -\frac{1}{3}x + 3$

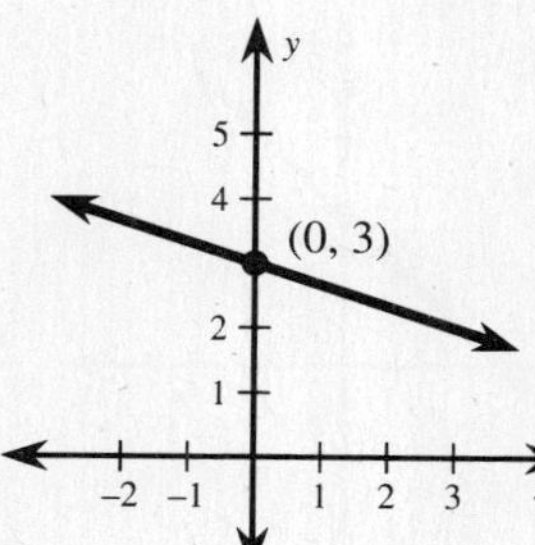

28.

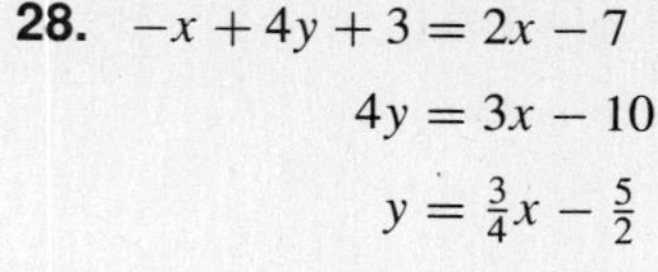

$-x + 4y + 3 = 2x - 7$

$4y = 3x - 10$

$y = \frac{3}{4}x - \frac{5}{2}$

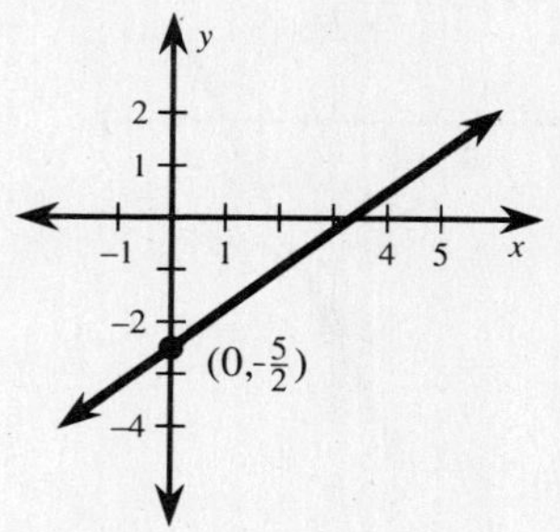

29. **d.** **30.** **c.** **31.** **a.** **32.** **b.**

33. Both lines have a slope of -3.

1st line: When $x = 0$, $y = 2$.
When $y = 0$, $x = \frac{2}{3}$.

2nd line: When $x = 0$, $y = -2$.
When $y = 0$, $x = -\frac{2}{3}$.

Therefore, the line $y = -3x + 2$ has an x-intercept of $\frac{2}{3}$ and a y-intercept of 2. The line $y = -3x - 2$ has an x-intercept of $-\frac{2}{3}$ and a y-intercept of -2.

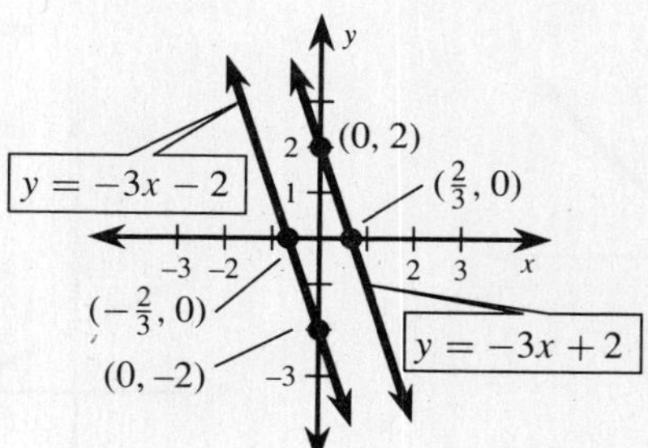

34. Both lines have a slope of -1.

1st line: When $x = 0$, $y = 6$.
When $y = 0$, $x = 6$.

2nd line: When $x = 0$, $y = 10$.
When $y = 0$, $x = 10$.

Therefore, the line $y = -x + 6$ has an x-intercept of 6 and a y-intercept of 6. The line $y = -x + 10$ has an x-intercept of 10 and a y-intercept of 10.

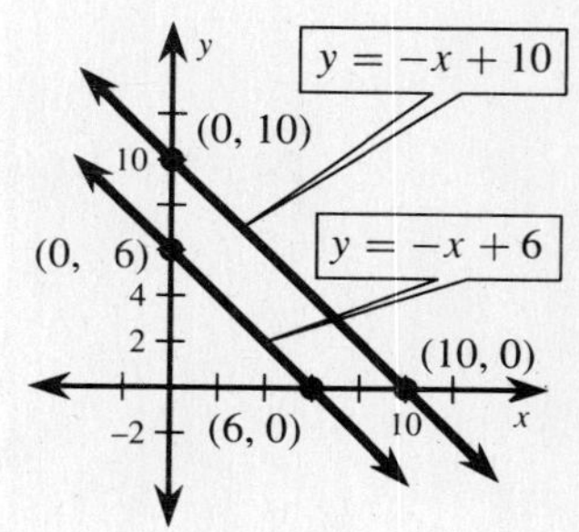

35. Both lines have a slope of 6.

1st line: When $x = 0$, $y = 8$.
When $y = 0$, $x = -\frac{4}{3}$.

2nd line: When $x = 0$, $y = -2$.
When $y = 0$, $x = \frac{1}{3}$.

Therefore, the line $y = 6x + 8$ has an x-intercept of $-\frac{4}{3}$ and a y-intercept of 8. The line $y = 6x - 2$ has an x-intercept of $\frac{1}{3}$ and y-intercept of -2.

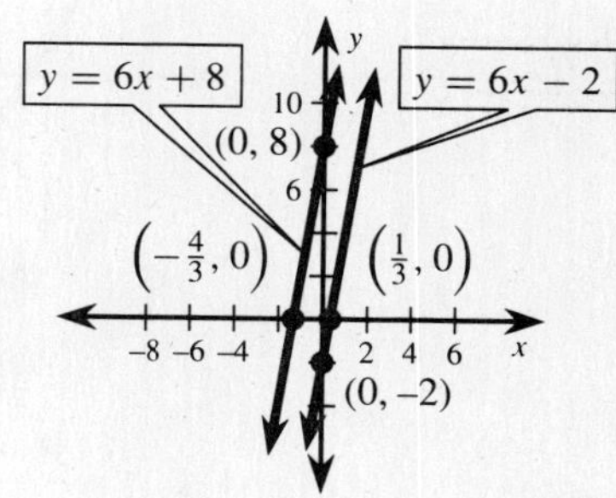

36. Both lines have a slope of $\frac{4}{3}$.

1st line: When $x = 0, y = -1$.
When $y = 0, x = \frac{3}{4}$.

2nd line: When $x = 0, y = 3$.
When $y = 0, x = -\frac{9}{4}$.

Therefore, the line $y = \frac{4}{3}x - 1$ has an x-intercept of $\frac{3}{4}$ and a y-intercept of -1. The line $y = \frac{4}{3}x + 3$ has an x-intercept of $-\frac{9}{4}$ and a y-intercept of 3.

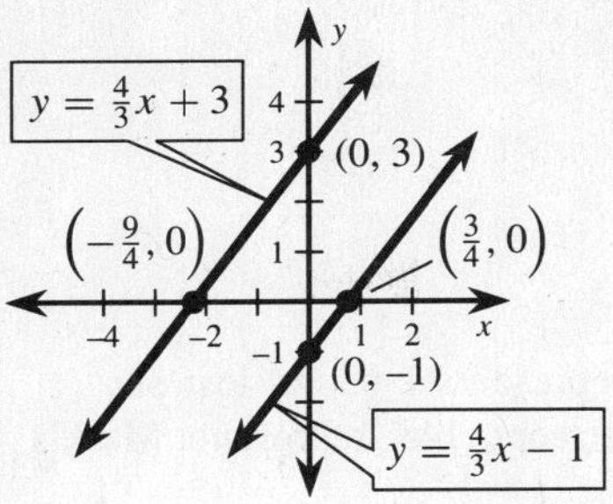

$y = \frac{4}{3}x + 3$ $(0, 3)$ $\left(-\frac{9}{4}, 0\right)$ $\left(\frac{3}{4}, 0\right)$ $(0, -1)$ $y = \frac{4}{3}x - 1$

37.
$$\frac{x}{50} = \frac{3}{200}$$
$$x = \frac{3}{200} \cdot 50$$
$$x = \frac{150}{200}$$
$$x = \frac{3}{4} \text{ foot}$$

38.
$$\frac{x}{10} = \frac{18}{45}$$
$$x = \frac{18}{45}(10)$$
$$x = \frac{180}{45}$$
$$x = 4 \text{ inches}$$

39.
$$\frac{48}{6} = \frac{x}{170.25}$$
$$(170.25)(8) = x$$
$$x = 1362 \text{ feet}$$

The World Trade Center is taller. You were correct.

40. #37
$$m = \frac{0 - \frac{3}{4}}{0 - 50} = \frac{-\frac{3}{4}}{-50} = \frac{3}{200}$$
$$m = \frac{0 - 3}{0 - 200} = \frac{-3}{-200} = \frac{3}{200}$$
$m = \frac{3}{200}$ for both triangles

#38
$$m = \frac{0 - 4}{0 - 10} = \frac{-4}{-10} = \frac{2}{5}$$
$$m = \frac{0 - 18}{0 - 45} = \frac{18}{45} = \frac{2}{5}$$
$m = \frac{2}{5}$ for both triangles

#39
$$m = \frac{0 - 48}{0 - 6} = \frac{-48}{-6} = 8$$
$$m = \frac{0 - 1362}{0 - 170.25} = \frac{-1362}{-170.25} = 8$$
$m = 8$ for both triangles

Similar triangles have the same ratio of "rise" to "run." Using the two coordinates of the vertices will give the slope of a line.

41. **b.**

42. **a.**

43. $m = \dfrac{148 - 147}{0 - 1}$

$= \dfrac{1}{-1}$

$= -1$

The slope, -1, represents 1 pound lost per week. The w-intercept, 148, represents Mark's initial weight.

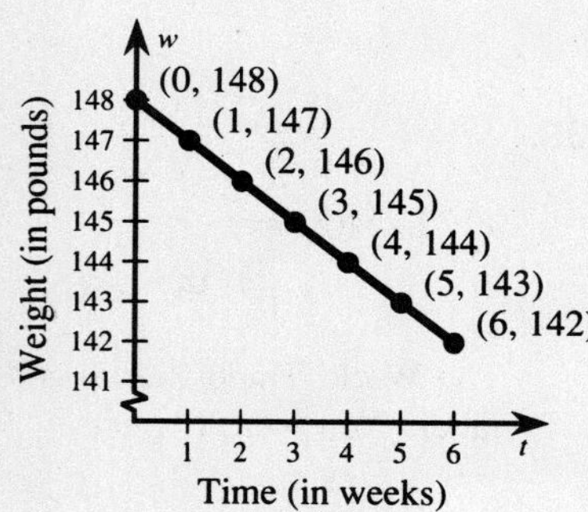

44. $m = \dfrac{2.01 - 0.46}{6 - 1}$

$= \dfrac{1.55}{5}$

$= 0.31$

The slope, 0.31, represents the cost for each additional minute.

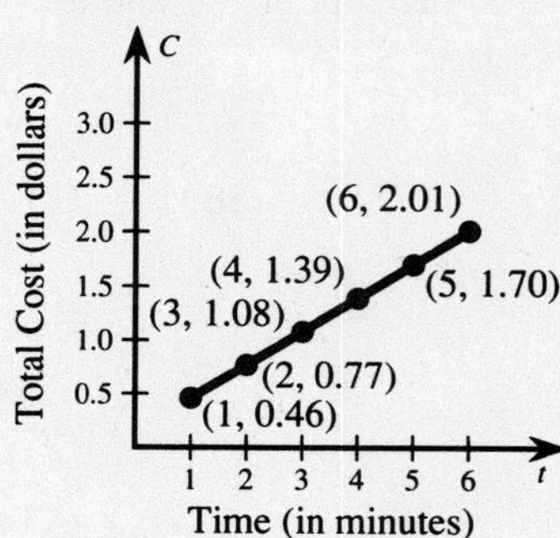

45. $\dfrac{-3 - (-4)}{5 - (-1)} = \dfrac{-3 + 4}{5 + 1}$

$= \dfrac{1}{6}$

46. $\dfrac{0 - 3}{9 - 3} = \dfrac{-3}{6}$

$= -\dfrac{1}{2}$

47. $\dfrac{-2 - (-2)}{8 - 1} = \dfrac{-2 + 2}{7}$

$= \dfrac{0}{7}$

$= 0$

48. $\dfrac{6 - 10}{0 - (-4)} = \dfrac{-4}{4}$

$= -1$

In Exercises 49–52, solutions vary.

49.

$y = -2(-1) + 4$	$y = -2(0) + 4$	$y = -2(3) + 4$	$y = -2(1) + 4$	$y = -2(2) + 4$
$y = 2 + 4$	$y = 0 + 4$	$y = -6 + 4$	$y = -2 + 4$	$y = -4 + 4$
$y = 6$	$y = 4$	$y = -2$	$y = 2$	$y = 0$
$(-1,\ 6)$	$(0,\ 4)$	$(3,\ -2)$	$(1,\ 2)$	$(2,\ 0)$

50.

$y = 5(-3) - 2$	$y = 5(0) - 2$	$y = 5(2) - 2$	$y = 5(1) - 2$	$y = 5(-1) - 2$
$y = -15 - 2$	$y = 0 - 2$	$y = 10 - 2$	$y = 5 - 2$	$y = -5 - 2$
$y = -17$	$y = -2$	$y = 8$	$y = 3$	$y = -7$
$(-3, -17)$	$(0, -2)$	$(2,\ 8)$	$(1,\ 3)$	$(-1,\ -7)$

51.

$y = -\frac{5}{7}(-7)$	$y = \left(-\frac{5}{7}\right)(0)$	$y = \left(-\frac{5}{7}\right)(7)$	$y = -\frac{5}{7}(14)$	$y = -\frac{5}{7}(-14)$
$y = 5$	$y = 0$	$y = -5$	$y = -10$	$y = 10$
$(-7,\ 5)$	$(0,\ 0)$	$(7, -5)$	$(14,\ -10)$	$(-14,\ 10)$

52. $y = \frac{1}{2}(-4)$ $\quad y = \frac{1}{2}(0)$ $\quad y = \frac{1}{2}(6)$ $\quad y = \frac{1}{2}(2)$ $\quad y = \frac{1}{2}(-2)$

$y = -2$ $\quad y = 0$ $\quad y = 3$ $\quad y = 1$ $\quad y = -1$

$(-4, -2)$ $\quad (0, 0)$ $\quad (6, 3)$ $\quad (2, 1)$ $\quad (-2, -1)$

53.

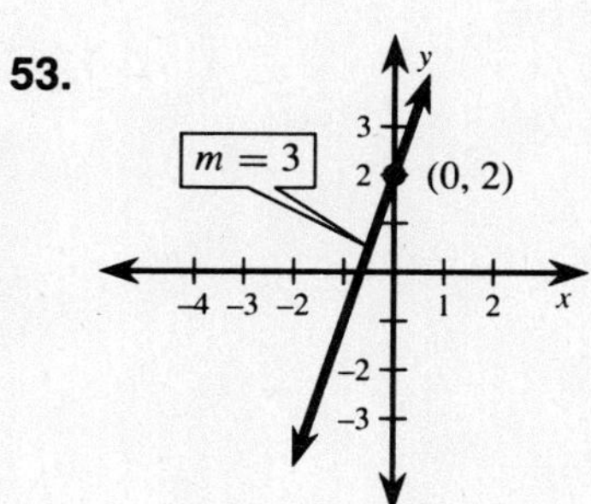

54.

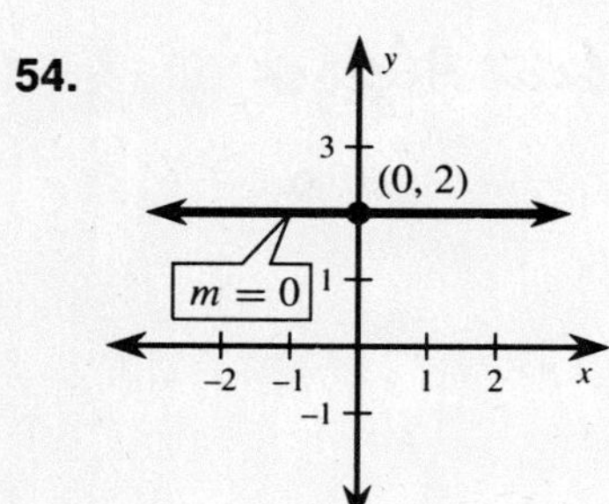

55.

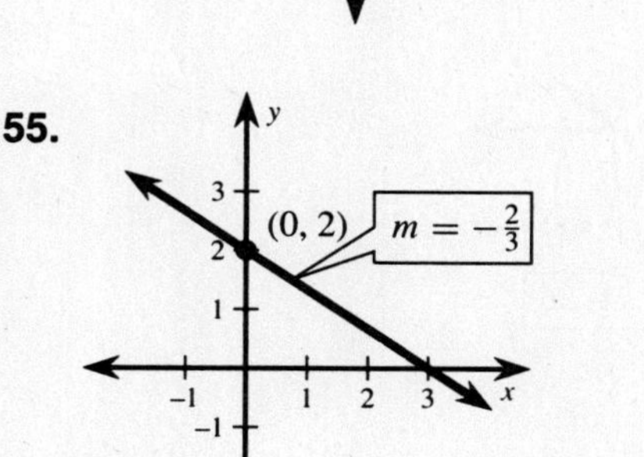
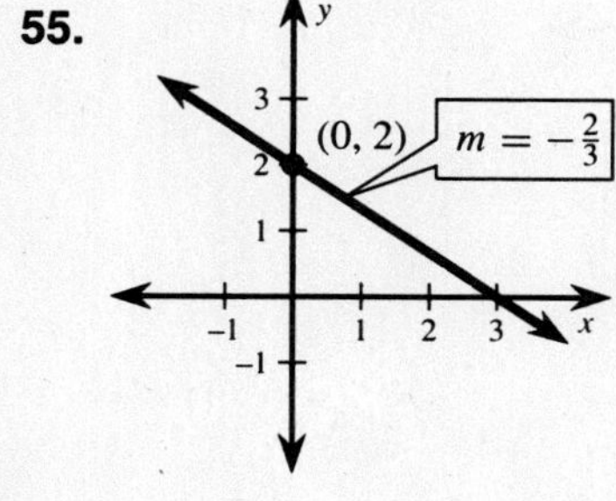

56.

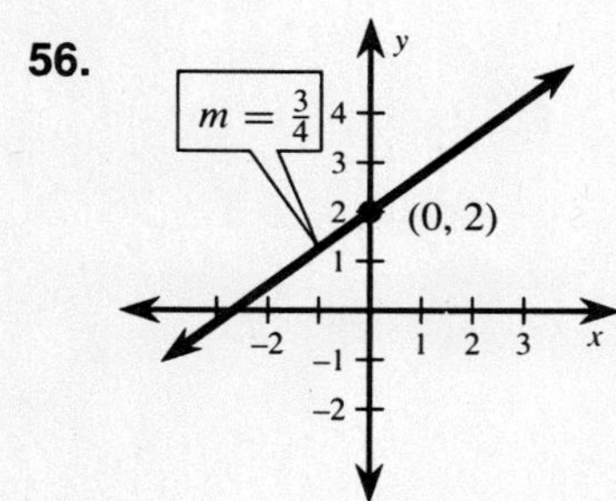

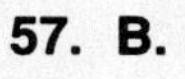

57. B.

58. A.

59.

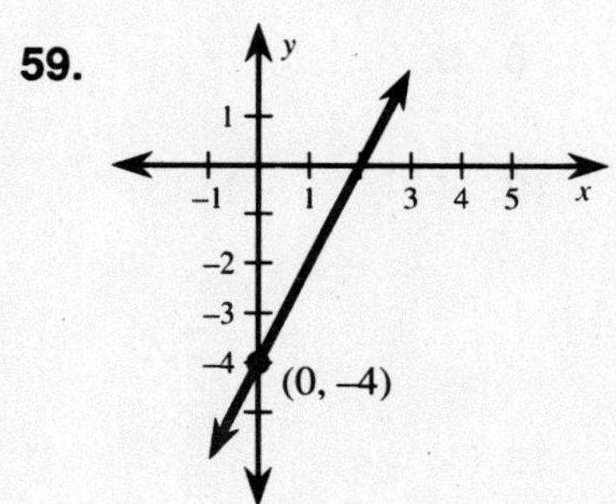

60.

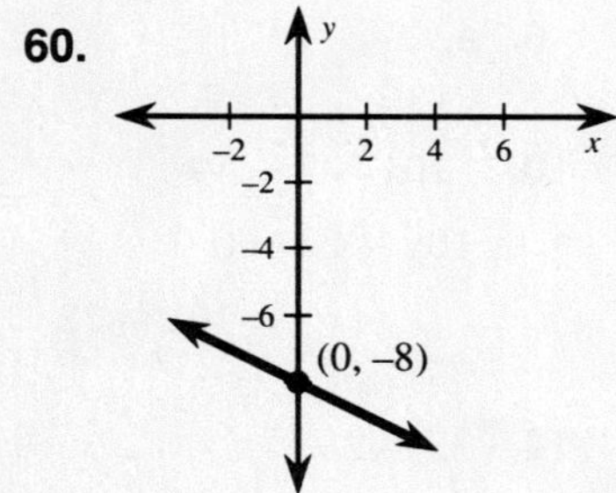

61.

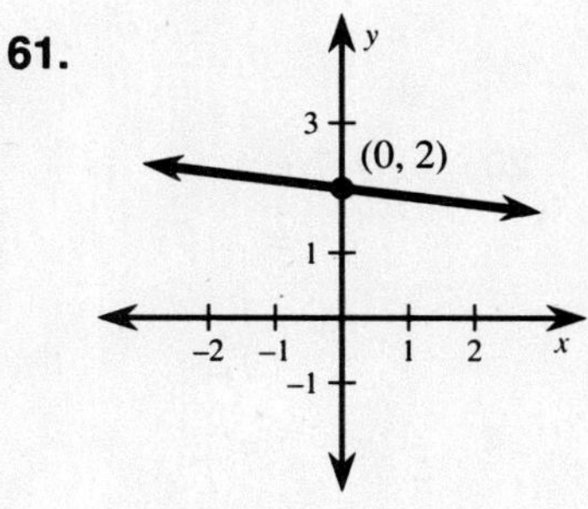

62.

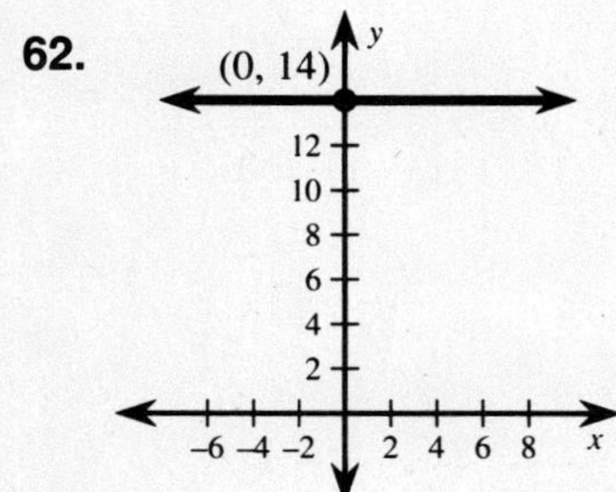

4.6 Connections: Solutions and x-Intercepts

Communicating about Algebra

A. a. **B.** c. **C.** b.

EXERCISES

1. $9x - 36 = 0$

$9x = 36$

$x = 4$

2. $y = 9x - 36$

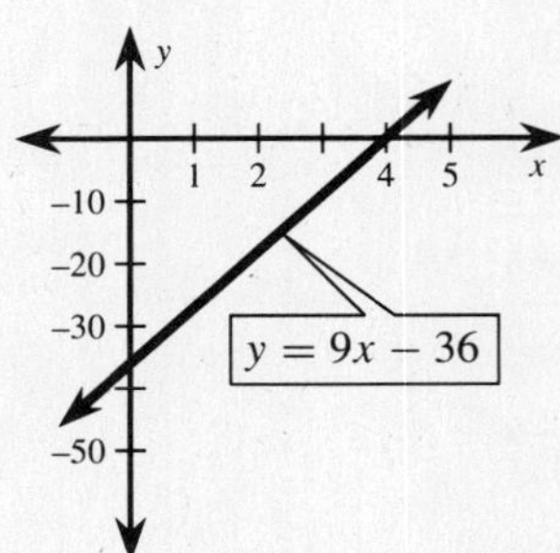

3. The x-intercept of the graph is 4.

4. True; the x-intercept of $y = ax + b$ is the value of x when $y = 0$. This value of x is the solution of $ax + b = 0$.

5. d. **6.** a. **7.** c. **8.** b.

9. $9x + 4 = -4$

$9x + 8 = 0$

$y = 9x + 8$

10. $10x - 3 = 19$

$10x - 22 = 0$

$y = 10x - 22$

11. $5 - 3x = 16$

$-11 - 3x = 0$

$y = -3x - 11$

12. $14 + 4x = 15$

$4x - 1 = 0$

$y = 4x - 1$

13. $2x + 3 = 7$

$2x = 4$

$x = 2$

14. $3x - 2 = -5$

$3x = -3$

$x = -1$

15. $4x - 7 = -23$

$4x = -16$

$x = -4$

16. $x - 9 = -6$

$x = 3$

17. $5x + 17 = -13$

$5x = -30$

$x = -6$

18. $5x - 17 = 8$

$5x = 25$

$x = 5$

19. $4x + 3 = 5$

$4x = 2$

$x = \frac{1}{2}$

20. $5x + 7 = 9$

$5x = 2$

$x = \frac{2}{5}$

21. $9x - 6 = -10$

$9x = -4$

$x = -\frac{4}{9}$

22. $8x - 5 = 1$

$8x = 6$

$x = \frac{3}{4}$

23. $4x - 6 = 10$

$4x = 16$

$x = 4$

24. $-2x + 5 = 9$

$-2x = 4$

$x = -2$

25. $6x + 18 = 2x + 10$

$4x = -8$

$x = -2$

26. $6(x + 2) = 5(x + 2)$

$6x + 12 = 5x + 10$

$x = -2$

27. $\frac{6}{5}(x + 2) = 5x + \frac{1}{2}$

$6(x + 2) = 5\left(5x + \frac{1}{2}\right)$

$6x + 12 = 25x + \frac{5}{2}$

$12 - \frac{5}{2} = 19x$

$\frac{19}{2} = 19x$

$x = \frac{1}{2}$

28. $x - \frac{1}{3} = \frac{5}{4}(x - 6)$

$4\left(x - \frac{1}{3}\right) = 5(x - 6)$

$4x - \frac{4}{3} = 5x - 30$

$30 - \frac{4}{3} = x$

$x = \frac{86}{3}$

$= 28\frac{2}{3}$

29. $\frac{3}{8}(x + 7) = \frac{1}{3}(x + 16)$

$9(x + 7) = 8(x + 16)$

$9x + 63 = 8x + 128$

$x = 65$

30. $\frac{3}{2}(x - 10) = \frac{2}{3}(x - 12)$

$9(x - 10) = 4(x - 12)$

$9x - 90 = 4x - 48$

$5x = 42$

$x = 8\frac{2}{5}$

31. $16{,}034{,}000 = 1{,}100{,}000t + 10{,}534{,}000$

$5{,}500{,}000 = 1{,}100{,}000t$

$t = 5$ or 1985

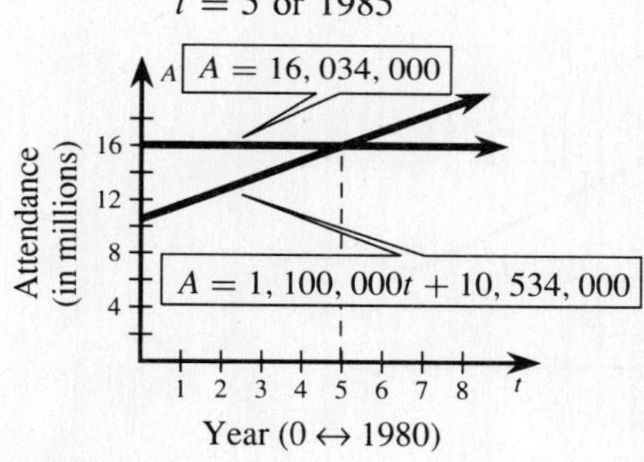

32. $7625 = 35x + 5000$

$2625 = 35x$

$x = 75$ units

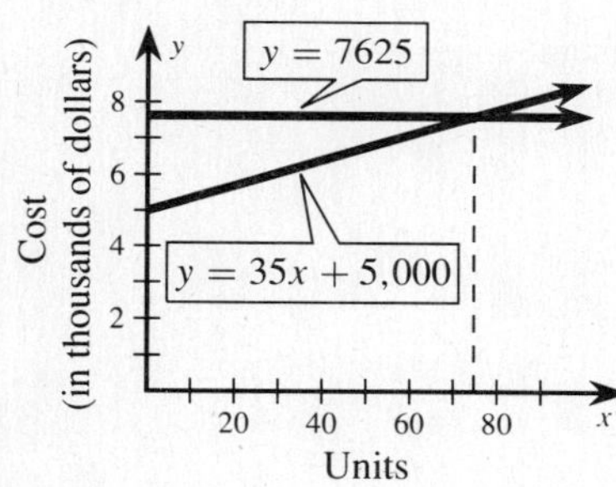

33. 4

34. -6

35. $4 - |-3| = 4 - 3$

$= 1$

36. $3|-5 + 2| = 3|-3|$

$= 3(3)$

$= 9$

37. $|1 - 2| + 3 = |-1| + 3$

$= 1 + 3$

$= 4$

38. $16 - |-11 + 9| = 16 - |-2|$

$= 16 - 2$

$= 14$

39. $-2|-8 + 2| + 7 = -2|-6| + 7$

$= -2(6) + 7$

$= -12 + 7$

$= -5$

40. $-12 + |3 - 7| = -12 + |-4|$

$= -12 + 4$

$= -8$

41.

x	-3	-2	-1	0	1	2	3
y	-13	-9	-5	-1	3	7	11

$y = 4(-3) - 1$ $\quad y = 4(-2) - 1$ $\quad y = 4(-1) - 1$ $\quad y = 4(0) - 1$

$y = -12 - 1$ $\quad y = -8 - 1$ $\quad y = -4 - 1$ $\quad y = 0 - 1$

$y = -13$ $\quad y = -9$ $\quad y = -5$ $\quad y = -1$

$y = 4(1) - 1$ $\quad y = 4(2) - 1$ $\quad y = 4(3) - 1$

$y = 4 - 1$ $\quad y = 8 - 1$ $\quad y = 12 - 1$

$y = 3$ $\quad y = 7$ $\quad y = 11$

42.

x	-3	-2	-1	0	1	2	3
y	30	24	18	12	6	0	-6

$y = -6(-3) + 12$ $\quad y = -6(-2) + 12$ $\quad y = -6(-1) + 12$ $\quad y = -6(0) + 12$

$y = 18 + 12$ $\quad y = 12 + 12$ $\quad y = 6 + 12$ $\quad y = 0 + 12$

$y = 30$ $\quad y = 24$ $\quad y = 18$ $\quad y = 12$

$y = -6(1) + 12$ $\quad y = -6(2) + 12$ $\quad y = -6(3) + 12$

$y = -6 + 12$ $\quad y = -12 + 12$ $\quad y = -18 + 12$

$y = 6$ $\quad y = 0$ $\quad y = -6$

43. **d.** remains constant

44.

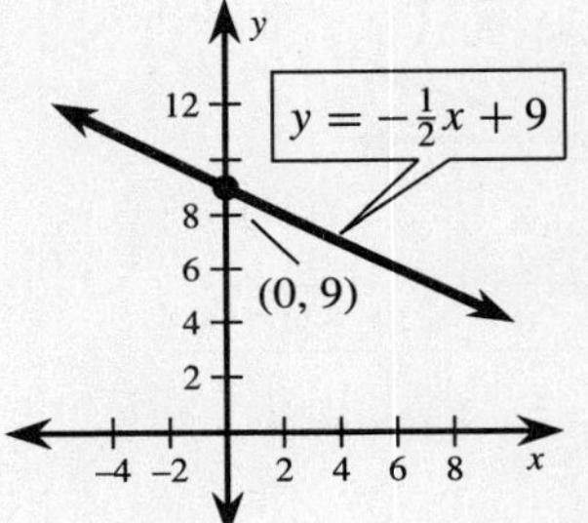

45. 1999; Trace the graph until the y-coordinate is equal to 205,000.

46. 2000; Trace the graph until the y-coordinate is equal to 43,000.

Mixed REVIEW

1. $-6 - |-3| = -6 - 3$
$= -9$

2. $6 - 2 = 4$

3. $|-7| - (-2) = 7 + 2$
$= 9$

4. $4 - (-\frac{1}{3}) = 4 + \frac{1}{3}$
$= 4\frac{1}{3}$

5. $\left(\frac{\text{dollars}}{\text{pound}}\right) \cdot (\text{pound}) = \text{dollars}$

6. $\left(\frac{\text{kilometers}}{\text{second}}\right) \cdot (\text{second}) = \text{kilometers}$

7. $|-3| + 2(x - 2) = 3 + 2x - 4$
$= 2x - 1$

8. $2y - 3(y + 2) = 2y - 3y - 6$
$= -y - 6$

9. $3x^2 + x = 3(-4)^2 + (-4)$
$= 3(16) - 4$
$= 48 - 4$
$= 44$

10. $3(n-1) + 2n = 3(5-1) + 2 \cdot 5$
$= 3(4) + 10$
$= 12 + 10$
$= 22$

11. $4a - 2b = 0$
$4a = 2b$
$a = \frac{1}{2}b$

12. $-3(1-y) + 4x = 1$
$-3 + 3y + 4x = 1$
$3y = 4 - 4x$
$y = \frac{1}{3}(4 - 4x)$

13. $|x| + 2 = 7$
$|5| + 2 \stackrel{?}{=} 7$
$5 + 2 \stackrel{?}{=} 7$
$7 = 7$

5 is a solution.

14. $|x| + 2 = 7$
$|-5| + 2 \stackrel{?}{=} 7$
$5 + 2 \stackrel{?}{=} 7$
$7 = 7$

-5 is a solution.

15. ≈ -12.11

16. $\frac{1}{3}(x-2) = \frac{1}{3}(3-2)$
$= \frac{1}{3}(1)$
$= \frac{1}{3}$

17. $x - 6 \le 10$

18. $6 + y = x \div 3$

19. $3(-10) - 1$

20. $2(x + y) = 20$

4.7 Graphs of Absolute Value Equations

Communicating about Algebra

Use the following graph to find **A, B, C.**

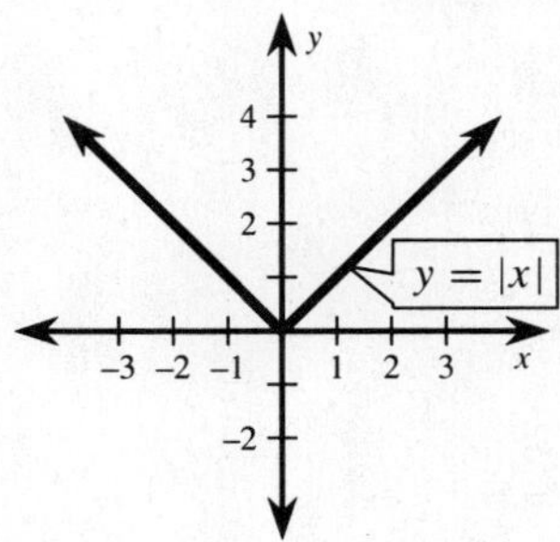

A.

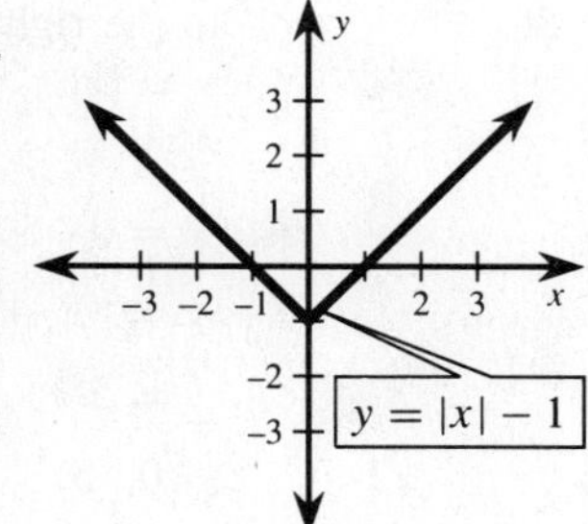

Compared to $y = |x|$, $y = |x| - 1$ is shifted one unit down on the y-axis.

B.

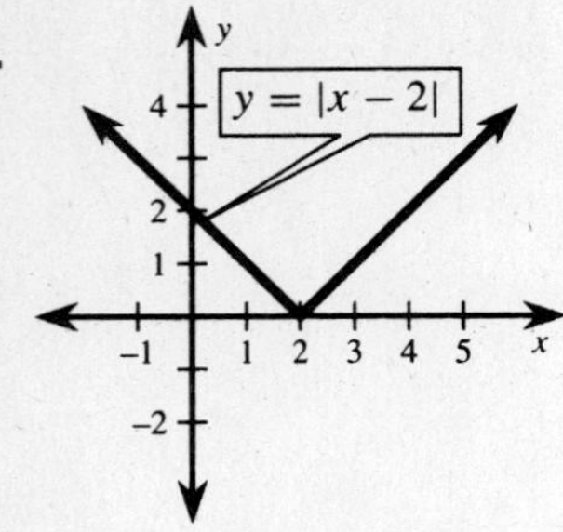

Compared to $y = |x|$,
$y = |x - 2|$ is shifted two units to the right of the y-axis.

C.

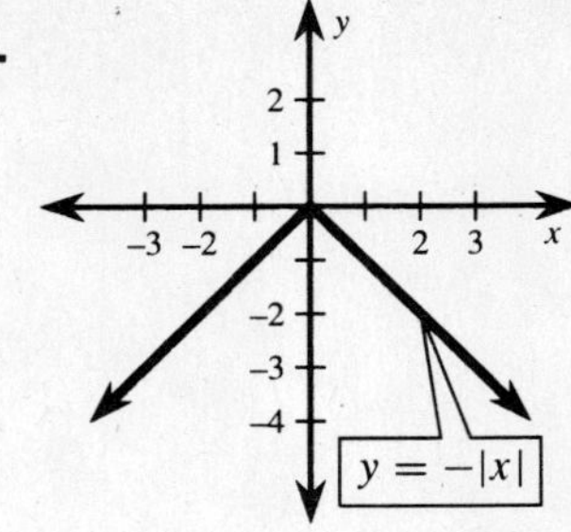

$y = -|x|$ opens down while $y = |x|$ opens up.

D. $y = 2|x|$ has the sharper corner.

EXERCISES

1. True

2. Since the absolute value gives a positive result, its opposite will give a negative result. Therefore, the highest point is the vertex (0, 0).

3. $x + 4 = 0$

$x = -4$

$(-4, -2)$

4. To find the x-coordinate of the vertex set the expression in the absolute value to zero and solve the equation. Construct a table choosing x-values to the left and right of the vertex. Plot the points.

5. **c.** The graph is one unit below graph of $y = |x|$.

6. **b.** The graph is one unit above graph of $y = |x|$.

7. **d.** The graph is two units below graph of $y = |x|$.

8. **a.** The graph is two units above graph of $y = |x|$.

9. **b.** The graph is one unit to the right graph of $y = |x|$.

10. **d.** The graph is one unit to the left of the graph of $y = |x|$.

11. **c.** The graph is two units to the right of the graph of $y = |x|$.

12. **a.** The graph is two units to the left of the graph of $y = |x|$.

13. $x = 0$

$y = |0| - 6$

$y = -6$

$(0, -6)$

14. $x = 0$

$y = |0| + 5$

$y = 5$

$(0, 5)$

15. $x = 0$

$y = -|0| - 3$

$y = -3$

$(0, -3)$

16. $x + 6 = 0$

$x = -6$

$y = |-6 + 6|$

$y = 0$

$(-6, 0)$

17. $x - 2 = 0$

$x = 2$

$y = -2|2 - 2|$

$y = 0$

$(2, 0)$

18. $x - 3 = 0$

$x = 3$

$y = \frac{1}{2}|3 - 3|$

$y = 0$

$(3, 0)$

19. $x+3=0$

$x=-3$

$y=|-3+3|-2$

$y=-2$

$(-3,-2)$

20. $x-3=0$

$x=3$

$y=|3-3|+1$

$y=1$

$(3,\ 1)$

21. $x-9=0$

$x=9$

$y=-|9-9|+10$

$y=10$

$(9,\ 10)$

22. $x+6=0$

$x=-6$

$y=|-6+6|-8$

$y=-8$

$(-6,-8)$

23. $x-2=0$

$x=2$

$y=2|2-2|+8$

$y=8$

$(2,\ 8)$

24. $x-3=0$

$x=3$

$y=-\frac{1}{2}|3-3|+5$

$y=5$

$(3,\ 5)$

25. **c.**

26. **d.**

27. **a.**

28. **b.**

29.

x	−2	−1	0	1	2	3	4
y	−3	−1	1	3	1	−1	−3

$$\begin{aligned} y &= -2|-2-1|+3 \\ &= -2|-3|+3 \\ &= -2(3)+3 \\ &= -6+3 \\ &= -3 \end{aligned}$$

$$\begin{aligned} y &= -2|-1-1|+3 \\ &= -2|-2|+3 \\ &= -2(2)+3 \\ &= -4+3 \\ &= -1 \end{aligned}$$

$$\begin{aligned} y &= -2|0-1|+3 \\ &= -2|-1|+3 \\ &= -2(1)+3 \\ &= -2+3 \\ &= 1 \end{aligned}$$

$$\begin{aligned} y &= -2|1-1|+3 \\ &= -2(0)+3 \\ &= 0+3 \\ &= 3 \end{aligned}$$

$$\begin{aligned} y &= -2|2-1|+3 \\ &= -2|1|+3 \\ &= -2+3 \\ &= 1 \end{aligned}$$

$$\begin{aligned} y &= -2|3-1|+3 \\ &= -2|2|+3 \\ &= -4+3 \\ &= -1 \end{aligned}$$

$$\begin{aligned} y &= -2|4-1|+3 \\ &= -2|3|+3 \\ &= -6+3 \\ &= -3 \end{aligned}$$

30.

x	−7	−6	−5	−4	−3	−2	−1
y	8	5	2	−1	2	5	8

$$\begin{aligned} y &= 3|-7+4|-1 \\ &= 3|-3|-1 \\ &= 3\cdot 3-1 \\ &= 9-1 \\ &= 8 \end{aligned}$$

$$\begin{aligned} y &= 3|-6+4|-1 \\ &= 3|-2|-1 \\ &= 3\cdot 2-1 \\ &= 6-1 \\ &= 5 \end{aligned}$$

$$\begin{aligned} y &= 3|-5+4|-1 \\ &= 3|-1|-1 \\ &= 3\cdot 1-1 \\ &= 3-1 \\ &= 2 \end{aligned}$$

$$\begin{aligned} y &= 3|-4+4|-1 \\ &= 3\cdot 0-1 \\ &= -1 \end{aligned}$$

$$\begin{aligned} y &= 3|-3+4|-1 \\ &= 3\cdot 1-1 \\ &= 3-1 \\ &= 2 \end{aligned}$$

$$\begin{aligned} y &= 3|-2+4|-1 \\ &= 3\cdot 2-1 \\ &= 6-1 \\ &= 5 \end{aligned}$$

$$\begin{aligned} y &= 3|-1+4|-1 \\ &= 3\cdot 3-1 \\ &= 9-1 \\ &= 8 \end{aligned}$$

31.

x	-6	-5	-4	-3	-2	-1	0
y	$\frac{1}{2}$	-1	$-\frac{5}{2}$	-4	$-\frac{5}{2}$	-1	$\frac{1}{2}$

$y = \frac{3}{2}|-6+3| - 4$
$= \frac{3}{2}|-3| - 4$
$= \frac{3}{2} \cdot 3 - 4$
$= \frac{9}{2} - \frac{8}{2}$
$= \frac{1}{2}$

$y = \frac{3}{2}|-5+3| - 4$
$= \frac{3}{2}|-2| - 4$
$= \frac{3}{2} \cdot 2 - 4$
$= 3 - 4$
$= -1$

$y = \frac{3}{2}|-4+3| - 4$
$= \frac{3}{2}|-1| - 4$
$= \frac{3}{2} \cdot 1 - 4$
$= \frac{3}{2} - \frac{8}{2}$
$= -\frac{5}{2}$

$y = \frac{3}{2}|-3+3| - 4$
$= \frac{3}{2} \cdot 0 - 4$
$= -4$

$y = \frac{3}{2}|-2+3| - 4$
$= \frac{3}{2}|1| - 4$
$= \frac{3}{2} - \frac{8}{2}$
$= -\frac{5}{2}$

$y = \frac{3}{2}|-1+3| - 4$
$= \frac{3}{2}|2| - 4$
$= 3 - 4$
$= -1$

$y = \frac{3}{2}|0+3| - 4$
$= \frac{3}{2}|3| - 4$
$= \frac{9}{2} - \frac{8}{2}$
$= \frac{1}{2}$

32.

x	-1	0	1	2	3	4	5
y	$\frac{15}{4}$	$\frac{9}{2}$	$\frac{21}{4}$	6	$\frac{21}{4}$	$\frac{9}{2}$	$\frac{15}{4}$

$y = -\frac{3}{4}|-1-2| + 6$
$= -\frac{3}{4}|-3| + 6$
$= -\frac{3}{4}(3) + 6$
$= -\frac{9}{4} + \frac{24}{4}$
$= \frac{15}{4}$

$y = -\frac{3}{4}|0-2| + 6$
$= -\frac{3}{4}|-2| + 6$
$= -\frac{3}{4}(2) + 6$
$= -\frac{3}{2} + \frac{12}{2}$
$= \frac{9}{2}$

$y = -\frac{3}{4}|1-2| + 6$
$= -\frac{3}{4}|-1| + 6$
$= -\frac{3}{4}(1) + 6$
$= -\frac{3}{4} + \frac{24}{4}$
$= \frac{21}{4}$

$y = -\frac{3}{4}|2-2| + 6$
$= -\frac{3}{4}|0| + 6$
$= 6$

$y = -\frac{3}{4}|3-2| + 6$
$= -\frac{3}{4}|1| + 6$
$= -\frac{3}{4} + \frac{24}{4}$
$= \frac{21}{4}$

$y = -\frac{3}{4}|4-2| + 6$
$= -\frac{3}{4}|2| + 6$
$= -\frac{3}{2} + \frac{12}{2}$
$= \frac{9}{2}$

$y = -\frac{3}{4}|5-2| + 6$
$= -\frac{3}{4}|3| + 6$
$= -\frac{9}{4} + \frac{24}{4}$
$= \frac{15}{4}$

33.

x	-1	0	1
y	4	3	4

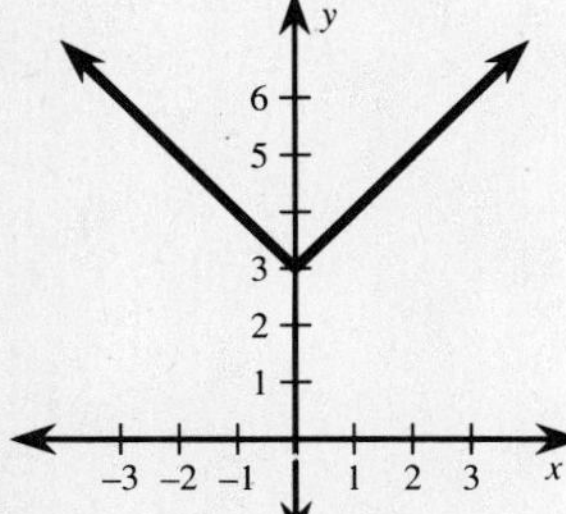

34.

x	-1	0	1
y	-3	-4	-3

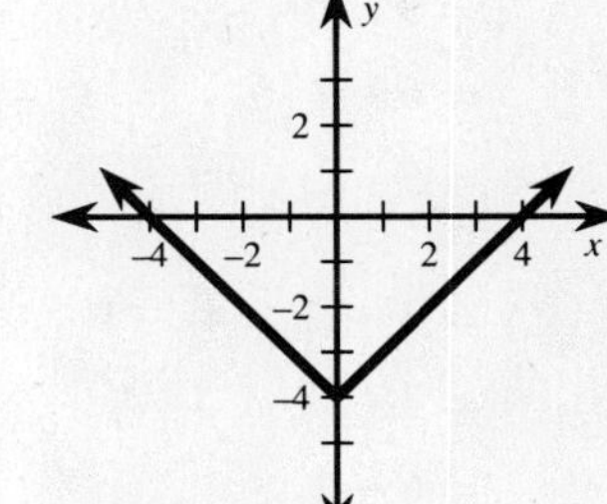

35.

x	−6	0	6
y	3	−3	3

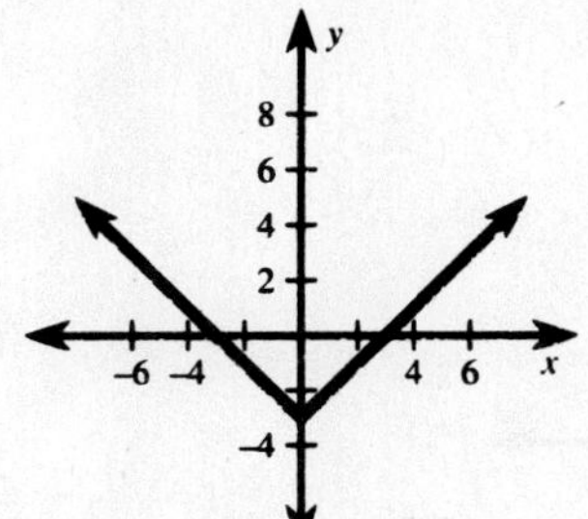

36.

x	−4	0	4
y	8	4	8

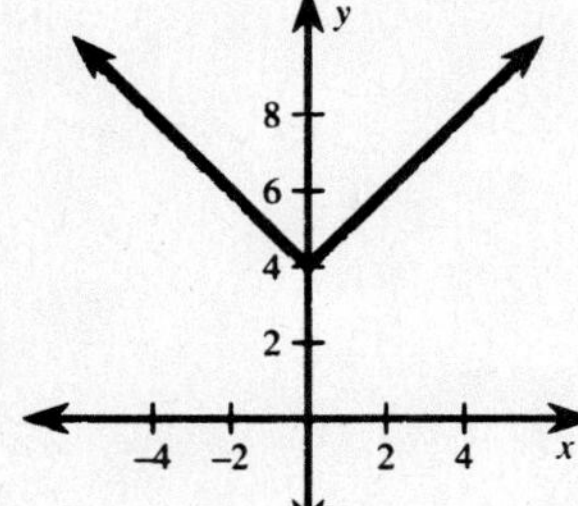

37.

x	−6	−3	0
y	3	0	3

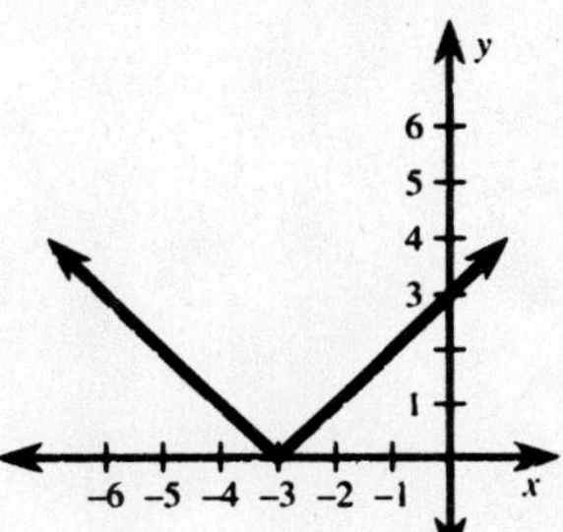

38.

x	−5	5	15
y	10	0	10

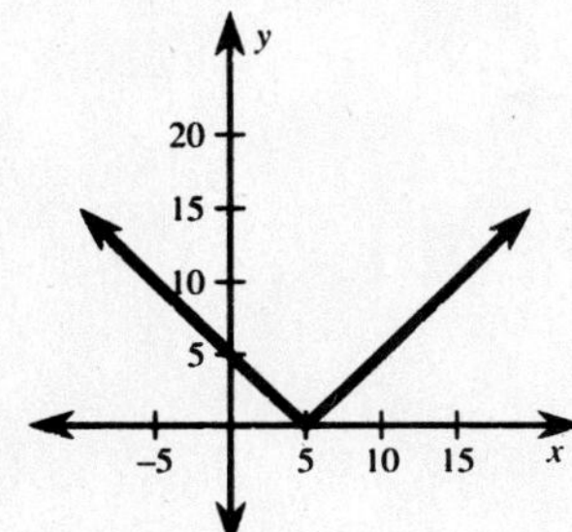

39.

x	6	3	0
y	3	0	3

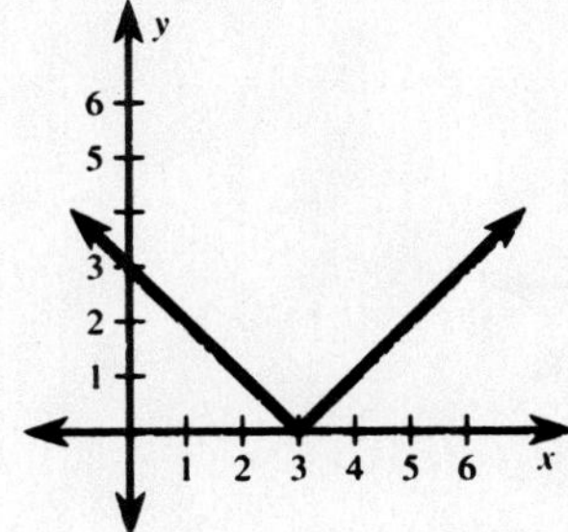

40.

x	−8	−4	0
y	4	0	4

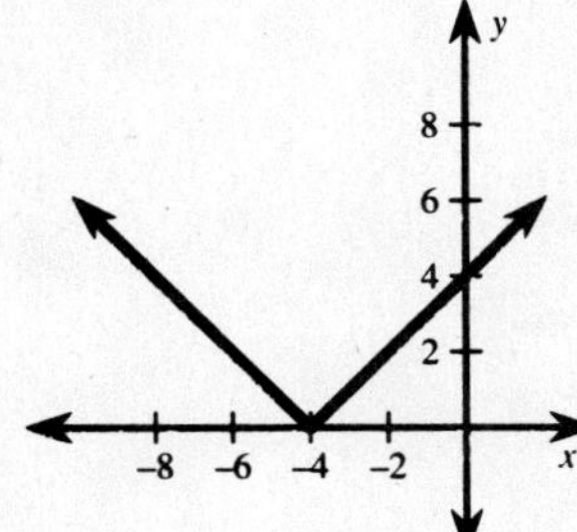

41.

x	−2	0	2
y	4	0	4

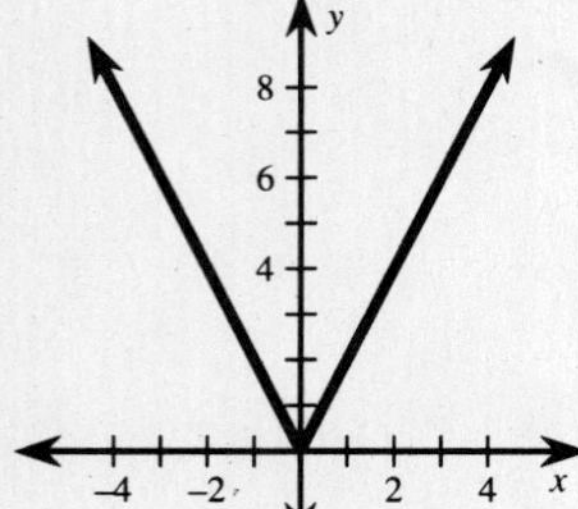

42.

x	−1	0	1
y	3	0	3

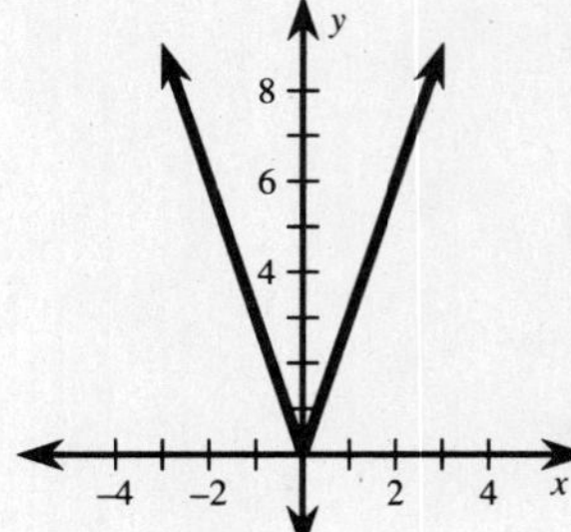

43.

x	−1	0	1
y	−2	0	−2

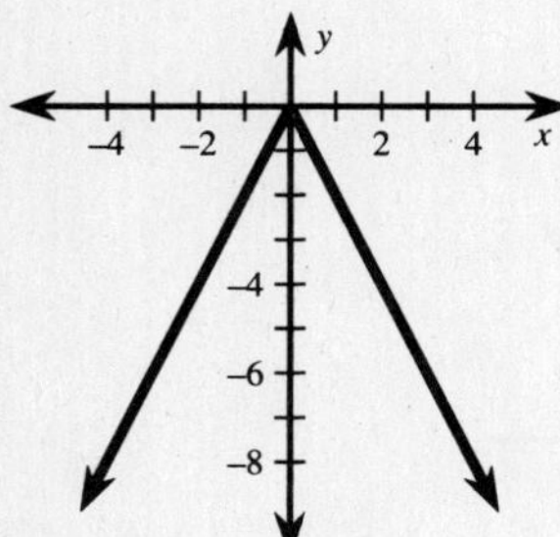

44.

x	−2	0	2
y	−1	0	−1

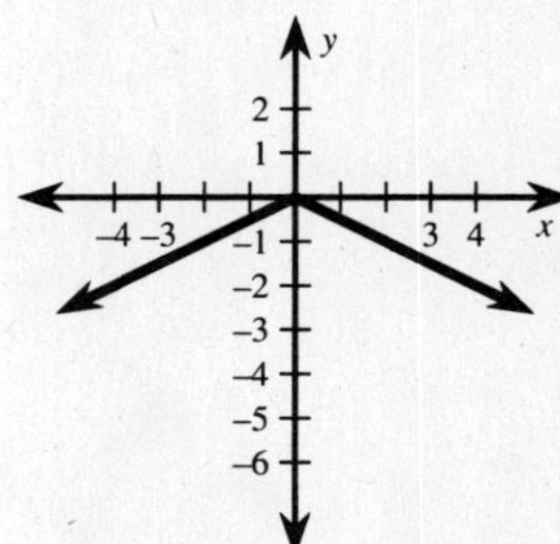

45.

x	−1	−3	−5
y	0	−2	0

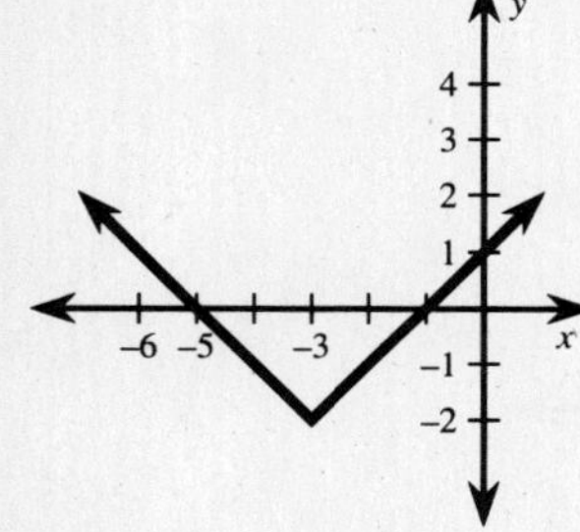

46.

x	−2	1	4
y	1	4	1

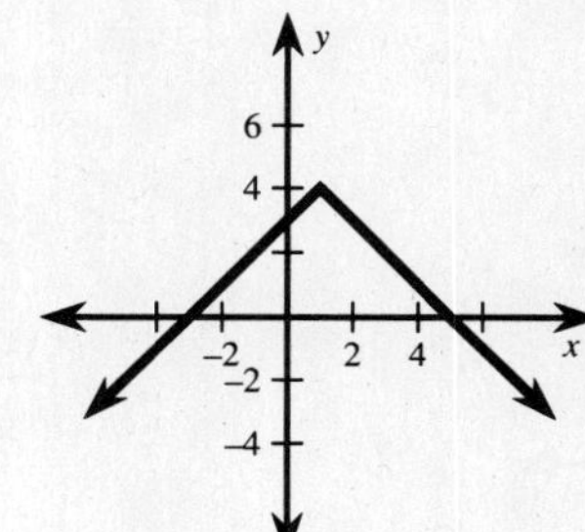

47.

x	-5	-3	-1
y	1	5	1

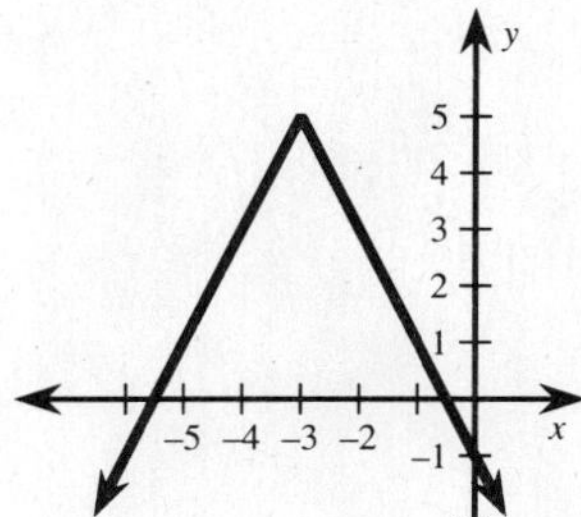

48.

x	-6	-4	-2
y	-1	-2	-1

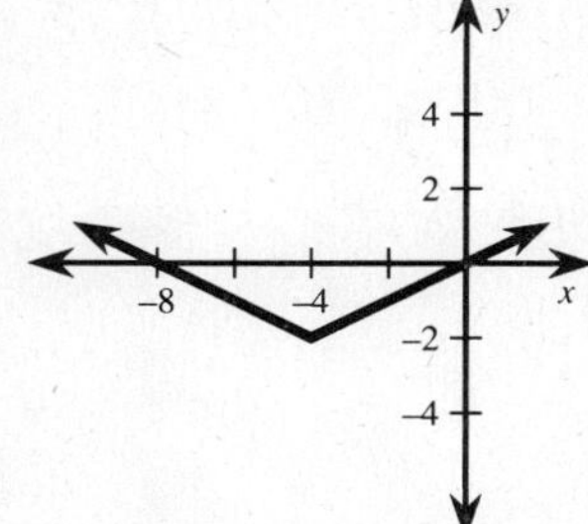

49.

x	0	2	4
y	5	-1	5

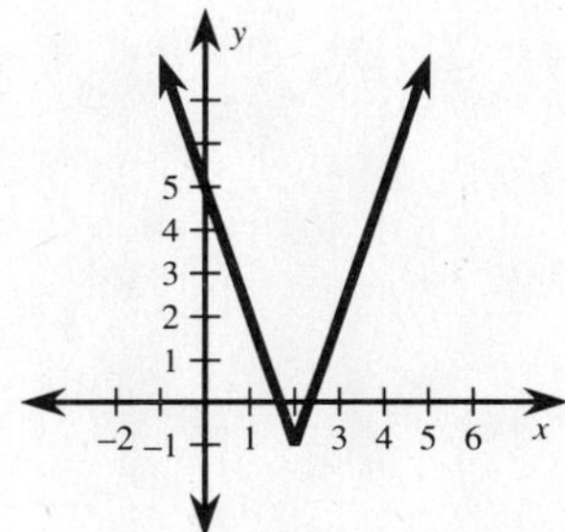

50.

x	-1	1	3
y	-5	1	-5

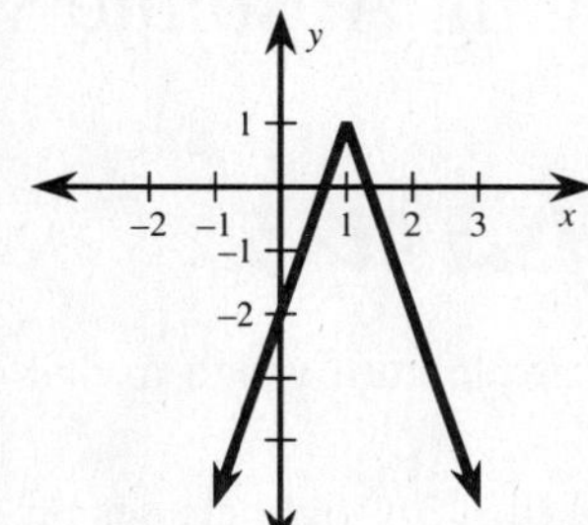

51. True, both graphs have the vertex (3, 4). The first one opens down. The second one opens up.

52. **a**: $y = |x + 2| + \frac{1}{2}$
b: $y = |x - 2| + \frac{1}{2}$
c: $y = -|x + 2| - \frac{1}{2}$
d: $y = -|x - 2| - \frac{1}{2}$

53. $y = \frac{4}{3}|x - 30|$
$y = \frac{4}{3}|72 - 30|$
$y = \frac{4}{3}|42|$
$y = \frac{4}{3}(42)$
$y = 56$ feet

54. $|-6+4| - 3 = |-2| - 3$
$= 2 - 3$
$= -1$

55. $-2|9 - 12| + 1 = -2|-3| + 1$
$= -2(3) + 1$
$= -6 + 1$
$= -5$

56. $-|-2-(-1)| + 4 = -|-2+1| + 4$
$= -|-1| + 4$
$= -1 + 4$
$= 3$

57. $|-5-(-5)| - 2 = |-5+5| - 2$
$= |0| - 2$
$= -2$

58. $|x-2|-5 = |-2-2|-5$
$= |-4|-5$
$= 4-5$
$= -1$

59. $-|x+3|-4 = -|-5+3|-4$
$= -|-2|-4$
$= -2-4$
$= -6$

60. $|-x+1|+3 = |-3+1|+3$
$= |-2|+3$
$= 2+3$
$= 5$

61. $-\frac{1}{2}|x+2|+4 = -\frac{1}{2}|-1+2|+4$
$= -\frac{1}{2}|1|+4$
$= -\frac{1}{2}+\frac{8}{2}$
$= \frac{7}{2}$

62. Each horizontal and vertical scale unit is 5.

63. The horizontal scale unit is 6.
The vertical scale unit is 5.

4.8 *Solving Absolute Value Equations*

Communicating about Algebra

A. To pass certification, the scale must weigh from 159 to 161 ounces.

B. To be eligible for one of the 13 weight classes on the wrestling team, you must weigh between 103 and 275 pounds.

C. To obtain a bonus, the pizza delivery driver must deliver the pizza in 20 to 40 minutes.

EXERCISES

1. $x+1=2$ or $x+1=-2$
$x=1$ $\quad x=-3$

2. $y=|x+1|-2$

3. $x+1=32$ and
$x+1=-32$

4. The mast rises 82.5 feet above the deck.
$0 = 82.5 - 0.92|x|$
$0.92|x| = 82.5$
$|x| \approx 90$
$x = 90$
$x = -90$

5. $x+4=3$ or $x+4=-3$
$x=-1$ $\quad x=-7$

6. $9-x=4$ or $9-x=-4$
$9-4=x$ $\quad 9+4=x$
$x=5$ $\quad x=13$

7. $6-x=9$ or $6-x=-9$
$6-9=x$ $\quad 6+9=x$
$x=-3$ $\quad x=15$

8. $x+12=8$ or $x+12=-8$
$x=8-12$ $\quad x=-8-12$
$x=-4$ $\quad x=-20$

9. $2x + 6 = 14$ or $2x + 6 = -14$

$2x = 8$ $\quad 2x = -20$

$x = 4$ $\quad x = -10$

10. $3x - 4 = 7$ or $3x - 4 = -7$

$3x = 11$ $\quad 3x = -3$

$x = \frac{11}{3}$ $\quad x = -1$

11. $6 + |x + 1| = 9$

$|x + 1| = 3$

12. $|x - 17| + 9 = 1$

$|x - 17| = -8$

13. $7 - |4 - x| = 12$

$-|4 - x| = 5$

$|4 - x| = -5$

14. We begin by graphing $y = |x - 5| - 7$.

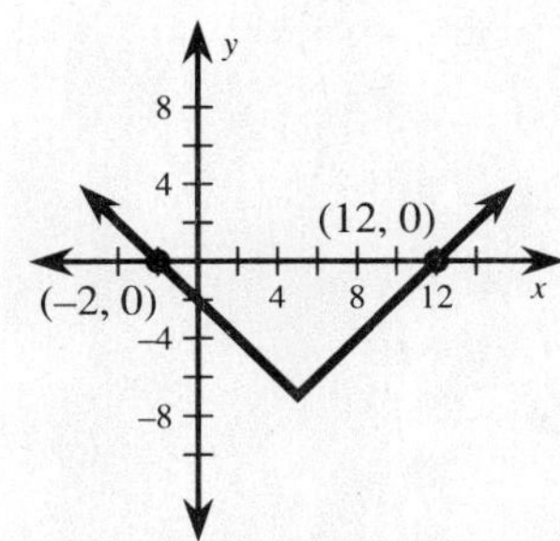

Since $(-2,\ 0)$ is an x-intercept of $y = |x - 5| - 7$, then -2 is a solution of $|x - 5| = 7$.

15. We begin by graphing $y = |x + 4| - 9$.

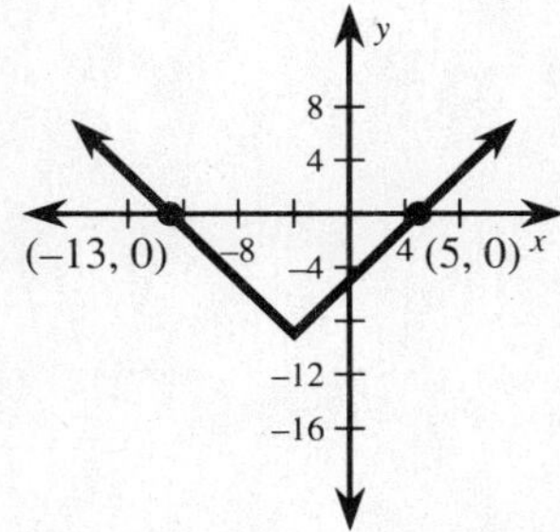

Since $(-13,\ 0)$ is an x-intercept of $y = |x + 4| - 9$, then -13 is a solution of $|x + 4| = 9$.

16. $x + 1 = 7$ or $x + 1 = -7$

$x = 6$ $\quad x = -8$

17. $x - 1 = 7$ or $x - 1 = -7$

$x = 8$ $\quad x = -6$

18. $|3x - 2| - 2 = 5$

$|3x - 2| = 7$

$3x - 2 = 7$ or $3x - 2 = -7$

$3x = 9$ $\quad 3x = -5$

$x = 3$ $\quad x = -\frac{5}{3}$

19. $|4x + 3| - 4 = 8$

$|4x + 3| = 12$

$4x + 3 = 12$ or $4x + 3 = -12$

$4x = 9$ $\quad 4x = -15$

$x = \frac{9}{4}$ $\quad x = -\frac{15}{4}$

20. $3 + |-2x + 9| = 10$

$|-2x + 9| = 7$

$-2x + 9 = 7$ or $-2x + 9 = -7$

$-2x = -2$ $\quad -2x = -16$

$x = 1$ $\quad x = 8$

21. $6 + |-x - 5| = 9$

$|-x - 5| = 3$

$-x - 5 = 3$ or $-x - 5 = -3$

$-x = 8$ $\quad -x = 2$

$x = -8$ $\quad x = -2$

22. $|4 - 5x| - 8 = 15$

$|4 - 5x| = 23$

$4 - 5x = 23$ or $4 - 5x = -23$

$-5x = 19$ $\quad -5x = -27$

$x = -\frac{19}{5}$ $\quad x = \frac{27}{5}$

23. $|7 - 3x| - 10 = 4$

$|7 - 3x| = 14$

$7 - 3x = 14$ or $7 - 3x = -14$

$-3x = 7$ $\quad -3x = -21$

$x = -\frac{7}{3}$ $\quad x = 7$

24. $2|3x - 7| + 2 = 4$

$2|3x - 7| = 2$

$|3x - 7| = 1$

$3x - 7 = 1$ or $3x - 7 = -1$

$3x = 8$ $\quad 3x = 6$

$x = \frac{8}{3}$ $\quad x = 2$

25. $|x - 9| = 4$

$x - 9 = 4$ or $x - 9 = -4$

$x = 13$ $\quad x = 5$

26. $|x + 7| = 16$

$x + 7 = 16$ or $x + 7 = -16$

$x = 9$ $\quad x = -23$

27. $|2x - 4| + 6 = 9$

$|2x - 4| = 3$

$2x - 4 = 3$ or $2x - 4 = -3$

$2x = 7$ $\quad 2x = 1$

$x = \frac{7}{2}$ $\quad x = \frac{1}{2}$

28. $4 + |x - 10| = 14$

$|x - 10| = 10$

$x - 10 = 10$ or $x - 10 = -10$

$x = 20$ $\quad x = 0$

29. $10 + |3x + 1| = 24$

$|3x + 1| = 14$

$3x + 1 = 14$ or $3x + 1 = -14$

$3x = 13$ $\quad 3x = -15$

$x = \frac{13}{3}$ $\quad x = -5$

30. $|2x + 9| - 15 = 36$

$|2x + 9| = 51$

$2x + 9 = 51$ or $2x + 9 = -51$

$2x = 42$ $\quad 2x = -60$

$x = 21$ $\quad x = -30$

31. $2\left|x + \frac{1}{2}\right| - 1 = 9$

$2\left|x + \frac{1}{2}\right| = 10$

$\left|x + \frac{1}{2}\right| = 5$

$x + \frac{1}{2} = 5$ or $x + \frac{1}{2} = -5$

$x = \frac{9}{2}$ $\quad x = -\frac{11}{2}$

32. $3\left|x + \frac{1}{6}\right| + 5 = 17$

$3\left|x + \frac{1}{6}\right| = 12$

$\left|x + \frac{1}{6}\right| = 4$

$x + \frac{1}{6} = 4$ or $x + \frac{1}{6} = -4$

$x = \frac{23}{6}$ $\quad x = -\frac{25}{6}$

33. $3|4x + 9| - 2 = 6$

$3|4x + 9| = 8$

$|4x + 9| = \frac{8}{3}$

$4x + 9 = \frac{8}{3}$ or $4x + 9 = \frac{-8}{3}$

$4x = \frac{-19}{3}$ $\quad 4x = \frac{-35}{3}$

$x = -\frac{19}{12}$ $\quad x = -\frac{35}{12}$

34. The tent is 10 feet tall.

35. $y = -2|x - 5| + 10$

$0 = -2|x - 5| + 10$

$2|x - 5| = 10$

$|x - 5| = 5$

$x - 5 = 5$ or $x - 5 = -5$

$x = 10$ $\quad$ $x = 0$

The tent is 10 feet wide.

36. $y = -\frac{1}{3}|x - 5| + 6$

$0 = -\frac{1}{3}|x - 5| + 6$

$\frac{1}{3}|x - 5| = 6$

$|x - 5| = 18$

$x - 5 = 18$ or $x - 5 = -18$

$x = 23$ $\quad$ $x = -13$

37. $|23 - 10| = 13$

$|-13 - 0| = |-13|$

$= 13$

The stakes are 13 feet from the edge of the tent.

38. $|x - 92{,}950{,}000| = 1{,}550{,}000$

$x - 92{,}950{,}000 = 1{,}550{,}000$

$x = 94{,}500{,}000$

or

$x - 92{,}950{,}000 = -1{,}550{,}000$

$x = 91{,}400{,}000$

Maximum distance is 94,500,000 miles.
Minimum distance is 91,400,000 miles.

39. $|x - 183| = 7$

$x - 183 = 7$ or $x - 183 = -7$

$x = 190$ $\quad$ $x = 176$

Maximum weight is 190 pounds.
Minimum weight is 176 pounds.

40. $2|4| + 6 = 8 + 6$

$= 14$

41. $3 - |8 - 4| = 3 - |4|$

$= 3 - 4$

$= -1$

42. $3^2 - |-4| = 9 - 4$

$= 5$

43. $6^2 - 2|14 - 19| = 36 - 2|-5|$

$= 36 - 2 \cdot 5$

$= 36 - 10$

$= 26$

44. $|3 - 9| \cdot 2^2 + 1 = |-6| \cdot 4 + 1$

$= 6 \cdot 4 + 1$

$= 24 + 1$

$= 25$

45. $-4| - 5 + 1| - 12 = -4|-4| - 12$

$= -4 \cdot 4 - 12$

$= -16 - 12$

$= -28$

46. $y = 4$

47. $x = 5$

48. $x + 2y = 18$

$2y = -x + 18$

$y = -\frac{1}{2}x + 9$

Slope: $-\frac{1}{2}$

y-intercept: 9

49. $6x - y = 3$

$-y = -6x + 3$

$y = 6x - 3$

Slope: 6

y-intercept: -3

50.

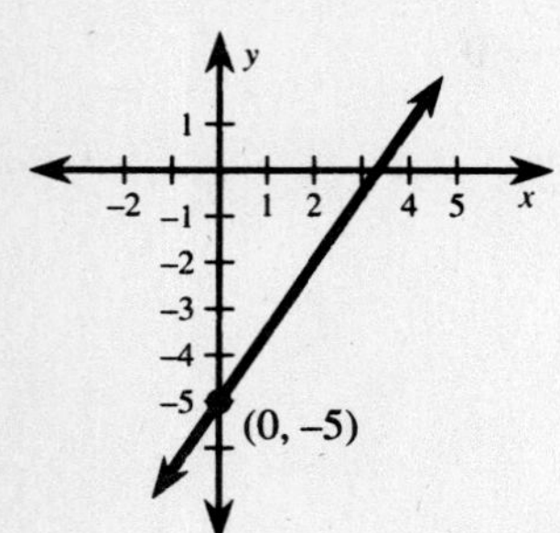

51.

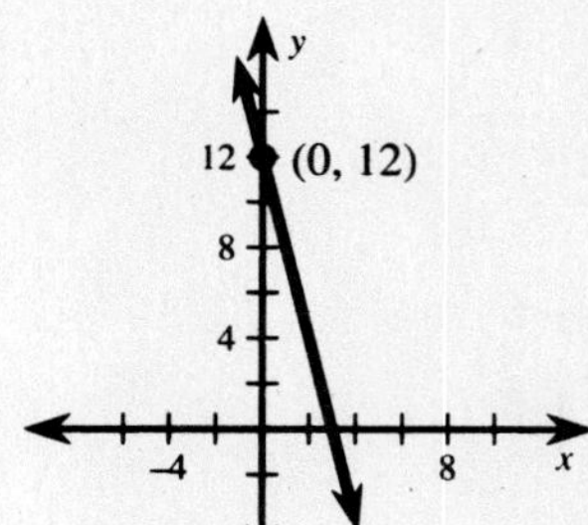

52. $m = \dfrac{2-(-2)}{-2-4} = \dfrac{2+2}{-6} = -\dfrac{4}{6} = -\dfrac{2}{3}$ $\qquad m = \dfrac{-2-0}{4-7} = \dfrac{-2}{-3} = \dfrac{2}{3}$

Left slope: $-\frac{2}{3}$

Right slope: $\frac{2}{3}$

53. $m = \dfrac{-2-4}{-12-(-10)} = \dfrac{-6}{-2} = 3$ $\qquad m = \dfrac{4-(-8)}{-10-(-6)} = \dfrac{12}{-4} = -3$

Left slope: 3

Right slope: -3

54. $(-282 + 20{,}320)\frac{1}{2} = 20{,}038\left(\frac{1}{2}\right)$

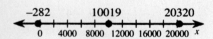

$= 10{,}019$ feet

−282 10019 20320

0 4000 8000 12000 16000 20000 x

55. −282 20320

0 4000 8000 12000 16000 20000 x

56. $|20{,}320 - 10{,}019| = 10{,}301$

$|10{,}019 - (-282)| = 10{,}301$

The distance between the midpoint and endpoint is 10,301.

$|x - 10{,}019| \leq 10{,}301$

57.

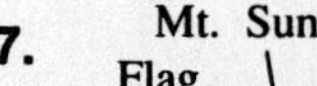

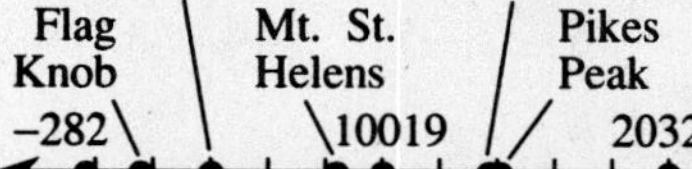

Chapter REVIEW

1. (0, −3)

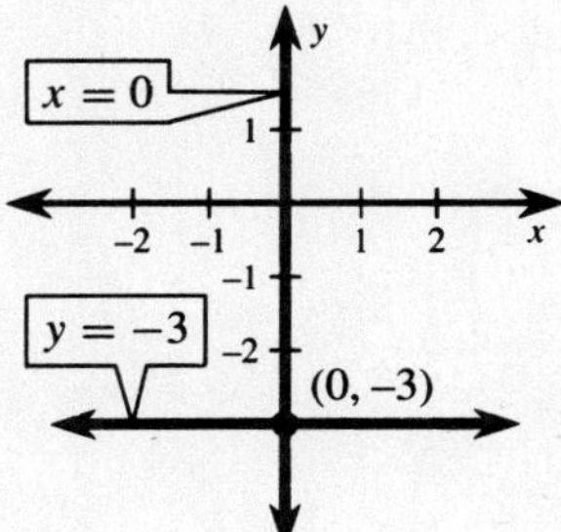

2. (7, −5)

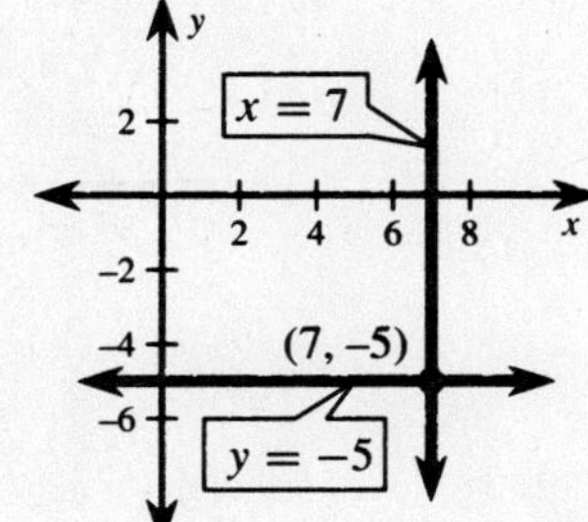

3. (−6, 4)

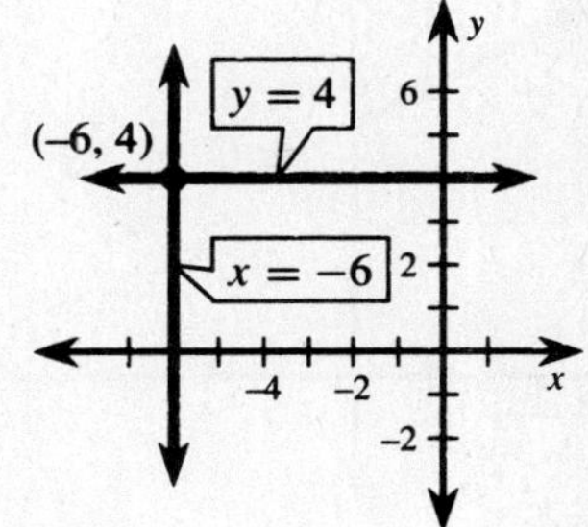

4. (−2, 0)

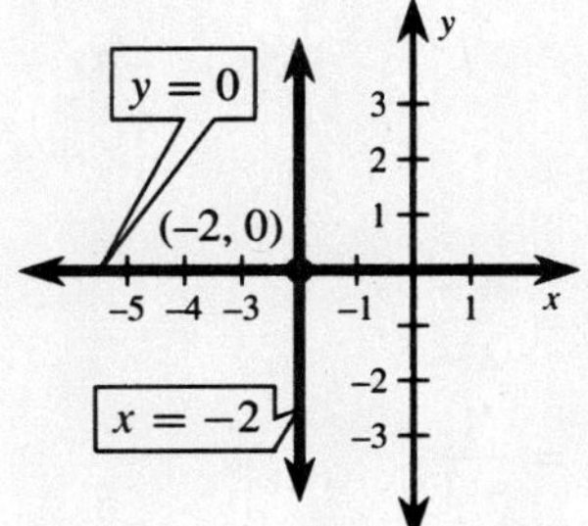

5. Yes

6. No

7. No

8. No

9.

x	−1	0	1
y	0	−2	−4

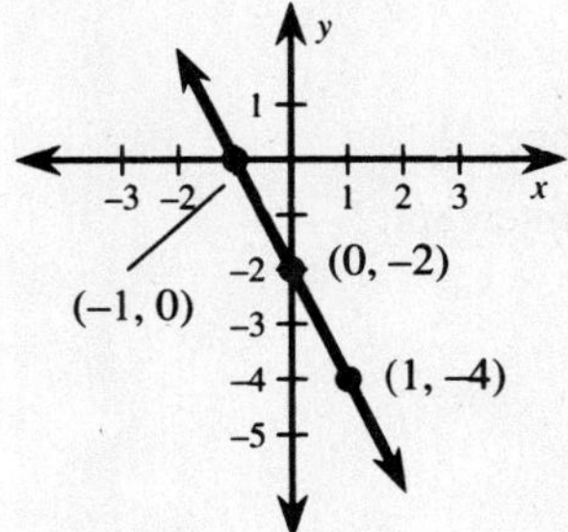

10.

x	−3	0	3
y	−3	−2	−1

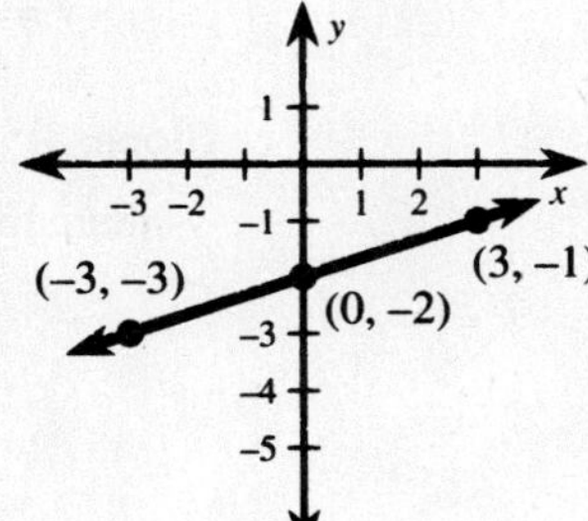

11.

x	-2	0	2
y	8	7	6

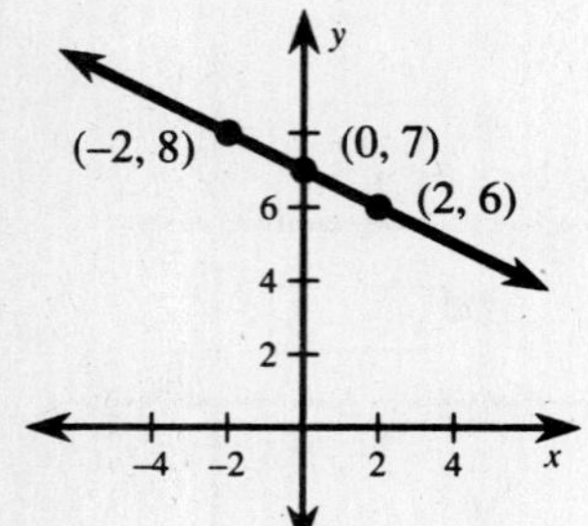

12.

x	-2	0	1
y	4	-4	-8

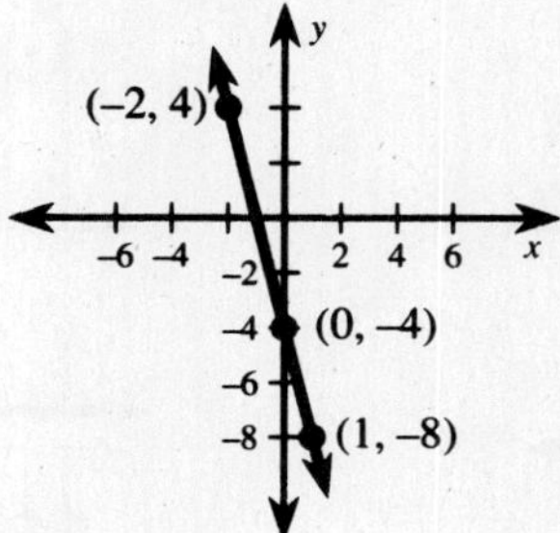

13. c.

$2x + 3y = 10$

$3y = -2x + 10$

$y = -\frac{2}{3}x + \frac{10}{3}$

14. b.

$-x + 4y = 8$

$4y = x + 8$

$y = \frac{1}{4}x + 2$

15. d.

$3x - 5y = 15$

$-5y = -3x + 15$

$y = \frac{3}{5}x - 3$

16. a.

$4x - 5y = -20$

$-5y = -4x - 20$

$y = \frac{4}{5}x + 4$

17. $m = \dfrac{-1-4}{2-3}$

$= \dfrac{-5}{-1}$

$= 5$

18. $m = \dfrac{8-2}{0-(-1)}$

$= \dfrac{6}{1}$

$= 6$

19. $m = \dfrac{4-0}{2-5}$

$= \dfrac{4}{-3}$

$= -\dfrac{4}{3}$

20. $x + 11y = 2$

$11y = -x + 2$

$y = -\frac{1}{11}x + \frac{2}{11}$

Slope: $-\frac{1}{11}$

y-intercept: $\frac{2}{11}$

21. $x - 4y = 12$

$-4y = -x + 12$

$y = \frac{1}{4}x - 3$

Slope: $\frac{1}{4}$

y-intercept: -3

22. $-x + 6y = -24$

$6y = x - 24$

$y = \frac{1}{6}x - 4$

Slope: $\frac{1}{6}$

y-intercept: -4

23. $x = 10,\ y = -5$

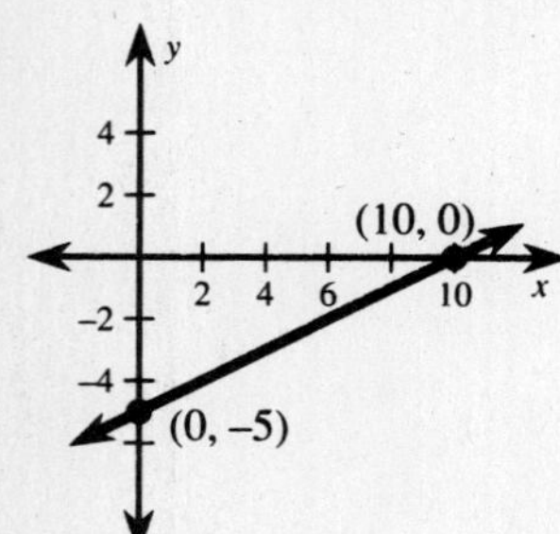

24. $x = -8,\ y = -6$

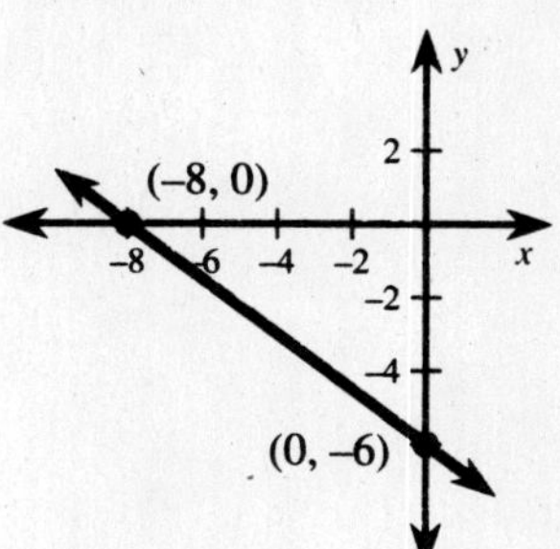

25. $3x - 6 = 0$

$3x = 6$

$x = 2$

26. $5x - 3 = 0$

$5x = 3$

$x = \frac{3}{5}$

27. $-x + 8 = 0$

$-x = -8$

$x = 8$

28. $-4x - 1 = 7$

$-4x = 8$

$x = -2$

29.

x	2	0	−2
y	−2	−4	−2

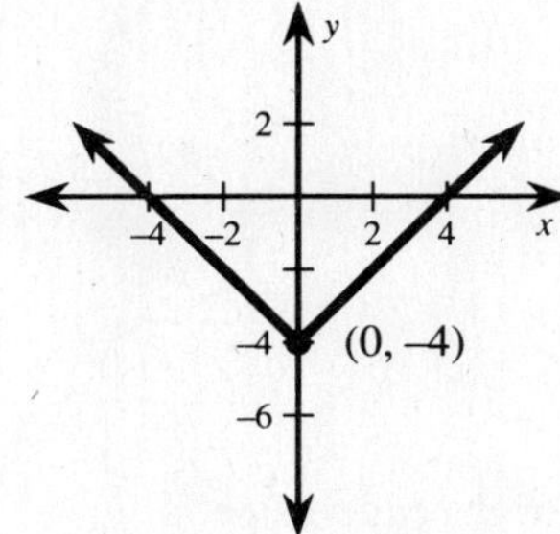

30.

x	−5	−3	−1
y	3	−1	3

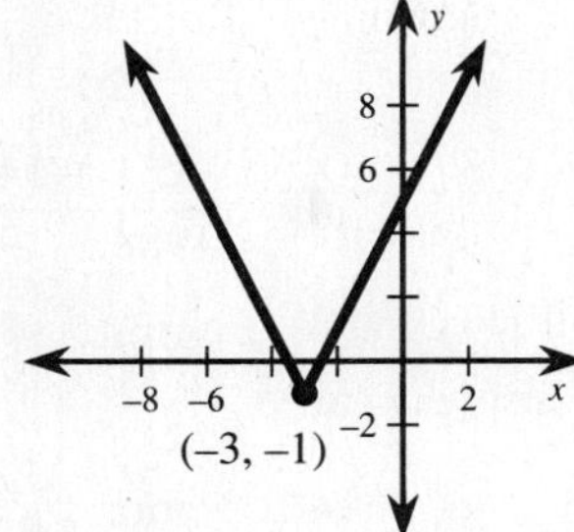

31.

x	−3	−1	2
y	−1	5	−4

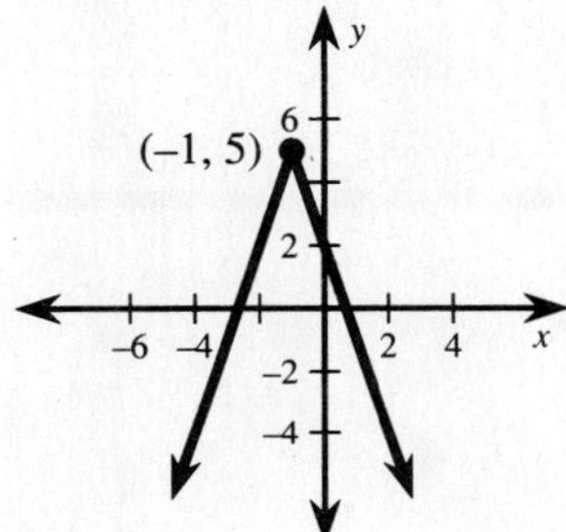

32.

x	8	6	4
y	3	2	3

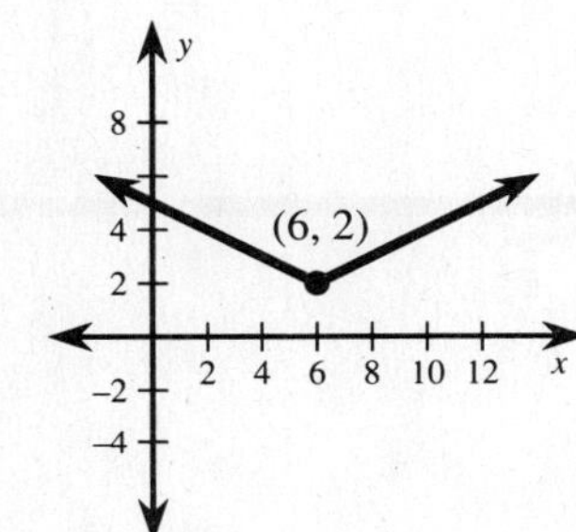

33. d.

34. a.

35. b.

36. c.

37. $4 + |x + 2| = 7$

$|x + 2| = 3$

$x + 2 = 3$ or $x + 2 = -3$

$x = 1$ $\quad x = -5$

38. $6 - 5|x - 1| = 1$

$-5|x - 1| = -5$

$|x - 1| = 1$

$x - 1 = 1$ or $x - 1 = -1$

$x = 2$ $\quad x = 0$

39. $7 - |2x + 6| = 4$

$-|2x + 6| = -3$

$|2x + 6| = 3$

$2x + 6 = 3$ or $2x + 6 = -3$

$2x = -3$ $\quad 2x = -9$

$x = -\frac{3}{2}$ $\quad x = -\frac{9}{2}$

40. $|x + 8| - 6 = 2$

$|x + 8| = 8$

$x + 8 = 8$ or $x + 8 = -8$

$x = 0$ $\quad x = -16$

41. The measure of success of being a good spouse and parent is being tallied.

42. $m = \dfrac{45 - 0}{100 - 0} = \dfrac{45}{100} = \dfrac{9}{20}$

43. 1987 and 1988

44. 1986 and 1987

45. $\dfrac{15.1 - 13.0}{1988 - 1983} = \dfrac{2.1}{5} = 0.42$ million boats per year

46. $\dfrac{15.1 - 14.3}{1988 - 1986} = \dfrac{0.8}{2} = 0.4$ million boats per year

47. The sails are 30 feet tall.

48.

$$y = -2.2|x| + 30$$
$$0 = -2.2|x| + 30$$
$$2.2|x| = 30$$
$$|x| \approx 14$$
$$x = 14 \text{ or } x = -14$$

$|14 - (-14)| = 28$ feet

49. Ratio: $\frac{30}{28} = \frac{15}{14}$

50. The right edge slope is negative: -2.2

The left edge slope is positive: 2.2

Chapter TEST

1. $(7,\ -1)$

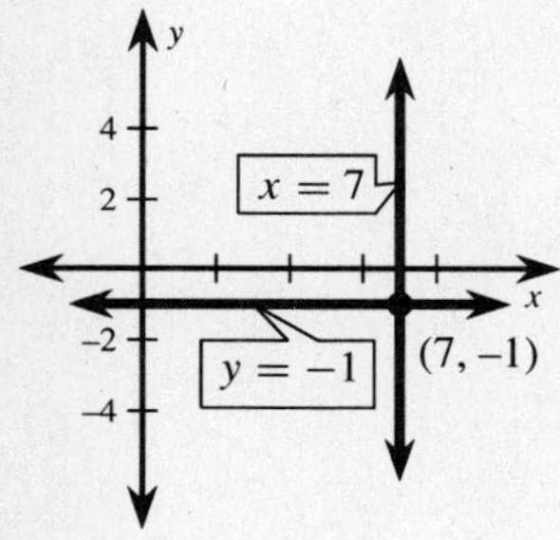

2. $x = 3$

3. a.

$$\tfrac{5}{3}x + y \stackrel{?}{=} 1$$
$$\tfrac{5}{3}(4) + \left(-\tfrac{17}{3}\right) \stackrel{?}{=} 1$$
$$\tfrac{20}{3} - \tfrac{17}{3} \stackrel{?}{=} 1$$
$$\tfrac{3}{3} \stackrel{?}{=} 1$$
$$1 = 1$$

$$\tfrac{5}{3}x + y \stackrel{?}{=} 1$$
$$\tfrac{5}{3}(2) + \tfrac{10}{3} \stackrel{?}{=} 1$$
$$\tfrac{10}{3} + \tfrac{10}{3} \stackrel{?}{=} 1$$
$$\tfrac{20}{3} \neq 1$$

4.

x	−9	−6	−3	0	3	6	9
y	−5	−4	−3	−2	−1	0	1

5. $\frac{3}{8}x + 0 = 3$ $\quad\quad$ $\frac{3}{8}(0) + y = 3$

$\frac{3}{8}x = 3$ $\quad\quad$ $y = 3$

$x = 8$

(8, 0), (0, 3)

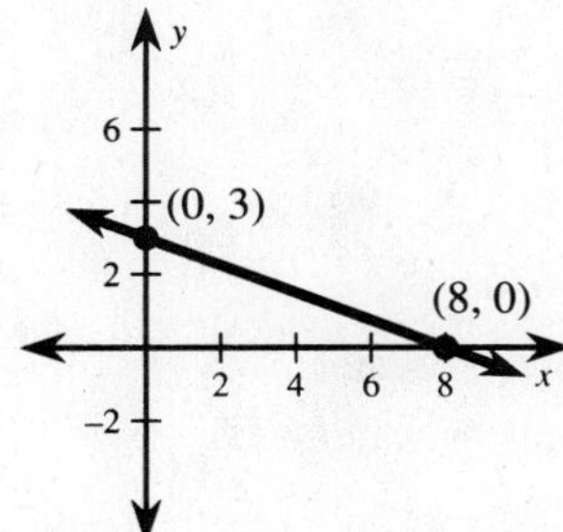

6. $0 = -x + 3$ $\quad\quad$ $y = -0 + 3$

$x = 3$ $\quad\quad$ $y = 3$

(3, 0), (0, 3)

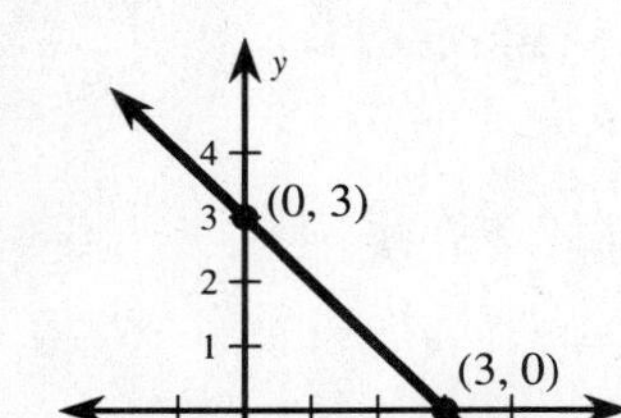

7. $m = \dfrac{6 - 6}{5 - (-9)}$

$= \dfrac{0}{14}$

$= 0$

8. $m = \dfrac{0 - (-2)}{4 - 1}$

$= \dfrac{2}{3}$

9. $m = \dfrac{-\frac{1}{2} - \left(-\frac{1}{4}\right)}{-3 - (-6)}$

$= \dfrac{-\frac{1}{2} + \frac{1}{4}}{-3 + 6}$

$= \dfrac{-\frac{1}{4}}{3}$

$= -\frac{1}{12}$

10. $m = \dfrac{70 - 76}{5 - 5}$

$= \dfrac{-6}{0}$

Undefined

11. $3y + 4x = 7$

$3y = -4x + 7$

$y = -\frac{4}{3}x + \frac{7}{3}$

12. $3(y - 1) = x - 3$

$y - 1 = \frac{1}{3}x - 1$

$y = \frac{1}{3}x$

13. $\frac{1}{3}(y - 9) - (x - 1) = 6$

$\frac{1}{3}y - 3 - x + 1 = 6$

$\frac{1}{3}y = x + 8$

$y = 3x + 24$

14. $\frac{1}{4}x + 4y = 4$

$4y = -\frac{1}{4}x + 4$

$y = -\frac{1}{16}x + 1$

15. $2x - 3 = 7$

$2x = 10$

$x = 5$

16. $2(x - 3) = -4$

$x - 3 = -2$

$x = 1$

17. $x - 1 = 0$

$x = 1$

x	0	1	2
y	4	2	4

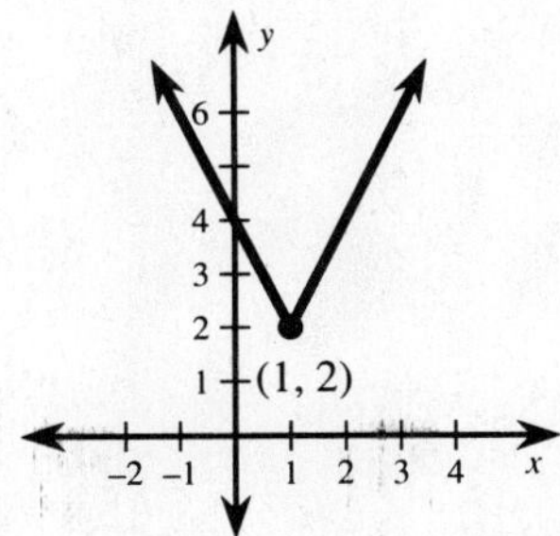

18. $x + 2 = 0$

$x = -2$

x	−3	−2	−1
y	−4	−1	−4

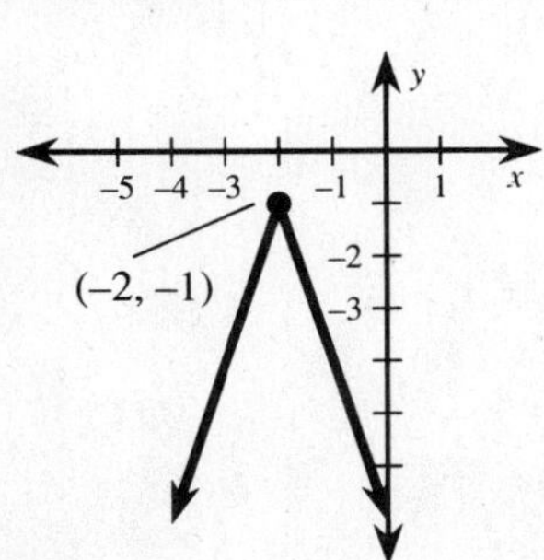

19. $|3x + 6| - 7 = 3$

$$|3x + 6| = 10$$

$$3x + 6 = 10 \quad \text{or} \quad 3x + 6 = -10$$

$$3x = 4 \qquad 3x = -16$$

$$x = \tfrac{4}{3} \qquad x = -\tfrac{16}{3}$$

20. $|x + 5| - 4 = 4$

$$|x + 5| = 8$$

$$x + 5 = 8 \quad \text{or} \quad x + 5 = -8$$

$$x = 3 \qquad x = -13$$

21. $1.50x + 1.25y = 375$

$$1.50x = 375 \qquad 1.25y = 375$$

$$x = 250 \qquad y = 300$$

(250, 0), (0, 300)

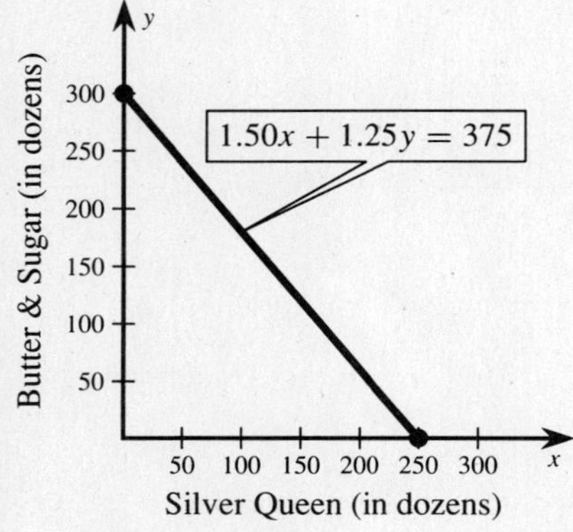

22. $|t - 122| = 90$

$$t - 122 = 90 \qquad t - 122 = -90$$

$$t = 212 \qquad t = 32$$

212° F is the boiling point of water.

32° F is the freezing point of water.

Chapter 5

Writing Linear Equations

5.1 Equations of Lines Using Slope-Intercept Form

Communicating about Algebra

A. $c = 0.45m + 1.25$

B. $y = 0.75 + 0.5(6)$

$y = 3.75$

$c = 0.45(6) + 1.25$

$c = 3.95$

A 7-minute call to the second number would cost more.

C. $y = 0.75 + 0.5(11)$

$y = 6.25$

$c = 0.45(11) + 1.25$

$c = 6.20$

A 12-minute call to the first number would cost more.

EXERCISES

1. Slope-intercept form

2. 5 is the y-intercept.

3. The slope is -1. The y-intercept is 0.

4. $y = -7x - \frac{2}{3}$

5. $P = 23{,}668{,}000 + 617{,}100 \cdot 14$

$P = 32{,}307{,}400$ people

The estimated population of California in 1994 would be 32,307,400.

6. $y = 1.50x + 11$

7.

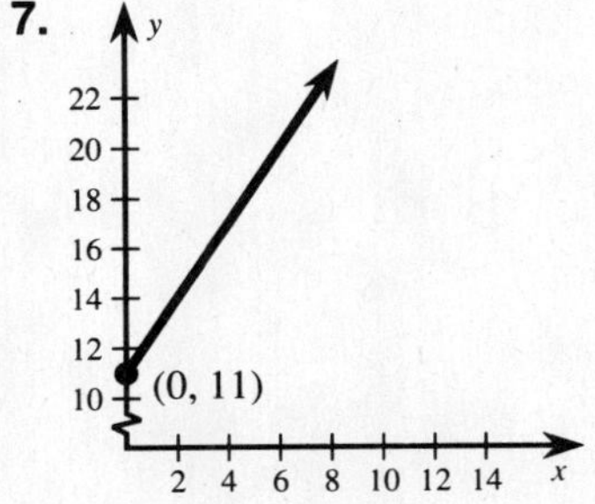

8. $y = 1.50 \cdot 12 + 11$

$y = 18 + 11$

$y = \$29$

9. $y = 3x - 2$

10. $y = x + 2$

11. $y = -x + 3$

12. $y = -2x$

13. $y = \frac{3}{2}x + 3$

14. $y = -\frac{1}{4}x + 1$

15. $y = 2x + 2$

16. $y = x - 3$

17. $y = -\frac{2}{3}x + 2$

18. $y = -x + 4$

19. a: $y = 2x + 3$
b: $y = 2x$
c: $y = 2x - 4$

20. a: $y = -x + 4$
b: $y = -x + 2$
c: $y = -x$

21. $y = 0.25x + 30$

22. $y = 0.35x + 45$

23.

Miles, *x*	25	50	75	100
Cost, *y*	36.25	42.50	48.75	55.00

$y = 0.25 \cdot 25 + 30$
$y = 6.25 + 30$
$y = 36.25$

$y = 0.25 \cdot 50 + 30$
$y = 12.50 + 30$
$y = 42.50$

$y = 0.25 \cdot 75 + 30$
$y = 18.75 + 30$
$y = 48.75$

$y = 0.25 \cdot 100 + 30$
$y = 25.00 + 30$
$y = 55.00$

24.

Miles, *x*	25	50	75	100
Cost, *y*	53.75	62.50	71.25	80.00

$y = 0.35 \cdot 25 + 45$
$y = 8.75 + 45$
$y = 53.75$

$y = 0.35 \cdot 50 + 45$
$y = 17.50 + 45$
$y = 62.50$

$y = 0.35 \cdot 75 + 45$
$y = 26.25 + 45$
$y = 71.25$

$y = 0.35 \cdot 100 + 45$
$y = 35.00 + 45$
$y = 80.00$

25. $P = 38{,}400t + 3{,}122{,}000$

26. $P = 38{,}400 \cdot 6 + 3{,}122{,}000$
$P = 230{,}400 + 3{,}122{,}000$
$P = 3{,}352{,}400$ people

The estimated population of South Carolina in 1986 is 3,352,400.

27. $y = -50t + 200$

The line given by this equation has a negative slope because as time increases, the distance from home decreases.

28.

Miles, *x*	1	2	3	4
Cost, *y*	150	100	50	0

$y = -50 \cdot 1 + 200$
$y = -50 + 200$
$y = 150$

$y = -50 \cdot 2 + 200$
$y = -100 + 200$
$y = 100$

$y = -50 \cdot 3 + 200$
$y = -150 + 200$
$y = 50$

$y = -50 \cdot 4 + 200$
$y = -200 + 200$
$y = 0$

29. $y = 100{,}000 \cdot 15 \cdot 5x$
$y = 7{,}500{,}000x$

$y = 7{,}500{,}000 \cdot 365$
$y = 2{,}737{,}500{,}000$ gallons per year

30. $y = 100{,}000 \cdot 15 \cdot (5 \cdot 0.50)x$
$y = 3{,}750{,}000x$

$y = 3{,}750{,}000 \cdot 365$
$y = 1{,}368{,}750{,}000$ gallons per year

$2{,}737{,}500{,}000 - 1{,}368{,}750{,}000 = 1{,}368{,}750{,}000$ gallons per year

31. Slope: -3
y-intercept: 6

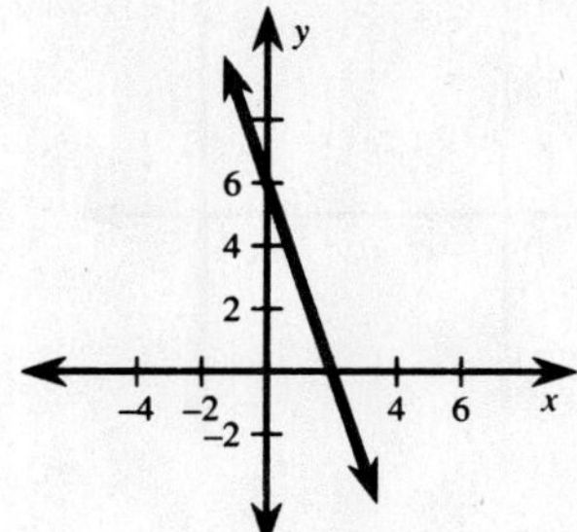

32. Slope: 2
y-intercept: -5

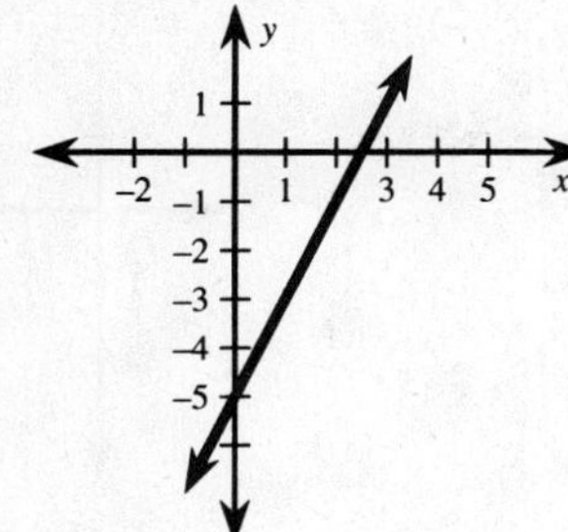

33. $y + 2x = 2$

$$y = -2x + 2$$

Slope: -2
y-intercept: 2

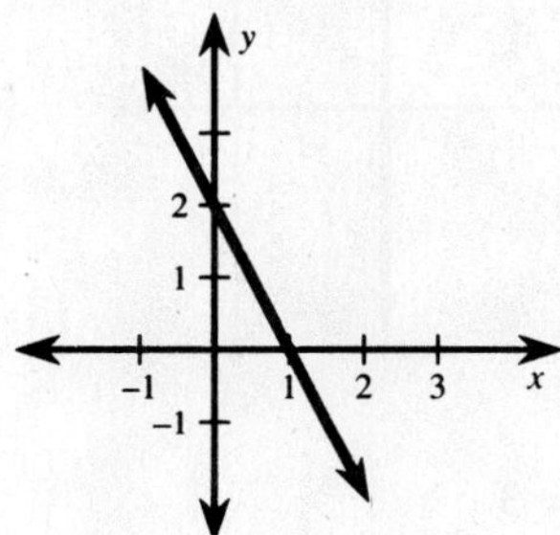

34. $-y + 3x = -5$

$$-y = -3x - 5$$
$$y = 3x + 5$$

Slope: 3
y-intercept: 5

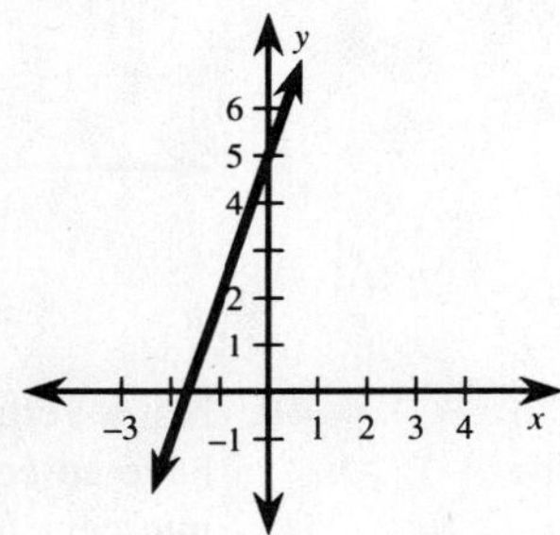

35. $2y - 3x = 6$

$$2y = 3x + 6$$
$$y = \frac{3}{2}x + 3$$

Slope: $\frac{3}{2}$
y-intercept: 3

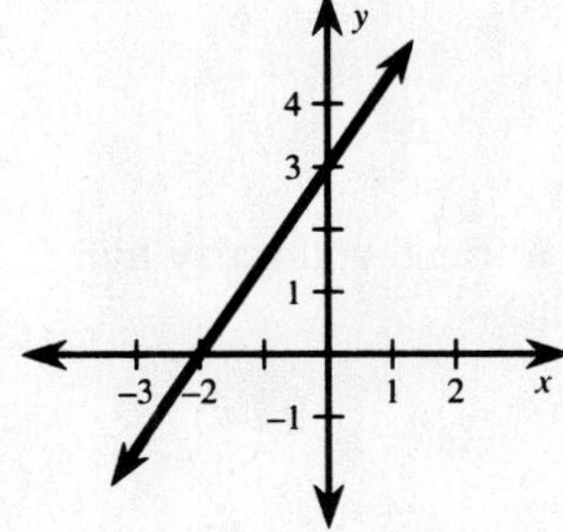

36. $2y + 4x = 6$

$$2y = -4x + 6$$
$$y = -2x + 3$$

Slope: -2
y-intercept: 3

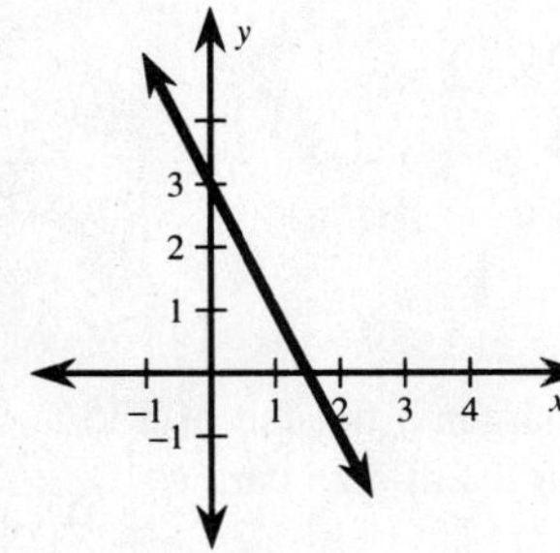

37. The line is horizontal.

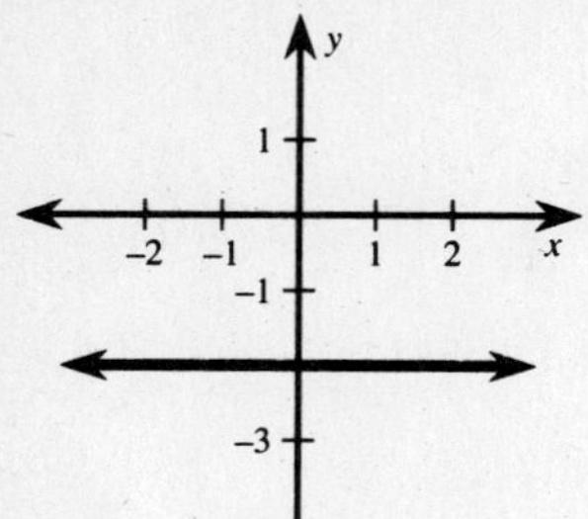

38. The line is vertical.

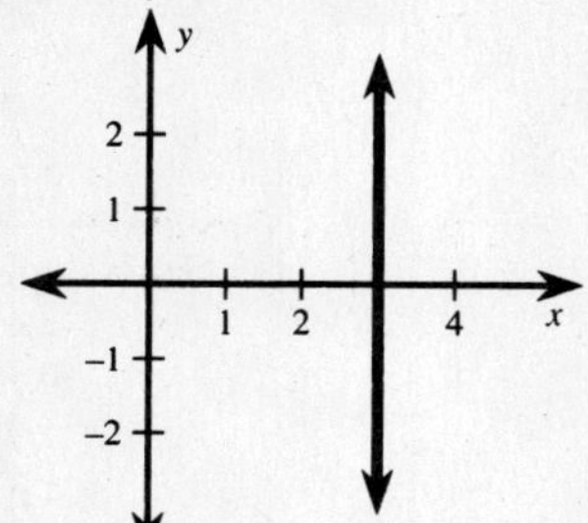

39. The line is vertical.

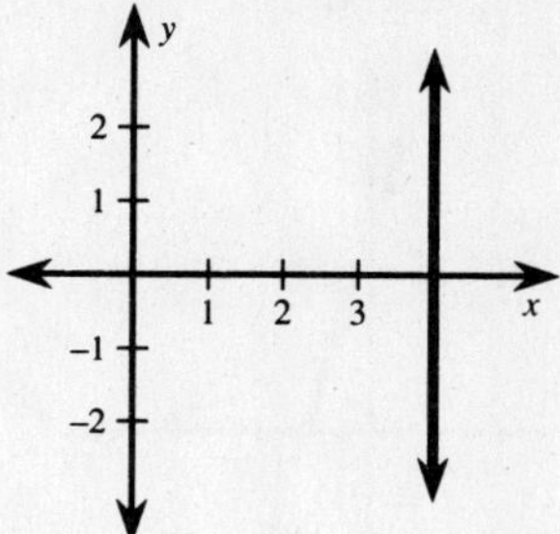

40. The line is horizontal.

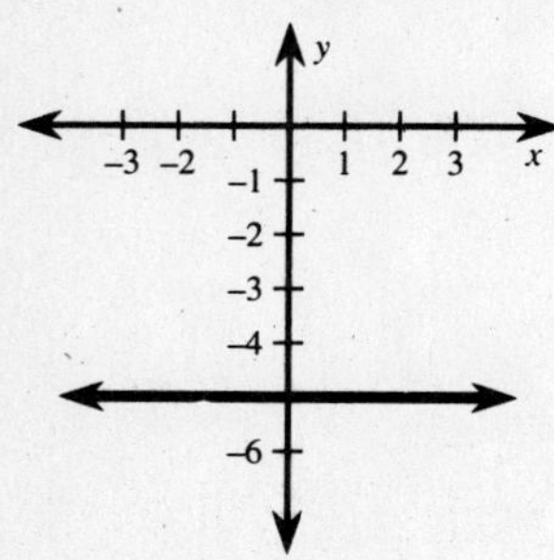

41. The line is horizontal.

$2y = 6$

$y = 3$

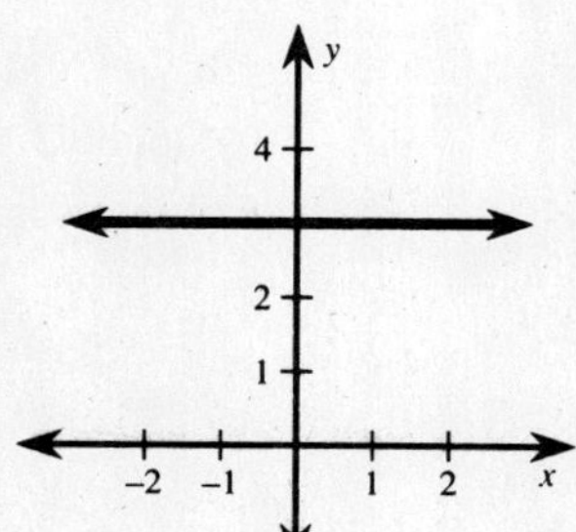

42. The line is vertical.

$3x = -6$

$x = -2$

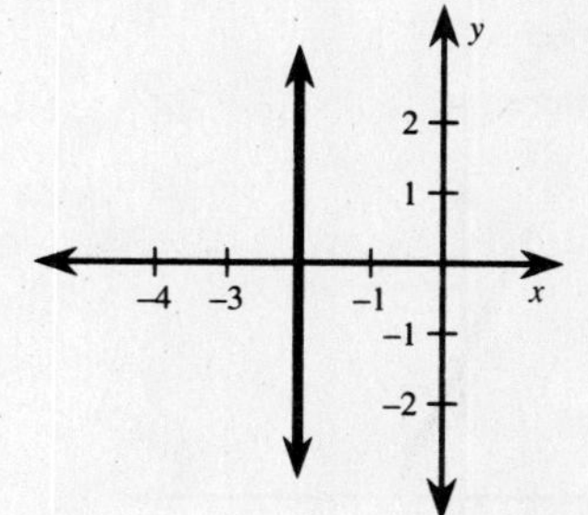

43. Yes, a horizontal line can have an equation in slope-intercept form.

44. No, a vertical line cannot have an equation in slope-intercept form.

45. $y = 3$

46. $x = -4$

47. $y = 10x$

48. $y = 10$

49.

$$m = \frac{75 - 35}{100 - 0} = \frac{40}{100} = \frac{2}{5} = 0.4$$

y-intercept: 35

$y = 0.4x + 35$

A car rental company charges a flat fee of $35 plus 40¢ per mile to rent a full-size car.

50.

$$m = \frac{200 - 0}{0 - 5} = \frac{200}{-5} = -40$$

y-intercept: 200

$y = -40x + 200$

You borrow $200 from a friend and repay him at a rate of $40 a month.

51. $y = -\frac{2}{5}x - 3$

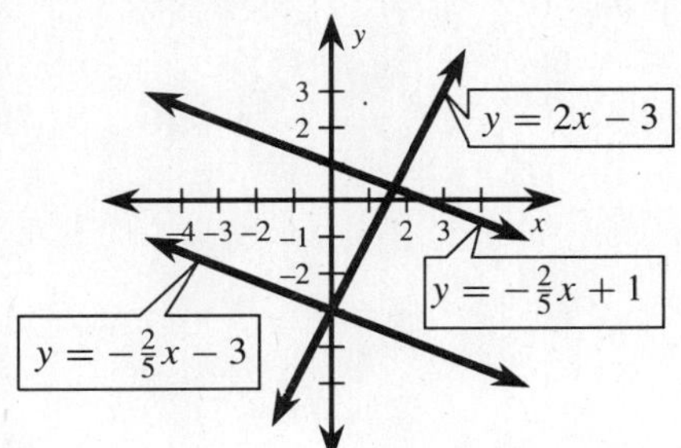

52. $y = \frac{3}{2}x + 3$

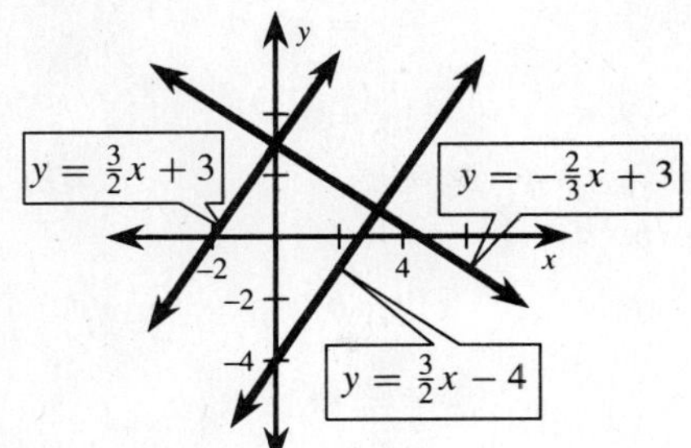

5.2 Equations of Lines Given the Slope and a Point

Communicating about Algebra

A. $y = 15(10) + 265 = 415$ million

B. $y = 15(17) + 265 = 520$ million

C. $400 = 15t + 265$

$15t = 135$

$t = 9$

During 1989 there will be about 400 million vacation trips.

D. No; extending the graph to the left would decrease the number of vacation trips to zero.

EXERCISES

1. Substitute the slope and point into the slope-intercept form. ⇒ Solve for b (y-intercept). ⇒ Substitute the slope and the y-intercept into the slope-intercept form.

2. $m = \frac{1}{3}$

$x = -2$

$y = 4$

These substitutions permit you to find b (the y-intercept).

3. $y = mx + b$

$3 = (-2)1 + b$

$5 = b$

$y = -2x + 5$

4. $y = mx + b$

$7 = 0 \cdot (-6) + b$

$7 = b$

$y = 0 \cdot x + 7$

$y = 7$

5. $y = mx + b$

$-2 = \frac{1}{2}(8) + b$

$-6 = b$

$y = \frac{1}{2}x - 6$

6. $y = mx + b$

$-\frac{3}{2} = 9\left(\frac{1}{2}\right) + b$

$-\frac{12}{2} = b$

$-6 = b$

$y = 9x - 6$

7. $y = mx + b$

$116{,}000 = 6{,}000(5) + b$

$86{,}000 = b$

$y = 6000x + 86{,}000$

8. $y = 6{,}000 \cdot 10 + 86{,}000$

$y = 146{,}000$

9. $6 = 2(-3) + b$

$12 = b$

$y = 2x + 12$

10. $2 = 1(3) + b$

$-1 = b$

$y = x - 1$

11. $-2 = -1(4) + b$

$2 = b$

$y = -x + 2$

12. $1 = -3(3) + b$

$10 = b$

$y = -3x + 10$

13. $-5 = -2(-2) + b$

$-9 = b$

$y = -2x - 9$

14. $4 = 4(1) + b$

$0 = b$

$y = 4x$

15. $-2 = \frac{1}{2}(4) + b$

$-4 = b$

$y = \frac{1}{2}x - 4$

16. $5 = \frac{1}{3}(-6) + b$

$7 = b$

$y = \frac{1}{3}x + 7$

17. $-1 = 3(0) + b$

$-1 = b$

$y = 3x - 1$

18. $4 = 2(0) + b$

$4 = b$

$y = 2x + 4$

19. $5 = 0 \cdot 2 + b$

$5 = b$

$y = 0 \cdot x + 5$

20. $-3 = 0 \cdot 1 + b$

$-3 = b$

$y = 0 \cdot x - 3$

21. $4 = \frac{2}{3}(-3) + b$

$4 = -2 + b$

$6 = b$

$y = \frac{2}{3}x + 6$

22. $3 = -\frac{1}{4}(8) + b$

$3 = -2 + b$

$5 = b$

$y = -\frac{1}{4}x + 5$

23. y-intercept: $(0, -2)$

$m = \dfrac{2 - (-2)}{-2 - 0}$

$= -2$

$y = -2x - 2$

24. y-intercept: $(0, 2)$

$m = \dfrac{3 - 2}{3 - 0}$

$= \dfrac{1}{3}$

$y = \dfrac{1}{3}x + 2$

25. y-intercept: $(0, 2)$

$m = \dfrac{3 - 2}{2 - 0}$

$= \dfrac{1}{2}$

$y = \dfrac{1}{2}x + 2$

26. y-intercept: $(0, 1)$

$m = \dfrac{-2 - 1}{-3 - 0}$

$= 1$

$y = x + 1$

27. $0 = -\frac{1}{3}(3) + b$

$1 = b$

$y = -\frac{1}{3}x + 1$

28. $0 = 2(-2) + b$

$4 = b$

$y = 2x + 4$

29. $20{,}434{,}000 = (1{,}100{,}000)(9) + b$

$10{,}534{,}000 = b$

$y = 1{,}100{,}000x + 10{,}534{,}000$

30. $41{,}100 = (3600)(7) + b$

$15{,}900 = b$

$y = 3600x + 15{,}900$

31. $30 = 2 \cdot 8 + b$

$14 = b$

$m = 2n + 14$

32. $452 = -7.50(12) + b$

$452 = -90 + b$

$542 = b$

$y = -7.50x + 542$

33. $y = \frac{1}{2}x$

34. $y = \frac{1}{2}(15)(8)$

$y = 60$ feet

35. $0.46 = 0.31(1) + b$

$0.15 = b$

$C = 0.31t + 0.15$

(Note: t is an integer greater than or equal to 1, since phone calls are billed in minutes.)

36. $2.50 = 1.30(1) + b$

$1.20 = b$

$y = 1.30x + 1.20,\ x \geq 1$

37. $-2 = \frac{3}{2}(-4) + b$

$-2 = -6 + b$

$4 = b$

38. $4 = \left(-\frac{2}{3}\right)(-6) + b$

$4 = 4 + b$

$0 = b$

39. $\frac{3}{2} = \left(-\frac{1}{6}\right)(3) + b$

$\frac{3}{2} = -\frac{1}{2} + b$

$2 = b$

40. $-\frac{2}{3} = \left(-\frac{1}{6}\right)(2) + b$

$-\frac{2}{3} = -\frac{1}{3} + b$

$-\frac{1}{3} = b$

41. $4 = -\frac{1}{2}(2) + b$

$4 = -1 + b$

$5 = b$

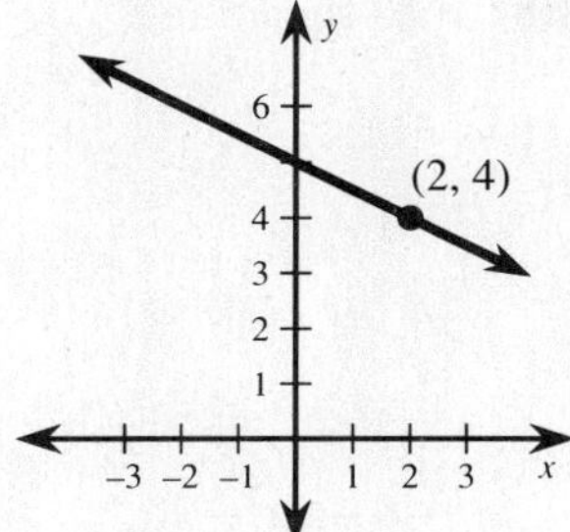

42. $8 = -2(4) + b$

$16 = b$

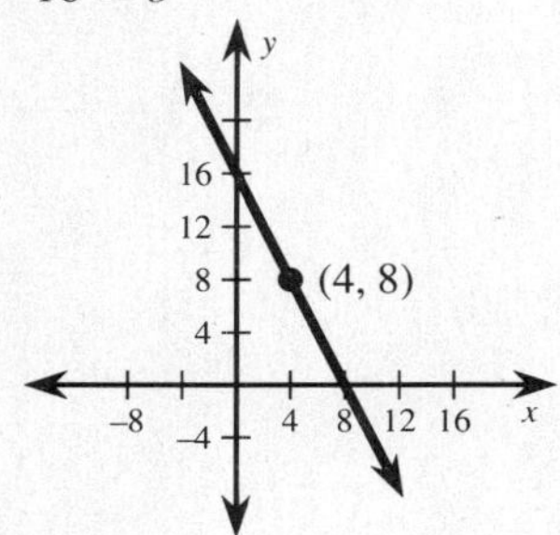

43. $6 = 2(3) + b$

$0 = b$

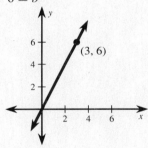

44. $0 = \frac{1}{2}(4) + b$

$-2 = b$

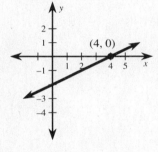

45. $4 = -2(-1) + b$

$2 = b$

$y = -2x + 2$

46. $6 = (1)(2) + b$

$4 = b$

$y = x + 4$

47. $P = 0.25n - 19.75$

48.

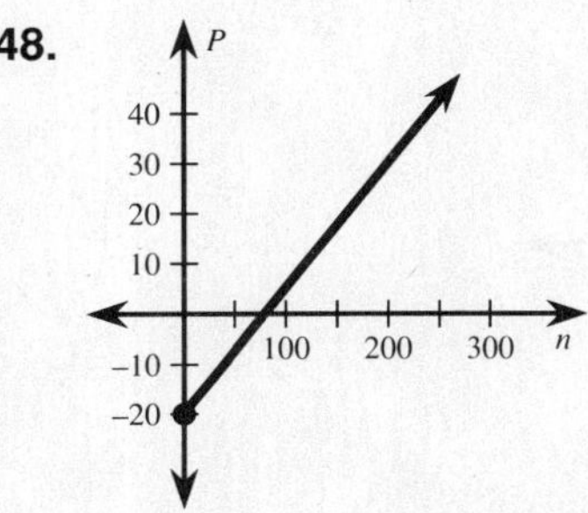

49. n cannot be negative, zero, or a fraction.

50. Yes, it is possible for the club to not make a profit.

$0 = 0.25n - 19.75$

$19.75 = 0.25n$

$n = 79$ people

79 people must attend the movie so that the club will get \$19.75 back.

51. The attendence at the movie was 242 people.

$40.75 = 0.25n - 19.75$

$60.50 = 0.25n$

$n = 242$ people

Mixed **REVIEW**

1. $-\frac{1}{3}$

2. $\frac{2}{3} + \frac{3}{2} = \frac{4}{6} + \frac{9}{6}$
$= \frac{13}{6}$

3. $(2)(8) = 16$ square feet

4. $\frac{1}{4}(3 + 6 + 8 + 13) = \frac{1}{4}(30)$
$= \frac{30}{4}$
$= \frac{15}{2}$

5. 11

6. $(0.35)(130) = 45.5$

7. $-(x - 4) + 2x = -x + 4 + 2x$
$= x + 4$

8. $2(3x - 4) - 5(x - 4) = 6x - 8 - 5x + 20$
$= x + 12$

9. $2x = 3y \qquad 3x = 2y$

$\frac{2}{3}x = y \qquad \frac{3}{2}x = y$

No, the lines are not parallel.

10. No, the lines are not parallel.

11. $2x - 4 = -x + 11$

$3x = 15$

$x = 5$

12. $3(x + 4) = -(x + 1) - 2$

$3x + 12 = -x - 1 - 2$

$4x = -15$

$x = -\frac{15}{4}$

13. $-3x + 15 = -3(-1) + 15$
$= 3 + 15$
$= 18$

14. $|2x + 3| = |2(-2) + 3|$
$= |-4 + 3|$
$= |-1|$
$= 1$

15.

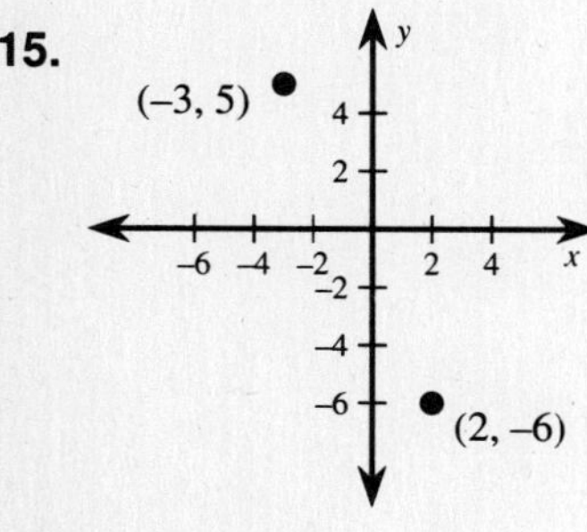

16.

(–3, 4)

(2, 1)

17.

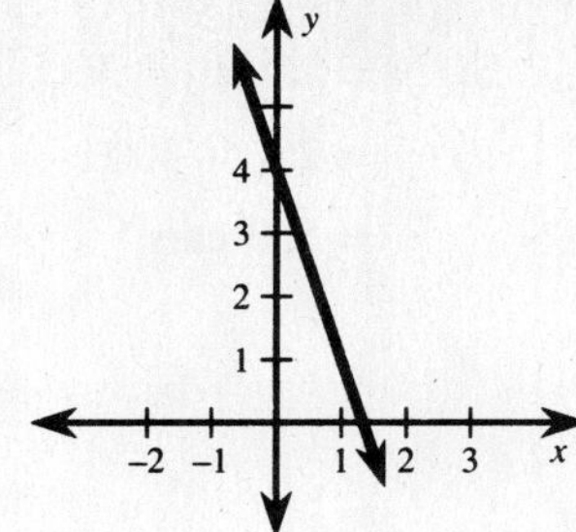

18.

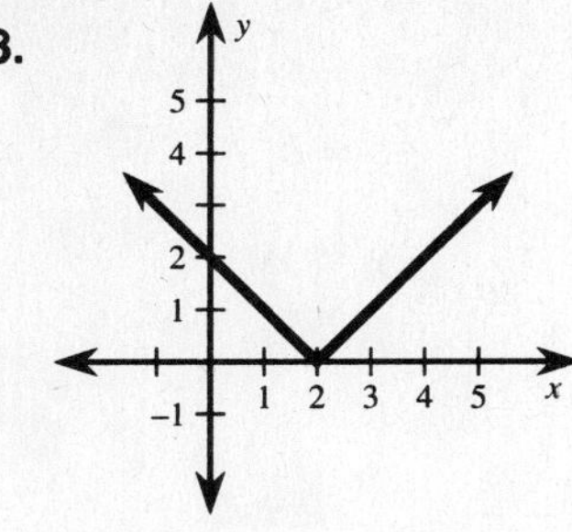

19. $y = 2x + 3$

20. $-3 = -1(1) + b$

$-2 = b$

$y = -x - 2$

5.3 Equations of Lines Given Two Points

Communicating about Algebra

A. The store sold 255 more jeans each year.

B. $y = 255(11) + 2650$

$= 5455$

C. $y = 255x + 2650$

$x = \frac{1}{255}(y - 2650)$

$x = \frac{1}{255}(6475 - 2650)$

$x = 15$

The store will sell 6475 pairs of jeans in the year 1995.

D. $y = 255(10) + 2650$

$= 5200$

$5200(35.95) = \$186{,}940.00$

EXERCISES

1. Find the slope by substituting the coordinates of the two given points into the formula for slope. $\Rightarrow$ Find the y-intercept by substituting the slope and the coordinates of one of the points into the slope-intercept form. $\Rightarrow$ Substitute the slope and the y-intercept values into the slope-intercept from of the equation.

2. To write the equation of a line, you need to know the slope and one of the points on the line.

3. $m = \frac{-1-3}{1-2}$

$= \frac{-4}{-1}$

$= 4$

4. $-1 = 4 \cdot 1 + b$

$-5 = b$

$y = 4x - 5$

5. $m = \frac{450-600}{6-12}$

$= \frac{-150}{-6}$

$= 25$

$450 = 25(6) + b$

$450 = 150 + b$

$300 = b$

$y = 25x + 300$

6. $y = 25(10) + 300$

$y = 250 + 300$

$y = 550$ cars

7. $m = \frac{-3-3}{-2-4}$

$= \frac{-6}{-6}$

$= 1$

$-3 = 1 \cdot (-2) + b$

$-1 = b$

$y = x - 1$

8. $m = \frac{5-(-3)}{-1-3}$

$= \frac{8}{-4}$

$= -2$

$5 = -2(-1) + b$

$3 = b$

$y = -2x + 3$

9. $m = \frac{1-16}{-4-1}$

$= \frac{-15}{-5}$

$= 3$

$1 = 3(-4) + b$

$13 = b$

$y = 3x + 13$

10. $m = \frac{\frac{1}{2}-(-1)}{-3-0}$

$= \frac{\frac{3}{2}}{-3}$

$= \frac{3}{2}\left(-\frac{1}{3}\right)$

$= -\frac{1}{2}$

y-intercept: $(0, -1)$

$y = -\frac{1}{2}x - 1$

11. $m = \frac{-1-8}{-1-2}$

$= \frac{-9}{-3}$

$= 3$

$-1 = 3(-1) + b$

$2 = b$

$y = 3x + 2$

12. $m = \frac{2-(-1)}{1-4}$

$= \frac{3}{-3}$

$= -1$

$2 = (-1)(1) + b$

$3 = b$

$y = -x + 3$

13. $m = \frac{0-(-3)}{2-(-4)}$

$= \frac{3}{6}$

$= \frac{1}{2}$

$0 = \frac{1}{2} \cdot 2 + b$

$-1 = b$

$y = \frac{1}{2}x - 1$

14. $m = \frac{1-5}{3-(-3)}$

$= \frac{-4}{6}$

$= -\frac{2}{3}$

$1 = -\frac{2}{3}(3) + b$

$3 = b$

$y = -\frac{2}{3}x + 3$

15. $m = \frac{-4-8}{1-(-2)}$

$= \frac{-12}{3}$

$= -4$

$-4 = (-4)(1) + b$

$0 = b$

$y = -4x$

16. $m = \frac{-4-2}{0-3}$

$= \frac{-6}{-3}$

$= 2$

$-4 = 2(0) + b$

$-4 = b$

$y = 2x - 4$

17. $m = \frac{-5-1}{2-(-1)}$

$= \frac{-6}{3}$

$= -2$

$-5 = (-2)(2) + b$

$-1 = b$

$y = -2x - 1$

18. $m = \frac{-1-2}{-2-4}$

$= \frac{-3}{-6}$

$= \frac{1}{2}$

$-1 = \frac{1}{2}(-2) + b$

$0 = b$

$y = \frac{1}{2}x$

19. $m = \frac{1-4}{1-4}$

$= \frac{-3}{-3}$

$= 1$

$1 = 1(1) + b$

$0 = b$

$y = x$

20. $m = \frac{2-4}{1-2}$

$= \frac{-2}{-1}$

$= 2$

$2 = 2 \cdot 1 + b$

$0 = b$

$y = 2x$

21. $m = \frac{3-3}{1-3}$

$= \frac{0}{-2}$

$= 0$

$3 = 0(1) + b$

$3 = b$

$y = 0 \cdot x + 3$

$y = 3$

22. $m = \frac{-2-(-2)}{-1-3}$

$= \frac{0}{-4}$

$= 0$

$-2 = 0(-1) + b$

$-2 = b$

$y = 0 \cdot x - 2$

$y = -2$

23. $m = \frac{6-3}{2-(-4)}$

$= \frac{3}{6}$

$= \frac{1}{2}$

$6 = \frac{1}{2}(2) + b$

$5 = b$

$y = \frac{1}{2}x + 5$

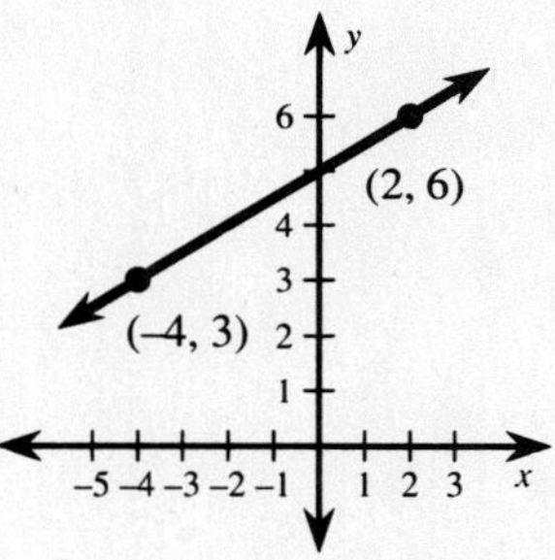

24. $m = \frac{-3-1}{3-(-3)}$

$= \frac{-4}{6}$

$= -\frac{2}{3}$

$-3 = -\frac{2}{3}(3) + b$

$-1 = b$

$y = -\frac{2}{3}x - 1$

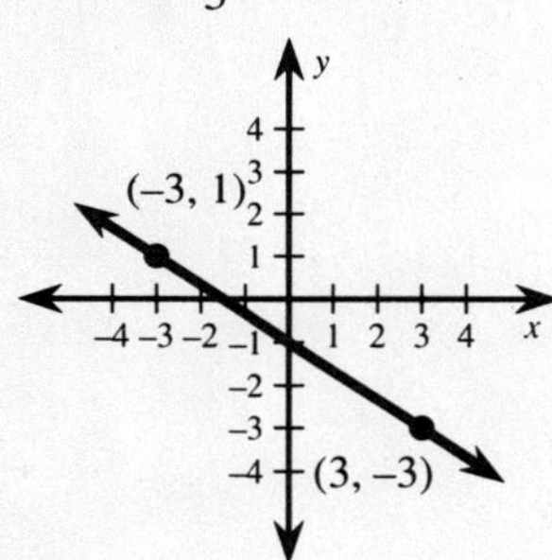

25. $m = \frac{0-(-4)}{-6-0}$

$= \frac{4}{-6}$

$= -\frac{2}{3}$

$y = -\frac{2}{3}x - 4$

26. $m = \frac{0-3}{-1-0}$

$= \frac{-3}{-1}$

$= 3$

$y = 3x + 3$

27. $m = \frac{665-532}{35-28}$

$= \frac{133}{7}$

$= 19$

$665 = 19 \cdot 35 + b$

$665 = 665 + b$

$0 = b$

$y = 19x$

28.

Square yards, x	15	26	41	63	104
Cost, y	285	494	779	1197	1976

29. $m = \dfrac{60 - (-70)}{0 - 15,000}$

$= -\dfrac{130}{15,000}$

$= -\dfrac{13}{1500}$

$60 = -\dfrac{13}{1500}(0) + b$

$60 = b$

$y = -\dfrac{13}{1500}x + 60$

Slope: $-\dfrac{13}{1500}$

30. $m = \dfrac{-90 - 0}{38,000 - 50,000}$

$= \dfrac{3}{400}$

$0 = \dfrac{3}{400}(50,000) + b$

$-375 = b$

$y = \dfrac{3}{400}x - 375$

Slope: $\dfrac{3}{400}$

The Chunnel is steeper on the English side.

31. $m = \dfrac{14,510 - 21,260}{8 - 13}$

$= \dfrac{-6750}{-5}$

$= 1350$

$14,510 = 1350(8) + b$

$14,510 = 10,800 + b$

$3710 = b$

$y = 1350x + 3710$

32. $m = \dfrac{576 - 792}{4 - 12}$

$= \dfrac{-216}{-8}$

$= 27$

$576 = 27(4) + b$

$468 = b$

$d = 27t + 468$

33. $m = \dfrac{51,096,000 - 58,826,000}{5 - 15}$

$= \dfrac{-7,730,000}{-10}$

$= 773,000$

$51,096,000 = 773,000(5) + b$

$47,231,000 = b$

$y = 773,000x + 47,231,000$

34. $m = \dfrac{20,190,000 - 43,200,000}{0 - 30}$

$= \dfrac{-23,010,000}{-30}$

$= 767,000$

$20,190,000 = 767,000 \cdot 0 + b$

$20,190,000 = b$

$y = 767,000x + 20,190,000$

35. $m = \dfrac{-3 - 0}{3 - (-6)}$

$= \dfrac{-3}{9}$

$= -\dfrac{1}{3}$

$-3 = -\dfrac{1}{3}(3) + b$

$-2 = b$

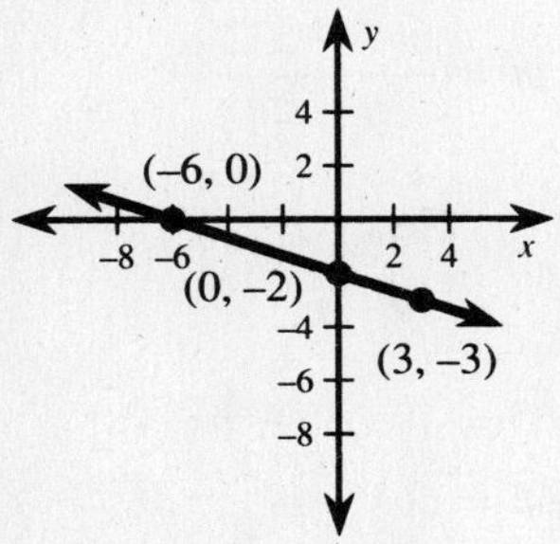

36. $m = \dfrac{1 - (-1)}{1 - (-3)}$

$= \dfrac{2}{4}$

$= \dfrac{1}{2}$

$1 = \dfrac{1}{2}(1) + b$

$\dfrac{1}{2} = b$

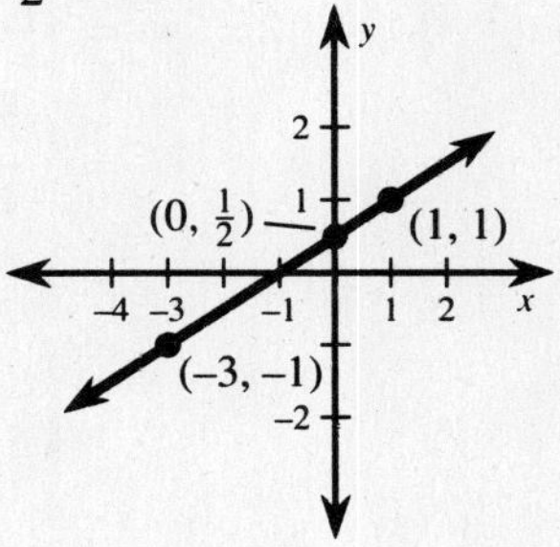

37. $m = \dfrac{1-(-3)}{1-(-5)}$

$= \dfrac{4}{6}$

$= \dfrac{2}{3}$

$1 = \dfrac{2}{3}(1) + b$

$\dfrac{1}{3} = b$

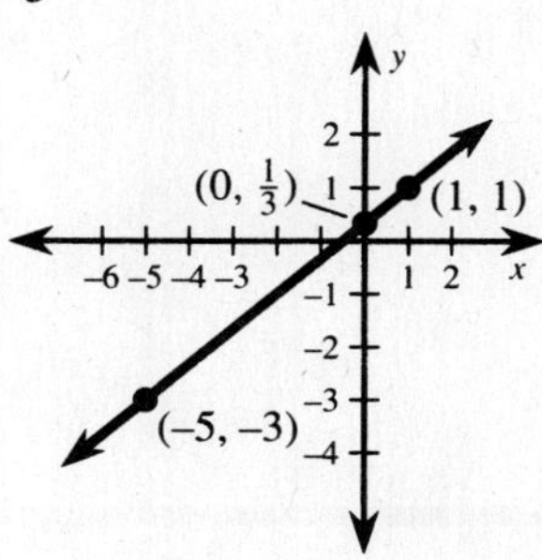

38. $m = \dfrac{2-7}{1-(-4)}$

$= \dfrac{-5}{5}$

$= -1$

$2 = -1(1) + b$

$3 = b$

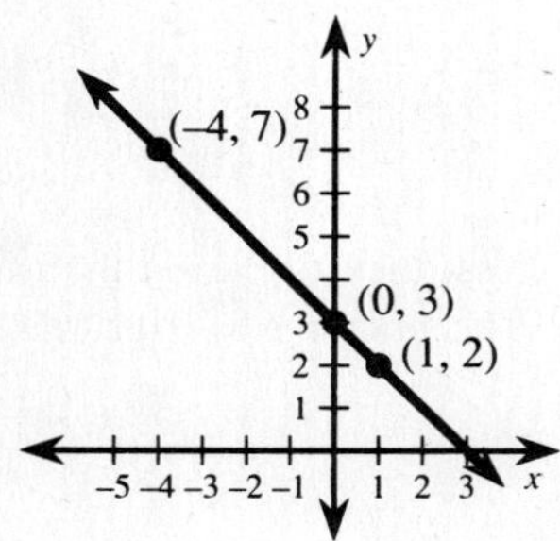

39. $m = \dfrac{11-3}{-4-0}$

$= \dfrac{8}{-4}$

$= -2$

$y = -2x + 3$

40. $m = \dfrac{7-(-5)}{3-0}$

$= \dfrac{12}{3}$

$= 4$

$y = 4x - 5$

41. $m = \dfrac{-1-5}{-4-2}$

$= \dfrac{-6}{-6}$

$= 1$

$-4 = 1 \cdot 3 + b$

$-7 = b$

$y = x - 7$

42. $m = \dfrac{0-(-2)}{2-(-2)}$

$= \dfrac{2}{4}$

$= \dfrac{1}{2}$

$-5 = \dfrac{1}{2} \cdot 4 + b$

$-7 = b$

$y = \dfrac{1}{2}x - 7$

43. $m = \dfrac{-1-1}{-3-0} = \dfrac{-2}{-3} = \dfrac{2}{3}$ $\quad m = \dfrac{1-9}{0-12} = \dfrac{-8}{-12} = \dfrac{2}{3}$ $\quad m = \dfrac{-1-9}{-3-12} = \dfrac{-10}{-15} = \dfrac{2}{3}$

Yes, they do lie on the same line. The line is $y = \frac{2}{3}x + 1$.

44. $m = \dfrac{-2-2}{4-(-1)} = \dfrac{-4}{5}$ $\quad m = \dfrac{2-9}{-1-(-8)} = \dfrac{-7}{7} = -1$ $\quad m = \dfrac{-2-9}{4-(-8)} = \dfrac{-11}{12}$

No, they do not lie on the same line.

45. $m = \dfrac{-1-2}{-2-3} = \dfrac{-3}{-5} = \dfrac{3}{5}$ $\quad m = \dfrac{2-5}{3-7} = \dfrac{-3}{-4} = \dfrac{3}{4}$ $\quad m = \dfrac{-1-5}{-2-7} = \dfrac{-6}{-9} = \dfrac{2}{3}$

No, they do not lie on the same line.

46. $m = \dfrac{-3-13}{3-(-1)} = \dfrac{-16}{4} = -4$ $\quad m = \dfrac{13-5}{-1-1} = \dfrac{8}{-2} = -4$ $\quad m = \dfrac{-3-5}{3-1} = \dfrac{-8}{2} = -4$

$-3 = -4(3) + b$

$9 = b$

$y = -4x + 9$

Yes, they do lie on the same line. The line is $y = -4x + 9$.

47. Choose (5, 13) and (−5, −6) because the slope is more easily determined using integer numbers.

5.4 Exploring Data: Fitting a Line to Data

Communicating about Algebra

A.

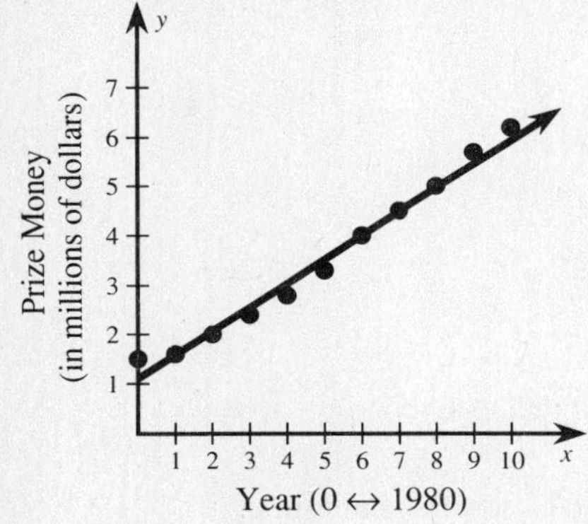

B. From the scatter plot, x and y appear to have a positive correlation.

C. See Exercise **A.**

D. (6, 4,001,450) and (2, 2,067,475)

E. $m = \dfrac{4{,}001{,}450 - 2{,}067{,}475}{6-2}$

$= 483{,}493.75$

$2{,}067{,}475 = 483{,}493.75(2) + b$

$2{,}067{,}475 = 966{,}987.5 + b$

$1{,}100{,}487.5 = b$

$y = 483{,}493.75x + 1{,}100{,}487.5$

F. In 1996, $t = 16$.

$y = 483{,}493.75(16) + 1{,}100{,}487.5$

$y = 8{,}836{,}387.5$ dollars

EXERCISES

1. The graph showing the data points for this experiment is called a scatter plot.

2. The line shown on the graph is called the best-fitting line.

3. $m = \dfrac{80.5 - 89}{0.4 - 0.9}$

$= \dfrac{-8.5}{-0.5}$

$= 17$

4. $80.5 = 17(0.4) + b$

$73.7 = b$

$y = 17x + 73.7$

5. $y = 17(0.80) + 73.7$

$y = 87.3$

It would feel like 87.3° F.

6. $90 = 17x + 73.7$

$16.3 = 17x$

$x \approx 0.96$

7. Suggest a linear relationship

8. Do not suggest a linear relationship

9. Do not suggest a linear relationship

10. Suggest a linear relationship

11. Points: $(0, -1), (3, \frac{1}{2})$

$m = \dfrac{-1 - \frac{1}{2}}{0 - 3}$

$= \dfrac{-\frac{3}{2}}{-3}$

$= \dfrac{1}{2}$

$y - (-1) = \dfrac{1}{2}(x - 0)$

$y = \dfrac{1}{2}x - 1$

There is a postive correlation.

12. Points: $(-2, -\frac{1}{2}), (0, \frac{3}{2})$

$m = \dfrac{-\frac{1}{2} - \frac{3}{2}}{-2 - 0}$

$= 1$

$y - \dfrac{3}{2} = 1(x - 0)$

$y = x + \dfrac{3}{2}$

There is a postive correlation.

13. Points: $(0, 1), (3, -1)$

$m = \dfrac{1 - (-1)}{0 - 3}$

$= -\dfrac{2}{3}$

$y - 1 = -\dfrac{2}{3}(x - 0)$

$y = -\dfrac{2}{3}x + 1$

There is a negative correlation.

14. Points: (2.0, 5.5), (4.0, 8.5)

$m = \dfrac{5.5 - 8.5}{2.0 - 4.0}$

$= \dfrac{3}{2}$

$y - 5.5 = \dfrac{3}{2}(x - 2.0)$

$y = \dfrac{3}{2}x + \dfrac{5}{2}$

x and y have a positive correlation.

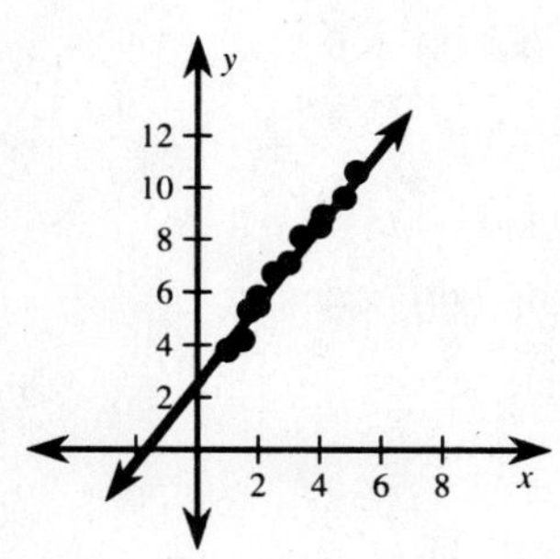

15. Points: (4.0, 8.5), (6.0, 5.5)

$$m = \frac{8.5 - 5.5}{4.0 - 6.0}$$
$$= -\frac{3}{2}$$
$$y - 8.5 = -\frac{3}{2}(x - 4.0)$$
$$y = -\frac{3}{2}x + \frac{29}{2}$$

x and y have a negative correlation.

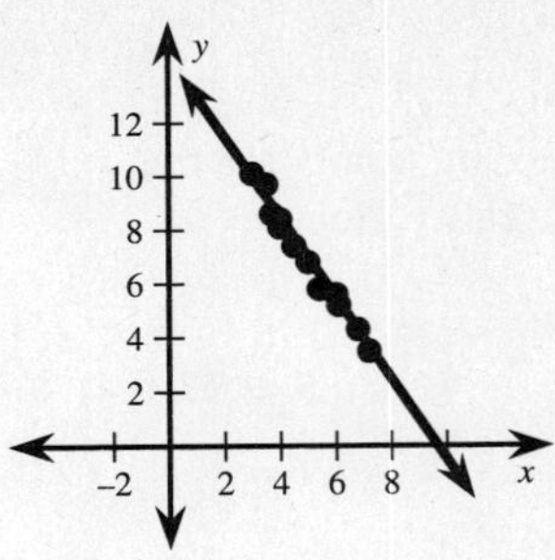

16. $m = \dfrac{200{,}000 - 80{,}000}{8 - 3}$
$$= \frac{120{,}000}{5}$$
$$= 24{,}000$$
$$80{,}000 = 24{,}000(3) + b$$
$$b = 8000$$
$$y = 24{,}000x + 8000$$
$$= 24{,}000(15) + 8000$$
$$= 368{,}000 \text{ dollars}$$

17. $m = \dfrac{95 - 155}{65 - 80}$
$$= \frac{-60}{-15}$$
$$= 4$$
$$95 = 4(65) + b$$
$$-165 = b$$
$$y = 4x - 165$$
$$= 4(85) - 165$$
$$= 340 - 165$$
$$= 175 \text{ chirps per minute}$$

18. $m = \dfrac{116{,}600{,}000 - 107{,}300{,}000}{10 - 5}$
$$= \frac{9{,}300{,}000}{5}$$
$$= 1{,}860{,}000$$
$$107{,}300{,}000 = 1{,}860{,}000(5) + b$$
$$b = 98{,}000{,}000$$
$$y = 1{,}860{,}000t + 98{,}000{,}000$$
$$= 1{,}860{,}000(30) + 98{,}000{,}000$$
$$= 153{,}800{,}000 \text{ people}$$

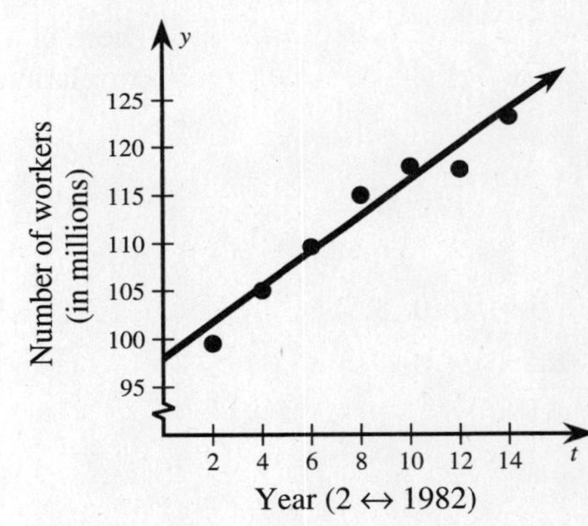

19. $m = \dfrac{80-72}{33-41}$

$= \dfrac{8}{-8}$

$= -1$

$80 = (-1)33 + b$

$113 = b$

$y = -x + 113$

$= -40 + 113$

$= 73°\text{F}$

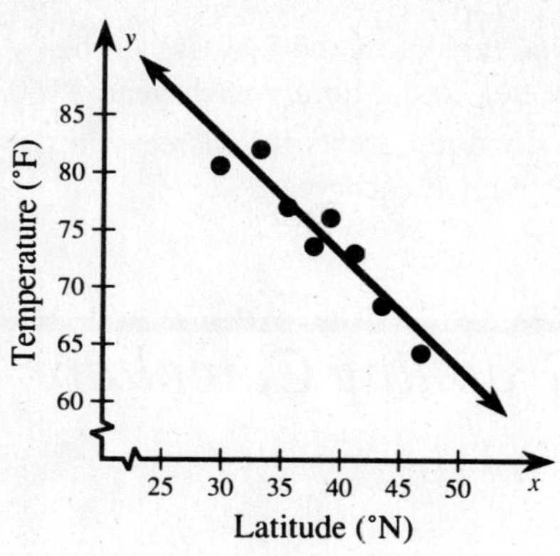

20. $m = \dfrac{4-5}{1-3}$

$= \dfrac{-1}{-2}$

$= \dfrac{1}{2}$

The slope is positive.

21. $m = \dfrac{5-1}{2-4}$

$= \dfrac{4}{-2}$

$= -2$

The slope is negative.

22. $m = \dfrac{1-8}{6-3}$

$= \dfrac{-7}{3}$

$= -\dfrac{7}{3}$

The slope is negative.

23. $m = \dfrac{2-3}{5-4}$

$= \dfrac{-1}{1}$

$= -1$

The slope is negative.

24. $m = \dfrac{5-4}{2-6}$

$= \dfrac{1}{-4}$

$= -\dfrac{1}{4}$

$5 = -\dfrac{1}{4}(2) + b$

$\dfrac{11}{2} = b$

$y = -\dfrac{1}{4}x + \dfrac{11}{2}$

25. $m = \dfrac{4-7}{1-3}$

$= \dfrac{-3}{-2}$

$= \dfrac{3}{2}$

$4 = \dfrac{3}{2}(1) + b$

$\dfrac{5}{2} = b$

$y = \dfrac{3}{2}x + \dfrac{5}{2}$

26. $m = \dfrac{7-3}{3-7}$

$= \dfrac{4}{-4}$

$= -1$

$7 = (-1)(3) + b$

$10 = b$

$y = -x + 10$

27. $m = \dfrac{6-4}{2-5}$

$= \dfrac{2}{-3}$

$= -\dfrac{2}{3}$

$6 = -\dfrac{2}{3}(2) + b$

$\dfrac{22}{3} = b$

$y = -\dfrac{2}{3}x + \dfrac{22}{3}$

28. $m = \dfrac{18{,}000 - 17{,}200}{10-5}$

$= \dfrac{800}{5}$

$= 160$

$18{,}000 = 160(10) + b$

$18{,}000 - 1600 = b$

$b = 16{,}400$

$y = 160t + 16{,}400$

29. $m = \dfrac{30.00 - 24.00}{6-3}$

$= \dfrac{6.00}{3}$

$= 2$

$30.00 = 2(6) + b$

$b = 18.00$

$y = 2t + 18$

30. The first slope represents the increase in the amount allocated to the library each year, \$160. The second slope represents the increase in the price of a new book each year, \$2.

31. The rate of increase in allocated funds in 1990 was $160 \div 18{,}000$ or 0.9%. The rate of increase of the cost of books that same year was $2 \div 38$ or 5.3%, -6 times the amount allocated.

Using a Graphing Calculator

1. $y = 0.95x + 1.4$

2. $y = -1.1x + 8.1$

Mid-Chapter SELF-TEST

1. $y = -\frac{1}{3}x + 4$

2. $m = \dfrac{1-(-3)}{2-0}$

$= \dfrac{4}{2}$

$= 2$

$y = 2x - 3$

3. $C = 0.40x + 35$

4. $4 = 3(-2) + b$

$4 = -6 + b$

$10 = b$

$y = 3x + 10$

5. $-2 = \left(-\frac{2}{3}\right)(3) + b$

$-2 = -2 + b$

$0 = b$

$y = -\frac{2}{3}x$

6. $y = 3$

7. $A = 8.14t + b$

$88.1 = 8.14(4) + b$

$55.54 = b$

$A = 8.14t + 55.54$

8. $m = \dfrac{5-1}{-3-4}$

$= \dfrac{4}{-7}$

$= -\dfrac{4}{7}$

$5 = -\dfrac{4}{7}(-3) + b$

$\dfrac{35}{7} = \dfrac{12}{7} + b$

$b = \dfrac{23}{7}$

$y = -\dfrac{4}{7}x + \dfrac{23}{7}$

9. Points: (5, 0), (0, 4)

$m = \dfrac{0-4}{5-0}$

$= -\dfrac{4}{5}$

$y = -\dfrac{4}{5}x + 4$

10. $m = \dfrac{49-77}{7-11}$

$= \dfrac{-28}{-4}$

$= 7$

$49 = 7(7) + b$

$b = 0$

$y = 7x$

$= 7(10)$

$= 70$ pounds

11. The best-fitting line varies.

$$m = \frac{3600 - 1200}{1500 - 500}$$
$$= \frac{2400}{1000}$$
$$= \frac{12}{5}$$

$$3600 = \frac{12}{5}(1500) + b$$
$$0 = b$$

$$y = \frac{12}{5}x$$
$$= \frac{12}{5} \cdot 400$$
$$= 960 \text{ square centimeters}$$

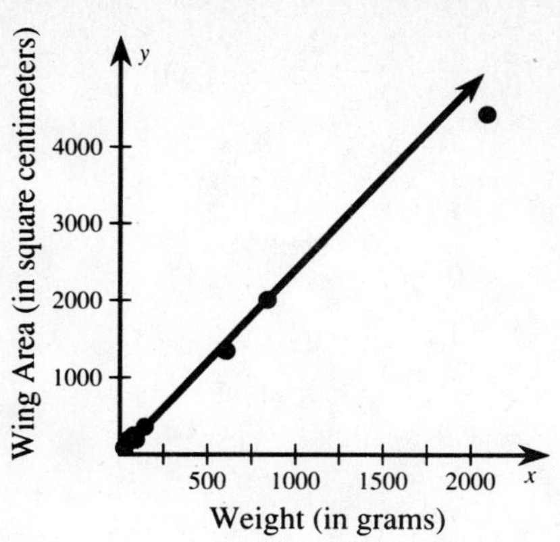

5.5 Standard Form of a Linear Equation

Communicating about Algebra

A. $4x + 3y = 12$

B. $y = -\frac{4}{3}x + 4$

C.

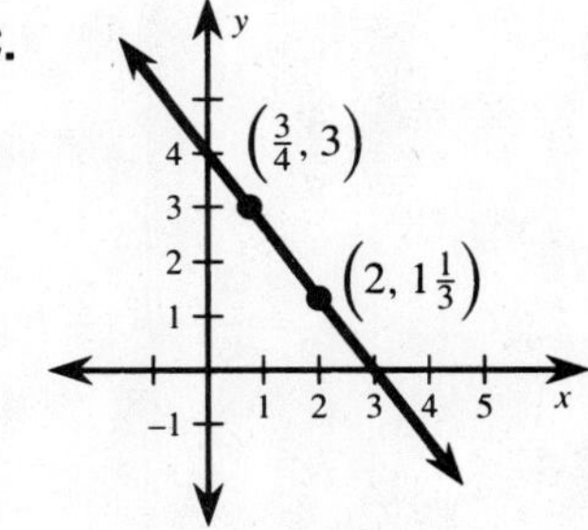

D. $\left(\frac{3}{4}, 3\right), \left(2, 1\frac{1}{3}\right)$

E. A package that contains all peat moss would have a volume of $\frac{12}{3}$ or 4 cubic feet. A package that contains all topsoil would have a volume of $\frac{12}{4}$ or 3 cubic feet. So any 12 pound package of potting soil would have a volume greater than 3 cubic feet and less than 4 cubic feet.

EXERCISES

1. Slope-intercept form

2. Standard form

3.
$$y = -\frac{1}{2} + 5$$
$$2y = -x + 10$$
$$x + 2y = 10$$

4. $y = -\frac{2}{3}x + 3$ for graphing

$2x + 3y = 9$ when creating a model

5. $1.25x + 2y = 10$

6. $2y = 10 - 1.25x$

$y = 5 - 0.625x$

Tomatoes, x	0 lb	1.6 lb	4 lb	6.4 lb	8 lb
Avocadoes, y	5 lb	4 lb	2.5 lb	1 lb	0 lb

7. $3x - y - 6 = 0$

$3x - y = 6$

8. $x + 2y - 4 = 0$

$x + 2y = 4$

9. $-4x + 3y + 18 = 0$

$-4x + 3y = -18$

$4x - 3y = 18$

10. $2x - 3y - 12 = 0$

$2x - 3y = 12$

11. $x - 3 = 0$

$x = 3$

12. $y + 4 = 0$

$y = -4$

13. $y = -3x + 4$

$3x + y = 4$

14. $y = 2x - 7$

$-2x + y = -7$

15. $y = -\frac{1}{3}x - 2$

$3y = -x - 6$

$x + 3y = -6$

16. $y = -\frac{3}{4}x + \frac{5}{4}$

$4y = -3x + 5$

$3x + 4y = 5$

17. $y = -\frac{1}{8}x + \frac{3}{8}$

$8y = -x + 3$

$x + 8y = 3$

18. $y = -0.4x + 1.2$

$10y = -4x + 12$

$4x + 10y = 12$

$2x + 5y = 6$

19. $x = -1$

$y = 3$

20. $x = 2$

$y = -4$

21. $3 = (-1)(-4) + b$

$-1 = b$

$y = -x - 1$

$x + y = -1$

22. $5 = 2(0) + b$

$5 = b$

$y = 2x + 5$

$-2x + y = 5$

23. $-1 = 0(3) + b$

$-1 = b$

$y = 0 \cdot x - 1$

$y = -1$

24. $-2 = \frac{1}{2}(-4) + b$

$-2 = -2 + b$

$0 = b$

$y = \frac{1}{2}x$

$2y = x$

$x - 2y = 0$

25. $m = \dfrac{4-6}{2-5}$

$= \dfrac{-2}{-3}$

$= \dfrac{2}{3}$

$4 = \dfrac{2}{3}(2) + b$

$4 - \dfrac{4}{3} = b$

$b = \dfrac{8}{3}$

$y = \dfrac{2}{3}x + \dfrac{8}{3}$

$3y = 2x + 8$

$-2x + 3y = 8$

26. $m = \dfrac{3-7}{-3-6}$

$= \dfrac{-4}{-9}$

$= \dfrac{4}{9}$

$3 = \dfrac{4}{9}(-3) + b$

$3 + \dfrac{4}{3} = b$

$\dfrac{13}{3} = b$

$y = \dfrac{4}{9}x + \dfrac{13}{3}$

$9y = 4x + 39$

$-4x + 9y = 39$

27. $m = \dfrac{-1-(-3)}{-2-2}$

$= \dfrac{2}{-4}$

$= -\dfrac{1}{2}$

$-1 = -\dfrac{1}{2}(-2) + b$

$-2 = b$

$y = -\dfrac{1}{2}x - 2$

$2y = -x - 4$

$x + 2y = -4$

28. $m = \dfrac{4-(-6)}{-5-2}$

$= \dfrac{10}{-7}$

$= -\dfrac{10}{7}$

$4 = -\dfrac{10}{7}(-5) + b$

$\dfrac{28}{7} - \dfrac{50}{7} = b$

$b = -\dfrac{22}{7}$

$y = -\dfrac{10}{7}x - \dfrac{22}{7}$

$7y = -10x - 22$

$10x + 7y = -22$

29. $3p + 4c = 24$

30. $4c = -3p + 24$

$c = -\frac{3}{4}p + 6$

Pounds of peanuts, *p*	0	2	4	6	8
Pounds of cashews, *c*	6	$4\frac{1}{2}$	3	$1\frac{1}{2}$	0

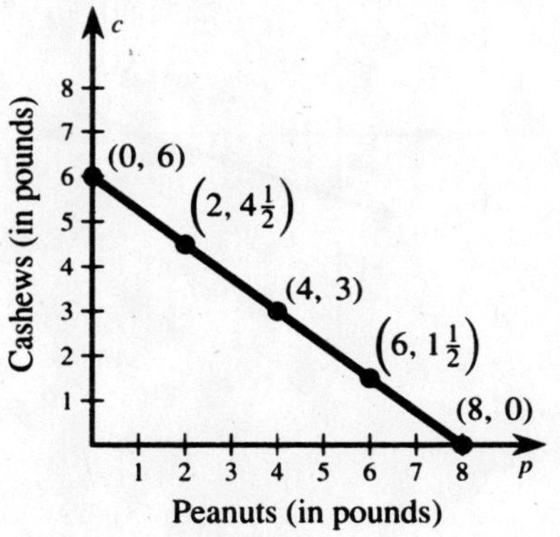

31. $4x + 6y = 48$

32. $6y = -4x + 48$

$y = -\frac{2}{3}x + 8$

Pounds of \$4 seed, *x*	0	3	6	9	12
Pounds of \$6 seed, *y*	8	6	4	2	0

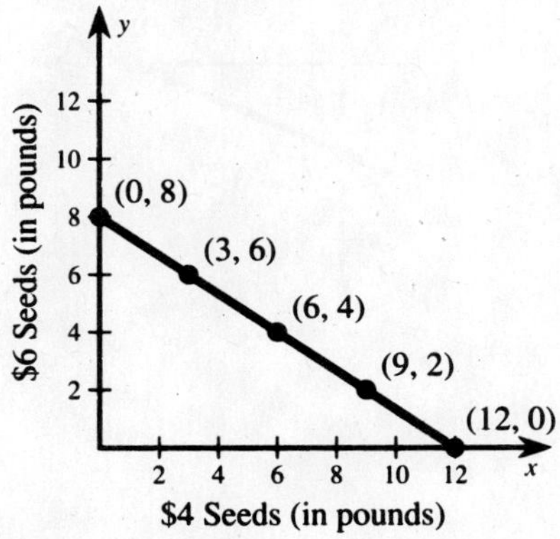

33. $x + y = 60$

34.

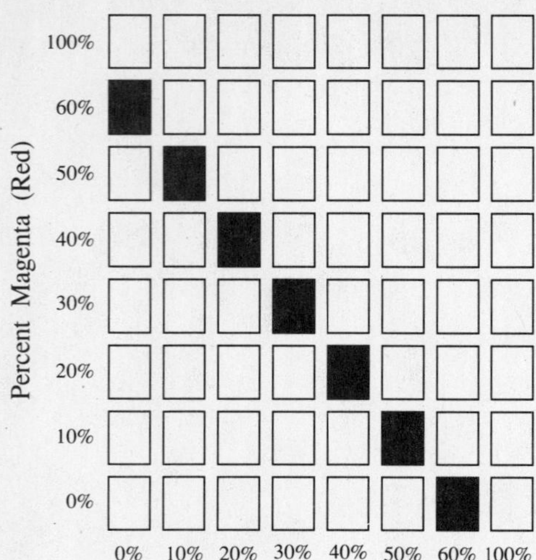

As the percent of red, x, increases, the percent of blue, y, decreases. When the percent of blue, y, increases, the percent of red, x, decreases.

35. $2x + y = 7$

$y = -2x + 7$

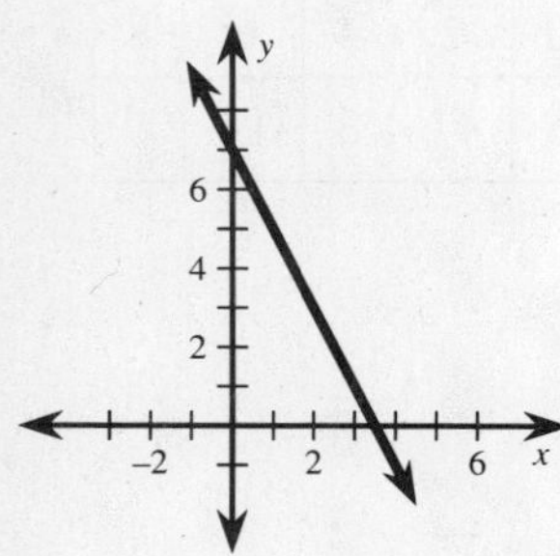

36. $x + 2y = 6$

$2y = -x + 6$

$y = -\frac{1}{2}x + 3$

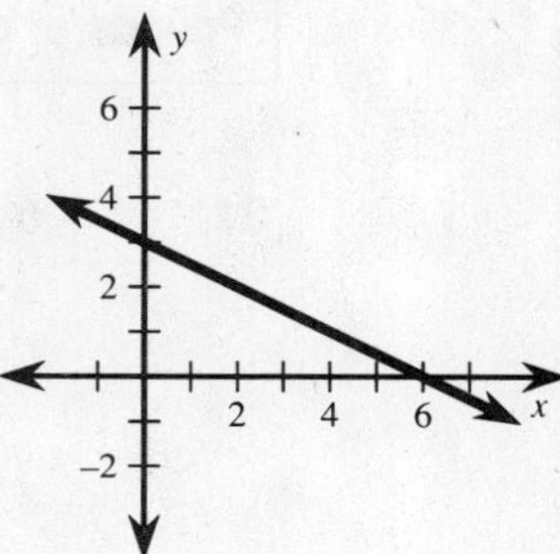

37. $-x + 3y = -6$

$3y = x - 6$

$y = \frac{1}{3}x - 2$

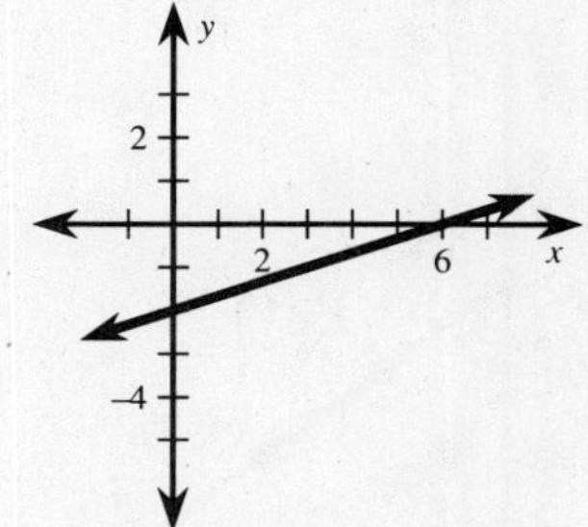

38. $6x - 2y = 1$

$-2y = -6x + 1$

$y = 3x - \frac{1}{2}$

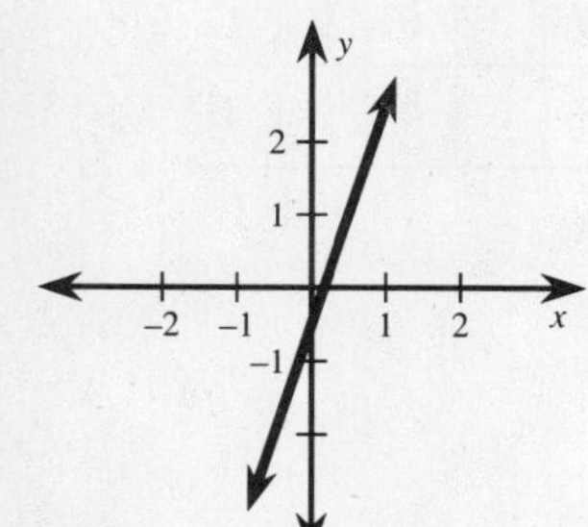

39. $2x + 3y = 6$

$3y = -2x + 6$

$y = -\frac{2}{3}x + 2$

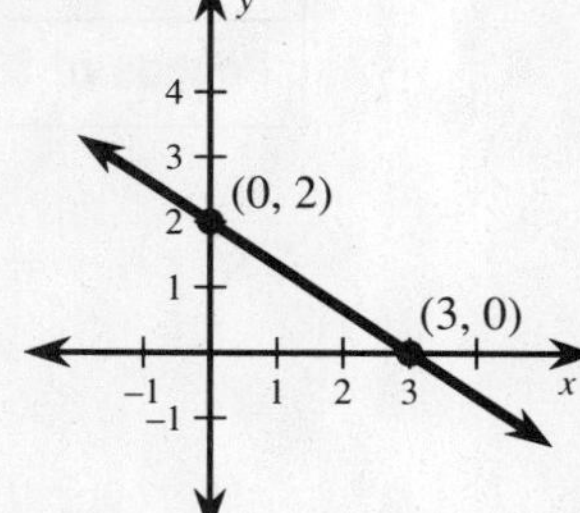

40. $3x - 7y = 21$

$-7y = -3x + 21$

$y = \frac{3}{7}x - 3$

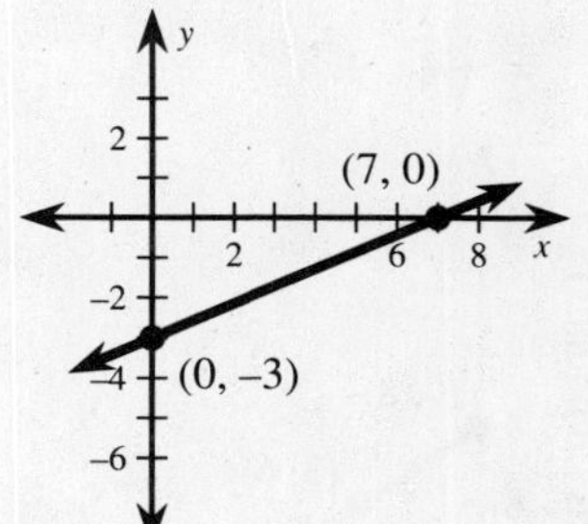

41. $-x + 4y = 8$

$4y = x + 8$

$y = \frac{1}{4}x + 2$

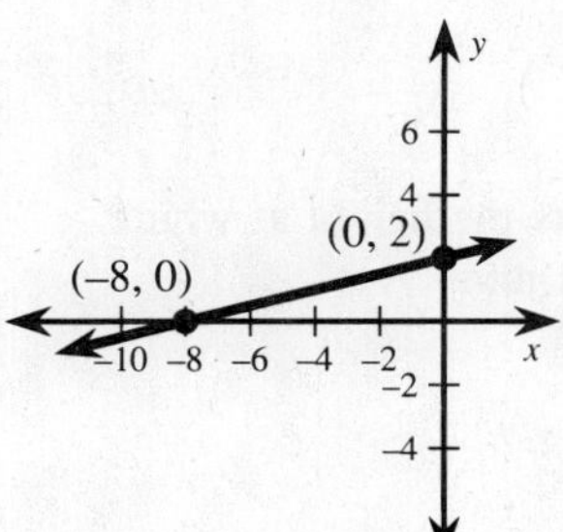

42. $-5x - 8y = 40$

$-8y = 5x + 40$

$y = -\frac{5}{8}x - 5$

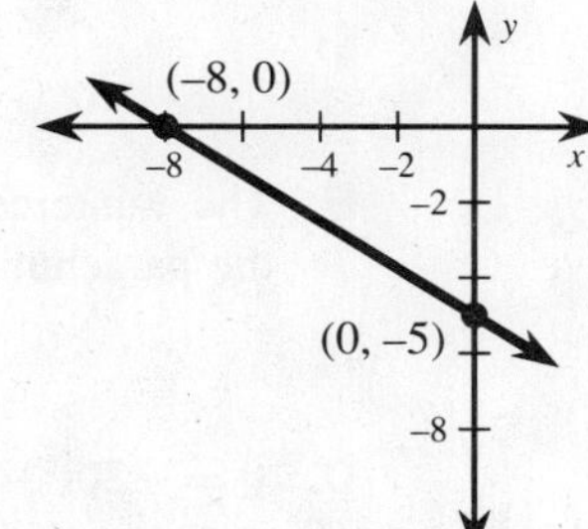

43. $m = \dfrac{52 - 12}{6 - 1}$

$= \dfrac{40}{5}$

$= 8$

$12 = 8(1) + b$

$4 = b$

$y = 8x + 4$

$-8x + y = 4$

44. $m = \dfrac{2 - 2.25}{2 - 3}$

$= \dfrac{1}{4}$

$2 = \dfrac{1}{4}(2) + b$

$\dfrac{3}{2} = b$

$y = \dfrac{1}{4}x + \dfrac{3}{2}$

$4y = x + 6$

$-x + 4y = 6$

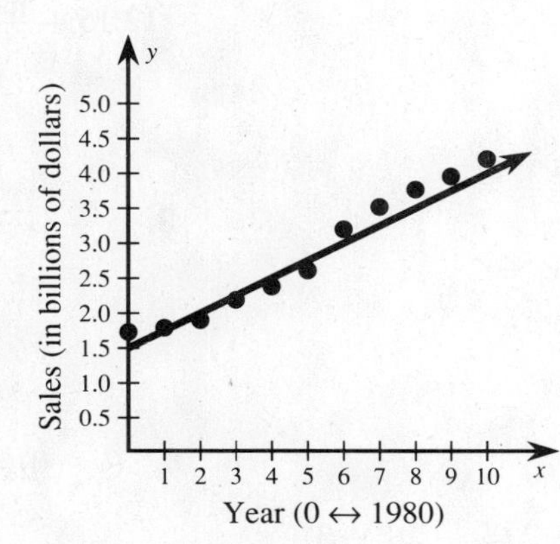

45. $2x + 7 \cdot 0 = 14$

$x = 7$

(7, 0)

46. $2 \cdot 0 + 7y = 14$

$y = 2$

(0, 2)

47. $2x + 7y = 14$

$\frac{1}{14}(2x) + \frac{1}{14}(7y) = \frac{1}{14}(14)$

$\frac{1}{7}x + \frac{1}{2}y = 1$

48. The denominator of the coefficient of x is the x-intercept; the denominator of the coefficient of y is the y-intercept.

49. $\dfrac{x}{2} + \dfrac{y}{3} = 1$

$3x + 2y = 6$

5.6 Point-Slope Form of the Equation of a Line

Communicating about Algebra

A. The slope represents the number of feet per second the parachutist is falling. It is negative because the parachutist is falling.

B. The y-intercept represents the height at which the parachutist began his jump.

C. $y = -20(30) + 2160$

$y = 1560$ feet

D. $0 = -20t + 2160$

$t = 108$ seconds

$12{:}15 + \frac{108}{60} = 12{:}16{:}48$

EXERCISES

1. Point-slope form

2. $m = 2$

$x_1 = 2$

$y_1 = -3$

3. $y - (-3) = 2(x - 2)$

$y + 3 = 2x - 4$

$y = 2x - 7$

4. $y - 4 = -\frac{1}{2}(x + 2)$

$y - 4 = -\frac{1}{2}x - 1$

$y = -\frac{1}{2}x + 3$

5. a. $(-1,\ 6)$

$6 + 2 \stackrel{?}{=} -2(-1 - 3)$ $\qquad$ $2 + 2 \stackrel{?}{=} -2(2 - 3)$

$8 \stackrel{?}{=} -2(-4)$ $\qquad$ $4 \stackrel{?}{=} -2(-1)$

$8 = 8$ $\qquad$ $4 \neq 2$

Therefore, only the point $(-1,\ 6)$ lies on the line.

6. $(y - 0) = \dfrac{62}{\frac{1}{2}}(t - 0)$

$y = 124t$

7. $300 = 124t$

$t = \frac{300}{124}$

≈ 2.4 hours

The mountain climber will reach the top of the cliff about 2:25.

8. The slope, 124, represents the number of feet climbed in an hour.

9. $y - 3 = \frac{1}{3}(x - 1)$

$y = \frac{1}{3}x - \frac{1}{3} + 3$

$y = \frac{1}{3}x + \frac{8}{3}$

10. $y - 4 = -2(x - 2)$

$y = -2x + 4 + 4$

$y = -2x + 8$

11. $y - 2 = -1[x - (-1)]$

$y - 2 = -1(x + 1)$

$y = -x - 1 + 2$

$y = -x + 1$

12. $y - 3 = 2[x - (-2)]$
$y - 3 = 2(x + 2)$
$y = 2x + 4 + 3$
$y = 2x + 7$

13. $y - (-1) = \frac{1}{2}(x - 1)$
$y + 1 = \frac{1}{2}(x - 1)$
$y = \frac{1}{2}x - \frac{1}{2} - 1$
$y = \frac{1}{2}x - \frac{3}{2}$

14. $y - (-2) = -\frac{1}{2}(x - 3)$
$y + 2 = -\frac{1}{2}(x - 3)$
$y = -\frac{1}{2}x + \frac{3}{2} - 2$
$y = -\frac{1}{2}x - \frac{1}{2}$

15. $m = \dfrac{-2 - 2}{3 - 0}$
$= -\dfrac{4}{3}$

$y - (-2) = -\dfrac{4}{3}(x - 3)$

$y + 2 = -\dfrac{4}{3}(x - 3)$ or $y - 2 = -\dfrac{4}{3}(x - 0)$

16. $m = \dfrac{0 - (-2)}{-4 - 2}$
$= -\dfrac{1}{3}$

$y - 0 = \dfrac{1}{3}[x - (-4)]$ or $y - (-2) = \dfrac{1}{3}(x - 2)$

$y - 0 = \dfrac{1}{3}(x + 4)$ $\quad y + 2 = \dfrac{1}{3}(x - 2)$

17. $m = \dfrac{-3 - 0}{0 - 5}$
$= \dfrac{3}{5}$

$y - (-3) = \dfrac{3}{5}(x - 0)$

$y + 3 = \dfrac{3}{5}(x - 0)$ or $y - 0 = \dfrac{3}{5}(x - 5)$

18. $m = \dfrac{0 - 4}{-1 - 2}$
$= \dfrac{4}{3}$

$y - 0 = \dfrac{4}{3}[x - (-1)]$

$y - 0 = \dfrac{4}{3}(x + 1)$ or $y - 4 = \dfrac{4}{3}(x - 2)$

19. $y - 0 = \dfrac{1.7 \cdot 470}{1.25}(x - 0)$

$y = \dfrac{799}{1.25}(x - 0)$

$y = 639.2x$

$470(1.7 + 3.2) = 639.2x$

$2303 = 639.2x$

$x \approx 3.6$ or 3 hours, 36 minutes

You will reach Miami at about 11:36 A.M.

20.

Mrs. Peacock:	$y = x + 7$
Prof. Plum:	$y = x + 2$
Mrs. White:	$y = x - 1$
Miss Scarlet:	$y = -x + 22$
Col. Mustard:	$y = -x + 14$

21. Slope-intercept form; the slope and y-intercept are given.

$y = \frac{2}{3}x + 4$

22. Point-slope form; two points are given, so the slope can be determined.

$m = \dfrac{3 - 4}{1 - (-2)}$
$= \dfrac{-1}{3}$

$y - 3 = -\dfrac{1}{3}(x - 1)$

23. Slope-intercept form; the slope and y-intercept are given.

$y = 2x - 3$

24. Vertical line; the points have the same x-coordinate.

$x = 1$

25. Point-slope form; the slope and a point are given.

$y - (-4) = 1(x - 1)$

$y + 4 = x - 1$

26. Horizontal line; the line has a slope of 0.

$y = 5$

27. b. **28.** d. **29.** c. **30.** a.

31. $y - 3 = -\frac{5}{3}[x - (-6)]$

$y - 3 = -\frac{5}{3}x - 10$

$y = -\frac{5}{3}x - 7$

Integer coordinates fall five units up and three units left of the previous integer coordinate or five units down and three units to the right. The two closest points are $(-9, 8)$ and $(-3, -2)$.

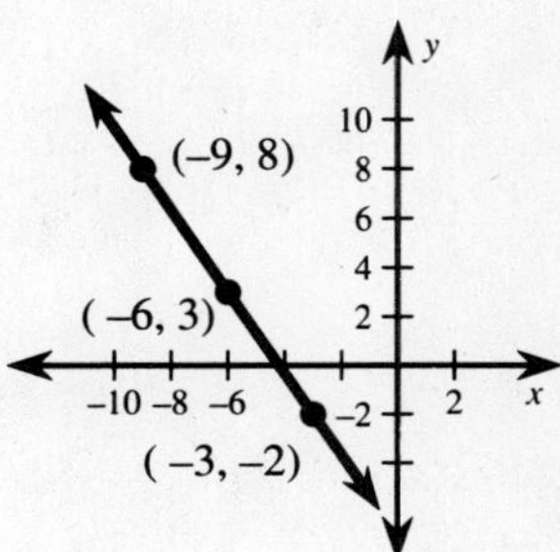

32. $m = \dfrac{2.9 - 3.9}{5 - 10}$

$= \dfrac{-1}{-5}$

$= \dfrac{1}{5}$

$(y - 2.9) = \dfrac{1}{5}(t - 5)$

$y = \dfrac{1}{5}t - 1 + 2.9$

$y = \dfrac{1}{5}t + 1.9$

$y = \dfrac{1}{5}(15) + 1.9$

$y = 3 + 1.9$

$y = 4.9$ million

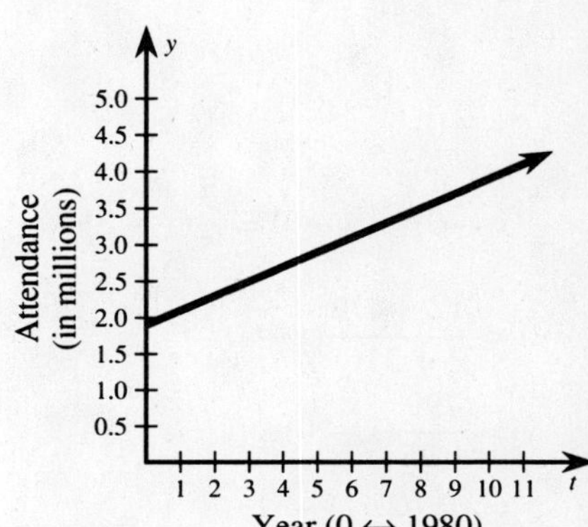

Mixed **REVIEW**

1. $\frac{1}{2}\left(x - \frac{1}{2}\right) = \frac{1}{2}\left(\frac{1}{4} - \frac{1}{2}\right)$

$= \frac{1}{2}\left(-\frac{1}{4}\right)$

$= -\frac{1}{8}$

2. $\frac{3}{4}(3y - 2) = \frac{3}{4}\left(3 \cdot \frac{1}{3} - 2\right)$

$= \frac{3}{4}(1 - 2)$

$= \frac{3}{4}(-1)$

$= -\frac{3}{4}$

3. $3a + 2b = 4$

$2b = -3a + 4$

$b = -\frac{3}{2}a + 2$

4. $8m - 9n = 10$

$8m = 9n + 10$

$m = \frac{1}{8}(9n + 10)$

5. $x(x - 3) < 21$

$7(7 - 3) \stackrel{?}{<} 21$

$7 \cdot 4 \stackrel{?}{<} 21$

$28 \not< 21$

7 is not a solution.

6. $\frac{1}{4}(10 - x) \geq 4$

$\frac{1}{4}[10 - (-6)] \stackrel{?}{\geq} 4$

$\frac{1}{4}(16) \stackrel{?}{\geq} 4$

$4 \geq 4$

-6 is a solution.

7. $3 \div 4 + 2 = \frac{3}{4} + 2$
$= 2\frac{3}{4}$

$3 \div (4 + 2) = 3 \div 6$
$= \frac{3}{6}$
$= \frac{1}{2}$

No, they are not equivalent.

8. $m = \dfrac{1-3}{-2-(-1)}$
$= \dfrac{-2}{-1}$
$= 2$

$y - 1 = 2[x - (-2)]$
$y - 1 = 2x + 4$
$y = 2x + 5$

9. $m = \dfrac{0-4}{2-(-3)}$
$= -\dfrac{4}{5}$

$y - 0 = -\dfrac{4}{5}(x - 2)$
$y = -\dfrac{4}{5}x + \dfrac{8}{5}$

10. $y - 4 = 4(x - 5)$

11. $y = 5x - 3$

5.7 Problem Solving Using Linear Models

Communicating about Algebra

A. No; the y-intercept is negative.

B. $y = 292{,}500(10) - 580{,}000$
$= 2{,}345{,}000$

There were 2,345,000 personal computers used in classrooms in 1990.

C. The number introduced each year is the slope of the model, 292,500.

EXERCISES

1. $y = 0.02x + 1000$

2. $y = 0.02(25{,}000) + 1000$
$y = 500 + 1000$
$y = 1500$ dollars

3.

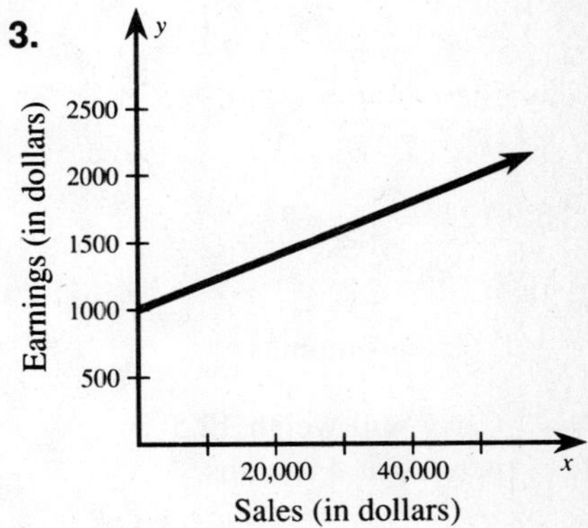

4. Slope: 0.02
The slope represents the commission rate.

5. y-intercept: 1000
The y-intercept is the amount of base pay.

6. $2000 = 0.02x + 1000$
$1000 = 0.02x$
$1000 = \frac{2}{100}x$
$x = 1000\left(\frac{100}{2}\right)$
$x = 50{,}000$ dollars

7. $y = 0.15x + 750$

8. $y = 0.15(5000) + 750$

$y = 750 + 750$

$y = 1500$ dollars

9.

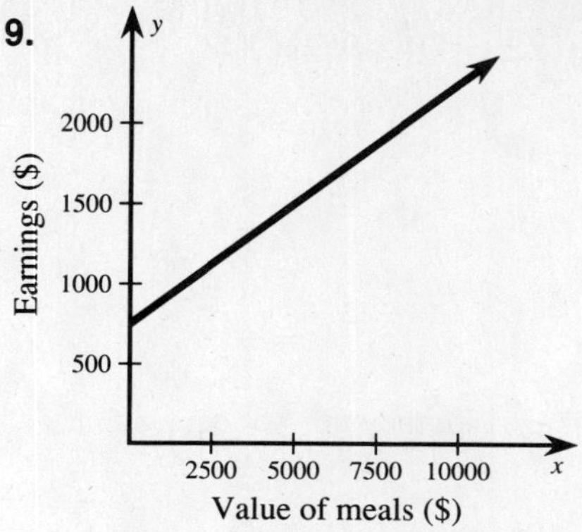

10. Slope: 0.15

The slope represents the rate of earning based on the value of the meals served.

11. y-intercept: 750

The y-intercept is the amount of base pay.

12. $2000 = 0.15x + 750$

$1250 = \frac{15}{100}x$

$x = 1250\left(\frac{100}{15}\right)$

$x = 8333.33$ dollars

13. $\left(0,\ 7\frac{1}{2}\right), \left(12,\ 22\frac{1}{2}\right)$

$$m = \frac{7\frac{1}{2} - 22\frac{1}{2}}{0 - 12} = \frac{-15}{-12} = \frac{5}{4}$$

$$y - 7\frac{1}{2} = \frac{5}{4}(x - 0)$$

$$y = \frac{5}{4}x + 7\frac{1}{2}$$

14.

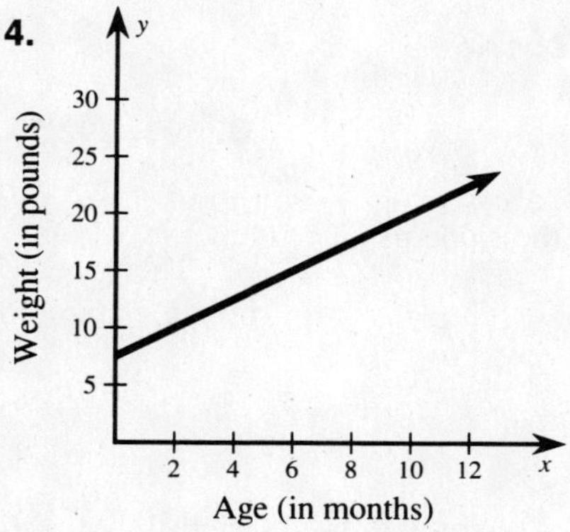

The slope represents the amount of weight gained per month.

15. y-intercept: $7\frac{1}{2}$

The y-intercept represents the weight at birth.

16. $12\frac{1}{2} = \frac{5}{4}x + 7\frac{1}{2}$

$5 = \frac{5}{4}x$

$x = 4$ months

Carly will weigh 12.5 pounds at 4 months.

17. $4.50(48) + 6.00x = 288$

$216 + 6.00x = 288$

$6.00x = 72$

$x = 12$ nonstudent tickets

Twelve nonstudent tickets were purchased.

18. $0.055x + 0.06(400) = 40.50$

$0.055x + 24 = 40.50$

$0.055x = 16.50$

$x = 300$ dollars

He has \$300 in his savings account.

19. $2x + y = 84$

20. $y = -2x + 84$

21.

Field goals, x	20	25	30	35	40
Free throws, y	44	34	24	14	4

$y = -2(20) + 84$, $y = 44$

$y = -2(25) + 84$, $y = 34$

$y = -2(30) + 84$, $y = 24$

$y = -2(35) + 84$, $y = 14$

$y = -2(40) + 84$, $y = 4$

22.

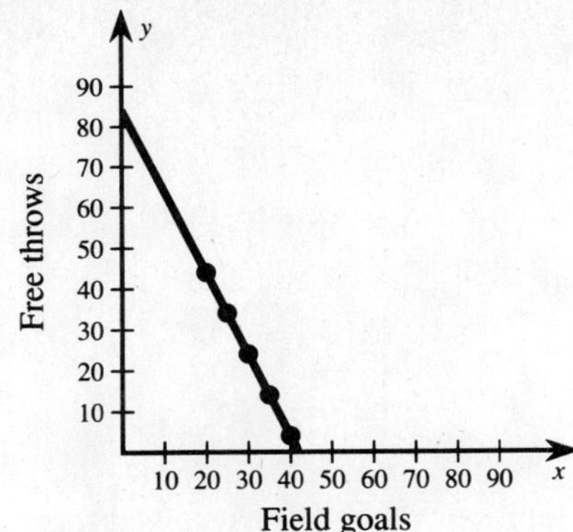

23. (0, 58), (18, 46)

$$m = \frac{58 - 46}{0 - 18} = \frac{12}{-18} = -\frac{2}{3}$$

$$y = -\frac{2}{3}t + 58$$

24.

Year, t	0	5	10	15	20
Model, y	58%	54.7%	51.3%	48%	44.7%

$y = -\frac{2}{3} \cdot 0 + 58$

$y = 58\%$

$y = -\frac{2}{3}(5) + 58$

$y = -\frac{10}{3} + \frac{174}{3}$

$y = \frac{164}{3}$

$\approx 54.7\%$

$y = -\frac{2}{3}(10) + 58$

$y = -\frac{20}{3} + \frac{174}{3}$

$y = \frac{154}{3}$

$\approx 51.3\%$

$y = -\frac{2}{3}(15) + 58$

$y = -10 + 58$

$y = 48\%$

$y = -\frac{2}{3}(20) + 58$

$y = -\frac{40}{3} + \frac{174}{3}$

$y = \frac{134}{3}$

$\approx 44.7\%$

25. See graph for Exercise 26.

26. Points: (0, 42), (18, 54)

$$m = \frac{42 - 54}{0 - 18} = \frac{-12}{-18} = \frac{2}{3}$$

$$y = \frac{2}{3}t + 42$$

The slopes of the equations are opposites and the y-intercepts sum to 100.

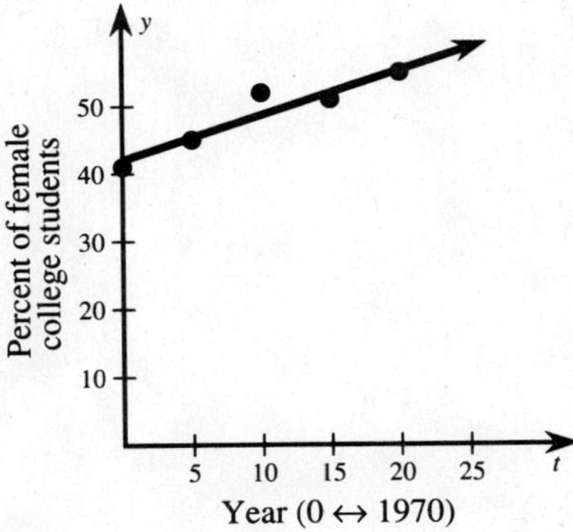

27. Points: (0, 90), (8, 160)

$$m = \frac{90 - 160}{0 - 8} = \frac{-70}{-8} = \frac{70}{8} = \frac{35}{4}$$

$$y = \frac{35}{4}t + 90$$

28.

Year, t	0	2	5	8	10
Model, y	90	107.5	133.75	160	177.5

$y = \frac{35}{4} \cdot 0 + 90$
$y = 90$

$y = \frac{35}{4} \cdot 2 + 90$
$y = \frac{35}{2} + \frac{180}{2}$
$y = \frac{215}{2}$
$= 107.5$

$y = \frac{35}{4} \cdot 5 + 90$
$y = \frac{175}{4} + \frac{360}{4}$
$y = \frac{535}{4}$
$= 133.75$

$y = \frac{35}{4} \cdot 8 + 90$
$y = 70 + 90$
$y = 160$

$y = \frac{35}{4} \cdot 10 + 90$
$y = \frac{175}{2} + \frac{180}{2}$
$y = \frac{355}{2}$
$= 177.5$

29. **b.** The slope represents the amount paid back each week.

30. **c.** The slope represents the salary received for each number of units produced per hour.

31. **a.** The slope represents the amount received for each mile driven.

32.

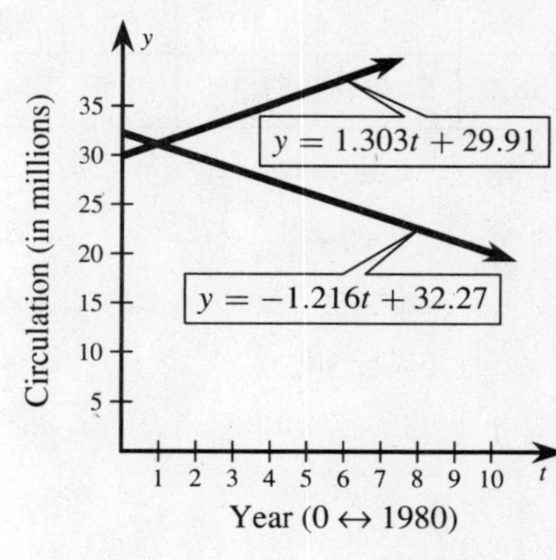

33. The slope represents the rate of change of circulation per year.
Morning newspapers had an increasing circulation and evening papers had a decreasing circulation.

34. In 1983 and 1989, there were more morning papers sold.

35. The two circulations were the same in 1981.

Chapter REVIEW

1. $y = 2x - 6$

2. $y = -x + 3$

3. $y = -\frac{1}{3}x - 1$

4. $y = \frac{2}{5}x - 5$

5. Points: (0, 3), (2, 0)

$m = \frac{3-0}{0-2}$
$= -\frac{3}{2}$

$y = -\frac{3}{2}x + 3$

6. Points: (0, −2), (1, 0)

$m = \frac{-2-0}{0-1}$
$= 2$

$y = 2x - 2$

7. Points: (0, 5), (−4, 0)

$m = \frac{5-0}{0-(-4)}$
$= \frac{5}{4}$

$y = \frac{5}{4}x + 5$

8. Points: (1, −3), (−5, 0)

$m = \frac{-3-0}{1-(-5)}$
$= -\frac{1}{2}$

$y - 0 = -\frac{1}{2}[x - (-5)]$
$y = -\frac{1}{2}x - \frac{5}{2}$

9. Slope: -4

y-intercept: 3

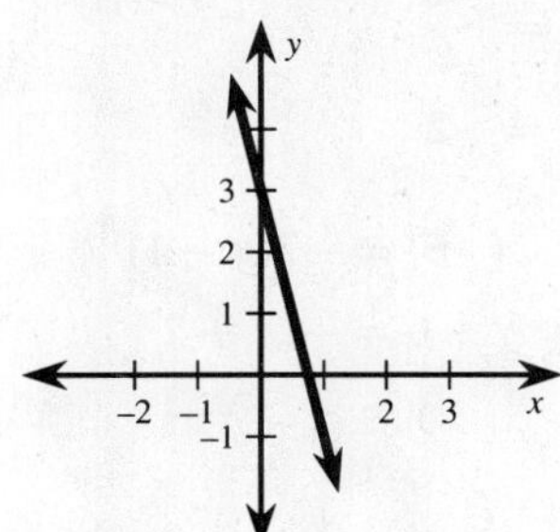
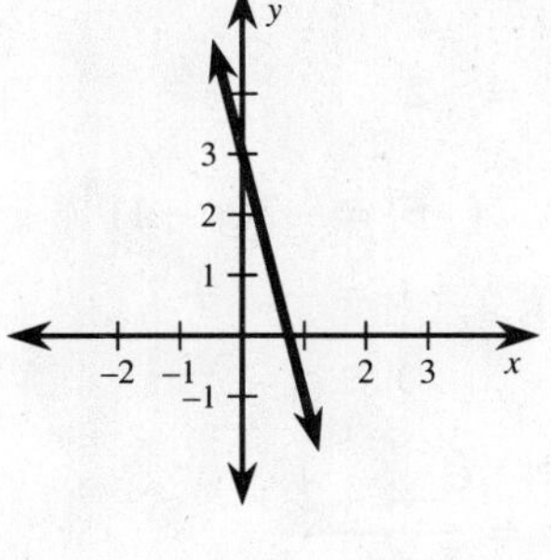

10. Slope: 1

y-intercept: -7

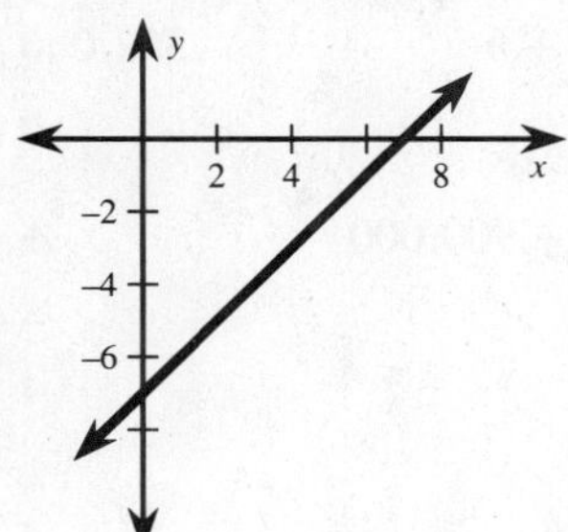

11. $y = -3000x + 32{,}000$

12. $y = -3000(6) + 32{,}000$

$y = -18{,}000 + 32{,}000$

$y = 14{,}000$ dollars

The value of the car will be \$14,000 in 1996.

13. $y - (-1) = 3(x - 6)$

$y + 1 = 3x - 18$

$y = 3x - 19$

14. $y - 4 = 2[x - (-9)]$

$y - 4 = 2(x + 9)$

$y - 4 = 2x + 18$

$y = 2x + 22$

15. $y - 2 = -1[x - (-3)]$

$y - 2 = -x - 3$

$y = -x - 1$

16. $y - (-6) = \frac{1}{3}[x - (-1)]$

$y + 6 = \frac{1}{3}x + \frac{1}{3}$

$y = \frac{1}{3}x - \frac{17}{3}$

17. $y = 4$

18. $y - (-1) = -3(x - 2)$

$y + 1 = -3x + 6$

$y = -3x + 5$

19. $y - (-3) = \frac{1}{5}(x - 5)$

$y + 3 = \frac{1}{5}x - 1$

$y = \frac{1}{5}x - 4$

20. $y - (-4) = \frac{1}{2}(x - 2)$

$y + 4 = \frac{1}{2}x - 1$

$y = \frac{1}{2}x - 5$

21. Points: (0, 3), (4, 0)

$m = \dfrac{3 - 0}{0 - 4}$

$= -\dfrac{3}{4}$

$y = -\dfrac{3}{4}x + 3$

22. Points: $(-2, 0)$, $(0, -1)$

$m = \dfrac{0 - (-1)}{-2 - 0}$

$= -\dfrac{1}{2}$

$y = -\dfrac{1}{2}x - 1$

23. Points: $(-2, -2)$, $(0, 6)$

$m = \dfrac{-2 - 6}{-2 - 0}$

$= 4$

$y = 4x + 6$

24. $y - (-6) = -1(x - 2)$

$y + 6 = -x + 2$

$y = -x - 4$

25. $y - 2 = 3[x - (-1)]$

$y - 2 = 3x + 3$

$y = 3x + 5$

26.
$$\begin{aligned} P &= 50{,}000t + b \\ 1{,}300{,}000 &= 50{,}000(8) + b \\ 1{,}300{,}000 &= 400{,}000 + b \\ b &= 900{,}000 \end{aligned}$$
$$P = 50{,}000t + 900{,}000$$

27.
$$\begin{aligned} A &= 32{,}000t + b \\ 352{,}000 &= 32{,}000(2) + b \\ 352{,}000 &= 64{,}000 + b \\ b &= 288{,}000 \end{aligned}$$
$$A = 32{,}000t + 288{,}000$$

28.
$$\begin{aligned} m &= \frac{-6-2}{1-(-3)} \\ &= \frac{-8}{4} \\ &= -2 \end{aligned}$$
$$\begin{aligned} y-(-6) &= -2(x-1) \\ y+6 &= -2x+2 \\ y &= -2x-4 \end{aligned}$$

29.
$$\begin{aligned} m &= \frac{8-(-1)}{1-(-2)} \\ &= \frac{9}{3} \\ &= 3 \end{aligned}$$
$$\begin{aligned} y-8 &= 3(x-1) \\ y-8 &= 3x-3 \\ y &= 3x+5 \end{aligned}$$

30.
$$\begin{aligned} m &= \frac{5-1}{2-(-4)} \\ &= \frac{4}{6} \\ &= \frac{2}{3} \end{aligned}$$
$$\begin{aligned} y-5 &= \frac{2}{3}(x-2) \\ y-5 &= \frac{2}{3}x - \frac{4}{3} \\ y &= \frac{2}{3}x + \frac{11}{3} \end{aligned}$$

31.
$$\begin{aligned} m &= \frac{-4-2}{3-(-6)} \\ &= \frac{-6}{9} \\ &= -\frac{2}{3} \end{aligned}$$
$$\begin{aligned} y-(-4) &= -\frac{2}{3}(x-3) \\ y+4 &= -\frac{2}{3}x+2 \\ y &= -\frac{2}{3}x-2 \end{aligned}$$

32.
$$\begin{aligned} m &= \frac{-3-(-1)}{-3-3} \\ &= \frac{-2}{-6} \\ &= \frac{1}{3} \end{aligned}$$
$$\begin{aligned} y-(-1) &= \frac{1}{3}(x-3) \\ y &= \frac{1}{3}x-2 \end{aligned}$$

33.
$$\begin{aligned} m &= \frac{3-(-2)}{-1-4} \\ &= \frac{5}{-5} \\ &= -1 \end{aligned}$$
$$\begin{aligned} y-(-2) &= -1(x-4) \\ y &= -x+2 \end{aligned}$$

34.
$$\begin{aligned} m &= \frac{3-1}{-4-4} \\ &= \frac{2}{-8} \\ &= -\frac{1}{4} \end{aligned}$$
$$\begin{aligned} y-3 &= -\frac{1}{4}[x-(-4)] \\ y &= -\frac{1}{4}x+2 \end{aligned}$$

35.
$$\begin{aligned} m &= \frac{-7-(-3)}{-2-6} \\ &= \frac{-4}{-8} \\ &= \frac{1}{2} \end{aligned}$$
$$\begin{aligned} y-(-3) &= \frac{1}{2}(x-6) \\ y &= \frac{1}{2}x-6 \end{aligned}$$

36. $m = \dfrac{1-2}{1-5}$

$= \dfrac{-1}{-4}$

$= \dfrac{1}{4}$

$y - 1 = \dfrac{1}{4}(x - 1)$

$y - 1 = \dfrac{1}{4}x - \dfrac{1}{4}$

$y = \dfrac{1}{4}x + \dfrac{3}{4}$

y-intercept: $\dfrac{3}{4}$

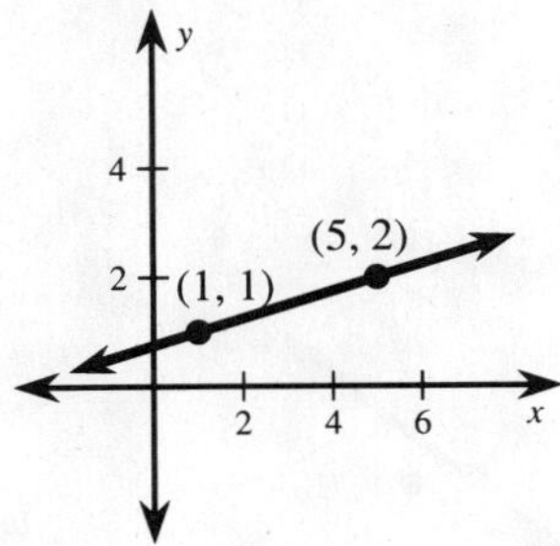

37. $m = \dfrac{-2-8}{-1-5}$

$= \dfrac{-10}{-6}$

$= \dfrac{5}{3}$

$y - (-2) = \dfrac{5}{3}[x - (-1)]$

$y + 2 = \dfrac{5}{3}(x + 1)$

$y = \dfrac{5}{3}x + \dfrac{5}{3} - 2$

$y = \dfrac{5}{3}x - \dfrac{1}{3}$

y-intercept: $-\dfrac{1}{3}$

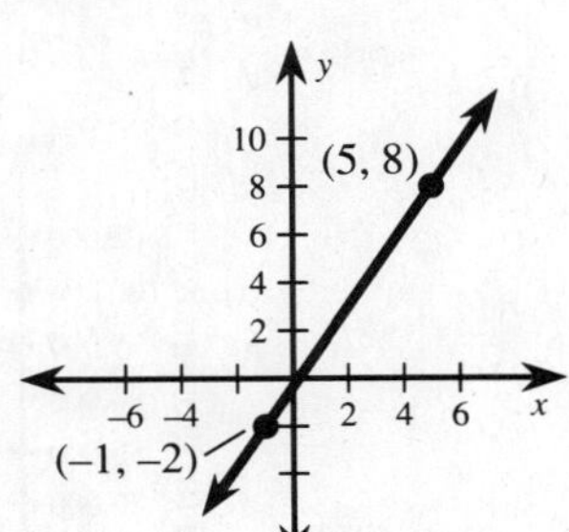

38. $m = \dfrac{-3-4}{-2-2}$

$= \dfrac{-7}{-4}$

$= \dfrac{7}{4}$

$y - (-3) = \dfrac{7}{4}[x - (-2)]$

$y + 3 = \dfrac{7}{4}(x + 2)$

$y = \dfrac{7}{4}x + \dfrac{7}{2} - 3$

$y = \dfrac{7}{4}x + \dfrac{1}{2}$

y-intercept: $\dfrac{1}{2}$

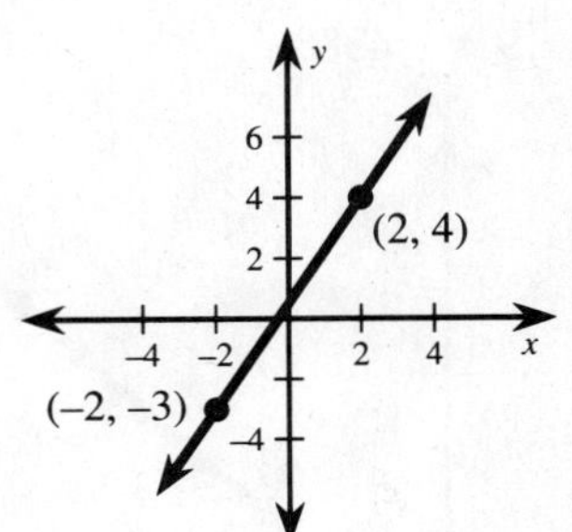

39. $m = \dfrac{-1-(-1)}{-1-4}$

$= \dfrac{0}{-5}$

$= 0$

$y = -1$

y-intercept: -1

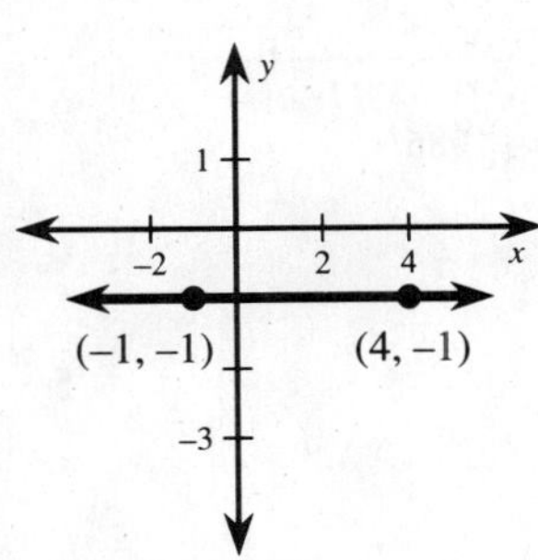

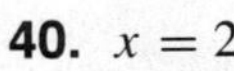

40. $x = 2$

41. $x = -1$

42. $y = -3$

43. $y = 6$

44. $m = \dfrac{45{,}200{,}000 - 84{,}900{,}000}{0 - 25}$

$= \dfrac{-39{,}700{,}000}{-25}$

$= 1{,}588{,}000$

$H = 1{,}588{,}000t + 45{,}200{,}000$

45. $m = \dfrac{350 - 650}{5 - 7}$

$= \dfrac{-300}{-2}$

$= 150$

$R - 350 = 150(t - 5)$

$R = 150t - 750 + 350$

$R = 150t - 400$

46. Points: $(-20,\ 21), (20,\ -19)$

$$m = \frac{21 - (-19)}{-20 - 20}$$
$$= -1$$
$$y - 21 = -1[x - (-20)]$$
$$y = -x + 1$$

47. Points: $(0,\ 1), (4,\ 4.2)$

$$m = \frac{1 - 4.2}{0 - 4}$$
$$= \frac{-3.2}{-4}$$
$$= \frac{4}{5}$$
$$y = \frac{4}{5}x + 1$$

48. Points: $(2, 4570), (7, 5025)$

$$m = \frac{5025 - 4570}{7 - 2}$$
$$= 91$$
$$4570 = 91(2) + b$$
$$b = 4388$$
$$y = 91t + 4388$$

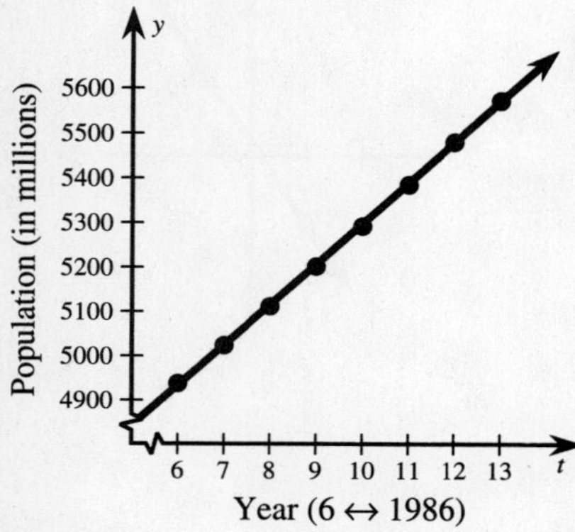

49. Points: $(4, 69{,}015), (14, 80{,}275)$

$$m = \frac{80{,}275 - 69{,}015}{14 - 4}$$
$$= 1126$$
$$69{,}015 = 1126(4) + b$$
$$b = 64{,}511$$
$$y = 1126t + 64{,}511$$

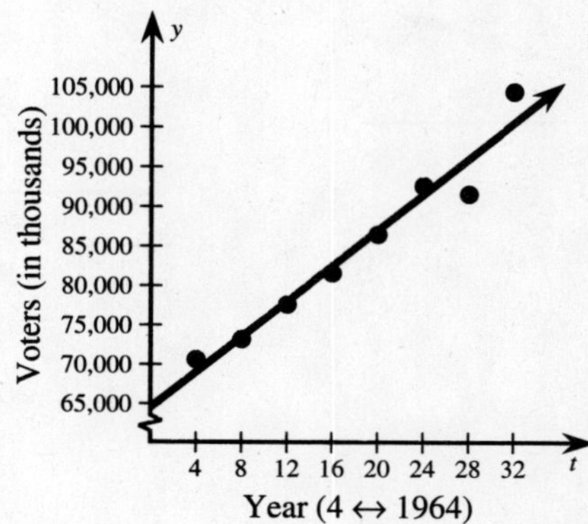

50. $x + 9y = 7$

$$9y = -x + 7$$
$$y = -\tfrac{1}{9}x + \tfrac{7}{9}$$

51. $3x + 5y = 5$

$$5y = -3x + 5$$
$$y = -\tfrac{3}{5}x + 1$$

52. $y = -\tfrac{1}{3}x + \tfrac{2}{3}$

$$3y = -x + 2$$
$$x + 3y = 2$$

53. $y = \tfrac{3}{4}x + \tfrac{1}{2}$

$$4y = 3x + 2$$
$$-3x + 4y = 2$$

54. $2B + 1.25C = 10$

55. $10x + 5y = 30$

56.

Broccoli, B	0	1	2	3	4	5
Cauliflower, C	8	6.4	4.8	3.2	1.6	0

$5C = -8B + 40$ $\quad C = -\frac{8}{5}B + 8$

$C = -\frac{8}{5} \cdot 0 + 8$ $\quad C = 8$

$C = -\frac{8}{5} \cdot 1 + 8$ $\quad C = \frac{32}{5}$ $\quad C = 6.4$

$C = -\frac{8}{5} \cdot 2 + 8$ $\quad C = \frac{24}{5}$ $\quad C = 4.8$

$C = -\frac{8}{5} \cdot 3 + 8$ $\quad C = \frac{16}{5}$ $\quad C = 3.2$

$C = -\frac{8}{5} \cdot 4 + 8$ $\quad C = \frac{8}{5}$ $\quad C = 1.6$

$C = -\frac{8}{5} \cdot 5 + 8$ $\quad C = 0$

57.

Racquetball, x	0	1	2	3
Tennis, y	6	4	2	0

$y = -2x + 6$

$y = -2 \cdot 0 + 6$ $\quad y = 6$

$y = -2 \cdot 1 + 6$ $\quad y = 4$

$y = -2 \cdot 2 + 6$ $\quad y = 2$

$y = -2 \cdot 3 + 6$ $\quad y = 0$

58. Points: (4, 0), (9, 850,000)

$$m = \frac{850{,}000 - 0}{9 - 4}$$

$$= 170{,}000$$

$$N - 0 = 170{,}000(t - 4)$$

$$N = 170{,}000t - 680{,}000$$

59. $N = 170{,}000t - 680{,}000$

When $t = 4$: $N = 170{,}000(4) - 680{,}000 = 0$
When $t = 5$: $N = 170{,}000(5) - 680{,}000 = 170{,}000$
When $t = 6$: $N = 170{,}000(6) - 680{,}000 = 340{,}000$
When $t = 7$: $N = 170{,}000(7) - 680{,}000 = 510{,}000$
When $t = 8$: $N = 170{,}000(8) - 680{,}000 = 680{,}000$
When $t = 9$: $N = 170{,}000(9) - 680{,}000 = 850{,}000$
When $t = 10$: $N = 170{,}000(10) - 680{,}000 = 1{,}020{,}000$

Year, t	4	5	6	7	8	9	10
Model, N	0	170,000	340,000	510,000	680,000	850,000	1,020,000

60. Points: (2, 0), (10, 2,400,000)

$$m = \frac{2{,}400{,}000}{10 - 2}$$

$$= 300{,}000$$

$$N - 0 = 300{,}000(t - 2)$$

$$N = 300{,}000t - 600{,}000$$

61. Using the model developed in Exercise 58, the approximate rate of change is 170,000 per year.

62. Using the model developed in Exercise 60, the approximate rate of change is 300,000 per year.

63. Those without networks were increasing at a faster rate.

Chapter TEST

1. $y = \frac{1}{4}x - 3$

2. $y - 3 = -2[x - (-2)]$

$y = -2x - 4 + 3$

$y = -2x - 1$

3. $m = \dfrac{3 - (-3)}{-4 - 2}$

$= \dfrac{6}{-6}$

$= -1$

$y - 3 = -1[x - (-4)]$

$y = -x - 4 + 3$

$y = -x - 1$

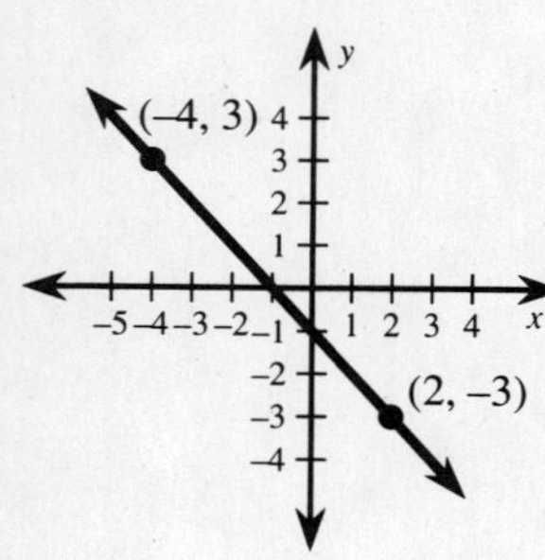

4. Points: $(1, \; -1), (-3, \; 2)$

$m = \dfrac{-1 - 2}{1 - (-3)}$

$= -\dfrac{3}{4}$

$y - (-1) = -\dfrac{3}{4}(x - 1)$

$y = -\dfrac{3}{4}x - \dfrac{1}{4}$

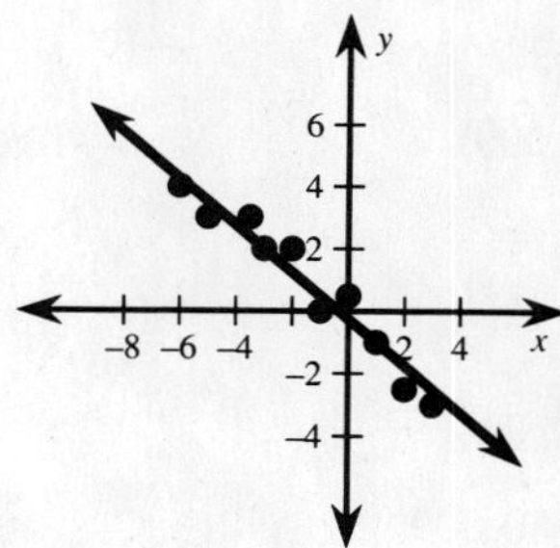

5. $y = 5$

6. $x = 2$

7. $-x + 5y = 20$

$5y = x + 20$

$y = \frac{1}{5}x + 4$

8.

(0, 5)

(−2, 0)

9. $y = \frac{2}{17}x + 3$

$17y = 2x + 51$

$-2x + 17y = 51$

10. $-5x - 2y = 18$

$-2y = 5x + 18$

$y = -\frac{5}{2}x - 9$

$2x + 5y = 12$

$5y = -2x + 12$

$y = -\frac{2}{5}x + \frac{12}{5}$

$5x + 2y = 6$

$2y = -5x + 6$

$y = -\frac{5}{2}x + 3$

a. and **c.** are parallel.

11. $1.20f + 2.40c = 24$

12. $y - 1 = \frac{1}{3}[x - (-3)]$

$y - 1 = \frac{1}{3}(x + 3)$

13. $m = \dfrac{77.5 - 55}{0.5 - 1}$

$= \dfrac{22.5}{-0.5}$

$= -45$

$y - 55 = -45(x - 1)$

$y = -45x + 100$

$0 = -45x + 100$

$45x = 100$

$x \approx 2.2$ hours

14. $y = 0.04x + 1250$

15. $6x + 4y = 150 - 30$

$6x + 4y = 120$

Chapter 6

Solving and Graphing Linear Inequalities

6.1 *Solving Inequalities in One Variable*

Communicating about Algebra

A. b. Add the same quantity to both sides.

B. a. Divide both sides by the same positive quantity.

C. b. Multiply both sides by the same negative quantity and reverse the inequality.

D. a. Both are equivalent inequalities.

EXERCISES

1. $x \geq 4$

2. All real numbers less than or equal to negative two

3.

4 5 6 7 8 x

4. $5 - 2x \geq 3$

$-2x \geq -2$

$x \leq 1$

5. Yes; it is a solution because $4.78 < 5$.

No; it is not a solution because $6 \nless 6$.

6. $x > 2$

7. You must reverse the direction of an inequality when multiplying or dividing by a negative number to maintain a true statement.

8. $x \leq 4$

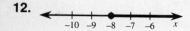

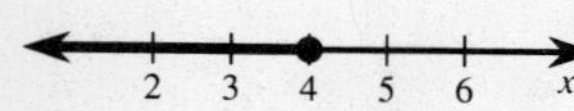

9.

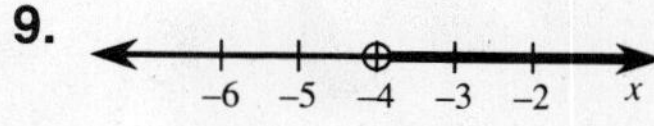

10.

13 14 15 16 17 x

11.

7 8 9 10 11 x

12.

−10 −9 −8 −7 −6 x

13.

0 1 2 3 4 x

14. 

15. $x + 5 < 7$

$x < 2$

16. $4 + x > -12$

$x > -16$

17. $-x - 8 > -17$

$-x > -9$

$x < 9$

18. $-3 + x < 19$

$x < 22$

19. $6 + x \le -8$

$x \le -14$

20. $x - 10 \ge -6$

$x \ge 4$

21. $2x + 7 \ge 4$

$2x \ge -3$

$x \ge -\frac{3}{2}$

22. $6 - 3x \le 15$

$-3x \le 9$

$x \ge -3$

23. $-4x - 2 \ge 10$

$-4x \ge 12$

$x \le -3$

24. $2x + 5 \le -13$

$2x \le -18$

$x \le -9$

25. $-3 \le 6x - 1$

$-2 \le 6x$

$-\frac{1}{3} \le x$

26. $17 \ge 4x + 11$

$6 \ge 4x$

$\frac{3}{2} \ge x$

27. $-x - 4 > 3x - 2$

$-x > 3x + 2$

$-4x > 2$

$x < -\frac{1}{2}$

28. $3x + 5 < -7x - 9$

$3x < -7x - 14$

$10x < -14$

$x < -\frac{7}{5}$

29. $x + 3 \le 2(x - 4)$

$x + 3 \le 2x - 8$

$x \le 2x - 11$

$-x \le -11$

$x \ge 11$

30. $2x + 10 \ge 7(x + 1)$

$2x + 10 \ge 7x + 7$

$2x \ge 7x - 3$

$-5x \ge -3$

$x \le \frac{3}{5}$

31. $-x + 4 < -2(x - 8)$

$-x + 4 < -2x + 16$

$-x < -2x + 12$

$x < 12$

32. $-x + 6 > -(2x + 4)$

$-x + 6 > -2x - 4$

$-x > -2x - 10$

$x > -10$

33. d.

$3x - 1 \le -7$

$3x \le -6$

$x \le -2$

34. a.

$10 \le x + 6$

$4 \le x$

35. e.

$5x - 7 < 3x + 9$

$5x < 3x + 16$

$2x < 16$

$x < 8$

36. c.

$12 - 2x > 10$

$-2x > -2$

$x < 1$

37. f.

$3x + 2 \le 14$

$3x \le 12$

$x \le 4$

38. g.

$-3 \ge 6x - 1$

$-2 \ge 6x$

$-\frac{1}{3} \ge x$

39. h.

$-9x + 2 < 14$

$-9x < 12$

$x > -\frac{4}{3}$

40. b.

$2x - 6 < -x + 6$

$2x < -x + 12$

$3x < 12$

$x < 4$

41. i.

$2x \ge -x + 6$

$3x \ge 6$

$x \ge 2$

42. $T \le 0$

43. $E \ge -282$

44. $P \geq 1200$

45. $V < 95$

93 94 95 96 97 V

46. $d \geq 14{,}000{,}000$

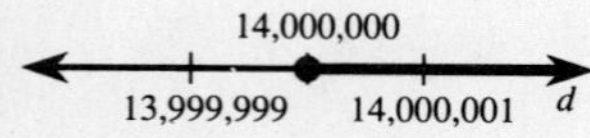

47. $x + 2 = 8$ or $x + 2 = -8$

$x = 6$ $\quad x = -10$

48. $12 - x = 6$ or $12 - x = -6$

$-x = -6$ $\quad -x = -18$

$x = 6$ $\quad x = 18$

49. $x - 3 = 9$ or $x - 3 = -9$

$x = 12$ $\quad x = -6$

50. $2x - 1 = 10$ or $2x - 1 = -10$

$2x = 11$ $\quad 2x = -9$

$x = \frac{11}{2}$ $\quad x = -\frac{9}{2}$

51. $45 = 5 \cdot 6 + b$

$45 = 30 + b$

$b = 15$

$t = 5w + 15$

52. $598 = 6.25 \cdot 15 + c$

$598 = 93.75 + c$

$c = 504.25$

$b = 6.25w + 504.25$

53. $y - (-4) = \frac{3}{2}(x - 2)$

$y = \frac{3}{2}x - 3 - 4$

$y = \frac{3}{2}x - 7$

54. $m = \dfrac{6 - 1}{-3 - 9}$

$= \dfrac{5}{-12}$

$y - 6 = -\dfrac{5}{12}[x - (-3)]$

$y = -\dfrac{5}{12}x - \dfrac{5}{4} + 6$

$y = -\dfrac{5}{12}x + \dfrac{19}{4}$

55. $x < 3$; for values of $x < 3$, the value of y is less than zero. Therefore, any value of x which results in $y < 0$ (where the line is below the x-axis) is a solution to $\frac{2}{3}x - 2 < 0$.

56. $x < 2$; for values of $x < 2$, the value of y is greater than zero. Therefore, any value of x which results in $y > 0$ (where the line is above the x-axis) is a solution to $-2x + 4 > 0$.

6.2 Problem Solving Using Inequalities

Communicating about Algebra

A. $\frac{\text{Distance}}{\text{Speed}} \le \text{Time}$

Distance $= 2$ (miles)
Speed $= r$ (miles per hour)
Time $= \frac{12}{60} = \frac{1}{5}$ (hour)

$\frac{2}{r} \le \frac{1}{5}$

$2 \cdot 5 \le 1 \cdot r$

$r \ge 10$ miles per hour

B. $10L \ge 100$

$L \ge 10$ inches

C. $7.50x - (48 + 3.50x) \ge 300$

$7.50x$ is the income, $48 + 3.50x$ is the total cost, and the difference is the profit; $x \ge 87$.

EXERCISES

1. [Cost per tape] $\cdot$ [Number of tapes] $+$ [Shipping and handling] $\le$ [Amount to spend]

2. Number of tapes $= x$ (tapes)
Cost per tape $= 3$ (dollars)
Shipping and handling $= 2$ (dollars)
Amount to spend $= 20$ (dollars)

3. $3x + 2 \le 20$

4. $3x + 2 \le 20$

$3x \le 18$

$x \le 6$

5. $m > -37.8°\text{F}$

6. $l < 1700$ feet

7. $x < 250 \cdot 10$

$x < 2500$ feet

8. $x < \frac{3}{30.2} \cdot \frac{60}{1}$

$x < 5.96$ miles per hour

9. $5 + 0.8x \le 13$

$0.8x \le 8$

$x \le 10$ rides

You can go on 10 rides for \$13.

10. $8 + 0.4x \le 12$

$0.4x \le 4$

$x \le 10$ toppings

You can afford 10 toppings for \$12.

11. $0.48 + 0.22(t - 1) \le 4.00$

$0.26 + 0.22t \le 4.00$

$0.22t \le 3.74$

$t \le 17$ minutes

12. $F = \dfrac{13{,}000{,}000 - 4{,}900{,}000}{30 - 0}t + 4{,}900{,}000$

$F = 270{,}000t + 4{,}900{,}000$

$J = \dfrac{7{,}747{,}000 - 6{,}067{,}000}{30 - 0}t + 6{,}067{,}000$

$J = 56{,}000t + 6{,}067{,}000$

$270{,}000t + 4{,}900{,}000 > 56{,}000t + 6{,}067{,}000$

$214{,}000t > 1{,}167{,}000$

$t > 5.5$

For the years 1966–1990, the population of Florida exceeded New Jersey.

13. $P = 62 - \dfrac{62 - 52}{30}t$

$P = 62 - \dfrac{1}{3}t$

$C = 31 + \dfrac{66 - 31}{30}t$

$C = 31 + \dfrac{7}{6}t$

$31 + \dfrac{7}{6}t > 62 - \dfrac{1}{3}t$

$\dfrac{3}{2}t > 31$

$3t > 62$

$t > 20\frac{2}{3}$ years

Therefore, from 1981 to 1990 the consumption of chicken exceeded the consumption of pork.

14. $x \ge \dfrac{1 \text{ hour}}{\text{frame}} \cdot \dfrac{24 \text{ frames}}{\text{second}} \cdot \dfrac{60 \text{ seconds}}{\text{minute}} \cdot \dfrac{90 \text{ minutes}}{\text{film}}$

$x \ge 1 \cdot 24 \cdot 60 \cdot 90$

$x \ge 129{,}600$ hours per film

15. $t \ge \left(\dfrac{129{,}000 \text{ hours}}{\text{film}}\right) \div \left(36 \cdot \dfrac{40 \text{ hours}}{\text{week}} \cdot \dfrac{45 \text{ weeks}}{\text{years}}\right)$

$t \ge \left(\dfrac{129{,}600 \text{ hours}}{\text{film}}\right) \div \left(\dfrac{64{,}800 \text{ hours}}{\text{year}}\right)$

$t \ge \left(\dfrac{129{,}600 \text{ hours}}{\text{film}}\right) \cdot \left(\dfrac{\text{year}}{64{,}800 \text{ hours}}\right)$

$t \ge 2$ years per film

16. $9 \cdot x \ge 36$

$x \ge 4$ meters

17. $2x - 4 + 12 + 21 \le 65$

$2x + 29 \le 65$

$2x \le 36$

$x \le 18$ feet

18. $4x < -28$

$x < -7$

19. $6 \ge x + 1$

$5 \ge x$

20. $9y - 4 \ge 59$

$9y \ge 63$

$y \ge 7$

21. $13 + 5x < 8$

$5x < -5$

$x < -1$

22. $5 - 3x > 11$

$-3x > 6$

$x < -2$

23. $-2x + 3 > 3x - 7$

$-2x > 3x - 10$

$-5x > -10$

$x < 2$

24. $4 + x \le 16 - x$

$x \le 12 - x$

$2x \le 12$

$x \le 6$

25. $-9x - 2 \le 16$

$-9x \le 18$

$x \ge -2$

26. **d.**

$4 - x > 5$

$-x > 1$

$x < -1$

27. c. The closest estimate of the radius of Earth is 4000 miles.

28. b. The closest estimate of the weight of a car is 2000 pounds.

29. b. $x > 0$ **30. c.** $x < -1000$ **31. a.** $x < -221$ **32. d.** $x > 618$

Mixed REVIEW

1. $\frac{3}{8} \div 2 = \frac{3}{8} \cdot \frac{1}{2}$

$= \frac{3}{16}$

2. $\frac{1}{3} - \frac{1}{4} = \frac{4}{12} - \frac{3}{12}$

$= \frac{1}{12}$

3. $-\left|x - \frac{2}{3}\right| + 2x = -\left|\frac{1}{6} - \frac{2}{3}\right| + 2\left(\frac{1}{6}\right)$

$= -\left|\frac{1}{6} - \frac{4}{6}\right| + \frac{2}{6}$

$= -\left|-\frac{3}{6}\right| + \frac{2}{6}$

$= -\frac{3}{6} + \frac{2}{6}$

$= -\frac{1}{6}$

4. $y^2 + y(4 - y) = 3^2 + 3(4 - 3)$

$= 9 + 3 \cdot 1$

$= 9 + 3$

$= 12$

5. $3(a - b) = 7$

$a - b = \frac{7}{3}$

$-b = -a + \frac{7}{3}$

$b = a - \frac{7}{3}$

6. $\frac{1}{2}(x - 2) + 3y = 6$

$x - 2 + 6y = 12$

$6y = 12 - (x - 2)$

$6y = 14 - x$

$y = \frac{1}{6}(14 - x)$

7. $b = a - \frac{7}{3}$

$b = \frac{1}{3} - \frac{7}{3}$

$b = \frac{-6}{3}$

$b = -2$

8. $y = \frac{1}{6}(14 - x)$

$y = \frac{1}{6}(14 - 0)$

$y = \frac{14}{6}$

$y = \frac{7}{3}$

9. $5x - 3 < 2$

$5(1) - 3 \stackrel{?}{<} 2$

$5 - 3 \stackrel{?}{<} 2$

$2 \not< 2$

1 is not a solution.

10. $x^2 + 2 \geq 11$

$3^2 + 2 \stackrel{?}{\geq} 11$

$9 + 2 \stackrel{?}{\geq} 11$

$11 \geq 11$

3 is a solution.

11. $\frac{1}{4}(x - 2) + \frac{3}{4}(6 - 3x) = \frac{1}{4}x - \frac{2}{4} + \frac{18}{4} - \frac{9}{4}x$

$= \frac{16}{4} - \frac{8}{4}x$

$= 4 - 2x$

12. $24 \div 6 + 3(x - 2) = 4 + 3x - 6$

$= 3x - 2$

13. $|x - 2| + 3 = 5$

$|x - 2| = 2$

$x - 2 = 2$ or $x - 2 = -2$

$x = 4$ $\quad x = 0$

14. $|16 - x| - 30 = -4$

$|16 - x| = 26$

$16 - x = 26$ or $16 - x = -26$

$-x = 10$ $\quad -x = -42$

$x = -10$ $\quad x = 42$

15.

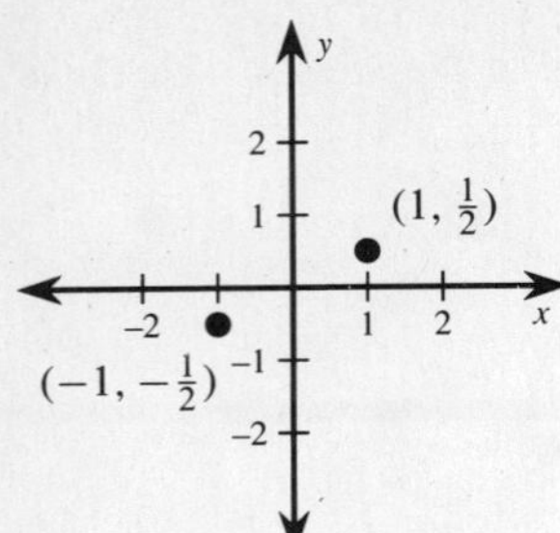

16.

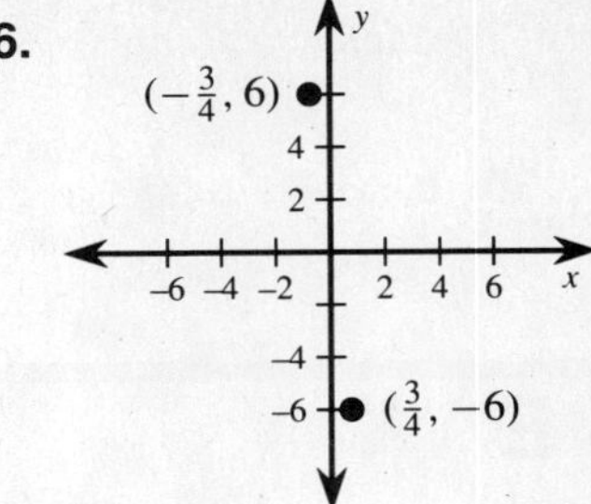

17. $|x + 2| - 3 = y$

Vertex: $(-2, -3)$

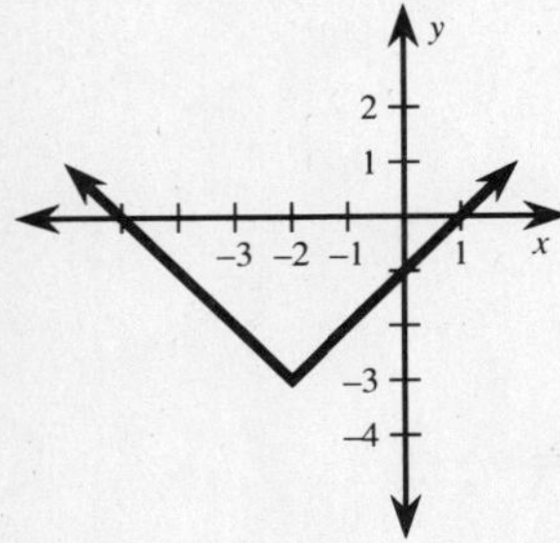

18.

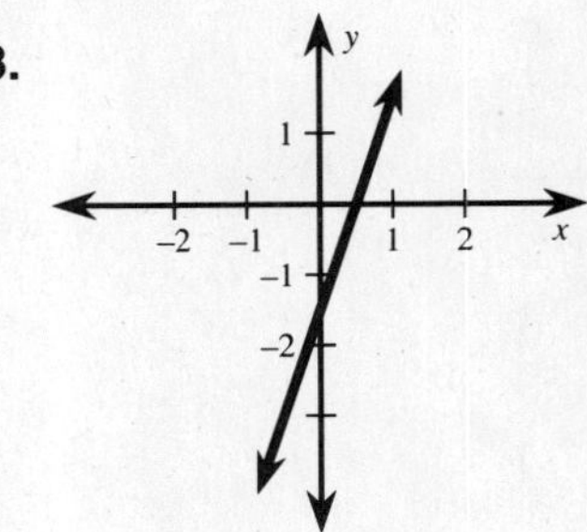

19. $m = \dfrac{0-2}{-3-1}$

$= \dfrac{-2}{-4}$

$= \dfrac{1}{2}$

$y - 0 = \dfrac{1}{2}[x - (-3)]$

$y = \dfrac{1}{2}(x + 3)$

$y = \dfrac{1}{2}x + \dfrac{3}{2}$

20. $y - 3 = -\frac{1}{3}[x - (-4)]$

$y = -\frac{1}{3}x - \frac{4}{3} + 3$

$y = -\frac{1}{3}x + \frac{5}{3}$

6.3 Compound Inequalities

Communicating about Algebra

A. a. Subtract the same quantity from each part.

B. b. Divide each part by the same positive quantity.

C. b. Multiply each part by the same negative quantity and reverse the inequalities.

D. a. Subtract the same quantity from each part and divide each part by the same positive quantity.

EXERCISES

1. c.

2. a.

3. d.

4. b.

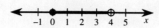

5. $-2 \le 3x - 2 < 10$

$0 \le 3x < 12$

$0 \le x < 4$

6. $2x - 3 < 5 \quad \text{or} \quad x - 4 \ge 0$

$2x < 8 \qquad x \ge 4$

$x < 4$

The solution consists of all real numbers.

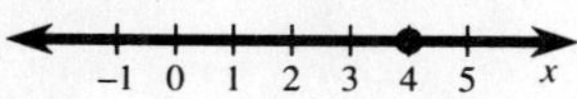

7. $-6 < x - 4 \le 4$

$-2 < x \le 8$

8. $-5 < x - 6 < 4$

$1 < x < 10$

9. $-4 < 3 - x < 2$

$-7 < -x < -1$

$7 > x > 1$

$1 < x < 7$

10. $-10 \le 6 - 2x < 8$

$-16 \le -2x < 2$

$8 \ge x > -1$

$-1 < x \le 8$

11. $-10 \le -4x - 18 \le 30$

$8 \le -4x \le 48$

$-2 \ge x \ge -12$

$-12 \le x \le -2$

12. $7 \le -3x + 4 \le 19$

$3 \le -3x \le 15$

$-1 \ge x \ge -5$

$-5 \le x \le -1$

13. $6 - 2x > 20 \quad \text{or} \quad 8 - x \le 0$

$-2x > 14 \qquad -x \le -8$

$x < -7 \qquad x \ge 8$

14. $-3x - 7 \ge 8 \quad \text{or} \quad -2x - 11 \le -31$

$-3x \ge 15 \qquad -2x \le -20$

$x \le -5 \qquad x \ge 10$

15. $2 \le x < 5$

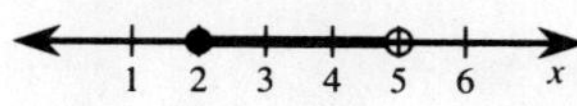

16. $-3 < x \le -1$

17. $-12 < 2x - 6 < 4$

$-6 < 2x < 10$

$-3 < x < 5$

18. $-3 \le 6x - 1 < 3$

$-2 \le 6x < 4$

$-\frac{1}{3} \le x < \frac{2}{3}$

19. $-8 \le 1 - 3(x - 2) < 13$

$-8 \le 1 - 3x + 6 < 13$

$-8 \le -3x + 7 < 13$

$-15 \le -3x < 6$

$5 \ge x > -2$

$-2 < x \le 5$

20. $-19 < 3 - 4(x + 7) \le 5$

$-19 < 3 - 4x - 28 \le 5$

$-19 < -4x - 25 \le 5$

$6 < -4x \le 30$

$-\frac{3}{2} > x \ge -\frac{15}{2}$

$-7\frac{1}{2} \le x < -\frac{3}{2}$

21. $4 < x < 7$

22. $-9 < x < 2$

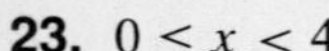

23. $0 \le x < 4$

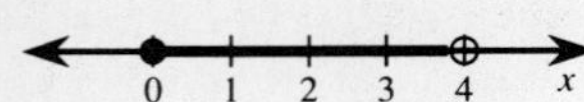

24. $-7 \le x < 2$

25. $-2 < 5x - 7 < 13$

$5 < 5x < 20$

$1 < x < 4$

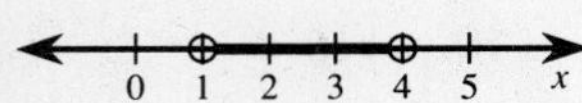

1 is not a solution.

26. $-4 < 8x - 20 \le 12$

$16 < 8x \le 32$

$2 < x \le 4$

4 is a solution.

27. $-3 < 3 - 4x < 3$

$-6 < -4x < 0$

$\frac{6}{4} > x > 0$

$0 < x < \frac{3}{2}$

$\frac{1}{2}$ is a solution.

28. $7 \le -2x + 21 < 31$

$-14 \le -2x < 10$

$7 \ge x > -5$

$-5 < x \le 7$

0 is a solution.

29. $4 \cdot 0.24 \le x \le 550{,}000$

$0.96 \le x \le 550{,}000$

30. $7 \le x \le 2000$

31. a. $10^7 < d < 10^{10}$

32. a. $10^{13} < d < 10^{18}$

33. $1 + \frac{1}{2} + \frac{1}{2} \le x \le 1 + 1\frac{1}{2} + \frac{1}{2}$

$2 \le x \le 3$

34. $\frac{1}{2} \le x \le 1\frac{1}{2}$

35. e.

36. $x \le 2$

37. $x > -1$

38. $x \le -1$ or $x > 3$

39. $x - 1 = 7$ or $x - 1 = -7$

$x = 8$ $\quad$ $x = -6$

40. $x - 3 = 9$ or $x - 3 = -9$

$x = 12$ $\quad$ $x = -6$

41. $2x + 1 = 11$ or $2x + 1 = -11$

$2x = 10$ $\quad$ $2x = -12$

$x = 5$ $\quad$ $x = -6$

42. $3x - 2 = 5$ or $3x - 2 = -5$

$3x = 7$ $\quad$ $3x = -3$

$x = \frac{7}{3}$ $\quad$ $x = -1$

43. $5x - 2 = 17$ or $5x - 2 = -17$

$5x = 19$ $\quad$ $5x = -15$

$x = \frac{19}{5}$ $\quad$ $x = -3$

44. $6x + 8 = 24$ or $6x + 8 = -24$

$6x = 16$ $\quad$ $6x = -32$

$x = \frac{8}{3}$ $\quad$ $x = -\frac{16}{3}$

45. $2 < x < 10$

46. $1 < x < 17$

47. $4 < x < 10$

48. $6 < x < 16$

Using a Graphing Calculator

1. $-2x + 3 \geq 7$

$-2x \geq 4$

$x \leq -2$

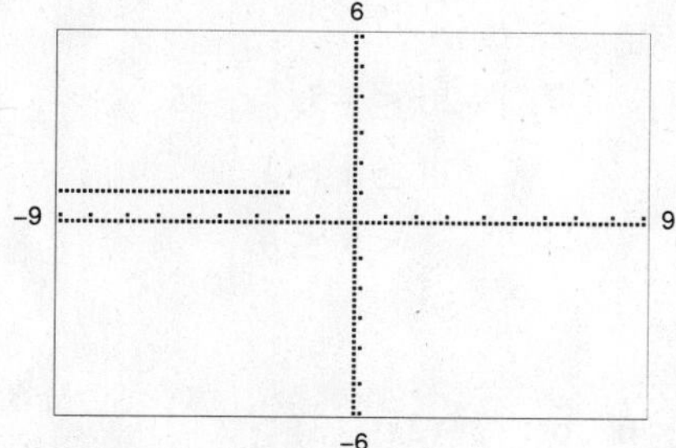

2. $-3 < -x + 5$

$-8 < -x$

$8 > x$

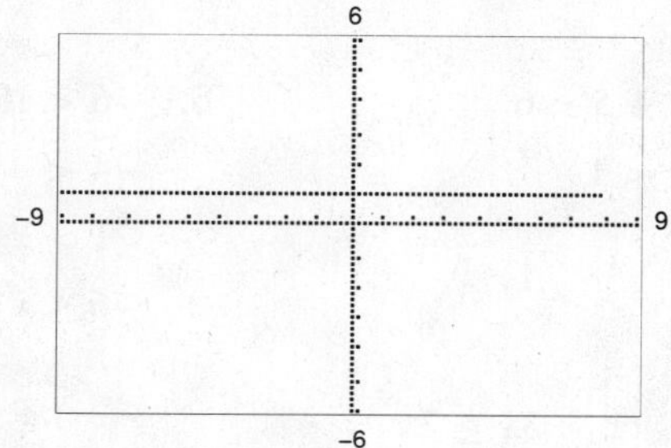

3. $-3x + 2 \leq 4$

$-3x \leq 2$

$x \geq -\frac{2}{3}$

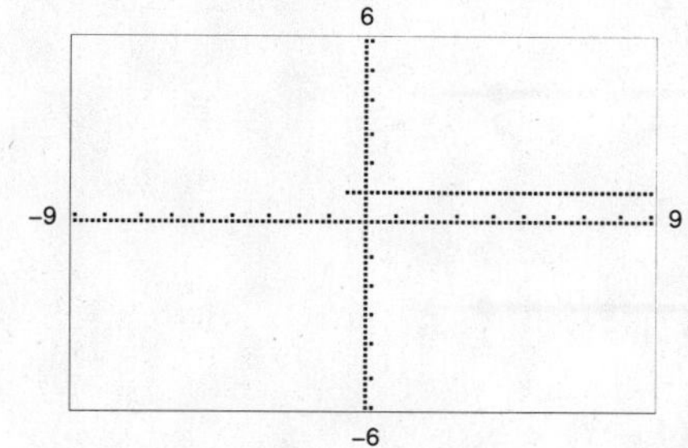

4. $5x + 1 < 4x + 5$

$5x < 4x + 4$

$x < 4$

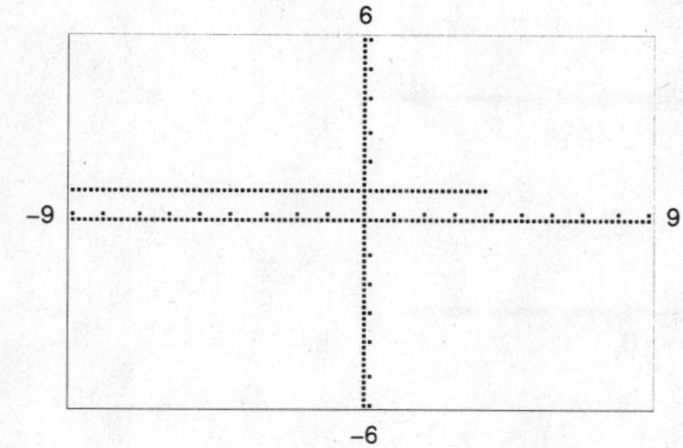

5. $-2x > -3x - 1$

$x > -1$

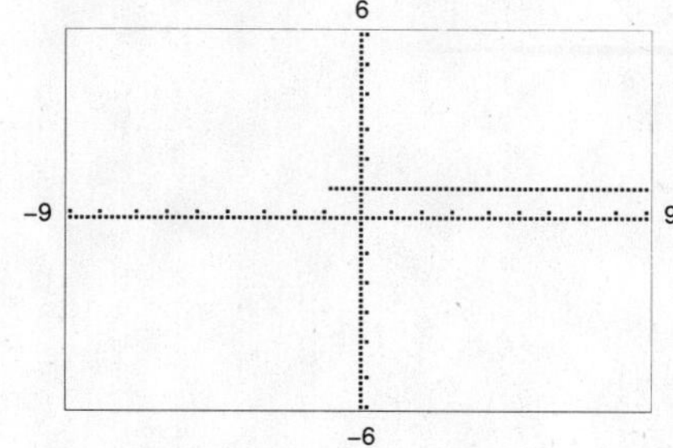

6. $-x - 2 \leq 3x + 6$

$-x \leq 3x + 8$

$-4x \leq 8$

$x \geq -2$

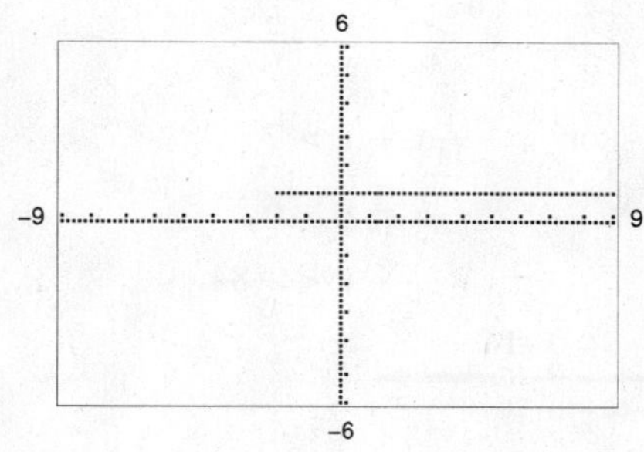

Mid-Chapter SELF-TEST

1. c.

$x + 2 > 4$

$x > 2$

2. a.

$x - 7 \le 6$

$x \le 13$

3. b.

$\frac{1}{4}x + 6 \ge 5$

$\frac{1}{4}x \ge -1$

$x \ge -4$

4. $-3 \le x + 2 \le 5$

$-5 \le x \le 3$

5. $-7 < 3x + 5 < 6$

$-12 < 3x < 1$

$-4 < x < \frac{1}{3}$

6. $6 < 10 - 4x \le 34$

$-4 < -4x \le 24$

$1 > x \ge -6$

$-6 \le x < 1$

7. $-20 \le -5x < -5$

$4 \ge x > 1$

$1 < x \le 4$

8. $-3x > 7$ or $3x \ge 7$

$x < -\frac{7}{3}$ $\quad x \ge \frac{7}{3}$

9. $\frac{3}{2}(x - 2) \le 6$ or $\frac{1}{5}(2x - 3) \ge 3$

$x - 2 \le 4$ $\quad 2x - 3 \ge 15$

$x \le 6$ $\quad 2x \ge 18$

$x \ge 9$

10. $5 < x < 8$

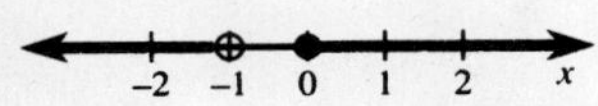

11. $-3 \le x \le 2$

12. $x < -1$ or $x \ge 0$

−2 −1 0 1 2 x

13. $-4 \le x \le 3$

−4 −3 −2 −1 0 1 2 3 x

14. $-3 < -3(x + 2) \le 5$

$1 > x + 2 \ge -\frac{5}{3}$

$-1 > x \ge -\frac{11}{3}$

$-\frac{11}{3} \le x < -1$

$-\frac{11}{3}$

−4 −3 −2 −1 0 x

15. $0 \le -2(4 - x) < 8$

$0 \ge 4 - x > -4$

$-4 \ge -x > -8$

$4 \le x < 8$

4 5 6 7 8 x

16. $\frac{1}{14}x > -1$ or $-\frac{1}{14}x + 1 > 7$

$x > -14$ $\quad -\frac{1}{14}x > 6$

$x < -84$

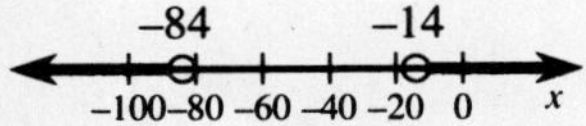

17. $x \ge 52$

18. $2\frac{1}{2} < x < 7\frac{1}{2}$

19. $1.96x + 0.69 \le 3.00$

$1.96x \le 2.31$

$x \le 1\frac{5}{28}$

20. $1 < x < 9$

6.4 Connections: Absolute Value and Inequalities

Communicating about Algebra

A. $|x - 1| < 4$

B. $|x + 2| \geq 1$

EXERCISES

1. True; $|x + 1| < 3$ is equivalent to the compound inequality $-3 < x + 1 < 3$.

2. True; $|x| \geq 5$ is equivalent to the compound inequality $x \leq -5$ or $x \geq 5$.

3. $-4 < x - 1 < 4$

$-3 < x < 5$

4. $x + 3 < -9$ or $x + 3 > 9$

$x < -12$ $\quad x > 6$

5. a.

6. b.

7. d.

$-3 < x - 1 < 3$

$-2 < x < 4$

8. e.

$-\frac{3}{2} \leq x - \frac{1}{2} \leq \frac{3}{2}$

$-1 \leq x \leq 2$

9. b.

$-2 \leq x + 1 \leq 2$

$-3 \leq x \leq 1$

10. c.

$x + 2 \leq -4$ or $x + 2 \geq 4$

$x \leq -6$ $\quad x \geq 2$

11. f.

$x - \frac{5}{2} < -\frac{3}{2}$ or $x - \frac{5}{2} > \frac{3}{2}$

$x < 1$ $\quad x > 4$

12. a.

$x + 2 < -1$ or $x + 2 > 1$

$x < -3$ $\quad x > -1$

13. $-5 < x - 2 < 5$

$-3 < x < 7$

14. $1 + x \leq -4$ or $1 + x \geq 4$

$x \leq -5$ $\quad x \geq 3$

15. $2x - 1 < -3$ or $2x - 1 > 3$

$2x < -2$ $\quad 2x > 4$

$x < -1$ $\quad x > 2$

16. $-9 \leq 4 + x \leq 9$

$-13 \leq x \leq 5$

17. $4 - x \leq -2$ or $4 - x \geq 2$

$-x \leq -6$ $\quad -x \geq -2$

$x \geq 6$ $\quad x \leq 2$

18. $-1 < -x + 1 < 1$

$-2 < -x < 0$

$2 > x > 0$

$0 < x < 2$

19. $-9 < x + 8 < 9$

$-17 < x < 1$

20. $-7 \le 9 + x \le 7$

$-16 \le x \le -2$

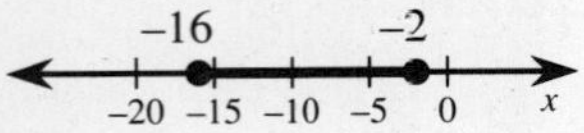

21. $-5 < 4 - x < 5$

$-9 < -x < 1$

$9 > x > -1$

$-1 < x < 9$

22. $-36 < x + 12 < 36$

$-48 < x < 24$

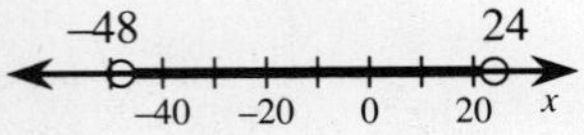

23. $x - 12 \le -6$ or $x - 12 \ge 6$

$x \le 6$ $\quad$ $x \ge 18$

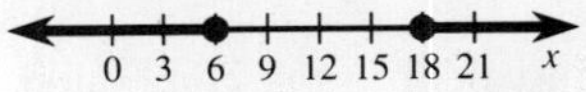

24. $5 - x < -18$ or $5 - x > 18$

$-x < -23$ $\quad$ $-x > 13$

$x > 23$ $\quad$ $x < -13$

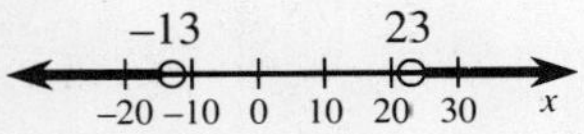

25. $x + 1 < -17$ or $x + 1 > 17$

$x < -18$ $\quad$ $x > 16$

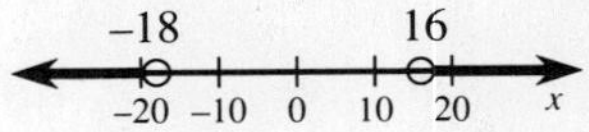

26. $x - 9 \le -4$ or $x - 9 \ge 4$

$x \le 5$ $\quad$ $x \ge 13$

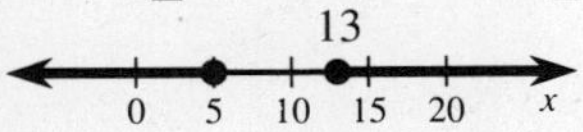

27. $3x - 6 \le 0$ or $3x - 6 \ge 0$

$3x \le 6$ $\quad$ $3x \ge 6$

$x \le 2$ $\quad$ $x \ge 2$

All real numbers

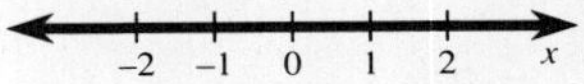

28. $-2 < 10 - 4x < 2$

$-12 < -4x < -8$

$3 > x > 2$

$2 < x < 3$

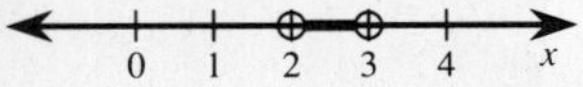

29. $-9 \le 1 + 2x \le 9$

$-10 \le 2x \le 8$

$-5 \le x \le 4$

30. $2x + 3 < -4$ or $2x + 3 > 4$

$2x < -7$ $\quad$ $2x > 1$

$x < -\frac{7}{2}$ $\quad$ $x > \frac{1}{2}$

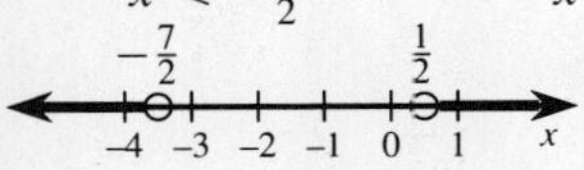

31. $-6 \le x \le 10$

$-6 - 2 \le x - 2 \le 10 - 2$

$-8 \le x - 2 \le 8$

$|x - 2| \le 8$

32. $-6 < x < 4$

$-6 + 1 < x + 1 < 4 + 1$

$-5 < x + 1 < 5$

$|x + 1| < 5$

33. $-6 < x < -2$

$-6 + 4 < x + 4 < -2 + 4$

$-2 < x + 4 < 2$

$|x + 4| < 2$

34. $-4 \le x \le -2$

$-4 + 3 \le x + 3 \le -2 + 3$

$-1 \le x + 3 \le 1$

$|x + 3| \le 1$

35. $x \le -4$ or $x \ge 4$

$|x| \ge 4$

36. $x < -10$ or

$x > 10$

$|x| > 10$

37. $|x - 14{,}000| < 1000$

38. $|x - 25| \le 4$

39.
$$60 \le x \le 100$$
$$60 - 80 \le x - 80 \le 100 - 80$$
$$-20 \le x - 80 \le 20$$
$$|x - 80| \le 20$$

40.
$$58 < x < 70$$
$$58 - 64 < x - 64 < 70 - 64$$
$$-6 < x - 64 < 6$$
$$|x - 64| < 6$$

41. $|w - 643| < 38$
$$-38 < w - 643 < 38$$
$$605 < w < 681$$

c. – d. orange-red

42. $|w - 455| < 23$
$$-23 < w - 455 < 23$$
$$432 < w < 478$$

a. blue

43. $|w - 519.5| < 12.5$
$$-12.5 < w - 519.5 < 12.5$$
$$507 < w < 532$$

b. green

44. $|w - 600| < 5$
$$-5 < w - 600 < 5$$
$$595 < w < 605$$

c. orange

45.
$$60 \le x \le 2100$$
$$60 - 1080 \le x - 1080 \le 2100 - 1080$$
$$-1020 \le x - 1080 \le 1020$$
$$|x - 1080| \le 1020$$

46.
$$x \le 66 \quad \text{or} \quad x \ge 74$$
$$x - 70 \le 66 - 70 \quad x - 70 \ge 74 - 70$$
$$x - 70 \le -4 \quad x - 70 \ge 4$$
$$|x - 70| \ge 4$$

47. $-6 < x - 4 < 3$
$$-2 < x < 7$$

48. $2 \le 9 + x \le 12$
$$-7 \le x \le 3$$

49. $-4 \le -x + 9 \le 6$
$$-13 \le -x \le -3$$
$$13 \ge x \ge 3$$
$$3 \le x \le 13$$

50. $-11 < -2x + 3 < 11$
$$-14 < -2x < 8$$
$$7 > x > -4$$
$$-4 < x < 7$$

51. $-7 < 6x - 5 < 4$
$$-2 < 6x < 9$$
$$-\tfrac{1}{3} < x < \tfrac{3}{2}$$

52. $2 \le 8x - 14 \le 58$
$$16 \le 8x \le 72$$
$$2 \le x \le 9$$

53. $3x + 7 > 1$
$$3x > -6$$
$$x > -2$$

54. $4x + 5 \ge 21$
$$4x \ge 16$$
$$x \ge 4$$

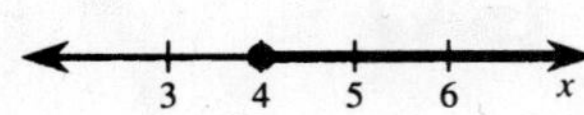

55. $2x + 4 \le x + 3$
$$x \le -1$$

56. $4x + 7 < 3x + 3$
$$x < -4$$

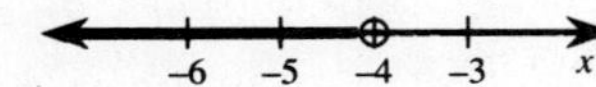

57. $-19 \le 2x - 9 \le -1$

$-10 \le 2x \le 8$

$-5 \le x \le 4$

58. $-4 < 5x - 9 < 26$

$5 < 5x < 35$

$1 < x < 7$

59. $440 \le x \le 580$

$440 - 510 \le x - 510 \le 580 - 510$

$-70 \le x - 510 \le 70$

$|x - 510| \le 70$

60. $475 \le x \le 515$

$475 - 495 \le x - 495 \le 515 - 495$

$-20 \le x - 495 \le 20$

$|x - 495| \le 20$

61. $85 < x < 1100$

$85 - 592.5 < x - 592.5 < 1100 - 592.5$

$-507.5 < x - 592.5 < 507.5$

$|x - 592.5| < 507.5$

62. $10{,}000 < x < 20{,}000$

$10{,}000 - 15{,}000 < x - 15{,}000 < 20{,}000 - 15{,}000$

$-5000 < x - 15{,}000 < 5000$

$|x - 15{,}000| < 5000$

63. $15 < x < 20$ and $20{,}000 < x < 50{,}000$

$15 - 17.5 < x - 17.5 < 20 - 17.5$ $\quad 20{,}000 - 35{,}000 < x - 35{,}000 < 50{,}000 - 35{,}000$

$-2.5 < x - 17.5 < 2.5$ $\quad -15{,}000 < x - 35{,}000 < 15{,}000$

$|x - 17.5| < 2.5$ $\quad |x - 35{,}000| < 15{,}000$

64. $60 < x < 760$ and $1520 < x < 65{,}000$

$60 - 410 < x - 410 < 760 - 410$ $\quad 1520 - 33{,}260 < x - 33{,}260 < 65{,}000 - 33{,}260$

$-350 < x - 410 < 350$ $\quad -31{,}740 < x - 33{,}260 < 31{,}740$

$|x - 410| < 350$ $\quad |x - 33{,}260| < 31{,}740$

65. $7000 < x < 20{,}000$

$7000 - 13{,}500 < x - 13{,}500 < 20{,}000 - 13{,}500$

$-6500 < x - 13{,}500 < 6500$

$|x - 13{,}500| < 6500$

66. $85 < x < 150$

$85 - 117.5 < x - 117.5 < 150 - 117.5$

$-32.5 < x - 117.5 < 32.5$

$|x - 117.5| < 32.5$

Mixed REVIEW

1. $35\% = 0.35$

2. x^2y^3

3. $(0.07)(3.40) = \$0.24$

4. $\left(\frac{2}{5}\right)(375) = 150$

5. $-\frac{3}{4}$

6. $-\frac{5}{6}$

7. $3x + 4y = -20$

$4y = -20 - 3x$

$y = \frac{1}{4}(-20 - 3x)$

8. $\frac{1}{4}m - 2n = 3$

$-2n = 3 - \frac{1}{4}m$

$n = -\frac{1}{2}(3 - \frac{1}{4}m)$

9. $x^2 + 2x - 3 = 4^2 + 2 \cdot 4 - 3$

$= 16 + 8 - 3$

$= 21$

10. $|3 - x| + |x| = |3 - (-1)| + |-1|$
$= |3 + 1| + 1$
$= 4 + 1$
$= 5$

11. $3(x - 2) + \frac{1}{2}(4x - 3) = 3x - 6 + 2x - \frac{3}{2}$
$= 5x - \frac{15}{2}$

12. $3(x - y) + \frac{3}{4}(4x + y) = 3x - 3y + 3x + \frac{3}{4}y$
$= 6x - \frac{9}{4}y$

13. $9x - 4 = \frac{1}{4}(3 - x)$
$36x - 16 = 3 - x$
$37x = 19$
$x = \frac{19}{37}$

14. $\frac{1}{4}(y - 4) = (2y + 6)\frac{3}{8}$
$2(y - 4) = (2y + 6)3$
$2y - 8 = 6y + 18$
$-4y = 26$
$y = -\frac{13}{2}$

15. $y = -3|x + 2| - 2$

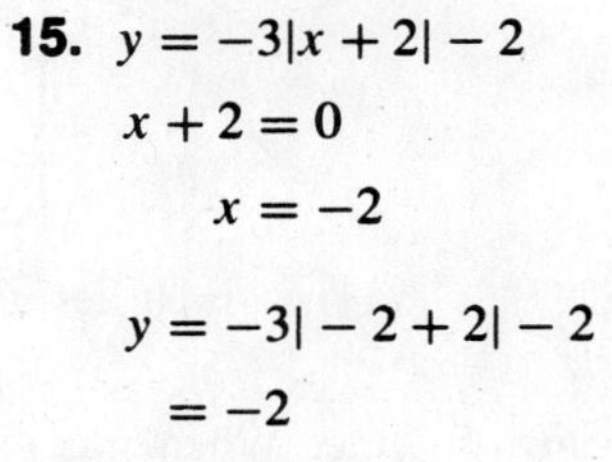

$x + 2 = 0$
$x = -2$

$y = -3|-2 + 2| - 2$
$= -2$

Vertex: $(-2, -2)$

x	-3	-2	-1
y	-5	-2	-5

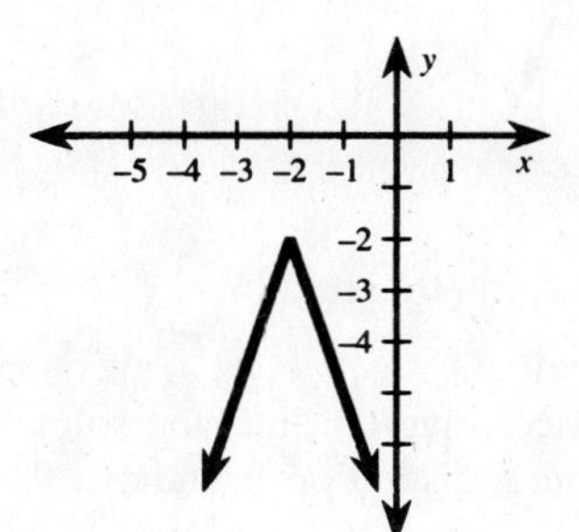

16. $6x = 42$ $7y = 42$
$x = 7$ $y = 6$

$(7, 0), (0, 6)$

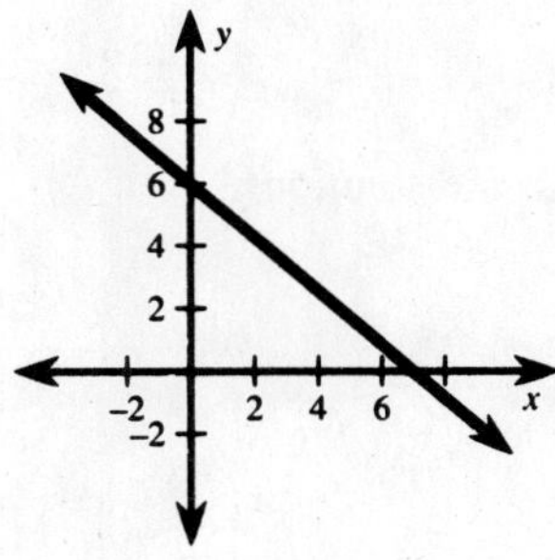

17. Yes, the lines are parallel.

18. $\frac{1}{9}x - 1 \geq -x - \frac{1}{3}$
$x - 9 \geq -9x - 3$
$10x \geq 6$
$x \geq \frac{3}{5}$

$\frac{3}{5}$
−1 0 1 2 3 x

19. Slope: $-\frac{1}{2}$
y-intercept: 3

20. $-3y = 6$ $2x = 6$
$y = -2$ $x = 3$

x-intercept: 3
y-intercept: -2

6.5 Graphing Linear Inequalities in Two Variables

Communicating about Algebra

A.

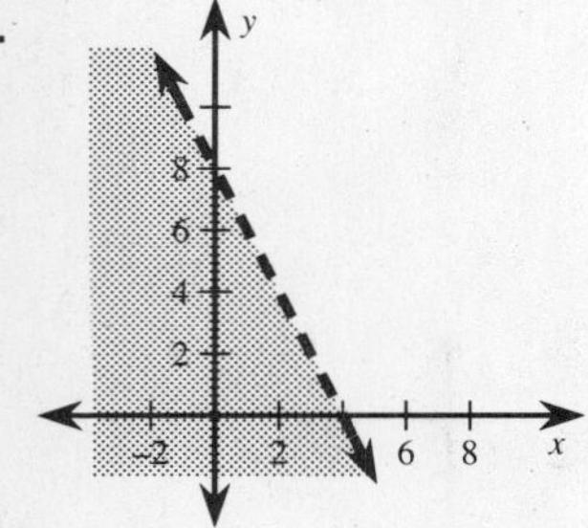

The graph lies below the line.

B.

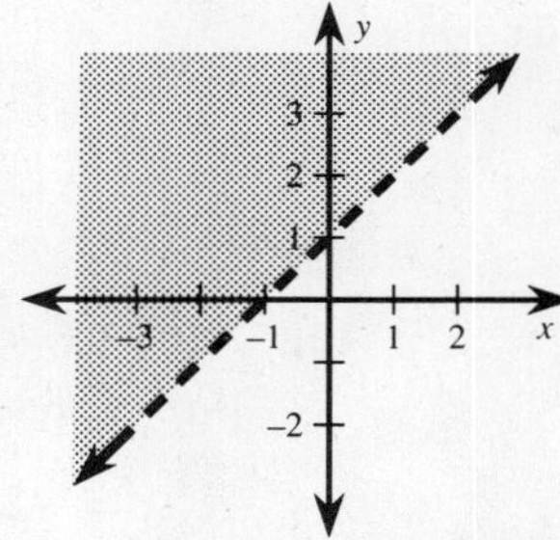

The graph lies above the line.

C. When y is less than the line, the solution lies below the line. When y is greater than the line, the solution lies above the line.

EXERCISES

1. $ax + by < c, \quad ax + by \le c$

$ax + by > c, \quad ax + by \ge c$

2. The graph of a linear inequality in x and y is a half-plane.

3. $2 \cdot 0 - 3(2) = 0 - 6$

$= -6 \le 4$

$2 \cdot 2 - 3 \cdot 1 = 4 - 3$

$= 1 \le 4$

Both are solutions.

4. $-0 + 4(2) = 0 + 8$

$= 8 > 0$

$-2 + 4 \cdot 1 = -2 + 4$

$= 2 > 0$

Both are solutions.

5. $2 - \frac{2}{3} \cdot 0 = 2 - 0$

$= 2 \ge -2$

$1 - \frac{2}{3} \cdot 2 = 1 - \frac{4}{3}$

$= -\frac{1}{3} \ge -2$

Both are solutions.

6. $y - 2x \le 2$

$y - 2x = 2$

$y = 2x + 2$

1. Write the corresponding equation.
2. Write in slope-intercept form.
3. Sketch the line.
4. Test the origin as a solution.
5. Shade the correct half-plane.

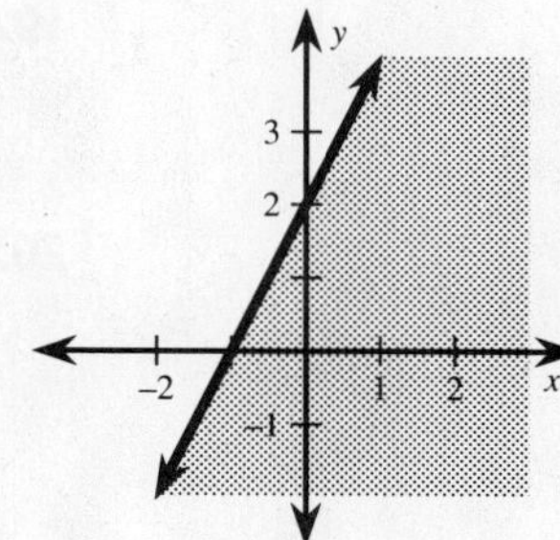

7. $3 \cdot 1 - 2 \cdot 3 = 3 - 6$
$= -3 < 2$

(1, 3) is a solution.

$3 \cdot 2 - 2 \cdot 0 = 6 - 0$
$= 6 > 2$

(2, 0) is not a solution.

8. $13 - 2 \cdot 4 = 13 - 8$
$= 5$

$1 - 2 \cdot 8 = 1 - 16$
$= -15 < 5$

Neither are solutions.

9. $5(-2) + 4 \cdot 4 = -10 + 16$
$= 6$

$5 \cdot 5 + 4 \cdot 5 = 25 + 20$
$= 45 \geq 6$

Both are solutions.

10. $5(8) + 8(-3) = 40 - 24$
$= 16 > 14$

$5(-6) + 8(7) = -30 + 56$
$= 26 > 14$

Neither are solutions.

11.

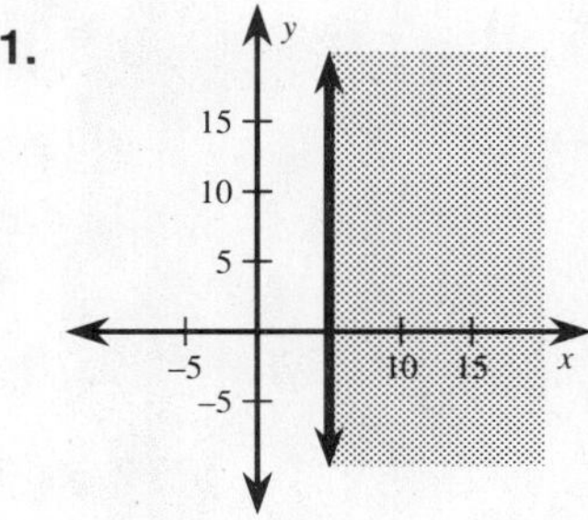

12.

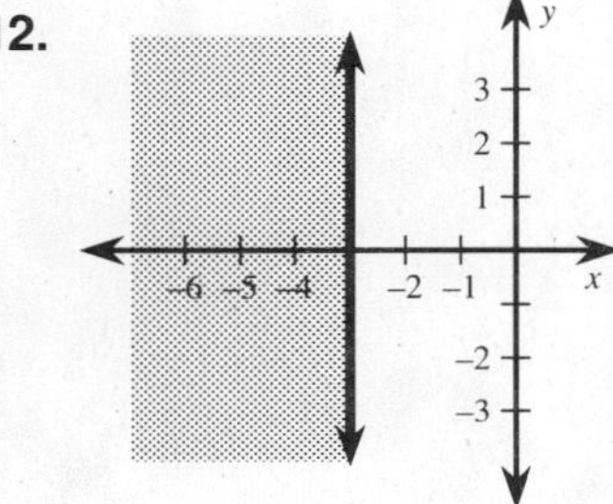

13.

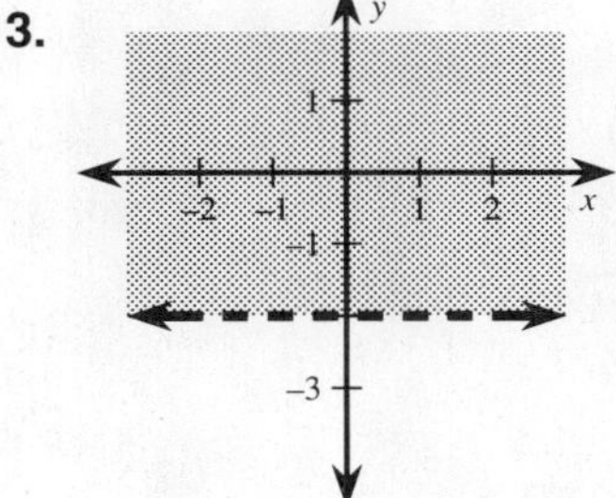

14.

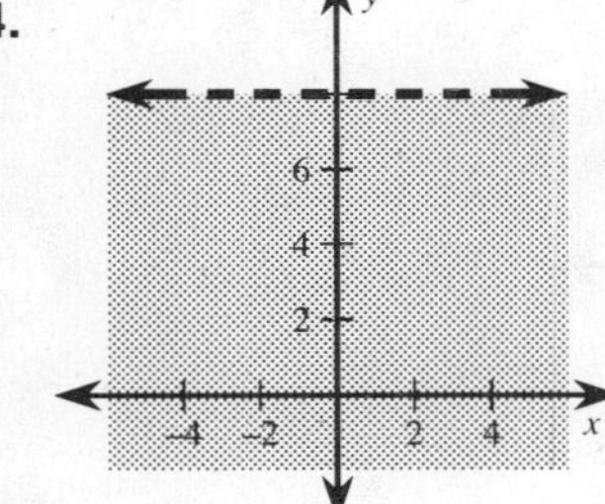

15. **c.**

16. **b.**

17. **d.**

18. **a.**

19.

20.

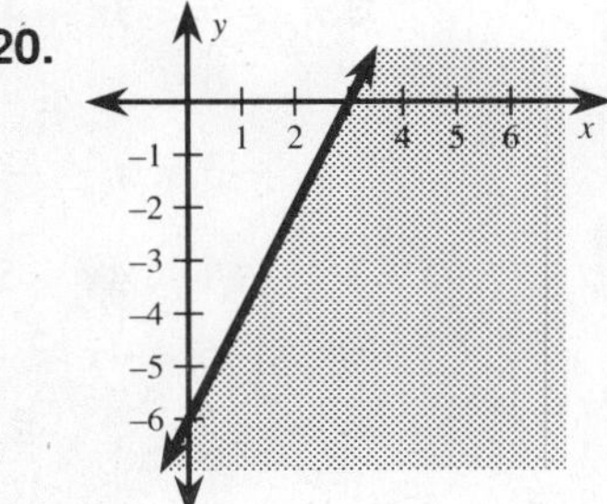

21.

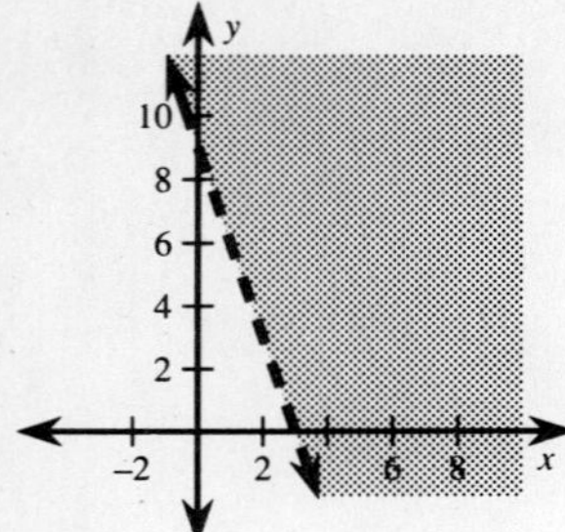

22.

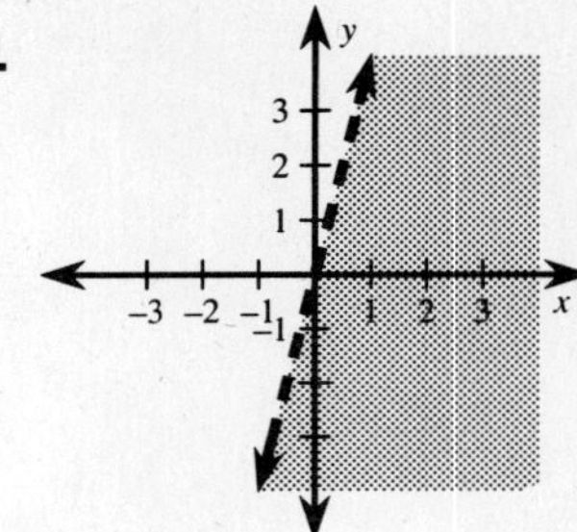

23. $y \leq -2x + 2$

24. $y \geq \frac{2}{5}x - 2$

25. $y < 2x$

26. $y < -\frac{1}{3}x + 1$

27. $0 \leq x + y \leq 6$

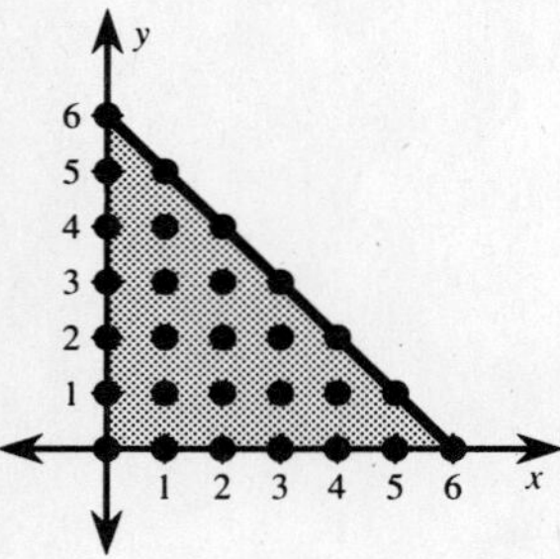

28. $x + y \leq 30$

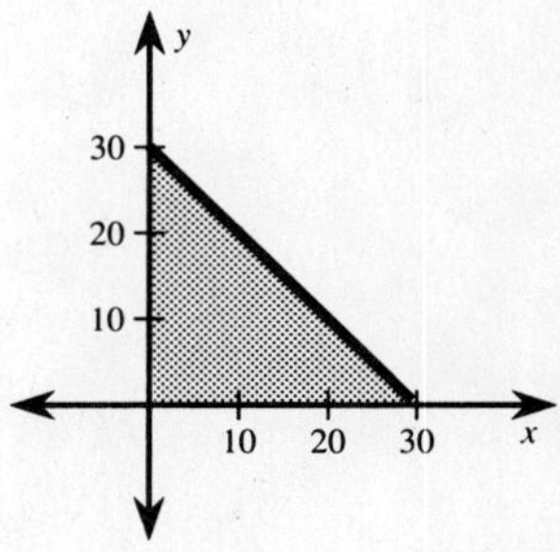

29. $3x + 2y \leq 42$

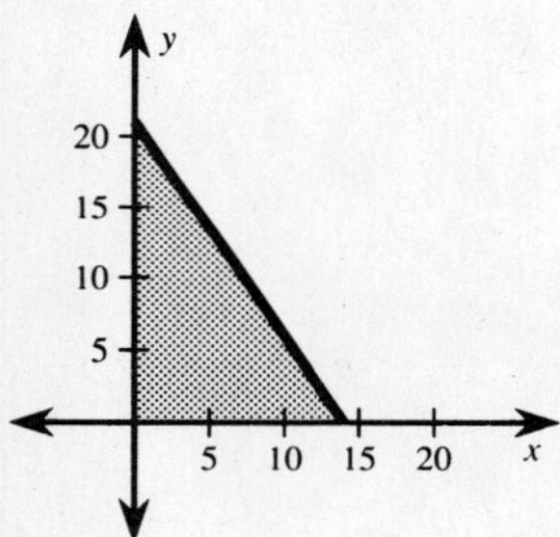

30. $20{,}000x + 12{,}000y \leq 1{,}200{,}000$

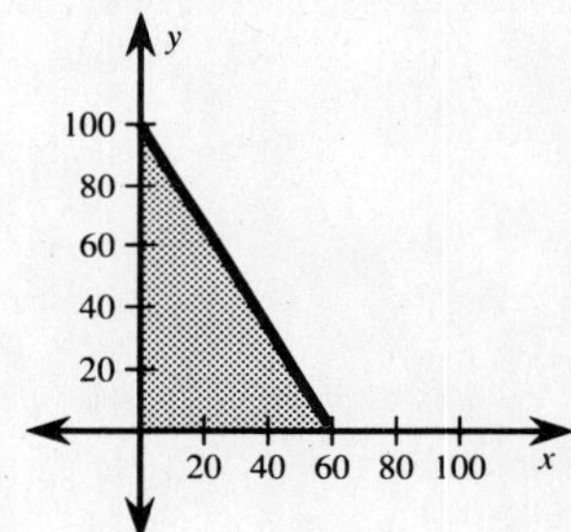

31. $3x - 1 > 7$
$3x > 8$
$x > \frac{8}{3}$

32. $6 - x \leq 28$
$-x \leq 22$
$x \geq -22$

33. $14x + 5 \leq 4x - 15$
$10x \leq -20$
$x \leq -2$

34. $-3x - 1 > -2x + 19$
$-x > 20$
$x < -20$

35. $-5 < 3x + 4 \leq 1$
$-9 < 3x \leq -3$
$-3 < x \leq -1$

36. $0 \leq 9x - 63 < 18$
$63 \leq 9x < 81$
$7 \leq x < 9$

37. $-10 \leq 3 - 2x \leq 9$
$-13 \leq -2x \leq 6$
$\frac{13}{2} \geq x \geq -3$
$-3 \leq x \leq \frac{13}{2}$

38. $-1 < 4x + 5 < 0$
$-6 < 4x < -5$
$-\frac{3}{2} < x < -\frac{5}{4}$

39. $5 \cdot 2 - 2(-2) = 10 + 4$
$= 14$
(2, −2) is not a solution.

40. $-5 - 3(-4) = -5 + 12$
$= 7 \leq 17$

$(-5, -4)$ is a solution.

41. $-4(-1) + 14 = 4 + 14$
$= 18 > 10$

$(-1, 14)$ is a solution.

42. $3(-4) + 9 \cdot 1 = -12 + 9$
$= -3$

$(-4, 1)$ is a solution.

43.

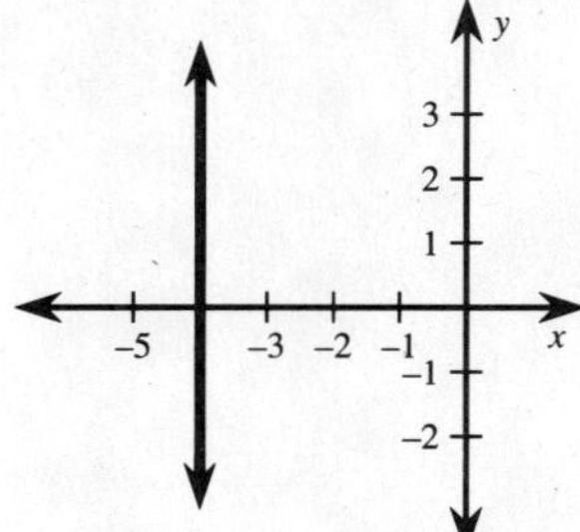

44.

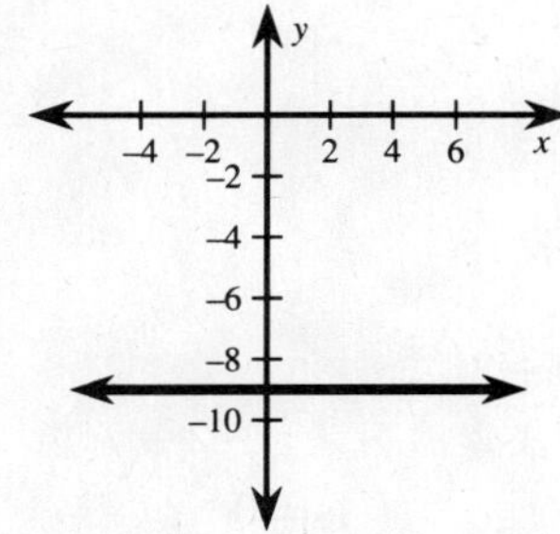

45.

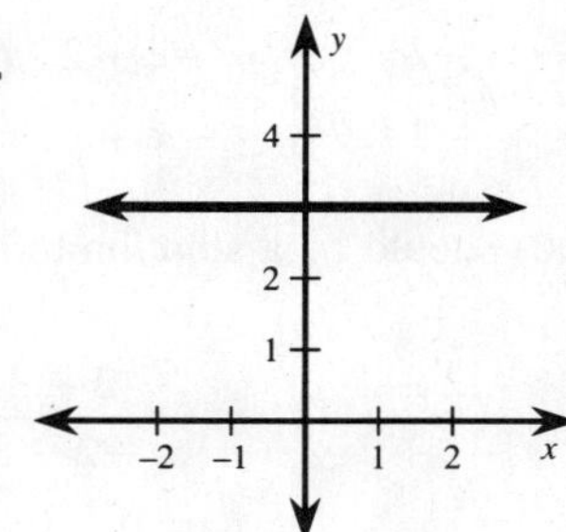

46.

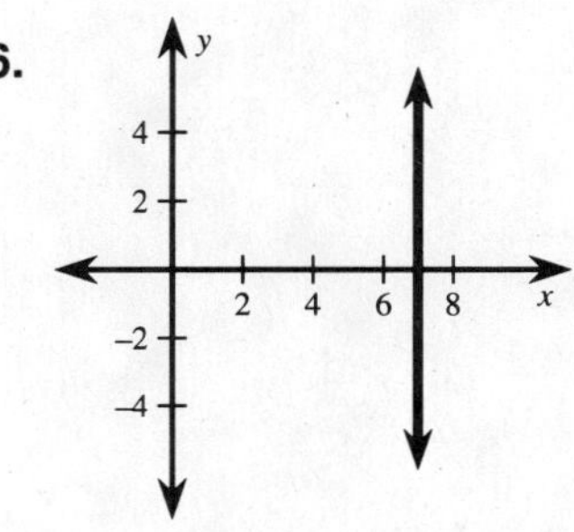

47. $x + y = 9$
$y = -x + 9$

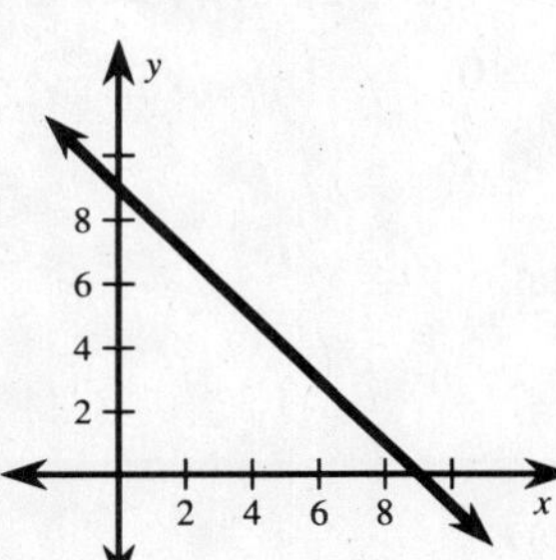

48. $-2x + y = 11$
$y = 2x + 11$

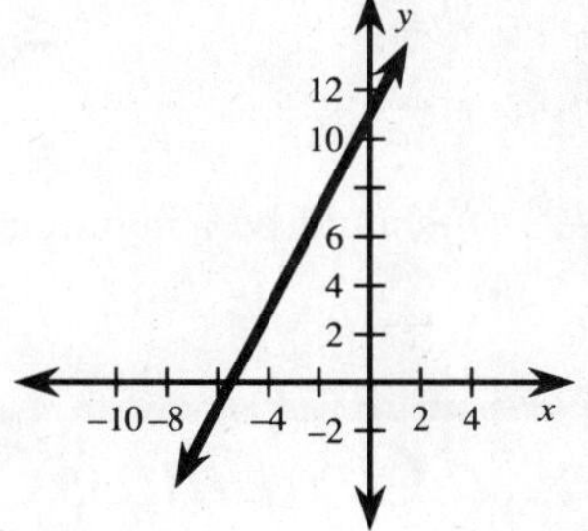

49. $3x - 2y = 12$
$-2y = -3x + 12$
$y = \frac{3}{2}x - 6$

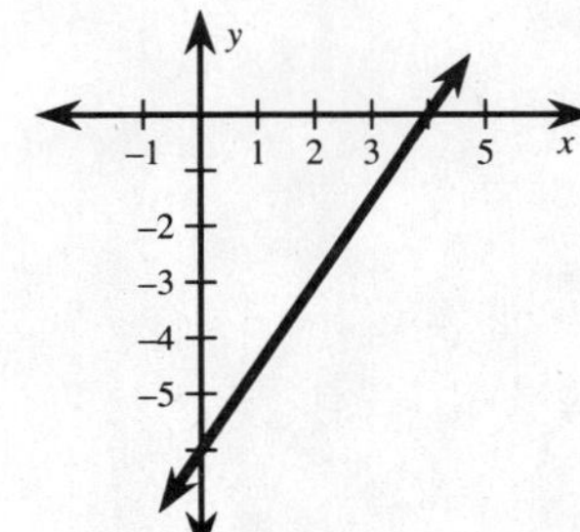

50. $x - 3y = 6$
$-3y = -x + 6$
$y = \frac{1}{3}x - 2$

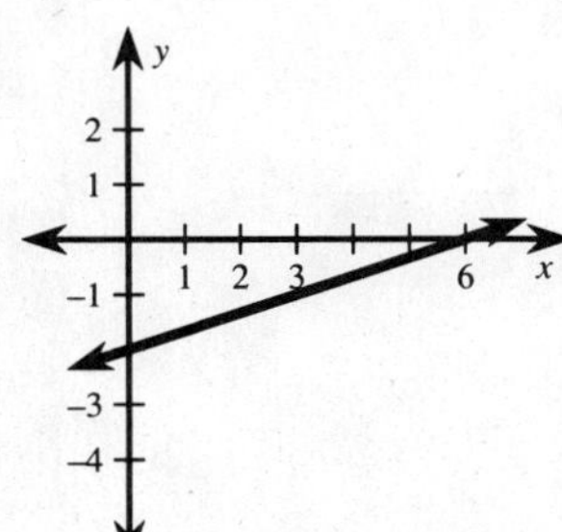

51. $m = \frac{0-2}{-2-0} = \frac{-2}{-2} = 1$ $\quad m = \frac{2-0}{0-2} = -1$ $\quad m = \frac{0-(-2)}{2-0} = \frac{2}{2} = 1$ $\quad m = \frac{-2-0}{0-(-2)} = \frac{-2}{2} = -1$

$y = x + 2 \qquad y = -x + 2 \qquad y = x - 2 \qquad y = -x - 2$

$y \le x + 2 \qquad y \le -x + 2 \qquad y \ge x - 2 \qquad y \ge -x - 2$

(0, 0) should be a solution to each inequality.

52. $m = \frac{-2-3}{-7+2} = \frac{-5}{-5} = 1$ $\quad m = \frac{3-3}{-2-3} = 0$ $\quad m = \frac{3+2}{3+2} = 1$ $\quad m = \frac{-2+2}{-2+7} = 0$

$y + 2 = 1(x + 7) \qquad y = 3 \qquad y + 2 = 1(x + 2) \qquad y = -2$

$-x + y = 5 \qquad y \le 3 \qquad -x + y = 0 \qquad y \ge -2$

$y \le x + 5 \qquad y \ge x$

(−2, 0) should be a solution to each inequality.

Using a Graphing Calculator

1.

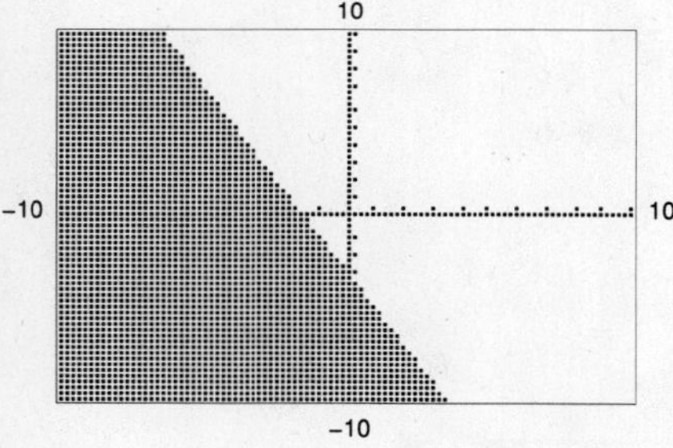

2.

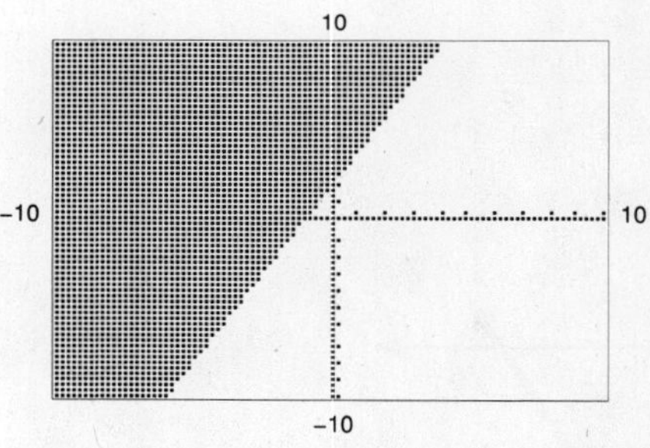

3. $x + 2y \le -1$

$2y \le -x - 1$

$y \le -\frac{1}{2}x - \frac{1}{2}$

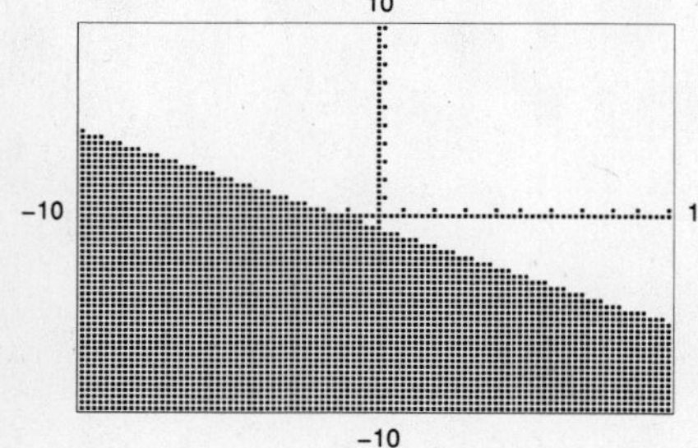

4. $x - 3y \ge 3$

$-3y \ge -x + 3$

$y \le \frac{1}{3}x - 1$

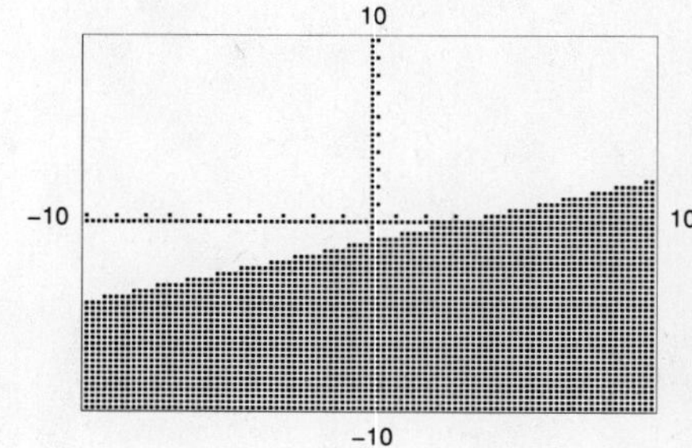

5.

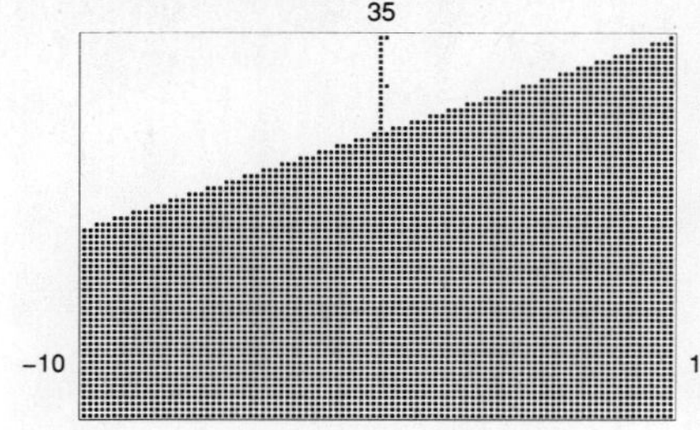

6.

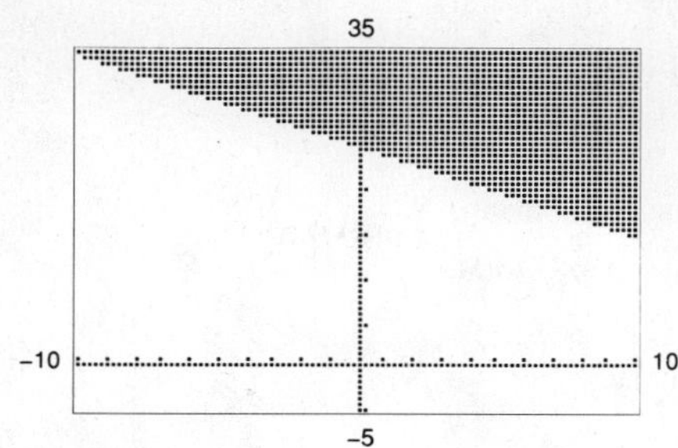

7.

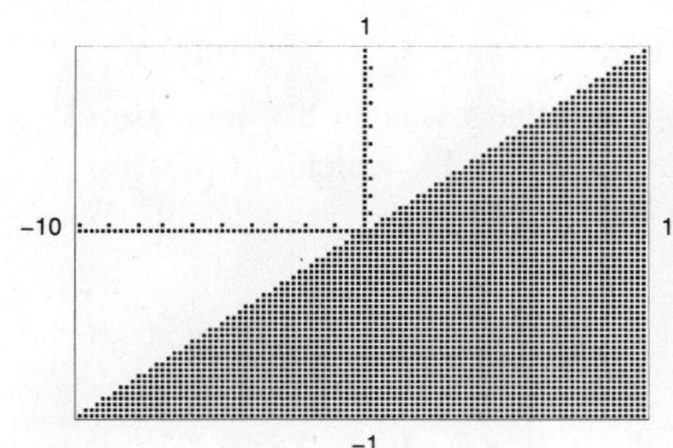

8.

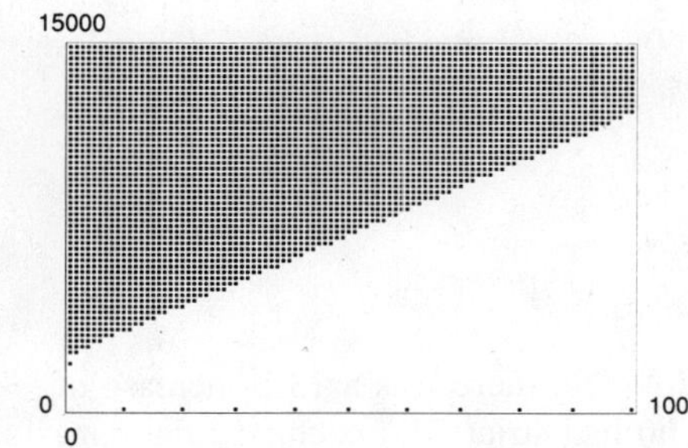

6.6 Exploring Data: Time Lines, Picture Graphs, and Circle Graphs

Communicating about Algebra

A. 9% of Japan's workforce was in construction.

B. $0.24(60{,}000{,}000) = 14{,}400{,}000$

There were approximately 14.4 million manufacturing workers.

C. $0.25(60{,}000{,}000) = 15{,}000{,}000$

There were approximately 15 million service workers.

D. $0.23(60{,}000{,}000) - 0.11(60{,}000{,}000) = 7{,}200{,}000$

7.2 million more people worked in distribution than in agriculture and fishing.

EXERCISES

1. No; the first automatic transmission was introduced in 1940.

2. 1985: 3.5 million gallons

1988: 7 million gallons

$$\frac{3.5}{7} = \frac{1}{2}$$

The ratio of Saudi Arabia's 1985 daily oil production to its 1988 daily oil production is approximately $\frac{1}{2}$.

3. The kittens left the box primarily when the mother was out of the box.

4. $0.36 \cdot 500 = 180$ (bored with arrangement)
$0.19 \cdot 500 = 95$ (moving to new home)
$0.16 \cdot 500 = 80$ (redecorating)
$0.15 \cdot 500 = 75$ (purchase new furniture)
$0.14 \cdot 500 = 70$ (other)

5. c. **6.** d. **7.** b. **8.** a.

9. Breakfast was at 7:30 A.M.
Lunch was at 12 noon.
Dinner was at 6:00 P.M.

10. The woman slept $7\frac{1}{2}$ hours.

11. Answers vary.

12. In 1990, 45% of parents had strict TV-watching rules for 13–17 year-olds.

13. In 1976, 60% of parents had strict TV-watching rules for 7–12 year-olds.

14. $45 - 37 = 8\%$

From 1976–1990 there was an 8% increase of parents who had strict TV-watching rules for 13–17 year-olds.

15. $62 - 49 = 13\%$

From 1976–1990 there was a 13% increase of parents who had strict TV-watching rules for children 6 and under.

16. Oil became the primary source in the 1960's.

17. In 1970, coal was the second most common source of energy.

18. Equivalent to 5 million barrels of natural gas were used in 1920.

19. Equivalent to 5 million barrels of electricity were used in 1970 than in 1960.

20. $24 + 36 = 50\%$

50% bought either queen or full-size beds.

21. $39 - 26 = 13\%$

The percentage difference between people who bought twin and full-size beds is 13%.

22. Total: $931 + 532 + 152 + 133 + 95 + 152 = 1995$

Romance: $\frac{931}{1995} \approx 46.7$ (%)

Get Well: $\frac{532}{1995} \approx 26.7$ (%)

Sympathy: $\frac{152}{1995} \approx 7.6$ (%)

Birthday: $\frac{133}{1995} \approx 6.7$ (%)

Congratulations: $\frac{95}{1995} \approx 4.8$ (%)

Other: $\frac{152}{1995} \approx 7.6$ (%)

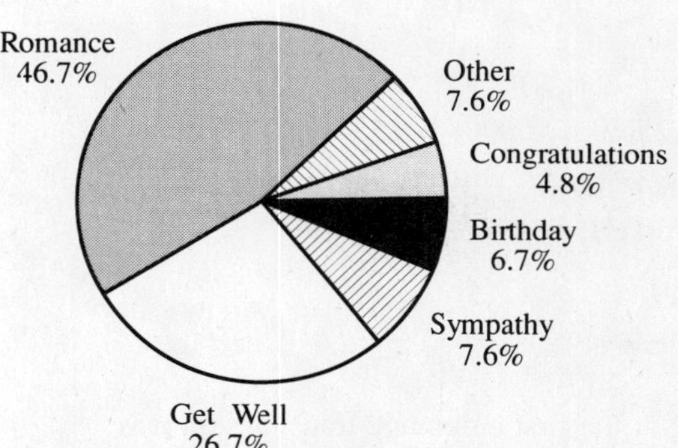

23. Total: $1810 + 1000 + 1540 + 1180 + 635 + 1180 = 7345$

Refrigeration: $\frac{1810}{7345} \approx 24.6$ (%)

Lighting: $\frac{1000}{7345} \approx 13.6$ (%)

Water Heating: $\frac{1540}{7345} \approx 21.0$ (%)

Air-Conditioning: $\frac{1180}{7345} \approx 16.1$ (%)

Cooking: $\frac{635}{7345} \approx 8.6$ (%)

Other: $\frac{1180}{7345} \approx 16.1$ (%)

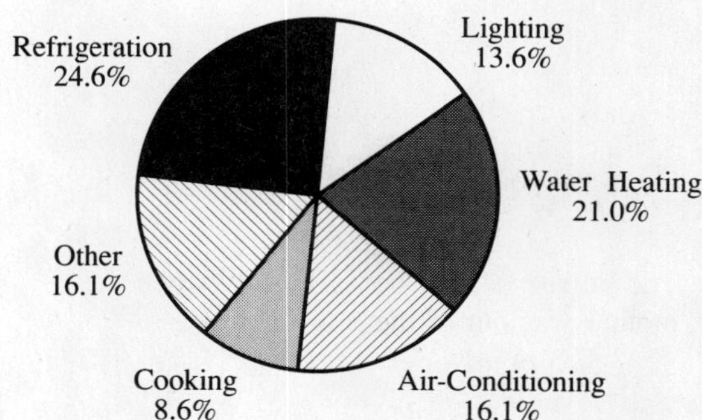

24. $0.23 \cdot 2{,}205{,}000 = 507{,}150$

$507,150 was spent on blue bicycles in 1989.

25. $(0.24 - 0.23)(2{,}205{,}000) = (0.01)(2{,}205{,}000)$

$= 22{,}050$

$22,050 more was spent on black bicycles than on blue bicycles.

26. $(0.72)(150) = 108$

You got 108 points on a 150-point test.

27. $24.99 + 24.99x = 26.74$

$24.99x = 1.75$

$x \approx 0.07$

The sales tax was 7%.

28. $(0.08)(240) = 192$

192 free throws were made in the season.

29. $(0.56)(25) = 14$

14 passes out of 25 would be completed in a game.

30. $3.50 + 3.50x = 5.00$

$3.50x = 1.50$

$x \approx 0.43$

You would make 43% profit on the baseball card.

31. $2x > 6$

$x > 3$

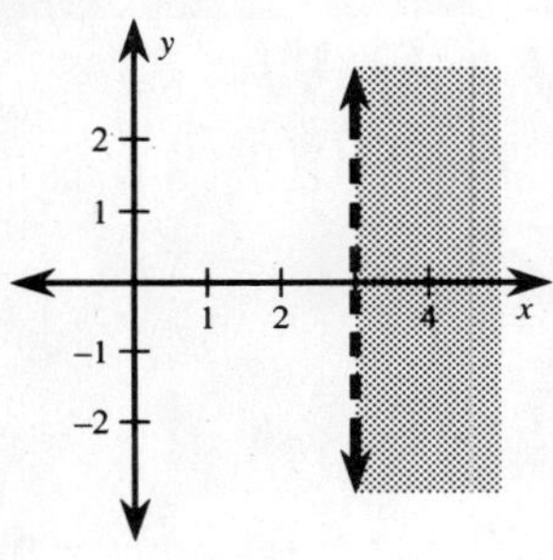

32. $y \leq 8$

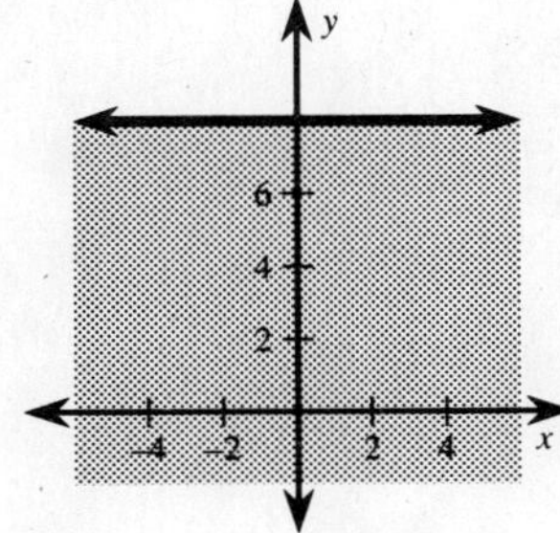

33. $x + y \leq 3$

$y \leq -x + 3$

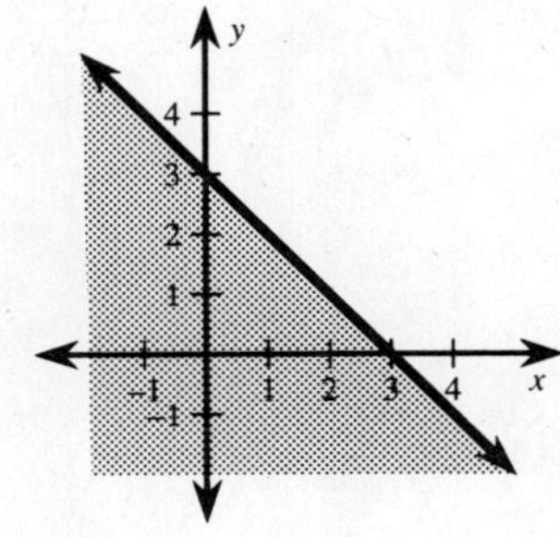

34. $x - y > 5$

$-y > -x + 5$

$y < x - 5$

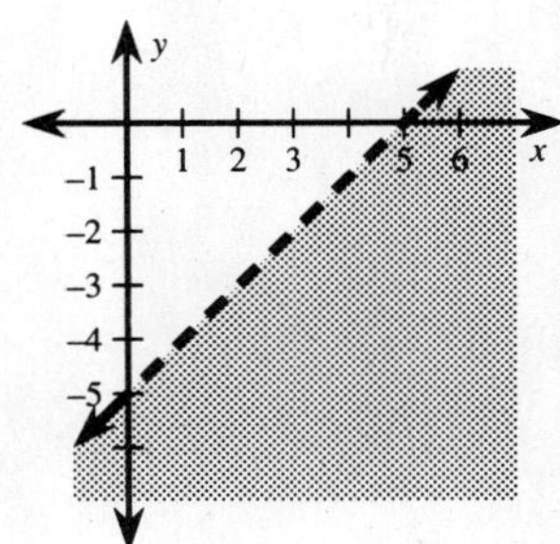

35. $x - 2y > 4$

$-2y > -x + 4$

$y < \frac{1}{2}x - 2$

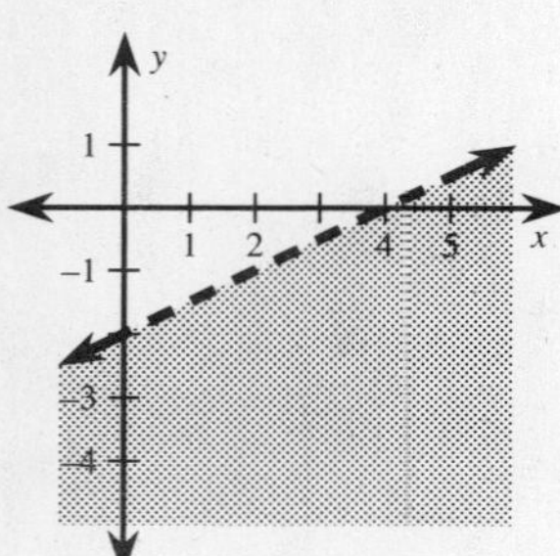

36. $2x + y < 6$

$y < -2x + 6$

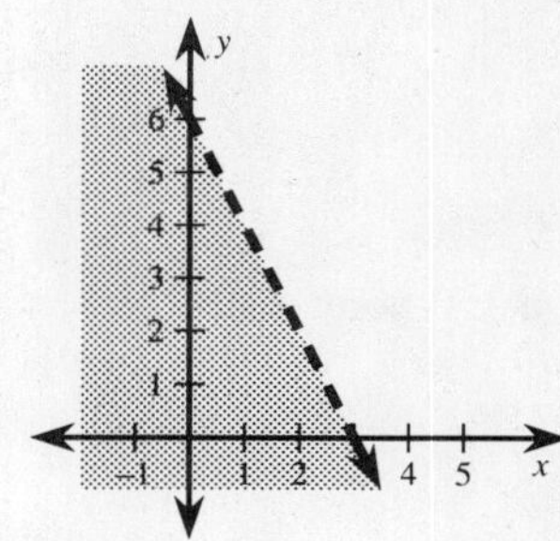

37. **b.**

38. **b.**

39. Amendments 13 and 14

40. Amendment 19

41. Amendment 22

42. Amendments 18 and 21

Chapter **REVIEW**

1. −4 −3 −2 −1 0 x

2.

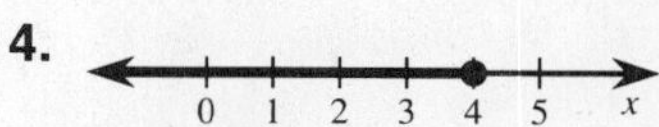

3. −5 −4 −3 −2 −1 0 x

4. 0 1 2 3 4 5 x

5. $3x + 5 \geq 4$

$3x \geq -1$

$x \geq -\frac{1}{3}$

6. $\frac{2}{3}(x - 6) \geq 0$

$x - 6 \geq 0$

$x \geq 6$

7. $6 \geq \frac{1}{4}(3 + x)$

$24 \geq 3 + x$

$21 \geq x$

$x \leq 21$

8. $75x - 50 < 55x - 30$

$20x < 20$

$x < 1$

9. $-x + 5 < 2(x - 4)$

$-x + 5 < 2x - 8$

$-3x < -13$

$x > \frac{13}{3}$

10. $(x - 6)4 > x + 30$

$4x - 24 > x + 30$

$3x > 54$

$x > 18$

11. $3 < 1 - 6x < 6$

$2 < -6x < 5$

$-\frac{1}{3} > x > -\frac{5}{6}$

$-\frac{5}{6} < x < -\frac{1}{3}$

12. $-53 < 37 - 5x < 42$

$-90 < -5x < 5$

$18 > x > -1$

$-1 < x < 18$

13. $0 \leq \frac{1}{4}(x - 8) \leq 20$

$0 \leq x - 8 \leq 80$

$8 \leq x \leq 88$

14. $2(x + 3) < -4$ or $14x + (-3) > 4$

$x + 3 < -2$ $\qquad 14x > 7$

$x < -5$ $\qquad x > \frac{1}{2}$

15. $-x + \frac{1}{2} \leq -\frac{3}{4}$ or $\frac{1}{4}(x + 2) < \frac{3}{4}$

$-x \leq -\frac{5}{4}$ $\qquad x + 2 < 3$

$x \geq \frac{5}{4}$ $\qquad x < 1$

16. $\frac{1}{3}(4 - x) > 6$ or $\frac{2}{5}(x + 7) \geq 4$

$4 - x > 18 \qquad x + 7 \geq 10$

$-x > 14 \qquad x \geq 3$

$x < -14$

17. $|2x - 4| \geq 3$

$2x - 4 \leq -3$ or $2x - 4 \geq 3$

$2x \leq 1 \qquad 2x \geq 7$

$x \leq \frac{1}{2} \qquad x \geq \frac{7}{2}$

18. $\left|x - \frac{1}{2}\right| \leq 3$

$-3 \leq x - \frac{1}{2} \leq 3$

$-\frac{5}{2} \leq x \leq \frac{7}{2}$

19. $\left|\frac{1}{3}x - \frac{2}{3}\right| > 6$

$\frac{1}{3}x - \frac{2}{3} < -6$ or $\frac{1}{3}x - \frac{2}{3} > 6$

$x - 2 < -18 \qquad x - 2 > 18$

$x < -16 \qquad x > 20$

20. $\left|\frac{25}{3} - 5x\right| < \frac{5}{3}$

$-\frac{5}{3} < \frac{25}{3} - 5x < \frac{5}{3}$

$-5 < 25 - 15x < 5$

$-30 < -15x < -20$

$2 > x > \frac{4}{3}$

$\frac{4}{3} < x < 2$

21. $5 - \frac{1}{2}x \leq -3$

$-\frac{1}{2}x \leq -8$

$x \geq 16$

14 15 16 17 18 x

22. $3(2x + 8) \geq 4(-2x - 4)$

$6x + 24 \geq -8x - 16$

$14x \geq -40$

$x \geq -\frac{20}{7}$

$-\frac{20}{7}$

−5 −4 −3 −2 −1 0 x

23. $-4 < 3x + 1 < 4$

$-5 < 3x < 3$

$-\frac{5}{3} < x < 1$

$-\frac{5}{3}$

−3 −2 −1 0 1 2 x

24. $\frac{1}{5}(x + 5) < \frac{2}{3}$ or $\frac{1}{5}(x + 5) > \frac{5}{4}$

$x + 5 < \frac{10}{3} \qquad x + 5 > \frac{25}{4}$

$x < -\frac{5}{3} \qquad x > \frac{5}{4}$

$-\frac{5}{3}$ $\frac{5}{4}$

−4 −2 0 2 4 x

25. $|4x - 5| < 20$

$-20 < 4x - 5 < 20$

$-15 < 4x < 25$

$-\frac{15}{4} < x < \frac{25}{4}$

$-\frac{15}{4}$ $\frac{25}{4}$

−6 −3 0 3 6 9 x

26. $\left|3 - \frac{1}{2}x\right| \geq 7$

$3 - \frac{1}{2}x \leq -7$ or $3 - \frac{1}{2}x \geq 7$

$-\frac{1}{2}x \leq -10 \qquad -\frac{1}{2}x \geq 4$

$x \geq 20 \qquad x \leq -8$

−8

−20 −10 0 10 20 30 x

27. b.

$|x - 2| \leq 3$

$-3 \leq x - 2 \leq 3$

$-1 \leq x \leq 5$

28. d.

$|x + 1| \geq 2$

$x + 1 \leq -2$ or $x + 1 \geq 2$

$x \leq -3 \qquad x \geq 1$

29. a.

$|x - 1| < 4$

$-4 < x - 1 < 4$

$-3 < x < 5$

30. c.

$|x + 2| > 1$

$x + 2 < -1$ or $x + 2 > 1$

$x < -3 \qquad x > -1$

31. $5 \le x \le 10$

$5 - 7.5 \le x - 7.5 \le 10 - 7.5$

$-2.5 \le x - 7.5 \le 2.5$

$|x - 7.5| \le 2.5$

32. $x < -2$ or $x > 0$

$x + 1 < -1 \qquad x + 1 > 1$

$|x + 1| > 1$

33. $-1 < x < 6$

$-1 - 2.5 < x - 2.5 < 6 - 2.5$

$-3.5 < x - 2.5 < 3.5$

$|x - 2.5| < 3.5$

34. $x \le -3$ or $x \ge 2$

$x + \frac{1}{2} \le -3 + \frac{1}{2} \qquad x + \frac{1}{2} \ge 2 + \frac{1}{2}$

$x + \frac{1}{2} \le -2\frac{1}{2} \qquad x + \frac{1}{2} \ge 2\frac{1}{2}$

$|x + \frac{1}{2}| \ge 2\frac{1}{2}$

35. $\frac{1}{4}(0) - 2(4) + 3 = 0 - 8 + 3$

$= -5 < 4$

(4, 0) is not a solution.

$\frac{1}{4}(-3) - 2(-4) + 3 = -\frac{3}{4} + 8 + 3$

$= 10\frac{1}{4} \ge 4$

(−4, −3) is a solution.

36. $2(0 - 0) = 2(0)$

$= 0$

(0, 0) is not a solution.

$2(-1 - 2) = 2(-3)$

$= -6 < 0$

(2, −1) is a solution.

37. $\frac{1}{2}(-2) + \frac{1}{3}(1) = -1 + \frac{1}{3}$

$= -\frac{2}{3} > -3$

(−2, 1) is a solution.

$\frac{1}{2}(-8) + \frac{1}{3}(-9) = -4 - 3$

$= -7 < -3$

(−8, −9) is not a solution.

38. $2(3)^2 + (-2) = 18 - 2$

$= 16 > 14$

(3, −2) is not a solution.

$2(2)^2 + 7 = 8 + 7$

$= 15 > 14$

(2, 7) is not a solution.

39. $-2x + y > 4$

$y > 2x + 4$

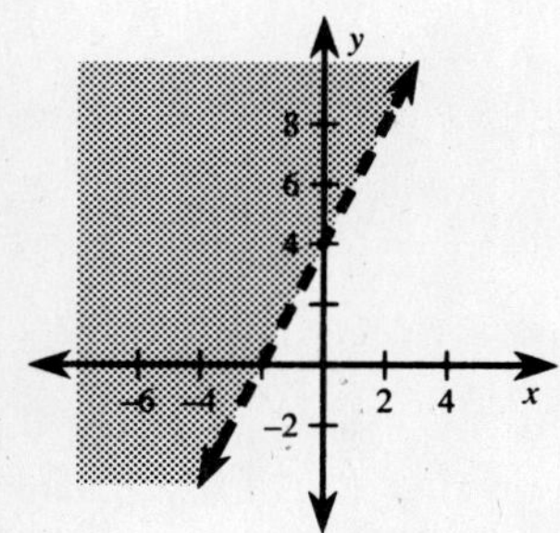

40. $-\left(\frac{1}{3}x + 3y\right) \le 3$

$\frac{1}{3}x + 3y \ge -3$

$3y \ge -\frac{1}{3}x - 3$

$y \ge -\frac{1}{9}x - 1$

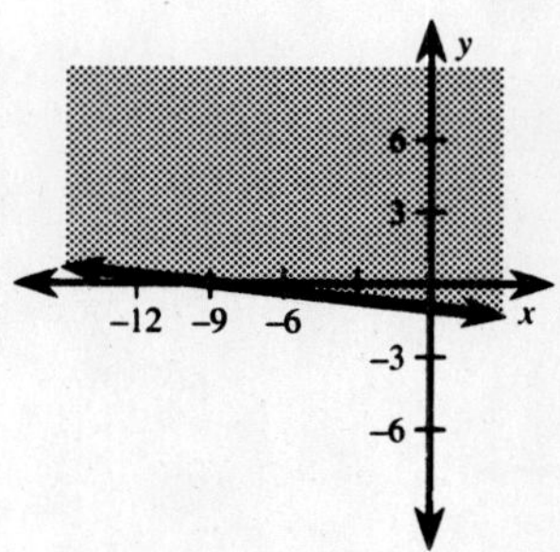

41. $\frac{3}{8}(x + y + 8) \geq \frac{1}{4}$

$3x + 3y + 24 \geq 2$

$3y \geq -3x - 22$

$y \geq -x - \frac{22}{3}$

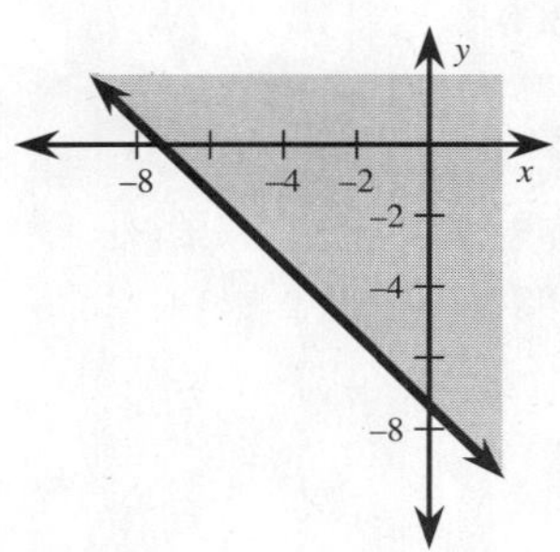

42. $13x + y \geq 10x - 10$

$y \geq -3x - 10$

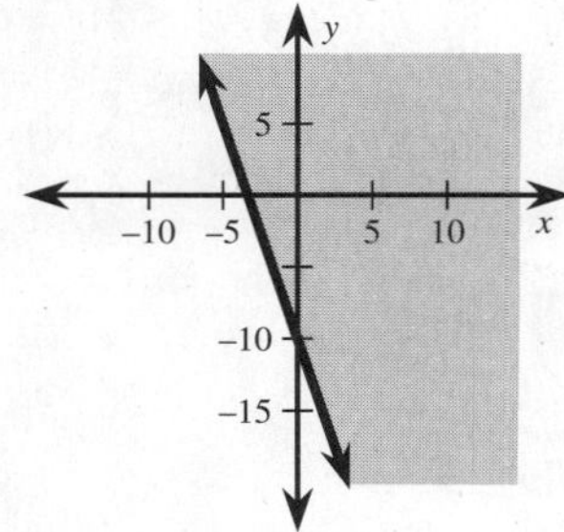

43. $1 \leq h \leq 40$

44. $5 \leq w \leq 100{,}000$

45. $3 \leq p \leq 12$

Tattarrattat is defined by the Oxford English Dictionary as a nonce word, which means the word was written for the occasion. James Joyce used the word in his 1922 work "Ulysses". "I knew his tattarrattat at the door."

46. $28 \leq t \leq 86$

47. $0.10d + 0.05n \leq 24.50$

48. $10d + 5n \leq 2450$

$2d + n \leq 490$

$n \leq -2d + 490$

$0.10(0) + 0.05(35) \stackrel{?}{\leq} 24.50$

$0 + 1.75 \stackrel{?}{\leq} 24.50$

$1.75 \leq 24.50$

Yes; there are 0 dimes and 35 nickels.

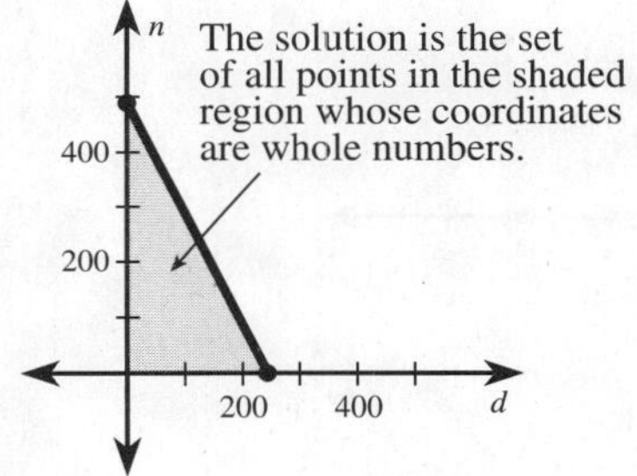

The solution is the set of all points in the shaded region whose coordinates are whole numbers.

49. $1.35x + 0.90y \leq 18.00$

50. $135x + 90y \leq 1800$

$3x + 2y \leq 40$

$2y \leq -3x + 40$

$y \leq -\frac{3}{2}x + 20$

$1.35(15) + 0.90(0) \stackrel{?}{\leq} 18.00$

$20.25 + 0 \stackrel{?}{\leq} 18.00$

$20.25 \not\leq 18.00$

(15, 0) is not a solution.

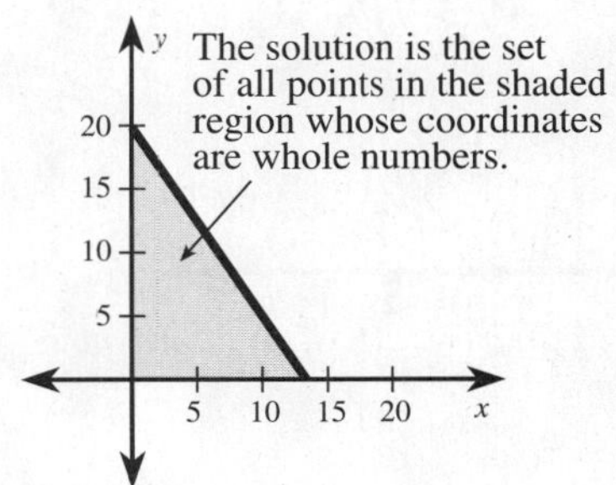

The solution is the set of all points in the shaded region whose coordinates are whole numbers.

No; the coach cannot afford large cones for everyone.

51. The Under 25 and 65-74 age groups spent approximately $650.

52. The 55-64 and 65-74 age groups spent nearly as much on live events as home entertainment.

53. $\approx \$550$

54. $\approx \$225$

55.

$|x - 25| \le 25$

$-25 \le x - 25 \le 25$

Stage 1: $0 \le x \le 50$

$|x - 100| \le 50$

$-50 \le x - 100 \le 50$

Stage 2: $50 \le x \le 150$

$|x - 225| \le 75$

$-75 \le x - 225 \le 75$

Stage 3: $150 \le x \le 300$

$x - 300 \ge 0$

Stage 4: $x \ge 300$

56.

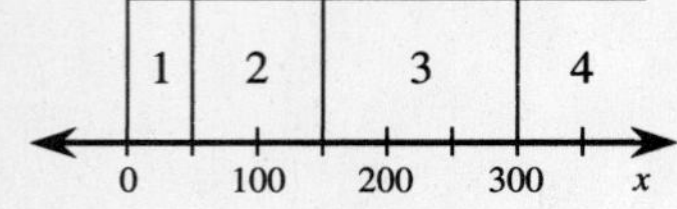

57. Approximately 45 forest fires occured in Yellowstone during 1988. About 87% of these were started by lightning.

58. 700,000 acres of Yellowstone forest burned in 1988. This is nearly 20 times the *total* number of fires between 1972 and 1987.

Chapter TEST

1. $\frac{3}{4}x + 6 \le 3$

$\frac{3}{4}x \le -3$

$x \le -4$

2. $7 - x > 12$

$-x > 5$

$x < -5$

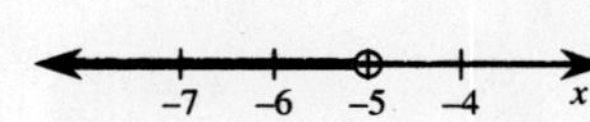

3. $4x + 3 \le 3x - 1$

$x \le -4$

4. $-(4 - x) \ge 2(3 - x)$

$-4 + x \ge 6 - 2x$

$3x \ge 10$

$x \ge \frac{10}{3}$

5. $-3x - 7 > 7x + 11$

$-10x > 18$

$x < -\frac{9}{5}$

6. $-6 \le \frac{1}{4}(3 - x) \le 12$

$-24 \le 3 - x \le 48$

$-27 \le -x \le 45$

$-45 \le x \le 27$

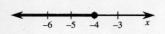

7. $8 < 3x - 4 < 17$

$12 < 3x < 21$

$4 < x < 7$

8. $2x + 1 \geq 7$ or $-3x - 4 \geq 2$

$2x \geq 6$ $\quad -3x \geq 6$

$x \geq 3$ $\quad x \leq -2$

9. $\left|\frac{3}{5}x - 2\right| < 7$

$-7 < \frac{3}{5}x - 2 < 7$

$-5 < \frac{3}{5}x < 9$

$-\frac{25}{3} < x < 15$

10. $|8 - 3x| \geq 12$

$8 - 3x \leq -12$ or $8 - 3x \geq 12$

$-3x \leq -20$ $\quad -3x \geq 4$

$x \geq \frac{20}{3}$ $\quad x \leq -\frac{4}{3}$

11. $x \leq -2$ or $x \geq 2$

$|x| \geq 2$

12. $-4 < x < 0$

$-4 + 2 < x + 2 < 0 + 2$

$-2 < x + 2 < 2$

$|x + 2| < 2$

13. a., b.

$2 \cdot 0 + 2 \cdot 4 \overset{?}{\geq} 3$ $\quad 2 \cdot \frac{3}{4} + 2 \cdot \frac{3}{4} \overset{?}{\geq} 3$ $\quad 2(-1) + 2\left(-\frac{1}{2}\right) \overset{?}{\geq} 3$

$0 + 8 \overset{?}{\geq} 3$ $\quad \frac{3}{2} + \frac{3}{2} \overset{?}{\geq} 3$ $\quad -2 - 1 \overset{?}{\geq} 3$

$8 \geq 3$ $\quad 3 = 3$ $\quad -3 \not\geq 3$

14. $-3y + 2x \geq 6$

$-3y \geq -2x + 6$

$y \leq \frac{2}{3}x - 2$

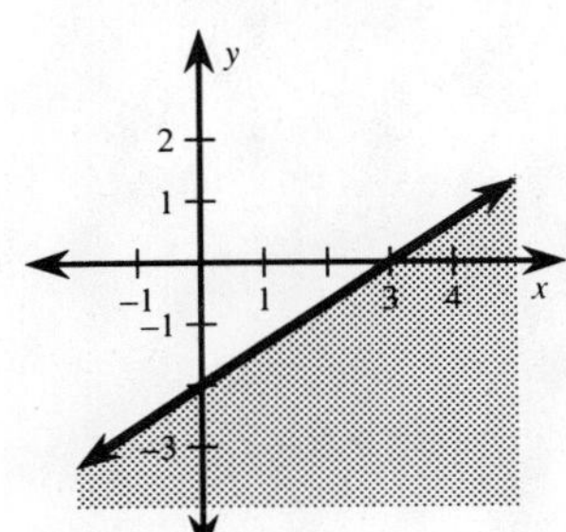

15. $6y - 2x + 2 < 8$

$6y < 2x + 6$

$y < \frac{1}{3}x + 1$

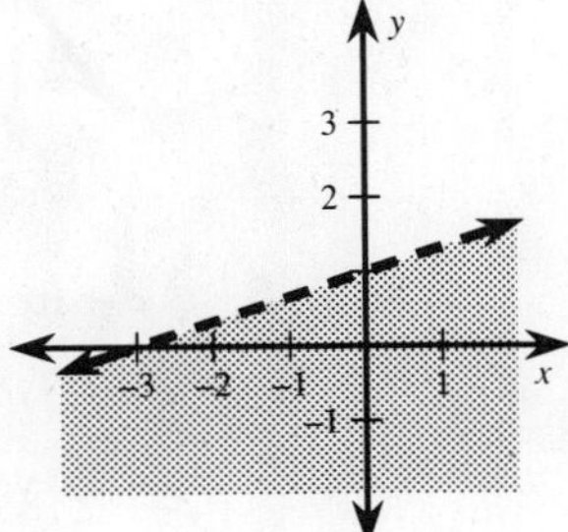

16. $2x + 4y \leq 6$

$4y \leq -2x + 6$

$y \leq -\frac{1}{2}x + \frac{3}{2}$

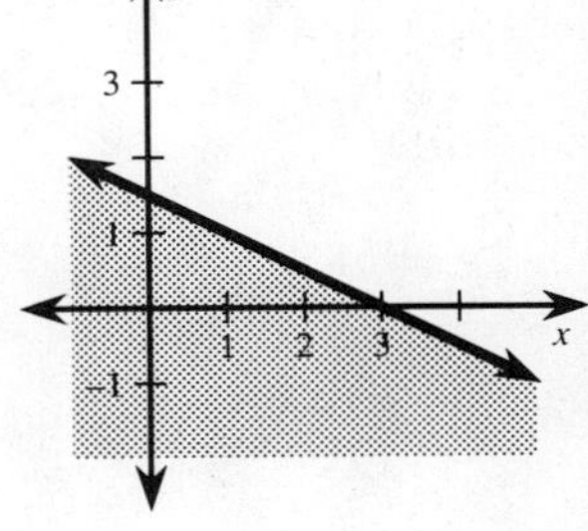

17. Total: $68.7 + 21.3 + 15.7 + 10.5 + 10.1 = 126.3$

United States: $\dfrac{68.7}{126.3} \approx 54.4 \quad (\%)$

Japan: $\dfrac{21.3}{126.3} \approx 16.9 \quad (\%)$

Canada: $\dfrac{15.7}{126.3} \approx 12.4 \quad (\%)$

Soviet Union: $\dfrac{10.5}{126.3} \approx 8.3 \quad (\%)$

West Germany: $\dfrac{10.1}{126.3} \approx 8.0 \quad (\%)$

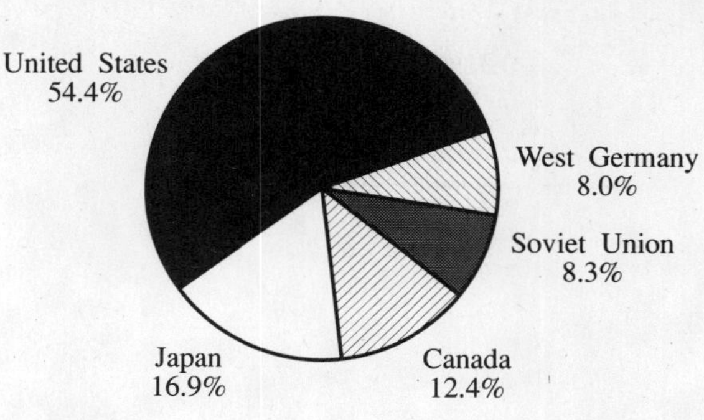

18. $\frac{1}{2} \le x \le 1$

19. $12 \le x \le 33$

20. $3 \div 1 \le x \le 3 \div \frac{3}{4}$

$3 \le x \le 3 \cdot \frac{4}{3}$

$3 \le x \le 4$

Cummulative REVIEW

1. Horizontal: $y = 4$
Vertical: $x = -3$

2. Horizontal: $y = -\frac{1}{2}$
Vertical: $x = -2$

3. Horizontal: $y = 6.2$
Vertical: $x = 7$

4. Horizontal: $y = -\frac{4}{3}$
Vertical: $x = 0$

5. Slope: -3
y-intercept: 2

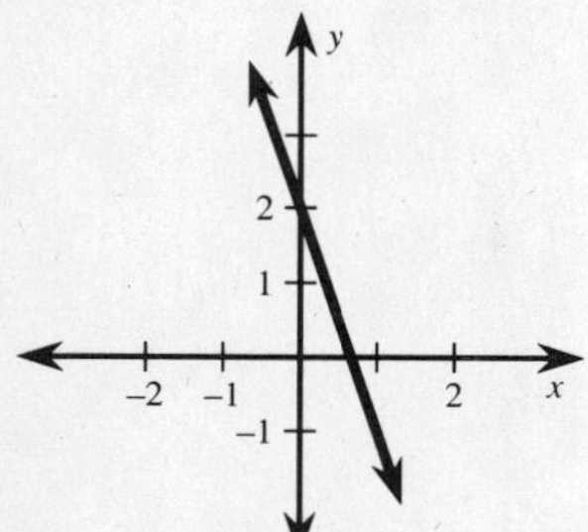

6. Slope: $2\left(\frac{2}{3}\right) = \frac{4}{3}$
y-intercept: $2(-4) = -8$

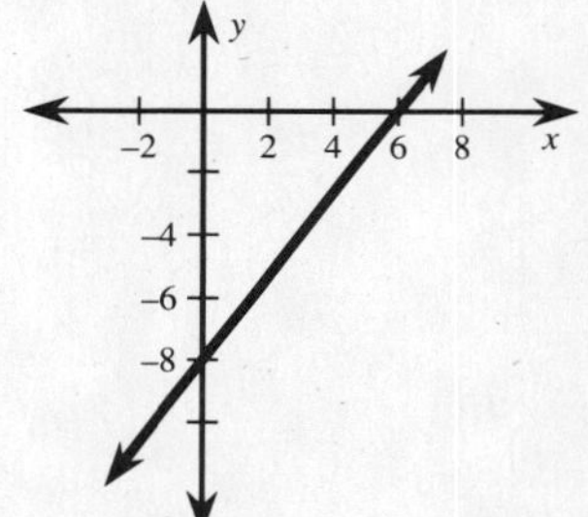

7. $3x + 2y = 14$

$2y = -3x + 14$

$y = -\frac{3}{2}x + 7$

Slope: $-\frac{3}{2}$
y-intercept: 7

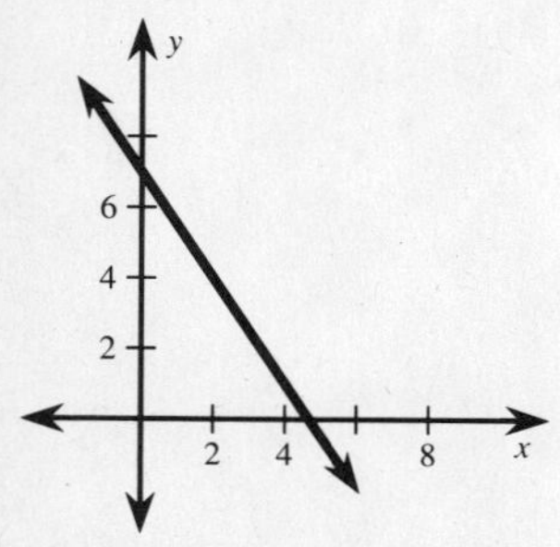

8. $\frac{1}{3}y - 6x = 4$

$\frac{1}{3}y = 6x + 4$

$y = 18x + 12$

Slope: 18
y-intercept: 12

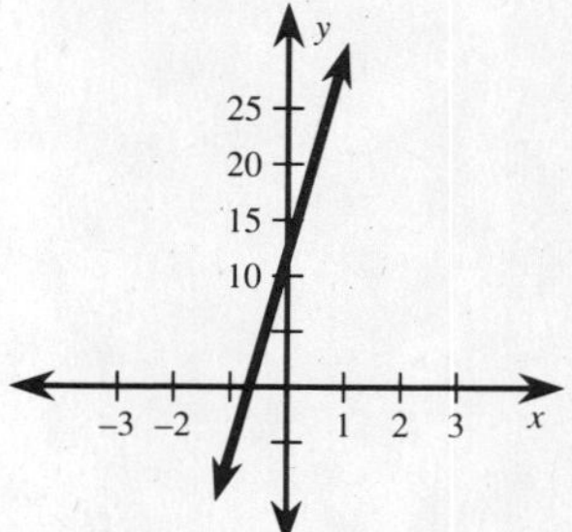

9. $m = \dfrac{-2-5}{6-0}$
$= -\dfrac{7}{6}$

10. $m = \dfrac{7-7}{3-(-6)}$
$= \dfrac{0}{9}$
$= 0$

11. $m = \dfrac{\frac{3}{4}-6}{\frac{1}{2}-(-3)}$
$= \dfrac{-\frac{21}{4}}{\frac{7}{2}}$
$= -\dfrac{21}{14}$
$= -\dfrac{3}{2}$

12. $m = \dfrac{5-25}{5-20}$
$= \dfrac{-20}{-15}$
$= \dfrac{4}{3}$

13. c.

14. a.

15. d.

16. b.

17. $y - 9 = 3(x - 4)$
$y = 3x - 12 + 9$
$y = 3x - 3$

18. $y - 0 = -\frac{1}{2}(x - 5)$
$y = -\frac{1}{2}x + \frac{5}{2}$

19. $y - 6 = -5[x - (-3)]$
$y - 6 = -5x - 15$
$y = -5x - 15 + 6$
$y = -5x - 9$

20. $y - 3 = \frac{7}{3}(x - 0)$
$y = \frac{7}{3}x + 3$

21. $m = \dfrac{6-9}{0-4}$
$= \dfrac{-3}{-4}$
$= \dfrac{3}{4}$

$y - 6 = \dfrac{3}{4}(x - 0)$
$y = \dfrac{3}{4}x + 6$

22. $m = \dfrac{-1-7}{\frac{2}{3}-\frac{4}{9}}$
$= \dfrac{-8}{\frac{2}{9}}$
$= -36$

$y - (-1) = -36\left(x - \frac{2}{3}\right)$
$y + 1 = -36x + 24$
$y = -36x + 23$

23. $m = \dfrac{-3.6-3.4}{4.2-7.0}$
$= \dfrac{-7.0}{-2.8}$
$= 2.5$

$y - (-3.6) = 2.5(x - 4.2)$
$y + 3.6 = 2.5x - 10.5$
$y = 2.5x - 14.1$

24. $m = \dfrac{19-(-19)}{56-37}$
$= \dfrac{38}{19}$
$= 2$

$y - 19 = 2(x - 56)$
$y = 2x - 112 + 19$
$y = 2x - 93$

25.

x	−4	−3	−2	−1	0	1
y	−5	−4	−3	−4	−5	−6

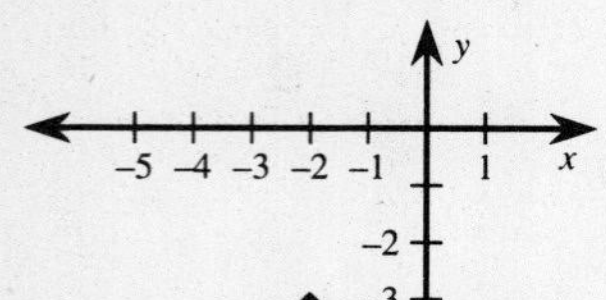
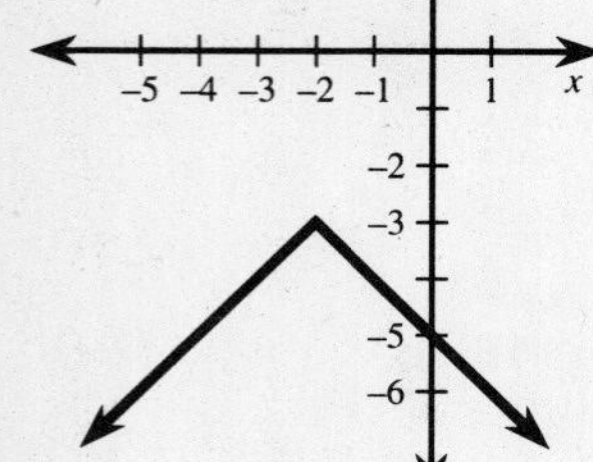

26.

x	1	2	3	4	5	6	7
y	7	$6\frac{2}{3}$	$6\frac{1}{3}$	6	$6\frac{1}{3}$	$6\frac{2}{3}$	7

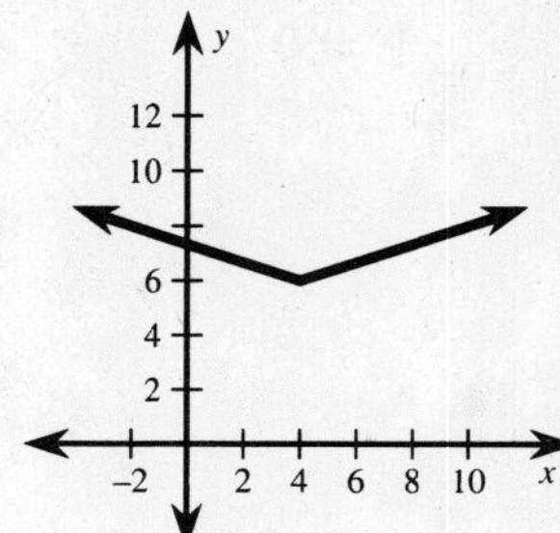

27.

x	−4	−3	−2	−1	0	1
y	−6	−4	−2	−4	−6	−8

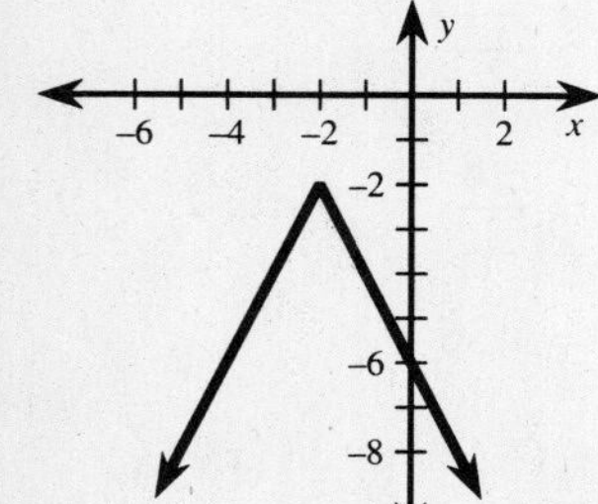

28.

x	−2	−1	0	1	2	3	4
y	18	14	10	6	10	14	18

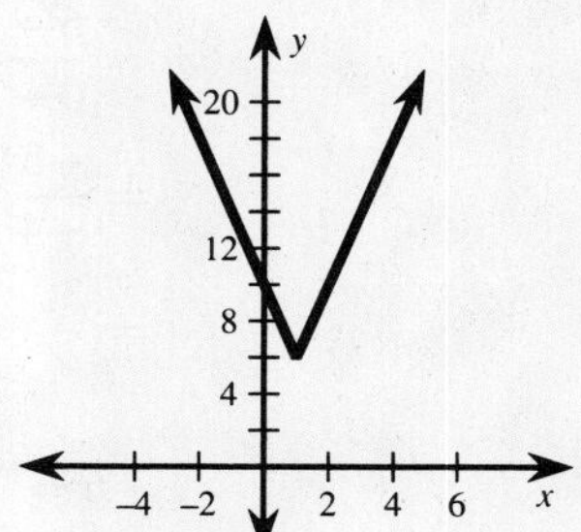

29. $x + 3 = 0$

$x = -3$

$y = |-3 + 3| - 6$

$y = -6$

$(-3, -6)$

30. $2x - 4 = 0$

$2x = 4$

$x = 2$

$y = |2(2) - 4| - 9$

$y = -9$

$(2, -9)$

31. $x + 4 = 0$

$x = -4$

$y = \frac{1}{2}|-4 + 4| + 4$

$y = 4$

$(-4, 4)$

32. $x + 6 = 0$

$x = -6$

$y = -3|-6 + 6| + 1$

$y = 1$

$(-6, 1)$

33. c.

34. d.

35. a.

36. b.

37. c.

$|x-2|<4$

$-4<x-2<4$

$-2<x<6$

38. d.

$|4x-6|\le 4$

$-4\le 4x-6\le 4$

$2\le 4x\le 10$

$\frac{1}{2}\le x\le \frac{5}{2}$

39. a.

$\left|\frac{1}{4}x+2\right|>1$

$\frac{1}{4}x+2<-1$ or $\frac{1}{4}x+2>1$

$\frac{1}{4}x<-3$ $\quad \frac{1}{4}x>-1$

$x<-12$ $\quad x>-4$

40. b.

$\left|x+\frac{3}{2}\right|\ge \frac{3}{2}$

$x+\frac{3}{2}\le -\frac{3}{2}$ or $x+\frac{3}{2}\ge \frac{3}{2}$

$x\le -3$ $\quad x\ge 0$

41. $-2x+3y\ge x+9$

$3y\ge 3x+9$

$y\ge x+3$

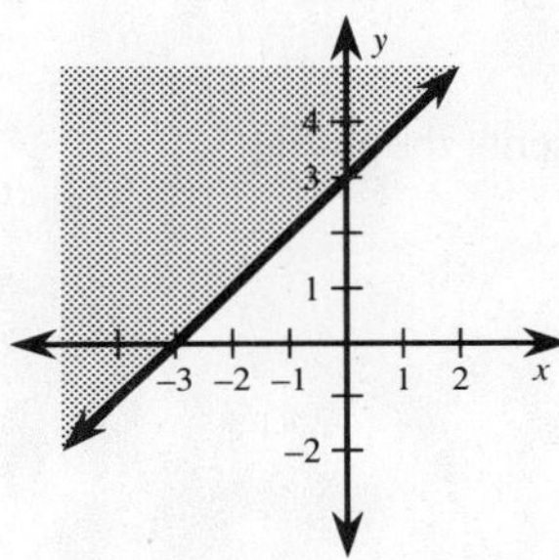

42. $\frac{1}{2}x+2y>4$

$2y>-\frac{1}{2}x+4$

$y>-\frac{1}{4}x+2$

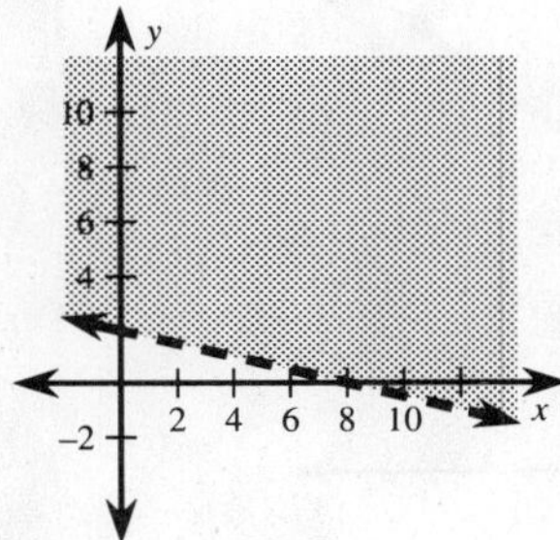

43. $-\frac{1}{2}(2x+y)<1$

$2x+y>-2$

$y>-2x-2$

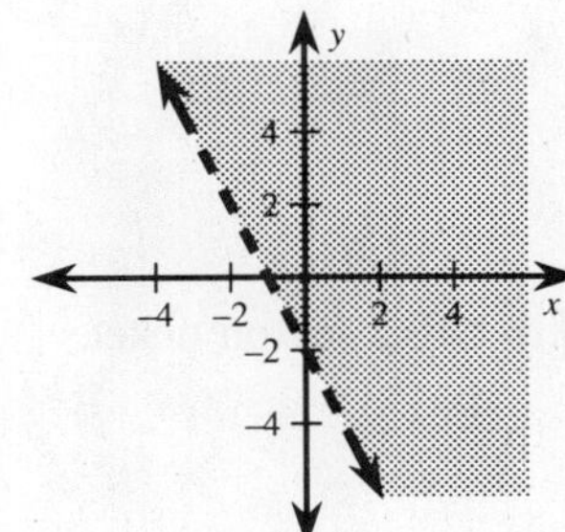

44. $-y\ge 3x-1$

$y\le -3x+1$

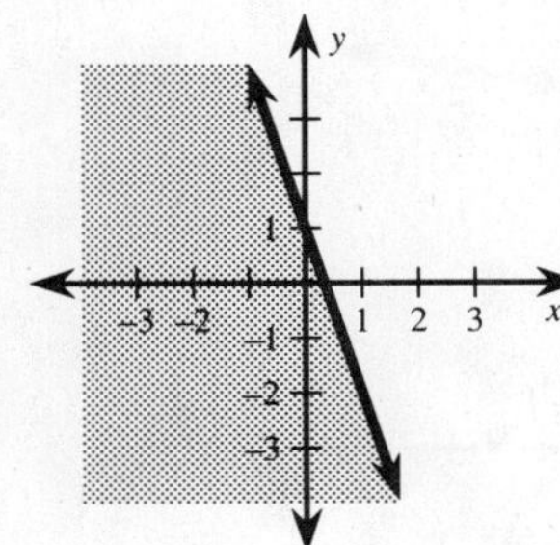

45. $1.00x + 1.50y = 150.00$

$$10x + 15y = 1500$$
$$15y = -10x + 1500$$
$$y = -\tfrac{2}{3}x + 100$$

Bags of peanuts

Boxes of popcorn

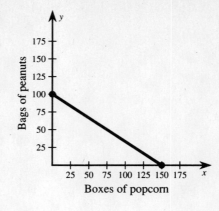

46. $1.00x + 1.50(36) = 150.00$

$$1.00x = 150.00 - 54.00$$
$$x = 96 \text{ boxes of popcorn}$$

47. $y = 3x + 20$

48. 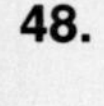

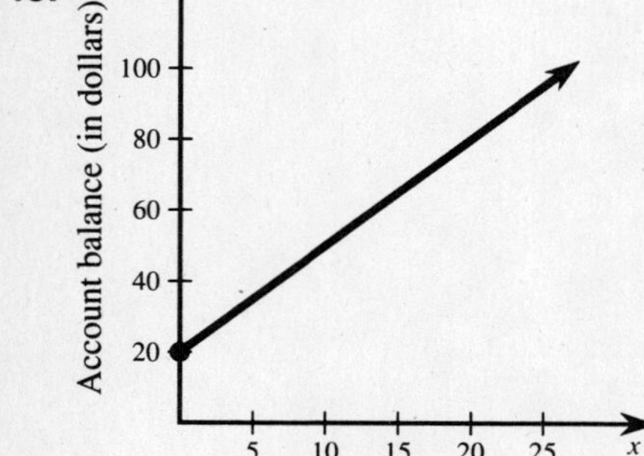

49. The slope represents an increase of \$3 each week.

50. The y-intercept represents the initial \$20 deposit.

51.

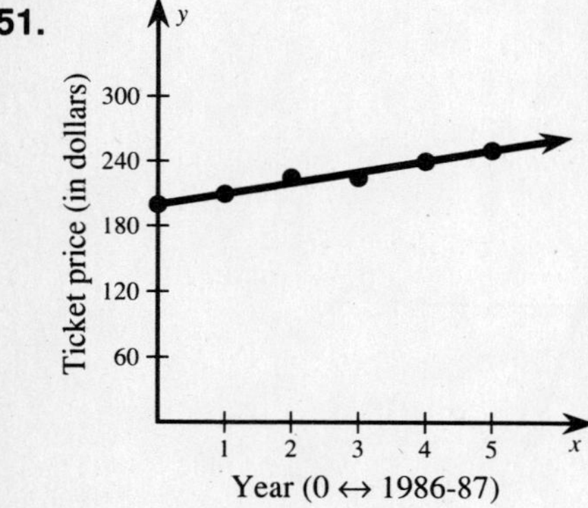

52. $y = 10x + 200$

53. The slope represents an average increase of \$10 per ticket each year.

54. $y = 10(6) + 200$

$y = \$260$

You should save \$260 to buy a season ticket.

55. **a.**

56. **b.**

57. **d.**

58. **c.**

59. $1972 - 1621 = 351$

The slide rule was used for 351 years in making calculations.

60. Dwight D. Eisenhower was elected in 1952.

61. $12(0.54) = 6.48$

6 or 7 out of 12 felt is was their responsibility to be serving on the jury.

62. $75(0.08) = 6$

6 jurors were unable to get out of jury duty.

63. $\dfrac{1700 \text{ miles}}{2\frac{1}{2} \text{ days}} = \dfrac{1700}{\frac{5}{2}}$

$= 1700\left(\frac{2}{5}\right)$

$= 680$ miles per day

64. 24 hours $= 1$ day: $\dfrac{975 \text{ miles}}{1 \text{ day}} = 975$ miles per day

The duck travels faster.

65. $3\frac{1}{4} < w < 8\frac{3}{4}$

66. $y = |x - 1| - 2$

67. $y = -|x - 1| - 2$

Chapter 7

Solving Systems of Linear Equations

7.1 Solving Linear Systems by Graphing

Communicating about Algebra

A. To solve a system of linear equations is to find an ordered pair (a, b) that satisfies each equation.

B. $-4(-3) + 5(1) \stackrel{?}{=} 17$ $\quad 9(-3) + 1 \stackrel{?}{=} -17$

$12 + 5 \stackrel{?}{=} 17$ $\quad -27 + 1 \stackrel{?}{=} -17$

$17 = 17$ $\quad -26 \neq -17$

$(-3, 1)$ is not a solution to the system.

C. $(5, 2)$

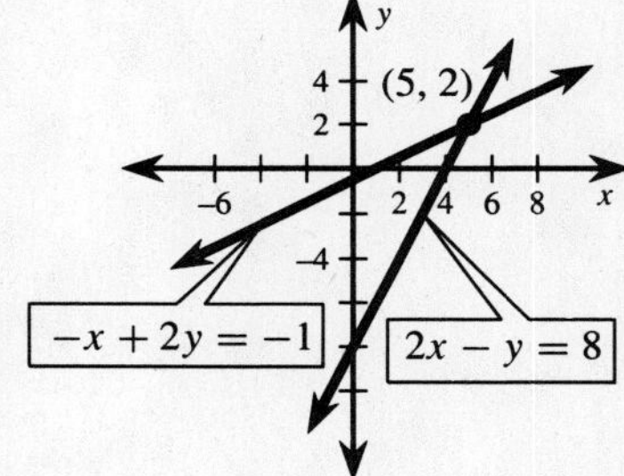

EXERCISES

1. $4x - 2y = 8$ $\quad -3x + 6y = 3$

$-2y = -4x + 8$ $\quad 6y = 3x + 3$

$y = 2x - 4$ $\quad y = \frac{1}{2}x + \frac{1}{2}$

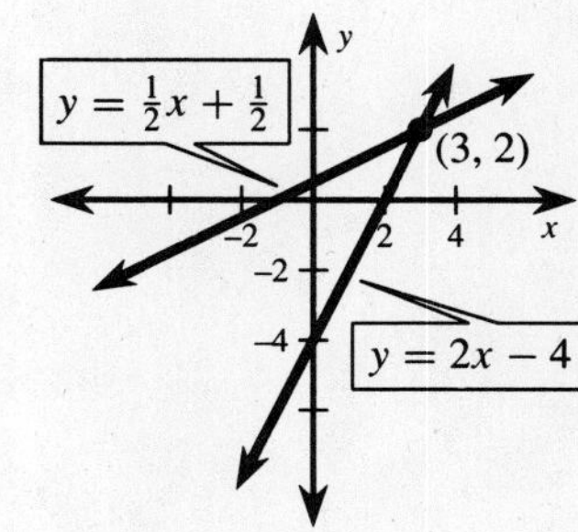

2. (3, 2)

3. $4(3) - 2(2) = 12 - 4$
$= 8$

$-3(3) + 6(2) = -9 + 12$
$= 3$

$4(3) - 2(-2) = 12 + 4$
$= 16 \neq 8$

$-3(3) + 6(-2) = -9 - 12$
$= -21 \neq 3$

4.  (2, 3)

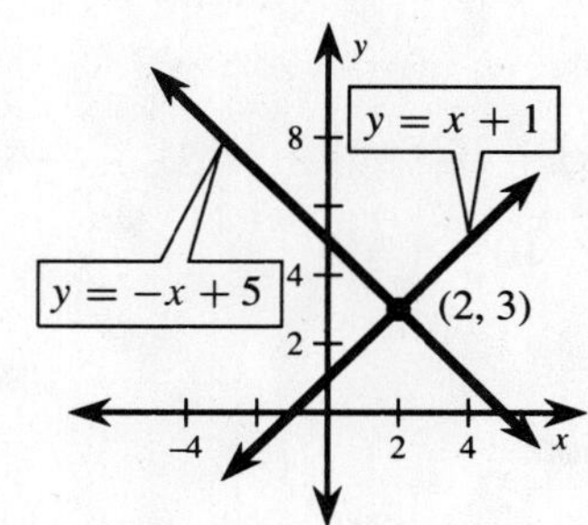

$3 = 2 + 1$ and $3 = -2 + 5$

5. (4, 2)

$2 = -\frac{1}{2}(4) + 4$ and $2 = 2(4) - 6$

6. (2, 1)

$$\begin{cases} y = 3x - 5 \\ y = \frac{1}{2}x \end{cases}$$

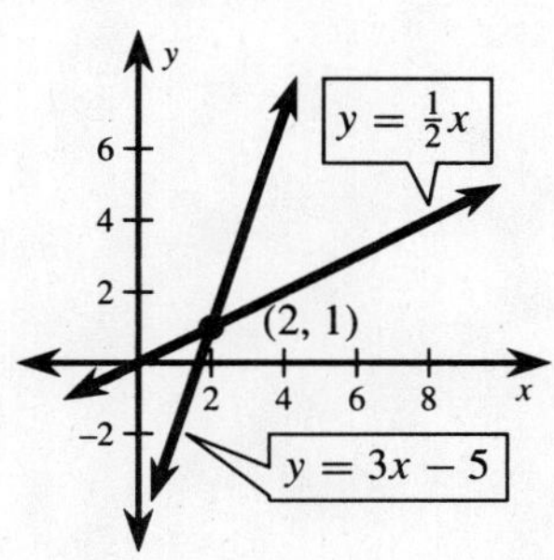

$3(2) - 1 = 5$ and $-2 + 2(1) = 0$

7. $3(2) + 2(-1) \stackrel{?}{=} 4$ $\qquad -2 + 3(-1) \stackrel{?}{=} -5$

$6 - 2 \stackrel{?}{=} 4$ $\qquad -2 - 3 \stackrel{?}{=} -5$

$4 = 4$ $\qquad -5 = -5$

(2, −1) is the solution.

$3(-3) + 2(2) \stackrel{?}{=} 4$ $\qquad -(-3) + 3(2) \stackrel{?}{=} 5$

$-9 + 4 \stackrel{?}{=} 4$ $\qquad 3 + 6 \stackrel{?}{=} 5$

$-5 \neq 4$ $\qquad 9 \neq 5$

(−3, 2) is not the solution.

8. $3+3 \stackrel{?}{=} 6$ $\qquad 2(3)-5(3) \stackrel{?}{=} 10$

$6=6 \qquad 6-15 \stackrel{?}{=} 10$

$-9 \neq 10$

(3, 3) is not the solution.

$4+2 \stackrel{?}{=} 6$ $\qquad 2(4)-5(2) \stackrel{?}{=} 10$

$6=6 \qquad 8-10 \stackrel{?}{=} 10$

$-2 \neq 10$

(4, 2) is not the solution.

Neither point is a solution.

9. $-2+3 \stackrel{?}{=} -2$ $\qquad 2(-2)-3(3) \stackrel{?}{=} -9$

$1 \neq -2 \qquad -4-9 \stackrel{?}{=} -9$

$-13 \neq -9$

(−2, 3) is not the solution.

$-3+1 \stackrel{?}{=} -2$ $\qquad 2(-3)-3(1) \stackrel{?}{=} -9$

$-2=-2 \qquad -6-3 \stackrel{?}{=} -9$

$-9=-9$

(−3, 1) is the solution.

10. $4(5)-5(4) \stackrel{?}{=} 0$ $\qquad 6(5)-5(4) \stackrel{?}{=} 10$

$20-20 \stackrel{?}{=} 0 \qquad 30-20 \stackrel{?}{=} 10$

$0=0 \qquad 10=10$

(5, 4) is the solution.

$4(10)-5(8) \stackrel{?}{=} 0$ $\qquad 6(10)-5(8) \stackrel{?}{=} 10$

$40-40 \stackrel{?}{=} 0 \qquad 60-40 \stackrel{?}{=} 10$

$0=0 \qquad 20 \neq 10$

(10, 8) is not the solution.

11. $2\left(\frac{5}{2}\right)+2 \stackrel{?}{=} 4$ $\qquad 4\left(\frac{5}{2}\right)+3(2) \stackrel{?}{=} 9$

$5+2 \stackrel{?}{=} 4 \qquad 10+6 \stackrel{?}{=} 9$

$7 \neq 4 \qquad 16 \neq 9$

$\left(\frac{5}{2}, 2\right)$ is not the solution.

$2\left(\frac{3}{2}\right)+1 \stackrel{?}{=} 4$ $\qquad 4\left(\frac{3}{2}\right)+3(1) \stackrel{?}{=} 9$

$3+1 \stackrel{?}{=} 4 \qquad 6+3 \stackrel{?}{=} 9$

$4=4 \qquad 9=9$

$\left(\frac{3}{2}, 1\right)$ is the solution.

12. $3(0)-2(2) \stackrel{?}{=} -4$ $\qquad -4(0)+3(2) \stackrel{?}{=} 5$

$0-4 \stackrel{?}{=} -4 \qquad 0+6 \stackrel{?}{=} 5$

$-4=-4 \qquad 6 \neq 5$

(0, 2) is not the solution.

$3(-2)-2(-1) \stackrel{?}{=} -4$ $\qquad -4(-2)+3(-1) \stackrel{?}{=} 5$

$-6+2 \stackrel{?}{=} -4 \qquad 8-3 \stackrel{?}{=} 5$

$-4=-4 \qquad 5=5$

(−2, −1) is the solution.

13. (2, 0)

14. (−1, 1)

15. (−1, −1)

16. (3, 4)

17. (1, 2)

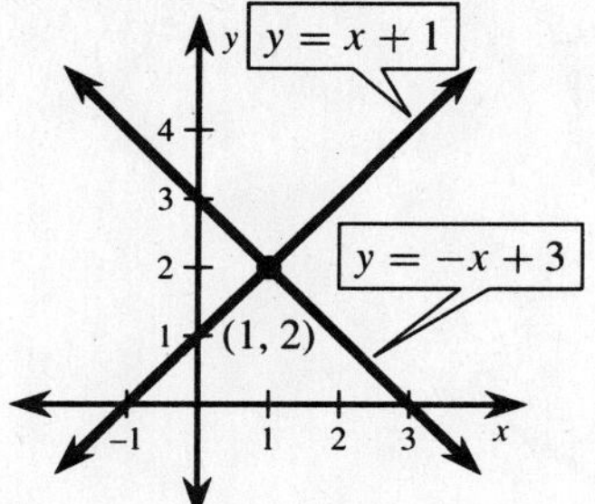

18. (0, 0)

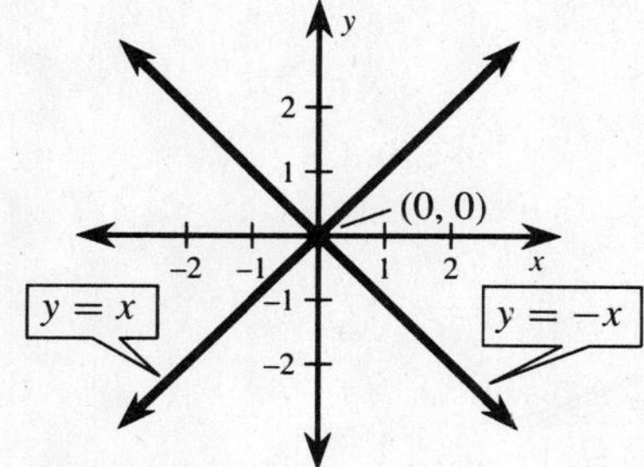

19. (2, 0)

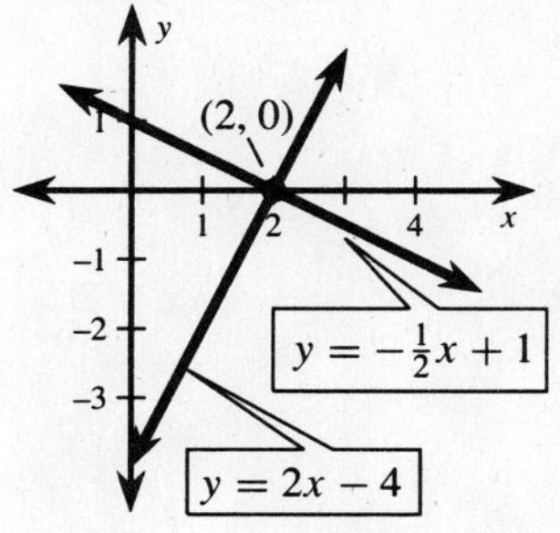

20. (1, 4)

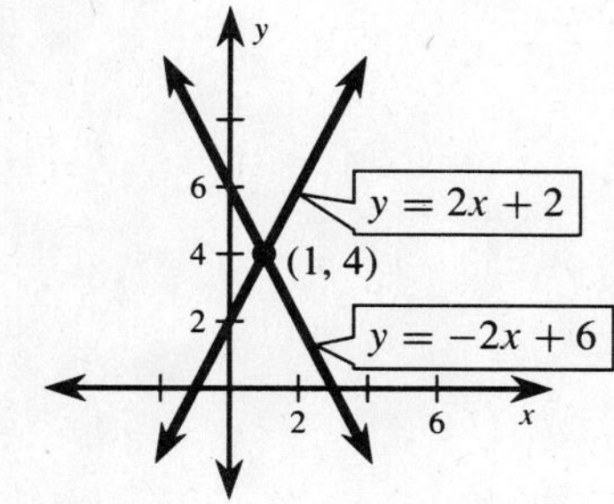

21. $3x - 4y = 5$

$$-4y = -3x + 5$$

$$y = \frac{3}{4}x - \frac{5}{4}$$

(3, 1)

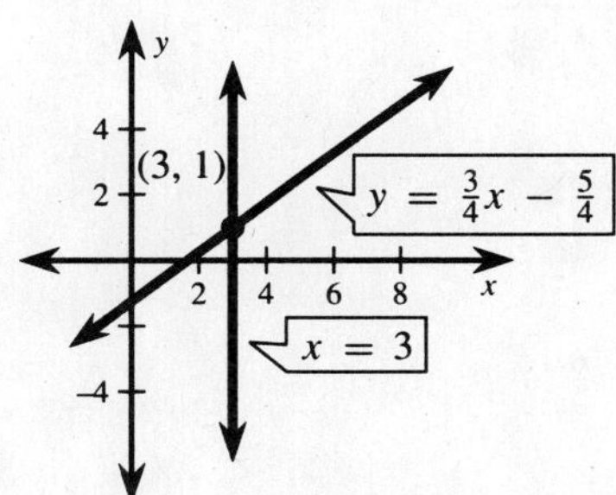

22. $5x + 4y = 18$

$$4y = -5x + 18$$

$$y = -\frac{5}{4}x + \frac{9}{2}$$

(2, 2)

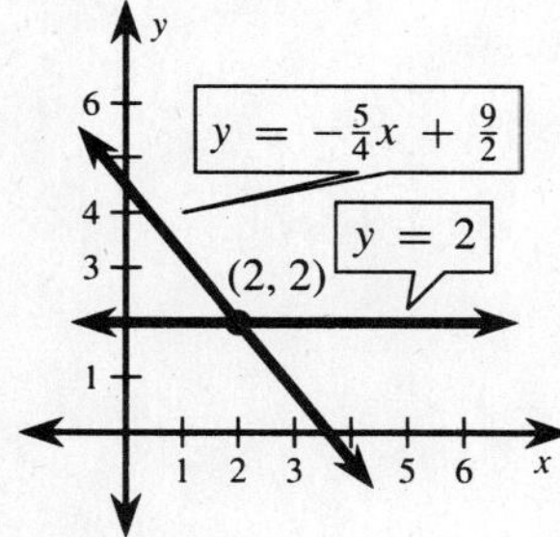

23. $4x - 3y = -6$ $\quad$ $4x - 2y = 0$

$-3y = -4x - 6$ $\quad$ $-2y = -4x$

$y = \frac{4}{3}x + 2$ $\quad$ $y = 2x$

(3, 6)

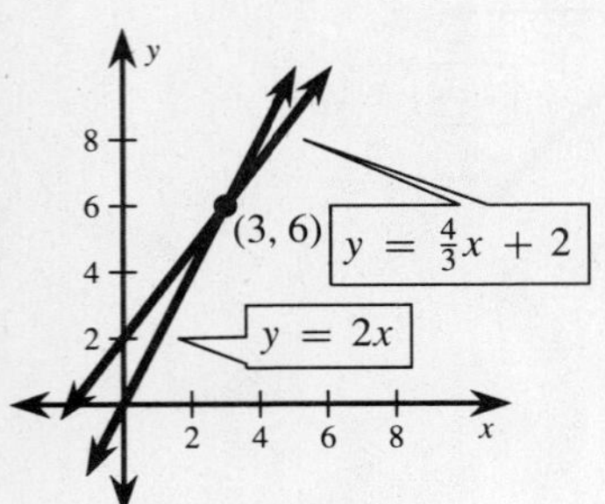

24. $3x + 6y = 15$ $\quad$ $-2x + 3y = -3$

$6y = -3x + 15$ $\quad$ $3y = 2x - 3$

$y = -\frac{1}{2}x + \frac{5}{2}$ $\quad$ $y = \frac{2}{3}x - 1$

(3, 1)

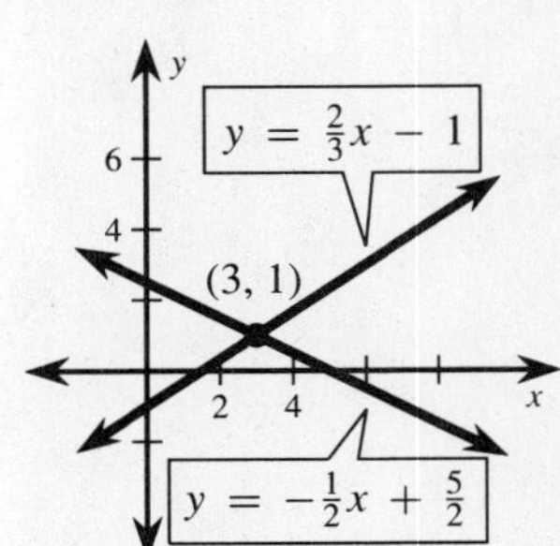

25. $2x - 3y = 8$ $\quad$ $4x + 3y = -2$

$-3y = -2x + 8$ $\quad$ $3y = -4x - 2$

$y = \frac{2}{3}x - \frac{8}{3}$ $\quad$ $y = -\frac{4}{3}x - \frac{2}{3}$

(1, −2)

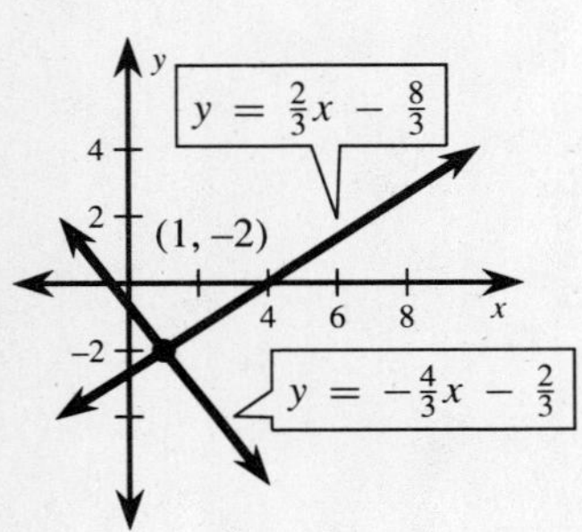

26. $-4x + 3y = 10$ $\quad$ $7x + y = 20$

$3y = 4x + 10$ $\quad$ $y = -7x + 20$

$y = \frac{4}{3}x + \frac{10}{3}$

(2, 6)

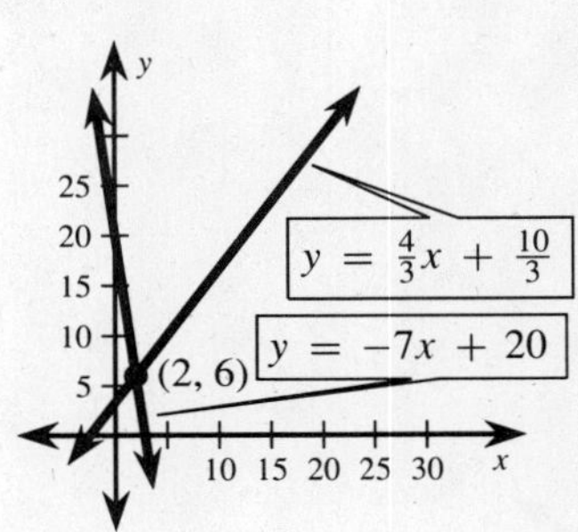

27. $x - 8y = -40$ $\quad$ $-5x + 8y = 8$

$-8y = -x - 40$ $\quad$ $8y = 5x + 8$

$y = \frac{1}{8}x + 5$ $\quad$ $y = \frac{5}{8}x + 1$

(8, 6)

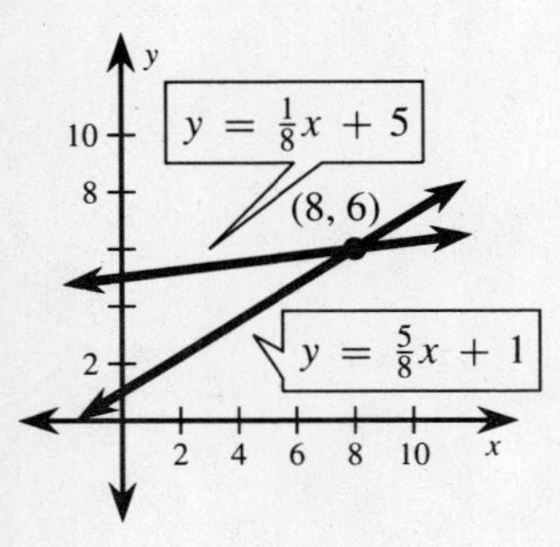

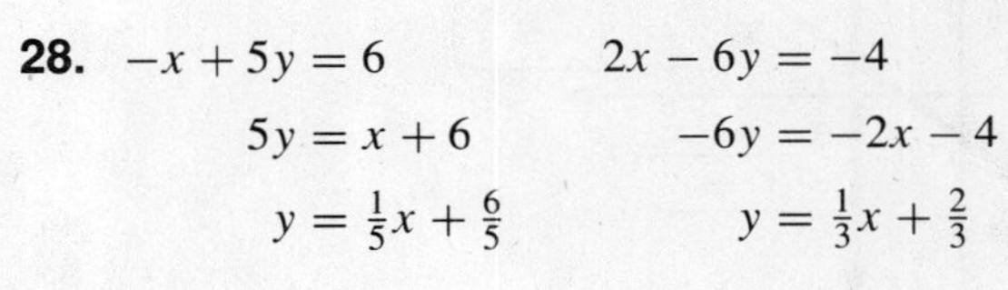

28. $-x + 5y = 6$ $\quad$ $2x - 6y = -4$

$5y = x + 6$ $\quad$ $-6y = -2x - 4$

$y = \frac{1}{5}x + \frac{6}{5}$ $\quad$ $y = \frac{1}{3}x + \frac{2}{3}$

(4, 2)

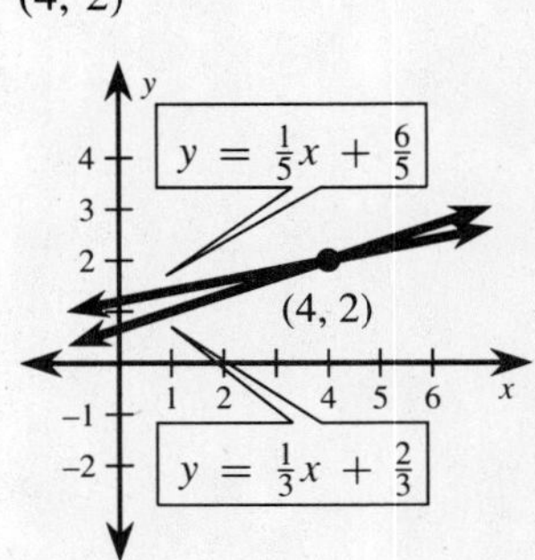

29. $4x + 5y = 20$

$5y = -4x + 20$

$y = -\frac{4}{5}x + 4$

$\frac{5}{4}x + y = 4$

$y = -\frac{5}{4}x + 4$

(0, 4)

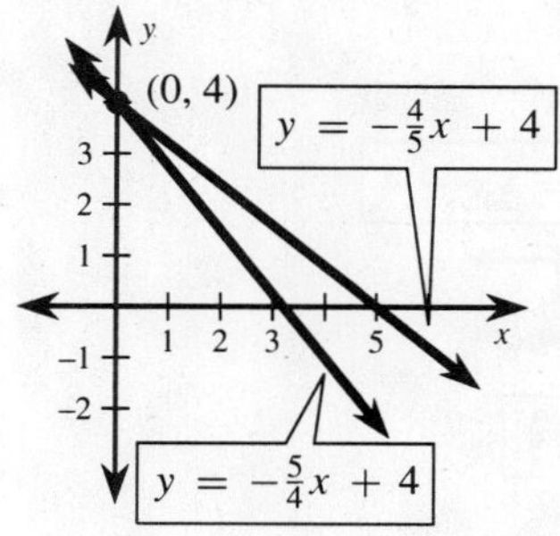

30. $-3x + 4y = -5$

$4y = 3x - 5$

$y = \frac{3}{4}x - \frac{5}{4}$

$4x + 2y = -8$

$2y = -4x - 8$

$y = -2x - 4$

(−1, −2)

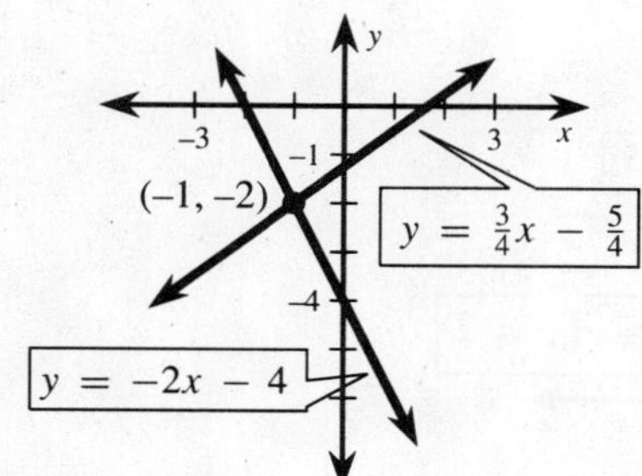

31. $x + y = -1$

$y = -x - 1$

$2x - y = -8$

$-y = -2x - 8$

$y = 2x + 8$

(−3, 2)

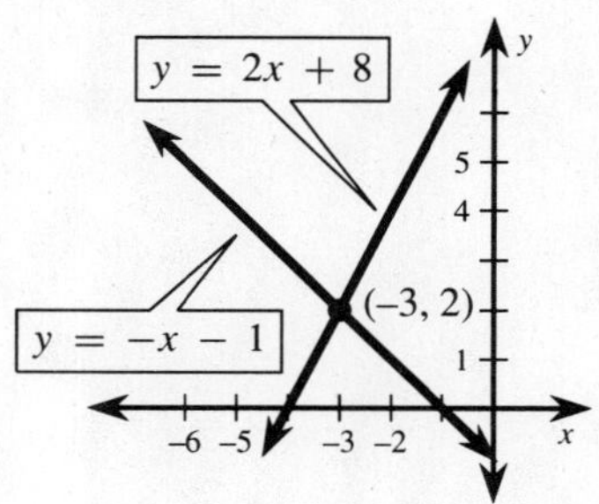

32. $-3x + y = 10$

$y = 3x + 10$

$-x + 2y = 0$

$2y = x$

$y = \frac{1}{2}x$

(−4, −2)

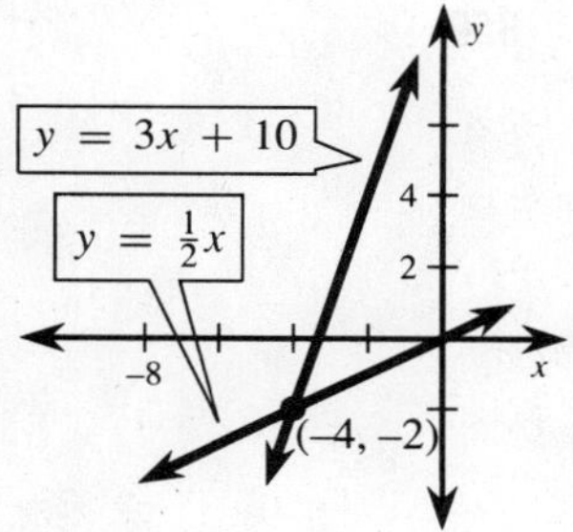

33. $x + 3y = 11$

$3y = -x + 11$

$y = -\frac{1}{3}x + \frac{11}{3}$

$-x + 3y = 7$

$3y = x + 7$

$y = \frac{1}{3}x + \frac{7}{3}$

(2, 3)

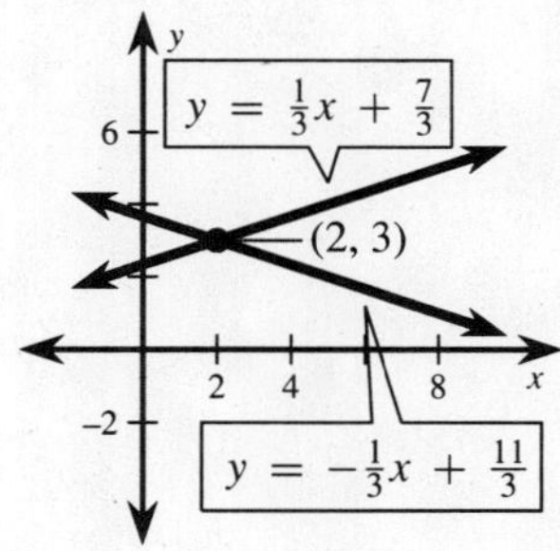

34. $3x - y = -2$

$-y = -3x - 2$

$y = 3x + 2$

$x - 3y = 2$

$-3y = -x + 2$

$y = \frac{1}{3}x - \frac{2}{3}$

(−1, −1)

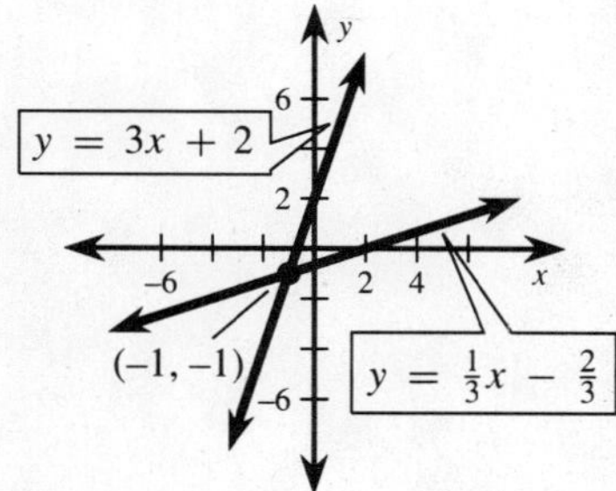

35. $2x + y = 5$ $\qquad$ $3x - 5y = 1$

$y = -2x + 5$ $\qquad$ $-5y = -3x + 1$

$y = \frac{3}{5}x - \frac{1}{5}$

(2, 1)

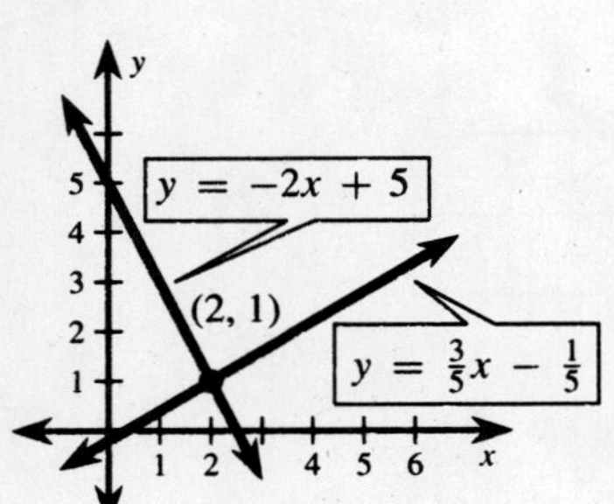

36. $x + 7y = -5$ $\qquad$ $3x - 2y = 8$

$7y = -x - 5$ $\qquad$ $-2y = -3x + 8$

$y = -\frac{1}{7}x - \frac{5}{7}$ $\qquad$ $y = \frac{3}{2}x - 4$

(2, −1)

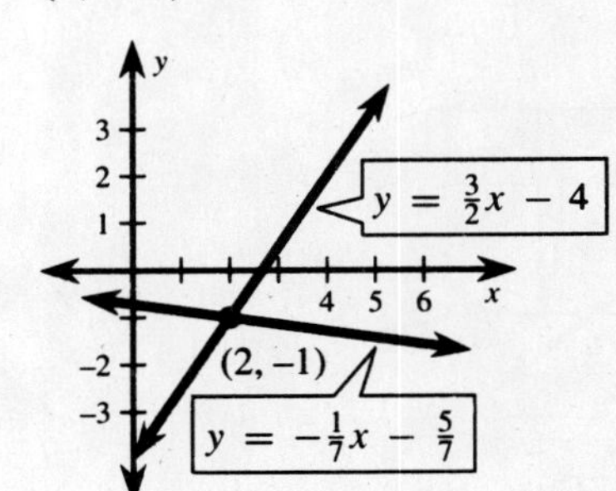

37. Amount in 5% fund = x (dollars)

Amount in $7\frac{1}{2}$% fund = y (dollars)

Total invested = 12,000 (dollars)

Total interest = 850 (dollars)

$$\begin{cases} x + y = 12{,}000 \\ 0.05x + 0.075y = 850 \end{cases}$$

$$50x + 75y = 850{,}000$$

$$2x + 3y = 34{,}000$$

$$\begin{cases} y = -x + 12{,}000 \\ y = -\frac{2}{3}x + \frac{34{,}000}{3} \end{cases}$$

(2000, 10,000)

38. $$\begin{cases} x + y = 25{,}000 \\ 0.05x + 0.06y = 1400 \end{cases}$$

$$\begin{cases} x + y = 25{,}000 \\ 5x + 6y = 140{,}000 \end{cases}$$

$$\begin{cases} y = -x + 25{,}000 \\ y = -\frac{5}{6}x + \frac{70{,}000}{3} \end{cases}$$

(10,000 15,000)

$10,000 at 5%

$15,000 at 6%

39. $m = \frac{53 - 46}{50}$ $\quad m = \frac{47 - 54}{50}$

$= \frac{7}{50}$ $\quad = -\frac{7}{50}$

$= 0.14$ $\quad = -0.14$

$p = 0.14t + 46$

$p = -0.14t + 54$

1968

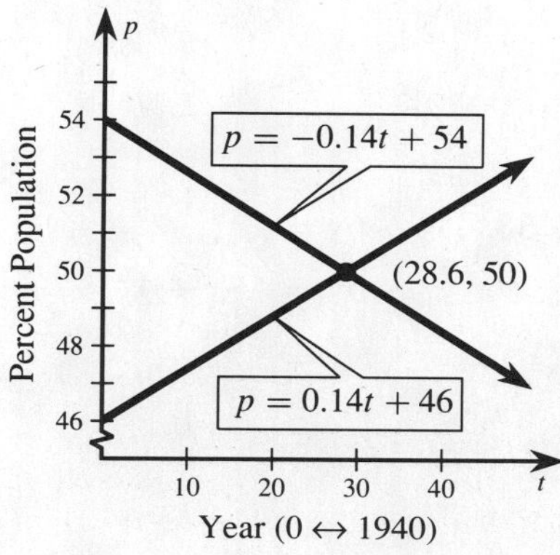

40. $y = 2.9t + 6.9$, monochrome

$y = 3.1t + 3.1$, color

(19, 62)

19 years or 2003

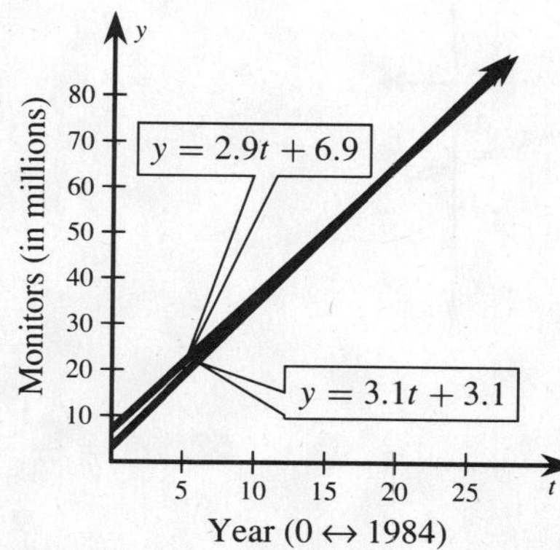

41. $2 \stackrel{?}{=} 3(3) + 11$

$2 \stackrel{?}{=} 9 + 11$

$2 \neq 20$

(3, 2) is not a solution.

42. $8 \stackrel{?}{=} 5(3) - 7$

$8 \stackrel{?}{=} 15 - 7$

$8 = 8$

(3, 8) is a solution.

43. $12 \stackrel{?}{=} 8(-1) - 4$

$12 \stackrel{?}{=} -8 - 4$

$12 \neq -12$

(−1, 12) is not a solution.

44. $-10 \stackrel{?}{=} 6(2) + 2$

$-10 \stackrel{?}{=} 12 + 2$

$-10 \neq 14$

(2, −10) is not a solution.

45. $2x + y = 4$

$y = -2x + 4$

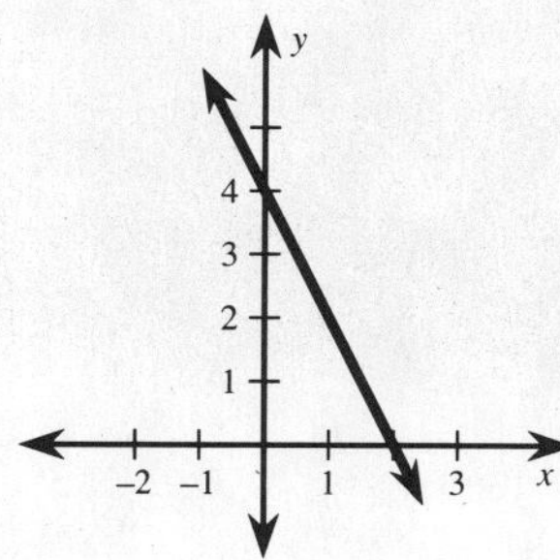

46. $5x - 2y = 3$

$-2y = -5x + 3$

$y = \frac{5}{2}x - \frac{3}{2}$

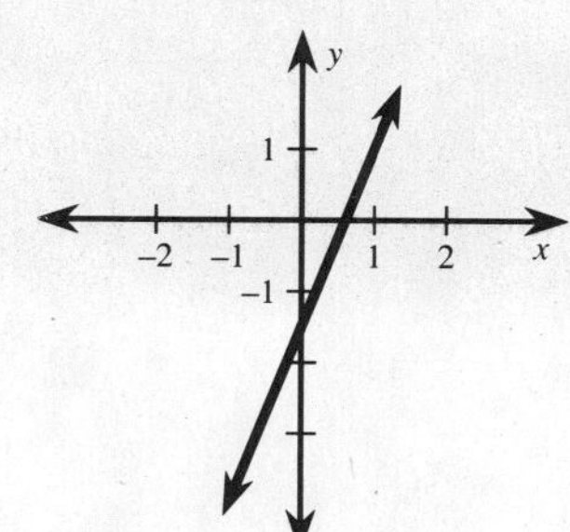

47. $x + 4y = 8$

$4y = -x + 8$

$y = -\frac{1}{4}x + 2$

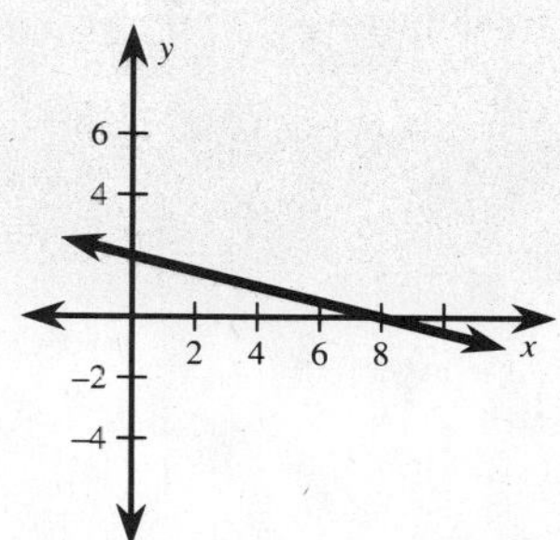

48. $-x - 3y = 12$

$-3y = x + 12$

$y = -\frac{1}{3}x - 4$

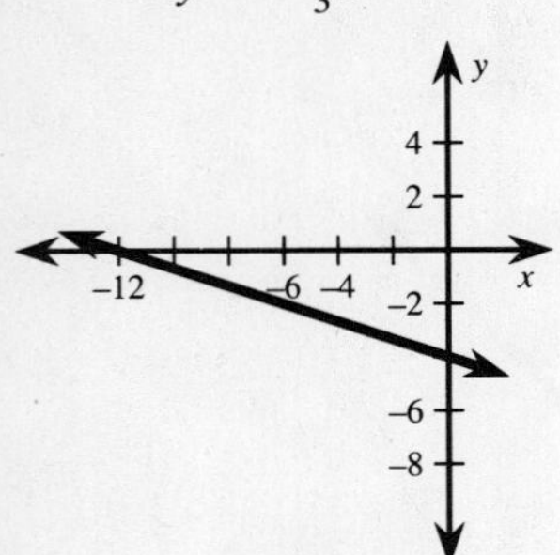

49. $m = \dfrac{3-8}{-1-4}$

$= \dfrac{-5}{-5}$

$= 1$

$y - 8 = 1(x - 4)$

$-x + y = 4$

50. $m = \dfrac{6-1}{2-5}$

$= -\dfrac{5}{3}$

$y - 1 = -\frac{5}{3}(x - 5)$

$3y - 3 = -5x + 25$

$5x + 3y = 28$

51. $m = \dfrac{-7-1}{-2-5}$

$= \dfrac{-8}{-7}$

$= \dfrac{8}{7}$

$y - 1 = \dfrac{8}{7}(x - 5)$

$7y - 7 = 8x - 40$

$-8x + 7y = -33$

52. $m = \dfrac{-1-8}{3-2}$

$= \dfrac{-9}{1}$

$= -9$

$y - 8 = -9(x - 2)$

$y - 8 = -9x + 18$

$9x + y = 26$

53. $3x + 6y = 4$

$6y = -3x + 4$

$y = -\frac{1}{2}x + \frac{2}{3}$

$m = -\frac{1}{2}$

54. $7x - 4y = 10$

$-4y = -7x + 10$

$y = \frac{7}{4}x - \frac{5}{2}$

$m = \frac{7}{4}$

55. $2x - 8y = 12$

$-8y = -2x + 12$

$y = \frac{1}{4}x - \frac{3}{2}$

$m = \frac{1}{4}$

56. $-5x + 2y = 7$

$2y = 5x + 7$

$y = \frac{5}{2}x + \frac{7}{2}$

$m = \frac{5}{2}$

57. $3x + y = 5$

$y = -3x + 5$

$y = -3(2) + 5$

$y = -6 + 5$

$y = -1$

58. $-x + 4y = 7$

$4y = x + 7$

$y = \frac{1}{4}x + \frac{7}{4}$

$y = \frac{1}{4}(9) + \frac{7}{4}$

$y = \frac{9}{4} + \frac{7}{4}$

$y = 4$

59. $-2x + 5y = 4$

$5y = 2x + 4$

$y = \frac{2}{5}x + \frac{4}{5}$

$y = \frac{2}{5}(-3) + \frac{4}{5}$

$y = -\frac{6}{5} + \frac{4}{5}$

$y = -\frac{2}{5}$

60. $6x - 8y = 22$

$$-8y = -6x + 22$$
$$y = \frac{3}{4}x - \frac{11}{4}$$
$$y = \frac{3}{4}(-1) - \frac{11}{4}$$
$$y = -\frac{14}{4}$$
$$y = -\frac{7}{2}$$

61. Red meat: $y = -0.75t + 150$

Poultry: $y = 2t + 45$

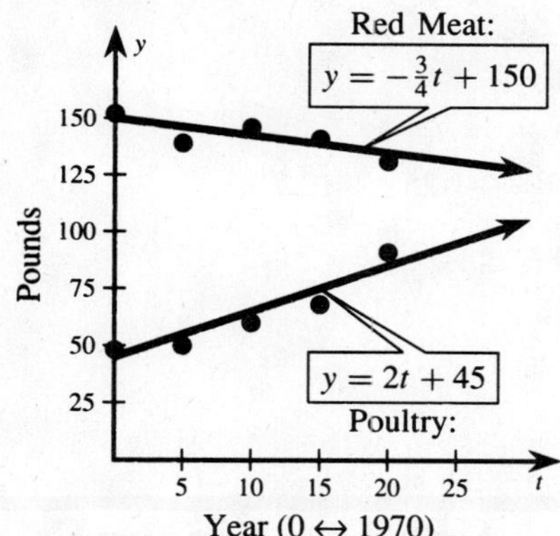

62. If the trends continue, the average number of pounds of poultry eaten will reach the number of pounds of read meat in the year 2008.

Using a Graphing Calculator

1. $2x - 5y = -6$

$$-5y = -2x - 6$$
$$y = \frac{2}{5}x + \frac{6}{5}$$

$3x - 2y = 2$

$$-2y = -3x + 2$$
$$y = \frac{3}{2}x - 1$$

(2, 2)

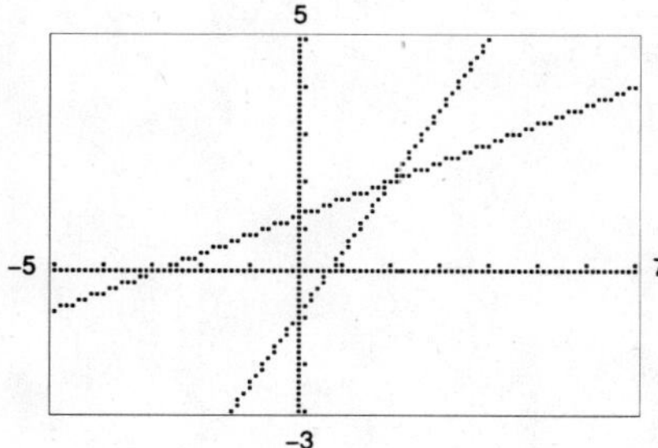

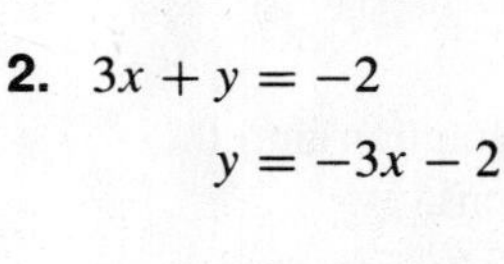

2. $3x + y = -2$

$$y = -3x - 2$$

$4x + y = -4$

$$y = -4x - 4$$

(−2, 4)

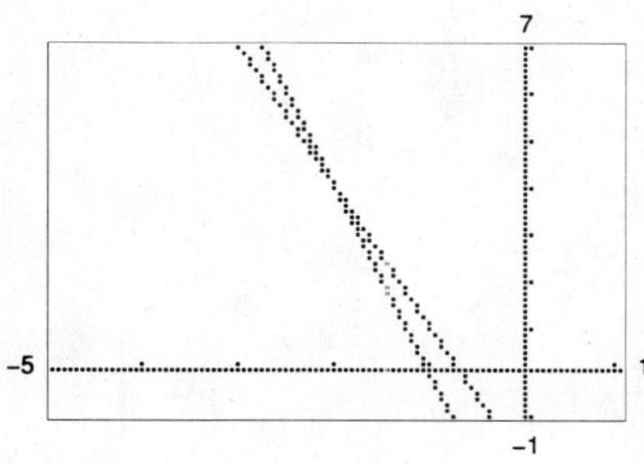

3. $-0.25x - y = 2.25$

$$-y = 0.25x + 2.25$$
$$y = -0.25x - 2.25$$

$-1.25x + 1.25y = -1.25$

$$1.25y = 1.25x - 1.25$$
$$y = x - 1$$

(−1, −2)

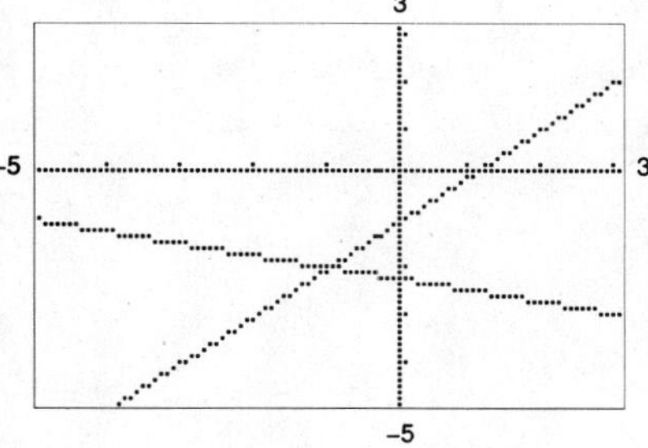

4. $0.8x + 0.6y = -1.2$

$$0.6y = -0.8x - 1.2$$

$$y = -\frac{4}{3}x - 2$$

$$1.25x - 1.5y = 12.75$$

$$-1.5y = -1.25x + 12.75$$

$$y = \frac{5}{6}x - \frac{17}{2}$$

(3, −6)

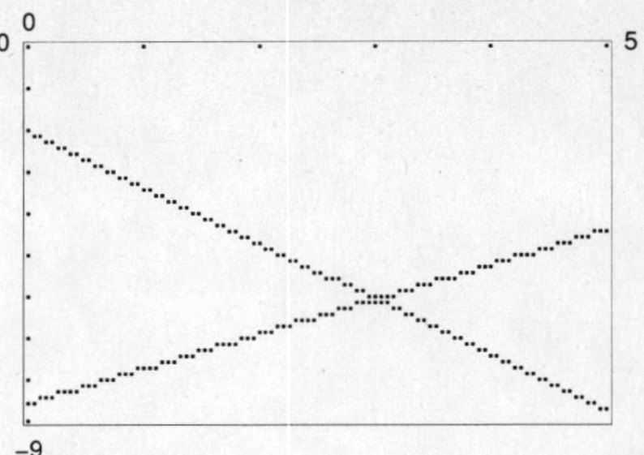

7.2 Solving Linear Systems by Substitution

Communicating about Algebra

A. Conventional: \$2394.24

Retrofit: \$1760.90

B. \$8,376,000,000 or 60% savings

EXERCISES

1. $y = -x + 9$

2. $2x + 5(-x + 9) = 30$

$$-3x + 45 = 30$$

$$-3x = -15$$

$$x = 5$$

3. $y = -5 + 9$

$y = 4$

(5, 4)

4. Algebraically: Substitute the solution into the original equations.

Graphically: Graph the equations and see if their intersection agrees with the solution.

5. $\begin{cases} x - y = 0 \\ x + y = 2 \end{cases}$

$x = y$

$y + y = 2$

$2y = 2$

$y = 1$

$x = 1$

(1, 1)

6. $\begin{cases} x + y = 1 \\ 2x - y = 2 \end{cases}$

$y = -x + 1$

$2x - (-x + 1) = 2$

$3x - 1 = 2$

$3x = 3$

$x = 1$

$y = -1 + 1$

$y = 0$

(1, 0)

7. $\begin{cases} 2x + y = 4 \\ -x + y = 1 \end{cases}$

$y = x + 1$

$2x + x + 1 = 4$

$3x = 3$

$x = 1$

$y = 1 + 1$

$y = 2$

(1, 2)

8. $\begin{cases} x - \ \ y = -5 \\ x + 2y = \ \ 4 \end{cases}$

$x = y - 5$

$y - 5 + 2y = 4$

$3y = 9$

$y = 3$

$x = 3 - 5$

$x = -2$

$(-2,\ 3)$

9. $\begin{cases} \quad\ \ y = \ x - 3 \\ 4x + y = 32 \end{cases}$

$4x + x - 3 = 32$

$5x = 35$

$x = 7$

$y = 7 - 3$

$y = 4$

$(7, 4)$

10. $\begin{cases} \quad\ \ y = \ x + 4 \\ 3x + y = 16 \end{cases}$

$3x + x + 4 = 16$

$4x = 12$

$x = 3$

$y = 3 + 4$

$y = 7$

$(3, 7)$

11. $\begin{cases} 4x + 3y = 31 \\ \quad\ \ y = 2x + 7 \end{cases}$

$4x + 3(2x + 7) = 31$

$10x + 21 = 31$

$10x = 10$

$x = 1$

$y = 2 \cdot 1 + 7$

$y = 9$

$(1, 9)$

12. $\begin{cases} 4x + 5y = 48 \\ \quad\ \ y = 3x + 2 \end{cases}$

$4x + 5(3x + 2) = 48$

$19x + 10 = 48$

$19x = 38$

$x = 2$

$y = 3 \cdot 2 + 2$

$y = 8$

$(2, 8)$

13. $\begin{cases} 2x \qquad = 5 \\ \ x + y = 1 \end{cases}$

$x = \frac{5}{2}$

$\frac{5}{2} + y = 1$

$y = -\frac{3}{2}$

$(\frac{5}{2},\ -\frac{3}{2})$

14. $\begin{cases} 3x - y = 0 \\ \qquad y = 6 \end{cases}$

$3x - 6 = 0$

$3x = 6$

$x = 2$

$(2, 6)$

15. $\begin{cases} \ \ x - y = 2 \\ 2x + y = 1 \end{cases}$

$x = y + 2$

$2(y + 2) + y = 1$

$3y + 4 = 1$

$3y = -3$

$y = -1$

$x = -1 + 2$

$x = 1$

$(1,\ -1)$

16. $\begin{cases} \ \ x - 2y = -10 \\ 3x - \ \ y = \quad 0 \end{cases}$

$x = 2y - 10$

$3(2y - 10) - y = 0$

$5y - 30 = 0$

$5y = 30$

$y = 6$

$x = 2 \cdot 6 - 10$

$x = 2$

$(2, 6)$

17. $\begin{cases} x - y = 0 \\ 2x + y = 0 \end{cases}$

$x = y$

$2y + y = 0$

$3y = 0$

$y = 0$

$x = 0$

$(0, 0)$

18. $\begin{cases} x - 2y = 0 \\ 3x - y = 0 \end{cases}$

$x = 2y$

$3(2y) - y = 0$

$5y = 0$

$y = 0$

$x = 2 \cdot 0$

$x = 0$

$(0, 0)$

19. $\begin{cases} x - y = 0 \\ 5x - 3y = 10 \end{cases}$

$x = y$

$5y - 3y = 10$

$2y = 10$

$y = 5$

$x = 5$

$(5, 5)$

20. $\begin{cases} x + 2y = 1 \\ 5x - 4y = -23 \end{cases}$

$x = -2y + 1$

$5(-2y + 1) - 4y = -23$

$-14y + 5 = -23$

$-14y = -28$

$y = 2$

$x = -2(2) + 1$

$x = -3$

$(-3, 2)$

21. $\begin{cases} 2x - y = -2 \\ 4x + y = 5 \end{cases}$

$y = -4x + 5$

$2x - (-4x + 5) = -2$

$6x - 5 = -2$

$6x = 3$

$x = \frac{1}{2}$

$y = -4\left(\frac{1}{2}\right) + 5$

$y = 3$

$\left(\frac{1}{2}, 3\right)$

22. $\begin{cases} -3x + 6y = 4 \\ 2x + y = 4 \end{cases}$

$y = -2x + 4$

$-3x + 6(-2x + 4) = 4$

$-15x + 24 = 4$

$-15x = -20$

$x = \frac{4}{3}$

$y = -2\left(\frac{4}{3}\right) + 4$

$y = \frac{4}{3}$

$\left(\frac{4}{3}, \frac{4}{3}\right)$

23. $\begin{cases} \frac{1}{5}x + \frac{1}{2}y = 8 \\ x + y = 20 \end{cases}$

$y = -x + 20$

$\frac{1}{5}x + \frac{1}{2}(-x + 20) = 8$

$-\frac{3}{10}x + 10 = 8$

$-\frac{3}{10}x = -2$

$x = \frac{20}{3}$

$y = -\frac{20}{3} + 20$

$y = \frac{40}{3}$

$\left(\frac{20}{3}, \frac{40}{3}\right)$

24. $\begin{cases} \frac{1}{2}x + \frac{3}{4}y = 10 \\ \frac{3}{2}x - y = 4 \end{cases}$

$y = \frac{3}{2}x - 4$

$\frac{1}{2}x + \frac{3}{4}\left(\frac{3}{2}x - 4\right) = 10$

$\frac{1}{2}x + \frac{9}{8}x - 3 = 10$

$\frac{13}{8}x = 13$

$x = 8$

$y = \frac{3}{2}(8) - 4$

$y = 8$

$(8, 8)$

25. $\begin{cases} -3x + y = 4 \\ -9x + 5y = 10 \end{cases}$

$y = 3x + 4$

$-9x + 5(3x + 4) = 10$

$6x + 20 = 10$

$6x = -10$

$x = -\frac{5}{3}$

$y = 3\left(-\frac{5}{3}\right) + 4$

$y = -5 + 4$

$y = -1$

$\left(-\frac{5}{3}, -1\right)$

26. $\begin{cases} 5x + 3y = 11 \\ x - 5y = 5 \end{cases}$

$x = 5y + 5$

$5(5y + 5) + 3y = 11$

$28y + 25 = 11$

$28y = -14$

$y = -\frac{1}{2}$

$x = 5\left(-\frac{1}{2}\right) + 5$

$x = \frac{5}{2}$

$\left(\frac{5}{2}, -\frac{1}{2}\right)$

27. $\begin{cases} x + 4y = 300 \\ x - 2y = 0 \end{cases}$

$x = 2y$

$2y + 4y = 300$

$6y = 300$

$y = 50$

$x = 2 \cdot 50$

$x = 100$

(100, 50)

28. $\begin{cases} 3x + y = 13 \\ 2x - 4y = 18 \end{cases}$

$y = -3x + 13$

$2x - 4(-3x + 13) = 18$

$14x - 52 = 18$

$14x = 70$

$x = 5$

$y = -3 \cdot 5 + 13$

$y = -2$

(5, −2)

29. Number of over 12 = x (people)
Number of 12 and under = y (people)
Price per over 12 = \$11.95 (dollars)
Price per 12 and under = \$6.95 (dollars)
Total number = 6 (people)
Total price = \$61.70 (dollars)

$\begin{cases} x + y = 6 \\ 11.95x + 6.95y = 61.70 \end{cases}$

$y = -x + 6$

$11.95x + 6.95(-x + 6) = 61.70$

$5.00x + 41.70 = 61.70$

$5.00x = 20.00$

$x = 4$

$y = -4 + 6$

$y = 2$

4: over 12

2: 12 and under

30. $\begin{cases} x + y = 1957 \\ 2x + 3y = 5035 \end{cases}$

$y = -x + 1957$

$2x + 3(-x + 1957) = 5035$

$-x + 5871 = 5035$

$x = 836$

$y = -836 + 1957$

$y = 1121$

836 students

1121 general admission

31. $\begin{cases} y = 12{,}000 + 0.10x \\ y = 14{,}000 + 0.08x \end{cases}$

$12{,}000 + 0.10x = 14{,}000 + 0.08x$

$0.02x = 2000$

$x = 100{,}000$ miles

32. $\begin{cases} y = 25 + x \\ y = 100 + 0.90x \end{cases}$

$25 + x = 100 + 0.90x$

$0.10x = 75$

$x = 750$

The two memberships would cost the same for \$750 worth of groceries.

33. $\begin{cases} y = -\frac{3}{2}x - 215 \\ y = 7x + 1026 \end{cases}$

$7x + 1026 = -\frac{3}{2}x - 215$

$\frac{17}{2}x = -1241$

$x = -\frac{2482}{17}$

$x = -146$

$y = -\frac{3}{2}(-146) - 215$

$y = 4$

(−146, 4)

34. $\begin{cases} y = -\frac{3}{2}x - 215 \\ 36x + 7y = -5483 \end{cases}$

$$36x + 7\left(-\tfrac{3}{2}x - 215\right) = -5483$$
$$\tfrac{51}{2}x - 1505 = -5483$$
$$\tfrac{51}{2}x = -3978$$
$$x = -156$$

$$y = -\tfrac{3}{2}(-156) - 215$$
$$y = 19$$

Hawaii: $(-156,\ 19)$

$\begin{cases} y = 7x + 1026 \\ 36x + 7y = -5483 \end{cases}$

$$36x + 7(7x + 1026) = -5483$$
$$85x + 7182 = -5483$$
$$85x = -12{,}665$$
$$x = -149$$

$$y = 7(-149) + 1026$$
$$y = -1043 + 1026$$
$$y = -17$$

Tahiti: $(-149,\ -17)$

35. Meters uphill $= x$ (meters)
Meters downhill $= y$ (meters)
Rate uphill $= 180$ (meters per minute)
Rate downhill $= 250$ (meters per minute)
Total meters $= 1557$ (meters)
Total time $= 7.6$ (minutes)

$\begin{cases} x + y = 1557 \\ \dfrac{x}{180} + \dfrac{y}{250} = 7.6 \end{cases}$

$$y = -x + 1557$$
$$\frac{x}{180} + \frac{-x + 1557}{250} = 7.6$$
$$25x + 18(-x + 1557) = 34{,}200$$
$$7x + 28{,}026 = 34{,}200$$
$$7x = 6174$$
$$x = 882 \text{ meters uphill}$$

$$y = -882 + 1557$$
$$y = 675 \text{ meters downhill}$$

36. $\begin{cases} x + y = 29 \\ 2x + 5y = 100 \end{cases}$

$$y = -x + 29$$
$$2x + 5(-x + 29) = 100$$
$$-3x + 145 = 100$$
$$-3x = -45$$
$$x = 15 \text{ 2-point problems}$$

$$y = -15 + 29$$
$$y = 14 \text{ 5-point problems}$$

37. $2x + 3y = 8$
$$y = -\tfrac{2}{3}x + \tfrac{8}{3}$$

38. $x - 5y = 9$
$$y = \tfrac{1}{5}x - \tfrac{9}{5}$$

39. $9x - 2y = 24$
$$y = \tfrac{9}{2}x - 12$$

40. $2x - 2y = 19$
$$y = x - \tfrac{19}{2}$$

41. $3x - 4y = 14$
$$y = \tfrac{3}{4}x - \tfrac{7}{2}$$

42. $-6x + 8y = 36$
$$y = \tfrac{3}{4}x + \tfrac{9}{2}$$

43. $(2x + 3y) + (-2x + 5y) = 8y$

44. $26 - (16y + 4) + (9y - x) = -x - 7y + 22$

45. $(x - 4y) - 14(3 - x) + y = 15x - 3y - 42$

46. $(5y + 6x) - (4x - 3y) = 2x + 8y$

47. $2x(4 + x) - (y - 5) = 2x^2 + 8x - y + 5$

48. $9(y + 6) + (7x + y)(-3) = -21x + 6y + 54$

49. (3, 2)

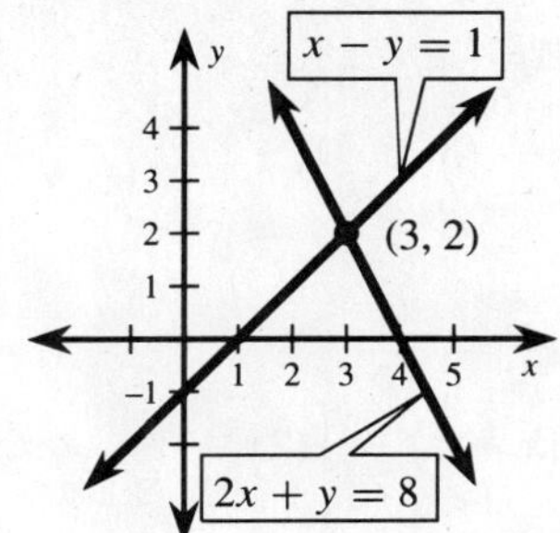

50. (−2, 4)

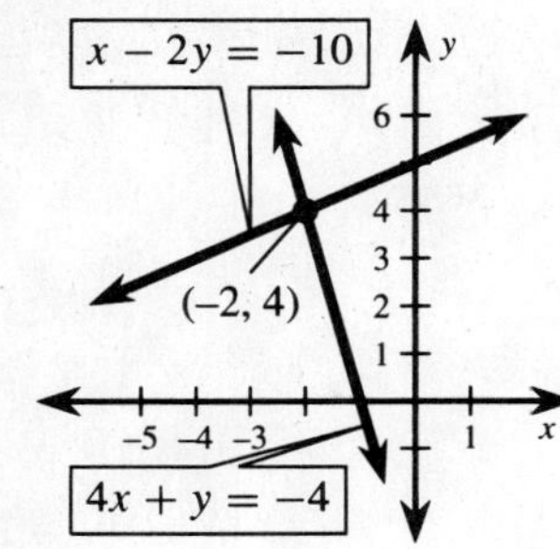

51. (−6, −2)

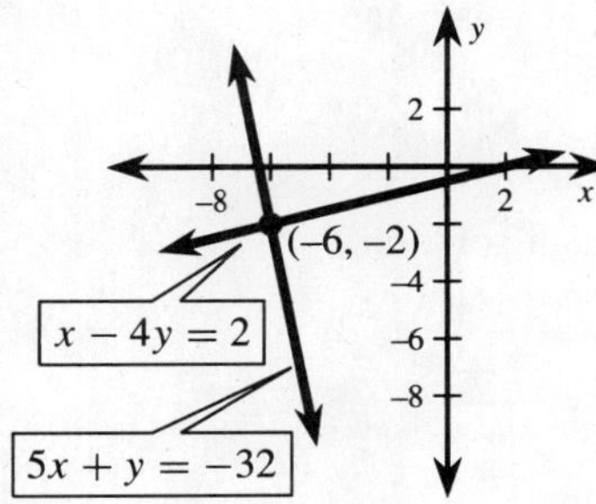

52. (1, −4)

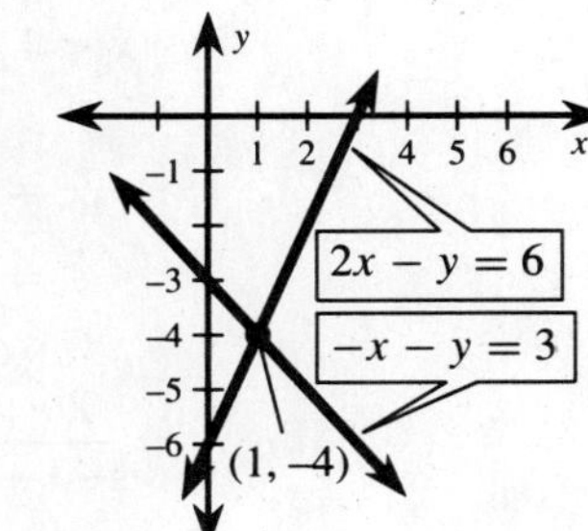

53. $(x+5)15 = y$

$y = 15x + 75$

$2(x+5+15) = 2y+2$

$2x + 40 = 2y + 2$

$2y = 2x + 38$

$y = x + 19$

$15x + 75 = x + 19$

$14x = -56$

$x = -4$

15×1

54. $\frac{1}{2}(2y)4 = 3x$

$4y = 3x$

$y = \frac{3}{4}x$

$(y+2) + (y+2) + 2y = 5x - 4$

$4y + 4 = 5x - 4$

$4y = 5x - 8$

$y = \frac{5}{4}x - 2$

$\frac{3}{4}x = \frac{5}{4}x - 2$

$-\frac{2}{4}x = -2$

$x = -2\left(-\frac{4}{2}\right)$

$x = 4$

$y = \frac{3}{4}(4)$

$= 3$

$y = \frac{5}{4}(4) - 2$

$= 5 - 2$

$= 3$

The length of each side of the triangle is 5, 5, 6.

Mixed **REVIEW**

1. $3x + 10$

2. $7x - 4y$

3. $\frac{1}{3}(4-x) + 2x = \frac{1}{3}\left(4 - \frac{1}{2}\right) + 2\left(\frac{1}{2}\right)$

$= \frac{1}{3}\left(\frac{7}{2}\right) + 1$

$= \frac{7}{6} + 1$

$= 2\frac{1}{6}$

4. $(|x| + 3)(x) + 2 = (|-3| + 3)(-3) + 2$

$= -18 + 2$

$= -16$

5. $m(n+1)+2n=\frac{1}{2}$

$mn+m+2n=\frac{1}{2}$

$n(m+2)=\frac{1}{2}-m$

$n=\dfrac{\frac{1}{2}-m}{m+2}$ or $\dfrac{1-2m}{2m+4}$

6. $\frac{2}{3}r+3s=4$

$\frac{2}{3}r=4-3s$

$r=\frac{3}{2}(4-3s)$

7. $3y+\frac{1}{2}(4-y)=3$

$3y+2-\frac{1}{2}y=3$

$\frac{5}{2}y=1$

$y=\frac{2}{5}$

8. $\left|x+\frac{3}{4}\right|\le 3$

$-3\le x+\frac{3}{4}\le 3$

$-3\frac{3}{4}\le x\le 2\frac{1}{4}$

9. $|x-2|-\frac{1}{4}>0$

$|x-2|>\frac{1}{4}$

$x-2<-\frac{1}{4}$ or $x-2>\frac{1}{4}$

$x<1\frac{3}{4}$ $\quad$ $x>2\frac{1}{4}$

10. $3\left(x-\frac{2}{3}\right)=\frac{1}{4}(2x+3)$

$3x-2=\frac{1}{2}x+\frac{3}{4}$

$\frac{5}{2}x=\frac{11}{4}$

$x=\frac{11}{10}$

11. $\frac{3}{4}\cdot\frac{8}{9}=\frac{2}{3}$

12. $\frac{27}{5}\div\frac{9}{10}=\frac{27}{5}\cdot\frac{10}{9}$

$=6$

13. $\frac{7}{8}(16)=14$

18 is a solution.

14. $\frac{1}{4}|-3|-(-3)=\frac{3}{4}+3$

$=3\frac{3}{4}>0$

-3 is a solution.

15. $m=\dfrac{2-6}{-3+4}$

$=\dfrac{-4}{1}$

$=-4$

$y-2=-4(x+3)$

$4x+y=-10$

16. $m=\dfrac{2+3}{-4+1}$

$=-\dfrac{5}{3}$

$y-2=-\dfrac{5}{3}(x+4)$

$3y-6=-5x-20$

$5x+3y=-14$

17. $m=\dfrac{-1+4}{-1+3}$

$=\dfrac{3}{2}$

$y+1=\frac{3}{2}(x+1)$

$2y+2=3x+3$

$-3x+2y=1$

18. $y+2=-\frac{3}{2}(x-0)$

$2y+4=-3x$

$3x+2y=-4$

19. $y+8=\frac{1}{4}(x-4)$

$4y+32=x-4$

$-x+4y=-36$

20. $y=5$

7.3 Solving Linear Systems by Linear Combinations

Communicating about Algebra

If the crown were pure gold, the gold block would displace the same amount of water as the crown. The same holds true for silver. However, the silver displaces more water than the gold. Since the crown displaces an amount of water between the silver and gold, the crown is not pure gold.

EXERCISES

1. $\begin{cases} 2x + 3y = 7 \\ -2x + 2y = -2 \end{cases}$

$$5y = 5$$
$$y = 1$$

$2x + 3(1) = 7$

$2x = 4$

$x = 2$

(2, 1)

2. $\begin{cases} 3x - 4y = 7 \\ 2x - y = 3 \end{cases}$

$$3x - 4y = 7$$
$$-8x + 4y = -12$$
$$-5x = -5$$

$x = 1$

$3(1) - 4y = 7$

$-4y = 4$

$y = -1$

(1, −1)

3. $\begin{cases} 2x + 3y = 1 \\ 5x - 4y = 14 \end{cases}$

$$8x + 12y = 4$$
$$15x - 12y = 42$$
$$23x = 46$$

$x = 2$

$2(2) + 3y = 1$

$3y = -3$

$y = -1$

(2, −1)

4. $\begin{cases} 4x + 2y = 6 \\ -4x + 5y = 1 \end{cases}$

$$7y = 7$$
$$y = 1$$

$4x + 2(1) = 6$

$4x = 4$

$x = 1$

(1, 1)

Linear combination; because x-coefficients are opposites.

5. $\begin{cases} y = -2x + 4 \\ y = \frac{1}{2}x - 1 \end{cases}$

$-2x + 4 = \frac{1}{2}x - 1$

$-\frac{5}{2}x = -5$

$x = 2$

$y = -2(2) + 4$

$y = 0$

(2, 0)

Substitution; because both equations are solved for y.

6. $\begin{cases} 4x + y = 9 \\ 7x - 8y = 6 \end{cases}$

$y = -4x + 9$

$7x - 8(-4x + 9) = 6$

$39x - 72 = 6$

$39x = 78$

$x = 2$

$y = -4 \cdot 2 + 9$

$y = 1$

(2, 1)

Substitution; because a y-coefficient is 1.

7. $\begin{cases} 2x + y = 4 \\ x - y = 2 \end{cases}$

$$3x = 6$$
$$x = 2$$

$2 \cdot 2 + y = 4$

$y = 0$

(2, 0)

8. $\begin{cases} x + 3y = 2 \\ -x + 2y = 3 \end{cases}$

$$5y = 5$$
$$y = 1$$

$x + 3 \cdot 1 = 2$

$x = -1$

(−1, 1)

9. $\begin{cases} x - y = 0 \\ 3x - 2y = -1 \end{cases}$

$$-3x + 3y = 0$$
$$3x - 2y = -1$$
$$y = -1$$

$x - (-1) = 0$

$x = -1$

(−1, −1)

10. $\begin{cases} 2x - y = 2 \\ 4x + 3y = 24 \end{cases}$

$$\begin{array}{r} 6x - 3y = 6 \\ 4x + 3y = 24 \\ \hline 10x \quad = 30 \end{array}$$

$x = 3$

$2(3) - y = 2$

$-y = -4$

$y = 4$

(3, 4)

11. $\begin{cases} x - y = 4 \\ x + y = 12 \end{cases}$

$$\begin{array}{r} \hline 2x \quad = 16 \end{array}$$

$x = 8$

$8 - y = 4$

$y = 4$

(8, 4)

12. $\begin{cases} -x + 2y = 12 \\ x + 6y = 20 \end{cases}$

$$\begin{array}{r} \hline 8y = 32 \end{array}$$

$y = 4$

$x + 6 \cdot 4 = 20$

$x = -4$

(−4, 4)

13. $\begin{cases} 3x - 5y = 1 \\ 2x + 5y = 9 \end{cases}$

$$\begin{array}{r} \hline 5x \quad = 10 \end{array}$$

$x = 2$

$3 \cdot 2 - 5y = 1$

$-5y = -5$

$y = 1$

(2, 1)

14. $\begin{cases} x + 2y = 14 \\ x - 2y = 10 \end{cases}$

$$\begin{array}{r} \hline 2x \quad = 24 \end{array}$$

$x = 12$

$12 + 2y = 14$

$2y = 2$

$y = 1$

(12, 1)

15. $\begin{cases} x + 7y = 12 \\ 3x - 5y = 10 \end{cases}$

$$\begin{array}{r} -3x - 21y = -36 \\ 3x - 5y = 10 \\ \hline -26y = -26 \end{array}$$

$y = 1$

$x + 7 \cdot 1 = 12$

$x = 5$

(5, 1)

16. $\begin{cases} 2x + 3y = 18 \\ 5x - y = 11 \end{cases}$

$$\begin{array}{r} 2x + 3y = 18 \\ 15x - 3y = 33 \\ \hline 17x \quad = 51 \end{array}$$

$x = 3$

$2 \cdot 3 + 3y = 18$

$3y = 12$

$y = 4$

(3, 4)

17. $\begin{cases} 5x + 2y = 7 \\ 3x - y = 13 \end{cases}$

$$\begin{array}{r} 5x + 2y = 7 \\ 6x - 2y = 26 \\ \hline 11x \quad = 33 \end{array}$$

$x = 3$

$5 \cdot 3 + 2y = 7$

$2y = -8$

$y = -4$

(3, −4)

18. $\begin{cases} 4x + 3y = 8 \\ x - 2y = 13 \end{cases}$

$$\begin{array}{r} 4x + 3y = 8 \\ -4x + 8y = -52 \\ \hline 11y = -44 \end{array}$$

$y = -4$

$4x + 3(-4) = 8$

$4x = 20$

$x = 5$

(5, −4)

19. $\begin{cases} 3x + 2y = 10 \\ 2x + 5y = 3 \end{cases}$

$$-6x - 4y = -20$$
$$\underline{6x + 15y = 9}$$
$$11y = -11$$
$$y = -1$$
$$3x + 2(-1) = 10$$
$$3x = 12$$
$$x = 4$$

$(4, -1)$

20. $\begin{cases} 4x + 5y = 7 \\ 6x - 2y = -18 \end{cases}$

$$8x + 10y = 14$$
$$\underline{30x - 10y = -90}$$
$$38x = -76$$
$$x = -2$$
$$4(-2) + 5y = 7$$
$$5y = 15$$
$$y = 3$$

$(-2, 3)$

21. $\begin{cases} 6x - 5y = 3 \\ -12x + 8y = 5 \end{cases}$

$$12x - 10y = 6$$
$$\underline{-12x + 8y = 5}$$
$$-2y = 11$$
$$y = -\tfrac{11}{2}$$
$$6x - 5\left(-\tfrac{11}{2}\right) = 3$$
$$6x = -\tfrac{49}{2}$$
$$x = -\tfrac{49}{12}$$

$\left(-\tfrac{49}{12}, -\tfrac{11}{2}\right)$

22. $\begin{cases} \tfrac{2}{3}x + \tfrac{1}{6}y = \tfrac{2}{3} \\ 3x - y = 12 \end{cases}$

$$4x + y = 4$$
$$\underline{3x - y = 12}$$
$$7x = 16$$
$$x = \tfrac{16}{7}$$
$$3\left(\tfrac{16}{7}\right) - y = 12$$
$$-y = \tfrac{84}{7} - \tfrac{48}{7}$$
$$y = -\tfrac{36}{7}$$

$\left(\tfrac{16}{7}, -\tfrac{36}{7}\right)$

23. $\begin{cases} 2u + v = 120 \\ u + 2v = 120 \end{cases}$

$$-4u - 2v = -240$$
$$\underline{u + 2v = 120}$$
$$-3u = -120$$
$$u = 40$$
$$2 \cdot 40 + v = 120$$
$$v = 40$$

$(40, 40)$

24. $\begin{cases} 5u + 6v = 14 \\ 3u + 5v = 7 \end{cases}$

$$-15u - 18v = -42$$
$$\underline{15u + 25v = 35}$$
$$7v = -7$$
$$v = -1$$
$$5u + 6(-1) = 14$$
$$5u = 20$$
$$u = 4$$

$(4, -1)$

25. $\begin{cases} 3a + 3b = 7 \\ 3a + 5b = 3 \end{cases}$

$$-3a - 3b = -7$$
$$\underline{3a + 5b = 3}$$
$$2b = -4$$
$$b = -2$$
$$3a + 3(-2) = 7$$
$$3a = 13$$
$$a = \tfrac{13}{3}$$

$\left(\tfrac{13}{3}, -2\right)$

26. $\begin{cases} 5a + 4b = 4 \\ 4a + 5b = \tfrac{31}{8} \end{cases}$

$$20a + 16b = 16$$
$$\underline{-20a - 25b = -\tfrac{155}{8}}$$
$$-9b = -\tfrac{27}{8}$$
$$b = \tfrac{3}{8}$$
$$5a + 4\left(\tfrac{3}{8}\right) = 4$$
$$5a + \tfrac{3}{2} = 4$$
$$5a = \tfrac{5}{2}$$
$$a = \tfrac{1}{2}$$

$\left(\tfrac{1}{2}, \tfrac{3}{8}\right)$

27. $\begin{cases} 10m + 16n = 140 \\ 5m - 8n = 60 \end{cases}$

$$10m + 16n = 140$$
$$\underline{-10m + 16n = -120}$$
$$32n = 20$$
$$n = \tfrac{5}{8}$$
$$10m + 16\left(\tfrac{5}{8}\right) = 140$$
$$10m = 130$$
$$m = 13$$

$\left(13, \tfrac{5}{8}\right)$

28. $\begin{cases} 7m - 13n = 14 \\ 28m - 39n = 35 \end{cases}$

$$-28m + 52n = -56$$
$$28m - 39n = 35$$
$$13n = -21$$
$$n = -\tfrac{21}{13}$$
$$7m - 13\left(-\tfrac{21}{13}\right) = 14$$
$$7m + 21 = 14$$
$$7m = -7$$
$$m = -1$$
$$\left(-1, -\tfrac{21}{13}\right)$$

29. Upper ray: $x + 3y = 1$

$\begin{cases} x + 3y = 1 \\ -x + 3y = -1 \end{cases}$

$$6y = 0$$
$$y = 0$$
$$x + 3(0) = 1$$
$$x = 1$$

The focal length is 1 inch.

30. $\begin{cases} y = \tfrac{4}{5}x \\ y = -2x + 3 \end{cases}$

$$\tfrac{4}{5}x = -2x + 3$$
$$\tfrac{14}{5}x = 3$$
$$x = \tfrac{15}{14}$$
$$y = \tfrac{4}{5}\left(\tfrac{15}{14}\right)$$
$$y = \tfrac{6}{7}$$
$$\left(\tfrac{15}{14}, \tfrac{6}{7}\right)$$

31. Air speed $= x$ (mph)
Wind speed $= y$ (mph)
Ground speed against wind $= 300$ (mph)
Ground speed with wind $= 450$ (mph)

$\begin{cases} x - y = 300 \\ x + y = 450 \end{cases}$

$$2x = 750$$
$x = 375$ mph air speed

$$375 - y = 300$$
$y = 75$ mph wind speed

32. Water speed $= x$ (mph)
Current $= y$ (mph)

$\begin{cases} x - y = 10 \\ x + y = 10 \div \tfrac{1}{2} \end{cases}$

$\begin{cases} x - y = 10 \\ x + y = 20 \end{cases}$

$$2x = 30$$
$x = 15$ mph water speed

$$15 - y = 10$$
$y = 5$ mph current

33. $x =$ volume of gold.
$y =$ volume of copper.

$\begin{cases} x + y = 15 \\ 19.3x + 9y = 238 \end{cases}$

$$-9x - 9y = -135$$
$$19.3x + 9y = 238$$
$$10.3x = 103$$
$x = 10$ cubic centimeters gold

$$10 + y = 15$$
$y = 5$ cubic centimeters copper

No; the bracelet is not 18-karat gold.

34. $x =$ number of liters 20% solution.
$y =$ number of liters 60% solution.

$\begin{cases} x + y = 5 \\ 0.20x + 0.60y = (0.40)(5) \end{cases}$

$$-0.20x - 0.20y = -1$$
$$0.20x + 0.60y = 2$$
$$0.40y = 1$$
$$y = 2.5$$
$$x + 2.5 = 5$$
$$x = 2.5$$

You must use 2.5 liters of each solution.

35. d. $\left(-\frac{1}{3}, -\frac{2}{3}\right)$

$$\begin{cases} 9x - 3y = -1 \\ 3x + 6y = -5 \end{cases}$$

$$\begin{aligned} 18x - 6y &= -2 \\ 3x + 6y &= -5 \\ \hline 21x &= -7 \\ x &= -\tfrac{1}{3} \end{aligned}$$

$$\begin{aligned} 9\left(-\tfrac{1}{3}\right) - 3y &= -1 \\ -3y &= 2 \\ y &= -\tfrac{2}{3} \end{aligned}$$

36. c. (3, 1)

$$\begin{cases} 5x + 3y = 18 \\ 2x - 7y = -1 \end{cases}$$

$$\begin{aligned} 35x + 21y &= 126 \\ 6x - 21y &= -3 \\ \hline 41x &= 123 \\ x &= 3 \end{aligned}$$

$$\begin{aligned} 5 \cdot 3 + 3y &= 18 \\ 3y &= 3 \\ y &= 1 \end{aligned}$$

37. b. $\left(\frac{12}{7}, -\frac{23}{14}\right)$

$$\begin{cases} x - 2y = 5 \\ 6x + 2y = 7 \end{cases}$$

$$\begin{aligned} 7x &= 12 \\ x &= \tfrac{12}{7} \end{aligned}$$

$$\begin{aligned} \tfrac{12}{7} - 2y &= 5 \\ -2y &= \tfrac{23}{7} \\ y &= -\tfrac{23}{14} \end{aligned}$$

38. a. $\left(\frac{4}{3}, -1\right)$

$$\begin{cases} -6x + 4y = -12 \\ 3x - 4y = 8 \end{cases}$$

$$\begin{aligned} -3x &= -4 \\ x &= \tfrac{4}{3} \end{aligned}$$

$$\begin{aligned} -6\left(\tfrac{4}{3}\right) + 4y &= -12 \\ 4y &= -4 \\ y &= -1 \end{aligned}$$

39. e. $\frac{2}{7}$

$$\begin{cases} 3x + 2y = 4 \\ 6x - 3y = 6 \end{cases}$$

$$\begin{aligned} 9x + 6y &= 12 \\ 12x - 6y &= 12 \\ \hline 21x &= 24 \\ x &= \tfrac{8}{7} \end{aligned}$$

$$\begin{aligned} 3\left(\tfrac{8}{7}\right) + 2y &= 4 \\ 2y &= \tfrac{4}{7} \\ y &= \tfrac{2}{7} \end{aligned}$$

40.

$$\begin{aligned} 3x + 2y &= 4 \\ 2y &= -3x + 4 \\ y &= -\tfrac{3}{2}x + 2 \end{aligned}$$

$$\begin{aligned} 6x - 3y &= 6 \\ -3y &= -6x + 6 \\ y &= 2x - 2 \end{aligned}$$

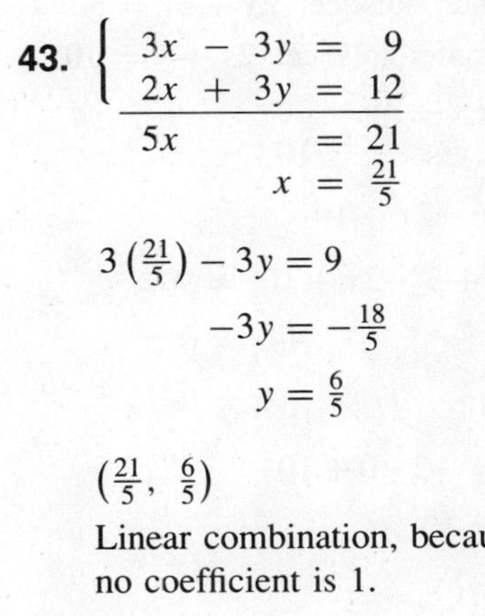

41. $\begin{cases} 2x - 4y = 8 \\ x + 2y = 5 \end{cases}$

$$\begin{aligned} x &= -2y + 5 \\ 2(-2y + 5) - 4y &= 8 \\ -8y &= -2 \\ y &= \tfrac{1}{4} \end{aligned}$$

$$\begin{aligned} x &= -2\left(\tfrac{1}{4}\right) + 5 \\ x &= \tfrac{9}{2} \end{aligned}$$

$\left(\frac{9}{2}, \frac{1}{4}\right)$

Substitution, because x has a coefficient of 1.

42. $\begin{cases} 2x - 3y = 6 \\ 4x + 9y = 8 \end{cases}$

$$\begin{aligned} 6x - 9y &= 18 \\ 4x + 9y &= 8 \\ \hline 10x &= 26 \\ x &= \tfrac{13}{5} \end{aligned}$$

$$\begin{aligned} 2\left(\tfrac{13}{5}\right) - 3y &= 6 \\ -3y &= \tfrac{4}{5} \\ y &= -\tfrac{4}{15} \end{aligned}$$

$\left(\frac{13}{5}, -\frac{4}{15}\right)$

Linear combination, because no coefficient is 1.

43. $\begin{cases} 3x - 3y = 9 \\ 2x + 3y = 12 \end{cases}$

$$\begin{aligned} 5x &= 21 \\ x &= \tfrac{21}{5} \end{aligned}$$

$$\begin{aligned} 3\left(\tfrac{21}{5}\right) - 3y &= 9 \\ -3y &= -\tfrac{18}{5} \\ y &= \tfrac{6}{5} \end{aligned}$$

$\left(\frac{21}{5}, \frac{6}{5}\right)$

Linear combination, because no coefficient is 1.

44. $\begin{cases} 5x + 2y = 10 \\ 3x - 6y = 12 \end{cases}$

$15x + 6y = 30$

$\underline{3x - 6y = 12}$

$18x = 42$

$x = \frac{7}{3}$

$5\left(\frac{7}{3}\right) + 2y = 10$

$2y = -\frac{5}{3}$

$y = -\frac{5}{6}$

$\left(\frac{7}{3}, -\frac{5}{6}\right)$

Linear combination, because no coefficient is 1.

45. $\begin{cases} 5x - y = 7 \\ x + 4y = 16 \end{cases}$

$x = -4y + 16$

$5(-4y + 16) - y = 7$

$-21y = -73$

$y = \frac{73}{21}$

$x = -4\left(\frac{73}{21}\right) + 16$

$x = -\frac{292}{21} + \frac{336}{21}$

$x = \frac{44}{21}$

$\left(\frac{44}{21}, \frac{73}{21}\right)$

Substitution, because an x-coefficient is 1.

46. $\begin{cases} 6x + y = 8 \\ -4x + 2y = 9 \end{cases}$

$y = -6x + 8$

$-4x + 2(-6x + 8) = 9$

$-16x = -7$

$x = \frac{7}{16}$

$y = -6\left(\frac{7}{16}\right) + 8$

$y = -\frac{21}{8} + \frac{64}{8}$

$y = \frac{43}{8}$

$\left(\frac{7}{16}, \frac{43}{8}\right)$

Substitution, because a y-coefficient is 1.

47. $\begin{cases} -4x + 5y = 20 \\ 2x + 3y = 8 \end{cases}$

$-4x + 5y = 20$

$\underline{4x + 6y = 16}$

$11y = 36$

$y = \frac{36}{11}$

$-4x + 5\left(\frac{36}{11}\right) = 20$

$-4x = \frac{40}{11}$

$x = -\frac{10}{11}$

$\left(-\frac{10}{11}, \frac{36}{11}\right)$

Linear combination, because no coefficient is 1.

48. $\begin{cases} 7x - 5y = 18 \\ 8x + y = 24 \end{cases}$

$y = -8x + 24$

$7x - 5(-8x + 24) = 18$

$47x = 138$

$x = \frac{138}{47}$

$y = -8\left(\frac{138}{47}\right) + 24$

$y = -\frac{1104}{47} + \frac{1128}{47}$

$y = \frac{24}{47}$

$\left(\frac{138}{47}, \frac{24}{47}\right)$

Substitution, because a y-coefficient is 1.

49. Winter solstice: $2x + 3y = 30$

Summer solstice: $2x + y = 10$

$\begin{cases} 2x + 3y = 30 \\ 2x + y = 10 \end{cases}$

$y = -2x + 10$

$2x + 3(-2x + 10) = 30$

$-4x = 0$

$x = 0$

$y = -2 \cdot 0 + 10$

$y = 10$

$(0, 10)$

The point of intersection is the top of the post.

50. $2x + 3 \cdot 0 = 30$ $\qquad$ $2x + 0 = 10$

$x = 15$ $\qquad$ $x = 5$

$15 - 5 = 10$ feet

To make a calendar that records the seasons, find the midpoint of the two points. The midpoint is the position of the shadow at the spring and fall equinoxes. Summer occurs as the shadow moves from the summer solstice to the fall equinox, fall occurs as the shadow moves from the fall equinox to the winter solstice, winter and spring occur as the shadow moves back again from the winter solstice to the summer solstice.

51. $\frac{1}{2}(8) + 6(12) = 76$

$4(8) - \frac{1}{3}(12) = 28$

52. $-5\left(\frac{3}{5}\right)+\frac{6}{5}\left(\frac{1}{2}\right)=-3+\frac{3}{5}$
$=-\frac{15}{5}+\frac{3}{5}$
$=-\frac{12}{5}$

$3\left(\frac{3}{5}\right)-\frac{2}{3}\left(\frac{1}{2}\right)=\frac{9}{5}-\frac{1}{3}$
$=\frac{27-5}{15}$
$=\frac{22}{15}$

53. $m=\frac{-4-2}{-2-6}$
$=\frac{-6}{-8}$
$=\frac{3}{4}$

$m=\frac{-2-5}{4+1}$
$=-\frac{7}{5}$

$y+4=\frac{3}{4}(x+2)$
$4y+16=3x+6$
$-3x+4y=-10$
$3x-4y=10$

$y+2=-\frac{7}{5}(x-4)$
$5y+10=-7x+28$
$7x+5y=18$

$$\begin{cases} 3x-4y=10 \\ 7x+5y=18 \end{cases}$$

$$\begin{aligned} 15x-20y &= 50 \\ 28x+20y &= 72 \\ \hline 43x &= 122 \\ x &= \frac{122}{43} \end{aligned}$$

$$\begin{aligned} 3\left(\frac{122}{43}\right)-4y &= 10 \\ -4y &= \frac{430}{43}-\frac{366}{43} \\ -4y &= \frac{64}{43} \\ y &= -\frac{16}{43} \end{aligned}$$

$\left(\frac{122}{43}, -\frac{16}{43}\right)$

54. $m=\frac{3-2}{-2-5}$
$=-\frac{1}{7}$

$m=\frac{3-4}{-1-2}$
$=\frac{-1}{-3}$
$=\frac{1}{3}$

$y-3=-\frac{1}{7}(x+2)$
$7y-21=-x-2$
$x+7y=19$

$y-3=\frac{1}{3}(x+1)$
$3y-9=x+1$
$-x+3y=10$

$$\begin{aligned} x+7y &= 19 \\ -x+3y &= 10 \\ \hline 10y &= 29 \\ y &= 2.9 \end{aligned}$$

$x+7(2.9)=19$
$x=-1.3$

$(-1.3,\ 2.9)$

7.4 Problem Solving Using Linear Systems

Communicating about Algebra

A. $r =$ speed of first plane.

$s =$ speed of second plane.

$s = 50 + r$

$2r + 1.5s = 1825$

The airplanes did not fly the same number of hours.

B. $2r + 1.5(50 + r) = 1825$

$3.5r = 1750$

$r = 500$

$s = 50 + 500$

$= 550$

Substitution is the best method for this system since one equation is already solved for s.

EXERCISES

1. [Number of gallons of regular unleaded] $\cdot$ [Cost per gallon of regular unleaded] $+$ [Number of gallons of premium unleaded] $\cdot$ [Cost per gallon of premium unleaded] $=$ [Total cost]

[Cost per gallon of regular unleaded] $+ 0.20 =$ [Cost per gallon of premium unleaded]

2.

Cost of gallons of regular unleaded = 15	(dollars)
Cost per gallon of regular unleaded = x	(dollars)
Number of gallons of premium unleaded = 10	(gallons)
Cost per gallon of premium unleaded = y	(dollars)
Total cost = 35.50	(dollars)

3. $\begin{cases} 15x + 10y = 35.50 \\ x + 0.20 = y \end{cases}$

4. $15x + 10(x + 0.20) = 35.50$

$25x = 33.50$

$x = 1.34$

$y = 1.34 + 0.20$

$y = 1.54$

The cost of regular unleaded is \$1.34 per gallon and the cost of premimum unleaded is \$1.54 per gallon.

5. $\begin{cases} x + y = 500 \\ 0.80x + 0.86y = 0.82(500) \end{cases}$

$-0.80x - 0.80y = -400$

$0.80x + 0.86y = 410$

$0.06y = 10$

$y = \frac{500}{3}$ gallons 86-octane

$x + \frac{500}{3} = 500$

$x = \frac{1000}{3}$ gallons 80-octane

6. $\begin{cases} x + y = 12 \\ 19.3x + 9y = 156.5 \end{cases}$

$$-9x - 9y = -108$$

$$\begin{array}{r} 19.3x + 9y = 156.5 \\ \hline 10.3x \quad = 48.5 \end{array}$$

$x \approx 4.7$ cubic centimeters gold

$$\frac{485}{103} + y = \frac{1236}{103}$$

$y \approx 7.3$ cubic centimeters copper

$$\frac{x}{24} = \frac{(4.7)(19.3)}{156.5}$$

$$\frac{x}{24} \approx 0.58$$

$x \approx 13.9$ or 14 karats

About 58 percent of the necklace's weight is gold.

7. Time for 1st runner $= x$ (minutes)
Time for 2nd runner $= y$ (minutes)
Distance for 1st runner $= 300x$ (meters per minute)
Distance for 2nd runner $= 360y$ (meters per minute)

$\begin{cases} x + y = 16 \\ 300x + 360y = 5160 \end{cases}$

$$-300x - 300y = -4800$$

$$\begin{array}{r} 300x + 360y = 5160 \\ \hline 60y = 360 \end{array}$$

$y = 6$ minutes

$$x + 6 = 16$$

$x = 10$ minutes

8. Time traveled at 40 mph $= 2$ (hours)
Time traveled at 55 mph $= x$ (hours)
Total time traveled $= y$ (hours)
Distance traveled at 40 mph $= (2)(40) = 80$ (miles)
Distance traveled at 55 mph $= 55x$ (miles)
Total distance traveled (to average 45 mph) $= 45y$ (miles)

The time traveled at 55 miles per hour is one hour. The total time traveled is three hours.

$\begin{cases} y = 2 + x \\ 45y = 80 + 55x \end{cases}$

$$45(2 + x) = 80 + 55x$$

$$90 + 45x = 80 + 55x$$

$$-10x = -10$$

$$x = 1$$

$$y = 2 + 1$$

$$y = 3$$

9. $\begin{cases} 2x + 3y = 7.80 \\ 3x + 5y = 12.70 \end{cases}$

$$-6x - 9y = -23.40$$

$$\begin{array}{r} 6x + 10y = 25.40 \\ \hline y = 2.00 \end{array}$$

$$2x + 3(2.00) = 7.80$$

$$2x = 1.80$$

$$x = 0.90$$

Taco: 90¢
Enchilada: \$2.00

10. $\begin{cases} 3x + 20y = 11.40 \\ 2x + 10y = 7.20 \end{cases}$

$$3x + 20y = 11.40$$

$$\begin{array}{r} -4x - 20y = -14.40 \\ \hline -x \quad = -3.00 \end{array}$$

$$x = 3.00$$

$$3(3) + 20y = 11.40$$

$$20y = 2.40$$

$$y = 0.12$$

Crepe paper: \$3.00 a roll
Balloon: 12¢ each

11. $2(L + W) = 22$ $\quad \frac{L}{2} + W + 5 = 12$

$L + W = 11$ $\quad \frac{L}{2} + W = 7$

$L + 2W = 14$

$$\begin{cases} L + W = 11 \\ L + 2W = 14 \end{cases}$$

$$\begin{array}{r} -L - W = -11 \\ L + 2W = 14 \\ \hline W = 3 \end{array} \qquad \begin{array}{r} L + 3 = 11 \\ L = 8 \end{array}$$

The dimensions of the rectangle are 8 meters by 3 meters.

12. $2(L + W) = 42$

$L + W = 21$

$L = W + 4$

$W + 4 + W = 21$ $\quad L = 8\frac{1}{2} + 4$

$2W = 17$ $\quad L = 12\frac{1}{2}$

$W = 8\frac{1}{2}$

The dimensions of the room are $8\frac{1}{2}$ feet by $12\frac{1}{2}$ feet.

13. $$\begin{cases} -2T + 302V = 546.4 \\ -T + 228V = 273.2 \end{cases} \qquad \begin{cases} -T + 228V = 273.2 \\ -3T + 1872V = 819.6 \end{cases} \qquad \begin{cases} -2T + 302V = 546.4 \\ -3T + 1872V = 819.6 \end{cases}$$

$$\begin{array}{r} -2T + 302V = 546.4 \\ 2T - 456V = -546.4 \\ \hline -154V = 0 \\ V = 0 \end{array} \qquad \begin{array}{r} 3T - 684V = -819.6 \\ -3T + 1872V = 819.6 \\ \hline 1188V = 0 \\ V = 0 \end{array} \qquad \begin{array}{r} -6T + 906V = 1639.2 \\ 6T - 3744V = -1639.2 \\ \hline -2838V = 0 \\ V = 0 \end{array}$$

$-2T + 302(0) = 546.4$ $\quad -T + 228(0) = 273.2$ $\quad -2T + 302(0) = 546.4$

$T = -273.2$ $\quad T = -273.2$ $\quad T = -273.2$

Absolute zero on the Celsius scale is -273.2°C.

14. Hemlock: $16 + 4x = y$
Spruce: $10 + 6(x - 5) = y$

$16 + 4x = 10 + 6(x - 5)$ $\quad 16 + 4(18) = y$

$16 + 4x = 6x - 20$ $\quad 16 + 72 = y$

$36 = 2x$ $\quad y = 88$ inches

$x = 18$ years

The two trees will be the same height of 88 inches in 18 years.

15. $2x - 5y = 2(3) - 5(-2)$ $\quad -x + 4y = -3 + 4(-2)$

$= 6 + 10$ $\quad = -3 - 8$

$= 16$ $\quad = -11$

$(3, -2)$ is a solution.

16. $x + 5y = 1 + 5(5)$

$= 1 + 25$

$= 26$

$3x - 6y = 3(1) - 6(5)$

$= 3 - 30$

$= -27 \neq 33$

$(1, 5)$ is not a solution.

17. $2x + 5y = 2(-6) + 5(1)$

$= -12 + 5$

$= -7$

$-3x - 6y = -3(-6) - 6(1)$

$= 18 - 6$

$= 12 \neq 24$

$(-6, 1)$ is not a solution.

18. $6x + 4y = 6(0) + 4(9)$

$= 36$

$3x - 6y = 3(0) - 6(9)$

$= -54$

$(0, 9)$ is a solution.

19. $\begin{cases} -3x + 2y = 6 \\ y = 1 \end{cases}$

$$-3x + 2(1) = 6$$
$$-3x = 4$$
$$x = -\tfrac{4}{3}$$

$(-\tfrac{4}{3}, 1)$

Substitution, because y is given.

20. $\begin{cases} x + 3y = -3 \\ x = -3 \end{cases}$

$$-3 + 3y = -3$$
$$3y = 0$$
$$y = 0$$

$(-3, 0)$

Substitution, because x is given.

21. $\begin{cases} 3x + y = 14 \\ -x + y = 2 \end{cases}$

$$y = x + 2$$
$$3x + x + 2 = 14$$
$$4x = 12$$
$$x = 3$$

$$y = 3 + 2$$
$$y = 5$$

$(3, 5)$

Substitution, because a y-coefficient is 1.

22. $\begin{cases} x + 5y = 45 \\ 2x - y = 2 \end{cases}$

$$x = -5y + 45$$
$$2(-5y + 45) - y = 2$$
$$-11y = -88$$
$$y = 8$$

$$x = -5 \cdot 8 + 45$$
$$x = 5$$

$(5, 8)$

Substitution, because an x-coefficient is 1.

23. $\begin{cases} 9x - 2y = 4 \\ -5x + y = 1 \end{cases}$

$$y = 5x + 1$$
$$9x - 2(5x + 1) = 4$$
$$-x = 6$$
$$x = -6$$

$$y = 5(-6) + 1$$
$$y = -29$$

$(-6, -29)$

Substitution, because a y-coefficient is 1.

24. $\begin{cases} 3x + 5y = 17 \\ \tfrac{1}{2}x + y = 3 \end{cases}$

$$y = -\tfrac{1}{2}x + 3$$
$$3x + 5\left(-\tfrac{1}{2}x + 3\right) = 17$$
$$\tfrac{1}{2}x = 2$$
$$x = 4$$

$$y = -\tfrac{1}{2}(4) + 3$$
$$y = 1$$

$(4, 1)$

Substitution, because a y-coefficient is 1.

25. $\begin{cases} 2x - 7y = -27 \\ 6x + 5y = -3 \end{cases}$

$-6x + 21y = 81$

$\underline{6x + 5y = -3}$

$26y = 78$

$y = 3$

$2x - 7(3) = -27$

$2x = -6$

$x = -3$

$(-3, 3)$

Linear combination, because no coefficient is 1.

26. $\begin{cases} 10x - 3y = 17 \\ -7x + y = 9 \end{cases}$

$y = 7x + 9$

$10x - 3(7x + 9) = 17$

$-11x = 44$

$x = -4$

$y = 7(-4) + 9$

$y = -19$

$(-4, -19)$

Substitution, because a y-coefficient is 1.

27. $\begin{cases} x + 4y = 9 \\ 3x + 8y = 32 \end{cases}$

$x = -4y + 9$

$3(-4y + 9) + 8y = 32$

$-4y = 5$

$y = -\frac{5}{4}$

$x = -4\left(-\frac{5}{4}\right) + 9$

$x = 14$

$\left(14, -\frac{5}{4}\right)$

Substitution, because an x-coefficient is 1.

28. $\begin{cases} 3x - 2y = 17 \\ -2x - 5y = 14 \end{cases}$

$6x - 4y = 34$

$\underline{-6x - 15y = 42}$

$-19y = 76$

$y = -4$

$3x - 2(-4) = 17$

$3x = 9$

$x = 3$

$(3, -4)$

Linear combination, because no coefficient is 1.

29. $\begin{cases} 9x - 5y = 45 \\ -2x + 21y = -10 \end{cases}$

$18x - 10y = 90$

$\underline{-18x + 189y = -90}$

$179y = 0$

$y = 0$

$9x - 5(0) = 45$

$x = 5$

$(5, 0)$

Linear combination, because no coefficient is 1.

30. $\begin{cases} 6x - y = -32 \\ 2x + 13y = 16 \end{cases}$

$y = 6x + 32$

$2x + 13(6x + 32) = 16$

$80x = -400$

$x = -5$

$y = 6(-5) + 32$

$y = 2$

$(-5, 2)$

Substitution, because a y-coefficient is 1.

31. b. The best estimate for the racing speed of a thoroughbred racehorse is 35 miles per hour.

32. d. The best estimate for the population of the United States is 250,000,000.

33. $\begin{cases} 24x - y = 24 \\ 6x + y = 9 \end{cases}$

$$\begin{aligned} 30x &= 33 \\ x &= \tfrac{11}{10} \end{aligned}$$

$$\begin{aligned} 24\left(\tfrac{11}{10}\right) - y &= 24 \\ -y &= \tfrac{240}{10} - \tfrac{264}{10} \\ y &= \tfrac{24}{10} \\ y &= \tfrac{12}{5} \end{aligned}$$

Point C $\left(\frac{11}{10}, \frac{12}{5}\right)$

Distance: $2\frac{2}{5}$ miles (y-coordinate)

Mid-Chapter SELF-TEST

1. $4(-3) - 4(-4) = -12 + 16$ $= 4$ $\quad -2(-3) + (-4) = 6 - 4$ $= 2$ $\quad 4(2) - 4(6) = 8 - 24$ $= -16$ $\quad -2(2) + 6 = -4 + 6$ $= 2$

$(-3, -4)$

2. $\frac{1}{2}(-1) + 2(7) = -\frac{1}{2} + 14$ $= \frac{27}{2}$ $\quad 12(-1) + 7 = -12 + 7$ $= -5$ $\quad \frac{1}{2}(4) + 2(-5) = 2 - 10$ $= -8$ $\quad 12(4) + (-5) = 48 - 5$ $= 43$

$(-1, 7)$

3. $3(-2) + 5(3) = -6 + 15$ $= 9$ $\quad -(-2) + 2(3) = 2 + 6$ $= 8$ $\quad 3(4) + 5(6) = 12 + 30$ $= 42$ $\quad -4 + 2(6) = -4 + 12$ $= 8$

$(-2, 3)$

4. $3(1) + 2(3) = 3 + 6$ $= 9$ $\quad 11(1) + 8(3) = 11 + 24$ $= 35$ $\quad 3(9) + 2(-8) = 27 - 16$ $= 11$ $\quad 11(9) + 8(-8) = 99 - 64$ $= 35$

$(9, -8)$

5. $-12\left(-\frac{3}{2}\right) + (-3) = 18 - 3$ $= 15$ $\quad 6\left(-\frac{3}{2}\right) - 2(-3) = -9 + 6$ $= -3$ $\quad -12\left(-\frac{5}{6}\right) + (5) = 10 + 5$ $= 15$

$6\left(-\frac{5}{6}\right) - 2(5) = -5 - 10$ $= -15$ $\quad \left(-\frac{5}{6}, 5\right)$

6. $\frac{1}{2} + 7\left(\frac{1}{2}\right) = \frac{1}{2} + \frac{7}{2}$ $= 4$ $\quad \frac{1}{2} + \frac{1}{2} = 1$ $\quad \frac{1}{4} + 7\left(\frac{3}{4}\right) = \frac{1}{4} + \frac{21}{4}$ $= \frac{11}{2}$ $\quad \frac{1}{4} + \frac{3}{4} = 1$

$\left(\frac{1}{2}, \frac{1}{2}\right)$

7. $-2x + 3y = 6$

$3y = 2x + 6$

$y = \frac{2}{3}x + 2$

$2x + y = 10$

$y = -2x + 10$

$(3,\ 4)$

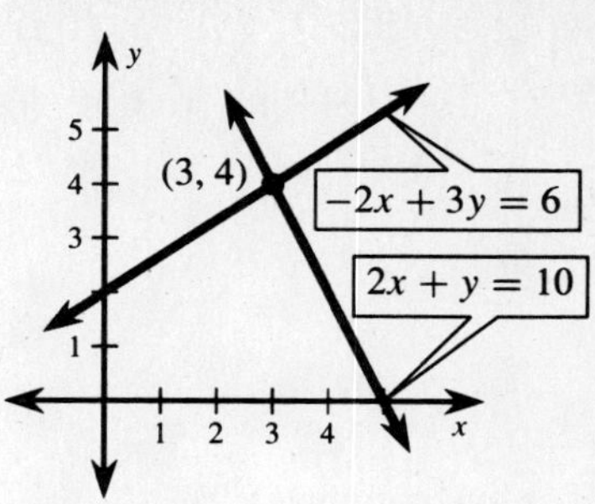

8. $-2x + y = 2$

$y = 2x + 2$

$x - y = 1$

$-y = -x + 1$

$y = x - 1$

$(-3,\ -4)$

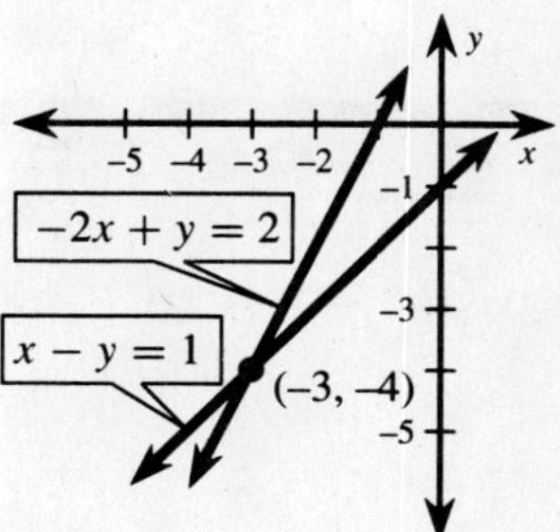

9. $\begin{cases} x + 3y = 7 \\ 4x - 7y = -10 \end{cases}$

$x = -3y + 7$

$4(-3y + 7) - 7y = -10$

$-19y = -38$

$y = 2$

$x = -3(2) + 7$

$x = 1$

$(1, 2)$

10. $\begin{cases} -6x - 5y = 28 \\ x - 2y = 1 \end{cases}$

$x = 2y + 1$

$-6(2y + 1) - 5y = 28$

$-17y = 34$

$y = -2$

$x = 2(-2) + 1$

$x = -3$

$(-3,\ -2)$

11. $\begin{cases} \frac{1}{2}x + \frac{3}{4}y = 9 \\ -2x + y = -4 \end{cases}$

$y = 2x - 4$

$\frac{1}{2}x + \frac{3}{4}(2x - 4) = 9$

$2x = 12$

$x = 6$

$y = 2(6) - 4$

$y = 8$

$(6,\ 8)$

12. $\begin{cases} 4x + y = -1 \\ -5x - y = 0 \end{cases}$

$y = -4x - 1$

$-5x - (-4x - 1) = 0$

$-x = -1$

$x = 1$

$y = -4(1) - 1$

$y = -5$

$(1,\ -5)$

13. $\begin{cases} x - 6y = -19 \\ 3x - 2y = -9 \end{cases}$

$x = 6y - 19$

$3(6y - 19) - 2y = -9$

$16y = 48$

$y = 3$

$x = 6(3) - 19$

$x = -1$

$(-1,\ 3)$

14. $\begin{cases} 4x + y = 14 \\ 3x + 2y = 8 \end{cases}$

$y = -4x + 14$

$3x + 2(-4x + 14) = 8$

$-5x = -20$

$x = 4$

$y = -4(4) + 14$

$y = -2$

$(4,\ -2)$

15. $\begin{cases} -2x - 3y = 4 \\ 2x - 4y = 3 \end{cases}$

$$\begin{array}{r} -7y = 7 \\ y = -1 \end{array}$$

$-2x - 3(-1) = 4$

$-2x = 1$

$x = -\frac{1}{2}$

$\left(-\frac{1}{2},\ -1\right)$

16. $\begin{cases} 5x + 7y = 35 \\ 4x - 7y = 1 \end{cases}$

$$\begin{array}{r} 9x = 36 \\ x = 4 \end{array}$$

$5(4) + 7y = 35$

$7y = 15$

$y = \frac{15}{7}$

$\left(4,\ \frac{15}{7}\right)$

17. $\begin{cases} 4x + 3y = 1 \\ -2x + 9y = -4 \end{cases}$

$$\begin{array}{r} 4x + 3y = 1 \\ -4x + 18y = -8 \\ \hline 21y = -7 \end{array}$$

$y = -\frac{1}{3}$

$4x + 3\left(-\frac{1}{3}\right) = 1$

$4x = 2$

$x = \frac{1}{2}$

$\left(\frac{1}{2},\ -\frac{1}{3}\right)$

18. $\begin{cases} 10x + 3y = 2 \\ 8x + 6y = 16 \end{cases}$

$$\begin{array}{r} -20x - 6y = -4 \\ 8x + 6y = 16 \\ \hline -12x = 12 \end{array}$$

$x = -1$

$10(-1) + 3y = 2$

$3y = 12$

$y = 4$

$(-1,\ 4)$

19. $\begin{cases} 3x - 5y = -4 \\ -9x + 7y = 8 \end{cases}$

$$\begin{aligned} 9x - 15y &= -12 \\ -9x + 7y &= 8 \\ \hline -8y &= -4 \\ y &= \tfrac{1}{2} \end{aligned}$$

$$\begin{aligned} 3x - 5\left(\tfrac{1}{2}\right) &= -4 \\ 3x &= -\tfrac{3}{2} \\ x &= -\tfrac{1}{2} \end{aligned}$$

$\left(-\frac{1}{2}, \frac{1}{2}\right)$

20. $\begin{cases} 3x + 7y = -4 \\ -15x - 14y = 6 \end{cases}$

$$\begin{aligned} 6x + 14y &= -8 \\ -15x - 14y &= 6 \\ \hline -9x &= -2 \\ x &= \tfrac{2}{9} \end{aligned}$$

$$\begin{aligned} 3\left(\tfrac{2}{9}\right) + 7y &= -4 \\ 7y &= -\tfrac{14}{3} \\ y &= -\tfrac{2}{3} \end{aligned}$$

$\left(\frac{2}{9}, -\frac{2}{3}\right)$

21. $\begin{cases} x + y = 8000 \\ 0.04x + 0.05y = 350 \end{cases}$

$$\begin{aligned} -0.04x - 0.04y &= -320 \\ 0.04x + 0.05y &= 350 \\ \hline 0.01y &= 30 \\ y &= 3000 \end{aligned}$$

$$\begin{aligned} x + 3000 &= 8000 \\ x &= 5000 \end{aligned}$$

\$5000 was invested in the 4% fund.
\$3000 was invested in the 5% fund.

22. $\begin{cases} x + y = 5 \\ 2x + 3y = 13 \end{cases}$

$$\begin{aligned} -2x - 2y &= -10 \\ 2x + 3y &= 13 \\ \hline y &= 3 \end{aligned}$$

$$\begin{aligned} x + 3 &= 5 \\ x &= 2 \end{aligned}$$

You rented (2) \$2.00 movies and (3) \$300 movies.

23. $\begin{cases} x + y = 46 \\ 3x + 5y = 150 \end{cases}$

$$\begin{aligned} -3x - 3y &= -138 \\ 3x + 5y &= 150 \\ \hline 2y &= 12 \\ y &= 6 \end{aligned}$$

$$\begin{aligned} x + 6 &= 46 \\ x &= 40 \end{aligned}$$

There are 40 3-point questions and 6 5-point questions.

24. $\begin{cases} x + y = 80 \\ 2.25x + 2.75y = 210 \end{cases}$

$$\begin{aligned} x &= -y + 80 \\ 2.25(-y + 80) + 2.75y &= 210 \\ 0.50y &= 30 \\ y &= 60 \end{aligned}$$

$$\begin{aligned} x + 60 &= 80 \\ x &= 20 \end{aligned}$$

You have 20 11-inch softballs and 60 12-inch softballs.

7.5 Special Types of Linear Systems

Communicating about Algebra

Assuming they knew their own heights, they could have used the ratio of their height to their shadow's length, then compared them to the ratio of the height and shadow length of one of the statues.

EXERCISES

1. The graphical model for a linear system that has no solution is 2 parallel lines.

2. The graphical model for a linear system that has many solutions is 1 line.

3. The graphical model for a linear system that has exactly one solution is 2 intersecting lines.

4. 2 parallel lines

5. 2 intersecting lines

6. 1 line

7. b.

8. d.

9. f.

10. c.

11. e.

12. a.

13. No solution

$x + y = -1$

$x + y = 8$

14. No solution

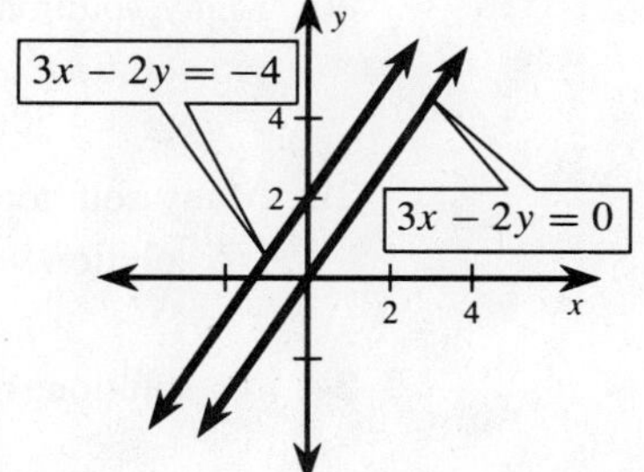

15. Many solutions

$3x - 2y = 3$

$-6x + 4y = -6$

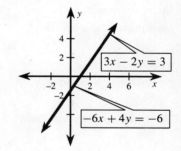

16. No solution

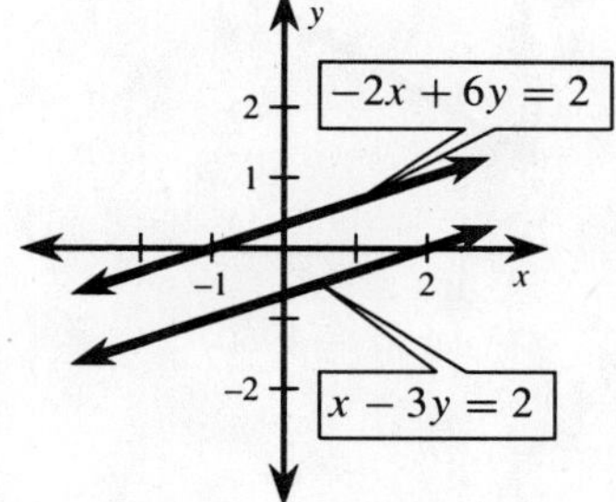

17. No solution

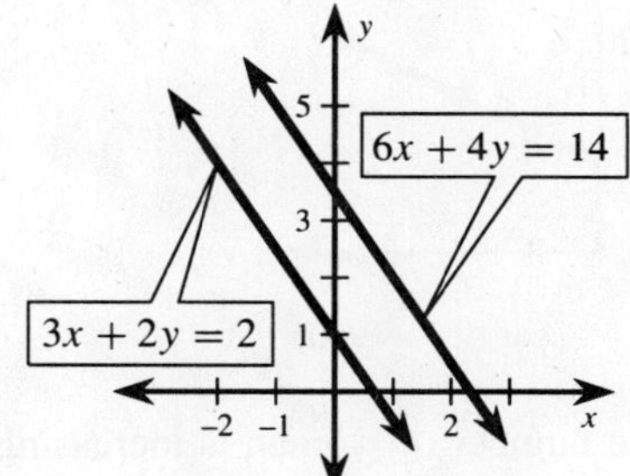

18. Many solutions

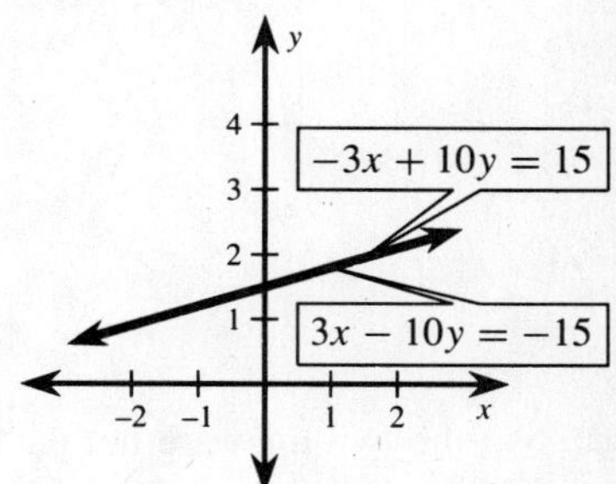

19. No solution

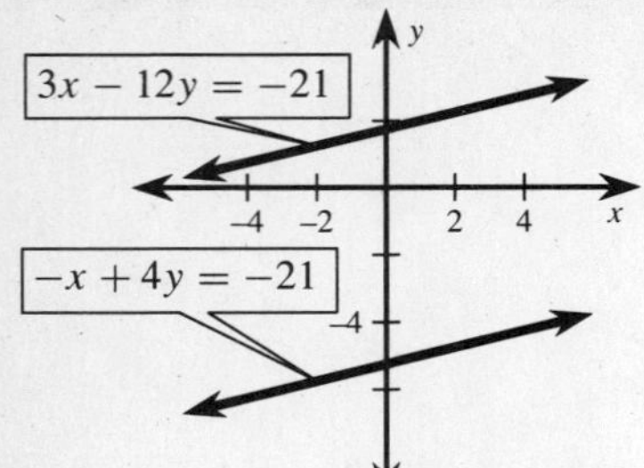

20. No solution

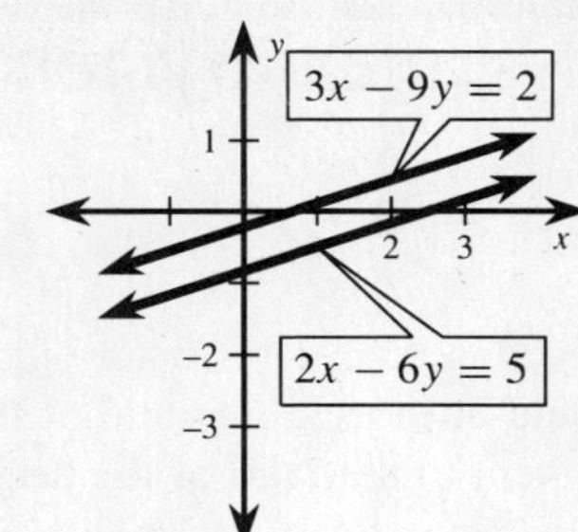

21. Many solutions

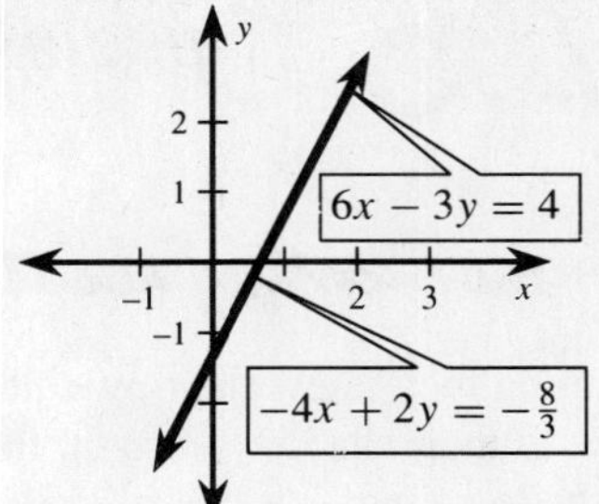

22. No solution

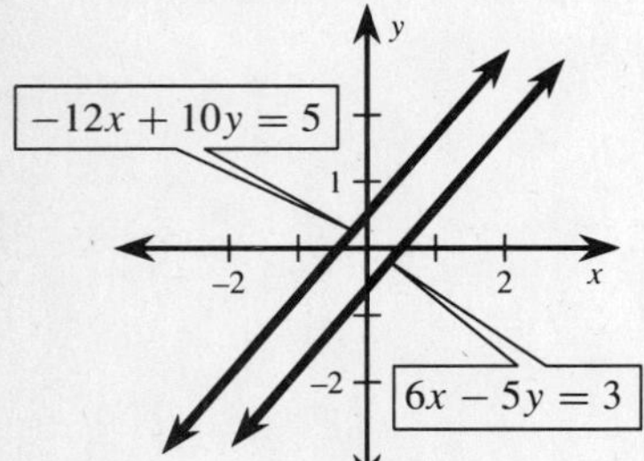

23. No solution

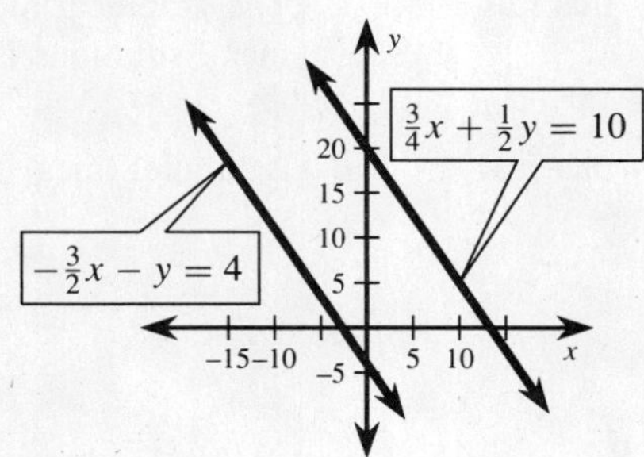

24. Many solutions

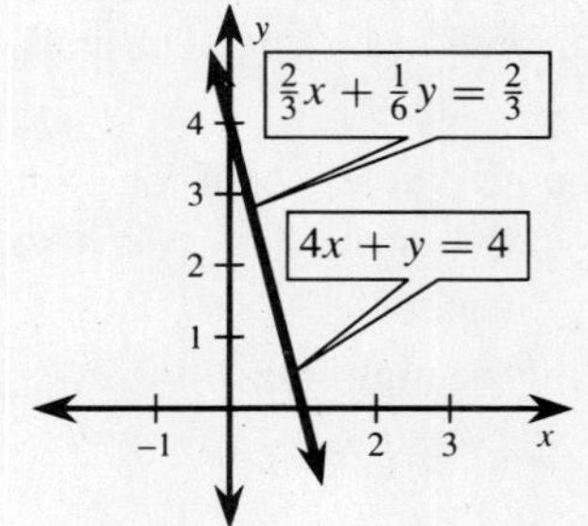

25. $\begin{cases} y = 4x - 2 \\ 3y = 12x - 6 \end{cases}$

26. $\begin{cases} y = \frac{2}{3}x + 2 \\ y = \frac{2}{3}x - 1 \end{cases}$

27. $\begin{cases} y = -\frac{1}{2}x + 4 \\ y = -\frac{1}{2}x - 4 \end{cases}$

28. $\begin{cases} y = \frac{1}{3}x + 1 \\ 3y = x + 3 \end{cases}$

29. Many solutions: $n = 8$
No solution: $n \neq 8$

30. Many solutions: $n = -6$
No solution: $n \neq -6$

31. Many solutions: $n = -6$
No solution: $n \neq -6$

32. Many solutions: $n = 20$
No solution: $n \neq 20$

33. Horizontal and vertical lines

34. No solution; the lines are parallel.

35. Male: $y = 89 + 1.1x$
Female: $y = 91 + 1.3x$

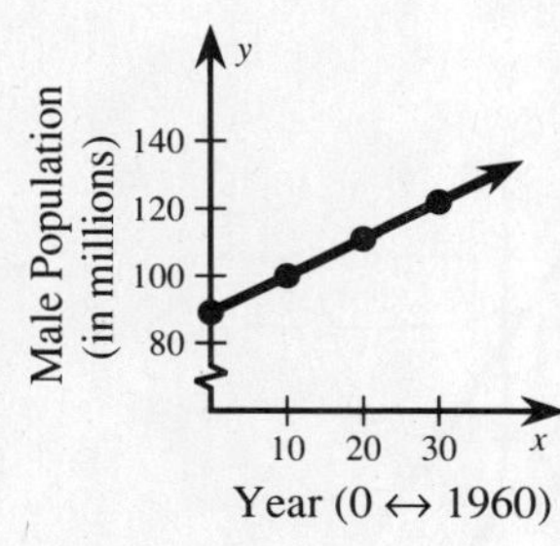

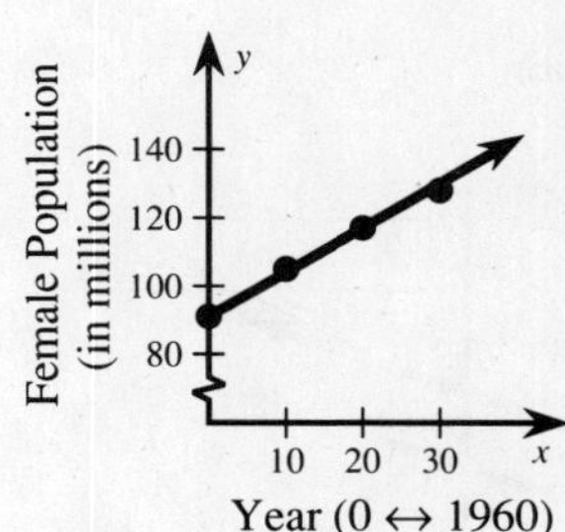

36. No; the two lines are not parallel. No; the number of women is increasing more rapidly than the number of men.

37. Married couples with children is decreasing to 25% and the single- person household is increasing to 25%, so they will intersect during the 1990s.

38.

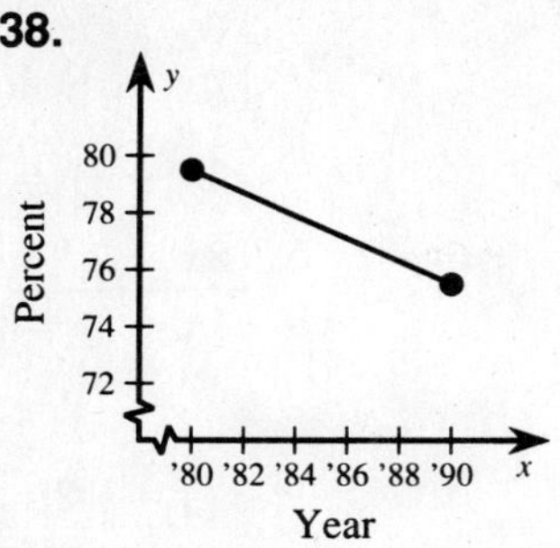

39. $\begin{cases} y = [(x+10)2 - 18]\frac{1}{2} - x \\ y = 1 \end{cases}$

$1 = [2x + 20 - 18]\frac{1}{2} - x$

$1 = x + 1 - x$

$1 = 1$

Any number x can be chosen that will give the final result of 1.

40. $\begin{cases} 2x - y = -4 \\ x + 2y = 3 \end{cases}$

$x = -2y + 3$

$2(-2y + 3) - y = -4$

$-5y = -10$

$y = 2$

$x = -2 \cdot 2 + 3$

$x = -1$

$(-1,\ 2)$

41. $\begin{cases} x + y = 22 \\ x - y = 8 \end{cases}$

$x = y + 8$

$y + 8 + y = 22$

$2y = 14$

$y = 7$

$x = 7 + 8$

$x = 15$

$(15, 7)$

42. $\begin{cases} y - 2x = 1 \\ y - 2x = -3 \end{cases}$

$y = 2x + 1$

$2x + 1 - 2x = -3$

$1 \neq -3$

No solution

43. $\begin{cases} 3x + 2y = 18 \\ 5x - 2y = 14 \end{cases}$

$8x = 32$

$x = 4$

$3 \cdot 4 + 2y = 18$

$2y = 6$

$y = 3$

$(4, 3)$

44. $\begin{cases} 2x + y = 4 \\ -2x + 3y = -12 \end{cases}$

$4y = -8$

$y = -2$

$2x - 2 = 4$

$2x = 6$

$x = 3$

$(3,\ -2)$

45. $\begin{cases} 2x - 5y = 3 \\ 4y - x = -3 \end{cases}$

$2x - 5y = 3$

$-2x + 8y = -6$

$3y = -3$

$y = -1$

$2x - 5(-1) = 3$

$2x = -2$

$x = -1$

$(-1,\ -1)$

46. $\begin{cases} \frac{1}{2}y = x + 3 \\ \phantom{\frac{1}{2}}y = 2x + 6 \end{cases}$

$\frac{1}{2}(2x + 6) = x + 3$

$x + 3 = x + 3$

Any point on the line $y = 2x + 6$

47. $\begin{cases} x + y = 5 \\ x - y = 3 \end{cases}$

$2x = 8$

$x = 4$

$4 + y = 5$

$y = 1$

$(4, 1)$

48. $\begin{cases} 3x - y = 9 \\ 6x - 2y = 10 \end{cases}$

$$\begin{aligned} -6x + 2y &= -18 \\ 6x - 2y &= 10 \\ \hline 0 &= -8 \end{aligned}$$

No solution

49. $\begin{cases} 3x + 2y = 10 \\ 4x - y = -1 \end{cases}$

$$\begin{aligned} 3x + 2y &= 10 \\ 8x - 2y &= -2 \\ \hline 11x \quad &= 8 \\ x &= \tfrac{8}{11} \\ 3\left(\tfrac{8}{11}\right) + 2y &= 10 \\ 2y &= \tfrac{86}{11} \\ y &= \tfrac{43}{11} \end{aligned}$$

$\left(\frac{8}{11}, \frac{43}{11}\right)$

50. $\begin{cases} 7 = 2x - y \\ 5 = x + y \end{cases}$

$$\begin{aligned} 12 &= 3x \\ 4 &= x \end{aligned}$$

$7 = 2 \cdot 4 - y$

$y = 1$

$(4, 1)$

51. $\begin{cases} x + y = 2 \\ x - 3y = 5 \end{cases}$

$x = -y + 2$

$$\begin{aligned} -y + 2 - 3y &= 5 \\ -4y &= 3 \\ y &= -\tfrac{3}{4} \end{aligned}$$

$x = -\left(-\frac{3}{4}\right) + 2$

$x = 2\frac{3}{4}$

$\left(2\frac{3}{4}, -\frac{3}{4}\right)$

52.

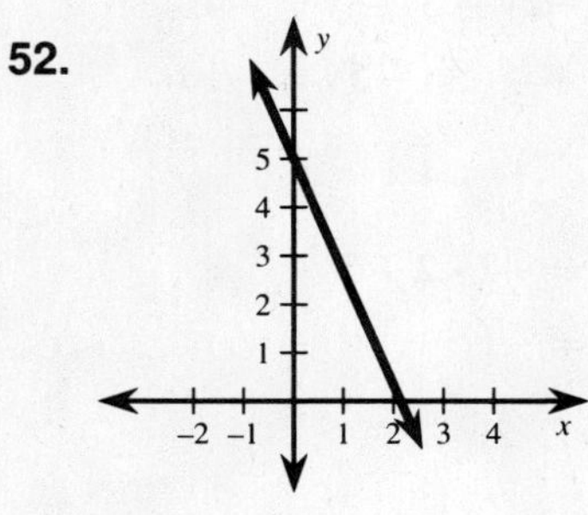

$$\begin{aligned} 7x + 3y &= 15 \\ 3y &= -7x + 15 \\ y &= -\tfrac{7}{3}x + 5 \end{aligned}$$

$$\begin{aligned} \tfrac{7}{3}x + y &= 5 \\ y &= -\tfrac{7}{3}x + 5 \end{aligned}$$

To correct the graphical model, delete the line on the left.

53.

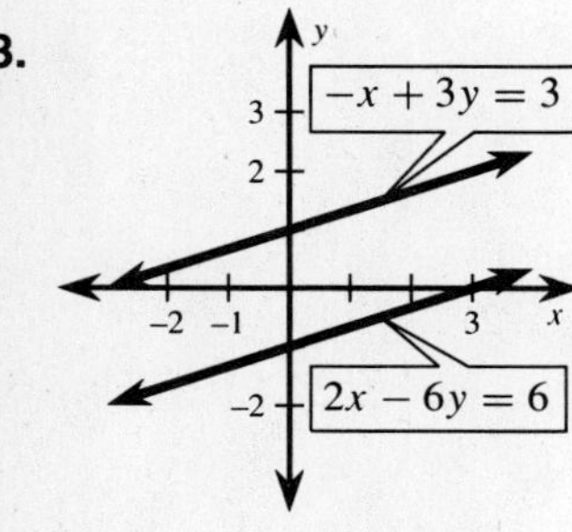

$$\begin{aligned} -x + 3y &= 3 \\ 3y &= x + 3 \\ y &= \tfrac{1}{3}x + 1 \end{aligned}$$

$$\begin{aligned} 2x - 6y &= 6 \\ -6y &= -2x + 6 \\ y &= \tfrac{1}{3}x - 1 \end{aligned}$$

To correct the graphical model, insert line parallel to the given line with y-intercept 1.

54. $\begin{cases} 200y - x = 200 \\ 199y - x = -198 \end{cases}$

$$\begin{aligned} 200y &= x + 200 \\ y &= \tfrac{1}{200}x + 1 \end{aligned}$$

$$\begin{aligned} 199y &= x - 198 \\ y &= \tfrac{1}{199}x - \tfrac{198}{199} \end{aligned}$$

Not parallel

$$\begin{aligned} -200y + x &= -200 \\ 199y - x &= -198 \\ \hline -y \quad &= -398 \\ y &= 398 \end{aligned}$$

$$\begin{aligned} 200(398) - x &= 200 \\ -x &= -79{,}400 \\ x &= 79{,}400 \end{aligned}$$

$(79{,}400, 398)$

55. $25x - 24y = 0$

$$y = \tfrac{25}{24}x$$

$$\begin{aligned} 13x - 12y &= 120 \\ -12y &= -13x + 120 \\ y &= \tfrac{13}{12}x - 10 \end{aligned}$$

Not parallel

$$\begin{aligned} 13x - 12\left(\tfrac{25}{24}\right)x &= 120 \\ 13x - \tfrac{25}{2}x &= 120 \\ \tfrac{1}{2}x &= 120 \\ x &= 240 \end{aligned}$$

$y = \frac{25}{24}(240)$

$y = 250$

$(240, 250)$

Mixed REVIEW

1. $3 + 6 \div 3 - 2 = 3 + 2 - 2$
$= 3$

2. $-\frac{5}{4} = -\frac{15}{12}$
$-\frac{4}{3} = -\frac{16}{12}$
$-\frac{5}{4}$ is larger than $-\frac{4}{3}$.

3. $\begin{bmatrix} -2 & 4 \\ 3 & 6 \end{bmatrix} + \begin{bmatrix} 6 & -2 \\ 3 & 8 \end{bmatrix} = \begin{bmatrix} 4 & 2 \\ 6 & 14 \end{bmatrix}$

4. $\begin{bmatrix} -3 & 7 \\ 4 & -5 \end{bmatrix} + \begin{bmatrix} 8 & 6 \\ -3 & -1 \end{bmatrix} = \begin{bmatrix} 5 & 13 \\ 1 & -6 \end{bmatrix}$

5. $3a + 4b - 6 = 0$
$4b = 6 - 3a$
$b = \frac{1}{4}(6 - 3a)$

6. $3m - 2n = 2n + 6$
$-4n = 6 - 3m$
$n = \frac{1}{4}(3m - 6)$

7. $3x + 2y = 3(-3) + 2(2)$
$= -9 + 4$
$= -5 < -4$
$(-3,\ 2)$ is a solution.

8. $\frac{1}{2}x - \frac{1}{6}y = \frac{1}{2}(4) - \frac{1}{6}(3)$
$= 2 - \frac{1}{2}$
$= \frac{3}{2} \geq 1$
(4, 3) is a solution.

9. $3x + \frac{1}{4}y = 6$
$\frac{1}{4}y = -3x + 6$
$y = -12x + 24$

10. $y = \frac{1}{4}(x + 4)$
$4y = x + 4$
$-x + 4y = 4$

11. $4a \div 3 = 4(6) \div 3$
$= 24 \div 3$
$= 8$
6 is a solution.

12. $3 \div b \cdot 7 = 3 \div \frac{7}{2} \cdot 7$
$= 3 \cdot \frac{2}{7} \cdot 7$
$= \frac{6}{7} \cdot 7$
$= 6$
$\frac{7}{2}$ is not a solution.

13. $-3 - (-6) = -3 + 6$
$= 3$

14. $\frac{1}{3} + \frac{1}{6} = \frac{2}{6} + \frac{1}{6}$
$= \frac{3}{6}$
$= \frac{1}{2}$

15. $3x^2 + x - 7 = 3(-1)^2 + (-1) - 7$
$= 3 - 1 - 7$
$= -5$

16. $\frac{1}{4}(8 + |y|) + 6 = \frac{1}{4}(8 + |4|) + 6$
$= \frac{1}{4}(12) + 6$
$= 3 + 6$
$= 9$

17. $6x + \frac{1}{2}(x + 2) = 5$
$12x + x + 2 = 10$
$13x = 8$
$x = \frac{8}{13}$

18. $\frac{1}{3}(3 - y) - \frac{2}{3}y = 8$
$3 - y - 2y = 24$
$-3y = 21$
$y = -7$

19. $y - (-3) = \frac{1}{4}(x - 0)$

$y = \frac{1}{4}x - 3$

20. $m = \dfrac{\frac{3}{2} - 2}{-\frac{1}{2} - 4}$

$= \dfrac{-\frac{1}{2}}{-\frac{9}{2}}$

$= \dfrac{1}{9}$

$y - 2 = \dfrac{1}{9}(x - 4)$

$9y - 18 = x - 4$

$-x + 9y = 14$

7.6 Solving Systems of Linear Inequalities

Communicating about Algebra

A. II

B.

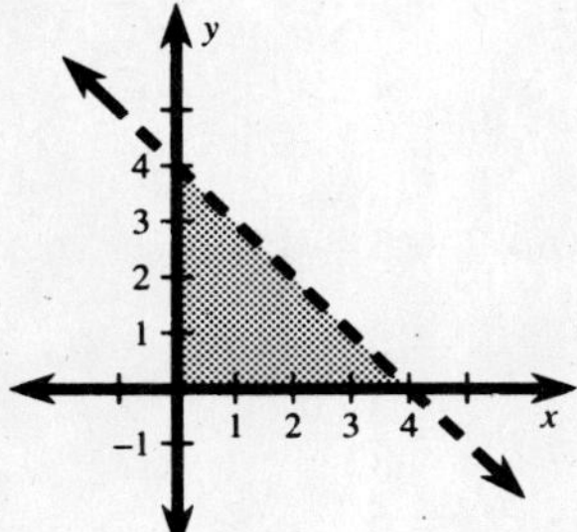

C.

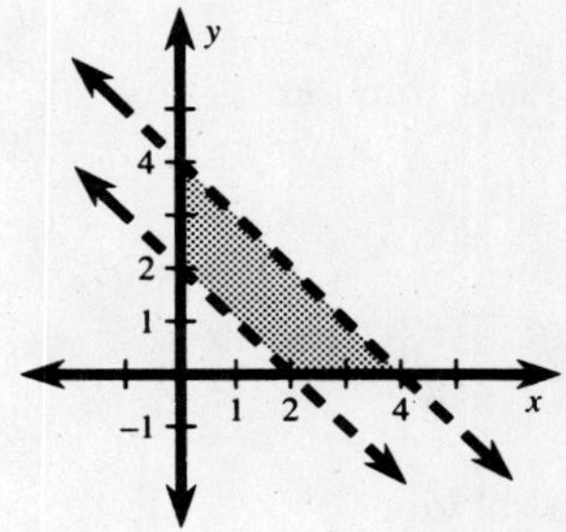

EXERCISES

1. False; "any" should be "each".

2. A vertex of the graph of a system of linear inequalities is the point of intersection of 2 lines in the system.

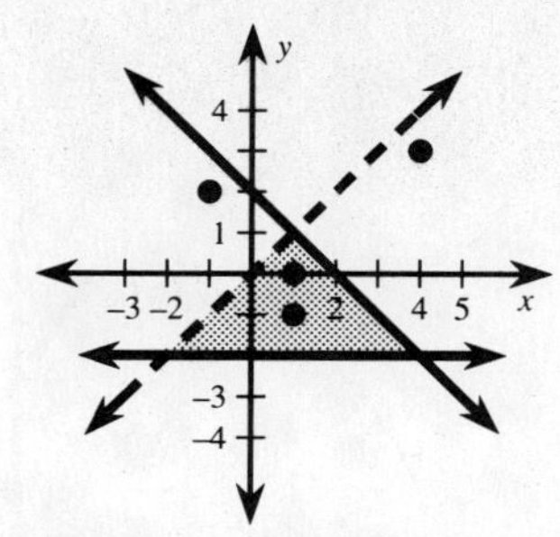

Use graph for Exercises 3–6

3. $1 + 0 = 1 \leq 2$

$1 - 0 = 1 > 0$

$0 \geq -2$

(1, 0) is a solution.

4. $4 + 3 = 7 \not\leq 2$

(4, 3) is not a solution.

5. $1 + (-1) = 0 \leq 2$

$1 - (-1) = 2 > 0$

$-1 \geq -2$

(1, −1) is a solution.

6. $-1 + 2 = 1 \leq 2$

$-1 - 2 = -3 \not> 0$

(−1, 2) is not a solution.

7. **c.**

8. **f.**

9. **d.**

10. **a.**

11. **e.**

12. **b.**

13.

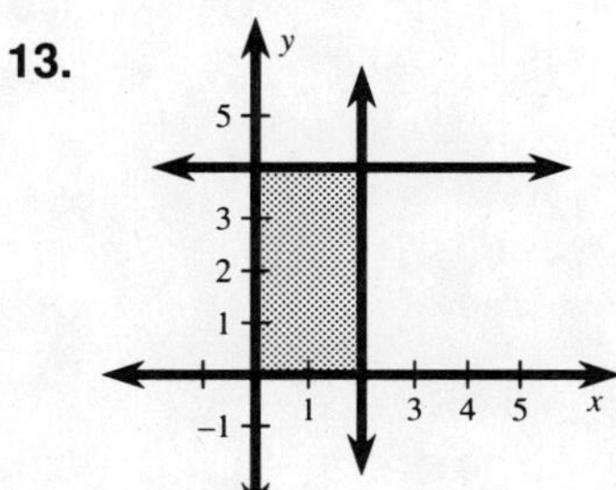

14.

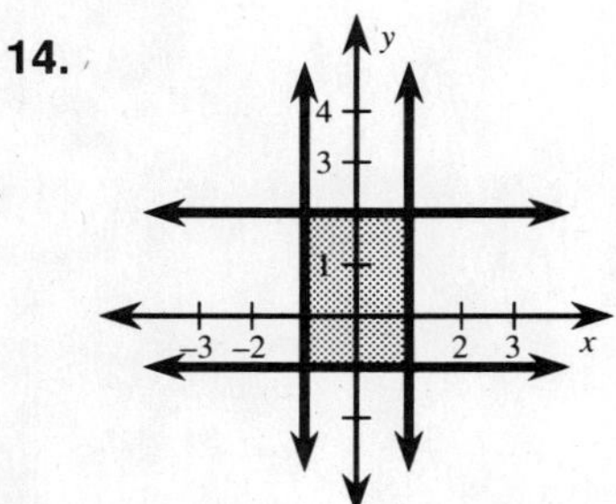

15. $x + y \le 1$

$y \le -x + 1$

$-x + y \le 1$

$y \le x + 1$

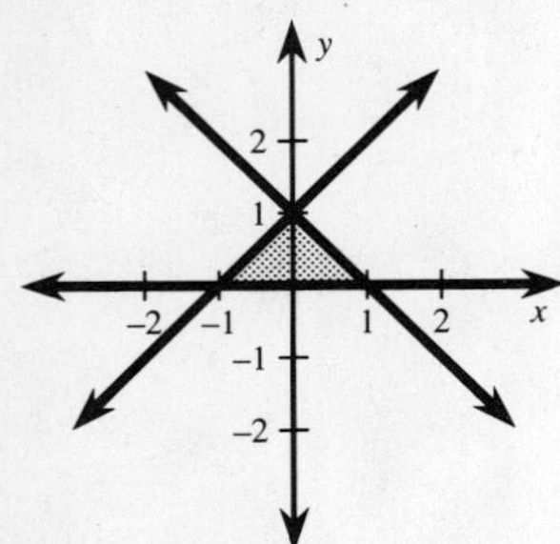

16. $\frac{3}{2}x + y < 3$

$y < -\frac{3}{2}x + 3$

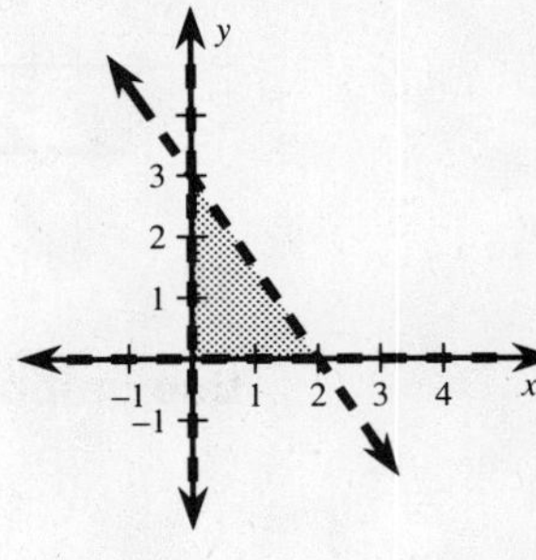

17. $x + y \le 5$

$y \le -x + 5$

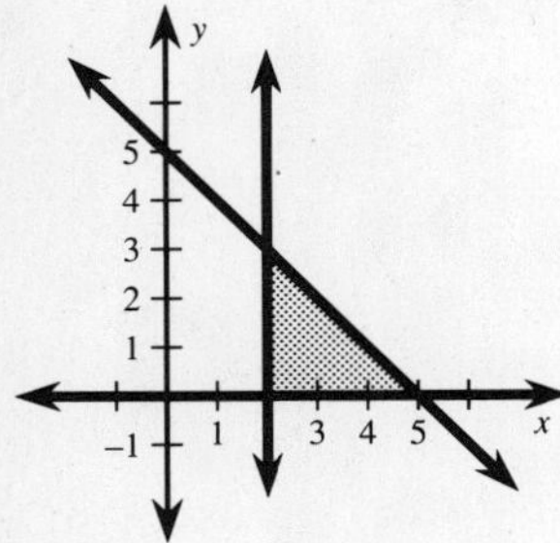

18. $2x + y \ge 2$

$y \ge -2x + 2$

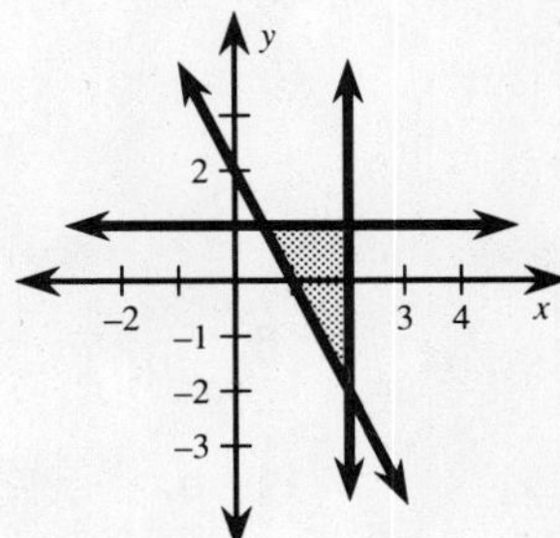

19. $-\frac{3}{2}x + y < 3$

$y < \frac{3}{2}x + 3$

$\frac{1}{4}x + y > -\frac{1}{2}$

$y > -\frac{1}{4}x - \frac{1}{2}$

$2x + y < 3$

$y < -2x + 3$

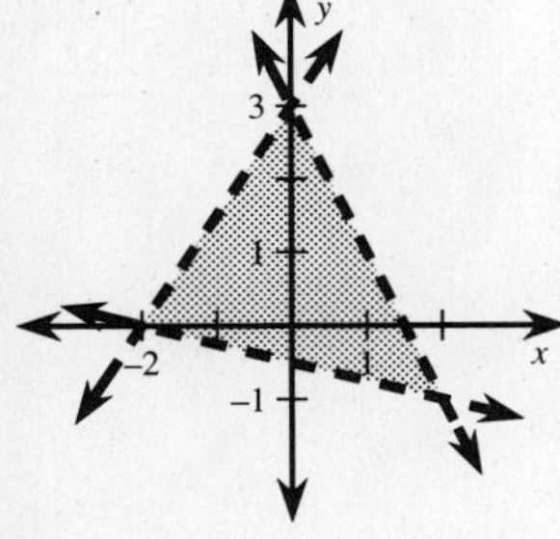

20. $-\frac{1}{7}x + y < \frac{36}{7}$

$y < \frac{1}{7}x + \frac{36}{7}$

$\frac{5}{2}x + y < \frac{5}{2}$

$y < -\frac{5}{2}x + \frac{5}{2}$

$\frac{6}{5}x + y > \frac{6}{5}$

$y > -\frac{6}{5}x + \frac{6}{5}$

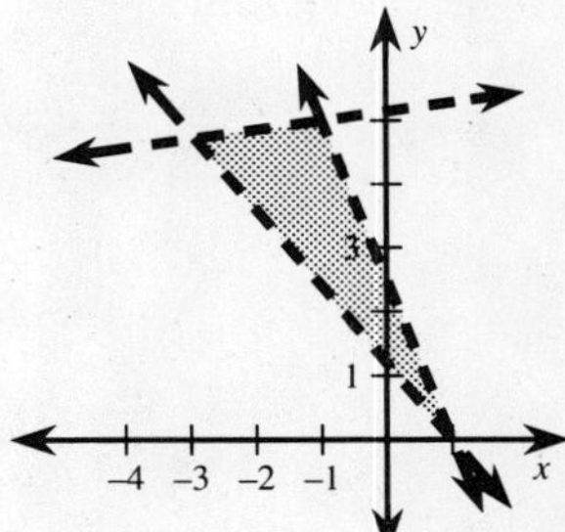

21. $x - 2y \le 3$

$-2y \le -x + 3$

$y \ge \frac{1}{2}x - \frac{3}{2}$

$3x + 2y \ge 9$

$2y \ge -3x + 9$

$y \ge -\frac{3}{2}x + \frac{9}{2}$

$x + y \le 6$

$y \le -x + 6$

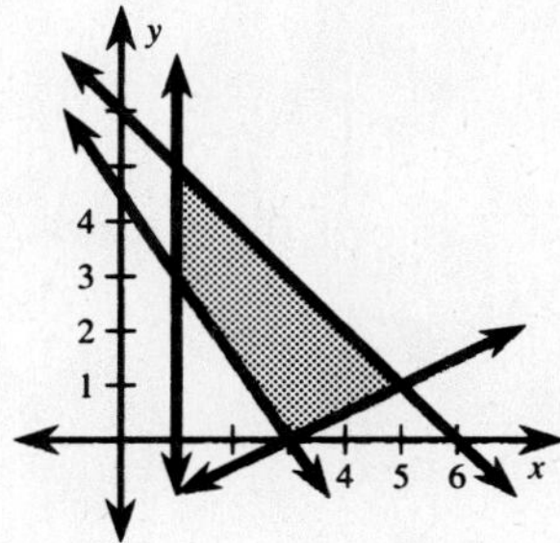

22. $x + y < 10$

$y < -x + 10$

$2x + y > 10$

$y > -2x + 10$

$x - y < 2$

$-y < -x + 2$

$y > x - 2$

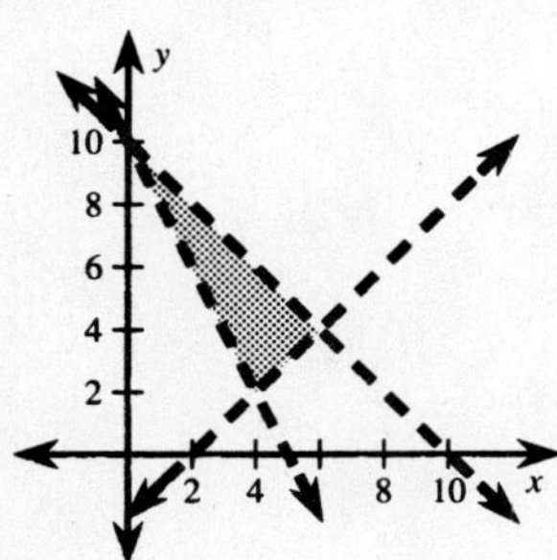

23. $x - 3y \ge 3$

$-3y \ge -x + 3$

$y \le \frac{1}{3}x - 1$

$x - 3y \le 12$

$-3y \le -x + 12$

$y \ge \frac{1}{3}x - 4$

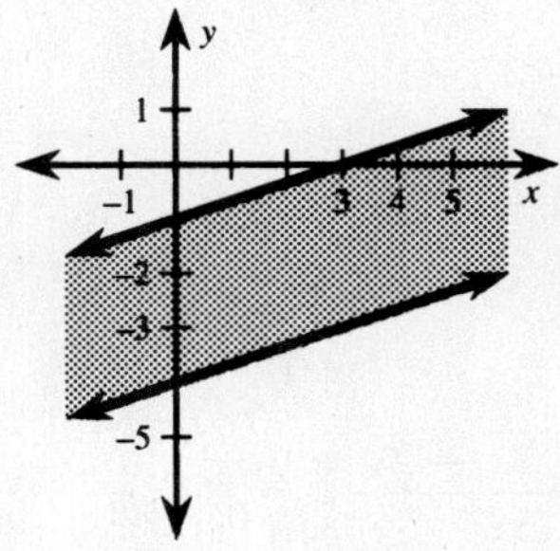

24. $x + y < 3$

$y < -x + 3$

$x + y > -1$

$y > -x - 1$

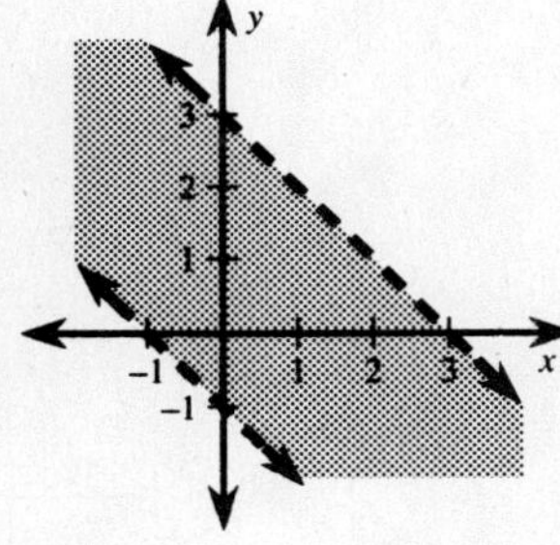

25. $\begin{cases} x + y = 12 \\ 3x - 4y = 15 \end{cases}$

$y = -x + 12$

$3x - 4(-x + 12) = 15$

$7x = 63$

$x = 9$

$y = -9 + 12$

$= 3$

(9, 3)

$\begin{cases} x + y = 12 \\ x = 0 \end{cases}$

$y = 12$

(0, 12)

$\begin{cases} 3x - 4y = 15 \\ y = 0 \end{cases}$

$3x = 15$

$x = 5$

(5, 0)

$\begin{cases} x = 0 \\ y = 0 \end{cases}$

(0, 0)

26. $\begin{cases} \frac{1}{2}x + y = 2 \\ x - y = 1 \end{cases}$

$\frac{3}{2}x = 3$

$x = 2$

$2 - y = 1$

$y = 1$

(2, 1)

$\begin{cases} \frac{1}{2}x + y = 2 \\ x = 0 \end{cases}$

$y = 2$

(0, 2)

$\begin{cases} x - y = 1 \\ y = 0 \end{cases}$

$x = 1$

(1, 0)

$\begin{cases} x = 0 \\ y = 0 \end{cases}$

(0, 0)

27. $\begin{cases} 5x - 3y = -7 \\ 3x + y = 7 \end{cases}$

$5x - 3y = -7$

$9x + 3y = 21$

$14x = 14$

$x = 1$

$y = 4$

(1, 4)

$\begin{cases} 3x + y = 7 \\ x + 5y = -7 \end{cases}$

$3x + y = 7$

$-3x - 15y = 21$

$-14y = 28$

$y = -2$

$x = 3$

(3, −2)

$\begin{cases} 5x - 3y = -7 \\ x + 5y = -7 \end{cases}$

$5x - 3y = -7$

$-5x - 25y = 35$

$-28y = 28$

$y = -1$

$x = -2$

(−2, −1)

28. $\begin{cases} x + 2y = 0 \\ 5x - 2y = 0 \end{cases}$

$6x = 0$

$x = 0$

$y = 0$

(0, 0)

$\begin{cases} x + 2y = 0 \\ -x + y = 3 \end{cases}$

$3y = 3$

$y = 1$

$x = -2$

(−2, 1)

$\begin{cases} 5x - 2y = 0 \\ -x + y = 3 \end{cases}$

$5x - 2y = 0$

$-2x + 2y = 6$

$3x = 6$

$x = 2$

$y = 5$

(2, 5)

29. $\begin{cases} x \geq 2 \\ y \geq 1 \\ x \leq 5 \\ y \leq 7 \end{cases}$

30. $\begin{cases} y \leq 4x \\ y \geq 0 \\ y \geq 4x - 16 \\ y \leq 4 \end{cases}$

31. $\begin{cases} y \geq 0 \\ y \leq \frac{3}{2}x \\ y \leq -x + 5 \end{cases}$

32. $\begin{cases} y \geq 0 \\ y \leq x + 1 \\ y \leq -x + 1 \end{cases}$

33. $x =$ stuffed mushroom

$y =$ cheese stick

$y \le -\frac{5}{3}x + 300$

$$\begin{cases} 0.25x + 0.15y \le 45 \\ x \ge 80 \\ y \ge 120 \end{cases}$$

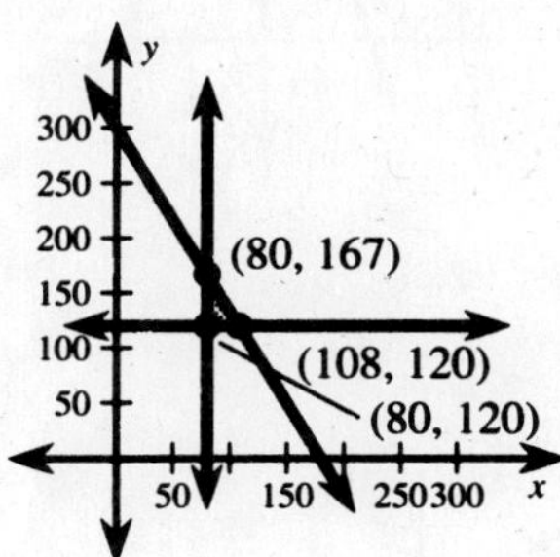

34. $$\begin{cases} x \ge 0 \\ y \ge 0 \\ x + y \le 20 \\ 3x + 5y \ge 80 \end{cases}$$

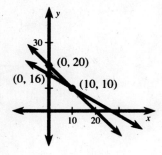

35. $$\begin{cases} x \ge 0 \\ y \ge 0 \\ y \le -x + 3 \end{cases}$$

36. $$\begin{cases} x \ge 0 \\ y \le 6 \\ y \ge x + 3 \end{cases}$$

37. $$\begin{cases} y \ge -x + 3 \\ y \le x + 3 \\ y \le -x + 9 \\ y \ge x - 3 \end{cases}$$

38. Corners: base = 3, height = 3

$A = \frac{1}{2}(3)(3)$

$A = \frac{9}{2}$

Center square

$(\text{side})^2 = 3^2 + 3^2$

$(\text{side})^2 = 18$

$\text{side} = \sqrt{18}$

$A = (\sqrt{18})(\sqrt{18})$

$A = 18$

Corner area $= \frac{9}{2}$

Center area $= 18$

39. $$m = \frac{6-8}{0-19} = \frac{-2}{-19} = \frac{2}{19}$$

$$y - 6 = \frac{2}{19}(x - 0)$$

$$19y - 114 = 2x$$

$$-2x + 19y = 114$$

$$\begin{cases} -2x + 19y \le 114 \\ x \ge 0 \\ x \le 19 \\ y \ge 0 \end{cases}$$

40. $2x - 6y = 18$

$-6y = -2x + 18$

$y = \frac{1}{3}x - 3$

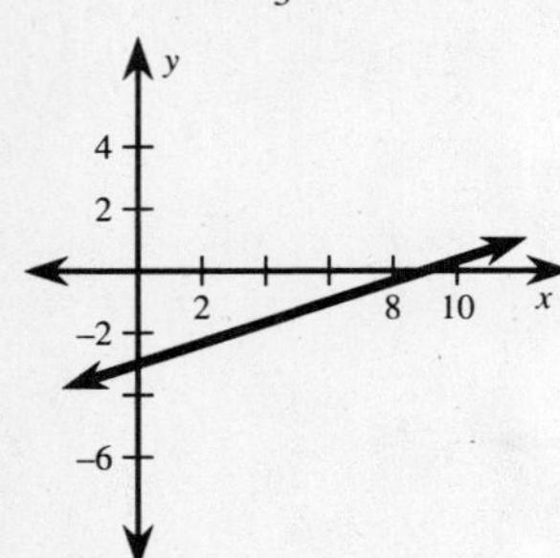

41. $x + 3y = -9$

$3y = -x - 9$

$y = -\frac{1}{3}x - 3$

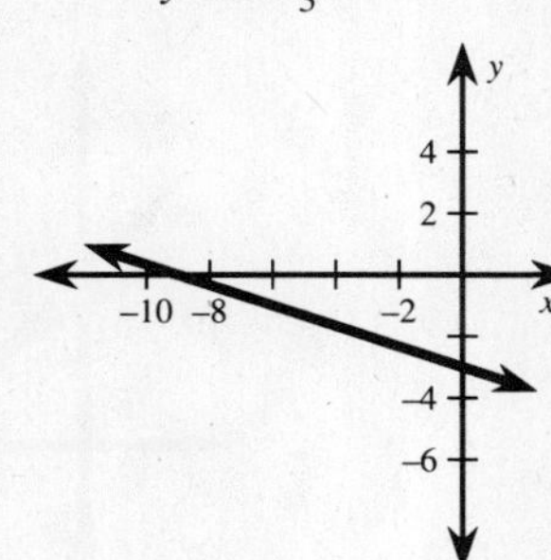

42. $-3x + y = 21$

$y = 3x + 21$

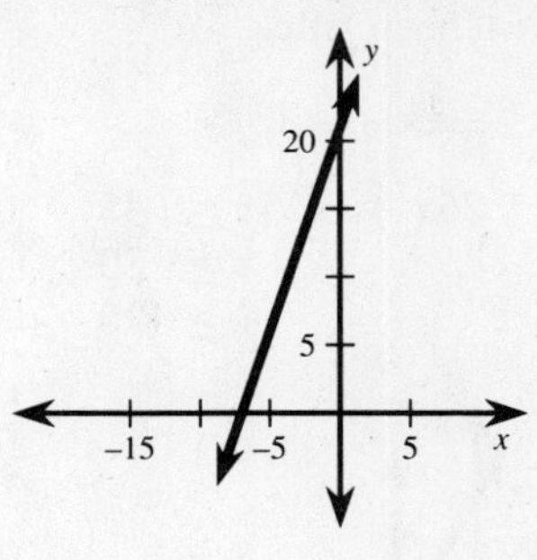

43. $7x + 2y = 28$

$2y = -7x + 28$

$y = -\frac{7}{2}x + 14$

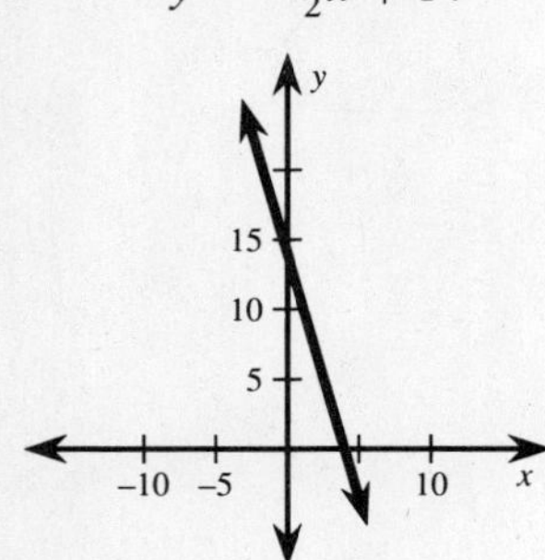

44. $x \geq 2$

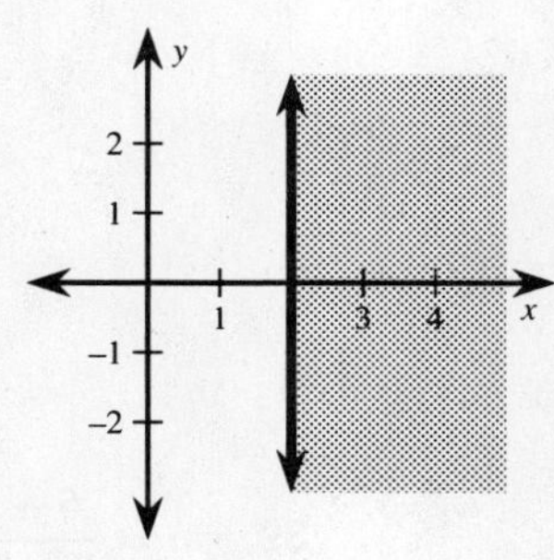

45. $y < 2 - x$

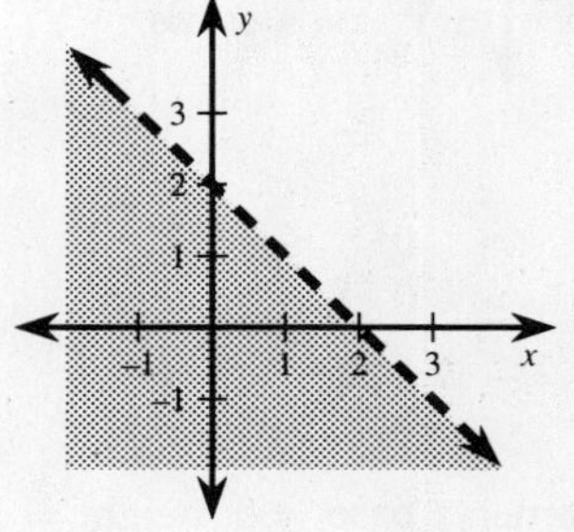

46. $2y - x \geq 4$

$2y \geq x + 4$

$y \geq \frac{1}{2}x + 2$

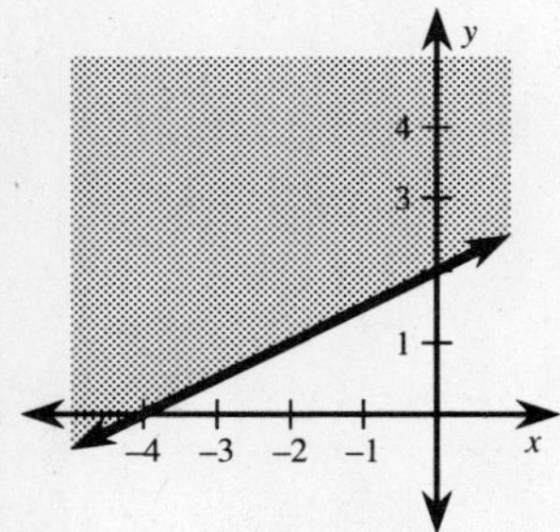

47. $4x - 2y \leq 12$

$-2y \leq -4x + 12$

$y \geq 2x - 6$

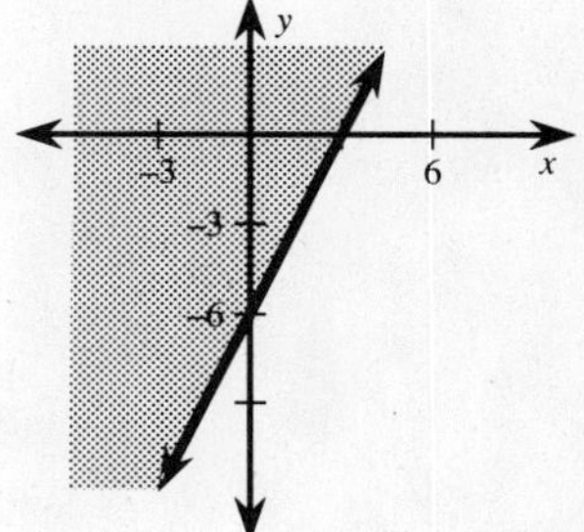

48. $\begin{cases} x \geq 1 \\ x \leq 19 \\ y \geq 1 \\ y \leq 11 \end{cases}$

49. No; each inequality describes a half-plane. When you form one point of a star, you eliminate 2 other points.

7.7 Exploring Data: Linear Programming

Communicating about Algebra

Process A: 0, Process B: 1200

EXERCISES

1. Constraints define the area of possible answers.

2. The objective quantity is evaluated at vertices formed by constraints.

3. The word *optimize* means to find the minimum or maximum value of some quantity.

4.

$C = 5x + 7y$

$C = 5 \cdot 0 + 7 \cdot 2$
$C = 14$

$C = 5 \cdot 0 + 7 \cdot 4$
$C = 28$

$C = 5 \cdot 1 + 7 \cdot 5$
$C = 40$

$C = 5 \cdot 6 + 7 \cdot 3$
$C = 51$

$C = 5 \cdot 5 + 7 \cdot 0$
$C = 25$

$C = 5 \cdot 3 + 7 \cdot 0$
$C = 15$

5. The minimum value of the objective quantity is $C = 14$.

6. The maximum value of the objective quantity is $C = 51$.

7. (0, 0), (0, 5), (3, 4), (4, 0)

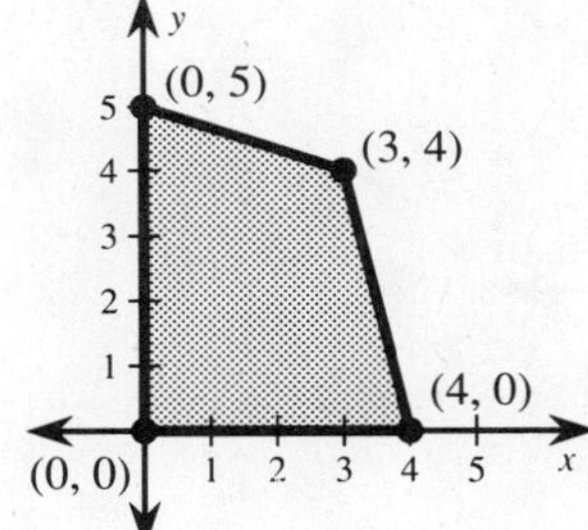

8. (0, 0), (0, 2), (2, 1), (3, 0)

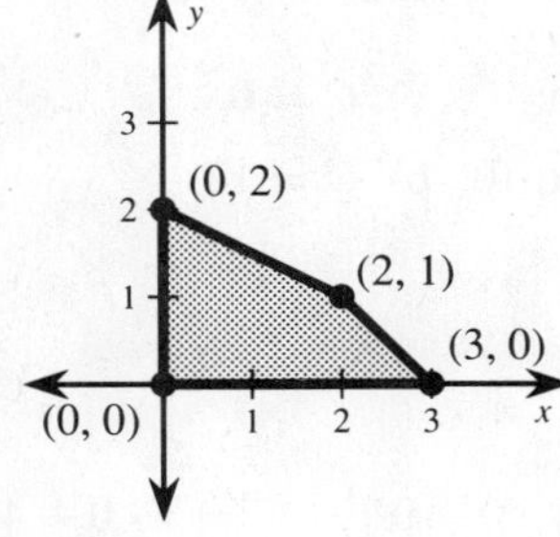

9. (0, 0), (0, 3), (4, 1), (5, 0)

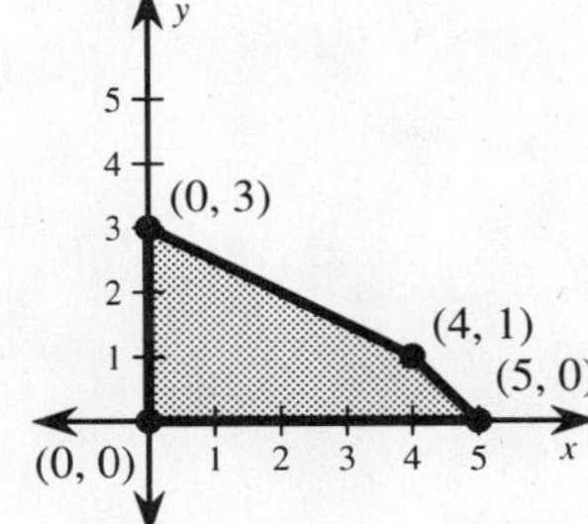

10. (0, 0), (0, 3), (2, 2), (3, 0)

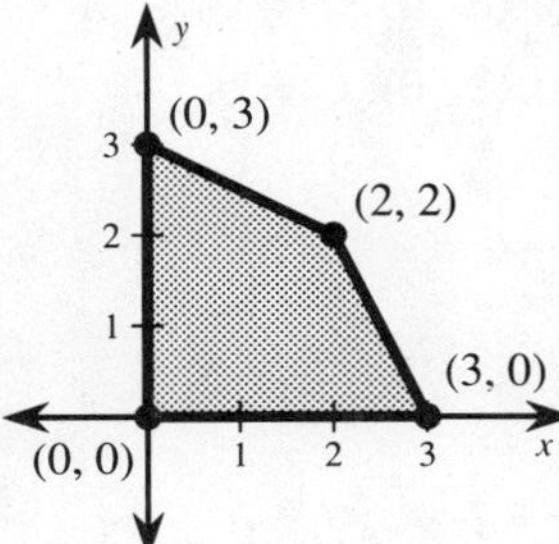

11. $C = 3x + 2y$ $\quad C = 3 \cdot 0 + 2 \cdot 0$ $\quad C = 3 \cdot 0 + 2 \cdot 5$ $\quad C = 3 \cdot 2 + 2 \cdot 5$

$C = 0$ $\quad C = 10$ $\quad C = 16$

$C = 3 \cdot 5 + 2 \cdot 2$ $\quad C = 3 \cdot 5 + 2 \cdot 0$ $\quad$ Min: $(0, 0), C = 0$

$C = 19$ $\quad C = 15$ $\quad$ Max: $(5, 2), C = 19$

12. $C = 3x + 4y$ $\quad C = 3 \cdot 0 + 4 \cdot 0$ $\quad C = 3 \cdot 0 + 4 \cdot 5$ $\quad C = 3 \cdot 4 + 4 \cdot 4$

$C = 0$ $\quad C = 20$ $\quad C = 28$

$C = 3 \cdot 5 + 4 \cdot 3$ $\quad C = 3 \cdot 6 + 4 \cdot 0$ $\quad$ Min: $(0, 0), C = 0$

$C = 27$ $\quad C = 18$ $\quad$ Max: $(4, 4), C = 28$

13. $C = 5x + 6y$ $\quad C = 5 \cdot 0 + 6 \cdot 2$ $\quad C = 5 \cdot 0 + 6 \cdot 5$ $\quad C = 5 \cdot 5 + 6 \cdot 4$

$C = 12$ $\quad C = 30$ $\quad C = 49$

$C = 5 \cdot 6 + 6 \cdot 0$ $\quad C = 5 \cdot 3 + 6 \cdot 0$ $\quad$ Min: $(0, 2), C = 12$

$C = 30$ $\quad C = 15$ $\quad$ Max: $(5, 4), C = 49$

14. $C = 6x + 7y$ $\quad C = 6 \cdot 0 + 7 \cdot 3$ $\quad C = 6 \cdot 0 + 7 \cdot 6$

$C = 21$ $\quad C = 42$

$C = 6 \cdot 5 + 7 \cdot 0$ $\quad C = 6 \cdot 2 + 7 \cdot 0$ $\quad$ Min: $(2, 0), C = 12$

$C = 30$ $\quad C = 12$ $\quad$ Max: $(0, 6), C = 42$

15. $C = x + 2y$ $\quad C = 0 + 2 \cdot 0$ $\quad C = 0 + 2 \cdot 6$

$C = 0$ $\quad C = 12$

$C = 6 + 2 \cdot 0$ $\quad$ Min: $(0, 0), C = 0$

$C = 6$ $\quad$ Max: $(0, 6), C = 12$

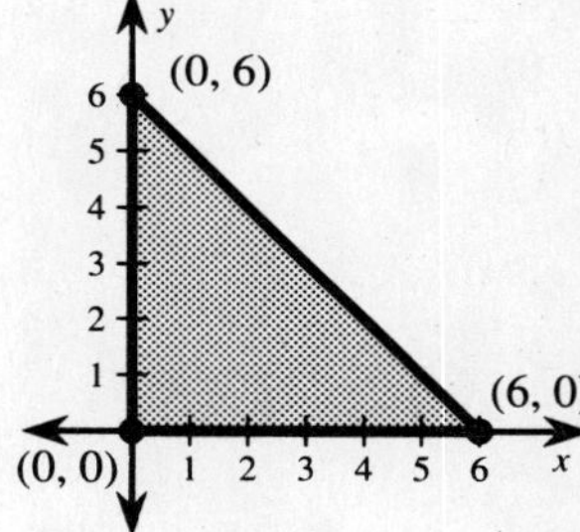

16. $C = 3x + y$ $\quad C = 3 \cdot 0 + 0$ $\quad C = 3 \cdot 0 + 4$

$C = 0$ $\quad C = 4$

$C = 3 \cdot 2 + 0$ $\quad$ Min: $(0, 0), C = 0$

$C = 6$ $\quad$ Max: $(2, 0), C = 6$

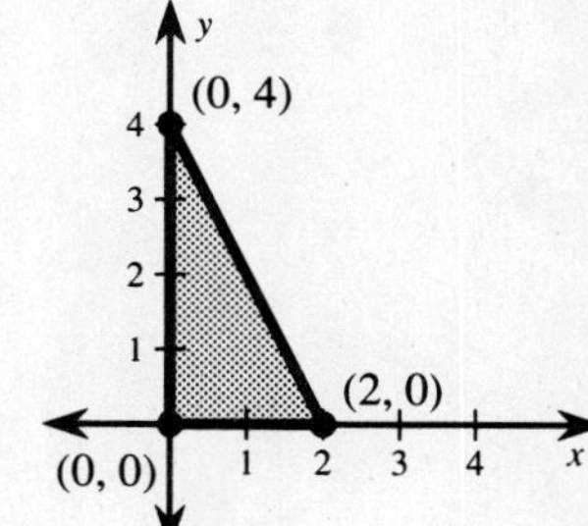

17. $C = 6x + 5y$ $\quad C = 6 \cdot 2 + 5 \cdot 3$ $\quad C = 6 \cdot 2 + 5 \cdot 4$

$C = 27$ $\quad C = 32$

$C = 6 \cdot 5 + 5 \cdot 4$ $\quad C = 6 \cdot 5 + 5 \cdot 3$

$C = 50$ $\quad C = 45$

Min: $(2,\ 3), C = 27$
Max: $(5,\ 4), C = 50$

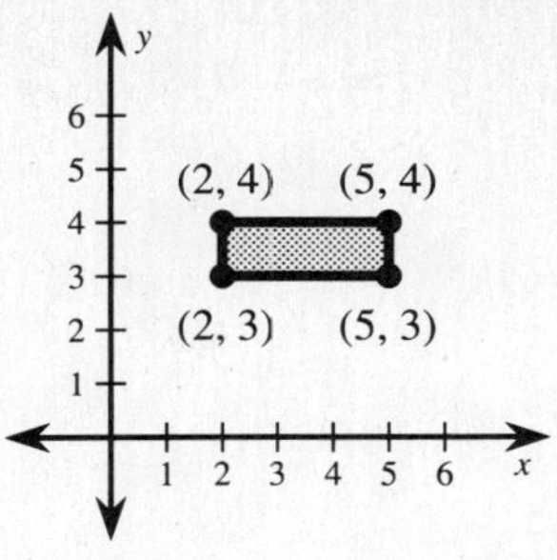

18. $C = 7x + 2y$ $\quad C = 7 \cdot 3 + 2 \cdot 2$ $\quad C = 7 \cdot 3 + 2 \cdot 5$

$C = 25$ $\quad C = 31$

$C = 7 \cdot 7 + 2 \cdot 5$ $\quad C = 7 \cdot 7 + 2 \cdot 2$

$C = 59$ $\quad C = 53$

Min: $(3,\ 2), C = 25$
Max: $(7,\ 5), C = 59$

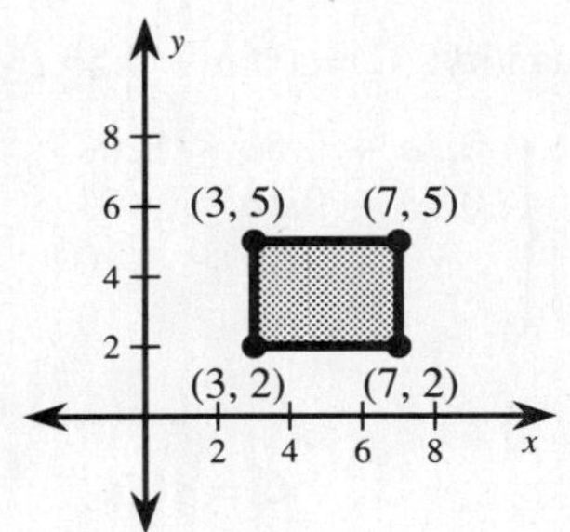

19. $C = 4x + y$ $\quad C = 4 \cdot 0 + 0$ $\quad C = 4 \cdot 0 + 4$

$C = 0$ $\quad C = 4$

$C = 4 \cdot 4 + 2$ $\quad C = 4 \cdot 6 + 0$

$C = 18$ $\quad C = 24$

Min: $(0,\ 0), C = 0$
Max: $(6,\ 0), C = 24$

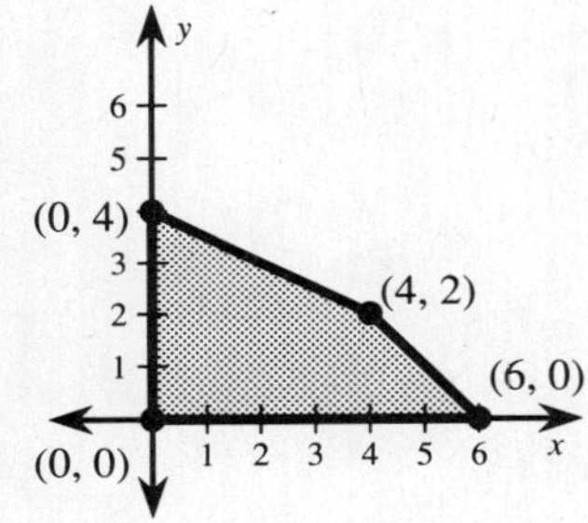

20. $C = 2x + 3y$ $\quad C = 2 \cdot 0 + 3 \cdot 0$ $\quad C = 2 \cdot 0 + 3 \cdot 3$

$C = 0$ $\quad C = 9$

$C = 2 \cdot 3 + 3 \cdot 2$ $\quad C = 2 \cdot 4 + 3 \cdot 0$

$C = 12$ $\quad C = 8$

Min: $(0,\ 0), C = 0$
Max: $(3,\ 2), C = 12$

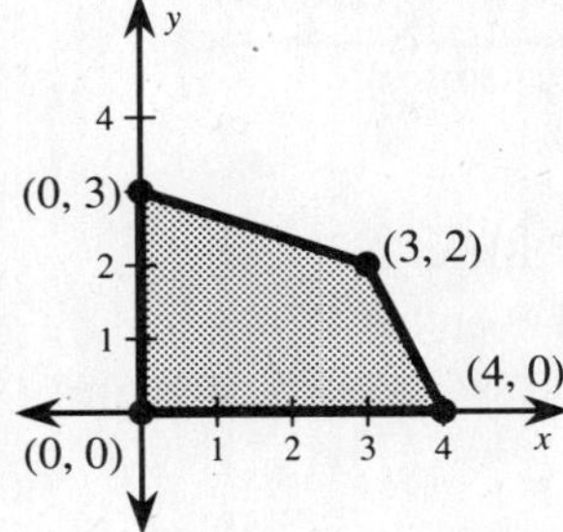

21. $C = 4x + 3y$ $\quad C = 4 \cdot 0 + 3 \cdot 2$ $\quad C = 4 \cdot 0 + 3 \cdot 4$

$C = 6$ $\quad C = 12$

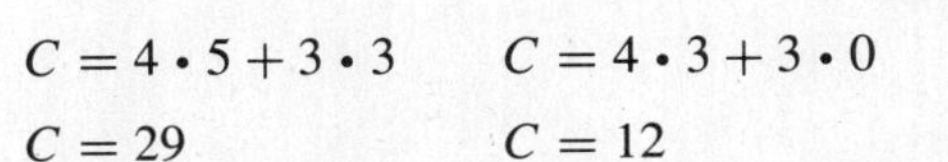

$C = 4 \cdot 5 + 3 \cdot 3$ $\quad C = 4 \cdot 3 + 3 \cdot 0$

$C = 29$ $\quad C = 12$

Min: $(0,\ 2), C = 6$
Max: $(5,\ 3), C = 29$

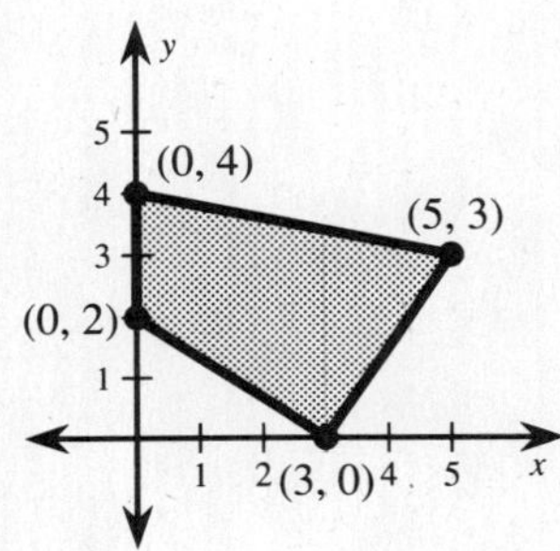

22. $C = x + 6y$ $\quad C = 0 + 6 \cdot 2$ $\quad C = 0 + 6 \cdot 4$

$C = 12$ $\quad C = 24$

$C = 5 + 6 \cdot 3$ $\quad C = 3 + 6 \cdot 0$

$C = 23$ $\quad C = 3$

Min: $(3,\ 0), C = 3$
Max: $(0,\ 4), C = 24$

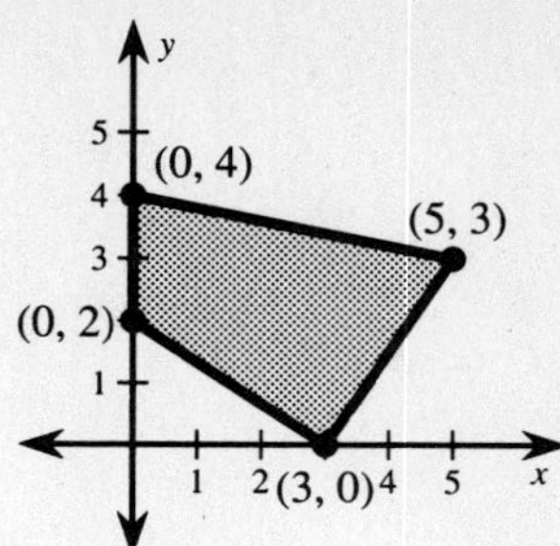

23. Objective quantity: $C = 0.6a + 0.5b$ (Max)

Constraints: $\begin{cases} 0.3a + 0.6b \leq 1200 \\ 0.7a + 0.4b \leq 1400 \\ a \geq 0 \\ b \geq 0 \end{cases}$

$C = 0.6(0) + 0.5(0)$ $\quad C = 0.6(0) + 0.5(2000)$

$C = 0$ $\quad C = 1000$

$C = 0.6(1200) + 0.5(1400)$

$C = 1420$

$C = 0.6(2000) + 0.5(0)$

$C = 1200$

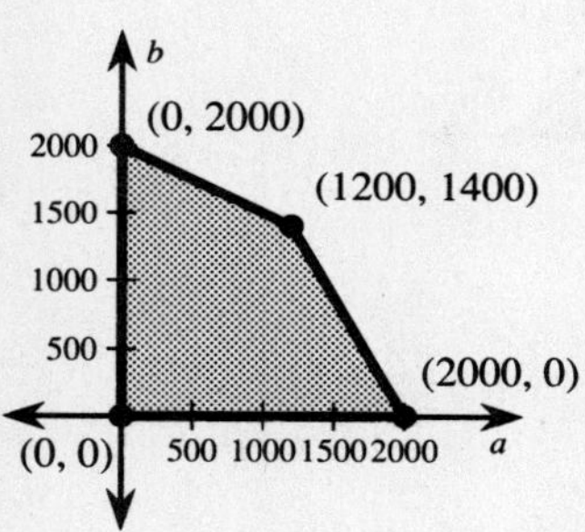

1200 liters of Blend A
1400 liters of Blend B
Profit: $1420

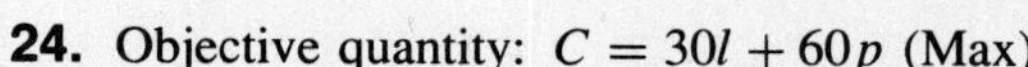

24. Objective quantity: $C = 30l + 60p$ (Max)

Constraints: $\begin{cases} l + p \leq 100 \\ 120l + 200p \leq 15{,}000 \\ l \geq 0 \\ p \geq 0 \end{cases}$

$C = 30 \cdot 0 + 60 \cdot 0$ $\quad C = 30 \cdot 0 + 60 \cdot 75$

$C = 0$ $\quad C = 4500$

$C = 30 \cdot 100 + 60 \cdot 0$

$C = 3000$

$C = 30 \cdot 62.5 + 60 \cdot 37.5$

$C = 4125$

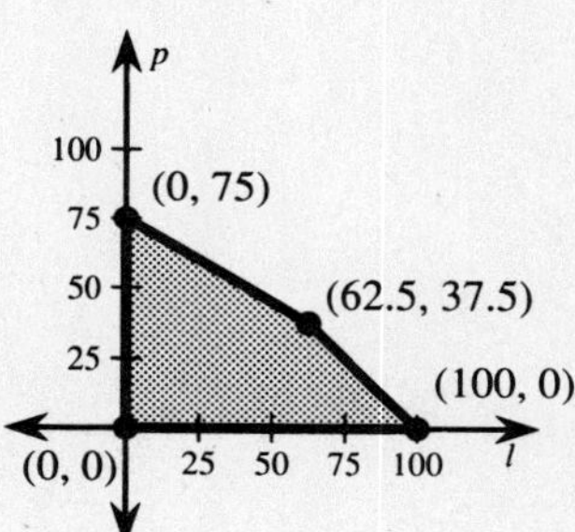

0 acres of lettuce
75 acres of peas
Profit: $4500

25. Objective quantity: $C = 45a + 50b$ (Max)

Constraints: $\begin{cases} 250a + 400b \le 70{,}000 \\ a + b \le 250 \\ a \ge 0 \\ b \ge 0 \end{cases}$

$C = 45 \cdot 0 + 50 \cdot 0$ $\qquad$ $C = 45 \cdot 0 + 50 \cdot 175$

$C = 0$ $\qquad$ $C = 8750$

$C = 45 \cdot 200 + 50 \cdot 50$ $\qquad$ $C = 45 \cdot 250 + 50 \cdot 0$

$C = 11{,}500$ $\qquad$ $C = 11{,}250$

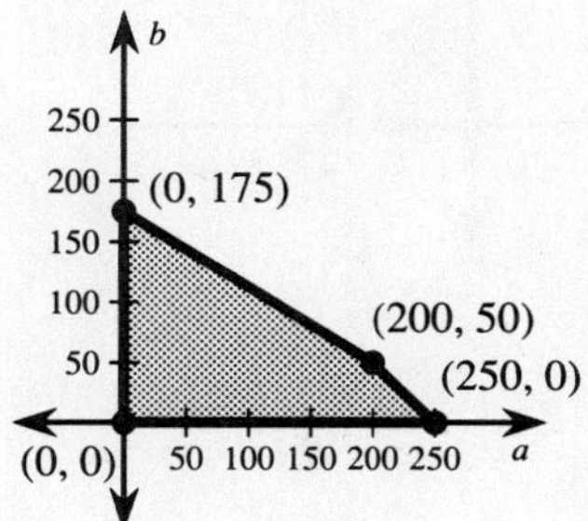

200 of Model A
50 of Model B
Profit: $11,500

26. Objective quantity: $C = 0.25a + 0.20b$ (Min)

Constraints: $\begin{cases} 0.25a + 0.50b \ge 3 \\ 0.75a + 0.50b \ge 5 \\ a \ge 0 \\ b \ge 0 \end{cases}$

$C = 0.25(0) + 0.20(10)$ $\qquad$ $C = 0.25(4) + 0.20(4)$

$C = 2.00$ $\qquad$ $C = 1.80$

$C = 0.25(12) + 0.20(0)$

$C = 3.00$

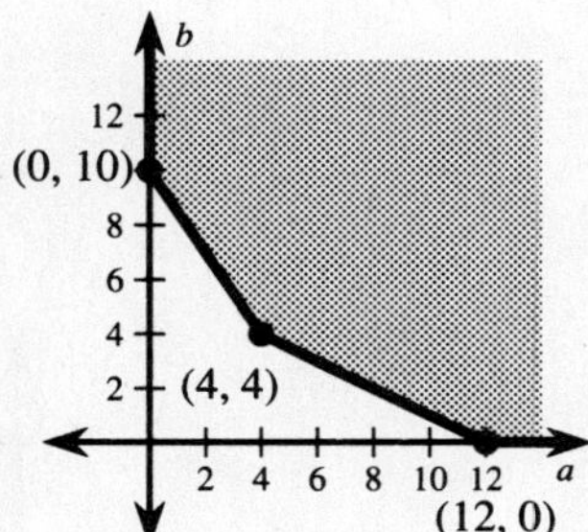

4 cups of Blend A
4 cups of Blend B
Minimum cost: $1.80

27.

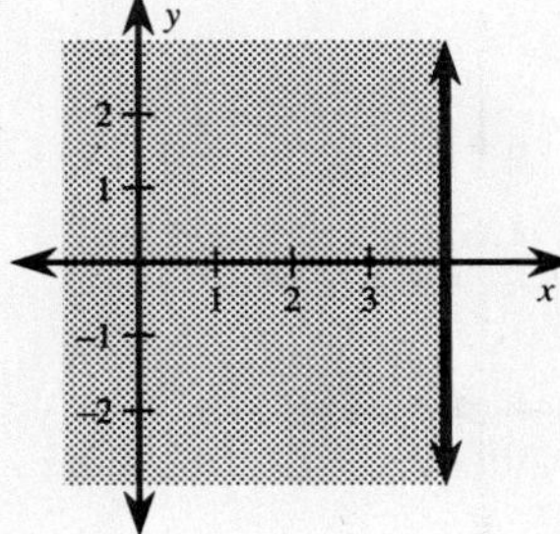

28.

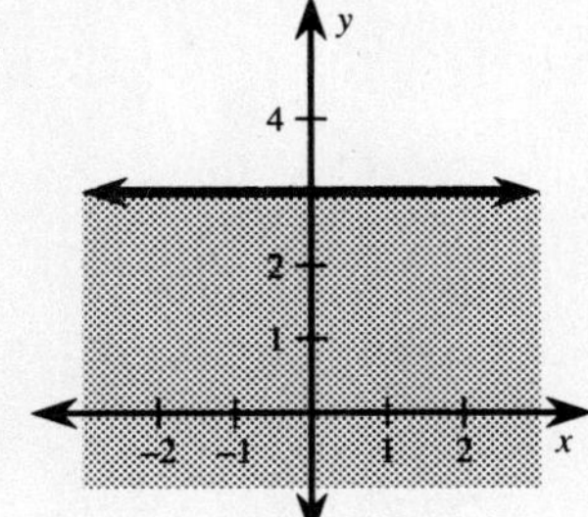

29.

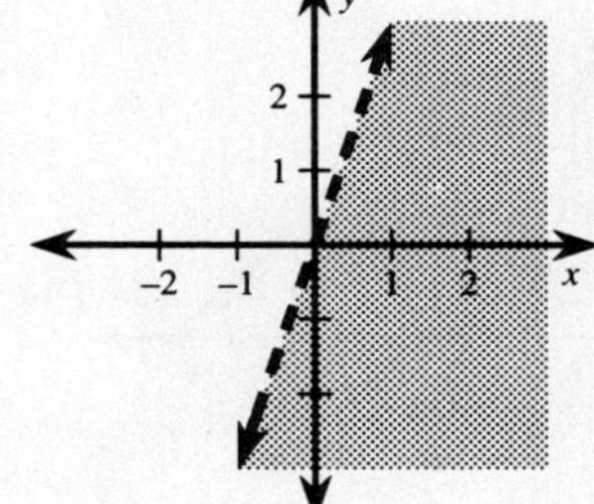

30.

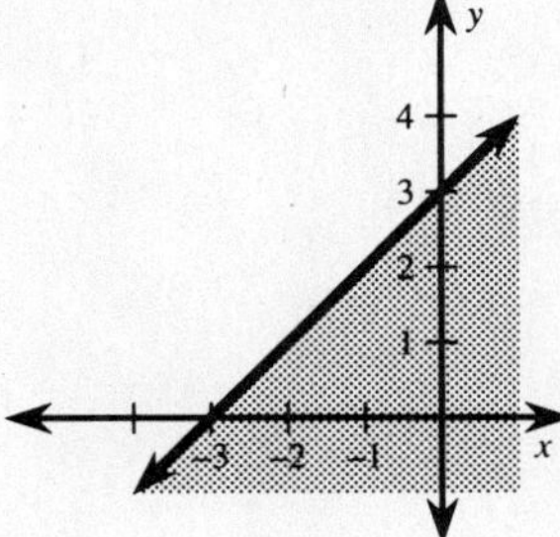

31.

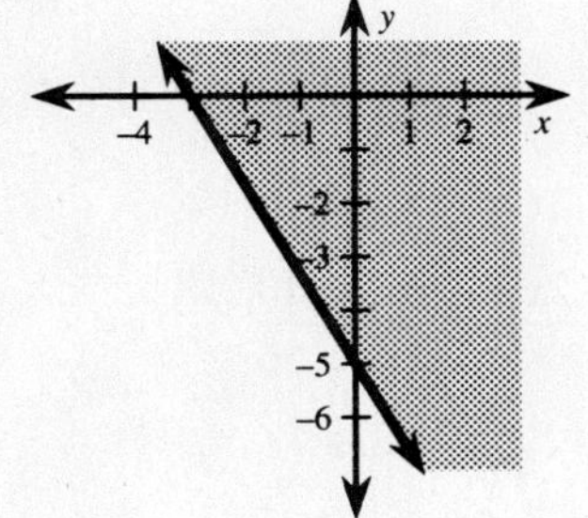

32. $6 - 2y < x$

$-2y < x - 6$

$y > -\frac{1}{2}x + 3$

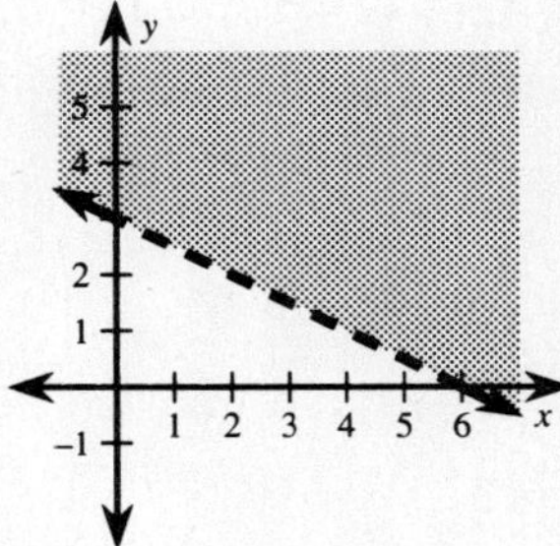

33. $y + 3x > 6$

$y > -3x + 6$

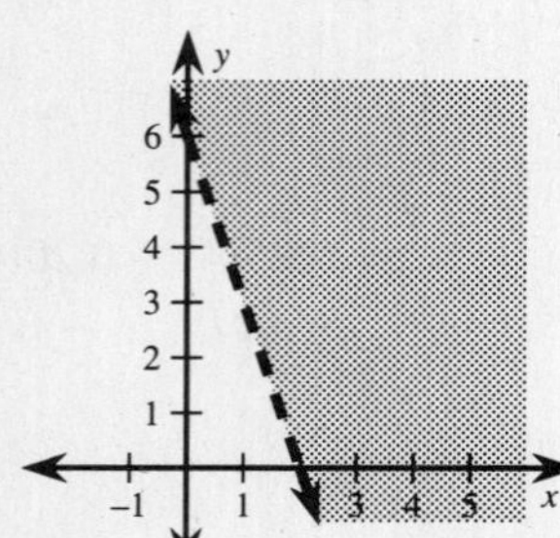

34.

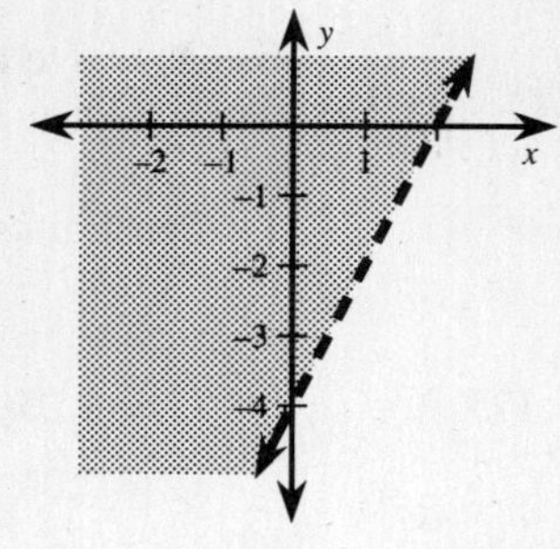

35. $2x + y \le 4$

$y \le -2x + 4$

$2x + 3y \le 6$

$3y \le -2x + 6$

$y \le -\frac{2}{3}x + 2$

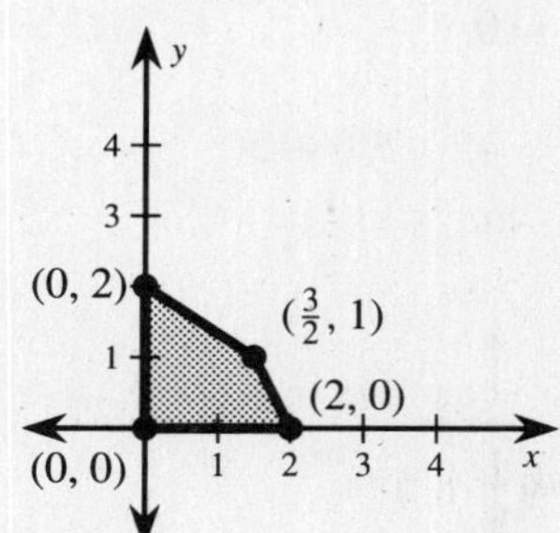

36. $x + y \le 27$

$y \le -x + 27$

$2x + 5y \le 90$

$5y \le -2x + 90$

$y \le -\frac{2}{5}x + 18$

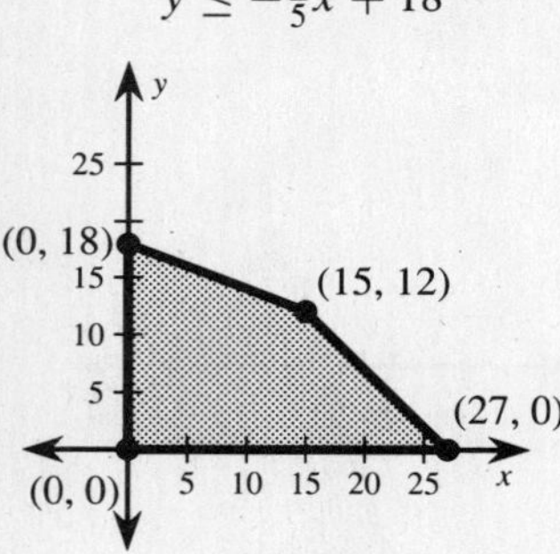

37.

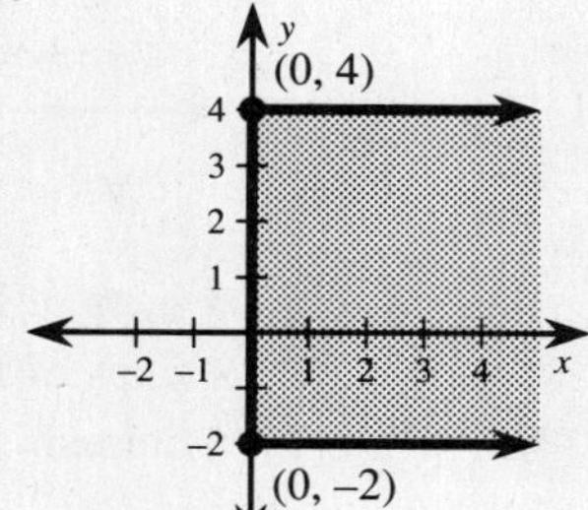

38. $2x - 3y \ge 0$

$-3y \ge -2x$

$y \le \frac{2}{3}x$

$2x - y \le 8$

$-y \le -2x + 8$

$y \ge 2x - 8$

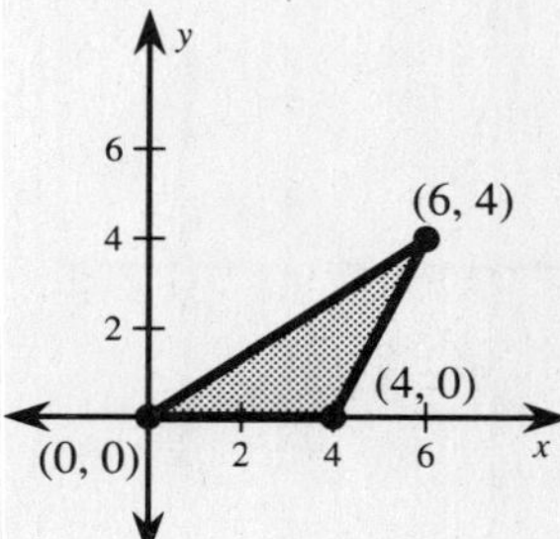

39. $\begin{cases} 3x - 2y = 18 \\ 4x + y = 13 \end{cases}$

$y = -4x + 13$

$3x - 2(-4x + 13) = 18$

$11x = 44$

$x = 4$

$y = -4 \cdot 4 + 13$

$y = -3$

$(4,\ -3)$

40. $\begin{cases} 2x + 5y = 26 \\ -x + 3y = 20 \end{cases}$

$2x + 5y = 26$

$\underline{-2x + 6y = 40}$

$11y = 66$

$y = 6$

$2x + 5 \cdot 6 = 26$

$2x = -4$

$x = -2$

$(-2,\ 6)$

41. $\begin{cases} -5x + y = 9 \\ 5x + 6y = 19 \end{cases}$

$y = 5x + 9$

$5x + 6(5x + 9) = 19$

$35x = -35$

$x = -1$

$y = 5(-1) + 9$

$y = 4$

$(-1,\ 4)$

42. $\begin{cases} 4x - 2y = 2 \\ 3x + 3y = 24 \end{cases}$

$12x - 6y = 6$

$\underline{6x + 6y = 48}$

$18x \quad = 54$

$x = 3$

$4 \cdot 3 - 2y = 2$

$-2y = -10$

$y = 5$

(3, 5)

43. $C = 2x + 2y$

$C = 2(0) + 2\left(\frac{5}{2}\right)$

$C = 5$

$C = 2(1) + 2(1)$

$C = 4$

$C = 2(3) + 2(0)$

$C = 6$

Minimum value: (1, 1), $C = 4$

The constraints are unbounded for $x \geq 0$ and $y \geq 0$.

44. $\begin{cases} x + 2y \leq 4 \\ x - \;\; y \leq 1 \\ x \geq 0 \\ y \geq 0 \end{cases}$

$C = x + y$

Chapter REVIEW

1. $3x + 8y = 4$

$8y = -3x + 4$

$y = -\frac{3}{8}x + \frac{1}{2}$

$\frac{3}{2}x + 4y = 2$

$4y = -\frac{3}{2}x + 2$

$y = -\frac{3}{8}x + \frac{1}{2}$

The solution is any point on the line $3x + 8y = 4$.

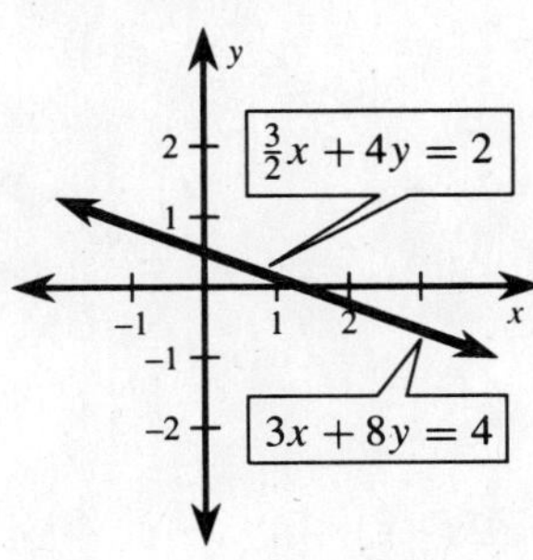

2. $-x + y = 3$

$y = x + 3$

$x + y = 7$

$y = -x + 7$

(2, 5)

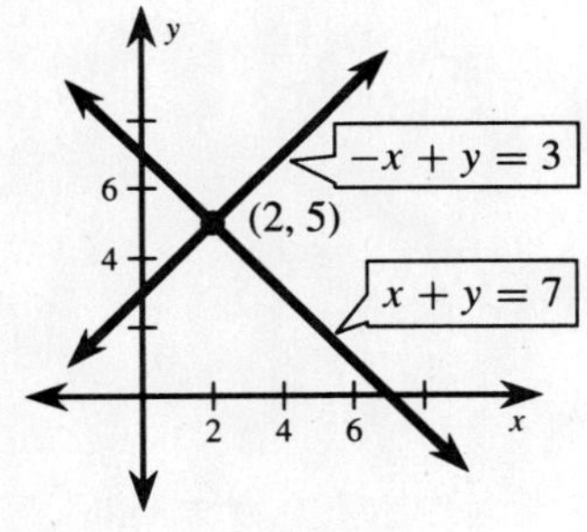

3. $2x - 3y = -3$

$-3y = -2x - 3$

$y = \frac{2}{3}x + 1$

$\frac{1}{3}x + 2y = -3$

$2y = -\frac{1}{3}x - 3$

$y = -\frac{1}{6}x - \frac{3}{2}$

(−3, −1)

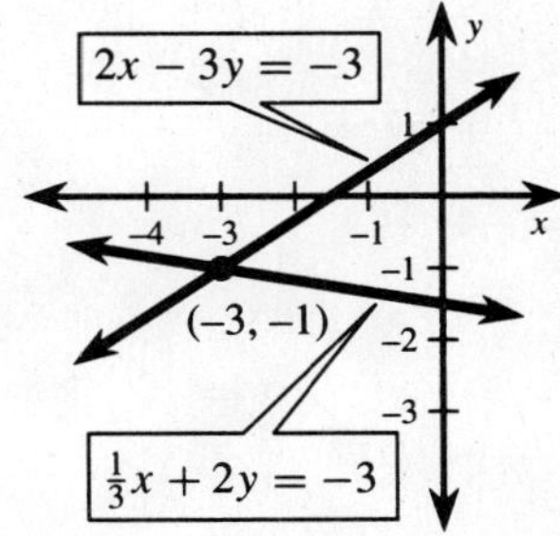

4. $3x + 5y = 7$

$5y = -3x + 7$

$y = -\frac{3}{5}x + \frac{7}{5}$

$6x + 10y = 8$

$10y = -6x + 8$

$y = -\frac{3}{5}x + \frac{4}{5}$

No solution

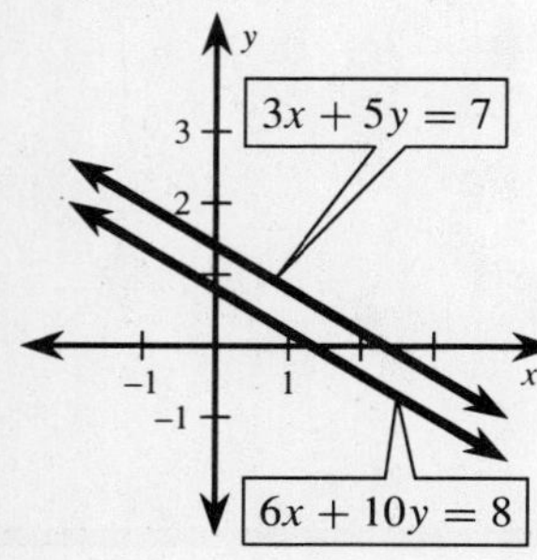

5. $-2x - 3y = -8$

$-3y = 2x - 8$

$y = -\frac{2}{3}x + \frac{8}{3}$

$6x + 2y = 24$

$2y = -6x + 24$

$y = -3x + 12$

(4, 0)

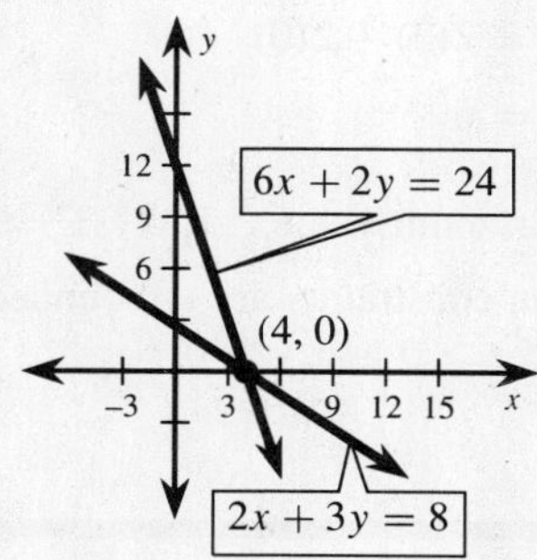

6. $5x - 2y = -17$

$-2y = -5x - 17$

$y = \frac{5}{2}x + \frac{17}{2}$

$3x + 6y = -3$

$6y = -3x - 3$

$y = -\frac{1}{2}x - \frac{1}{2}$

$(-3,\ 1)$

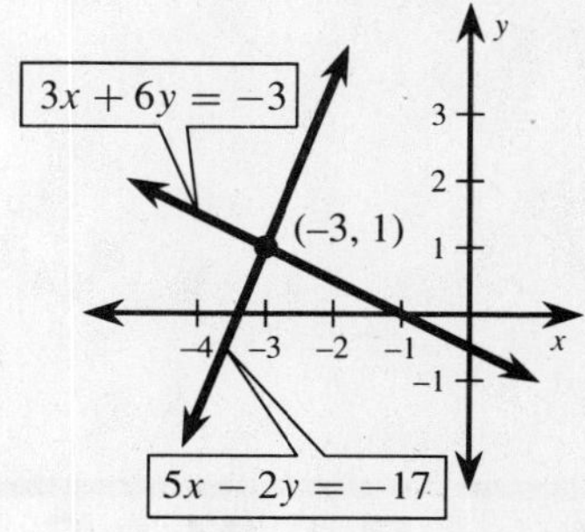

7. $\begin{cases} x + 3y = 0 \\ 4x - 2y = -14 \end{cases}$

$x = -3y$

$4(-3y) - 2y = -14$

$-14y = -14$

$y = 1$

$x = -3(1)$

$x = -3$

$(-3,\ 1)$

8. $\begin{cases} 3x - 4y = 6 \\ -x + y = -1 \end{cases}$

$y = x - 1$

$3x - 4(x - 1) = 6$

$-x = 2$

$x = -2$

$y = -2 - 1$

$y = -3$

$(-2,\ -3)$

9. $\begin{cases} \frac{1}{3}x + y = 2 \\ 2x + 6y = 12 \end{cases}$

$y = -\frac{1}{3}x + 2$

$2x + 6\left(-\frac{1}{3}x + 2\right) = 12$

$12 = 12$

The solution is any point on the line $x + 3y = 6$.

10. $\begin{cases} 4x - 3y = -2 \\ 4x + y = 4 \end{cases}$

$y = -4x + 4$

$4x - 3(-4x + 4) = -2$

$16x = 10$

$x = \frac{5}{8}$

$y = -4\left(\frac{5}{8}\right) + 4$

$y = \frac{3}{2}$

$\left(\frac{5}{8},\ \frac{3}{2}\right)$

11. $\begin{cases} x + \frac{3}{8}y = 1 \\ 8x + 3y = 4 \end{cases}$

$x = -\frac{3}{8}y + 1$

$8\left(-\frac{3}{8}y + 1\right) + 3y = 4$

$8 \neq 4$

No solution

12. $\begin{cases} -2x + y = 4 \\ 4x - 3y = -7 \end{cases}$

$y = 2x + 4$

$4x - 3(2x + 4) = -7$

$-2x = 5$

$x = -\frac{5}{2}$

$y = 2\left(-\frac{5}{2}\right) + 4$

$y = -1$

$\left(-\frac{5}{2},\ -1\right)$

13. $\begin{cases} x - y = 14 \\ 7x - 15y = 50 \end{cases}$

$x = y + 14$

$7(y + 14) - 15y = 50$

$-8y = -48$

$y = 6$

$x = 6 + 14$

$x = 20$

$(20, 6)$

14. $\begin{cases} 3x + y = 11 \\ x + 2y = -3 \end{cases}$

$x = -2y - 3$

$3(-2y - 3) + y = 11$

$-5y = 20$

$y = -4$

$x = -2(-4) - 3$

$x = 5$

$(5, -4)$

15. $\begin{cases} 5x - 2y = 4 \\ x - 0.4y = 0.8 \end{cases}$

$x = 0.4y + 0.8$

$5(0.4y + 0.8) - 2y = 4$

$4 = 4$

The solution is any point on the line $5x - 2y = 4$.

16. $\begin{cases} -2x - 5y = 7 \\ 7x + y = -8 \end{cases}$

$y = -7x - 8$

$-2x - 5(-7x - 8) = 7$

$33x = -33$

$x = -1$

$y = -7(-1) - 8$

$y = -1$

$(-1, -1)$

17. $\begin{cases} 0.25x - 1.25y = 10.25 \\ x - 5y = 20 \end{cases}$

$x = 5y + 20$

$0.25(5y + 20) - 1.25y = 10.25$

$5 \neq 10.25$

No solution

18. $\begin{cases} x + \frac{1}{2}y = 2 \\ 6x + 4y = 15 \end{cases}$

$x = -\frac{1}{2}y + 2$

$6\left(-\frac{1}{2}y + 2\right) + 4y = 15$

$y = 3$

$x = -\frac{1}{2}(3) + 2$

$x = \frac{1}{2}$

$\left(\frac{1}{2}, 3\right)$

19. $\begin{cases} 8x + 3y = 15 \\ 5x - 2y = -10 \end{cases}$

$$\begin{array}{r} 16x + 6y = 30 \\ 15x - 6y = -30 \\ \hline 31x = 0 \end{array}$$

$x = 0$

$8 \cdot 0 + 3y = 15$

$y = 5$

$(0, 5)$

20. $\begin{cases} 3x + 5y = -16 \\ -2x + 6y = -36 \end{cases}$

$$\begin{array}{r} 6x + 10y = -32 \\ -6x + 18y = -108 \\ \hline 28y = -140 \end{array}$$

$y = -5$

$3x + 5(-5) = -16$

$3x = 9$

$x = 3$

$(3, -5)$

21. $\begin{cases} 7x - 3y = -1 \\ 4x + 6y = -16 \end{cases}$

$$\begin{array}{r} 14x - 6y = -2 \\ 4x + 6y = -16 \\ \hline 18x = -18 \end{array}$$

$x = -1$

$7(-1) - 3y = -1$

$-3y = 6$

$y = -2$

$(-1, -2)$

22. $\begin{cases} 2x - 3y = 1 \\ -2x + 3y = 1 \end{cases}$

$$0 \neq 2$$

No solution

23. $\begin{cases} -4x - 5y = 7 \\ 3x + 10y = -24 \end{cases}$

$$-8x - 10y = 14$$
$$3x + 10y = -24$$
$$-5x = -10$$
$$x = 2$$
$$-4(2) - 5y = 7$$
$$-5y = 15$$
$$y = -3$$

(2, −3)

24. $\begin{cases} 4x - 5y = 2 \\ 600x - 750y = 300 \end{cases}$

$$-600x + 750y = -300$$
$$600x - 750y = 300$$
$$0 = 0$$

Any point on the line $4x - 5y = 2$.

25. $\begin{cases} -6x + 5y = 18 \\ 7x + 2y = 26 \end{cases}$

$$-42x + 35y = 126$$
$$42x + 12y = 156$$
$$47y = 282$$
$$y = 6$$
$$-6x + 5 \cdot 6 = 18$$
$$-6x = -12$$
$$x = 2$$

(2, 6)

26. $\begin{cases} 2x - 15y = -20 \\ -4x + 5y = 5 \end{cases}$

$$4x - 30y = -40$$
$$-4x + 5y = 5$$
$$-25y = -35$$
$$y = \tfrac{7}{5}$$
$$-4x + 5\left(\tfrac{7}{5}\right) = 5$$
$$-4x = -2$$
$$x = \tfrac{1}{2}$$

$\left(\frac{1}{2}, \frac{7}{5}\right)$

27. $\begin{cases} 2x + y = 0 \\ x - 4y = 24 \end{cases}$

$$8x + 4y = 0$$
$$x - 4y = 24$$
$$9x = 24$$
$$x = \tfrac{8}{3}$$
$$2\left(\tfrac{8}{3}\right) + y = 0$$
$$y = -\tfrac{16}{3}$$

$\left(\frac{8}{3}, -\frac{16}{3}\right)$

28. $\begin{cases} \frac{1}{2}x + \frac{1}{3}y = 8 \\ \frac{1}{4}x + \frac{1}{6}y = 12 \end{cases}$

$$-3x - 2y = -48$$
$$3x + 2y = 144$$
$$0 \neq 96$$

No solution

29. $\begin{cases} \frac{1}{9}x + \frac{1}{3}y = 4 \\ -\frac{1}{3}x - 3y = -18 \end{cases}$

$$x + 3y = 36$$
$$-x - 9y = -54$$
$$-6y = -18$$
$$y = 3$$
$$-\tfrac{1}{3}x - 3(3) = -18$$
$$-\tfrac{1}{3}x = -9$$
$$x = 27$$

(27, 3)

30. $\begin{cases} \frac{5}{12}x - \frac{2}{3}y = \frac{1}{3} \\ \frac{1}{3}x - \frac{8}{15}y = \frac{4}{15} \end{cases}$

$$x - \tfrac{8}{5}y = \tfrac{4}{5}$$
$$-x + \tfrac{8}{5}y = -\tfrac{4}{5}$$
$$0 = 0$$

Any point on the line $5x - 8y = 4$.

31.

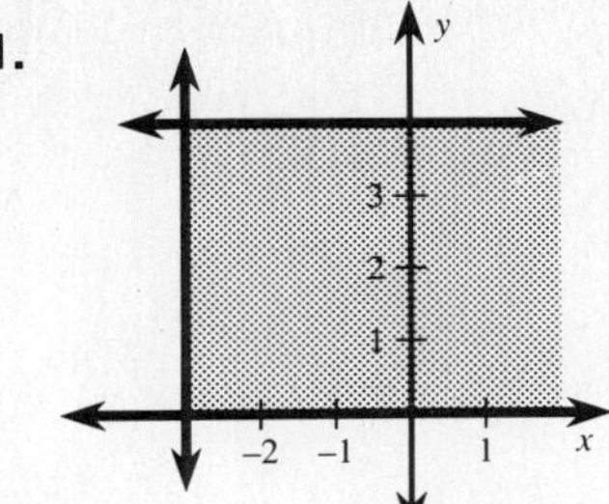

32. $\frac{1}{2}x + y > -2$

$y > -\frac{1}{2}x - 2$

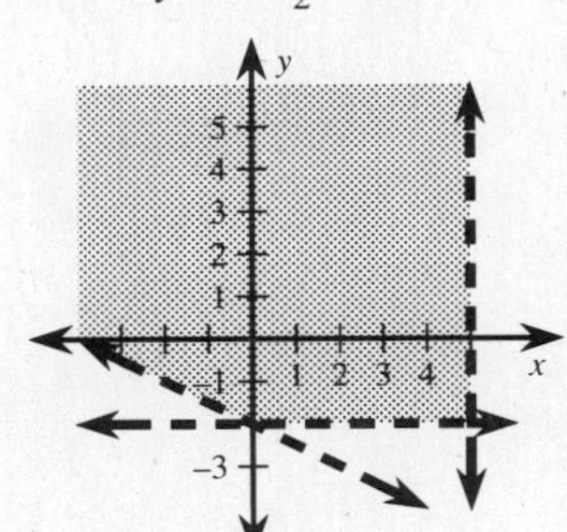

33. $3x - y \le 7$

$-y \le -3x + 7$

$y \ge 3x - 7$

$2x + y \le 2$

$y \le -2x + 2$

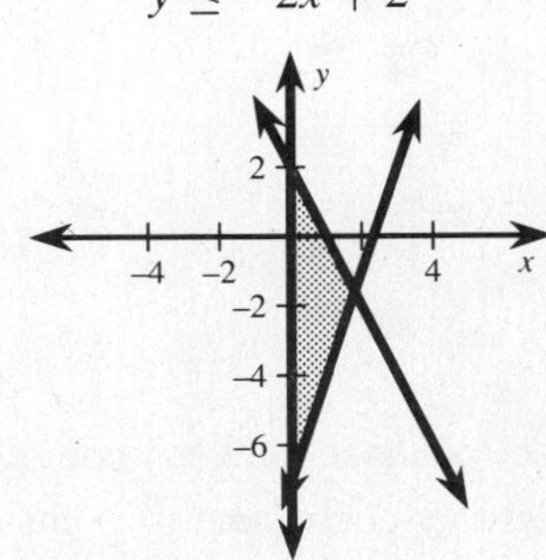

34.

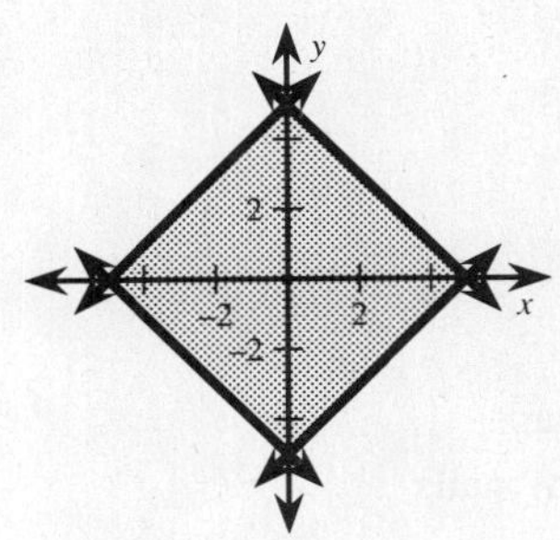

35. $3x + 2y \le 12$

$2y \le -3x + 12$

$y \le -\frac{3}{2}x + 6$

$x + 2y \le 8$

$2y \le -x + 8$

$y \le -\frac{1}{2}x + 4$

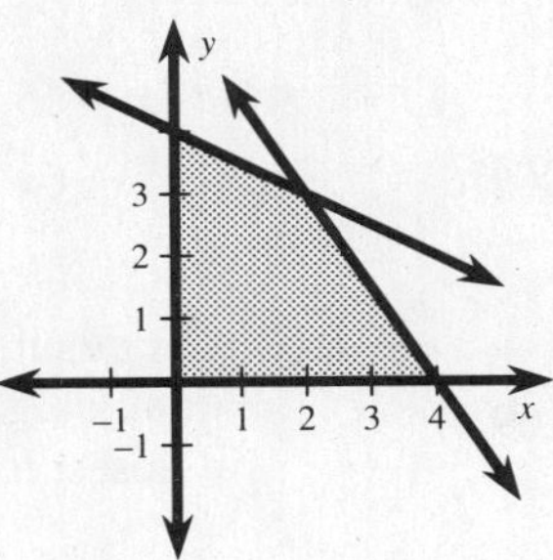

36. $\frac{2}{5}x + y \ge 4$

$y \ge -\frac{2}{5}x + 4$

$3x + y \ge 6$

$y \ge -3x + 6$

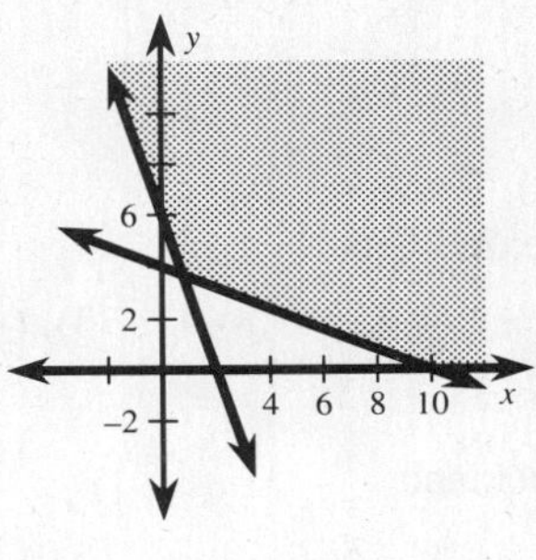

37. Vertices: (1, −3), (1, 2), (4, 2), (4, −3)

$C = 3x - 2y$ $\quad C = 3 \cdot 1 - 2(-3)$

$C = 9$

$C = 3 \cdot 1 - 2 \cdot 2$ $\quad C = 3 \cdot 4 - 2 \cdot 2$

$C = -1$ $\quad C = 8$

$C = 3 \cdot 4 - 2(-3)$ $\quad$ Min: (1, 2), $C = -1$

$C = 18$ $\quad$ Max: (4, −3), $C = 18$

38. Vertices: (0, 0), (0, 6), (3, 0)

$C = 4x + y$ $\quad C = 4 \cdot 0 + 0$ $\quad C = 4 \cdot 0 + 6$

$C = 0$ $\quad C = 6$

$C = 4 \cdot 3 + 0$ $\quad$ Min: (0, 0), $C = 0$

$C = 12$ $\quad$ Max: (3, 0), $C = 12$

39. Vertices: (0, 0), (0, 3), (4, 6), (5, 0)

$C = x + 3y$ $\quad C = 0 + 3 \cdot 0$ $\quad C = 0 + 3 \cdot 3$ $\quad C = 4 + 3 \cdot 6$ $\quad C = 5 + 3 \cdot 0$ $\quad$ Min: (0, 0), $C = 0$

$C = 0$ $\quad C = 9$ $\quad C = 22$ $\quad C = 5$ $\quad$ Max: (4, 6), $C = 22$

40. $\begin{cases} x - y = 1 \\ 3x + 2y = 18 \end{cases}$ $\begin{cases} x - y = 1 \\ y = 0 \end{cases}$ $\begin{cases} 3x + 2y = 18 \\ y = 0 \end{cases}$

$$\begin{aligned} 3x + 2y &= 18 \\ 2x - 2y &= 2 \\ \hline 5x &= 20 \\ x &= 4 \end{aligned}$$

$4 - y = 1$

$y = 3$

(4, 3)

$x = 1$

(1, 0)

$x = 6$

(6, 0)

41. Base (distance between coordinates on x-axis): 5

Height (y-coordinate of point not on x-axis): 3

$A = \frac{1}{2}bh$

$A = \frac{1}{2}(5)(3)$

$A = 7\frac{1}{2}$

42. $\begin{cases} x + y = 390 \\ 847x - 11y = 0 \end{cases}$

$$\begin{aligned} 847x - 11y &= 0 \\ 11x + 11y &= 4290 \\ \hline 858x &= 4290 \\ x &= 5 \end{aligned}$$

$5 + y = 390$

$y = 385$

5 pounds of 2-penny nails

385 pounds of 60-penny nails

43. Mexico City

(1, 68.6), (2, 69.8), (3, 73), (4, 76.2), (5, 79.4)

$y = 3x + 65$

Auckland

(1, 81.0), (2, 78.0), (3, 75.0), (4, 72.0), (5, 69.0)

$y = -3x + 84$

44. $3x + 65 = -3x + 84$

$6x = 19$

$x = 3\frac{1}{6}$

In month 3 or March it is most likely that the daily high temperatures for the two cities are closest together.

45. $\begin{cases} x + y = 12{,}500 \\ 15x + 25y = 225{,}000 \end{cases}$

$$\begin{aligned} -15x - 15y &= -187{,}500 \\ 15x + 25y &= 225{,}000 \\ \hline 10y &= 37{,}500 \\ y &= 3750 \end{aligned}$$

$x + 3750 = 12{,}500$

$x = 8750$

Vertices: (0, 12,500)
(8750, 3750)
(15,000, 0)

Objective quantity: $C = 5x + 7.5y$

$C = 5(0) + 7.5(12{,}500)$

$C = 93{,}750$

$C = 5(8750) + 7.5(3750)$

$C = 71{,}875$

$C = 5(15{,}000) + 7.5(0)$

$C = 75{,}000$

Minimum guaranteed the rock group is $71,875.00.

46. $\begin{cases} 3x - 2y = -2 \\ x + y = 6 \end{cases}$

$$\begin{aligned} 3x - 2y &= -2 \\ 2x + 2y &= 12 \\ \hline 5x &= 10 \\ x &= 2 \end{aligned} \qquad \begin{aligned} 2 + y &= 6 \\ y &= 4 \end{aligned}$$

(2, 4)

47. $3x - 2y = 3(10) - 2(17)$

$= 30 - 34$

$= -4 \neq -2$

The plane is off course.

48. $\begin{cases} d = 176t & \text{Beech} \\ 600 - d = 561t & \text{DC-9} \end{cases}$

$600 = 737t$

$t \approx 0.81$ or 49 minutes

49. Time of travel + time at game = 5 hours.

$$\frac{425 + 425}{266} + x = 5$$

$$\frac{850}{266} + x = 5$$

$$x = 1.8 \text{ hours}$$

She could have made the round-trip in 5 hours if the game only took less than 1.8 hours to play which is doubtful.

Chapter TEST

1. $x + 2y = 0$

$y = -\frac{1}{2}x$

$3x + 4y = 2$

$4y = -3x + 2$

$y = -\frac{3}{4}x + \frac{1}{2}$

(2, −1)

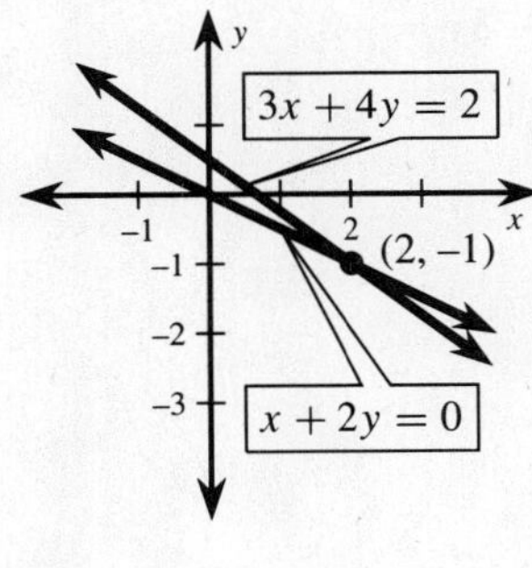

2. $5x - y = 12$

$-y = -5x + 12$

$y = 5x - 12$

$3x - 2y = 3$

$-2y = -3x + 3$

$y = \frac{3}{2}x - \frac{3}{2}$

(3, 3)

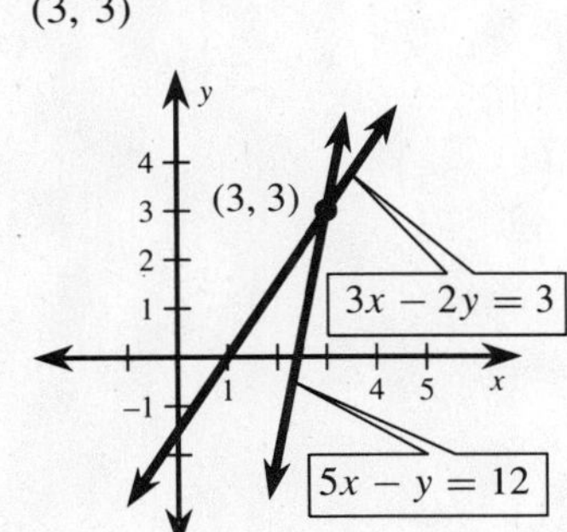

3. $-4x + 7y = -2$

$7y = 4x - 2$

$y = \frac{4}{7}x - \frac{2}{7}$

$-x - y = 5$

$-y = x + 5$

$y = -x - 5$

(−3, −2)

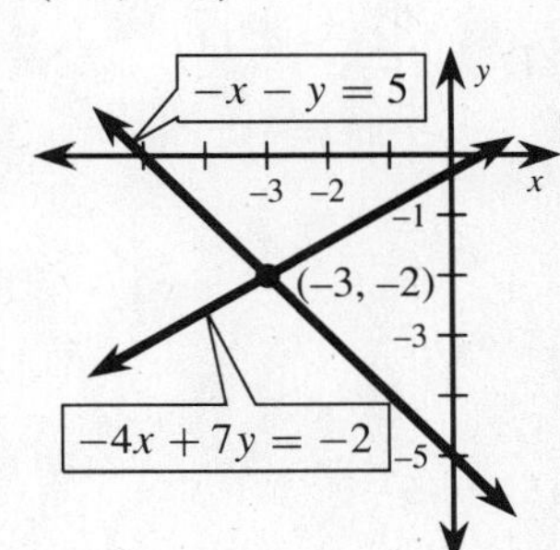

4. $\begin{cases} 2x - 5y = -12 \\ -4x + y = 6 \end{cases}$

$y = 4x + 6$

$2x - 5(4x + 6) = -12$

$-18x = 18$

$x = -1$

$y = 4(-1) + 6$

$y = 2$

$(-1,\ 2)$

5. $\begin{cases} -3x + 5y = 11 \\ x - 2y = -5 \end{cases}$

$x = 2y - 5$

$-3(2y - 5) + 5y = 11$

$-y = -4$

$y = 4$

$x = 2 \cdot 4 - 5$

$x = 3$

$(3, 4)$

6. $\begin{cases} -x + 3y = 4 \\ 2x - 6y = -8 \end{cases}$

$x = 3y - 4$

$2(3y - 4) - 6y = -8$

$-8 = -8$

Any point on the line $-x + 3y = 4$.

7. $\begin{cases} 5x + y = 3 \\ 10x + 2y = 0 \end{cases}$

$y = -5x + 3$

$10x + 2(-5x + 3) = 0$

$6 \neq 0$

No solution

8. $\begin{cases} 6x + y = 12 \\ -4x - 2y = 0 \end{cases}$

$y = -6x + 12$

$-4x - 2(-6x + 12) = 0$

$8x = 24$

$x = 3$

$y = -6 \cdot 3 + 12$

$y = -6$

$(3,\ -6)$

9. $\begin{cases} 7x + 4y = 5 \\ x - 6y = -19 \end{cases}$

$x = 6y - 19$

$7(6y - 19) + 4y = 5$

$46y = 138$

$y = 3$

$x = 6 \cdot 3 - 19$

$x = -1$

$(-1,\ 3)$

10. $\begin{cases} 8x - 4y = -11 \\ 6x + 2y = -2 \end{cases}$

$$\begin{array}{rl} 8x - 4y &= -11 \\ 12x + 4y &= -4 \\ \hline 20x \quad &= -15 \end{array}$$

$x = -\frac{3}{4}$

$8\left(-\frac{3}{4}\right) - 4y = -11$

$-4y = -5$

$y = \frac{5}{4}$

$\left(-\frac{3}{4},\ \frac{5}{4}\right)$

11. $\begin{cases} -7x + 2y = -5 \\ 10x - 2y = 6 \end{cases}$

$$\begin{array}{rl} -7x + 2y &= -5 \\ 10x - 2y &= 6 \\ \hline 3x \quad &= 1 \end{array}$$

$x = \frac{1}{3}$

$-7\left(\frac{1}{3}\right) + 2y = -5$

$2y = -\frac{8}{3}$

$y = -\frac{4}{3}$

$\left(\frac{1}{3},\ -\frac{4}{3}\right)$

12. $\begin{cases} \frac{1}{4}x - \frac{3}{4}y = -2 \\ 2x - 6y = -16 \end{cases}$

$$\begin{array}{rl} -2x + 6y &= 16 \\ 2x - 6y &= -16 \\ \hline 0 &= 0 \end{array}$$

Any point on the line $x - 3y = -8$.

13. $\begin{cases} 6x + 7y = 5 \\ 4x - 2y = -10 \end{cases}$

$12x + 14y = 10$

$\underline{-12x + 6y = 30}$

$20y = 40$

$y = 2$

$4x - 2 \cdot 2 = -10$

$4x = -6$

$x = -\frac{3}{2}$

$\left(-\frac{3}{2}, 2\right)$

14. $\begin{cases} 4x + 7y = -11 \\ 14x - 12y = -2 \end{cases}$

$28x + 49y = -77$

$\underline{-28x + 24y = 4}$

$73y = -73$

$y = -1$

$4x + 7(-1) = -11$

$4x = -4$

$x = -1$

$(-1, -1)$

15. $\begin{cases} -x + \frac{1}{3}y = -6 \\ 3x - y = -16 \end{cases}$

$-3x + y = -18$

$\underline{3x - y = -16}$

$0 \neq -34$

No solution

16.

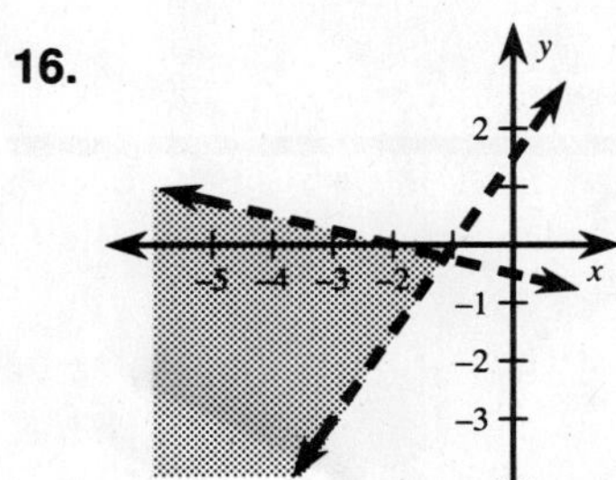

17.

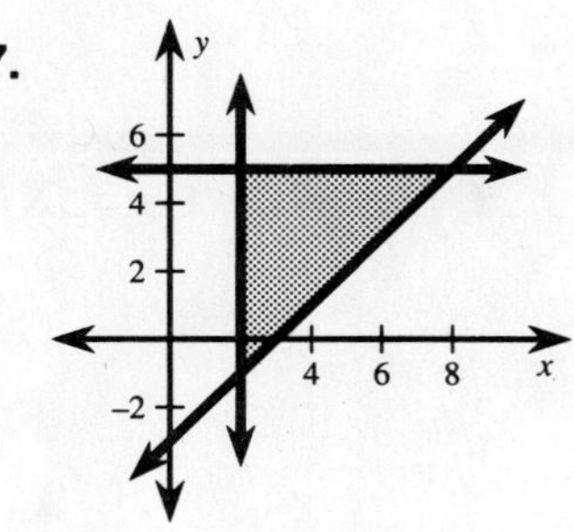

18.

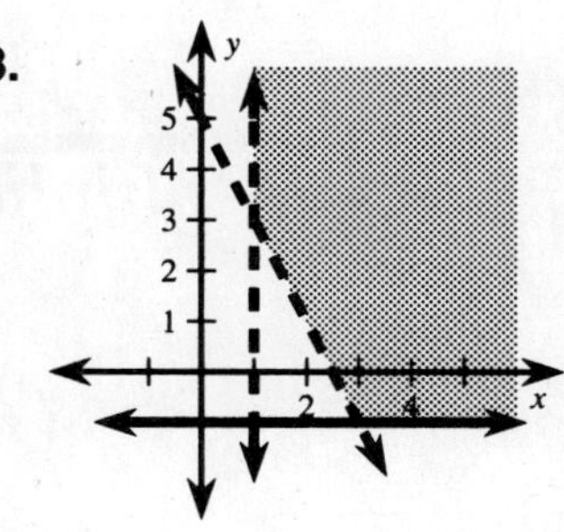

19. Vertices: (1, 2), (1, 6), (3, 6), (3, 2)

$C = 3x + 2y$ $\quad C = 3 \cdot 1 + 2 \cdot 2$

$C = 7$

$C = 3 \cdot 1 + 2 \cdot 6$ $\quad C = 3 \cdot 3 + 2 \cdot 6$

$C = 15$ $\quad C = 21$

$C = 3 \cdot 3 + 2 \cdot 2$ $\quad$ Min: (1, 2), $C = 7$

$C = 13$ $\quad$ Max: (3, 6), $C = 21$

20. Vertices: (0, 0), (0, 6), (2, 4), $\left(\frac{10}{3}, 0\right)$

$C = 4x + 5y$ $\quad C = 4 \cdot 0 + 5 \cdot 0$

$C = 0$

$C = 4 \cdot 0 + 5 \cdot 6$ $\quad C = 4 \cdot 2 + 5 \cdot 4$

$C = 30$ $\quad C = 28$

$C = 4\left(\frac{10}{3}\right) + 5(0)$ $\quad$ Min: (0, 0), $C = 0$

$C = \frac{40}{3}$ $\quad$ Max: (0, 6), $C = 30$

$C = 13\frac{1}{3}$

21. $\begin{cases} 2x + 1.5y \le 3000 \\ 3x + 6y \le 9000 \end{cases}$

$-8x - 6y = -12{,}000$

$\underline{3x + 6y = 9000}$

$-5x = -3000$

$x = 600$

$2(600) + 1.5y = 3000$

$1.5y = 1800$

$y = 1200$

$C = 4x + 5y$

Vertices: (0, 0), (0, 1500), (1500, 0), (600, 1200)

$C = 4 \cdot 0 + 5 \cdot 0$ $\quad C = 4 \cdot 0 + 5 \cdot 1500$ $\quad C = 4 \cdot 1500 + 5 \cdot 0$ $\quad C = 4 \cdot 600 + 5 \cdot 1200$

$C = 0$ $\quad C = 7500$ $\quad C = 6000$ $\quad C = 8400$

To produce the maximum profit of \$8400, you would need 600 bottles of Gentle Rose and 1200 bottles of Rich Gardenia.

Chapter 8

Powers and Exponents

8.1 Multiplication Properties of Exponents

Communicating about Algebra

A.

x	1	2	3
2x	2	4	6
2^x	2	4	8

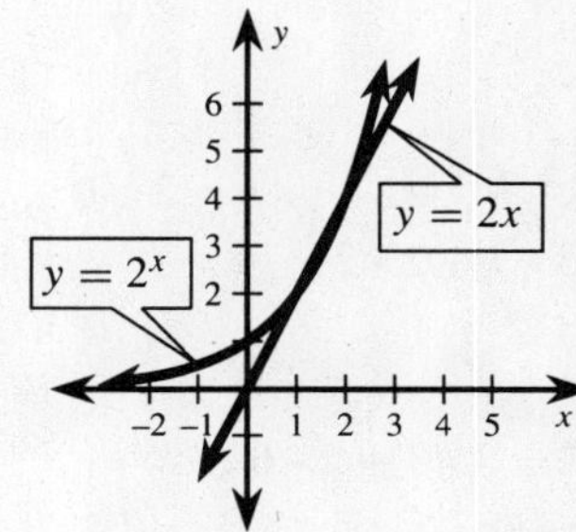

B. You would choose 2^x, because after 3 hours the $2x$ job pays \$6 and the 2^x job pays \$8.

C. After working 8 hours, you could make \$768 working 2 additional hours if your hourly rate is 2^x dollars.

EXERCISES

1. No; the base of each of the powers must be the same in order to simplify.

2. $(a^{10})^3 = a^{30}$
Power of the power

3. No
$a^5 \cdot a^3 = a^{5+3}$
$= a^8$

4. No
$(-3b)^4 = (-3)^4 b^4$
$= 81b^4$

5. $a^3 \cdot a^4 = a^7$
$2^3 \cdot 2^4 = 8 \cdot 16 = 128$
$a^7 = 2^7 = 128$

6. $(1.06)^{11} = 1.90$

7. $y = Ca^x$
If $a = 2$ and $x = 3$, then
$y = C(2)^3 = 8C$.
If x increases by $1 (x = 4)$, then
$y = C(2)^4 = 16C$.
Therefore, y is doubled.

8.
a. $y = 3^x$ (exponential growth)
b. $y = 0.5(3)^x$ (exponential growth)
c. $y = (0.5)^x$ (exponential decay)
d. $y = 2(0.5)^x$ (exponential decay)

9. $4^2 \cdot 4^3 = 4^5$

10. $6^5 \cdot 6^4 = 6^9$

11. $[(-9)^2]^4 = (-9)^8$

12. $10^2 \cdot 10^9 = 10^{11}$

13. $x \cdot x^5 = x^6$

14. $(5^5)^4 = 5^{20}$

15. $[(2x+3)^3]^2 = (2x+3)^6$

16. $(2x)^3 = 8x^3$

17. $(3 \cdot 7)^4 = 21^4$

18. $[(5+x)^3]^6 = (5+x)^{18}$

19. $(-5a)^2 = 25a^2$

20. $(16 \cdot 2)^2 = 32^2$

21. $(4a)^2 \cdot a = 16a^3$

22. $6^2 \cdot (6x^3)^2 = 6^4x^6$

23. $[(-3xy)^2]^3 = (-3xy)^6$

24. $(x \cdot x^2)^3 \cdot 3x = (x^3)^3 \cdot 3x$
$= x^9 \cdot 3x$
$= 3x^{10}$

25. $(3a)^2 \cdot (-4a)^4 = (3)^2(-4)^4a^6$

26. $(9a^3)^2 \cdot (2a)^3 = (2)^3(9)^2a^9$

27. $2x^3 \cdot (3x)^2 = 2 \cdot 3^2x^5$
$= 18x^5$

28. $3y^2 \cdot (2y)^3 = 3 \cdot 2^3y^5$
$= 24y^5$

29. $(-ab)(a^2b)^2 = -a^5b^3$

30. $(-rs)(rs^3)^2 = -r^3s^7$

31. $(-2xy)^3(-x^2) = (-8x^3y^3)(-x^2)$
$= 8x^5y^3$

32. $(-3cd)^3(-d^2) = (-27c^3d^3)(-d^2)$
$= 27c^3d^5$

33. $(4a^2)^3\left(\frac{1}{2}a^3\right)^2 = (64a^6)\left(\frac{1}{4}a^6\right)$
$= 16a^{12}$

34. $(8b^3)^2\left(\frac{1}{4}b^2\right)^2 = 8^2\left(\frac{1}{4}\right)^2 b^6 \cdot b^4$
$= 4b^{10}$

35. $(-x)^5(-x)^2(-x)^3 = (-x)^{10}$
$= x^{10}$

36. $(-y)^4(-y)^3(-y)^2 = (-y)^9$
$= -y^9$

37. $(2t)^3(-t^2) = -8t^5$

38. $(-w^3)(3w^2)^2 = -9w^7$

39. $(abc^2)^3(a^2b)^2 = a^7b^5c^6$

40. $(r^2st^3)^2(s^4t)^3 = r^4s^{14}t^9$

41. $(-3xy^2)^3(-2x^2y)^2 = -27 \cdot 4x^7y^8$
$= -108x^7y^8$

42. $(a^4)^3 = a^{12}$
$= 1^{12}$
$= 1$

43. $b^3 \cdot b^4 = b^7$
$= 2^7$
$= 128$

44. $(a^2 \cdot b)^3 = a^6 \cdot b^3$
$= 1^6 \cdot 2^3$
$= 1 \cdot 8$
$= 8$

45. $(a^2b)^5 = a^{10}b^5$
$= 1^{10} \cdot 2^5$
$= 1 \cdot 32$
$= 32$

46. $(b^2 \cdot b^3) \cdot (b^2)^4 = b^5 \cdot b^8$
$= b^{13}$
$= 2^{13}$
$= 8192$

47. $[(a+4)^2]^3 \cdot (a+4) = (a+4)^6 \cdot (a+4)$
$= (a+4)^7$
$= (1+4)^7$
$= 78{,}125$

48. $(5 \cdot 7)^3 = 35^3$ $\quad 5 \cdot 7^3 = 5 \cdot 343$

$= 42{,}875 \quad = 1715$

Therefore, $(5 \cdot 7)^3$ is larger.

49. $5^4 \cdot 2^5 = 625 \cdot 32$ $\quad (5 \cdot 2)^5 = 10^5$

$= 20{,}000 \quad = 1{,}000{,}000$

Therefore, $(5 \cdot 2)^5$ is larger.

50. $(4^5 \cdot 4^{10}) = 4^{15} < 4^{50}$

Therefore, 4^{50} is larger.

51. $4^2 \cdot 4^4 = 4^x$

$4^6 = 4^x$

$x = 6$

52. $(3^2)^9 = 3^x$

$3^{18} = 3^x$

$x = 18$

53. The power of a power property is $(a^m)^n = a^{m \cdot n}$.

$$(a^m)^n = \Big[\underbrace{a \cdot a \cdot a \cdots a}_{m \text{ times}}\Big]^n = \underbrace{\Big[\underbrace{a \cdot a \cdots a}_{m \text{ times}}\Big] \cdot \Big[\underbrace{a \cdot a \cdots a}_{m \text{ times}}\Big] \cdots \Big[\underbrace{a \cdot a \cdots a}_{m \text{ times}}\Big]}_{n \text{ times}}$$

Therefore, a is multiplied $m \cdot n$ times.

54. The power of a product property is $(a \cdot b)^m = a^m \cdot b^m$.

$$(a \cdot b)^m = \Big[\underbrace{(a \cdot b) \cdot (a \cdot b) \cdots (a \cdot b)}_{m \text{ times}}\Big]$$

Using the Commutative Property of Multiplication, we can write this as

$$\underbrace{a \cdot a \cdots a}_{m \text{ times}} \cdot \underbrace{b \cdot b \cdots b}_{m \text{ times}} = a^m \cdot b^m.$$

55. $(1.1 + 3.3)^3 = (4.4)^3$

≈ 85.18

56. $5.5^3 \cdot 5.5^4 = 5.5^7$

$\approx 152{,}243.52$

57. $2.4^4 \cdot 2.4^2 = 2.4^6$

≈ 191.10

58. $(4.0 + 3.9)^2 = 7.9^2$

$= 62.41$

59. $(2.9^3)^5 = 2.9^{15}$

$\approx 8{,}629{,}188.75$

60. $(9.1^2)^4 = 9.1^8$

$= 47{,}025{,}252.76$

61. Volume $= \frac{1}{3}\left(\frac{1}{2}\right)(800^3 - 600^3)$

Volume $= 49{,}333{,}333\frac{1}{3}$ cubic feet

62. $49{,}333{,}333\frac{1}{3}(90) =$ 4,440,000,000 pounds

63. $y = Ca^x$

$= 2(1)^{50}$

$= 2$

64. $y = Ca^x$

$= 1(2)^2$

$= 4$

65. $y = Ca^x$

$= 2\left(\frac{1}{2}\right)^3$

$= 2 \cdot \frac{1}{8}$

$= \frac{1}{4}$

66. $y = Ca^x$

$= 4 \cdot \left(\frac{3}{4}\right)^2$

$= 4 \cdot \frac{9}{16}$

$= \frac{9}{4}$

67. $y = 500(1.03)^8$

Exponential growth

68. $y = 10(0.99)^{10}$

Exponential decay

69. $y = 1000(0.03)^{25}$

Exponential decay

70. $y = 0.75(1.01)^{50}$

Exponential growth

71. $a^2 + 2 = 3^2 + 2$

$= 9 + 2$

$= 11$

72. $3x^2 - 5 = 3(5)^2 - 5$
$= 75 - 5$
$= 70$

73. $x^2 + y^3 = 1^2 + 4^3$
$= 1 + 64$
$= 65$

74. $2a^4 - b^3 = 2 \cdot 2^4 - 3^3$
$= 2^5 - 3^3$
$= 32 - 27$
$= 5$

75. $\begin{cases} 7y + 4 = 10x \\ 13y + 16 = 12x + 48 \end{cases}$

$$\begin{aligned} 60x - 42y &= 24 \\ -60x + 65y &= 160 \\ \hline 23y &= 184 \\ y &= 8 \end{aligned}$$

$7(8) + 4 = 10x$

$x = 6$

76. $13y + 16 = 13(8) + 16$
$= 120$

$12x + 48 = 12(6) + 48$
$= 120$

$7y + 4 = 7(8) + 4$
$= 60$

$10x = 10(6)$
$= 60$

The measures of the angles of the parallelogram are 60° and 120°.

77. $60 + 60 + 120 + 120 = 360$

78. $n = 3960 \cdot 1.7^t$
$= 3960 \cdot 1.7^7$
$\approx 162{,}494.11$

About 162,494 businesses used voice messages in 1992.

79.

Year, *t*	1981	1983	1985	1987	1990
Profit ($), *P*	188.99	241.32	308.15	393.47	567.74

The profit would be $925.69 million in 1994.

80. $567.74(0.09) = 51.10$

About $51.1 million of the $567.74 million profit for 1990 was due to the Star-Kist Tuna division.

8.2 Negative and Zero Exponents

Communicating about Algebra

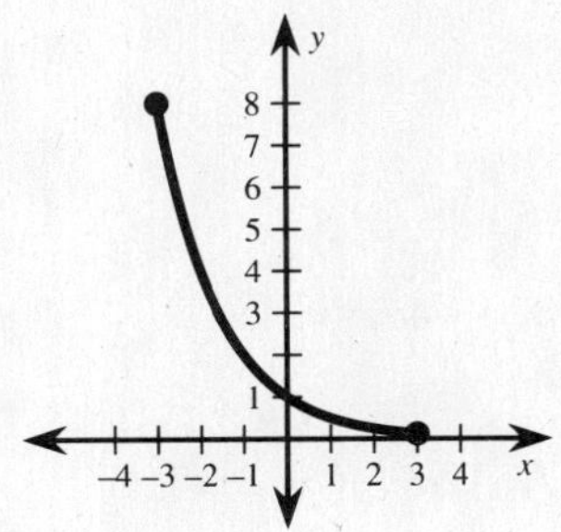

EXERCISES

1. True; the base of a power determines if the term is positive or negative.

2. $a^5 \cdot a^{-5} = a^{5-5}$
$= a^0$
$= 1$

The result implies that a^5 and a^{-5} are reciprocals of each other.

3. $5a^{-3}b^{-2} = \dfrac{5}{a^3b^2}$

Five does not have a negative exponent.

4. $3c^{-5} \cdot 4c^4 = 12c^{-1}$
$= \dfrac{12}{c}$

A simplified form cannot have a negative exponent.

5. All of the graphs of $y = a^x$ pass through the point (0, 1). The graphs of the form $y = 2(a)^x$ do not pass through (0, 1), but pass through (0, 2).

6. $x^{-7} = \dfrac{1}{x^7}$

7. $x^{-9} = \dfrac{1}{x^9}$

8. $5x^{-4} = \dfrac{5}{x^4}$

9. $3x^{-2} = \dfrac{3}{x^2}$

10. $\dfrac{1}{2x^{-3}} = \dfrac{x^3}{2}$

11. $\dfrac{1}{4x^{-5}} = \dfrac{x^5}{4}$

12. $x^{-2}y^3 = \dfrac{y^3}{x^2}$

13. $x^6y^{-7} = \dfrac{x^6}{y^7}$

14. $3x^{-3}y^{-8} = \dfrac{3}{x^3y^8}$

15. $6x^{-2}y^{-4} = \dfrac{6}{x^2y^4}$

16. $\dfrac{1}{7x^{-4}y^{-1}} = \dfrac{x^4y}{7}$

17. $\dfrac{1}{2x^{-10}y^{12}} = \dfrac{x^{10}}{2y^{12}}$

18. $3^{-2} = \frac{1}{9}$

19. $2^{-4} = \frac{1}{16}$

20. $-4^0 \cdot \dfrac{1}{2^{-2}} = -1 \cdot 4$
$= -4$

21. $4^{-3} \cdot 4^2 = 4^{-1}$
$= \frac{1}{4}$

22. $6^3 \cdot 6^{-1} = 6^2$
$= 36$

23. $8^4 \cdot 8^{-4} = 8^0$
$= 1$

24. $7^{-9} \cdot 7^9 = 7^0$
$= 1$

25. $(5^{-3})^2 = 5^{-6}$
$= \dfrac{1}{5^6}$
$= \dfrac{1}{15{,}625}$

26. $(-4^{-2})^{-1} = \left(-\dfrac{1}{4^2}\right)^{-1}$
$= -4^2$
$= -16$

27. $-6 \cdot (-6)^{-1} = (-6)^0$
$= 1$

28. $5 \cdot 5^{-1} = 5^0$
$= 1$

29. $2^0 \cdot 3^{-3} = 1 \cdot \frac{1}{27}$
$= \frac{1}{27}$

30. $(-3)^0x = x$

31. $(5y)^{-2} = \dfrac{1}{25y^2}$

32. $(-2x)^{-3} = -\dfrac{1}{8x^3}$

33. $(-4a)^0 = 1$

34. $(-3x)^{-1} \cdot 2y = -\dfrac{2y}{3x}$

35. $(4xy)^{-2} = \dfrac{1}{16x^2y^2}$

36. $(3x)^{-1} = \dfrac{1}{3x}$

37. $(2a^{-3})^3 = 2^3a^{-9}$
$= \dfrac{8}{a^9}$

38. $\dfrac{4}{b^{-2}} = 4b^2$

39. $\dfrac{5}{a^{-4}} = 5a^4$

40. $\dfrac{1}{(4x)^{-3}} = 64x^3$

41. $\dfrac{1}{(2y)^{-5}} = 32y^5$

42. $y = -3^x$

$1 \stackrel{?}{=} -3^0$

$1 \neq -1$

Since (0, 1) is not a solution point, the graph of $y = -3^x$ does not contain (0, 1).

43. $y = 4^x$

$1 \stackrel{?}{=} 4^0$

$1 = 1$

Since (0, 1) is a solution point, the graph of $y = 4^x$ does contain (0, 1).

44. $y = 3 \cdot 1^x$

$1 \stackrel{?}{=} 3 \cdot 1^0$

$1 \neq 3$

Since (0, 1) is not a solution point, the graph of $y = 3 \cdot 1^x$ does not contain (0, 1).

45. $y = 50^x$

$1 \stackrel{?}{=} 50^0$

$1 = 1$

Since (0, 1) is a solution point, the graph of $y = 50^x$ does contain (0, 1).

46. $P = 4{,}903{,}000 \cdot 1.0047^t$

1970: 4,678,406
1980: 4,903,000
1990: 5,138,376

47. $P = 1{,}025{,}000 \cdot 0.9918^t$

1970: 1,112,968
1980: 1,025,000
1990: 943,985

48.

Half-life periods, *h*	0	1	2
Grams, *W*	40	20	10

49. The age of the skull is about 8000 years.

50.

Year, *t*	0	2	4	6	8	10
Dollars, *A*	500,000	480,200	461,184.08	442,921.19	425,381.51	408,536.40

51. 1980: \$700,000.00
1990: \$633,067.45
2000: \$572,534.85

52. a. $p^8 \cdot q^4 \cdot p^4 \cdot q^8 = p^{12}q^{12}$

53. $4^3 = 64$

54. $(-2)^5 = -32$

55. $\left(-\frac{2}{3}\right)^2 = \frac{4}{9}$

56. $-8^2 = -64$

57. $25 - 3^2 \cdot 2 = 25 - 9 \cdot 2$
$= 25 - 18$
$= 7$

58. $(12 - 9)^3 \cdot 4 + 36 = 3^3 \cdot 4 + 36$
$= 27 \cdot 4 + 36$
$= 108 + 36$
$= 144$

59. $a^4 \cdot a^6 = a^{10}$

60. $x^2 \cdot y^4 \cdot x^3 = x^5y^4$

61. $(-t^2)^3 = -t^6$

62. $(4z)^2 = 16z^2$

63. $(m \cdot n)^5 = m^5n^5$

64. $(3a \cdot 2b)^3 = 216a^3b^3$

65. d.

66. a.

67. c.

68. b.

69.

Shoulder height (in.), *s*	50	60	70	80
Antler length (in.), *a*	47.5	66.6	90.0	118.5

70. The estimated antler length of the Irish elk is 62.5 inches.

71. The antler spread is greater than the elk's shoulder height.

Mixed REVIEW

1. $\frac{3}{7} - \frac{2}{5} = \frac{15}{35} - \frac{14}{35}$
$= \frac{1}{35}$

2. $2x + 3x = 5x$

3. $150(0.37) = 55.5$

4. $64\left(\frac{3}{4}\right) = 48$

5. $6a + 5b = 10$
$6a = -5b + 10$
$a = \frac{1}{6}(-5b + 10)$

6. $45r - 9s = -27$
$45r = 9s - 27$
$r = \frac{1}{5}s - \frac{3}{5}$

7. $x^2 - 3x + 12 = x(3 + x)$
$x^2 - 3x + 12 = 3x + x^2$
$12 = 6x$
$x = 2$

8. $\frac{1}{4}(8x + 2) = -\frac{1}{3}(4 - x)$
$3(8x + 2) = -4(4 - x)$
$24x + 6 = -16 + 4x$
$20x = -22$
$x = -\frac{11}{10}$

9. $3x + 2y = 6$
$2y = -3x + 6$
$y = -\frac{3}{2}x + 3$

10. $y = -\frac{1}{2}x + 2$
$2y = -x + 4$
$x + 2y = 4$

11. $3x + 4(3 - x) + 2 = 3x + 12 - 4x + 2$
$= 14 - x$

12. $\frac{1}{2} - \frac{3}{4}(y - 12) + \frac{3}{2} = \frac{1}{2} - \frac{3}{4}y + 9 + \frac{3}{2}$
$= -\frac{3}{4}y + 11$

13. $3x^2 + 4x^3 = 3(-1)^2 + 4(-1)^3$
$= 3 - 4$
$= -1$

14. $5p + 3p(4 - p) = 5 \cdot 3 + 3 \cdot 3(4 - 3)$
$= 15 + 9$
$= 24$

15. $3x + 2 = 3(3) + 2$
$= 11 > 9$

3 is a solution.

16. $4(x - 3) = 4\left(\frac{1}{4} - 3\right)$
$= 4\left(-\frac{11}{4}\right)$
$= -11 < -10$

$\frac{1}{4}$ is a solution.

17. $3x + 6y = 3(-2) + 6(3)$
$= -6 + 18$
$= 12 \geq 12$

$(-2, 3)$ is a solution.

18. $\frac{1}{2}x - y = \frac{1}{2}(4) - (-2)$

$= 2 + 2$

$= 4 > 3$

(4, −2) is a solution.

19. $\begin{cases} 3x - 2y = -4 \\ -5x + y = 3 \end{cases}$

$y = 5x + 3$

$3x - 2(5x + 3) = -4$

$3x - 10x - 6 = -4$

$-7x = 2$

$x = -\frac{2}{7}$

$y = 5\left(-\frac{2}{7}\right) + 3$

$y = -\frac{10}{7} + 3$

$y = \frac{11}{7}$

$\left(-\frac{2}{7}, \frac{11}{7}\right)$

20. $\begin{cases} 6x - 2y = 3 \\ 4x + 2y = 6 \end{cases}$

$10x = 9$

$x = \frac{9}{10}$

$6\left(\frac{9}{10}\right) - 2y = 3$

$-2y = \frac{30}{10} - \frac{54}{10}$

$-2y = -\frac{24}{10}$

$y = \frac{6}{5}$

$\left(\frac{9}{10}, \frac{6}{5}\right)$

8.3 Division Properties of Exponents

Communicating about Algebra

Personal choice

$$\left(\frac{a^{-2}}{b^5}\right)^{-3} = \frac{(a^{-2})^{-3}}{(b^5)^{-3}} = \frac{(b^5)^3}{(a^{-2})^3} = \frac{b^{15}}{a^{-6}} = a^6b^{15}$$

EXERCISES

1. No; the base of the power in the numerator is not the same as the base of the power in the denominator.

2. $\frac{x^{-4}}{x^{-5}} = x^{-4-(-5)}$

$= x^{-4+5}$

$= x$

3. You subtract exponents when you divide powers with the same base.

4. They are reciprocals. Their product is 1.

5. $\frac{6^6}{6^4} = 6^2$

$= 36$

6. $\frac{8^3}{8^1} = 8^2$

$= 64$

7. $\frac{(-4)^5}{(4)^5} = \left(-\frac{4}{4}\right)^5$

$= (-1)^5$

$= -1$

8. $\frac{(-3)^9}{(-3)^9} = \left(\frac{-3}{-3}\right)^9$

$= 1^9$

$= 1$

9. $\frac{2^2}{2^{-3}} = 2^{2-(-3)}$

$= 2^5$

$= 32$

10. $\frac{8^3 \cdot 8^2}{8^5} = \frac{8^5}{8^5}$

$= 1$

11. $\frac{7^4 \cdot 7}{7^7} = \frac{7^5}{7^7}$

$= \frac{1}{7^2}$

$= \frac{1}{49}$

12. $\left(\frac{3}{4}\right)^2 = \frac{9}{16}$

13. $\left(\frac{5}{3}\right)^3 = \frac{125}{27}$

14. $\left(-\frac{2}{3}\right)^3 = -\frac{8}{27}$

15. $\left(-\frac{4}{5}\right)^2 = \frac{16}{25}$

16. $\left(\frac{9}{6}\right)^{-1} = \frac{6}{9}$

$= \frac{2}{3}$

17. $\left(\frac{2}{x}\right)^4 = \frac{16}{x^4}$

18. $\frac{x^4}{x^5} = \frac{1}{x}$

19. $\left(\frac{1}{x}\right)^6 = \frac{1}{x^6}$

20. $x^3 \cdot \frac{1}{x^2} = x$

21. $x^7 \cdot \frac{1}{x^9} = \frac{1}{x^2}$

22. $\frac{3x^2y^2}{3xy} \cdot \frac{6xy^3}{3y} = 2x^2y^3$

23. $\frac{4xy^3}{2y} \cdot \frac{5xy^{-3}}{x^2} = \frac{10}{y}$

24. $\frac{16x^3y}{-4xy^3} \cdot \frac{-2xy}{-x} = \frac{-8x^2}{y}$

25. $\frac{-9x^5y^7}{x^2y^3} \cdot \frac{(2xy)^2}{-6x^2y^2} = 6x^3y^4$

26. $\frac{6x^{-2}y^2}{xy^{-3}} \cdot \frac{(4x^2y)^{-2}}{xy^2} = \frac{6}{16} \cdot \frac{y^5}{x^3} \cdot \frac{1}{x^5y^4}$

$= \frac{3y}{8x^8}$

27. $\frac{7x^{-1}y^3}{x^2y^{-2}} \cdot \frac{(3xy^2)^{-1}}{xy} = \frac{7y^5}{x^3} \cdot \frac{1}{3x^2y^3}$

$= \frac{7y^2}{3x^5}$

28. $\left(\frac{2xy^{-2}y^4}{3yx^{-1}}\right)^{-2} \cdot \left(\frac{4xy}{2x^{-1}y^3}\right)^2 = \left(\frac{3^2}{2^2x^4y^2}\right) \cdot \left(\frac{4^2x^4}{2^2y^4}\right)$

$= \frac{9}{y^6}$

29. $\frac{4 \cdot 10^{-3}}{4.5 \cdot 10^3} \approx \frac{0.9}{10^6}$

Yes, this fish meets FDA requirements.

30. $\frac{11 \cdot 10^{-3}}{9 \cdot 10^3} \approx \frac{1.2}{10^6}$

$\frac{11 \cdot 10^{-3}}{x} = \frac{1}{10^6}$

$x = 11 \cdot 10^{-3} \cdot 10^6$

$x = 11 \cdot 10^3$

No; the fish would have to weigh 11 kilograms for 11 milligrams of methylmercury to be acceptable.

31. $\frac{640\left(\frac{5}{4}\right)^9}{640\left(\frac{5}{4}\right)^4} = \left(\frac{5}{4}\right)^5$

$= \frac{5^5}{4^5}$

≈ 3.05

32.

Weeks, n	0	1	2	3	4	5	6	7	8
Words, S	200	160	128	102	82	66	52	42	34

It takes approximately 19 weeks to forget all but three words.

33. $\frac{16.3(1.0285)^8}{16.3(1.0285)^2} = (1.0285)^6$

≈ 1.1837

34. $\frac{83(1.026)^{28}}{83(1.026)^{-28}} = (1.026)^{56}$

≈ 4.210

35. $(x^3)^5 = x^{15}$

36. $(a^5)^3 = a^{15}$

37. $x^5 \cdot x^3 = x^8$

38. $n^3 \cdot n^{-5} = \frac{1}{n^2}$

39. $\frac{x^{-5}}{x^3} = \frac{1}{x^8}$

40. $\frac{b^3}{b^5} = \frac{1}{b^2}$

41. $x^3 \cdot x^2y = x^5y$

$2^5 \cdot 3 = 96$

42. $a^6b \cdot a^{-4}b^2 = a^2b^3$

$10^2 \cdot (-5)^3 = -12{,}500$

43. $(2x)^2 \cdot (3y^2)^2 = 36x^2y^4$

$36 \cdot (-1)^2(2)^4 = 576$

44. $(5n^3m)^4 \cdot (2nm)^2 = 2500n^{14}m^6$

$2500 \cdot (0)^{14} \cdot (2)^6 = 0$

45. $(xy^4)^{-1} \cdot \left(\frac{1}{x^2y^3}\right)^{-2} = \frac{1}{xy^4} \cdot x^4y^6$

$= x^3y^2$

$2^3 \cdot 5^2 = 8 \cdot 25$

$= 200$

46. $\left(\frac{1}{3a^3b^2}\right)^{-4} \cdot (-3a^{10}b^9)^{-1} = 3^4a^{12}b^8 \cdot \frac{1}{-3a^{10}b^9}$

$= \frac{-27a^2}{b}$

$\frac{-27 \cdot 4^2}{6} = -72$

47. $(10r^7s^{11})^0 \cdot \left(\frac{s^2}{rs^3}\right)^{-2} = r^2s^2$

$12^2 \cdot (-1)^2 = 144$

48. $-\left(\frac{x^2y^3}{x^4y^2}\right) \cdot \left(\frac{2x^7y^4}{x^5y^6}\right)^{-2} = -\left(\frac{y}{x^2}\right)\left(\frac{x^{10}y^{12}}{4x^{14}y^8}\right)$

$= -\frac{y^5}{4x^6}$

$-\frac{3^5}{4 \cdot 2^6} = -\frac{243}{256}$

49. $x^a \cdot x^a = x^{2a}$

50. $2^{7x+1} \cdot 2^{3x+4} = 2^{10x+5}$

51. $\frac{x^{a+2}}{x^{a-2}} = x^{a+2-(a-2)}$

$= x^4$

52. $\frac{x^b}{x^{b-1}} = x^{b-(b+1)}$

$= x^{-1}$

$= \frac{1}{x}$

53. $n(3.5) = 6^3$

$n \approx 61.7$

54. $n(55) = 6^3$

$n \approx 3.9$

55. $\frac{61.7}{3.9} \approx 15.8$

56. Long, pointed wings like a gulls excel at soaring and gliding while the narrow, tapered wings of a hummingbird provide speed.

8.4 Scientific Notation

Communicating about Algebra

A. $\dfrac{139 \times 10^6}{2.5 \times 10^9} = 5.56 \times 10^{-2}$

$= 0.0556$

5.56% of the crude oil produced in the U.S. in 1993 was produced in Louisiana.

B. $5^6 = 15{,}625$
$5^7 = 78{,}125$
$5^8 = 390{,}625$
$5^9 = 1{,}953{,}125$
$5^{10} = 9{,}765{,}625$
$5^{11} = 48{,}828{,}125$
$5^{12} = 244{,}140{,}625$
$5^{13} = 1{,}220{,}703{,}125$
$5^{14} = 6{,}103{,}515{,}625$
$5^{15} = 3.051757813 \times 10^{10}$
$5^{16} = 1.525878906 \times 10^{11}$
$5^{17} = 7.629394531 \times 10^{11}$

Your calculator displays scientific notation for power 15 or greater.

C. 1.147791×10^{-5} grams

EXERCISES

1. b.

2. Decimal point must be moved 5 places to the right.

3. 6.2×10^4

4. $10^3 \cdot 10^{-6} = 1 \times 10^{-3}$
One thousandth

5. 1,090,000

6. 234,500,000

7. 6.21

8. 94,675

9. 0.00852

10. 0.00007021

11. 0.0867

12. 4.73

13. 9.3×10^7

14. 9×10^8

15. 1.637×10^9

16. 6.78×10^1

17. 4.35×10^{-4}

18. 8.367×10^{-3}

19. 4.392×10^{-3}

20. 8.75×10^{-2}

21. $6 \times 10^{-2} \cdot 3 \times 10^4 = 18 \times 10^2$
$= 1800$

22. $5 \times 10^5 \cdot 5 \times 10^{-5} = 25 \times 10^0$
$= 25$

23. $4 \times 10^4 \cdot 2 \times 10^{-1} = 8 \times 10^3$
$= 8000$

24. $6 \times 10^{-3} \cdot 7 \times 10^{-4} = 42 \times 10^{-7}$
$= 0.0000042$

25. $9 \times 10^{-3} \cdot 4 \times 10^8 = 36 \times 10^5$
$= 3{,}600{,}000$

26. $8 \times 10^4 \cdot 10 \times 10^{-1} = 80 \times 10^4$
$= 80{,}000$

27. $8{,}000{,}000 \cdot 623{,}000 = 4{,}984{,}000{,}000{,}000$
$= 4.984 \times 10^{12}$

28. $3{,}000{,}000 \cdot 43{,}000 = 129{,}000{,}000{,}000$
$= 1.29 \times 10^{11}$

29. $0.000345 \cdot 8{,}980{,}000{,}000 = 3{,}098{,}100$
$= 3.0981 \times 10^6$

30. $345{,}000 \cdot 0.000086 = 29.67$
$= 2.967 \times 10$

31. $(3.28 \times 10^{-6})^4 \approx 0.000\,000\,000\,000\,000\,000\,000\,115\,7$
$= 1.157 \times 10^{-22}$

32. $(0.000045)^3 = 0.000\,000\,000\,000\,091\,125$
$= 9.1125 \times 10^{-14}$

33. 4×10^{-23}

34. 2.5×10^8

35. 4.8×10^6

36. 1×10^{-3}

37. $\dfrac{1.0 \times 10^5}{3.0 \times 10^{-4}} \approx 3.3 \times 10^8$

38. $\dfrac{2 \times 10^3}{8.5 \times 10^7} \approx 0.24 \times 10^{-4}$
$= 2.4 \times 10^{-5}$
$\approx 0.0002\%$

39. $\dfrac{1}{2.1 \times 10^{23}} \approx 0.476 \times 10^{-23}$
$= 4.76 \times 10^{-24}$

40. $\dfrac{1}{2.5 \times 10^{-3}} \approx 0.4 \times 10^3$
$= 4 \times 10^2$

41. $\dfrac{1 \times 10^{57}}{8.5 \times 10^{31}} \approx 0.12 \times 10^{26}$
$= 1.2 \times 10^{25}$

42. $\dfrac{9.3 \times 10^7}{1.1 \times 10^7} = \dfrac{9.3}{1.1} \times 10^0$
≈ 8.5

43. $76 \cdot 5.88 \times 10^{12} = 446.88 \times 10^{12}$
$= 4.4688 \times 10^{14}$ miles

44. $79 \cdot 1.67 \times 10^{-24} + 79 \cdot 1.67 \times 10^{-24} + (9.11 \times 10^{-28})79 = 131.93 \times 10^{-24} + 131.93 \times 10^{-24} + 719.69 \times 10^{-28}$
$= 26386 \times 10^{-26} + 7.1969 \times 10^{-26}$
$\approx 26400 \times 10^{-26}$
$= 2.64 \times 10^{-22}$

45. $\dfrac{1.6 \times 10^{10}}{365} \approx 0.0043835616 \times 10^{10}$
$= 43{,}835{,}616$
$\approx 4.4 \times 10^7$

46. $\dfrac{1.095 \times 10^{12}}{365} = 0.003 \times 10^{12}$
$= 3{,}000{,}000{,}000$
$= 3 \times 10^9$

47. $\dfrac{7.7 \times 10^{10}}{2.5 \times 10^8} = 3.08 \times 10^2$
≈ 308

48. $\dfrac{7.1 \times 10^9}{2.5 \times 10^8} \approx 2.8 \times 10^1$
$= 28$

49. $(9.1 \times 10^4)^4 \approx 6.9 \times 10^{19}$
$(9.1 \times 10^2)^{10} \approx 3.9 \times 10^{29}$
$(9.1 \times 10^5)^4 \approx 6.9 \times 10^{23}$
$(9.1 \times 10^{10})^2 \approx 8.3 \times 10^{21}$
$(9.1 \times 10^4)^4,\ (9.1 \times 10^{10})^2$
$(9.1 \times 10^5)^4,\ (9.1 \times 10^2)^{10}$

50. $\dfrac{1}{4 \times 10^5}$

51. $m = \dfrac{6.2 \times 10^5 - 9.0 \times 10^5}{3.4 \times 10^4 - 1.4 \times 10^4}$
$= \dfrac{-2.8 \times 10^5}{2 \times 10^4}$
$= -1.4 \times 10^1$
$= -14$

52. $m = \dfrac{4.6 \times 10^2 - 3.4 \times 10^2}{1.9 \times 10^9 - 9.9 \times 10^9}$
$= \dfrac{1.2 \times 10^2}{-8 \times 10^9}$
$= -0.15 \times 10^{-7}$
$= -1.5 \times 10^{-8}$

53. \$1.6 billion; $\$1.6 \times 10^9$

54. $(0.03)(1.6 \times 10^9) = 0.048 \times 10^9$
$= 4.8 \times 10^7$

55. $186{,}280.8697 \approx 1.86 \times 10^5$

56. $\dfrac{1.93 \times 10^5 \text{ feet}}{\text{minute}} \cdot \dfrac{1 \text{ minute}}{60 \text{ seconds}} \approx 3.22 \times 10^3$ feet per second

$\dfrac{1.93 \times 10^5 \text{ feet}}{\text{minute}} \cdot \dfrac{1 \text{ mile}}{5280 \text{ feet}} \cdot \dfrac{60 \text{ minutes}}{1 \text{ hour}} \approx 2.19 \times 10^3$ miles per hour

Mixed REVIEW

1. $(3 + 2) \div (27 - 2) = 5 \div 25$
$= 0.2$

2. $12 \div 3 \cdot (4 - 1) = 4 \cdot 3$
$= 12$

3. $|x + 2| = 3$
$x + 2 = -3$ or $x + 2 = 3$
$x = -5$ $\quad$ $x = 1$

4. $-3|x + 2| = -9$
$|x + 2| = 3$
$x = -5$ or $x = 1$

5. $3x \cdot (3x)^2 \cdot x^4 = 27x^7$

6. $p^2 \cdot q^3 \cdot p^2q^2 = p^4q^5$

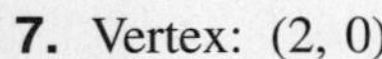

7. Vertex: (2, 0)

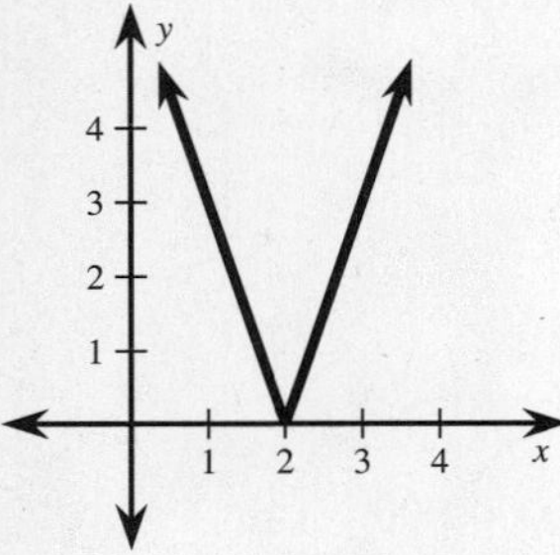

8. Intercepts: (9, 0), (0, 8)

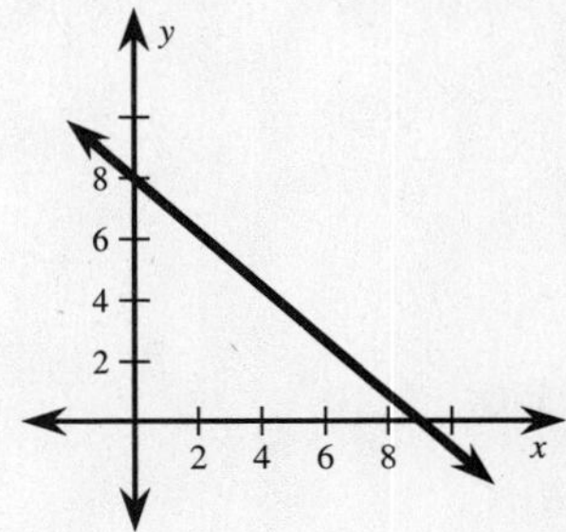

9. x^{-3} or $\dfrac{1}{x^3}$

10. $-3y$

11. $3y + 2(3 - 6y) = 12$
$-9y = 6$
$y = -\frac{2}{3}$

12. $(t - 2)\frac{1}{3} - 5t \geq 6$
$t - 2 - 15t \geq 18$
$-14t \geq 20$
$t \leq -\frac{10}{7}$

13. $3y + 2y^2 = 3(-3) + 2(-3)^2$
$= -9 + 18$
$= 9$

14. $\frac{1}{4}x \div (3 - x) = \left(\frac{1}{4}\right)\left(\frac{1}{2}\right) \div \left(3 - \frac{1}{2}\right)$
$= \frac{1}{8} \cdot \frac{2}{5}$
$= \frac{1}{20}$

Mid-Chapter SELF-TEST

1. $q^3 \cdot q^2 = q^5$

2. $x^2 \cdot x^2 \cdot x^3 = x^7$

3. $(n^5)^2 = n^{10}$

4. $-(t^3)^2 = -t^6$

5. $-3s^2 \cdot 8s^3 = -24s^5$ **6.** $5x^{-5} = \frac{5}{x^5}$ **7.** $(-2b)^{-2} = \frac{1}{4b^2}$ **8.** $4c^0 = 4$

9. $\frac{4x^2y}{2xy^2} = \frac{2x}{y}$ **10.** $\frac{p^{-3}}{p^2} = \frac{1}{p^5}$ **11.** $\frac{4q^4}{3q^{-3}} = \frac{4q^7}{3}$

12. $\frac{4w^2z^4}{5y^3z^2} \cdot \frac{10z^2}{2wy} = \frac{4wz^4}{y^4}$ **13.** $6^2 \cdot 6^0 = 36$ **14.** $4^3 \cdot 4^{-4} = \frac{1}{4}$

15. $\left(\frac{3}{4}\right)^2 = \frac{9}{16}$ **16.** $\left(\frac{5}{2}\right)^{-2} = \frac{4}{25}$ **17.** $(0.3 + 2.5)^4 \approx 61.5$ **18.** $(3^2)^3 = 3^6 = 729$

19. 10,079,000 **20.** 0.0005006 **21.** 3.78965×10^6 **22.** 1.79×10^{-6}

23. $(6.2 \times 10^5) \cdot (1.1 \times 10^{-7}) = 6.82 \times 10^{-2}$ **24.** $(5.9 \times 10^{-2}) \div (4.7 \times 10^{-4}) \approx 1.26 \times 10^2$

25. $V = \frac{4}{3}\pi\left(\frac{9}{2}\right)^3$
$= 381.51$

26. $V = \frac{4}{3}\pi 2^3$
$\approx 33.49 \text{ in.}^3$

27.

Half-life periods, *h*	0	1	2	3	4
Grams, *W*	16	8	4	2	1

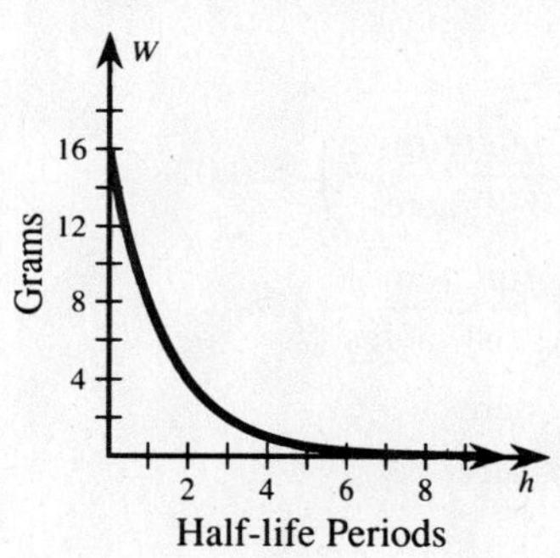

28. 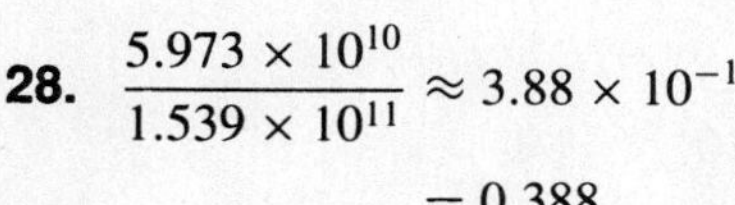
$\frac{5.973 \times 10^{10}}{1.539 \times 10^{11}} \approx 3.88 \times 10^{-1}$
$= 0.388$

38.8% of the total volume of mail is direct-mail advertising.

8.5 Problem Solving and Scientific Notation

Communicating about Algebra

$$\frac{1.622 \times 10^{23}}{(1080)^2} \div \frac{1.318 \times 10^{25}}{(3960)^2} \approx \frac{16.5}{100}$$
$$= 0.165$$

EXERCISES

1. 1. Write a verbal model.
2. Assign labels.
3. Write an algebraic model.
4. Solve algebraic model.
5. Answer the question.

2. | Number of flowers per year | = | Number of flowers per pound | • | Number of pounds per year |

3. Number of flowers per year $= n$

Number of flower per pound $= \dfrac{45 \times 10^6}{2.2}$ to $\dfrac{64 \times 10^6}{2.2}$

Number of pounds per year $= 500$

4. $n = \dfrac{45 \times 10^6}{2.2} \cdot 500$ to $n = \dfrac{64 \times 10^6}{2.2} \cdot 500$

5. $n \approx 1.0 \times 10^{10}$ to 1.5×10^{10}

6. The workers must visit between 1.0×10^{10} and 1.5×10^{10} flowers per year.

7. $\dfrac{7.8 \times 10^8}{3.0 \times 10^5} = 2.6 \times 10^3$

It takes $43\frac{1}{3}$ minutes for light to travel from the sun to Jupiter.

8. $(7.8 \times 10^8 - 1.5 \times 10^8) \leq d \leq (7.8 \times 10^8 + 1.5 \times 10^8)$

$6.3 \times 10^8 \leq d \leq 9.3 \times 10^8$

9. $\dfrac{15 \times 10^6}{8.28 \times 10^5} \approx 1.812 \times 10^1 = 18.12$

$\dfrac{10 \times 10^6}{2.94 \times 10^4} \approx 3.4014 \times 10^2 = 340.14$

Louisiana: \$18.12 per square mile

Gadsden: \$340.14 per square mile

10. $\left(\dfrac{18.12 \text{ dollars}}{\text{square mile}}\right)\left(\dfrac{\text{square mile}}{640 \text{ acres}}\right) \approx 0.028$

$\left(\dfrac{340.14 \text{ dollars}}{\text{square mile}}\right)\left(\dfrac{\text{square mile}}{640 \text{ acres}}\right) \approx 0.531$

Louisiana: 2.8¢ per acre

Gadsden: 53.1¢ per acre

11.

Year	1985	1986	1987	1988	1989
Number redeemed	6.497×10^9	7.094×10^9	7.197×10^9	7.100×10^9	7.091×10^9

12. $(1.14342 \times 10^{12})(0.25) \approx 2.859 \times 10^{11}$

13. $(2.5 \times 10^{-17})(10 \times 10^7) = 25 \times 10^{-10}$

$= 2.5 \times 10^{-9}$ cm^3

14. $\dfrac{80 \text{ beats}}{\text{minute}} \cdot \dfrac{60 \text{ minutes}}{\text{hour}} \cdot \dfrac{24 \text{ hours}}{\text{day}} \cdot \dfrac{365 \text{ days}}{\text{year}} \cdot 75 \text{ years} = 3.1536 \times 10^9$ heart beats

(excluding leap days)

15. $\dfrac{20 \text{ millimeters}}{\dfrac{36.9 \times 10^3 \text{ millimeters}}{\text{second}}} \approx 5.42 \times 10^{-4}$ second

16. $\dfrac{4.494 \times 10^9}{8.265 \times 10^{13}} \approx 0.5437 \times 10^{-4}$

$= 0.00005437$ or 0.005437%

17. $\dfrac{2.5 \times 10^8}{3.54 \times 10^6} \approx 0.71 \times 10^2$

$= 71$ people per square mile

18. $(5x^4)(2x^0) = 10x^4$

19. $(3y^2)(8y^3) = 24y^5$

20. $\dfrac{2a^2}{a^3} = \dfrac{2}{a}$

21. $\dfrac{4b^3}{b^7} = \dfrac{4}{b^4}$

22. $(-3xy^4)(4xy^{-3}) = -12x^2y$

23. $(6x^3y)(7x^{-1}y^8) = 42x^2y^9$

24. $\dfrac{12(x^2y^4)^0}{-6x^{-2}y^2} = \dfrac{-2x^2}{y^2}$

25. $\left(\dfrac{5x^3}{y}\right)^{-2} = \dfrac{y^2}{25x^6}$

26. $\left(\dfrac{3}{4}\right)^2 \cdot \left(\dfrac{2}{3}\right)^4 = \dfrac{1}{3^2}$

$= \dfrac{1}{9}$

27. 6.5×10^{-7}

28. 2.4×10^{10}

29. 2,650,000,000,000,000

30. 0.0000000004316

31. $(4.2 \times 10^{-5}) \cdot (6.1 \times 10^8) = 25.62 \times 10^3$

$= 2.562 \times 10^4$

32. $(5.04 \times 10^{12}) \cdot (8.97 \times 10^{-7}) = 45.2088 \times 10^5$

$= 4.52088 \times 10^6$

33. $(8 \times 10^6)(365) \approx 3 \times 10^9$ flashes/year

34. $\dfrac{8 \times 10^6}{44 \times 10^3} \approx 0.182 \times 10^3$

≈ 200

35. $\left(\dfrac{1100 \text{ feet}}{\text{second}}\right)(5 \text{ seconds}) = 5500$ feet

36. $300 \le x \le 4(5280)$

$300 \le x \le 21{,}120$

8.6 Problem Solving: Compound Interest and Exponential Growth

Communicating about Algebra

A. $y = 24{,}000(1.04)^t$, exponential

t	0	1	2	3	4
y	24,000	24,960	25,958.4	26,996.74	28,076.61

t	5	6	7	8	9
y	29,199.67	30,367.66	31,582.36	32,845.66	34,159.48

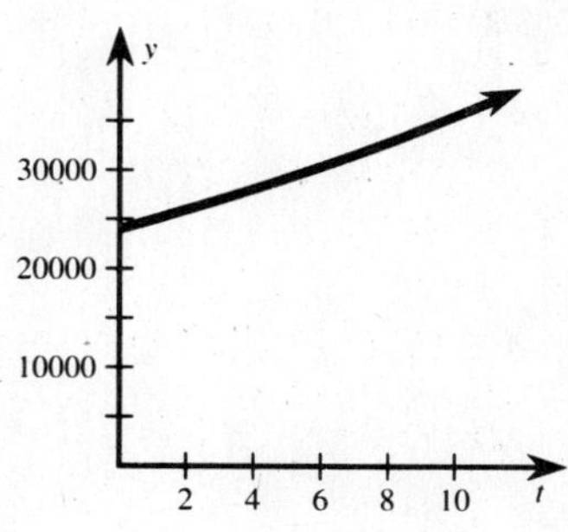

B. $y = 24{,}000 + 1000t$, linear

t	0	1	2	3	4
y	24,000	25,000	26,000	27,000	28,000

t	5	6	7	8	9
y	29,000	30,000	31,000	32,000	33,000

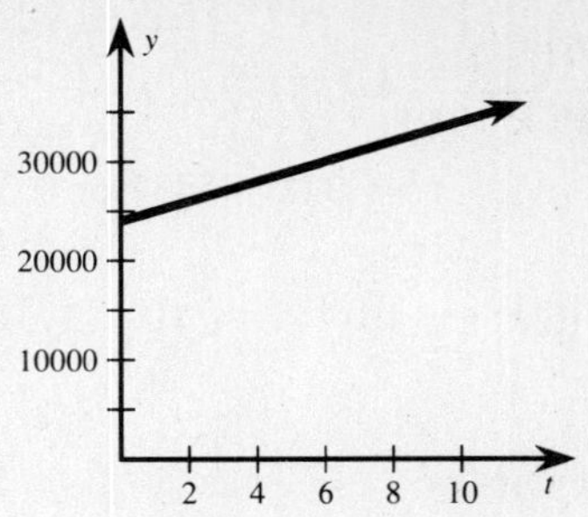

Choose plan A because in the long run you will make more money.

EXERCISES

1. True

2. $A = 1000(1.05)^{10}$

$A = 1628.89$

The balance after 10 years is $1628.89.

3. $(1 + r)$

4. r represents the percent the amount increases.

5. $A = 100(1.07)^5$

$A = \$140.26$

The balance after 5 years is $140.26.

6. $A = 1200(1.05)^{10}$

$A = \$1954.67$

The balance after 10 years is $1954.67.

7. $600 = P(1.065)^8$

$P = \$362.54$

You must deposit $362.54.

8. $200 = P(1.07)^5$

$P = \$142.60$

You must deposit $142.60.

9. **c.**

10. **b.**

11. **a.**

12. **d.**

13. $P = 9{,}580{,}000(1.0194)^t$

14. $P = 9{,}580{,}000(1.0194)^{10} = 11{,}609{,}454$

$P = 9{,}580{,}000(1.0194)^{20} = 14{,}068{,}834$

$P = 9{,}580{,}000(1.0194)^{30} = 17{,}049{,}215$

$1970 : 11{,}609{,}454 \approx 11{,}600{,}000$

$1980 : 14{,}068{,}834 \approx 14{,}100{,}000$

$1990 : 17{,}049{,}215 \approx 17{,}000{,}000$

15. **a.**

16. **b.** The profit of this business is increasing at a faster rate.

17. $y = 334{,}000(1.034)^x$

18. $y = 17 \times 10^9(1.10)^x$

19. $y = 17.46t + 266$

In 1990: $y = 527.90$

$y = 266(1.062)^t$

In 1990: $y = 655.77$

The workers' earnings did not keep up with inflation.

20. $y = 0.36t + 3.75$

In 1990: $y = 9.15$

$y = 3.75(1.062)^t$

In 1990: $y = 9.24$

The workers' earnings did keep up with inflation.

21. $-3x^3 = -3\left(\frac{1}{2}\right)^3 = -\frac{3}{8}$

22. $2^x = 2^5 = 32$

23. $(1 + y)^y = (1 + 3)^3 = 64$

24. $5x^4 - 9 = 5(1.1)^4 - 9 = -1.6795$

25. $a^2 - 4 = (4.9)^2 - 4 = 20.01$

26. $3^{2b} - 4(9^b) = 3^4 - 4(9^2) = -243$

27. $0.00462 = 4.62 \times 10^{-3}$

28. $54{,}000 = 5.4 \times 10^4$

29. $67{,}500{,}000 = 6.75 \times 10^7$

30. $0.000000751 = 7.51 \times 10^{-7}$

31. c.

$5\left(\frac{3}{2}\right) = x(1)$

$x = \frac{15}{2} = 7\frac{1}{2}$

32. b.

$(x^a)^b = x^{ab}$

33. b.

34. The estimated length of an adult house wren is 13.5 centimeters.

35. $L = 12 + (0.09)(1.237)^{14} = 13.8$

The estimated length of an adult house wren using the exponential growth model is 13.8 centimeters.

36. $\frac{12 + (0.09)(1.237)^{13}}{12 + (0.09)(1.237)^{23.8}} \approx 0.51$

The ratio of the length of a chickadee to the length of a robin using the exponential growth model is 0.51.

Using a Graphing Calculator

1. $y = 1.034 \cdot 1.629^x$

2. $y = 0.444 \cdot 1.347^x$

8.7 Exploring Data: Exponential Growth and Decay

Communicating about Algebra

A.

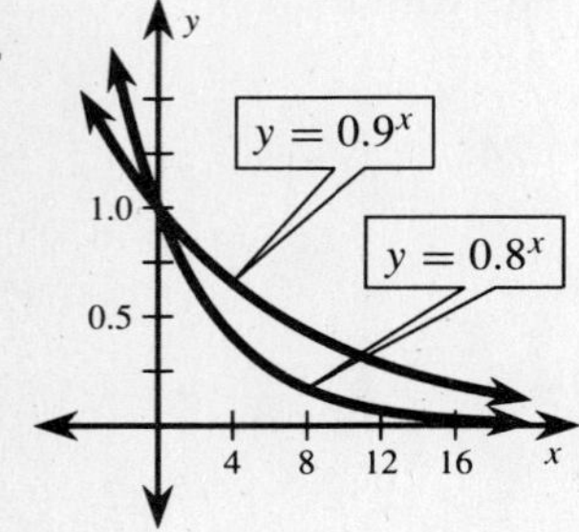

Both decrease, but $y = 0.9^x$ decreases less rapidly.

B. The adult mola mola weighs about 1006.6 pounds.

EXERCISES

1. **a.** and **d.**

The base of the power is less than 1.

2. The amount decreases 4% for each time period.

3. $E = 75{,}000(0.98)^t$

4. $y = 10{,}000(0.88)^t$

$y = 10{,}000(0.88)^{10}$

$y \approx 2800$

No; the number of hours never reaches zero.

5. $50(0.90)^3 \approx 36$

6. $50(0.95)^3 \approx 43$

$50 - 43 = 7$

7. $y = 1240(0.98)^t$

Year	1985	1986	1987	1988	1989	1990	1991	1992
Enrollment	1240	1215	1191	1167	1144	1121	1098	1076

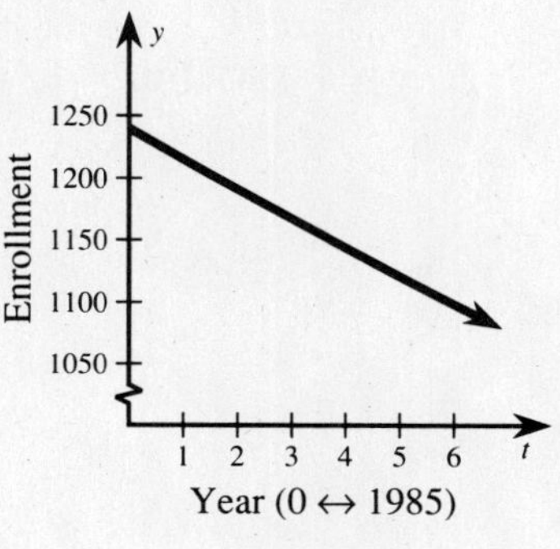

8. $E = 1{,}200{,}000(0.932)^t$

$E = 1{,}200{,}000(0.932)^{10}$

$E \approx 593{,}390$

9. $D = (56.3 - 37.5)(0.97)^t$

$D = 18.8(0.97)^t$

$D = 18.8(0.97)^{10}$

$D \approx 13.9$ million

10. c. **11.** d. **12.** a. **13.** b.

14. e., c., h., d., i., a., f., b., g.

15. Voyager I had a greater average speed.

16. By measuring the dollar bill pictured, we find its dimensions to be $2\frac{1}{16}$ inches by $\frac{7}{8}$ inch, or about 2.06 inches by 0.9 inch. Let l represent length, w represent width, and t represent the number of times you reduce the picture.

At 72%, $l = 6.1(0.72)^t$ and $w = 2.6(0.72)^t$.

After reducing three times at 72%, you must reduce again once at 90%. At 90%, $l = 2.3(0.90)^t$ and $w = 1.0(0.90)^t$.

t	1	2	3
l	4.4	3.2	2.3
w	1.9	1.3	1.0

t	1
l	2.07
w	0.9

17.

Mammal	Bear	Lion	Sheep	Deer	Seal	Cow	Giraffe	Elephant
Weight, *w*	0.5 kg	1.2 kg	4.1 kg	18 kg	33.5 kg	40 kg	68 kg	100 kg
Days, *t*	143	145	152	189	242	268	418	694

The gestation time for humans does not fit this model since the model predicts a gestation time of about 149 days or 5 months. The gestation time for humans is about 270 days or 9 months.

18. $P = 6{,}893{,}000 + 672{,}240t^2$

$t = 19$

$P \approx 249{,}600{,}000$

19. $t = 10 \quad P = 74{,}117{,}000$

$t = 13 \quad P = 120{,}501{,}560$

$t = 16 \quad P = 178{,}986{,}440$

$t = 19 \quad P = 249{,}571{,}640$

$\frac{120{,}501{,}560}{74{,}117{,}000} \approx 1.63$

$\frac{249{,}571{,}640}{178{,}986{,}440} \approx 1.39$

$\approx 63\%, \approx 39\%$

Exponential growth would have the same percentage growth during 1900 to 1930 and 1960 to 1990.

Chapter REVIEW

1. $b^2 \cdot b^7 = b^9$

2. $(p^3)^4 = p^{12}$

3. $(a^2)^3 \cdot a^3 = a^9$

4. $x^2 \cdot (xy)^2 = x^4y^2$

5. $(4m)^2 \cdot m^3 = 16m^5$

6. $(3a)^3 \cdot (2p)^2 = 108a^3p^2$

7. $8^2 \cdot (xy)^2 \cdot 2x = 128x^3y^2$

8. $w^3 \cdot (3w)^4 = 81w^7$

9. $q^0 = 1$

10. $p^{-2} = \frac{1}{p^2}$

11. $(a^2b)^0 = 1$

12. $(x^{-2}y^3)^{-2} = \frac{x^4}{y^6}$

13. $\frac{p^4}{p^2} = p^2$

14. $\frac{3b^2}{9b^5} = \frac{1}{3b^3}$

15. $\frac{(4x^2)^2}{4x^4} = 4$

16. $\frac{x^2 \cdot y^0 \cdot 3^2}{x^3 \cdot y^{-4}} = \frac{9y^4}{x}$

17. $\frac{(2p)^{-2} \cdot pq}{(p^2q)^4 \cdot p^0} = \frac{1}{4p^9q^3}$

18. $\left(\frac{m}{n}\right)^3 \cdot m^2n^{-4} = \frac{m^5}{n^7}$

19. $\left(\frac{3a^2}{b}\right)^3 \cdot \frac{2b^{-1}}{3^2 \cdot a} = \frac{6a^5}{b^4}$

20. $\left(\frac{w^{-2}}{z^4}\right)^{-3} = w^6z^{12}$

21. $\frac{(3pq)^2}{2p^{-2}} \cdot \frac{4p^{-1}q^4}{p^2} = 18pq^6$

22. $\frac{5m^2n}{m^4} \cdot \left(\frac{m^{-3}}{n}\right)^{-2} = 5m^4n^3$

23. $\frac{(3w)^4}{z^{-2}} \cdot (w^{-2}z)^{-2} = 81w^8$

24. $\frac{(3x)^{-3}}{3y^3} \cdot \frac{x^{-2}y^2}{x^{-4}} = \frac{1}{81xy}$

25. 0.006667

26. 0.375

27. 0.000000981

28. 129

29. 768,000

30. 5,440,000,000

31. 5.88×10^{-2}

32. 7.69×10^{-4}

33. 2.33×10^{-8}

34. 5.23×10^{8}

35. 7.95×10^{3}

36. 1.234×10^{9}

37. $\frac{3^2}{3^5} = \frac{1}{27}$

38. $2^{-1} \cdot 2^5 = 16$

39. $\left(\frac{2^{-1}}{3^2}\right)^{-2} \cdot \frac{1}{2 \cdot 3^3} = \frac{2^2 \cdot 1}{3^{-4} \cdot 2 \cdot 3^3}$

$= 6$

40. $(3^5 \cdot 5^2) \cdot 3^{-4} = 75$

41. $2^{-3} \cdot 4^2 \cdot 5^{-1} \cdot (3^2)^0 = \frac{2^4}{2^3 \cdot 5}$

$= \frac{2}{5}$

42. $\frac{(37 \cdot (24)^2)^2}{37 \cdot 24^4} = 37$

43. $\frac{2.4 \times 10^{-6}}{1.2 \times 10^{-12}} = 2.0 \times 10^6$

$= 2{,}000{,}000$

44. $(7.6 \times 10^2) \cdot (2.0 \times 10^4) = 15.2 \times 10^6$

$= 15{,}200{,}000$

45. $\frac{3.33 \times 10^4}{6.66 \times 10^{12}} = 0.5 \times 10^{-8}$

$= 5.0 \times 10^{-9}$

46. $\frac{9.6 \times 10^{-4} \cdot 4.8 \times 10^6}{2.4 \times 10^8 \cdot 2.4 \times 10^{-2}} = 8.0 \times 10^{-4}$

47. $\frac{3.6 \times 10^{-4}}{7.2 \times 10^6} \cdot 1.8 \times 10^{-2} = 0.9 \times 10^{-12}$

$= 9.0 \times 10^{-13}$

48. $\frac{9.9 \times 10^6}{1.1 \times 10^{-4}} = 9.0 \times 10^{10}$

49. $\frac{1.615 \times 10^{12}}{365} \approx 4.425 \times 10^9$

$\frac{1.615 \times 10^{12}}{2.5 \times 10^8} = 6.46 \times 10^3$

The average amount spent was $4.43 × 10⁹ per day.

The average amount spent per American in 1990 was $6460.

50. $\frac{4.425 \times 10^9}{2.5 \times 10^8} = 1.77 \times 10^1$

$= 17.70$

The average amount spent on retail purchases each day by an American in 1990 was $17.70.

51. A = 5^3 = 125 cubic meters

B = $\left(\frac{5}{2}\right)^3 = \frac{125}{8}$ cubic meters

52. $\frac{5}{\frac{5}{2}} = 2 \quad \frac{25}{\frac{25}{8}} = 8$

Eight equals two cubed.

53. $1.9 \times 10^{12} - 0.4178 \times 10^{12} = 1.4822 \times 10^{12}$

1,482,200,000,000 more miles were traveled by motor vehicle than by aircraft.

54. $1.9 \times 10^{12} + 0.4178 \times 10^{12} = 2.3178 \times 10^{12}$

The total traveled by motor vehicle and aircraft was 2,317,800,000,000 miles.

55. $\dfrac{0.4178 \times 10^{12}}{1.9 \times 10^{12}} \approx 0.22$

56. $\dfrac{1.9 \times 10^{12}}{2.5 \times 10^{8}} = 7.6 \times 10^3 = 7600$

The average number of miles traveled by motor vehicle per American in 1990 was approximately 7600 miles.

57. The annual percentage increase for sales of related items was 48%.

58. Graph A: $T = 60 + (50)(1.29)^t$

Graph B: $S = 20(1.48)^t$

59. 1988–1990

60. Using the graphs 1980: \$130 million
1990: \$1700 million

Using the models 1980: \$130 million
1990: \$1707 million

61. b. **62. c.** **63. d.** **64. a.**

65. $\dfrac{8.64 \times 10^5}{2.16 \times 10^3} = 4 \times 10^2$

$= 400$

66.

Moon to Earth Distance (in miles)	Sun to Earth Distance (in miles)	
	Minimum 9.15×10^7	*Maximum* 9.45×10^7
Minimum 2.2×10^5	Ratio $\approx$ 420	Ratio $\approx$ 430
Maximum 2.5×10^5	Ratio $\approx$ 370	Ratio $\approx$ 380

67. No; the ratio of the diameters stays the same (5) while the ratio of the distances decreases to 1 as you move further away.

68. When the ratio of the distances is greater than or equal to the ratio of the diameters, a total eclipse can occur. During the moon's Aphelion, the ratio of the distances is less than 400 and a total eclipse cannot occur.

Chapter TEST

1. $a^2 \cdot a^5 = a^7$

2. $x^0 \cdot x^3 = x^3$

3. $x^{-4} \cdot x^2 = \dfrac{1}{x^2}$

4. $y^{-3} = \dfrac{1}{y^3}$

5. $(b^2)^8 = b^{16}$

6. $(a^{-1})^2 = \dfrac{1}{a^2}$

7. $\dfrac{q^3}{q^6} = \dfrac{1}{q^3}$

8. $(3a)^2(a^{-3}) = \dfrac{9}{a}$

9. $(mn)^2 \cdot m^3 = m^5n^2$

10. $3x^4 \cdot 4x^{-2} \cdot x^3 = 12x^5$

11. $\left(\dfrac{m^3}{mn^2}\right)\left(\dfrac{n}{m}\right)^4 = \dfrac{n^2}{m^2}$

12. $\dfrac{x^{-1}y^2}{xy} \cdot \dfrac{x^2y^3}{y^{-2}} = y^6$

13. $3^4 = 81$

14. $5^{-2} = \frac{1}{25}$

15. $(375^2)^0 = 1$

16. $\frac{5 \cdot 2^5}{2^4} = 10$

17. $\left(\frac{3}{4}\right)^3 \cdot 4^2 \cdot 3^0 = \frac{27}{4}$

18. $(6 \cdot 2)^3 \cdot 6^{-2} = 48$

19. 3,650,000

20. 0.000000005779

21. 2.44×10^9

22. 1.29×10^{-7}

23. $\frac{6.3 \times 10^{10}}{1.2 \times 10^5} \approx 5.3 \times 10^5$

24. $V = \frac{1}{3}hb^2$

$V = \frac{1}{3}(177)(1400)^2$

$V = 115{,}640{,}000$

The volume of the pyramid is 115,640,000 cubic feet.

25. Savings $= 500(1.05)^6$

Savings = \$670.05

Stock $= 500(0.95)^6$

Stock = \$367.55

Sum = 670.05 + 367.55

Sum = \$1037.60

The sum is \$37.60 greater than the value of the original inheritance.

Chapter 9

Quadratic Equations

9.1 Square Roots and the Pythagorean Theorem

Communicating about Algebra

A. $2\sqrt{13} \approx 7.21$

B. $5 - 3\sqrt{2} \approx 0.76$

C. $\dfrac{-3 + \sqrt{(3)^2 - 4(2)(-1)}}{2} \approx 0.56$

$\dfrac{-3 - \sqrt{(3)^2 - 4(1)(-2)}}{2} \approx -3.56$

EXERCISES

1. True

2. a. True; -1
b. True; 0
c. True; the square roots of 25 are 5 and -5.
d. False

3. $\sqrt{25} = 5$
$-\sqrt{25} = -5$
$\pm\sqrt{25} = \pm 5$

4. 8 and -2

5. 9, $\frac{1}{4}$, 0.01

6. $\sqrt{2}$ is irrational. $\frac{144}{99}$ is not a square root of 2. $\frac{7064}{4995}$ is not a square root of 2. An irrational number cannot be represented by a fraction.

7. 8, -8

8. 12, -12

9. None

10. 0

11. $\frac{2}{3}$, $-\frac{2}{3}$

12. $\frac{5}{4}$, $-\frac{5}{4}$

13. 0.4, -0.4

14. 0.5, -0.5

15. -16

16. 7

17. 3.32

18. 11

19. 10

20. -13

21. 6

22. 4.80

23. 6.48

24. 0.87

25. 0.2

26. $-\frac{5}{10}$ or $-\frac{1}{2}$

27. $\frac{9}{18}$ or $\frac{1}{2}$

28. 2.5

29. $-\frac{1}{8}$

30. 5.10

31. $\sqrt{5^2 - 4(4)(1)} = \sqrt{9}$
$= 3$

32. $\sqrt{8^2 - 4(-2)(-8)} = \sqrt{0}$
$= 0$

33. $\sqrt{(-7)^2 - 4(3)(6)} = \sqrt{-23}$ is undefined.

34. $\sqrt{13^2 - 4(12)(3)} = \sqrt{25}$
$= 5$

35. $\dfrac{2 \pm 5\sqrt{6}}{2} \approx 7.12$ and -5.12

36. $\dfrac{3 \pm 4\sqrt{5}}{4} \approx 2.99$ and -1.49

37. $\dfrac{7 \pm 3\sqrt{2}}{-1} \approx -11.24$ and -2.76

38. $\dfrac{5 \pm 6\sqrt{3}}{3} \approx 5.13$ and -1.80

39. $\sqrt{27.04} = 5.2$

40. $\sqrt{12.96} = 3.6$

41. $\sqrt{\dfrac{50.24}{3.14}} = 4$

42. $\sqrt{\dfrac{153.86}{3.14}} = 7$

43. $\sqrt{130{,}000} \approx 360.6$ feet by ≈ 360.6 feet

44. $\sqrt{\dfrac{110{,}000}{25}} \approx 66$ feet

45. $\frac{1}{2}\sqrt{3}(2) = \sqrt{3}$ or ≈ 1.73 inches

46. $\frac{1}{2}(2)\sqrt{3} = \sqrt{3}$ or ≈ 1.73 square inches

47.
$$a^2 + b^2 = c^2$$
$$5^2 + 10^2 = c^2$$
$$25 + 100 = c^2$$
$$c \approx 11.2 \text{ feet}$$

48.
$$\sqrt{7^2 + 12^2} = \sqrt{49 + 144}$$
$$= \sqrt{193}$$
$$\approx 13.9 \text{ feet}$$

49. $\sqrt{360^2 + 45^2} \approx 362.8$ feet

50. $\sqrt{3^2 + 4^2} = 5$ feet

51. Miles

52. Inches

53. $(-3a)^2 = 9a^2$

54. $(7b)^2 = 49b^2$

55. $(2x^2y)^2 = 4x^4y^2$

56. $(3xy^3)^2 = 9x^2y^6$

57. $x = 3$ or -3

58. $y = 4$ or -4

59. $y = 2$

60. $x = 6$ or -6

61. $\sqrt{8} = 2\sqrt{2}$

62. $\sqrt{18} = 3\sqrt{2}$

63. $\sqrt{27} = 3\sqrt{3}$

64. $\sqrt{75} = 5\sqrt{3}$

9.2 Solving Quadratic Equations by Finding Square Roots

Communicating about Algebra

When $t = 3.52$
$h = 1.7536$

When $t = 3.53$
$h = 0.6256$

$$\text{Speed} = \frac{1.7536 - 0.6256}{3.52 - 3.53}$$
$$= \frac{1.128}{0.01}$$
$$\approx 113 \text{ feet per second}$$

EXERCISES

1. **b.** and **d.**

2. $-3x^2 + 5 = 0,\ -3$

3. $\frac{1}{2}x^2 + 9x - 3 = 0,\ \frac{1}{2}$

4. $-x^2 - 8x + 4 = 0, \ -1$

5. $x = \pm\sqrt{17}$

6. $x = 0$

7. No real solution

8. $x = \pm\sqrt{6}$

9. $x = \pm 3$

10. $h = \pm 5$

11. $x = \pm 10$

12. $x = \pm 5$

13. $x = \pm 11$

14. $b = \pm 7$

15. $t = \pm 3$

16. $t = \pm 12$

17. $x = \pm 4$

18. $t = \pm\frac{1}{2}$

19. $s = \pm 4$

20. $x = \pm\frac{5}{9}$

21. $3x^2 + 2 = 56$

$x^2 = 18$

$x \approx \pm 4.24$

22. $7y^2 - 12 = 23$

$y^2 = 5$

$y \approx \pm 2.24$

23. $2x^2 - 5 = 7$

$x^2 = 6$

$x \approx \pm 2.45$

24. $\frac{2}{3}n^2 - 6 = 2$

$n^2 = 12$

$n \approx \pm 3.46$

25. $\frac{1}{2}x^2 + 3 = 8$

$x^2 = 10$

$x \approx \pm 3.16$

26. $4x^2 + 9 = 41$

$x^2 = 8$

$x \approx \pm 2.83$

27. $6s^2 - 2 = 0$

$s^2 = \frac{1}{3}$

$s \approx \pm 0.58$

28. $5a^2 + 10 = 20$

$a^2 = 2$

$a \approx \pm 1.41$

29. $0 = -16t^2 + 64$

$t^2 = 4$

$t = 2$ seconds

30. $0 = -16t^2 + 144$

$t^2 = 9$

$t = 3$ seconds

31. $0 = -16t^2 + 500$

$t^2 = 31.25$

$t \approx 5.59$ seconds

32. $0 = -16t^2 + 600$

$t^2 = 37.5$

$t \approx 6.12$ seconds

33. $A = 6x^2$

$150 = 6x^2$

$x^2 = 25$

$x = 5$ feet

34. $80 = 4\pi r^2$

$r^2 = \frac{20}{\pi}$

$r \approx 2.52$ meters

35. $1736 = -7.75t^2 + 1860$

$7.75t^2 = 124$

$t = 4, \ -4$

During the years 1978 and 1986 there were 1736 million free lunches served.

$1364 = -7.75t^2 + 1860$

$7.75t^2 = 496$

$t = 8, \ -8$

During the years 1974 and 1990 there were 1364 million free lunches served.

36. $19.5 = 0.037t^2 + 10$

$0.037t^2 = 9.5$

$t \approx 16, \ -16$

In 1996 there will be 19.5 thousand motion picture theaters in the United States.

37. $180d^2 = 1.89$

$d^2 = 0.0105$

$d \approx 0.10$

$40d^2 = 1.89$

$d^2 = 0.04725$

$d \approx 0.22$

$85d^2 = 1.89$

$d^2 = 0.222352941$

$d \approx 0.15$

Fluorite: 0.10 mm

Sulfur: 0.22 mm

Wulfenite: 0.15 mm

38. Fluorite is the hardest mineral. Sulfur is the softest mineral. Diamond is the hardest known mineral.

39. $0 = -\frac{27}{10}t^2 + 5$

$t^2 = \frac{50}{27}$

$t \approx 1.36$

It would take about 1.36 seconds for both the hammer and the feather to hit the surface of the moon.

40. $h = -16t^2 + s$ $\quad t^2 = \frac{5}{16}$

$0 = -16t^2 + 5$ $\quad t \approx 0.6$

It would take the hammer about 6 seconds to hit the surface of the earth. No; air resistance would cause the feather to fall to earth more slowly than the hammer.

41. $4(3)^2 + 9(3) - 14 = 49$

42. $4^2 - 4(4) + 9 = 9$

43. $-4(5)(2) = -40$

44. $-16(4)^2 + 4 = -252$

45. $2x - 9 = 7$

$x = 8$

46. $5x - 9 = 11$

$x = 4$

47. $\frac{1}{4}x + 6 = 8$

$x = 8$

48. $\frac{1}{3}x - 4 = -1$

$x = 9$

49. $\sqrt{x} - 1 = 5$

$x = 36$

50. $\sqrt{x} + 3 = 4$

$x = 1$

51.

x	−3	−2	−1	0	1	2	3
y	11	6	3	2	3	6	11

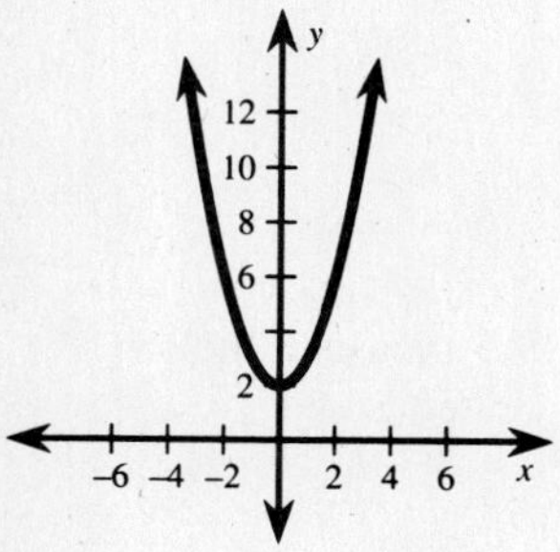

52. $7 = x^2 + 2$

$x^2 = 5$

$x \approx \pm 2.24$

$10 = x^2 + 2$

$x^2 = 8$

$x \approx \pm 2.83$

53. $\begin{cases} x + \quad y = 4 \\ -5 + 2x^2 = 27 \end{cases}$

$2x^2 = 32$

$x^2 = 16$

$x = \pm 4$

$4 + y = 4$

$y = 0$

$-4 + y = 4$

$y = 8$

$(4,\ 0), (-4,\ 8)$

54. $\begin{cases} 2x + y = 4 \\ \frac{1}{3}x^2 + 2 = 5 \end{cases}$

$\frac{1}{3}x^2 = 3$

$x^2 = 9$

$x = \pm 3$

$2(3) + y = 4$

$y = -2$

$2(-3) + y = 4$

$y = 10$

$(3,\ -2), (-3,\ 10)$

Mixed REVIEW

1. $\dfrac{1}{a^4}$

2. $\frac{1}{3}$

3. $p(1 + q) = 2 + q$

$p = \dfrac{2 + q}{1 + q}$

4. $3x - 4y = -20$

$-4y = -3x - 20$

$y = \frac{3}{4}x + 5$

5. $3(-2)^3 + 2(-2) - 2 = -24 - 4 - 2$

$= -30$

6. $3z^0 + 4z^{-1} = 3\left(\frac{1}{4}\right)^0 + 4\left(\frac{1}{4}\right)^{-1}$

$= 3 \cdot 1 + 4 \cdot 4$

$= 19$

7. 5

8. 0

9. 1.299×10^9

10. 4.96×10^{-7}

11. $1 + 2(2) \overset{?}{<} 4(2)$

$5 < 8$

2 is a solution.

12. $3(6) - 6 = 18 - 6$

$= 12 \neq 10$

6 is not a solution.

13. $10x - 4y = -16$

$-4y = -10x - 16$

$y = \frac{5}{2}x + 4$

14. $y = \frac{1}{3}x - 2$

$3y = x - 6$

$-x + 3y = -6$

$x - 3y = 6$

15. $3x(1+x) - x^2 + x = 2x^2 + 4x$

16. $(x^2y^{-3})^{-2} \cdot x^2y^{-4} = x^{-4+2} \cdot y^{6-4}$

$= \dfrac{y^2}{x^2}$

17. $x - 3 = 6$ or $x - 3 = -6$

$x = 9 \qquad x = -3$

18. $-12 \le 2x + 4 \le 12$

$-16 \le 2x \le 8$

$-8 \le x \le 4$

19. $2.2 \times 10^{-6} \cdot 3.6 \times 10^4 = 7.92 \times 10^{-2}$

20. $7.6 \times 10^{-6} \div (2.5 \times 10^8) = 3.04 \times 10^{-14}$

9.3 Graphs of Quadratic Equations

Communicating about Algebra

A.

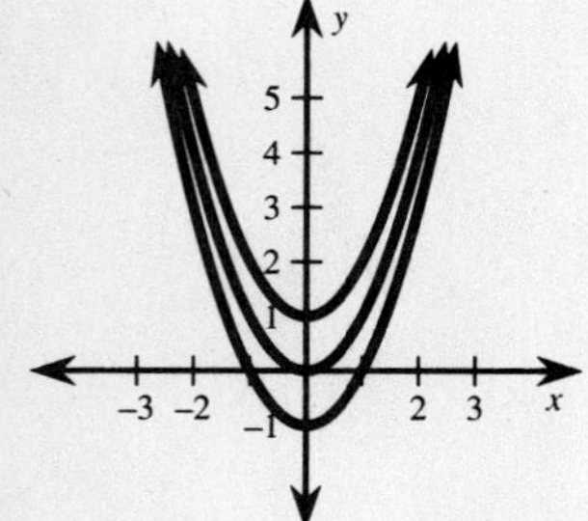

The axis of symmetry is the same, $x = 0$. The y intercepts are different. The graphs all open upward.

B.

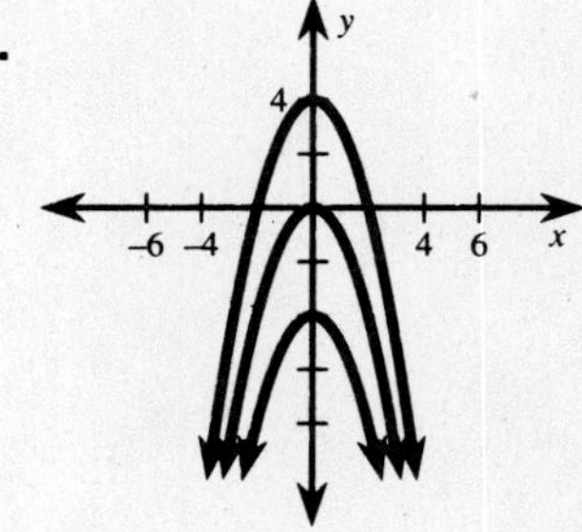

The axis of symmetry is the same, $x = 0$. The y intercepts are different. The graphs all open downward.

EXERCISES

1. $y = -x^2 + 4x - 3$

2. The graph of a quadratic equation is called a parabola.

3. If $a > 0$, the graph opens up.
If $a < 0$, the graph opens down.

4. True; $x = -\dfrac{b}{2a}$ is a vertical line.

5. $x = -\dfrac{b}{2a}$
$= -\dfrac{4}{2 \cdot 2}$
$= -1$

$y = 2(-1)^2 + 4(-1) - 2$
$= -4$

$(-1,\ -4)$

6. $x = -\dfrac{3}{2(-3)}$
$x = \dfrac{1}{2}$

7. Up; (0, 4)
$x = -\dfrac{-0}{2(4)}$
$= 0$
$y = 4$

8. Down; (0, 0)
$x = -\dfrac{0}{2(-5)}$
$= 0$
$y = 0$

9. Down; (0, 0)
$x = -\dfrac{0}{2(-4)}$
$= 0$
$y = 0$

10. Up; $\left(\dfrac{1}{3},\ -\dfrac{1}{3}\right)$
$x = -\dfrac{-2}{2(3)}$
$= \dfrac{1}{3}$
$y = -\dfrac{1}{3}$

11. Down; $\left(-\frac{1}{10}, \frac{201}{20}\right)$

$$x = -\frac{-1}{2(-5)}$$
$$= -\frac{1}{10}$$
$$y = \frac{201}{20}$$

12. Up; $\left(-\frac{1}{4}, \frac{93}{8}\right)$

$$x = -\frac{3}{2(6)}$$
$$= -\frac{1}{4}$$
$$y = 6\left(-\frac{1}{4}\right)^2 + 3\left(-\frac{1}{4}\right) + 12$$
$$= \frac{3}{8} - \frac{6}{8} + \frac{96}{8}$$
$$= \frac{93}{8}$$

13. $x = -\frac{2}{2 \cdot 3}$

$$= -\frac{1}{3}$$
$$y = 3\left(-\frac{1}{3}\right)^2 + 2\left(-\frac{1}{3}\right) + 4$$
$$= \frac{1}{3} - \frac{2}{3} + \frac{12}{3}$$
$$= \frac{11}{3}$$
$$x = -\frac{1}{3},\ \left(-\frac{1}{3}, \frac{11}{3}\right)$$

14. $x = -\frac{3}{2 \cdot 2}$

$$= -\frac{3}{4}$$
$$y = 2\left(-\frac{3}{4}\right)^2 + 3\left(-\frac{3}{4}\right) + 6$$
$$= \frac{9}{8} - \frac{18}{8} + \frac{48}{8}$$
$$= \frac{39}{8}$$
$$x = -\frac{3}{4},\ \left(-\frac{3}{4}, \frac{39}{8}\right)$$

15. $x = -\frac{-4}{2(-4)}$

$$= -\frac{1}{2}$$
$$y = -4\left(-\frac{1}{2}\right)^2 - 4\left(-\frac{1}{2}\right) + 8$$
$$= -1 + 2 + 8$$
$$= 9$$
$$x = -\frac{1}{2},\ \left(-\frac{1}{2}, 9\right)$$

16. $x = -\frac{-9}{2 \cdot 3}$

$$= \frac{3}{2}$$
$$y = 3\left(\frac{3}{2}\right)^2 - 9\left(\frac{3}{2}\right) - 12$$
$$= \frac{27}{4} - \frac{54}{4} - \frac{48}{4}$$
$$= -\frac{75}{4}$$
$$x = \frac{3}{2},\ \left(\frac{3}{2}, -\frac{75}{4}\right)$$

17. $x = -\frac{7}{2 \cdot 2}$

$$= -\frac{7}{4}$$
$$y = 2\left(-\frac{7}{4}\right)^2 + 7\left(-\frac{7}{4}\right) - 21$$
$$= \frac{49}{8} - \frac{98}{8} - \frac{168}{8}$$
$$= -\frac{217}{8}$$
$$x = -\frac{7}{4},\ \left(-\frac{7}{4}, -\frac{217}{8}\right)$$

18. $x = -\frac{4}{2(-1)}$

$$= 2$$
$$y = -(2)^2 + 4 \cdot 2 + 16$$
$$= -4 + 8 + 16$$
$$= 20$$
$$x = 2,\ (2,\ 20)$$

19. $x = -\dfrac{1}{2 \cdot 1}$

$= -\dfrac{1}{2}$

$y = \left(-\dfrac{1}{2}\right)^2 - \dfrac{1}{2} + 2$

$= \dfrac{1}{4} - \dfrac{2}{4} + \dfrac{8}{4}$

$= \dfrac{7}{4}$

$\left(-\dfrac{1}{2}, \dfrac{7}{4}\right)$

20. $x = -\dfrac{2}{2(-1)}$

$= 1$

$y = -1^2 + 2(1) - 1$

$= 0$

$(1, 0)$

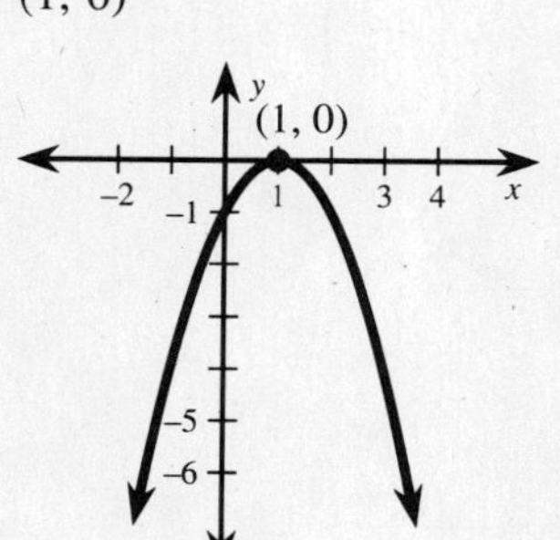

21. $x = -\dfrac{6}{2(-2)}$

$= \dfrac{3}{2}$

$y = -2\left(\dfrac{3}{2}\right)^2 + 6\left(\dfrac{3}{2}\right) - 9$

$= -\dfrac{9}{2} + \dfrac{18}{2} - \dfrac{18}{2}$

$= -\dfrac{9}{2}$

$\left(\dfrac{3}{2}, -\dfrac{9}{2}\right)$

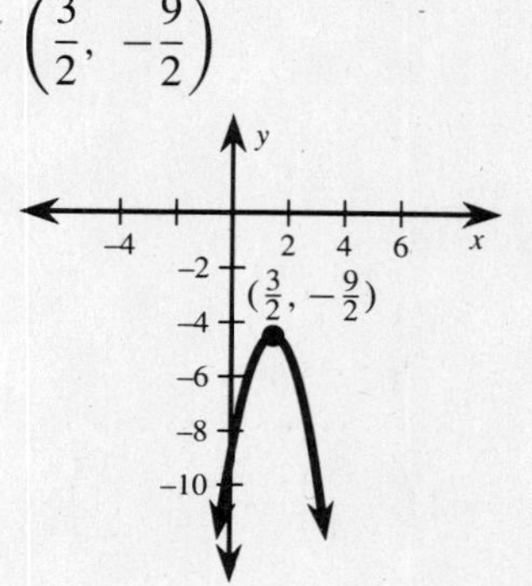

22. $x = -\dfrac{-3}{2 \cdot 2}$

$= \dfrac{3}{4}$

$y = 2\left(\dfrac{3}{4}\right)^2 - 3\left(\dfrac{3}{4}\right) + 4$

$= \dfrac{9}{8} - \dfrac{18}{8} + \dfrac{32}{8}$

$= \dfrac{23}{8}$

$\left(\dfrac{3}{4}, \dfrac{23}{8}\right)$

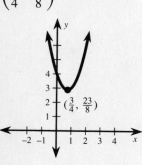

23. $x = -\dfrac{-3}{2 \cdot 6}$

$= \dfrac{1}{4}$

$y = 6\left(\dfrac{1}{4}\right)^2 - 3\left(\dfrac{1}{4}\right) + 4$

$= \dfrac{3}{8} - \dfrac{6}{8} + \dfrac{32}{8}$

$= \dfrac{29}{8}$

$\left(\dfrac{1}{4}, \dfrac{29}{8}\right)$

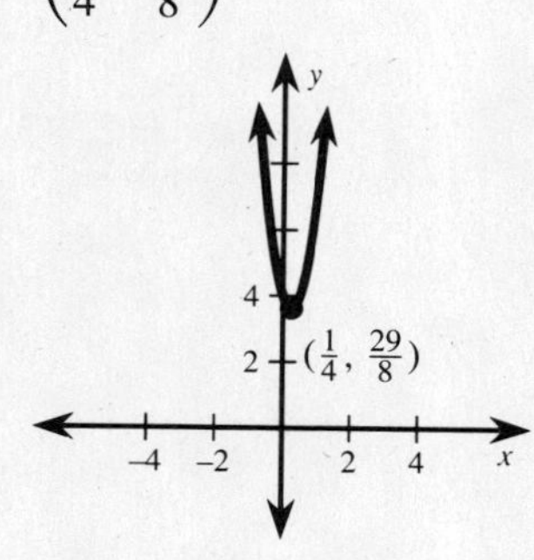

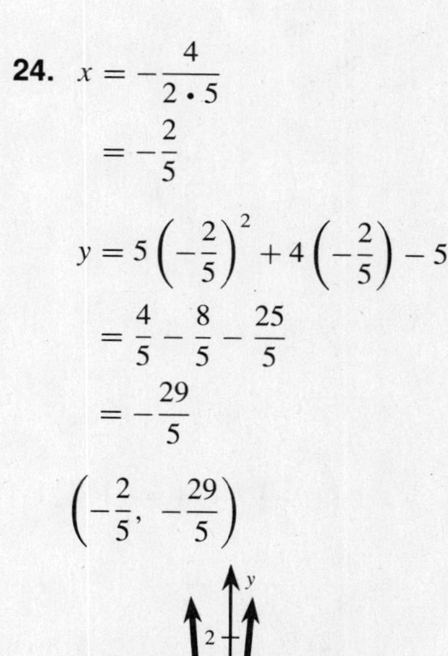

24. $x = -\dfrac{4}{2 \cdot 5}$

$= -\dfrac{2}{5}$

$y = 5\left(-\dfrac{2}{5}\right)^2 + 4\left(-\dfrac{2}{5}\right) - 5$

$= \dfrac{4}{5} - \dfrac{8}{5} - \dfrac{25}{5}$

$= -\dfrac{29}{5}$

$\left(-\dfrac{2}{5}, -\dfrac{29}{5}\right)$

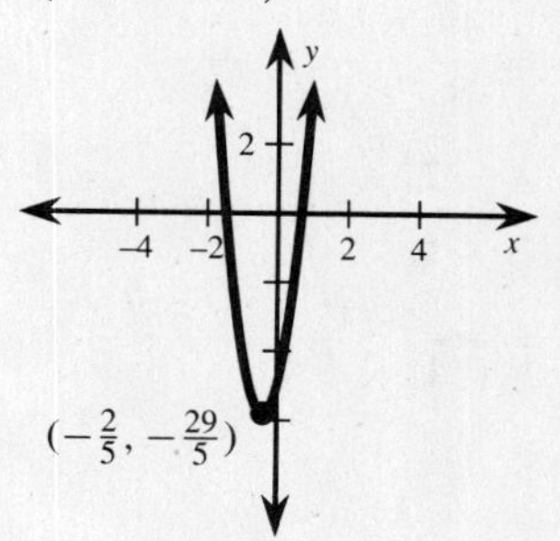

25. $x = -\dfrac{-1}{2 \cdot 4}$

$= \dfrac{1}{8}$

$y = 4\left(\dfrac{1}{8}\right)^2 - \dfrac{1}{8} + 6$

$= \dfrac{1}{16} - \dfrac{2}{16} + \dfrac{96}{16}$

$= \dfrac{95}{16}$

$\left(\dfrac{1}{8}, \dfrac{95}{16}\right)$

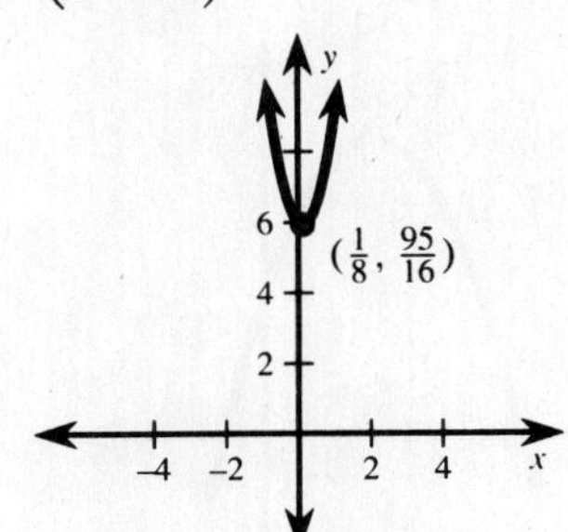

26. $x = -\dfrac{-1}{2(-3)}$

$= -\dfrac{1}{6}$

$y = -3\left(-\dfrac{1}{6}\right)^2 - \left(-\dfrac{1}{6}\right) + 7$

$= -\dfrac{1}{12} + \dfrac{2}{12} + \dfrac{84}{12}$

$= \dfrac{85}{12}$

$\left(-\dfrac{1}{6}, \dfrac{85}{12}\right)$

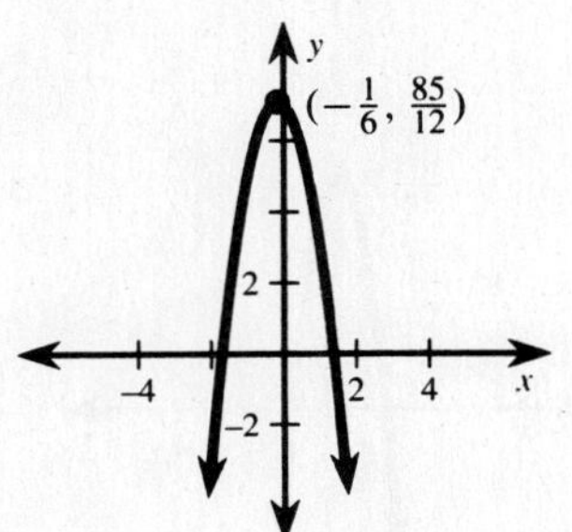

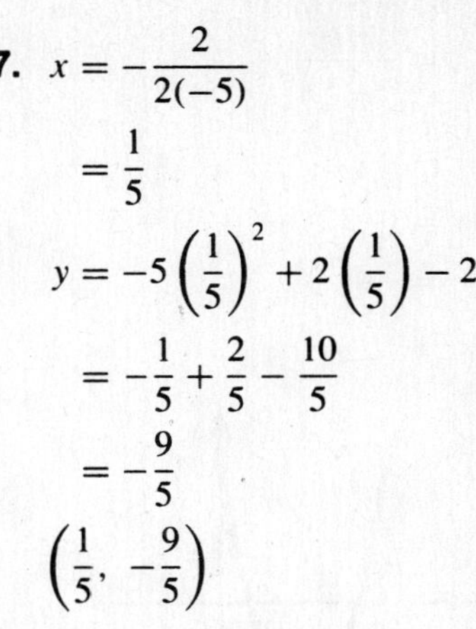

27. $x = -\dfrac{2}{2(-5)}$

$= \dfrac{1}{5}$

$y = -5\left(\dfrac{1}{5}\right)^2 + 2\left(\dfrac{1}{5}\right) - 2$

$= -\dfrac{1}{5} + \dfrac{2}{5} - \dfrac{10}{5}$

$= -\dfrac{9}{5}$

$\left(\dfrac{1}{5}, -\dfrac{9}{5}\right)$

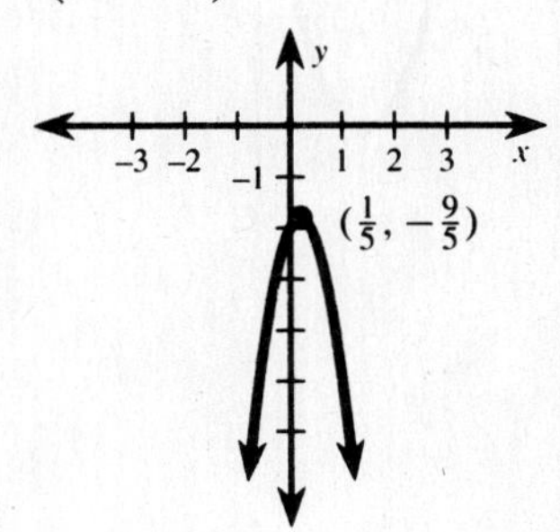

28. $x = -\dfrac{-4}{2 \cdot 6}$

$= \dfrac{1}{3}$

$y = 6\left(\dfrac{1}{3}\right)^2 - 4\left(\dfrac{1}{3}\right) - 1$

$= \dfrac{2}{3} - \dfrac{4}{3} - \dfrac{3}{3}$

$= -\dfrac{5}{3}$

$\left(\dfrac{1}{3}, -\dfrac{5}{3}\right)$

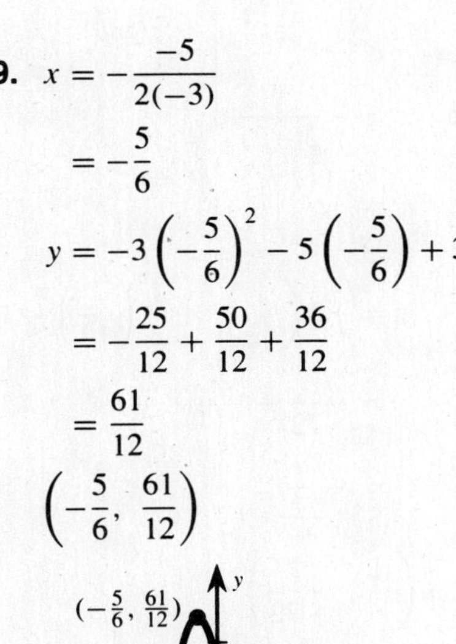

29. $x = -\dfrac{-5}{2(-3)}$

$= -\dfrac{5}{6}$

$y = -3\left(-\dfrac{5}{6}\right)^2 - 5\left(-\dfrac{5}{6}\right) + 3$

$= -\dfrac{25}{12} + \dfrac{50}{12} + \dfrac{36}{12}$

$= \dfrac{61}{12}$

$\left(-\dfrac{5}{6}, \dfrac{61}{12}\right)$

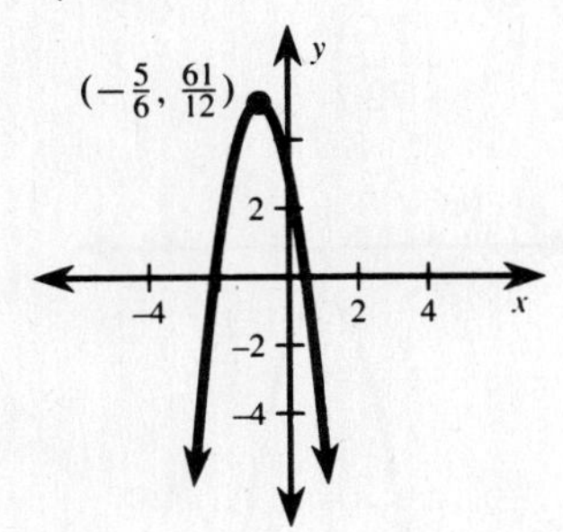

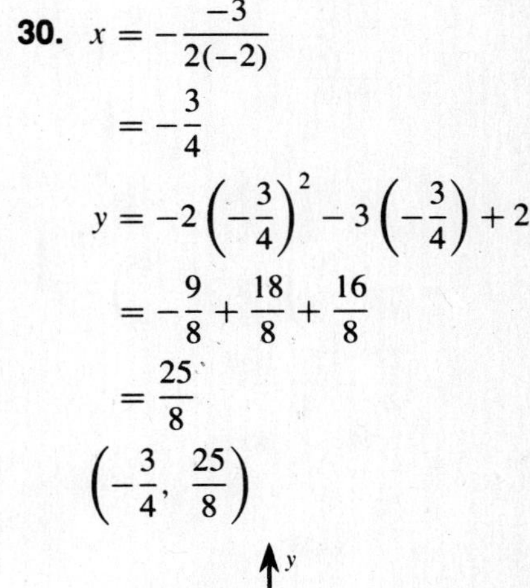

30. $x = -\dfrac{-3}{2(-2)}$

$= -\dfrac{3}{4}$

$y = -2\left(-\dfrac{3}{4}\right)^2 - 3\left(-\dfrac{3}{4}\right) + 2$

$= -\dfrac{9}{8} + \dfrac{18}{8} + \dfrac{16}{8}$

$= \dfrac{25}{8}$

$\left(-\dfrac{3}{4}, \dfrac{25}{8}\right)$

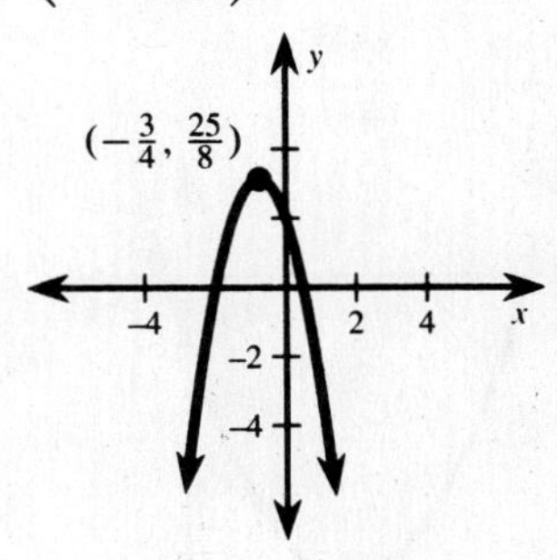

31. $x = -\dfrac{6}{2 \cdot 1}$
$= -3$

$y = (-3)^2 + 6(-3) + 5$
$= -4$

$(-3,\ -4)$

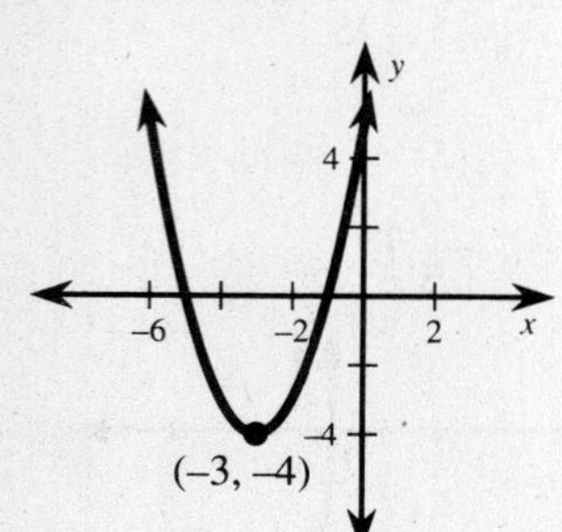

32. $x = -\dfrac{-3}{2(-4)}$
$= -\dfrac{3}{8}$

$y = -4\left(-\dfrac{3}{8}\right)^2 - 3\left(-\dfrac{3}{8}\right) + 6$
$= -\dfrac{9}{16} + \dfrac{18}{16} + \dfrac{96}{16}$
$= \dfrac{105}{16}$

$\left(-\dfrac{3}{8},\ \dfrac{105}{16}\right)$

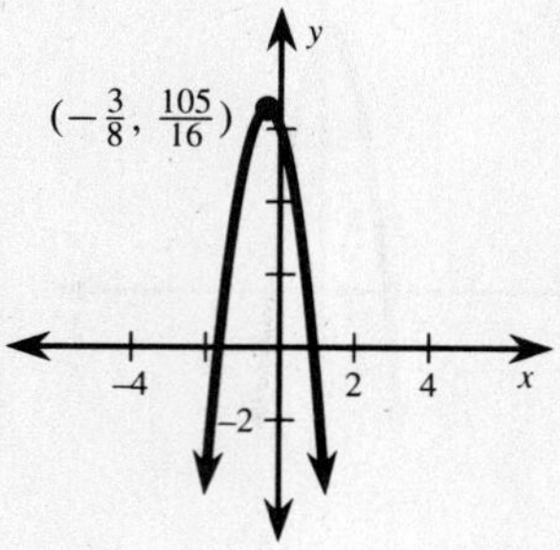

33. $x = -\dfrac{-3}{2\left(-\frac{1}{2}\right)}$
$= -3$

$y = -\dfrac{1}{2}(-3)^2 - 3(-3) + 4$
$= -\dfrac{9}{2} + 13$
$= \dfrac{17}{2}$

$\left(-3,\ \dfrac{17}{2}\right)$

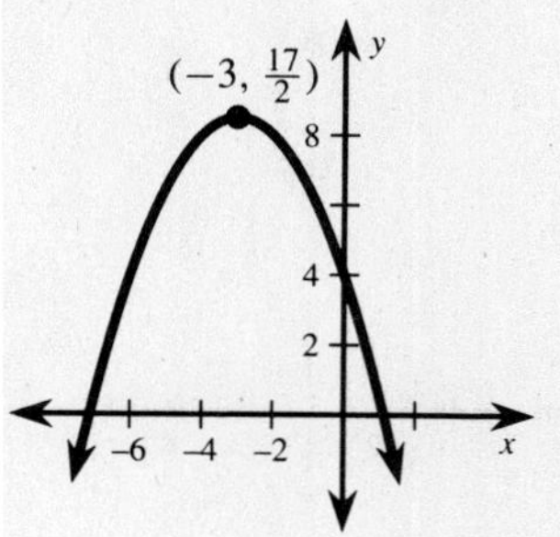

34. $x = -\dfrac{3}{2\left(\frac{1}{3}\right)}$
$= -\dfrac{9}{2}$

$y = \dfrac{1}{3}\left(-\dfrac{9}{2}\right)^2 + 3\left(-\dfrac{9}{2}\right) - 2$
$= \dfrac{27}{4} - \dfrac{54}{4} - \dfrac{8}{4}$
$= -\dfrac{35}{4}$

$\left(-\dfrac{9}{2},\ -\dfrac{35}{4}\right)$

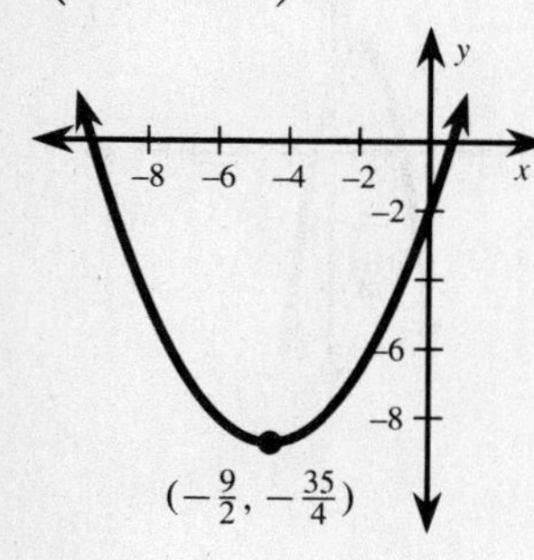

35. $x = -\dfrac{\frac{1}{3}}{2(-2)}$
$= \dfrac{1}{12}$

$y = -2\left(\dfrac{1}{12}\right)^2 + \dfrac{1}{3}\left(\dfrac{1}{12}\right) - 1$
$= -\dfrac{1}{72} + \dfrac{2}{72} - \dfrac{72}{72}$
$= -\dfrac{71}{72}$

$\left(\dfrac{1}{12},\ -\dfrac{71}{72}\right)$

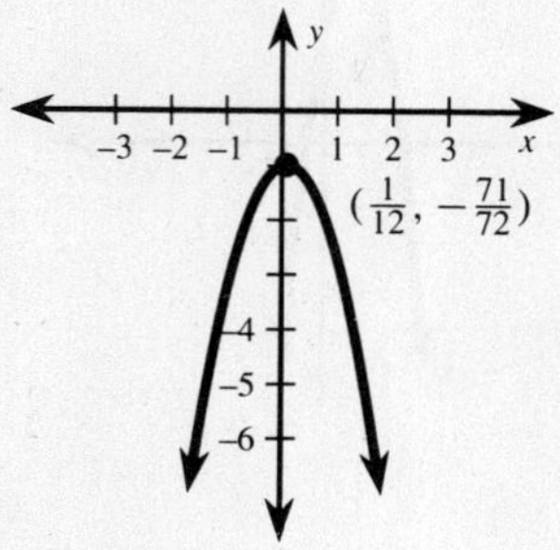

36. $x = -\dfrac{-\frac{1}{2}}{2 \cdot 3}$
$= \dfrac{1}{12}$

$y = 3\left(\dfrac{1}{12}\right)^2 - \dfrac{1}{2}\left(\dfrac{1}{12}\right) + 4$
$= \dfrac{1}{48} - \dfrac{2}{48} + \dfrac{192}{48}$
$= \dfrac{191}{48}$

$\left(\dfrac{1}{12},\ \dfrac{191}{48}\right)$

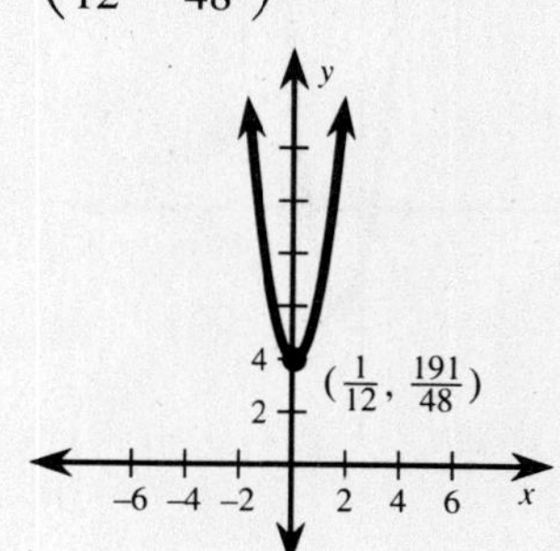

37. No; at 72 feet, the 50° shot is on the ground while the 45° shot is in the air; at 72.8 feet, the 40° shot is on the ground while the 45° shot is in the air.

38. $35° : x = -\dfrac{0.70}{2(-0.06)} = 5.8$ radius $\approx$ 12 feet

height $\approx$ 2.5 feet

$60° : x = -\dfrac{1.73}{2(-0.16)} = 5.4$ radius $\approx$ 11 feet

height $\approx$ 5.2 feet

$75° : x = -\dfrac{3.73}{2(-0.6)} = 3.1$ radius $\approx$ 6 feet

height $\approx$ 6.3 feet

39. $x = \dfrac{-1}{2(-0.08)} = 6.25$ radius $\approx$ 13 feet

height $\approx$ 3.6 feet

A 45° angle setting for the sprinkler will cover a greater area.

40. $x = -\dfrac{-2446}{2(167)} \approx 7.3$

During the years 1970 to 1977, the world gold production was decreasing. During the years 1978 to 1990, the world gold production was increasing. The vertex is the point where the decrease changes to an increase.

41. Gold production decreased when the U.S. went off the gold standard.

42. $x = -\dfrac{51.4}{2(-3.1)} \approx 8.3$

Yes; a decrease in consumption of cigarettes began in 1968.

43. $16 + t^2 = 32$
$t^2 = 16$
$t = \pm 4$

44. $s^2 - 40 = -4$
$s^2 = 36$
$s = \pm 6$

45. $2m^2 - 30 = 20$
$m^2 = 25$
$m = \pm 5$

46. $24 = 4n^2 - 12$
$4n^2 = 36$
$n^2 = 9$
$n = \pm 3$

47. $12 + 3a^2 = 2a^2 + 16$
$a^2 = 4$
$a = \pm 2$

48. $6a^2 = 3a^2 + 108$
$a^2 = 36$
$a = \pm 6$

49. **b.**

50. **c.**

51. **f.**

52. **e.**

53. **d.**

54. **a.**

55. $-4\left(\frac{1}{2}\right)(12) = -24$

56. $-4(-2)(7) = 56$

57. $6^2 - 4(6)(1) = 36 - 24$
$= 12$

58. $3^2 - 4(-5)(1) = 9 + 20$
$= 29$

59. $\sqrt{(-10)^2 - 4(8)(2)} = \sqrt{100 - 64}$
$= 6$

60. $\sqrt{(12.1)^2 - 4(6.2)(-4.3)} \approx 15.91$

61.

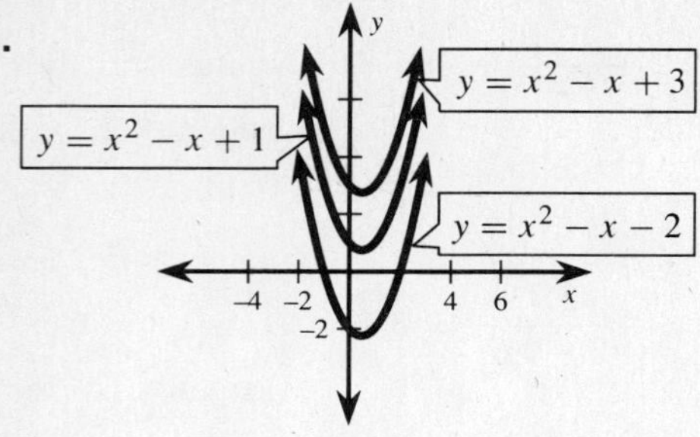

All 3 have their vertex on $x = \frac{1}{2}$. The y-coordinates vary.

62.

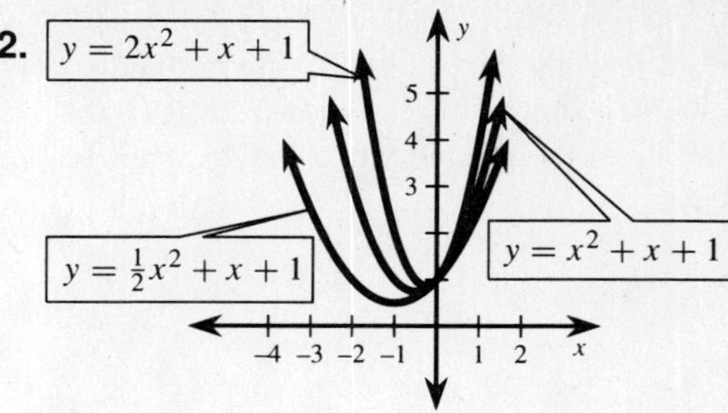

All intercept the y-axis at $y = 1$. The greater the leading coefficient, the narrower the parabola.

63.

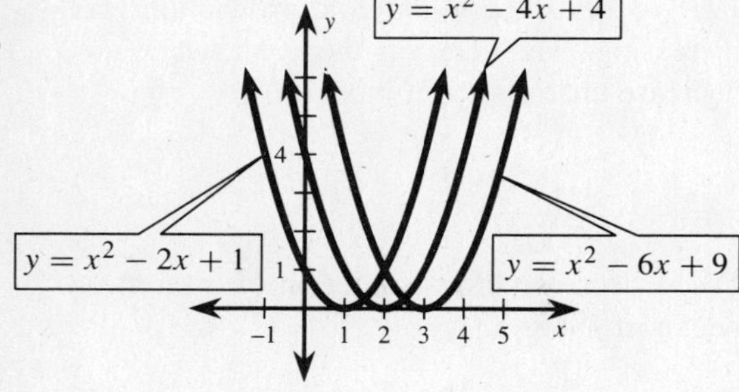

The equations shift to the right. All vertices have a y-coordinate of zero.

64. The value of c shifts the parabola up or down on its axis of symmetry. The greater the value of c, the higher the graph.

65. The value of $|a|$ widens or narrows the parabola. The greater the value of $|a|$, the narrower the graph.

Using a Graphing Calculator

1. 6.41 and 0.26

2. −0.77 and 2.27

3. 0.21 and 4.79

4. −44.16 and 1.16

5. 1.71 and 2

6. 3.71 and −0.43

9.4 The Quadratic Formula

Communicating about Algebra

$0 = -16t + 4000$

$t^2 = 250$

$t \approx 15.8$

The rock would hit the water in approximately 15.8 seconds.

EXERCISES

1. False

2. $h = -16t^2 + s$ Height after object is dropped.
$h = -16t^2 + vt + s$ Height after object is thrown.

3. $a = -1$
$b = 9$
$c = 1$

4. $x = \dfrac{-1 \pm \sqrt{1 - 4(1)(-2)}}{2 \cdot 1}$
$= \dfrac{-1 \pm 3}{2}$
$x = \dfrac{-1 + 3}{2} \qquad x = \dfrac{-1 - 3}{2}$
$= 1 \qquad = -2$

5. (1, 0), (−2, 0)

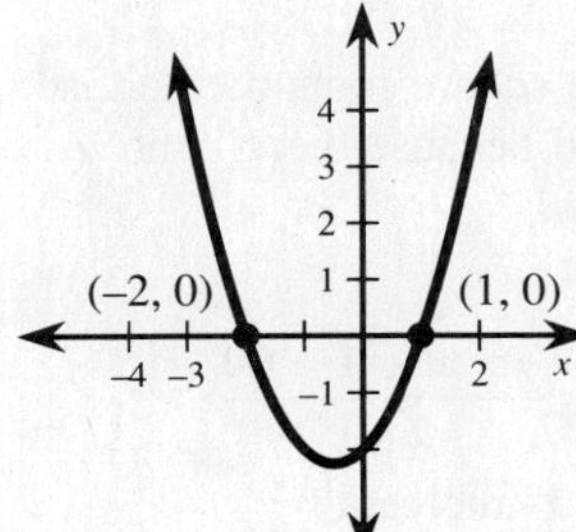

6. The x-intercepts are the solutions to the equation.

7. $-3x^2 + 5x - 9 = 0$

8. $x^2 - 2x + 5 = 0$

9. $x^2 + 3x - 9 = 0$

10. $-7x^2 + 9x - 16 = 0$

11. $(-3)^2 - 4(2)(-1) = 9 + 8$
$= 17$

12. $4^2 - 4(4)(1) = 0$

13. $(-2)^2 - 4(3)(-5) = 4 + 60$
$= 64$

14. $(-11)^2 - 4(1)(30) = 121 - 120$
$= 1$

15. $x = \dfrac{-(-13) \pm \sqrt{(-13)^2 - 4(4)(3)}}{2 \cdot 4}$
$= \dfrac{13 \pm \sqrt{121}}{8}$
$= \dfrac{13 \pm 11}{8}$
$= 3, \ \dfrac{1}{4}$

16. $y = \dfrac{-11 \pm \sqrt{11^2 - 4(3)(10)}}{2 \cdot 3}$
$= \dfrac{-11 \pm \sqrt{1}}{6}$
$= \dfrac{-11 \pm 1}{6}$
$= -\dfrac{5}{3}, \ -2$

17. $x = \dfrac{-7 \pm \sqrt{7^2 - 4(2)(3)}}{2 \cdot 2}$
$= \dfrac{-7 \pm \sqrt{25}}{4}$
$= \dfrac{-7 \pm 5}{4}$
$= -\dfrac{1}{2}, \ -3$

18. $x = \dfrac{-(-6) \pm \sqrt{(-6)^2 - 4(1)(7)}}{2 \cdot 1}$
$= \dfrac{6 \pm \sqrt{8}}{2}$
$= \dfrac{6 \pm 2\sqrt{2}}{2}$
$= 3 + \sqrt{2}, \ 3 - \sqrt{2}$

19. $y = \dfrac{-2 \pm \sqrt{4+40}}{2 \cdot 5}$

$x = \frac{1}{5}\left(-1 + \sqrt{11}\right) \approx 0.46$

or

$x = \frac{1}{5}\left(-1 - \sqrt{11}\right) \approx -0.86$

20. $x = \dfrac{-4 \pm \sqrt{16+24}}{2 \cdot 2}$

$x = -1 + \frac{1}{2}\sqrt{10}$

or

$x = -1 - \frac{1}{2}\sqrt{10}$

21. $x = \dfrac{-20 \pm \sqrt{400 - 120}}{2 \cdot 6}$

$= \dfrac{-20 \pm 2\sqrt{70}}{12}$

$x = -\frac{5}{3} + \frac{1}{6}\sqrt{70} \approx -0.27$

or

$x = -\frac{5}{3} - \frac{1}{6}\sqrt{70} \approx -3.06$

The quadratic formula is used because of the x term.

22. $t^2 = 27$

$t = \pm 3\sqrt{3}$

$\approx \pm 5.20$

The square roots method is used because there is no t term.

23. $x^2 = 625$

$x = \pm 25$

The square roots method is used because there is no x term.

24. $4u^2 - 49 = 0$

$u^2 = \frac{49}{4}$

$u = \pm\frac{7}{2}$

The square roots method is used because there is no u term.

25. $x = \dfrac{-6 \pm \sqrt{36+8}}{2(-2)}$

$x = \dfrac{-6 \pm 2\sqrt{11}}{-4}$

$\frac{3}{2} - \frac{1}{2}\sqrt{11} \approx -0.16$

$\frac{3}{2} + \frac{1}{2}\sqrt{11} \approx 3.16$

The quadratic formula is used because of the x term.

26. $x = \dfrac{-14 \pm \sqrt{196 - 196}}{2 \cdot 1}$

$x = -7$

The quadratic formula is used because of the x term.

27. $x = \dfrac{-2 \pm \sqrt{4 - 60}}{2 \cdot 1}$

No x-intercepts.

28. $x = \dfrac{6 \pm \sqrt{36+28}}{2 \cdot 1}$

$= \dfrac{6 \pm 8}{2}$

$= 3 \pm 4$

$x = 7,\ -1$

29. $x = \dfrac{-1 \pm \sqrt{1+80}}{2 \cdot 1}$

$= \dfrac{-1 \pm 9}{2}$

$x = 4,\ -5$

30. $x = \dfrac{-8 \pm \sqrt{64 - 48}}{2 \cdot 1}$

$= \dfrac{-8 \pm 4}{2}$

$= -4 \pm 2$

$x = -2,\ -6$

31. $x = \dfrac{-1 \pm \sqrt{1+3}}{2 \cdot 1}$

$= \dfrac{-1 \pm 2}{2}$

$x = \dfrac{1}{2}, -\dfrac{3}{2}$

32. $x = \dfrac{-\frac{7}{3} \pm \sqrt{\frac{49}{9} + 8}}{2 \cdot 1}$

$= \dfrac{-\frac{7}{3} \pm \frac{11}{3}}{2}$

$= \dfrac{-7 \pm 11}{6}$

$x = \dfrac{2}{3}, -3$

33. $-16t^2 + 1053 = 0$

$t^2 = 65.8125$

$t \approx \pm 8.1$

The rock would take 8.1 seconds to hit the water. Yes, because the rock would be traveling at 90 mph and could do a lot of damage to whatever it hit.

34. $-16t^2 - 30t + 1053 = 0$

$t = \dfrac{30 \pm \sqrt{900 + 67{,}392}}{2(-16)}$

$t \approx -9.1,\ 7.2$

$8.1 - 7.2 = 0.9$

The rock would hit the water 0.9 seconds sooner.

35. $-16t^2 - 10t + 100 = 0$

$t = \dfrac{10 \pm \sqrt{100 + 6400}}{2(-16)}$

$t \approx -2.8,\ 2.2$

The mouse has 2.2 seconds to escape.

36. $-4.9t^2 - 3t + 30.5 = 0$

$t = \dfrac{3 \pm \sqrt{9 + 597.8}}{2(-4.9)}$

$t \approx -2.8,\ 2.2$

The mouse has 2.2 seconds to escape.

37. $435^2 + 580^2 = c^2$

$c = \pm\sqrt{525{,}625}$

$c = \pm 725$

$\dfrac{725}{500} = 1.45$

It would take 1.45 hours to take a plane flying from Atlanta to Toronto.

38. $d^2 + d^2 = 3000^2$

$d^2 = 4{,}500{,}000$

$d = \pm\sqrt{4{,}500{,}000}$

$d \approx \pm 2121.3$

The submarine is 2121 feet below.

39. $19.2t^2 + 31.6t + 16{,}964.5 = 100{,}000$

$19.2t^2 + 31.6t - 83{,}035.5 = 0$

$t \approx 64.9,\ -66.6$

$1930 + 64.9 = 1994.9$

The population of Mexico will reach 100,000,000 in 1994.

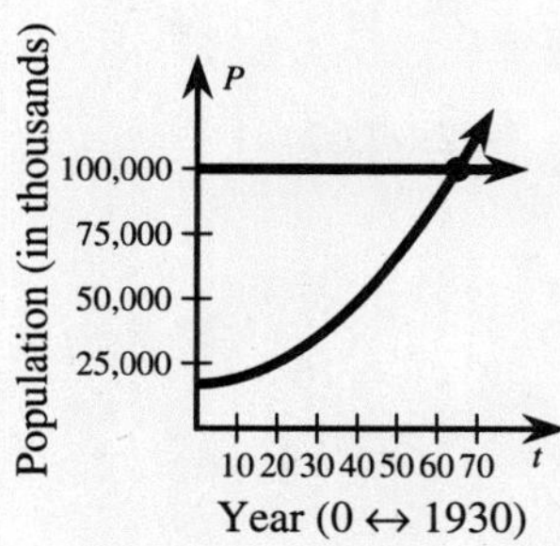

40. $500 = 27.4t^2 - 394.5t + 1831.3$

$27.4t^2 - 394.5t + 1331.3 = 0$

$t \approx 5.3, 9.0$

If $t = 7$ corresponds to 1987, then $t = 9$ corresponds to 1989.
Yes; in 1989 the average salary of a major league baseball player was $500,000.

41. 2

42. 8.25

43. $2 \cdot (2)^2 - 4 \cdot 2 + 9 = 8 - 8 + 9$

$= 9$

2 is a solution.

44. $3(-2)^2 + 3(-2) + 4 = 12 - 6 + 4$

$= 10 \neq 12$

-2 is not a solution.

45. $6^2 - 9(6) + 7 = 36 - 54 + 7$

$= -11 \neq 11$

6 is not a solution.

46. $(5,\ 0), (-9,\ 0)$

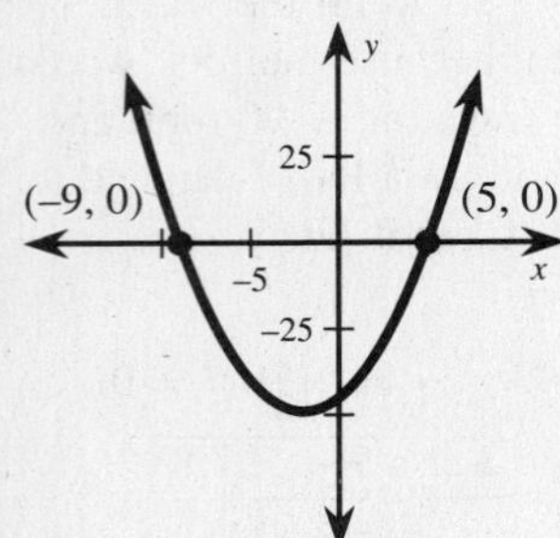

47. $(3,\ 0), (-2,\ 0)$

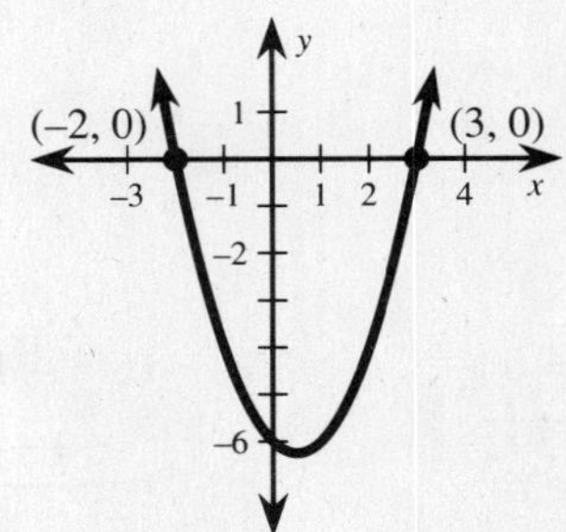

48. $(3,\ 0)\ (\frac{1}{2},\ 0)$

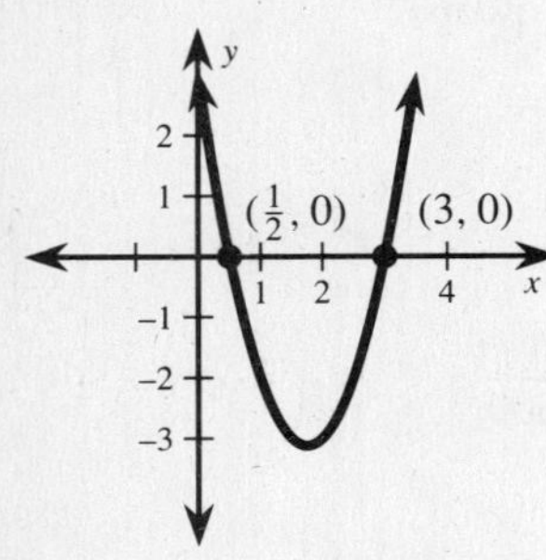

49. The axis $x = 3$ is 2 units from each of the x-intercepts, 1 and 5. The two-part form of the quadratic formula gives $x = 3 \pm 2$, where the "3" refers to the axis and the "± 2" refers to the distance to each x-intercept.

50. The axis $x = -\frac{3}{2}$ is $\frac{9}{2}$ units from each of the x-intercepts, 3 and -6. The two-part form of the quadratic formula gives $x = -\frac{3}{2} \pm \frac{9}{2}$, where the "$-\frac{3}{2}$" refers to the axis and the "$\pm\frac{9}{2}$" refers to the distance to each x-intercept.

Mid-Chapter SELF-TEST

1. ± 8

2. ± 11

3. ± 0.08

4. $\pm \frac{7}{10}$

5. $\pm \frac{1}{9}$

6. ± 0.1

7. 2

8. 1

9. 2.83

10. 1.5

11. 0.32

12. 7.07

13. $\frac{1}{3}x^2 - 27 = 0$

$x^2 = 81$

$x = \pm 9$

14. $25x^2 - 37 = 588$

$x^2 = 25$

$x = \pm 5$

15. $7x^2 - 81 = 31$

$x^2 = 16$

$x = \pm 4$

16. $\frac{3}{4}x^2 - 3 = 51$

$x^2 = 72$

$x \approx \pm 8.49$

17. $x^2 - \frac{1}{4} = 6$

$x^2 = \frac{25}{4}$

$x = \pm \frac{5}{2}$

18. $x^2 + 37 = 199$

$x^2 = 162$

$x \approx \pm 12.73$

19. Vertex: (0, −4)
Intercepts: 2, −2

20. Vertex: (1, 4)
Intercepts: −1, 3

21. Vertex: (0, 2)
Intercepts: 2, −2

22. Vertex: (0, −3)
Intercepts: 1, −1

23. $x = \frac{1 \pm \sqrt{1+120}}{2}$

$x = \frac{1 \pm 11}{2}$

$x = 6, -5$

24. $x = \frac{8 \pm \sqrt{64-64}}{2(-1)}$

$x = \frac{8 \pm 0}{-2}$

$x = -4$

25. $x = \frac{-3 \pm \sqrt{9+8}}{2(-1)}$

$x = \frac{3}{2} \pm \frac{\sqrt{17}}{2}$

$x \approx 3.56, -0.56$

26. $x = \frac{-5 \pm \sqrt{25+8}}{2 \cdot 1}$

$x = -\frac{5}{2} \pm \frac{\sqrt{33}}{2}$

$x \approx 0.37, -5.37$

27. $3^2 + 4^2 = c^2$

$c^2 = 25$

$c = \pm 5$

The length of the hypotenuse is 5 inches.

28. $1400 = 14b^2$

$b^2 = 100$

$b = \pm 10$

The length of an edge of the base is 10 centimeters.

29. $-16t^2 + 30 = 0$

$t^2 = 1.875$

$t \approx \pm 1.37$

The bag would hit the floor in 1.37 seconds.

30. $-16t^2 - 10t + 30 = 0$

$t = \frac{10 \pm \sqrt{100+1920}}{2(-16)}$

$t \approx -1.72, 1.09$

If the bag was thrown down, it would take 1.09 seconds to hit the floor.

9.5 Problem Solving Using the Discriminant

Communicating about Algebra

A. No solution: $c > 4$
One solution: $c = 4$
Two solutions: $c < 4$

B. No solution: The parabola does not touch or cross the x-axis.
One solution: The vertex of the parabola has a y-coordinate of 0 (one x-intercept).
Two solutions: The parabola has two x-intercepts.

EXERCISES

1. $x = \frac{-b \pm \sqrt{b^2 - 4ac}}{2a}$

Discriminant: $b^2 - 4ac$

2. If the discriminant is negative, there is no solution.
If the discriminant is 0, there is one solution.
If the discriminant is positive, there are two solutions.

3. $(-2)^2 - 4(3)(-5) = 4 + 60$

$= 64$

Equation has 2 solutions

4. b.

5. c.

6. a.

7. $3^2 - 4(2)(-2) = 25$

Equation has 2 solutions.

8. $(-2)^2 - 4(1)(4) = -12$

Equation has no solution.

9. $4^2 - 4(-2)(-2) = 0$

Equation has one solution.

10. $1^2 - 4\left(-\frac{1}{2}\right)(3) = 7$

Equation has two solutions.

11. $(-2)^2 - 4(5)(3) = -56$

Equation has no solution.

12. $(-6)^2 - 4(3)(3) = 0$

Equation has one solution.

13. $-16t^2 + 30t - 15 = 0$

$(30)^2 - 4(-16)(-15) = -60$

No, the discriminant is negative.

14. $-16t^2 + 30t - 14 = 0$

$30^2 - 4(-16)(-14) = 4$

Yes, the discriminant would be positive.

15. $(26 - x)x = 148.75$

$x^2 - 26x + 148.75 = 0$

$(-26)^2 - 4(1)(148.75) = 81$

Yes, discriminant is postive so there are two possible solutions.

16. $192 = \frac{1}{2}(4x)(6x)$

$192 = 12x^2$

$x^2 = 16$

$x = \pm 4$

$5x + 5x + 3x + 3x = 16x$

$= 16 \cdot 4$

$= 64$

The perimeter is 64 meters.

17. Chun: $-16t^2 + 13t - 2.6 = 0$

Discriminant: $13^2 - 4(-16)(-2.6) = 2.6$

Chun can dunk. The discriminant is positive.

R.J.: $-16t^2 + 15t - 3.6 = 0$

Discriminant: $15^2 - 4(-16)(-3.6) = -5.4$

R.J. cannot dunk. The discriminant is negative.

18. Chun: $-16t^2 + 12.5t - 2.6 = 0$

Discriminant: $12.5^2 - 4(-16)(-2.6) = -10.15$

Chun cannot dunk.

R.J.: $-16t^2 + 15.5t - 3.6 = 0$

Discriminant: $15.5^2 - 4(-16)(-3.6) = 9.85$

R.J. can dunk.

19. $P = 1.4t^2 + 2.2t + 258$

$t = 30,\ P = 1584$

$t = 35,\ P = 2050$

Increase of 10% per year

$P = 1584(1.1)^5 \approx 2551$

You need to change strategies. In 5 years the profit from the model would be $2,050,000. The board of directors expects a profit of $2,551,000 in 5 years.

20. $P = I - E$

$P = -4.2t^2 + 59.2t + 503$

$t = 0,\quad P = 503$

$t = 5,\quad P = 694$

$t = 7,\quad P = 711.6$

$t = 10,\quad P = 675$

$t = 15,\quad P = 446$

$t = 20,\quad P = 7$

During the first seven years, profits increased yearly. During the next three years, profits started to decrease. During the following ten years, the model suggests that profits will continue decreasing.

21. $195t^2 + 3480t + 41{,}540 = 350{,}000$

$195t^2 + 3480t - 308{,}460 = 0$

$t \approx 31.8, \ -49.7$

$1970 + 31.8 = 2001.8$

Annual spending will reach $350 million between 2001 and 2002.

22. $16^2 + 96t - 5000 = 0$

$t \approx 14.9, \ -20.9$

$1980 + 14.9 = 1994.9$

During 1994–1995, 5 million computers will be used in grades K–12.

23. c. **24.** e. **25.** b. **26.** b.

27. b.
$$x = \frac{2}{2 \cdot 3} = \frac{1}{3}$$

28. c.
$$x = \frac{-2}{2\left(\frac{3}{4}\right)} = -\frac{4}{3}$$

29. d.
$$x = \frac{2}{2\left(\frac{3}{4}\right)} = \frac{4}{3}$$

30. a.
$$x = \frac{-2}{2 \cdot 3} = -\frac{1}{3}$$

31. $32 = 0.005x^2 - 2x + 200$

$0.005x^2 - 2x + 168 = 0$

$x = 280, \ 120$

x-coordinate: 120

32. $0.005x^2 - 2x + 182 = 0$

$x = 260, \ 140$

x-coordinate: 140

33. $(140 - 120)^2 + (18 - 32)^2 = c^2$

$c^2 = 596$

$c \approx \pm 24.4$

The approximate length of the track is 24.4 feet.

34. $\dfrac{24.4 \text{ feet}}{0.23 \text{ second}} \approx 106.1$ feet per second

Mixed **REVIEW**

1. $\dfrac{x^2y}{xy^2} = \dfrac{x}{y}$

2. $\frac{3}{7} + \frac{1}{2} = \frac{6}{14} + \frac{7}{14} = \frac{13}{14}$

3. $|9| - \sqrt{9} = 9 - 3 = 6$

4. $|3(-6) + 2| - \frac{1}{2}(-6) = 16 + 3 = 19$

5. $\frac{6}{7}$

6. a^3

7. $y = |3x - 3| - 6$

$3x - 3 = 0$

$x = 1$

$y = -6$

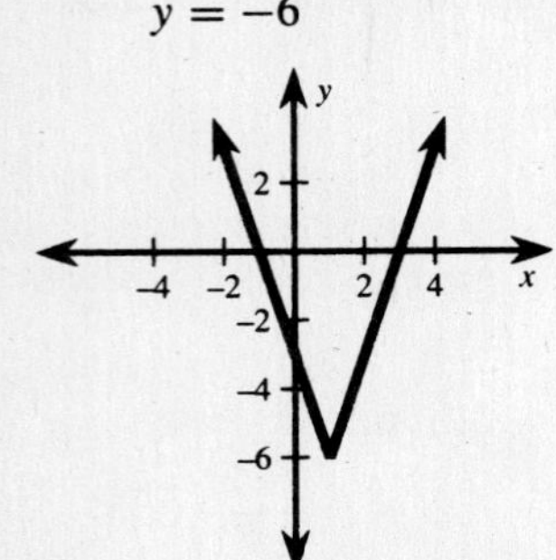

8.

9. $4\left[(3 \div 2) + \frac{1}{2}\right] = 4\left[\frac{3}{2} + \frac{1}{2}\right]$

$= 4(2)$

$= 8$

10. $(3 \cdot 4 - 2)\frac{1}{2} + 2 \cdot 4 = 5 + 8$

$= 13$

11. $2 \cdot 4 + 3 \cdot 6 = 8 + 18$

$= 26$

(4, 6) is a solution.

12. $4 \cdot 0 - 3 \cdot 3 = -9$

$5 \cdot 0 + 1 = 1$

$-9 < 1$

(0, 3) is a solution.

13. $\left|x + \frac{1}{4}\right| < 8$

$-8 < x + \frac{1}{4} < 8$

$-\frac{33}{4} < x < \frac{31}{4}$

14. $\frac{1}{3}(6x - 1) > 2$

$6x - 1 > 6$

$6x > 7$

$x > \frac{7}{6}$

15. $y + 1 = -\frac{1}{2}(x - 3)$

$2y + 2 = -x + 3$

$x + 2y = 1$

16. $y + 6 = 5(x - 8)$

$5x - y = 46$

17. $y - 6 = 0(x + 3)$

$y = 6$

18. $m = \dfrac{-5 - 7}{3 - 3}$

$= \dfrac{-12}{0}$

$x = 3$

19. $m = \dfrac{28 - 17}{44 - 33}$

$= \dfrac{11}{11}$

$= 1$

$y - 28 = x - 44$

$x - y = 16$

20. $m = \dfrac{-3 + 5}{-8 + 5}$

$= -\dfrac{2}{3}$

$y + 3 = -\dfrac{2}{3}(x + 8)$

$3y + 9 = -2x - 16$

$2x + 3y = -25$

9.6 Graphing Quadratic Inequalities

Communicating about Algebra

$108 - 4(13.5) = 54$

$13.5 \times 13.5 \times 54$ inches

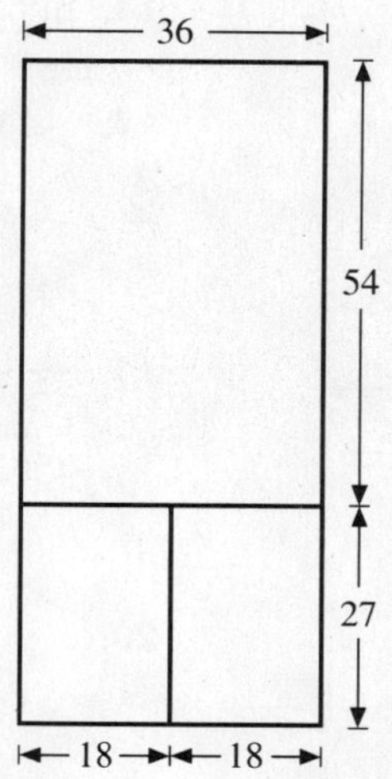

EXERCISES

1. 1. Sketch the graph of the parabola.

2. Test a point inside and outside the ∪-shape.

3. Shade the area that contains the point that is a solution.

2.

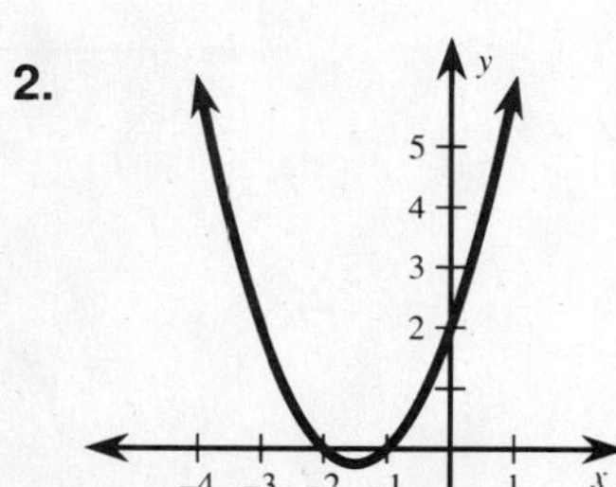

3. $(-2,\ 2), (0,\ 0)$

$2 \overset{?}{\leq} 4 - 6 + 2 \qquad 0 \overset{?}{\leq} 0 + 0 + 2$

$2 \not\leq 0 \qquad 0 \leq 2$

Points vary; (0, 0) is a solution.

4.

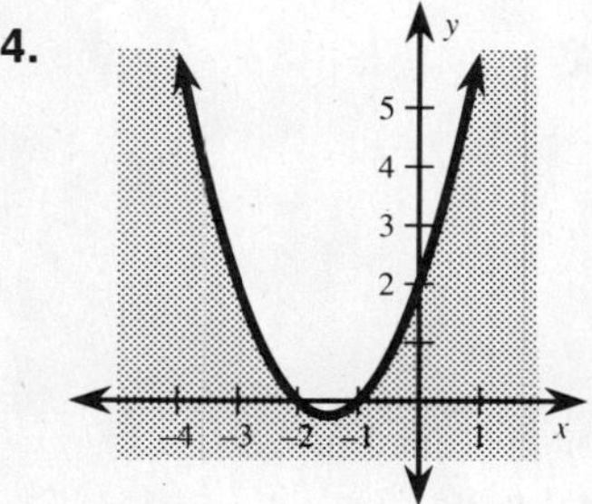

5.

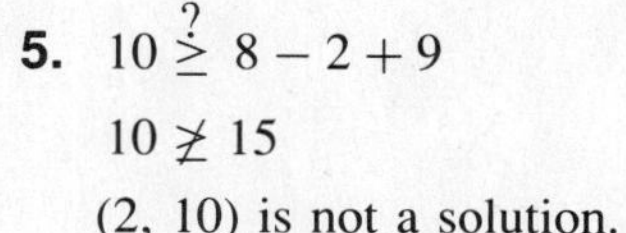

$10 \overset{?}{\geq} 8 - 2 + 9$

$10 \not\geq 15$

(2, 10) is not a solution.

6. $-60 \overset{?}{>} 4 \cdot 144 - 64 \cdot 12 + 115$

$-60 > -77$

(12, −60) is a solution.

7. $6 \stackrel{?}{<} 1 - 6 + 12$

$6 < 7$

$(-1,\ 6)$ is a solution.

8. $16 \stackrel{?}{\geq} 1 + 8 + 9$

$16 \not\geq 18$

$(-1,\ 16)$ is not a solution.

9. **d.**

10. **f.**

11. **a.**

12. **e.**

13. **c.**

14. **b.**

15.

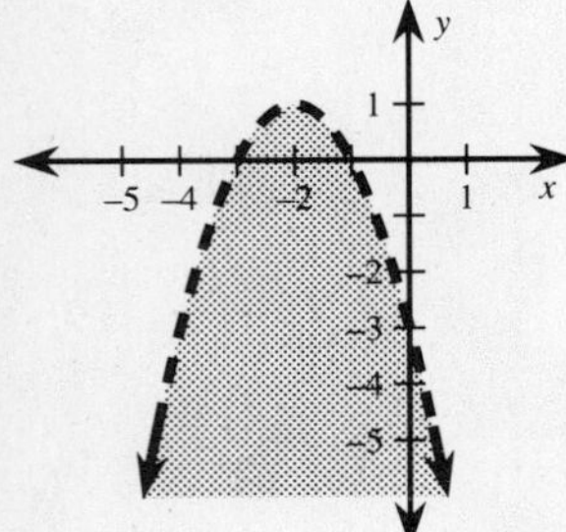

16.

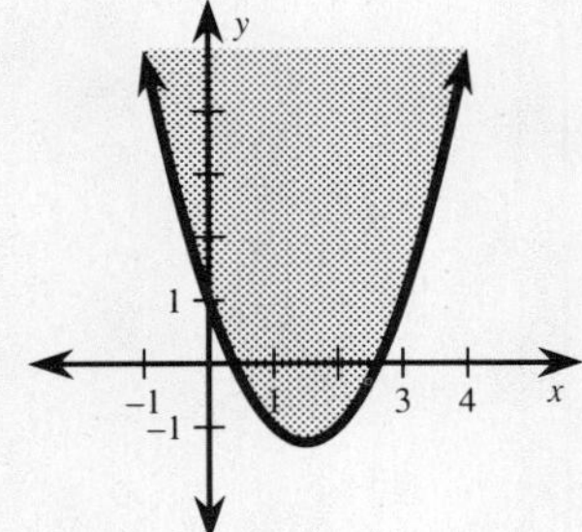

17.

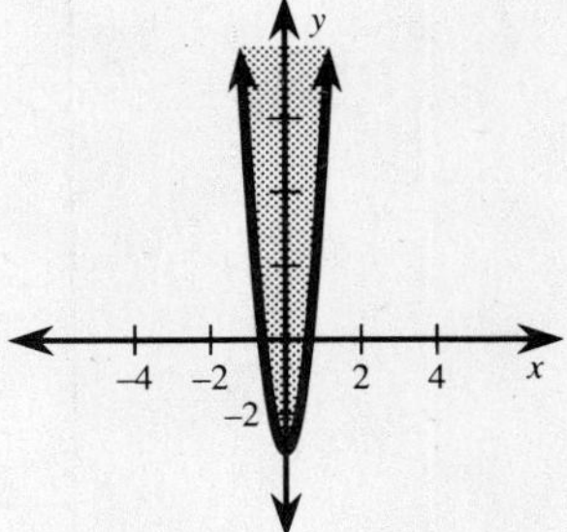

18.

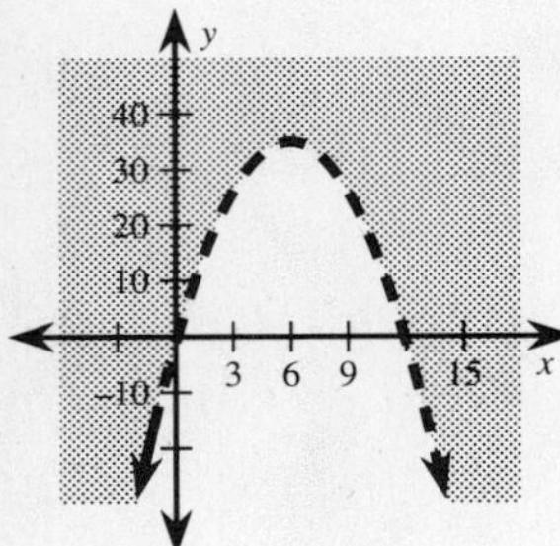

19.

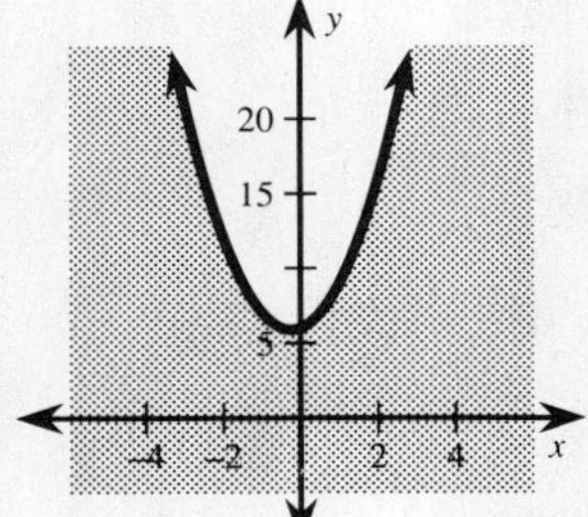

20.

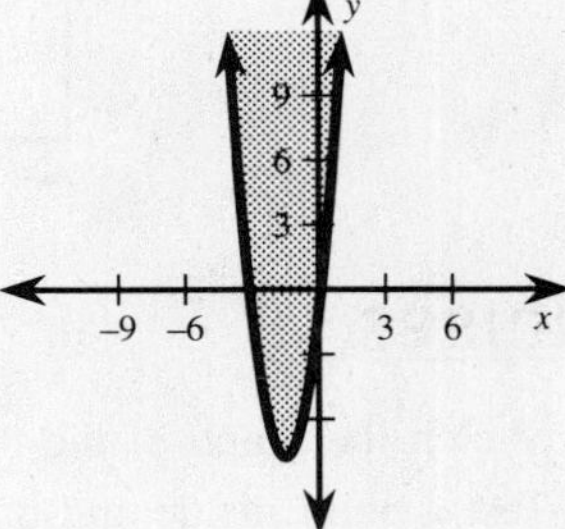

21.

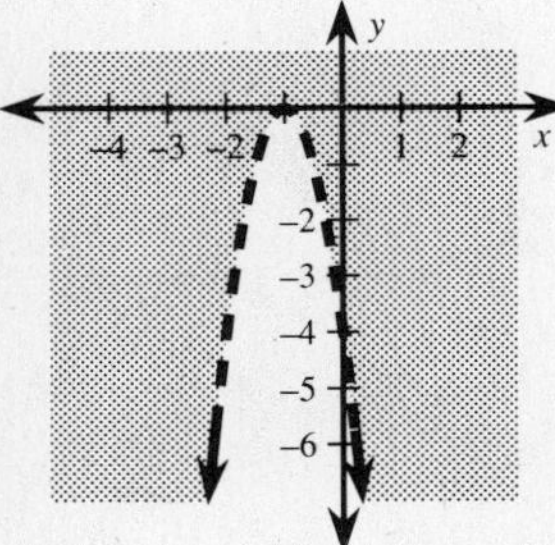

22.

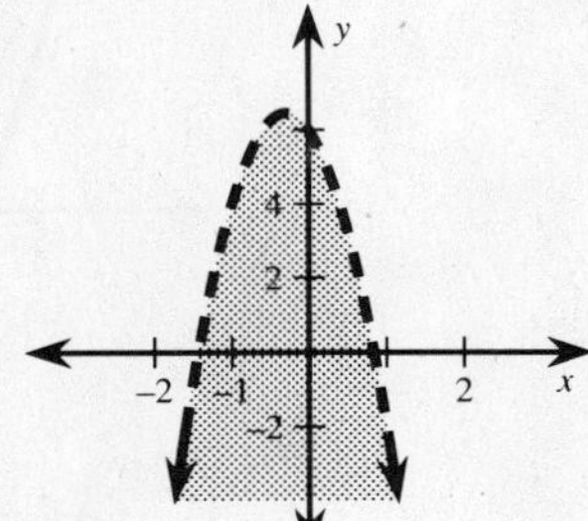

23.

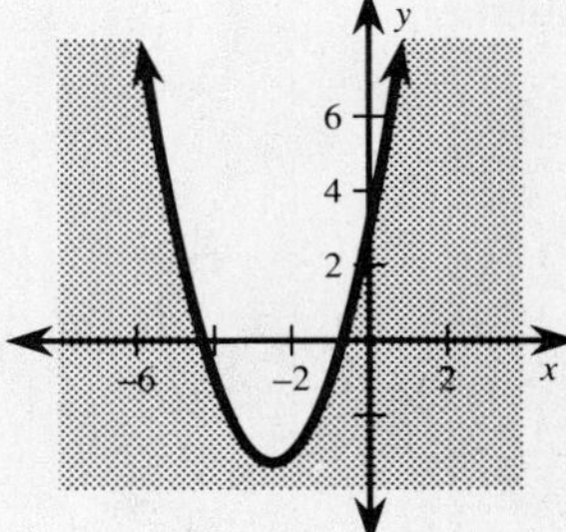

24. $y = 40 + 13{,}000(2)^2$

$= 52{,}040$

The wholesale price for the diamond was \$52,040. Your aunt paid more than the wholesale price.

25. **b.** $y < 31 + 10{,}160x^2$

$31 + 10{,}160\left(2\frac{1}{2}\right)^2 = 63{,}531$

The grade of the diamond is VVS2.

26. $T_a = 27 + 8670(3)^2 + 20 + 6660(1)^2$
$= 84{,}737$

$T_b = 40 + 13{,}000(2)^2 + 20 + 6660(2)^2$
$= 78{,}700$

$T_c = 40 + 13{,}000(1.5)^2 + 2[27 + 8670(1.25)^2]$
$= 56{,}437.75$

a. The value is \$84,737 compared to \$78,700 and \$56,437.75.

27. $y = 40 + 13{,}000(125)^2$
$y = 203{,}125{,}040$
$\approx \$200$ million

28. a. $y > \frac{1}{24}x^2 + 1$

29. a. $N < \frac{1}{2}t^2 + 46$

The number in North and South America will be less than the number in the world.

30. b. $N > \frac{1}{2}t^2 + 46$

$\frac{1}{2}(30)^2 + 46 = 496$

$2.25 \times 225 = 506.25$

No; if it were true, there would have been 506 million in the U.S. alone. The world, according to the model, had 496 million sets.

31. $9x - 20 > 61$
$9x > 81$
$x > 9$

32. $2x + 9 < 3$
$2x < -6$
$x < -3$

33. $3x + 5 \le 17$
$3x \le 12$
$x \le 4$

34. $\frac{1}{2}x - 2 \ge 6$
$\frac{1}{2}x \ge 8$
$x \ge 16$

35.

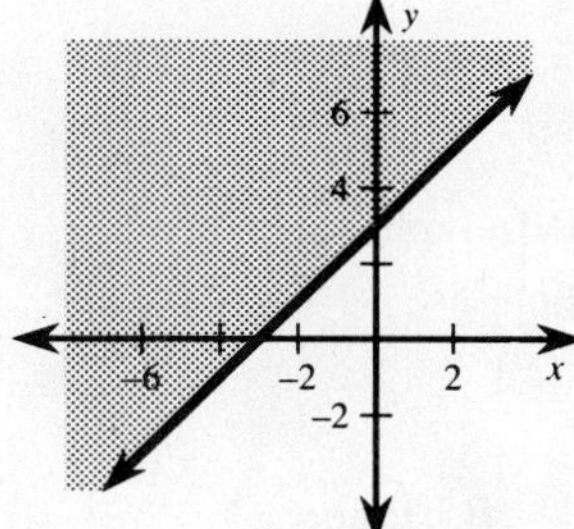

36.

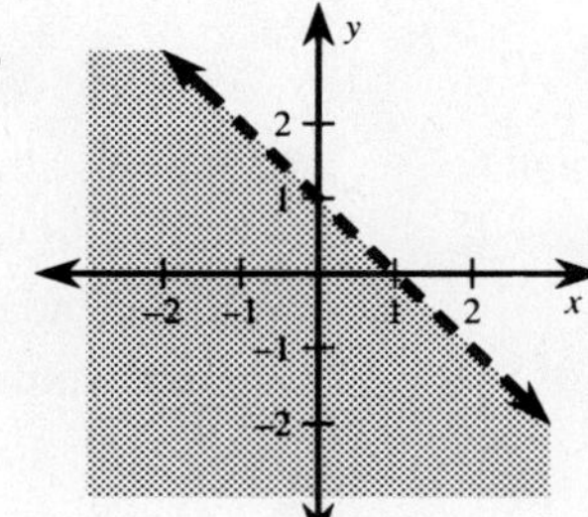

37.

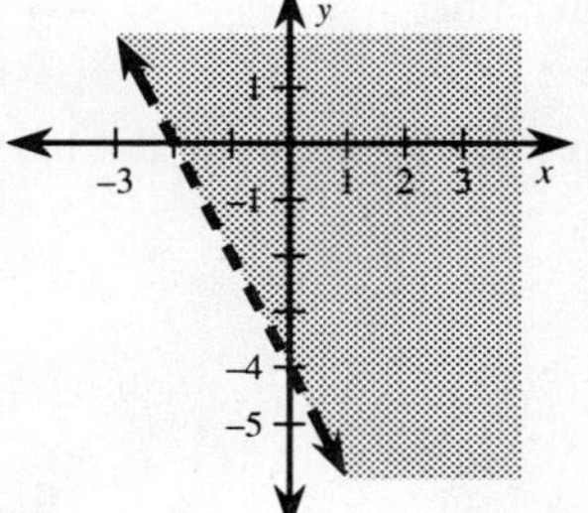

38.

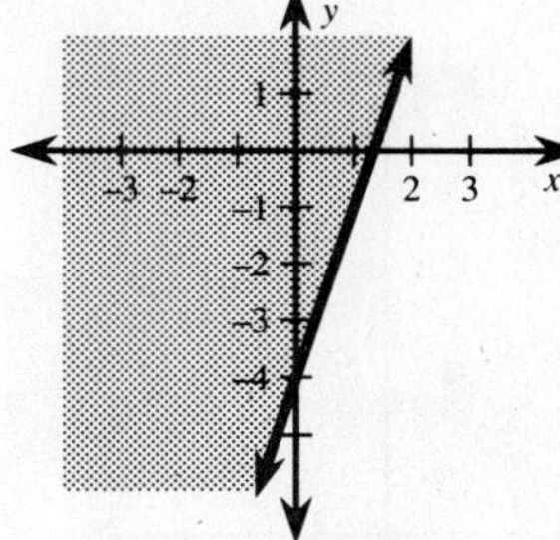

39.

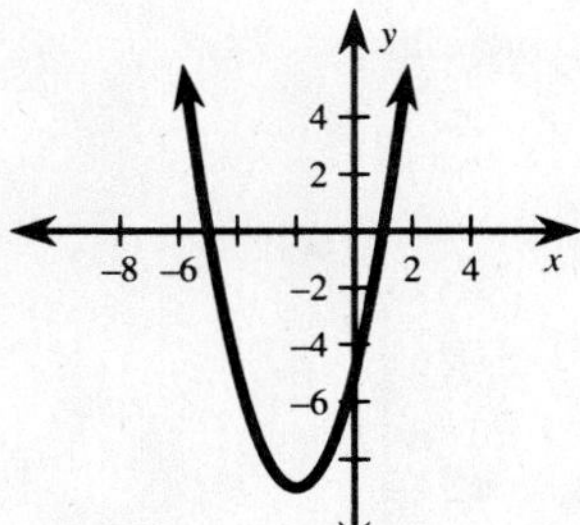

40.

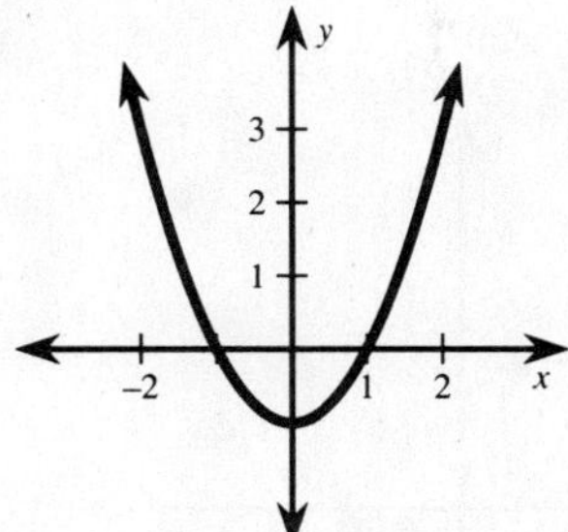

41.

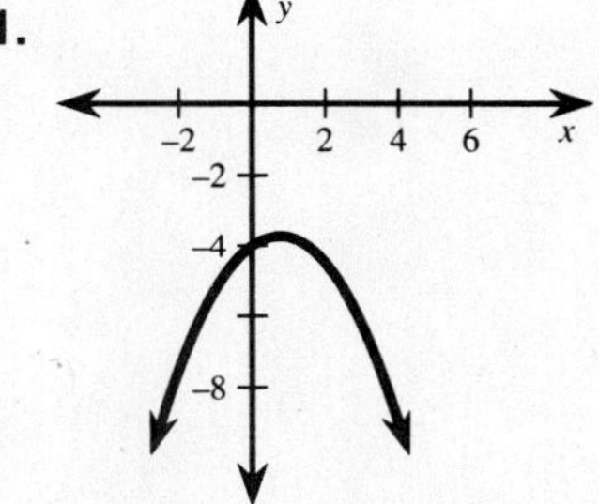

42.

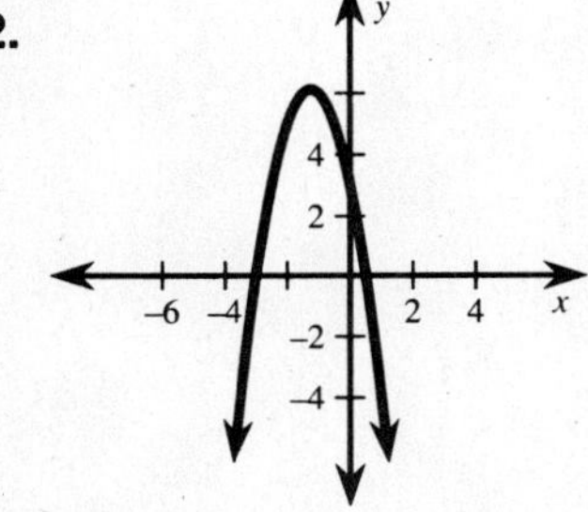

43.

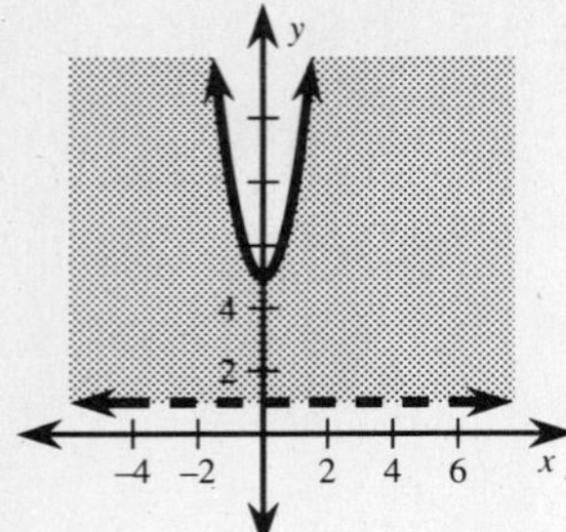

44.

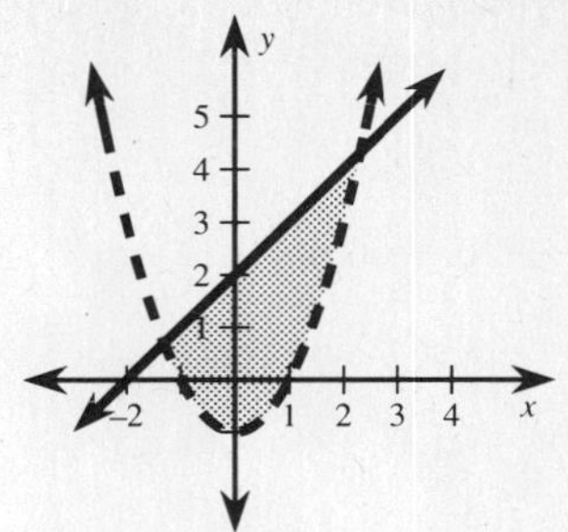

9.7 Exploring Data: Comparing Models

Communicating about Algebra

$A = \pi(r)(r+1)$

EXERCISES

1. Linear: $y = x + 1$
Absolute-value: $y = |x + 1| + 1$
Exponential: $y = 3(1.2)^x$
Quadratic: $y = x^2 - 3x - 4$

2. A quadratic model has a ∪-shaped graph.

3. An absolute-value model has a V-shaped graph.

4. Linear: straight line
Absolute-value: V-shaped graph
Exponential: curved graph
Quadratic: ∪-shaped graph

5. Quadratic

6. Exponential

7. Absolute-value

8. Linear

9. Quadratic

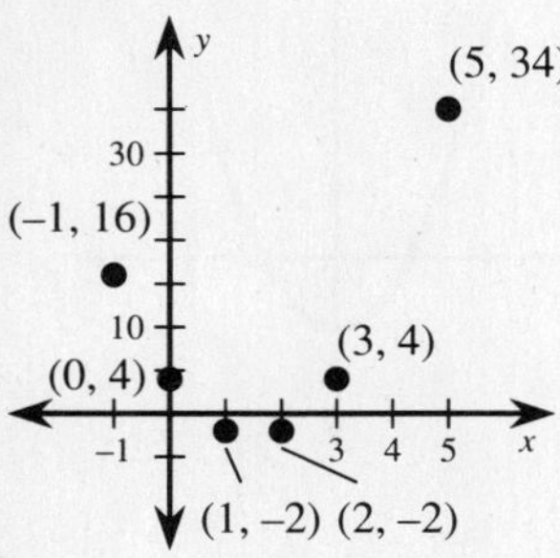

10. Exponential

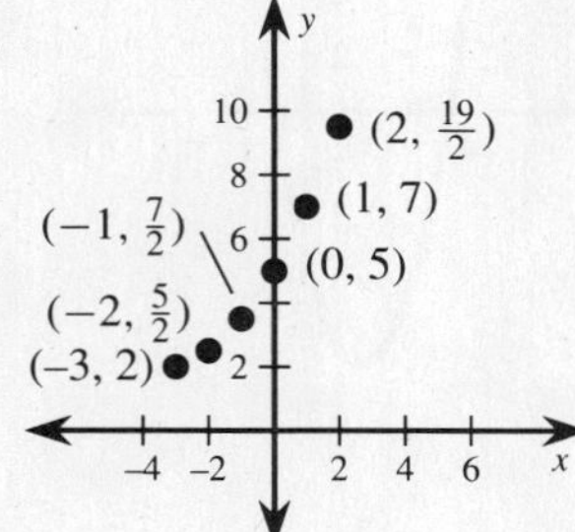

11. Linear

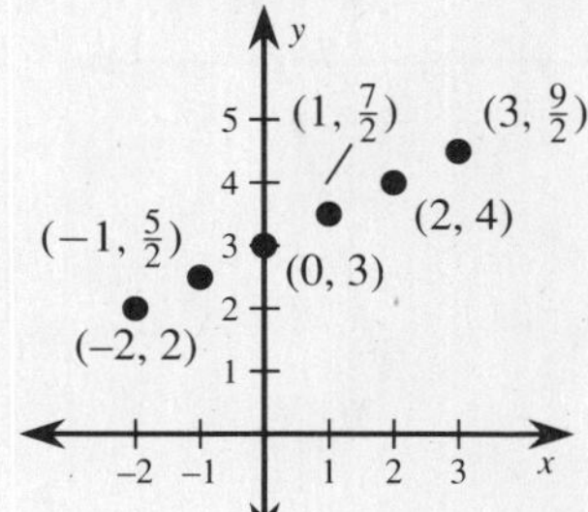

12. Absolute-value

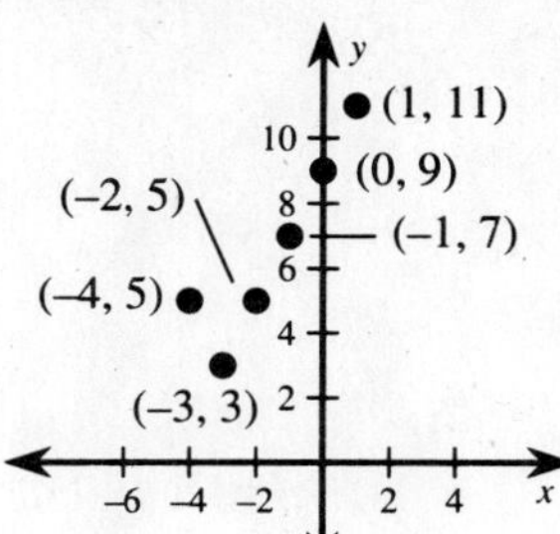

13. Quadratic

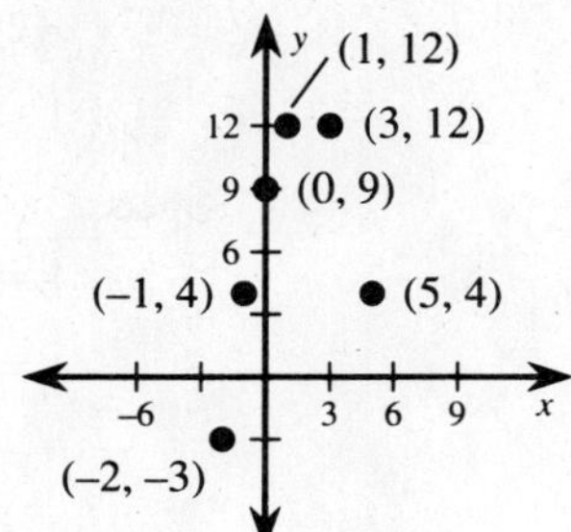

14. Linear

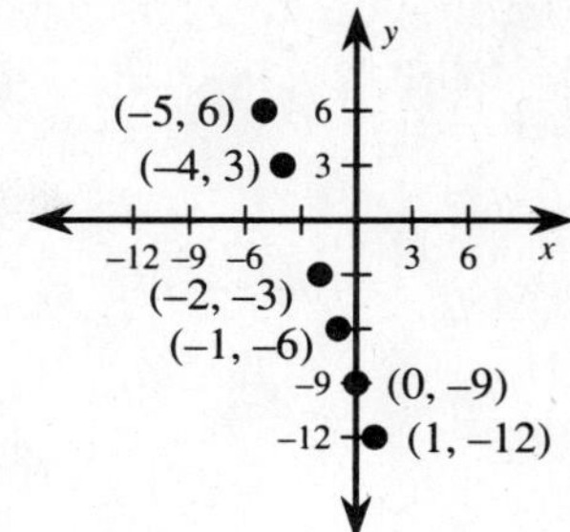

15. **c.**

16. Between 1950 and 1982 cotton consumption decreased. After 1982 consumption increased. The decline was caused by the increase of man-made fibers and increased after 1982 due to the rediscovery of the comfort of cotton.

17. Linear; $d = 2.6M$

18.

Year, t	4	5	6	7	8	9
Amount, A	61,400	67,500	75,000	83,900	94,200	105,900

Year, t	10	11	12	13	14
Amount, A	119,000	133,500	149,400	166,700	185,400

6100, 7500, 8900, 10,300, 11,700, 13,100, 14,500, 15,900, 17,300, 18,700

The difference between each is 1400.

19. $P = 38{,}680{,}000(1.027)^t$

20. Linear, $G = 88 + 13.3t$

21. $D = 2{,}766{,}000{,}000(1.12)^t$

22. $S = 4\pi r^2$

23.
$$m = \frac{-2-4}{3-5} = \frac{-6}{-2} = 3$$
$$y + 2 = 3(x - 3)$$
$$y + 2 = 3x - 9$$
$$3x - y = 11$$

24.
$$m = \frac{-9-7}{-3-5} = \frac{-16}{-8} = 2$$
$$y + 9 = 2(x + 3)$$
$$2x - y = 3$$

25.
$$m = \frac{3-6}{2+4} = \frac{-3}{6} = -\frac{1}{2}$$
$$y - 3 = -\frac{1}{2}(x - 2)$$
$$2y - 6 = -x + 2$$
$$x + 2y = 8$$

26.
$$t^2 + t - 30 = 0$$
$$t = \frac{-1 \pm \sqrt{1 + 120}}{2 \cdot 1}$$
$$t = \frac{-1 \pm 11}{2}$$
$$t = 5,\ -6$$

27.
$$\tfrac{1}{2}x^2 - 35 = 37$$
$$\tfrac{1}{2}x^2 = 72$$
$$x^2 = 144$$
$$x = \pm 12$$

28.
$$3t^2 - 4t = 0$$
$$t = \frac{4 \pm \sqrt{16 - 0}}{2 \cdot 3}$$
$$t = \frac{4 \pm 4}{6}$$
$$t = \frac{4}{3},\ 0$$

29. $A = 1000(1.04)^t$

30. $A = 160(0.92)^t$

31.
$$1 = a(1)^2 + b(1)$$
$$3 = a(2^2) + b(2)$$
$$-2(\ 1 = a + b\ )$$
$$3 = 4a + 2b$$
$$1 = 2a$$
$$a = \tfrac{1}{2}$$
$$b = \tfrac{1}{2}$$
$$S = \tfrac{1}{2}n^2 + \tfrac{1}{2}n$$

Check: $\frac{1}{2}(6^2) + \frac{1}{2}(6) = 18 + 3$
$= 21$

1, 3, 6, 10, 15, 21, . . . are the number of dots used in making successive triangular arrays.

Chapter REVIEW

1. 5 **2.** -0.24 **3.** 6.86 **4.** 0.5

5. 5.66 **6.** 28.77 **7.** $\frac{1}{3}$ **8.** -0.55

9.
$$w^2 - 144 = 0$$
$$w^2 = 144$$
$$w = \pm 12$$

10.
$$8y^2 = 968$$
$$y^2 = 121$$
$$y = \pm 11$$

11.
$$16t^2 - 81 = 0$$
$$16t^2 = 81$$
$$t^2 = \tfrac{81}{16}$$
$$t = \pm\tfrac{9}{4}$$

12.
$$4x^2 - 19 = 6$$
$$4x^2 = 25$$
$$x^2 = \tfrac{25}{4}$$
$$x = \pm\tfrac{5}{2}$$

13. d. **14.** a. **15.** c. **16.** b.

**17.**

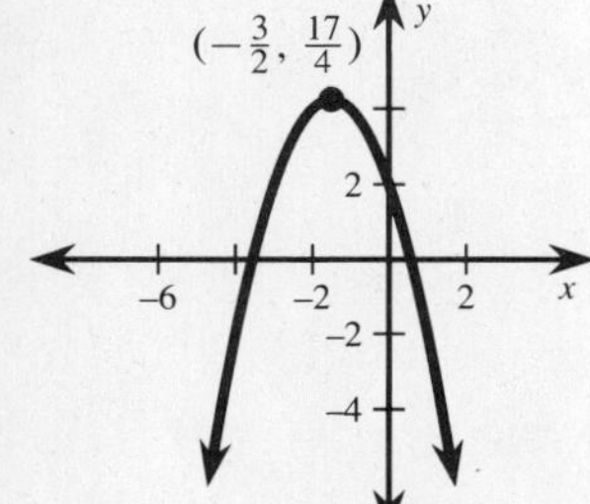

18.

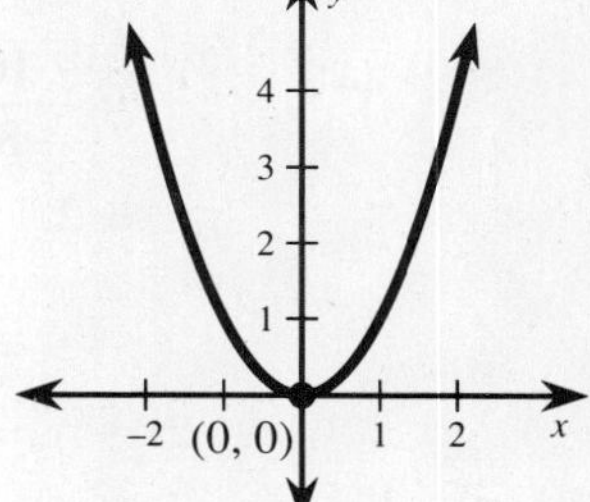

19.

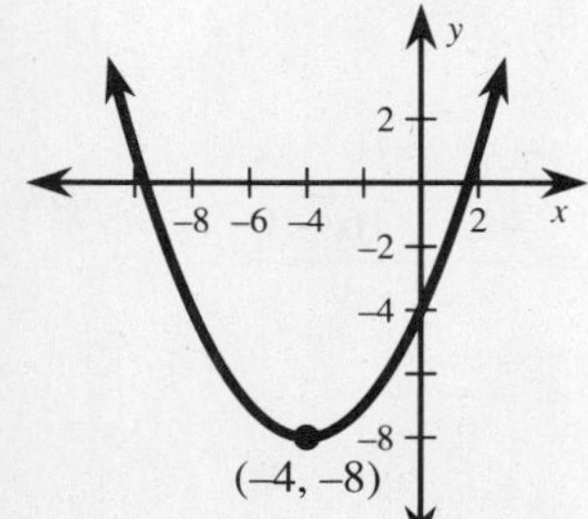

20.

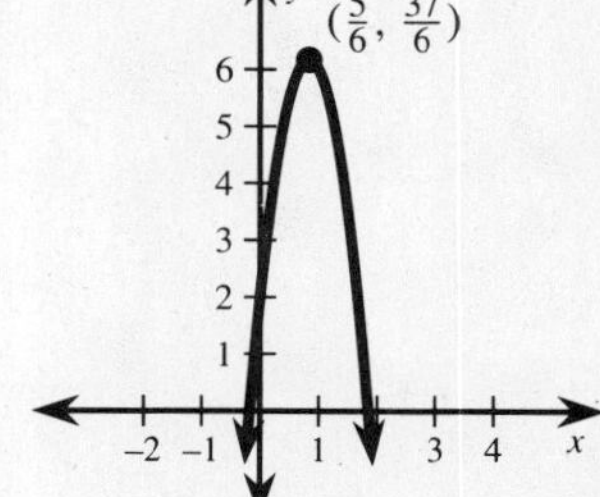

21. $x = \dfrac{\frac{1}{4} \pm \sqrt{\frac{1}{16} - \frac{1}{16}}}{2 \cdot 1}$

$x = \frac{1}{8}$

22. $x = \dfrac{4 \pm \sqrt{16 - 12}}{6}$

$x = \dfrac{4 \pm 2}{6}$

$x = 1,\ \frac{1}{3}$

23. $x = \dfrac{-3 \pm \sqrt{9 - 9}}{2\left(-\frac{1}{4}\right)}$

$x = \dfrac{-3 \pm 0}{-\frac{1}{2}}$

$x = 6$

24. $x = \dfrac{-1 \pm \sqrt{1 - \frac{1}{2}}}{2(-1)}$

$x = \dfrac{-1 \pm \sqrt{\frac{1}{2}}}{-2}$

$x = \frac{1}{2} + \frac{1}{2}\sqrt{\frac{1}{2}},\ \frac{1}{2} - \frac{1}{2}\sqrt{\frac{1}{2}}$

$x \approx 0.15,\ 0.85$

25. $x = \dfrac{-1 \pm \sqrt{1 + 48}}{2(-2)}$

$x = \dfrac{-1 \pm 7}{-4}$

$x = -\dfrac{3}{2},\ 2$

26. $x = \dfrac{-\frac{1}{4} \pm \sqrt{\frac{1}{16} + \frac{1}{2}}}{2\left(-\frac{1}{4}\right)}$

$x = \dfrac{-\frac{1}{4} \pm \frac{3}{4}}{-\frac{1}{2}}$

$x = \dfrac{-1 \pm 3}{-2}$

$x = -1,\ 2$

27.

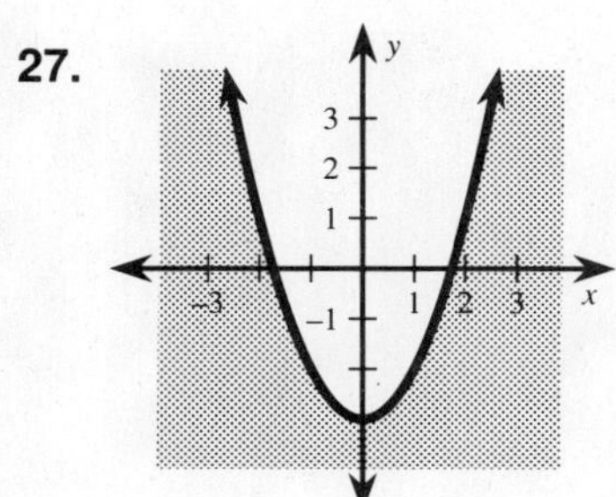

28.

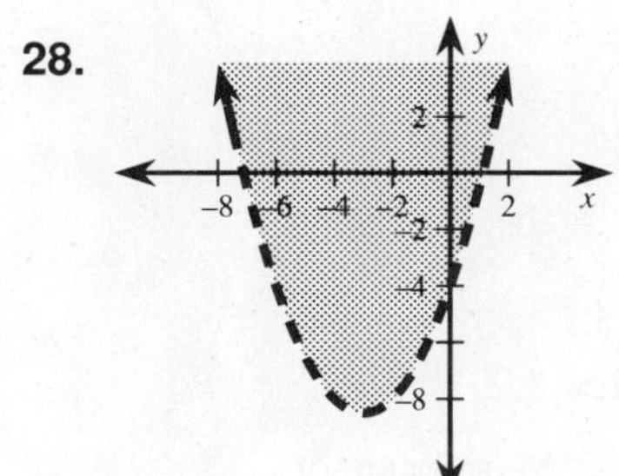

29.

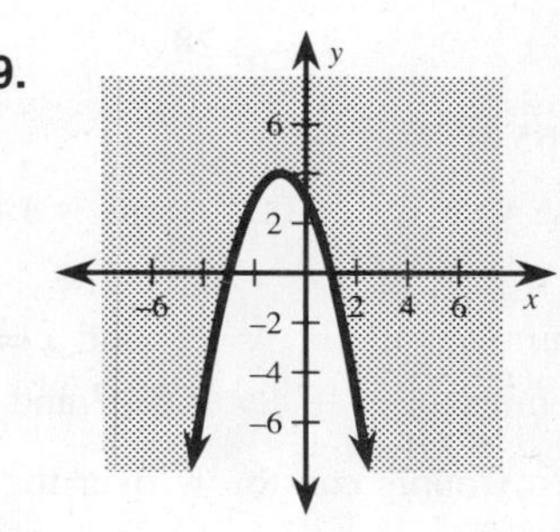

30.

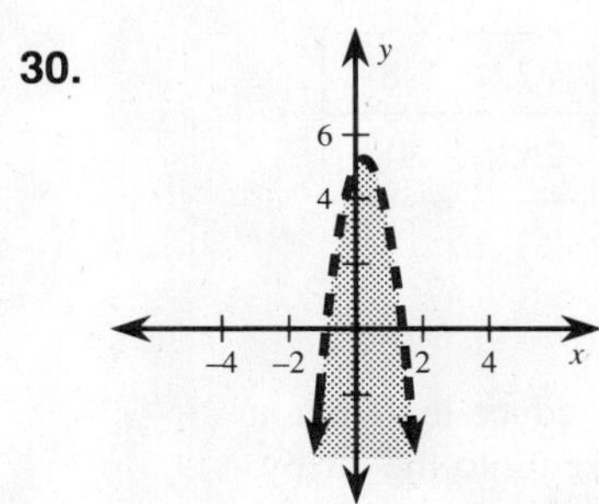

31. Quadratic

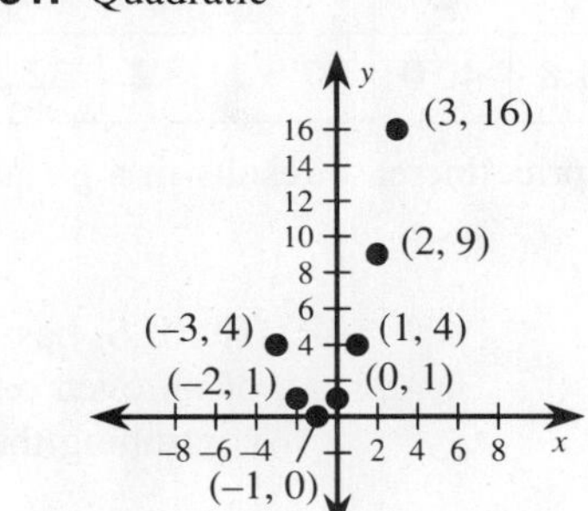

32. Linear

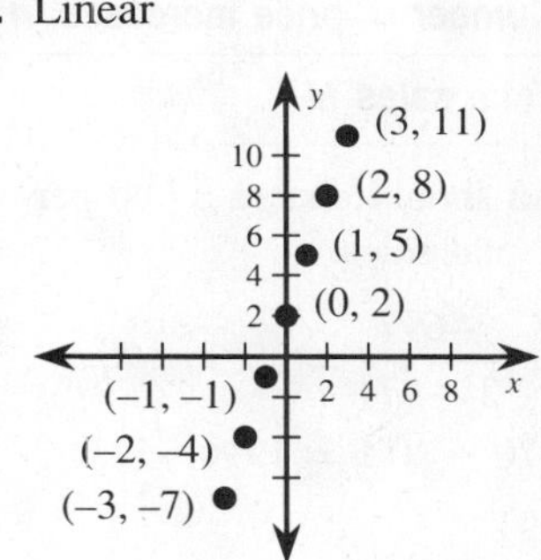

33. Exponential

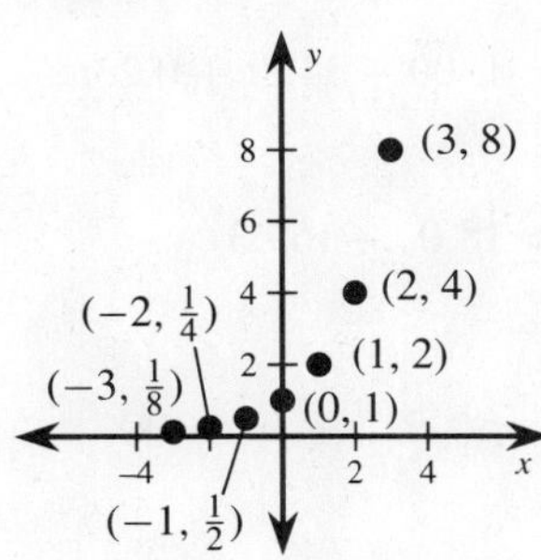

34. Absolute-value

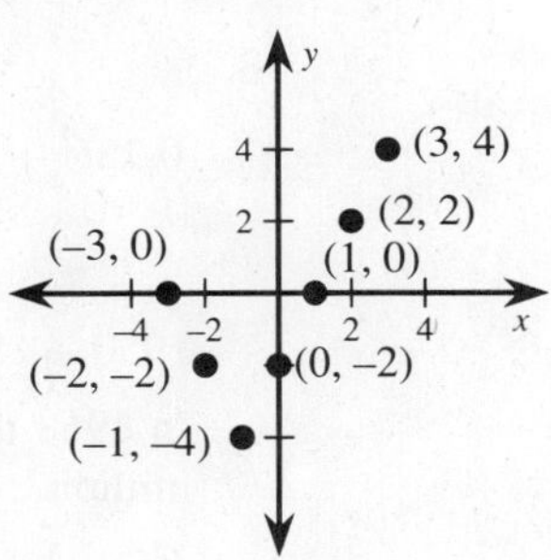

35. $3^2 + 3^2 = c^2$

$c^2 = 18$

$c \approx \pm 4.24$

$P \approx 3 + 3 + 4.24$

$P \approx 10.24$ feet

36. $-16t^2 + 180 = 0$

$t^2 = 11.25$

$t \approx \pm 3.4$

O'Neill was in the air 3.4 seconds.

37. $A = \pi r^2$ $\quad C = 2\pi r$

$3.27 = 3.14r^2$ $\quad C \approx 2(3.14)(1.02)$

$r^2 = 1.04$ $\quad C \approx 6.41$

$r \approx \pm 1.02$

A proton travels 6.41 kilometers in one trip around the tunnel.

38.

Year, t	0	5	10	15	20	25
Teams, S	1180	3055	8680	18,055	31,180	48,055

$0.075t^2 + 1.18 = 60$

$0.075t^2 = 58.82$

$t^2 \approx 784.27$

$t \approx \pm 28$

$1965 + 28 = 1993$

The year for 60,000 teams is 1993.

39. Muriel: $x = 10$, $y = 7$ and $x = 16$, $y = 5.2$
Connie: $x = 10$, $y \approx 8.17$ and $x = 16$, $y = 8.2$

Yes, Connie can throw over the building but Muriel cannot.

40.

Number of price increases, n	0	1	2	3	4	5	6	7	8
Total sales M	43.2	41.8	40.0	37.8	35.2	32.2	28.8	25.0	20.8

Bud should charge \$3.60 per dozen. Any price increase results in a greater loss of total sales.

41. $t = \dfrac{-697}{2(-17)} = 20.5$

$1970 + 20.5 = 1990.5$

1991

42. The U.S. has begun to reduce the amount of nitrogen oxide released into the air by controlling the amount of emissions.

43. South America

44. Asia

45. North America

46. Africa

47. $254 + 0.25t^2 = 110 + 3.5t + 0.03t^2$

$0.22t^2 - 3.5t + 144 = 0$

Negative discriminant, no solution

No, the population of South America will never exceed the population of Africa.

48. $2000 = 1300 + 34.8t + 0.23t^2$

$0.23t^2 + 34.8t - 700 = 0$

$t \approx 18.0, \ -169.3$

$1950 + 18 = 1968$

In 1968 the population of Asia reached 2000 million.

49. North America: $y = 278$ million

Density: $\dfrac{278 \times 10^6}{21{,}525} = 12{,}915$

Africa: $y = 654$ million

Density: $\dfrac{654 \times 10^6}{30{,}305} = 21{,}581$

South America: $y = 298$ million

Density: $\dfrac{298 \times 10^6}{17{,}819} = 16{,}724$

Asia: $y = 3090$ million

Density: $\dfrac{3090 \times 10^6}{27{,}582} = 112{,}030$

Asia: 112,030 people per square kilometer

North America: 12,915 people per square kilometer

50. Africa: $y = 879$ million

Density: 29,005

South America: $y = 360$ million

Density: 20,203

Africa's population density is increasing more rapidly.

Chapter TEST

1. -2

2. 0.09

3. $\frac{2}{5}$

4. No solution

5. 6.32

6. 0

7. $\frac{1}{2}x^2 - 8 = 0$

$x^2 = 16$

$x = \pm 4$

8. $-3x^2 + 243 = 0$

$x^2 = 81$

$x = \pm 9$

9. $x^2 - 8x + 7 = 0$

$x = \dfrac{8 \pm \sqrt{64 - 28}}{2}$

$x = \dfrac{8 \pm 6}{2}$

$x = 4 \pm 3$

$x = 7,\ 1$

10. $-2x^2 + 5x + 9 = 0$

$x = \dfrac{-5 \pm \sqrt{25 + 72}}{2(-2)}$

$x = \dfrac{-5 \pm \sqrt{97}}{-4}$

$x \approx -1.21,\ 3.71$

11. $x^2 + 9x - 3 = 0$

$x = \dfrac{-9 \pm \sqrt{81 + 12}}{2}$

$x = \dfrac{-9 \pm \sqrt{93}}{2}$

$x \approx 0.32,\ -9.32$

12. $x^2 + 3x + 3 = 0$

$x = \dfrac{-3 \pm \sqrt{9 - 12}}{2}$

No solution

13. c.

14. a.

15. d.

16. b.

17.

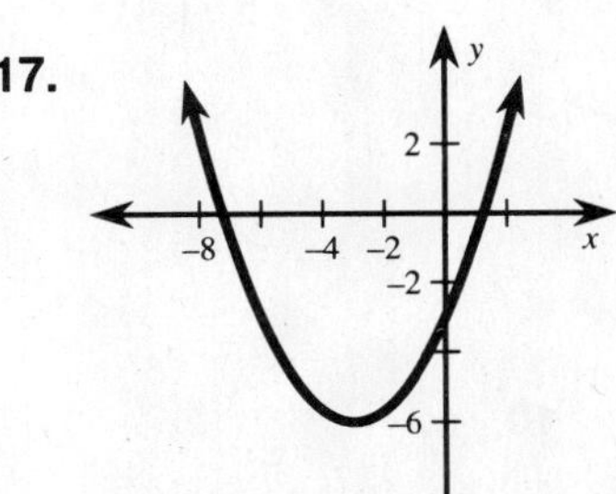

18.

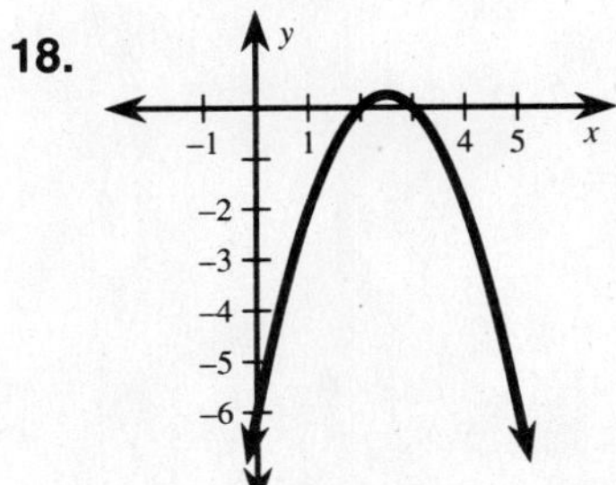

19.

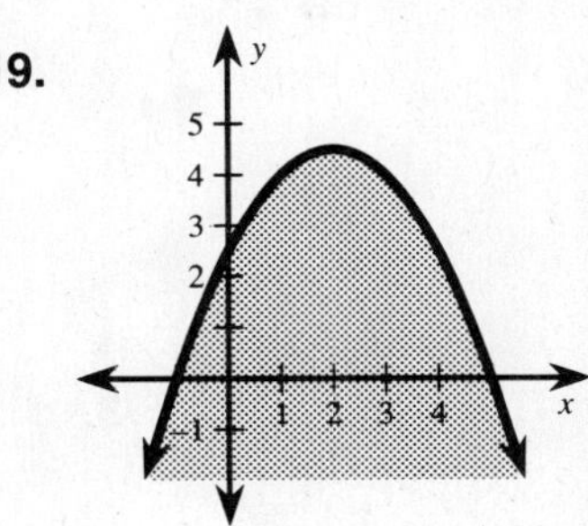

20. 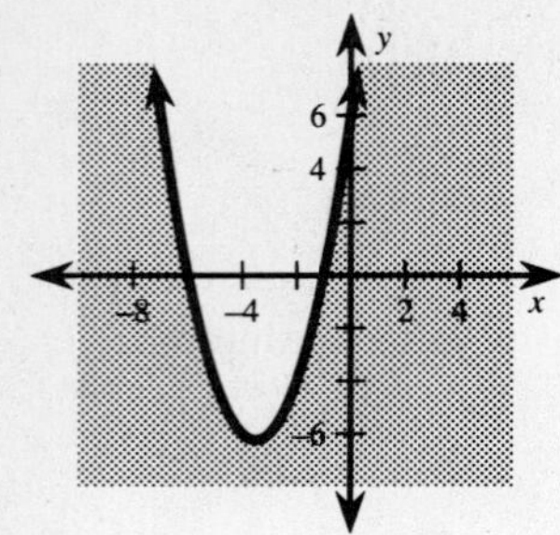

21. $\left(\frac{3}{2}\right)^2 + \left(\frac{3}{2}\right)^2 = c^2$

$c^2 = \frac{9}{2}$

$c = \pm\sqrt{\frac{9}{2}}$

$c \approx \pm 2.12$

No; the diagonal of the square peg is 2.12 inches.

22. $-16t^2 + 20 = 0$

$t^2 = \frac{5}{4}$

$t \approx \pm 1.12$

It will take the stone 1.12 seconds to hit the water.

23. $-16t^2 + 30t + 20 = 0$

$t \approx -0.52,\ 2.40$

It will take the stone 2.40 seconds to hit the water.

24. $-16t^2 + 50t + 20 = 60$

$-16t^2 + 50t - 40 = 0$

$50^2 - 4(-16)(-40) = -60$

No; the discriminant is negative.

Cummulative REVIEW

1. $\begin{cases} x + y = 5 \\ 2x + y = 9 \end{cases}$

$-x - y = -5$

$\underline{2x + y = 9}$

$x = 4$

$4 + y = 5$

$y = 1$

(4, 1)

2. $\begin{cases} \frac{1}{3}x - y = 4 \\ x + 3y = 0 \end{cases}$

$x = -3y$

$\frac{1}{3}(-3y) - y = 4$

$-2y = 4$

$y = -2$

$x = -3(-2)$

$x = 6$

(6, −2)

3. $\begin{cases} -2x + 16y = 10 \\ x - 4y = -4 \end{cases}$

$-2x + 16y = 10$

$\underline{2x - 8y = -8}$

$8y = 2$

$y = \frac{1}{4}$

$x - 4\left(\frac{1}{4}\right) = -4$

$x = -3$

$\left(-3,\ \frac{1}{4}\right)$

4. $\begin{cases} 3.2x + 1.1y = -19.3 \\ -32x + 4y = 148 \end{cases}$

$32x + 11y = -193$

$\underline{-32x + 4y = 148}$

$15y = -45$

$y = -3$

$-32x + 4(-3) = 148$

$-32x = 160$

$x = -5$

(−5, −3)

5. $\begin{cases} \frac{1}{4}x - \frac{1}{2}y = -\frac{5}{2} \\ -4x + 3y = 5 \end{cases}$

$\begin{cases} x - 2y = -10 \\ -4x + 3y = 5 \end{cases}$

$x = 2y - 10$

$-4(2y - 10) + 3y = 5$

$-8y + 40 + 3y = 5$

$-5y = -35$

$y = 7$

$x = 2(7) - 10$

$x = 4$

(4, 7)

6. $\begin{cases} 1.4x + 2.1y = 17.99 \\ 2.8x - 4.2y = -11.99 \end{cases}$

$2.8x + 4.2y = 35.98$

$\underline{2.8x - 4.2y = -11.99}$

$5.6x = 23.99$

$x \approx 4.28$

$1.4(4.28) + 2.1y = 17.99$

$2.1y = 11.998$

$y \approx 5.71$

(4.28, 5.71)

7. c.

8. d.

9. b.

10. a.

11.
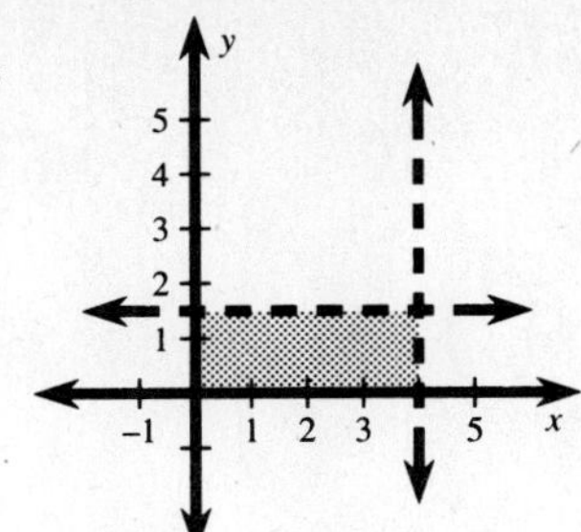

12.
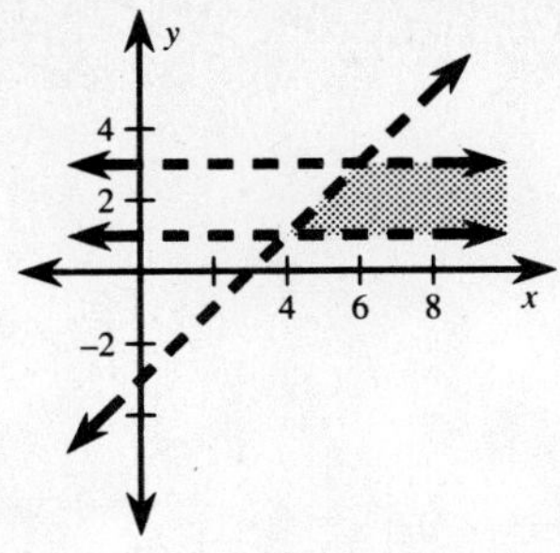

13.
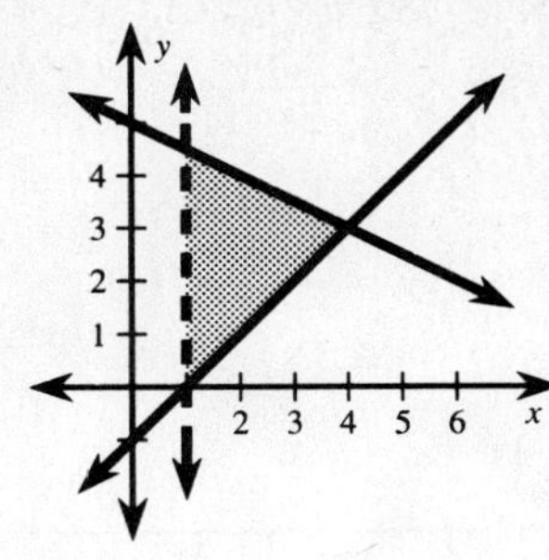

14.
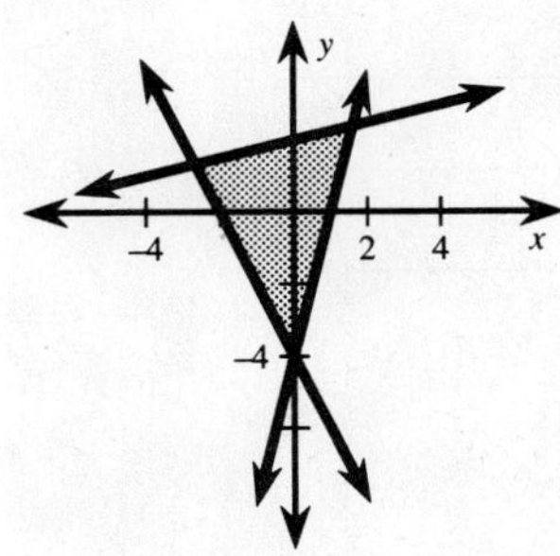

15. $\dfrac{(3w)^2}{2^2 \cdot w} \cdot w^{-3} = \dfrac{9}{4}w^{2-1-3}$

$= \dfrac{9}{4}w^{-2}$

$= \dfrac{9}{4w^2}$

16. $\dfrac{4ab^2}{2a^{-1}} \cdot (a^{-1}b)^4 = 2a^2b^2 \cdot a^{-4}b^4$

$= 2a^{-2}b^6$

$= \dfrac{2b^6}{a^2}$

17. $\dfrac{(37p)^0}{p^2} \cdot \dfrac{(q^2p)^4}{q^2p^2} = p^{-2} \cdot q^{8-2}p^{4-2}$

$= q^6p^0$

$= q^6$

18. $\dfrac{1}{4}r^2s^3t^{-1} \cdot 4r^{-3}t^4 = r^{2-3}s^3t^{-1+4}$

$= r^{-1}s^3t^3$

$= \dfrac{s^3t^3}{r}$

19. $(4.27 \times 10^3) \cdot (2.2 \times 10^2) = (4.27)(2.2) \times 10^{3+2}$

$= 9.394 \times 10^5$

or 939,400

20. $(3.6 \times 10^{-4}) \div (1.4 \times 10^{-3}) = \dfrac{3.6}{1.4} \times 10^{-4-(-3)}$

$\approx 2.57 \times 10^{-1}$

or 0.257

21. $3x^2 - 27 = 0$

$3x^2 = 27$

$x^2 = 9$

$x = \pm 3$

22. $-\frac{1}{2}x^2 + 2 = 0$

$-\frac{1}{2}x^2 = -2$

$x^2 = 4$

$x = \pm 2$

23. $x^2 - 2x - 63 = 0$

$(x - 9)(x + 7) = 0$

$x - 9 = 0$ or $x + 7 = 0$

$x = 9$ $\quad x = -7$

24. $3x^2 + 11x + 6 = 0$

$(3x + 2)(x + 3) = 0$

$3x + 2 = 0$ or $x + 3 = 0$

$3x = -2$ $\quad x = -3$

$x = -\frac{2}{3}$

25. $x^2 + 3x - 9 = 0$

$x = \dfrac{-3 \pm \sqrt{9 - 4(1)(-9)}}{2 \cdot 1}$

$x = \dfrac{-3 \pm \sqrt{45}}{2}$

26. $5x^2 - 24x - 5 = 0$

$(5x + 1)(x - 5) = 0$

$5x + 1 = 0$ or $x - 5 = 0$

$5x = -1$ $\quad x = 5$

$x = -\frac{1}{5}$

27. Vertex: $x = \dfrac{-2}{2(-1)}$

$= 1$

$y = -1^2 + 2(1)$

$= 1$

(1, 1)

x	−2	−1	0	1	2	3	4
y	−8	−3	0	1	0	−3	−8

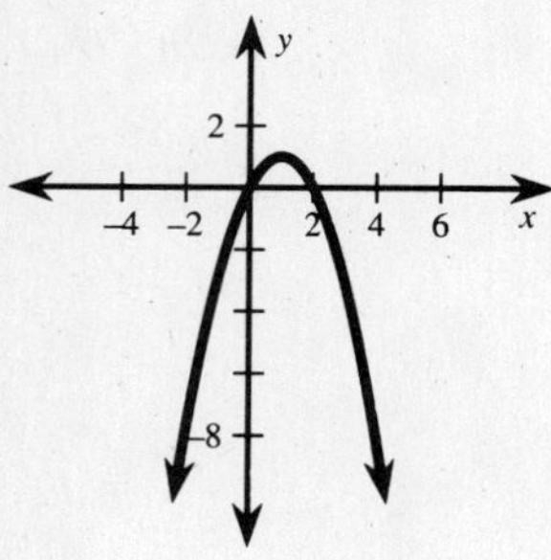

28. Vertex: $x = \dfrac{-(-3)}{2(1)}$

$= \frac{3}{2}$

$y = \left(\dfrac{3}{2}\right)^2 - 3\left(\dfrac{3}{2}\right) + 2$

$= -\dfrac{1}{4}$

$\left(\dfrac{3}{2}, -\dfrac{1}{4}\right)$

x	−1	0	1	$\frac{3}{2}$	2	3
y	6	2	0	$-\frac{1}{4}$	0	2

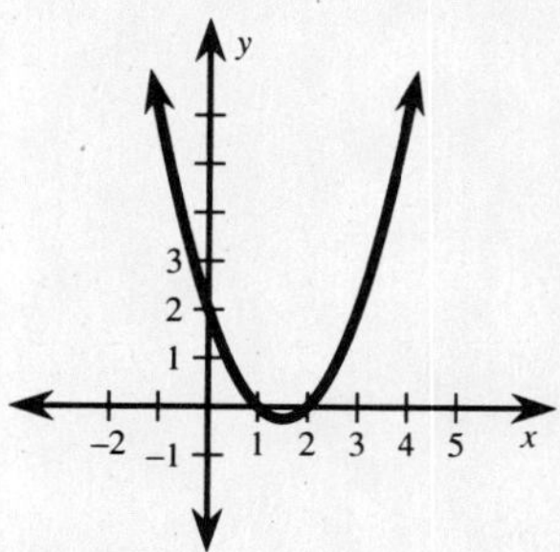

29. Vertex: $x = \dfrac{-6}{2(3)}$

$= -1$

$y = 3(-1)^2 + 6(-1) + 1$

$= -2$

(−1, −2)

x	−3	−2	−1	0	1
y	10	1	−2	1	10

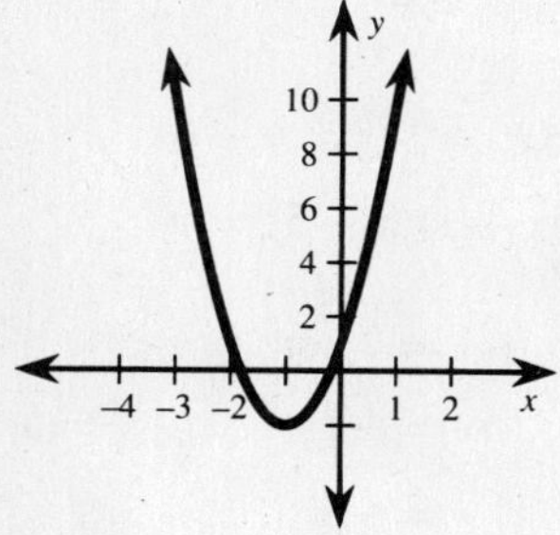

30. Vertex: $x = \dfrac{-(-2)}{2\left(\frac{1}{4}\right)}$

$= 4$

$y = \frac{1}{4}(4)^2 - 2(4) + 4$

$= 0$

(4, 0)

x	0	1	2	3	4	5	6	7	8
y	4	$2\frac{1}{4}$	1	$\frac{1}{4}$	0	$\frac{1}{4}$	1	$2\frac{1}{4}$	4

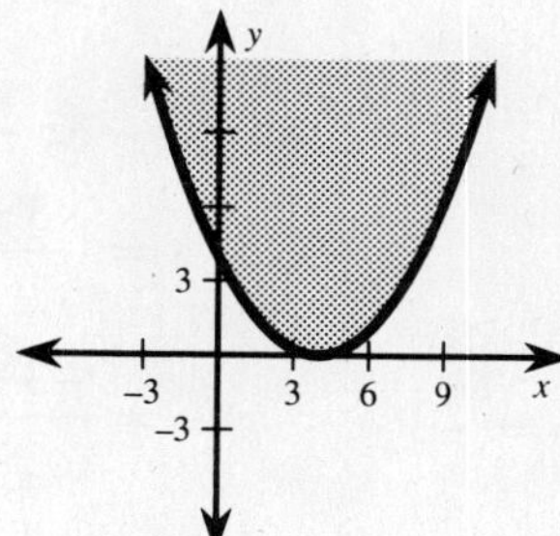

31. Vertex: $x = \dfrac{-4}{2(1)}$

$= -2$

$y = (-2)^2 + 4(-2) + 6$

$= 2$

$(-2,\ 2)$

x	−4	−3	−2	−1	0
y	6	3	2	3	6

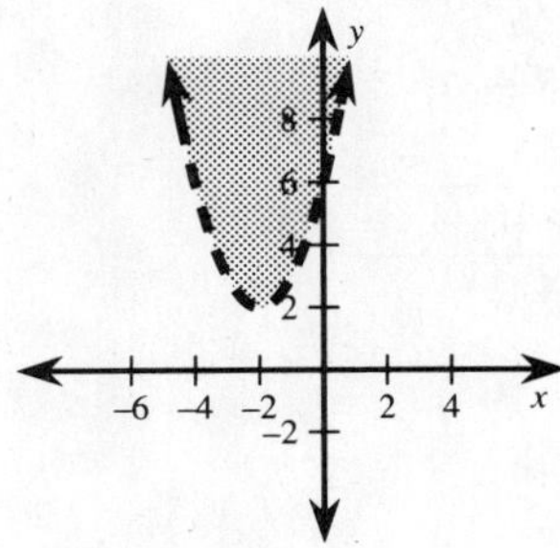

32. 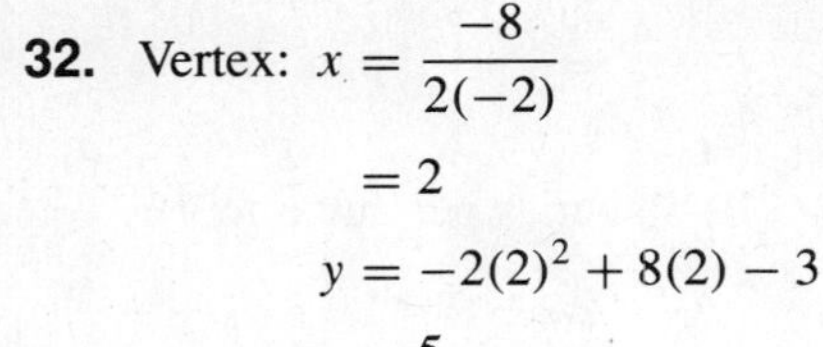

Vertex: $x = \dfrac{-8}{2(-2)}$

$= 2$

$y = -2(2)^2 + 8(2) - 3$

$= 5$

$(2,\ 5)$

x	−1	0	1	2	3	4	5
y	−13	−3	3	5	3	−3	−13

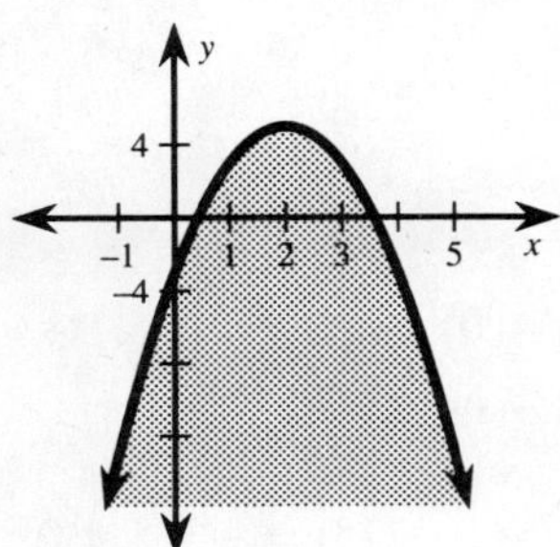

33. $\begin{cases} 2x + 4y \le 200 \\ 5(2x + 3y) \le 900 \\ x \ge 0 \\ y \ge 0 \end{cases}$

$P = 6x + 10y$

Vertices: (0, 0), (0, 50), (60, 20), (90, 0)

$P = 6(0) + 10(0)$
$= 0$

$P = 6(0) + 10(50)$
$= 500$

$P = 6(60) + 10(20)$
$= 560$

$P = 6(90) + 10(0)$
$= 540$

To obtain the maximum profit, 60 dresses of Style X and 20 dresses of Style Y must be produced.

34. Objective equation: $P = 6x + 10y$

Constraints: $\begin{cases} 2x + 4y \le 200 \\ 5(2x + 3y) \le 900 \\ x \ge 0 \\ y \ge 0 \end{cases}$

35. $V = \frac{4}{3}\pi r^3$

$\approx \frac{4}{3}(3.14)(4)^3$

≈ 268 cubic feet

Scientific notation: 2.68×10^2 cubic feet

Decimal form: 268 cubic feet

36. $(16 \text{ tons})\left(\dfrac{2000 \text{ pounds}}{1 \text{ ton}}\right) = 32{,}000 \text{ pounds}$

$\dfrac{32{,}000 \text{ pounds}}{268 \text{ cubic feet}} \approx 119.4 \text{ pounds per cubic foot}$

37. $A = 567(1.048)^5$ $\quad$ $A = 567(1.051)^5$

$= 716.79$ $\quad$ $= 727.10$

In 5 years: $727.10 - 716.79 = \$10.31$

$A = 567(1.048)^{10}$ $\quad$ $A = 567(1.051)^{10}$

$= 906.14$ $\quad$ $= 932.42$

In 10 years: $932.42 - 906.14 = \$26.28$

38. $A = 3700(1 - 0.15)^4$

$= 3700(0.85)^4$

$\approx \$1931$

39.

$$1100 = -16x^2 + 300x + 0$$
$$-16x^2 + 300x - 1100 = 0$$
$$-4x^2 + 75x - 275 = 0$$

$$x = \frac{-75 \pm \sqrt{(75)^2 - 4(-4)(-275)}}{2(-4)}$$

$$x = \frac{-75 \pm 35}{-8}$$

$x = 5,\ 13.75$

It will take 5 seconds for the rocket to reach an altitude of 1100 feet. Note that on the rocket's descent, it will be at an altitude of 1100 feet again, 13.75 seconds after takeoff.

40.

$$1500 = -16x^2 + 300x + 0$$
$$-16x^2 + 300x - 1500 = 0$$
$$-4x^2 + 75x - 375 = 0$$

Discriminant: $75^2 - 4(-4)(-375) = -375 < 0$

No, the rocket reaches its maximum height prior to 1500 feet.

Chapter 10

Polynomials and Factoring

10.1 Adding and Subtracting Polynomials

Communicating about Algebra

A. Polygon–many sided figure
Monopoly–a commodity controlled by one party
Binocular–relating to the use of both eyes
Tricycle–a vehicle with three wheels

B. $(x^3+2x+1)+(-x^3+3x^2-3)=3x^2+2x-2$

EXERCISES

1. An expression whose terms are of the form ax^k, where k is a nonnegative integer.

2. $-3x^3,\ -2x^2,\ 4x,\ -5$

3. $-7,\ 0,\ 12,\ -31$

4. $10y^3-3y^2+15y-6$

5. 3

6. $(x^2+8)-(2x^2-4x+1)=-x^2+4x+7$

7. Linear
Binomial

8. Constant
Monomial

9. Quadratic
Polynomial

10. Quadratic
Trinomial

11. $(x^2+3x^2)+(-3+5)=4x^2+2$

12. $y^2+(-3y+3y)+(2+2)=y^2+4$

13. $(2x^2+x^2)+(3x-2x)+(1+2)=3x^2+x+3$

14. $(2x^2+3x^2)+(-x-4x)+(3+7)=5x^2-5x+10$

15. $12x^3+(2x^2+9x^2)+3x+(-4-8)=12x^3+11x^2+3x-12$

16. $(-4x^3+2x^3)+(-2x^2)+(x+3x)+(-5+4)=-2x^3-2x^2+4x-1$

17.
$$\begin{array}{r} -8z^2+2z-3 \\ \underline{z^2+5z} \\ -7z^2+7z-3 \end{array}$$

18.
$$\begin{array}{r} 6x^2+5 \\ \underline{-2x^2+3} \\ 4x^2+8 \end{array}$$

19.
$$\begin{array}{r} 5x^4-2x+7 \\ \underline{-3x^4+6x^2-5} \\ 2x^4+6x^2-2x+2 \end{array}$$

20. $\begin{array}{r} 4x^2 - 7x + 2 \\ -x^2 + x - 2 \\ \hline 3x^2 - 6x \end{array}$

21. $z^3 + (z^2 - z^2) + 1 = z^3 + 1$

22. $-u^2 + (10 - 5) = -u^2 + 5$

23. $(2x^2 - x^2) + (3x - x) + (-4 + 1) = x^2 + 2x - 3$

24. $(3x^3 - x^3) + (-4x^2 - 3x^2) + (0 + x) + (3 + 4) = 2x^3 - 7x^2 + x + 7$

25. $\begin{array}{r} 10x^3 \qquad\quad + 15 \\ -(17x^3 - 4x + 5) \\ \hline -7x^3 + 4x + 10 \end{array}$

26. $\begin{array}{r} 3y^4 + y^2 \\ -(y^5 - y^4 \qquad) \\ \hline -y^5 + 4y^4 + y^2 \end{array}$

27. $\begin{array}{r} -2x^3 + 5x^2 - x + 8 \\ -(-2x^3 \qquad + 3x - 4) \\ \hline 5x^2 - 4x + 12 \end{array}$

28. $\begin{array}{r} 3x^2 + 7x - 6 \\ -(3x^2 + 7x \qquad) \\ \hline -6 \end{array}$

29. $(6x - 8x + 3x) + (-5 - 15 - 4) = x - 24$

30. $(2x^2 + x^2 - 2x^2) + (0 - 2x - 0) + (1 + 1 - 8) = x^2 - 2x - 6$

31. $(-x^3 + 4x^3 + 0) + (0 + 0 - 2x^2) + (0 - 2x + 0) + (2 + 0 - 3) = 3x^3 - 2x^2 - 2x - 1$

32. $(-5x^2 + 3x^2 - x^2) + (0 + 0 + x) + (1 - 5 - 0) = -3x^2 + x - 4$

33. $(2t^2 - 3t^2 + 5t^2) + (10 - 15 + 25) = 4t^2 + 20$

34. $(-10u + 8u - 3u) + (-10 - 8 - 18) = -5u - 36$

35. $x(2x) - 4\left(\frac{x}{2}\right) = 2x^2 - 2x$

36. $x(3x) - 5\left(\frac{x}{3}\right) = 3x^2 - \frac{5}{3}x$

37. $P = -0.19t^2 + 4.60t + 31.37$

38. $F = -0.116t^2 - 0.376t + 253.558$

39. $F = 1267.2t + 77{,}601$

40. $N = -0.47t^2 + 28.7t + 323.1$

41. $5x - 2y$

42. $\frac{1}{6}x + 8$

43. $\frac{9}{2}x - \frac{3}{2}y$

44. $4y$

45. $\begin{bmatrix} 2x^2 & -x \\ -7 + 9x & -3x^2 + 4 \end{bmatrix}$

46. $\begin{bmatrix} 3x^2 + 3 & -2x \\ 5x^2 + 3x & 3x - 1 \end{bmatrix}$

47. $\begin{bmatrix} 20x - 13 & 10 - 3x \\ x^3 + 7y^3 & 4y^2 - 11y + 2 \end{bmatrix}$

48. $\begin{bmatrix} 7x^3 + 2x^2 & -x^2 - 4x \\ 2x - 4 & 4 - 7x - x^2 \end{bmatrix}$

49. $$\begin{aligned} 4x(3x + 1) - 6(x^2 - 3x) &= 260 \\ 12x^2 + 4x - (6x^2 - 18x) &= 260 \\ 6x^2 + 22x - 260 &= 0 \\ 3x^2 + 11x - 130 &+ 0 \\ (x - 5)(3x + 26) &= 0 \\ x &= 5, -\tfrac{26}{3} \end{aligned}$$

$x = 5$ units.

50. $6x(5x - 1) - 4(2x^2 - 2) = 84$

$$30x^2 - 6x - 8x^2 + 8 = 84$$
$$22x^2 - 6x - 76 = 0$$
$$(x - 2)(22x + 38) = 0$$
$$x = 2,\ -\tfrac{19}{11}$$

$x = 2$ units.

51. $-3x^2 + 4x + 6$

52. $-4x^2 + 9x - 4$

53. $-9x^2 + 8x - 15$

10.2 Multiplying Polynomials

Communicating about Algebra

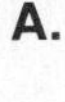
A.

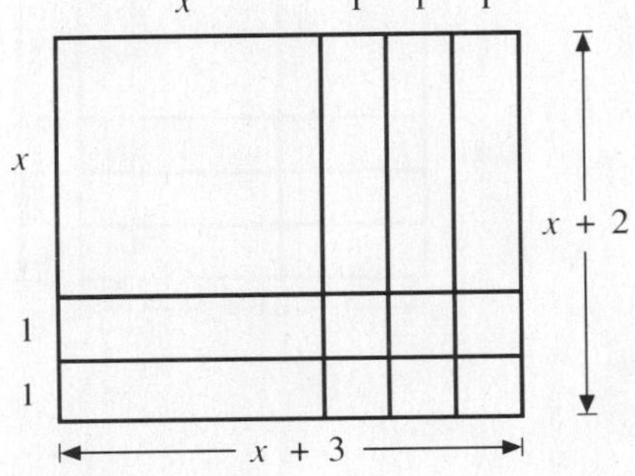

B.

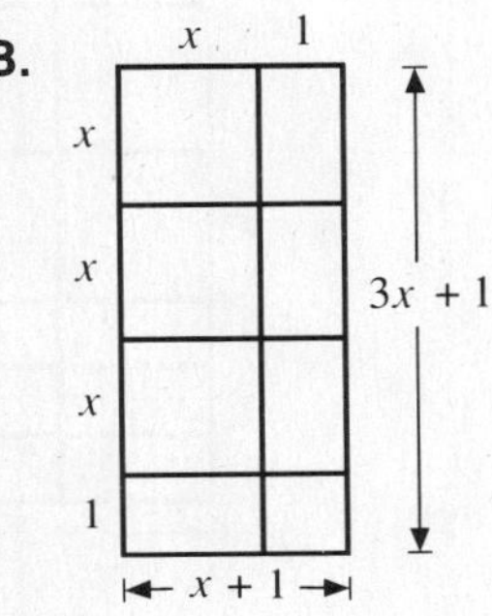

EXERCISES

1. $(2x - 3)(x + 4) = 2x(x + 4) - 3(x + 4)$
$$= 2x^2 + 8x - 3x - 12$$
$$= 2x^2 + 5x - 12$$

2. $(x + 1)(x^2 - x + 1) = x^3 - x^2 + x + (x^2 - x + 1)$
$$= x^3 + 1$$

3. $(x - 3)(2x + 5) = 2x^2 - x - 15$

4. Product of the **F**irst terms
Product of the **O**uter terms
Product of the **I**nner terms
Product of the **L**ast terms

5. $(3x - 7)(-2x) = -6x^2 + 14x$

6. $3x^2(5x - x^3 + 2) = 15x^3 - 3x^5 + 6x^2$

7. $(-x)(2x^2 - 3x) = -2x^3 + 3x^2$

8. $2x(3x^2 - 4x + 1) = 6x^3 - 8x^2 + 2x$

9. $4x^2(5x^3 - 2x^2 + x) = 20x^5 - 8x^4 + 4x^3$

10. $-x^2(6x^3 - 14x + 9) = -6x^5 + 14x^3 - 9x^2$

11. $(3x - 2)(5x + 7) = 15x^2 + 11x - 14$

12. $(3x + 5)(2x + 1) = 6x^2 + 13x + 5$

13. $(x - 4)(x + 4) = x^2 - 16$

14. $(2x - 3)(x + 3) = 2x^2 + 3x - 9$

15. $(x - 5)(2x + 10) = 2x^2 - 50$

16. $(3x - 5)(2x + 1) = 6x^2 - 7x - 5$

17. $x^2 + 6x + 5$

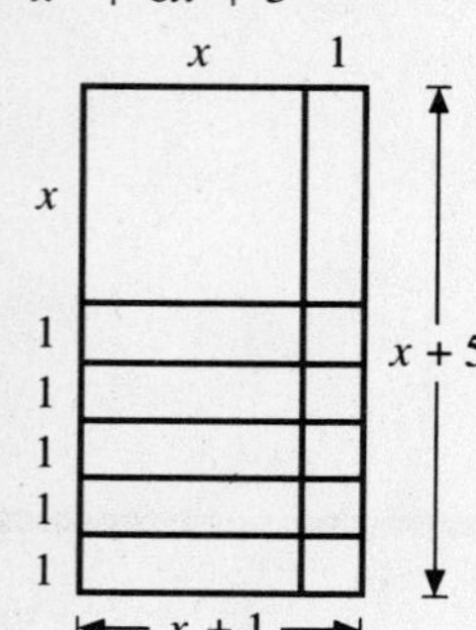

18. $x^2 + 8x + 12$

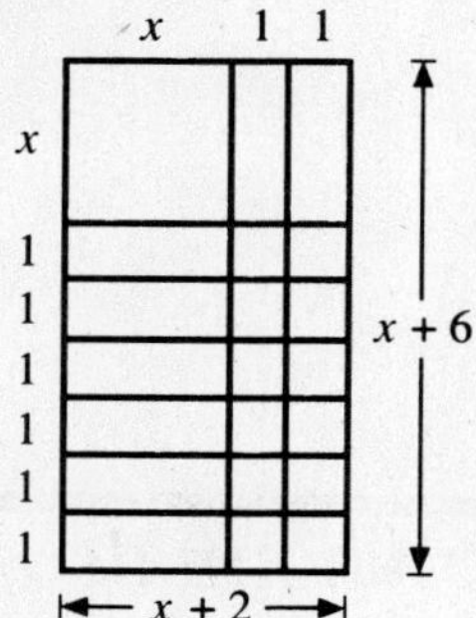

19. $x^2 + 3x + 2$

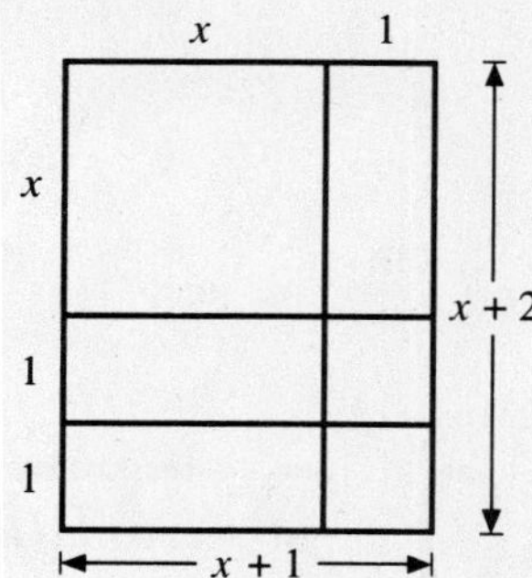

20. $6x^2 + 8x + 2$

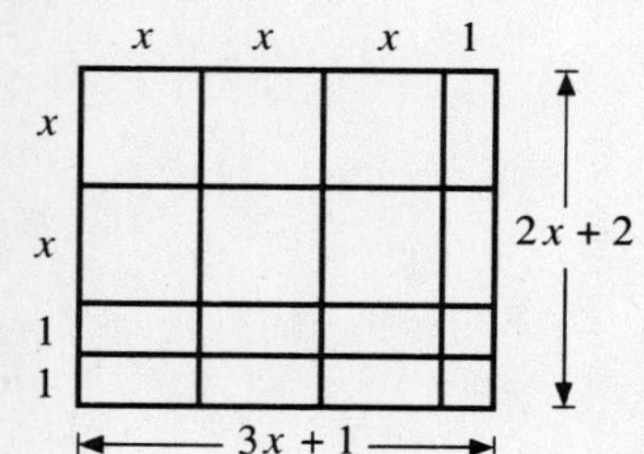

21. $2x^2 + 7x + 6$

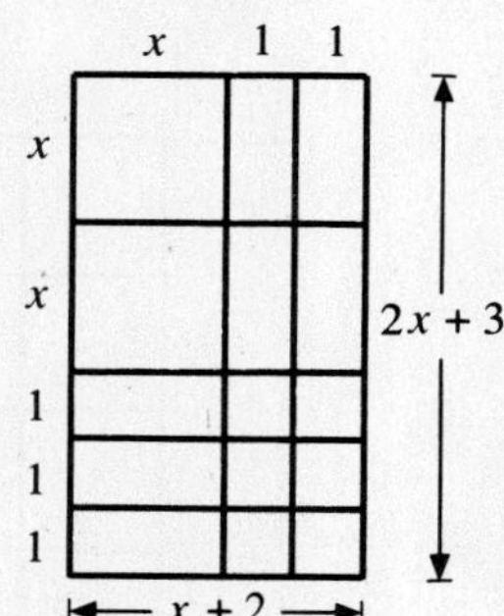

22. $2x^2 + 7x + 3$

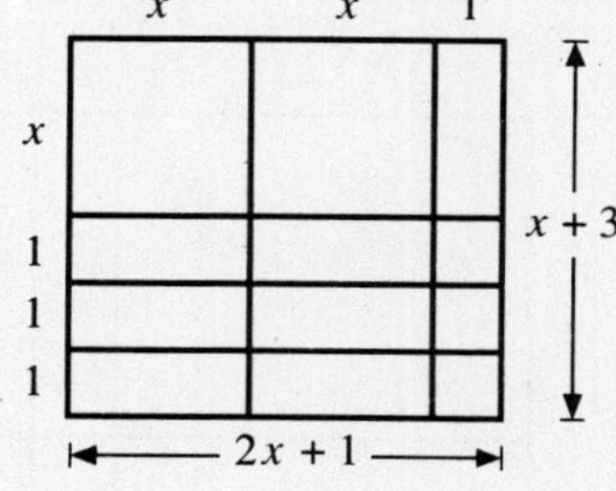

23. $(x - 3)(3x + 1) = x(3x + 1) - 3(3x + 1)$
$= 3x^2 + x - 9x - 3$
$= 3x^2 - 8x - 3$

24. $(2x + 1)(3x + 1) = 2x(3x + 1) + 1(3x + 1)$
$= 6x^2 + 2x + 3x + 1$
$= 6x^2 + 5x + 1$

25. $(3x^2 + x - 5)(2x - 1) = 3x^2(2x - 1) + x(2x - 1) - 5(2x - 1)$
$= 6x^3 - 3x^2 + 2x^2 - x - 10x + 5$
$= 6x^3 - x^2 - 11x + 5$

26. $(2x^2 - 7x + 1)(4x + 3) = 2x^2(4x + 3) - 7x(4x + 3) + 1(4x + 3)$
$= 8x^3 + 6x^2 - 28x^2 - 21x + 4x + 3$
$= 8x^3 - 22x^2 - 17x + 3$

27. $(x^2 + 9)(x^2 - x - 4) = x^2(x^2 - x - 4) + 9(x^2 - x - 4)$
$= x^4 - x^3 - 4x^2 + 9x^2 - 9x - 36$
$= x^4 - x^3 + 5x^2 - 9x - 36$

28. $(x + 3)(x^2 - 6x + 2) = x(x^2 - 6x + 2) + 3(x^2 - 6x + 2)$
$= x^3 - 6x^2 + 2x + 3x^2 - 18x + 6$
$= x^3 - 3x^2 - 16x + 6$

29. $(x+3)(x-4) = x^2 - x - 12$

30. $(2x-1)(x+9) = 2x^2 + 17x - 9$

31. $(2x-5)(x+6) = 2x^2 + 7x - 30$

32. $(3x-4)\left(\frac{1}{3}x+1\right) = x^2 + \frac{5}{3}x - 4$

33. $\left(x+\frac{6}{5}\right)(4x-5) = 4x^2 - \frac{1}{5}x - 6$

34. $\left(x+\frac{1}{4}\right)\left(x-\frac{5}{4}\right) = x^2 - x - \frac{5}{16}$

35. $\left(\frac{1}{2}x+3\right)\left(\frac{1}{2}x-2\right) = \frac{1}{4}x^2 + \frac{1}{2}x - 6$

36. $$\begin{aligned}(-3x^2+x-1)(x+3) &= -3x^2(x+3) + x(x+3) - 1(x+3)\\ &= -3x^3 - 9x^2 + x^2 + 3x - x - 3\\ &= -3x^3 - 8x^2 + 2x - 3\end{aligned}$$

37. $$\begin{aligned}(x^2+4x-9)(x-4) &= x^2(x-4) + 4x(x-4) - 9(x-4)\\ &= x^3 - 4x^2 + 4x^2 - 16x - 9x + 36\\ &= x^3 - 25x + 36\end{aligned}$$

38. $A = \frac{1}{2}(x)\left(\frac{1}{2}x+5\right)$

$A = \frac{1}{4}x^2 + \frac{5}{2}x$

39.

Base, x	5	6	7	8	9	10
Area, A	$18\frac{3}{4}$	24	$29\frac{3}{4}$	36	$42\frac{3}{4}$	50

40. $A = \pi(4x+28)(4x-28)$

$A = \pi(16x^2 - 784)$

$A = \pi(16(9)^2 - 784)$

≈ 1608.5 square feet

41. No. From Exercise 40, we know that when $x = 9$, $A = 512\pi$. However, if $x = 18$, $A = 4400\pi \neq 2(512\pi)$.

42. $$\begin{aligned}(x+b)(x+a) &= x^2 + bx + ax + ab\\ 1(x^2) + 1(bx) + 1(ax) + 1(ab) &= x^2 + bx + ax + ab\end{aligned}$$

Each term of one side of the large rectangle is multiplied by each term of the other side. This is the same as each term in the first binomial is multiplied by each term in the second binomial.

43. **d.**

44. $A = \frac{1}{2}(x+1)(3x+4+5x+7)$

$A = 4x^2 + \frac{19}{2}x + \frac{11}{2}$

45. $A = \frac{1}{2}(6x-5)(x+4)$

$A = 3x^2 + \frac{19}{2}x - 10$

46. $T = (900t + 11{,}800)(228 + 2.2t)$

$= 1980t^2 + 231{,}160t + 2{,}690{,}400$

Year	0	5	10
S	11,800	16,300	20,800
P	228	239	250
T	2,690,400	3,895,700	5,200,000

47. $(-3)^4$

48. x^3

49. $(-2)^2x^3$

50. 4^2y^2

51. $\frac{4}{5} \cdot \frac{4}{5} \cdot \frac{4}{5} \cdot \frac{4}{5}$

52. $4.5 \cdot 4.5 \cdot 4.5 \cdot 4.5 \cdot 4.5$

53. $x^2 \cdot x^2 \cdot x^2$

54. $y^2 \cdot y^2$

55. $2(x-4)+5x = 7x-8$

56. $4(3-y)+2(y+1) = -2y+14$

57. $-3(z-2)-(z-6) = -4z+12$

58. $(u-2)-3(2u+1) = -5u-5$

59. $\dfrac{x^4}{3x^{-3}} = \dfrac{1}{3}x^7$

60. $\dfrac{6x^{-1}}{2x} = \dfrac{3}{x^2}$

61. $\dfrac{5x^2y^0}{xy^3} = \dfrac{5x}{y^3}$

62. $\dfrac{x^3y^3}{x^0y} = x^3y^2$

63.
$$\begin{aligned}(x+1)(2x-3)(x-7) &= (2x^2-x-3)(x-7)\\ &= 2x^2(x-7)-x(x-7)-3(x-7)\\ &= 2x^3-14x^2-x^2+7x-3x+21\\ &= 2x^3-15x^2+4x+21\end{aligned}$$

64.
$$\begin{aligned}(3x+7)(x+4)(2x-3) &= (3x^2+19x+28)(2x-3)\\ &= 3x^2(2x-3)+19x(2x-3)+28(2x-3)\\ &= 6x^3-9x^2+38x^2-57x+56x-84\\ &= 6x^3+29x^2-x-84\end{aligned}$$

65. $(x-1)(x+1) = x^2-1$

$$\begin{aligned}(x-1)(x^2+x+1) &= x^3+x^2+x-x^2-x-1\\ &= x^3-1\end{aligned}$$

$$\begin{aligned}(x-1)(x^3+x^2+x+1) &= x^4+x^3+x^2+x-x^3-x^2-x-1\\ &= x^4-1\end{aligned}$$

$$\begin{aligned}(x-1)(x^4+x^3+x^2+x+1) &= x^5+x^4+x^3+x^2+x-x^4-x^3-x^2-x-1\\ &= x^5-1\end{aligned}$$

Mixed REVIEW

1. $4242.00 \times 0.22 = \$933.24$

2. $\frac{1}{4} \cdot \left(\frac{2}{3}\right) = \frac{2}{12}$
$= \frac{1}{6}$

3. $\dfrac{1}{x^2y}$

4. -2

5.
$$\begin{aligned}6^{x+3} &= (3+3)^2\\ x+3 &= 2\\ x &= -1\end{aligned}$$

6.
$$\begin{aligned}3x^2-2x-1 &= 0\\ (3x+1)(x-1) &= 0\\ x = -\tfrac{1}{3},\ x &= 1\end{aligned}$$

7.
$$\begin{aligned}x^2+4x+4 &= 0\\ (x+2)(x+2) &= 0\\ x &= -2\end{aligned}$$

8.
$$\begin{aligned}y^{x+3} &= y^7\\ x+3 &= 7\\ x &= 4\end{aligned}$$

9. $(-1)^2-5(-1)-7 = 1+5-7$
$= -1$

10. $|-4+2|+3(-4) = 2-12$
$= -10$

11. $(0.9)(3.2)^2 = 9.216$

12. $(7.29)(6.2)^{-1} \approx 1.18$

13. $3(3) + 2^3 = 9 + 8$

$= 17 > 15$

3 is a solution.

14. $-(-4) + 7(-4)^2 - 14 = 4 + 112 - 14$

$= 102 \nless 18$

-4 is not a solution.

15. $5 + 2 = 7$

$|-3(-3)| = 9$

$7 \neq 9$

$(5, -3)$ is not a solution.

16. $2^{-4} = \frac{1}{2^4}$ $(2^{-1})^2 = 2^{-2}$

$= \frac{1}{16}$ $= \frac{1}{2^2}$

$= \frac{1}{4}$

$\frac{1}{16} < \frac{1}{4}$

$(-4, -1)$ is a solution.

17. 7.94×10^{-3}

18. 32,900

19. $2x - 5y = 10$

$-5y = -2x + 10$

$y = \frac{2}{5}x - 2$

Slope: $\frac{2}{5}$

20. $y = 3x - 2$ $0 = 3x - 2$

$y = -2$ $3x = 2$

$x = \frac{2}{3}$

x-intercept: $\left(\frac{2}{3}, 0\right)$

y-intercept: $(0, -2)$

10.3 Multiplying Polynomials: Two Special Cases

Communicating about Algebra

A. $(x - 2)^2$

Yes, the trinomial is the square of a binomial.

B. No, the coefficient of x^2 is not a perfect square.

C. $4(x + 3)^2$

Yes, factor out a common factor of 4.

EXERCISES

1. False

$(a - b)(a - b) = a^2 - ab - ab + b^2$

$= a^2 - 2ab + b^2$

$\neq a^2 - b^2$

2. $2ab$

3. $(x - 4)^2$

$x^2 - 8x + 16$

4. $(x - 3)(x + 3) = x^2 - 9$

$(x + 3)^2 = x^2 + 6x + 9$

$(x - 3)^2 = x^2 - 6x + 9$

5. $x^2 + 4x + 4$

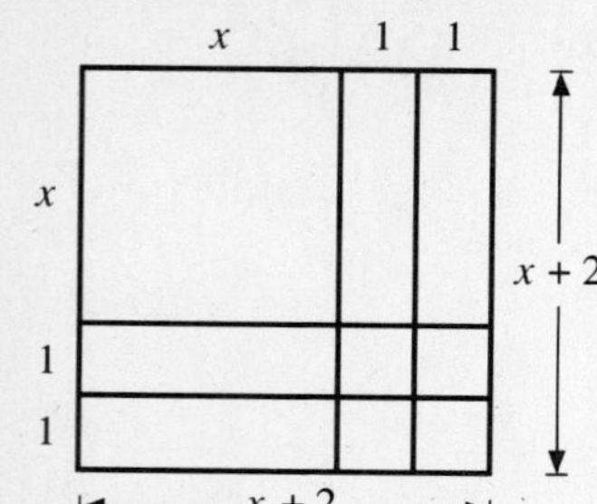

6. $x^2 + 6x + 9$

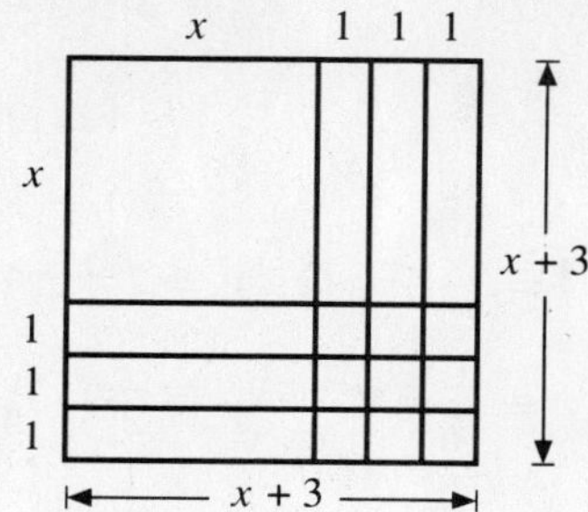

7. $4n^2 + 4n + 1$

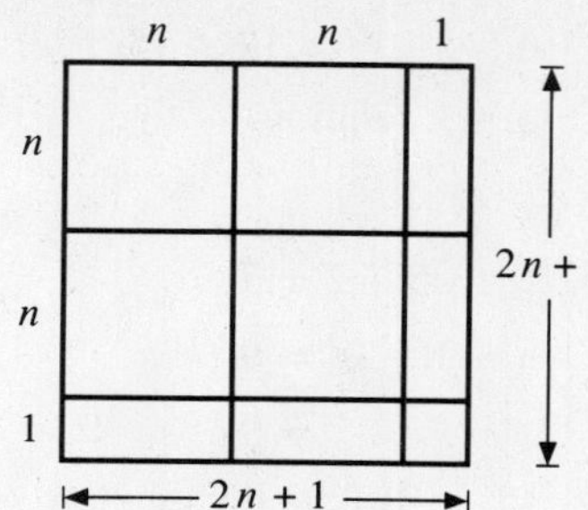

8. $9a^2 + 12a + 4$

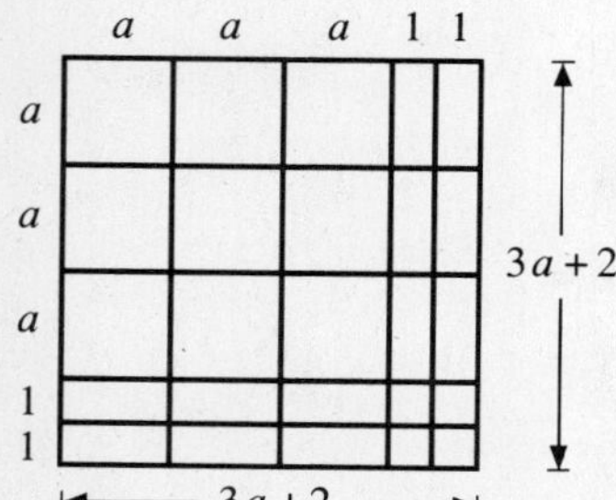

9. $4x^2 + 8x + 4$

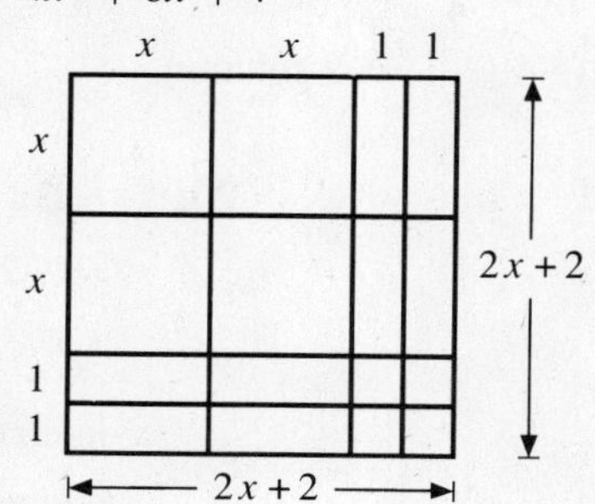

10. $9x^2 + 6x + 1$

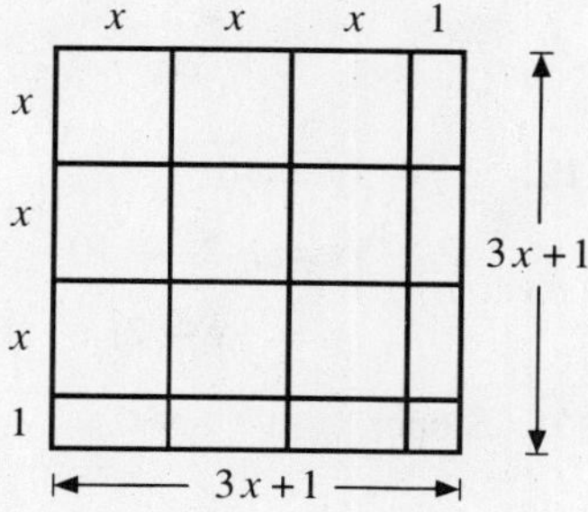

11. $n^2 + 12n + 36$

12. $x^2 + 8x + 16$

13. $4x^2 + 4x + 1$

14. $4m^2 - 12m + 9$

15. $9t^2 - 12t + 4$

16. $x^2 - 18x + 81$

17. $x^2 - 25$

18. $x^2 - 4$

19. $4x^2 - 4$

20. $25x^2 - 36$

21. $a^2 - 4b^2$

22. $16x^2 - 49y^2$

23. $x^2 + 12x + 36$

24. $x^2 + 20x + 100$

25. $a^2 - 4a + 4$

26. $4x^2 - 20x + 25$

27. $4x^2 - 20xy + 25y^2$

28. $16s^2 + 24st + 9t^2$

29. $(x + 2)^2$

$x^2 + 4x + 4$

Square of a binomial

30. $(2x + 3)(2x - 3)$

$4x^2 - 9$

Product of a sum and difference of two terms

31. $0.25 + 0.5 = 0.75$ or 75%, normal colored

0.25 or 25%, albino

32. 25%, normal feathers

50%, mildly frizzled feathers

25%, extremely frizzled feathers

33. $\dfrac{w}{\frac{3}{2}w} = \dfrac{x}{w}$

$\dfrac{3}{2}wx = w^2$

$x = \dfrac{2}{3}w$

Large: $P = 5w, \ A = \dfrac{3}{2}w^2$

Small: $P = \dfrac{10}{3}w, \ A = \dfrac{2}{3}w^2$

34. Triangle: $A = \frac{3}{2}x^2 + \frac{15}{2}x$
Rectangle: $A = 5x^2 + 25x$

35. $1000(1 + r)^2 = 1000 + 2000r + 1000r^2$

36. $2000(1 + 0.06)^2 = 2247.2$
$2000 + 2000(0.12) + 2000(0.0036) = 2247.2$

37. $(3 + 4)^2 = 7^2 = 49$ $\quad 3^2 + 4^2 = 9 + 16 = 25$
$49 \neq 25$

38. $(5 - 4)^2 = 1^2 = 1$
$5^2 - 4^2 = 25 - 16 = 9$
$1 \neq 9$

39. $(4 + 5)^2 = 9^2 = 81$

40. $(2 \cdot 1 - 4)^2 = (-2)^2 = 4$

41. $(-3 \cdot 0 + 5)^2 = 5^2 = 25$

42. $(-6 + 3)^2 = (-3)^2 = 9$

43. $\left(\frac{1}{4}(-40) + 9\right)^2 = (-1)^2 = 1$

44. $\left(6\left(\frac{1}{3}\right) - 5\right)^2 = (-3)^2 = 9$

45. $\dfrac{x^2y}{xy^2} = \dfrac{x}{y}$

46. $\dfrac{4x^6y^8}{2y^2} = 2x^6y^6$

47. $\dfrac{9x^5y^3}{3x^2y} = 3x^3y^2$

48. $4x - (x + 5)(x - 5) = -x^2 + 4x + 25$

49. $(4 - x)^2 + 8 = 24 - 8x + x^2$

50. $(x + 2)^2 - x^2 + 9 = 4x + 13$

51. **e.** **52.** **b.** **53.** **b.** **54.** **d.**

55. a. $(a + b)(a + b)(a - b) = (a + b)(a^2 - b^2)$
$= a^3 + a^2b - ab^2 - b^3$

b. $(a + b)(a + b)(a - b) = (a^2 + 2ab + b^2)(a - b)$
$= a^3 + 2a^2b + ab^2 - a^2b - 2ab^2 - b^3$
$= a^3 + a^2b - ab^2 - b^3$

c. Personal choice, methods give the same results.

56. $(a + b + c)^2 = a(a + b + c) + b(a + b + c) + c(a + b + c)$
$= a^2 + ab + ac + ab + b^2 + bc + ac + bc + c^2$
$= a^2 + b^2 + c^2 + 2ab + 2ac + 2bc$

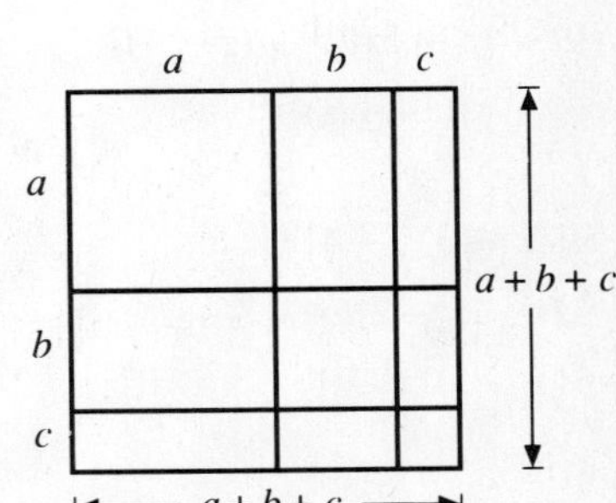

10.4 Factoring: Special Products

Communicating about Algebra

A. $9t^2 - 49 = (3t + 7)(3t - 7)$

Difference of two squares pattern

B. $x^2 - 16x + 64 = (x - 8)^2$

Perfect square trinomial pattern

C. $4y^2 + 36y + 81 = (2y + 9)^2$

Perfect square trinomial pattern

D. $121x^2 - 100 = (11x + 100)(11x - 100)$

Difference of two squares pattern

EXERCISES

1. Multiplying polynomials is the reverse of factoring polynomials.

2. $3(x^3 - 2x^2 + 3)$

3. $2x(2x - 3) + 3(2x - 3) = (2x - 3)(2x + 3)$

4. $4x^2 - 25 = (2x - 5)(2x + 5)$

$x^2 + 14x + 49 = (x + 7)^2$

$x^2 - 16x + 64 = (x - 8)^2$

5. $6x^3$ **6.** $7x$ **7.** $8x^2$ **8.** $9x^3$

9. $4xy$ **10.** $5xy$ **11.** $2(x^2 - 2)$ **12.** $3(x + 2)$

13. $4(a - 3)$ **14.** $7(2z^3 + 3)$ **15.** $6(4x^2 - 3)$ **16.** $-a(a^2 + 4)$

17. $7u(3u - 2)$ **18.** $12y^2(3y^2 + 2)$ **19.** $4(x^2 - 2x + 2)$ **20.** $(x - 8)(x + 8)$

21. $(y - 12)(y + 12)$ **22.** $2(x + 4)^2$ **23.** $(3x - 5y)^2$ **24.** $(2y + 5z)^2$

25. $\left(u - \frac{1}{4}\right)\left(u + \frac{1}{4}\right)$ **26.** $\left(v - \frac{3}{5}\right)\left(v + \frac{3}{5}\right)$

27. $[9 - (z + 5)][9 + (z + 5)]$

$(4 - z)(14 + z)$

28. $3[(x - 3)^2 - 4]$

$3(x - 3 - 2)(x - 3 + 2)$

$3(x - 5)(x - 1)$

29. $R = 800x - 0.05x^2$

$xp = 800x - 0.05x^2$

$xp = x(800 - 0.05x)$

$p = 800 - 0.05x$

The graph of the price model has a negative slope; therefore, as the price, p, decreases, the number of units sold, x, increases.

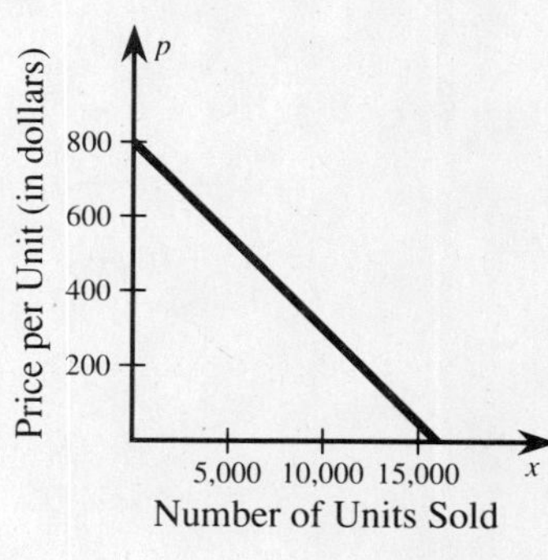

30. The maximum revenue occurs when

$$x = \frac{-b}{2a} = \frac{-800}{-0.1} = 8000 \text{ units.}$$

The price per unit when $x = 8000$ is

$$p = 800 - 0.05x = 800 - 0.05(8000) = 400 \text{ dollars per unit.}$$

31. $4^2 = 16 = (2)(8)$ $\quad (2)(8) = (5-3)(5+3) = 5^2 - 3^2$

$4^2 = 5^2 - 3^2$ $\quad 4^2 + 3^2 = 5^2$ $\quad a = 4$, $b = 3$, $c = 5$

32. $6^2 = 36 = (2)(18)$ $\quad (2)(18) = (10-8)(10+8) = 10^2 - 8^2$ $\quad 6^2 = 10^2 - 8^2$ $\quad 6^2 + 8^2 = 10^2$ $\quad a = 6$, $b = 8$, $c = 10$

33. $8^2 = 64 = (2)(32) = 4(16)$ $\quad (2)(32) = (17-15)(17+15) = 17^2 - 15^2$ $\quad 8^2 = 17^2 - 15^2$ $\quad 8^2 + 15^2 = 17^2$ $\quad a = 8$, $b = 15$, $c = 17$

$(4)(16) = (10-6)(10+6) = 10^2 - 6^2$ $\quad 8^2 = 10^2 - 6^2$ $\quad 8^2 + 6^2 = 10^2$ $\quad a = 8$, $b = 6$, $c = 10$

34. $A = \pi R^2 - \pi r^2 = \pi(30^2 - 5^2) \approx 2748.9 \text{ cm}^2$

35. $kQx - kx^2 = kx(Q - x)$

36.

$$\begin{aligned} (60-2x)(60+2x) &= 3200 \\ 3600 - 4x^2 &= 3200 \\ 400 - 4x^2 &= 0 \\ 4(100 - x^2) &= 0 \\ 4(10-x)(10+x) &= 0 \end{aligned}$$

$x = 10$ or $x = -10$

40 feet by 80 feet

$80 \div 4 = 20$ rows

The length of the region the band is allotted is 80 feet. 20 rows are possible for 160 band members. Yes, all the members can be in the parade.

37.

$$\begin{aligned} (25x^2 - 1)7 &= 161 \\ 25x^2 - 1 &= 23 \\ 25x^2 &= 24 \\ x^2 &= \tfrac{24}{25} \\ x &= \pm\sqrt{\tfrac{24}{25}} \\ x &\approx 0.98, \ -0.98 \end{aligned}$$

$(7)(5x+1)(5x-1)$

The package dimensions were 7 inches $\times \approx 5.9$ inches $\times 3.9$ inches. You will have to pick it up at the post office.

38. $24x^2 - 36x$

39. $28y - 21y^2$

40. $t^3 + t - t^3 + t = 2t$

41. $2z(z+5) - 7(z+5) = 2z^2 + 3z - 35$

42. $121 - x^2$

43. $36r^2 - 25s^2$

44. $x^2 + 4x + 4 - x^2 = 8$
$4x = 4$
$x = 1$

45. $x^2 - 2x + 1 + 2x = 4$
$x^2 + 1 = 4$
$x^2 = 3$
$x = \pm\sqrt{3}$

46. $x^2 - 8x + 16 + 8x = 32$
$x^2 + 16 = 32$
$x^2 = 16$
$x = \pm 4$

47. $x^2 - 12x + 36 - x^2 = 0$
$12x = 36$
$x = 3$

48. $x^2 - 9 + 5 = 0$
$x^2 = 4$
$x = \pm 2$

49. $x^2 - 16 = -7$
$x^2 = 9$
$x = \pm 3$

50. $h = -16(2)^2 + 57(2)$
$= 50$ feet

51. $5^2 + b^2 = 13^2$
$b^2 = 144$
$b = 12$

52. $P = 2[(x + 7) + (x - 7)]$
$= 4x$

53. $P = 2[(x + 3) + (x + 3)]$
$= 4x + 12$

Mid-Chapter SELF-TEST

1. $(x^2 - 4x^2) + (2x + 3x) + (-1 + 2) = -3x^2 + 5x + 1$

2. $(-2x^2 - x^2) + (4x + 7x) + (-5 - 3) = -3x^2 + 11x - 8$

3. $\begin{array}{r} 3x^2 - x + 2 \\ \underline{x^2 - 3x + 2} \\ 4x^2 - 4x + 4 \end{array}$

4. $\begin{array}{r} (7x^2 - 5x + 10) \\ \underline{-(3x^2 + 2x + 5)} \\ 4x^2 - 7x + 5 \end{array}$

5. $9x^2 + 21x + 10$

6. $8x^2 + 30x - 50$

7. $2x^3 - 3x^2 + 2x + 2x^2 - 3x + 2 = 2x^3 - x^2 - x + 2$

8. $10x^3 + 14x^2 - 6x + 5x^2 + 7x - 3 = 10x^3 + 19x^2 + x - 3$

9. $x^2 - x - 6$

10. $x^2 - 9x + 18$

11. $-2x^2 + 5x + 12$

12. $x^2 + 7x + 12$

13. $4x^2 + 12x + 9$

14. $16x^2 - 40x + 25$

15. $4x^2 - 36$

16. $x^2 - 49$

17. $(2x - 7)(2x + 7)$

18. $3(x - 6)(x + 6)$

19. $(x - 1)^2$

20. $7(x + 3)^2$

21. $(3x + 2)^2$

22. $(x - 13)(x + 13)$

23. $M = F + J$
$= 50{,}262 + 99.2t^2 + (33{,}045 + 140.7t^2)$
$M = 83{,}307 + 239.9t^2$

24. $V = (x + 1)^3 + (x + 3)^3 + (x + 5)^3$

25. $A = (3x + 2)^2$

26. $A = (2x + 16)(2x + 20)$

10.5 Factoring Quadratic Trinomials

Communicating about Algebra

A. $(x + 4)(x + 3)$

B. $(a - 5)(a - 1)$

C. $(3n - 2)(n + 2)$

EXERCISES

1. $(x - 1)(x - 3)$

Since c is positive, its factors must have the same sign.

2. $(x + 3)(x - 1)$

Since c is negative, its factors must have opposite signs.

3. $b^2 - 4ac$

4. No; the discriminant must be the square of an integer.

5. **a.**

6. **b.**

7. **a.**

8. **a.**

9. **b.**

10. Neither
$(x + 1)(2x - 9)$

11. $(x + 4)(x - 1)$

12. $(x - 2)(x - 3)$

13. $(x + 6)(x - 3)$

14. $(y - 18)(y + 2)$

15. $(x - 6)(x - 4)$

16. $(x + 2)(x + 11)$

17. $(x + 10)(x + 5)$

18. $(y + 12)(y + 18)$

19. $(y - 15)(y - 20)$

20. $(t - 7)(t + 3)$

21. $(3x + 5)(x + 1)$

22. $(2x - 1)(3x + 4)$

23. $(2x - 7)(x + 3)$

24. $(3x + 5)(x + 2)$

25. $(y - 12)(y - 4)$

26. $(x + 4)(x + 8)$

27. $(2x + 3)(x - 2)$

28. $(-7x - 1)(x - 5)$

29. $(-11)^2 - 4(12)(3) = 121 - 144$
$= -23$

Cannot factor

30. $(-5)^2 - 4(2)(-12) = 25 + 96$
$= 121$

$(2x + 3)(x - 4)$

31. $(-10)^2 - 4(6)(4) = 100 - 96$
$= 4$

$2(3x - 2)(x - 1)$

32. $(-9)^2 - 4(10)(6) = 81 - 240$
$= -159$

Cannot factor

33. $(-19)^2 - 4(14)(-40) = 361 + 2240$
$= 2601$

$(7x + 8)(2x - 5)$

34. $(3)^2 - 4(24)(-11) = 9 + 1065$
$= 1065$

Cannot factor

35. $(x + 5)$, $(x - 1)$

36. $(2x + 3)$

Use the tables for Exercises 37–46

Letter	A	B	C	D	E	F	G	H	I	J	K	L
Code Number	1	−4	8	−3	9	−8	10	−7	2	−9	5	−6

Letter	M	N	O	P	Q	R	S	T	U	V	Y	Z
Code Number	3	−10	4	−1	6	−11	7	−2	11	−12	12	−5

37. A = 1
B = −4
C = 8
D = −3

38. E = 9
F = −8
G = 10
H = −7

39. I = 2
J = −9
K = 5
L = −6

40. M = 3
N = −10
O = 4
P = −1

41. Q = 6
R = −11
S = 7
T = −2

42. U = 11
V = −12
Y = 12
Z = −5

43. **a.** Ivory mask

44. **b.** Carved stool

45. **c.** Patterned vessel

46. **d.** Masai necklace

47. $(x+3)(x+1)$

48. $(x+4)(x+1)$

49. Revenue each week: $R = \frac{1}{100}(-40t^2 + 740t + 1200)$

Sales each week: $S = 8t + 12$

Price of a hot dog each week: $P = \frac{R}{S}$

t	0	1	2	3	4	5	6	7
P	\$1.00	95¢	90¢	85¢	80¢	75¢	70¢	65¢

$$= \frac{\frac{1}{100}(-40t^2 + 740t + 1200)}{8t + 12}$$

$$= \frac{\frac{1}{100}(8t + 12)(-5t + 100)}{(8t + 12)}$$

$$= \frac{1}{100}(-5t + 100)$$

$$P = -\frac{1}{20}t + 1$$

50. $t^2 + 11t + 30 = (t+6)(t+5)$

Average number of players: $t + 5$; 6, 7, 8, 9, 10

51. $-2y^2 - 2y$

52. $x^2 + 8x + 16$

53. $v^2 - 7v + 6$

54. $3x + 6 = 5$
$3x = -1$
$x = -\frac{1}{3}$

55. $-4x + 5 = x$
$5 = 5x$
$x = 1$

56. $5y - 15 = -y - 6$
$6y = 9$
$y = \frac{3}{2}$

57. $x(2x+1)(x-3)$

58. $2x(3x-2)(8x+5)$

59. $(x^2-1)(x^2-4) = (x+1)(x-1)(x+2)(x-2)$

60. $(x^2-4)(x^2-9) = (x-2)(x+2)(x-3)(x+3)$

10.6 Solving Quadratic Equations by Factoring

Communicating about Algebra

A. Solve by factoring.

$(x-2)(x-1)=0$

$x=2,\ x=1$

The graph shows the x-intercepts of (2, 0) and (1, 0).

B. Solve by quadratic formula.

$$x=\frac{-(-2)\pm\sqrt{(-2)^2-4(1)(-1)}}{2\cdot 1}$$

$$=\frac{2\pm\sqrt{8}}{2}$$

$$=1\pm\sqrt{2}$$

$x\approx 2.4,\ -0.4$

The graph shows the x-intercepts.

C. Solve by square roots, since there is no x-term.

$x=\pm\sqrt{3}$

The graph shows the x-intercepts.

EXERCISES

1. $a=0$ or $b=0$

2. $x=2$ or $x=-1$

3. $x=0$ or $x=-\frac{4}{3}$

4. 0 and -1

5. False; the product of any number and its reciprocal is 1; so neither factor has to equal 1.

6. True; a product cannot equal 0 unless one of the factors is 0.

7. $x=-1$ or $x=-2$

8. $x=3$ or $x=-7$

9. $x=-3$ or $x=-4$

10. $x=-6$ or $x=5$

11. $(x+6)(x-1)=0$
$x=-6$ or $x=1$

12. $(3x-1)(x+4)=0$
$x=\frac{1}{3}$ or $x=-4$

13. $(2x+3)(x+1)=0$
$x=-\frac{3}{2}$ or $x=-1$

14. $(2x+1)(3x+5)=0$
$x=-\frac{1}{2}$ or $x=-\frac{5}{3}$

15. $(3x+1)(x+2)=0$
$x=-\frac{1}{3}$ or $x=-2$

16. $(4x-3)(3x+1)=0$
$x=\frac{3}{4}$ or $x=-\frac{1}{3}$

17. **f.**

18. **b.**

19. **g.**

20. **a.**

21. **d.**

22. **c.**

23. **e.**

24. **h.**

25. $x=0$
$x=9$

26. $y=0$
$y=-6$

27. $y^2-7y+12=0$
$(y-3)(y-4)=0$
$y=3$ or $y=4$

28. $x^2=9$
$x=\pm 3$

29. $x^2-8x+16=0$
$(x-4)^2=0$
$x=4$

30. $x^2 + 4x + 4 = 0$

$(x + 2)^2 = 0$

$x = -2$

31. $2x(2x + 1) = 0$

$x = 0$ or $x = -\frac{1}{2}$

32. $2y(2y - 9) = 0$

$y = 0$ or $y = \frac{9}{2}$

33. $x^2 - 12x + 36 = 0$

$(x - 6)^2 = 0$

$x = 6$

34. $8x^2 + 32x + 24 = 0$

$8(x^2 + 4x + 3) = 0$

$8(x + 1)(x + 3) = 0$

$x = -1$ or $x = -3$

35. $23x^2 - 54x + 16 = 0$

$(23x - 8)(x - 2) = 0$

$x = \frac{8}{23}$ or $x = 2$

36. $x(x + 8) = 33$

$x^2 + 8x - 33 = 0$

$(x + 11)(x - 3) = 0$

$x = -11$ or $x = 3$

The dimensions of the scale are 3 feet by 11 feet.

37. $w^2 - 38w + 361 = 0$

$(w - 19)^2 = 0$

$w = 19$

$1900 - 0.38(1900) = 1178$

The male elephant seal weighed 1178 pounds at the end of the season.

38. $(x + 140)^2 = 102{,}400$

$x^2 + 280x + 19{,}600 = 102{,}400$

$x^2 + 280x - 82{,}800 = 0$

$(x - 180)(x + 460) = 0$

$x = 180$ or $x = -460$

Platform: 320 feet by 320 feet
Building: 180 feet by 180 feet

39. **b.**

40. $x^2 - 3x - 18$

41. $4x^2 + 33x - 27$

42. $-x^2 + x + 42$

43. $9x^2 + 18x - 7$

44. $12x^2 + 32x - 11$

45. $x^2 + \frac{7}{4}x + \frac{9}{2}$

46. $2^2 - 3 \cdot 2 + 4 = 2 \neq 0$

2 is not a solution.

47. $(-1)^2 + 5(-1) + 4 = 0$

-1 is a solution.

48. $\frac{1}{3}(6)^2 + 2 \cdot 6 - 36 = -12 \neq 0$

6 is not a solution.

49. $2 \cdot 2^2 - 3 \cdot 2 - 4 = -2 \neq 0$

2 is not a solution.

50. $4(-3)^2 + 3(-3) - 27 = 0$

-3 is a solution.

51. $\frac{1}{2} \cdot 4^2 - 4 + 8 = 12 \neq 0$

4 is not a solution.

52. $x = \dfrac{-4 \pm \sqrt{16 - 4(1)(3)}}{2 \cdot 1}$

$x = \dfrac{-4 \pm \sqrt{4}}{2}$

$x = -1, \ -3$

53. $x = \dfrac{7 \pm \sqrt{49 - 4(1)(9)}}{2 \cdot 1}$

$x = \dfrac{7 \pm \sqrt{13}}{2}$

$x \approx 5.30, \ 1.70$

54. $x = \dfrac{5 \pm \sqrt{25 - 4(2)3}}{2 \cdot 2}$

$x = \dfrac{5 \pm \sqrt{1}}{4}$

$x = \frac{3}{2}, \ 1$

55. $x = \dfrac{11 \pm \sqrt{121 - 4(3)(-24)}}{2 \cdot 3}$

$x = \dfrac{11 \pm \sqrt{409}}{6}$

$x \approx 5.20, \ -1.54$

56. $x = \dfrac{16 \pm \sqrt{256 - 4(5)(-12)}}{2 \cdot 5}$

$x = \dfrac{16 \pm \sqrt{496}}{10}$

$x \approx 3.83, \ -0.63$

57. $x = \dfrac{17 \pm \sqrt{289 - 4(9)(6)}}{2 \cdot 9}$

$x = \dfrac{17 \pm \sqrt{73}}{18}$

$x \approx 1.42, \ 0.47$

58. The diver will hit the water in 2 seconds. One of the factors must equal zero. The factor $(t-2)$ will give a positive answer.

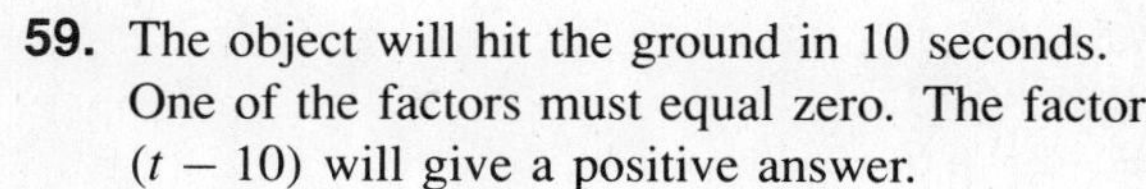

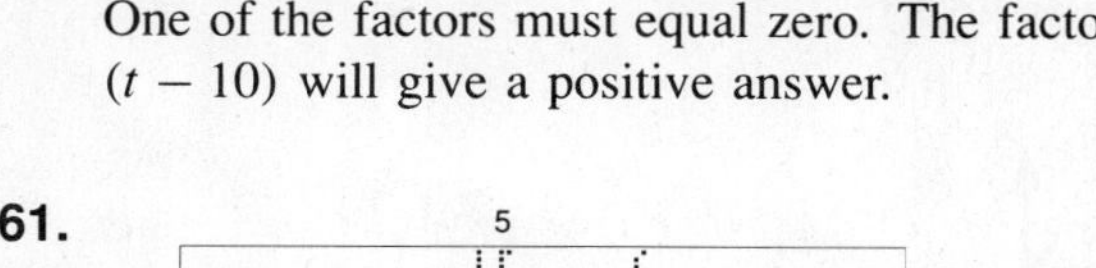

59. The object will hit the ground in 10 seconds. One of the factors must equal zero. The factor $(t - 10)$ will give a positive answer.

60.

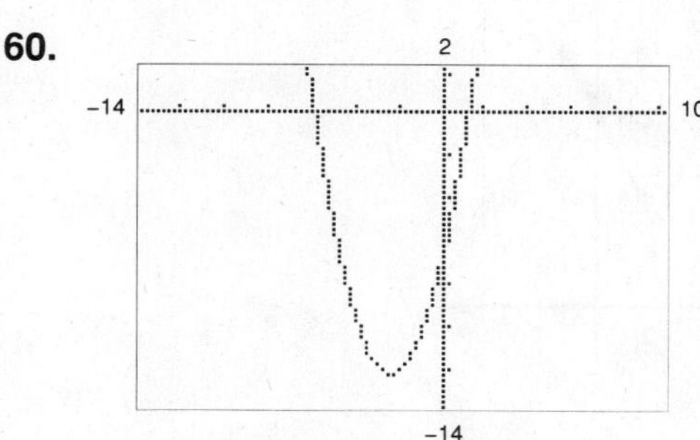

They are the same graph.

61.

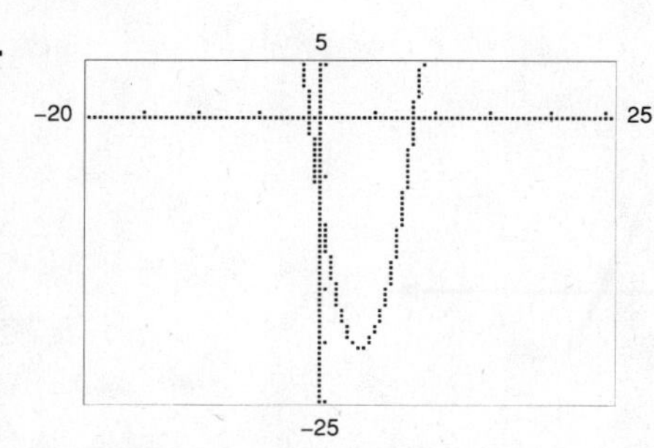

They are the same graph.

62. $(x - 4)(x + 3) = 0$

$x^2 - x - 12 = 0$

63. $(x - 5)(x - 5) = 0$

$x^2 - 10x + 25 = 0$

64. $(x + 2)(x + 5) = 0$

$x^2 + 7x + 10 = 0$

65. $x(x + 1) = 0$

$x^2 + x = 0$

66. $ax^2 + bx = 0$

$x(ax + b) = 0$

$x = 0 \text{ or } x = -\dfrac{b}{a}$

67. $ax^2 - ax = 0$

$ax(x - 1) = 0$

$x = 0 \text{ or } x = 1$

68. $2x(x) = 5000$

$x^2 = 2500$

$x = 50$

Weft: 100 per square inch

Warp: 50 per square inch

Mixed REVIEW

1. $\dfrac{x^2y^{-1}}{3x} \cdot y^2 = \dfrac{1}{3}xy$

2. $\dfrac{p^2q^4}{2p} \cdot \dfrac{4p^{-2}}{q^{-2}} = \dfrac{2q^6}{p}$

3. $3x^2 \div 9x = \dfrac{x}{3}$

4. $2p + (-4p) = -2p$

5. $4m + 2n = 3$

$4m = -2n + 3$

$m = -\frac{1}{2}n + \frac{3}{4}$

6. $ab + a = 5$

$a(b + 1) = 5$

$a = \dfrac{5}{b + 1}$

7. $2x^4$

8. 1.2×10^{-4}

9. $8 \times 10^1 = 80$

10. 2×10^7

11. $|x + 3| \le 4$

$-4 \le x + 3 \le 4$

$-7 \le x \le 1$

12. $2|3 - x| > 1$

$|3 - x| > \frac{1}{2}$

$3 - x < -\frac{1}{2}$ or $3 - x > \frac{1}{2}$

$-x < -\frac{7}{2}$ $\quad -x > -\frac{5}{2}$

$x > \frac{7}{2}$ $\quad x < \frac{5}{2}$

13. 8, -8

14. x, $-x$

15. $y = -2x + 6$

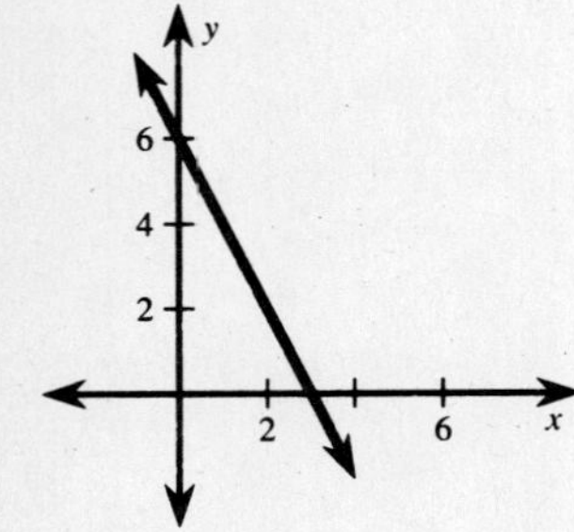

16. Vertex: $(-2, 3)$

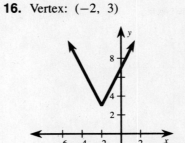

17. $2^{-(-6)} = 2^6$ $\quad -7(-6) = 42$

$= 64$

$64 \not< 42$

-6 is not a solution.

18. $y = -2$ $\quad -|2x| = -|2(-1)|$

$= -2$

$(-1, -2)$ is a solution.

19. $\begin{cases} x - 7y = -17 \\ 3x + y = -7 \end{cases}$

$x = 7y - 17$

$3(7y - 17) + y = -7$

$21y - 51 + y = -7$

$22y = 44$

$y = 2$

$x = 7 \cdot 2 - 17$

$x = -3$

$(-3, 2)$

20. $\begin{cases} 4x + 3y = -1 \\ 5x - 6y = 28 \end{cases}$

$8x + 6y = -2$

$5x - 6y = 28$

$13x = 26$

$x = 2$

$4 \cdot 2 + 3y = -1$

$3y = -9$

$y = -3$

$(2, -3)$

Using a Graphing Calculator

1. $y_1 = x - 1$

$y_2 = \frac{1}{2}x + 2$

$y_3 = 1\frac{1}{2}x + 1$

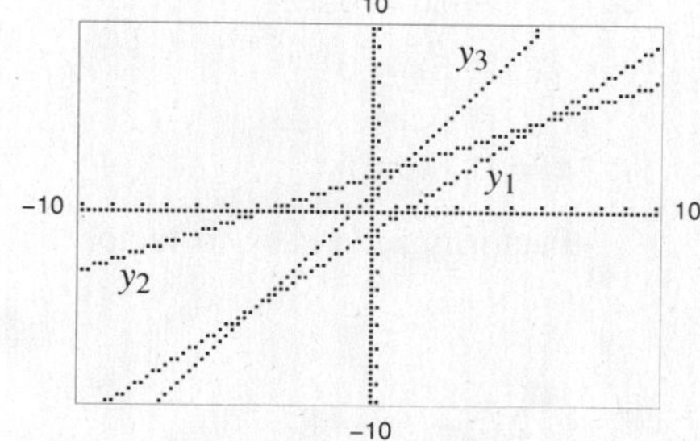

2. $y_1 = x^2 + x$

$y_2 = 1$

$y_3 = x^2 + x + 1$

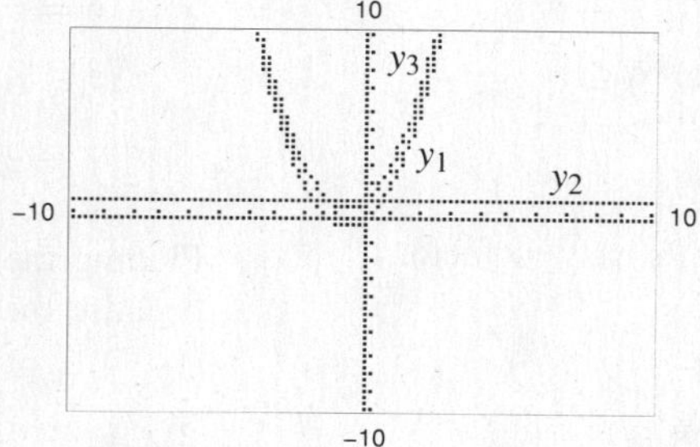

3. $y_1 = \frac{1}{2}x^2 - 1$

$y_2 = \frac{1}{2}x^2 + 1$

$y_3 = x^2$

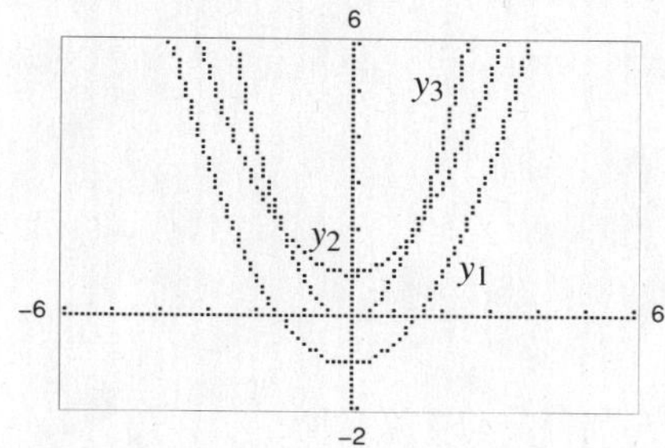

4. $y_1 = 2x + 1$

$y_2 = x + 1$

$y_3 = x$

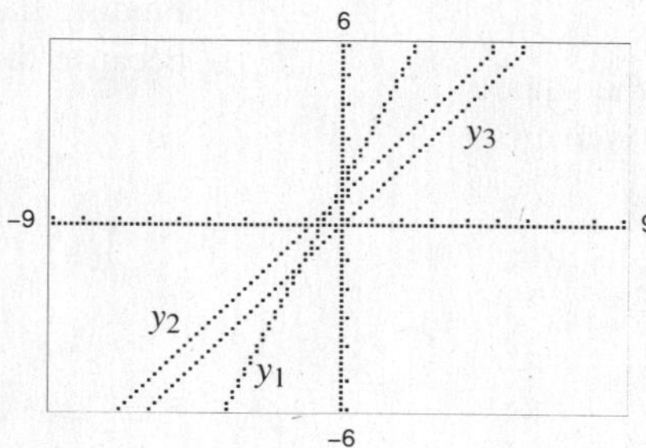

5. $y_1 = x^2 + 3$

$y_2 = \frac{1}{2}x^2$

$y_3 = \frac{1}{2}x^2 + 3$

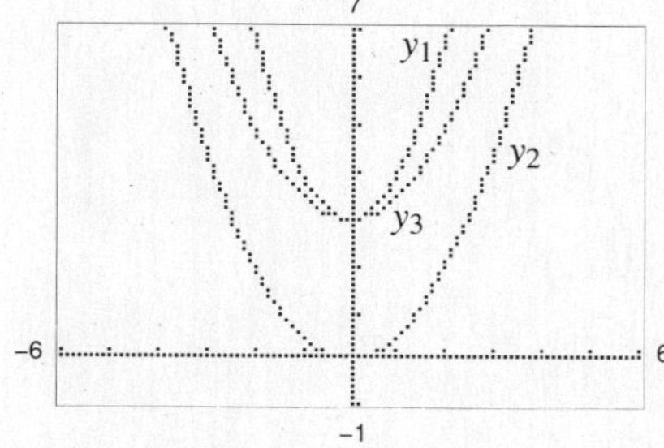

6. $y_1 = \frac{1}{3}x^2 + x$

$y_2 = 1$

$y_3 = \frac{1}{3}x^2 + x - 1$

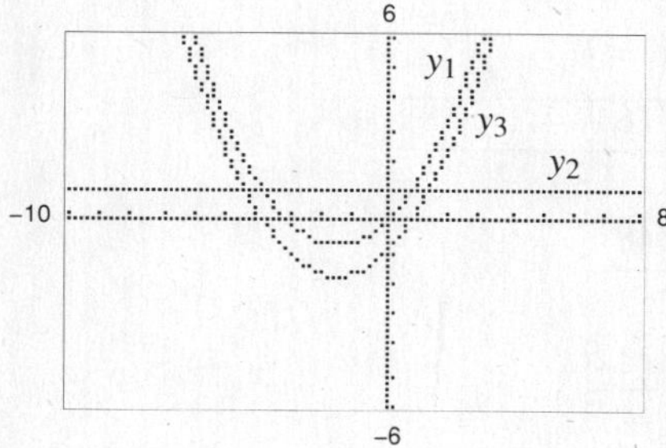

10.7 Solving Quadratic Equations by Completing the Square

Communicating about Algebra

A. $x^2 - 6x + 8 = 0$

$(x-4)(x-2) = 0$

$x = 4,\ x = 2$

Factoring; it's easy to factor.

B. $x^2 - 6 = 0$

$x^2 = 6$

$x = \pm\sqrt{6}$

Finding the square roots; because there is no x-term.

C. $x^2 - 6x = 0$

$x(x-6) = 0$

$x = 0,\ x = 6$

Factoring; it's easy to factor.

D. $x^2 - 6x - 8 = 0$

$x^2 - 6x + 9 = 8 + 9$

$(x-3)^2 = 17$

$x - 3 = \pm\sqrt{17}$

$x = 3 \pm \sqrt{17}$

Completing the square; $a = 1$ and b is even.

E. $2(x-3)^2 = 12$

$(x-3)^2 = 6$

$x - 3 = \pm\sqrt{6}$

$x = 3 \pm \sqrt{6}$

Finding the square roots; because there is no x-term.

F. $2x^2 - 6x - 8 = 0$

$2(x^2 - 3x - 4) = 0$

$2(x-4)(x+1) = 0$

$x = 4,\ x = -1$

Factoring; it's easy to factor.

EXERCISES

1. **b.**

2. $x^2 - 4x + 4 = 12$

$(x-2)^2 = 12$

$x - 2 = \pm\sqrt{12}$

$x = 2 \pm \sqrt{12}$

$x^2 - 4x - 8 = 0$

$$x = \frac{4 \pm \sqrt{16 - 4(1)(-8)}}{2 \cdot 1}$$

$$= \frac{4 \pm \sqrt{48}}{2}$$

$$= \frac{4 \pm 2\sqrt{12}}{2}$$

$$= 2 \pm \sqrt{12}$$

There is no difference.

3. 9

4.
1. Find square roots
2. Graphing
3. Quadratic Formula
4. Factoring
5. Completing the square

5. 81

6. 9

7. 36

8. 25

9. $\frac{49}{4}$

10. $\frac{25}{4}$

11. $x^2 + 10x - 11 = 0$

$$x^2 + 10x + 25 = 11 + 25$$
$$(x + 5)^2 = 36$$
$$x + 5 = \pm 6$$
$$x = \pm 6 - 5$$

$x = 1$ or $x = -11$

12. $x^2 + 14x - 15 = 0$

$$x^2 + 14x + 49 = 15 + 49$$
$$(x + 7)^2 = 64$$
$$x + 7 = \pm 8$$
$$x = \pm 8 - 7$$

$x = 1$ or $x = -15$

13. $y^2 - 24y + 63 = 0$

$$y^2 - 24y + 144 = -63 + 144$$
$$(y - 12)^2 = 81$$
$$y - 12 = \pm 9$$
$$y = \pm 9 + 12$$

$y = 21$ or $y = 3$

14. $y^2 - 8y + 12 = 0$

$$y^2 - 8y + 16 = -12 + 16$$
$$(y - 4)^2 = 4$$
$$y - 4 = \pm 2$$
$$y = \pm 2 + 4$$

$y = 6$ or $y = 2$

15. $t^2 + 3t - \frac{7}{4} = 0$

$$t^2 + 3t + \tfrac{9}{4} = \tfrac{7}{4} + \tfrac{9}{4}$$
$$\left(t + \tfrac{3}{2}\right)^2 = 4$$
$$t + \tfrac{3}{2} = \pm 2$$
$$t = \pm 2 - \tfrac{3}{2}$$

$t = \frac{1}{2}$ or $t = -\frac{7}{2}$

16. $y^2 + 9y + \frac{17}{4} = 0$

$$y^2 + 9y + \tfrac{81}{4} = -\tfrac{17}{4} + \tfrac{81}{4}$$
$$\left(y + \tfrac{9}{2}\right)^2 = 16$$
$$y + \tfrac{9}{2} = \pm 4$$
$$y = \pm 4 - \tfrac{9}{2}$$

$y = -\frac{1}{2}$ or $y = -\frac{17}{2}$

17. $x^2 - \dfrac{2}{3}x - 3 = 0$

$$x^2 - \frac{2}{3}x + \frac{1}{9} = 3 + \frac{1}{9}$$
$$\left(x - \frac{1}{3}\right)^2 = \frac{28}{9}$$
$$x - \frac{1}{3} = \pm\frac{\sqrt{28}}{3}$$
$$x = \pm\frac{\sqrt{28}}{3} + \frac{1}{3}$$
$$x = \frac{1 \pm \sqrt{28}}{3}$$

18. $x^2 + \dfrac{4}{5}x - 1 = 0$

$$x^2 + \frac{4}{5}x + \frac{4}{25} = 1 + \frac{4}{25}$$
$$\left(x + \frac{2}{5}\right)^2 = \frac{29}{25}$$
$$x + \frac{2}{5} = \pm\frac{\sqrt{29}}{5}$$
$$x = \pm\frac{\sqrt{29}}{5} - \frac{2}{5}$$
$$x = \frac{-2 \pm \sqrt{29}}{5}$$

19. $x^2 + x - 1 = 0$

$$x^2 + x + \frac{1}{4} = 1 + \frac{1}{4}$$
$$\left(x + \frac{1}{2}\right)^2 = \frac{5}{4}$$
$$x + \frac{1}{2} = \pm\frac{\sqrt{5}}{2}$$
$$x = \pm\frac{\sqrt{5}}{2} - \frac{1}{2}$$
$$x = \frac{-1 \pm \sqrt{5}}{2}$$

20. $x^2 - x - 1 = 0$

$$x^2 - x + \frac{1}{4} = 1 + \frac{1}{4}$$
$$\left(x - \frac{1}{2}\right)^2 = \frac{5}{4}$$
$$x - \frac{1}{2} = \pm\frac{\sqrt{5}}{2}$$
$$x = \frac{1 \pm \sqrt{5}}{2}$$

21. $4y^2 + 4y - 9 = 0$

$$y^2 + y + \frac{1}{4} = \frac{9}{4} + \frac{1}{4}$$
$$\left(y + \frac{1}{2}\right)^2 = \frac{10}{4}$$
$$y + \frac{1}{2} = \pm\frac{\sqrt{10}}{2}$$
$$y = \pm\frac{\sqrt{10}}{2} - \frac{1}{2}$$
$$y = \frac{-1 \pm \sqrt{10}}{2}$$

22. $3x^2 - 24x - 5 = 0$

$$x^2 - 8x + 16 = \frac{5}{3} + 16$$
$$(x - 4)^2 = \frac{53}{3}$$
$$x - 4 = \pm\sqrt{\frac{53}{3}}$$
$$x = \pm\frac{\sqrt{159}}{3} + 4$$
$$x = 4 \pm \frac{\sqrt{159}}{3}$$

23. $2x^2 - 6x - 15 = 5$

$$x^2 - 3x + \frac{9}{4} = 10 + \frac{9}{4}$$
$$\left(x - \frac{3}{2}\right)^2 = \frac{49}{4}$$
$$x - \frac{3}{2} = \pm\frac{7}{2}$$
$$x = \pm\frac{7}{2} + \frac{3}{2}$$

$x = 5$ or $x = -2$

24. $5x^2 - 20x - 20 = 5$

$$x^2 - 4x + 4 = 5 + 4$$
$$(x - 2)^2 = 9$$
$$x - 2 = \pm 3$$
$$x = \pm 3 + 2$$

$x = -1$ or $x = 5$

25. $3x^2 + 4x + 4 = 3$

$$x^2 + \tfrac{4}{3}x + \tfrac{4}{9} = -\tfrac{1}{3} + \tfrac{4}{9}$$
$$\left(x + \tfrac{2}{3}\right)^2 = \tfrac{1}{9}$$
$$x + \tfrac{2}{3} = \pm\tfrac{1}{3}$$
$$x = \pm\tfrac{1}{3} - \tfrac{2}{3}$$

$x = -\tfrac{1}{3}$ or $x = -1$

26. $4x^2 + 6x - 6 = 2$

$$x^2 + \frac{3}{2}x + \frac{9}{16} = 2 + \frac{9}{16}$$
$$\left(x + \frac{3}{4}\right)^2 = \frac{41}{16}$$
$$x + \frac{3}{4} = \pm\frac{\sqrt{41}}{4}$$
$$x = \pm\frac{\sqrt{41}}{4} - \frac{3}{4}$$
$$x = \frac{-3 \pm \sqrt{41}}{4}$$

27. $x^2 + 2x + 1 = 2 + 1$

$$(x + 1)^2 = 3$$
$$x + 1 = \pm\sqrt{3}$$
$$x = \pm\sqrt{3} - 1$$
$$x = -1 \pm \sqrt{3}$$

28. $x^2 - 2x + 1 = 2 + 1$

$$(x - 1)^2 = 3$$
$$x - 1 = \pm\sqrt{3}$$
$$x = \pm\sqrt{3} + 1$$
$$x = 1 \pm \sqrt{3}$$

29. $x^2 - 3x - 1 = 0$

$$x^2 - 3x + \frac{9}{4} = 1 + \frac{9}{4}$$
$$\left(x - \frac{3}{2}\right)^2 = \frac{13}{4}$$
$$x - \frac{3}{2} = \pm\frac{\sqrt{13}}{2}$$
$$x = \pm\frac{\sqrt{13}}{2} + \frac{3}{2}$$
$$x = \frac{3 \pm \sqrt{13}}{2}$$

30. $4x^2 - 12 = 0$

$$x^2 = 3$$
$$x = \pm\sqrt{3}$$

31. $y^2 + 6y - 24 = 0$ $\quad y = \dfrac{-6 \pm \sqrt{36 - 4(1)(-24)}}{2(1)}$

$$= \frac{-6 \pm \sqrt{132}}{2}$$
$$= -3 \pm \frac{\sqrt{132}}{2}$$

32. $4x^2 - 25 = 0$

$$x^2 = \tfrac{25}{4}$$
$$x = \pm\tfrac{5}{2}$$

33. $x^2 + 7x + 10 = 0$

$(x+5)(x+2) = 0$

$x = -5$ or $x = -2$

34. $u^2 + 5u + 2 = 0$

$$u^2 + 5u + \frac{25}{4} = -2 + \frac{25}{4}$$

$$\left(u + \frac{5}{2}\right)^2 = \frac{17}{4}$$

$$u + \frac{5}{2} = \pm\frac{\sqrt{17}}{2}$$

$$u = \pm\frac{\sqrt{17}}{2} - \frac{5}{2}$$

$$u = \frac{-5 \pm \sqrt{17}}{2}$$

35. $3x^2 - 5x = 0$

$x(3x - 5) = 0$

$x = 0$ or $x = \frac{5}{3}$

36. $y^2 + 2y - 26 = 0$

$y^2 + 2y + 1 = 26 + 1$

$(y+1)^2 = 27$

$y + 1 = \pm\sqrt{27}$

$y = \pm\sqrt{27} - 1$

$y = -1 \pm \sqrt{27}$

37. $9z^2 + 10z - 4 = 0$

$$z = \frac{-10 \pm \sqrt{100 - 4(9)(-4)}}{2 \cdot 9}$$

$$z = \frac{-10 \pm \sqrt{244}}{18}$$

$$z = -\frac{5}{9} \pm \frac{\sqrt{244}}{18}$$

38. $4x^2 + 4x + 1 = 0$

$(2x+1)(2x+1) = 0$

$2x + 1 = 0$

$x = -\frac{1}{2}$

39. $7x^2 - 14x = 0$

$7x(x - 2) = 0$

$x = 0$ or $x = 2$

40. $4x^2 - 13x + 3 = 0$

$$x = \frac{13 \pm \sqrt{169 - 4(4)(3)}}{2 \cdot 4}$$

$$x = \frac{13 \pm 11}{8}$$

$$x = 3 \text{ or } x = \frac{1}{4}$$

41. $8x^2 - 10x + 3 = 0$

$$x = \frac{10 \pm \sqrt{100 - 4(8)3}}{16}$$

$$x = \frac{10 \pm \sqrt{4}}{16}$$

$$x = \frac{10 \pm 2}{16}$$

$$x = \frac{3}{4} \text{ or } x = \frac{1}{2}$$

42. $7x^2 - 14 = 0$

$7(x^2 - 2) = 0$

$x = \pm\sqrt{2}$

43. $y^2 + 20y + 10 = 0$

$$y = \frac{-20 \pm \sqrt{400 - 40}}{2}$$

$$y = \frac{-20 \pm \sqrt{360}}{2}$$

$$y = -10 \pm \frac{\sqrt{360}}{2}$$

44. $228.98 = 200(1 + r)^2$

$(1 + r)^2 = 1.1449$

$1 + r = 1.07$

$r = 0.07$

$200(1.08^2) = 233.28$

Your balance after two years is \$233.28.

45. Vertex of wave is $(-10, 3)$.

$y = \frac{1}{5}(-10)$

$= -2$ feet in water

5 feet 4 inches $-$ 2 feet $=$ 3 feet 4 inches

No, Jared was still 4 inches taller than the height of the wave.

46. $-\frac{1}{400}x^2 + \frac{4}{5}x - 52 = 0$

$$x = \frac{-\frac{4}{5} \pm \sqrt{\frac{16}{25} - 4\left(-\frac{1}{400}\right)(-52)}}{-\frac{2}{400}}$$

$$x = \frac{-\frac{4}{5} \pm \frac{\sqrt{12}}{10}}{-\frac{1}{200}}$$

$$x = 160 \pm 20\sqrt{12}$$

$x \approx 229.28$ or $x \approx 90.72$

$$-\frac{b}{2a} = \frac{-\frac{4}{5}}{-\frac{2}{400}}$$
$$= 160 \text{ feet}$$

$160 - 90.72 = 69.28$ feet

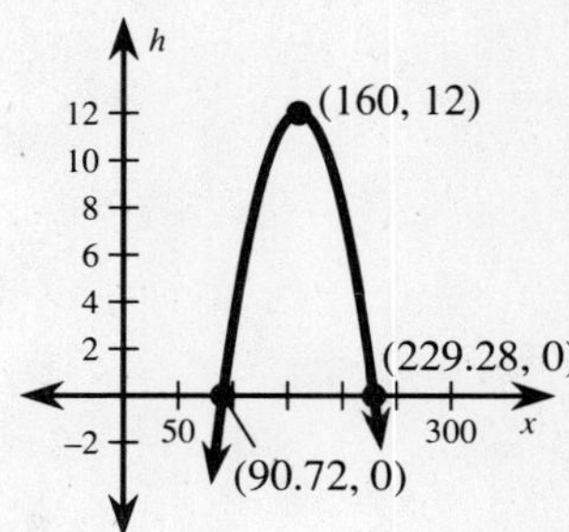

47. $0 = -\frac{1}{30}(x - 10)^2 + 900$

$(x - 10)^2 = 27{,}000$

$x - 10 \approx \pm 164.32$

$x \approx 10 \pm 164.32$

$x \approx -154.32,\ 174.32$

The water hits the river at approximately 174 feet from the base of the cliff.

48. $-16t^2 + 900 = 0$

$16t^2 = 900$

$t^2 = 56.25$

$t = 7.5$

It takes the water 7.5 seconds to hit the lower river.

49. $x^2 = 16$

$x = \pm 4$

50. $x^2 + 3 = 7$

$x^2 = 4$

$x = \pm 2$

51. $x^2 + 4 = 29$

$x^2 = 25$

$x = \pm 5$

52. $\frac{1}{7}x^2 + 8 = 15$

$\frac{1}{7}x^2 = 7$

$x^2 = 49$

$x = \pm 7$

53. $2x^2 - 7 = 11$

$2x^2 = 18$

$x^2 = 9$

$x = \pm 3$

54. $3x^2 - 8 = 100$

$3x^2 = 108$

$x^2 = 36$

$x = \pm 6$

55. $y = x^2 - 6x + 8$

x-intercepts: (2, 0) (4, 0)

Vertex: $\dfrac{-(-6)}{2} = 3$

$y = 9 - 18 + 8 = -1$

Vertex: (3, −1)

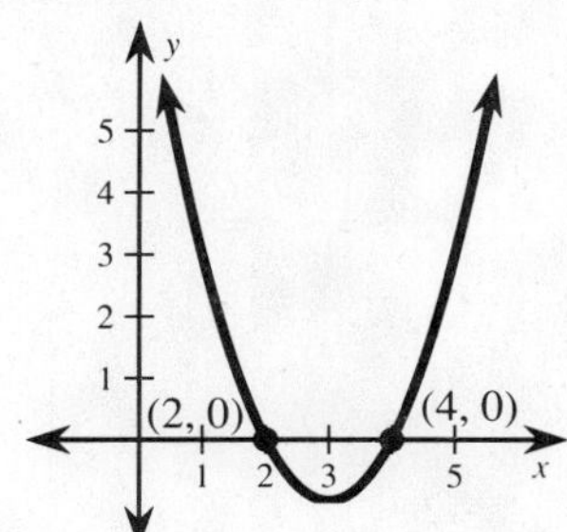

56. $y = -2x^2 - 8x - 6$

$y = -2(x^2 + 4x + 3)$

$y = -2(x + 1)(x + 3)$

x-intercepts: (−1, 0)(−3, 0)

Vertex: $-\frac{4}{2} = -2$

$y = -8 + 16 - 6 = 2$

Vertex: (−2, 2)

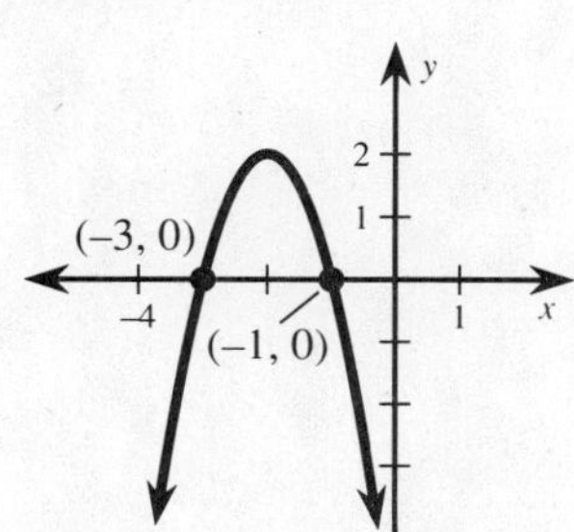

57. $y = -x^2 - 2x - 1$

$y = -(x + 1)^2$

x-intercept: (−1, 0)

Vertex: (−1, 0)

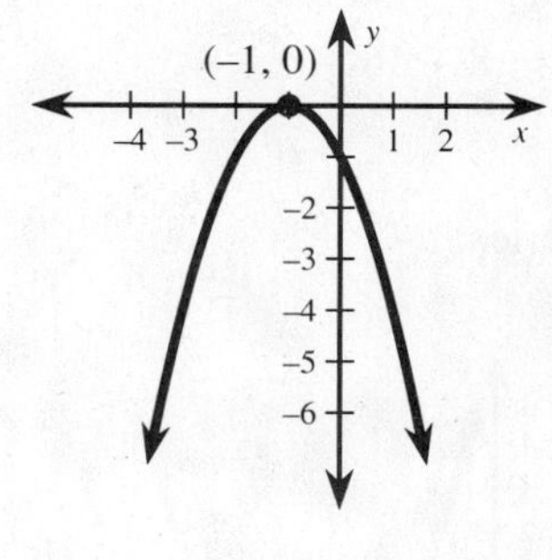

58. $y = x^2 + 8x + 16$

$y = (x + 4)^2$

x-intercept: (−4, 0)

Vertex: $-\frac{8}{2} = -4$

$y = 16 - 32 + 16 = 0$

Vertex: (−4, 0)

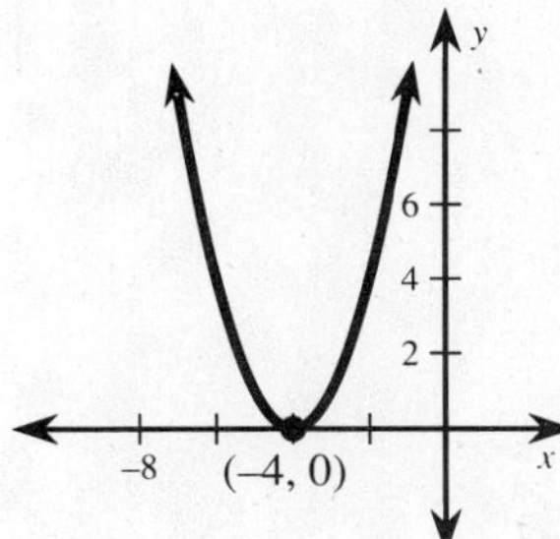

59. $y = 2x^2 - x - 10$

$y = (2x - 5)(x + 2)$

x-intercepts: $\left(\frac{5}{2}, 0\right)$ (−2, 0)

Vertex: $\frac{1}{4}$

$y = \frac{1}{8} - \frac{1}{4} - 10 = -10\frac{1}{8}$

Vertex: $\left(\frac{1}{4}, -10\frac{1}{8}\right)$

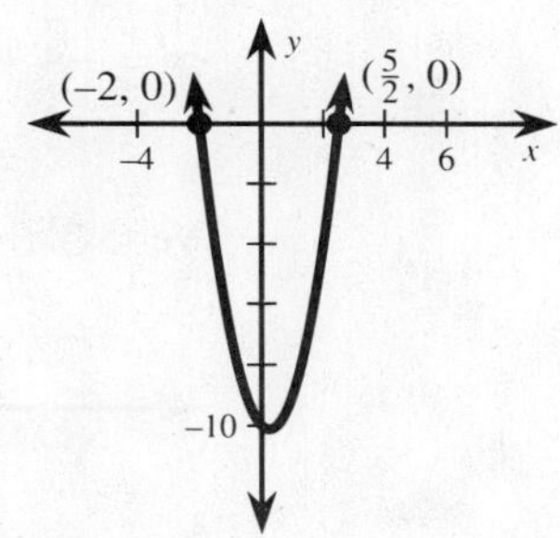

60. $y = x^2 + 5x - 6$

$y = (x + 6)(x - 1)$

x-intercepts: (−6, 0)(1, 0)

Vertex: $-\frac{5}{2}$

$y = \frac{25}{4} - \frac{25}{2} - 6 = -12\frac{1}{4}$

Vertex: $\left(-2\frac{1}{2}, -12\frac{1}{4}\right)$

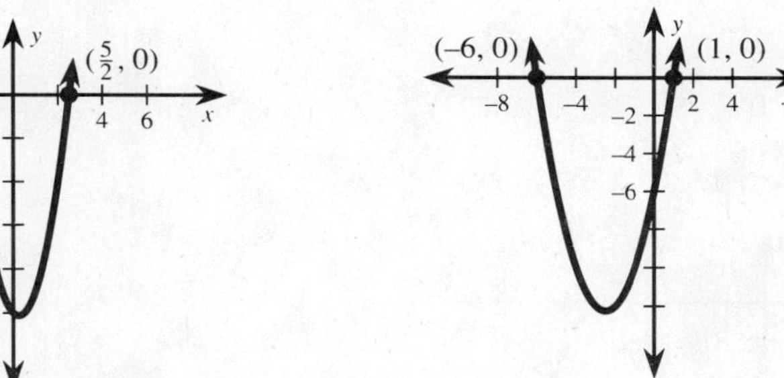

61. $3(x^2 - 5x - 6) = 3(x - 6)(x + 1)$

62. $2(6x^2 + 23x - 4) = 2(6x - 1)(x + 4)$

63. $20(7y^2 + 17y + 6) = 20(7y + 3)(y + 2)$

64. $-6(3y^2 - 26y - 9) = -6(3y + 1)(y - 9)$

65. $12(a^2 + 3a + 2) = 12(a + 1)(a + 2)$

66. $5(2x^2 + 3x + 1) = 5(2x + 1)(x + 1)$

67. d. **68.** a. **69.** b. **70.** c.

71. $y \geq \frac{1}{2}x^2 - 4x + 6$

$$-\frac{b}{2a} = \frac{4}{1}$$
$$= 4$$

$$y = 8 - 16 + 6$$
$$= -2$$

Vertex: $(4, -2)$

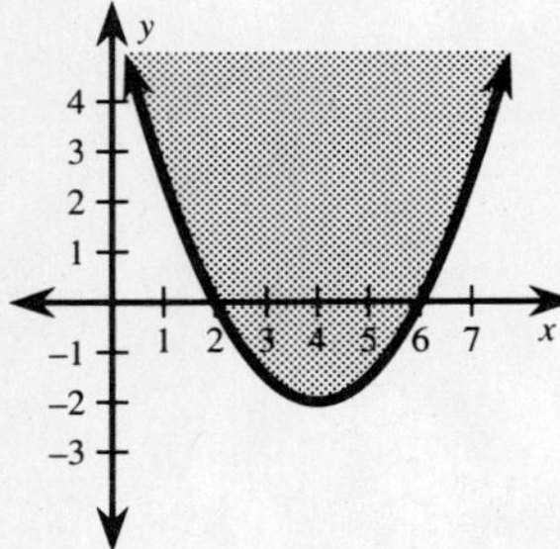

72. $y < \frac{1}{3}x^2 + 2x + 1$

$$-\frac{b}{2a} = \frac{-2}{\frac{2}{3}}$$
$$= -\frac{6}{2}$$
$$= -3$$

$$y = 3 - 6 + 1$$
$$= -2$$

Vertex: $(-3, -2)$

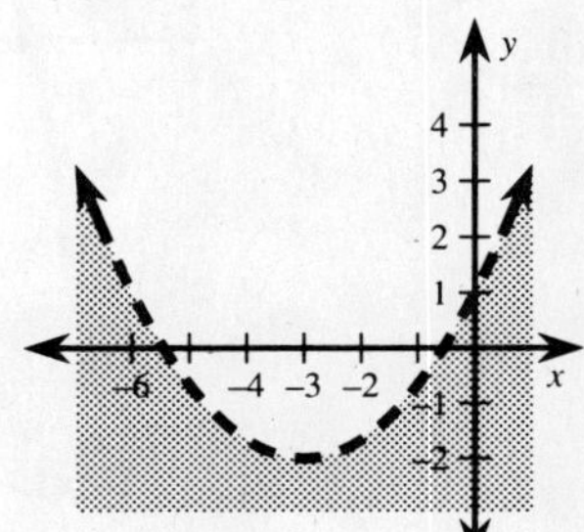

73. $y > -x^2 + 8x - 16$

$$-\frac{b}{2a} = \frac{-8}{-2}$$
$$= 4$$

$$y = -16 + 32 - 16$$
$$= 0$$

Vertex: $(4, 0)$

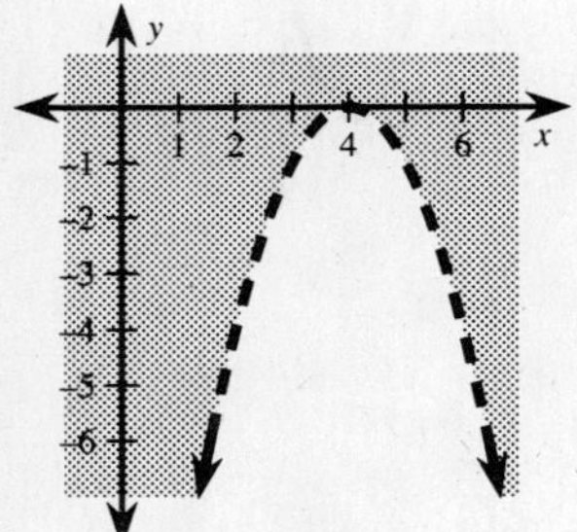

74. $y \leq -x^2 - 4x - 5$

$$-\frac{b}{2a} = -\frac{4}{2}$$
$$= -2$$

$$y = -4 + 8 - 5$$
$$= -1$$

Vertex: $(-2, -1)$

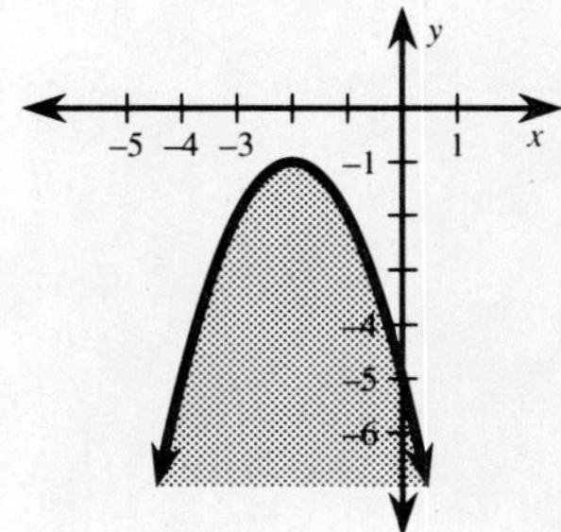

75.

$$1218 = x\left(50 - \tfrac{1}{2}x\right)$$
$$\tfrac{1}{2}x^2 - 50x + 1218 = 0$$
$$x^2 - 100x + 2436 = 0$$
$$(x - 58)(x - 42) = 0$$

$x = 58,\ x = 42$

76.

$$990 = x\left(100 - \tfrac{1}{10}x\right)$$
$$\tfrac{1}{10}x^2 - 100x + 990 = 0$$
$$x^2 - 1000x + 9900 = 0$$
$$(x - 10)(x - 990) = 0$$

$x = 10,\ x = 990$

77. a.

$$y^2 = 25 - x^2$$

$$\begin{aligned} x^2 - (25 - x^2) &= 7 \\ 2x^2 &= 32 \\ x^2 &= 16 \\ x &= 4 \end{aligned} \qquad \begin{aligned} y^2 &= 25 - 16 \\ y^2 &= 9 \\ y &= 3 \end{aligned}$$

Chapter REVIEW

1. Quadratic Binomial

2. Quadratic Trinomial

3. Constant Monomial

4. Linear Monomial

5. Quadratic Polynomial

6. Linear Binomial

7. Cubic Binomial

8. Cubic Polynomial

9. $(-x^2+3x^2)+(x+4x)+(2+5) = 2x^2+5x+7$

10. $4x^3+(x^2-x^2)+(-x)+(-1+2) = 4x^3-x+1$

11. $(-x^2+4x^2)+(3x-2x)+(15-10) = 3x^2+x+5$

12. $-x^3-x^2+(3x-x)+(2+4) = -x^3-x^2+2x+6$

13. $(x^2-4x^2)+(3x+5x)+(-1-6) = -3x^2+8x-7$

14. $(x^2+3x^2)+(9x-8x)+(2-5) = 4x^2+x-3$

15. $-(-x^3)+3x^2+(-2x-2x)+(4+6) = x^3+3x^2-4x+10$

16. $x^3+(5x^2-3x^2)+(-4x+6x)+(-2) = x^3+2x^2+2x-2$

17. $\begin{aligned} x(x-10)-5(x-10) &= x^2-10x-5x+50 \\ &= x^2-15x+50 \end{aligned}$

18. $\begin{aligned} 2x(x+4)+2(x+4) &= 2x^2+8x+2x+8 \\ &= 2x^2+10x+8 \end{aligned}$

19. $\begin{aligned} 6(x^2-2x+3)+x(x^2-2x+3) &= 6x^2-12x+18+x^3-2x^2+3x \\ &= x^3+4x^2-9x+18 \end{aligned}$

20. $\begin{aligned} 7(3x^2+2x-6)-x(3x^2+2x-6) &= 21x^2+14x-42-3x^3-2x^2+6x \\ &= -3x^3+19x^2+20x-42 \end{aligned}$

21. $\begin{array}{r} 6x^2+2x-1 \\ x^2-2 \\ \hline 7x^2+2x-3 \end{array}$

22. $\begin{array}{r} x-2 \\ 4x^2-7x+5 \\ \hline 4x^2-6x+3 \end{array}$

23. $\begin{array}{r} -x^2-x+2 \\ x^2+2x-4 \\ \hline x-2 \end{array}$

24. $\begin{array}{r} x^2+3x+5 \\ 3x^2-4x+6 \\ \hline 4x^2-x+11 \end{array}$

25. $\begin{array}{r} x^2-3 \\ -(4x^2-3x+2) \\ \hline -3x^2+3x-5 \end{array}$

26. $\begin{array}{r} x^2+3x-7 \\ -(-2x^2+x+14) \\ \hline 3x^2+2x-21 \end{array}$

27.
$$\begin{array}{r} x^2 - 4x + 2 \\ -(\ 6x^2 + 4x - 3\ ) \\ \hline -5x^2 - 8x + 5 \end{array}$$

28.
$$\begin{array}{r} 10x^2 + 3x - 4 \\ -(\ 5x^2 + 2x - 6\ ) \\ \hline 5x^2 + x + 2 \end{array}$$

29.
$$\begin{array}{r} 3x^2 + 4x - 1 \\ \times \qquad x - 2 \\ \hline -6x^2 - 8x + 2 \\ 3x^3 + 4x^2 - x \qquad \\ \hline 3x^3 - 2x^2 - 9x + 2 \end{array}$$

30.
$$\begin{array}{r} x^2 + x + 1 \\ \times \qquad -x + 10 \\ \hline 10x^2 + 10x + 10 \\ -x^3 - x^2 - x \qquad \\ \hline -x^3 + 9x^2 + 9x + 10 \end{array}$$

31.
$$\begin{array}{r} 4x^2 - 6x + 2 \\ \times \qquad 2x + 2 \\ \hline 8x^2 - 12x + 4 \\ 8x^3 - 12x^2 + 4x \qquad \\ \hline 8x^3 - 4x^2 - 8x + 4 \end{array}$$

32.
$$\begin{array}{r} 6x^2 - 4x + 1 \\ \times \qquad 3x + 4 \\ \hline 24x^2 - 16x + 4 \\ 18x^3 - 12x^2 + 3x \qquad \\ \hline 18x^3 + 12x^2 - 13x + 4 \end{array}$$

33. $x^2 - 225$

34. $9x^2 - 4$

35. $x^2 + 4x + 4$

36. $25x^2 - 60x + 36$

37. $(-2)^2 - 4(1)(-15) = 4 + 60$
$= 64$

$(x - 5)(x + 3)$

38. $3^2 - 4(1)(-70) = 9 + 280$
$= 289$

$(x + 10)(x - 7)$

39. $0^2 - 4(1)(-64) = 256$

$(x - 8)(x + 8)$

40. $0^2 - 4(4)(25) = -400$

Cannot factor

41. $(-8)^2 - 4(1)(8) = 64 - 32$
$= 32$

Cannot factor

42. $12^2 - 4(9)(4) = 144 - 144$
$= 0$

$(3x + 2)(3x + 2) = (3x + 2)^2$

43. $10^2 - 4(1)(25) = 100 - 100$
$= 0$

$(x + 5)(x + 5) = (x + 5)^2$

44. $(-8)^2 - 4(1)(16) = 64 - 64$
$= 0$

$(x - 4)(x - 4) = (x - 4)^2$

45. $(-32)^2 - 4(4)(60) = 1024 - 960$
$= 64$

$4(x - 5)(x - 3)$

46. $21^2 - 4(3)(30) = 441 - 360$
$= 81$

$3(x + 2)(x + 5)$

47. $x^2 - 21x + 108 = 0$
$(x - 9)(x - 12) = 0$

$x = 9$ or $x = 12$

48. $x^2 - 8x - 240 = 0$
$(x - 20)(x + 12) = 0$

$x = 20$ or $x = -12$

49. $-x^2 + 30x - 200 = 0$
$-(x^2 - 30x + 200) = 0$
$-(x - 10)(x - 20) = 0$

$x = 10$ or $x = 20$

50. $-15x^2 + 45x + 150 = 0$
$-15(x^2 - 3x - 10) = 0$
$-15(x - 5)(x + 2) = 0$

$x = 5$ or $x = -2$

51. $36x^2 - 49 = 0$
$36x^2 = 49$
$x^2 = \frac{49}{36}$
$x = \pm\frac{7}{6}$

52. $x^2 + 26x + 169 = 0$
$(x + 13)(x + 13) = 0$
$x = -13$

53. $x^2 - 14x + 36 = 0$
$$x = \frac{14 \pm \sqrt{196 - 4(36)}}{2}$$
$$x = 7 \pm \frac{\sqrt{52}}{2}$$

54. $x^2 + 10x - 3 = 0$
$$x = \frac{-10 \pm \sqrt{100 - 4(-3)}}{2}$$
$$x = -5 \pm \frac{\sqrt{112}}{2}$$

55. $(11)^2 = 121$

$= (1)(121)$

$= (61 - 60)(61 + 60)$

$= 61^2 - 60^2$

$11^2 = 61^2 - 60^2$

11, 60, 61

56. $(17)^2 = 289$

$= (1)(289)$

$= (145 - 144)(145 - 144)$

$= 145^2 - 144^2$

$17^2 = 145^2 - 144^2$

17, 144, 145

57. $t = \dfrac{-12 \pm \sqrt{144 - 4(-16)(10)}}{2(-16)}$

$t = \dfrac{-12 \pm 28}{-32}$

$t = -0.5,\ 1.25$

It will take 1.25 seconds for the ball to reach the ground.

58. $R = -2t^2 + 37t + 60$

$R = (2t + 3)(-t + 20)$

No, the price of the T-shirts decreased by $1.00 each week.

59. $V = \left(\dfrac{1}{6}\right)\pi(x - 3)(x^2 - 6x + 9)$

$V = \dfrac{1}{6}\pi(x^3 - 9x^2 + 27x - 27)$

$V = \dfrac{\pi}{6}x^3 - \dfrac{3\pi}{2}x^2 + \dfrac{9\pi}{2}x - \dfrac{9\pi}{2}$

60. $V = \dfrac{\pi}{6}(11)^3 - \dfrac{3\pi}{2}(11)^2 + \dfrac{9\pi}{2} \cdot 11 - \dfrac{9\pi}{2}$

≈ 268 cubic inches

61. $S = 1.1x + 0.14x^2 - 4.43x + 58.4$

$S = 0.14x^2 - 3.33x + 58.4$

62. $S = 0.14 \cdot 15^2 - 3.33 \cdot 15 + 58.4$

$= 39.95$

$S = 0.14 \cdot 30^2 - 3.33 \cdot 30 + 58.4$

$= 84.50$

$S = 0.14 \cdot 55^2 - 3.33 \cdot 55 + 58.4$

$= 298.75$

15 mph: 39.95 feet
30 mph: 84.5 feet
55 mph: 298.75 feet

63. No; it's related by a quadratic model since the x term is squared. The distance needed to stop increases quadratically with an increase in speed.

64. $F = 1.8(55) = 99$

There should be 99 feet between cars traveling at 55 miles per hour.

65. $129{,}874{,}900 = 20{,}500t^2 + 1{,}460{,}100t + 25{,}942{,}500$

$20{,}500t^2 + 1{,}460{,}100t - 103{,}932{,}400 = 0$

$t = 44$ or $t = -115.2$

$1940 + 44 = 1984$

In 1984 there were 129,874,900 cars registered.

66. $C = 20{,}500(55)^2 + 1{,}460{,}100(55) + 25{,}942{,}500$

$C = 168{,}260{,}500$

There will be 168,260,500 cars registered in 1995.

Chapter TEST

1. $(x^2 + 4x^2) + 3x + (-1 + 2) = 5x^2 + 3x + 1$

2. $(x^4 + 2x^4) + (3x^2 - 3x^2) + (2 + 6) = 3x^4 + 8$

3. $5x^2 + (-2x - 7x) + (1 - 10) = 5x^2 - 9x - 9$

4. $(5x^3 - 4x^3) - (2x^2) + (2x + 5x) + (-4) = x^3 - 2x^2 + 7x - 4$

5. $81x^2 - 4$ **6.** $25x^2 - 16$ **7.** $x^2 - 28x + 196$

8. $9x^2 + 30x + 25$ **9.** $3x^2 + 11x + 10$ **10.** $26x^2 - 3x - 5$

11. $$\begin{aligned} x(4x^2 + 3x - 5) - 6(4x^2 + 3x - 5) &= 4x^3 + 3x^2 - 5x - 24x^2 - 18x + 30 \\ &= 4x^3 - 21x^2 - 23x + 30 \end{aligned}$$

12. $$\begin{aligned} 4x^3(x + 1) - 6x(x + 1) + 7(x + 1) &= 4x^4 + 4x^3 - 6x^2 - 6x + 7x + 7 \\ &= 4x^4 + 4x^3 - 6x^2 + x + 7 \end{aligned}$$

13. $(x - 12)(x + 12)$ **14.** $(6x - 5)(6x + 5)$ **15.** $(x - 6)^2$

16. $(x + 5)^2$ **17.** $(3x - 1)(x + 1)$ **18.** $(5x + 2)(x - 1)$

19. $x(x^2 + 2x + 1) = x(x + 1)^2$ **20.** $2(x^2 - 14x + 48) = 2(x - 6)(x - 8)$

21.
$$\begin{aligned} x^2 + 4x + 4 &= 0 \\ (x + 2)^2 &= 0 \\ x &= -2 \end{aligned}$$

22.
$$\begin{aligned} x^2 - 7x + 6 &= 0 \\ (x - 1)(x - 6) &= 0 \end{aligned}$$
$x = 1,\ x = 6$

23.
$$\begin{aligned} x^2 - 5x - 150 &= 0 \\ (x - 15)(x + 10) &= 0 \end{aligned}$$
$x = 15,\ x = -10$

24.
$$\begin{aligned} x^2 + 6x - 91 &= 0 \\ (x - 7)(x + 13) &= 0 \end{aligned}$$
$x = 7,\ x = -13$

25.
$$\begin{aligned} 12x^2 + 15x + 3 &= 0 \\ 3(4x + 1)(x + 1) &= 0 \end{aligned}$$
$x = -\frac{1}{4},\ x = -1$

26.
$$\begin{aligned} 4x^2 - 10x - 36 &= 0 \\ 2(2x - 9)(x + 2) &= 0 \end{aligned}$$
$x = \frac{9}{2},\ x = -2$

27.
$$\begin{aligned} x^2 - 4x + 1 &= 0 \\ x^2 - 4x + 4 &= -1 + 4 \\ (x - 2)^2 &= 3 \\ x - 2 &= \pm\sqrt{3} \\ x &= 2 \pm \sqrt{3} \end{aligned}$$

28.
$$\begin{aligned} x^2 + 6x - 9 &= 0 \\ x^2 + 6x + 9 &= 9 + 9 \\ (x + 3)^2 &= 18 \\ x + 3 &= \pm\sqrt{18} \\ x &= -3 \pm \sqrt{18} \end{aligned}$$

29.
$$\begin{aligned} x^2 + 20x + 3 &= 0 \\ x^2 + 20x + 100 &= -3 + 100 \\ (x + 10)^2 &= 97 \\ x + 10 &= \pm\sqrt{97} \\ x &= -10 \pm \sqrt{97} \end{aligned}$$

30.
$$\begin{aligned} x^2 - 2x - 5 &= 0 \\ x^2 - 2x + 1 &= 5 + 1 \\ (x - 1)^2 &= 6 \\ x - 1 &= \pm\sqrt{6} \\ x &= 1 \pm \sqrt{6} \end{aligned}$$

31.
$$\begin{aligned} 5^2 &= (1)(25) \\ &= (13 - 12)(13 + 12) \\ &= 13^2 - 12^2 \end{aligned}$$
$5^2 = 12^2 - 13^2$

5, 12, 13

32. $l = 2w - 3$
$$\begin{aligned} (2w - 3)w &= 135 \\ 2w^2 - 3w - 135 &= 0 \\ (2w + 15)(w - 9) &= 0 \end{aligned}$$
$w = -\frac{15}{2},\ w = 9$

Width = 9 feet

Length = 15 feet

33. $5644.53 = 5000(1 + r)^2$

$1.128906 = (1 + r)^2$

$1 + r = 1.0625$

$r = .0625$

The rate of interest is 6.25%.

34. $25y = 2x^2 - 20x + 1$

$25(0) = 2x^2 - 20x + 1$

$2x^2 - 20x + 1 = 0$

$$x = \frac{20 \pm \sqrt{400 - 4(2)(1)}}{2 \cdot 2}$$

$$x = \frac{20 \pm \sqrt{392}}{4}$$

$$x = 5 \pm \frac{\sqrt{392}}{4}$$

$$w = 5 + \frac{\sqrt{392}}{4} - \left(5 - \frac{\sqrt{392}}{4}\right)$$

$$w = \frac{2\sqrt{392}}{4}$$

$$\approx 9.9$$

The width of the pond is approximately 9.9 meters.

Chapter 11

Using Proportions and Rational Equations

11.1 Problem Solving Using Ratios and Proportions

Communicating about Algebra

A. $\frac{x}{4} = \frac{9}{2}$

$x = 18$ Multiply both sides by 4

B. $\frac{5}{x} = \frac{4}{5}$

$\frac{x}{5} = \frac{5}{4}$ Reciprocal property

$x = \frac{25}{4}$ Multiply both sides by 5

C. $\frac{x}{x+1} = \frac{10}{x+7}$

$x(x+7) = 10(x+1)$ Cross multiply

$x^2 - 3x - 10 = 0$ Write in standard form

$(x-5)(x+2) = 0$ Factor

$x = 5$ or $x = -2$ Zero-product property

EXERCISES

1. a and d are extremes. b and c are means.

2. c.

3. b.

4. $\frac{x}{4} = \frac{2}{5}$

$x = \frac{8}{5}$

5. $\frac{5}{x} = \frac{3}{2}$

$\frac{x}{5} = \frac{2}{3}$

$x = \frac{10}{3}$

6. $\frac{1}{x+1} = \frac{x}{2}$

$x^2 + x = 2$

$x^2 + x - 2 = 0$

$(x+2)(x-1) = 0$

$x = -2$ or $x = 1$

7. $\frac{2}{x} = \frac{3}{4}$

$\frac{x}{2} = \frac{4}{3}$

$x = \frac{8}{3}$

8. $$\frac{3x}{4x-1} = \frac{1}{x}$$
$$3x^2 = 4x - 1$$
$$3x^2 - 4x + 1 = 0$$
$$(3x-1)(x-1) = 0$$
$$x = \frac{1}{3} \text{ or } x = 1$$

9. $$\frac{7x}{x+1} = \frac{5x}{2}$$
$$5x^2 + 5x = 14x$$
$$5x^2 - 9x = 0$$
$$x(5x-9) = 0$$
$$x = 0 \text{ or } x = \frac{9}{5}$$

10. $$\frac{8x}{6} = \frac{2x}{x+3}$$
$$8x^2 + 24x = 12x$$
$$8x^2 + 12x = 0$$
$$4x(2x+3) = 0$$
$$x = 0 \text{ or } x = -\frac{3}{2}$$

11. $$\frac{6}{2y} = \frac{5}{8}$$
$$\frac{2y}{6} = \frac{8}{5}$$
$$y = \frac{24}{5}$$

12. $$\frac{4}{5} = \frac{7}{y}$$
$$\frac{5}{4} = \frac{y}{7}$$
$$y = \frac{35}{4}$$

13. $$\frac{4}{x} = \frac{6}{8}$$
$$\frac{x}{4} = \frac{4}{3}$$
$$x = \frac{16}{3}$$

14. $$\frac{2}{x} = \frac{6}{3}$$
$$\frac{x}{2} = \frac{1}{2}$$
$$x = 1$$

15. $$\frac{-3}{x} = \frac{5}{6}$$
$$\frac{x}{-3} = \frac{6}{5}$$
$$x = -\frac{18}{5}$$

16. $$\frac{4}{x} = \frac{14}{-7}$$
$$\frac{x}{4} = -\frac{1}{2}$$
$$x = -2$$

17. $$\frac{9}{2} = \frac{18}{y}$$
$$\frac{2}{9} = \frac{y}{18}$$
$$y = 4$$

18. $$\frac{10}{8} = \frac{5}{y}$$
$$\frac{4}{5} = \frac{y}{5}$$
$$y = 4$$

19. $$\frac{x}{5x+6} = \frac{1}{x}$$
$$x^2 = 5x + 6$$
$$x^2 - 5x - 6 = 0$$
$$(x-6)(x+1) = 0$$
$$x = 6 \text{ or } x = -1$$

20. $$\frac{5}{x+1} = \frac{4x}{x}$$
$$\frac{5}{x+1} = 4$$
$$\frac{x+1}{5} = \frac{1}{4}$$
$$x + 1 = \frac{5}{4}$$
$$x = \frac{1}{4}$$

21. $$\frac{6}{x+2} = \frac{x+1}{x}$$
$$x^2 + 3x + 2 = 6x$$
$$x^2 - 3x + 2 = 0$$
$$(x-1)(x-2) = 0$$
$$x = 1 \text{ or } x = 2$$

22. $$\frac{6}{19x} = \frac{-2}{x^2+2}$$
$$6x^2 + 12 = -38x$$
$$6x^2 + 38x + 12 = 0$$
$$2(3x^2 + 19x + 6) = 0$$
$$2(3x+1)(x+6) = 0$$
$$x = -\frac{1}{3} \text{ or } x = -6$$

23. $$\frac{x+6}{x-2} = \frac{2}{x}$$
$$x^2 + 6x = 2x - 4$$
$$x^2 + 4x + 4 = 0$$
$$(x+2)^2 = 0$$
$$x = -2$$

24. $$\frac{x-3}{x} = \frac{2x}{-3}$$
$$2x^2 = -3x + 9$$
$$2x^2 + 3x - 9 = 0$$
$$(2x-3)(x+3) = 0$$
$$x = \frac{3}{2} \text{ or } x = -3$$

25. $\dfrac{x}{6{,}508{,}000} = \dfrac{301}{485}$

$x \approx 4{,}038{,}986$

The 1990 population of Alabama was approximately 4,039,000.

26. $\dfrac{300}{W} = \dfrac{15}{200}$

$\dfrac{W}{300} = \dfrac{200}{15}$

$W = 4000$

They estimated the blue whale population to be 4000.

27. $\dfrac{x}{3} = \dfrac{140}{1}$

$x = 420$

The diameter of the horse's nostril is estimated to be 420 inches or 35 feet.

28. $\dfrac{x}{\frac{5}{2}} = \dfrac{20}{1}$

$x = 20\left(\frac{5}{2}\right)$

$x = 50$

The estimated length of the horse's head is 50 feet.

29. The Boilermakers have to travel approximately 65 miles.

30. You will be traveling approximately 20 miles in Delaware.

31. 3

32. $\frac{5}{4}$

33. $-\frac{7}{2}$

34. $\frac{6}{7}$

35. 0.23

36. 0.064

37. 0.0025

38. 0.03

39. 75%

40. 66.7%

41. 300%

42. 20%

43. 6

44. $\dfrac{y}{3x}$

45. $\dfrac{-y}{7x}$

46. $-\dfrac{y^2}{x^2}$

47. b.

48. c.

49. Experimental results vary.

50. $\pi \approx 3.1415929$

$\dfrac{3195}{x} = \dfrac{3.1415929}{2}$

$x = 2034$

11.2 Problem Solving Using Percents

Communicating about Algebra

Centimeter: $\frac{1}{100}$ of a meter.

Cent: $\frac{1}{100}$ of a dollar.

Centennial: occuring once every hundred years.

EXERCISES

1. 160, $16 = 0.10(160)$

2. $30 = 0.15x$

$x = 200$

3. $x = 0.26(450)$

$x = 117$

4. $19 = x(10)$

$x = 1.9$

$x = 190\%$

5. $x = 0.23(90)$
$x = 20.7$

6. $x = 0.71(310)$
$x = 220.1$

7. $13 = x(50)$
$x = 0.26$
$x = 26\%$

8. $48 = 0.60x$
$x = 80$

9. $x = 0.06(400)$
$x = 24$ meters

10. $x = 0.32(625)$
$x = \$200$

11. $x = 0.21(580)$
$x = 121.8$ miles

12. $x = 0.86(950)$
$x = 817$ students

13. $35 = 0.50x$
$x = 70$ feet

14. $54 = 0.45x$
$x = 120$ degrees

15. $3 = 0.02x$
$x = 150$ dollars

16. $9 = 0.12x$
$x = 75$ grams

17. $11 = x(50)$
$x = 0.22$ or 22%

18. $13 = x(20)$
$x = 0.65$ or 65%

19. $24 = x(600)$
$x = 0.04$ or 4%

20. $486 = x(900)$
$x = 0.54$ or 54%

21. $78 = x(39)(7)$
$x \approx 0.286$ or 28.6%

22. $52 = x(20)(12)$
$x \approx 0.217$ or 21.7%

23. $\dfrac{(20)(20)}{(60)(50)} \approx 0.133$
13.3% shaded blue
$\dfrac{(60)(50) - (20)(20)}{(60)(50)} \approx 0.867$
86.7% shaded yellow

24. $\dfrac{\frac{1}{2}(8)(12)}{(8)(15)} = 0.4$
40% shaded blue
$\dfrac{(8)(15) - \frac{1}{2}(8)(12)}{(8)(15)} = 0.6$
60% shaded yellow

25. $\dfrac{\frac{1}{2}(18)(80)}{36(80)} = 0.25$
25% shaded blue
$\dfrac{36(80) - \frac{1}{2}(18)80}{36(80)} = 0.75$
75% shaded yellow

26. $\dfrac{2(5)(5)}{(5+5)(5+7+5)} \approx 0.294$
29.4% shaded blue
$\dfrac{(10)(17) - 2(5)(5)}{(10)(17)} \approx 0.706$
70.6% shaded yellow

27. $x = 0.48(1010)$
$x \approx 485$

28. $x = 0.48(1500)$
$x \approx 720$

29. $13{,}698{,}630 = 0.12x$
$x = 114{,}155{,}250$

$114{,}155{,}250 - 13{,}698{,}630 = 100{,}456{,}620$
$100{,}456{,}620 = x(114{,}155{,}250$
$x = 0.88$

The average number of bottles and jars produced each day was 114,155,250. 100,456,620 or 88% were not recycled.

30. a. $(37.08 - 24.72) = x(37.08)$
$x = 33\frac{1}{3}\%$

b. $37.08 = x(24.72)$
$x = 1.5$

c. $24.72 = x(37.08)$
$x = 66\frac{2}{3}\%$

All statements are correct.

31. $\dfrac{5{,}023{,}561}{8{,}714{,}521 + 2{,}498{,}630 + 2{,}129{,}315 + 5{,}023{,}561 + 315{,}616 + 517{,}260} \approx 0.262$ or 26.2%

32. $\dfrac{20(5{,}023{,}561)}{1(8{,}714{,}521) + 5(2{,}498{,}630) + 10(2{,}129{,}315) + 20(5{,}023{,}561) + 50(315{,}616) + 100(517{,}260)} \approx 0.477$
or 47.7%

33. a. $(2.45 - 1.96) = x(1.96)$ or 25%

c. $2.45 = x(1.96)$ or 125%

34. $748 = 0.174x$

$x = \$4298.85$

35. $x = 19.95 - 0.20(19.95)$

$x = \$15.96$

36. $107.50 = x - 0.15(x)$

$107.50 = 0.85x$

$x = \$126.47$

37. 0.04

38. 0.18

39. 0.69

40. 134%

41. 13.4%

42. 1.34%

43. $6x = 3$

$x = \frac{1}{2}$

44. $5x = 2$

$x = \frac{2}{5}$

45. $108x = 100$

$x = \frac{25}{27}$

46. $96x = 50$

$x = \frac{25}{48}$

47. $16x = 9$

$x = \frac{9}{16}$

48. $110x = 9$

$x = \frac{9}{110}$

49. $\frac{2}{x} = \frac{x}{8}$

$x^2 = 16$

$x = \pm 4$

50. $\frac{x}{3} = \frac{3}{x}$

$x^2 = 9$

$x = \pm 3$

51. $\frac{x+1}{3} = \frac{1}{4x}$

$4x^2 + 4x - 3 = 0$

$(2x + 3)(2x - 1) = 0$

$x = -\frac{3}{2}$ or $x = \frac{1}{2}$

52. $\frac{3}{x-6} = \frac{1}{x}$

$3x = x - 6$

$2x = -6$

$x = -3$

53. $\frac{2}{2x-3} = \frac{x}{7}$

$2x^2 - 3x = 14$

$2x^2 - 3x - 14 = 0$

$(2x - 7)(x + 2) = 0$

$x = \frac{7}{2}$ or $x = -2$

54. $\frac{3x+1}{9} = \frac{10}{3x}$

$9x^2 + 3x = 90$

$3(3x^2 + x - 30) = 0$

$3(3x + 10)(x - 3) = 0$

$x = -\frac{10}{3}$ or $x = 3$

55. No; if your sister earns \$20, you earn $20 + 0.1(20)$ or \$22. The percent of your earnings that your sister receives is $22(x) = 20$ or $x \approx 0.909$ (90.9% of your salary). This means your sister earns 100 − 90.9 or 9.1% less than you.

56. Discount before tax:

$48(0.75) = \$36$ discount
$36(1.07) = \$38.52$ discount then tax

Discount after tax:

$48(1.07) = \$51.36$ tax
$51.36(0.75) = \$38.52$ tax then discount

Neither; the cost would be the same.

Mixed REVIEW

1. $y - 3 = 2x + 6$

$-2x + y = 9$

2. $3x - 9 + 2x^2 = 0$

$2x^2 + 3x - 9 = 0$

3. −4

4. $(2x-3)(x+3)=0$

$x=\frac{3}{2}$ or $x=-3$

5. $(x-1)(x+2)+3x-5=x^2+x-2+3x-5$

$=x^2+4x-7$

6. $(xy^2 \div 3xy)(4x^{-2} \div 8x)=\left(\frac{xy^2}{3xy}\right)\left(\frac{4}{8x^3}\right)$

$=\frac{y}{6x^3}$

7. $8x+2=3(4-x)$

$8x+2=12-3x$

$11x=10$

$x=\frac{10}{11}$

8. $8|x-2|-3=0$

$8|x-2|=3$

$|x-2|=\frac{3}{8}$

$x-2=\frac{3}{8}$ or $x-2=-\frac{3}{8}$

$x=\frac{19}{8}$ $\quad x=\frac{13}{8}$

9. $y=3(1.6)^4$

$y=19.6608$

10. $|x+3|+x^2=|-2+3|+(-2)^2$

$=1+4$

$=5$

11. $m^2-3m=12^2-3 \cdot 12$

$=144-36$

$=108 \not\cong 110$

12 is not a solution.

12. $-\frac{1}{4}x^2=-\frac{1}{4}(4)^2$

$=-4 \not\cong -3$

$(4, -3)$ is not a solution.

13. $b^2-4ac=4^2-4(1)(-7)$

$=16+28$

$=44$

14. $x^2+4x-7=0$

$x=\frac{-4 \pm \sqrt{44}}{(2)(1)}$

$x=-2 \pm \frac{\sqrt{44}}{2}$

15. $2x+3y=6$

$3y=-2x+6$

$y=-\frac{2}{3}x+2$

Slope: $-\frac{2}{3}$

16. $3x=16$ $\quad -y=16$

$x=\frac{16}{3}$ $\quad y=-16$

$\left(\frac{16}{3}, 0\right)$ $(0, -16)$

17. $\frac{3}{8}=0.375$

18. $0.92=92\%$

19. $(3 \times 10^{-6})(6 \times 10^{10})=18 \times 10^4$

$=1.8 \times 10^5$

20. $(2.9 \times 10^{-3}) \div (4.6 \times 10^4) \approx 0.630 \times 10^{-7}$

$=6.3 \times 10^{-8}$

11.3 Direct and Inverse Variation

Communicating about Algebra

A. $W=kV$

$5120=k(88{,}300)$

$k \approx 0.058$

$W=0.058(7{,}060{,}000)$

$W=409{,}480$ pounds

B. Hydrogen is flammable.

EXERCISES

1. Examples vary. Distance and rate when time is constant; circumference and diameter of a circle.

2. Examples vary. Rate and time when distance is constant.

3. Direct variation

4. Neither

5. Direct variation

6. Inverse variation

7. Direct variation

8. Inverse variation

9. Neither

10. Direct variation

11. $8 = k \cdot 4$

$k = 2$

$y = 2x$

12. $24 = k \cdot 6$

$k = 4$

$y = 4x$

13. $4 = k \cdot 18$

$k = \frac{4}{18}$

$= \frac{2}{9}$

$y = \frac{2}{9}x$

14. $6 = k \cdot 22$

$k = \frac{6}{22}$

$= \frac{3}{11}$

$y = \frac{3}{11}x$

15. $k = (1)(4)$

$k = 4$

$xy = 4$

16. $k = (10)(3)$

$k = 30$

$xy = 30$

17. $k = \left(\frac{1}{2}\right)(7)$

$k = \frac{7}{2}$

$xy = \frac{7}{2}$

18. $k = \left(\frac{3}{4}\right)(4)$

$k = 3$

$xy = 3$

19. $VP = k$

$(100)(25) = k$

$k = 2500$

$VP = 2500$

20. $tr = 2500$

21. $g = 2n$

22. $p = 5n$

23. $16 = k \cdot 4$

$k = 4$

$8 = 4 \cdot x$

$x = 2$

24. $c = kd$

$6 = k3$

$k = 2$

$c = 2 \cdot 5$

$c = 10$

25. $(2)(7) = k$

$k = 14$

$m(2) = 14$

$m = 7$

26. $\left(\frac{1}{2}\right)\left(\frac{1}{3}\right) = k$

$k = \frac{1}{6}$

$q(6) = \frac{1}{6}$

$q = \frac{1}{36}$

27. $b = kp$

$b = 0.006(p)$

Answers will vary.

28. $\frac{x}{54} = \frac{360}{60}$

$x = 324$

She would have weighed 324 pounds on Earth, with equipment.

29. $t = kc$

$12 = k(0.02)$

$k = 600$

$t = 600(0.05)$

$t = 30$

An explosion could occur in 30 minutes.

30. $PA = k$

$4(29) = k$

$k = 116$

$P(29 \cdot 11) = 116$

$P \approx 0.36$

Denise's weight is 116 pounds.

31. $p = \frac{k}{t}$

$p = 38$

$t = 3$

$k = (38)(3)$

$= 114$

$pt = 114$

$p = \frac{114}{6.5}$

≈ 17.5

Approximately 17.5% of the oil remained after $6\frac{1}{2}$ years after the spill.

32. $Td = k$

$(2)(2000) = k$

$k = 4000$

$Td = 4000$

$T(4385) = 4000$

$T \approx 0.93°C$

33. $\frac{a}{20} = \frac{1}{5}$

$a = 4$

34. $\frac{3}{x} = \frac{4}{9}$

$x = \frac{27}{4}$

35. $\frac{3}{8} = \frac{3}{2d}$

$d = 4$

36. $\frac{5}{17} = \frac{r}{9}$

$r = \frac{45}{17}$

37. $50\% = 0.5$

38. $10\% = 0.1$

39. $120\% = 1.20$

40. $3\% = 0.03$

41. $58 = x(70)$

$x \approx 0.8286$ or 82.86%

$100 - 82.86 = 17.14\%$

42. $43.96 = (1 - 0.2)x$

$x = \$54.95$

43. $l = 0.25L$

$w = 0.25W$

$lw = (0.25L)(0.25W)$

$= 0.0625LW$

$1 - 0.0625 = 0.9375$

No, the area is reduced by 93.75%.

11.4 Exploring Data: Probability

Communicating about Algebra

A. Of all days on record with comparable meteorological conditions, rain occurred 80% of the days.

B. Of all the time in a comparable situation, a person won 50% of the time.

EXERCISES

1. Zero; the sun sets in the morning.

2. One; the sun rises in the morning.

3. The denominator is the total possible number of times an event can occur. The numerator is the number of times the event did occur.

4. $\frac{12}{25} = 0.48$

5. $\frac{13}{25} = 0.52$

6. $\frac{25}{25} = 1$

7. $\frac{12}{64} = \frac{3}{16}$
$= 0.1875$

8. $\frac{2}{10} = \frac{1}{5}$
$= 0.2$

9. $\frac{3}{16}$

10. $0.95(827{,}000) = 785{,}650$

11. $1700(0.006) \approx 10$

Ten poems were published (without her permission) when she was living.

12. $$\frac{200 - 24 - 125 - 39}{200} = \frac{12}{200} = \frac{3}{50}$$

13. $$\frac{57{,}510{,}000}{57{,}510{,}000 + 139{,}440{,}000} = \frac{57{,}510{,}000}{196{,}950{,}000} = \frac{5751}{19{,}695} = \frac{1917}{6565}$$

14. $$\frac{139{,}440{,}000}{196{,}950{,}000} = \frac{13{,}944}{19{,}695} = \frac{4648}{6565}$$

15. $$\frac{\pi(1)^2}{\pi(9)^2} = \frac{1}{81}$$

16. $$\frac{\pi(9)^2 - \pi(5)^2}{\pi(9)^2} = \frac{81 - 25}{81} = \frac{56}{81}$$

17. $$\frac{1000}{1000 + 3951 + 421 + 1528 + 1305 + 697} = \frac{500}{4451}$$

18. $$\frac{8{,}902{,}000}{246{,}329{,}000} = \frac{8902}{246{,}329}$$

19. $$\frac{8{,}795{,}000 + 5{,}736{,}000 + 4{,}107{,}000 + 528{,}000}{8{,}795{,}000 + 5{,}736{,}000 + 4{,}107{,}000 + 528{,}000 + 1{,}035{,}000 + 2{,}515{,}000 + 3{,}322{,}000 + 4{,}493{,}000 + 6{,}161{,}000}$$
$$= \frac{19{,}166{,}000}{36{,}692{,}000} = \frac{19{,}166}{36{,}692} = \frac{9583}{18{,}346}$$

20. $$\frac{18{,}346 - 9583}{18{,}346} = \frac{8763}{18{,}346}$$

21. $\frac{82}{100} = \frac{41}{50}$

22. $\frac{49}{100}$

23. $\frac{2x}{9} \div \frac{x}{3} = \frac{2x}{9} \cdot \frac{3}{x}$
$= \frac{2}{3}$

24. $\frac{x^2 - 1}{x} \div \frac{x + 1}{3} = \frac{(x + 1)(x - 1)}{x} \cdot \frac{3}{x + 1}$
$= \frac{3(x - 1)}{x}$

25. $\frac{32x + x^2}{x} \div \frac{x}{4} = \frac{x(32 + x)}{2} \cdot \frac{4}{x}$
$= 2(32 + x)$

26. $0.90(50) = 45$

27. $11 = x(185)$
$x \approx 0.059$ or 5.9%

28. $159 = 0.75x$
$x = 212$

29. $\frac{12}{600 - 12} = \frac{12}{588}$
$= \frac{1}{49}$

30. $\frac{6}{18 - 6} = \frac{6}{12}$
$= \frac{1}{2}$

Mid-Chapter SELF-TEST

1. $\frac{4}{x} = \frac{5}{6}$
$x = \frac{24}{5}$

2. $\frac{3}{7} = \frac{12}{x}$
$x = 28$

3. $\frac{a}{3} = \frac{5}{27}$
$a = \frac{15}{27}$
$= \frac{5}{9}$

4. $\frac{a}{26} = \frac{5}{13}$
$a = 10$

5. $\frac{y}{27} = \frac{3}{y}$
$y^2 = 81$
$y = \pm 9$

6. $\frac{2y}{5} = \frac{40}{y}$
$2y^2 = 200$
$y^2 = 100$
$y = \pm 10$

7. $\frac{x}{2x + 1} = \frac{-1}{x}$
$x^2 + 2x + 1 = 0$
$(x + 1)^2 = 0$
$x = -1$

8. $\frac{x + 4}{x} = \frac{-6}{x - 4}$
$x^2 + 6x - 16 = 0$
$(x + 8)(x - 2) = 0$
$x = -8$ or $x = 2$

9. $\frac{x - 3}{-3} = \frac{2x - 3}{x - 3}$
$x^2 - 6x + 9 = -6x + 9$
$x^2 = 0$
$x = 0$

10. $\frac{y + 2}{5} = \frac{4}{y + 3}$
$y^2 + 5y + 6 = 20$
$y^2 + 5y - 14 = 0$
$(y + 7)(y - 2) = 0$
$y = -7$ or $y = 2$

11. $\frac{y + 7}{6} = \frac{y + 5}{3}$
$3y + 21 = 6y + 30$
$3y = -9$
$y = -3$

12. $\frac{5}{y - 3} = \frac{6}{y + 2}$
$6y - 18 = 5y + 10$
$y = 28$

13. $0.065(4.00) = \$0.26$

14. $0.75(1248) = 936$ students

15. $24 = 0.80x$
$x = 30$ feet

16. $100 = 0.26x$
$x \approx 385$ bottles

17. $38 = x(56)$
$x = 0.679$ or 67.9%

18. $17 = x(68)$
$x = 0.25$ or 25%

19. $j = 4a$
$a = \frac{1}{4}j$
$b = 2a$
$a = \frac{1}{2}b$

$\frac{1}{4}j = \frac{1}{2}b$
$j = 2b$

20. $1540(0.55) + 1540(0.26) \approx 847 + 400$
≈ 1247

$1540(0.11) \approx 169$

21. $ab = k$
$7(35) = k$
$k = 245$
$ab = 245$

$5b = 245$
$b = 49$

22. $\frac{1}{6}, \frac{1}{4}$

23. $60 = 0.80x$
$75 = x$ regular retail price
$60 + 5 = 65$ discount catalog price

$75 - 65 = 10$ amount saved
$10 = y(75)$
$y = \frac{2}{15}$
$= 13\frac{1}{3}\%$

You really saved $13\frac{1}{3}\%$.

11.5 Simplifying Rational Expressions

Communicating about Algebra

A.

x-values	−2	−1	0	1	2	3	4
$\frac{x^2 - x - 6}{x - 3}$	0	1	2	3	4	$\frac{0}{0}$ or undefined	6
$x + 2$	0	1	2	3	4	5	6

B. $\dfrac{x^2 - x - 6}{x - 3}$ is undefined at $x = 3$.

$x + 2$ is defined for all real numbers.

The two expressions are equivalent for all values of x except $x = 3$.

EXERCISES

1. A fraction whose numerator and denominator are polynomials.

2. The set of all real numbers except those for which the denominator is zero; all real numbers except 2 and -1.

3. **c.**

4. True

5. All real numbers except 4

6. All real numbers except 6

7. All real numbers except 1 and -1.

8. All real numbers except 2 and -2.

9. All real numbers except 2 and -3.

10. All real numbers except 1 and -6.

11. $3x$

12. $2x^2$

13. $(x+2)$

14. $5x$

15. $(x+2)$

16. $(z+1)$

17. $\dfrac{4x}{12} = \dfrac{x}{3}$

18. $\dfrac{18y}{36} = \dfrac{y}{2}$

19. $\dfrac{15x^2}{10x} = \dfrac{3x}{2}$

20. $\dfrac{18y^2}{60y^5} = \dfrac{3}{10y^3}$

21. $\dfrac{3x}{10x + x^2} = \dfrac{3}{10+x}$

22. $\dfrac{x + 2x^2}{2x+1} = x$

23. $\dfrac{y^2 - 16}{3y + 12} = \dfrac{(y+4)(y-4)}{3(y+4)} = \dfrac{y-4}{3}$

24. $\dfrac{x^2 - 25z^2}{x - 5z} = \dfrac{(x-5z)(x+5z)}{(x-5z)} = (x+5z)$

25. $\dfrac{3-x}{x^2 - 5x + 6} = \dfrac{-(x-3)}{(x-3)(x-2)} = \dfrac{-1}{x-2}$

26. $\dfrac{y^2 - 7y + 12}{y^2 + 3y - 18} = \dfrac{(y-3)(y-4)}{(y+6)(y-3)} = \dfrac{y-4}{y+6}$

27. $\dfrac{x^3 + 5x^2 + 6x}{x^2 - 4} = \dfrac{x(x+3)(x+2)}{(x-2)(x+2)} = \dfrac{x(x+3)}{x-2}$

28. $\dfrac{t^3 - t}{t^3 + 5t^2 - 6t} = \dfrac{t(t+1)(t-1)}{t(t+6)(t-1)} = \dfrac{t+1}{t+6}$

29. **e.**

30. **d.**

31. $w = \dfrac{(7 - 23x)(1+x)}{(10 - 0.022x + 0.005x^2)(1+x)}$

$w = \dfrac{7 - 23x}{10 - 0.022x + 0.005x^2}$

32. $w = \dfrac{7 - 23(15)}{10 - 0.022(15) + 0.005(15)^2}$

$\approx -31.3°\text{F}$

33. $C = \dfrac{116 + 68t + 5t^2}{(10 - 0.8t + 0.0592t^2)(2+t)}$

$C = \dfrac{(58 + 5t)(2+t)}{(10 - 0.8t + 0.0592t^2)(2+t)}$

$C = \dfrac{58 + 5t}{10 - 0.8t + 0.0592t^2}$

34. $c = \dfrac{58 + 5(10)}{10 - 0.8(10) + 0.0592(10)^2}$

≈ 13.6

There were approximately 13.6 billion catalogs mailed in 1990.

35. $\dfrac{13.6 \times 10^9}{94 \times 10^6} \approx 145$

36. 1980: 5.80 1982: 7.87 1984: 10.07
1986: 12.00 1988: 13.26 1990: 13.64

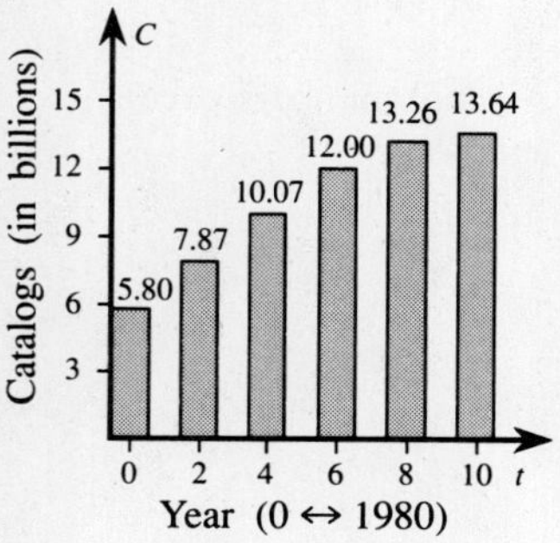

37. $3x^2 \cdot x^4 = 3x^6$

38. $\frac{1}{4}x^3 \cdot x^{10} = \frac{1}{4}x^{13}$

39. $xy^3 \cdot y^2 = xy^5$

40. $12xy^3 \cdot \frac{1}{2}x^4y = 6x^5y^4$

41. $\dfrac{5xy^2}{15x^3y} = \dfrac{y}{3x^2}$

42. $\dfrac{a^2b^2}{5ab} = \dfrac{ab}{5}$

43. $\dfrac{2x^2 - 1}{x^2 + 3} = \dfrac{2(1)^2 - 1}{1^2 + 3}$

$= \dfrac{1}{4}$

44. $\dfrac{3x + 4}{x - 5} = \dfrac{3(-2) + 4}{-2 - 5}$

$= \dfrac{-2}{-7}$

$= \dfrac{2}{7}$

45. $\dfrac{9 + x^2}{(x + 3)(x - 3)} = \dfrac{9 + 4^2}{(4 + 3)(4 - 3)}$

$= \dfrac{25}{7}$

46. $\dfrac{x + y^2}{x^2 - 1} = \dfrac{2 + (-3)^2}{2^2 - 1}$

$= \dfrac{11}{3}$

47. $\dfrac{x^2 + y^2}{x^2 - y^2} = \dfrac{(-4)^2 + (2)^2}{(-4)^2 - (2)^2}$

$= \dfrac{20}{12}$

$= \dfrac{5}{3}$

48. $\dfrac{3 + x^2}{3 + y^2} = \dfrac{3 + 2^2}{3 + 1^2}$

$= \dfrac{7}{4}$

49. Write the product of two binomials as a trinomial in the numerator; then write the product of a third binomial times one of the previous two binomials as a trinomial in the denominator.

50.
$$\frac{x^2 + 5x + 6}{x^2 - 2x - 8} = \frac{x^2 - 4x - 5}{x^2 - 8x + 15}$$
$$\frac{(x + 3)\cancel{(x + 2)}}{(x - 4)\cancel{(x + 2)}} = \frac{\cancel{(x - 5)}(x + 1)}{(x - 3)\cancel{(x - 5)}}$$
$$\frac{x + 3}{x - 4} = \frac{x + 1}{x - 3}$$
$$x^2 - 9 = x^2 - 3x - 4$$
$$-9 = -3x - 4$$
$$-5 = -3x$$
$$\frac{-5}{-3} = x$$
$$x = \frac{5}{3}$$

Mixed REVIEW

1. 4.675×10^9

2. 6.49×10^{-4}

3. 0.000006209

4. 42,550

5. $-m^3$

6. m^{-3} or $\frac{1}{m^3}$

7. $0.072(69) = \$4.97$

8. $\frac{4}{9}(36) = 16$ inches

9.
$$4|x - 3| \geq 8$$
$$|x - 3| \geq 2$$
$$x - 3 \geq 2 \quad \text{or} \quad x - 3 \leq -2$$
$$x \geq 5 \qquad x \leq 1$$

10.
$$|3x + 2| < 6$$
$$-6 < 3x + 2 < 6$$
$$-8 < 3x < 4$$
$$-\tfrac{8}{3} < x < \tfrac{4}{3}$$

11. $(x^2y^{-3})^2 \cdot 4x^{-4}y^2 \cdot \frac{1}{8}x = \frac{x}{2y^4}$

12. $3(x - 2) + x(-6 - x) = -x^2 - 3x - 6$

13.
$$2^y = 2^6$$
$$= 64$$
$$x^2 + x = 5^2 + 5$$
$$= 30$$
(5, 6) is not a solution.

14.
$$y = 5$$
$$2x^2 - 1 = 2(-2)^2 - 1$$
$$= 7$$
(−2, 5) is not a solution.

15. $\pm\sqrt{81} = \pm 9$

16.
$$5x^2 = 720$$
$$x^2 = 144$$
$$x = \pm 12$$

17.
$$x^2 - 3\sqrt{x} + 3 = 4^2 - 3\sqrt{4} + 3$$
$$= 16 - 6 + 3$$
$$= 13$$

18.
$$\sqrt{3x} + 2^x = \sqrt{3 \cdot 3} + 2^3$$
$$= 3 + 8$$
$$= 11$$

19.
$$y + 6 = \tfrac{3}{5}(x - 4)$$
$$5y + 30 = 3x - 12$$
$$-3x + 5y + 42 = 0$$

20.
$$m = \frac{-2 - (-2)}{6 - 27}$$
$$= 0$$
$$y = -2$$

11.6 Multiplying and Dividing Rational Expressions

Communicating about Algebra

A. $\frac{x^2-1}{x} \cdot \frac{2x}{x-1} = \frac{(x+1)(x-1)(2x)}{x(x-1)}$ *Multiply numerators and denominators.*

$= 2(x+1)$ *Divide out common factors.*

B. $\frac{x^2-4x+3}{2x} \div \frac{x-1}{2} = \frac{(x-1)(x-3)}{2x} \cdot \frac{2}{(x-1)}$ *Multiply by reciprocal.*

$= \frac{x-3}{x}$ *Divide out common factors.*

C. $\frac{2}{x^2-4} \cdot (x+2) = \frac{2(x+2)}{(x-2)(x+2)}$ *Multiply.*

$= \frac{2}{(x-2)}$ *Divide out common factors.*

EXERCISES

1. Multiply numerators, multiply denominators, and write the new fraction in reduced form.

2. Multiply the first by the reciprocal of the second and write the new fraction in reduced form.

3. $\frac{3x}{2x^2} \cdot \frac{-4x^2}{12x^3} = \frac{-12x^3}{24x^5}$

$= \frac{-1}{2x^2}$

4. $\frac{4x^2-25}{4x} \div (2x-5) = \frac{(2x+5)(2x-5)}{4x} \cdot \frac{1}{(2x-5)}$

$= \frac{2x+5}{4x}$

5. The reciprocal of the first rational expression was used rather than the reciprocal of the second.

$\frac{x^2-4}{5x} \div \frac{x+2}{x-2} \neq \frac{5x}{x^2-4} \cdot \frac{x+2}{x-2}$

$\frac{x^2-4}{5x} \div \frac{x+2}{x-2} = \frac{x^2-4}{5x} \cdot \frac{x-2}{x+2}$

6. The reciprocal of the second rational expression was used and it shouldn't have been. (Reciprocals are only used when dividing.)

$(2x+2) \cdot \frac{x^2-2x-3}{x+4} \neq \frac{2x+2}{1} \cdot \frac{x+4}{x^2-2x-3}$

$(2x+2) \cdot \frac{x^2-2x-3}{x+4} = \frac{2x+2}{1} \cdot \frac{x^2-2x-3}{x+4}$

7. $\frac{6}{5}$ **8.** $\frac{3x}{2}$ **9.** $3x^2$ **10.** 3

11. $5y$ **12.** $11x^2$ **13.** $\frac{5-4x}{4} \cdot \frac{48}{2(5-4x)} = 6$

14. $\frac{4x}{(x+3)(x-3)} \cdot \frac{(x-3)}{4x(2x+3)} = \frac{1}{(x+3)(2x+3)}$

15. $\frac{3x}{(x-6)(x+4)} \cdot \frac{x-6}{3x(2x+3)} = \frac{1}{(x+4)(2x+3)}$

16. $\dfrac{5}{(x-1)} \cdot \dfrac{(x-1)}{25(x-2)} = \dfrac{1}{5(x-2)}$

17. $\dfrac{x(x-3)}{(x-3)(x-2)} \cdot \dfrac{(x-2)^2}{2x} = \dfrac{x-2}{2}$

18. $\dfrac{x+1}{x^3(3-x)} \cdot \dfrac{x(x-3)}{5} = -\dfrac{x+1}{5x^2}$

19. $\dfrac{x}{(2x-3)(x+1)} \cdot (2x-3) = \dfrac{x}{x+1}$

20. $\dfrac{8}{2+3x} \cdot 4(2+3x) = 32$

21. $3(a+2) \cdot \dfrac{1}{3(a+2)} = 1$

22. $(4x-3)(x+1) \cdot \dfrac{1}{(4x+3)(x-1)} = \dfrac{(4x-3)(x+1)}{(4x+3)(x-1)}$

23. $\dfrac{x}{x+4} \div \dfrac{x+3}{x+4} = \dfrac{x}{x+4} \cdot \dfrac{x+4}{x+3}$

$= \dfrac{x}{x+3}$

24. $\dfrac{7x^2}{10} \div \dfrac{14x^3}{15} = \dfrac{7x^2}{10} \cdot \dfrac{15}{14x^3}$

$= \dfrac{3}{4x}$

25. $\dfrac{2(x+2)}{5(x-3)} \div \dfrac{4(x-2)}{5x-15} = \dfrac{2(x+2)}{5(x-3)} \cdot \dfrac{5(x-3)}{4(x-2)}$

$= \dfrac{x+2}{2(x-2)}$

26. $\dfrac{3x+12}{4x} \div \dfrac{x+4}{2x} = \dfrac{3(x+4)}{4x} \cdot \dfrac{2x}{x+4}$

$= \dfrac{3}{2}$

27. $\dfrac{x^2-6x+8}{x^2-2x} \div 3x - 12 = \dfrac{(x-4)(x-2)}{x(x-2)} \cdot \dfrac{1}{3(x-4)}$

$= \dfrac{1}{3x}$

28. $\dfrac{5x^2-30x+45}{x+2} \div (5x-15) = \dfrac{5(x-3)(x-3)}{x+2} \cdot \dfrac{1}{5(x-3)}$

$= \dfrac{x-3}{x+2}$

29. $\left(\dfrac{x^2}{5} \cdot \dfrac{x+2}{2}\right) \div \dfrac{x}{30} = \dfrac{x^2}{5} \cdot \dfrac{x+2}{2} \cdot \dfrac{30}{x}$

$= 3x(x+2)$

30. $\left(\dfrac{2u^2}{3} \cdot \dfrac{5}{u}\right) \div \dfrac{6u^2}{25} = \dfrac{2u^2}{3} \cdot \dfrac{5}{u} \cdot \dfrac{25}{6u^2}$

$= \dfrac{125}{9u}$

31. $S = \dfrac{390(9+20)}{30-20}$ $\quad H = \dfrac{21(9+20)}{32-20}$

$S = \$1131$ billion $\quad H = \$50.75$ billion

$A = \dfrac{27(8+20)}{34-20}$

$A = \$54$ billion

32. $\dfrac{H}{S} = \dfrac{21(9+t)}{32-t} \div \dfrac{390(9+t)}{30-t}$

$= \dfrac{21(9+t)}{32-t} \cdot \dfrac{30-t}{390(9+t)}$

$\dfrac{H}{S} = \dfrac{7(30-t)}{130(32-t)}$

The ratio was decreasing from 1970 to 1990.

33. $\dfrac{A}{S} = \dfrac{27(8+t)}{34-t} \div \dfrac{390(9+t)}{30-t}$

$= \dfrac{27(8+t)}{34-t} \cdot \dfrac{30-t}{390(9+t)}$

$\dfrac{A}{S} = \dfrac{9(8+t)(30-t)}{130(9+t)(34-t)}$

The ratio was decreasing from 1970 to 1990.

34. **a.** A

b. S

c. H

35. $\dfrac{S}{P} = \dfrac{2200+400t}{24-t} \div \dfrac{10{,}000+5500t}{35-t}$

$\dfrac{S}{P} = \dfrac{200(11+2t)}{24-t} \cdot \dfrac{35-t}{500(20+11t)}$

$\dfrac{S}{P} = \dfrac{2(11+2t)(35-t)}{5(24-t)(20+11t)}$

36.

Year, t	0	5	10	15	20
Average Sales	0.32	0.18	0.17	0.20	0.32

37. $\frac{9}{25}$

38. $\frac{32}{35}$

39. $4x$

40. $\dfrac{2}{x^2}$

41. $\dfrac{(x-1)(x+1)}{(x+1)(x+3)} = \dfrac{x-1}{x+3}$

42. $\dfrac{(x+2)(x-2)}{(x-2)(x+6)} = \dfrac{x+2}{x+6}$

43. $\dfrac{8x}{8(x+3)} = \dfrac{x}{x+3}$

44. $\dfrac{10x}{5(x^2+4x+4)} = \dfrac{2x}{x^2+4x+4}$

45. $\dfrac{9}{6} = \dfrac{4}{x}$

$x = \dfrac{8}{3}$

46. $\dfrac{7}{3} = \dfrac{18}{y}$

$y = \dfrac{54}{7}$

47. $\dfrac{16}{2y} = \dfrac{3}{4}$

$y = \dfrac{32}{3}$

48. $\dfrac{8}{3x} = \dfrac{12}{18}$

$x = 4$

49. $15 = x^2 + 2x$

$0 = x^2 + 2x - 15$

$0 = (x+5)(x-3)$

$x = -5,\ 3$

50. $2x - 2 = x^2 - x - 2$

$0 = x^2 - 3x$

$0 = x(x-3)$

$x = 0,\ 3$

51. $x^2 - 3x - 4 = 36$

$x^2 - 3x - 40 = 0$

$(x-8)(x+5) = 0$

$x = 8,\ -5$

52. $12 = x^2 + 11x$

$0 = x^2 + 11x - 12$

$0 = (x+12)(x-1)$

$x = -12,\ 1$

53. $8x^2 + 12x = 4x(2x+3)$

The domain is all real numbers except 0 and $-\frac{3}{2}$.

54. $x^2 - 9 = (x-3)(x+3)$

The domain is all real numbers except 3 and -3.

55. $x^2 - 5x + 6 = (x-3)(x-2)$

The domain is all real numbers except 2 and 3.

56. $2x^2 - 3x - 20 = (2x+5)(x-4)$

The domain is all real numbers except 4 and $-\frac{5}{2}$.

57. $\frac{(x+1)(x+2)}{(3x+6)(2x+2)} = \frac{(x+1)(x+2)}{3(x+2)2(x+1)}$

$= \frac{1}{6}$

58. $\frac{3x(2x+2) - x(x+1)}{3x(2x+2)} = \frac{6x^2+6x-x^2-x}{3x(2x+2)}$

$= \frac{5x^2+5x}{3x(2)(x+1)}$

$= \frac{5x(x+1)}{6x(x+1)}$

$= \frac{5}{6}$

59. $2x^2 - 2 = 2(x^2-1)$

$= 2(x-1)(x+1)$

$x = -1$ is not in the domain.

60. $y^2 - 5y + 6 = (y-3)(y-2)$

$y = 2,\ 3$ is not in the domain.

61. $y^3 + 3y^2 - 10y = y(y+5)(y-2)$

$y = 0,\ 2,\ -5$ is not in the domain.

62. $x^3 - 8x^2 + 7x = x(x-7)(x-1)$

$x = 0$ is not in the domain.

$x = -3,\ -2$ is in the domain.

63. $\frac{3(2x-1)}{(x+9)}$ and $\frac{x-6}{x-4}$

$\frac{3(x-6)}{x+9}$ and $\frac{2x-1}{x-4}$

11.7 Dividing Polynomials

Communicating about Algebra

$$\begin{array}{r} -120{,}000 \\ -p+1 \overline{)\ 120{,}000p \qquad\qquad} \\ \underline{120{,}000p - 120{,}000} \\ 120{,}000 \end{array}$$

Thus, $\frac{120{,}000}{-p+1} = -120{,}000 + \frac{120{,}000}{1-p}$.

C gets larger

EXERCISES

1. a. 5469
b. 42
c. 130
d. 9

2. a. $x^2 + 2$
b. $x - 3$
c. $x + 3$
d. 11

3.

$$\begin{array}{r} 7 \\ 52 \overline{)\ 365} \\ \underline{364} \\ 1 \end{array}$$

Thus, $\frac{365}{52} = 7 + \frac{1}{52}$.

4.

$$\begin{array}{r} 1666 \\ 15\overline{)25001} \\ \underline{15} \\ 100 \\ \underline{90} \\ 100 \\ \underline{90} \\ 101 \\ \underline{90} \\ 11 \end{array}$$

Thus, $\frac{25,001}{15} = 1666 + \frac{11}{15}$.

5.

$$\begin{array}{r} x + 1 \\ x+2\overline{)\,x^2 + 3x - 1} \\ \underline{x^2 + 2x\phantom{{}-1}} \\ x - 1 \\ \underline{x + 2} \\ -3 \end{array}$$

Thus, $\dfrac{x^2 + 3x - 1}{x + 2} = x + 1 - \dfrac{3}{x + 2}$.

6.

$$\begin{array}{r} 3x^2 - 3x - 1 \\ x+1\overline{)\,3x^3 + 0x^2 - 4x - 1} \\ \underline{3x^3 + 3x^2\phantom{{}-4x-1}} \\ -3x^2 - 4x\phantom{{}-1} \\ \underline{-3x^2 - 3x\phantom{{}-1}} \\ -x - 1 \\ \underline{-x - 1} \\ 0 \end{array}$$

Thus, $\dfrac{3x^3 - 4x - 1}{x + 1} = 3x^2 - 3x - 1$.

7. $\dfrac{10x^2}{2x(5x + 2)} = \dfrac{5x}{5x + 2}$

8. $\dfrac{33x^3(x + 1)}{27x^4(x + 2)} = \dfrac{11(x + 1)}{9x(x + 2)}$

9. $(6z + 10) \div 2 = 3z + 5$

10. $(9x + 10) \div 3 = 3x + \frac{10}{3}$

11. $(10z^2 + 4z - 12) \div 4 = \frac{5}{2}z^2 + z - 3$

12. $(4u^2 + 8u - 24) \div 16 = \frac{1}{4}u^2 + \frac{1}{2}u - \frac{3}{2}$

13. $(7x^3 - 2x^2) \div 14x = \frac{1}{2}x^2 - \frac{1}{7}x$

14. $(6a^2 + 7a) \div a = 6a + 7$

15. $(m^4 + 2m^2 - 7) \div m = m^3 + 2m - \dfrac{7}{m}$

16. $(x^2 - 8) \div (-x) = -x + \dfrac{8}{x}$

17. Quotient: $x^2 + 3x + 9$
Remainder: 0
Divisor: $x - 3$

18. Quotient: $2x^2 + x + 3$
Remainder: 3
Divisor: $2x - 1$

19.

$$\begin{array}{r} x - 5 \\ x-3\overline{)\,x^2 - 8x + 15} \\ \underline{x^2 - 3x\phantom{{}+15}} \\ -5x + 15 \\ \underline{-5x + 15} \\ 0 \end{array}$$

Thus, $\dfrac{x^2 - 8x + 15}{x - 3} = x - 5$.

20.

$$\begin{array}{r} t - 12 \\ t-6\overline{)\,t^2 - 18t + 72} \\ \underline{t^2 - 6t\phantom{{}+72}} \\ -12t + 72 \\ \underline{-12t + 72} \\ 0 \end{array}$$

Thus, $\dfrac{t^2 - 18t + 72}{t - 6} = t - 12$.

21.

$$\begin{array}{r} x + 10 \\ x+5 \overline{) x^2 + 15x + 50} \\ \underline{x^2 + 5x} \\ 10x + 50 \\ \underline{10x + 50} \\ 0 \end{array}$$

Thus, $\dfrac{x^2 + 15x + 50}{x + 5} = x + 10.$

22.

$$\begin{array}{r} y - 8 \\ y+2 \overline{) y^2 - 6y - 16} \\ \underline{y^2 + 2y} \\ -8y - 16 \\ \underline{-8y - 16} \\ 0 \end{array}$$

Thus, $\dfrac{y^2 - 6y - 16}{y + 2} = y - 8.$

23.

$$\begin{array}{r} x + 3 \\ x-3 \overline{) x^2 - 0x - 4} \\ \underline{x^2 - 3x} \\ 3x - 4 \\ \underline{3x - 9} \\ 5 \end{array}$$

Thus, $\dfrac{x^2 - 4}{x - 3} = x + 3 + \dfrac{5}{x - 3}.$

24.

$$\begin{array}{r} y + 4 \\ y+1 \overline{) y^2 + 5y + 0} \\ \underline{y^2 + y} \\ 4y + 0 \\ \underline{4y + 4} \\ -4 \end{array}$$

Thus, $\dfrac{y^2 + 5y}{y + 1} = y + 4 - \dfrac{4}{y + 1}.$

25.

$$\begin{array}{r} 4x + 20 \\ x-2 \overline{) 4x^2 + 12x - 10} \\ \underline{4x^2 - 8x} \\ 20x - 10 \\ \underline{20x - 40} \\ 30 \end{array}$$

Thus, $\dfrac{4x^2 + 12x - 10}{x - 2} = 4x + 20 + \dfrac{30}{x - 2}.$

26.

$$\begin{array}{r} 5y + 5 \\ y-1 \overline{) 5y^2 + 0y + 2} \\ \underline{5y^2 - 5y} \\ 5y + 2 \\ \underline{5y - 5} \\ 7 \end{array}$$

Thus, $\dfrac{5y^2 + 2}{y - 1} = 5y + 5 + \dfrac{7}{y - 1}.$

27. $\dfrac{C}{B} = \dfrac{90{,}000(t + 15)}{360{,}000(t + 33)}$

$= \dfrac{t + 15}{4t + 132}$

$$\begin{array}{r} \frac{1}{4} \\ 4t+132 \overline{) t + 15} \\ \underline{t + 33} \\ -18 \end{array}$$

Thus, $\dfrac{C}{B} = \dfrac{1}{4} - \dfrac{18}{4t + 132} = \dfrac{1}{4} - \dfrac{9}{2t + 66}.$

28.

Year, *t*	3	5	7	9	11	13
Ratio of *C* to *B*	0.125	0.132	0.138	0.143	0.148	0.152

Canoeing was becoming more popular compared to the total.

29. $\dfrac{S}{A} = \dfrac{800(t+1.06)}{3600(t+2.8)}$

$= \dfrac{2t+2.12}{9t+25.2}$

$$\begin{array}{r|l} & \frac{2}{9} \\ 9t+25.2 & 2t + 2.12 \\ & 2t + 5.6 \\ \hline & -\ 3.48 \end{array}$$

Thus, $\dfrac{S}{A} = \dfrac{2}{9} - \dfrac{3.48}{9t+25.2}$

30.

Year, t	8	9	10	11	12	13
Ratio of S to A	0.186	0.189	0.192	0.194	0.196	0.198

Commercial sports revenue is not increasing as rapidly as amusement and recreation services revenue. The ratio $\dfrac{S}{A}$ will always be less than $\dfrac{2}{9}$.

31. $\dfrac{(2z-1)(z-4)}{z-4} = 2z-1$

32. $\dfrac{(2x-6)(x+5)}{2x-6} = x+5$

33. $\dfrac{2y(3+y)}{2y} = 3+y$

34. $\dfrac{3p(4p-5)}{3p^2} = \dfrac{4p-5}{p}$

35. $\dfrac{(2m-10)(m+1)}{m+1} = 2m-10$

36. $\dfrac{2(t+3)(t+2)}{4(t+3)} = \dfrac{t+2}{2}$

In Exercises 37– 42, in most cases, use long division so you won't have to take time looking for factors that don't exist.

37.

$$\begin{array}{r|l} & x + 5 \\ x-2 & x^2 + 3x + 2 \\ & x^2 - 2x \\ \hline & 5x + 2 \\ & 5x - 10 \\ \hline & 12 \end{array}$$

Thus, $\dfrac{x^2+3x+2}{x-2} = x+5+\dfrac{12}{x-2}$.

38.

$$\begin{array}{r|l} & a - 3 \\ a+7 & a^2 + 4a - 77 \\ & a^2 + 7a \\ \hline & -3a - 77 \\ & -3a - 21 \\ \hline & -56 \end{array}$$

Thus, $\dfrac{a^2+4a-77}{a+7} = a-3-\dfrac{56}{a+7}$.

39. $\dfrac{(3y+2)(2y-1)}{3y+2} = 2y-1$

40.

$$\begin{array}{r|l} & z \\ 3z-2 & 3z^2 - 2z - 2 \\ & 3z^2 - 2z \\ \hline & 0z - 2 \end{array}$$

Thus, $\dfrac{3z^2-2z-2}{3z-2} = z - \dfrac{2}{3z-2}$.

41.

$$\begin{array}{r}
2b + 41 \\
b - 10 \overline{\smash{\big)}\, 2b^2 + 21b + 10} \\
\underline{2b^2 - 20b} \\
41b + 10 \\
\underline{41b - 410} \\
420
\end{array}$$

Thus, $\dfrac{2b^2 + 21b + 10}{b - 10} = 2b + 41 + \dfrac{420}{b - 10}$.

42.

$$\begin{array}{r}
c + 10 \\
2c - 1 \overline{\smash{\big)}\, 2c^2 + 19c - 10} \\
\underline{2c^2 - c} \\
20c - 10 \\
\underline{20c - 10} \\
0
\end{array}$$

Thus, $\dfrac{2c^2 + 19c - 10}{2c - 1} = c + 10$.

43. c.

44. d.

45.

x	0	20	40	60	80	100
$\dfrac{x^2+6}{x+2}$	3	18.45	38.24	58.16	78.12	98.10
$x - 2$	−2	18	38	58	78	98
$\dfrac{10}{x+2}$	5	0.45	0.24	0.16	0.12	0.10

The first two are increasing and the last one is decreasing.

46. A: $y = \dfrac{x^2 + 6}{x + 2}$

B: $y = x - 2$

47.

$$\begin{array}{r}
1 \\
t + 14 \overline{\smash{\big)}\, t + 4} \\
\underline{t + 14} \\
-10
\end{array}$$

Thus, $\dfrac{t + 4}{t + 14} = 1 - \dfrac{10}{t + 14}$.

The ratio is getting larger as the years go by.

Using a Graphing Calculator

1.

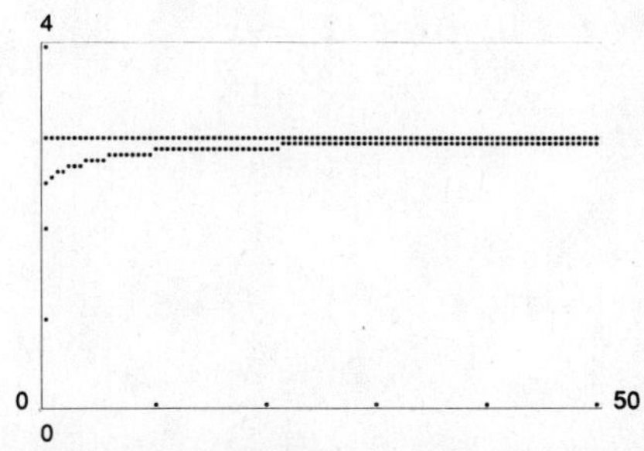

The graphs resemble each other when $x > 20$.

2.

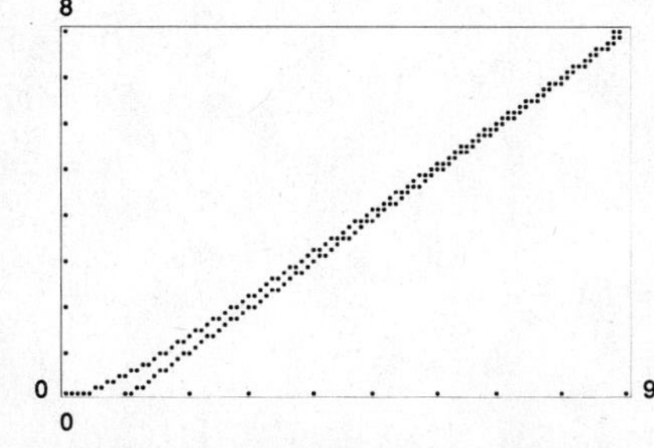

The graphs resemble each other when $x > 6$.

11.8 Solving Rational Equations

Communicating about Algebra

A. $\dfrac{4}{x^2-2x} = \dfrac{4}{3x-6}$

$12x - 24 = 4x^2 - 8x$

$0 = 4x^2 - 20x + 24$

$0 = 4(x^2 - 5x + 6)$

$0 = 4(x-3)(x-2)$

$x = 3$ or $x = 2$

False solution: $x = 2$

B. $\dfrac{4}{x(x+1)} = \dfrac{3}{x}$

$3x^2 + 3x = 4x$

$3x^2 - x = 0$

$x(3x-1) = 0$

$x = 0$ or $x = \frac{1}{3}$

False solution: $x = 0$

EXERCISES

1. $3x$

2. $x^2 = 36$

$x = \pm 6$

3. $36 = x^2$

$x = \pm 6$

4. $\dfrac{1}{x} + \dfrac{x}{3} = \dfrac{4}{3}$

$3 + x^2 = 4x$

$x^2 - 4x + 3 = 0$

$(x-1)(x-3) = 0$

$x = 1$ or $x = 3$

5. $\dfrac{16}{x} = \dfrac{4}{2}$

$4x = 32$

$x = 8$

6. $\dfrac{x}{9} - \dfrac{1}{3} = \dfrac{6}{x}$

$x^2 - 3x = 54$

$x^2 - 3x - 54 = 0$

$(x-9)(x+6) = 0$

$x = 9$ or $x = -6$

7. $12x$

8. $12x^2$

9. $4x^2$

10. $6x^2$

11. $24x^2$

12. $15x^3$

13. $\dfrac{x}{3} = \dfrac{5}{2}$

$2x = 15$

$x = \dfrac{15}{2}$

14. $\dfrac{x}{10} = \dfrac{12}{5}$

$5x = 120$

$x = 24$

15. $6x + 12 = 9x$

$3x = 12$

$x = 4$

16. $15x + 15 = 5x + 20$

$10x = 5$

$x = \frac{1}{2}$

17. $3x + 3 = 2x + 10$

$x = 7$

18. $7x - 21 = 5x + 5$

$2x = 26$

$x = 13$

19. $\frac{1}{2} + \frac{2}{x} = \frac{1}{x}$

$x + 4 = 2$

$x = -2$

20. $\frac{1}{3} - \frac{2}{3x} = \frac{1}{x}$

$x - 2 = 3$

$x = 5$

21. $\frac{x}{3} - \frac{1}{x} = \frac{2}{3}$

$x^2 - 3 = 2x$

$x^2 - 2x - 3 = 0$

$(x - 3)(x + 1) = 0$

$x = 3$ or $x = -1$

22. $\frac{x}{4} - \frac{5}{x} = \frac{1}{4}$

$x^2 - 20 = x$

$x^2 - x - 20 = 0$

$(x - 5)(x + 4) = 0$

$x = 5$ or $x = -4$

23. $\frac{25}{t} = 10 - t$

$25 = 10t - t^2$

$t^2 - 10t + 25 = 0$

$(t - 5)^2 = 0$

$t = 5$

24. $x + 4 = -\frac{4}{x}$

$x^2 + 4x = -4$

$x^4 + 4x + 4 = 0$

$(x + 2)^2 = 0$

$x = -2$

25. $\frac{x}{x + 4} = \frac{4}{x + 4} + 2$

$x = 4 + 2x + 8$

$x = -12$

26. $\frac{7}{3x - 12} - \frac{1}{x - 4} = \frac{2}{3}$

$7 - 3 = 2x - 8$

$2x = 12$

$x = 6$

27. $\frac{1}{x - 3} + \frac{1}{x + 3} = \frac{10}{x^2 - 9}$

$x + 3 + x - 3 = 10$

$2x = 10$

$x = 5$

28. $\frac{1}{x - 2} + 3 = -\frac{16}{x^2 + x - 6}$

$x + 3 + 3x^2 + 3x - 18 = -16$

$3x^2 + 4x + 1 = 0$

$(3x + 1)(x + 1) = 0$

$x = -\frac{1}{3}$ or $x = -1$

29. $5 + \frac{6}{x - 3} = \frac{x + 3}{x^2 - 9}$

$5x^2 - 45 + 6x + 18 = x + 3$

$5x^2 + 5x - 30 = 0$

$5(x + 3)(x - 2) = 0$

$x = 2$

($x = -3$ is a false solution.)

30. $\frac{2}{(x - 2)^2} = 1 - \frac{1}{x - 2}$

$2 = x^2 - 4x + 4 - x + 2$

$x^2 - 5x + 4 = 0$

$(x - 4)(x - 1) = 0$

$x = 4$ or $x = 1$

31. $\frac{3x}{x + 1} = \frac{2}{x - 1}$

$3x^2 - 3x = 2x + 2$

$3x^2 - 5x - 2 = 0$

$(3x + 1)(x - 2) = 0$

$x = -\frac{1}{3}$ or $x = 2$

32. $\frac{20 - x}{x} = x$

$x^2 + x - 20 = 0$

$(x + 5)(x - 4) = 0$

$x = -5$ or $x = 4$

33. $\frac{4}{x} - \frac{x}{6} = \frac{5}{3}$

$24 - x^2 = 10x$

$x^2 + 10x - 24 = 0$

$(x + 12)(x - 2) = 0$

$x = -12$ or $x = 2$

34. $x + \frac{1}{x} = \frac{5}{2}$

$2x^2 + 2 = 5x$

$2x^2 - 5x + 2 = 0$

$(2x - 1)(x - 2) = 0$

$x = \frac{1}{2}$ or $x = 2$

35. $\dfrac{x+30}{x} = x$

$x + 30 = x^2$

$x^2 - x - 30 = 0$

$(x-6)(x+5) = 0$

$x = 6$ or $x = -5$

36. $\dfrac{3}{x+5} = \dfrac{2}{x+1}$

$2x + 10 = 3x + 3$

$x = 7$

37. $\dfrac{18}{u} = \dfrac{u}{2}$

$u^2 = 36$

$u = \pm 6$

38. $\dfrac{4}{x+2} - \dfrac{1}{x} = \dfrac{1}{x}$

$4x - x - 2 = x + 2$

$2x = 4$

$x = 2$

39. $\dfrac{15}{x} - 4 = \dfrac{6}{x} + 3$

$15 - 4x = 6 + 3x$

$7x = 9$

$x = \dfrac{9}{7}$

40. $\dfrac{5}{u+8} = \dfrac{1}{4}$

$u + 8 = 20$

$u = 12$

41. $\dfrac{2}{x+3} + \dfrac{1}{x} = \dfrac{4}{3x}$

$6x + 3x + 9 = 4x + 12$

$5x = 3$

$x = \dfrac{3}{5}$

42. $\dfrac{10}{x+3} - \dfrac{3}{5} = \dfrac{10x+1}{3x+9}$

$150 - 9x - 27 = 50x + 5$

$59x = 118$

$x = 2$

43. $0.250 = \dfrac{0.160(50) + x}{50 + x}$

$12.5 + 0.25x = 8 + x$

$0.75x = 4.5$

$x = 6$

44. $130 = \dfrac{12(120) + 6(x)}{18}$

$2340 = 1440 + 6x$

$6x = 900$

$x = 150$

45. $y = \dfrac{36 + 3.50n}{n}$

$6.50 = \dfrac{36 + 3.50n}{n}$

$6.50n = 36 + 3.50n$

$3n = 36$

$n = 12$

46. $y = \dfrac{120{,}000 + 0.50x}{x}$

$1 = \dfrac{120{,}000 + 0.50x}{x}$

$x = 120{,}000 + 0.50x$

$0.50x = 120{,}000$

$x = 240{,}000$

47. $\dfrac{210}{x} + \dfrac{210}{2x} = 21$

$420 + 210 = 42x$

$42x = 630$

$x = 15$ pages per day

$2x = 30$ pages per day

48. $\dfrac{45}{x} + \dfrac{45}{3x} = 40$

$135 + 45 = 120x$

$120x = 180$

$x = 1.5$ papers per minute

$3x = 4.5$ papers per minute

49. b. $\dfrac{D}{d} = 118.2$

$\dfrac{13{,}000}{d} = 118.2$

$\dfrac{13{,}000}{118.2} = d$

$d \approx 110$ feet

50. $\dfrac{5}{n+25} = \dfrac{3}{n-7}$

$5n - 35 = 3n + 75$

$2n = 110$

$n = 55$

$1977 - 55 = 1922$

51. $\dfrac{6}{5} - \dfrac{3}{6} = \dfrac{36-15}{30}$

$= \dfrac{21}{30}$

$= \dfrac{7}{10}$

$x = 6$ is a solution.

52. $-\frac{6}{5} + \frac{10}{5} = \frac{4}{5}$

$x = -2$ is a solution.

53. $\frac{5}{2 \cdot 0} - \frac{4}{0}$

$x = 0$ is not a solution.

54. $(2x + 3)(x - 9) = 0$

$x = -\frac{3}{2}$ or $x = 9$

55. $x^2 + x - 56 = 0$

$(x + 8)(x - 7) = 0$

$x = -8$ or $x = 7$

56. $t^2 - 5t = 0$

$t(t - 5) = 0$

$t = 0$ or $t = 5$

57. $\frac{3}{4} = \frac{2}{x}$

$x = \frac{8}{3}$

58. $\frac{5}{x} = \frac{1}{3}$

$x = 15$

59. $\frac{1}{x + 1} = \frac{1}{6}$

$x + 1 = 6$

$x = 5$

60. $\frac{1}{2x - 3} = \frac{1}{9}$

$2x - 3 = 9$

$x = 6$

61. $\frac{1}{3 - y} = -\frac{1}{10}$

$3 - y = -10$

$y = 13$

62. $\frac{5}{u + 8} = \frac{1}{4}$

$u + 8 = 20$

$u = 12$

63. $\frac{1}{x^2 - x} = \frac{1}{2x - 2}$

$x^2 - 3x + 2 = 0$

$(x - 1)(x - 2) = 0$

$x = 2$ is a solution.

$x = 1$ is a false solution.

64. $\frac{1}{x(x + 4)} = \frac{2}{x + 4}$

$2x^2 + 8x = x + 4$

$2x^2 + 7x - 4 = 0$

$(2x - 1)(x + 4) = 0$

$x = \frac{1}{2}$ is a solution.

$x = -4$ is a false solution.

65. $\frac{5}{x^2} = -\frac{1}{x}$

$-x^2 = 5x$

$x^2 + 5x = 0$

$x(x + 5) = 0$

$x = -5$ is a solution.

$x = 0$ is a false solution.

Chapter REVIEW

1. $\frac{x}{2} = \frac{4}{7}$

$x = \frac{8}{7}$

2. $\frac{5}{x} = \frac{6}{11}$

$x = \frac{55}{6}$

3. $\frac{7}{10} = \frac{9 + x}{x}$

$7x = 90 + 10x$

$-3x = 90$

$x = -30$

4. $\frac{8x}{4 + x} = 2$

$8x = 8 + 2x$

$6x = 8$

$x = \frac{4}{3}$

5. $\frac{x + 3}{x} = \frac{4}{x - 1}$

$4x = x^2 + 2x - 3$

$x^2 - 2x - 3 = 0$

$(x - 3)(x + 1) = 0$

$x = 3$ or $x = -1$

6. $\frac{5}{x + 6} = \frac{x - 6}{x}$

$x^2 - 36 = 5x$

$x^2 - 5x - 36 = 0$

$(x - 9)(x + 4) = 0$

$x = 9$ or $x = -4$

7. $6 = k19$

$k = \frac{6}{19}$

$a = \frac{6}{19}b$

8. $3 = \frac{6}{19}b$

$b = \frac{19}{2}$

9. $a = \frac{6}{19}(14)$

$a = \frac{84}{19}$

10. $2(9) = k$

$k = 18$

$pq = 18$

11. $30q = 18$

$q = \frac{3}{5}$

12. $p(27) = 18$

$p = \frac{2}{3}$

13. $\frac{8}{1} = \frac{x}{24}$

$x = 192$ pounds

14. $\frac{1}{50} = \frac{x}{1500}$

$50x = 1500$

$x = 30$ inches

15. $$\frac{4x(3)(x+1) - \frac{1}{2}x(x+1)}{(4x)(3)(x+1)} = \frac{24x^2 + 24x - x^2 - x}{24x^2 + 24x} = \frac{23x^2 + 23x}{24x^2 + 24x} = \frac{23(x^2 + x)}{24(x^2 + x)} = \frac{23}{24}$$

16. $$\frac{x(x+1)}{\frac{1}{2}(4x)(3)(x+1)} = \frac{x^2 + x}{6x^2 + 6x} = \frac{1(x^2 + x)}{6(x^2 + x)} = \frac{1}{6}$$

17. $\frac{7.0}{18.3} = \frac{70}{183}$

18. $\frac{9.4}{25.4} = \frac{94}{254} = \frac{47}{127}$

19. $\frac{3x}{9x^2 + 3} = \frac{x}{3x^2 + 1}$

20. $\frac{4x^2 - 2x}{8x^2} = \frac{2x - 1}{4x}$

21. $$\frac{5x^2 + 10x - 5}{25x + 100} = \frac{5(x^2 + 2x - 1)}{25(x + 4)} = \frac{x^2 + 2x - 1}{5(x + 4)}$$

22. $\frac{6x^2}{12x^4 + 18x^2} = \frac{1}{2x^2 + 3}$

23. $\frac{8x^2 - 4x}{16x^3} = \frac{2x - 1}{4x^2}$

24. $\frac{7x^4}{49x^2 + x^2} = \frac{7x^2}{50}$

25. $\frac{12x^2}{5x^3} \cdot \frac{25x^4}{3x} = 20x^2$

26. $\frac{2x^3}{4x} \cdot \frac{3x^2}{12x^4} = \frac{1}{8}$

27. $\frac{14x}{x^3} \cdot \frac{2x^2}{7x^4} = \frac{4}{x^4}$

28. $\frac{2x}{x^2 + 2x + 1} \cdot \frac{x + 1}{2x^2 - 2x} = \frac{1}{(x + 1)(x - 1)}$

29. $\frac{3x^2 - 3}{x - 1} \cdot \frac{4}{x + 1} = 12$

30. $\frac{x^2 - 6x - 7}{6x + 30} \cdot \frac{2x^2 - 50}{2x - 14} = \frac{(x + 1)(x - 5)}{6}$

31. $$\frac{3x}{x + 4} \div \frac{x^2}{x + 4} = \frac{3x}{x + 4} \cdot \frac{x + 4}{x^2} = \frac{3}{x}$$

32. $$\frac{6x^3 - 6x}{3x^2} \div \frac{x + 1}{2x^3} = \frac{6x(x - 1)(x + 1)}{3x^2} \cdot \frac{2x^3}{x + 1} = 4x^2(x - 1)$$

33. $$\frac{x^2 + 5x + 6}{x + 3} \div \frac{x + 5}{x^2 + 4x + 3} = \frac{(x + 2)(x + 3)}{x + 3} \cdot \frac{(x + 3)(x + 1)}{x + 5} = \frac{(x + 1)(x + 2)(x + 3)}{x + 5}$$

34. $$\frac{9x^3}{x^3 - x^2} \div \frac{x - 8}{x^2 - 9x + 8} = \frac{9x^3}{x^2(x - 1)} \cdot \frac{(x - 8)(x - 1)}{(x - 8)} = 9x$$

35. $\dfrac{8x+4}{32x^2} \div \dfrac{2x^2+x}{x^3} = \dfrac{4(2x+1)}{32x^2} \cdot \dfrac{x^3}{x(2x+1)}$

$= \dfrac{1}{8}$

36. $\dfrac{x^2+3x+2}{x^2+7x+12} \div \dfrac{x^2+5x+4}{x^2+5x+6} = \dfrac{(x+1)(x+2)}{(x+4)(x+3)} \cdot \dfrac{(x+2)(x+3)}{(x+1)(x+4)}$

$= \dfrac{(x+2)^2}{(x+4)^2}$

37. $(12x^2+2x-3) \div 2x = \dfrac{12x^2}{2x} + \dfrac{2x}{2x} - \dfrac{3}{2x}$

$= 6x + 1 - \dfrac{3}{2x}$

38. $(8x^2-6x+9) \div 2x = \dfrac{8x^2}{2x} - \dfrac{6x}{2x} + \dfrac{9}{2x}$

$= 4x - 3 + \dfrac{9}{2x}$

39. $(9x^2+3x+1) \div 3x = \dfrac{9x^2}{3x} + \dfrac{3x}{3x} + \dfrac{1}{3x}$

$= 3x + 1 + \dfrac{1}{3x}$

40. $(4x^2+10x-3) \div 2x = \dfrac{4x^2}{2x} + \dfrac{10x}{2x} - \dfrac{3}{2x}$

$= 2x + 5 - \dfrac{3}{2x}$

41. $(3x^2-15x-10) \div 3x = \dfrac{3x^2}{3x} - \dfrac{15x}{3x} - \dfrac{10}{3x}$

$= x - 5 - \dfrac{10}{3x}$

42. $(6x^2-36x+5) \div 6x = \dfrac{6x^2}{6x} - \dfrac{36x}{6x} + \dfrac{5}{6x}$

$= x - 6 + \dfrac{5}{6x}$

43.

$$\begin{array}{r|l} & 3x + 5 \\ \hline x-1 & 3x^2 + 2x - 1 \\ & 3x^2 - 3x \\ \hline & 5x - 1 \\ & 5x - 5 \\ \hline & 4 \end{array}$$

Thus, $\dfrac{3x^2+2x-1}{x-1} = 3x + 5 + \dfrac{4}{x-1}$.

44.

$$\begin{array}{r|l} & x - 6 \\ \hline x+2 & x^2 - 4x + 2 \\ & x^2 + 2x \\ \hline & -6x + 2 \\ & -6x - 12 \\ \hline & 14 \end{array}$$

Thus, $\dfrac{x^2-4x+2}{x+2} = x - 6 + \dfrac{14}{x+2}$.

45.

$$\begin{array}{r|l} & 2x + \frac{11}{2} \\ \hline 2x-1 & 4x^2 + 9x + 5 \\ & 4x^2 - 2x \\ \hline & 11x + 5 \\ & 11x - \frac{11}{2} \\ \hline & \frac{21}{2} \end{array}$$

Thus, $\dfrac{4x^2+9x+5}{2x-1} = 2x + \dfrac{11}{2} + \dfrac{21}{2(2x-1)}$.

46.

$$\begin{array}{r|l} & 2x - 5 \\ \hline 3x+6 & 6x^2 - 3x - 4 \\ & 6x^2 + 12x \\ \hline & -15x - 4 \\ & -15x - 30 \\ \hline & 26 \end{array}$$

Thus, $\dfrac{6x^2-3x-4}{3x+6} = 2x - 5 + \dfrac{26}{3x+6}$.

47.

$$\begin{array}{r}
x + 1 \\
5x - 2 \overline{\smash{\big)}\, 5x^2 + 3x + 6} \\
\underline{5x^2 - 2x} \\
5x + 6 \\
\underline{5x - 2} \\
8
\end{array}$$

Thus, $\dfrac{5x^2 + 3x + 6}{5x - 2} = x + 1 + \dfrac{8}{5x - 2}$.

48.

$$\begin{array}{r}
3x - \frac{13}{2} \\
4x + 6 \overline{\smash{\big)}\, 12x^2 - 8x - 2} \\
\underline{12x^2 + 18x} \\
-26x - 2 \\
\underline{-26x - 39} \\
37
\end{array}$$

Thus, $\dfrac{12x^2 - 8x - 2}{4x + 6} = 3x - \dfrac{13}{2} + \dfrac{37}{4x + 6}$.

49. $\dfrac{3}{x} + \dfrac{2}{3} = \dfrac{5}{x}$

$9 + 2x = 15$

$2x = 6$

$x = 3$

50. $\dfrac{1}{4} + \dfrac{6}{x} = \dfrac{3}{x}$

$x + 24 = 12$

$x = -12$

51. $\dfrac{x}{5} - \dfrac{6}{x} = \dfrac{1}{5}$

$x^2 - 30 = x$

$x^2 - x - 30 = 0$

$(x - 6)(x + 5) = 0$

$x = 6$ or $x = -5$

52. $\dfrac{x}{4} + \dfrac{7}{4} = -\dfrac{3}{x}$

$x^2 + 7x = -12$

$x^2 + 7x + 12 = 0$

$(x + 4)(x + 3) = 0$

$x = -4$ or $x = -3$

53. $\dfrac{x + 2}{2} = \dfrac{4}{x}$

$x^2 + 2x = 8$

$x^2 + 2x - 8 = 0$

$(x + 4)(x - 2) = 0$

$x = -4$ or $x = 2$

54. $\dfrac{x}{5} = \dfrac{7}{x - 2}$

$x^2 - 2x = 35$

$x^2 - 2x - 35 = 0$

$(x - 7)(x + 5) = 0$

$x = 7$ or $x = -5$

55. $13(0.56) = k$

$k = 7.28$

$c(0.75) = 7.28$

$c = 9.7$

The annual per capita consumption would be 9.7 pounds.

56. $x = 80a$

$558 = 80a$

$a \approx 7$

You ate approximately 7 apples in one week.

57. $\frac{6}{231} \approx 0.026$ or $= 2.6$

Approximately 2.6% of the apples were processed as dried apples.

58. $\frac{50}{231}$

The probability that an apple was picked for apple juice is $\frac{50}{231}$.

59. $635(0.78) \approx 495$

Approximately 495 adults have eaten at a Chinese restaurant.

60. $336 = 0.74x$

$x \approx 454$

You surveyed 454 people.

Chapter TEST

1. $\frac{3}{x} = \frac{15}{4}$

$15x = 12$

$x = \frac{4}{5}$

2. $\frac{7}{3} = \frac{5}{y}$

$7y = 15$

$y = \frac{15}{7}$

3. $\frac{x+2}{5} = \frac{-1}{x-4}$

$x^2 - 2x - 8 = -5$

$x^2 - 2x - 3 = 0$

$(x-3)(x+1) = 0$

$x = 3$ or $x = -1$

4. $\frac{x+8}{x} = \frac{x+2}{2}$

$x^2 + 2x = 2x + 16$

$x^2 = 16$

$x = \pm 4$

5. $x = 0.22(200)$

$x = 44$ gallons

6. $x = 0.18(4700)$

$x = 846$ people

7. $37 = 0.74x$

$x = 50$ meters

8. $230 = x(500)$

$x = 0.46$ or 46%

9. $14 = k3$

$k = \frac{14}{3}$

$y = \frac{14}{3}x$

$y = \frac{14}{3}(5)$

$y = \frac{70}{3}$

10. $(12)(42) = k$

$k = 504$

$mn = 504$

$m \cdot 2 = 504$

$m = 252$

11. $\frac{5}{15} = \frac{1}{3}$

12. Fork: $\frac{7}{16}$

Spoon: $\frac{9}{16}$

13. $\frac{3x}{x^2 + 2x} = \frac{3}{x+2}$

14. $\frac{x^2 + 2x + 1}{(x^2 - 1)} = \frac{(x+1)}{(x-1)}$

15. $\frac{4x^2}{10x^4} \cdot \frac{-3x^2}{6x} = \frac{-1}{5x}$

16. $\frac{x^3 + x^2}{x^2 - 9} \cdot \frac{x+3}{4x^3 + x^2 - 3x} = \frac{x}{(x-3)(4x-3)}$

17. $\frac{x+5}{3x^2} \div \frac{4x}{x+5} = \frac{x+5}{3x^2} \cdot \frac{x+5}{4x}$

$= \frac{(x+5)^2}{12x^3}$

18. $\frac{x+5}{x^3 - x^2 - 6x} \div \frac{x^2 - 25}{x^2 + x - 12} = \frac{x+5}{x(x-3)(x+2)} \cdot \frac{(x+4)(x-3)}{(x+5)(x-5)}$

$= \frac{x+4}{x(x+2)(x-5)}$

19.

$$\begin{array}{r} 3x - 5 \\ x+2\overline{)\,3x^2 + x - 1} \\ \underline{3x^2 + 6x} \\ -5x - 1 \\ \underline{-5x - 10} \\ 9 \end{array}$$

Thus, $\dfrac{3x^2+x-1}{x+2} = 3x - 5 + \dfrac{9}{x+2}$.

20.

$$\begin{array}{r} x + 1 \\ x-3\overline{)\,x^2 - 2x + 6} \\ \underline{x^2 - 3x} \\ x + 6 \\ \underline{x - 3} \\ 9 \end{array}$$

Thus, $\dfrac{x^2-2x+6}{x-3} = x + 1 + \dfrac{9}{x-3}$.

21. $\dfrac{6}{x} + \dfrac{1}{2} = \dfrac{4}{x}$

$12 + x = 8$

$x = -4$

22. $\dfrac{x}{4} - \dfrac{21}{4x} = 5$

$x^2 - 21 = 20x$

$x^2 - 20x - 21 = 0$

$(x - 21)(x + 1) = 0$

$x = 21$ or $x = -1$

23. $1.80 = \dfrac{30{,}000 + 1.20d}{d}$

$1.80d = 30{,}000 + 1.20d$

$0.60d = 30{,}000$

$d = 50{,}000$ dozen

24. $92 = \dfrac{4(88) + 2x}{6}$

$552 = 352 + 2x$

$x = 100$ points

Chapter 12

Functions

12.1 Functions and Relations

Communicating about Algebra

A. $f(x) = 5x - 7$

$f(3) = 5(3) - 7$

$= 8$

$f\left(\frac{2}{3}\right) = 5\left(\frac{2}{3}\right) - 7$

$= -3\frac{2}{3}$

B. $f(x) = -x^2 + 2x + 4$

$f(1) = -(1)^2 + 2(1) + 4$

$= 5$

$f\left(-\frac{1}{2}\right) = -\left(-\frac{1}{2}\right)^2 + 2\left(-\frac{1}{2}\right) + 4$

$= 2\frac{3}{4}$

C. $f(x) = \dfrac{1}{x}$

$f(2) = \dfrac{1}{2}$

$f\left(-\dfrac{3}{4}\right) = -\dfrac{4}{3}$

EXERCISES

1. $f(4) = 1$

Domain: $\{1, 2, 3, 4\}$

2. $f(2) = 4$

Domain: $\{1, 2, 3, 4\}$

3. $f(3) = 2$

Domain: $\{1, 2, 3, 4\}$

4. $f(1) = 3(1)^2 + 2(1) - 1$

$= 3 + 2 - 1$

$= 4$

Substitute 1 in the equation and simplify.

$f(2) = 3(2)^2 + 2(2) - 1$

$= 12 + 4 - 1$

$= 15$

Substitute 2 in the equation and simplify.

5. y is a function of x, since no two ordered pairs have the same first coordinates.

6. y is not a function of x, since two ordered pairs have the same first coordinates.

7. y is not a function of x, since two ordered pairs have the same first coordinates.

8. y is a function of x, since no two ordered pairs have the same first coordinates.

9. Function

Domain: $\{1, 2, 3, 4\}$

10. Not a function

11. Function

Domain: {1, 2, 3, 4}

12. Function

Domain: {0, 1, 2, 3}

13. Function

Domain: {0, 1, 2, 3, 4}

14. Not a function

15. Not a function

16. Function

Domain: {2, 4, 6, 8, 10}

17. $f(0) = 1$

$f(2) = 21$

18. $f(-1) = -10$

$f(1) = 6$

19. $f(2) = 5$

$f(3) = 11$

20. $f(0) = 1$

$f(2) = 5$

21. $f(-1) = -1$

$f(4) = 29$

22. $f(2) = 17$

$f(-4) = 53$

23. $f(-1) = 18$

$f(1) = -2$

24. $f(-2) = 16$

$f(3) = 56$

25. $f(-5) = 85$

$f(5) = -15$

26. $f(4) = 32$

$f(5) = 55$

27. {0, 2, 4, 6, 8, 10}

$f(0) = 0$

$f(2) = 1$

28. {−3, −2, −1, 0, 1, 2, 3}

$f(0) = 0$

$f(2) = -4$

29. $f(x) = \frac{1}{2}x$

30. $f(x) = -2x$

31. Yes, each pulse rate corresponds to only one animal.

32. No, the number 1311 corresponds to 2 different years.

33. Yes, no two ordered pairs have the same first coordinate.

34. No, two ordered pairs have the same first coordinate.

35. Yes, no two ordered pairs have the same first coordinate.

36. Yes, no two ordered pairs have the same first coordinate.

37. $f(1993) \approx 13{,}100$

38. $f(1993) \approx 13{,}600$

39. $y = \frac{3}{2}x - \frac{1}{2}$

$y = \frac{3}{2}(-2) - \frac{1}{2}$

$y = -3\frac{1}{2}$

40. $3y - 5 = x$

$y = \frac{1}{3}x + \frac{5}{3}$

$y = \frac{1}{3}(-2) + \frac{5}{3}$

$y = 1$

41. $y - 5 = 2x^2$

$y = 2x^2 + 5$

$y = 2(-2)^2 + 5$

$y = 13$

42. $y - 10 = 3x^2 - 2x$

$y = 3x^2 - 2x + 10$

$y = 3(-2)^2 - 2(-2) + 10$

$y = 26$

43. **c.**

44. **d.**

45. **b.**

46. **a.**

47. $f(1) = 10\sqrt{3(1) - 1}$

$= 10\sqrt{2}$

≈ 14.1

48. $f(12) = 25\sqrt{12 - 3}$

$= 25\sqrt{9}$

$= 75$

12.2 Linear Functions

Communicating about Algebra

Answers vary. For example, height above sea level of a city and the average daily temperature of that city's outdoor air. Or, someone's present salary for work and the number of past years that someone has worked at the same company.

EXERCISES

1. A vertical line, because all ordered pairs have the same first coordinate.

2. $(-3,\ 5)$; when $x = -3$, $y = 5$.

3. 5; when $x = 1$, $y = 5$.

4. Points on the linear function are $(1,\ 2)$, $(3,\ -1)$. Use the slope formula to determine slope.

5. c.

6. a.

7. d.

8. b.

9. $m = \dfrac{-3-5}{2+2}$
$= -\dfrac{8}{4}$
$= -2$

10. $m = \dfrac{1-0}{0-1}$
$= -1$

11. $m = \dfrac{-9-4}{-3-3}$
$= \dfrac{13}{6}$

12. $m = \dfrac{-1-8}{6-3}$
$= -\dfrac{9}{3}$
$= -3$

13. $m = \dfrac{-1-2}{9+1}$
$= -\dfrac{3}{10}$

14. $m = \dfrac{1-6}{-1-1}$
$= \dfrac{-5}{-2}$
$= \dfrac{5}{2}$

15. $m = \dfrac{1-1}{0-2}$
$= 0$

$f(x) = 1$

16. $m = \dfrac{-2-1}{2+4}$
$= -\dfrac{3}{6}$
$= -\dfrac{1}{2}$

$-2 = -\dfrac{1}{2}(2) + b$

$b = -1$

$f(x) = -\dfrac{1}{2}x - 1$

17. $m = \dfrac{-4-2}{3-5} = \dfrac{-6}{-2} = 3$

$-4 = 3(3) + b$

$b = -13$

$f(x) = 3x - 13$

18. $m = \dfrac{5-3}{0+6} = \dfrac{2}{6} = \dfrac{1}{3}$

$5 = \dfrac{1}{3}(0) + b$

$b = 5$

$f(x) = \dfrac{1}{3}x + 5$

19. $m = \dfrac{1+4}{-1+2} = \dfrac{5}{1} = 5$

$1 = 5(-1) + b$

$b = 6$

$f(x) = 5x + 6$

20. $m = \dfrac{6-1}{4-9} = -\dfrac{5}{5} = -1$

$6 = (-1)4 + b$

$b = 10$

$f(x) = -x + 10$

21. $m = \dfrac{4-6}{0+3} = -\dfrac{2}{3}$

$4 = -\dfrac{2}{3}(0) + b$

$b = 4$

$f(x) = -\dfrac{2}{3}x + 4$

22. $m = \dfrac{-2+2}{3-5} = 0$

$f(x) = -2$

23. $m = \dfrac{2+1}{6-9} = -\dfrac{3}{3} = -1$

$2 = -1(6) + b$

$b = 8$

$f(x) = -x + 8$

24. $m = \dfrac{10-16}{2+4} = -\dfrac{6}{6} = -1$

$10 = -1(2) + b$

$b = 12$

$f(x) = -x + 12$

25. $m = \dfrac{5+3}{-5-5} = -\dfrac{8}{10} = -\dfrac{4}{5}$

$5 = -\dfrac{4}{5}(-5) + b$

$b = 1$

$f(x) = -\dfrac{4}{5}x + 1$

26. $m = \dfrac{2+8}{7-3} = \dfrac{10}{4} = \dfrac{5}{2}$

$2 = \dfrac{5}{2}(7) + b$

$b = -\dfrac{31}{2}$

$f(x) = \dfrac{5}{2}x - \dfrac{31}{2}$

27.

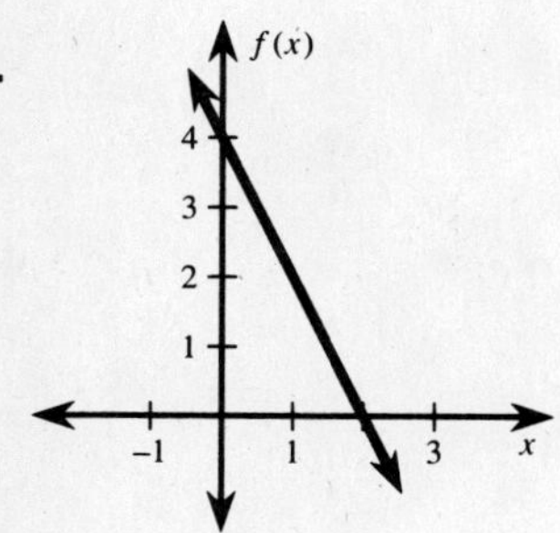

28.

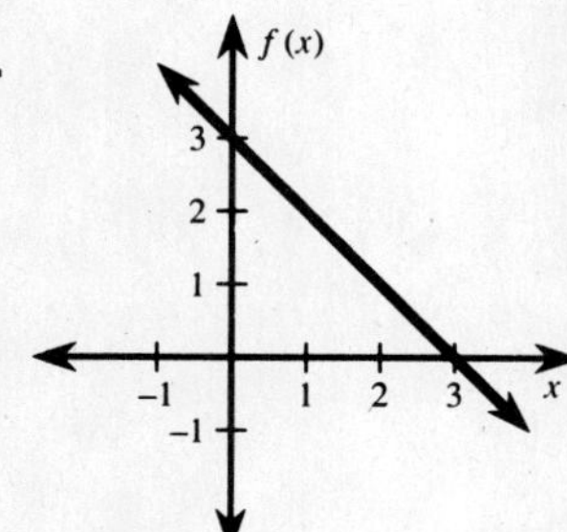

29.

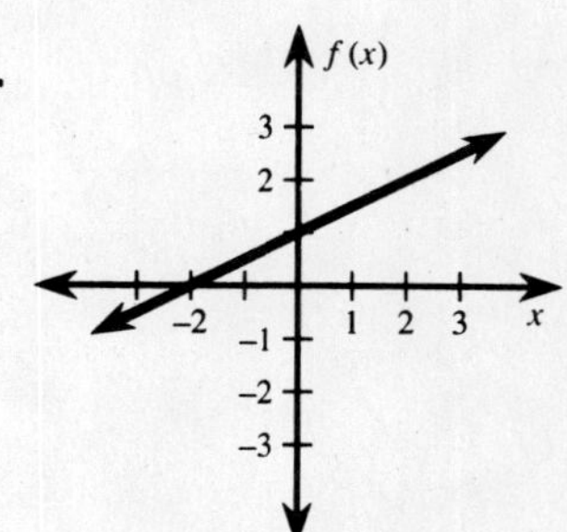

30.

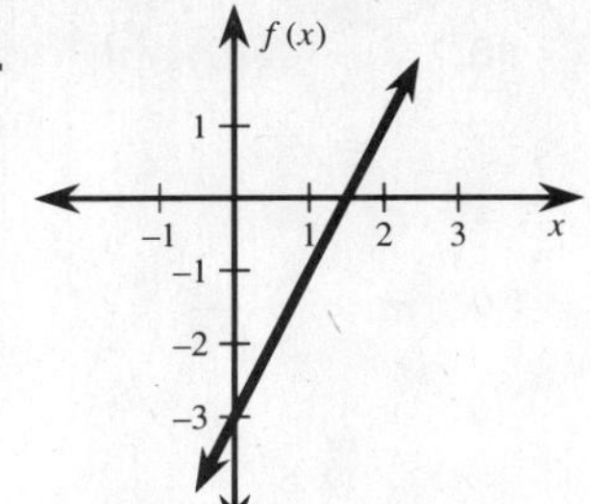

31.

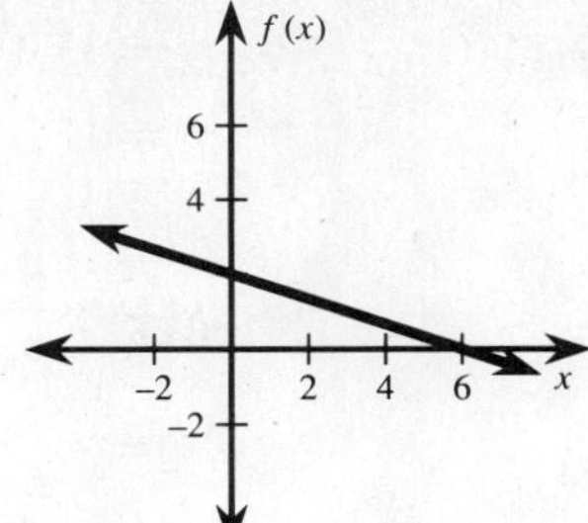

32.

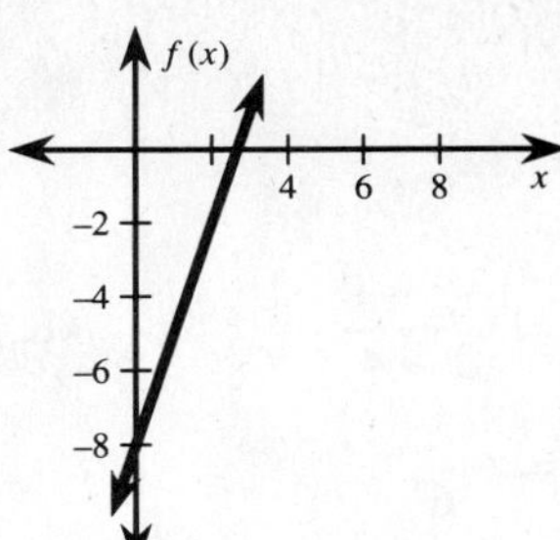

33.
$$f(x) = \tfrac{28}{980}x$$
$$f(x) = \tfrac{1}{35}x$$
$$f(430) = \tfrac{1}{35} \cdot 430$$
$$f(430) = 12\tfrac{2}{7}$$

It would take $12\frac{2}{7}$ days to go from Kansas City to Indianapolis.

34. $f(t) = \dfrac{12.2}{133}t$

35. Points: (0, 63), (70, 70)

$$m = \frac{63 - 70}{0 - 70} = \frac{-7}{-70} = \frac{1}{10}$$

$$f(x) = \frac{1}{10}x + 63$$
$$f(90) = \frac{1}{10}(90) + 63 = 72°\text{F}$$

36. $f(t) = 3300 + 600t$

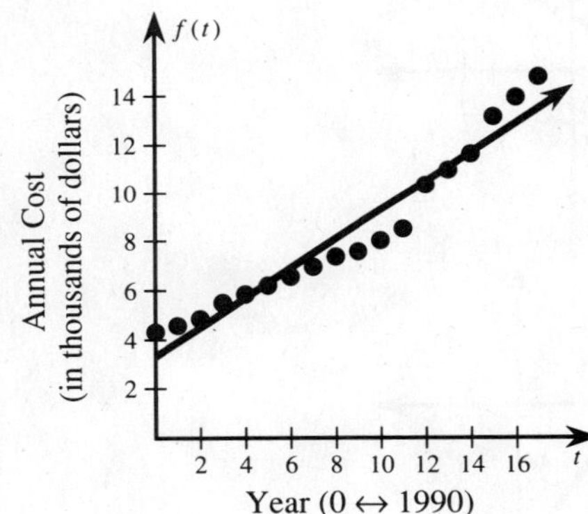

37. $f(t) = 4900 + 800t$

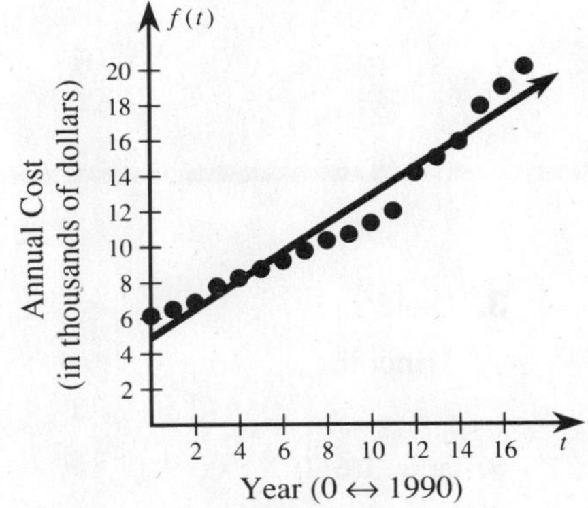

38. $f(t) = 7100 + 1100t$

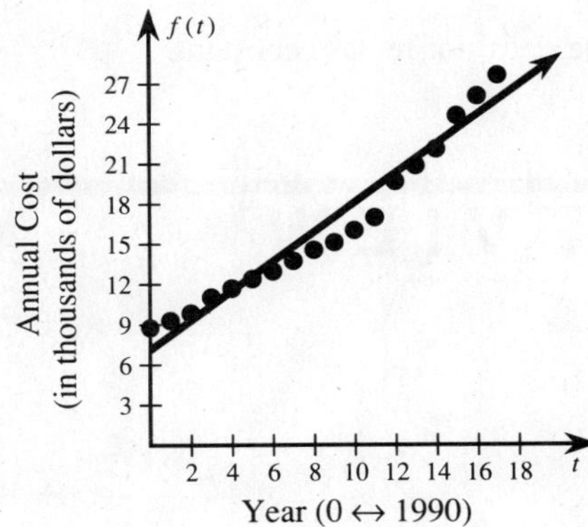

39. b. **40.** a. **41.** c. **42.** d.

43. $y = 6\left(\frac{1}{2}\right) + 9$

$= 12$

44. $y = 3(-4) - 1$

$= -13$

45. $y = 13 + 0$

$= 13$

46. $y = -\frac{1}{3}(9) + 1$

$= -2$

47. $m = \frac{-5-0}{2+4}$

$= -\frac{5}{6}$

$-5 = -\frac{5}{6}(2) + b$

$b = -\frac{10}{3}$

$y = -\frac{5}{6}x - \frac{10}{3}$

48. $m = \frac{7-2}{-1-0}$

$= -\frac{5}{1}$

$= -5$

$7 = -5(-1) + b$

$b = 2$

$y = -5x + 2$

49. $m = \frac{3-1}{0-6}$

$= -\frac{2}{6}$

$= -\frac{1}{3}$

$3 = -\frac{1}{3} \cdot 0 + b$

$b = 3$

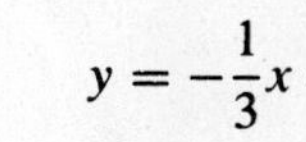

$y = -\frac{1}{3}x + 3$

50. $m = \frac{4-1}{5+3}$

$= \frac{3}{8}$

$4 = \frac{3}{8}(5) + b$

$b = \frac{17}{8}$

$y = \frac{3}{8}x + \frac{17}{8}$

51.

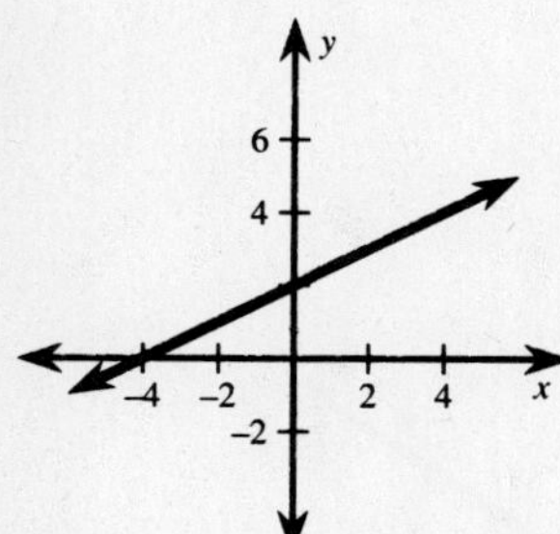

52.

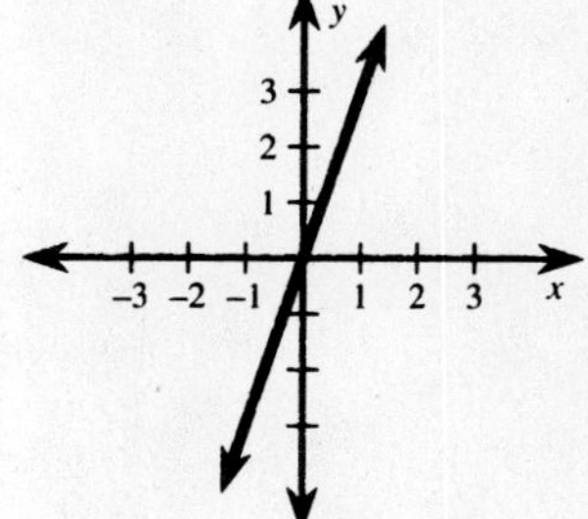

53.

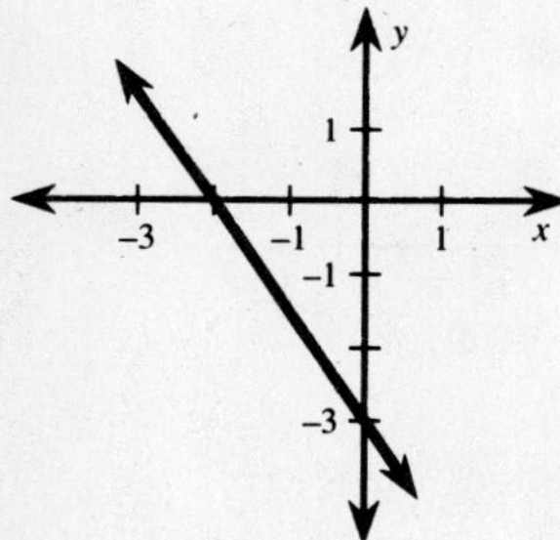

54.

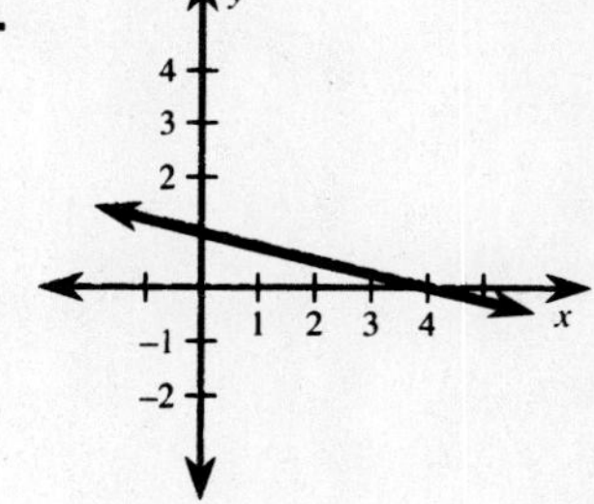

55. No, the slope does not remain constant.

Mixed REVIEW

1. 4.24×10^6

2. 6.2×10^{-7}

3. Quadratic
Trinomial

4. -4

5. $y = 3 + 14(1.2)^3$

$= 27.192$

6. $y = 3(6.2)^{-2}$

≈ 0.078

7.

$$\begin{array}{r} 3x + 8 \\ x-2\overline{\big)\, 3x^2 + 2x - 6} \\ \underline{3x^2 - 6x} \\ 8x - 6 \\ \underline{8x - 16} \\ 10 \end{array}$$

$$3x + 8 + \frac{10}{x-2}$$

8. $(4x^2-2)(4x^2+2) = 16x^4-4$

9. $x - 3 = 0$

$x = 3$

$y = -3|x - 3| + 2$

$y = 2$

$(3, 2)$

10. $x = -\frac{b}{2a}$

$= -\frac{0}{2 \cdot 2}$

$= 0$

$y = 2 \cdot 0^2 + 3$

$= 3$

$(0, 3)$

11. $x^2 - 3x - 7 = 0$

$x = \frac{3 \pm \sqrt{9 - 4(1)(-7)}}{2 \cdot 1}$

$x = \frac{3 \pm \sqrt{37}}{2}$

12. $x^2 + 8x + 5 = 0$

$x^2 + 8x + 16 = -5 + 16$

$(x + 4)^2 = 11$

$x + 4 = \pm\sqrt{11}$

$x = -4 \pm \sqrt{11}$

13. $x^2 - x + 2 = (-1)^2 - (-1) + 2$

$= 4$

$1 < 4$

$(-1,\ 1)$ is a solution.

14. $y + 2 = 2 + 2$

$= 4$

$\frac{1}{3}(x + 5) = \frac{1}{3}(7 + 5)$

$= 4$

$(7,\ 2)$ is a solution.

15. $-x^2 - 3x + 4 = 0$

$x^2 + 3x - 4 = 0$

$(x + 4)(x - 1) = 0$

$x = -4$ or $x = 1$

16. $3x^2 = 27$

$x^2 = 9$

$x = \pm 3$

17. $3x^2 + 14x + 8 = 0$

$(3x + 2)(x + 4) = 0$

$x = -\frac{2}{3}$ or $x = -4$

$\left(-\frac{2}{3},\ 0\right), (-4,\ 0)$

18. $3x + 2y = -6$

$3(0) + 2y = -6$

$y = -3$

$(0,\ -3)$

19. $x = 0.28(490)$

$x = 137.2$

20. $99 = x(450)$

$x = 0.22$ or 22%

12.3 Exponential Functions

Communicating about Algebra

A.

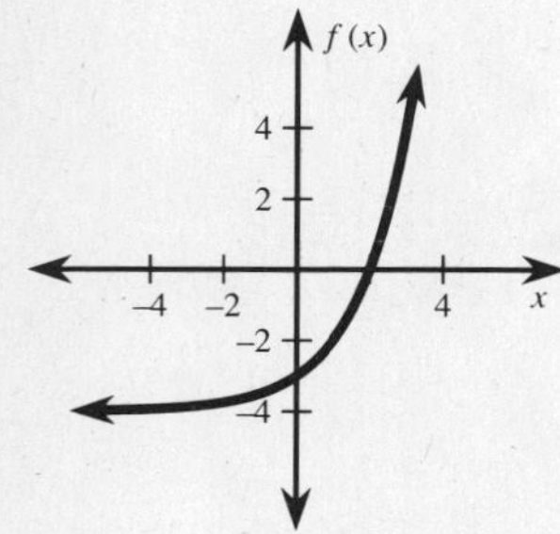

Shift the graph of $f(x) = 2^x$ four units down.

B.

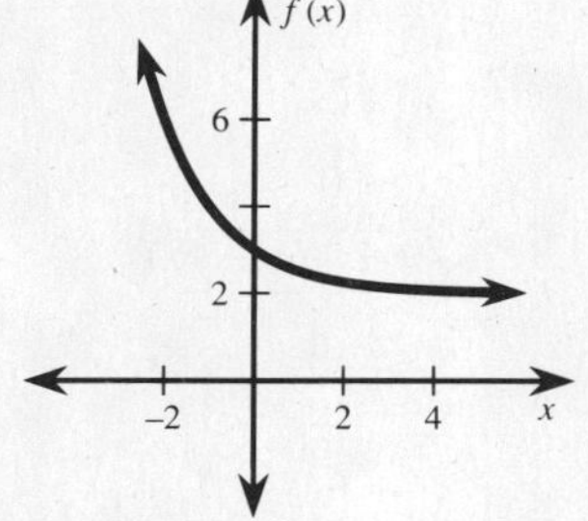

Shift the graph of $f(x) = \left(\frac{1}{2}\right)^x$ two units up.

C.

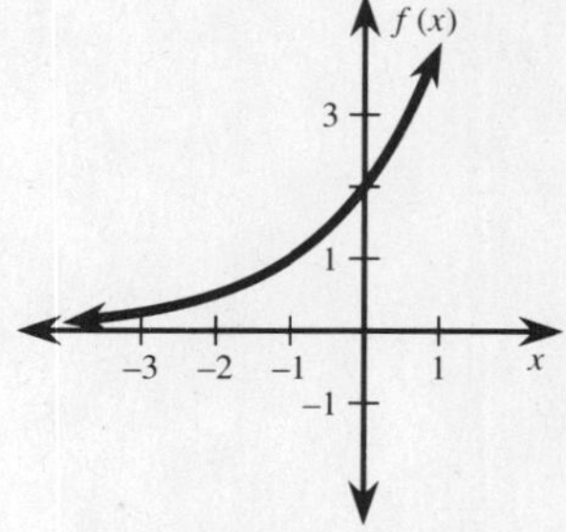

Shift the graph of $f(x) = 2^x$ one unit to the left.

D.

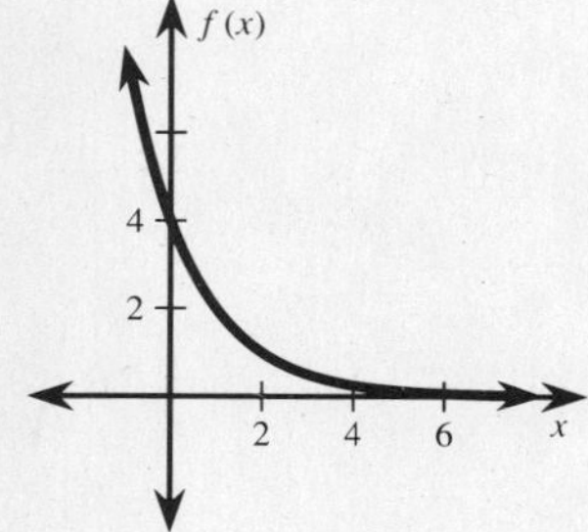

Shift the graph of $f(x) = \left(\frac{1}{2}\right)^x$ two units to the right.

E.

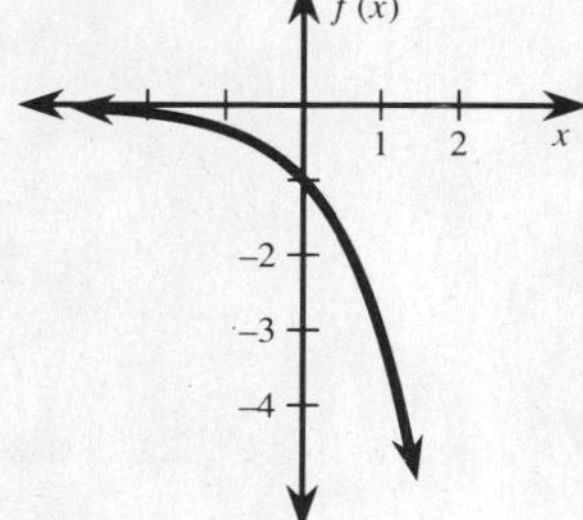

Reflect the graph of $f(x) = 3^x$ in the x-axis.

F.

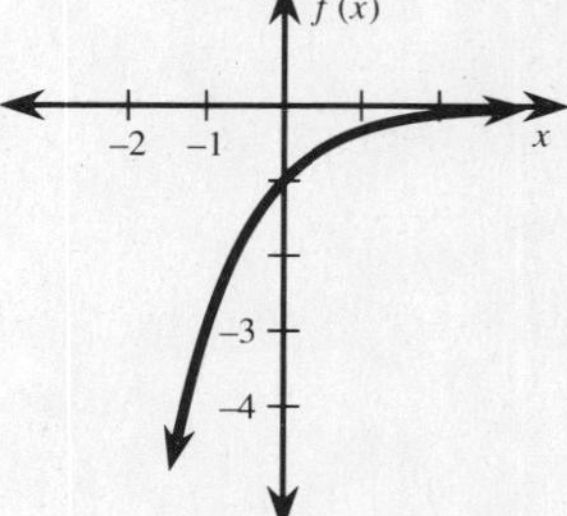

Reflect the graph of $f(x) = \left(\frac{1}{3}\right)^x$ in the x-axis.

EXERCISES

1. Exponential decay

$0 < \frac{1}{4} < 1$

2. Exponential growth

$5 > 1$

3. Horizontal shift

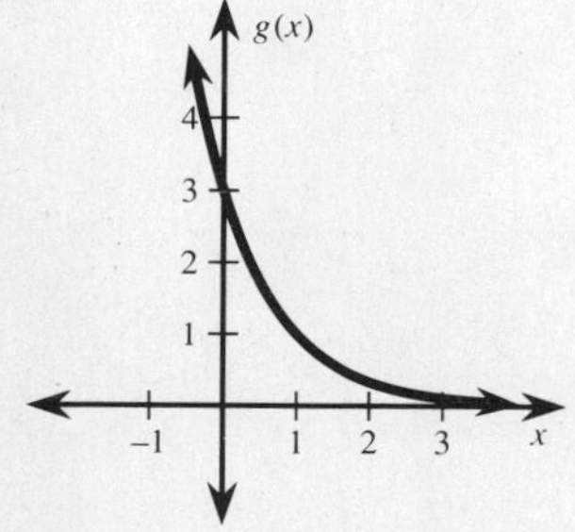

4. Vertical shift

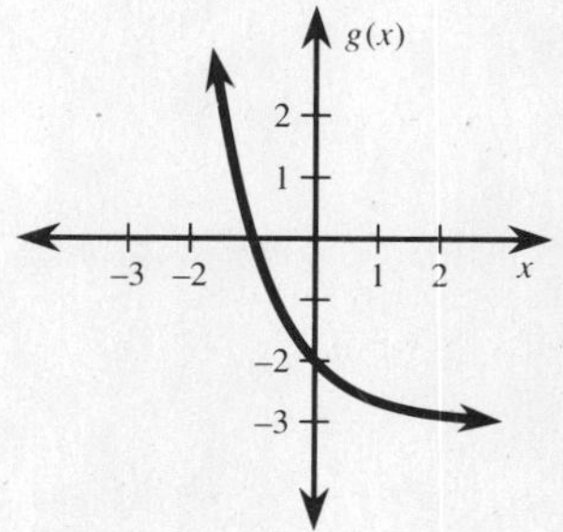

5. Reflection

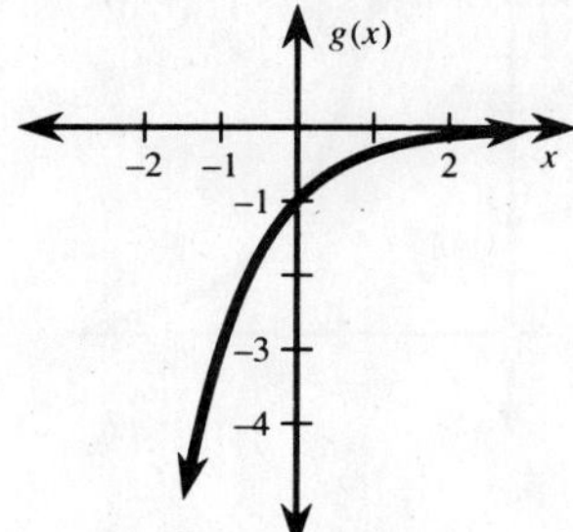

6. Vertical shift

7. Reflection

8. Vertical shift

9. Horizontal shift

10. Horizontal shift

11. Vertical shift

12. Reflection

13. Vertical shift

14. Reflection

15. Vertical shift

16. Horizontal shift

17. Reflection

18. Horizontal shift

19.

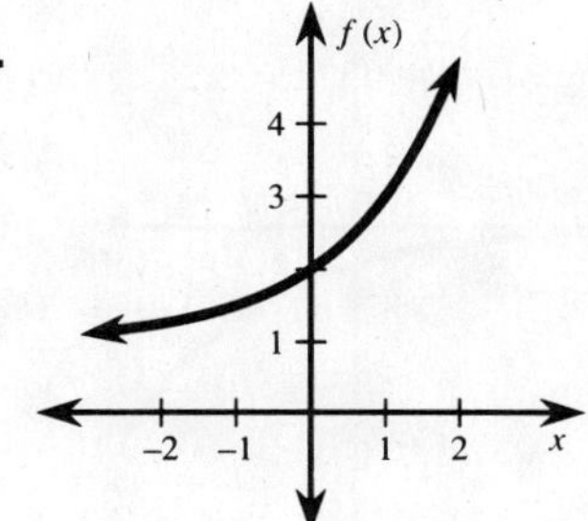

20.

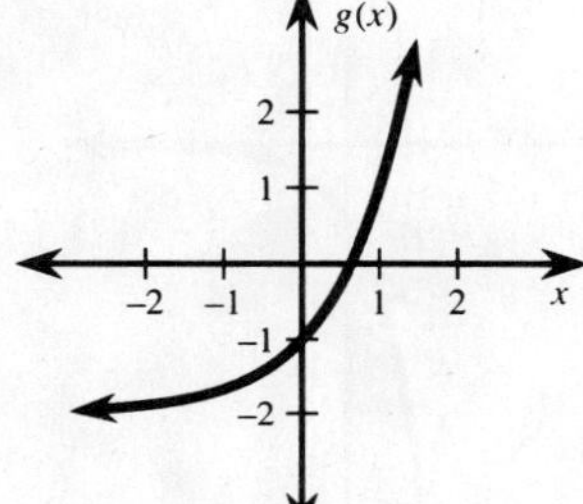

21.

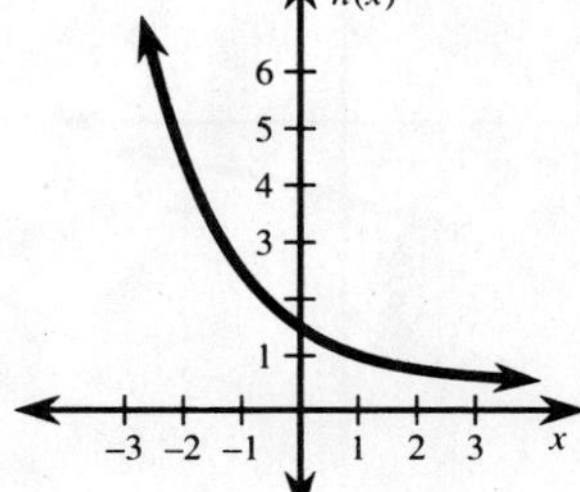

22.

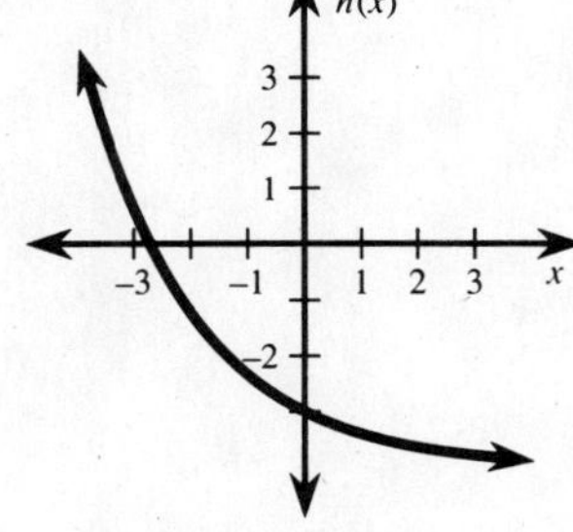

23.

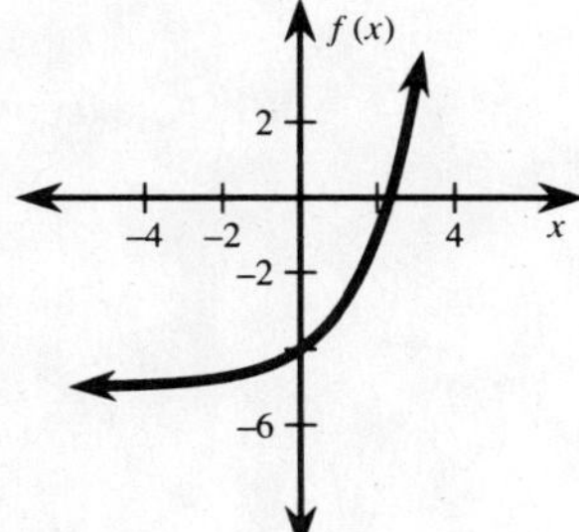

24.

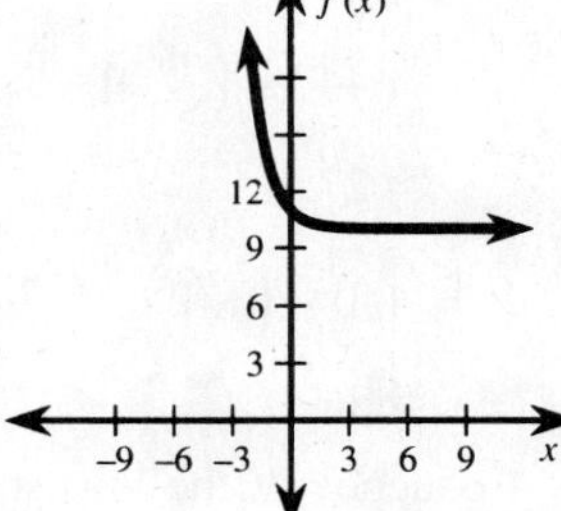

25.

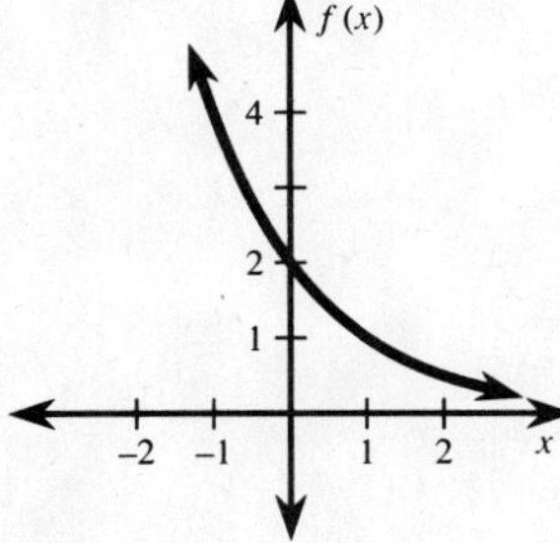

26.

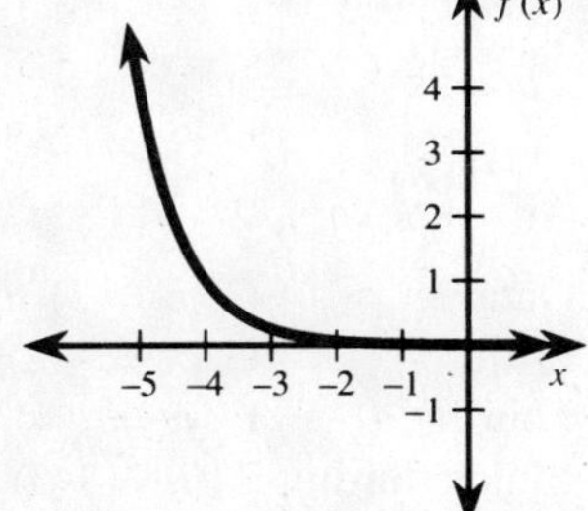

27.

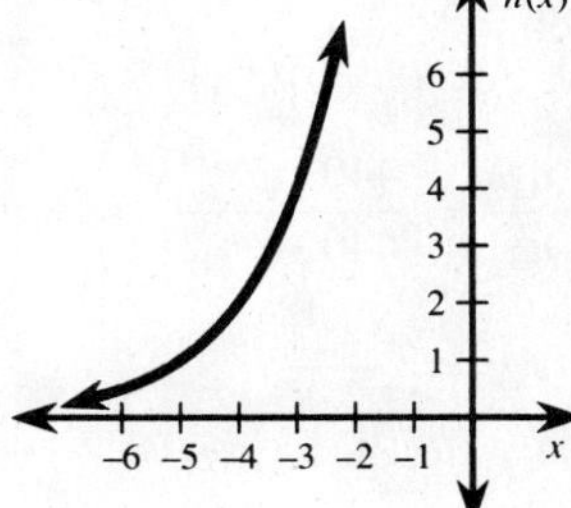

28. 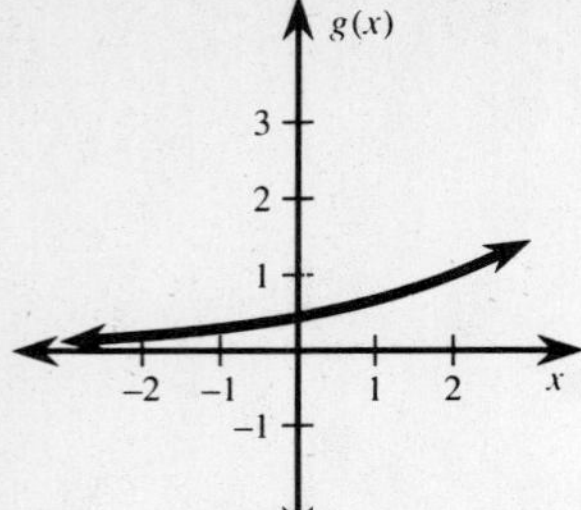

29. 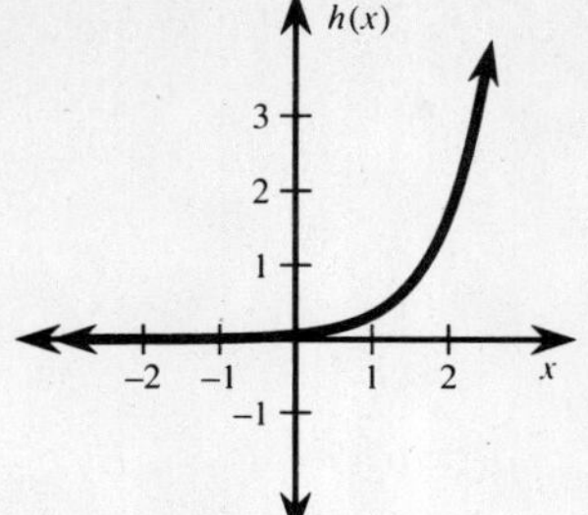

30. 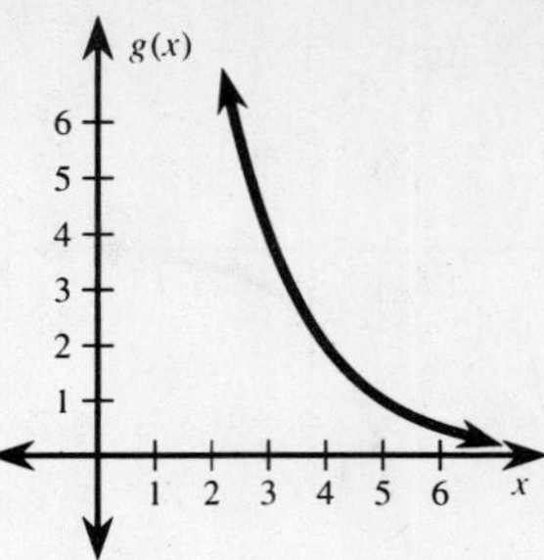

31. 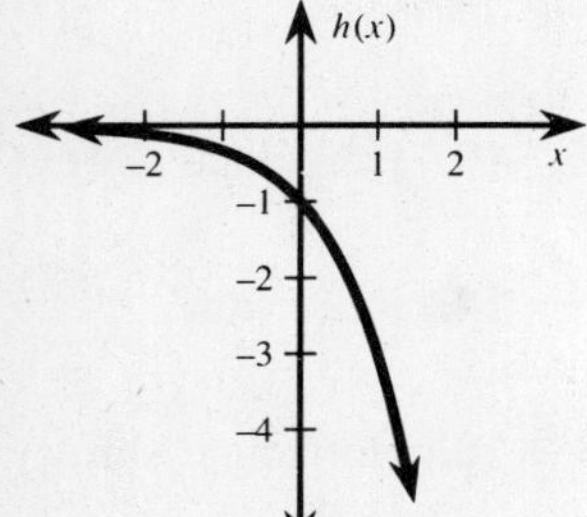

32. 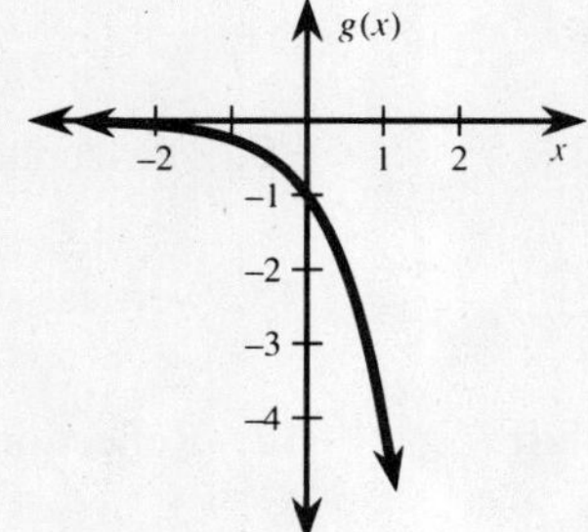

33. 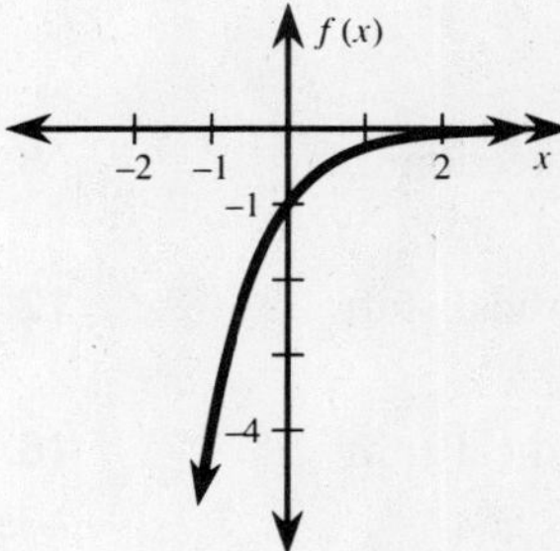

34. 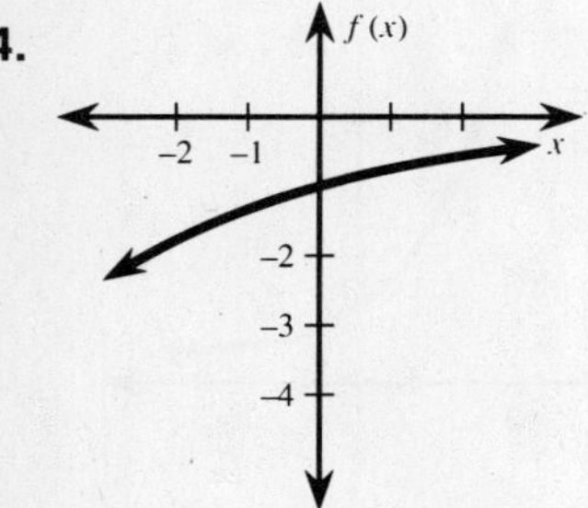

35. 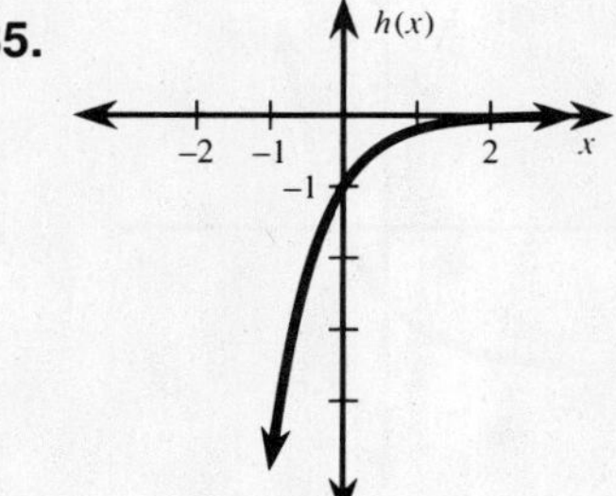

36. 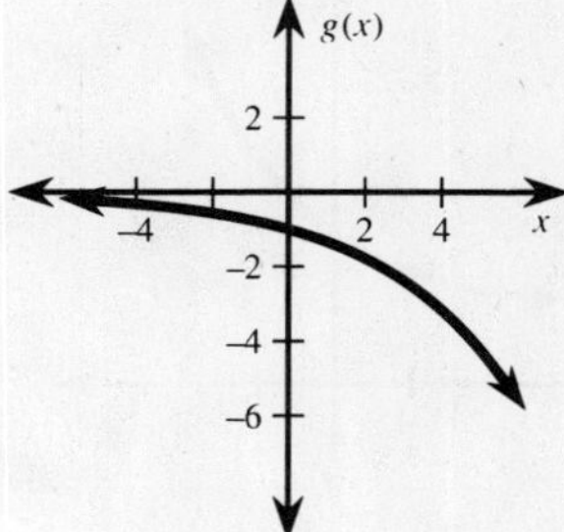

37. $f(-48) = 440 \cdot \left(\sqrt[12]{2}\right)^{-48}$

≈ 27.5

$f(39) = 440 \cdot \left(\sqrt[12]{2}\right)^{39}$

≈ 4186.0

The frequency of the lowest note on the piano is approximately 27.5. The frequency of the highest note on the piano is approximately 4186.0.

38. A, except the lowest A

39. $\dfrac{f(n_1)}{f(n_2)} = \dfrac{440 \cdot 2^{n_1/12}}{440 \cdot 2^{n_2/12}}$

$= \dfrac{2^{n_1/12}}{2^{n_2/12}}$

$= 2^{(n_1-n_2)/12}$

$n_1 > n_2$

Answers vary.

Octave:	C ($n = 3$) to C ($n = -9$)
Fifth:	G ($n = -2$) to C ($n = -9$)
Fourth:	F ($n = -4$) to C ($n = -9$)
Major third:	E ($n = -5$) to C ($n = -9$)
Minor third:	G ($n = -2$) to E ($n = -5$)
Major sixth:	A ($n = 0$) to C ($n = -9$)
Minor sixth:	C ($n = 3$) to E ($n = -5$)

40. $W = 0.00235$

$L = 5$

$F = 27.5$

$T = 4(0.00235)(27.5)^2(5)^2$

≈ 177.7 pounds per foot

41. $f(0) = 1$ $\quad f(1) = \frac{4}{3} \approx 1.33$ $\quad f(2) = \left(\frac{4}{3}\right)^2 \approx 1.78$

$f(3) = \left(\frac{4}{3}\right)^3 \approx 2.37$ $\quad f(4) = \left(\frac{4}{3}\right)^4 \approx 3.16$ $\quad f(5) = \left(\frac{4}{3}\right)^5 \approx 4.21$

42. $f(15) = \left(\frac{4}{3}\right)^{15}$

≈ 74.83

43. **d.**

44. **c.**

45. **a.**

46. **b.**

47. $f(3) = (0.05)^3$

$= 1.25 \times 10^{-4}$

48. $f(5) = \frac{1}{7}(10)^5$

$= 14{,}285.71$

49. $f(2) = 6^2 - 12$

$= 24$

50. $f(8) = 21\left(\frac{1}{3}\right)^8$

$= 0.003$

51. $f(5) = \frac{1}{11}(2^5) + 4$

$= 6.91$

52. $f(9) = 6\left(\frac{1}{6}\right)^9$

$= 5.95 \times 10^{-7}$

53. **d.**

54. **e.**

55. $g(t) = 100 - [75 + 37.25(0.615)^t]$

$g(t) = 25 - 37.25(0.615)^t$

56.

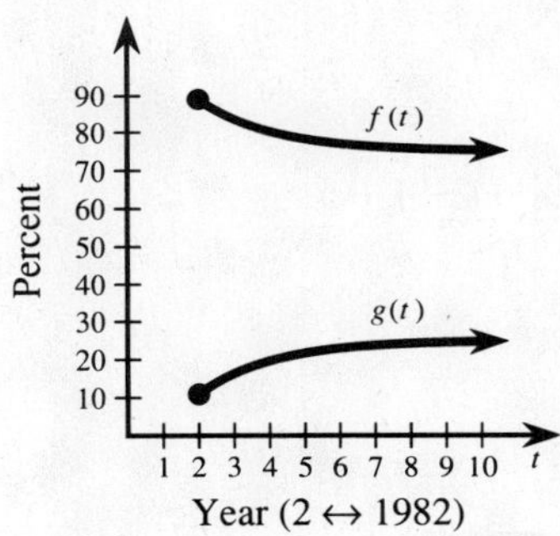

The percent of sugar compared to the percent of nonsugar sweeteners appear to be stabilizing.

57.

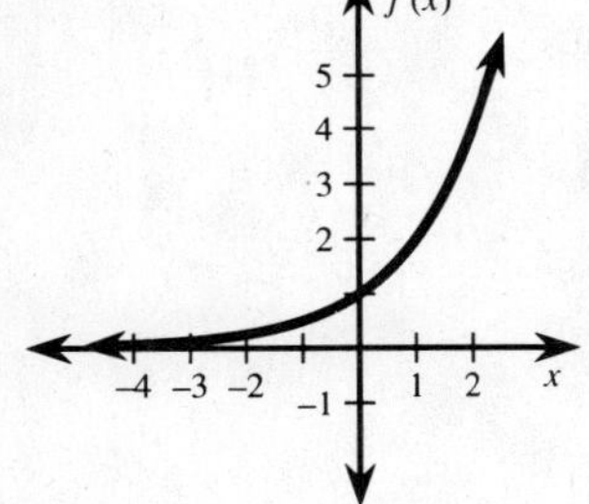

No, there are no solutions.

12.4 Quadratic Functions

Communicating about Algebra

A. $f(x) = x^2 - 4x + 2$

$= x^2 - 4x + 4 - 4 + 2$

$f(x) = (x - 2)^2 - 2$

Vertex: $(2, -2)$

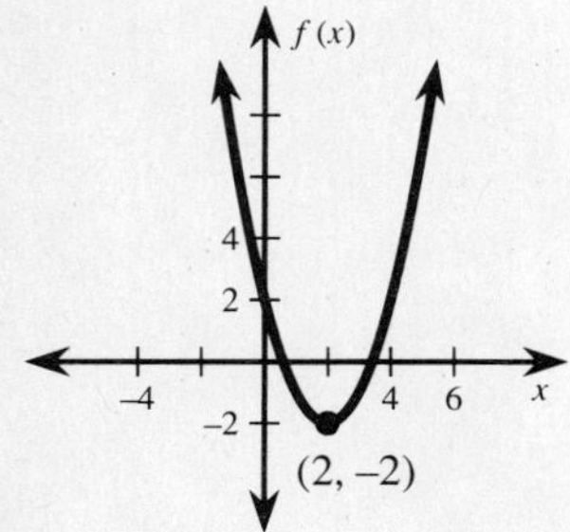

B. $f(x) = -x^2 - 2x - 5$

$= -(x^2 + 2x + 1) - 5 + 1$

$f(x) = -(x + 1)^2 - 4$

Vertex: $(-1, -4)$

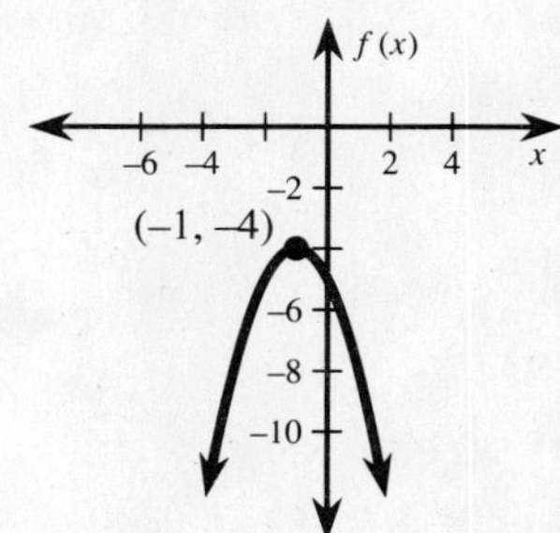

C. $f(x) = 2x^2 - 4x + 7$

$= 2(x^2 - 2x + 1) + 7 - 2$

$f(x) = 2(x - 1)^2 + 5$

Vertex: $(1, 5)$

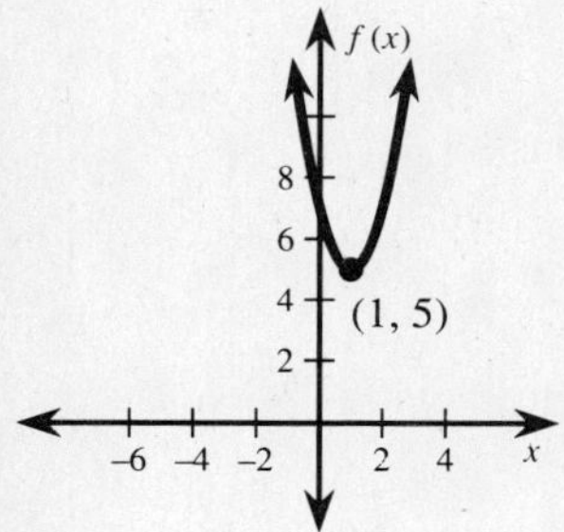

D. $f(x) = -3x^2 - 6x - 4$

$= -3(x^2 + 2x + 1) - 4 + 3$

$f(x) = -3(x + 1)^2 - 1$

Vertex: $(-1, -1)$

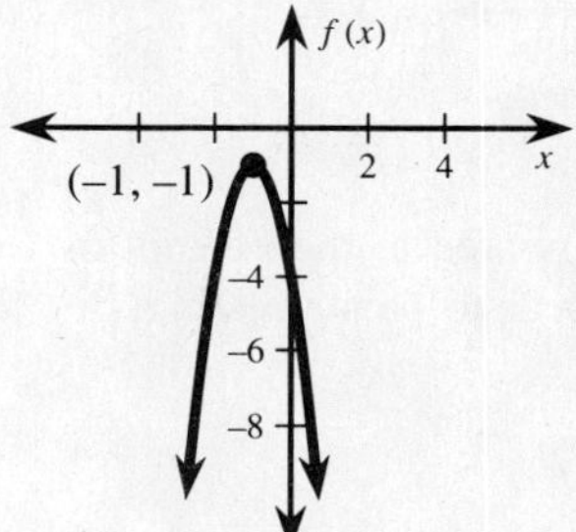

EXERCISES

1. $f(x) = x^2 - 6x + 6$

$= x^2 - 6x + 9 - 9 + 6$

$f(x) = (x - 3)^2 - 3$

2. $(-4, -3)$

3. Since a is positive 1, the graph opens upward and the vertex is the point where the graph reverses direction from downward to upward.

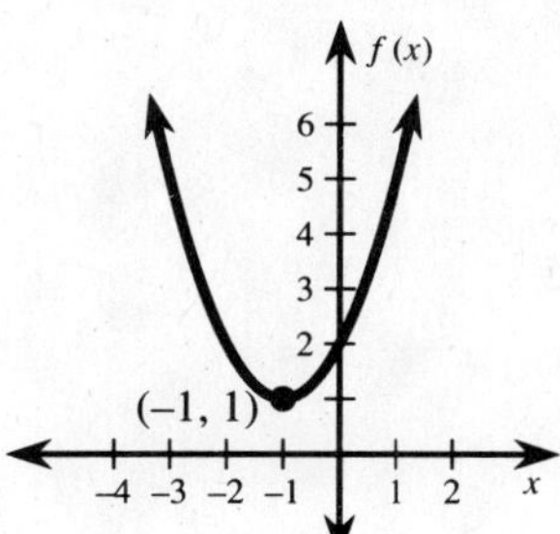

4. Since a is negative 1, the graph opens downward and the vertex is the point where the graph reverses direction from upward to downward.

(1, −1)

5. (1, 5), highest

6. (3, −5), highest

7. (3, −2), lowest

8. (7, 0), lowest

9. (−2, 6), lowest

10. (−5, 9), lowest

11. c.

12. a.

13. b.

14. d.

15.

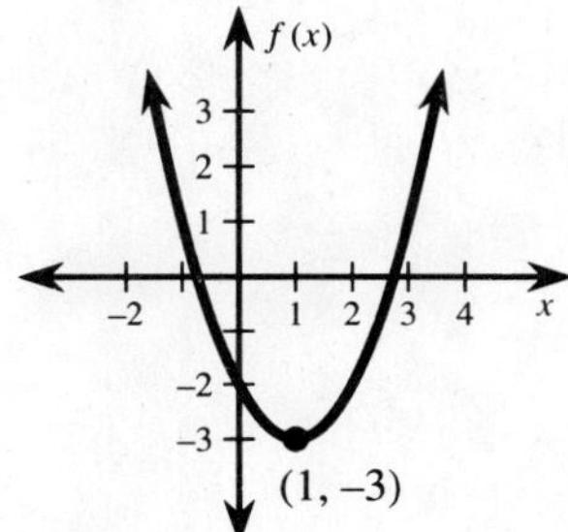

16.

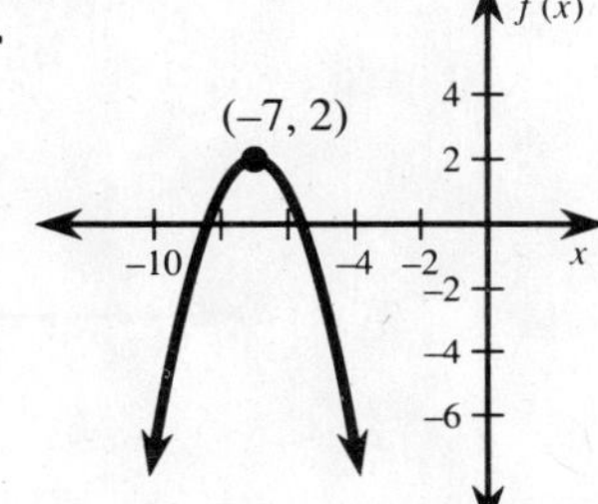

17.

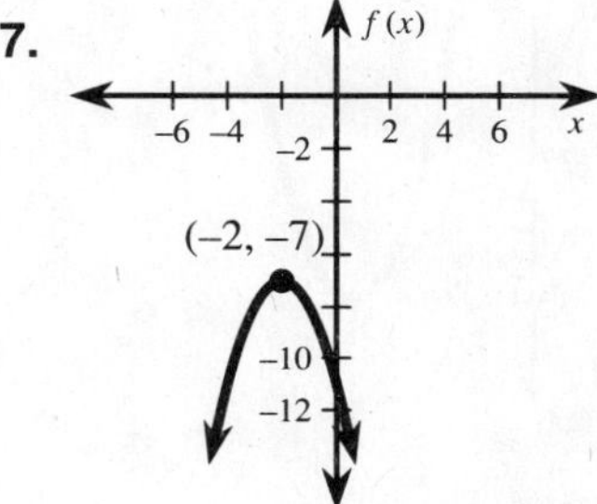

18.

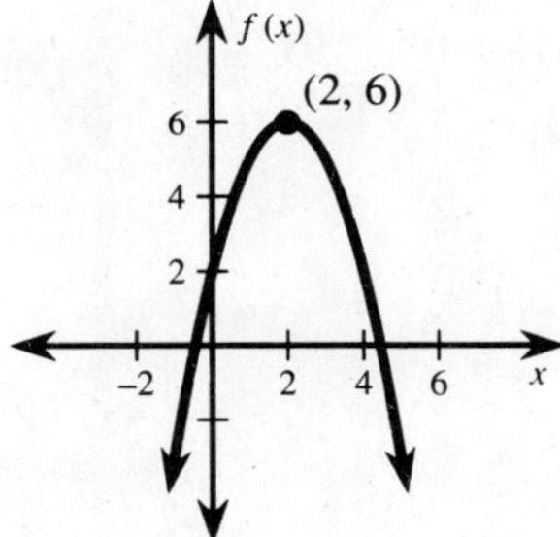

19.

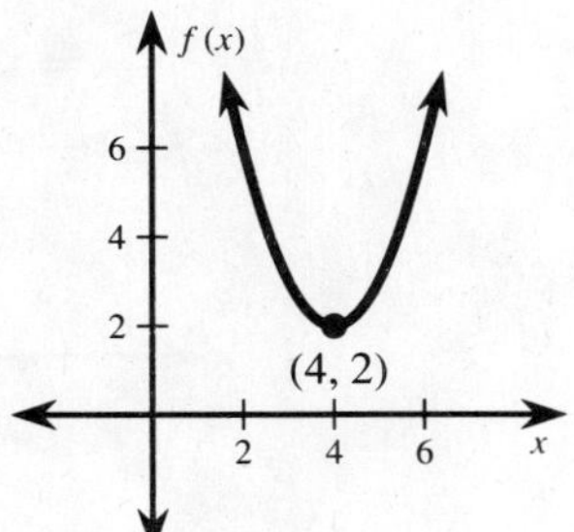

20.

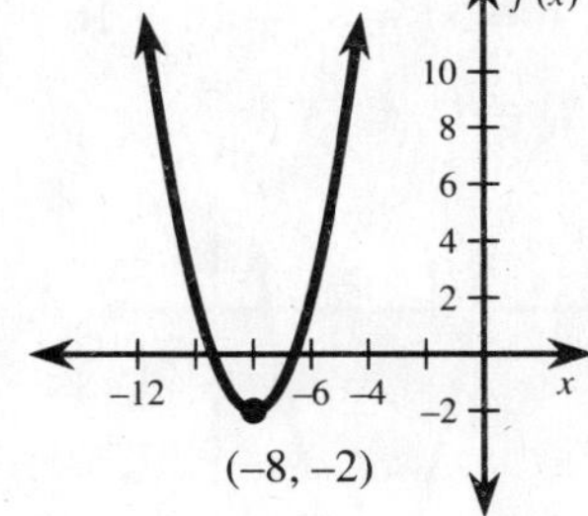

21. $f(x) = x^2 - 18x + 79$

$= x^2 - 18x + 81 - 81 + 79$

$f(x) = (x - 9)^2 - 2$

(9, −2)

22. $f(x) = x^2 + 8x + 11$

$= x^2 + 8x + 16 - 16 + 11$

$f(x) = (x + 4)^2 - 5$

(−4, −5)

23. $f(x) = x^2 - 4x + 16$

$= x^2 - 4x + 4 - 4 + 16$

$f(x) = (x - 2)^2 + 12$

(2, 12)

24. $f(x) = x^2 + 10x + 33$

$= x^2 + 10x + 25 - 25 + 33$

$f(x) = (x + 5)^2 + 8$

(−5, 8)

25. $f(x) = x^2 + 16x + 62$

$= x^2 + 16x + 64 - 64 + 62$

$f(x) = (x + 8)^2 - 2$

$(-8,\ -2)$

26. $f(x) = x^2 - 24x + 151$

$= x^2 - 24x + 144 - 144 + 151$

$f(x) = (x - 12)^2 + 7$

$(12,\ 7)$

27. $f(x) = -x^2 - 6x - 1$

$= -(x^2 + 6x + 9) + 9 - 1$

$f(x) = -(x + 3)^2 + 8$

$(-3,\ 8)$

28. $f(x) = -x^2 + 8x - 25$

$= -(x^2 - 8x + 16) + 16 - 25$

$f(x) = -(x - 4)^2 - 9$

$(4,\ -9)$

29. $f(x) = x^2 - 10x + 19$

$= x^2 - 10x + 25 - 25 + 19$

$f(x) = (x - 5)^2 - 6$

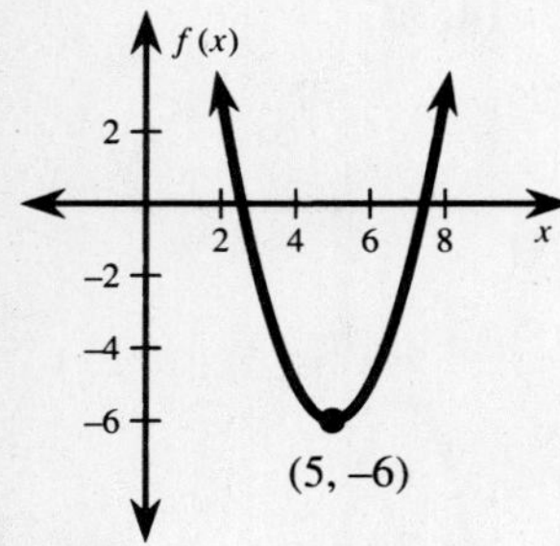

30. $f(x) = x^2 - 8x + 25$

$= x^2 - 8x + 16 - 16 + 25$

$f(x) = (x - 4)^2 + 9$

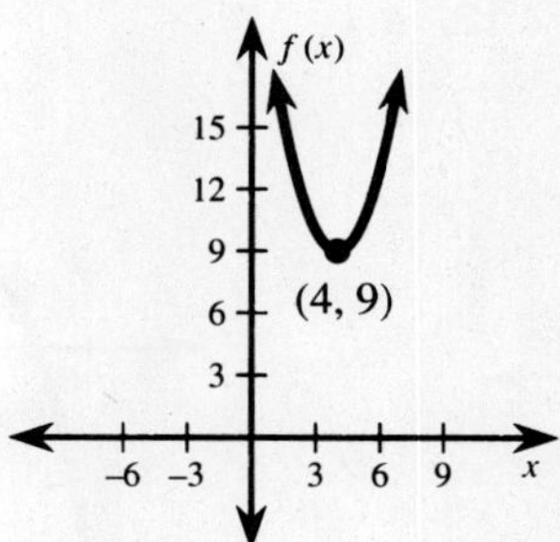

31. $f(x) = x^2 + 8x + 9$

$= x^2 + 8x + 16 - 16 + 9$

$f(x) = (x + 4)^2 - 7$

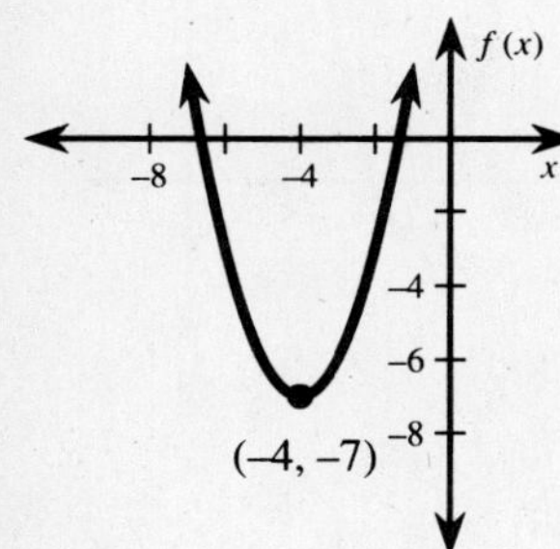

32. $f(x) = x^2 - 20x - 50$

$= x^2 - 20x + 100 - 100 - 50$

$f(x) = (x - 10)^2 - 150$

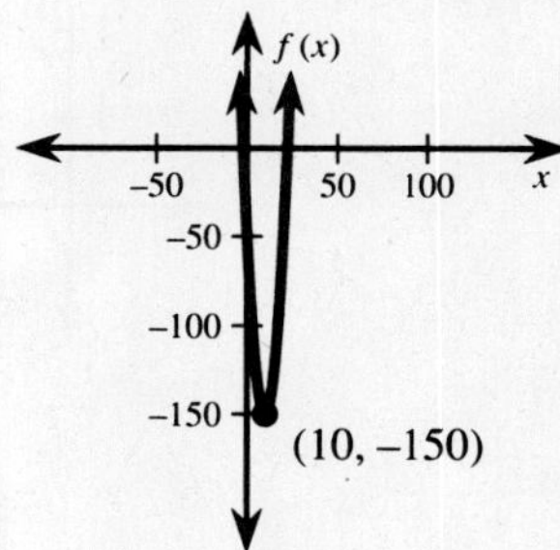

33. $f(x) = 2x^2 + 32x + 121$

$= 2(x^2 + 16x + 64) - 128 + 121$

$f(x) = 2(x + 8)^2 - 7$

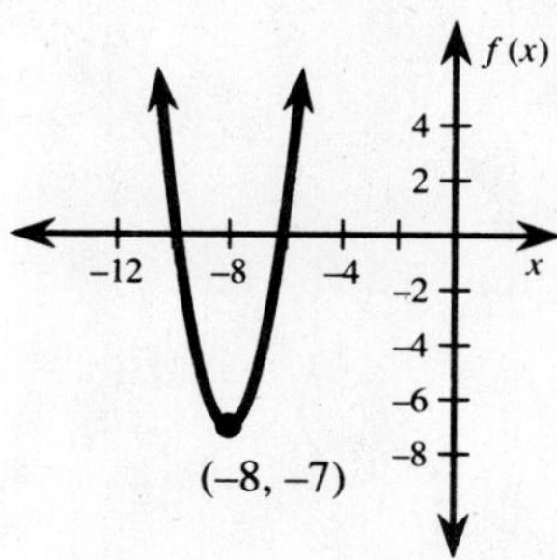

34. $f(x) = -3x^2 + 30x - 81$

$= -3(x^2 - 10x + 25) + 75 - 81$

$f(x) = -3(x - 5)^2 - 6$

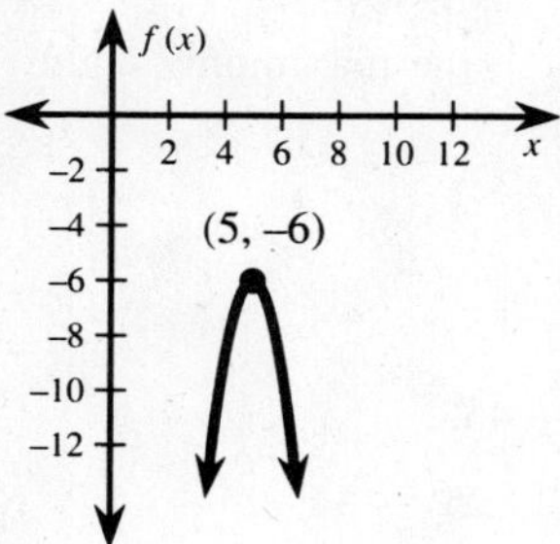

35. $f(x) = 3x^2 - 12x + 6$

$= 3(x^2 - 4x + 4) - 12 + 6$

$f(x) = 3(x - 2)^2 - 6$

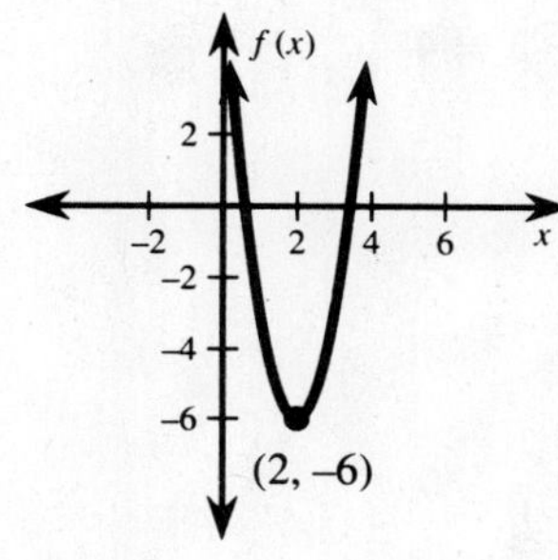

36. $f(x) = 2x^2 - 4x + 5$

$= 2(x^2 - 2x + 1) - 2 + 5$

$f(x) = 2(x - 1)^2 + 3$

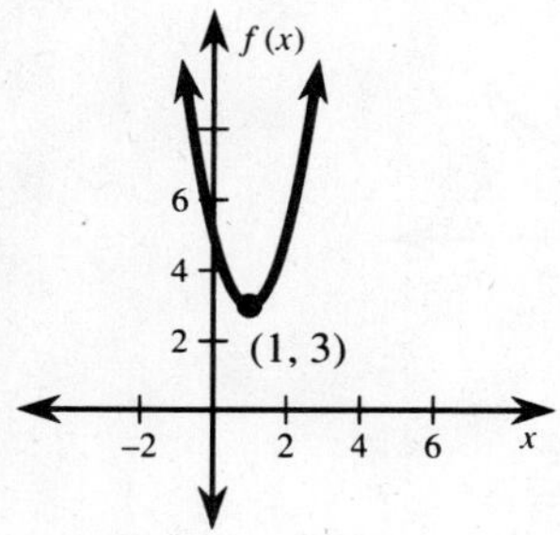

37. $f(x) = x(48 - 2x)$

$= 48x - 2x^2$

$= -2(x^2 - 24 + 144) + 288$

$f(x) = -2(x - 12)^2 + 288$

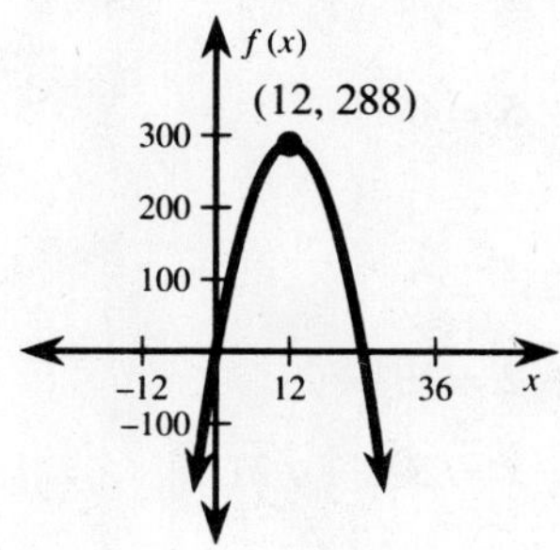

38. The box should be 12 inches tall. The dimensions of its base is 24 inches by 24 inches.

39. $h(x) = -\frac{1}{100}x^2 + x + 8$

$= -\frac{1}{100}(x^2 - 100x + 2500) + 25 + 8$

$h(x) = -\frac{1}{100}(x - 50)^2 + 33$

The vertex is (50, 33), so the maximum height is 33 feet above ground.

40. $8 = -\frac{1}{100}x^2 + x + 8$

$x\left(-\frac{1}{100}x + 1\right) = 0$

$x = 0$ or $-\frac{1}{100}x + 1 = 0$

$\frac{1}{100}x = 1$

$x = 100$

The human cannonball traveled 100 feet.

41. $f(t) = 1.7t^2 - 15.3t + 45.2$

$= 1.7(t^2 - 9t + 20.25) - 34.425 + 45.2$

$f(t) = 1.7(t - 4.5)^2 + 10.775$

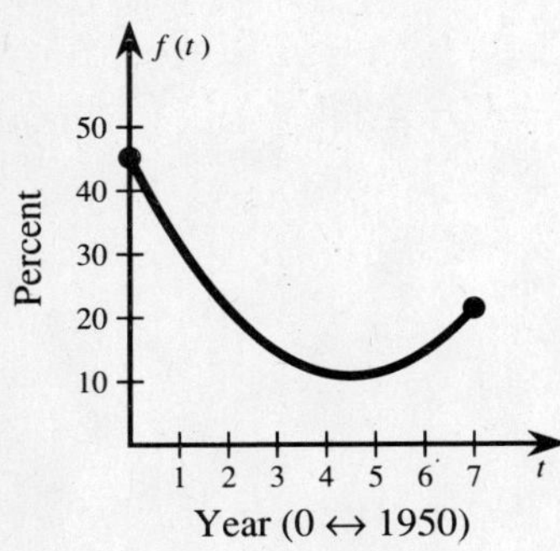

42. 1995

43. $x^2 + 6x - 7 = 0$

$x^2 + 6x + 9 - 9 - 7 = 0$

$(x + 3)^2 = 16$

$x + 3 = \pm 4$

$x + 3 = -4$ or $x + 3 = 4$

$x = -7$ $\quad x = 1$

44. $x^2 - 2x - 35 = 0$

$x - 2x + 1 - 1 - 35 = 0$

$(x - 1)^2 = 36$

$x - 1 = \pm 6$

$x - 1 = -6$ or $x - 1 = 6$

$x = -5$ $\quad x = 7$

45. $x^2 - 4x - 9 = 0$

$x^2 - 4x + 4 - 4 - 9 = 0$

$(x - 2)^2 = 13$

$x - 2 = \pm\sqrt{13}$

$x = 2 \pm \sqrt{13}$

46. $x^2 + 12x - 16 = 0$

$x^2 + 12x + 36 - 36 - 16 = 0$

$(x + 6)^2 = 52$

$x + 6 = \pm\sqrt{52}$

$x = -6 \pm \sqrt{52}$

47. $4x^2 - 16x - 5 = 0$

$4(x^2 - 4x + 4) - 16 - 5 = 0$

$4(x - 2)^2 = 21$

$x - 2 = \pm\frac{1}{2}\sqrt{21}$

$x = 2 \pm \frac{1}{2}\sqrt{21}$

48. $3x^2 + 24x - 131 = 0$

$3(x^2 + 8x + 16) - 48 - 131 = 0$

$3(x + 4)^2 = 179$

$(x + 4)^2 = \frac{179}{3}$

$x + 4 = \pm\sqrt{\frac{179}{3}}$

$x = -4 \pm \sqrt{\frac{179}{3}}$

49. $x = -\dfrac{b}{2a}$ $\quad y = 4 - 8 + 11$

$= \dfrac{4}{2}$ $\quad = 7$

$= 2$

$y = (x^2 - 4x + 4) - 4 + 11$

$y = (x - 2)^2 + 7$

$(2, 7)$

50. $x = -\frac{18}{2}$ $\quad y = 81 - 162 + 90$

$= -9$ $\quad = 9$

$y = (x^2 + 18x + 81) - 81 + 90$

$y = (x + 9)^2 + 9$

$(-9, 9)$

51. $x = -\frac{2}{2}$ $\quad y = 1 - 2 - 2$

$= -1$ $\quad = -3$

$y = (x^2 + 2x + 1) - 1 - 2$

$y = (x + 1)^2 - 3$

$(-1, -3)$

52. $x = \frac{8}{2}$ $\quad y = 16 - 32 + 22$

$= 4$ $\quad = 6$

$y = (x^2 - 8x + 16) - 16 + 22$

$= (x - 4)^2 + 6$

$(4, 6)$

53. $x = \frac{72}{6}$ $\quad y = 432 - 864 + 428$

$= 12$ $\quad = -4$

$y = 3(x^2 - 24x + 144) - 432 + 428$

$y = 3(x - 12)^2 - 4$

$(12, -4)$

54. $x = \frac{4}{4}$ $\quad y = 2 - 4 + 3$

$= 1$ $\quad = 1$

$y = 2(x^2 - 2x + 1) - 2 + 3$

$y = 2(x - 1)^2 + 1$

$(1, 1)$

55. $y = x^2 + 2x - 2$

$y = (x^2 + 2x + 1) - 2 - 1$

$y = (x + 1)^2 - 3$

Vertex: $(-1, -3)$

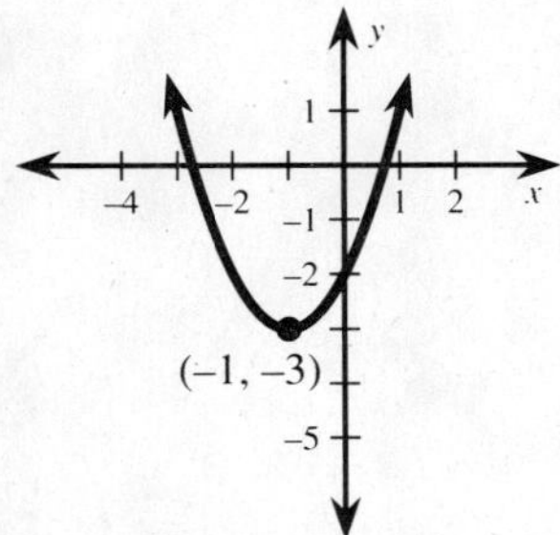

56. $y = x^2 - 14x + 53$

$y = (x^2 - 14x + 49) + 53 - 49$

$y = (x - 7)^2 + 4$

Vertex: (7, 4)

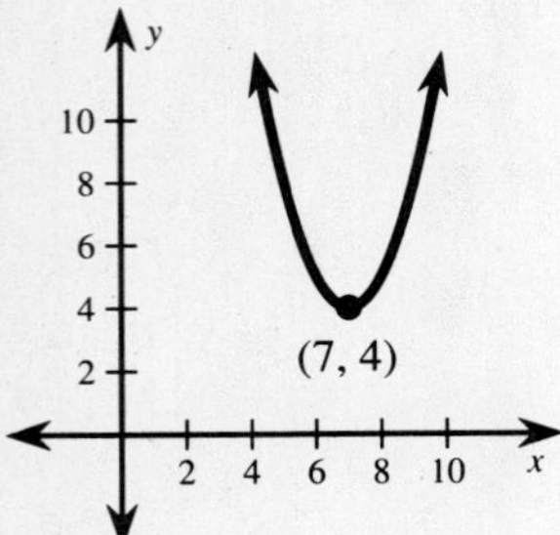

57. $y = x^2 + 10x + 18$

$y = (x^2 + 10x + 25) + 18 - 25$

$y = (x + 5)^2 - 7$

Vertex: $(-5, \ -7)$

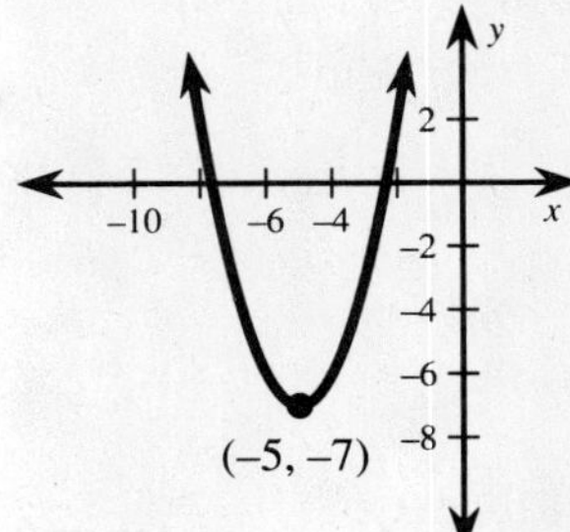

58. $y = x^2 + 2x - 9$

$y = (x^2 + 2x + 1) - 9 - 1$

$y = (x + 1)^2 - 10$

Vertex: $(-1, \ -10)$

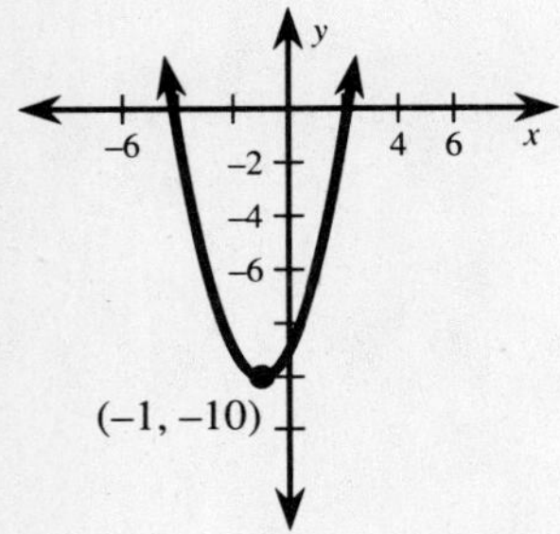

59. $y = 2x^2 - 4x + 18$

$y = 2(x^2 - 2x + 1) + 18 - 2$

$y = 2(x - 1)^2 + 16$

Vertex: (1, 16)

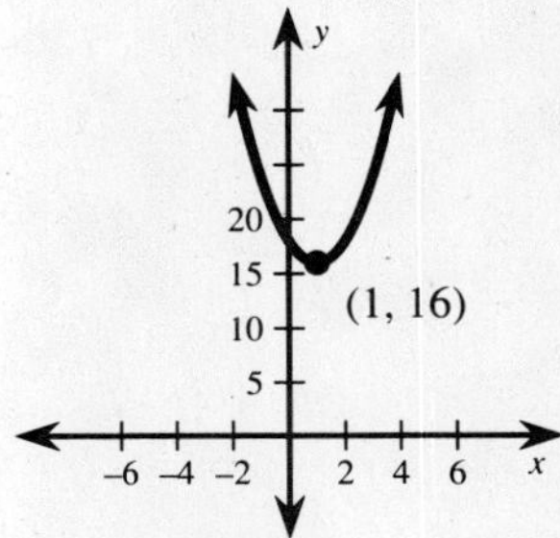

60. $y = 4x^2 + 24x + 33$

$y = 4(x^2 + 6x + 9) + 33 - 36$

$y = 4(x + 3)^2 - 3$

Vertex: $(-3, \ -3)$

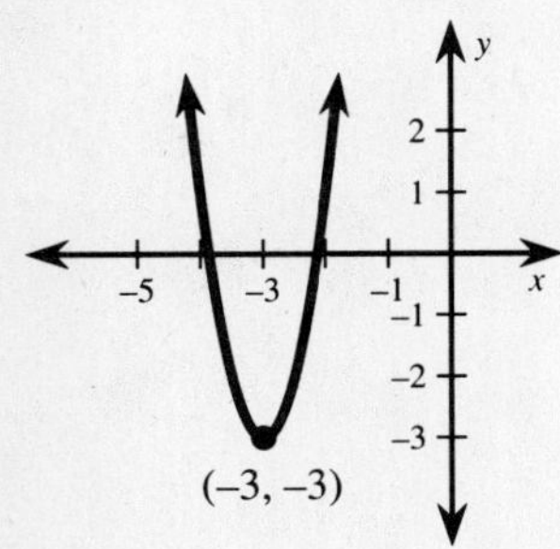

61. $\frac{9}{100}$

62. $\frac{21}{100}$

63. **b.** and **c.**

b. opens downward and the y of the vertex is negative.

c. opens upward and the y of the vertex is positive.

Mid-Chapter SELF-TEST

1. Not a function

2. Function

3. $f(-2) = -4$
$f(0) = 2$
$f(2) = 8$

4. $f(-2) = 0$
$f(0) = -4$
$f(2) = -8$

5. $f(-2) = 3$
$f(0) = -1$
$f(2) = 3$

6. $f(-2) = -7$
$f(0) = 5$
$f(2) = -7$

7. $f(-2) = 21$
$f(0) = 1$
$f(2) = 13$

8. $f(-2) = -10$
$f(0) = 6$
$f(2) = 6$

9. $m = \dfrac{3-9}{0-3}$
$= \dfrac{-6}{-3}$
$= 2$

$y - 3 = 2(x - 0)$
$y = 2x + 3$
$f(x) = 2x + 3$

10. $m = \dfrac{6+6}{-2-2}$
$= -3$

$6 = -3(-2) + b$
$b = 0$
$f(x) = -3x$

11. $m = \dfrac{4-4}{-1-5}$
$= 0$

$f(x) = 4$

12. Vertical shift

13. Vertical shift

14. Horizontal shift

15. $f(x) = (x^2 - 4x + 4) - 4 + 9$
$f(x) = (x - 2)^2 + 5$

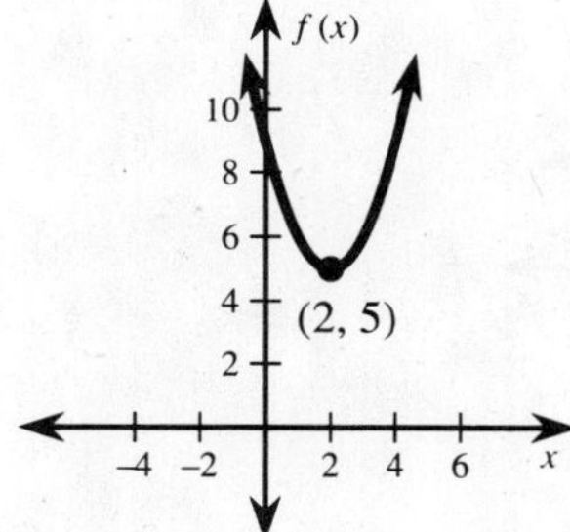

16. $f(x) = -(x^2 + 2x + 1) + 1 - 4$
$f(x) = -(x + 1)^2 - 3$

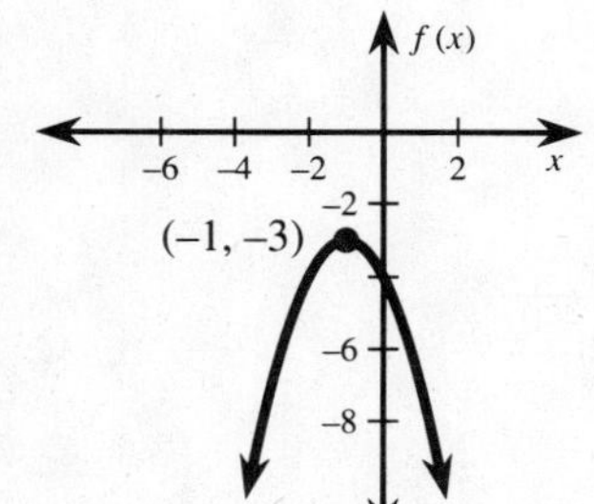

17. $f(x) = 2(x^2 - 2x + 1) - 2 - 7$
$f(x) = 2(x - 1)^2 - 9$

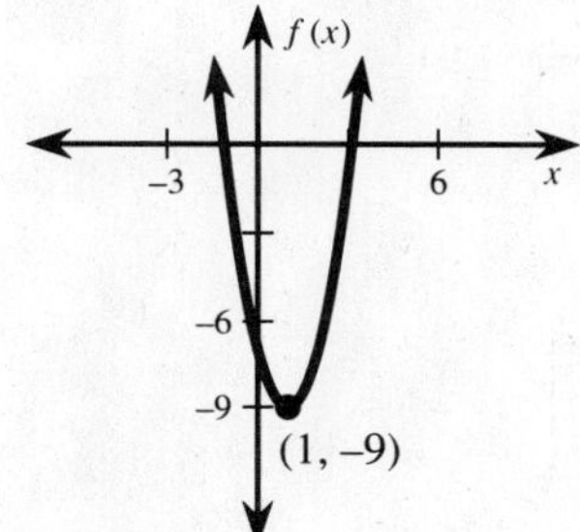

18. Yes, the number of bowling lanes is a function of the number of bowling establishments.

19. $f(x) = 5x$

$f(x) = 5(12)$

$= 60$

60 feet is the distance traveled in 12 seconds.

20. $A = x(20 - 2x)$

$A = -2(x^2 - 10x + 25) + 50$

$A = -2(x - 5)^2 + 50$

Vertex: (5, 50)

5 centimeters should be folded up to obtain a maximum cross section area.

12.5 Rational Functions

Communicating about Algebra

A.

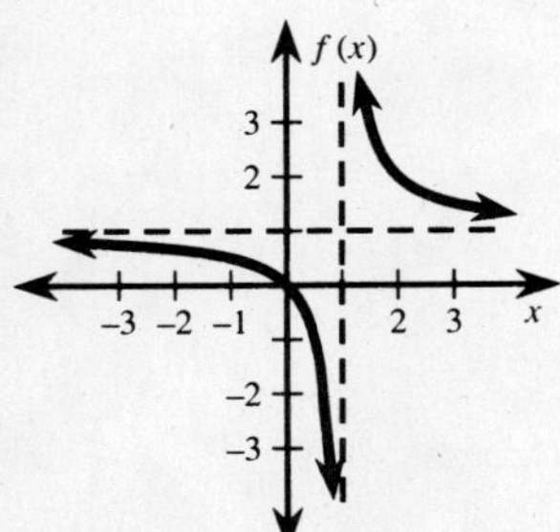

B.

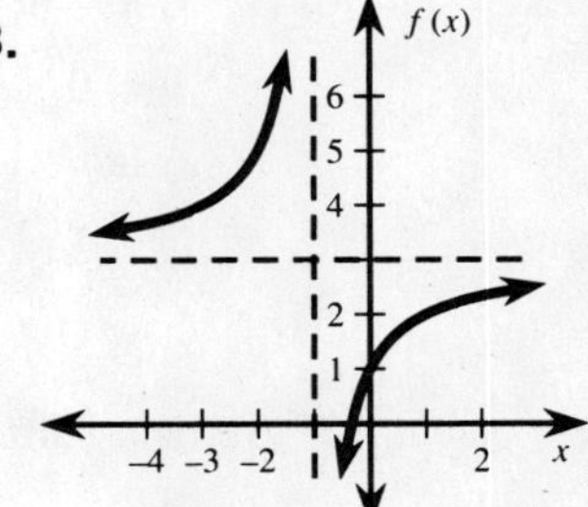

C.

$$\begin{array}{r} 3 \\ x-2 \overline{)\ 3x + 1} \\ \underline{3x - 6} \\ 7 \end{array}$$

Thus, $\dfrac{3x+1}{x-2} = 3 + \dfrac{7}{x-2}$.

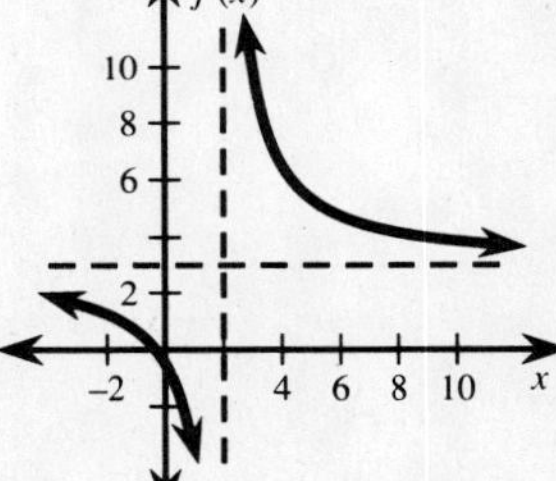

D.

$$\begin{array}{r} 3 \\ x+1 \overline{)\ 3x - 1} \\ \underline{3x + 3} \\ -\ 4 \end{array}$$

Thus, $\dfrac{3x-1}{x+1} = 3 - \dfrac{4}{x+1}$.

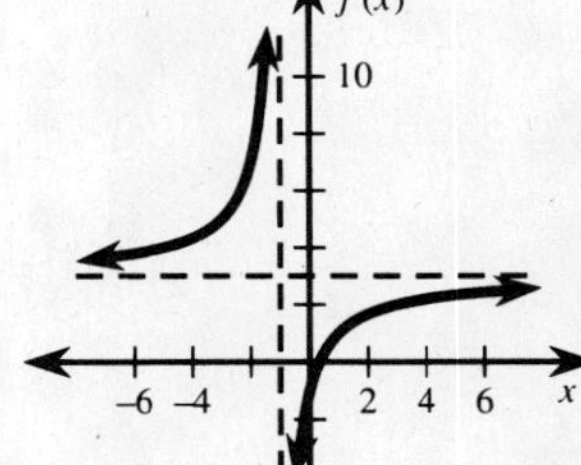

EXERCISES

In Exercises 1– 4, $f(x) = \dfrac{a}{x-h} + k$ is a hyperbola whose center is $(h,\ x)$ and whose asymptotes are the vertical and horizontal lines through the center.

1. Center: $(-5,\ -3)$
$x = -5,\ y = -3$

2. Center: $(10, 4)$
$x = 10,\ y = 4$

3. Center: $(3, 16)$
$x = 3,\ y = 16$

4. Center: $(-1,\ -9)$
$x = -1,\ y = -9$

5.

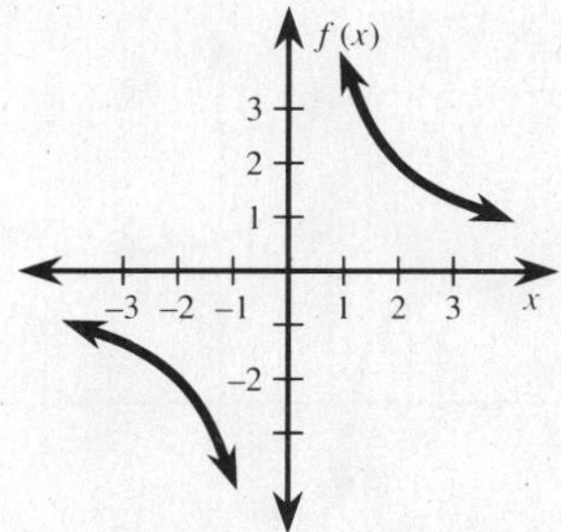

6.

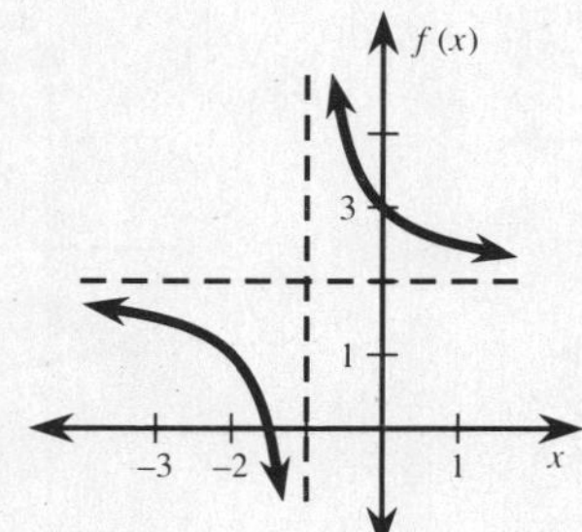

7. Center: $(5, 2)$
$x = 5,\ y = 2$

8. Center: $(3,\ -8)$
$x = 3,\ y = -8$

9. Center: $(4, 6)$
$x = 4,\ y = 6$

10. Center: $(-1,\ 8)$
$x = -1,\ y = 8$

11. Center: $(-9,\ -7)$
$x = -9,\ y = -7$

12. Center: $(-1,\ -4)$
$x = -1,\ y = -4$

13. **c.**

14. **f.**

15. **d.**

16. **a.**

17. **b.**

18. **e.**

19.

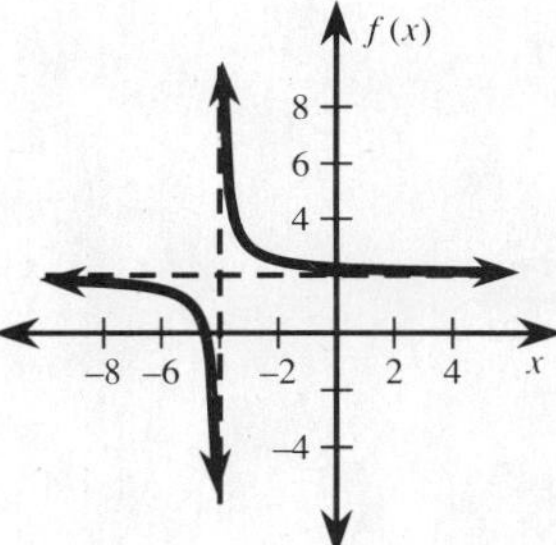

20.

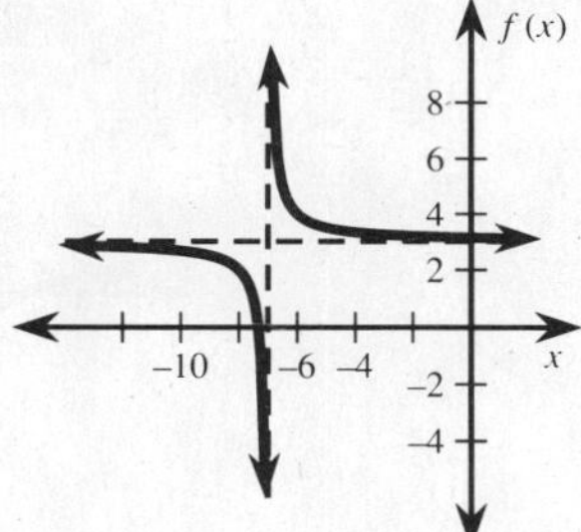

21.

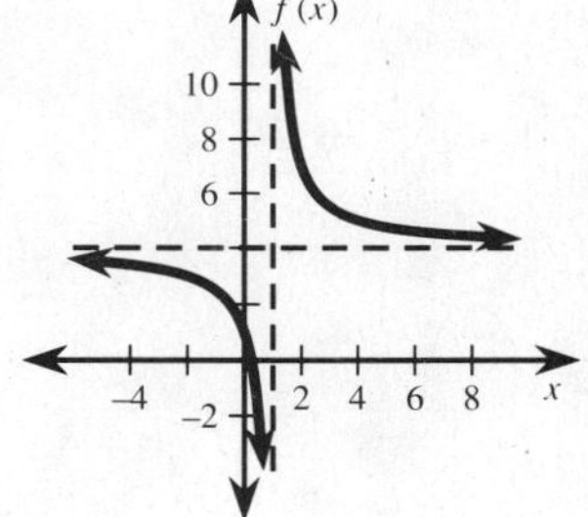

22.

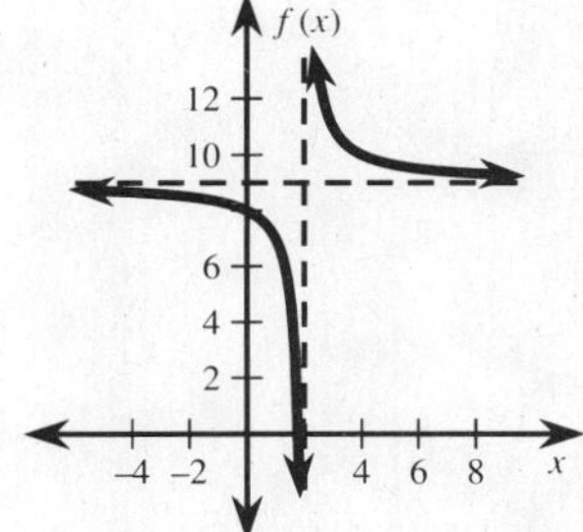

23.

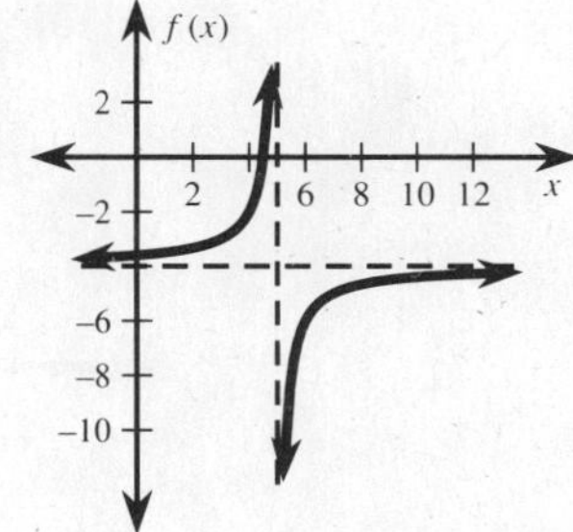

24.

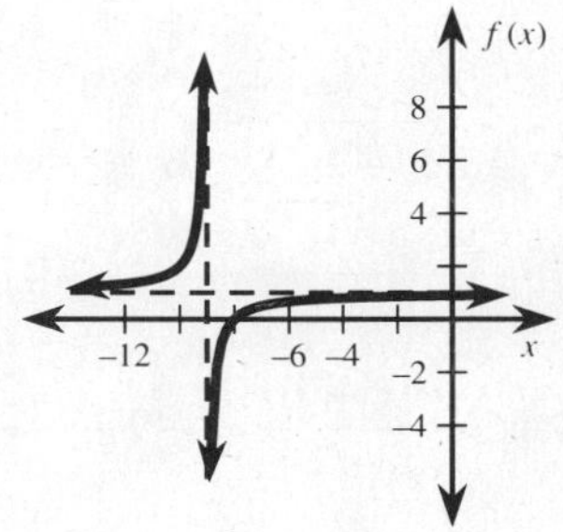

25.

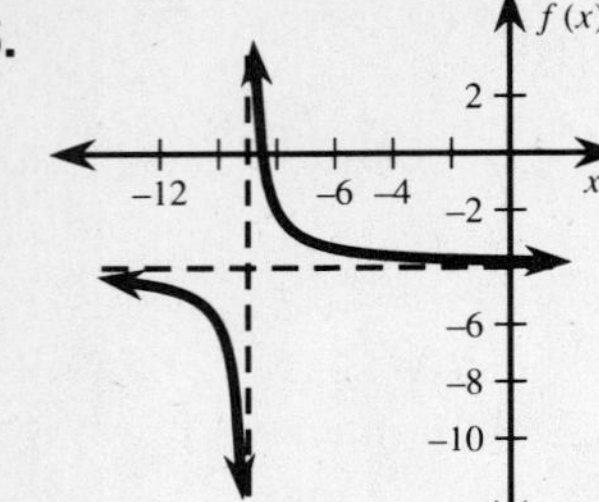

26.

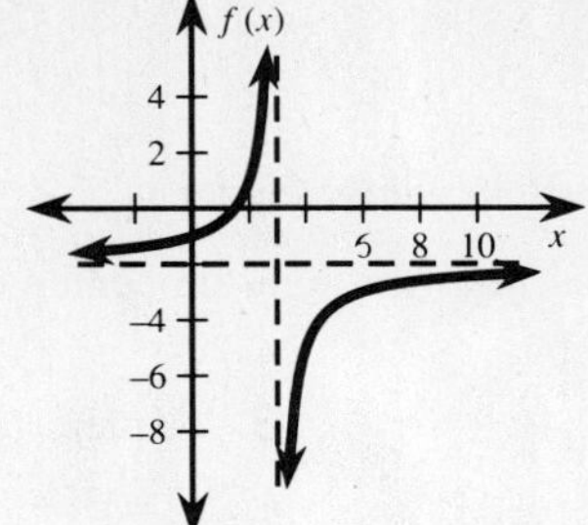

27.

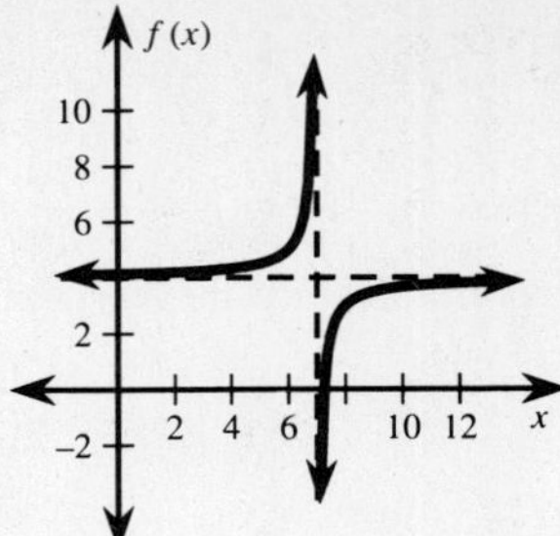

28.

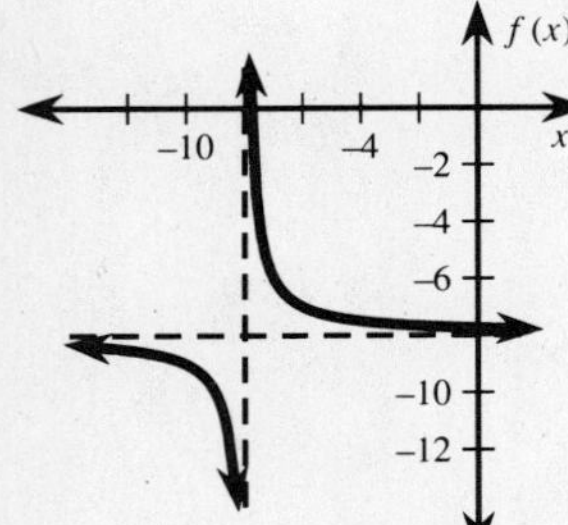

29.

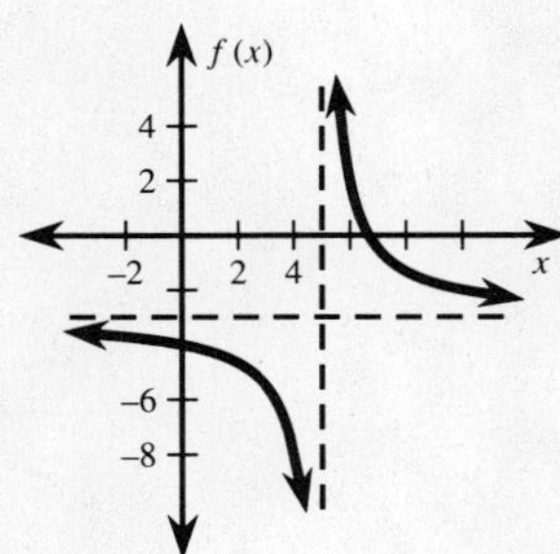

30.

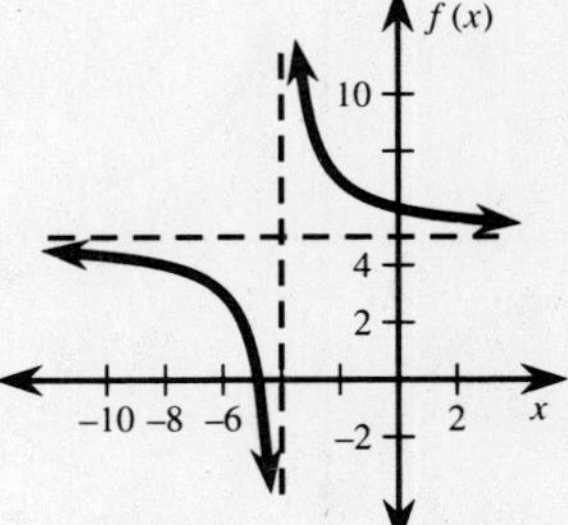

31.

$$
\begin{array}{r@{}l}
 & \quad\;\; -\;\;2 \\
\cline{2-2}
x-5 \big) & \;-2x + 11 \\
 & \;-2x + 10 \\
\cline{2-2}
 & \qquad\quad\;\; 1
\end{array}
$$

Thus, $\dfrac{-2x+11}{x-5} = -2 + \dfrac{1}{x-5}.$

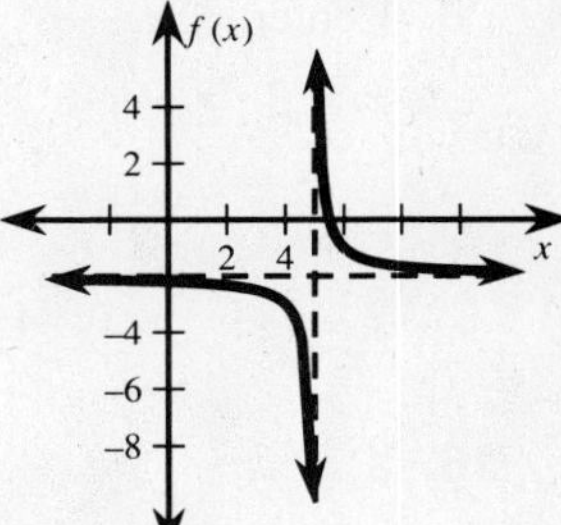
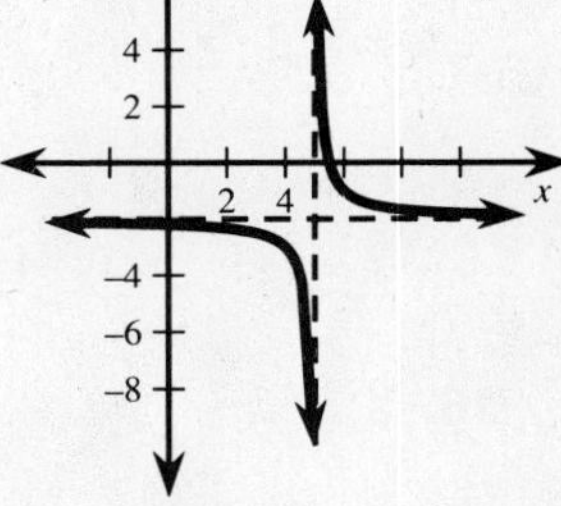

32.

$$
\begin{array}{r@{}l}
 & \qquad\quad 1 \\
\cline{2-2}
x+8 \big) & \; x + 10 \\
 & \; x + \;\,8 \\
\cline{2-2}
 & \qquad\quad 2
\end{array}
$$

Thus, $\dfrac{x+10}{x+8} = 1 + \dfrac{2}{x+8}.$

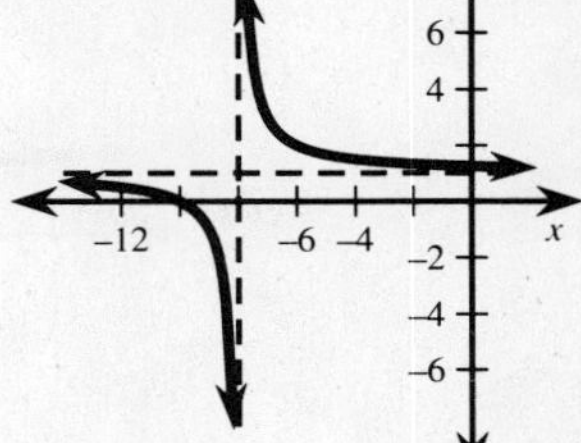

33.

$$
\begin{array}{r@{}l}
 & \qquad -\;\;9 \\
\cline{2-2}
x-2 \big) & \;-9x + 16 \\
 & \;-9x + 18 \\
\cline{2-2}
 & \qquad -\;\;2
\end{array}
$$

Thus, $\dfrac{-9x+16}{x-2} = -9 - \dfrac{2}{x-2}.$

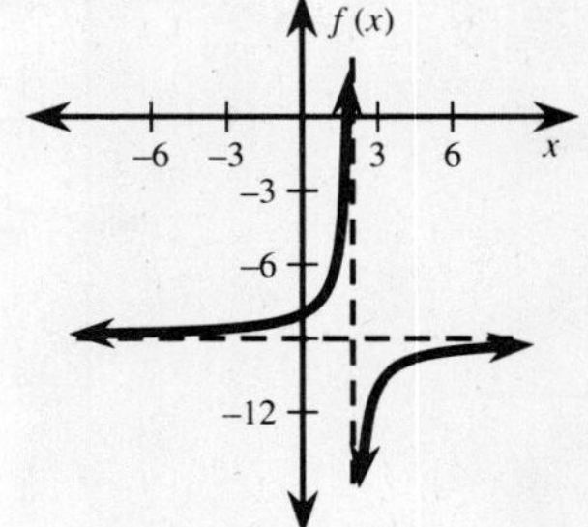

34.

$$x - 1\overline{\smash{)}\,9x - 6}$$
quotient: 9

$$\begin{array}{r} 9x - 9 \\ \hline 3 \end{array}$$

Thus, $\dfrac{9x - 6}{x - 1} = 9 + \dfrac{3}{x - 1}$.

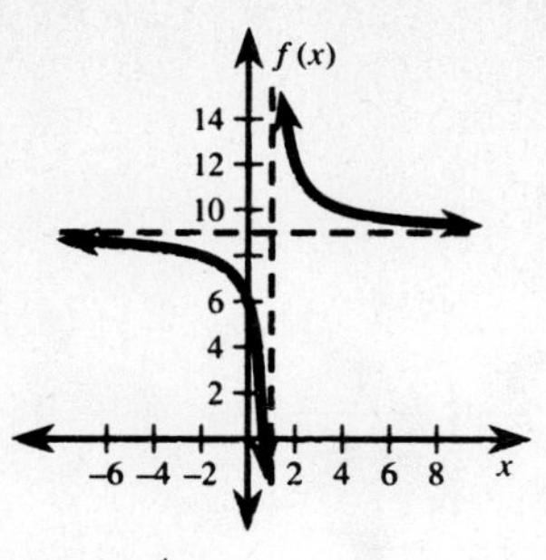

35.

$$x - 3\overline{\smash{)}\,-5x + 19}$$
quotient: -5

$$\begin{array}{r} -5x + 15 \\ \hline 4 \end{array}$$

Thus, $\dfrac{-5x + 19}{x - 3} = -5 + \dfrac{4}{x - 3}$.

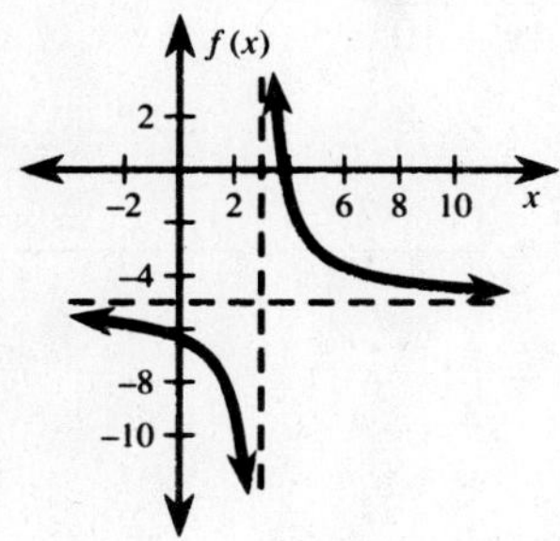

36.

$$x + 8\overline{\smash{)}\,-6x + 50}$$
quotient: -6

$$\begin{array}{r} -6x - 48 \\ \hline 98 \end{array}$$

Thus, $\dfrac{-6x + 50}{x + 8} = -6 + \dfrac{98}{x + 8}$.

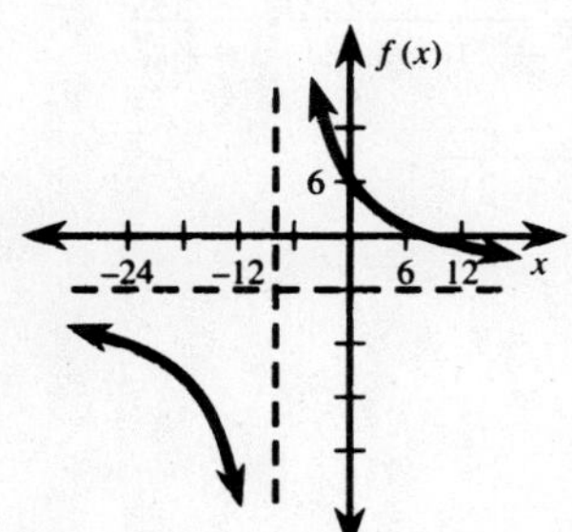

37.

$$-t + 1997\overline{\smash{)}\,t - 1898}$$
quotient: -1

$$\begin{array}{r} t - 1997 \\ \hline 99 \end{array}$$

Thus, $\dfrac{t - 1898}{-t + 1997} = -1 - \dfrac{99}{t - 1997}$.

1997, the year the lease is up.

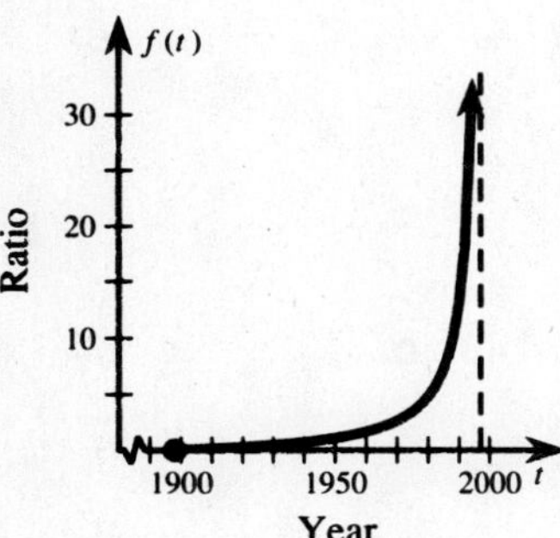

38. $1997 - t = t - 1898$

$2t = 3895$

$t = 1947.5$

1947, half of the time of the lease.

39. $f(x) = \dfrac{20 + x}{5 + 2x}$

40.

$$\begin{array}{r} \tfrac{1}{2} \\ 2x+5\,\overline{\smash{)}\,x + 20} \\ \underline{x + \tfrac{5}{2}} \\ \tfrac{35}{2} \end{array}$$

Thus, $\dfrac{x+20}{2x+5} = \dfrac{1}{2} + \dfrac{35}{2}\left(\dfrac{1}{2x+5}\right)$

$$f(x) = \frac{1}{2} + \frac{35}{4x+10}.$$

41. $\dfrac{x^2-2x-3}{4} \div \dfrac{x-3}{2} = \dfrac{(x-3)(x+1)}{4} \cdot \dfrac{2}{x-3}$

$= \dfrac{1}{2}(x+1)$

42. $\dfrac{x^2+3x-10}{14} \div \dfrac{x+5}{2} = \dfrac{(x+5)(x-2)}{14} \cdot \dfrac{2}{x+5}$

$= \dfrac{1}{7}(x-2)$

43. $\dfrac{1}{x^2-4} \div \dfrac{x+2}{x-2} = \dfrac{1}{(x-2)(x+2)} \cdot \dfrac{x-2}{x+2}$

$= \dfrac{1}{(x+2)^2}$

44. $\dfrac{1}{x^2} = \dfrac{1}{4}$

$x^2 = 4$

$x = \pm 2$

45. $\dfrac{x-3}{4} = \dfrac{1}{x}$

$x^2 - 3x - 4 = 0$

$(x-4)(x+1) = 0$

$x = 4$ or $x = -1$

46. $\dfrac{1}{x} - \dfrac{5}{x-5} = 16$

$x - 5 - 5x = 16x^2 - 80x$

$16x^2 - 76x + 5 = 0$

$x = \dfrac{76 \pm \sqrt{5776 - 320}}{32}$

$x = \dfrac{19}{8} \pm \dfrac{\sqrt{5456}}{32}$

47. b.

48. c.

49. d.

50. a.

51. $f(t) = \dfrac{431.5t + 4189}{1836t + 1954}$

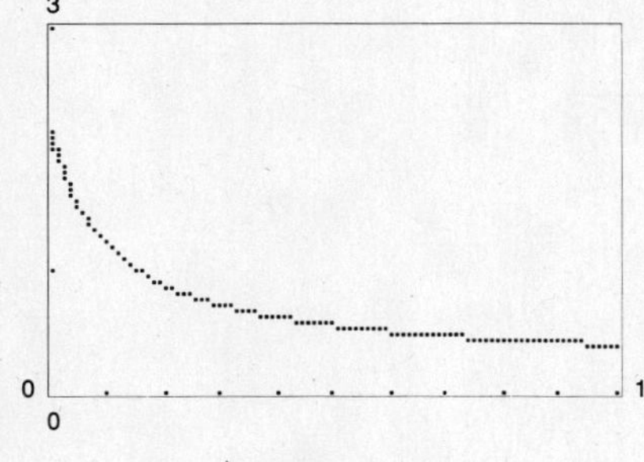

52. $y \approx \frac{1}{4}$; ratio of state payroll to federal payroll

Mixed REVIEW

1. $\frac{1}{2}x^{-2}y$

2.
$$\frac{1}{x} - \frac{2x}{3} = \frac{5}{3}$$
$$3 - 2x^2 = 5x$$
$$2x^2 + 5x - 3 = 0$$
$$(x+3)(2x-1) = 0$$
$$x = -3 \text{ or } x = \frac{1}{2}$$

3. $3^3 + 4 \cdot 3 = 39$

4.
$$3|4 - m| \le 3$$
$$|4 - m| \le 1$$
$$-1 \le 4 - m \le 1$$
$$-5 \le -m \le -3$$
$$5 \ge m \ge 3$$
$$3 \le m \le 5$$

5.
$$(x^2y^{-2})^{-1} \div 3(xy^4)^2 = \frac{y^2}{x^2} \cdot \frac{1}{3x^2y^8}$$
$$= \frac{1}{3x^4y^6}$$

6.
$$x = 0.69(43)$$
$$x = 29.67$$

7. $(6.7 \times 10^{-3}) \div (2.0 \times 10^5) = 3.35 \times 10^{-8}$

8.
$$x = \frac{-6}{2 \cdot 1} \qquad y = 9 - 18 - 25$$
$$= -3 \qquad = -34$$
$$(-3,\ -34)$$

9.
$$512 = 8(1+p)^2$$
$$64 = (1+p)^2$$
$$1 + p = \pm 8$$
$$p = -1 \pm 8$$
$$p = 7 \text{ or } p = -9$$

10.
$$\begin{cases} 2x - 3y = 4 \\ -2x - 4y = 10 \end{cases}$$
$$-7y = 14$$
$$y = -2$$
$$2x - 3(-2) = 4$$
$$2x = -2$$
$$x = -1$$
$$(-1,\ -2)$$

12.6 Exploring Data: Stem-and-Leaf Plots, Box-and-Whisker Plots

Communicating about Algebra

2	2 8 3 5 9 9 4 6 2
3	0 8 3 0 6 7
4	3 7 1
5	9
6	
7	5

2	2 2 3 4 5 6 8 9 9
3	0 0 3 6 7 8
4	1 3 7
5	9
6	
7	5

$Q_1 = 25.5$

$Q_2 = 30$

$Q_3 = 39.5$

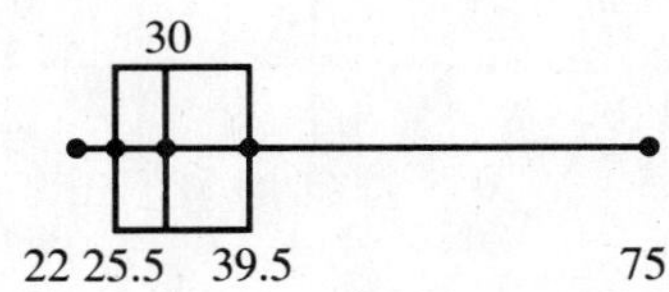

EXERCISES

1. A stem-and-leaf plot is used to order data in increasing or decreasing order.

2. Mean is the average of a collection of numbers. Median is the middle number of a collection. Answers vary.

3. **a.** 2, 2, 3 $\rightarrow$ 1st quarter
4, 4, 5 $\rightarrow$ 2nd quarter
6, 6, 7 $\rightarrow$ 3rd quarter
8, 8, 9 $\rightarrow$ 4th quarter

b. 1st quartile $= 3.5$
2nd quartile $= 5.5$
3rd quartile $= 7.5$

c. 2nd

4.

1	2 7 2 3
2	5 9 0 4
3	8 2 9 2
4	3 9 4 6
5	5 1 1 4

1	2 2 3 7
2	0 4 5 9
3	2 2 8 9
4	3 4 6 9
5	1 1 4 5

$Q_1 = 22$
$Q_2 = 35$
$Q_3 = 47.5$

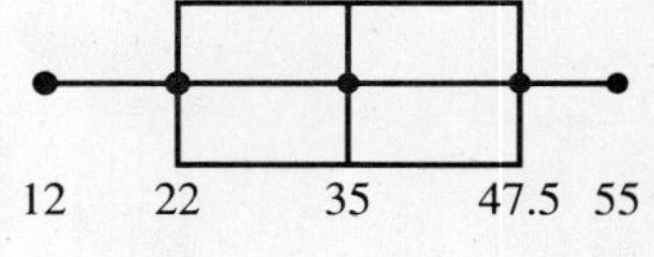

5. 7.5

6. 151

7. 10

8. 4.40

9.

1	0 3 7 8 9 3 2 3 5
2	5 3 1 1 5 6
3	5 3 1
4	8 8 0 2 4 6 1 8
5	0 0 7 9

10, 12, 13, 13, 13, 15, 17, 18, 19, 21, 21, 23, 25, 25, 26, 31, 33, 35, 40, 41, 42, 44, 46, 48, 48, 48, 50, 50, 57, 59

10.

3	0 3 0 7
4	2
5	5 2
6	1 8 1 8
7	8 9 6 6 0
8	5 6 7 2 4 9 0

30, 30, 33, 37, 42, 52, 55, 61, 61, 68, 68, 70, 76, 76, 78, 79, 80, 82, 84, 85, 86, 87, 89

11.

2	0 4 2
3	4 5 5 6
4	8 0 7 1 9 5 8 8 0
5	1 7 3 2 3
6	0 8 5 1 5 3 5 5 4 6 6

2	0 2 4
3	4 5 5 6
4	0 0 1 5 7 8 8 8 9
5	1 2 3 3 7
6	0 1 3 4 5 5 5 6 6 8

$Q_1 = 40$
$Q_2 = 50$
$Q_3 = 63.5$

20 40 50 63.5 68

12.

15	4 5 7 8
16	7 6 1 3 9 7 0 1
17	4 2 6 4
18	8 0 2 4
19	1 0 2 2

15	4 5 7 8
16	0 1 1 3 6 7 7 9
17	2 4 4 6
18	0 2 4 8
19	0 1 2 2

$Q_1 = 161$
$Q_2 = 170.5$
$Q_3 = 183$

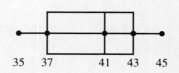

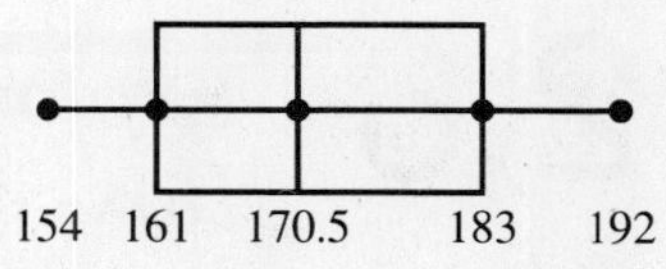

13. $Q_1 = 3$
$Q_2 = 4.5$
$Q_3 = 6$

0 3 4.5 6 10

14. $Q_1 = 37$
$Q_2 = 41$
$Q_3 = 43$

35 37 41 43 45

15. Answers vary. 10, 11, 12, 13, 13, 14, 15, 16, 22, 23, 24, 25, 29, 32, 35, 38

16. Answers vary. 106, 112, 118, 124, 124, 132, 140, 148, 152, 155, 158, 161, 163, 173, 183, 193

17. Answers vary. 81, 84, 87, 90, 94, 94, 94, 96, 96, 97, 97, 99, 104, 109, 114

18. Answers vary. 284, 290, 296, 302, 302, 309, 316, 323, 327, 345, 363, 381, 383, 390, 397, 404

19.

1	24 3 25
2	22 7
3	17
4	14 15 30 30 1
5	10
6	5 13
7	31
8	21 26
9	12
10	11 17
11	11
12	28 9 15

1–3, 1–24, 1–25, 2–7, 2–22, 3–17, 4–1, 4–14, 4–15, 4–30, 4–30, 5–10, 6–5, 6–13, 7–31, 8–21, 8–26, 9–12, 10–11, 10–17, 11–11, 12–9, 12–15, 12–28

20.

9	8 9
10	
11	
12	0 9 6 2 1
13	6 3 9
14	
15	0 5

98, 99, 120, 121, 122, 126, 129, 133, 136, 139, 150, 155

21.

1	6 0
2	2
3	6 6
4	9 5
5	4
6	9
8	5
9	6 7
10	7
15	2
25	8
26	3
28	7
34	7
50	7

50.7, 34.7, 28.7, 26.3, 25.8, 15.2, 10.7, 9.7, 9.6, 8.5, 6.9, 5.4, 4.9, 4.5, 3.6, 3.6, 2.2, 1.6, 1.0

22.

0	8
1	5 2 5 9 2 2
2	5 9 5 9
3	2 9
4	
5	1
6	8
7	
8	
9	5
10	
13	2

13.2, 9.5, 6.8, 5.1, 3.9, 3.2, 2.9, 2.9, 2.5, 2.5, 1.9, 1.5, 1.5, 1.2, 1.2, 1.2, 0.8

23.

Stem	Leaves
1	9 8
2	4 3 3 3 4 0 9 0 4
3	4
4	7 8 0
5	9 0 0
6	
7	1
8	
9	
10	8

Stem	Leaves
1	8 9
2	0 0 3 3 3 4 4 4 9
3	4
4	0 7 8
5	0 0 9
7	1
10	8

$Q_1 = 2.3$

$Q_2 = 2.65$

$Q_3 = 4.9$

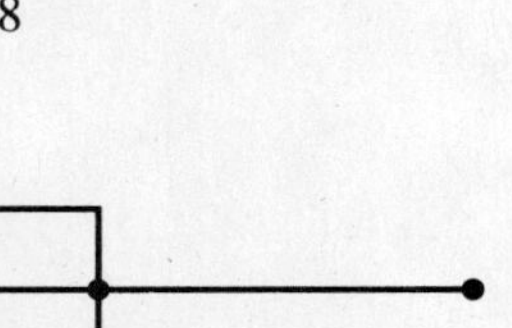

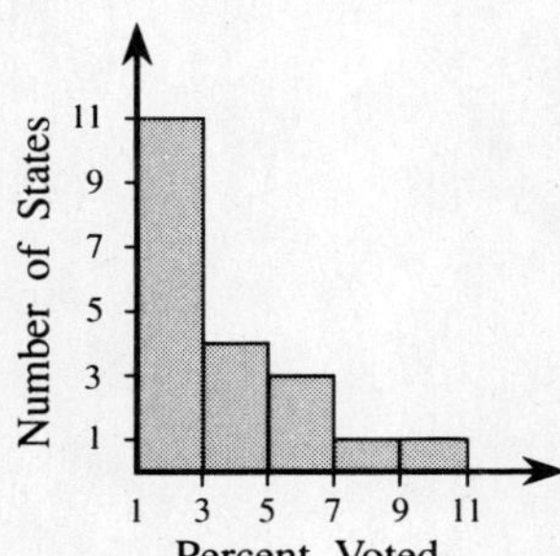

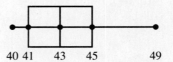

The box-and-whisker plot is better in showing how the data is clustered or spread out, while the bar graph is better in showing specific relationships among the data.

24.

40	|||	3
41	||||	4
42	||	2
43	||	2
44	||	2
45	~~||||~~	5
46	|	1
47		
48		
49	|	1

$Q_1 = 41$

$Q_2 = 43$

$Q_3 = 45$

40 41 43 45 49

The "greatest number" and the "greatest percent" produce different data.

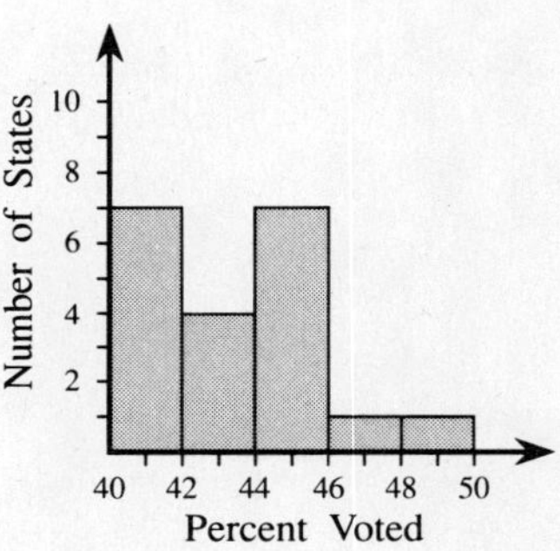

25. $W = 91.6 \times 10^6(0.02)$

$= 1{,}832{,}000$

$1{,}832{,}000 = 0.40P$

$P = 4{,}580{,}000$

The 1988 population of Washington was 4,580,000.

26. $N = 91.6 \times 10^6(0.034)$

$= 3{,}114{,}400$

$3{,}114{,}400 = 0.40P$

$P = 7{,}786{,}000$

The 1988 population of New Jersey was 7,786,000.

27. Answers vary.

12.7 Exploring Data: Measures of Central Tendency

Communicating about Algebra

Mean of 180: **A., B., D.**

Median of 180: **D.**

Mode of 180: **C., D.**

EXERCISES

1. The mean of n numbers is the sum of the numbers divided by n.

The median of n numbers is the middle number when the numbers are written in order. (If n is even, the median is the average of the two middle numbers.)

The mode is the number that occurs most frequently.

2. Mean: 233.7

Median: 235

Mode: 235

3. Answers vary. The collection 1, 2, 99 has a mean of 34.

4. The bar graph shows the frequency of each number.

The box plot shows the median and quartiles.

5.

Stem	Leaves
60	9
61	3 0 7 7
62	5 8 8 6 8
63	2 1 0 1 9
64	2 0 3 5 6

Stem	Leaves
60	9
61	0 3 7 7
62	5 6 8 8 8
63	0 1 1 2 9
64	0 2 3 5 6

No; the mean and the median are 62.9, the mode is 62.8.

6. Mean: $27{,}783\frac{1}{3}$

Median: 21,700

The mean and median are not equal.

7. Mean: 7.25 $Q_1 = 6$

Median: 7.5 $Q_3 = 8$

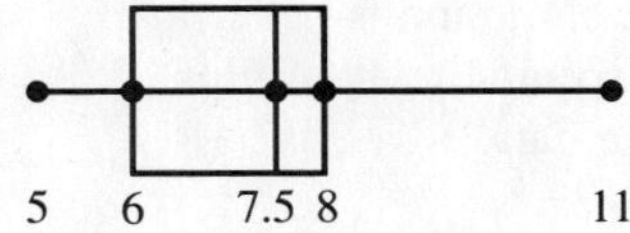

8. Mean: 3.675 $Q_1 = 2$

Median: 3 $Q_3 = 5$

Mode: 2

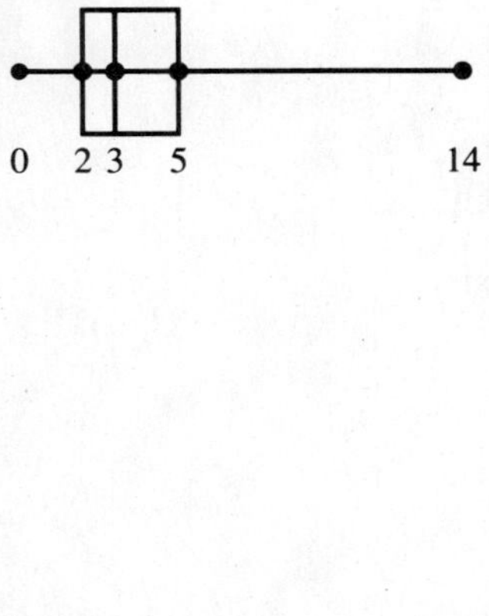

0 2 3 5 14

9.

0	2 9 2 5
4	0 7 6 3 4 2
5	4 0 1 5
6	3 2 1

0	2 2 5 9
4	0 2 3 4 6 7
5	0 1 4 5
6	1 2 3

Mean: 3.98

Median: 4.6

Mode: 0.2

Since the mode is the smallest length and the mean is smaller than most of the lengths, the median of 4.6 inches is the most representative.

10.

0	246 708 246
1	696 225
2	228 444 314
4	922

Mean: 1781

Median: 1696

Mode: 246

The mode is the smallest number, the mean is smaller than 4 numbers, and the median is smaller than 4 numbers and larger than 4 numbers. Thus, the median is most representative.

11. No, this is not a fair measure of a typical salary in the town.

$$x = \frac{(74{,}750)100 - 5{,}000{,}000}{99}$$

$x = 25{,}000$

The mean salary of the other 99 adults is $25,000.

12. Answers will vary.

Example 1: 7, 7, 8, 10, 14, 18, 18, 19, 19, 20

Example 2: 10, 12, 13, 13, 14, 14, 16, 20, 24, 24

13. $20 = x(80)$

$x = 0.25$

$= 25\%$

14. $x = 0.5(11.3)$

$x = 5.65$

15. $7.3 = x(9.5)$

$x \approx 0.768$

$= 76.8\%$

16. $0.5 = 0.1(x)$

$x = 5$

17. $x = 0.27(21.4)$

$x = 5.778$

18. $1.2 = 0.06x$

$x = 20$

19. **b.**

20. **c.**

21. The mean cost is $126.40.

22. The mean cost is $98.20.

23. The mean riding time is 14.175 minutes.

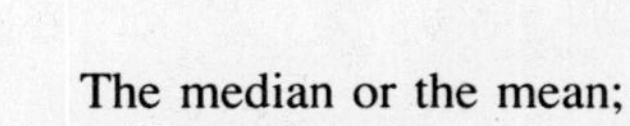

24. The mean delivery time is 9.27 minutes.

25. Mean: 2.0–2.5

Median: 2.0–2.5

Mode: 3.0–3.5

$Q_1 = 1.5$

$Q_2 = 2.25$

$Q_3 = 3.25$

The median or the mean; they are the same.

26.

Number of Days

Study Hours

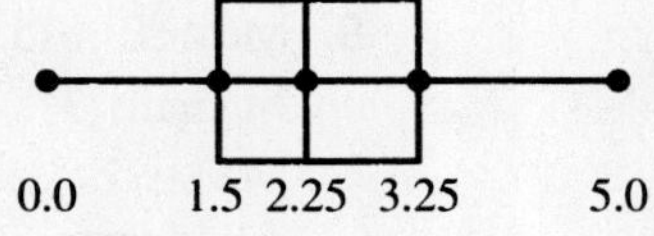

The box-and-whisker plot is better in showing how the data is clustered or spread out, while the bar graph is better in showing specific relationships among the data.

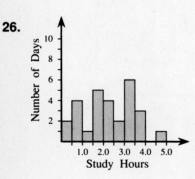

Using a Graphing Calculator

1.

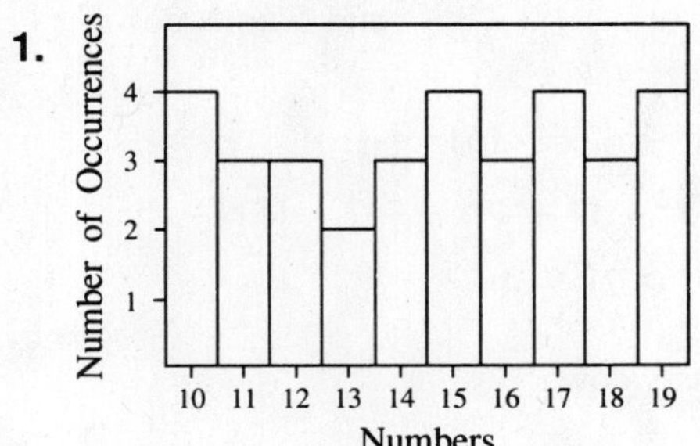

2.

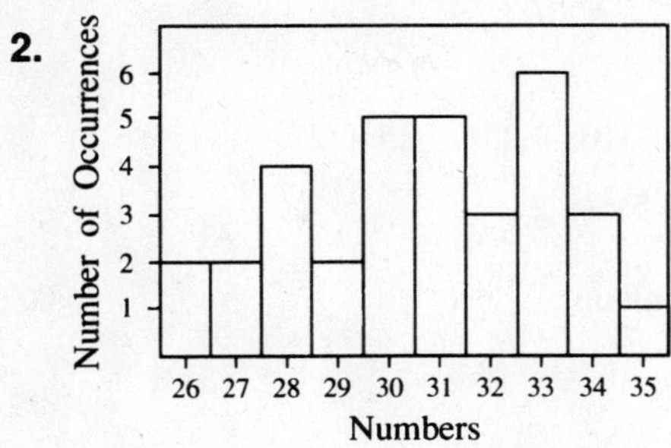

Chapter **REVIEW**

1. Function

Domain: {a, b, c, d}

2. Not a function

3. Function

Domain: {3, 4, 6, 8}

4. Function

Domain: {3, 6, 9, 12}

5. $m = \dfrac{-6+1}{-3-2}$

$= \dfrac{-5}{-5}$

$= 1$

$-6 = 1(-3) + b$

$b = -3$

$f(x) = x - 3$

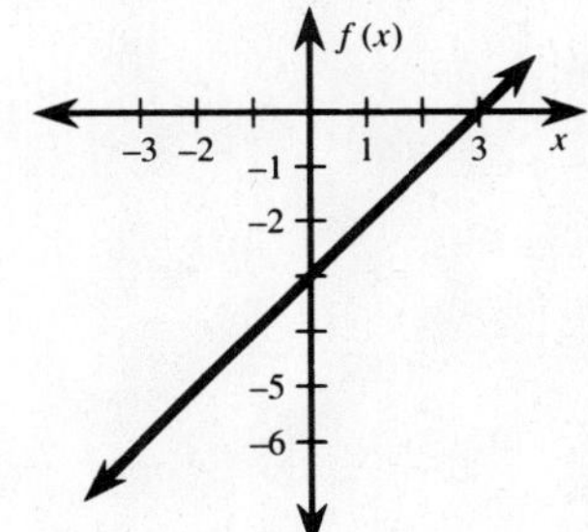

6. $m = \dfrac{0+3}{0-5}$

$= -\dfrac{3}{5}$

$0 = -\dfrac{3}{5} \cdot 0 + b$

$b = 0$

$f(x) = -\dfrac{3}{5}x$

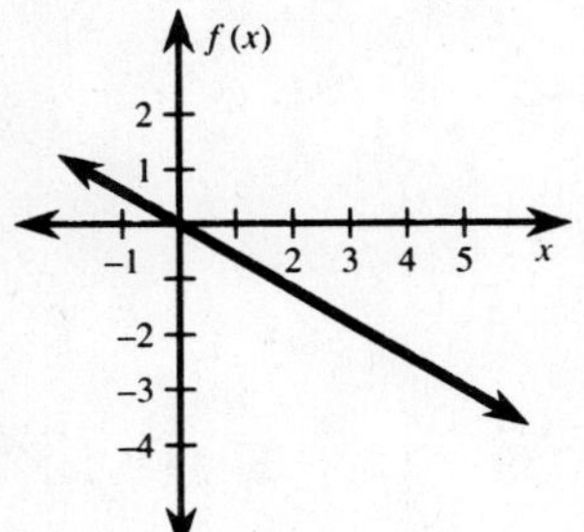

7. $m = \dfrac{2-6}{-3-1}$

$= \dfrac{-4}{-4}$

$= 1$

$2 = 1 \cdot (-3) + b$

$b = 5$

$f(x) = x + 5$

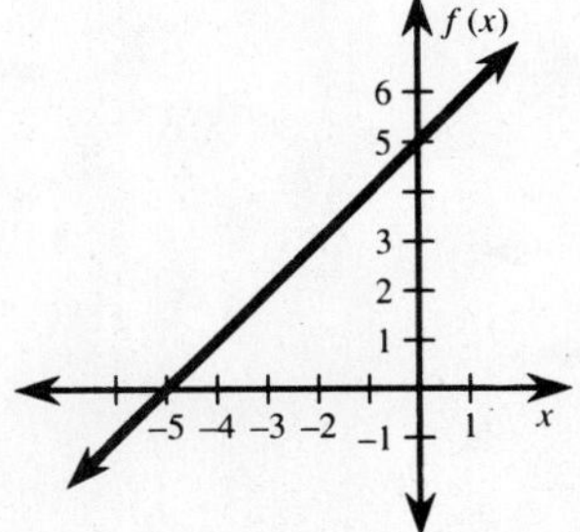

8. $m = \dfrac{3-2}{3-7}$

$= -\dfrac{1}{4}$

$3 = -\dfrac{1}{4}(3) + b$

$b = \dfrac{15}{4}$

$f(x) = -\dfrac{1}{4}x + \dfrac{15}{4}$

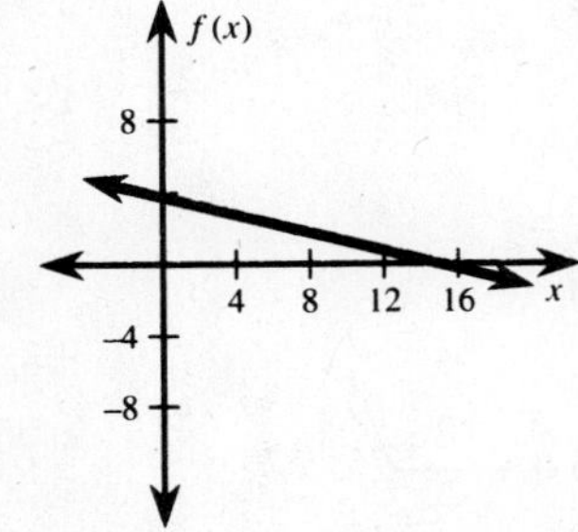

9. b. **10.** a. **11.** d. **12.** c.

13. Shift 2 units down

14. Shift 5 units right

15. Reflection

16. Shift 2 units left and 5 units down

17. $f(x) = (x^2 + 10x + 25) - 25 + 27$

$f(x) = (x + 5)^2 + 2$

$(-5,\ 2)$, opens up

18. $g(x) = -3x^2 + 42x - 151$

$= -3(x^2 - 14 + 49) + 147 - 151$

$g(x) = -3(x - 7)^2 - 4$

$(7,\ -4)$, opens down

19. $h(x) = -\frac{1}{3}x^2 - \frac{4}{3}x - \frac{22}{3}$

$= -\frac{1}{3}(x^2 + 4x + 4) + \frac{4}{3} - \frac{22}{3}$

$h(x) = -\frac{1}{3}(x + 2)^2 - 6$

$(-2,\ -6)$, opens down

20. $g(x) = \frac{1}{2}x^2 - 10x + 55$

$= \frac{1}{2}(x^2 - 20x + 100) - 50 + 55$

$g(x) = \frac{1}{2}(x - 10)^2 + 5$

$(10,\ 5)$, opens up

21. c. **22.** b. **23.** d. **24.** a.

25.

$$\begin{array}{r|l} & \ \ 3 \\ x - 4 & 3x - 8 \\ & 3x - 12 \\ \hline & \quad\ \ 4 \end{array}$$

Thus, $\frac{3x - 8}{x - 4} = 3 + \frac{4}{x - 4}$.

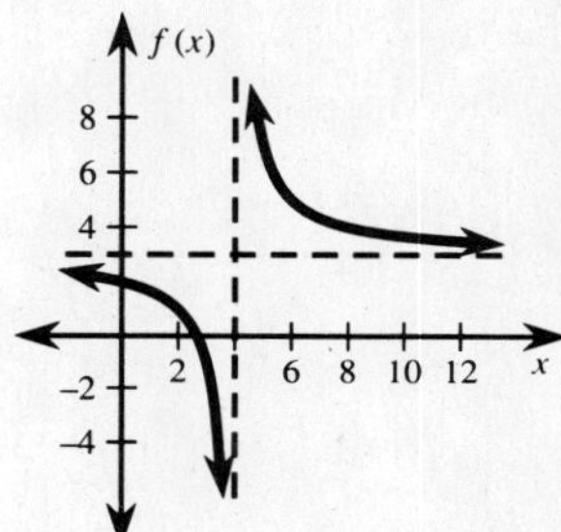

26.

$$\begin{array}{r|l} & \ \ 2 \\ x + 1 & 2x + 3 \\ & 2x + 2 \\ \hline & \quad\ \ 1 \end{array}$$

Thus, $\frac{2x + 3}{x + 1} = 2 + \frac{1}{x + 1}$.

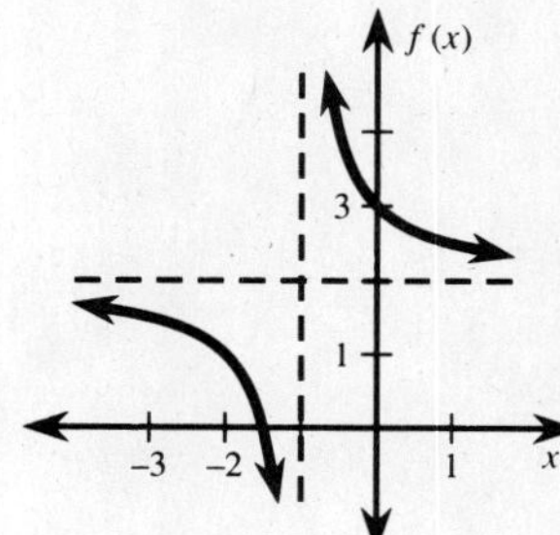

27.

$$\begin{array}{r|l} & \quad -5 \\ x - 2 & -5x + 12 \\ & -5x + 10 \\ \hline & \qquad\ \ 2 \end{array}$$

Thus, $\frac{-5x + 12}{x - 2} = -5 + \frac{2}{x - 2}$.

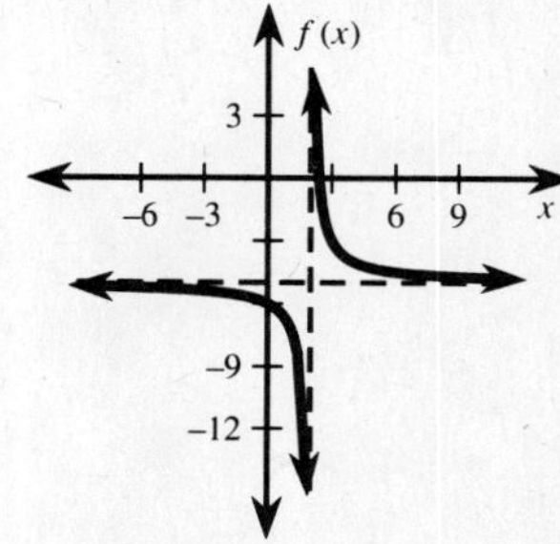

28.

$$\begin{array}{r|l} & \quad -3 \\ \cline{2-2} x+5 & -3x - 12 \\ & \underline{-3x - 15} \\ & \qquad\ 3 \end{array}$$

Thus, $\dfrac{-3x-12}{x+5} = -3 + \dfrac{3}{x+5}$.

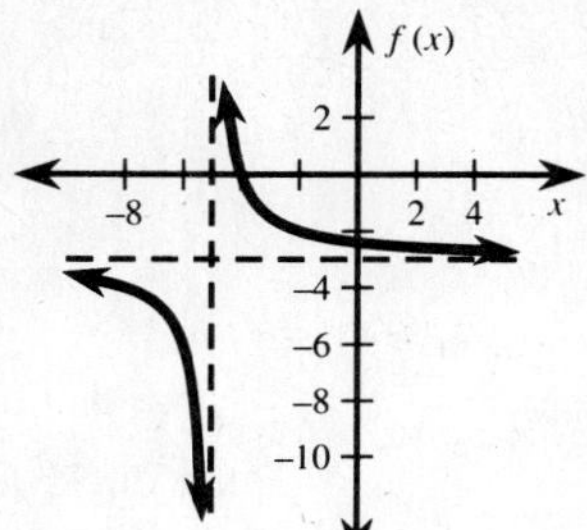

29.

$$\begin{array}{r|l} & \qquad 2 \\ \cline{2-2} x-2 & 2x + 0 \\ & \underline{2x - 4} \\ & \qquad 4 \end{array}$$

Thus, $\dfrac{2x}{x-2} = 2 + \dfrac{4}{x-2}$.

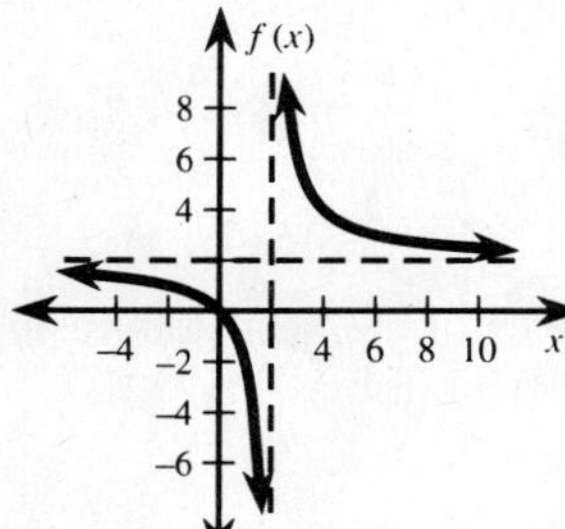

30.

$$\begin{array}{r|l} & \quad -3 \\ \cline{2-2} x+3 & -3x - 2 \\ & \underline{-3x - 9} \\ & \qquad 7 \end{array}$$

Thus, $\dfrac{-3x-2}{x+3} = -3 + \dfrac{7}{x+3}$.

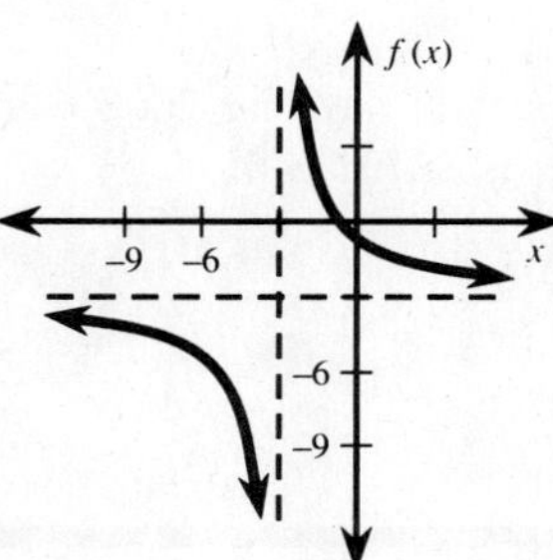

31.

Stem	Leaves
3	7 6 5 7
4	0 9 3 4 5 4 5 6 9 7
5	6 3 0 4
6	0 9 7 8 8 4
7	5 0 2 0 1 2

32. Mean: 54.5

Median: 51.5

No mode

33. $Q_1 = 44$

$Q_2 = 51.5$

$Q_3 = 68$

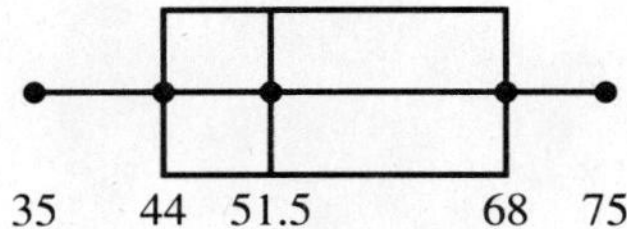

34. 35–45: 8

45–55: 9

55–65: 3

65–75: 10

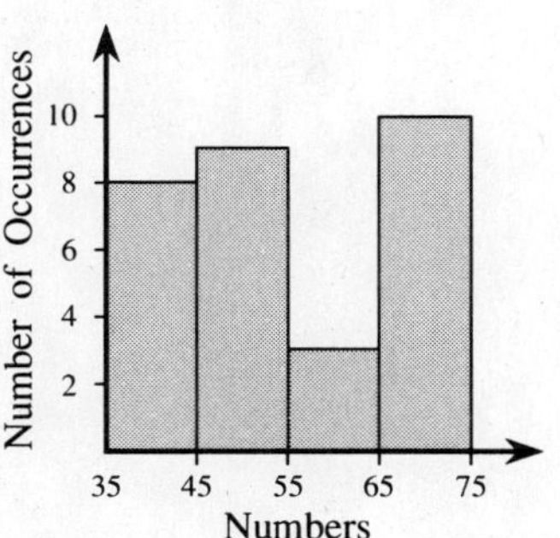

35. $f(x) = \dfrac{x}{30}$

$$f(x) = \frac{100}{30} = 3\frac{1}{3}$$

The speed of the ship would be $3\frac{1}{3}$ feet per second.

36.

0	7 9 6 2 2 7 3 5 8 3 8
1	2 0 0 0 2 1 0 1 2 3 1 1
2	2 2
3	5 0
4	5

0	2 2 3 3 5 6 7 7 8 8 9
1	0 0 0 0 1 1 1 1 2 2 2 3
2	2 2
3	0 5
4	5

$Q_1 = 7$

$Q_2 = 10$

$Q_3 = 12$

2 7 10 12 45

Deer, duck, lion, pig, sheep, cat, cow, dog, goat, pigeon, and wolf

37. $f(t) = 1040 + 70(20)$

$= 2440$

The total wholesale sales in the year 2000 using the linear model is $2440 billion.

38. $f(t) = 1.25(20)^2 + 51.9(20) + 1083$

$= 2621$

The total wholesale sales in the year 2000 using the quadratic model is $2621 billion.

39. $f(t) = 1090(1.047)^{20}$

≈ 2731

The total wholesale sales in the year 2000 using the exponential model is $2731 billion.

40. $f(t) = \dfrac{22.85(20) + 1098.6}{-0.023(20) + 1}$

≈ 2881

The total wholesale sales in the year 2000 using the rational model is $2881 billion.

41. Answers will vary.

Chapter TEST

1. Yes, y is a function of x.

2. No, x is not a function of y.

3. $f(-3) = 17(-3) - 25$

$= -76$

$f(2) = 17(2) - 25$

$= 9$

4. $m = \dfrac{-4 - 3}{-2 - 3}$

$= \dfrac{-7}{-5}$

$= \dfrac{7}{5}$

$-4 = \dfrac{7}{5}(-2) + b$

$b = -4 + \dfrac{14}{5}$

$b = -\dfrac{6}{5}$

$f(x) = \dfrac{7}{5}x - \dfrac{6}{5}$

5. b.

6. d.

7. a.

8. c.

9. $f(x) = x^2 + 6x + 15$

$= x^2 + 6x + 9 - 9 + 15$

$f(x) = (x + 3)^2 + 6$

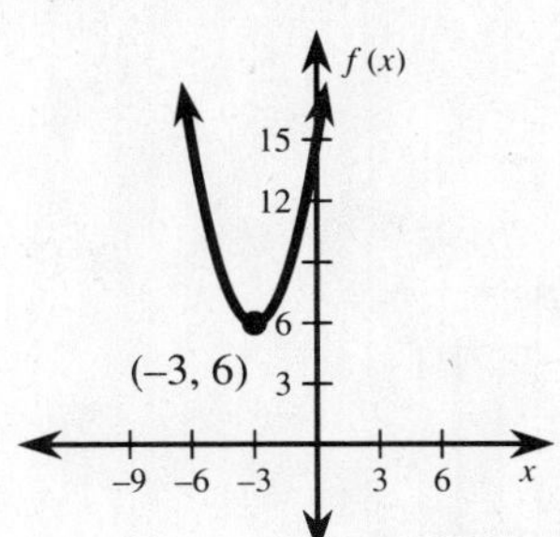

10.

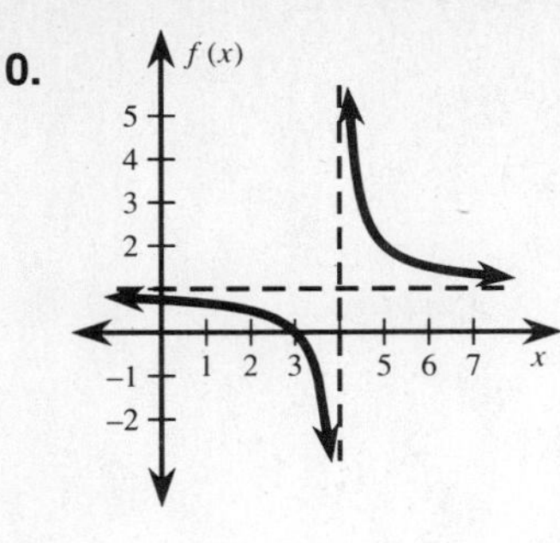

11.

$$\begin{array}{r} 3 \\ x-1 \overline{)\ 3x + 2} \\ \underline{3x - 3} \\ 5 \end{array}$$

Thus, $\dfrac{3x+2}{x-1} = 3 + \dfrac{5}{x-1}$.

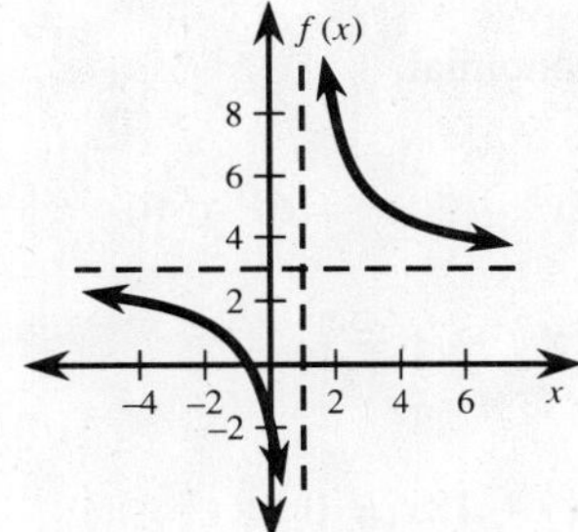

12.

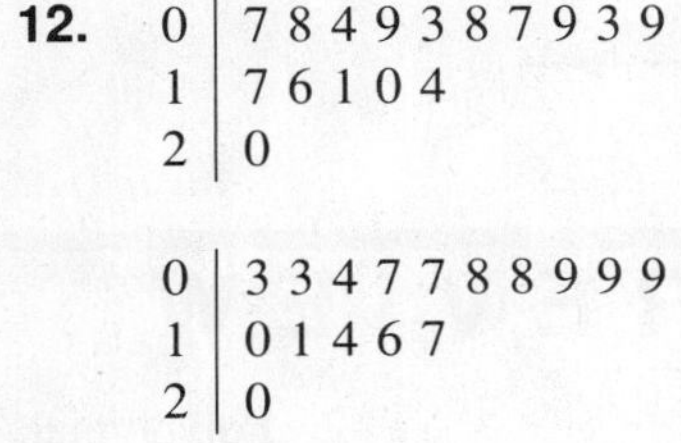

0	7 8 4 9 3 8 7 9 3 9
1	7 6 1 0 4
2	0

0	3 3 4 7 7 8 8 9 9 9
1	0 1 4 6 7
2	0

13. $Q_1 = 7$

$Q_2 = 9$

$Q_3 = 12.5$

14. Mean: 9.6875

Median: 9

Mode: 9

15.

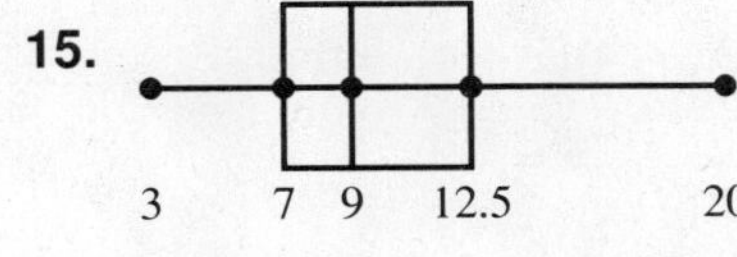

16. $f(x) = 2000x$

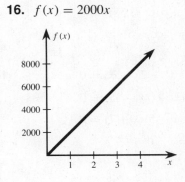

17. $f(t) = \dfrac{5 + 4t}{12 + 3t}$

$$\begin{array}{r} \frac{4}{3} \\ 3t + 12 \overline{\smash{)}\, 4t + 5} \\ \underline{4t + 16} \\ -11 \end{array}$$

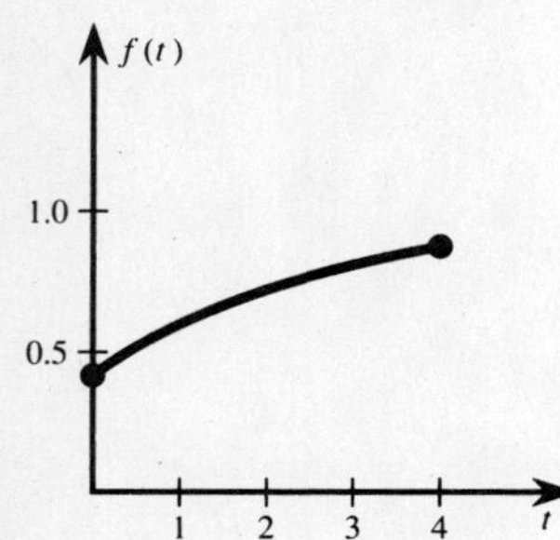

18. Mean: $7\frac{11}{12}$
Median: $8\frac{1}{2}$
Mode: 6

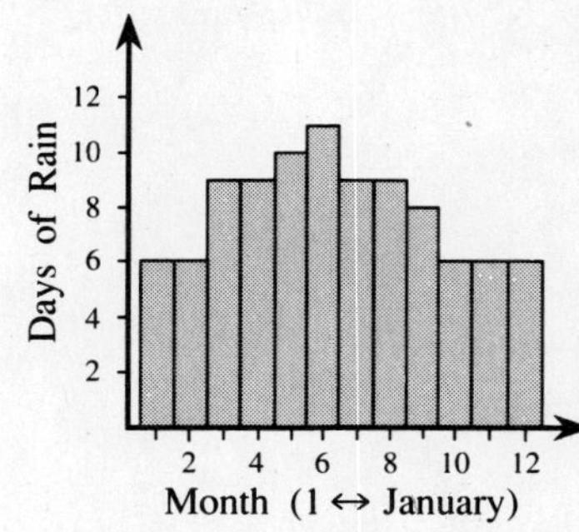

Cummulative REVIEW

1. Monomial, 0

2. Polynomial, 3

3. Trinomial, 2

4. Binomial, 4

5. Binomial, 1

6. Monomial, 1

7. $3x^3 + 9x^2 + 12$

8. $2x^2 + 3x - 2$

9. $12x^3 + 20x^2 + 6x + 10$

10. $-\frac{1}{2}x^2 + 4x - 6$

11. $4x^2 - 16$

12. $4x^2 + 28x + 49$

13.
$$\begin{aligned} x^2 - 9x + 5 &= -13 \\ x^2 - 9x + 18 &= 0 \\ (x - 3)(x - 6) &= 0 \\ x = 3,\ x &= 6 \end{aligned}$$

14.
$$\begin{aligned} 3x^2 + 8x - 4 &= 12 \\ 3x^2 + 8x - 16 &= 0 \\ (3x - 4)(x + 4) &= 0 \\ x = \tfrac{4}{3},\ x &= -4 \end{aligned}$$

15.
$$\begin{aligned} 3x^2 + 18x &= 0 \\ 3x(x + 6) &= 0 \\ x = 0,\ x &= -6 \end{aligned}$$

16.
$$\begin{aligned} -x^2 - 2x + 35 &= 0 \\ -(x^2 + 2x - 35) &= 0 \\ -(x - 5)(x + 7) &= 0 \\ x = 5,\ x &= -7 \end{aligned}$$

17.
$$\begin{aligned} 4x^2 - 37 &= 12 \\ 4x^2 - 49 &= 0 \\ (2x + 7)(2x - 7) &= 0 \\ x = -\tfrac{7}{2},\ x &= \tfrac{7}{2} \end{aligned}$$

18.
$$\begin{aligned} 9x^2 + 30x + 24 &= -1 \\ 9x^2 + 30x + 25 &= 0 \\ (3x + 5)^2 &= 0 \\ x &= -\tfrac{5}{3} \end{aligned}$$

19.
$$\begin{aligned} x^2 + 3x - 5 &= 0 \\ x &= \frac{-3 \pm \sqrt{3^2 - 4(1)(-5)}}{2(1)} \\ &= \frac{-3 \pm \sqrt{9 + 20}}{2} \\ &= \frac{-3 \pm \sqrt{29}}{2} \end{aligned}$$

20.
$$\begin{aligned} x^2 - 6x + 7 &= 0 \\ (x^2 - 6x + 9) - 9 + 7 &= 0 \\ (x - 3)^2 &= 2 \\ x - 3 &= \pm\sqrt{2} \\ x &= 3 \pm \sqrt{2} \end{aligned}$$

21.
$$\begin{aligned} x^2 - 4x - 13 &= 0 \\ x^2 - 4x + 4 - 4 - 13 &= 0 \\ (x - 2)^2 &= 17 \\ x - 2 &= \pm\sqrt{17} \\ x &= 2 \pm \sqrt{17} \end{aligned}$$

22.
$$x^2 + 8x - 1 = 0$$
$$(x^2 + 8x + 16) - 1 - 16 = 0$$
$$(x + 4)^2 = 17$$
$$x + 4 = \pm\sqrt{17}$$
$$x = -4 \pm \sqrt{17}$$

23. $2x^2 - 12x + 7 = 0$
$$x = \frac{12 \pm \sqrt{(-12)^2 - 4(2)(7)}}{2(2)}$$
$$= \frac{12 \pm \sqrt{144 - 56}}{4}$$
$$= \frac{12 \pm \sqrt{88}}{4}$$
$$= 3 \pm \frac{\sqrt{88}}{4}$$

24. $3x^2 - 24x + 6 = 0$
$$x = \frac{24 \pm \sqrt{(-24)^2 - 4(3)(6)}}{2(3)}$$
$$= \frac{24 \pm \sqrt{576 - 72}}{6}$$
$$= \frac{24 \pm \sqrt{504}}{6}$$
$$= 4 \pm \frac{\sqrt{504}}{6}$$

25.
$$\frac{3}{4m} = \frac{5}{2}$$
$$6 = 20m$$
$$\frac{3}{10} = m$$

26.
$$\frac{x+5}{3} = \frac{2}{x}$$
$$x^2 + 5x = 6$$
$$x^2 + 5x - 6 = 0$$
$$(x + 6)(x - 1) = 0$$
$$x = -6, \ x = 1$$

27.
$$\frac{x+5}{x-8} = \frac{1}{3x}$$
$$3x^2 + 15x = x - 8$$
$$3x^2 + 14x + 8 = 0$$
$$(3x + 2)(x + 4) = 0$$
$$x = -\frac{2}{3}, \ x = -4$$

28.
$$\frac{\frac{1}{2}(10)(10) + \frac{1}{2}(5)(5)}{(10+10)(10+10)} = \frac{62.5}{400}$$
$$\approx 15.6\%$$

29.
$$\frac{\frac{1}{2}(6)(8)}{\frac{1}{2}(6)(8) + 4(10)} = \frac{24}{64}$$
$$= 37.5\%$$

30.
$$\frac{30(20)}{50(50)} = \frac{600}{2500}$$
$$= 24\%$$

31. $24 \times 1.3 = 31.2$ yards

32. $40 \div 36 \approx 111.1\%$

33. $120 \div 840 \approx 14.3\%$

34. $4 \div 180 \approx 2.2\%$

35.
$$y = kx$$
$$5 = k3$$
$$k = \tfrac{5}{3}$$
$$y = \tfrac{5}{3}x$$
$$3y = 5x$$

36.
$$y = kx$$
$$\tfrac{1}{3} = k\left(\tfrac{1}{2}\right)$$
$$k = \tfrac{2}{3}$$
$$y = \tfrac{2}{3}x$$
$$3y = 2x$$

37.
$$y = kx$$
$$3.1 = k(4.2)$$
$$k = \frac{3.1}{4.2}$$
$$y = \frac{3.1}{4.2}x$$
$$4.2y = 3.1x$$

38.
$$xy = k$$
$$(12)(2) = k$$
$$k = 24$$
$$xy = 24$$

39.
$$xy = k$$
$$\left(\tfrac{3}{2}\right)6 = k$$
$$k = 9$$
$$xy = 9$$

40.
$$xy = k$$
$$(6.3)(10.1) = k$$
$$k = 63.63$$
$$xy = 63.63$$

41. $\frac{13}{25}$

42. $\frac{12}{25}$

43. $\frac{1}{5}$

44. $\frac{1}{25}$

45. $\frac{3y}{4} \cdot \frac{2}{6y^2} = \frac{1}{4y}$

46. $\frac{8x^3}{3} \cdot 5x^2 = \frac{40x^5}{3}$

47.
$$\frac{5p^4}{3} \cdot \frac{2}{3p^3} = \frac{10p^4}{9p^3} = \frac{10p}{9}$$

48.
$$\frac{(x-2)}{3x} \cdot \frac{15x^2}{4} = \frac{x-2}{1} \cdot \frac{5x}{4} = \frac{5x^2 - 10x}{4}$$

49. $\frac{m}{(m-2)^2} \cdot m - 2 = \frac{m}{m-2}$

50.
$$\frac{3n^2 - 2n - 5}{n+1} \cdot \frac{1}{n+1} = \frac{(3n-5)(n+1)}{(n+1)^2} = \frac{3n-5}{n+1}$$

51. $(6z^2 + 4z) \div 2z = 3z + 2$

52. $(8x^2 + 4x - 7) \cdot \frac{1}{4} = 2x^2 + x - \frac{7}{4}$

53.
$$\begin{array}{r} y + 8 \\ y - 2 \overline{) y^2 + 6y - 2} \\ \underline{y^2 - 2y} \\ 8y - 2 \\ \underline{8y - 16} \\ 14 \end{array}$$

$$\frac{y^2 + 6y - 2}{y - 2} = y + 8 + \frac{14}{y - 2}$$

54.
$$\begin{array}{r} 4m^2 - 8m + 17 \\ m + 2 \overline{) 4m^3 + 0m^2 + m + 6} \\ \underline{4m^3 + 8m^2} \\ -8m^2 + m \\ \underline{-8m^2 - 16m} \\ 17m + 6 \\ \underline{17m + 34} \\ -28 \end{array}$$

$$\frac{4m^3 + m + 6}{m + 2} = 4m^2 - 8m + 17 - \frac{28}{m + 2}$$

55.
$$\begin{array}{r} \frac{1}{3}z^2 - 7 \\ z + 3 \overline{) \frac{1}{3}z^3 + z^2 - 7z + 0} \\ \underline{\frac{1}{3}z^3 + z^2} \\ -7z + 0 \\ \underline{-7z - 21} \\ 21 \end{array}$$

$$\frac{\frac{1}{3}z^3 + z^2 - 7z}{z + 3} = \frac{1}{3}z^2 - 7 + \frac{21}{z + 3}$$

56.

$$\begin{array}{r} 9x + 4 \\ 3x - 1 \overline{)\, 27x^2 + 3x - 2} \\ \underline{27x^2 - 9x} \\ 12x - 2 \\ \underline{12x - 4} \\ 2 \end{array}$$

$$\frac{27x^2 + 3x - 2}{3x - 1} = 9x + 4 + \frac{2}{3x - 1}$$

57. $\dfrac{5}{x+3} = \dfrac{6}{x+1}$

$5x + 5 = 6x + 18$

$-x = 13$

$x = -13$

58. $\dfrac{4}{2x+1} = \dfrac{1}{x}$

$4x = 2x + 1$

$2x = 1$

$x = \dfrac{1}{2}$

59. $\dfrac{2}{x} - \dfrac{1}{2} = \dfrac{5}{x}$

$4 - x = 10$

$-x = 6$

$x = -6$

60. $120 + 29x = 6x^2$

$0 = 6x^2 - 29x - 120$

$x = \dfrac{29 \pm \sqrt{(-29)^2 - 4(6)(-120)}}{2(6)}$

$= \dfrac{29 \pm \sqrt{3721}}{12}$

$= \dfrac{29 \pm 61}{12}$

$x = \dfrac{90}{12} \qquad x = -\dfrac{32}{12}$

$= \dfrac{15}{2} \qquad = -\dfrac{8}{3}$

61. $4x + 4 = 6x + 3$

$-2x = -1$

$x = \frac{1}{2}$

62. $\dfrac{4x^2}{x-1} - \dfrac{4x}{x-1} = \dfrac{-3}{4x-4}$

$16x^2 - 16x = -3$

$16x^2 - 16x + 3 = 0$

$(4x - 3)(4x - 1) = 0$

$x = \frac{3}{4},\ x = \frac{1}{4}$

63. $f(4) = 4(4) + 2$

$= 18$

64. $f(3) = 2^3 + 14$

$= 22$

65. $f(-5) = (-5)^2 + 4(-5) - 3$

$= 25 - 20 - 3$

$= 2$

66. $f(1) = -3(1 - 7)^2$

$= -3(-6)^2$

$= -108$

67. $f(6) = \frac{3}{6}$

$= \frac{1}{2}$

68. $f(-10) = \dfrac{6}{-10-2} + 4$

$= \dfrac{6}{-12} + 4$

$= -\dfrac{1}{2} + 4$

$= 3\dfrac{1}{2}$

69. b.

70. c.

71. d.

72. a.

73. $\dfrac{5}{7\frac{1}{2}} = \dfrac{12}{x}$

$5x = 90$

$x = 18$

74. $\dfrac{x}{13.5} = \dfrac{7.6}{19}$

$19x = 102.6$

$x = 5.4$

75. $x(1 - 0.20) = 18.80$

$0.80x = 18.80$

$x = \$23.50$

The original price was \$23.50.

76. Let c = cups of cereal.
Let p = cups of pretzel sticks.
Since c and p vary directly,

$c = kp$

$5 = k\left(\frac{3}{2}\right)$

$k = \frac{10}{3}$.

Therefore, $c = \frac{10}{3}p$.

77. $\dfrac{10 + (3 - 1)x}{x} = 2.50$

$10 + 2x = 2.50x$

$10 = 0.5x$

$x = 20$ games

78. $\dfrac{10 + (3 - 1)x}{x} > 3$

$10 + 2x > 3x$

$10 > x$

$x < 10$

Maximum number of games attended: 9

79.

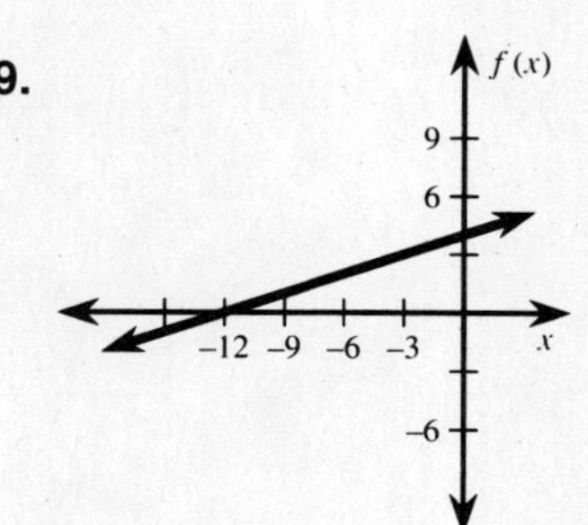

80.

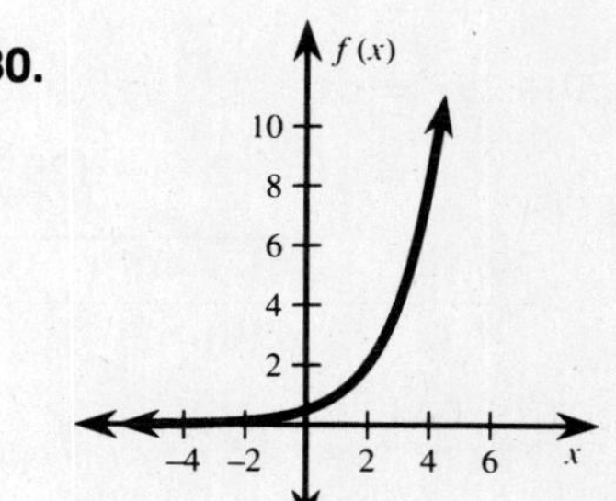

81.

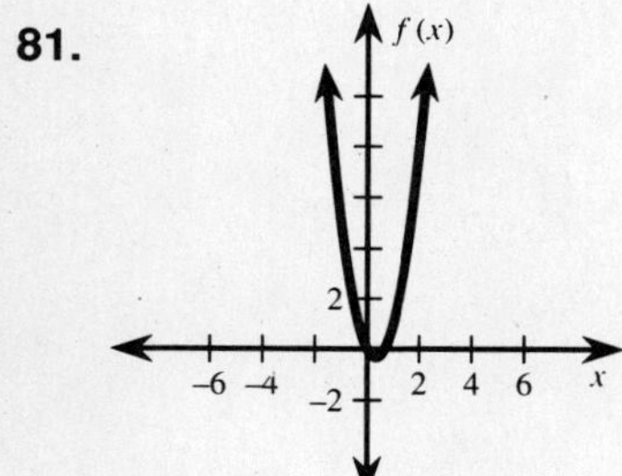

82.

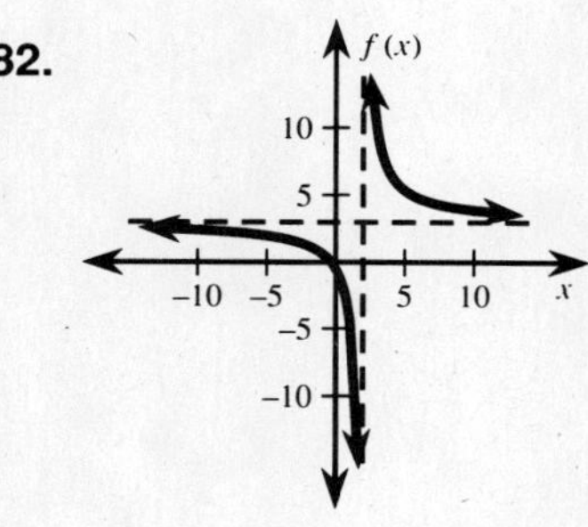

83. $\dfrac{F}{P} = \dfrac{54{,}420 + 2900t}{31{,}665 + 1545t}$

$0 \le t \le 10$

84. Increasing; when $t = 0$, the ratio is approximately 1.719 and when $t = 10$, the ratio is approximately 1.771.

85.

Stem	Leaves
0	1 3 1 7 9 2 6 3 2 4
1	8 1
2	9
4	0
6	4
8	2

Stem	Leaves
0	1 1 2 2 3 3 4 6 7 9
1	1 8
2	9
4	0
6	4
8	2

86. Mean: 1.8 inches

87. Median: 0.65 inches

88. The usual daily snowfall in December is less than an inch, half the time the snowfall is less than 0.65 inch, and three-fourths of the time the snowfall is less than 2.35 inches.

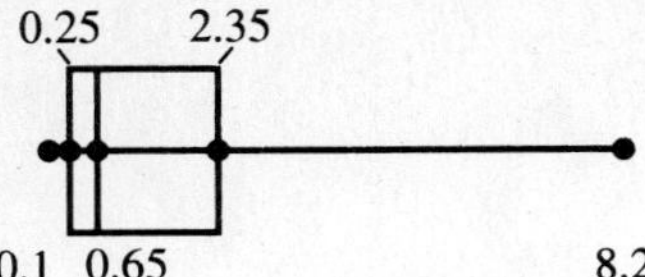

89. The area cleared in terms of x (the width of the sidewalk) is

$$\begin{aligned}(133x+1+x+x)(80x+x+x)-(133x+1)(80x) &= (135x+1)(82x)-(133x+1)(80x)\\ &= 11{,}070x^2+82x-10{,}640x^2-80x\\ &= 430x^2+2x.\end{aligned}$$

Let $x = 3$. Then $430(3)^2 + 2(3) = 3870 + 6$

$= 3876$ square feet.

90. $(3876 \text{ square feet})(6.4 \text{ inches})\left(\dfrac{1 \text{ foot}}{12 \text{ inches}}\right) = 2067.2 \text{ cubic feet}$

91. Since each week you gain one more client, your charge is determined by the coefficient of t: \$2.00.

92. $\sum_{0}^{7} 2t + 6 = (8)\left(\dfrac{6+20}{2}\right)$

$= \$104$

Chapter 13

Radicals and More Connections to Geometry

13.1 The Distance Formula

Communicating about Algebra

In the Distance Formula, squaring a positive difference gives the same result as squaring a negative difference. In the Midpoint Formula, addition of coordinates is commutative.

EXERCISES

1. $d = \sqrt{(3+3)^2 + (6+2)^2}$
$d = \sqrt{6^2 + 8^2}$
$d = \sqrt{100}$
$d = 10$

2. $x = \dfrac{6-4}{2} = \dfrac{2}{2} = 1$ $\quad y = \dfrac{-1+5}{2} = \dfrac{4}{2} = 2$

$(1, 2)$

3. If the lengths of the sides of a triangle satisfy the equation $a^2 + b^2 = c^2$, then the triangle is a right triangle.

4. $d = \sqrt{(-3-1)^2 + (1-5)^2}$
$d = \sqrt{16+16}$
$d = \sqrt{32}$
$d \approx 5.66$

5. $d = \sqrt{(-2-2)^2 + (2-1)^2}$
$d = \sqrt{16+1}$
$d = \sqrt{17}$
$d \approx 4.12$

6. $d = \sqrt{(-3-4)^2 + (-2-1)^2}$
$d = \sqrt{49+9}$
$d = \sqrt{58}$
$d \approx 7.62$

7. $d = \sqrt{(5+1)^2 + (-2-1)^2}$
$d = \sqrt{36+9}$
$d = \sqrt{45}$
$d \approx 6.71$

8. $d = \sqrt{(1-9)^2 + (0+4)^2}$
$d = \sqrt{64+16}$
$d = \sqrt{80}$
$d \approx 8.94$

9. $d = \sqrt{(1+2)^2 + (-7-2)^2}$
$d = \sqrt{9+81}$
$d = \sqrt{90}$
$d \approx 9.49$

10. $d = \sqrt{(3-0)^2 + (-1-3)^2}$

$d = \sqrt{9+16}$

$d = \sqrt{25}$

$d = 5$

11. $d = \sqrt{(1+4)^2 + (-4-6)^2}$

$d = \sqrt{25+100}$

$d = \sqrt{125}$

$d \approx 11.18$

12. $d = \sqrt{(6+3)^2 + (9-1)^2}$

$d = \sqrt{81+64}$

$d = \sqrt{145}$

$d \approx 12.04$

13. $d = \sqrt{(-2-1)^2 + (2-5)^2}$

$d = \sqrt{9+9}$

$d = \sqrt{18}$

$d \approx 4.24$

14. $d = \sqrt{\left(\frac{1}{2}+\frac{1}{2}\right)^2 + \left(\frac{1}{4}-\frac{5}{4}\right)^2}$

$d = \sqrt{1+1}$

$d = \sqrt{2}$

$d \approx 1.41$

15. $d = \sqrt{\left(\frac{1}{2}-1\right)^2 + \left(\frac{3}{2}-1\right)^2}$

$d = \sqrt{\frac{1}{4}+\frac{1}{4}}$

$d = \sqrt{\frac{1}{2}}$

$d \approx 0.71$

16. $d_1 = \sqrt{(4-2)^2 + (0-1)^2}$
$= \sqrt{4+1}$
$= \sqrt{5}$

$d_2 = \sqrt{(2+1)^2 + (1+5)^2}$
$= \sqrt{9+36}$
$= \sqrt{45}$

$d_3 = \sqrt{(4+1)^2 + (0+5)^2}$
$= \sqrt{25+25}$
$= \sqrt{50}$

$d_1{}^2 + d_2{}^2 = 5 + 45$
$= 50$
$= d_3{}^2$

Yes, they are vertices of a right triangle.

17. $d_1 = \sqrt{(4-1)^2 + (5-0)^2}$
$= \sqrt{9+25}$
$= \sqrt{34}$

$d_2 = \sqrt{(1+1)^2 + (0-2)^2}$
$= \sqrt{4+4}$
$= \sqrt{8}$

$d_3 = \sqrt{(4+1)^2 + (5-2)^2}$
$= \sqrt{25+9}$
$= \sqrt{34}$

$d_1{}^2 + d_2{}^2 = 34 + 8$
$= 42 \neq d_3{}^2$

No, they are not vertices of a right triangle.

18. $d_1 = \sqrt{(1-3)^2 + (-3-2)^2}$
$= \sqrt{4+25}$
$= \sqrt{29}$

$d_2 = \sqrt{(3+2)^2 + (2-4)^2}$
$= \sqrt{25+4}$
$= \sqrt{29}$

$d_3 = \sqrt{(1+2)^2 + (-3-4)^2}$
$= \sqrt{9+49}$
$= \sqrt{58}$

$d_1{}^2 + d_2{}^2 = 29 + 29$
$= 58$
$= d_3{}^2$

Yes, they are vertices of a right triangle.

19. $d_1 = \sqrt{(-1-10)^2 + (-1-7)^2}$
$= \sqrt{121+64}$
$= \sqrt{185}$

$d_2 = \sqrt{(10-2)^2 + (7-18)^2}$
$= \sqrt{64+121}$
$= \sqrt{185}$

$d_3 = \sqrt{(-1-2)^2 + (-1-18)^2}$
$= \sqrt{9+361}$
$= \sqrt{370}$

$d_1{}^2 + d_2{}^2 = 185 + 185$
$= 370$
$= d_3{}^2$

Yes, they are vertices of a right triangle.

20. $\left(\frac{-4+2}{2}, \frac{4+0}{2}\right) = (-1, 2)$

21. $\left(\frac{0+0}{2}, \frac{0+10}{2}\right) = (0, 5)$

22. $\left(\frac{2+14}{2}, \frac{1+6}{2}\right) = \left(8, \frac{7}{2}\right)$

23. $\left(\frac{-1+6}{2}, \frac{0+2}{2}\right) = \left(\frac{5}{2}, 1\right)$

24. $\left(\frac{-2+3}{2}, \frac{2-10}{2}\right) = \left(\frac{1}{2}, -4\right)$

25. $\left(\frac{1+4}{2}, \frac{6+2}{2}\right) = \left(\frac{5}{2}, 4\right)$

26. $d_1 = \sqrt{(0-2)^2 + (0-6)^2} = \sqrt{4+36} = \sqrt{40}$

$d_2 = \sqrt{(2-8)^2 + (6-8)^2} = \sqrt{36+4} = \sqrt{40}$

$d_3 = \sqrt{(8-14)^2 + (8-0)^2} = \sqrt{36+64} = \sqrt{100} = 10$

$d_4 = \sqrt{(14-0)^2 + (0-0)^2} = \sqrt{14^2+0} = 14$

$D = \sqrt{40} + \sqrt{40} + 10 + 14 = 24 + 2\sqrt{40}$

27. $d_1 = \sqrt{(0+8)^2 + (-8+6)^2} = \sqrt{64+4} = \sqrt{68}$

$d_2 = \sqrt{(-8+6)^2 + (-6+2)^2} = \sqrt{4+16} = \sqrt{20}$

$d_3 = \sqrt{(-6-4)^2 + (-2-4)^2} = \sqrt{100+36} = \sqrt{136}$

$d_4 = \sqrt{(4-6)^2 + (4-0)^2} = \sqrt{4+16} = \sqrt{20}$

$d_5 = \sqrt{(6-0)^2 + (0+8)^2} = \sqrt{36+64} = \sqrt{100} = 10$

$D = \sqrt{68} + \sqrt{20} + \sqrt{136} + \sqrt{20} + 10 = 10 + 2\sqrt{20} + \sqrt{68} + \sqrt{136}$

28. Let the location of Pierre be represented by (0.2, 4.3) and the location of Sante Fe be represented by (−3.1, −1.6).

$d = \sqrt{(0.2+3.1)^2 + (4.3+1.6)^2} \approx 6.8$

Therefore, the distance is $(6.8)(95) \approx 646$ miles.

29. Let the location of Wichita be represented by (1.7, −0.25) and the location of Cheyenne be represented by (−2.4, 2.25).

$d = \sqrt{(1.7+2.4)^2 + (-0.25-2.25)^2} \approx 4.8$

Therefore, the distance is $(4.8)(95) \approx 456$ miles.

30. Let the location of Oklahoma City be represented by (2, −2.2) and the lcoation of Des Moines be represented by (4, 2.5).

$d = \sqrt{(4-2)^2 + (2.5+2.2)^2} \approx 5.1$

Therefore, the distance is $(5.1)(95) \approx 485$ miles.

31. $d = \sqrt{(0-24)^2 + (-1-31)^2} = \sqrt{576+1024} = \sqrt{1600} = 40$ feet

32.

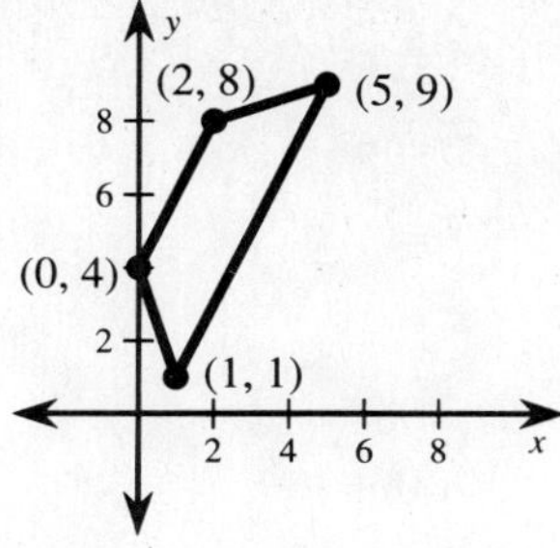

$$m = \frac{4-8}{0-2} = \frac{-4}{-2} = 2 \qquad m = \frac{9-1}{5-1} = \frac{8}{4} = 2$$

$$d_1 = \sqrt{(1-0)^2 + (1-4)^2} = \sqrt{1+9} = \sqrt{10}$$

$$d_2 = \sqrt{(5-2)^2 + (9-8)^2} = \sqrt{9+1} = \sqrt{10}$$

$m = 2,\ d = \sqrt{10}$

33.

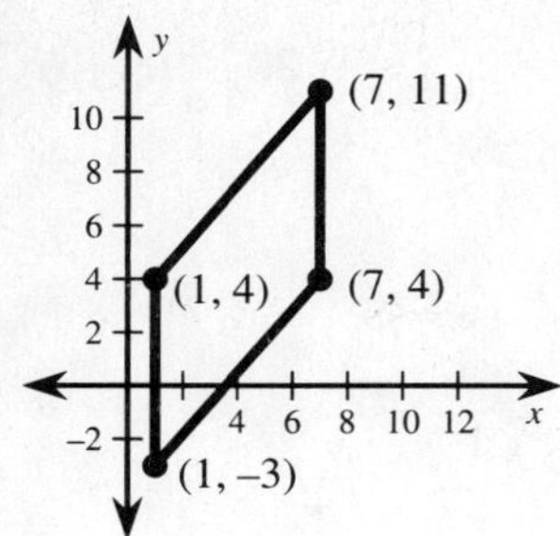

$$d_1 = \sqrt{(1-1)^2 + (-3-4)^2} = \sqrt{49} = 7$$

$$d_3 = \sqrt{(7-7)^2 + (11-4)^2} = \sqrt{49} = 7$$

$d_1 = d_3$

$$d_2 = \sqrt{(1-7)^2 + (4-11)^2} = \sqrt{36+49} = \sqrt{85}$$

$$d_4 = \sqrt{(1-7)^2 + (-3-4)^2} = \sqrt{36+49} = \sqrt{85}$$

$d_2 = d_4$

34.

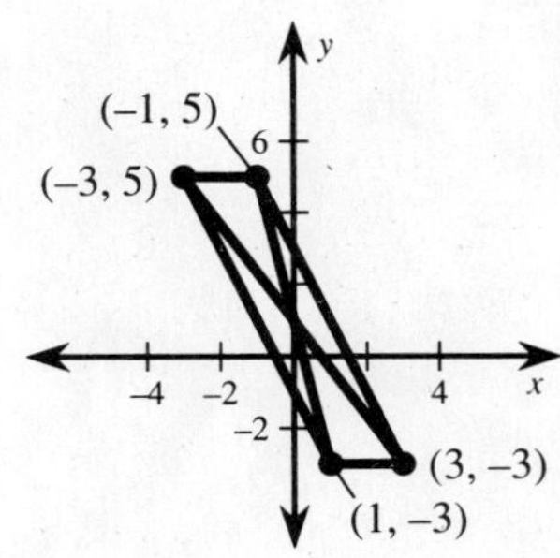

$$\left(\frac{-1+1}{2}, \frac{5-3}{2}\right) = (0, 1)$$

$$\left(\frac{-3+3}{2}, \frac{5-3}{2}\right) = (0, 1)$$

Midpoints are the same, (0, 1).

35. $\sqrt{4^2 + 9^2} = \sqrt{16+81} = \sqrt{97}$

36. $13^2 - 6^2 = 169 - 36 = 133$

37. $(4-2)^2 + (-2+3)^2 = 2^2 + 1^2 = 4 + 1 = 5$

38. $\sqrt{1^2 + 6^2} = \sqrt{1 + 36}$
$= \sqrt{37}$

39. $10^2 + b^2 = 26^2$
$b^2 = 676 - 100$
$b^2 = 576$
$b = 24$

40. $8^2 + 6^2 = c^2$
$c^2 = 64 + 36$
$c^2 = 100$
$c = 10$

41. $a^2 + 11^2 = 61^2$
$a^2 = 3721 - 121$
$a^2 = 3600$
$a = 60$

42. $24^2 + 7^2 = c^2$
$c^2 = 576 + 49$
$c^2 = 625$
$c = 25$

43. $m = \dfrac{1 - 11}{3 - 2}$
$= \dfrac{-10}{1}$
$= -10$

$1 = -10(3) + b$
$b = 31$

$y = -10x + 31$

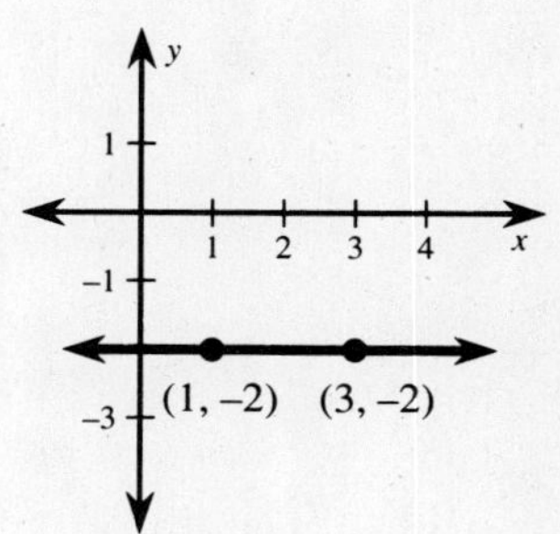

44. $m = \dfrac{6 - 3}{-1 - 5}$
$= \dfrac{3}{-6}$
$= -\dfrac{1}{2}$

$6 = -\dfrac{1}{2}(-1) + b$
$b = \dfrac{11}{2}$

$y = -\dfrac{1}{2}x + \dfrac{11}{2}$

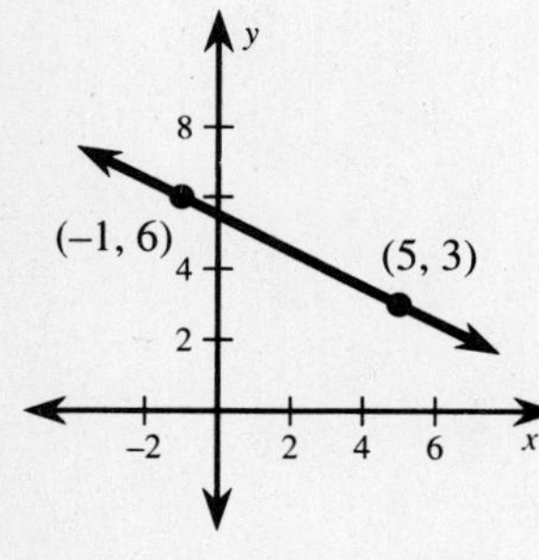

45. $m = \dfrac{-2 - (-2)}{3 - 1}$
$= 0$

$y - (-2) = 0(x - 1)$
$y + 2 = 0$
$y = -2$

46. $m = \dfrac{2-0}{9+1}$ $\quad 2 = \dfrac{1}{5}(9) + b$

$= \dfrac{2}{10}$ $\quad b = \dfrac{1}{5}$

$= \dfrac{1}{5}$

$y = \dfrac{1}{5}x + \dfrac{1}{5}$

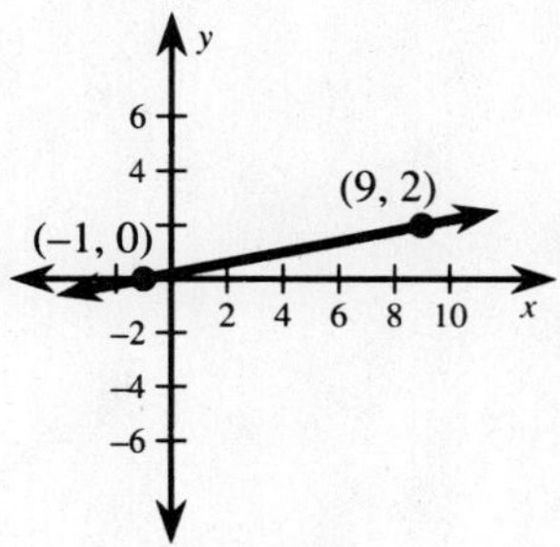

47. $m = \dfrac{7+4}{2-6}$ $\quad 7 = -\dfrac{11}{4}(2) + b$

$= -\dfrac{11}{4}$ $\quad b = \dfrac{25}{2}$

$y = -\dfrac{11}{4}x + \dfrac{25}{2}$

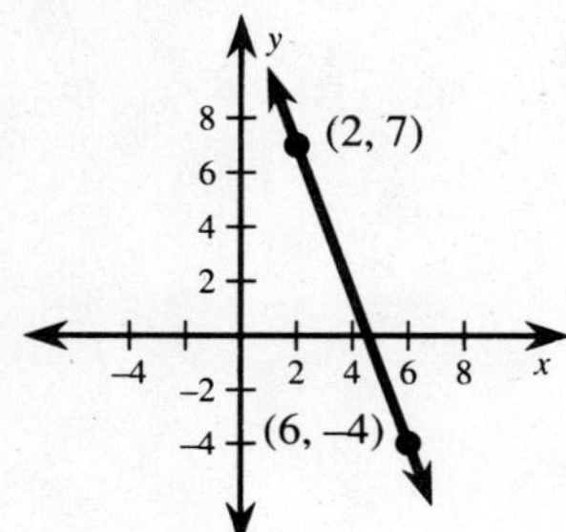

48. $m = \dfrac{-5-0}{8-8}$

$= \dfrac{-5}{-0}$ undefined

$x = 8$

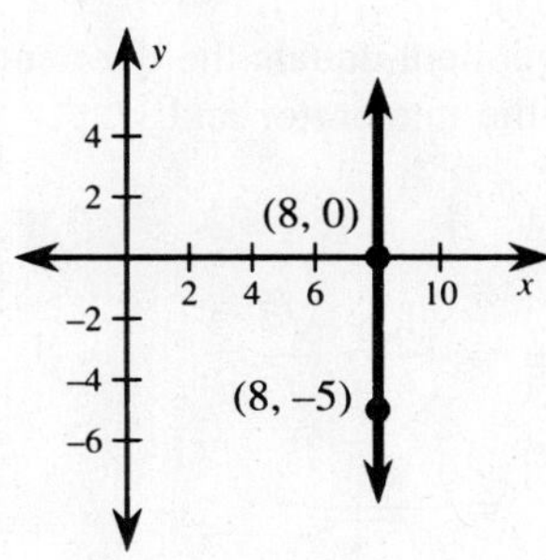

49. $s = \dfrac{12+16+20}{2}$

$= 24$

area $= \sqrt{24(24-12)(24-16)(24-20)}$

$= \sqrt{24(12)(8)(4)}$

$= \sqrt{9216}$

$= 96$

50. $\sqrt{(-16+11)^2 + (6-18)^2} = \sqrt{25+144}$

$= \sqrt{169}$

$= 13$

$\sqrt{(-11-16)^2 + (18+18)^2} = \sqrt{729+1296}$

$= \sqrt{2025}$

$= 45$

$\sqrt{(16+16)^2 + (-18-6)^2} = \sqrt{1024+576}$

$= \sqrt{1600}$

$= 40$

$s = \dfrac{13+45+40}{2}$

$= \dfrac{98}{2}$

$= 49$

area $= \sqrt{49(49-13)(49-45)(49-40)}$

$= \sqrt{49 \cdot 36 \cdot 4 \cdot 9}$

$= \sqrt{63{,}504}$

$= 252$

13.2 Simplifying Radicals

Communicating about Algebra

A. $r_1, r_2, r_4, r_5, r_6, r_9, r_{10}, r_{12}, r_{13}$, and r_{14} are simplified.

$r_0 = 1$

$r_3 = 2$

$r_7 = 2\sqrt{2}$

$r_8 = 3$

$r_{11} = 2\sqrt{3}$

$r_{15} = 4$

B. $A_n = \frac{1}{2}(1)(r_{n-1})$

C.
$$\frac{A_8}{A_7} = \frac{\left(\frac{1}{2}\right)(1)(r_7)}{\left(\frac{1}{2}\right)(1)(r_6)} = \frac{r_7}{r_6} = \frac{2\sqrt{2}}{\sqrt{7}} = \frac{2\sqrt{14}}{7}$$

EXERCISES

1. No radicands have perfect square factors other than the number one.

No radicands contain fractions.

No radicals appear in the denominator of a fraction.

2. The square root of a product equals the product of the square roots of the factors.

3. The square root of a quotient equals the quotient of the square roots of the numerator and denominator.

4. $\sqrt{28} = \sqrt{4 \cdot 7} = \sqrt{4}\sqrt{7} = 2\sqrt{7}$

5. $\sqrt{6} \cdot \sqrt{24} = \sqrt{6 \cdot 24} = \sqrt{144} = 12$

6. $\frac{1}{\sqrt{3}} = \frac{1}{\sqrt{3}} \cdot \frac{\sqrt{3}}{\sqrt{3}} = \frac{\sqrt{3}}{\sqrt{3 \cdot 3}} = \frac{\sqrt{3}}{3}$

7. $\sqrt{40} = 2\sqrt{10}$

8. $\sqrt{18} = 3\sqrt{2}$

9. $\sqrt{48} = 4\sqrt{3}$

10. $\sqrt{75} = 5\sqrt{3}$

11. $\sqrt{\frac{7}{9}} = \frac{\sqrt{7}}{3}$

12. $\sqrt{\frac{11}{16}} = \frac{\sqrt{11}}{4}$

13. $\sqrt{\frac{2}{50}} = \frac{1}{5}$

14. $\sqrt{\frac{20}{12}} = \sqrt{\frac{5}{3}} = \frac{\sqrt{15}}{3}$

15. $\frac{1}{2}\sqrt{80} = 2\sqrt{5}$

16. $\frac{1}{3}\sqrt{27} = \sqrt{3}$

17. $2\sqrt{\frac{5}{4}} = \sqrt{5}$

18. $18\sqrt{\frac{5}{81}} = 2\sqrt{5}$

19. $\sqrt{\frac{1}{12}} = \frac{1}{2\sqrt{3}} = \frac{\sqrt{3}}{6}$

20. $\sqrt{\frac{4}{5}} = \frac{2}{\sqrt{5}} = \frac{2\sqrt{5}}{5}$

21. $2\sqrt{\frac{1}{2}} = \sqrt{2}$

22. $3\sqrt{\frac{5}{6}} = 3\sqrt{\frac{30}{36}} = \frac{\sqrt{30}}{2}$

23. $\sqrt{5}\sqrt{15} = \sqrt{5 \cdot 5 \cdot 3}$
$= 5\sqrt{3}$

24. $\sqrt{10}\sqrt{20} = \sqrt{10 \cdot 10 \cdot 2}$
$= 10\sqrt{2}$

25. $\sqrt{2}\sqrt{6}\sqrt{3} = \sqrt{2 \cdot 2 \cdot 3 \cdot 3}$
$= 6$

26. $\sqrt{2}\sqrt{3}\sqrt{5} = \sqrt{30}$

27. $\left(2\sqrt{13}\right)^2 = 52$

28. $(7\sqrt{3})^2 = 147$

29. $\left(\frac{1}{2}\sqrt{8}\right)^2 = 2$

30. $\left(\frac{2}{3}\sqrt{3}\right)^2 = \frac{4}{3}$

31. $\frac{1}{\sqrt{18}} = \frac{1}{3\sqrt{2}}$
$= \frac{\sqrt{2}}{6}$

32. $\frac{2\sqrt{5}}{\sqrt{4}} = \sqrt{5}$

33. $\frac{\sqrt{6}}{\sqrt{2}} = \sqrt{3}$

34. $\frac{6}{\sqrt{3}} = 2\sqrt{3}$

35. $\sqrt{10} \cdot \sqrt{20} = \sqrt{10 \cdot 10 \cdot 2}$
$= 10\sqrt{2}$

14.14

36. $\frac{1}{2}\sqrt{3} \cdot \sqrt{\frac{27}{2}} = \frac{\sqrt{81}}{2\sqrt{2}}$
$= \frac{9\sqrt{2}}{4}$

3.18

37. $\frac{1}{2}\left(6\sqrt{3}\right)\left(4\sqrt{2}\right) = 12\sqrt{6}$

29.39

38. $\left(7\sqrt{2}\right)^2 = 98$

98

39. $x^2 + \left(\sqrt{2}\right)^2 = \left(\sqrt{20}\right)^2$
$x^2 + 2 = 20$
$x^2 = 18$
$x = \sqrt{18}$
$= 3\sqrt{2}$

40. $x^2 + 2^2 = 8^2$
$x^2 + 4 = 64$
$x^2 = 60$
$x = \sqrt{60}$
$= 2\sqrt{15}$

41. $s = 3.1\sqrt{60}$
$s = 3.1\sqrt{4 \cdot 15}$
$s = 6.2\sqrt{15}$

42. $s = 3.1\sqrt{200}$
$s = 3.1\sqrt{100 \cdot 2}$
$s = 31\sqrt{2}$

43. $\sqrt{\frac{24{,}200}{18\pi^2}} = \sqrt{\frac{12{,}100}{9\pi^2}}$
$= \frac{110}{3\pi}$

44. $d = \sqrt{(1.5 - 0)^2 + (3.7 - 0)^2}$
$= \sqrt{2.25 + 13.69}$
≈ 3.99

The distance from New Castle to Booths Corners is $3.99(3) = 11.97$ miles. Since this distance is greater than the distance from New Castle to the northern boundary of Delaware $\left(\frac{110}{3\pi} \approx 11.67 \text{ miles}\right)$, we conclude that Booths Corner is in Pennsylvania.

45. $d = \sqrt{(-1.6 - 0)^2 + (3.4 - 0)^2}$
$= \sqrt{2.56 + 11.56}$
≈ 3.76

The distance from New Castle to Yorklyn is $3.76(3) = 11.28$ miles. Since this distance is less than the distance from New Castle to the northern boundary of Delaware $\left(\frac{110}{3\pi} \approx 11.67 \text{ miles}\right)$, we conclude that Yorklyn is in Delaware.

46. $d = \sqrt{(2.1-0)^2 + (3-0)^2}$
$= \sqrt{4.41 + 9}$
≈ 3.66

The distance from New Castle to Naamans Garden is $3.66(3) = 10.98$ miles. Since this distance is less than the distance from New Castle to the northern boundary of Delaware $\left(\frac{110}{3\pi} \approx 11.67 \text{ miles}\right)$, we conclude that Naamans Gardens is in Delaware.

47. $f\left(\sqrt{6}\right) = \left(\sqrt{6}\right)^2 - 7$
$= 6 - 7$
$= -1$

48. $f\left(\sqrt{10}\right) = 2\left(\sqrt{10}\right)^2 + 2$
$= 20 + 2$
$= 22$

49. $f(8) = \sqrt{2}\sqrt{8}$
$= \sqrt{16}$
$= 4$

50. $f(12) = \sqrt{3}\sqrt{12}$
$= \sqrt{36}$
$= 6$

51. $f\left(2\sqrt{5}\right) = \left(2\sqrt{5}\right)^2 - 5$
$= 20 - 5$
$= 15$

52. $f\left(4\sqrt{2}\right) = \left(4\sqrt{2}\right)^2 - 10$
$= 32 - 10$
$= 22$

53. $x = \dfrac{-6 \pm \sqrt{6^2 - 4\left(\frac{1}{2}\right)(-6)}}{2\left(\frac{1}{2}\right)}$
$= -6 \pm \sqrt{48}$
$= -6 \pm 4\sqrt{3}$

54. $x = \dfrac{-10 \pm \sqrt{10^2 - 4\left(\frac{1}{2}\right)10}}{2\left(\frac{1}{2}\right)}$
$= -10 \pm \sqrt{80}$
$= -10 \pm 4\sqrt{5}$

55. $x = \dfrac{-2 \pm \sqrt{2^2 - 4(1)(-1)}}{2 \cdot 1}$
$= \dfrac{-2 \pm \sqrt{8}}{2}$
$= \dfrac{-2 \pm 2\sqrt{2}}{2}$
$= -1 \pm \sqrt{2}$

56. $x = \dfrac{-6 \pm \sqrt{6^2 - 4(1)(-6)}}{2 \cdot 1}$
$= \dfrac{-6 \pm \sqrt{60}}{2}$
$= \dfrac{-6 \pm 2\sqrt{15}}{2}$
$= -3 \pm \sqrt{15}$

57. $x = \dfrac{4 \pm \sqrt{(-4)^2 - 4(1)(-5)}}{2 \cdot 1}$
$= \dfrac{4 \pm \sqrt{36}}{2}$
$= \dfrac{4 \pm 6}{2}$
$= 2 \pm 3$

5, -1

58. $x = \dfrac{3 \pm \sqrt{(-3)^2 - 4(1)(-4)}}{2 \cdot 1}$
$= \dfrac{3 \pm \sqrt{25}}{2}$
$= \dfrac{3 \pm 5}{2}$

4, -1

59. $\dfrac{B}{G} = \dfrac{2\left(\frac{1}{2}\right)\sqrt{5}\sqrt{10}}{\sqrt{10}\sqrt{10}}$
$= \dfrac{5\sqrt{2}}{10}$
$= \dfrac{\sqrt{2}}{2}$

60. $\dfrac{B}{G} = \dfrac{\frac{1}{2}\left(\sqrt{3} + 2\sqrt{3}\right)\sqrt{3}}{\frac{1}{2}\sqrt{3}\sqrt{3}}$
$= \dfrac{3\sqrt{3} \cdot \sqrt{3}}{3}$
$= 3$

61. $d = \sqrt{\left(0 - \sqrt{12}\right)^2 + (9-3)^2}$
$= \sqrt{12 + 36}$
$= \sqrt{48}$
$= 4\sqrt{3}$

62. $d = \sqrt{\left(\sqrt{5} - 0\right)^2 + (5-10)^2}$
$= \sqrt{5 + 25}$
$= \sqrt{30}$

63. $T = 2\pi\sqrt{\frac{1}{32}}$
$= 2\pi\sqrt{\frac{2}{64}}$
$= 2\pi\frac{\sqrt{2}}{8}$
$= \frac{\pi\sqrt{2}}{4}$

64. When one is set in motion, its partner does *not* begin to move.

Mixed REVIEW

1. $(x + 7)(x + 1)$

2. No factors

3. $x = \frac{6 \pm \sqrt{36 + 80}}{8}$
$= \frac{6 \pm 2\sqrt{29}}{8}$
$= \frac{3 \pm \sqrt{29}}{4}$

4. $x = \frac{-5 \pm \sqrt{25 - 8}}{2}$
$= \frac{-5 \pm \sqrt{17}}{2}$

5. $f(6) = 3 \cdot 6 + 2$
$= 18 + 2$
$= 20$

6. $f(0) = 300(1.07)^0$
$= 300$

7. 4.23×10^9

8. 2.6×10^{-3}

9. $x^2 + y^2 = 3^2 + 4^2$
$= 9 + 16$
$= 25 \neq 5$
(3, 4) is not a solution.

10. $4 \cdot 3^{-2} = \frac{4}{9} < 3$
(2, 3) is a solution.

11.

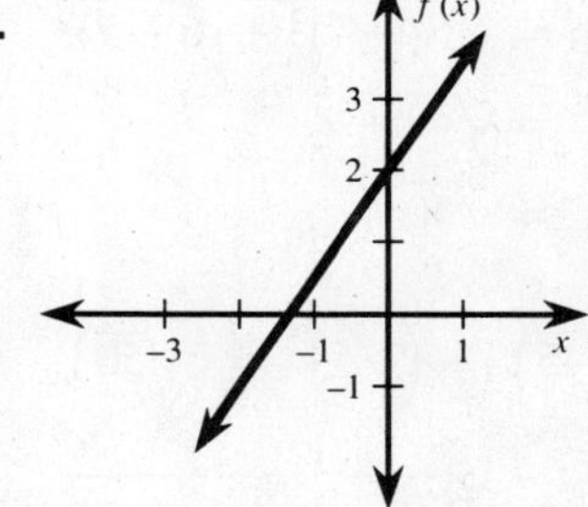

12. Vertex (3, −16)

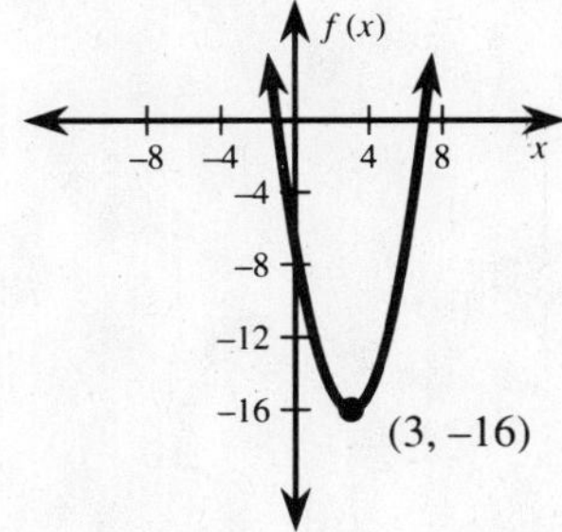

13. $\frac{1}{x} + \frac{x}{5} = \frac{6}{5}$
$5 + x^2 = 6x$
$x^2 - 6x + 5 = 0$
$(x - 1)(x - 5) = 0$
$x = 1$ or $x = 5$

14. $\frac{1}{y} + \frac{3}{5} = \frac{2}{y}$
$5 + 3y = 10$
$3y = 5$
$y = \frac{5}{3}$

15. $-(3x^2 - 2) = -3x^2 + 2$

16. $2x^{-2}y$

17. $3m^4$

18. $\dfrac{4x^2z^4}{y^3} \div \dfrac{6x^4y}{z^2} = \dfrac{4x^2z^4}{y^3} \cdot \dfrac{z^2}{6x^4y}$

$= \dfrac{2z^6}{3x^2y^4}$

19. $\begin{bmatrix} 3 & 4 \\ -2a & b \end{bmatrix} + \begin{bmatrix} 2b & 3 \\ 4 & 2b \end{bmatrix} = \begin{bmatrix} 3+2b & 7 \\ 4-2a & 3b \end{bmatrix}$

20. $\begin{bmatrix} 7 & 9 \\ 6 & -4 \end{bmatrix} - \begin{bmatrix} 3 & 6 \\ -2 & 5 \end{bmatrix} = \begin{bmatrix} 4 & 3 \\ 8 & -9 \end{bmatrix}$

13.3 Operations with Radicals

Communicating about Algebra

A. See graph on page 690.

B. $d_{AE} = \sqrt{(0-6)^2 + (6-9)^2}$
$= \sqrt{36+9}$
$= \sqrt{45}$

$d_{AB} = \sqrt{(0-2)^2 + (6-2)^2}$
$= \sqrt{4+16}$
$= \sqrt{20}$

$d_{BE} = \sqrt{(6-2)^2 + (9-2)^2}$
$= \sqrt{16+49}$
$= \sqrt{65}$

$(\sqrt{45})^2 + (\sqrt{20})^2 = \left(\sqrt{65}\right)^2$

$d_{AD} = \sqrt{(0-7)^2 + (6-7)^2}$
$= \sqrt{49+1}$
$= \sqrt{50}$

$d_{DE} = \sqrt{(7-6)^2 + (7-9)^2}$
$= \sqrt{1+4}$
$= \sqrt{5}$

$\left(\sqrt{45}\right)^2 + \left(\sqrt{5}\right)^2 = \left(\sqrt{50}\right)^2$

$d_{BC} = \sqrt{(2-4)^2 + (2-1)^2}$
$= \sqrt{4+1}$
$= \sqrt{5}$

$d_{CD} = \sqrt{(4-7)^2 + (1-7)^2}$
$= \sqrt{9+36}$
$= \sqrt{45}$

$d_{BD} = \sqrt{(2-7)^2 + (2-7)^2}$
$= \sqrt{25+25}$
$= \sqrt{50}$

$\left(\sqrt{5}\right)^2 + \left(\sqrt{45}\right)^2 = \left(\sqrt{50}\right)^2$

C. Area $= \frac{1}{2}(d_{AB} + d_{DE})(d_{AE}) + \frac{1}{2}(d_{BC})(d_{CD})$
$= \frac{1}{2}\left(\sqrt{20} + \sqrt{5}\right)\left(\sqrt{45}\right) + \frac{1}{2}\left(\sqrt{5}\right)\left(\sqrt{45}\right)$
$= \frac{1}{2}\left(\sqrt{45}\right)\left(\sqrt{45}\right) + \frac{1}{2}(15)$
$= \frac{45}{2} + \frac{15}{2}$
$= \frac{60}{2}$
$= 30$ square units or 6750 square feet

EXERCISES

1. Like: $3\sqrt{5},\ \sqrt{5}$
Unlike: $2\sqrt{5},\ \sqrt{2}$

2. $\sqrt{2},\ 3\sqrt{2}$

3. $3\sqrt{6}+\sqrt{24} = 3\sqrt{6}+2\sqrt{6}$
$= 5\sqrt{6}$

4. $\sqrt{72}-5\sqrt{2} = 6\sqrt{2}-5\sqrt{2}$
$= \sqrt{2}$

5. $\sqrt{3}\left(5\sqrt{3}-2\sqrt{6}\right) = 15-6\sqrt{2}$

6. $\left(3+\sqrt{6}\right)^2 - 6\left(3+\sqrt{6}\right)+3 = 9+6\sqrt{6}+6-18-6\sqrt{6}+3$
$= 0$

$3+\sqrt{6}$ is a solution.

7. $4\sqrt{7}+3\sqrt{7} = 7\sqrt{7}$

8. $\sqrt{5}+3\sqrt{5} = 4\sqrt{5}$

9. $9\sqrt{3}-12\sqrt{3} = -3\sqrt{3}$

10. $2\sqrt{6}-\sqrt{6} = \sqrt{6}$

11. $\sqrt{2}+\sqrt{18} = \sqrt{2}+3\sqrt{2}$
$= 4\sqrt{2}$

12. $\sqrt{27}+\sqrt{3} = 3\sqrt{3}+\sqrt{3}$
$= 4\sqrt{3}$

13. $4\sqrt{5}+\sqrt{80}+\sqrt{20} = 4\sqrt{5}+4\sqrt{5}+2\sqrt{5}$
$= 10\sqrt{5}$

14. $5\sqrt{5}+\sqrt{405}+\sqrt{5} = 5\sqrt{5}+9\sqrt{5}+\sqrt{5}$
$= 15\sqrt{5}$

15. $\sqrt{44}-2\sqrt{11} = 2\sqrt{11}-2\sqrt{11}$
$= 0$

16. $\sqrt{72}-9\sqrt{2} = 6\sqrt{2}-9\sqrt{2}$
$= -3\sqrt{2}$

17. $\sqrt{20}-\sqrt{45}+\sqrt{5} = 2\sqrt{5}-3\sqrt{5}+\sqrt{5}$
$= 0$

18. $\sqrt{243}+\sqrt{75}-\sqrt{300} = 9\sqrt{3}+5\sqrt{3}-10\sqrt{3}$
$= 4\sqrt{3}$

19. $\sqrt{3}\left(3\sqrt{2}+\sqrt{3}\right) = 3\sqrt{6}+3$

20. $\sqrt{6}\left(5\sqrt{2}+6\right) = 10\sqrt{3}+6\sqrt{6}$

21. $\left(\sqrt{5}+4\right)^2 = 5+8\sqrt{5}+16$
$= 21+8\sqrt{5}$

22. $\left(2\sqrt{3}-5\right)^2 = 12-20\sqrt{3}+25$
$= 37-20\sqrt{3}$

23. $\left(\sqrt{2}+4\right)\left(1-5\sqrt{2}\right) = \sqrt{2}-10+4-20\sqrt{2}$
$= -6-19\sqrt{2}$

24. $\left(\sqrt{7}+3\right)\left(\sqrt{7}-3\right) = 7-3\sqrt{7}+3\sqrt{7}-9$
$= -2$

25. Area $= \left(\sqrt{17}+9\right)\left(\sqrt{68}\right)$
$= \left(\sqrt{17}+9\right)\left(2\sqrt{17}\right)$
$= 34+18\sqrt{17}$

Perimeter $= 2\left(\sqrt{17}+9+2\sqrt{17}\right)$
$= 6\sqrt{17}+18$

26. Area $= \frac{1}{2}\left(\sqrt{99}+2\right)\left(\sqrt{44}+12\right)$
$= \frac{1}{2}\left(3\sqrt{11}+2\right)\left(2\sqrt{11}+12\right)$
$= \frac{1}{2}\left(66+36\sqrt{11}+4\sqrt{11}+24\right)$
$= \frac{1}{2}\left(90+40\sqrt{11}\right)$
$= 45+20\sqrt{11}$

27. $f\left(\sqrt{10}\right) = \left(\sqrt{10}\right)^2 + 5\left(\sqrt{10}\right) - 4$
$= 6 + 5\sqrt{10}$

28. $f\left(2\sqrt{3}\right) = \left(2\sqrt{3}\right)^2 - 2\sqrt{3} - 6$
$= 6 - 2\sqrt{3}$

29. $\left(2 - \sqrt{19}\right)^2 - 4\left(2 - \sqrt{19}\right) - 15 = 4 - 4\sqrt{19} + 19 - 8 + 4\sqrt{19} - 15$
$= 0$

$2 - \sqrt{19}$ is a solution.

30. $2\left(-4 + \sqrt{106}\right)^2 + 16\left(-4 + \sqrt{106}\right) - 21 = 2\left(16 - 8\sqrt{106} + 106\right) - 64 + 16\sqrt{106} - 21$
$= 32 - 16\sqrt{106} + 212 - 64 + 16\sqrt{106} - 21$
$= 159$

$-4 + \sqrt{106}$ is not a solution.

31. $d_{AB} = \sqrt{(0+2)^2 + (0-2)^2}$
$= \sqrt{4+4}$
$= \sqrt{8}$
$= 2\sqrt{2}$

$d_{BC} = \sqrt{(-2+2)^2 + (2-4)^2}$
$= \sqrt{0+4}$
$= \sqrt{4}$
$= 2$

$d_{CD} = \sqrt{(-2-0)^2 + (4-6)^2}$
$= \sqrt{4+4}$
$= \sqrt{8}$
$= 2\sqrt{2}$

$d_{DE} = \sqrt{(0-2)^2 + (6-6)^2}$
$= \sqrt{4+0}$
$= \sqrt{4}$
$= 2$

$d_{EF} = \sqrt{(2-7)^2 + (6-1)^2}$
$= \sqrt{25+25}$
$= \sqrt{50}$
$= 5\sqrt{2}$

$d_{FG} = \sqrt{(7-7)^2 + (1+1)^2}$
$= \sqrt{0+4}$
$= \sqrt{4}$
$= 2$

$d_{GH} = \sqrt{(7-5)^2 + (-1+1)^2}$
$= \sqrt{4+0}$
$= \sqrt{4}$
$= 2$

$d_{HI} = \sqrt{(5-3)^2 + (-1-1)^2}$
$= \sqrt{4+4}$
$= \sqrt{8}$
$= 2\sqrt{2}$

$d_{IJ} = \sqrt{(3-1)^2 + (1-1)^2}$
$= \sqrt{4+0}$
$= \sqrt{4}$
$= 2$

$d_{JA} = \sqrt{(1-0)^2 + (1-0)^2}$
$= \sqrt{1+1}$
$= \sqrt{2}$

Perimeter $= 2\left(2\sqrt{2} + 2 + 2\sqrt{2} + 2 + 5\sqrt{2} + 2 + 2 + 2\sqrt{2} + 2 + \sqrt{2}\right)$
$= 2\left(12\sqrt{2} + 10\right)$
$= 24\sqrt{2} + 20$ feet

32. $\sqrt{(0-5)^2+(8-3)^2} = \sqrt{25+25}$ $\quad P_1 = 8+5+3+5\sqrt{2}$

$= 5\sqrt{2}$ $\quad = 16+5\sqrt{2}$

$\sqrt{(0-5)^2+(10-5)^2} = \sqrt{25+25}$ $\quad P_2 = 5\sqrt{2}+5+5+10$

$= 5\sqrt{2}$ $\quad = 20+5\sqrt{2}$

$\sqrt{(11-16)^2+(5-10)^2} = \sqrt{25+25}$ $\quad P_3 = 5+5+5\sqrt{2}$

$= 5\sqrt{2}$ $\quad = 10+5\sqrt{2}$

$\sqrt{(8-18)^2+(0-10)^2} = \sqrt{100+100}$

$= 10\sqrt{2}$

$\sqrt{(15-20)^2+(0-5)^2} = \sqrt{25+25}$ $\quad P_4 = 7+5\sqrt{2}+2+5+10\sqrt{2}$

$= 5\sqrt{2}$ $\quad = 14+15\sqrt{2}$

Total perimeter of all 4 pieces $= 16+5\sqrt{2}+20+5\sqrt{2}+10+5\sqrt{2}+14+15\sqrt{2}$

$= 60+30\sqrt{2}$

Perimeter of T = 60. To find the area of all four pieces, count the squares in the assembled T.

33.

Year	Number of Households (in millions)	Increase from previous year
1970	≈ 63.07	–
1971	≈ 64.95	1.88
1972	≈ 66.78	1.83
1973	≈ 68.56	1.78

34.

Week	Number Sold
1	7
2	12
3	15
4	18
5	21
6	23
7	25
8	27
9	29
10	30

Week	Number Sold
11	32
12	33
13	35
14	36
15	37
16	39
17	40
18	41
19	42
20	43

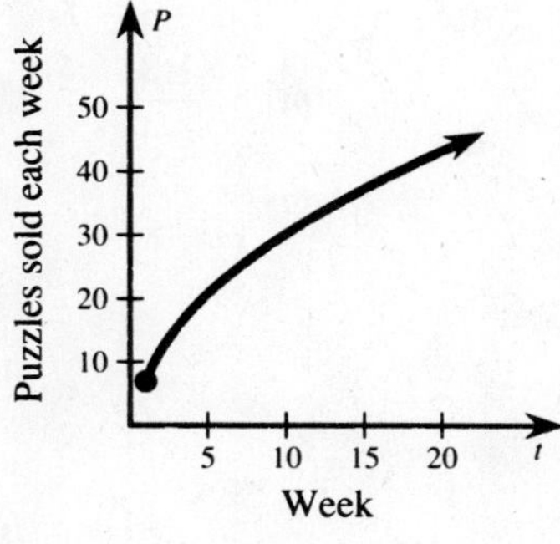

Total sold $= 585$

$(585)4 = 2340$

Profit $=$ \$2340.00

35. $\sqrt{(8-5)^2 + \left(\sqrt{5} - 6\sqrt{5}\right)^2} = \sqrt{9 + 125}$

$= \sqrt{134}$

36. $\sqrt{\left(6\sqrt{2} - \sqrt{2}\right)^2 + (5-3)^2} = \sqrt{50 + 4}$

$= \sqrt{54}$

$= 3\sqrt{6}$

37. $\sqrt{\left(\sqrt{2} + 2\sqrt{2}\right)^2 + (3-2)^2} = \sqrt{18 + 1}$

$= \sqrt{19}$

38. $\sqrt{(3-4)^2 + \left(\sqrt{3} - 4\sqrt{3}\right)^2} = \sqrt{1 + 27}$

$= \sqrt{28}$

$= 2\sqrt{7}$

39. $\sqrt{4+5} + \sqrt{4} = \sqrt{9} + \sqrt{4}$

$= 3 + 2$

$= 5$

4 is a solution.

40. $\sqrt{-2+6} + \sqrt{14-(-2)} = \sqrt{4} + \sqrt{16}$

$= 2 + 4$

$= 6$

-2 is not a solution.

41. $\dfrac{\sqrt{243} \times 10^4}{\sqrt{27} \times 10^{-2}} = 3 \times 10^6$

42. $\dfrac{\sqrt{112} \times 10^{-1}}{2\sqrt{7} \times 10^3} = 2 \times 10^{-4}$

43. **e.**

44. $\sqrt{(-3-1)^2 + (-4-4)^2} = \sqrt{16 + 64}$

$= \sqrt{80}$

$= 4\sqrt{5}$

$\sqrt{(1-5)^2 + (4-2)^2} = \sqrt{16 + 4}$

$= \sqrt{20}$

$= 2\sqrt{5}$

$\sqrt{(-3-5)^2 + (-4-2)^2} = \sqrt{64 + 36}$

$= \sqrt{100}$

$= 10$

$\left(4\sqrt{5}\right)^2 + \left(2\sqrt{5}\right)^2 = 10^2$

$m_1 = \dfrac{-4-4}{-3-1}$

$m_1 = \dfrac{-8}{-4}$

$m_1 = 2$

$m_2 = \dfrac{4-2}{1-5}$

$m_2 = \dfrac{2}{-4}$

$m_2 = -\dfrac{1}{2}$

$m_1 \cdot m_2 = -1$

45. $\sqrt{(1+5)^2+(-7-1)^2} = \sqrt{36+64}$
$= \sqrt{100}$
$= 10$

$\sqrt{(-5+2)^2+(1-2)^2} = \sqrt{9+1}$
$= \sqrt{10}$

$\sqrt{(1+2)^2+(-7-2)^2} = \sqrt{9+81}$
$= \sqrt{90}$
$= 3\sqrt{10}$

$\left(\sqrt{10}\right)^2 + \left(3\sqrt{10}\right)^2 = 10^2$

$m_1 = \frac{-7-2}{1+2}$
$m_1 = \frac{-9}{3}$
$m_1 = -3$

$m_2 = \frac{1-2}{-5+2}$
$m_2 = \frac{-1}{-3}$
$m_2 = \frac{1}{3}$

$m_1 \bullet m_2 = -1$

46. The slope of the shortest path is $-\frac{3}{5}$.

$y - 7 = -\frac{3}{5}(x+4)$
$y = -\frac{3}{5}x - \frac{12}{5} + 7$
$y = -\frac{3}{5}x - \frac{12}{5} + \frac{35}{5}$
$y = -\frac{3}{5}x + \frac{23}{5}$

$$\begin{cases} y = \frac{5}{3}x \\ y = -\frac{3}{5}x + \frac{23}{5} \end{cases}$$

$\frac{5}{3}x = -\frac{3}{5}x + \frac{23}{5}$
$\frac{25}{15}x + \frac{9}{15}x = \frac{23}{5}$
$\frac{34}{15}x = \frac{23}{5}$
$x = \frac{69}{34}$

$y = \frac{5}{3}\left(\frac{69}{34}\right)$
$= \frac{115}{34}$

$\left(\frac{69}{34}, \frac{115}{34}\right)$ is the point of intersection of the shoreline and the shortest path.

$d = \sqrt{\left(-4 - \frac{69}{34}\right)^2 + \left(7 - \frac{115}{34}\right)^2}$
$= \sqrt{\left(\frac{-136-69}{34}\right)^2 + \left(\frac{238-115}{34}\right)^2}$
$= \sqrt{\left(-\frac{205}{34}\right)^2 + \left(\frac{123}{34}\right)^2}$
$= \sqrt{\frac{42{,}025}{34^2} + \frac{15{,}129}{34^2}}$
$= \sqrt{\frac{57{,}154}{34^2}}$
$= \frac{41}{34}\sqrt{34}$

The distance between the point of intersection and the point describing your position is $\frac{41}{34}\sqrt{34}$ units.

13.4 Solving Radical Equations

Communicating about Algebra

A. $\sqrt{x} - 5 = 0$ — *Add 5 to both sides.*

$\sqrt{x} = 5$ — *Square both sides.*

$x = 25$

B. $\sqrt{x} + 5 = 0$

$\sqrt{x} = -5$ — *Subtract 5 from both sides.*

$x = 25$ — *Square both sides.*

No solution

C. $\sqrt{3x+4} - 2 = 5$

$\sqrt{3x+4} = 7$ — *Add 2 to both sides.*

$3x + 4 = 49$ — *Square both sides.*

$3x = 45$ — *Subtract 4 from both sides.*

$x = 15$ — *Divide both sides by 3.*

D. $x - 2 = \sqrt{8-x}$

$x^2 - 4x + 4 = 8 - x$ — *Square both sides.*

$x^2 - 3x - 4 = 0$ — *Add $x - 8$ to both sides.*

$(x-4)(x+1) = 0$ — *Factor.*

$x = 4$ or $x = -1$

EXERCISES

1. Isolate the radical, then square both sides.

$\sqrt{2x} - 10 = 0$

$\sqrt{2x} = 10$

$2x = 100$

$x = 50$

2. $\sqrt{25} = 5$

$x = 25$ is not a solution.

It does not check.

3. You could have a false solution.

4. $6 = \sqrt{12 \cdot x}$

$36 = 12x$

$x = 3$

5. $\sqrt{x} - 10 = 0$

$\sqrt{x} = 10$

$x = 100$

6. $\sqrt{x} - 1 = 0$

$\sqrt{x} = 1$

$x = 1$

7. $\sqrt{-x} - \frac{1}{2} = \frac{3}{2}$

$\sqrt{-x} = 2$

$-x = 4$

$x = -4$

8. $\sqrt{3x} - 4 = 6$

$\sqrt{3x} = 10$

$3x = 100$

$x = \frac{100}{3}$

9. $\sqrt{3x+2} + 2 = 3$

$\sqrt{3x+2} = 1$

$3x + 2 = 1$

$3x = -1$

$x = -\frac{1}{3}$

10. $\sqrt{4-x} - 5 = 1$

$\sqrt{4-x} = 6$

$4 - x = 36$

$-x = 32$

$x = -32$

11. $4 = 6 - \sqrt{21x-3}$

$-2 = -\sqrt{21x-3}$

$2 = \sqrt{21x-3}$

$4 = 21x - 3$

$21x = 7$

$x = \frac{1}{3}$

12. $10 = 17 + \sqrt{6x+7}$

$-7 = \sqrt{6x+7}$

No solution

13. $\sqrt{\frac{1}{2}x - 5} - 1 = 11$

$\sqrt{\frac{1}{2}x - 5} = 12$

$\frac{1}{2}x - 5 = 144$

$\frac{1}{2}x = 149$

$x = 298$

14. $\sqrt{\frac{1}{9}x + 1} - \frac{2}{3} = \frac{5}{3}$

$\sqrt{\frac{1}{9}x + 1} = \frac{7}{3}$

$\frac{1}{9}x + 1 = \frac{49}{9}$

$\frac{1}{9}x = \frac{40}{9}$

$x = 40$

15. $-5 - \sqrt{10x - 2} = 5$

$\sqrt{10x - 2} = -10$

No solution

16. $6 - \sqrt{7x - 9} = 3$

$\sqrt{7x - 9} = 3$

$7x - 9 = 9$

$7x = 18$

$x = \frac{18}{7}$

17. $x = \sqrt{20 - x}$

$x^2 = 20 - x$

$x^2 + x - 20 = 0$

$(x + 5)(x - 4) = 0$

$x = -5$ or $x = 4$

$x = 4$

18. $x = \sqrt{6 - x}$

$x^2 = 6 - x$

$x^2 + x - 6 = 0$

$(x + 3)(x - 2) = 0$

$x = -3$ or $x = 2$

$x = 2$

19. $\sqrt{-10x - 4} = 2x$

$-10x - 4 = 4x^2$

$4x^2 + 10x + 4 = 0$

$2(2x^2 + 5x + 2) = 0$

$2(2x + 1)(x + 2) = 0$

$x = -\frac{1}{2}$ or $x = -2$

No solution

20. $x = \sqrt{100 - 15x}$

$x^2 = 100 - 15x$

$x^2 + 15x - 100 = 0$

$(x + 20)(x - 5) = 0$

$x = -20$ or $x = 5$

$x = 5$

21. $\sqrt{77 - 4x} = x$

$77 - 4x = x^2$

$x^2 + 4x - 77 = 0$

$(x + 11)(x - 7) = 0$

$x = -11$ or $x = 7$

$x = 7$

22. $2x = \sqrt{-13x - 10}$

$4x^2 = -13x - 10$

$4x^2 + 13x + 10 = 0$

$(x + 2)(4x + 5) = 0$

$x = -2$ or $x = -\frac{5}{4}$

No solution

23. $\frac{1}{2}x = \sqrt{x + 3}$

$\frac{1}{4}x^2 = x + 3$

$\frac{1}{4}x^2 - x - 3 = 0$

$x^2 - 4x - 12 = 0$

$(x - 6)(x + 2) = 0$

$x = 6$ or $x = -2$

$x = 6$

24. $x = \sqrt{4x + 32}$

$x^2 = 4x + 32$

$x^2 - 4x - 32 = 0$

$(x - 8)(x + 4) = 0$

$x = 8$ or $x = -4$

$x = 8$

25. $a = \sqrt{8 \cdot 32}$

$a = \sqrt{256}$

$a = 16$

26. $a = \sqrt{4 \cdot 32}$

$a = \sqrt{128}$

$a = 8\sqrt{2}$

27. $15 = \sqrt{5 \cdot x}$

$225 = 5x$

$x = 45$

28. $6 = \sqrt{9 \cdot x}$

$36 = 9x$

$x = 4$

29. $10^2 + (x-2)^2 = x^2$

$100 + x^2 - 4x + 4 = x^2$

$-4x = -104$

$x = 26$

30. $7^2 + \left(\sqrt{3}x\right)^2 = (2x)^2$

$49 + 3x^2 = 4x^2$

$x^2 = 49$

$x = 7$

31. $10 = \sqrt{\dfrac{\pi^2(115)(20)}{8F}}$

$100 = \dfrac{\pi^2 575}{2F}$

$F = \dfrac{\pi^2 575}{200}$

$F \approx 28.38$

The person feels approximately 28.38 pounds of centrifugal force.

32. As r decreases, t decreases. The skater spins at a faster rate.

33. $\dfrac{170}{0.5} = 20\sqrt{t+273}$

$115{,}600 = 400(t+273)$

$t + 273 = 289$

$t = 16°\text{C}$

34. $v = 20\sqrt{-273+273}$

$v = 20(0)$

$v = 0$ meters per second

35. $v = \dfrac{3200}{\frac{1}{8}+1}$

$v = \dfrac{3200}{\frac{9}{8}}$

$v = 2844\frac{4}{9}$

The bullet is moving $2844\frac{4}{9}$ feet per second when it hits the target.

36. $\frac{1}{8} = \frac{1}{4}\sqrt{h}$

$\sqrt{h} = \frac{1}{2}$

$h = \frac{1}{4}$

The bullet fell $\frac{1}{4}$ foot before hitting the target.

37. $3 - \sqrt{9} = 3 - 3$

$= 0$

$-3 - \sqrt{9} = -3 - 3$

$= -6$

Solution: $x = 3$

38. $2(2) - \sqrt{16} = 4 - 4$

$= 0$

$2(-2) - \sqrt{16} = -4 - 4$

$= -8$

Solution: $x = 2$

39. $\sqrt{80 - 2(-10)} = \sqrt{80+20}$

$= \sqrt{100}$

$= 10$

$\sqrt{80 - 2(8)} = \sqrt{64}$

$= 8$

Solution: $x = 8$

40. $\sqrt{12 - 11(-12)} = \sqrt{12+132}$

$= \sqrt{144}$

$= 12$

$\sqrt{12 - 11(1)} = \sqrt{1}$

$= 1$

Solution: $x = 1$

41. $4x^2 + 22x + 30 = 0$

$(2x+5)(2x+6) = 0$

$x = -\frac{5}{2}$ or $x = -3$

42. $3x^2 - 4x + 1 = 0$

$(3x - 1)(x - 1) = 0$

$x = \frac{1}{3}$ or $x = 1$

43. $x^2 - 3x - 9 = 0$

$x = \dfrac{3 \pm \sqrt{9 + 36}}{2}$

$x = \dfrac{3}{2} \pm \dfrac{3\sqrt{5}}{2}$

44. $x^2 + 14x - 12 = 0$

$x = \dfrac{-14 \pm \sqrt{196 + 48}}{2}$

$x = -7 \pm \sqrt{61}$

45. $x^2 - 14x + 33 = 0$

$(x - 11)(x - 3) = 0$

$x = 11$ or $x = 3$

46. $10x^2 + \dfrac{5}{8}x - 2 = 0$

$80x^2 + 5x - 16 = 0$

$x = \dfrac{-5 \pm \sqrt{25 + 5120}}{2 \cdot 80}$

$x = \dfrac{-5 \pm \sqrt{5145}}{160}$

$x = -\dfrac{1}{32} \pm \dfrac{7\sqrt{105}}{160}$

47. $x^2 + \frac{5}{3}x + \frac{4}{9} = 0$

$9x^2 + 15x + 4 = 0$

$(3x + 4)(3x + 1) = 0$

$x = -\frac{4}{3}$ or $x = -\frac{1}{3}$

48. $\frac{1}{21}x^2 - \frac{3}{7}x - \frac{10}{21} = 0$

$x^2 - 9x - 10 = 0$

$(x - 10)(x + 1) = 0$

$x = 10$ or $x = -1$

49. $\frac{1}{6}x^2 + \frac{2}{3}x + \frac{1}{3} = 0$

$x^2 + 4x + 2 = 0$

$x = \dfrac{-4 \pm \sqrt{16 - 4(2)}}{2 \cdot 1}$

$x = \dfrac{-4 \pm \sqrt{8}}{2}$

$x = -2 \pm \sqrt{2}$

50. $\frac{1}{4}x^2 + \frac{5}{8}x - 2 = 0$

$2x^2 + 5x - 16 = 0$

$x = \dfrac{-5 \pm \sqrt{25 + 128}}{2 \cdot 2}$

$x = \dfrac{-5 \pm \sqrt{153}}{4}$

51.

	Mercury	Venus	Earth	Mars	Jupiter	Saturn
x^3	0.058	0.378	1.0	3.533	140.852	868.524
y^2	0.058	0.378	1.0	3.538	140.683	867.715

$y^2 = x^3$

$y = \sqrt{x^3}$

Using a Graphing Calculator

1.

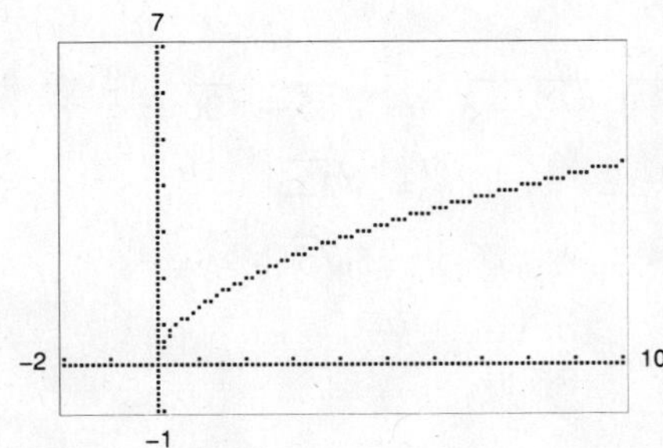

Domain is $x \geq 0$.

2.

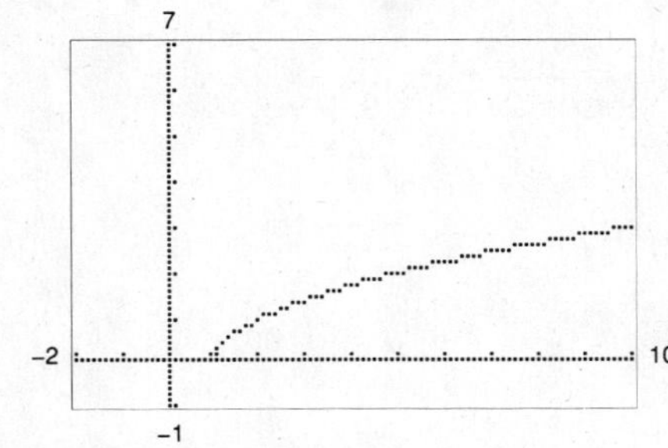

Domain is $x \geq 1$.

3.

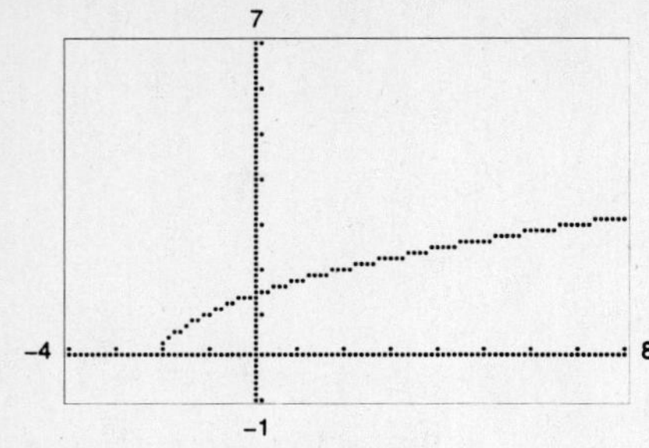

Domain is $x \geq -2$

4.

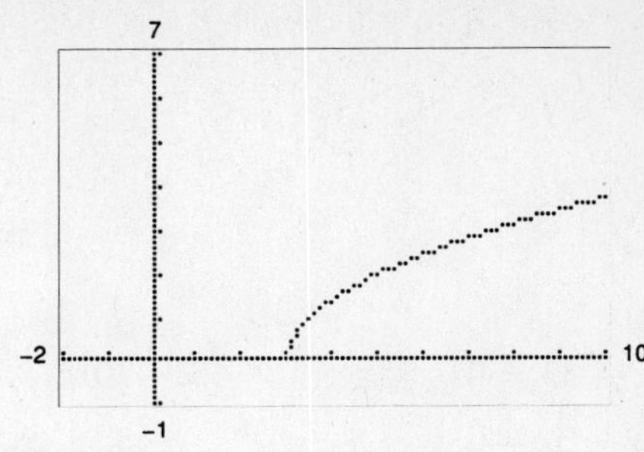

Domain is $x \geq 3$.

5.

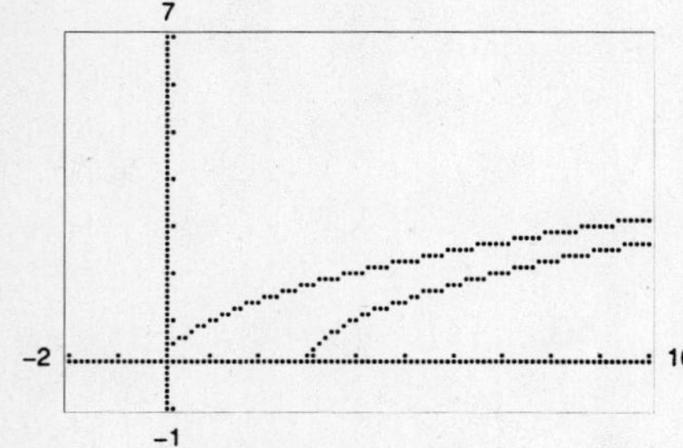

Shifted 3 units to the right

6.

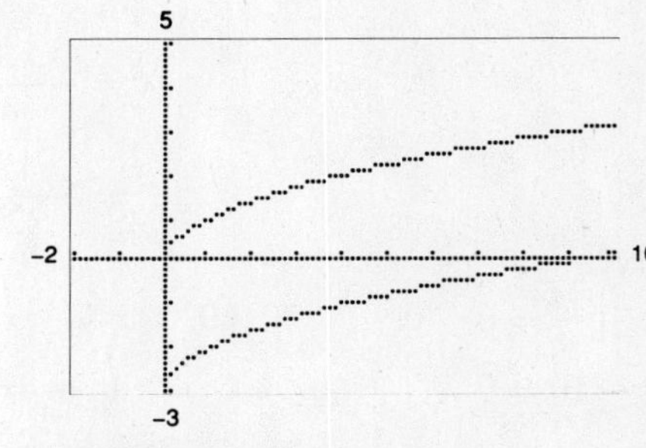

Shifted 3 units down

7.

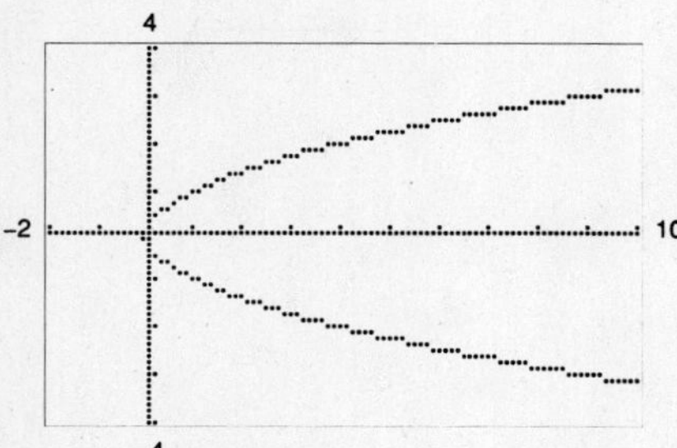

Reflection about the x-axis

8.

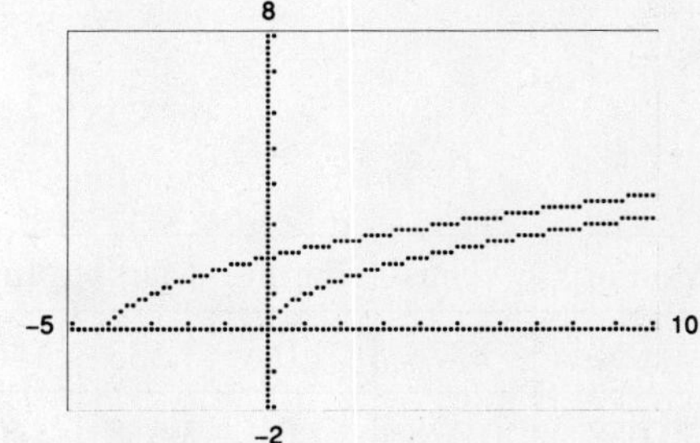

Shifted 4 units to the left

Mid-Chapter SELF-TEST

1. $\sqrt{(4-7)^2+(5-2)^2} = \sqrt{9+9}$
$= \sqrt{18}$
$= 3\sqrt{2}$

2. $\sqrt{(1+4)^2+(-2-8)^2} = \sqrt{25+100}$
$= \sqrt{125}$
$= 5\sqrt{5}$

3. $\sqrt{(3-4)^2+(-2-6)^2} = \sqrt{1+64}$
$= \sqrt{65}$

$\sqrt{(4-11)^2+(6+1)^2} = \sqrt{49+49}$
$= \sqrt{98}$
$= 7\sqrt{2}$

$\sqrt{(3-11)^2+(-2+1)^2} = \sqrt{64+1}$
$= \sqrt{65}$

No, it is not a right triangle.

4. $\sqrt{(1-2)^2+(5-8)^2} = \sqrt{1+9}$
$= \sqrt{10}$

$\sqrt{(2+2)^2+(8-6)^2} = \sqrt{16+4}$
$= \sqrt{20}$
$= 2\sqrt{5}$

$\sqrt{(1+2)^2+(5-6)^2} = \sqrt{9+1}$
$= \sqrt{10}$

$(\sqrt{10})^2 + (\sqrt{10})^2 = (2\sqrt{5})^2$

Yes, it is a right triangle.

5. $\left(\frac{4+5}{2}, \frac{2-6}{2}\right) = \left(\frac{9}{2}, -2\right)$

6. $\left(\frac{0-12}{2}, \frac{10+5}{2}\right) = \left(-6, \frac{15}{2}\right)$

7. $\sqrt{98} = 7\sqrt{2}$

8. $\sqrt{432} = 12\sqrt{3}$

9. $\sqrt{\frac{5}{36}} = \frac{\sqrt{5}}{6}$

10. $\sqrt{\frac{7}{20}} = \frac{\sqrt{7}}{2\sqrt{5}}$
$= \frac{\sqrt{35}}{10}$

11. $5\sqrt{3}+\sqrt{3}-\sqrt{2} = 6\sqrt{3}-\sqrt{2}$

12. $3\sqrt{3}\left(4\sqrt{3}+\sqrt{6}\right) = 36+9\sqrt{2}$

13. $\sqrt{2}\left(8\sqrt{2}-2\sqrt{10}\right) = 16-4\sqrt{5}$

14. $\left(2\sqrt{3}-3\right)^2 = 12-12\sqrt{3}+9$
$= 21-12\sqrt{3}$

15. $\sqrt{x}-3=0$
$\sqrt{x}=3$
$x=9$

16. $\sqrt{3x-2}-6=0$
$\sqrt{3x-2}=6$
$3x-2=36$
$3x=38$
$x=\frac{38}{3}$

17. $x = \sqrt{5x+6}$
$x^2 = 5x+6$
$x^2-5x-6=0$
$(x-6)(x+1)=0$
$x=6$ or $x=-1$

$x=6$

18. $x = \sqrt{-3x+4}$
$x^2 = -3x+4$
$x^2+3x-4=0$
$(x+4)(x-1)=0$
$x=-4$ or $x=1$

$x=1$

19. $a = \sqrt{4 \cdot 9}$
$a = \sqrt{36}$
$a = 6$

20. $8 = \sqrt{32a}$
$64 = 32a$
$a = 2$

21. $\sqrt{(-1+4)^2+(-2-4)^2} = \sqrt{9+36}$
$= \sqrt{45}$
$= 3\sqrt{5}$
$\sqrt{(-4+2)^2+(4-5)^2} = \sqrt{4+1}$
$= \sqrt{5}$
$\sqrt{(-2-4)^2+(5-2)^2} = \sqrt{36+9}$
$= \sqrt{45}$
$= 3\sqrt{5}$
$\sqrt{(4-3)^2+(2-0)^2} = \sqrt{1+4}$
$= \sqrt{5}$
$\sqrt{(3+1)^2+(0+2)^2} = \sqrt{16+4}$
$= \sqrt{20}$
$= 2\sqrt{5}$

Perimeter $= 10\sqrt{5}$

22. Area $= \left(\sqrt{3}+2\sqrt{2}\right)\sqrt{6}$
$= \sqrt{18}+2\sqrt{12}$
$= 3\sqrt{2}+4\sqrt{3}$

Perimeter $= 2\left(\sqrt{3}+2\sqrt{2}\right)+2\sqrt{6}$
$= 2\sqrt{3}+4\sqrt{2}+2\sqrt{6}$

23. $\left(\dfrac{-79-15}{2}, \dfrac{68+112}{2}\right) = (-47, 90)$

24. $d = \sqrt{(43+245)^2+(0+285)^2}$
$= \sqrt{164{,}169}$
≈ 405.2

Yes, it is a home run.

13.5 The Tangent of an Angle

Communicating about Algebra

A. Solve $\tan 50° = \dfrac{a}{10}$ for a, substitute for a in $a^2 + 10^2 = c^2$, and solve for c.

B. Solve $\tan 40° = \dfrac{10}{b}$ for b, substitute for b in $10^2 + b^2 = c^2$ and solve for c.

C. Solve $a^2 + b^2 = 2^2$ for a in terms of b, substitute for a in $\tan 45° = \dfrac{a}{b}$ and solve for b, substitute for b in $a^2 + b^2 = 2^2$ and solve for a.

EXERCISES

1. An acute angle is an angle whose measure is greater than 0° and less than 90°.

2. $\tan A = \frac{14}{25}$

3. $\tan 28° = \dfrac{8}{b}$
$b \approx 15$
$8^2 + 15^2 = c^2$
$c = 17$

4. 0.70

5. $\tan A = \frac{4}{5}$

$\tan B = \frac{5}{4}$

6. $a^2 = 25 - 16$

$a = 3$

$\tan A = \frac{3}{4}$

$\tan B = \frac{4}{3}$

7. $b^2 = 100 - 25$

$b = 5\sqrt{3}$

$\tan A = \dfrac{\sqrt{3}}{3}$

$\tan B = \sqrt{3}$

8. $\tan A \approx 0.87$

$\tan B \approx 1.15$

9. $\tan A \approx 0.36$

$\tan B \approx 2.75$

10. $\tan A \approx 1.88$

$\tan B \approx 0.53$

11. 0.21

12. 1.11

13. 9.51

14. 0.46

15. 0.03

16. 2.08

17. $\dfrac{2}{3} = \dfrac{8}{b}$

$2b = 24$

$b = 12$

$8^2 + 12^2 = c^2$

$c^2 = 208$

$c \approx 14.42$

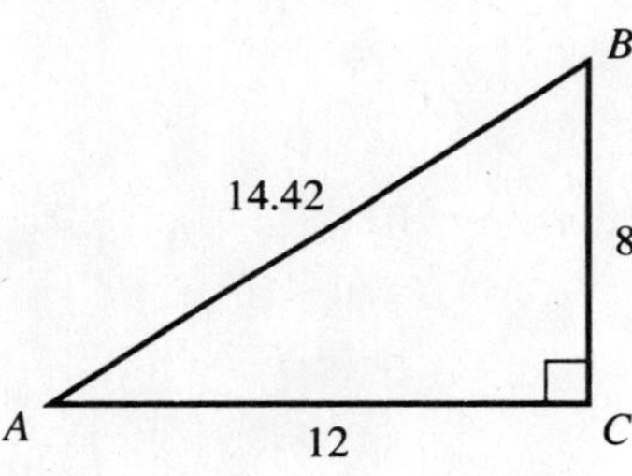

18. $\dfrac{7}{2} = \dfrac{a}{3}$

$2a = 21$

$a = \dfrac{21}{2}$

$\left(\dfrac{21}{2}\right)^2 + 3^2 = c^2$

$c^2 = \dfrac{477}{4}$

$c \approx 10.92$

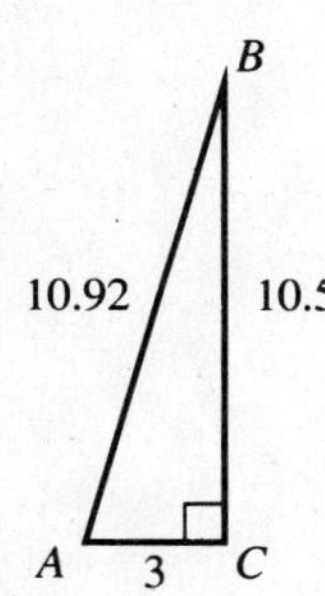

19. $\tan 38° = \dfrac{10}{b}$

$b \approx 12.8$

$10^2 + (12.8)^2 = c^2$

$c \approx 16.2$

$38° + B = 90°$

$B = 52°$

20. $\tan 59° = \dfrac{20}{b}$

$b \approx 12.0$

$20^2 + 12^2 = c^2$

$c \approx 23.3$

$59° + B = 90°$

$B = 31°$

21. $\tan 21° = \dfrac{a}{12}$

$a \approx 4.6$

$(4.6)^2 + 12^2 = c^2$

$c \approx 12.9$

$21° + B = 90°$

$B = 69°$

22. $\tan 63° = \dfrac{19}{a}$

$a \approx 9.7$

$(9.7)^2 + 19^2 = c^2$

$c \approx 21.3$

$A + 63° = 90°$

$A = 27°$

23. $\tan 38° = \dfrac{45}{a}$

$a \approx 57.6$

$(57.6)^2 + 45^2 = c^2$

$c \approx 73.1$

$A + 38° = 90°$

$A = 52°$

24. $\tan 57° = \dfrac{b}{102}$

$b \approx 157.1$

$102^2 + (157.1)^2 = c^2$

$c \approx 187.3$

$A + 57° = 90°$

$A = 33°$

25. $\tan 45° = \frac{b}{a}$

$= \frac{a}{a}$

$= 1$

26. $a^2 + b^2 = c^2$

$\frac{1}{4}c^2 + b^2 = c^2$

$b^2 = \frac{3}{4}c^2$

$b = \frac{\sqrt{3}}{2}c$

$\tan 30° = \frac{a}{b}$

$= \frac{\frac{1}{2}c}{\frac{\sqrt{3}}{2}c}$

$= \frac{\sqrt{3}}{3}$

$\tan 60° = \frac{b}{a}$

$= \frac{\frac{\sqrt{3}}{2}c}{\frac{1}{2}c}$

$= \sqrt{3}$

27. Let x = half the distance between the tips of two consecutive cylinders.

Angle between blades $= \frac{360°}{7}$.

Half of the angle between blades $= \frac{1}{2}\left(\frac{360}{7}\right) = \frac{180}{7}$.

$x^2 + y^2 = (28)^2$

$y = \sqrt{784 - x}$

$\tan\left(\frac{180}{7}\right) = \frac{x}{y}$

$\tan\left(\frac{180}{7}\right) = \frac{x}{\sqrt{784 - x^2}}$

$\sqrt{784 - x^2} = \frac{x}{\left[\tan\left(\frac{180}{7}\right)\right]}$

$784 - x^2 = \frac{x^2}{\left[\tan\left(\frac{180}{7}\right)\right]^2}$

$784 - x^2 \approx 4.3119x^2$

$784 \approx 5.3119x^2$

$\sqrt{\frac{784}{5.3119}} \approx x$

$12.15 \approx x$

Then the distance between the tips of two consecutive cylinders $= 2x$. $2x \approx 24.3$ inches.

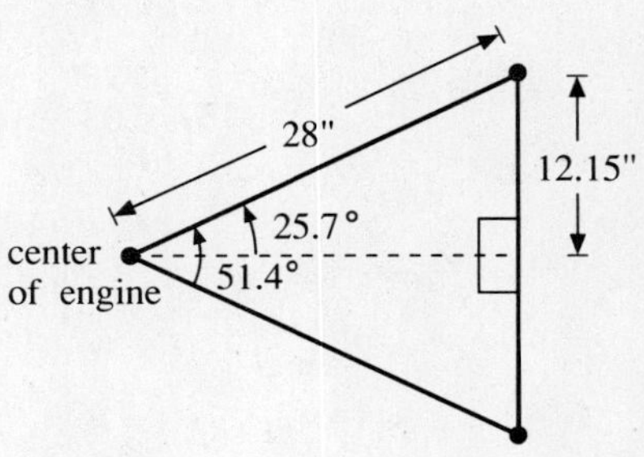

28. Since the blades are of equal length, $a = b$. From Exercise 25, we know that the measure of the angles in one of the triangles whose legs are consecutive blades is 45° – 45° – 90°.

$a^2 + a^2 = (32.5)^2$

$a^2 = 528.125$

$a \approx 23$ feet

29. $\tan 20° = \frac{x}{20}$

$x \approx 7.28$

$\tan 35° = \frac{x + y}{20}$

$x + y \approx 14.00$

$y \approx 14.00 - 7.28$

$y \approx 6.72$

30. $\tan 10° = \frac{x}{20}$

$x \approx 3.53$

$\tan 30° = \frac{x + y}{20}$

$x + y \approx 11.55$

$y \approx 11.55 - 3.53$

$y \approx 8.02$

31. $\tan 38^\circ = \frac{x}{75}$

$x \approx 58.6$ feet

32. $\tan 29^\circ = \frac{x}{75}$

$x \approx 41.6$

Thickness $\approx 58.6 - 41.6$

≈ 17 feet

33. $\tan 65^\circ = \frac{x}{100}$

$x \approx 214.5$ feet

34. $\tan A = \frac{214.5}{120}$

$\tan A \approx 1.79$

35. $a^2 + 4^2 = 8^2$

$a^2 = 64 - 16$

$a^2 = 48$

$a = \pm 4\sqrt{3}$

36. $6^2 + b^2 = 9^2$

$b^2 = 81 - 36$

$b^2 = 45$

$b = \pm 3\sqrt{5}$

37. $c^2 = 4^2 + 5^2$

$c^2 = 16 + 25$

$c^2 = 41$

$c = \pm\sqrt{41}$

38. $\frac{2}{5} = \frac{a}{3}$

$5a = 6$

$a = \frac{6}{5}$

39. $\frac{7}{3} = \frac{4}{b}$

$7b = 12$

$b = \frac{12}{7}$

40. $\tan 20^\circ = \frac{3}{b}$

$b \approx 8.2$

41. $m = \frac{0-2}{1-3}$

$= \frac{-2}{-2}$

$= 1$

Slope is the tangent of the angle.

42. $m = \frac{0-2}{2-5}$

$= \frac{-2}{-3}$

$= \frac{2}{3}$

Slope is the tangent of the angle.

43. **b.**

$\text{Area} = \frac{1}{2}bh$

$25 = \frac{1}{2}(2h)(h)$

$25 = h^2$

$h = 5$

$5^2 + 10^2 = c^2$

$c = \sqrt{125}$

$c = 5\sqrt{5}$

44. Slope $= \tan 60^\circ = \sqrt{3}$

Slope is positive.

$y = \sqrt{3}x$

45. Slope $= \tan 60^\circ = \sqrt{3}$

Slope is negative.

$y = -\sqrt{3}x$

Mixed REVIEW

1. $2x(x+3) - x(4 - x^2) = 2x^2 + 6x - 4x + x^3$

$= x^3 + 2x^2 + 2x$

2. $\frac{3x}{4x} + \frac{1}{4} = \frac{3}{4} + \frac{1}{4}$

$= 1$

3. $3^2 - 2 \cdot 3 + 4 = 9 - 6 + 4$

$= 7 > 5$

3 is not a solution.

4. $|3(-4) + 2| + (-4) = 10 - 4$

$= 6 > 5$

-4 is a solution.

5. $3p^2 - 6q = 0$

$$3p^2 = 6q$$
$$p^2 = 2q$$
$$p = \pm\sqrt{2q}$$

6. $3m + 3mn - 6x = 0$

$$3m + 3mn = 6x$$
$$3m(1+n) = 6x$$
$$m = \frac{2x}{1+n}$$

7. $36\left(\frac{1}{4}\right)^2 + 2\left(\frac{1}{4}\right) - 6 = \frac{36}{16} + \frac{1}{2} - 6$

$$= \frac{9}{4} + \frac{2}{4} - \frac{24}{4}$$
$$= -\frac{13}{4}$$

8. $3\left(\frac{2}{9}\right) + 9 = \frac{2}{3} + \frac{27}{3}$

$$= \frac{29}{3}$$

9. $\dfrac{2+3+5+7+8}{5} = 5$

10. 35

11. $216 = x(360)$

$x = 0.6$ or 60%

12. $212.5 = 0.25x$

$$x = 850$$

13. $-4x + 5y = -5$

$$5y = 4x - 5$$
$$y = \frac{4}{5}x - 1$$

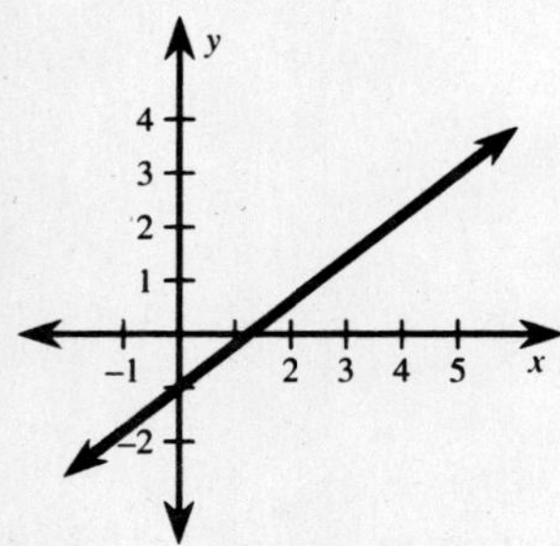

14. $3x + 2 = 0$

$$3x = -2$$
$$x = -\frac{2}{3}$$

Vertex: $\left(-\frac{2}{3}, -4\right)$

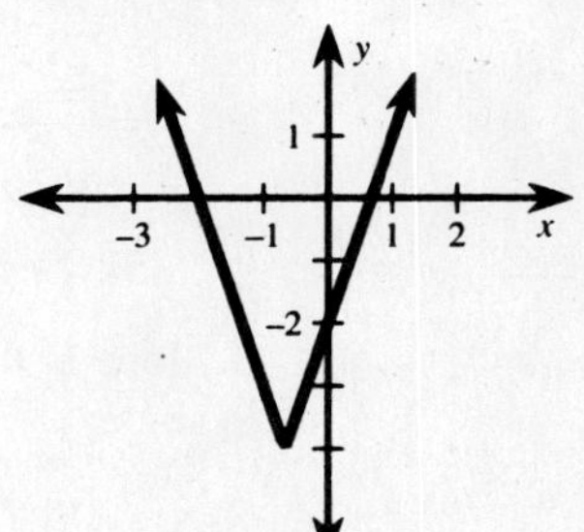

15. $f(x) = \left(\frac{1}{4}\right)^x + 2$

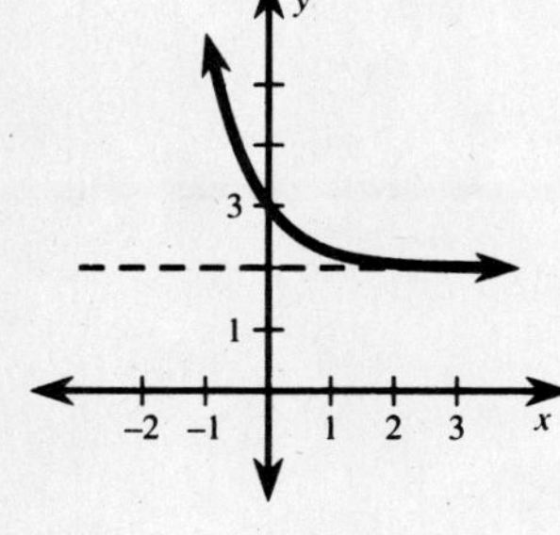

16.

$$\begin{array}{r} 1 + \dfrac{1}{x+1} \\ x+1 \overline{)\ x + 2} \\ \underline{x + 1} \\ 1 \end{array}$$

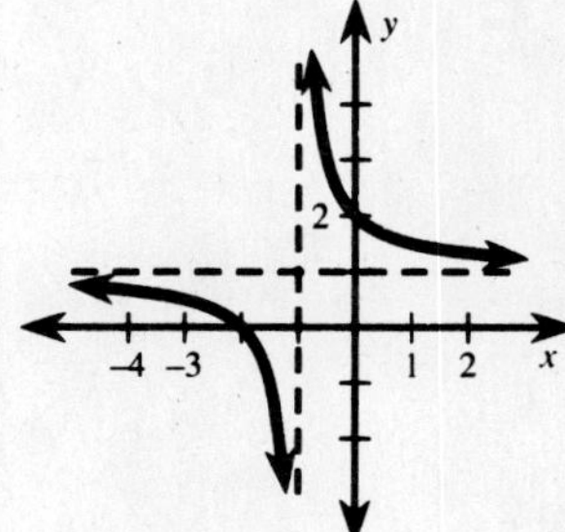

17. $y < 3x + 2$

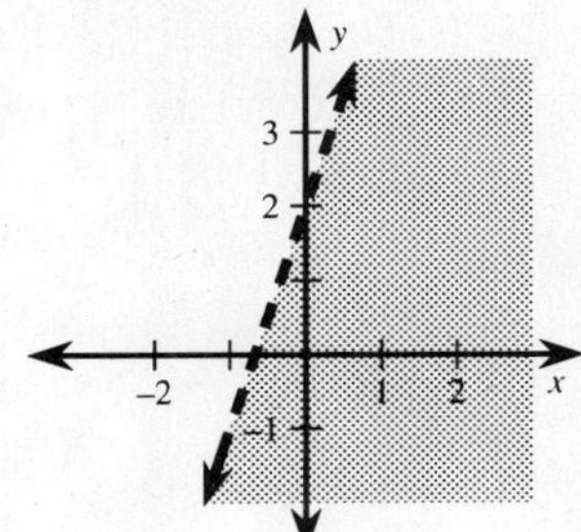

18. $y \geq x^2 - 4$

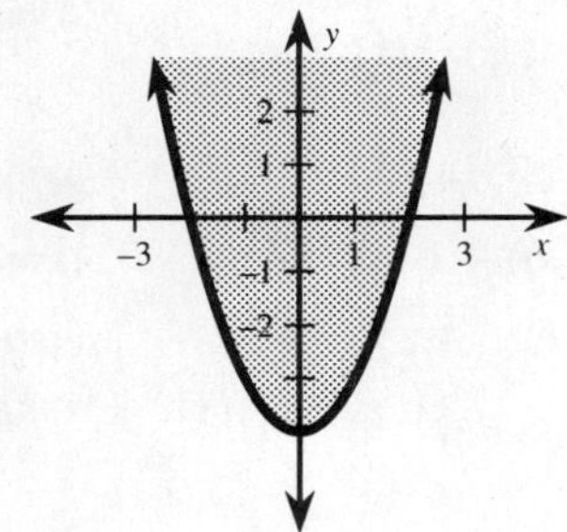

19. $\begin{cases} x + 2y = -15 \\ 5x - 4y = 9 \end{cases}$

$x = -2y - 15$

$5(-2y - 15) - 4y = 9$

$-14y = 84$

$y = -6$

$x = -2(-6) - 15$

$x = -3$

$(-3, -6)$

20. $\begin{cases} 4x + 2y = 8 \\ 6x - 5y = 28 \end{cases}$

$12x + 6y = 24$

$-12x + 10y = -56$

$16y = -32$

$y = -2$

$4x + 2(-2) = 8$

$4x = 12$

$x = 3$

$(3, -2)$

13.6 Formal Use of Properties of Algebra

Communicating about Algebra

Euler found a counterexample to Fermat's conjecture; so Fermat's conjecture was false.

EXERCISES

1. $a - b = a + (-b)$

No; a definition needs to be consistent with other definitions and with axioms, but is accepted as true rather than having to be proved true.

2.

$(a - b)c = (a + (-b))c$	*Definition of subtraction*
$= (a)(c) + (-b)(c)$	*Distributive axiom*
$= ac + (-bc)$	$(-b)c = -bc$
$= ac - bc$	*Definition of subtraction*

3. No; in order to prove her conjecture she would need to give every example (to avoid a counterexample) which would be impossible.

4. Yes, the map serves as a counterexample to the proposal. The map cannot be colored as proposed.

5. $a - b = a + (-b)$ *Definition of subtraction*

$= -b + a$ *Commutative axiom*

6. $(a - b) - c = (a + (-b)) + (-c)$ *Definition of subtraction*

$= a + [(-b) + (-c)]$ *Associative axiom*

$= a + (-1)(b + c)$ *Distributive axiom*

$= a - (b + c)$ *Definition of subtraction*

7. Answers vary. Let $a = 3$ and $b = 4$.

$(3+4)^2 \stackrel{?}{=} 3^2 + 4^2$

$49 \neq 25$

8. Answers vary. Let $a = 3$ and $b = 4$.

$(3-4)^2 \stackrel{?}{=} 3^2 - 4^2$

$1 \neq -7$

9. Answers vary. Let $a = 0$, b and c any real number.

$0 \cdot 1 = 0 \cdot 2$

$1 \neq 2$

10. Answers vary. Let $a = 12$, $b = 6$, and $c = 2$.

$(12 \div 6) \div 2 \stackrel{?}{=} 12 \div (6 \div 2)$

$1 \neq 4$

11. She drew a plan of the patio and colored it like a checkerboard.

12. Each rectangular tile must cover a red and a white square. The two that could not be covered were both red.

13. Each additional L-shape contains the next odd number of dots. The dots can be lined up in a square form.

14. Add 4 triangles of height a and base b to $a^2 + b^2$ and you have an area equal to $(a+b)^2$. Add 4 triangles of height a and base b to c^2 and you have an area equal to $(a+b)^2$. Therefore, $a^2 + b^2 + 4\left(\frac{1}{2}ab\right) = c^2 + 4\left(\frac{1}{2}ab\right)$ and $a^2 + b^2 = c^2$.

15. $ab - ac = 12$

$a(b - c) = 12$

$a = \dfrac{12}{b - c}$

16. $a^2 - 2a = 12$

$a^2 - 2a - 12 = 0$

$a = \dfrac{2 \pm \sqrt{4 - 4(1)(-12)}}{2 \cdot 1}$

$a = \dfrac{2 \pm \sqrt{52}}{2}$

$a = 1 \pm \sqrt{13}$

17. $ab - b^2 = 12$

$$ab = b^2 + 12$$

$$a = b + \frac{12}{b}$$

18. $\frac{1}{a} + a = 12$

$$1 + a^2 = 12a$$

$$a^2 - 12a + 1 = 0$$

$$a = \frac{12 \pm \sqrt{144 - 4(1)(1)}}{2 \cdot 1}$$

$$a = \frac{12 \pm \sqrt{140}}{2}$$

$$a = \frac{12 \pm 2\sqrt{35}}{2}$$

$$a = 6 \pm \sqrt{35}$$

19. $\sqrt{(12 - 0)^2 + (14 - 0)^2} = \sqrt{144 + 196}$

$$= \sqrt{340}$$

$$= 2\sqrt{85}$$

$$\approx 18.4 \text{ feet}$$

20. $\tan 50° = \frac{a}{20}$

$$a \approx 23.8 \text{ feet}$$

21. b.

22. b.

23. Start at the goal and count squares horizontally and vertically until the number of the square matches the count. This is the previous square. Continue until you reach the number 3 in the upper left hand corner.

Chapter REVIEW

1. $d = \sqrt{(-6 + 9)^2 + (0 + 1)^2}$

$$= \sqrt{9 + 1}$$

$$= \sqrt{10}$$

$$\left(\frac{-6 - 9}{2}, \frac{0 - 1}{2}\right) = \left(-\frac{15}{2}, -\frac{1}{2}\right)$$

2. $d = \sqrt{(-3 - 1)^2 + (6 - 7)^2}$

$$= \sqrt{16 + 1}$$

$$= \sqrt{17}$$

$$\left(\frac{-3 + 1}{2}, \frac{6 + 7}{2}\right) = \left(-1, \frac{13}{2}\right)$$

3. $d = \sqrt{(0 + 8)^2 + (0 - 9)^2}$

$$= \sqrt{64 + 81}$$

$$= \sqrt{145}$$

$$\left(\frac{0 - 8}{2}, \frac{0 + 9}{2}\right) = \left(-4, \frac{9}{2}\right)$$

4. $d = \sqrt{(-3 - 1)^2 + (-2 - 7)^2}$

$$= \sqrt{16 + 81}$$

$$= \sqrt{97}$$

$$\left(\frac{-3 + 1}{2}, \frac{-2 + 7}{2}\right) = \left(-1, \frac{5}{2}\right)$$

5. $d = \sqrt{(-3-6)^2 + (-3-7)^2}$

$= \sqrt{81 + 100}$

$= \sqrt{181}$

$\left(\frac{-3+6}{2}, \frac{-3+7}{2}\right) = \left(\frac{3}{2}, 2\right)$

6. $d = \sqrt{(-9-5)^2 + (17+7)^2}$

$= \sqrt{196 + 576}$

$= \sqrt{772}$

$= 2\sqrt{193}$

$\left(\frac{-9+5}{2}, \frac{17-7}{2}\right) = (-2, 5)$

7. $\sqrt{(0-1)^2 + (0-2)^2} = \sqrt{5}$

$\sqrt{(1-2)^2 + (2+1)^2} = \sqrt{10}$

$\sqrt{(0-2)^2 + (0+1)^2} = \sqrt{5}$

$\left(\sqrt{5}\right)^2 + \left(\sqrt{5}\right)^2 = \left(\sqrt{10}\right)^2$

8. $\sqrt{(-4-8)^2 + (2-5)^2} = \sqrt{153}$

$= 3\sqrt{17}$

$\sqrt{(8+2)^2 + (5+6)^2} = \sqrt{221}$

$\sqrt{(-4+2)^2 + (2+6)^2} = \sqrt{68}$

$= 2\sqrt{17}$

$\left(2\sqrt{17}\right)^2 + \left(3\sqrt{17}\right)^2 = \left(\sqrt{221}\right)^2$

9. $\sqrt{216} = 6\sqrt{6}$

10. $\sqrt{175} = 5\sqrt{7}$

11. $\sqrt{18} = 3\sqrt{2}$

12. $\sqrt{\frac{4}{17}} = \frac{2\sqrt{17}}{17}$

13. $\sqrt{\frac{8}{9}} = \frac{2\sqrt{2}}{3}$

14. $\sqrt{\frac{25}{125}} = \frac{\sqrt{5}}{5}$

15. $\sqrt{5} + 2\sqrt{5} - \sqrt{3} = 3\sqrt{5} - \sqrt{3}$

16. $3\sqrt{3} - 6\sqrt{3} + \sqrt{2} = -3\sqrt{3} + \sqrt{2}$

17. $\sqrt{6}(2\sqrt{3} - 4\sqrt{2}) = 6\sqrt{2} - 8\sqrt{3}$

18. $\sqrt{2}(2\sqrt{2} - 6) = 4 - 6\sqrt{2}$

19. $(3\sqrt{5} - \sqrt{10})^2 = 45 - 3\sqrt{50} - 3\sqrt{50} + 10$

$= 55 - 6\sqrt{50}$

$= 55 - 30\sqrt{2}$

20. $(2\sqrt{3} - 2)(2\sqrt{3} + 2) = 12 - 4$

$= 8$

21. $2\sqrt{x} - 4 = 0$

$\sqrt{x} = 2$

$x = 4$

22. $\frac{1}{3}\sqrt{x} + 2 = 8$

$\sqrt{x} = 18$

$x = 324$

23. $x = \sqrt{-4x - 4}$

$x^2 + 4x + 4 = 0$

$(x+2)^2 = 0$

No solution

24. $\sqrt{3x - 2} = x$

$x^2 - 3x + 2 = 0$

$(x-2)(x-1) = 0$

$x = 2$ or $x = 1$

25. $\sqrt{11x + 12} = x$

$x^2 - 11x - 12 = 0$

$(x-12)(x+1) = 0$

$x = 12$

26. $x = \sqrt{3x}$

$x^2 = 3x$

$x^2 - 3x = 0$

$x(x-3) = 0$

$x = 0$ or $x = 3$

27. $a = \sqrt{6 \cdot 30}$

$a = \sqrt{180}$

$a = 6\sqrt{5}$

28. $a = \sqrt{7 \cdot 35}$

$a = \sqrt{7 \cdot 7 \cdot 5}$

$a = 7\sqrt{5}$

29. $\sqrt{(-1+4)^2 + (-2+1)^2} = \sqrt{9+1} = \sqrt{10}$

$\sqrt{(-4+3)^2 + (-1-2)^2} = \sqrt{1+9} = \sqrt{10}$

$\sqrt{(-3-0)^2 + (2-3)^2} = \sqrt{9+1} = \sqrt{10}$

$\sqrt{(0-3)^2 + (3-2)^2} = \sqrt{9+1} = \sqrt{10}$

$\sqrt{(3-2)^2 + (2+1)^2} = \sqrt{1+9} = \sqrt{10}$

$\sqrt{(2+1)^2 + (-1+2)^2} = \sqrt{9+1} = \sqrt{10}$

$\sqrt{10} + \sqrt{10} + \sqrt{10} + \sqrt{10} + \sqrt{10} + \sqrt{10} = 6\sqrt{10}$

30. $\sqrt{(-1+1)^2 + (2-4)^2} = \sqrt{4} = 2$

$\sqrt{(-1-1)^2 + (4-5)^2} = \sqrt{4+1} = \sqrt{5}$

$\sqrt{(1-3)^2 + (5-3)^2} = \sqrt{4+4} = 2\sqrt{2}$

$\sqrt{(3-1)^2 + (3-1)^2} = \sqrt{4+4} = 2\sqrt{2}$

$\sqrt{(1+1)^2 + (1-2)^2} = \sqrt{4+1} = \sqrt{5}$

$2 + \sqrt{5} + 2\sqrt{2} + 2\sqrt{2} + \sqrt{5} = 2 + 4\sqrt{2} + 2\sqrt{5}$

31. Perimeter $= 2\left(3\sqrt{3} + 3\sqrt{3} + 2\right)$

$= 2\left(6\sqrt{3} + 2\right)$

$= 12\sqrt{3} + 4$

Area $= 3\sqrt{3}\left(3\sqrt{3} + 2\right)$

$= 27 + 6\sqrt{3}$

32. Perimeter $= 2(5 + 2\sqrt{5} - 1)$

$= 2\left(2\sqrt{5} + 4\right)$

$= 4\sqrt{5} + 8$

Area $= 5\left(2\sqrt{5} - 1\right)$

$= 10\sqrt{5} - 5$

33. $\tan 60^\circ = \dfrac{a}{1}$

$a = \sqrt{3}$

$\left(\sqrt{3}\right)^2 + 1^2 = c^2$

$c = 2$

$60 + B = 90$

$B = 30^\circ$

34. $\tan 24^\circ = \dfrac{4}{a}$

$a \approx 8.98$

$(8.98)^2 + 4^2 = c^2$

$c \approx 9.83$

$A + 24 = 90$

$A = 66^\circ$

35. $\tan 67^\circ = \dfrac{7}{b}$

$b \approx 2.97$

$7^2 + (2.97)^2 = c^2$

$c \approx 7.60$

$67 + B = 90$

$B = 23^\circ$

36. $6^2 + 4^2 = c^2$

$c = 2\sqrt{13}$

$\tan A = \frac{6}{4}$

Using guess and check, we find that the measure of angle A is approximately 56°.

$56° + B \approx 90°$

$B \approx 34°$

37. Answers vary.

Example: $3 + 6 = 9 = 3^2$

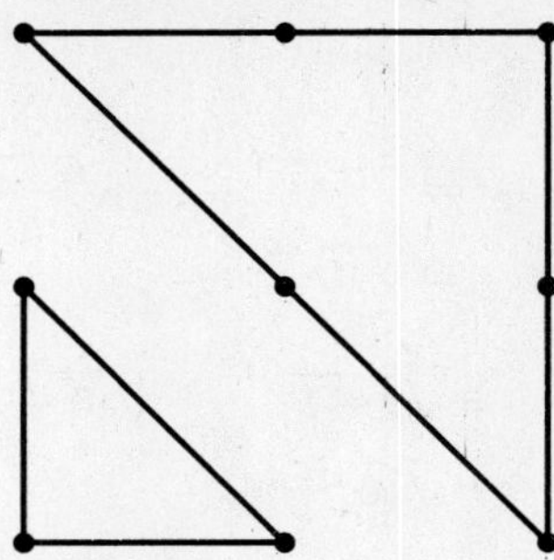

38. $\tan 58° = \dfrac{x}{10}$

$x \approx 16$ meters

39. $x = \sqrt{36 \cdot 40}$

$x \approx 37.9$ grams

40. $37.9 = \sqrt{37 \cdot a}$

$1436.41 = 37a$

$a \approx 38.8$ grams

41. $\tan 30° = \dfrac{a}{b}$

42. $b = \dfrac{a}{\tan 30°}$

43. $a^2 + \left(\dfrac{a}{\tan 30°}\right)^2 = 70^2$

$a^2\left[1 + \left(\dfrac{1}{\tan 30}\right)^2\right] = 70^2$

$a = \sqrt{\dfrac{4900}{1 + \left(\dfrac{1}{\tan 30}\right)^2}}$

$a = 35$

44. You should set your fishing lines 35 feet deep to be at the same depth as the fish.

45. M(4, 6) A(−3, 7)

$d = \sqrt{(4 + 3)^2 + (6 - 7)^2}$

$= \sqrt{49 + 1}$

$= \sqrt{50}$

$= 5\sqrt{2}$

$D = 5\sqrt{2}(100)$

$= 500\sqrt{2}$

≈ 707 miles

No; Green's closest piece (an armored unit at (−3, 7)) to one of pink's missiles is approximately 707 miles away from its location at (4, 6).

46. M(−3, 8) A(1, 4)

$$d = \sqrt{(-3-1)^2 + (8-4)^2}$$
$$= \sqrt{16+16}$$
$$= \sqrt{32}$$
$$= 4\sqrt{2}$$

$$D = 4\sqrt{2}(100)$$
$$= 400\sqrt{2}$$
$$\approx 566 \text{ miles}$$

M(−5, 5) A(1, 4)

$$d = \sqrt{(-5-1)^2 + (5-4)^2}$$
$$= \sqrt{36+1}$$
$$= \sqrt{37}$$

$$D = \sqrt{37}(100) \approx 608 \text{ miles}$$

M(−3, 8) A(3, 6)

$$d = \sqrt{(-3-3)^2 + (8-6)^2}$$
$$= \sqrt{36+4}$$
$$= \sqrt{40}$$
$$D = \sqrt{40}(100)$$
$$\approx 632 \text{ miles}$$

Yes; Pink's armored unit at (3, 6) is approximately 632 miles from Green's missile at (−3, 8). Pink's armored unit at (1, 4) is approximately 608 miles from Green's missile at (−5, 5) and approximately 566 miles from Green's missile at (−3, 8).

48. F(−3, 2) A(6, 6)

$$d = \sqrt{(-3-6)^2 + (2-6)^2}$$
$$= \sqrt{81+16}$$
$$= \sqrt{97}$$

$$D = 100\sqrt{97}$$
$$= 984$$

M(4, 6), A(3, 6), A(6, 6), A(4, 5), A(1, 4), A(6, 4), A(3, 3), F(2, 4), Port City (7, 2)

47. F(2, 4) F(−7, −1) M(−3, 8) T(−5, 0)

$$d_1 = \sqrt{(2+7)^2 + (4+1)^2}$$
$$= \sqrt{81+25}$$
$$= \sqrt{106}$$

$$d_2 = \sqrt{(2+3)^2 + (4-8)^2}$$
$$= \sqrt{25+16}$$
$$= \sqrt{41}$$

$$d_3 = \sqrt{(2+5)^2 + (4-0)^2}$$
$$= \sqrt{49+16}$$
$$= \sqrt{65}$$

$$D_1 = 100\sqrt{106}$$
$$\approx 1030$$

$$D_2 = 100\sqrt{41}$$
$$\approx 640$$

$$D_3 = 100\sqrt{65}$$
$$\approx 806$$

M(−3, 8), M(−5, 5), A(−3, 7), A(−4, 5), A(−5, 3), F(−3, 2), T(−5, 0), Port City (−5, 1)

Chapter TEST

1. $\sqrt{(-6-0)^2+(-4+4)} = \sqrt{36}$
$= 6$

$\sqrt{(0+6)^2+(-4-0)^2} = \sqrt{36+16}$
$= 2\sqrt{13}$

$\sqrt{(-6+6)^2+(-4+0)^2} = \sqrt{16}$
$= 4$

$4^2+6^2 = \left(2\sqrt{13}\right)^2$

2. $\sqrt{(5+5)^2+(2-0)^2} = \sqrt{100+4}$
$= \sqrt{104}$
$= 2\sqrt{26}$

$\sqrt{(-5-1)^2+(0-22)^2} = \sqrt{36+484}$
$= \sqrt{520}$
$= 2\sqrt{130}$

$\sqrt{(5-1)^2+(2-22)^2} = \sqrt{16+400}$
$= \sqrt{416}$
$= 4\sqrt{26}$

$\left(2\sqrt{26}\right)^2+\left(4\sqrt{26}\right)^2 = \left(2\sqrt{130}\right)^2$

3. $\sqrt{500} = 10\sqrt{5}$

4. $\sqrt{384} = 8\sqrt{6}$

5. $\sqrt{\frac{1}{8}} = \frac{1}{2\sqrt{2}}$
$= \frac{\sqrt{2}}{4}$

6. $\sqrt{\frac{25}{27}} = \frac{5}{3\sqrt{3}}$
$= \frac{5\sqrt{3}}{9}$

7. $4\sqrt{3}-\sqrt{2}-\sqrt{3} = 3\sqrt{3}-\sqrt{2}$

8. $6\sqrt{6}+\sqrt{6}+\sqrt{2} = 7\sqrt{6}+\sqrt{2}$

9. $3\sqrt{5}\left(2\sqrt{5}-6\sqrt{10}\right) = 30-90\sqrt{2}$

10. $\left(4\sqrt{5}+1\right)^2 = 80+8\sqrt{5}+1$
$= 81+8\sqrt{5}$

11. $\sqrt{y}+6 = 10$
$\sqrt{y} = 4$
$y = 16$

12. $\sqrt{2m+3}-6 = 4$
$\sqrt{2m+3} = 10$
$2m+3 = 100$
$2m = 97$
$m = \frac{97}{2}$

13. $n = \sqrt{9n-18}$
$n^2-9n+18 = 0$
$(n-6)(n-3) = 0$
$n = 6$ or $n = 3$

14. $p = \sqrt{-3p+18}$
$p^2+3p-18 = 0$
$(p+6)(p-3) = 0$
$p = 3$

15. Area $= 2\sqrt{2}\left(3\sqrt{5}+4\sqrt{2}\right)$
Area $= 6\sqrt{10}+16$
Perimeter $= 2\left(2\sqrt{2}+3\sqrt{5}+4\sqrt{2}\right)$
Perimeter $= 12\sqrt{2}+6\sqrt{5}$

16. $\sqrt{(-3+3)^2+(1-5)^2} = \sqrt{16}$
$= 4$

$\sqrt{(-3-3)^2+(5-7)^2} = \sqrt{36+4}$
$= \sqrt{40}$
$= 2\sqrt{10}$

$\sqrt{(3-3)^2+(3-7)^2} = \sqrt{16}$
$= 4$

$\sqrt{(3+3)^2+(3-1)^2} = \sqrt{36+4}$
$= 2\sqrt{10}$

Perimeter $= 8 + 4\sqrt{10}$

17. $\frac{6}{b} = \frac{3}{4}$
$b = 8$

$b = 8$
$6^2 + 8^2 = c^2$
$c = 10$

18. $\tan 36° = \frac{a}{20}$
$a \approx 14.5$

$(14.5)^2 + (20)^2 = c^2$
$c \approx 24.7$

19. Answers vary.
Let $a = 2$, $b = 3$, and $c = -1$. Then $2 < 3$, but $\frac{2}{-1} \not< \frac{3}{-1}$.

20. $\frac{l}{w} = \frac{w}{h}$
$\frac{6}{w} = \frac{w}{3}$
$w^2 = 18$
$w = 3\sqrt{2}$ feet

21. $\tan 78° = \frac{x}{134}$
$x \approx 630$ feet